CONTENTS

KT-377-510

ABBREVIATIONS

adj	adjective		*MED*	medicine
abl	ablative		*MIL*	military
acc	accusative		*mod*	modern
adv	adverb		*n*	noun
AGR	agriculture		*NAUT*	nautical
ARCH	architecture		*neg*	negative
art	article		*nom*	nominative
ASTR	astronomy		*nt*	neuter
AUG	augury		*num*	numeral
COMM	business		*occ*	occasionally
CIRCS	circumstances		*p*	participle
compar	comparative		*pass*	passive
conj	conjunction		*perf*	perfect
cpd	compound		*perh*	perhaps
dat	dative		*pers*	person
defec	defective		*PHILOS*	philosophy
ECCL	ecclesiastical		*pl*	plural
esp	especially		*POL*	politics
excl	exclamatory		*ppa*	perfect participle active
f	feminine		*ppp*	perfect participle passive
fig	figurative		*prep*	preposition
fut	future		*pres*	present
gen	genitive		*pron*	pronoun
GEOG	geography		*prop*	properly
GRAM	grammar		*PROV*	proverb
impers	impersonal		*relat*	relative
imperf	imperfect		*RHET*	rhetoric
impv	imperative		*sg*	singular
indecl	indeclinable		*sim*	similarly
indic	indicative		*subj*	subjunctive
inf	informal		*superl*	superlative
infin	infinitive		*THEAT*	theatre
interj	interjection		*UNIV*	university
interrog	interrogative		*usu*	usually
LIT	literature		*vi*	intransitive verb
loc	locative		*voc*	vocative
m	masculine		*vt*	transitive verb
MATH	mathematics			

INTRODUCTION

Whether you are learning Latin for the first time or wish to "brush up" what you learned some time ago, this dictionary is designed to help you understand Latin and to express yourself in Latin, if you so wish.

HOW TO USE THE DICTIONARY

Entries are laid out as follows:

Headword

This is shown in **bold type**. On the Latin-English side all long vowels are shown by placing a ¯ above them. Latin nouns show the genitive singular form in bold. Latin verbs show the first person singular of the present indicative as the headword, followed by the infinitive, the first person singular of the perfect indicative and usually the past participle, all in bold type:

elegīa, -ae
elementum, -ī
ēlevō, āre
ēmātūrēscō, -ēscere, -uī

Part of Speech

Next comes the part of speech (noun, verb, adjective etc), shown in *italics*. Part of speech abbreviations used in the dictionary are shown in the abbreviations list (*p iv*). Where a word has more than one part of speech, each new part of speech is preceded by a black lozenge (♦). If a Latin headword is a preposition, the case taken by the preposition comes immediately after the part of speech, in *italics* and in brackets.

era, -ae *f*
ticklish *adj*
thunder *n* tonitrus *m* ♦ *vi* tonare, intonare.
ērgā *prep* (*with acc*) towards; against.

Meanings

Where a word or a part of speech has only one meaning, the translation comes immediately after the part of speech. However, many words have more than one meaning. Where the context is likely to show which translation is correct, variations in meaning are simply separated by a semi-colon. But usually there will also be an "indicator" in *italics* and in brackets. Some meanings relate to specific subject areas, for example religion, politics, military matters etc –

these indicators are in small italic capitals.

ēnsiger, -ī *adj* with his sword.
toy *n* crepundia *ntpl* ♦ *vi* ludere.
toll collector *n* exactor *m*; portitor *m*.
eō, -īre, īvī *and* **iī, ītum** *vi* to go; (*MIL*) to march; (*time*) to pass; (*event*) to proceed, turn out.

Translations

Most words can be translated directly. On the English-Latin side, translations of nouns include the gender of the Latin noun in *italics*. However, sometimes a phrase is needed to show how a word is used, but in some cases a direct translation of a phrase would be meaningless: the symbol ~ in front of a translation shows that the translation is natural English, but does not mean word for word what the Latin means. Sometimes, even an approximate translation would not be very helpful (for place names, for example) – in these cases, an explanation in *italics* is given instead. In other cases, the user will need more information than simply the translation; in these cases, "indicators" are included in the translation(s), giving, for instance, the case required by a Latin verb or preposition or further details about a place or person.

thumb *n* pollex *m*; **have under one's** ~ in potestate sua habere.
elephantomacha, -ae *m fighter mounted on an elephant.*
Erymanthus, -ī *m* mountain range in Arcadia (*where Hercules killed the bear*).
thwart *vt* obstare (*dat*), officere (*dat*).

Pronunciation

Since Latin pronunciation is regular, once the basic rules have been learned (*see pp viii, ix*), the dictionary does not show phonetic transcriptions against each headword, but does show all long vowels.

Other Information

The dictionary also includes:

- a basic grammar section
- information about life in Roman times:
  – how government and the army were organized – how numbers and dates were calculated and expressed – family relationships – geographical names – major Roman authors – key events in Roman history – (*important historical and mythological characters and events are listed within the body of the main text*).
- a section on Latin poetry and scansion
- a list of Latin expressions commonly used in English today

LATIN ALPHABET

The Latin alphabet is the one which has been almost universally adopted by the modern languages of Europe and America. In the Classical period it had 23 letters, namely the English alphabet without letters **j, v** and **w**.

Letter v
The symbol **v** was the capital form of the letter **u**, but in a later age the small **v** came into use to represent the consonantal **u**, and as it is commonly so employed in modern editions of Latin authors, it has been retained as a distinct letter in this dictionary for convenience.

Letter j
The symbol **j** came to be used as the consonantal **i**, and is found in older editions of the Classics, but as it has been almost entirely discarded in modern texts, it is not used in this dictionary, and words found spelt with a **j** must therefore be looked up under **i**.

Letters w, y, z
The letter **w** may be seen in the Latinized forms of some modern names, *e.g.* **Westmonasterium**, Westminster. The letters **y** and **z** occur only in words of Greek origin.

ORTHOGRAPHY

Many Latin words which begin with a prefix can be spelled in two ways. The prefix can retain its original spelling, or it can be assimilated, changing a letter depending on the letter which follows it. Compare the following:

ad before **g, l, r** and **p**:

adpropinquare	appropinquare
adgredi	aggredi
adloquor	alloquor
adrogans	arrogans

ad is also often assimilated before **f** and **n**:

adfectus	affectus
adnexus	annexus

and **ad** is often shortened to **a** before **sc**:

adscendere	ascendere

in changes to **il** before **l**, to **im** before **m** or **p** and to **ir** before **r**.

con becomes **cor** when followed by another **r** and **col** when followed by **l**.

We have provided cross-references in the text to draw your attention to the alternative forms of words. Thus, although **arrogantia** does not appear in the Latin-English section, the cross-reference at **arr-** will point you to the entry for **adrogantia**, where the translation is given.

PRONUNCIATION

The ancient pronunciation of Latin has been established with a fair degree of certainty from the evidence of ancient authorities and inscriptions and inferences from the modern Romance languages. It is not possible, of course, to recapture the precise nuances of Classical Latin speech, but what follows is now generally accepted and generally understood as a reasonably accurate guide to the sounds of Latin as spoken by educated Romans during the two centuries from Cicero to Quintilian.

ACCENT

The Latin accent in the Classical period was a weak stress, perhaps with an element of pitch in it. It falls, as in English, on the second last syllable of the word, if that syllable is long, and on the third last syllable if the second last is short. Disyllabic words take the accent on the first syllable, unless they have already lost a final syllable, *e.g.* **illīc(e)**.

Inflected words are commonly learned with the accent wrongly placed on the last syllable, for convenience in memorizing the inflexions. But it is advisable to get the accent as well as the ending right.

The correct accent of other words can easily be found by noting carefully the quantity of the second last syllable and then accenting the word as in English, according to the rule given above. Thus **fuērunt** is accented on the second last syllable because the **e** is long, whereas **fuerant** is accented on the third last, because the **e** is short.

VOWELS

Vowels are pure and should not be diphthongized as in certain sounds of Southern English. They may be long or short. Throughout this Dictionary all vowels known or believed by the best authorities to be long are marked with a line above them; those unmarked are either known to be short or of uncertain quantity.

Short		Long	
agricolạ	rạt	rāmus	rạther
hederā	pẹn	avē	pạy
ītaque	kīn	cīvis	kẹẹn
favor	rọb	ampliō	rọbe
nebulā	fụll	lūna	fọol

y is a Greek sound and is pronounced (both short and long) as **u** in French *ie* rụe.

DIPHTHONGS

_ae_stas	tr_y_	
_au_diō	to_wn_	
he_i_	pa_yee_	
me_us_	_ay-oo_	with the accent on first sound
m_oe_cha	to_y_	
t_ui_tus	Lo_ui_s	

CONSONANTS

_b_alneae	_b_a_b_y	
ab_s_tēmius	a_ps_e	
su_b_tractus	a_pt_	
_c_astra	_c_ar	
_ch_orda	sepul_ch_re	
inter_d_o	_d_og	
cōn_f_lō	_f_ortune	
in_g_redior	_g_o	
_h_abeō	_h_and	(but faintly)
_i_aceo	_y_es	(consonantal i = j)
_K_alendae	oa_k_	
conge_l_ō	_l_et	
co_m_es	_m_an	(final m was hardly sounded and may have simply nasalized the preceding vowel)
pā_n_is	_n_o	
pa_n_go	fi_n_ger	
stu_p_eō	a_p_t	
rap_h_anus	_p_ill	
exse_qu_or	_qu_ite	
suprē_m_us	_br_ae	(Scottish)
māgnu_s_	_s_ister	(never as in ro_s_e)
lae_t_us	_s_top	
_th_eātrum	_t_ake	
_v_apor (and consonantal u)	_w_in	
de_x_tra	si_x_	(ks, not gs)
_z_ōna	_z_ero	

Double consonants lengthen the sound of the consonant.

Quick Reference Grammar

DECLENSIONS OF NOUNS

1st Declension

	mainly f		*m*	
SING				
Nom.	terra	crambē	Aenēās	Anchīsēs
Voc.	terra	crambē	Aenēā	Anchīsā, -ē
Acc.	terram	crambēn	Aenēam, -ān	Anchīsam, -ēn
Gen.	terrae	crambes	Aenēae	Anchīsae
Dat.	terrae	crambae	Aenēae	Anchīsae
Abl.	terra	cramba	Aenēā	Anchīsā

PLURAL		
Nom.	terrae	crambae
Voc.	terrae	crambae
Acc.	terrās	crambās
Gen.	terrārum	crambārum
Dat.	terrīs	crambīs
Abl.	terrīs	crambīs

2nd Declension

mainly m

SING					
Nom.	modus	Lūcius	Dēlos (*f*)	puer	liber
Voc.	mode	Lūcī	Dēle	puer	liber
Acc.	modum	Lūcium	Dēlon	puerum	librum
Gen.	modī	Lūcī	Dēlī	puerī	librī
Dat.	modō	Lūciō	Dēlō	puerō	librō
Abl.	modō	Lūciō	Dēlō	puerō	librō

PLURAL				
Nom.	modī		puerī	librī
Voc.	modī		puerī	librī
Acc.	modōs		puerōs	librōs
Gen.	modōrum		puerōrum	librōrum
Dat.	modīs		puerīs	librīs
Abl.	modīs		puerīs	librīs

SING	
Nom.	dōnum
Voc.	dōnum
Acc.	dōnum
Gen.	dōnī
Dat.	dōnō
Abl.	dōnō

PLURAL	
Nom.	dōna
Voc.	dōna
Acc.	dōna
Gen.	dōnōrum
Dat.	dōnīs
Abl.	dōnīs

3rd Declension

Group I: *Vowel stems, with gen pl in* **-ium**

	m and f		*nt*	
SING				
Nom.	clādēs	nāvis	rēte	animal
Voc.	clādēs	nāvis	rēte	animal
Acc.	clādem	nāvem, -im	rēte	animal
Gen.	clādis	nāvis	rētis	animālīs
Dat.	clādī	nāvī	rētī	animālī
Abl.	clāde	nāve, -ī	rētī	animālī
PLURAL				
Nom.	clādēs	nāvēs	rētia	animālia
Voc.	clādēs	nāvēs	rētia	animālia
Acc.	clādēs, -īs	nāvēs, -īs	rētia	animālia
Gen.	clādium	nāvium	rētium	animālium
Dat.	clādibus	nāvibus	rētibus	animālibus
Abl.	clādibus	nāvibus	rētibus	animālibus

Group II: *Consonant stems, some with gen pl in* **-ium**, *some in* **-um** *and some in either. Monosyllabic nouns ending in two consonants (e.g.* **urbs** *below) regularly have* **-ium**.

	m and f			*f*	*nt*
SING					
Nom.	urbs	amāns	laus	aetās	os
Voc.	urbs	amāns	laus	aetās	os
Acc.	urbem	amantem	laudem	aetātem	os
Gen.	urbis	amantis	laudis	aetātis	ossis
Dat.	urbī	amantī	laudī	aetātī	ossī
Abl.	urbe	amante	laude	aetāte	osse
PLURAL					
Nom.	urbēs	amantēs	laudēs	aetātēs	ossa
Voc.	urbēs	amantēs	laudēs	aetātēs	ossa

Acc.	urbēs	amantēs	laudēs	aetātēs	ossa
Gen.	urbium	amantium, -um	laudum, -ium	aetātum, -ium	ossium
Dat.	urbibus	amantibus	laudibus	aetātibus	ossibus
Abl.	urbibus	amantibus	laudibus	aetātibus	ossibus

Group III: *Consonant stems, with gen pl in* -um

	m and f			*nt*	
SING					
Nom.	mōs	ratiō	pater	nōmen	opus
Voc.	mōs	ratiō	pater	nōmen	opus
Acc.	mōrem	ratiōnem	patrem	nōmen	opus
Gen.	mōris	ratiōnis	patris	nōminis	operis
Dat.	mōrī	ratiōnī	patrī	nōminī	operī
Abl.	mōre	ratiōne	patre	nōmine	opere
PLURAL					
Nom.	mōrēs	ratiōnēs	patrēs	nōmina	opera
Voc.	mōrēs	ratiōnēs	patrēs	nōmina	opera
Acc.	mōrēs	ratiōnēs	patrēs	nōmina	opera
Gen.	mōrum	ratiōnum	patrum	nōminum	operum
Dat.	mōribus	ratiōnibus	patribus	nōminibus	operibus
Abl.	mōribus	ratiōnibus	patribus	nōminibus	operibus

Group IV: *Greek nouns*

	m			*f*	*nt*
SING					
Nom.	āēr	hērōs	Periclēs	Naias	poēma
Voc.	āēr	hērōs	Periclē	Naias	poēma
Acc.	āera	hērōa	Periclem, Periclea	Naiada	poēma
Gen.	āeris	hērōis	Periclis, -ī	Naiadis, -os	poēmatis
Dat.	āerī	hērōī	Periclī	Naiadī	poēmatī
Abl.	āere	hērōe	Periclē	Naiade	poēmate
PLURAL					
Nom.	āeres	hērōes		Naiades	poēmata
Voc.	āeres	hērōes		Naiades	poēmata
Acc.	āeras	hērōas		Naiadas	poēmata
Gen.	āerum	hērōum		Naiadum	poēmatōrum
Dat.	āeribus	hērōibus		Naiadibus	poēmatīs
Abl.	āeribus	hērōibus		Naiadibus	poēmatīs

	4th Declension		**5th Declension**	
	mainly m	*nt*	*mainly f*	
SING				
Nom.	portus	genū	diēs	rēs
Voc.	portus	genū	diēs	rēs
Acc.	portum	genū	diem	rem
Gen.	portūs	genūs	diēī	reī
Dat.	portuī	genū	diēī	reī
Abl.	portū	genū	diē	rē
PLURAL				
Nom.	portūs	genua	diēs	rēs
Voc.	portūs	genua	diēs	rēs
Acc.	portūs	genua	diēs	rēs
Gen.	portuum	genuum	diērum	rērum
Dat.	portibus, -ubus	genibus, -ubus	diēbus	rēbus
Abl.	portibus, -ubus	genibus, -ubus	diēbus	rēbus

CONJUGATIONS OF VERBS

ACTIVE

PRESENT TENSE

	First **parāre** *prepare*	Second **habēre** *have*	Third **sūmere** *take*	Fourth **audīre** *hear*
Indicative				
SING				
1st pers	parō	habeō	sūmō	audiō
2nd pers	parās	habēs	sūmis	audīs
3rd pers	parat	habet	sūmit	audit
PLURAL				
1st pers	parāmus	habēmus	sūmimus	audīmus
2nd pers	parātis	habētis	sūmitis	audītīs
3rd pers	parant	habent	sūmunt	audiunt
Subjunctive				
SING				
1st pers	parem	habeam	sūmam	audiam
2nd pers	parēs	habeās	sūmās	audiās
3rd pers	paret	habeat	sūmat	audiat
PLURAL				
1st pers	parēmus	habeāmus	sūmāmus	audiāmus
2nd pers	parētis	habeātis	sūmātis	audiātis
3rd pers	parent	habeant	sūmant	audiant

IMPERFECT TENSE
Indicative

SING

1st pers	parābam	habēbam	sūmēbam	audiēbam
2nd pers	parābās	habēbās	sūmēbās	audiēbās
3rd pers	parābat	habēbat	sūmēbat	audiēbat

PLURAL

1st pers	parābāmus	habēbāmus	sūmēbāmus	audiēbāmus
2nd pers	parābātis	habēbātis	sūmēbātis	audiēbātis
3rd pers	parābant	habēbant	sūmēbant	audiēbant

Subjunctive

SING

1st pers	parārem	habērem	sūmerem	audīrem
2nd pers	parārēs	habērēs	sūmerēs	audīrēs
3rd pers	parāret	habēret	sūmeret	audīret

PLURAL

1st pers	parārēmus	habērēmus	sūmerēmus	audīrēmus
2nd pers	parārētis	habērētis	sūmerētis	audīrētis
3rd pers	parārent	habērent	sūmerent	audīrent

FUTURE TENSE
Indicative

SING

1st pers	parābō	habēbō	sūmam	audiam
2nd pers	parābis	habēbis	sūmēs	audiēs
3rd pers	parābit	habēbit	sūmet	audiet

PLURAL

1st pers	parābimus	habēbimus	sūmēmus	audiēmus
2nd pers	parābitis	habēbitis	sūmētis	audiētis
3rd pers	parābunt	habēbunt	sūment	audient

Subjunctive

SING

parātūrus, -a, -um	sim	*or*	essem
habitūrus, -a, -um	sīs		essēs
sūmptūrus, -a, -um	sit		esset
audītūrus, -a, -um			

PLURAL

parātūrī, -ae, -a	simus	*or*	essēmus
habitūrī, -ae, -a	sītis		essētis
sūmptūrī, -ae, -a	sint		essent
audītūrī, -ae, -a			

PERFECT TENSE
Indicative

SING
1st pers	parāvī	habuī	sūmpsī	audīvī
2nd pers	parāvistī	habuistī	sūmpsistī	audīvistī
3rd pers	parāvit	habuit	sūmpsit	audīvit

PLURAL
1st pers	parāvimus	habuimus	sūmpsimus	audīvimus
2nd pers	parāvistis	habuistis	sūmpsistis	audīvistis
3rd pers	parāvērunt, -e	habuērunt, -e	sūmpsērunt, -e	audīvērunt, -e

Subjunctive

SING
1st pers	parāverim	habuerim	sūmpserim	audīverim
2nd pers	parāveris	habueris	sūmpseris	audīveris
3rd pers	parāverit	habuerit	sūmpserit	audīverit

PLURAL
1st pers	parāverimus	habuerimus	sūmpserimus	audīverimus
2nd pers	parāveritis	habueritis	sūmpseritis	audīveritis
3rd pers	parāverint	habuerint	sūmpserint	audīverint

PLUPERFECT TENSE
Indicative

SING
1st pers	parāveram	habueram	sūmpseram	audīveram
2nd pers	parāverās	habuerās	sūmpserās	audīverās
3rd pers	parāverat	habuerat	sūmpserat	audīverat

PLURAL
1st pers	parāverāmus	habuerāmus	sūmpserāmus	audīverāmus
2nd pers	parāverātis	habuerātis	sūmpserātis	audīverātis
3rd pers	parāverant	habuerant	sūmpserant	audīverant

Subjunctive

SING
1st pers	parāvissem	habuissem	sūmpsissem	audīvissem
2nd pers	parāvissēs	habuissēs	sūmpsissēs	audīvissēs
3rd pers	parāvisset	habuisset	sūmpsisset	audīvisset

PLURAL
1st pers	parāvissēmus	habuissēmus	sūmpsissēmus	audīvissēmus
2nd pers	parāvissētis	habuissētis	sūmpsissētis	audīvissētis
3rd pers	parāvissent	habuissent	sūmpsissent	audīvissent

FUTURE PERFECT TENSE
Indicative

SING				
1st pers	parāverō	habuerō	sūmpserō	audīverō
2nd pers	parāveris	habueris	sūmpseris	audīveris
3rd pers	parāverit	habuerit	sūmpserit	audīverit
PLURAL				
1st pers	parāverimus	habuerimus	sūmpserimus	audīverimus
2nd pers	parāveritis	habueritis	sūmpseritis	audīveritis
3rd pers	parāverint	habuerint	sūmpserint	audīverint

IMPERATIVE
Present

SING	parā	habē	sūme	audī
PLURAL	parāte	habēte	sūmite	audīte

Future

SING				
2nd pers	parātō	habētō	sūmitō	audītō
3rd pers	parātō	habētō	sūmitō	audītō
PLURAL				
2nd pers	parātōte	habētōte	sūmitōte	audītōte
3rd pers	parantō	habentō	sūmuntō	audiuntō

INFINITIVE
Present

parāre	habēre	sūmere	audīre

Perfect

parāvisse	habuisse	sūmpsisse	audīvisse

Future

parātūrus,	-a, -um, esse
habitūrus,	-a, -um, esse
sūmptūrus,	-a, -um, esse
audītūrus,	-a, -um, esse

PASSIVE

PRESENT TENSE
Indicative

SING
1st pers	paror	habeor	sūmor	audior
2nd pers	parāris	habēris	sūmeris	audīris
3rd pers	parātur	habētur	sūmitur	audītur

PLURAL
1st pers	parāmur	habēmur	sūmimur	audīmur
2nd pers	parāminī	habēminī	sūmiminī	audīminī
3rd pers	parantur	habentur	sūmuntur	audiuntur

Subjunctive

SING
1st pers	parer	habear	sūmar	audiar
2nd pers	parēris	habeāris	sūmāris	audiāris
3rd pers	parētur	habeātur	sūmātur	audiātur

PLURAL
1st pers	parēmur	habeāmur	sūmāmur	audiāmur
2nd pers	parēminī	habeāminī	sūmāminī	audiāminī
3rd pers	parentur	habeantur	sūmantur	audiantur

IMPERFECT TENSE
Indicative

SING
1st pers	parābar	habēbar	sūmēbar	audiēbar
2nd pers	parābāris	habēbāris	sūmēbāris	audiēbāris
3rd pers	parābātur	habēbātur	sūmēbātur	audiēbātur

PLURAL
1st pers	parābāmur	habēbāmur	sūmēbāmur	audiēbāmur
2nd pers	parābāmini	habēbāmini	sūmēbāminī	audiēbāminī
3rd pers	parābāntur	habēbantur	sūmēbantur	audiēbantur

Subjunctive

SING
1st pers	parārer	habērer	sūmerer	audīrer
2nd pers	parārēris	habērēris	sūmerēris	audīrēris
3rd pers	parārētur	habērētur	sūmerētur	audīrētur

1st pers	pararēmur	habērēmur	sūmerēmur	audīrēmur
2nd pers	pararēminī	habērēminī	sūmerēminī	audīrēminī
3rd pers	pararentur	habērentur	sūmerentur	audīrentur

FUTURE TENSE

Indicative

SING

1st pers	parābor	habēbor	sūmar	audiar
2nd pers	parāberis	habēberis	sūmēris	audiēris
3rd pers	parābitur	habēbitur	sūmētur	audiētur

PLURAL

1st pers	parābimur	habēbimur	sūmēmur	audiēmur
2nd pers	parābimini	habēbimini	sūmēminī	audiēminī
3rd pers	parābuntur	habēbuntur	sūmentur	audientur

PERFECT TENSE

Indicative

SING		PLURAL	
parātus, -a, -um	sum/es/est	parātī, -ae, -a	sumus/estis/sunt
habitus, -a, -um	sum/es/est	habītī, -ae, -a	sumus/estis/sunt
sūmptus, -a, -um	sum/es/est	sūmptī, -ae, -a	sumus/estis/sunt
audītus, -a, -um	sum/es/est	audītī, -ae, -a	sumus/estis/sunt

Subjunctive

SING		PLURAL	
parātus, -a, -um	sim/sīs/sit	parātī, -ae, -a	sīmus/sītis/sint
habitus, -a, -um	sim/sīs/sit	habītī, -ae, -a	sīmus/sītis/sint
sūmptus, -a, -um	sim/sīs/sit	sūmptī, -ae, -a	sīmus/sītis/sint
audītus, -a, -um	sim/sīs/sit	audītī, -ae, -a	sīmus/sītis/sint

PLUPERFECT TENSE

Indicative

SING		PLURAL	
parātus, -a, -um	eram/eras/erat	parātī, -ae, -a	eramus/eratis/erant
habitus, -a, -um	eram/eras/erat	habītī, -ae, -a	eramus/eratis/erant
sūmptus, -a, -um	eram/eras/erat	sūmptī, -ae, -a	eramus/eratis/erant
audītus, -a, -um	eram/eras/erat	audītī, -ae, -a	eramus/eratis/erant

Subjunctive

SING		PLURAL	
parātus, -a, -um	essem/essēs/esset	parātī, -ae, -a	essēmus/essētis/essent
habitus, -a, -um	essem/essēs/esset	habītī, -ae, -a	essēmus/essētis/essent
sūmptus, -a, -um	essem/essēs/esset	sūmptī, -ae, -a	essēmus/essētis/essent
audītus, -a, -um	essem/essēs/esset	audītī, -ae, -a	essēmus/essētis/essent

FUTURE PERFECT TENSE
Indicative

SING		PLURAL	
parātus, -a, -um	erō/eris/erit	parātī, -ae, -a	erimus/eritis/erunt
habitus, -a, -um	erō/eris/erit	habītī, -ae, -a	erimus/eritis/erunt
sūmptus, -a, -um	erō/eris/erit	sūmptī, -ae, -a	erimus/eritis/erunt
audītus, -a, -um	erō/eris/erit	audītī, -ae, -a	erimus/eritis/erunt

IMPERATIVE
Present

SING	parāre	habēre	sūmere	audīre
PLURAL	parāminī	habēminī	sūmiminī	audīminī

Future

SING				
2nd pers	parātor	habētor	sūmitor	audītor
3rd pers	parātor	habētor	sūmitor	audītor
PLURAL				
3rd pers	parantor	habentor	sūmuntor	audiuntor

INFINITIVE
Present

parārī	habērī	sūmī	audīrī

Perfect

parātus -a, -um, esse	habitus -a, -um, esse	sūmptus -a, -um, esse	audītus, -a, -um, esse

Future

parātum īrī	habitum īrī	sūmptum īrī	audītum īrī

VERBAL NOUNS AND ADJECTIVES

Present Participle Active

parāns	habēns	sūmēns	audiēns

Perfect Participle Passive

parātus	habitus	sūmptus	audītus

Future Participle Active

parātūrus	habitūrus	sūmptūrus	audītūrus

Gerund
(acc, gen, dat and abl)

parandum, -ī, -ō	habendum, -ī, -ō	sūmendum, -ī, -ō	audiendum, -ī, -ō

Gerundive

parandus	habendus	sūmendus	audiendus

Supines

1st	parātum	habitum	sūmptum	audītum
2nd	parātū	habitū	sūmptū	audītū

Note. *Some verbs of the 3rd conjugation have the present indicative ending in* -io; *e.g.* **capio,** *I capture.*

PRESENT TENSE

INDICATIVE

SUBJUNCTIVE

Active	Passive	Active	Passive
capio	capior	capiam	capiar
capis	caperis	capias	capiāris
capit	capitur	capiat	capiātur
capimus	capimur	capiāmus	capiāmur
capitis	capiminī	capiātis	capiāminī
capiunt	capiuntur	capiant	capiantur

IMPERFECT TENSE

capiēbam *etc.*	capiēbar *etc.*	caperem *etc.*	caperer *etc.*

FUTURE TENSE

INFINITIVE MOOD

capiam	capiar	Present Active	capere
capiēs *etc.*	capiēris *etc.*	Present Passive	capī

PRESENT IMPERATIVE

	Active		**Passive**
cape	capite	capere	capiminī

	PARTICIPLE	*GERUND*	*GERUNDIVE*
Pres.	capiēns	capiendum	capiendus, -a, um

In all other tenses and moods **capere** *is similar to* **sumere**.

IRREGULAR VERBS

	Esse *be*	**Posse** *be able*	**Velle** *wish*	**Ire** *go*
Present Indicative				
SING				
1st Pers	sum	possum	volō	eō
2nd Pers	es	potes	vīs	īs
3rd Pers	est	potest	vult, volt	it
PLURAL				
1st Pers	sumus	possumus	volumus	īmus
2nd Pers	estis	potestis	vultis, voltis	ītis
3rd Pers	sunt	possunt	volunt	eunt
Present Subjunctive				
SING				
1st Pers	sim	possim	velim	eam
2nd Pers	sīs	possīs	velīs	eās
3rd Pers	sit	possit	velit	eat
PLURAL				
1st Pers	sīmus	possīmus	velīmus	eāmus
2nd Pers	sītis	possītis	velītis	eātis
3rd Pers	sint	possint	velint	eant
Imperfect Indicative				
1st Pers	eram	poteram	volēbam	ībam
Imperfect Subjunctive				
1st Pers	essem	possem	vellem	īrem
Future Indicative				
1st Pers	erō	poterō	volam	ībō
Future Subjunctive				
1st Pers	futūrus, -a, -um sim *or* essem	—	—	itūrus, -a, -um sim *or* essem
Perfect Indicative				
1st Pers	fuī	potuī	voluī	īvī, iī
Perfect Subjunctive				
1st Pers	fuerim	potuerim	voluerim	īverim, ierim

Pluperfect Indicative

1st Pers	fueram	potueram	volueram	īveram, ieram

Pluperfect Subjunctive

1st Pers	fuissem	potuissem	voluissem	īvissem, iissem

Future Perfect Indicative

1st Pers	fuerō	potuerō	voluerō	īverō, ierō

Present Imperative

SING	es	—	—	ī
PLURAL	este	—	—	īte

Future Imperative

SING	estō	—	—	ītō
PLURAL	estōte	—	—	ītōte

Infinitives

PRES	esse	posse	velle	īre
PERF	fuisse	potuisse	voluisse	īvisse, iisse
FUT	futūrus, -a, -um, esse	—	—	itūrus, -a, -um, esse

Participles

PRES	—	—	—	iēns, euntis
FUT	futūrus	—	—	itūrus

Gerund and Supine

GERUND	—	—	—	eundum
SUPINE	—	—	—	itum

Latin-English

A, a

ā *prep (with abl)* from; after, since; by, in respect of; **ab epistulīs**, **ā manū** secretary; **ab hāc parte** on this side; **ab integrō** afresh; **ā nōbīs** on our side; **ā tergō** in the rear; **cōpiōsus ā frūmentō** rich in corn; **usque ab** ever since.

ā *interj* ah!

ab *prep see* **ā**.

abāctus *ppp of* **abigō**.

abacus, -ī *m* tray; sideboard; gaming board; panel; counting table.

abaliēnō, -āre, -āvī, -ātum *vt* to dispose of; to remove, estrange.

Abantiadēs *m* Acrisius *or* Perseus.

Abās, -antis *m a king of Argos*.

abavus, -ī *m* great-great-grandfather.

abbās, -ātis *m* abbot.

abbātia *f* abbey.

abbātissa *f* abbess.

Abdēra, -ōrum *or* **-ae** *ntpl or fs a town in Thrace*.

Abdērītānus *adj see n*.

Abdērītēs *m* Democritus *or* Protagoras.

abdicātiō, -ōnis *f* disowning, abdication.

abdicō, -āre, -āvī, -ātum *vt* to disown; to resign; **sē ~** abdicate.

abdīcō, -īcere, -īxī, -ictum *vt* (AUG) to be unfavourable to.

abditus *ppp of* **abdō**.

abdō, -ere, -idī, -itum *vt* to hide; to remove.

abdōmen, -inis *nt* paunch, belly; gluttony.

abdūcō, -ūcere, -ūxi, -uctum *vt* to lead away, take away; to seduce.

abductus *ppp of* **abdūcō**.

abecedārium, -iī *nt* alphabet.

abēgī *perf of* **abigō**.

abeō, -īre, -iī, -itum *vi* to go away, depart; to pass away; to be changed; to retire (*from an office*); **sīc ~** turn out like this.

abequitō, -āre, -āvī, -ātum *vi* to ride away.

aberrātiō, -ōnis *f* relief (*from trouble*).

aberrō, -āre, -āvī, -ātum *vi* to stray; to deviate; to have respite.

abfore *fut infin of* **absum**.

abfuī *perf of* **absum**.

abfutūrus *fut p of* **absum**.

abhinc *adv* since, ago.

abhorreō, -ēre, -uī *vi* to shrink from; to differ; to be inconsistent.

abiciō, -icere, -iēcī, -iectum *vt* to throw away, throw down; to abandon, degrade.

abiectus *ppp of* **abiciō** ♦ *adj* despondent; contemptible.

abiēgnus *adj* of fir.

abiēns, -euntis *pres p of* **abeō**.

abiēs, -etis *f* fir; ship.

abigō, -igere, -ēgī, -āctum *vt* to drive away.

abitus, -ūs *m* departure; exit.

abiūdicō, -āre, -āvī, -ātum *vt* to take away (*by judicial award*).

abiūnctus *ppp of* **abiungō**.

abiungō, -ungere, -ūnxī, -ūnctum *vt* to unyoke; to detach.

abiūrō, -āre, -āvī, -ātum *vt* to deny on oath.

ablātus *ppp of* **auferō**.

ablēgātiō, -ōnis *f* sending away.

ablēgō, -āre, -āvī, -ātum *vt* to send out of the way.

abligurriō, -īre, -īvī, -ītum *vt* to spend extravagantly.

ablocō, -āre, -āvī, -ātum *vt* to let (a house).

ablūdō, -dere, -sī, -sum *vi* to be unlike.

abluō, -uere, -uī, -ūtum *vt* to wash clean; to remove.

abnegō, -āre, -āvī, -ātum *vt* to refuse.

abnepōs, -ōtis *m* great-great-grandson.

abneptis *f* great-great-granddaughter.

abnoctō, -āre *vi* to stay out all night.

abnōrmis *adj* unorthodox.

abnuō, -uere, -uī, -ūtum *vt* to refuse; to deny.

aboleō, -ēre, -ēvī, -itum *vt* to abolish.

abolēscō, -ēscere, -ēvī *vi* to vanish.

abolitiō, -ōnis *f* cancelling.

abolla, -ae *f* greatcoat.

abōminātus *adj* accursed.

abōminor, -ārī, -ātus *vt* to deprecate; to detest.

Aborīginēs, -um *mpl* original inhabitants.

aborior, -īrī, -tus *vi* to miscarry.

abortiō, -ōnis *f* miscarriage.

abortīvus *adj* born prematurely.

abortus, -ūs *m* miscarriage.

abrādō, -dere, -sī, -sum *vt* to scrape off, shave.

abrāsus *ppp of* **abrādō**.

abreptus *ppp of* **abripiō**.

abripiō, -ipere, -ipuī, -eptum *vt* to drag away, carry off.

Noun declensions and verb conjugations are shown on pp xiii to xxv. The present infinitive ending of a verb shows to which conjugation it belongs: **-āre** = 1st; **-ēre** = 2nd; **-ere** = 3rd and **-īre** = 4th. Irregular verbs are shown on p xxvi

abrogātiō, -ōnis _f_ repeal.
abrogō, -āre, -āvī, -ātum _vt_ to annul.
abrotonum, -ī _nt_ southernwood.
abrumpō, -umpere, -ūpī, -uptum _vt_ to break off.
abruptus _ppp of_ **abrumpō** ♦ _adj_ steep; abrupt, disconnected.
abs _etc see_ **ā**.
abscēdō, -ēdere, -essi, -essum _vi_ to depart, withdraw; to cease.
abscīdō, -dere, -dī, -sum _vt_ to cut off.
abscindō, -ndere, -dī, -ssum _vt_ to tear off, cut off.
abscissus _ppp of_ **abscindō**.
abscīsus _ppp of_ **abscīdō** ♦ _adj_ steep; abrupt.
abscondō, -ere, -ī _and_ **idī, -itum** _vt_ to conceal; to leave behind.
absēns, -entis _pres p of_ **absum** ♦ _adj_ absent.
absentia, -ae _f_ absence.
absiliō, -īre, -iī _and_ **uī** _vi_ to spring away.
absimilis _adj_ unlike.
absinthium, -ī _and_ **iī** _nt_ wormwood.
absis, -īdis _f_ vault; (_ECCL_) chancel.
absistō, -istere, -titī _vi_ to come away; to desist.
absolūte _adv_ fully, unrestrictedly.
absolūtiō, -ōnis _f_ acquittal; perfection.
absolūtus _ppp of_ **absolvō** ♦ _adj_ complete; (_RHET_) unqualified.
absolvō, -vere, -vī, -ūtum _vt_ to release, set free; (_law_) to acquit; to bring to completion, finish off; to pay off, discharge.
absonus _adj_ unmusical; incongruous; **~ ab** not in keeping with.
absorbeō, -bēre, -buī, -ptum _vt_ to swallow up; to monopolize.
absp- _etc see_ **asp-**.
absque _prep_ (_with abl_) without, but for.
abstēmius _adj_ temperate.
abstergeō, -gēre, -sī, -sum _vt_ to wipe away; (_fig_) to banish.
absterreō, -ēre, -ui, -itum _vt_ to scare away, deter.
abstinēns, -entis _adj_ continent.
abstinenter _adv_ with restraint.
abstinentia, -ae _f_ restraint, self-control; fasting.
abstineō, -inēre, -inuī, -entum _vt_ to withhold, keep off ♦ _vi_ to abstain, refrain; **sē ~** refrain.
abstitī _perf of_ **absistō**.
abstō, -āre _vi_ to stand aloof.
abstractus _ppp of_ **abstrahō**.
abstrahō, -here, -xī, -ctum _vt_ to drag away, remove; to divert.
abstrūdō, -dere, -sī, -sum _vt_ to conceal.
abstrūsus _ppp of_ **abstrūdō** ♦ _adj_ deep, abstruse; reserved.
abstulī _perf of_ **auferō**.
absum, abesse, āfuī _vi_ to be away, absent, distant; to keep clear of; to be different; to be missing, fail to assist; **tantum abest ut** so far from; **haud multum āfuit quīn** I was (they

were _etc_) within an ace of.
absūmō, -ere, -psī, -ptum _vt_ to consume; to ruin, kill; (_time_) to spend.
absurdē _adv_ out of tune; absurdly.
absurdus _adj_ unmusical; senseless, absurd.
Absyrtus, -ī _m_ brother of Medea.
abundāns, -antis _adj_ overflowing; abundant; rich; abounding in.
abundanter _adv_ copiously.
abundantia, -ae _f_ abundance, plenty; wealth.
abundē _adv_ abundantly, more than enough.
abundō, -āre, -āvī, -ātum _vi_ to overflow; to abound, be rich in.
abūsiō, -ōnis _f_ (_RHET_) catachresis.
abusque _prep_ (_with abl_) all the way from.
abūtor, -tī, -sus _vi_ (_with abl_) to use up; to misuse.
Abydēnus _adj see n._
Abȳdos, Abȳdus, -ī _m_ a town on Dardanelles.
ac _etc see_ **atque**.
Acadēmia, -ae _f_ Plato's Academy at Athens; Plato's philosophy; Cicero's villa.
Acadēmica _ntpl_ Cicero's book on the Academic philosophy.
Acadēmus, -ī _m_ an Athenian hero.
acalanthis, -dis _f_ thistlefinch.
acanthus, -ī _m_ bear's-breech.
Acarnānes, -um _mpl_ the Acarnanians.
Acarnānia, -iae _f_ a district of N.W. Greece.
Acarnānicus _adj see n._
Acca Larentia, -ae, -ae _f_ Roman goddess.
accēdō, -ēdere, -essī, -essum _vi_ to come, go to, approach; to attack; to be added; to agree with; (_duty_) to take up; **ad rem pūblicam ~** to enter politics; **prope ~ ad** to resemble; **~ēdit quod, hūc ~ēdit ut** moreover.
accelerō, -āre, -āvī, -ātum _vt, vi_ to hasten.
accendō, -endere, -endī, -ēnsum _vt_ to set on fire, light; to illuminate; (_fig_) to inflame, incite.
accēnseō, -ēre, -uī, -um _vt_ to assign.
accēnsī _mpl_ (_MIL_) supernumeraries.
accēnsus _ppp of_ **accendō** _and_ **accēnseō**.
accēnsus, -ī _m_ officer attending a magistrate.
accentus, -ūs _m_ accent.
accēpī _perf of_ **accipiō**.
acceptiō, -ōnis _f_ receiving.
acceptum _nt_ credit side (of ledger); **in ~ referre** place to one's credit.
acceptus _ppp of_ **accipiō** ♦ _adj_ acceptable.
accersō _etc see_ **accessō**.
accessiō, -ōnis _f_ coming, visiting; attack; increase, addition.
accessus, -ūs _m_ approach, visit; flood tide; admittance, entrance.
Acciānus _adj see_ **Accius**.
accīdō, -dere, -dī, -sum _vt_ to fell, cut into; to eat up, impair.
accidō, -ere, -ī _vi_ to fall (at, on); (_senses_) to strike; (_usu misfortune_) to befall, happen.
accingō, -gere, -xī, -ctum _vt_ to gird on, arm; (_fig_) to make ready.
acciō, -īre, -īvī, -ītum _vt_ to summon; to

procure.

accipiō, -ipere, -ēpī, -eptum *vt* to take, receive, accept; (*guest*) to treat; (*information*) to hear; to interpret, take as; to suffer; to approve.

accipiter, -ris *m* hawk.

accīsus *ppp of* **accīdō.**

accītus *ppp of* **acciō.**

accītus, -ūs *m* summons.

Accius, -ī *m Roman tragic poet.*

acclāmātiō, -ōnis *f* shout (*of approval or disapproval*).

acclāmō, -āre, -āvī, -ātum *vi* to cry out against; to hail.

acclārō, -āre, -āvī, -ātum *vt* to make known.

acclīnātus *adj* sloping.

acclīnis *adj* leaning against; inclined.

acclīnō, -āre, -āvī, -ātum *vt* to lean against; **sē ~ incline** towards.

acclīvis *adj* uphill.

acclīvitās, -ātis *f* gradient.

accola, -ae *m* neighbour.

accolō, -olere, -oluī, -ultum *vt* to live near.

accommodātē *adv* suitably.

accommodātiō, -ōnis *f* fitting together; compliance.

accommodātus *adj* suited.

accommodō, -āre, -āvī, -ātum *vt* to fit, put on; to adjust, adapt, bring to; to apply; **sē ~** devote oneself.

accommodus *adj* suitable.

accrēdō, -ere, -idī, -itum *vi* to believe.

accrēscō, -ēscere, -ēvī, -ētum *vi* to increase, be added.

accrētiō, -ōnis *f* increasing.

accubitiō, -ōnis *f* reclining (*at meals*).

accubō, -āre *vi* to lie near; to recline (*at meals*).

accumbō, -mbere, -buī, -bitum *vi* to recline at table; **in sinū ~** sit next to.

accumulātē *adv* copiously.

accumulō, -āre, -āvī, -ātum *vt* to pile up, amass; to load.

accūrātē *adv* painstakingly.

accūrātiō, -ōnis *f* exactness.

accūrātus *adj* studied.

accūrō, -āre, -āvī, -ātum *vt* to attend to.

accurrō, -rrere, -currī *and* **rrī, -rsum** *vi* to hurry to.

accursus, -ūs *m* hurrying.

accūsābilis *adj* reprehensible.

accūsātiō, -ōnis *f* accusation.

accūsātor, -ōris *m* accuser, prosecutor.

accūsātōriē *adv* like an accuser.

accūsātōrius *adj* of the accuser.

accūsō, -āre, -āvī, -ātum *vt* to accuse, prosecute; to reproach; **ambitūs ~** prosecute for bribery.

acer, -is *nt* maple.

ācer, -ris *adj* sharp; (*sensation*) keen, pungent;

(*emotion*) violent; (*mind*) shrewd; (*conduct*) eager, brave; hasty, fierce; (*circumstances*) severe.

acerbē *adv see* **acerbus.**

acerbitās, -ātis *f* bitterness; (*fig*) harshness, severity; sorrow.

acerbō, -āre, -āvī, -ātum *vt* to aggravate.

acerbus *adj* bitter, sour; harsh; (*fig*) premature; (*person*) rough, morose, violent; (*things*) troublesome, sad.

acernus *adj* of maple.

acerra, -ae *f* incense box.

acervātim *adv* in heaps.

acervō, -āre, -āvī, -ātum *vt* to pile up.

acervus, -ī *m* heap.

acēscō, -ere, acuī *vt* to turn sour.

Acestēs, -ae *m a mythical Sicilian.*

acētum, -ī *nt* vinegar; (*fig*) wit.

Achaemenēs, -is *m first Persian king; type of Oriental wealth.*

Achaeus *adj* Greek.

Achāia, -ae *f a district in W. Greece; Greece; Roman province.*

Achāicus *adj see n.*

Achātēs, -ae *m companion of Aeneas.*

Achelōius *adj see n.*

Achelōus, -ī *m river in N.W. Greece; river god.*

Acherōn, -ontis *m river in Hades.*

Acherūsius *adj see* **Acherōn.**

Achillēs, -is *m Greek epic hero.*

Achillēus *adj see n.*

Achīvus *adj* Greek.

Acidālia, -ae *f* Venus.

Acidālius *adj see n.*

acidus *adj* sour, tart; (*fig*) disagreeable.

aciēs, -ēī *f* sharp edge or point; (*eye*) sight, keen glance, pupil; (*mind*) power, apprehension; (*MIL*) line of troops, battle order, army, battle; (*fig*) debate; **prīma ~** van; **novissima ~** rearguard.

acīnacēs, -is *m* scimitar.

acinum, -ī *nt* berry, grape; fruit seed.

acinus, -ī *m* berry, grape; fruit seed.

acipēnser, -eris *m* sturgeon.

acipēnsis, -is *m* sturgeon.

aclys, -dis *f* javelin.

aconītum, -ī *nt* monkshood; poison.

acor, -ōris *m* sour taste.

acquiēscō, -ēscere, -ēvī, -ētum *vi* to rest, die; to find pleasure (in); to acquiesce.

acquīrō, -rere, -sīvī, -sītum *vt* to get in addition, acquire.

Acragās, -antis *m see* **Agrigentum.**

acrātophorum, -ī *nt* wine jar.

acrēdula, -ae *f* a bird (*unidentified*).

ācriculus *adj* peevish.

ācrimōnia, -ae *f* pungent taste; (*speech, action*) briskness, go.

Acrisiōniadēs, -ae *m* Perseus.

Acrisius, -ī *m father of Danae.*

Noun declensions and verb conjugations are shown on pp xiii to xxv. The present infinitive ending of a verb shows to which conjugation it belongs: **-āre** = 1st; **-ēre** = 2nd; **-ere** = 3rd and **-īre** = 4th. Irregular verbs are shown on p xxvi

ācriter _adv see_ **ācer.**

ācroāma, -tis _nt_ entertainment, entertainer.

ācroāsis, -is _f_ public lecture.

Ācroceraunia, -ōrum _ntpl_ a promontory in N.W. Greece.

Ācrocorinthus, -ī _f_ fortress of Corinth.

acta, -ae _f_ beach.

ācta, -ōrum _ntpl_ public records, proceedings; ~ **diurna,** ~ **pūblica** daily gazette.

Actaeus _adj_ Athenian.

āctiō, -ōnis _f_ action, doing; official duties, negotiations; (_law_) action, suit, indictment, pleading, case, trial; (_RHET_) delivery; (_drama_) plot; ~ **grātiārum** expression of thanks; ~**ōnem intendere, īnstituere** bring an action.

āctitō, -āre, -āvī, -ātum _vt_ to plead, act often.

Actium, -ī _and_ **iī** _nt_ a town in N.W. Greece; Augustus's great victory.

Actius -iacus _adj see n._

āctivus _adj_ of action, practical.

āctor, -ōris _m_ driver, performer; (_law_) plaintiff, pleader; (_COMM_) agent; (_RHET_) orator; (_drama_) actor; ~ **pūblicus** manager of public property; ~ **summārum** cashier.

āctuāria _f_ pinnace.

āctuāriolum, -ī _m_ small barge.

āctuārius _adj_ fast (ship).

āctuōsē _adv_ actively.

āctuōsus _adj_ very active.

āctus _ppp of_ **agō.**

āctus, -ūs _m_ moving, driving; right of way for cattle _or_ vehicles; performance; (_drama_) playing a part, recital, act of a play.

āctūtum _adv_ immediately.

acuī _perf of_ **acēscō;** _perf of_ **acuō.**

acula, -ae _f_ small stream.

aculeātus _adj_ prickly; (_words_) stinging; quibbling.

aculeus, -ī _m_ sting, prickle barb; (_fig_) sting.

acūmen, -inis _nt_ point, sting; (_fig_) shrewdness, ingenuity; trickery.

acuō, -uere, -uī, -ūtum _vt_ to sharpen; to exercise; (_the mind_) to stimulate; to rouse (to action).

acus, -ūs _f_ needle, pin; **acū pingere** embroider; **rem acū tangere** ≈ _hit the nail on the head._

acūtē _adv see_ **acūtus.**

acūtulus _adj_ rather subtle.

acūtus _adj_ sharp, pointed; (_senses_) keen; (_sound_) high-pitched; severe; intelligent.

ad _prep_ (_with acc_) to, towards, against; near, at; until; (_num_) about; with regard to, according to; for the purpose of, for; compared with; besides; **ad Castoris** to the temple of Castor; **ad dextram** on the right; **ad hōc** besides; **ad locum** on the spot; **ad manum** at hand; **ad rem** to the point; **ad summam** in short; **ad tempus** in time; **ad ūnum omnes** all without exception; **ad urbem esse** wait outside the city gates; **ad verbum** literally; **nīl ad** nothing to do with; **usque ad** right up to.

adāctiō, -ōnis _f_ enforcing.

adāctus _ppp of_ **adigō.**

adāctus, -ūs _m_ snapping (_of teeth_).

adaequē _adv_ equally.

adaequō, -āre, -āvī, -ātum _vt_ to make equal, level; to equal, match ♦ _vi_ to be equal.

adamantēus, adamantinus _adj see_ **adamās.**

adamās, -antis _m_ adamant, steel; diamond.

adamō, -āre, -āvī, -ātum _vt_ to fall in love with.

adaperiō, -īre, -uī, -tum _vt_ to throw open.

adapertilis _adj_ openable.

adaquō, -āre, -āvī, -ātum _vt_ (_plants, animals_) to water.

adaquor _vi_ to fetch water.

adauctus, -ūs _m_ growing.

adaugeō, -gēre, -xī, -ctum _vt_ to aggravate; (_sacrifice_) to consecrate.

adaugēscō, -ere _vi_ to grow bigger.

adbibō, -ere, -ī _vt_ to drink; (_fig_) to drink in.

adbītō, -ere _vi_ to come near.

adc- _etc see_ **acc-.**

addecet, -ēre _vt_ it becomes.

addēnseō, -ēre _vt_ to close (ranks).

addīcō, -īcere, -īxī, -ictum _vi_ (_AUG_) to be favourable ♦ _vt_ (_law_) to award; (_auction_) to knock down; (_fig_) to sacrifice, devote.

addictiō, -ōnis _f_ award (_at law_).

addictus _ppp of_ **addīcō** ♦ _m_ bondsman.

addiscō, -scere, -dicī _vt_ to learn more.

additāmentum, -ī _nt_ increase.

additus _ppp of_ **addō.**

addō, -ere, -idī, -itum _vt_ to add, put to, bring to; to impart; to increase; ~ **gradum** quicken pace; ~**e quod** besides.

addoceō, -ēre, -uī, -tum _vt_ to teach new.

addubitō, -āre, -āvī, -ātum _vi_ to be in doubt ♦ _vt_ to question.

addūcō, -ūcere, -ūxī, -uctum _vt_ to take, bring to; to draw together, pull taut, wrinkle; (_fig_) to induce; (_pass_) to be led to believe.

adductus _ppp of_ **addūcō** ♦ _adj_ contracted; (_fig_) severe.

adedō, -edere, -ēdī, -ēsum _vt_ to begin to eat; to eat up; to use up; to wear away.

adēmī _perf of_ **adimō.**

ademptiō, -ōnis _f_ taking away.

ademptus _ppp of_ **adimō.**

adeō, -īre, -iī, -itum _vt, vi_ to go to, approach; to address; to undertake, submit to, enter upon.

adeō _adv_ so; (_after pron_) just; (_after conj, adv, adj: for emphasis_) indeed, very; (_adding an explanation_) for, in fact, thus; or rather; ~ **nōn ... ut** so far from; **atque** ~, **sīve** ~ or rather; **usque** ~ so far, so long, so much.

adeps, -ipis _m/f_ fat; corpulence.

adeptiō, -ōnis _f_ attainment.

adeptus _ppa of_ **adipīscor.**

adequitō, -āre, -āvī, -ātum _vi_ to ride up (to).

adesdum come here!

adesse _infin of_ **adsum.**

adēsus _ppp of_ **adedō.**

adfābilis *adj* easy to talk to.
adfābilitās, -ātis *f* courtesy.
adfabrē *adv* ingeniously.
adfatim *adv* to one's satisfaction, enough, ad nauseam.
adfātur, -rī, -tus *vt* (*defec*) to speak to.
adfātus *ppa of* **adfātur.**
adfātus, -ūs *m* speaking to.
adfectātiō, -ōnis *f* aspiring; (*RHET*) affectation.
adfectātus *adj* (*RHET*) studied.
adfectiō, -ōnis *f* frame of mind, mood; disposition; goodwill; (*ASTRO*) relative position.
adfectō, -āre, -āvī, -ātum *vt* to aspire to, aim at; to try to win over; to make pretence of; **viam ~ ad** try to get to.
adfectus *ppp of* **adficiō ♦** *adj* affected with, experienced (*abl*); (*person*) disposed; (*things*) weakened; (*undertakings*) well-advanced.
adfectus, -ūs *m* disposition, mood; fondness; (*pl*) loved ones.
adferō, adferre, attulī, adlātum *and* **allātum** *vt* to bring, carry to; to bring to bear, use against; to bring news; (*explanation*) to bring forward; to contribute (*something useful*).
adficiō, -icere, -ēcī, -ectum *vt* to affect; to endow, afflict with (*abl*); **exsiliō ~** banish; **honōre ~** honour; *also used with other nouns to express the corresponding verbs.*
adfictus *ppp of* **adfingō.**
adfīgō, -gere, -xī, -xum *vt* to fasten, attach; to impress (*on the mind*).
adfingō, -ngere, -nxī, -ctum *vt* to make, form (*as part of*); to invent.
adfīnis, -is *m/f* neighbour; relation (*by marriage*) **♦** *adj* neighbouring; associated with (*dat or gen*).
adfīnitās, -ātis *f* relationship (*by marriage*).
adfirmātē *adv* with assurance.
adfirmātiō, -ōnis *f* declaration.
adfirmō, -āre, -āvī, -ātum *vt* to declare; to confirm.
adfīxus *ppp of* **adfīgō.**
adflātus, -ūs *m* breath, exhalation; (*fig*) inspiration.
adfleō, -ēre *vi* to weep (at).
adflīctātiō, -ōnis *f* suffering.
adflīctō, -āre, -āvī, -ātum *vt* to harass, distress.
adflīctor, -ōris *m* destroyer.
adflīctus *ppp of* **adflīgō ♦** *adj* distressed, ruined; dejected; depraved.
adflīgō, -īgere, -īxī, -īctum *vt* to dash against, throw down; (*fig*) to impair, crush.
adflō, -āre, -āvī, -ātum *vt, vi* to blow on, breathe upon.
adfluēns, -entis *adj* rich (in).
adfluenter *adv* copiously.

adfluentia, -ae *f* abundance.
adfluō, -ere, -xī, -xum *vi* to flow; (*fig*) to flock in, abound in.
adfore *fut infin of* **adsum.**
adforem *imperf subj of* **adsum.**
adfuī *perf of* **adsum.**
adfulgeō, -gēre, -sī *vi* to shine on; to appear.
adfundō, -undere, -ūdī, -ūsum *vt* to pour in; to rush (troops) in.
adfūsus *adj* prostrate.
adfutūrus *fut p of* **adsum.**
adgemō, -ere *vi* to groan at.
adglomerō, -āre *vt* to add on.
adglūtinō, -āre *vt* to stick on.
adgravēscō, -ere *vi* to become worse.
adgravō, -āre, -āvī, -ātum *vt* to aggravate.
adgredior, -dī, -ssus *vt* to approach, accost; to attack; (*a task*) to undertake, take up.
adgregō, -āre, -āvī, -ātum *vt* to add, attach.
adgressiō, -ōnis *f* introductory remarks.
adgressus *ppa of* **adgredior.**
adhaereō, -rēre, -sī, -sum *vi* to stick to; (*fig*) to cling to, keep close to.
adhaerēscō, -ere *vi* to stick to *or* in; (*speech*) to falter.
adhaesiō, -ōnis *f* clinging.
adhaesus, -ūs *m* adhering.
adhibeō, -ēre, -uī, -itum *vt* to bring, put, add; to summon, consult, treat; to use, apply (*for some purpose*).
adhinniō, -īre, -īvī, -ītum *vi* to neigh to; (*fig*) to go into raptures over.
adhortātiō, -ōnis *f* exhortation.
adhortātor, -ōris *m* encourager.
adhortor, -ārī, -ātus *vt* to encourage, urge.
adhūc *adv* so far; as yet, till now; still **~ nōn** not yet.
adiaceō, -ēre, -uī *vi* to lie near, border on.
adiciō, -icere, -iēcī, -iectum *vt* to throw to; to add; to turn (mind, eyes) towards.
adiectiō, -ōnis *f* addition.
adiectus *ppp of* **adiciō.**
adiectus, -ūs *m* bringing close.
adigō, -igere, -ēgī, -āctum *vt* to drive (to); to compel; **iūs iūrandum ~** put on oath; **in verba ~** force to owe allegiance.
adimō, -imere, -ēmī, -emptum *vt* to take away (from *dat*).
adipātum *nt* pastry.
adipātus *adj* fatty; (*fig*) florid.
adipīscor, -ipīscī, -eptus *vt* to overtake; to attain, acquire.
aditus, -ūs *m* approach, access (*to a person*); entrance; (*fig*) avenue.
adiūdicō, -āre, -āvī, -ātum *vt* to award (*in arbitration*); to ascribe.
adiūmentum, -ī *nt* aid, means of support.
adiūncta *ntpl* collateral circumstances.
adiūnctiō, -ōnis *f* uniting; addition; (*RHET*) proviso; repetition.

Noun declensions and verb conjugations are shown on pp xiii to xxv. The present infinitive ending of a verb shows to which conjugation it belongs: **-āre** = 1st; **-ēre** = 2nd; **-ere** = 3rd and **-īre** = 4th. Irregular verbs are shown on p xxvi

adiūnctus *ppp of* **adiungō** ♦ *adj* connected.

adiungō, -ungere, -ūnxī, -ūnctum *vt* to yoke; to attach; (*suspicion etc*) to direct; (*remark*) to add.

adiūrō, -āre, -āvī, -ātum *vt, vi* to swear, swear by.

adiūtō, -āre, -āvī, -ātum *vt* to help.

adiūtor, -ōris *m* helper; (*MIL*) adjutant; (*POL*) official; (*THEAT*) supporting cast.

adiūtrīx, -rīcis *f see* **adiūtor**.

adiūtus *ppp of* **adiuvō**.

adiuvō, -uvāre, -ūvī, -ūtum *vt* to help; to encourage.

adj- *etc see* **adi-**.

adlābor, -bī, -psus *vi* to fall, move towards, come to.

adlabōrō, -āre, -āvī, -ātum *vi* to work hard; to improve by taking trouble.

adlacrimō, -āre, -āvī, -ātum *vi* to shed tears.

adlāpsus *ppa of* **adlābor**.

adlāpsus, -ūs *m* stealthy approach.

adlātrō, -āre, -āvī, -ātum *vt* to bark at; (*fig*) to revile.

adlātus *ppp of* **adferō**.

adlaudō, -āre, -āvī, -ātum *vt* to praise highly.

adlectō, -āre, -āvī, -ātum *vt* to entice.

adlēctus *ppp of* **adlegō**.

adlectus *ppp of* **adliciō**.

adlēgātī *mpl* deputies.

adlēgātiō, -ōnis *f* mission.

adlēgō, -āre, -āvī, -ātum *vt* to despatch, commission; to mention.

adlegō, -egere, -ēgī, -ēctum *vt* to elect.

adlevāmentum, -ī *nt* relief.

adlevātiō, -ōnis *f* easing.

adlevō, -āre, -āvī, -ātum *vt* to lift up; to comfort; to weaken.

adliciō, -icere, -exī, -ectum *vt* to attract.

adlīdō, -dere, -sī, -sum *vt* to dash (against); (*fig*) to hurt.

adligō, -āre, -āvī, -ātum *vt* to tie up, bandage; (*fig*) to bind, lay under an obligation.

adlinō, -inere, -ēvī, -itum *vt* to smear; (*fig*) to attach.

adlīsus *ppp of* **adlīdō**.

adlocūtiō, -ōnis *f* address; comforting words.

adlocūtus *ppa of* **adloquor**.

adloquium, -ī *and* **iī** *nt* talk; encouragement.

adloquor, -quī, -cūtus *vt* to speak to, address.

adlūdiō, -āre, -āvī, -ātum *vi* to play (with).

adlūdō, -dere, -sī, -sum *vi* to joke, play.

adluō, -ere, -ī *vt* to wash.

adluviēs, -ēī *f* pool left by flood water.

adluviō, -ōnis *f* alluvial land.

admātūrō, -āre, -āvī, -atum *vt* to hurry on.

admētior, -tīrī, -nsus *vt* to measure out.

adminiculor, -ārī, -ātus *vt* to prop.

adminiculum, -ī *nt* (*AGR*) stake; (*fig*) support.

administer, -rī *m* assistant.

administrātiō, -ōnis *f* services; management.

administrātor, -ōris *m* manager.

administrō, -āre, -āvī, -ātum *vt* to manage, govern.

admīrābilis *adj* wonderful, surprising.

admīrābilitās, -ātis *f* wonderfulness.

admīrābiliter *adv* admirably; paradoxically.

admīrātiō, -ōnis *f* wonder, surprise, admiration.

admīror, -ārī, -ātus *vt* to wonder at, admire; to be surprised at.

admisceō, -scēre, -scuī, -xtum *vt* to mix in with, add to; (*fig*) to involve; **sē ~** interfere.

admissārius, -ī *and* **iī** *m* stallion.

admissum, -ī *nt* crime.

admissus *ppp of* **admittō**.

admittō, -ittere, -īsī, -issum *vt* to let in, admit; to set at a gallop; to allow; to commit (a crime); **equō ~issō** charging.

admixtiō, -ōnis *f* admixture.

admixtus *ppp of* **admisceō**.

admoderātē *adv* suitably.

admoderor, -ārī, -ātus *vt* to restrain.

admodum *adv* very, quite; fully; yes; (*with neg*) at all.

admoneō, -ēre, -uī, -itum *vt* to remind, suggest, advise, warn.

admonitiō, -ōnis *f* reminder, suggestion, admonition.

admonitor, -ōris *m* admonisher (*male*).

admonitrīx, -rīcis *f* admonisher (*female*).

admonitū at the suggestion, instance.

admordeō, -dēre, -sum *vt* to bite into; (*fig*) to cheat.

admorsus *ppp of* **admordeō**.

admōtiō, -ōnis *f* applying.

admōtus *ppp of* **admoveō**.

admoveo, -ovēre, -ōvī, -ōtum *vt* to move, bring up, apply; to lend (an ear), direct (the mind).

admurmurātiō, -ōnis *f* murmuring.

admurmurō, -āre, -āvī, -ātum *vi* to murmur (*of a crowd approving or disapproving*).

admutilō, -āre, -āvī, -ātum *vt* to clip close; (*fig*) to cheat.

adnectō, -ctere, -xuī, -xum *vt* to connect, tie.

adnexus, -ūs *m* connection.

adnīsus *ppp of* **adnītor**.

adnītor, -tī, -sus *and* **-xus** *vi* to lean on; to exert oneself.

adnīxus *ppp of* **adnītor**.

adnō, -āre *vt, vi* to swim to.

adnotō, -āre, -āvī, -ātum *vt* to comment on.

adnumerō, -āre, -āvī, -ātum *vt* to pay out; to reckon along with.

adnuō, -uere, -uī, -ūtum *vi* to nod; to assent, promise; to indicate.

adoleō, -olēre, -oluī, -ultum *vt* to burn; to pile with gifts.

adolēscen- *etc see* **adulēscen-**.

adolēscō, -ēscere, -ēvī *vi* to grow up, increase; to burn.

Adōnis, -is and **idis** m a beautiful youth loved by Venus.
adopertus adj covered.
adoptātiō, -ōnis f adopting.
adoptiō, -ōnis f adoption.
adoptīvus adj by adoption.
adoptō, -āre, -āvī, -ātum vt to choose; to adopt.
ador, -ōris and **oris** nt spelt.
adōreus adj see n.
adōrea f glory.
adorior, -īrī, -tus vt to accost; to attack; to set about.
adōrnō, -āre, -āvī, -ātum vt to get ready.
adōrō, -āre, -āvī, -ātum vt to entreat; to worship, revere.
adortus ppa of **adorior.**
adp- etc see **app-.**
adrādō, -dere, -sī, -sum vt to shave close.
Adrastus, -ī m a king of Argos.
adrāsus ppp of **adrādō.**
adrēctus ppp of **adrigō** ♦ adj steep.
adrēpō, -ere, -sī, -tum vi to creep, steal into.
adreptus ppp of **adripiō.**
Adria etc see **Hadria** etc.
adrīdeō, -dēre, -sī, -sum vt, vi to laugh, smile at; to please.
adrigō, -igere, -ēxī, -ēctum vt to raise; (fig) to rouse.
adripiō, -ipere, -ipuī, -eptum vt to seize; to appropriate; to take hold of; to learn quickly; (law) to arrest; to satirize.
adrōdō, -dere, -sī, -sum vt to gnaw, nibble at.
adrogāns, -antis adj arrogant, insolent.
adroganter adv see **adrogāns.**
adrogantia, -ae f arrogance, presumption, haughtiness.
adrogātiō, -ōnis f adoption.
adrogō, -āre, -āvī, -ātum vt to ask; to associate; to claim, assume; (fig) to award.
adsc- etc see **asc-.**
adsecla etc see **adsecula.**
adsectātiō, -ōnis f attendance.
adsectātor, -ōris m follower.
adsector, -ārī, -ātus vt to attend on, follow (esp a candidate).
adsecula, -ae m follower (derogatory).
adsēdī perf of **adsideō;** perf of **adsīdō.**
adsēnsiō, -ōnis f assent, applause; (PHILOS) acceptance of the evidence of the senses.
adsēnsor, -ōris m one in agreement.
adsēnsus ppa of **adsentior.**
adsēnsus, -ūs m assent, approval; echo; (PHILOS) acceptance of the evidence of the senses.
adsentātiō, -ōnis f flattery.
adsentātiuncula f trivial compliments.
adsentātor, -ōris m flatterer (male).
adsentātōriē adv ingratiatingly.

adsentātrīx, -rīcis f flatterer (female).
adsentiō, -entīre, -ēnsī, -ēnsum; -entior, -entīrī, -ēnsus vi to agree, approve.
adsentor, -ārī, -ātus vi to agree, flatter.
adsequor, -quī, -cūtus vt to overtake; to attain; to grasp (by understanding).
adserō, -ere, -uī, -tum vt (law) to declare free (usu with manū), liberate (a slave); to lay claim to, appropriate; ~ **in servitūtem** claim as a slave.
adserō, -erere, -ēvī, -itum vt to plant near.
adsertiō, -ōnis f declaration of status.
adsertor, -ōris m champion.
adserviō, -īre vi to assist.
adservō, -āre, -āvī, -ātum vt to watch carefully; to keep, preserve.
adsessiō, -ōnis f sitting beside.
adsessor, -ōris m counsellor.
adsessus, -ūs m sitting beside.
adsevēranter adv emphatically.
adsevērātiō, -ōnis f assertion; earnestness.
adsevērō, -āre, -āvī, -ātum vt to do in earnest; to assert strongly.
adsideō, -idēre, -ēdī, -essum vi to sit by; to attend, assist; to besiege; to resemble.
adsīdō, -īdere, -ēdī vi to sit down.
adsiduē adv continually.
adsiduitās, -ātis f constant attendance; continuance, frequent recurrence.
adsiduō adv continually.
adsiduus adj constantly in attendance, busy; continual, incessant.
adsiduus, -ī m taxpayer.
adsignātiō, -ōnis f allotment (of land).
adsignō, -āre, -āvī, -ātum vt to allot (esp land); to assign; to impute, attribute; to consign.
adsiliō, -ilīre, -iluī, -ultum vi to leap at or on to.
adsimilis adj like.
adsimiliter adv similarly.
adsimulātus adj similar; counterfeit.
adsimulō, -āre, -āvī, -ātum vt, vi to compare; to pretend, imitate.
adsistō, -istere, -titī vi to stand (by); to defend.
adsitus ppp of **adserō.**
adsoleō, -ēre vi to be usual.
adsonō, -āre vi to respond.
adsp- etc see **asp-.**
adsternō, -ere vt to prostrate.
adstipulātor, -ōris m supporter.
adstipulor, -ārī, -ātus vi to agree with.
adstitī perf of **adsistō;** perf of **adstō.**
adstō, -āre, -itī vi to stand near, stand up; to assist.
adstrepō, -ere vi to roar.
adstrictē adv concisely.
adstrictus ppp of **adstringō** ♦ adj tight, narrow; concise; stingy.

Noun declensions and verb conjugations are shown on pp xiii to xxv. The present infinitive ending of a verb shows to which conjugation it belongs: **-āre** = 1st; **-ēre** = 2nd; **-ere** = 3rd and **-īre** = 4th. Irregular verbs are shown on p xxvi

adstringō, -ngere, -nxī, -ctum *vt* to draw close, tighten; to bind, oblige; to abridge.

adstruō, -ere, -xī, -ctum *vt* to build on; to add.

adstupeō, -ēre *vi* to be astonished.

adsuēfaciō, -acere, -ēcī, -actum *vt* to accustom, train.

adsuēscō, -scere, -vī, -tum *vi* to accustom, train.

adsuētūdō, -inis *f* habit.

adsuētus *ppp of* **adsuēscō** ♦ *adj* customary.

adsultō, -āre, -āvī, -ātum *vi* to jump; to attack.

adsultus, -ūs *m* attack.

adsum, -esse, -fuī *vi* to be present; to support, assist (*esp at law*); to come; to appear before (a tribunal); **animō ~** pay attention; **iam aderō** I'll be back soon.

adsūmō, -ere, -psī, -ptum *vt* to take for oneself, receive; to take also.

adsūmptiō, -ōnis *f* taking up; (*logic*) minor premise.

adsūmptīvus *adj* (*law*) which takes its defence from extraneous circumstances.

adsūmptum, -ī *nt* epithet.

adsūmptus *ppp of* **adsūmō**.

adsuō, -ere *vt* to sew on.

adsurgō, -gere, -rēxī, -rēctum *vi* to rise, stand up; to swell, increase.

adt- *etc see* **att-**.

adulātiō, -ōnis *f* (*dogs*) fawning; servility.

adulātor, -ōris *m* sycophant.

adulātōrius *adj* flattering.

adulēscēns, -entis *m/f* young man *or* woman (*usu from 15 to 30 years*).

adulēscentia, -ae *f* youth (*age 15 to 30*).

adulēscentula, -ae *f* girl.

adulēscentulus, -ī *m* quite a young man.

adulō, -āre, -āvī, -ātum; adulor, -ārī, -ātus *vt, vi* to fawn upon, flatter, kowtow.

adulter, -ī *m*, **-a, -ae** *f* adulterer, adulteress ♦ *adj* adulterous.

adulterīnus *adj* forged.

adulterium, -ī *and* **iī** *nt* adultery.

adulterō, -āre, -āvī, -ātum *vt, vi* to commit adultery; to falsify.

adultus *ppp of* **adolēscō** ♦ *adj* adult, mature.

adumbrātim *adv* in outline.

adumbrātiō, -ōnis *f* sketch; semblance.

adumbrātus *adj* false.

adumbrō, -āre, -āvī, -ātum *vt* to sketch; to represent, copy.

aduncitās, -ātis *f* curvature.

aduncus *adj* hooked, curved.

adurgeō, -ēre *vt* to pursue closely.

adūrō, -rere, -ssī, -stum *vt* to burn; to freeze; (*fig*) to fire.

adusque *prep* (*with acc*) right up to ♦ *adv* entirely.

adūstus *ppp of* **adūrō** ♦ *adj* brown.

advectīcius *adj* imported.

advectō, -āre *vt* to carry frequently.

advectus *ppp of* **advehō**.

advectus, -ūs *m* bringing.

advehō, -here, -xī, -ctum *vt* to carry, convey; (*pass*) to ride.

advēlō, -āre *vt* to crown.

advena, -ae *m/f* stranger ♦ *adj* foreign.

adveniō, -enīre, -ēnī, -entum *vi* to arrive, come.

adventīcius *adj* foreign, extraneous; unearned.

adventō, -āre, -āvī, -ātum *vi* to come nearer and nearer, advance rapidly.

adventor, -ōris *m* visitor.

adventus, -ūs *m* arrival, approach.

adversāria *ntpl* daybook.

adversārius, -ī *and* **iī** *m* opponent ♦ *adj* opposing.

adversātrīx, -īcis *f* antagonist.

adversiō, -ōnis *f* turning (the attention).

adversor, -ārī, -ātus *vi* to oppose, resist.

adversum, -ī *nt* opposite; misfortune ♦ *prep* (+ *acc*) towards, against ♦ *adv* to meet.

adversus *ppp of* **advertō** ♦ *adj* opposite, in front; hostile; **~ō flūmine** upstream; **~ae rēs** misfortune ♦ *prep* (+ *acc*) towards, against ♦ *adv* to meet.

advertō, -tere, -tī, -sum *vt* to turn, direct towards; to call attention; **animum ~** notice, perceive; (*with ad*) to attend to; (*with in*) to punish.

advesperāscit, -scere, -vit *vi* it is getting dark.

advigilō, -āre *vi* to keep watch.

advocātiō, -ōnis *f* legal assistance, counsel.

advocātus, -ī *m* supporter in a lawsuit; advocate, counsel.

advocō, -āre, -āvī, -ātum *vt* to summon; (*law*) to call in the assistance of.

advolō, -āre, -āvī, -ātum *vi* to fly to, swoop down upon.

advolvō, -vere, -vī, -ūtum *vt* to roll to; to prostrate.

advor- *etc see* **adver-**.

adytum, -ī *nt* sanctuary.

Aeacidēs, -idae *m* Achilles; Pyrrhus.

Aeacus, -ī *m* father of Peleus, and judge of the dead.

Aeaea, -ae *f* Circe's island.

Aeaeus *adj* of Circe.

aedēs, -is *f* temple; (*pl*) house.

aedicula, -ae *f* shrine; small house, room.

aedificātiō, -ōnis *f* building.

aedificātiuncula, -ae *f* little house.

aedificātor, -ōris *m* builder.

aedificium, -ī *and* **iī** *nt* building.

aedificō, -āre, -āvī, -ātum *vt* to build, construct.

aedīlicius *adj* aedile's ♦ *m* ex-aedile.

aedīlis, -is *m* aedile.

aedīlitās, -ātis *f* aedileship.

aedis, -is *see* **aedēs**.

aeditumus, aedituus, -ī *m* temple-keeper.

Aeduī, -ōrum *mpl a tribe of central Gaul*.

Aeētēs, -ae *m father of Medea*.

Aegaeus *adj* Aegean ♦ *nt* Aegean Sea.
Aegātēs, -um *fpl* islands off Sicily.
aeger, -rī *adj* ill, sick; sorrowful; weak.
Aegīna, -ae *f* a Greek island.
Aegīnēta, -ae *m* inhabitant of Aegina.
aegis, -dis *f* shield of Jupiter or Athena, aegis.
Aegisthus, -ī *m* paramour of Clytemnestra.
aegocerōs, -ōtis *m* Capricorn.
aegrē *adv* painfully; with displeasure; with
    difficulty; hardly; **~ ferre** be annoyed.
aegrēscō, -ere *vi* to become ill; to be
    aggravated.
aegrimōnia, -ae *f* distress of mind.
aegritūdō, -inis *f* sickness; sorrow.
aegror, -ōris *m* illness.
aegrōtātiō, -ōnis *f* illness, disease.
aegrōtō, -āre, -āvī, -ātum *vi* to be ill.
aegrōtus *adj* ill, sick.
Aegyptius *adj see n.*
Aegyptus, -ī *f* Egypt ♦ *m* brother of Danaus.
aelinos, -ī *m* dirge.
Aemiliānus *adj esp* Scipio, destroyer of Carthage.
Aemilius, -ī Roman family name; **Via ~ia** road in
    N. Italy.
aemulātiō, -ōnis *f* rivalry (good or bad);
    jealousy.
aemulātor, -ōris *m* zealous imitator.
aemulor, -ārī, -ātus *vt* to rival, copy; to be
    jealous.
aemulus, -ī *m* rival ♦ *adj* rivalling; jealous.
Aeneadēs, -ae *m* Trojan; Roman.
Aenēās, -ae *m* Trojan leader and hero of Virgil's
    epic.
Aenēis, -idis *and* **idos** *f* Aeneid.
Aenēius *adj see n.*
aēneus *adj* of bronze.
aenigma, -tis *nt* riddle, mystery.
aēnum, -ī *nt* bronze vessel.
aēnus *adj* of bronze.
Aeolēs, -um *mpl* the Aeolians.
Aeolia *f* Lipari Island.
Aeolidēs *m* a descendant of Aeolus.
Aeolis, -idis *f* Aeolia (N.W. of Asia Minor).
Aeolis, -idis *f* daughter of Aeolus.
Aeolius *adj see n.*
Aeolus, -ī *m* king of the winds.
aequābilis *adj* equal; consistent, even;
    impartial.
aequābilitās, -ātis *f* uniformity; impartiality.
aequābiliter *adv* uniformly.
aequaevus *adj* of the same age.
aequālis *adj* equal, like; of the same age,
    contemporary; uniform.
aequālitās, -ātis *f* evenness; (in politics, age)
    equality, similarity.
aequāliter *adv* evenly.
aequanimitās, -ātis *f* goodwill; calmness.
aequātiō, -ōnis *f* equal distribution.
aequē *adv* equally; just as (with **ac, atque, et,
    quam**); justly.
Aequī, -ōrum *mpl* a people of central Italy.

Aequicus, Aequiculus *adj see n.*
Aequimaelium, -ī *and* **iī** *nt* an open space in
    Rome.
aequinoctiālis *adj see n.*
aequinoctium, -ī *and* **iī** *nt* equinox.
aequiperābilis *adj* comparable.
aequiperō, -āre, -āvī, -ātum *vt* to compare;
    to equal.
aequitās, -ātis *f* uniformity; fair dealing,
    equity; calmness of mind.
aequō, -āre, -āvī, -ātum *vt* to make equal,
    level; to compare; to equal; **solō ~** raze to the
    ground.
aequor, -is *nt* a level surface, sea.
aequoreus *adj* of the sea.
aequum, -ī *nt* plain; justice.
aequus *adj* level, equal; favourable, friendly,
    fair, just; calm; **~ō animō** patiently; **~ō Marte**
    without deciding the issue; **~um est** it is
    reasonable; **ex ~ō** equally.
āēr, āeris *m* air, weather; mist.
aerāria *f* mine.
aerārium *nt* treasury.
aerārius *adj* of bronze; of money ♦ *m* a citizen
    of the lowest class at Rome; **tribūnī ~ī**
    paymasters; a wealthy middle class at Rome.
aerātus *adj* of bronze.
aereus *adj* of copper or bronze.
aerifer, -ī *adj* carrying cymbals.
aeripēs, -edis *adj* bronze-footed.
āerius *adj* of the air; lofty.
aerūgō, -inis *f* rust; (fig) envy, avarice.
aerumna, -ae *f* trouble, hardship.
aerumnōsus *adj* wretched.
aes, aeris *nt* copper, bronze; money; (pl)
    objects made of copper or bronze (esp
    statues, instruments, vessels; soldiers' pay); **~
    aliēnum** debt; **~ circumforāneum** borrowed
    money; **~ grave** Roman coin, as.
Aeschylus, -ī *m* Greek tragic poet.
Aesculāpius, -ī *m* god of medicine.
aesculētum, -ī *nt* oak forest.
aesculeus *adj see* **aesculus.**
aesculus, -ī *f* durmast oak.
Aesōn, -onis *m* father of Jason.
Aesonidēs, -ae *m* Jason.
Aesōpius *adj see n.*
Aesōpus, -ī *m* Greek writer of fables.
aestās, -ātis *f* summer.
aestifer, -ī *adj* heat-bringing.
aestimātiō, -ōnis *f* valuation, assessment;
    lītis ~ assessment of damages.
aestimātor, -ōris *m* valuer.
aestimō, -āre, -āvī, -ātum *vt* to value,
    estimate the value of; **māgnī ~** think highly
    of.
aestīva, -ōrum *ntpl* summer camp, campaign.
aestīvus *adj* summer.
aestuārium, -ī *and* **iī** *nt* tidal waters, estuary.
aestuō, -āre, -āvī, -ātum *vi* to boil, burn;

Noun declensions and verb conjugations are shown on pp xiii to xxv. The present infinitive ending of a verb shows
to which conjugation it belongs: **-āre** = 1st; **-ēre** = 2nd; **-ere** = 3rd and **-īre** = 4th. Irregular verbs are shown on p xxvi

(*movement*) to heave, toss; (*fig*) to be excited; to waver.
aestuōsus *adj* very hot; agitated.
aestus, -ūs *m* heat; surge of the sea; tide; (*fig*) passion; hesitation.
aetās, -ātis *f* age, life; time.
aetātem *adv* for life.
aetātula, -ae *f* tender age.
aeternitās, -ātis *f* eternity.
aeternō, -āre *vt* to immortalize.
aeternus *adj* eternal, immortal; lasting; in ~um for ever.
aethēr, -eris *m* sky, heaven; air.
aetherius *adj* ethereal, heavenly; of air.
Aethiops, -is *adj* Ethiopian; (*fig*) stupid.
aethra, -ae *f* sky.
Aetna, -ae *f* Etna (*in Sicily*).
Aetnaeus, Aetnēnsis *adj see n*.
Aetōlia, -iae *f* a district of N. Greece.
Aetōlus, -icus *adj see n*.
aevitās, -ātis old form of **aetās**.
aevum, -ī *nt* age, lifetime; eternity; in ~ for ever.
Āfer, -rī *adj* African.
āfore *fut infin of* **absum**.
Āfrānius, -ī *m* Latin comic poet.
Āfrica, -ae *f* Roman province (*now* Tunisia).
Āfricānae *fpl* panthers.
Āfricānus *adj* name of two Scipios.
Āfricus *adj* African ♦ *m* south-west wind.
āfuī, āfutūrus *perf, fut p of* **absum**.
Agamēmnōn, -onis *m* leader of Greeks against Troy.
Agamēmnonius *adj see n*.
Aganippē, -ēs *f* a spring on Helicon.
agāsō, -ōnis *m* ostler, footman.
age, agedum come on!, well then.
agellus, -ī *m* plot of land.
Agēnōr, -oris *m* father of Europa.
Agēnoreus *adj see n*.
Agēnoridēs, -ae *m* Cadmus; Perseus.
agēns, -entis *adj* (*RHET*) effective.
ager, -rī *m* land, field; countryside; territory.
agg- *etc see* **adg-**.
agger, -is *m* rampart; mound, embankment, any built-up mass.
aggerō, -āre, -āvī, -ātum *vt* to pile up; to increase.
aggerō, -rere, -ssi, -stum *vt* to carry, bring.
aggestus, -ūs *m* accumulation.
agilis *adj* mobile; nimble, busy.
agilitās, -ātis *f* mobility.
agitābilis *adj* light.
agitātiō, -ōnis *f* movement, activity.
agitātor, -ōris *m* driver, charioteer.
agitō, -āre, -āvī, -ātum *vt* (*animals*) to drive; to move, chase, agitate; (*fig*) to excite (to action); to persecute, ridicule; to keep (*a ceremony*) ♦ *vi* to live; to deliberate.
agmen, -inis *nt* forward movement, procession, train; army on the march; ~ claudere bring up the rear; **novissimum ~** rearguard; **prīmum ~** van.

agna, -ae *f* ewe lamb; lamb (flesh).
agnāscor, -scī, -tus *vi* to be born after.
agnātus, -ī *m* relation (*by blood on father's side*).
agnellus, -ī *m* little lamb.
agnīnus *adj* of lamb.
agnitiō, -ōnis *f* recognition, knowledge.
agnitus *ppp of* **agnōscō**.
agnōmen, -inis *nt* an extra surname (*eg Africanus*).
agnōscō, -ōscere, -ōvī, -itum *vt* to recognize; to acknowledge, allow; to understand.
agnus, -ī *m* lamb.
agō, agere, ēgī, āctum *vt* to drive, lead; to plunder; to push forward, put forth; (*fig*) to move, rouse, persecute; to do, act, perform; (*time*) to pass, spend; (*undertakings*) to manage, wage; (*public speaking*) to plead, discuss; to negotiate, treat; (*THEAT*) to play, act the part of; ~ **cum populō** address the people; **age** come on!, well then; **age age** all right!; **āctum est dē** it is all up with; **aliud** ~ not attend; **animam** ~ expire; **annum quartum** ~ be three years old; **causam** ~ plead a cause; **hōc age** pay attention; **id** ~ **ut** aim at; **lēge** ~ go to law; **nīl agis** it's no use; **quid agis?** how are you?; **rēs agitur** interests are at stake; **sē** ~ go, come.
agrāriī *mpl* the land reform party.
agrārius *adj* of public land; **lēx** ~**a** land law.
agrestis *adj* rustic; boorish, wild, barbarous ♦ *m* countryman.
agricola, -ae *m* countryman, farmer.
Agricola, -ae *m* a Roman governor of Britain; his biography by Tacitus.
Agrigentīnus *adj see n*.
Agrigentum, -ī *nt* a town in Sicily.
agripeta, -ae *m* landgrabber.
Agrippa, -ae *m* Roman surname (*esp Augustus's minister*).
Agrippīna, -ae *f* mother of Nero; **Colōnia** ~**a** *or* ~**ēnsis** Cologne.
Agyīeus, -eī *and* **eos** *m* Apollo.
āh *interj* ah! (*in sorrow or joy*).
aha *interj* expressing reproof *or* laughter.
ahēn- *etc see* **aēn-**.
Āiāx, -ācis *m* Ajax (*name of two Greek heroes at Troy*).
āiō *vt* (*defec*) to say, speak; **ain tū?/ain vērō?** really?; **quid ais?** I say!
āla, -ae *f* wing; armpit; (*MIL*) wing of army.
alabaster, -rī *m* perfume box.
alacer, -ris *adj* brisk, cheerful.
alacritās, -ātis *f* promptness, liveliness; joy, rapture.
alapa, -ae *f* slap on the face; a slave's freedom.
ālāriī *mpl* allied troops.
ālārius *adj* (*MIL*) on the wing.
ālātus *adj* winged.
alauda, -ae *f* lark; name of a legion of Caesar's.
alāzōn, -onis *m* braggart.

Alba Longa, -ae, -ae *f* a Latin town (*precursor of Rome*).
Albānus *adj* Alban; **Lacus ~, Mōns ~** *lake and mountain near Alba Longa.*
albātus *adj* dressed in white.
albeō, -ēre *vi* to be white; to dawn.
albēscō, -ere *vi* to become white; to dawn.
albicō, -āre *vi* to be white.
albidus *adj* white.
Albiōn, -ōnis *f* ancient name for Britain.
albitūdō, -inis *f* whiteness.
Albula, -ae *f* old name for the Tiber.
albulus *adj* whitish.
album, -ī *nt* white; records.
Albunea, -ae *f* a spring at Tibur; a sulphur spring near Alban Lake.
albus *adj* white, bright.
Alcaeus, -ī *m* Greek lyric poet.
alcēdō, -inis *f* kingfisher.
alcēdōnia *ntpl* halcyon days.
alcēs, -is *f* elk.
Alcibiadēs, -is *m* brilliant Athenian politician.
Alcīdēs, -ae *m* Hercules.
Alcinous, -ī *m* king of Phaeacians in the Odyssey.
ālea, -ae *f* gambling, dice; (*fig*) chance, hazard; **iacta ~ est** the die is cast; **in ~am dare** to risk.
āleātor, -ōris *m* gambler.
āleātōrius *adj* in gambling.
ālēc *etc see* **allēc.**
āleō, -ōnis *m* gambler.
āles, -itis *adj* winged; swift ♦ *m/f* bird; omen.
alēscō, -ere *vi* to grow up.
Alexander, -rī *m* a Greek name; Paris (*prince of Troy*); Alexander the Great (*king of Macedon*).
Alexandrēa (*later* **-īa**), **-ēae** *f* Alexandria in Egypt.
alga, -ae *f* seaweed.
algeō, -gēre, -sī *vi* to feel cold; (*fig*) to be neglected.
algēscō, -ere *vi* to catch cold.
Algidus, -ī *m* mountain in Latium.
algidus *adj* cold.
algor, -ōris *m* cold.
algū *abl sg m* with cold.
aliā *adv* in another way.
aliās *adv* at another time; at one time ... at another.
alibī *adv* elsewhere; otherwise; in one place ... in another.
alicubī *adv* somewhere.
alicunde *adv* from somewhere.
alid *old form of* **aliud.**
aliēnātiō, -ōnis *f* transfer; estrangement.
aliēnigena, -ae *m* foreigner.
aliēnigenus *adj* foreign; heterogeneous.
aliēnō, -āre, -āvī, -ātum *vt* to transfer (property by sale); to alienate, estrange; (*mind*) to derange.

aliēnus *adj* of another, of others; alien, strange; (*with abl or* **ab**) unsuited to, different from; hostile ♦ *m* stranger.
āliger, -ī *adj* winged.
alimentārius *adj* about food.
alimentum, -ī *nt* nourishment, food; obligation of children to parents; (*fig*) support.
alimōnium, -i *and* **ī ī** *nt* nourishment.
aliō *adv* in another direction, elsewhere; one way ... another way.
aliōquī, aliōquīn *adv* otherwise, else; besides.
aliōrsum *adv* in another direction; differently.
ālipēs, -edis *adj* wing-footed; fleet.
alīptēs, -ae *m* sports trainer.
aliquā *adv* some way or other.
aliquam *adv*: **~ diū** for sometime; **~ multī** a considerable number.
aliquandō *adv* sometime, ever; sometimes; once, for once; now at last.
aliquantisper *adv* for a time.
aliquantō *adv* (*with comp*) somewhat.
aliquantulum *nt* a very little ♦ *adv* somewhat.
aliquantulus *adj* quite small.
aliquantum *adj* a good deal ♦ *adv* somewhat.
aliquantus *adj* considerable.
aliquātenus *adv* to some extent.
aliquī, -qua, -quod *adj* some, any; some other.
aliquid *adv* at all.
aliquis, -quid *pron* somebody, something; someone *or* something important.
aliquō *adv* to some place, somewhere else.
aliquot *adj* (*indecl*) some.
aliquotiēns *adv* several times.
aliter *adv* otherwise, differently; in one way ... in another.
alitus *ppp of* **alō.**
ālium, -i *and* **ī ī** *nt* garlic.
aliunde *adv* from somewhere else.
alius, alia, aliud *adj* other, another; different; **alius ... alius** some ... others; **alius ex aliō** one after the other; **in alia omnia īre** oppose a measure; **nihil aliud quam** only.
all- *etc see* **adl-.**
allēc, -is *nt* fish pickle.
allex, -icis *m* big toe.
Allia, -ae *f* tributary of the Tiber (*scene of a great Roman defeat*).
Alliēnsis *adj see* **Allia.**
Allobrogēs, -um *mpl* a people of S.E. Gaul.
Allobrogicus *adj see n.*
almus *adj* nourishing; kindly.
alnus, -ī *f* alder.
alō, -ere, -uī, -tum *and* **-itum** *vt* to nourish, rear; to increase, promote.
Alpēs, -ium *fpl* Alps.
Alphēus, -ī *m* river of Olympia in S.W. Greece.
Alpīnus *adj see n.*

Noun declensions and verb conjugations are shown on pp xiii to xxv. The present infinitive ending of a verb shows to which conjugation it belongs: **-āre** = 1st; **-ēre** = 2nd; **-ere** = 3rd and **-īre** = 4th. Irregular verbs are shown on p xxvi

alsī *perf of* **algeō.**
alsius, alsus *adj* cold.
altāria, -ium *ntpl* altars, altar; altar top.
altē *adv* on high, from above; deep; from afar.
alter, -īus *adj* the one, the other (*of two*);
second, the next; fellow man; different; ~
ego, ~ **īdem** a second self; **~um tantum** twice
as much; **ūnus et** ~ one or two.
altercātiō, -ōnis *f* dispute, debate.
altercor, -ārī, -ātus *vi* to wrangle, dispute; to
cross-examine.
alternīs *adv* alternately.
alternō, -āre, -āvī, -ātum *vt* to do by turns,
alternate.
alternus *adj* one after the other, alternate;
elegiac (verses).
alteruter, -īusutrīus *adj* one or the other.
altilis *adj* fat (*esp fowls*).
altisonus *adj* sounding on high.
altitonāns, -antis *adj* thundering on high.
altitūdō, -inis *f* height, depth; (*fig*) sublimity,
(*mind*) secrecy.
altivolāns, -antis *adj* soaring on high.
altor, -ōris *m* foster father.
altrīnsecus *adv* on the other side.
altrīx, -īcis *f* nourisher, foster mother.
altum, -ī *nt* heaven; sea (*usu out of sight of
land*); **ex ~ō repetītus** far-fetched.
altus *adj* high, deep; (*fig*) noble; profound.
ālūcinor, -ārī, -ātus *vi* to talk wildly; (*mind*) to
wander.
aluī *perf of* **alō.**
alumnus, -ī *m/f* foster child; pupil.
alūta, -ae *f* soft leather; shoe, purse, face
patch.
alveārium, -ī *and* **iī** *nt* beehive.
alveolus, -ī *m* basin.
alveus, -eī *m* hollow; trough; (*ship*) hold; bath
tub; riverbed.
alvus, -ī *f* bowels; womb; stomach.
amābilis *adj* lovely, lovable.
amābilitās, -ātis *f* charm.
amābiliter *adv see* **amābilis.**
Amalthēa, -ae *f* nymph or she-goat; **cornū
~ae** horn of plenty.
Amalthēum, -ī *nt* Atticus's library.
āmandātiō *f* sending away.
āmandō, -āre, -āvī, -ātum *vt* to send away.
amāns, -antis *adj* fond ♦ *m* lover.
amanter *adv* affectionately.
āmanuēnsis, -is *m* secretary.
amāracinum, -inī *nt* marjoram ointment.
amāracum, -ī *nt*, **amāracus, -ī** *m/f* sweet
marjoram.
amārē *adv see* **amārus.**
amāritiēs, -ēī *f*, **amāritūdō, -inis** *f*, **amāror,
-ōris** *m* bitterness.
amārus *adj* bitter; (*fig*) sad; ill-natured.
amāsius, -ī *and* **iī** *m* lover.
Amathūs, -ūntis *f* town in Cyprus.
Amathūsia *f* Venus.
amātiō, -ōnis *f* lovemaking.
amātor, -ōris *m* lover, paramour.

amātorculus *m* poor lover.
amātōriē *adv* amorously.
amātōrius *adj* of love, erotic.
amātrīx, -rīcis *f* mistress.
Amāzōn, -onis *f* Amazon, warrior woman.
Amāzonidēs *fpl* Amazons.
Amāzonius *adj see n.*
ambāctus, -ī *m* vassal.
ambāgēs, -is *f* windings; (*speech*)
circumlocution, quibbling; enigma.
ambedō, -edere, -ēdī, -ēsum *vt* to consume.
ambēsus *ppp of* **ambedō.**
ambigō, -ere *vt, vi* to wander about; to be in
doubt; to argue; to wrangle.
ambiguē *adv* doubtfully.
ambiguitās, -ātis *f* ambiguity.
ambiguus *adj* changeable, doubtful,
unreliable; ambiguous.
ambiō, -īre, -īī, -ītum *vt* to go round, encircle;
(*POL*) to canvass for votes; (*fig*) to court (for a
favour).
ambitiō, -ōnis *f* canvassing for votes;
currying favour; ambition.
ambitiōsē *adv* ostentatiously.
ambitiōsus *adj* winding; ostentatious,
ambitious.
ambītus *ppp of* **ambiō.**
ambitus, -ūs *m* circuit, circumference;
circumlocution; canvassing, bribery; **lēx de
~ū** a law against bribery.
ambō, ambae, ambō *num* both, two.
Ambracia, -ae *f* district of N.W. Greece.
Ambraciēnsis, -us *adj see n.*
ambrosia, -ae *f* food of the gods.
ambrosius *adj* divine.
ambūbāia, -ae *f* Syrian flute-girl.
ambulācrum, -ī *nt* avenue.
ambulātiō, -ōnis *f* walk, walking; walk
(*place*).
ambulātiuncula *f* short walk.
ambulō, -āre, -āvī, -ātum *vi* to walk, go; to
travel.
ambūrō, -rere, -ssī, -stum *vt* to burn up; to
make frostbitten; (*fig*) to ruin.
ambūstus *ppp of* **ambūrō.**
amellus, -ī *m* Michaelmas daisy.
āmēns, -entis *adj* mad, frantic; stupid.
āmentia, -ae *f* madness; stupidity.
āmentum, -ī *nt* strap (for throwing javelin).
ames, -itis *m* fowler's pole.
amfr- *etc see* **anfr-.**
amīca, -ae *f* friend; mistress.
amiciō, -īre, -tus *vt* to clothe, cover.
amīciter, -ē *adv see* **amīcus.**
amīcitia, -ae *f* friendship; alliance.
amictus *ppp of* **amiciō.**
amictus, -ūs *m* (manner of) dress; clothing.
amiculum, -ī *nt* cloak.
amīculus, -ī *m* dear friend.
amīcus, -ī *m* friend ♦ *adj* friendly, fond.
āmissiō, -ōnis *f* loss.
āmissus *ppp of* **āmittō.**
amita, -ae *f* aunt (*on father's side*).

āmittō, -ittere, -īsī, -issum *vt* to let go, lose.
Ammōn, -is *m Egyptian god identified with Jupiter.*
Ammōniacus *adj see n.*
amnicola, -ae *m/f* sth growing by a river.
amniculus *m* brook.
amnicus *adj see n.*
amnis, -is *m* river.
amō, -āre, -āvī, -ātum *vt* to love, like; (*colloq*) to be obliged to; **ita mē dī ament!** ≈ *bless my soul!*; **amābō** please!
amoenitās, -ātis *f* delightfulness (*esp of scenery*).
amoenus *adj* delightful.
āmōlior, -īrī, -ītus *vt* to remove.
amōmum, -ī *nt* cardamom.
amor, -ōris *m* love; (*fig*) strong desire; term of endearment; Cupid; (*pl*) love affairs.
āmōtiō, -ōnis *f* removal.
āmōtus *ppa of* **āmoveō.**
āmoveō, -ovēre, -ōvī, -ōtum *vt* to remove; to banish.
amphibolia, -ae *f* ambiguity.
Amphīōn, -onis *m musician and builder of Thebes.*
Amphīonius *adj see n.*
amphitheātrum, -ī *nt* amphitheatre.
Amphitrītē, -ēs *f sea goddess; the sea.*
Amphitryō, -ōnis *m husband of Alcmena.*
Amphitryōniadēs *m Hercules.*
amphora, -ae *f* a two-handled jar; liquid measure; (*NAUT*) measure of tonnage.
Amphrȳsius *adj of Apollo.*
Amphrȳsus, -ī *m river in Thessaly.*
ample *adv see* **amplūs.**
amplector, -ctī, -xus *vt* to embrace, encircle; (*mind*) to grasp; (*speech*) to deal with; (*fig*) to cherish.
amplexor, -ārī, -ātus *vt* to embrace, love.
amplexus *ppa of* **amplector.**
amplexus, -ūs *m* embrace, encircling.
amplificātiō, -ōnis *f* enlargement; (*RHET*) a passage elaborated for effect.
amplificē *adv* splendidly.
amplificō, -āre, -āvī, -ātum *vt* to increase, enlarge; (*RHET*) to enlarge upon.
ampliō, -āre, -āvī, -ātum *vt* to enlarge; (*law*) to adjourn.
ampliter *adv see* **amplūs.**
amplitūdō, -inis *f* size; (*fig*) distinction; (*RHET*) fullness.
amplius *adv* more (*esp amount or number*), further, longer; ~ **ducentī** more than 200; ~ **nōn petere** take no further legal action; ~ **prōnūntiāre** adjourn a case.
amplūs *adj* large, spacious; great, abundant; powerful, splendid, eminent; (*sup*) distinguished.
ampulla, -ae *f* a two-handled flask; (*fig*) high-flown language.

ampullārius, -ārī *m* flask-maker.
ampullor, -ārī *vi* to use high-flown language.
amputātiō, -ōnis *f* pruning.
amputātus *adj* (*RHET*) disconnected.
amputō, -āre, -āvī, -ātum *vt* to cut off, prune; (*fig*) to lop off.
Amūlius, -ī *m king of Alba Longa, grand-uncle of Romulus.*
amurca, -ae *f* lees of olive oil.
amussitātus *adj* nicely adjusted.
Amȳclae, -ārum *fpl town in S. Greece.*
Amȳclaeus *adj see n.*
amygdalum, -ī *nt* almond.
amystis, -dis *f* emptying a cup at a draught.
an *conj* or; perhaps; (*with single question*) surely not; **haud sciō** ~ I feel sure.
Anacreōn, -ontis *m Greek lyric poet.*
anadēma, -tis *nt* headband.
anagnōstēs, -ae *m* reader.
anapaestum, -ī *nt* poem in anapaests.
anapaestus *adj*: ~ **pēs** anapaest.
anas, -tis *f* duck.
anaticula, -ae *f* duckling.
anatīnus *adj see n.*
anatocismus, -ī *m* compound interest.
Anaxagorās, -ae *m early Greek philosopher.*
Anaximander, -rī *m early Greek philosopher.*
anceps, -ipitis *adj* two-headed; double; wavering, doubtful; dangerous ♦ *nt* danger.
Anchīsēs, -ae *m father of Aeneas.*
Anchīsēus *adj* Aeneas.
Anchīsiadēs *m* Aeneas.
ancīle, -is *nt* oval shield (*esp one said to have fallen from heaven in Numa's reign*).
ancilla, -ae *f* servant.
ancillāris *adj* of a young servant.
ancillula *f* young servant.
ancīsus *adj* cut round.
ancora, -ae *f* anchor.
ancorārius *adj see n.*
ancorāle, -is *nt* cable.
Ancus Marcius, -ī, -ī *m 4th king of Rome.*
Ancȳra, -ae *f* Ankara (*capital of Galatia*).
andabata, -ae *m* blindfold gladiator.
Andrius *adj see* **Andros.**
androgynē, -ēs *f* hermaphrodite.
androgynus, -ī *m* hermaphrodite.
Andromachē, -ēs *f wife of Hector.*
Andromeda, -ae *f wife of Perseus; a constellation.*
Andronicus, -ī *m* Livius (*earliest Latin poet*).
Andros (-us), -ī *m* Aegean island.
ānellus, -ī *m* little ring.
anēthum, -ī *nt* fennel.
ānfrāctus, -ūs *m* bend, orbit; roundabout way; (*words*) digression, prolixity.
angelus, -ī *m* angel.
angina, -ae *f* quinsy.
angiportum, -ī *nt* alley.
angiportus, -ūs *m* alley.

Noun declensions and verb conjugations are shown on pp xiii to xxv. The present infinitive ending of a verb shows to which conjugation it belongs: **-āre** = 1st; **-ēre** = 2nd; **-ere** = 3rd and **-īre** = 4th. Irregular verbs are shown on p xxvi

angō, -ere _vt_ to throttle; (_fig_) to distress, torment.

angor, -ōris _m_ suffocation; (_fig_) anguish, torment.

anguicomus _adj_ with snakes for hair.

anguiculus, -ī _m_ small snake.

anguifer, -ī _adj_ snake-carrying.

anguigena, -ae _m_ one born of serpents; Theban.

anguīlla, -ae _f_ eel.

anguimanus _adj_ with a trunk.

anguipēs, -edis _adj_ serpent-footed.

anguis, -is _m/f_ snake, serpent; (_constellation_) Draco.

Anguitenēns, -entis _m_ Ophiuchus.

angulātus _adj_ angular.

angulus, -ī _m_ angle, corner; out-of-the-way place; **ad parēs ~ōs** at right angles.

angustē _adv_ close, within narrow limits; concisely.

angustiae, -ārum _fpl_ defile, strait; (_time_) shortness; (_means_) want; (_CIRCS_) difficulty; (_mind_) narrowness; (_words_) subtleties.

angusticlāvius _adj_ wearing a narrow purple stripe.

angustō, -āre _vt_ to make narrow.

angustum, -ī _nt_ narrowness; danger.

angustus _adj_ narrow, close; (_time_) short; (_means_) scanty; (_mind_) mean; (_argument_) subtle; (_CIRCS_) difficult.

anhēlitus, -ūs _m_ panting; breath, exhalation.

anhēlō, -āre, -āvī, -ātum _vi_ to breathe hard, pant; to exhale.

anhēlus _adj_ panting.

anicula, -ae _f_ poor old woman.

Aniēnsis, Aniēnus _adj_ of the river Anio.

Aniēnus _m_ Anio.

anīlis _adj_ of an old woman.

anīlitās, -tātis _f_ old age.

anīliter _adv_ like an old woman.

anima, -ae _f_ wind, air; breath; life; soul, mind; ghost, spirit; **~am agere, efflāre** expire; **~am comprimere** hold one's breath.

animadversiō, -ōnis _f_ observation; censure, punishment.

animadversor, -ōris _m_ observer.

animadvertō, -tere, -tī, -sum _vt_ to pay attention to, notice; to realise; to censure, punish; **~ in** punish.

animal, -ālis _nt_ animal; living creature.

animālis _adj_ of air; animate.

animāns, -antis _m/f/nt_ living creature; animal.

animātiō, -ōnis _f_ being.

animātus _adj_ disposed, in a certain frame of mind; courageous.

animō, -āre, -āvī, -ātum _vt_ to animate; to give a certain temperament to.

animōsē _adv_ boldly, eagerly.

animōsus _adj_ airy; lifelike; courageous, proud.

animula, -ae _f_ little soul.

animulus, -ī _m_ darling.

animus, -ī _m_ mind, soul; consciousness; reason, thought, opinion, imagination; heart, feelings, disposition; courage, spirit, pride, passion; will, purpose; term of endearment; **~ī** in mind, in heart; **~ī causā** for amusement; **~ō fingere** imagine; **~ō male est** I am fainting; **aequō ~ō esse** be patient, calm; **bonō ~ō esse** take courage; be well-disposed; **ex ~ō** sincerely; **ex ~ō effluere** be forgotten; **in ~ō habēre** purpose; **meō ~ō** in my opinion.

Aniō, -ēnis _m tributary of the Tiber._

Anna Perenna, -ae, -ae _f Roman popular goddess._

annālēs, -ium _mpl_ annals, chronicle.

annālis _adj_ of a year; **lēx ~** law prescribing ages for public offices.

anne _etc see_ **an.**

anniculus _adj_ a year old.

anniversārius _adj_ annual.

annōn or not.

annōna, -ae _f_ year's produce; grain; price of corn; the market.

annōsus _adj_ aged.

annōtinus _adj_ last year's.

annus, -ī _m_ year; **~ māgnus** astronomical great year; **~ solidus** a full year.

annuus _adj_ a year's; annual.

anquīrō, -rere, -sīvī, -sītum _vt_ to search for; to make inquiries; (_law_) to institute an inquiry (**dē**) or prosecution (_abl or gen_).

ānsa, -ae _f_ handle; (_fig_) opportunity.

ānsātus _adj_ with a handle; (_comedy_) with arms akimbo.

ānser, -is _m_ goose.

ānserīnus _adj see_ **n.**

ante _prep_ (_with acc_) before (_in time, place, comparison_) ♦ _adv_ (_place_) in front; (_time_) before.

anteā _adv_ before, formerly.

antecapiō, -apere, -ēpī, -eptum _vt_ to take beforehand, anticipate.

antecēdō, -ēdere, -essī, -essum _vt_ to precede; to surpass.

antecellō, -ere _vi_ to excel, be superior.

anteceptus _ppp of_ **antecapiō.**

antecessiō, -ōnis _f_ preceding; antecedent cause.

antecessor, -ōris _m_ forerunner.

antecursor, -ōris _m_ forerunner, pioneer.

anteeō, -īre, -iī _vi_ to precede, surpass.

anteferō, -ferre, -tulī, -lātum _vt_ to carry before; to prefer; to anticipate.

antefīxus _adj_ attached (in front) ♦ _ntpl_ ornaments on roofs of buildings.

antegredior, -dī, -ssus _vt_ to precede.

antehabeō, -ēre _vt_ to prefer.

antehāc _adv_ formerly, previously.

antelātus _ppp of_ **anteferō.**

antelūcānus _adj_ before dawn.

antemerīdiānus _adj_ before noon.

antemittō, -ittere, -īsī, -issum _vt_ to send on in front.

antenna, -ae _f_ yardarm.

antepīlānī, -ōrum *mpl* (*MIL*) the front ranks.
antepōnō, -ōnere, -osuī, -ositum *vt* to set before; to prefer.
antequam *conj* before.
Anterōs, -ōtis *m* avenger of slighted love.
antēs, -ium *mpl* rows.
antesignānus, -ī *m* (*MIL*) leader; (*pl*) defenders of the standards.
antestō, antistō, -āre, -ētī *vi* to excel, distinguish oneself.
antestor, -ārī, -ātus *vi* to call a witness.
anteveniō, -enīre, -ēnī, -entum *vt, vi* to anticipate; to surpass.
antevertō, -tere, -tī, -sum *vt* to precede; to anticipate; to prefer.
anticipātiō, -ōnis *f* foreknowledge.
anticipō, -āre, -āvī, -ātum *vt* to take before, anticipate.
antīcus *adj* in front.
Antigonē, -ēs *f* daughter of Oedipus.
Antigonus, -ī *m* name of Macedonian kings.
Antiochēnsis *adj see n.*
Antiochīa, -īae *f* Antioch (*capital of Syria*).
Antiochus, -ī *m* name of kings of Syria.
antīquārius, -ī *and* **iī** *m* antiquary.
antīquē *adv* in the old style.
antīquitās, -ātis *f* antiquity, the ancients; integrity.
antīquitus *adv* long ago, from ancient times.
antīquō, -āre, -āvī, -ātum *vt* to vote against (a bill).
antīquus *adj* ancient, former, old; good old-fashioned, honest, illustrious; **antīquior** more important; **antīquissimus** most important.
antistēs, -itis *m/f* high priest, chief priestess; (*fig*) master (*in any art*).
Antisthenēs, -is *and* **ae** *m* founder of Cynic philosophy.
antistita, -ae *f* chief priestess.
antistō *etc see* **antestō**.
antitheton, -ī *nt* (*RHET*) antithesis.
Antōnīnus, -ī *m* name of Roman emperors (*esp Pius and Marcus Aurelius*).
Antōnius, -ī *m* Roman name (*esp the famous orator, and Mark Antony*).
antrum, -ī *nt* cave, hollow.
ānulārius, -ī *m* ringmaker.
ānulātus *adj* with rings on.
ānulus, -ī *m* ring; equestrian rank.
ānus, -ī *m* rectum; ring.
anus, -ūs *f* old woman ♦ *adj* old.
ānxiē *adv see* **anxius**.
ānxietās, -ātis *f* anxiety, trouble (*of the mind*).
ānxifer, -ī *adj* disquieting.
ānxitūdō, -inis *f* anxiety.
ānxius *adj* (*mind*) troubled; disquieting.
Āones, -um *adj* Boeotian.
Āonia *f* part of Boeotia.
Āonius *adj* of Boeotia, of Helicon.

Aornos, -ī *m* lake Avernus.
apage *interj* away with!, go away!
apēliōtēs, -ae *m* east wind.
Apellēs, -is *m* Greek painter.
aper, -rī *m* boar.
aperiō, -īre, -uī, -tum *vt* to uncover, disclose, open; (*country*) to open up; (*fig*) to unfold, explain, reveal.
apertē *adv* clearly, openly.
apertum, -ī *nt* open space; **in ~ō esse** be well known; be easy.
apertus *ppp of* **aperiō** ♦ *adj* open, exposed; clear, manifest; (*person*) frank.
aperuī *perf of* **aperiō**.
apex, -icis *m* summit; crown, priest's cap; (*fig*) crown.
aphractus, -ī *f* a long open boat.
apiārius, -ī *and* **iī** *m* beekeeper.
Apīcius, -ī *m* Roman epicure.
apicula, -ae *f* little bee.
apis, -is *f* bee.
apīscor, -īscī, -tus *vt* to catch, get, attain.
apium, -ī *and* **iī** *nt* celery.
aplustre, -is *nt* decorated stern of a ship.
apoclētī, -ōrum *mpl* committee of the Aetolian League.
apodytērium, -ī *and* **iī** *nt* dressing room.
Apollināris, -ineus *adj*: **lūdī ~ inārēs** Roman games in July.
Apollō, -inis *m* Greek god of music, archery, prophecy, flocks and herds, and often identified with the sun.
apologus, -ī *m* narrative, fable.
apophorēta, -ōrum *ntpl* presents for guests to take home.
apoproēgmena, -ōrum *ntpl* (*PHILOS*) what is rejected.
apostolicus *adj see n.*
apostolus, -ī *m* (*ECCL*) apostle.
apothēca, -ae *f* storehouse, wine store.
apparātē *adv see* **apparātus**.
apparātiō, -ōnis *f* preparation.
apparātus *adj* ready, well-supplied, sumptuous.
apparātus, -ūs *m* preparation; equipment, munitions; pomp, ostentation.
appāreō, -ēre, -uī, -itum *vi* to come in sight, appear; to be seen, show oneself; to wait upon (*an official*); **~et** it is obvious.
appāritiō, -ōnis *f* service; domestic servants.
appāritor, -ōris *m* attendant.
apparō, -āre, -āvī, -ātum *vt* to prepare, provide.
appellātiō, -ōnis *f* accosting, appeal; title; pronunciation.
appellātor, -ōris *m* appellant.
appellitātus *adj* usually called.
appellō, -āre, -āvī, -ātum *vt* to speak to; to appeal to; (*for money*) to dun; (*law*) to sue; to call, name; to pronounce.

Noun declensions and verb conjugations are shown on pp xiii to xxv. The present infinitive ending of a verb shows to which conjugation it belongs: **-āre** = 1st; **-ēre** = 2nd; **-ere** = 3rd and **-īre** = 4th. Irregular verbs are shown on p xxvi

appellō, -ellere, -ulī, -ulsum *vt* to drive, bring (to); (NAUT) to bring to land.
appendicula, -ae *f* small addition.
appendix, -icis *f* supplement.
appendō, -endere, -endī, -ensum *vt* to weigh, pay.
appetēns, -entis *adj* eager; greedy.
appetenter *adv see* **appetēns**.
appetentia, -ae *f* craving.
appetītiō, -ōnis *f* grasping, craving.
appetītus *ppp of* **appetō**.
appetītus, -ūs *m* craving; natural desire (*as opposed to reason*).
appetō, -ere, -īvī, -ītum *vt* to grasp, try to get at; to attack; to desire ♦ *vi* to approach.
appingō, -ere *vt* to paint (in); (*colloq*) to write more.
Appius, -ī *m* Roman first name; Via ~ia *main road from Rome to Capua and Brundisium.*
applaudō, -dere, -sī, -sum *vt* to strike, clap ♦ *vi* to applaud.
applicātiō, -ōnis *f* applying (*of the mind*); **iūs** ~ōnis *the right of a patron to inherit a client's effects.*
applicātus *and* **itus** *ppp of* **applicō**.
applicō, -āre, -āvī *and* **uī, -ātum** *and* **itum** *vt* to attach, place close (to); (NAUT) to steer, bring to land; **sē, animum** ~ devote self, attention (to).
applōrō, -āre *vt* to deplore.
appōnō, -ōnere, -osuī, -ositum *vt* to put (to, beside); (*meal*) to serve; to add, appoint; to reckon.
apporrēctus *adj* stretched nearby.
apportō, -āre, -āvī, -ātum *vt* to bring, carry (to).
apposcō, -ere *vt* to demand also.
apposītē *adv* suitably.
appositus *ppp of* **appōnō** ♦ *adj* situated near; (*fig*) bordering on; suitable.
apposuī *perf of* **appōnō**.
appōtus *adj* drunk.
apprecor, -ārī, -ātus *vt* to pray to.
apprehendō, -endere, -endī, -ēnsum *vt* to take hold of; (MIL) to occupy; (*argument*) to bring forward.
apprīmē *adv* especially.
apprimō, -imere, -essī, -essum *vt* to press close.
approbātiō, -ōnis *f* acquiescence; proof.
approbātor, -ōris *m* approve.
approbē *adv* very well.
approbō, -āre, -āvī, -ātum *vt* to approve; to prove; to perform to someone's satisfaction.
apprōmittō, -ere *vt* to promise also.
approperō, -āre, -āvī, -ātum *vt* to hasten ♦ *vi* to hurry up.
appropinquātiō, -ōnis *f* approach.
appropinquō, -āre, -āvī, -ātum *vi* to approach.
appugnō, -āre *vt* to attack.
appulsus *ppp of* **appellō**.
appulsus, -ūs *m* landing; approach.

aprīcātiō, -ōnis *f* basking.
aprīcor, -ārī *vi* to bask.
aprīcus *adj* sunny; basking; **in ~um prōferre** bring to light.
Aprīlis *adj* April, of April.
aprūgnus *adj* of the wild boar.
aps- *etc see* **abs-**.
aptē *adv* closely; suitably, rightly.
aptō, -āre, -āvī, -ātum *vt* to fit, put on; (*fig*) to adapt; to prepare, equip.
aptus *adj* attached, joined together, fitted (with); suitable.
apud *prep* (*with acc*) 1. (*with persons*) beside, by, with, at the house of, among, in the time of; (*speaking*) in the presence of, to; (*judgment*) in the opinion of; (*influence*) with; (*faith*) in; (*authors*) in. 2. (*with places*) near, at, in; **est ~ mē** I have; **sum ~ mē** I am in my senses.
Āpūlia, -iae *f* district of S.E. Italy.
Āpūlus *adj see n.*
aput *prep see* **apud**.
aqua, -ae *f* water; ~ **mihī haeret** I am in a fix; ~ **intercus** dropsy; ~**m adspergere** revive; ~**m praebēre** entertain; ~**m et terram petere** demand submission; ~**ā et ignī interdīcere** outlaw.
aquae *fpl* medicinal waters, spa.
aquaeductus, -ūs *m* aqueduct; right of leading water.
aquāliculus *m* belly.
aquālis, -is *m/f* washbasin.
aquārius *adj* of water ♦ *m* water carrier, water inspector; a constellation.
aquāticus *adj* aquatic; humid.
aquātilis *adj* aquatic.
aquātiō, -ōnis *f* fetching water; watering place.
aquātor, -ōris *m* water carrier.
aquila, -ae *f* eagle; standard of a legion; (ARCH) gable; a constellation; ~**ae senectūs** a vigorous old age.
Aquileia, -ae *f* town in N. Italy.
Aquileiēnsis *adj see n.*
aquilifer, -ī *m* chief standard-bearer.
aquilīnus *adj* eagle's.
aquilō, -ōnis *m* north wind; north.
aquilōnius *adj* northerly.
aquilus *adj* swarthy.
Aquīnās, ātis *adj see n.*
Aquīnum, -ī *nt* town in Latium.
Aquītānia, -iae *f* district of S.W. Gaul.
Aquītānus *adj see n.*
aquor, -ārī, -ātus *vi* to fetch water.
aquōsus *adj* humid, rainy.
aquula, -ae *f* little stream.
āra, -ae *f* altar; (*fig*) refuge; a constellation; ~**ae et focī** hearth and home.
arabarchēs, -ae *m* customs officer in Egypt.
Arabia, -iae *f* Arabia.
Arabicē *adv* with all the perfumes of Arabia.
Arabicus, Arabicius, Arabus *adj see n.*
Arachnē, -s *f* Lydian woman changed into a spider.

arānea, -ae f spider; cobweb.
arāneola f, **-olus** m small spider.
arāneōsus adj full of spiders' webs.
arāneum, -ī nt spider's web.
arāneus, -i m spider ♦ adj of spiders.
Arar, -is m river Saône.
Arātēus adj see **Arātus**.
arātiō, -ōnis f ploughing, farming; arable land.
arātiuncula f small plot.
arātor -ōris m ploughman, farmer; (pl) cultivators of public land.
arātrum, -ī nt plough.
Arātus, -ī m Greek astronomical poet.
Araxēs, -is m river in Armenia.
arbiter, -rī m witness; arbiter, judge, umpire; controller; ~ **bibendī** president of a drinking party.
arbitra, -ae f witness.
arbitrāriō adv with some uncertainty.
arbitrārius adj uncertain.
arbitrātus, -ūs m decision; **meō ~ū** in my judgment.
arbitrium, -ī and **iī** nt decision (of an arbitrator), judgment; mastery, control.
arbitror, -ārī, -ātus vt, vi to be a witness of; to testify; to think, suppose.
arbor, (arbōs), -oris f tree; ship, mast, oar; ~ **īnfēlix** gallows.
arboreus adj of trees, like a tree.
arbustum, -ī nt plantation, orchard; (pl) trees.
arbustus adj wooded.
arbuteus adj of the strawberry tree.
arbutum, -ī nt fruit of strawberry tree.
arbutus, -ī f strawberry tree.
arca, -ae f box; moneybox, purse; coffin; prison cell; **ex ~ā absolvere** pay cash.
Arcadēs, -um mpl Arcadians.
Arcadia, -iae f district of S. Greece.
Arcadicus, -ius adj see **Arcadia**.
arcānō adv privately.
arcānum, -ī nt secret, mystery.
arcānus adj secret; able to keep secrets.
arceō, -ēre, -uī, -tum vt to enclose; to keep off, prevent.
arcessītū abl sg m at the summons.
arcessītus ppp of **arcessō** ♦ adj far-fetched.
arcessō, -ere, -īvī, -ītum vt to send for, fetch; (law) to summon, accuse; (fig) to derive.
archetypus, -ī m original.
Archilochus, -ī m Greek iambic and elegiac poet.
archimagīrus, -ī m chief cook.
Archimēdēs, -is m famous mathematician of Syracuse.
archipīrāta, -ae m pirate chief.
architectōn, -onis m master builder; master in cunning.
architector, -ārī, -ātus vt to construct; (fig) to devise.
architectūra, -ae f architecture.

architectus, -ī m architect; (fig) author.
archōn, -ontis m Athenian magistrate.
Archytās, -ae m Pythagorean philosopher of Tarentum.
arcitenēns, -entis adj holding a bow ♦ m Apollo.
Arctophylax, -cis m (constellation) Bootes.
arctos, -ī f Great Bear, Little Bear; north, north wind; night.
Arctūrus, -ī m brightest star in Boötes.
arctus etc see **artus** etc.
arcuī perf of **arceō**.
arcula, -ae f casket; (RHET) ornament.
arcuō, -āre, -āvī, -ātum vt to curve.
arcus, -ūs m bow; rainbow; arch, curve; (MATH) arc.
ardea, -ae f heron.
Ardea, -ae f town in Latium.
ardeliō, -ōnis m busybody.
ārdēns, -entis adj hot, glowing, fiery; (fig) eager, ardent.
ārdenter adv passionately.
ārdeō, -dēre, -sī, -sum vi to be on fire, burn, shine; (fig) to be fired, burn.
ārdēscō, -ere vi to catch fire, gleam; (fig) to become inflamed, wax hotter.
ārdor, -ōris m heat, brightness; (fig) ardour, passion.
arduum, -ī nt steep slope; difficulty.
arduus adj steep, high; difficult, troublesome.
ārea, -ae f vacant site, open space, playground; threshing-floor; (fig) scope (for effort).
ārefaciō, -acere, -ēcī, -actum vt to dry.
arēna etc see **harēna**.
ārēns, -entis adj arid; thirsty.
āreō, -ēre vi to be dry.
āreola, -ae f small open space.
Arēopagītēs m member of the court.
Arēopagus, -ī m Mars' Hill in Athens; a criminal court.
Arēs, -is m Greek god of war.
ārēscō, -ere vi to dry, dry up.
Arestoridēs, -ae m Argus.
aretālogus, -ī m braggart.
Arethūsa, -ae f spring near Syracuse.
Arethūsis adj Syracusan.
Argēī, -ōrum mpl sacred places in Rome; effigies thrown annually into the Tiber.
argentāria, -ae f bank, banking; silver mine.
argentārius adj of silver, of money ♦ m banker.
argentātus adj silver-plated; backed with money.
argenteus adj of silver, adorned with silver; silvery (in colour); of the silver age.
argentum, -ī nt silver, silver plate; money.
Argēus, -īvus, -olicus adj Argive; Greek.
Argīlētānus adj see n.
Argīlētum, -ī nt part of Rome (noted for

bookshops).
argilla, -ae _f_ clay.
Argō, -ūs _f_ Jason's ship.
Argolis, -olidis _f_ district about Argos.
Argonautae, -ārum _mpl_ Argonauts.
Argonauticus _adj see n._
Argos _nt, -ī, -ōrum_ _mpl_ town in S.E. Greece.
Argōus _adj see_ **Argō.**
argūmentātiō, -ōnis _f_ adducing proofs.
argūmentor, -ārī, -ātus _vt, vi_ to prove, adduce as proof; to conclude.
argūmentum, -ī _nt_ evidence, proof; (_LIT_) subject matter, theme, plot (_of a play_); (_art_) subject, motif.
arguō, -uere, -uī, -ūtum _vt_ to prove, make known; to accuse, blame, denounce.
Argus, -ī _m_ monster with many eyes.
argūtē _adv_ subtly.
argūtiae, -ārum _fpl_ nimbleness, liveliness; wit, subtlety, slyness.
argūtor, -ārī, -ātus _vi_ to chatter.
argūtulus _adj_ rather subtle.
argūtus _adj_ (_sight_) clear, distinct, graceful; (_sound_) clear, melodious, noisy; (_mind_) acute, witty, sly.
argyraspis, -dis _adj_ silver-shielded.
Ariadna, -ae _f_ daughter of Minos of Crete.
Ariadnaeus _adj see n._
āridulus _adj_ rather dry.
āridum, -ī _nt_ dry land.
āridus _adj_ dry, withered; meagre; (_style_) flat.
ariēs, -etis _m_ ram; 1st sign of Zodiac; battering ram; beam used as a breakwater.
arietō, -āre _vt, vi_ to butt, strike hard.
Ariōn, -onis _m_ early Greek poet and musician.
Ariōnius _adj see n._
arista, -ae _f_ ear of corn.
Aristaeus, -ī _m_ legendary founder of beekeeping.
Aristarchus, -ī _m_ Alexandrian scholar; a severe critic.
Aristīdēs, -is _m_ Athenian statesman noted for integrity.
Aristippēus _adj see n._
Aristippus, -ī _m_ Greek hedonist philosopher.
aristolochia, -ae _f_ birthwort.
Aristophanēs, -is _m_ Greek comic poet.
Aristophanēus, and īus _adj see n._
Aristotelēs, -is _m_ Aristotle (_founder of Peripatetic school of philosophy_).
Aristotelēus, and īus _adj see n._
arithmētica, -ōrum _ntpl_ arithmetic.
āritūdō, -inis _f_ dryness.
Ariūsius _adj_ of Ariusia in Chios.
arma, -ōrum _ntpl_ armour, shield; arms, weapons (_of close combat only_); warfare, troops; (_fig_) defence, protection; implements, ship's gear.
armāmenta, -ōrum _ntpl_ implements, ship's gear.
armāmentārium, -ī and iī _nt_ arsenal.
armāriolum, -ī _nt_ small chest.
armārium, -ī and iī _nt_ chest, safe.
armātū _m abl_ armour; **gravī ~** with heavy-

armed troops.
armātūra, -ae _f_ armour, equipment; **levis ~** light-armed troops.
armātus _adj_ armed.
Armenia, -ae _f_ Armenia.
Armeniaca, -acae _f_ apricot tree.
Armeniacum, -acī _nt_ apricot.
Armenius _adj see_ **Armenia.**
armentālis _adj_ of the herd.
armentārius, -ī and iī _m_ cattle herd.
armentum, -ī _nt_ cattle (_for ploughing_), herd (_cattle etc_).
armifer, -ī _adj_ armed.
armiger, -ī _m_ armour-bearer ♦ _adj_ armed; productive of warriors.
armilla, -ae _f_ bracelet.
armillātus _adj_ wearing a bracelet.
armipotēns, -entis _adj_ strong in battle.
armisonus _adj_ resounding with arms.
armō, -āre, -āvī, -ātum _vt_ to arm, equip; to rouse to arms (against).
armus, -ī _m_ shoulder (_esp of animals_).
Arniēnsis _adj see_ **Arnus.**
Arnus, -ī _m_ river Arno.
arō, -āre, -āvī, -ātum _vt_ to plough, cultivate; to live by farming; (_fig: sea, brow_) to furrow.
Arpīnās, -ātis _adj see n._
Arpīnum, -ī _nt_ town in Latium (_birthplace of Cicero_).
arquātus _adj_ jaundiced.
arr- _etc see_ **adr-.**
arrabō, -ōnis _m_ earnest money.
ars, artis _f_ skill (_in any craft_); the art (_of any profession_); science, theory; handbook; work of art; moral quality, virtue; artifice, fraud.
ārsī _perf of_ **ārdeō.**
ārsus _ppp of_ **ārdeō.**
artē _adv_ closely, soundly, briefly.
artēria, -ae _f_ windpipe; artery.
artēria, -ōrum _ntpl_ trachea.
arthrīticus _adj_ gouty.
articulātim _adv_ joint by joint; (_speech_) distinctly.
articulō, -āre, -āvī, -ātum _vt_ to articulate.
articulōsus _adj_ minutely subdivided.
articulus, -ī _m_ joint, knuckle; limb; (_words_) clause; (_time_) point, turning point; **in ipsō ~ō temporis** in the nick of time.
artifex, -icis _m_ artist, craftsman, master; (_fig_) maker, author ♦ _adj_ ingenious, artistic, artificial.
artificiōsē _adv_ skilfully.
artificiōsus _adj_ ingenious, artistic, artificial.
artificium, -ī and iī _nt_ skill, workmanship; art, craft; theory, rule of an art; ingenuity, cunning.
artō, -āre _vt_ to compress, curtail.
artolaganus, -ī _m_ kind of cake.
artopta, -ae _m_ baker; baking tin.
artus _adj_ close, narrow, tight; (_sleep_) deep; (_fig_) strict, straitened.
artus, -ūs _m_ joint; (_pl_) limbs, body; (_fig_) strength.

ārula, -ae *f* small altar.
arundō *etc see* **harundō** *etc*.
arvīna, -ae *f* grease.
arvum, -ī *nt* field; land, country, plain.
arvus *adj* ploughed.
arx, arcis *f* fortress, castle; height, summit; (*fig*) bulwark, stronghold; **arcem facere ē cloācā** make a mountain out of a molehill.
ās, assis *m* (*weight*) pound; (*coin*) bronze unit, of low value; (*inheritance*) the whole (*subdivided into 12 parts*); **ad assem** to the last farthing; **hērēs ex asse** sole heir.
Ascānius, -ī *m son of Aeneas.*
ascendō, -endere, -endī, -ēnsum *vt, vi* to go up, climb, embark; (*fig*) to rise.
ascēnsiō, -ōnis *f* ascent; (*fig*) sublimity.
ascēnsus, -ūs *m* ascent, rising; way up.
ascia, -ae *f* axe; mason's trowel.
asciō, -īre *vt* to admit.
ascīscō, -īscere, -īvī, -ītum *vt* to receive with approval; to admit (*to some kind of association*); to appropriate, adopt (*esp customs*); to arrogate to oneself.
ascītus *adj* acquired, alien.
Ascra, -ae *f birthplace of Hesiod in Boeotia.*
Ascraeus *adj* of Ascra; of Hesiod; of Helicon.
ascrībō, -bere, -psī, -ptum *vt* to add (*in writing*); to attribute, ascribe; to apply (*an illustration*); to enrol, include.
ascrīptīcius *adj* enrolled.
ascrīptiō, -ōnis *f* addition (*in writing*).
ascrīptīvus *adj* (*MIL*) supernumerary.
ascrīptor, -ōris *m* supporter.
ascrīptus *ppp of* **ascrībō**.
asella, -ae *f* young ass.
asellus, -ī *m* young ass.
Āsia, -ae *f* Roman province; Asia Minor; Asia.
asīlus, -ī *m* gad fly.
asinus, -ī *m* ass; fool.
Āsis, -dis *f* Asia.
Āsius (Āsiānus, Āsiāticus) *adj see n.*
Āsōpus, -ī *m river in Boeotia.*
asōtus, -ī *m* libertine.
asparagus, -ī *m* asparagus.
aspargō *etc see* **aspergō**.
aspectābilis *adj* visible.
aspectō, -āre *vt* to look at, gaze at; to pay heed to; (*places*) to face.
aspectus *ppp of* **aspiciō**.
aspectus, -ūs *m* look, sight; glance, sense of sight; aspect, appearance.
aspellō, -ere *vt* to drive away.
asper, -ī *adj* rough; (*taste*) bitter; (*sound*) harsh; (*weather*) severe; (*style*) rugged; (*person*) violent, exasperated, unkind, austere; (*animal*) savage; (*CIRCS*) difficult.
asperē *adv see adj.*
aspergō, -gere, -sī, -sum *vt* to scatter, sprinkle; to bespatter, besprinkle; **aquam ~** revive.
aspergō, -inis *f* sprinkling; spray.

asperitās, -ātis *f* roughness, unevenness, harshness, severity; (*fig*) ruggedness, fierceness; trouble, difficulty.
aspernātiō, -ōnis *f* disdain.
aspernor, -ārī, -ātus *vt* to reject, disdain.
asperō, -āre, -āvī, -ātum *vt* to roughen, sharpen; to exasperate.
aspersiō, -ōnis *f* sprinkling.
aspersus *ppp of* **aspergō**.
aspiciō, -icere, -exī, -ectum *vt* to catch sight of, look at; (*places*) to face; (*fig*) to examine, consider.
aspīrātiō, -ōnis *f* breathing (on); evaporation; pronouncing with an aspirate.
aspīrō, -āre, -āvī, -ātum *vi* to breathe, blow; to favour; to aspire, attain (to) ♦ *vt* to blow, instil.
aspis, -dis *f* asp.
asportātiō, -ōnis *f* removal.
asportō, -āre *vt* to carry off.
asprēta, -ōrum *ntpl* rough country.
ass- *etc see* **ads-**.
Assaracus, -ī *m* Trojan ancestor of Aeneas.
asser, -is *m* pole, stake.
assula, -ae *f* splinter.
assulātim *adv* in splinters.
assum, -ī *nt* roast; (*pl*) sweating-bath.
assus *adj* roasted.
Assyria, -ae *f* country in W. Asia.
Assyrius *adj* Assyrian; oriental.
ast *conj* (*laws*) and then; (*vows*) then; (*strong contrast*) and yet.
ast- *etc see* **adst-**.
Astraea, -ae *f* goddess of Justice.
Astraeus, -ī *m* father of winds; **~ī frātrēs** the winds.
astrologia, -ae *f* astronomy.
astrologus, -ī *m* astronomer; astrologer.
astrum, -ī *nt* star, heavenly body, constellation; a great height; heaven, immortality, glory.
astu *nt* (*indecl*) city (*esp Athens*).
astus, -ūs *m* cleverness, cunning.
astūtē *adv* cleverly.
astūtia, -ae *f* slyness, cunning.
astūtus *adj* artful, sly.
Astyanax, -ctis *m* son of Hector and Andromache.
asȳlum, -ī *nt* sanctuary.
asymbolus *adj* with no contribution.
at *conj* (*adversative*) but, on the other hand; (*objecting*) but it may be said; (*limiting*) at least, but at least; (*continuing*) then, thereupon; (*transitional*) now; (*with passionate appeals*) but oh!, look now!; **~ enim** yes, but; **~ tamen** nevertheless.
Atābulus, -ī *m* sirocco.
atat *interj* (*expressing fright, pain, surprise*) oh!
atavus, -ī *m* great-great-great-grandfather; ancestor.

Noun declensions and verb conjugations are shown on pp xiii to xxv. The present infinitive ending of a verb shows to which conjugation it belongs: **-āre** = 1st; **-ēre** = 2nd; **-ere** = 3rd and **-īre** = 4th. Irregular verbs are shown on p xxvi

Atella, -ae f Oscan town in Campania.
Ātellānicus, Atellānius adj see n.
Atellānus adj: **fābula ~āna** kind of comic show popular in Rome.
āter, -rī adj black, dark; gloomy, dismal; malicious; **diēs ~rī** unlucky days.
Athamantēus adj see **Athamās.**
Athamantiadēs m Palaemon.
Athamantis f Helle.
Athamās, -antis m king of Thessaly (who went mad).
Athēnae, -ārum fpl Athens.
Athēnaeus, -iēnsis adj see n.
atheos, -ī m atheist.
athlēta, -ae m wrestler, athlete.
athlēticē adv athletically.
Athos (dat -ō, acc -ō, -on, -ōnem) m mount Athos in Macedonia.
Atlanticus adj: **mare ~anticum** Atlantic Ocean.
Atlantiadēs m Mercury.
Atlantis f lost Atlantic island; a Pleiad.
Atlās, -antis m giant supporting the sky; Atlas mountains.
atomus, -ī m atom.
atque (before consonants **ac**) conj (connecting words) and, and in fact; (connecting clauses) and moreover, and then, and so, and yet; (in comparison) as, than, to, from; **~ adeō** and that too; or rather; **~ nōn** and not rather; **~ sī** as if; **alius ~** different from; **contrā ~** opposite to; **īdem ~** same as; **plūs ~** more than.
atquī conj (adversative) and yet, nevertheless, yes but; (confirming) by all means; (minor premise) now; **~ sī** if now.
ātrāmentum, -ī nt ink; blacking.
ātrātus adj in mourning.
Atreus, -eī m son of Pelops (king of Argos).
Atrīdēs m Agamemnon; Meneleaus.
ātriēnsis, -is m steward, major-domo.
ātriolum, -ī nt anteroom.
ātrium, -ī and **iī** nt hall, open central room in Roman house; forecourt of a temple; hall (in other buildings).
atrōcitās, -ātis f hideousness; (mind) brutality; (PHILOS) severity.
atrōciter adv savagely.
Atropos, -ī f one of the Fates.
atrōx, -ōcis adj hideous, dreadful; fierce, brutal, unyielding.
attāctus ppp of **attingō.**
attāctus, -ūs m contact.
attagēn, -is m heathcock.
Attalica ntpl garments of woven gold.
Attalicus adj of Attalus; of Pergamum; ornamented with gold cloth.
Attalus, -ī m king of Pergamum (who bequeathed his kingdom to Rome).
attamen conj nevertheless.
attat etc see **atat.**
attegia, -ae f hut.
attemperātē adv opportunely.
attempto etc see **attentō.**

attendō, -dere, -dī, -tum vt to direct (the attention); to attend to, notice.
attenē adv carefully.
attentiō, -ōnis f attentiveness.
attentō, -āre, -āvī, -ātum vt to test, try; (loyalty) to tamper with; to attack.
attentus ppp of **attendō** ♦ adj attentive, intent; businesslike, careful (esp about money).
attentus ppp of **attineō.**
attenuātē adv simply.
attenuātus adj weak; (style) brief; refined; plain.
attenuō, -āre, -āvī, -ātum vt to weaken, reduce; to diminish; to humble.
atterō, -erere, -rīvī, -rītum vt to rub; to wear away; (fig) to impair, exhaust.
attestor, -ārī, -ātus vt to confirm.
attexō, -ere, -uī, -tum vt to weave on; (fig) to add on.
Atthis, -dis f Attica.
Attiānus adj see **Attius.**
Attica, -ae f district of Greece about Athens.
Atticē adv in the Athenian manner.
Atticissō vi to speak in the Athenian manner.
Atticus adj Attic, Athenian; (RHET) of a plain and direct style.
attigī perf of **attingō.**
attigō see **attingō.**
attineō, -inēre, -inuī, -entum vt to hold fast, detain; to guard; to reach for ♦ vi to concern, pertain, be of importance, avail.
attingō, -ingere, -igī, -āctum vt to touch; to strike, assault; to arrive at; to border on; to affect; to mention; to undertake; to concern, resemble.
Attis, -dis m Phrygian priest of Cybele.
Attius, -ī m Latin tragic poet.
attollō, -ere vt to lift up, erect; (fig) to exalt, extol.
attondeō, -ondēre, -ondī, -ōnsum vt to shear, prune, crop; (fig) to diminish; (comedy) to fleece.
attonitus adj thunderstruck, terrified, astonished; inspired.
attonō, -āre, -uī, -itum vt to stupefy.
attōnsus ppp of **attondeō.**
attorqueō, -ēre vt to hurl upwards.
attractus ppp of **attrahō.**
attraho, -here, -xī, -ctum vt to drag by force, attract; (fig) to draw, incite.
attrectō, -āre vt to touch, handle; to appropriate.
attrepidō, -āre vi to hobble along.
attribuō, -uere, -uī, -ūtum vt to assign, bestow; to add; to impute, attribute; to lay as a tax.
attribūtiō, -ōnis f (money) assignment; (GRAM) predicate.
attribūtum, -ī nt (GRAM) predicate.
attribūtus ppp of **attribuō** ♦ adj subject.
attrītus ppp of **atterō** ♦ adj worn; bruised; (fig) impudent.
attulī perf of **adferō.**

au *interj* (*expressing pain, surprise*) oh!
auceps, -upis *m* fowler; (*fig*) eavesdropper; a
    pedantic critic.
auctārium, -ī *and* **iī** *nt* extra.
auctificus *adj* increasing.
auctiō, -ōnis *f* increase; auction sale.
auctiōnārius *adj* auction; **tabulae ~ae**
    catalogues.
auctiōnor, -ārī, -ātus *vi* to hold an auction.
auctitō, -āre *vt* to greatly increase.
auctō, -āre *vt* to increase.
auctor, -ōris *m/f* **1.** (*originator: of families*)
    progenitor; (: *of buildings*) founder; (: *of
    deeds*) doer. **2.** (*composer: of writings*) author,
    historian; (: *of knowledge*) investigator,
    teacher; (: *of news*) informant. **3.** (*instigator:
    of action*) adviser; (: *of measures*) promoter;
    (: *of laws*) proposer, supporter; ratifier. **4.**
    (*person of influence: in public life*) leader; (: *of
    conduct*) model; (: *of guarantees*) witness,
    bail; (: *of property*) seller; (: *of women and
    minors*) guardian; (: *of others' welfare*)
    champion; **mē ~ōre** at my suggestion.
auctōrāmentum, -ī *nt* contract; wages.
auctōrātus *adj* bound (*by a pledge*); hired out
    (*for wages*).
auctōritās, -ātis *f* **1.** source; lead,
    responsibility. **2.** judgment; opinion; advice,
    support; bidding, guidance; (*of senate*)
    decree; (*of people*) will. **3.** power; (*person*)
    influence, authority, prestige; (*things*)
    importance, worth; (*conduct*) example;
    (*knowledge*) warrant, document, authority;
    (*property*) right of possession.
auctumn- *etc see* **autumn-**.
auctus *ppp of* **augeō** ♦ *adj* enlarged, great.
auctus, -ūs *m* growth, increase.
aucupium, -ī *and* **iī** *nt* fowling; birds caught;
    (*fig*) hunting (after), quibbling.
aucupō, -āre *vt* to watch for.
aucupor, -ārī, -ātus *vi* to go fowling ♦ *vt* to
    chase; (*fig*) to try to catch.
audācia, -ae *f* daring, courage; audacity,
    impudence; (*pl*) deeds of daring.
audācter, audāciter *adv see* **audāx**.
audāx, -ācis *adj* bold, daring; rash, audacious;
    proud.
audēns, -entis *adj* bold, brave.
audenter *adv see* **audēns**.
audentia, -ae *f* boldness, courage.
audeō, -dēre, -sus *vt*, *vi* to dare, venture; to
    be brave.
audiēns, -entis *m* hearer ♦ *adj* obedient.
audientia, -ae *f* hearing; **~m facere** gain a
    hearing.
audiō, -īre, -īvī *and* **iī, -ītum** *vt* to hear; to
    learn, be told; to be called; to listen, attend
    to, study under (a teacher); to examine a
    case; to agree with; to obey, heed; **bene/
    male ~** have a good/bad reputation.

audītiō, -ōnis *f* listening; hearsay, news.
audītor, -ōris *m* hearer; pupil.
audītōrium, -ī *and* **iī** *nt* lecture room, law
    court; audience.
audītus, -ūs *m* (sense of) hearing; a hearing;
    rumour.
auferō, auferre, abstulī, ablātum *vt* to take
    away, carry away; to mislead, lead into a
    digression; to take by force, steal; to win,
    obtain (*as the result of effort*); **aufer** away
    with!
Aufidus, -ō *m* river in Apulia.
aufugiō, -ugere, -ūgī *vi* to run away ♦ *vt* to
    flee from.
Augēās, -ae *m* king of Elis (*whose stables
    Hercules cleaned*).
augeō, -gēre, -xī, -ctum *vt* to increase; to
    enrich, bless (with); to praise, worship ♦ *vi*
    to increase.
augēscō, -ere *vi* to begin to grow, increase.
augmen, -inis *nt* growth.
augur, -is *m/f* augur; prophet, interpreter.
augurāle, -is *nt* part of camp where auspices
    were taken.
augurālis *adj* augur's.
augurātiō, -ōnis *f* soothsaying.
augurātō *adv* after taking auspices.
augurātus, -ūs *m* office of augur.
augurium, -ī *and* **iī** *nt* augury; an omen;
    prophecy, interpretation; presentiment.
augurius *adj* of augurs.
augurō, -āre *vt*, *vi* to take auguries; to
    consecrate by auguries; to forebode.
auguror, -ārī, -ātus *vt*, *vi* to take auguries; to
    foretell by omens; to predict, conjecture.
Augusta, -ae *f* title of the emperor's wife,
    mother, daughter *or* sister.
Augustālis *adj* of Augustus; **lūdī ~ēs** games in
    October; **praefectus ~is** governor of Egypt;
    sodālēs ~ēs priests of deified Augustus.
augustē *adv see* **augustus**.
augustus *adj* venerable, august, majestic.
Augustus, -ī *m* title given to C Octavius, first
    Roman emperor, and so to his successors ♦ *adj*
    imperial; (*month*) August, of August.
aula, -ae *f* courtyard of a Greek house; hall of a
    Roman house; palace, royal court; courtiers;
    royal power.
aula *etc see* **olla**.
aulaeum, -ī *nt* embroidered hangings,
    canopy, covering; (*THEAT*) curtain.
aulicī, -ōrum *mpl* courtiers.
aulicus *adj* of the court.
Aulis, -idis *and* **is** *f* port in Boeotia from which the
    Greeks sailed for Troy.
auloedus, -ī *m* singer accompanied by flute.
aura, -ae *f* breath of air, breeze, wind; air,
    upper world; vapour, odour, sound, gleam;
    (*fig*) winds (*of public favour*), breeze (*of
    prosperity*), air (*of freedom*), daylight (*of*

publicity).

aurāria, -ae _f_ gold mine.

aurārius _adj_ of gold.

aurātus _adj_ gilt, ornamented with gold; gold.

Aurēlius, -ī _m_ Roman name; **lēx ~ia** _law on the composition of juries;_ **via ~ia** _main road running NW from Rome._

aureolus _adj_ gold; beautiful, splendid.

aureus _adj_ gold, golden; gilded; (_fig_) beautiful splendid ♦ _m_ gold coin.

aurichalcum, -ī _nt_ a precious metal.

auricomus _adj_ golden-leaved.

auricula, -ae _f_ the external ear; ear.

aurifer, -ī _adj_ gold-producing.

aurifex, -icis _m_ goldsmith.

aurīga, -ae _m_ charioteer, driver; groom; helmsman; a constellation.

aurigena, -ae _adj_ gold-begotten.

auriger, -ī _adj_ gilded.

aurigō, -āre _vi_ to compete in the chariot race.

auris, -is _f_ ear; (_RHET_) judgment; (_AGR_) earthboard (_of a plough_); **ad ~em admonēre** whisper; **in utramvis ~em dormīre** sleep soundly.

aurītulus, -ī _m_ "Long-Ears".

aurītus _adj_ long-eared; attentive.

aurōra, -ae _f_ dawn, morning; _goddess of dawn;_ the East.

aurum, -ī _nt_ gold; gold plate, jewellery, bit, fleece _etc;_ money; lustre; the Golden Age.

auscultātiō, -ōnis _f_ obedience.

auscultātor, -ōris _m_ listener.

auscultō, -āre, -āvī, -ātum _vt_ to listen to; to overhear ♦ _vi_ (_of servants_) to wait at the door; to obey.

ausim _subj of_ **audeō.**

Ausones, -um _mpl indigenous people of central Italy._

Ausonia _f_ Italy.

Ausonidae _mpl_ Italians.

Ausonius, -is _adj_ Italian.

auspex, -icis _m_ augur, soothsayer; patron, commander; witness of a marriage contract.

auspicātō _adv_ after taking auspices; at a lucky moment.

auspicātus _adj_ consecrated; auspicious, lucky.

auspicium, -ī _and_ **iī** _nt_ augury, auspices; right of taking auspices; power, command; omen; **~ facere** give a sign.

auspicō, -āre _vi_ to take the auspices.

auspicor, -ārī, -ātus _vi_ to take the auspices; to make a beginning ♦ _vt_ to begin, enter upon.

auster, -rī _m_ south wind; south.

austērē _adv see_ **austērus.**

austēritās, -ātis _f_ severity.

austērus _adj_ severe, serious; gloomy, irksome.

austrālis _adj_ southern.

austrīnus _adj_ from the south.

ausum, -ī _nt_ enterprise.

ausus _ppa of_ **audeō.**

aut _conj_ or; either ... or; or else _or_ at least, or rather.

autem _conj_ (_adversative_) but, on the other hand; (_in transitions, parentheses_) moreover, now, and; (_in dialogue_) indeed.

authepsa, -ae _f_ stove.

autographus _adj_ written with his own hand.

Autolycus, -ī _m_ a robber.

automaton, -ī _nt_ automaton.

automatus _adj_ spontaneous.

Automedōn, -ontis _m_ a charioteer.

autumnālis _adj_ autumn, autumnal.

autumnus, -ī _m_ autumn ♦ _adj_ autumnal.

autumō, -āre _vt_ to assert.

auxī _perf of_ **augeō.**

auxilia, -iōrum _ntpl_ auxiliary troops; military force.

auxiliāris _adj_ helping, auxiliary; of the auxiliaries ♦ _mpl_ auxiliary troops.

auxiliārius _adj_ helping; auxiliary.

auxiliātor, -ōris _m_ helper.

auxiliātus, -ūs _m_ aid.

auxilior, -ārī, -ātus _vi_ to aid, support.

auxilium, -ī _and_ **iī** _nt_ help, assistance.

avārē, avāliter _adv see_ **avārus.**

avāritia, -ae _f_ greed, selfishness.

avāritiēs, -ēī _f_ avarice.

avārus _adj_ greedy, covetous; eager.

avē, avēte, avētō _impv_ hail!, farewell!

āvehō, -here, -xī, -ctum _vt_ to carry away; (_pass_) to ride away.

āvellō, -ellere, -ellī _and_ **ulsī (-olsī), -ulsum (-olsum)** _vt_ to pull away, tear off; to take away (by force), remove.

avēna, -ae _f_ oats; (_music_) reed, shepherd's pipe.

Aventīnum, -ī _nt_ Aventine hill.

Aventīnus, -ī _m_ Aventine hill in Rome ♦ _adj_ of Aventine.

avēns, -entis _adj_ eager.

aveō, -ēre _vt_ to desire, long for.

Avernālis _adj_ of lake Avernus.

Avernus, -ī _m_ lake near Cumae (_said to be an entrance to the lower world_); the lower world ♦ _adj_ birdless; of Avernus; infernal.

āverruncō, -āre _vt_ to avert.

āversābilis _adj_ abominable.

āversor, -ārī, -ātus _vi_ to turn away ♦ _vt_ to repulse, decline.

āversor, -ōris _m_ embezzler.

āversum, -ī _nt_ back.

āversus _ppp of_ **āvertō** ♦ _adj_ in the rear, behind, backwards; hostile, averse.

āvertō, -tere, -tī, -sum _vt_ to turn aside, avert; to divert; to embezzle; to estrange ♦ _vi_ to withdraw.

avia, -ae _f_ grandmother.

avia, -ōrum _ntpl_ wilderness.

aviārium, -ī _nt_ aviary, haunt of birds.

aviārius _adj_ of birds.

avidē _adv see_ **avidus.**

avidītās, -ātis _f_ eagerness, longing; avarice.

avidus *adj* eager, covetous; avaricious, greedy; hungry; vast.

avis, -is *f* bird; omen; ~ **alba** a rarity.

avītus *adj* of a grandfather; ancestral.

āvius *adj* out of the way, lonely, untrodden; wandering, astray.

āvocāmentum, -ī *nt* relaxation.

āvocātiō, -ōnis *f* diversion.

āvocō, -āre *vt* to call off; to divert, distract; to amuse.

āvolō, -āre *vi* to fly away, hurry away; to depart, vanish.

āvolsus, avulsus *ppp of* **avellō**.

avunculus, -ī *m* uncle (*on mother's side*); ~ **māgnus** great-uncle.

avus, -ī *m* grandfather; ancestor.

Axenus, -ī *m* Black Sea.

axicia, axitia, -ae *f* scissors.

āxilla -ae *f* armpit.

axis, -is *m* axle, chariot; axis, pole, sky, clime; plank.

azȳmus *adj* unleavened.

B, b

babae *interj* (*expressing wonder or joy*) oho!

Babylōn, -ōnis *f* ancient city on the Euphrates.

Babylōnia *f* the country under Babylon.

Babylōnicus, (-)ōniēnsis *adj see n.*

Babylōnius *adj* Babylonian; Chaldaean, versed in astrology.

bāca, -ae *f* berry; olive; fruit; pearl.

bācātus *adj* of pearls.

bacca *etc see* **bāca.**

baccar, -is *nt* cyclamen.

Baccha, -ae *f* Bacchante.

Bacchānal, -ālis *nt* place consecrated to Bacchus; (*pl*) festival of Bacchus.

bacchātiō, -ōnis *f* revel.

Bacchēus, -icus, -ius *adj see n.*

Bacchiadae, -ārum *mpl* kings of Corinth (*founders of Syracuse*).

bacchor, -ārī, -ātus *vi* to celebrate the festival of Bacchus; to revel, rave; to rage.

Bacchus, -ī *m* god of wine, vegetation, poetry, and religious ecstasy; vine, wine.

bācifer, -ī *adj* olive-bearing.

bacillum, -ī *nt* stick, lictor's staff.

Bactra, -ōrum *ntpl* capital of Bactria in central Asia (*now* Balkh).

Bactriāna *f* Bactria.

Bactriānus *and* **ius** *adj* Bactrian.

baculum, -ī *nt*, **-us, -ī** *m* stick, staff.

Baetica *f* Roman province (*now* Andalusia).

Baeticus *adj see* **Baetis.**

Baetis, -is *m* river in Spain (*now* Guadalquivir).

Bagrada, -ae *m* river in Africa (*now* Mejerdah).

Bāiae, -ārum *fpl* Roman spa on Bay of Naples.

Bāiānus *adj see n.*

bāiulō, -āre *vt* to carry (*something heavy*).

bāiulus, -ī *m* porter.

bālaena, -ae *f* whale.

balanus, -ī *f* balsam (*from an Arabian nut*); a shellfish.

balatrō, -ōnis *m* jester.

bālātus, -ūs *m* bleating.

balbus *adj* stammering.

balbūtiō, -īre *vt, vi* to stammer, speak indistinctly; (*fig*) to speak obscurely.

Baliārēs, -ium *fpl* Balearic islands.

Baliāris, Baliāricus *adj see n.*

balineum *etc see* **balneum** *etc.*

ballista, -ae *f* (MIL) catapult for shooting stones and other missiles; (*fig*) weapon.

ballistārium, -ī *and* **iī** *nt* catapult.

balneae, -ārum *fpl* bath, baths.

balneāria, -ōrum *ntpl* bathroom.

balneārius *adj* of the baths.

balneātor, -ōris *m* bath superintendent.

balneolum, -ī *nt* small bath.

balneum, -ī *nt* bath.

bālō, -āre *vi* to bleat.

balsamum, -ī *nt* balsam, balsam tree.

baltea, -ōrum *ntpl* belt (*esp swordbelt; woman's girdle; strapping*).

balteus, -ī *m* belt (*esp swordbelt; woman's girdle; strapping*).

Bandusia, -ae *f* spring near Horace's birthplace.

baptisma, -tis *nt* baptism.

baptizō, -āre *vt* (ECCL) to baptize.

barathrum, -ī *nt* abyss; the lower world; (*fig*) a greedy person.

barba, -ae *f* beard.

barbarē *adv* in a foreign language, in Latin; in an uncivilized way; roughly, cruelly.

barbaria, -ae, -ēs *acc, and* **-em** *f* a foreign country (*outside Greece or Italy*); (*words*) barbarism; (*manners*) rudeness, stupidity.

barbaricus *adj* foreign, outlandish; Italian.

barbarus *adj* foreign, barbarous; (*to a Greek*) Italian; rude, uncivilized; savage, barbarous ♦ *m* foreigner, barbarian.

barbātulus *adj* with a little beard.

barbātus *adj* bearded, adult; ancient (Romans); of philosophers.

barbiger, -ī *adj* bearded.

barbitos (*acc* **-on**) *m* lyre, lute.

barbula, -ae *f* little beard.

Barcās, -ae *m* ancestor of Hannibal.

Barcīnus *adj see n.*
bardus *adj* dull, stupid.
bardus, -ī *m* Gallic minstrel.
bārō, -ōnis *m* dunce.
barrus, -ī *m* elephant.
bascauda, -ae *f* basket (*for the table*).
bāsiātiō, -ōnis *f* kiss.
basilica, -ae *f* public building used as exchange and law court.
basilicē *adv* royally, in magnificent style.
basilicum, -ī *nt* regal robe.
basilicus *adj* royal, magnificent ♦ *m* highest throw at dice.
bāsiō, -āre *vt* to kiss.
basis, -is *f* pedestal, base.
bāsium, -ī *and* **ī ī** *nt* kiss.
Bassareus, -eī *m* Bacchus.
Batāvī, -ōrum *mpl* people of Batavia (*now* Holland).
batillum, -ī *nt* firepan.
Battiadēs, -ae *m* Callimachus.
bātuō, -ere, -ī *vt* to beat.
baubor, -ārī *vi* (*of dogs*) to howl.
Baucis, -idis *f* wife of Philemon.
beātē *adv see* **beātus.**
beātitās, -ātis *f* happiness.
beātitūdō, -inis *f* happiness.
beātulus, -ī *m* the blessed man.
beātus *adj* happy; prosperous, well-off; rich, abundant.
Bēdriacēnsis *adj see n.*
Bēdriācum, -ī *nt* village in N. Italy.
Belgae, -ārum *mpl* people of N. Gaul (*now* Belgium).
Bēlidēs, -idae *m* Danaus, Aegyptus, Lynceus.
Bēlides, -um *fpl* Danaids.
bellāria, -ōrum *ntpl* dessert, confectionery.
bellātor, -ōris *m* warrior, fighter ♦ *adj* warlike.
bellātōrius *adj* aggressive.
bellātrīx, -īcis *f* warrioress ♦ *adj* warlike.
bellē *adv* well, nicely; ~ **habēre** be well (in health).
Bellerophōn, -ontis *m* slayer of Chimaera, rider of Pegasus.
Bellerophontēus *adj see n.*
bellicōsus *adj* warlike.
bellicus *adj* of war, military; ~**um canere** give the signal for marching or attack.
belliger, -ī *adj* martial.
belligerō, -āre, -āvī, -ātum *vi* to wage war.
bellipotēns, -entis *adj* strong in war.
bellō, -āre, -āvī, -ātum *vi* to fight, wage war.
Bellōna, -ae *f* goddess of war.
bellor, -ārī *vi* to fight.
bellulus *adj* pretty.
bellum, -ī *nt* war, warfare; battle; ~ **gerere** wage war; ~**ī** in war.
bellus *adj* pretty, handsome; pleasant, nice.
bēlua, -ae *f* beast, monster (*esp large and fierce*); any animal; (*fig*) brute; ~ **Gaetula** India elephant.
bēluātus *adj* embroidered with animals.

bēluōsus *adj* full of monsters.
Bēlus, -ī *m* Baal; an oriental king.
Bēnācus, -ī *m* lake in N. Italy (*now* Garda).
bene *adv* (*compar* **melius,** *superl* **optimē**) well; correctly; profitably; very ♦ *interj* bravo!, good!; ~ **dīcere** speak well; speak well of, praise; ~ **emere** buy cheap; ~ **est tibi** you are well off; ~ **facere** do well; do good to; ~ **facis** thank you; **rem** ~ **gerere** be successful; ~ **sē habēre** have a good time; ~ **habet** all is well, it's all right; ~ **merērī dē** do a service to; ~ **partum** honestly acquired; ~ **tē!** your health!; ~ **vēndere** sell at a high price; ~ **vīvere** live a happy life.
benedīcō, -īcere, -īxī, -ictum *vt* to speak well of, praise; (*ECCL*) to bless.
benedictiō, -ōnis *f* (*ECCL*) blessing.
beneficentia, -ae *f* kindness.
beneficiāriī, -ōrum *mpl* privileged soldiers.
beneficium, -ī *and* **ī ī** *nt* benefit, favour; (*POL, MIL*) promotion; ~**ō tuō** thanks to you.
beneficus *adj* generous, obliging.
Beneventānus *adj see n.*
Beneventum, -ī *nt* town in S. Italy (*now* Benevento).
benevolē *adv see* **benevolus.**
benevolēns, -entis *adj* kind-hearted.
benevolentia, -ae *f* goodwill, friendliness.
benevolus *adj* kindly, friendly; (*of servants*) devoted.
benīgnē *adv* willingly, courteously; generously; (*colloq*) no thank you; ~ **facere** do a favour.
benīgnitās, -ātis *f* kindness; liberality; bounty.
benīgnus *adj* kind, friendly; favourable; liberal, lavish; fruitful, bounteous.
beō, -āre, -āvī, -ātum *vt* to gladden, bless, enrich.
Berecyntia *f* Cybele.
Berecyntius *adj* of Berecyntus; of Cybele.
Berecyntus, -ī *m* mountain in Phrygia sacred to Cybele.
Berenīcē, -ēs *f* a queen of Egypt; **coma ~ēs** a constellation.
bēryllus, -ī *m* beryl.
bēs, bessis *m* two-thirds of the as; two-thirds.
bēstia, -ae *f* beast; wild animal for the arena.
bēstiārius *adj* of beasts ♦ *m* beast fighter in the arena.
bēstiola, -ae *f* small animal.
bēta, -ae *f* beet.
bēta *nt indecl* Greek letter beta.
bibī *perf of* **bibō.**
bibliopōla, -ae *m* bookseller.
bibliothēca, -ae, -ē, -ēs *f* library.
bibō, -ere, -ī *vt* to drink; to live on the banks of (a river); to drink in, absorb; (*fig*) to listen attentively, be imbued; ~ **aquas** be drowned; **Graecō mōre** ~ drink to one's health.
bibulus *adj* fond of drink, thirsty; (*things*) thirsty.
Bibulus, -ī *m* consul with Caesar in 59 BC.

biceps, -ipitis *adj* two-headed.
biclīnium, -ī *and* **iī** *nt* dining couch for two.
bicolor, -ōris *adj* two-coloured.
bicorniger, -ī *adj* two-horned.
bicornis *adj* two-horned, two-pronged; (*rivers*) two-mouthed.
bicorpor, -is *adj* two-bodied.
bidēns, -entis *adj* with two teeth *or* prongs ♦ *m* hoe ♦ *f* sheep (*or other sacrificial animal*).
bidental, -ālis *nt* a place struck by lightning.
biduum, -ī *nt* two days.
biennium, -ī *and* **iī** *nt* two years.
bifāriam *adv* in two parts, twice.
bifer, -ī *adj* flowering twice a year.
bifidus *adj* split in two.
biforis *adj* double-doored; double.
bifōrmātus, bifōrmis *adj* with two forms.
bifrōns, -ontis *adj* two-headed.
bifurcus *adj* two-pronged, forked.
bīgae, -ārum *fpl* chariot and pair.
bīgātus *adj* stamped with a chariot and pair.
biiugī, -ōrum *mpl* two horses yoked abreast; chariot with two horses.
biiugis, biiugus *adj* yoked.
bilībra, -ae *f* two pounds.
bilībris *adj* holding two pounds.
bilinguis *adj* double-tongued; bilingual; deceitful.
bīlis, -is *f* bile, gall; (*fig*) anger, displeasure; ~ **ātra, nigra** melancholy; madness.
bilīx, -īcis *adj* double-stranded.
bilūstris *adj* ten years.
bimaris *adj* between two seas.
bimarītus, -ī *m* bigamist.
bimāter, -ris *adj* having two mothers.
bimembris *adj* half man, half beast; (*pl*) Centaurs.
bimēstris *adj* of two months, two months old.
bīmulus *adj* only two years old.
bīmus *adj* two years old, for two years.
bīnī, bīnae, bīna *num* two each, two by two; a pair; (*with pl nouns having a meaning*) two.
binoctium, -ī *and* **iī** *nt* two nights.
binōminis *adj* with two names.
Biōn, -ōnis *m* satirical philosopher.
Biōnēus *adj* satirical.
bipalmis *adj* two spans long.
bipartītō *adv* in two parts, in two directions.
bipartītus *adj* divided in two.
bipatēns, -entis *adj* double-opening.
bipedālis *adj* two feet long broad *or* thick.
bipennifer, -ī *adj* wielding a battle-axe.
bipennis *adj* two-edged ♦ *f* battle-axe.
bipertītō *etc see* **bipartītō**.
bipēs, -edis *adj* two-footed ♦ *m* biped.
birēmis *adj* two-oared; with two banks of oars ♦ *f* two-oared skiff; galley with two banks of oars.
bis *adv* twice, double; ~ **ad eundem** make the same mistake twice; ~ **diē, in diē** twice a day;

~ **tantō, tantum** twice as much; ~ **terque** frequently; ~ **terve** seldom.
bissextus, -ī *m* intercalary day after 24th Feb.
Bistones, -um *mpl* people of Thrace.
Bistonis *f* Thracian woman, Bacchante.
Bistonius *adj* Thracian.
bisulcilingua, -ae *adj* fork-tongued, deceitful.
bisulcus *adj* cloven.
Bīthȳnia, -iae *f* province of Asia Minor.
Bīthȳnicus, Bīthȳnius, -us *adj see* **Bīthȳnia**.
bītō, -ere *vi* to go.
bitūmen, -inis *nt* bitumen, a kind of pitch.
bitūmineus *adj see* **bitūmen**.
bivium *nt* two ways.
bivius *adj* two-way.
blaesus *adj* lisping, indistinct.
blandē *adv see* **blandus**.
blandidicus *adj* fair-spoken.
blandiloquentia, -ae *f* attractive language.
blandiloquus, -entulus *adj* fair-spoken.
blandīmentum, -ī *nt* compliment, allurement.
blandior, -īrī, -ītus *vi* to coax, caress; to flatter, pay compliments; (*things*) to please, entice.
blanditia, -ae *f* caress, flattery; charm, allurement.
blandītim *adv* caressingly.
blandus *adj* smooth-tongued, flattering, fawning; charming, winsome.
blaterō, -āre *vi* to babble.
blatiō, -īre *vt* to babble.
blatta, -ae *f* cockroach.
blennus, -ī *m* idiot.
bliteus *adj* silly.
blitum, -ī *nt* kind of spinach.
boārius *adj* of cattle; **forum -um** *cattle market in Rome.*
Bodotria, -ae *f* Firth of Forth.
Boeōtarchēs *m* chief magistrate of Boeotia.
Boeōtia, -iae *f* district of central Greece.
Boeōtius, -us *adj see n.*
boiae, -ārum *fpl* collar.
Boiī, -ōrum *mpl* people of S.E. Gaul.
Boiohaemī, -ōrum *mpl* Bohemians.
bōlētus, -ī *m* mushroom.
bolus, -ī *m* (*dice*) throw; (*net*) cast; (*fig*) haul, piece of good luck; titbit.
bombus, -ī *m* booming, humming, buzzing.
bombȳcinus *adj* of silk.
bombȳx, -ȳcis *m* silkworm; silk.
Bona Dea, -ae, -ae *f* goddess worshipped by women.
bonitās, -ātis *f* goodness; honesty, integrity; kindness, affability.
Bonōnia, -ae *f* town in N. Italy (*now* Bologna).
Bonōniēnsis *adj see n.*
bonum, -ī *nt* a moral good; advantage, blessing; (*pl*) property; **cuī ~ō?** who was the

---

Noun declensions and verb conjugations are shown on pp xiii to xxv. The present infinitive ending of a verb shows to which conjugation it belongs: **-āre** = 1st; **-ēre** = 2nd; **-ere** = 3rd and **-īre** = 4th. Irregular verbs are shown on p xxvi

gainer?

bonus *adj (compar* **melior,** *superl* **optimus)** good; kind; brave; loyal; beneficial; lucky ♦ *mpl* upper class party, conservatives; **~a** **aetās** prime of life; **~ō animō** of good cheer; well-disposed; **~ae artēs** integrity; culture, liberal education; **~ a dicta** witticisms; **~a** **fidēs** good faith; **~ī mōrēs** morality; **~ī nummī** genuine money; **~a pars** large part; conservative party; **~ae rēs** comforts, luxuries; prosperity; morality; **~ā veniā** with kind permission; **~a verba** words of good omen; well-chosen diction; **~a vōx** loud voice.

boō, -āre *vi* to cry aloud.

Boōtēs, -ae *nt constellation containing Arcturus.*

Boreās, -ae *m* north wind; north.

Boreus *adj see n.*

Borysthenēs, -is *m river Dnieper.*

Borysthenidae *mpl dwellers near the Dnieper.*

Borysthenius *adj see* **Borysthenidae.**

bōs, bovis *m/f* ox, cow; kind of turbot; **~ Lūca** elephant; **bovī clitellās impōnere** ≈ *put a round peg in a square hole.*

Bosporānus *adj see n.*

Bosporius *adj:* **~ Cimmerius** *strait from Sea of Azov to Black Sea.*

Bosporus, -ī *m strait from Black Sea to Sea of Marmora.*

Boudicca, -ae *f* British queen *(falsely called Boadicea).*

bovārius *etc see* **boārius.**

Bovillae, -ārum *fpl ancient Latin town.*

Bovillānus *adj see n.*

bovillus *adj* of oxen.

brācae, -ārum *fpl* trousers.

brācātus *adj* trousered; barbarian *(esp of tribes beyond the Alps).*

bracchiālis *adj* of the arm.

bracchiolum, -ī *nt* dainty arm.

bracchium, -ī *and* **iī** *nt* arm, forearm; *(shellfish)* claw; *(tree)* branch; *(sea)* arm; *(NAUT)* yardarm; *(MIL)* outwork, mole; **levī,** **mollī bracchiō** casually.

bractea *etc see* **brattea.**

brassica, -ae *f* cabbage.

brattea, -ae *f* gold leaf.

bratteola, -ae *f* very fine gold leaf.

Brennus, -ī *m Gallic chief who defeated the Romans.*

brevī *adv* shortly, soon; briefly, in a few words.

brevia, -ium *ntpl* shoals.

breviārium, -ī *and* **iī** *nt* summary, statistical survey, official report.

breviculus *adj* shortish.

breviloquēns, -ēntis *adj* brief.

brevis *adj* short, small, shallow; brief, short-lived; concise.

brevitās, -ātis *f* shortness, smallness; brevity, conciseness.

breviter *adv* concisely.

Brigantēs, -um *mpl British tribe in N. England.*

Briganticus *adj see n.*

Brīsēis, -idos *f captive of Achilles.*

Britannia, -iae *f* Britain; the British Isles.

Britannicus *m son of emperor Claudius.*

Britannus, (-icus) *adj see n.*

Bromius, -ī *and* **iī** *m Bacchus.*

brūma, -ae *f* winter solstice, midwinter; winter.

brūmālis *adj* of the winter solstice; wintry; **~ flexus** tropic of Capricorn.

Brundisīnus *adj see n.*

Brundisium, -ī *and* **iī** *nt* port in S.E. Italy *(now Brindisi).*

Bruttiī, -ōrum *mpl people of the toe of Italy.*

Bruttius *adj see n.*

brūtus *adj* heavy, unwieldy; stupid, irrational.

Brūtus, -ī *m liberator of Rome from kings; murderer of Caesar.*

bubīle, -is *nt* stall.

būbo, -ōnis *m/f* owl.

būbula, -ae *f* beef.

bubulcitor, -ārī *vi* to drive oxen.

bubulcus, -ī *m* ploughman.

būbulus *adj* of cattle.

būcaeda, -ae *m* flogged slave.

bucca, -ae *f* cheek; mouth; ranter.

buccō, -ōnis *m* babbler.

buccula, -ae *f* visor.

bucculentus *adj* fat-cheeked.

būcerus *adj* horned.

būcina, -ae *f* shepherd's horn; military trumpet; night watch.

būcinātor, -ōris *m* trumpeter.

būcolica, -ōrum *ntpl* pastoral poetry.

būcula, -ae *f* young cow.

būfō, -ōnis *m* toad.

bulbus, -ī *m* bulb; onion.

būlē, -es *f* Greek senate.

būleuta *m* senator.

būleutērium *nt* senate house.

bulla, -ae *f* bubble; knob, stud; *gold charm worn round the neck by children of noblemen.*

bullātus *adj* wearing the bulla; still a child.

būmastus, -ī *f* kind of vine.

būris, -is *m* plough-beam.

Burrus old form of **Pyrrhus.**

Busīris, -idis *m Egyptian king killed by Hercules.*

bustirapus, -ī *m* graverobber.

bustuārius *adj* at a funeral.

bustum, -ī *nt* funeral place; tomb, grave.

buxifer, -ī *adj* famed for its box trees.

buxum, -ī *nt* boxwood; flute, top, comb, tablet.

buxus, -ī *f* box tree; flute.

Byzantius, -ī *and* **iī** *nt* city on Bosporus *(later Constantinople, now Istanbul).*

Byzantius *adj see n.*

C, c

caballīnus *adj* horse's.
caballus, -ī *m* horse.
cacātus *adj* impure.
cachinnātiō, -ōnis *f* loud laughter.
cachinnō, -āre *vi* to laugh, guffaw.
cachinnō, -ōnis *m* scoffer.
cachinnus, -ī *m* laugh, derisive laughter;
(*waves*) splashing.
cacō, -āre *vi* to evacuate the bowels.
cacoēthes, -is *nt* (*fig*) itch.
cacula, -ae *m* soldier's slave.
cacūmen, -inis *nt* extremity, point, summit,
treetop; (*fig*) height, limit.
cacūminō, -āre *vt* to make pointed.
Cācus, -ī *m* giant robber, son of Vulcan.
cadāver, -is *nt* corpse, carcass.
cadāverōsus *adj* ghastly.
Cadmēa, -ēae *f* fortress of Thebes.
Cadmēis, -ēidis *f* Agave; Ino; Semele.
Cadmēus, (-ēius) *adj* of Cadmus; Theban.
Cadmus, -ī *m* founder of Thebes.
cadō, -ere, cecidī, cāsum *vi* to fall; to droop,
die, be killed; (*ASTRO*) to set; (*dice*) to be
thrown; (*events*) to happen, turn out; (*money*)
to be due; (*strength, speech, courage*) to
diminish, cease, fail; (*wind, rage*) to subside;
(*words*) to end; **~ in** suit, agree with; come
under; **~ sub** be exposed to; **animīs ~** be
disheartened; **causā ~** lose one's case.
cādūceātor, -ōris *m* officer with flag of truce.
cādūceus, -ī *m* herald's staff; Mercury's
wand.
cādūcifer, -ī *adj* with herald's staff.
cadūcus *adj* falling, fallen; (*fig*) perishable,
fleeting, vain; (*law*) without an heir ♦ *nt*
property without an heir.
Cadurcī, -ōrum *mpl* Gallic tribe.
Cadurcum, -ī *nt* linen coverlet.
cadus, -ī *m* jar, flask (*esp for wine*); urn.
caecigenus *adj* born blind.
Caeciliānus *adj see n.*
Caecilius, -ī *m* Roman name (*esp early Latin
comic poet*).
caecitās, -ātis *f* blindness.
caecō, -āre, -āvī, -ātum *vt* to blind; to make
obscure.
Caecubum, -ī *nt* choice wine from the Ager
Caecubus in S. Latium.
caecus *adj* blind; invisible, secret; dark,
obscure; (*fig*) aimless, unknown, uncertain;
appāret ~ō ≈ it's as clear as daylight; **domus ~a**
a house with no windows; **~ā diē emere** buy

on credit; **~um corpus** the back.
caedēs, -is *f* murder, massacre; gore; the
slain.
caedō, -ere, cecīdī, caesum *vt* to cut; to
strike; to kill, cut to pieces; (*animals*) to
sacrifice.
caelāmen, -inis *nt* engraved work.
caelātor, -ōris *m* engraver.
caelātūra, -ae *f* engraving in bas-relief.
caelebs, -ibis *adj* unmarried (bachelor *or*
widower); (*trees*) with no vine trained on.
caeles, -itis *adj* celestial ♦ *mpl* the gods.
caelestis, -is *adj* of the sky, heavenly; divine;
glorious ♦ *mpl* the gods ♦ *ntpl* the heavenly
bodies.
Caeliānus *adj see n.*
caelibātus, -ūs *m* celibacy.
caelicola, -ae *m* god.
caelifer, -ī *adj* supporting the sky.
Caelius, -ī *m* Roman name; Roman hill.
caelō, -āre, -āvī, -ātum *vt* to engrave (*in relief
on metals*), carve (*on wood*); (*fig*) to compose.
caelum, -ī *nt* engraver's chisel.
caelum, -ī *nt* sky, heaven; air, climate,
weather; (*fig*) height of success, glory; **~um
ac terrās miscēre** create chaos; **ad ~um ferre**
extol; **dē ~ō dēlāpsus** a messiah; **dē ~ō
servāre** watch for omens; **dē ~ō tangī** be
struck by lightning; **digitō ~um attingere** ≈
be in the seventh heaven; **in ~ō esse** be
overjoyed.
caementum, -ī *nt* quarrystone, rubble.
caenōsus *adj* muddy.
caenum, -ī *nt* mud, filth.
caepa, -ae *f*, **caepe, -is** *nt* onion.
Caere *nt indecl* (*gen* **-itis**, *abl* **-ēte**) *f* ancient
Etruscan town.
Caeres, -itis *and* **ētis** *adj*: **~ite cērā dignī** like
the disfranchised masses.
caerimōnia, -ae *f* sanctity; veneration (*for
gods*); religious usage, ritual.
caeruleus, caerulus *adj* blue, dark blue, dark
green, dusky ♦ *ntpl* the sea.
Caesar, -is *m* Julius (*great Roman soldier,
statesman, author*); Augustus; the emperor.
Caesareus, *and* iānus, *and* īnus *adj see n.*
caesariātus *adj* bushy-haired.
caesariēs, -ēī *f* hair.
caesīcius *adj* bluish.
caesim *adv* with the edge of the sword; (*RHET*)
in short clauses.
caesius *adj* bluish grey, blue-eyed.
caespes, -itis *m* sod, turf; mass of roots.
caestus, -ūs *m* boxing glove.
caesus *ppp of* **caedō**.
caetra, -ae *f* targe.
caetrātus *adj* armed with a targe.
Caīcus, -ī *m* river in Asia Minor.
Cāiēta, -ae, -ē, -ēs *f* town in Latium.
Cāius *etc see* **Gaius**.

Calaber, -rī *adj* Calabrian.
Calabria *f S.E. peninsula of Italy.*
Calamis, -idis *m Greek sculptor.*
calamister, -rī *m,* **-rum, -rī** *nt* curling iron;
(*RHET*) flourish.
calamistrātus *adj* curled; foppish.
calamitās, -ātis *f* disaster; (*MIL*) defeat; (*AGR*)
damage, failure.
calamitōsē *adv see* **calamitōsus.**
calamitōsus *adj* disastrous, ruinous; blighted,
unfortunate.
calamus, -ī *m* reed; stalk; pen, pipe, arrow,
fishing rod.
calathiscus, -ī *m* small basket.
calathus, -ī *m* wicker basket; bowl, cup.
calātor, -ōris *m* servant.
calcāneum, -ī *nt* heel.
calcar, -āris *nt* spur.
calceāmentum, -ī *nt* shoe.
calceātus *ppp* shod.
calceolārius, -ī *and* **iī** *m* shoemaker.
calceolus, -ī *m* small shoe.
calceus, -ī *m* shoe.
Calchās, -antis *m Greek prophet at Troy.*
calcitrō, -āre *vi* to kick; (*fig*) to resist.
calcō, -āre, -āvī, -ātum *vt* to tread, trample
on; (*fig*) to spurn.
calculus, -ī *m* pebble, stone; draughtsman,
counting stone, reckoning, voting stone;
~um redūcere take back a move; **~ōs**
subdūcere compute; **ad ~ōs vocāre** subject to
a reckoning.
caldārius *adj* with warm water.
caldus *etc see* **calidus.**
Calēdonia, -ae *f the Scottish Highlands.*
Calēdonius *adj see* n.
calefaciō, (calfaciō), -facere, -fēcī, -factum
vt to warm, heat; (*fig*) to provoke, excite.
calefactō, -āre *vt* to warm.
Calendae *see* **Kalendae.**
Calēnus *adj of Cales* ♦ *nt* wine of Cales.
caleō, -ēre *vi* to be warm, be hot, glow; (*mind*)
to be inflamed; (*things*) to be pursued with
enthusiasm; to be fresh.
Calēs, -ium *fpl town in Campania.*
calēscō, -ere, -uī *vi* to get hot; (*fig*) to become
inflamed.
calidē *adv* promptly.
calidus *adj* warm, hot; (*fig*) fiery, eager; hasty;
prompt ♦ *f* warm water ♦ *nt* warm drink.
caliendrum, -ī *nt* headdress of hair.
caliga, -ae *f* soldier's boot.
caligātus *adj* heavily shod.
cālīginōsus *adj* misty, obscure.
cālīgō, -inis *f* mist, fog; dimness, darkness;
(*mind*) obtuseness; (*CIRCS*) trouble.
cālīgō, -āre *vi* to be misty, be dim; to cause
dizziness.
Caligula, -ae *m emperor Gaius.*
calix, -cis *m* wine cup; cooking pot.
calleō, -ēre *vi* to be thick-skinned; (*fig*) to be
unfeeling; to be wise, be skilful ♦ *vt* to know,
understand.

callidē *adv see* **callidus.**
calliditās, -ātis *f* skill; cunning.
callidus *adj* skilful, clever; crafty.
Callimachus, -ī *m Greek poet of Alexandria.*
Calliopē, -ēs, *and* **ēa, -ēae** *f Muse of epic*
poetry.
callis, -is *m* footpath, mountain track; pass;
hill pastures.
Callistō, -ūs *f daughter of Lycaon;* (*constellation*)
Great Bear.
callōsus *adj* hard-skinned; solid.
callum, -ī *nt* hard *or* thick skin; firm flesh; (*fig*)
callousness.
calō, -āre, -āvī, -ātum *vt* to convoke.
cālō, -ōnis *m* soldier's servant; drudge.
calor, -ōris *m* warmth, heat; (*fig*) passion,
love.
Calpē, -ēs *f* Rock of Gibraltar.
Calpurniānus *adj see* n.
Calpurnius, -ī *m Roman name.*
caltha, -ae *f* marigold.
calthula, -ae *f* yellow dress.
caluī *perf of* **calēscō.**
calumnia, -ae *f* chicanery, sharp practice;
subterfuge; misrepresentation; (*law*)
dishonest accusation, blackmail; being
convicted of malicious prosecution; **~am**
iūrāre swear that an action is brought in
good faith.
calumniātor, -ōris *m* legal trickster,
slanderer.
calumnior, -ārī, -ātus *vt* to misrepresent,
slander; (*law*) to bring an action in bad faith;
sē ~ deprecate oneself.
calva, -ae *f* bald head.
calvitium, -ī *and* **iī** *nt* baldness.
calvor, -ārī *vt* to deceive.
calvus *adj* bald.
calx, -cis *f* heel; foot; **~ce petere, ferīre** kick;
adversus stimulum ~cēs ≈ *kicking against the*
pricks.
calx, -cis *f* pebble; lime, chalk; finishing line,
end; **ad carcerēs ā ~ce revocārī** have to begin
all over again.
Calydōn, -ōnis *f town in Aetolia.*
Calydōnis *adj* Calydonian.
Calydōnius *f* Deianira; **~ōnius amnis**
Achelous; **~** **hērōs** Meleager; **~ōnia rēgna**
Daunia in S. Italy.
Calypsō, -ūs (*acc* -**ō**) *f nymph who detained*
Ulysses in Ogygia.
camēlīnus *adj* camel's.
camella, -ae *f* wine cup.
camēlus, -ī *m* camel.
Camēna, -ae *f* Muse; poetry.
camera, -ae *f* arched roof.
Camerīnum, -ī *nt town in Umbria.*
Camers, -tis, *and* **tīnus** *adj* of Camerinum.
Camillus, -ī *m Roman hero* (*who saved Rome*
from the Gauls).
camīnus, -ī *m* furnace, fire; forge; **oleum**
addere ~ō ≈ *add fuel to the flames.*
cammarus, -ī *m* lobster.

Campānia, -iae f district of W. Italy.
Campānicus, and ius, and us adj Campanian, Capuan.
campē, -ēs f evasion.
campester, -ris adj of the plain; of the Campus Martius ♦ nt loincloth ♦ ntpl level ground.
campus, -ī m plain; sports field; any level surface; (fig) theatre, arena (of action, debate); ~ **Martius** level ground by the Tiber (used for assemblies, sports, military drills).
Camulodūnum, -ī nt town of Trinobantes (now Colchester).
camur, -ī adj crooked.
canālis, -is m pipe, conduit, canal.
cancellī, -ōrum mpl grating, enclosure; barrier (in public places), bar of law court.
cancer, -rī m crab; (constellation) Cancer; south, tropical heat; (MED) cancer.
candefaciō, -ere vt to make dazzlingly white.
candēla, -ae f taper, tallow candle; waxed cord; ~**am appōnere valvīs** set the house on fire.
candēlābrum, -ī nt candlestick, chandelier, lampstand.
candēns, -entis adj dazzling white; white-hot.
candeō, -ēre vi to shine, be white; to be white-hot.
candēscō, -ere vi to become white; to grow white-hot.
candidātōrius adj of a candidate.
candidātus adj dressed in white ♦ m candidate for office.
candidē adv in white; sincerely.
candidulus adj pretty white.
candidus adj white, bright; radiant, beautiful; clothed in white; (style) clear; (mind) candid, frank; (CIRCS) happy; ~**a sententia** acquittal.
candor, -ōris m whiteness, brightness, beauty; (fig) brilliance, sincerity.
cānēns, -entis adj white.
cāneō, -ēre, -uī vi to be grey, be white.
cānescō, -ere vi to grow white; to grow old.
canīcula, -ae f bitch; Dog Star, Sirius.
canīnus adj dog's, canine; snarling, spiteful; ~ **littera** letter R.
canis, -is m/f dog, bitch; (fig) shameless or angry person; hanger-on; (dice) lowest throw; (ASTRO) Canis Major, Canis Minor; (myth) Cerberus.
canistrum, -ī nt wicker basket.
cānitiēs, -ēī f greyness; grey hair; old age.
canna, -ae f reed; pipe; gondola.
cannabis, -is f hemp.
Cannae, -ārum fpl village in Apulia (scene of great Roman defeat by Hannibal).
Cannēnsis adj see n.
canō, canere, cecinī vt, vi to sing; to play; to sing about, recite, prophesy; (MIL) to sound; (birds) to sing, crow.

canor, -ōris m song, tune, sound.
canōrus adj musical, melodious; singsong ♦ nt melodiousness.
Cantaber, -rī m Cantabrian.
Cantabria, -riae f district of N Spain.
Cantabricus adj see n.
cantāmen, -inis nt charm.
cantharis, -idis f beetle; Spanish fly.
cantharus, -ī m tankard.
canthērīnus adj of a horse.
canthērius, -ī m gelding.
canticum, -ī nt aria in Latin comedy; song.
cantilēna, -ae f old song, gossip; ~**am eandem canere** keep harping on the same theme.
cantiō, -ōnis f song; charm.
cantitō, -āre, -āvī, -atum vt to sing or play often.
Cantium, -ī and iī nt Kent.
cantiunculae, -ārum fpl fascinating strains.
cantō, -āre, -āvī, -ātum vt, vi to sing; to play; to sing about, recite, celebrate; to proclaim, harp on; to use magic spells; to sound; to drawl.
cantor, -ōris m, **-rīx, -rīcis** f singer, musician, poet; actor.
cantus, -ūs m singing, playing, music; prophecy; magic spell.
cānus adj white, grey, hoary; old ♦ mpl grey hairs.
Canusīnus adj see n.
Canusium, -ī nt town in Apulia (famous for wool).
capācitās, -ātis f spaciousness.
capāx, -ācis adj capable of holding, spacious, roomy; capable, able, fit.
capēdō, -inis f sacrificial dish.
capēduncula f small dish.
capella, -ae f she-goat; (ASTRO) bright star in Auriga.
Capēna, -ae f old Etruscan town.
Capēnās, -us adj: **Porta ~a** Roman gate leading to the Via Appia.
caper, -rī m goat; odour of the armpits.
caperrō, -āre vi to wrinkle.
capessō, -ere, -īvī, -ītum vt to seize, take hold of, try to reach, make for; to take in hand, engage in; **rem pūblicam ~** go in for politics.
capillātus adj long-haired; ancient.
capillus, -ī m hair (of head or beard); a hair.
capiō, -ere, cēpī, captum vt to take, seize; to catch, capture; (MIL) to occupy, take prisoner; (NAUT) to make, reach (a goal); (fig) to captivate, charm, cheat; (pass) to be maimed, lose the use of; to choose; (appearance) to assume; (habit) to cultivate; (duty) to undertake; (ideas) to conceive, form; (feeling) to experience; (harm) to suffer; to receive, get, inherit; to contain, hold; (fig) to bear; (mind) to grasp; **cōnsilium**

Noun declensions and verb conjugations are shown on pp xiii to xxv. The present infinitive ending of a verb shows to which conjugation it belongs: **-āre** = 1st; **-ēre** = 2nd; **-ere** = 3rd and **-īre** = 4th. Irregular verbs are shown on p xxvi

~ come to a decision; **impetum** ~ gather momentum; **initium** ~ start; **oculō capī** lose an eye; **mente captus** insane; **cupīdō eum cēpit** he felt a desire.

capis, -dis *f sacrificial bowl with one handle.*

capistrātus *adj* haltered.

capistrum, -ī *nt* halter, muzzle.

capital, -ālis *nt* capital crime.

capitālis *adj* mortal, deadly, dangerous; (*law*) capital; important, excellent.

capitō, -ōnis *m* bighead.

Capitōlīnus *adj* of the Capitol; of Jupiter.

Capitōlium, -ī *nt Roman hill with temple of Jupiter.*

capitulātim *adv* summarily.

capitulum, -ī *nt* small head; person, creature.

Cappadocia, -ae *f country of Asia Minor.*

capra, -ae *f* she-goat; odour of armpits; (*ASTRO*) Capella.

caprea, -ae *f* roe.

Capreae, -ārum *fpl island of Capri.*

capreolus, -ī *m* roebuck; (*pl*) crossbeams.

Capricornus, -ī *m* (*constellation*) Capricorn (*associated with midwinter*).

caprifīcus, -ī *f* wild fig tree.

caprigenus *adj* of goats.

caprimulgus, -ī *m* goatherd, rustic.

caprīnus *adj* of goats.

capripēs, -edis *adj* goat-footed.

capsa, -ae *f* box (*esp for papyrus rolls*).

capsō *archaic fut of* **capiō.**

capsula, -ae *f* small box; **dē ~ā tōtus** ≈ *out of a bandbox.*

Capta, -ae *f* Minerva.

captātiō, -ōnis *f* catching at.

captātor, -ōris *m* one who courts; legacy hunter.

captiō, -ōnis *f* fraud; disadvantage; (*argument*) fallacy, sophism.

captiōsē *adv see* **captiōsus.**

captiōsus *adj* deceptive; dangerous; captious.

captiuncula, -ae *f* quibble.

captīvitās, -ātis *f* captivity; capture.

captīvus *adj* captive, captured; of captives ♦ *m/f* prisoner of war.

captō, -āre, -āvī, -ātum *vt* to try to catch, chase; to try to win, court, watch for; to deceive, trap.

captus *ppp of* **capiō** ♦ *m* prisoner.

captus, -ūs *m* grasp, notion.

Capua, -ae *f chief town of Campania.*

capulāris *adj* due for a coffin.

capulus, -ī *m* coffin; handle, hilt.

caput, -itis *nt* head; top, extremity; (*rivers*) source; (*more rarely*) mouth; person, individual; life; civil rights; (*person*) chief, leader; (*towns*) capital; (*money*) principal; (*writing*) substance, chapter; principle, main point, the great thing; **~ cēnae** main dish; **~itis accūsāre** charge with a capital offence; **~itis damnāre** condemn to death; **~itis dēminūtiō** loss of political rights; **~itis poena** capital punishment; **~ita cōnferre** confer in

secret; **in ~ita** per head; **suprā ~ut esse** be imminent.

Cār, -is *m* Carian.

carbaseus *adj* linen, canvas.

carbasus, -ī *f* (*pl* **-a, -ōrum** *nt*) Spanish flax, fine linen; garment, sail, curtain.

carbō, -ōnis *m* charcoal, embers.

carbōnārius, -ī *and* **iī** *m* charcoal burner.

carbunculus, -ī *m* small coal; precious stone.

carcer, -is *m* prison; jailbird; barrier, starting place (*for races*); **ad ~ēs ā calce revocārī** have to begin all over again.

carcerārius *adj* of a prison.

carchēsium, -ī *and* **iī** *nt* drinking cup; (*NAUT*) masthead.

cardiacus, -ī *m* dyspeptic.

cardō, -inis *m* hinge; (*ASTRO*) pole, axis, cardinal point; (*fig*) juncture, critical moment.

carduus, -ī *m* thistle.

cārē *adv see* **cārus.**

cārectum, -ī *nt* sedge.

cāreō, -ēre, -uī *vi* (*with abl*) to be free from, not have, be without; to abstain from, be absent from; to want, miss.

cārex, -icis *f* sedge.

Cāria, -ae *f district of S.W. Asia Minor.*

Cāricus *adj* Carian ♦ *f* dried fig.

cariēs (*acc* **-em**, *abl* **-ē**) *f* dry rot.

carīna, -ae *f* keel; ship.

Carīnae, -ārum *fpl district of Rome.*

carīnārius, -ī *and* **iī** *m* dyer of yellow.

cariōsus *adj* crumbling; (*fig*) withered.

cāris, -idis *f* kind of crab.

cāritās, -ātis *f* dearness, high price; esteem, affection.

carmen, -inis *nt* song, tune; poem, poetry, verse; prophecy; (*in law, religion*) formula; moral text.

Carmentālis *adj see* n.

Carmentis, -is, *and* **a, -ae** *f prophetess, mother of Evander.*

carnārium, -ī *and* **iī** *nt* fleshhook; larder.

Carneadēs, -is *m Greek philosopher (founder of the New Academy).*

Carneadēus *adj see* n.

carnifex, -icis *m* executioner, hangman; scoundrel; murderer.

carnificīna, -ae *f* execution; torture; **~am facere** be an executioner.

carnificō, -āre *vt* to behead, mutilate.

carnuf- *etc see* **carnif-.**

carō, -nis *f* flesh.

cārō, -ere *vt* to card.

Carpathius *adj see* n.

Carpathus, -ī *f island between Crete and Rhodes.*

carpatina, -ae *f* leather shoe.

carpentum, -ī *nt* two-wheeled coach.

carpō, -ere, -sī, -tum *vt* to pick, pluck, gather; to tear off; to browse, graze on; (*wool*) to card; (*fig*) to enjoy, snatch; to carp at, slander; to weaken, wear down; to divide up; (*journey*) to go, travel.

carptim *adv* in parts; at different points; at different times.

carptor, -ōris *m* carver.

carptus *ppp of* **carpō**.

carrus, -ī *m* waggon.

Carthāginiēnsis *adj see n.*

Carthāgō, -inis *f* Carthage (*near Tunis*); ~ **Nova** town in Spain (*now* Cartagena).

caruncula, -ae *f* piece of flesh.

cārus *adj* dear, costly; dear, beloved.

Carystēus *adj see n.*

Carystos, -ī *f* town in Euboea (*famous for marble*).

casa, -ae *f* cottage, hut.

cascus *adj* old.

cāseolus, -ī *m* small cheese.

cāseus, -ī *m* cheese.

casia, -ae *f* cinnamon; spurge laurel.

Caspius *adj* Caspian.

Cassandra, -ae *f* Trojan princess and prophetess, doomed never to be believed.

cassēs, -ium *mpl* net, snare; spider's web.

Cassiānus *adj see n.*

cassida, -ae *f* helmet.

Cassiepēa, -ae, Cassiopē, -ēs *f* mother of Andromeda; a constellation.

cassis, -idis *f* helmet.

Cassius, -ī *m* Roman family name.

cassō, -āre *vi* to shake.

cassus *adj* empty; devoid of, without (*abl*); vain, useless; ~ **lūmine** dead; **in ~um** in vain.

Castalia, -ae *f* spring on Parnassus, (*sacred to Apollo and the Muses*).

Castalides, -dum *fpl* Muses.

Castalius, -s *adj see n.*

castanea, -ae *f* chestnut tree; chestnut.

castē *adv see* **castus**.

castellānus *adj* of a fortress ♦ *mpl* garrison.

castellātim *adv* in different fortresses.

castellum, -ī *nt* fortress, castle; (*fig*) defence, refuge.

castēria, -ae *f* rowers' quarters.

castīgābilis *adj* punishable.

castīgātiō, -ōnis *f* correction, reproof.

castīgātor, -ōris *m* reprover.

castīgātus *adj* small, slender.

castīgō, -āre, -āvī, -ātum *vt* to correct, punish; to reprove; to restrain.

castimōnia, -ae *f* purity, morality; chastity, abstinence.

castitās, -ātis *f* chastity.

castor, -oris *m* beaver.

Castor, -oris *m* twin brother of Pollux (*patron of sailors*); star in Gemini.

castoreum, -ī *nt* odorous secretion of the beaver.

castra, -ōrum *ntpl* camp; day's march; army life; (*fig*) party, sect; ~ **movēre** strike camp; ~ **mūnīre** construct a camp; ~ **pōnere** pitch camp; **bīna ~** two camps.

castrēnsis *adj* of the camp, military.

castrō, -āre *vt* to castrate; (*fig*) to weaken.

castrum, -ī *nt* fort.

castus *adj* clean, pure, chaste, innocent; holy, pious.

cāsū *adv* by chance.

casula, -ae *f* little cottage.

cāsus, -ūs *m* fall, downfall; event, chance, accident; misfortune, death; opportunity; (*time*) end; (*GRAM*) case.

Catadūpa, -ōrum *ntpl* Nile cataract near Syene.

catagraphus *adj* painted.

Catamītus, -ī *m* Ganymede.

cataphractēs, -ae *m* coat of mail.

cataphractus *adj* wearing mail.

cataplus, -ī *m* ship arriving.

catapulta, -ae *f* (*MIL*) catapult; (*fig*) missile.

catapultārius *adj* thrown by catapult.

cataracta, -ae *f* waterfall; sluice; drawbridge.

catasta, -ae *f* stage, scaffold.

catē *adv see* **catus**.

catēia, -ae *f* javelin.

catella, -ae *f* small chain.

catellus, -ī *m* puppy.

catēna, -ae *f* chain; fetter; (*fig*) bond, restraint; series.

catēnātus *adj* chained, fettered.

caterva, -ae *f* crowd, band; flock; (*MIL*) troop, body; (*THEAT*) company.

catervātim *adv* in companies.

cathedra, -ae *f* armchair, sedan chair; teacher's chair.

catholicus *adj* (*ECCL*) orthodox, universal.

Catilīna, -ae *m* Catiline (*conspirator suppressed by Cicero*).

Catilīnārius *adj see n.*

catillo, -āre *vt* to lick a plate.

catillus, -ī *m* small dish.

catīnus, -ī *m* dish, pot.

Catō, -ōnis *m* famous censor and author, idealised as the pattern of an ancient Roman; famous Stoic and republican leader against Caesar.

Catoniānus *adj see n.*

Catōnīnī *mpl* Cato's supporters.

catōnium, -ī and iī *nt* the lower world.

Catulliānus *adj see n.*

Catullus, -ī *m* Latin lyric poet.

catulus, -ī *m* puppy; cub, young of other animals.

catus *adj* clever, wise; sly, cunning.

Caucasius *adj see n.*

Caucasus, -ī *m* Caucasus mountains.

cauda, -ae *f* tail; ~**am iactāre** fawn; ~**am trahere** be made a fool of.

caudeus *adj* wooden.

caudex, -icis *m* trunk; block of wood; book, ledger; (*fig*) blockhead.

caudicālis *adj* of woodcutting.

Caudīnus *adj see n.*

Noun declensions and verb conjugations are shown on pp xiii to xxv. The present infinitive ending of a verb shows to which conjugation it belongs: **-āre** = 1st; **-ēre** = 2nd; **-ere** = 3rd and **-īre** = 4th. Irregular verbs are shown on p xxvi

Caudium, -ī *nt Samnite town.*
caulae, -ārum *fpl* opening; sheepfold.
caulis, -is *m* stalk; cabbage.
Cauneus *adj* Caunian.
Caunus, -ī *f town in Caria* ♦ *fpl* dried figs.
caupō, -ōnis *m* shopkeeper, innkeeper.
caupōna, -ae *f* shop, inn.
caupōnius *adj see n.*
caupōnor, -ārī *vt* to trade in.
caupōnula, -ae *f* tavern.
Caurus, -ī *m* north-west wind.
causa, -ae *f* cause, reason; purpose, sake; excuse, pretext; opportunity; connection, case, position; (*law*) case, suit; (*POL*) cause, party; (*RHET*) subject matter; **~am agere, ōrāre** plead a case; **~am dēfendere** speak for the defence; **~am dīcere** defend oneself; **~ā** for the sake of; **cum ~ā** with good reason; **quā dē ~ā** for this reason; **in ~ā esse** be responsible; **per ~am** under the pretext.
causārius *adj* (*MIL*) unfit for service.
causia, -ae *f* Macedonian hat.
causidicus, -ī *m* advocate.
causificor, -ārī *vi* to make a pretext.
causor, -ārī, -ātus *vt, vi* to pretend, make an excuse of.
caussa *etc see* **causa.**
causula, -ae *f* petty lawsuit; slight cause.
cautē *adv* carefully, cautiously; with security.
cautēla, -ae *f* caution.
cautēs, -is *f* rock, crag.
cautim *adv* warily.
cautiō, -ōnis *f* caution, wariness; (*law*) security, bond, bail; **mihi ~ est** I must take care; **mea ~ est** I must see to it.
cautor, -ōris *m* wary person; surety.
cautus *ppp of* **caveō** ♦ *adj* wary, provident; safe, secure.
cavaedium, -ī *and* **iī** *nt* inner court of a house.
cavea, -ae *f* cage, stall, coop, hive; (*THEAT*) auditorium; theatre; **prīma ~** upper class seats; **ultima ~** lower class seats.
caveō, -ēre, cāvī, cautum *vt* to beware of, guard against ♦ *vi* (*with ab or abl*) to be on one's guard against; (*with dat*) to look after; (*with nē*) to take care that … not; (*with ut*) to take good care that; (*with subj or inf*) to take care not to, do not; (*law*) to stipulate, decree; (*COMM*) to get a guarantee, give a guarantee, stand security; **cavē!** look out!
caverna, -ae *f* hollow, cave, vault; (*NAUT*) hold.
cavilla, -ae *f* jeering.
cavillātiō, -ōnis *f* jeering, banter; sophistry.
cavillātor, -ōris *m* scoffer.
cavillor, -ārī, -ātus *vt* to scoff at ♦ *vi* to jeer, scoff; to quibble.
cavō, -āre, -āvī, -ātum *vt* to hollow, excavate.
cavus *adj* hollow, concave, vaulted; (*river*) deep-channelled ♦ *nt* cavity, hole.
Caystros, -us, -ī *m* river in Lydia (*famous for swans*).
-ce *demonstrative particle appended to pronouns and adverbs.*

Cēa, -ae *f* Aegean island (*birthplace of Simonides*).
cecidī *perf of* **cadō.**
cecīdī *perf of* **caedō.**
cecinī *perf of* **canō.**
Cecropidēs, -idae *m* Theseus; Athenian.
Cecropis, -idis *f* Aglauros; Procne; Philomela; Athenian, Attic.
Cecropius *adj* Athenian ♦ *f* Athens.
Cecrops, -is *m ancient king of Athens.*
cēdō, -ere, cessī, cessum *vi* to go, walk; to depart, withdraw, retreat; to pass away, die; (*events*) to turn out; to be changed (into); to accrue (to); to yield, be inferior (to) ♦ *vt* to give up, concede, allow; **~ bonīs, possessiōne** make over property (to); **~ forō** go bankrupt; **~ locō** leave one's post; **~ memoriā** be forgotten.
cedo (*pl* **cette**) *impv* give me, bring here; tell me; let me; look at!
cedrus, -ī *f* cedar, perfumed juniper; cedar oil.
Celaenō, -ūs *f* a Harpy; a Pleiad.
cēlāta *ntpl* secrets.
celeber, -ris *adj* crowded, populous; honoured, famous; repeated.
celebrātiō, -ōnis *f* throng; celebration.
celebrātus *adj* full, much used; festive; famous.
celebritās, -ātis *f* crowd; celebration; fame.
celebrō, -āre, -āvī, -ātum *vt* to crowd, frequent; to repeat, practise; to celebrate, keep (*a festival*); to advertise, glorify.
celer, -is *adj* quick, swift, fast; hasty.
Celerēs, -um *mpl* royal bodyguard.
celeripēs, -edis *adj* swift-footed.
celeritās, -ātis *f* speed, quickness.
celeriter *adv see* **celer.**
celerō, -āre *vt* to quicken ♦ *vi* to make haste.
cella, -ae *f* granary, stall, cell; garret, hut, small room; sanctuary of a temple.
cellārius *adj* of the storeroom ♦ *m* steward.
cellula, -ae *f* little room.
cēlō, -āre, -āvī, -ātum *vt* to hide, conceal, keep secret; **id mē ~at** he keeps me in the dark about it.
celōx, -ōcis *adj* swift ♦ *f* fast ship, yacht.
celsus *adj* high, lofty; (*fig*) great, eminent; haughty.
Celtae, -ārum *mpl* Celts (*esp of central Gaul*) ♦ *nt* the Celtic nation.
Celtibērī, -ōrum *mpl* people of central Spain.
Celtibēria, -iae *f* Central Spain.
Celtibēricus *adj see n.*
Celticus *adj* Celtic.
cēna, -ae *f* dinner (*the principal Roman meal*); **inter ~am** at table.
cēnāculum, -ī *nt* dining-room; upper room, garret.
cēnāticus *adj* of dinner.
cēnātiō, -ōnis *f* dining-room.
cēnātus *ppa* having dined, after dinner ♦ *ppp* spent in feasting.

Cenchreae, -ārum *fpl* harbour of Corinth.
cēnitō, -āre *vi* to be accustomed to dine.
cēnō, -āre, -āvī, -ātum *vi* to dine ♦ *vt* to eat, dine on.
cēnseō, -ēre, -uī, -um *vt* (*census*) to assess, rate, take a census, make a property return; (*fig*) to estimate, appreciate, celebrate; (*senate or other body*) to decree, resolve; (*member*) to express an opinion, move, vote; to advise; to judge, think, suppose, consider; **cēnsuī ~endō** for census purposes.
cēnsiō, -ōnis *f* punishment; expression of opinion.
cēnsor, -ōris *m* censor; (*fig*) severe judge, critic.
cēnsōrius *adj* of the censors, to be dealt with by the censors; (*fig*) severe; **homō ~** an ex-censor.
cēnsūra, -ae *f* censorship; criticism.
cēnsus *ppp of* **cēnseō; capite ~ī** the poorest class of Roman citizens.
cēnsus, -ūs *m* register of Roman citizens and their property, census; registered property; wealth; **~um agere, habēre** hold a census; **sine ~ū** poor.
centaurēum, -ī *nt* centaury.
Centaurēus *adj see n.*
Centaurus, -ī *m* Centaur, half man half horse.
centēnī, -um *num* a hundred each, a hundred.
centēsimus *adj* hundredth ♦ *f* hundredth part; (*interest*) 1 per cent monthly (*12 per cent per annum*).
centiceps *adj* hundred-headed.
centiēns, -ēs *adv* a hundred times.
centimanus *adj* hundred-handed.
centō, -ōnis *m* patchwork; **~ōnēs sarcīre** ≈ tell tall stories.
centum *num* a hundred.
centumgeminus *adj* hundred-fold.
centumplex *adj* hundred-fold.
centumpondium, -ī and iī *nt* a hundred pounds.
centumvirālis *adj* of the centumviri.
centumvirī, -ōrum *mpl* a bench of judges who heard special civil cases in Rome.
centunculus, -ī *m* piece of patchwork, saddlecloth.
centuria, -ae *f* (*MIL*) company; (*POL*) century (*a division of the Roman people according to property*).
centuriātim *adv* by companies, by centuries.
centuriātus *adj* divided by centuries; **comitia ~a** assembly which voted by centuries.
centuriātus, -ūs *m* division into centuries; rank of centurion.
centuriō, -āre, -āvī, -ātum *vt* (*MIL*) to assign to companies; (*POL*) to divide by centuries.
centuriō, -ōnis *m* (*MIL*) captain, centurion.
centussis, -is *m* a hundred asses.
cēnula, -ae *f* little dinner.

Ceōs, *acc* **-ō** *see* **Cea.**
Cēphēis *f* Andromeda.
Cēphēius *adj* of Cepheus.
Cēpheus *adj* Ethiopian.
Cēpheus, -eī (*acc* **-ea**) *m* king of Ethiopia (*father of Andromeda*).
Cēphīsis *adj see n.*
Cēphīsius *m* Narcissus.
Cēphīsus, -ī *m* river in central Greece.
cēpī *perf of* **capiō.**
cēra, -ae *f* wax; honey cells; writing tablet, notebook; seal; portrait of an ancestor; **prīma ~** first page.
Cerāmīcus, -ī *m* Athenian cemetery.
cērārium, -ī and iī *nt* seal-duty.
cerastēs, -ae *m* a horned serpent.
cerasus, -ī *f* cherry tree; cherry.
cērātus *adj* waxed.
Ceraunia, -ōrum *nt*, **Cerauniī** *m* mountains in Epirus.
Cerbereus *adj see n.*
Cerberus, -ī *m* three-headed watchdog of Hades.
cercopithēcus, -ī *m* monkey.
cercūrus, -ī *m* Cyprian type of ship.
cerdō, -ōnis *m* tradesman.
Cereālia, -ium *ntpl* festival of Ceres.
Cereālis *adj* of Ceres; of corn, of meal.
cerebrōsus *adj* hot-headed.
cerebrum, -ī *nt* brain; understanding; quick temper.
Cerēs, -eris *f* goddess of agriculture; (*fig*) grain, bread.
cēreus *adj* waxen; wax-coloured; (*fig*) supple, easily led ♦ *m* a taper.
cēriāria, -ae *f* taper maker.
cērina, -ōrum *ntpl* wax-coloured clothes.
cērintha, -ae *f* honeywort.
cernō, -ere, -crēvī, crētum *vt* to see, discern; to understand, perceive; to decide, determine; (*law*) to decide to take up (an inheritance).
cernuus *adj* face downwards.
cērōma, -atis *nt* wrestlers' ointment.
cērōmaticus *adj* smeared with wax ointment.
cerrītus *adj* crazy.
certāmen, -inis *nt* contest, match; battle, combat; (*fig*) struggle, rivalry.
certātim *adv* emulously.
certātiō, -ōnis *f* contest; debate; rivalry.
certē *adv* assuredly, of course; at least.
certō *adv* certainly, really.
certō, -āre, -āvī, -ātum *vi* to contend, compete; (*MIL*) to fight it out; (*law*) to dispute; (*with inf*) to try hard.
certus *adj* determined, fixed, definite; reliable, unerring; sure, certain; **mihi ~um est** I have made up my mind; **~um scīre, prō ~ō habēre** know for certain, be sure; **~iōrem facere** inform.
cērula, -ae *f* piece of wax; **~ miniāta** red

pencil.

cērussa, -ae *f* white lead.

cērussātus *adj* painted with white lead.

cerva, -ae *f* hind, deer.

cervīcal, -ālis *nt* pillow.

cervīcula, -ae *f* slender neck.

cervīnus *adj* deer's.

cervīx, -īcis *f* neck; **in ~īcibus esse** be a burden (to), threaten.

cervus, -ī *m* stag, deer; (*MIL*) palisade.

cessātiō, -ōnis *f* delaying; inactivity, idleness.

cessātor, -ōris *m* idler.

cessī *perf of* **cēdō.**

cessiō, -ōnis *f* giving up.

cessō, -āre, -āvī, -ātum *vi* to be remiss, stop; to loiter, delay; to be idle, rest, do nothing; (*land*) to lie fallow; to err.

cestrosphendonē, -ēs *f* (*MIL*) engine for shooting stones.

cestus, -ī *m* girdle (*esp of Venus*).

cētārium, -ī *and* **iī** *nt* fishpond.

cētārius, -ī *and* **iī** *m* fishmonger.

cētera *adv* in other respects.

cēterī, -ōrum *adj* the rest, the others; (*sg*) the rest of.

cēterōquī, -n *adv* otherwise.

cēterum *adv* for the rest, otherwise; but for all that; besides.

Cethēgus, -ī *m* a conspirator with Catiline.

cētr- *etc see* **caetr-.**

cette *etc see* **cedo.**

cētus, -ī *m* (-ē *ntpl*) sea monster, whale.

ceu *adv* just as, as if.

Cēus *adj see* **Cēa.**

Cēyx, -ycis *m* husband of Alcyone, changed to a kingfisher.

Chalcidēnsis, (-discus) *adj see n.*

Chalcis, -dis *f* chief town of Euboea.

Chaldaeī, -aeōrum *mpl* Chaldeans; astrologers.

Chaldāicus *adj see n.*

chalybēius *adj* of steel.

Chalybes, -um *mpl* a people of Pontus (*famous as ironworkers*).

chalybs, -is *m* steel.

Chāones, -um *mpl* a people of Epirus.

Chāonia, -iae *f* Epirus.

Chāonius, -is *adj see n.*

Chaos (*abl* -ō) *nt* empty space, the lower world, chaos.

chara, -ae *f* an unidentified vegetable.

charistia, -ōrum *ntpl* a Roman family festival.

Charites, -um *fpl* the Graces.

Charōn, -ontis *m* Charon (*ferryman of Hades*).

charta, -ae *f* sheet of papyrus, paper; writing.

chartula, -ae *f* piece of paper.

Charybdis, -is *f* monster personifying a whirlpool in the Straits of Messina; (*fig*) peril.

Chattī, -ōrum *mpl* a people of central Germany.

Chēlae, -ārum *fpl* (*ASTRO*) the Claws (of Scorpio), Libra.

chelydrus, -ī *m* watersnake.

chelys (*acc* -yn) *f* tortoise; lyre.

cheragra, -ae *f* gout in the hands.

Cherronēsus, Chersonēsus, -ī *f* Gallipoli peninsula; Crimea.

chīliarchus, -ī *m* officer in charge of 1000 men; chancellor of Persia.

Chimaera, -ae *f* fire-breathing monster formed of lion, goat and serpent.

Chimaeriferus *adj* birthplace of Chimaera.

Chios, -ī *f* Aegean island (*famous for wine*).

Chīus *adj* Chian ♦ *nt* Chian wine; Chian cloth.

chīrographum, -ī *nt* handwriting; document.

Chīrōn, -ōnis *m* a learned Centaur (*tutor of heroes*).

chīronomos, -ī *m/f,* **chīronomōn, -untis** *m* mime actor.

chiūrūrgia, -ae *f* surgery; (*fig*) violent measures.

chlamydātus *adj* wearing a military cloak.

chlamys, -dis *f* Greek military cloak.

Choerilus, -ī *m* inferior Greek poet.

chorāgium, -ī *and* **iī** *nt* producing of a chorus.

chorāgus, -ī *m* one who finances a chorus.

choraulēs, -ae *m* flute-player (accompanying a chorus).

chorda, -ae *f* string (of an instrument); rope.

chorēa, -ae *f* dance.

chorēus, -ī *m* trochee.

chorus, -ī *m* choral dance; chorus, choir of singers or dancers; band, troop.

Christiānismus, -ī *m* Christianity.

Christiānus *adj* Christian.

Christus, -ī *m* Christ.

Chrȳsēis, -ēidis *f* daughter of Chrȳsēs.

Chrȳsēs, -ae *m* priest of Apollo in the Iliad.

Chrȳsippēus *adj see n.*

Chrȳsippus, -ī *m* Stoic philosopher.

chrȳsolithos, -ī *m/f* topaz.

chrȳsos, -ī *m* gold.

cibārius *adj* food (*in cpds*); common ♦ *ntpl* rations.

cibātus, -ūs *m* food.

cibōrium, -ī *and* **iī** *nt* kind of drinking cup.

cibus, -ī *m* food, fodder, nourishment.

cicāda, -ae *f* cicada, cricket.

cicātrīcōsus *adj* scarred.

cicātrīx, -īcis *f* scar; (*plants*) mark of an incision.

ciccus, -ī *m* pomegranate pip.

cicer, -is *nt* chickpea.

Cicerō, -ōnis *m* great Roman orator and author.

Cicerōniānus *adj see n.*

cichorēum, -ī *nt* chicory.

Cicōnes, -um *mpl* people of Thrace.

cicōnia, -ae *f* stork.

cicur, -is *adj* tame.

cicūta, -ae *f* hemlock; pipe.

cieō, ciēre, cīvī, citum *vt* to move, stir, rouse; to call, invoke; (*fig*) to give rise to, produce; **calcem ~** make a move (in chess).

Cilicia, -ae *f* country in S. Asia Minor (*famous for piracy*).

Ciliciēnsis, (-us) *adj see n.*

Cilix, -cis, -ssa *adj* Cilician ♦ *nt* goats' hair garment.
Cimbrī, -ōrum *mpl people of N. Germany.*
Cimbricus *adj see n.*
cīmex, -icis *m* bug.
Cimmeriī, -ōrum *mpl people of the Crimea; mythical race in caves near Cumae.*
Cimmerius *adj see n.*
cinaedius *adj* lewd.
cinaedus, -ī *m* sodomite; lewd dancer.
cincinnātus *adj* with curled hair.
Cincinnātus, -ī *m* ancient Roman dictator.
cincinnus, -ī *m* curled hair; (*fig*) rhetorical ornament.
Cincius, -ī *m* Roman tribune; Roman historian.
cincticulus, -ī *m* small girdle.
cinctus *ppp of* **cingō.**
cinctus, -ūs *m* girding; ~ **Gabīnus** *a ceremonial style of wearing the toga.*
cinctūtus *adj* girded.
cinefactus *adj* reduced to ashes.
cinerārius, -ī *and* **iī** *m* hair curler.
cingō, -gere, -xī, -ctum *vt* to surround, enclose; to gird, crown; (*MIL*) to besiege, fortify; to cover, escort; **ferrum ~or** I put on my sword.
cingula, -ae *f* girth (*of animals*).
cingulum, -ī *nt* belt.
cingulus, -ī *m* zone.
ciniflō, -ōnis *m* hair curler.
cinis, -eris *m* ashes; (*fig*) ruin.
Cinna, -ae *m* colleague of Marius; poet friend of Catullus.
cinnamōmum, cinnamum, -ī *nt* cinnamon.
cinxī *perf of* **cingō.**
Cīnyphius *adj* of the Cinyps, river of N. Africa; African.
Cinyrās, -ae *m* father of Adonis.
Cinyrēius *adj see n.*
cippus, -ī *m* tombstone; (*pl*) palisade.
circā *adv* around, round about ♦ *prep* (*with acc*) (*place*) round, in the vicinity of, in; (*time, number*) about; with regard to.
Circaeus *adj see* **Circē.**
circamoerium, -ī *and* **iī** *nt* space on both sides of a wall.
Circē, -ēs *and* **ae** *f goddess with magic powers living in Aeaea.*
circēnsēs, -ium *mpl* the games.
circēnsis *adj* of the Circus.
circinō, -āre *vt* to circle through.
circinus, -ī *m* pair of compasses.
circiter *adv* (*time, number*) about ♦ *prep* (*with acc*) about, near.
circueō, circumeō, -īre, -īvī *and* **iī, -itum** *vt, vi* to go round, surround; (*MIL*) to encircle; to visit, go round canvassing; to deceive.
circuitiō, -ōnis *f* (*MIL*) rounds; (*speech*) evasiveness.
circuitus *ppp of* **circueō.**

circuitus, -ūs *m* revolution; way round, circuit; (*RHET*) period, periphrasis.
circulātor, -ōris *m* pedlar.
circulor, -ārī *vi* to collect in crowds.
circulus, -ī *m* circle; orbit; ring; social group.
circum *adv* round about ♦ *prep* (*with acc*) round, about; near; ~ **īnsulās mittere** send to the islands round about.
circumagō, -agere, -ēgī, -āctum *vt* to turn, move in a circle, wheel; (*pass: time*) to pass; (*: mind*) to be swayed.
circumarō, -āre *vt* to plough round.
circumcaesūra, -ae *f* outline.
circumcīdō, -dere, -dī, -sum *vt* to cut round, trim; to cut down, abridge.
circumcircā *adv* all round.
circumcīsus *ppp of* **circumcīdō** ♦ *adj* precipitous.
circumclūdō, -dere, -sī, -sum *vt* to shut in, hem in.
circumcolō, -ere *vt* to live round about.
circumcursō, -āre *vi* to run about.
circumdō, -are, -edī, -atum *vt* to put round; to surround, enclose.
circumdūcō, -ūcere, -ūxī, -uctum *vt* to lead round, draw round; to cheat; (*speech*) to prolong, drawl.
circumductus *ppp of* **circumdūcō.**
circumeō *etc see* **circueō.**
circumequitō, -āre *vt* to ride round.
circumferō, -ferre, -tulī, -lātum *vt* to carry round, pass round; to spread, broadcast; to purify; (*pass*) to revolve.
circumflectō, -ctere, -xī, -xum *vt* to wheel round.
circumflō, -āre *vt* (*fig*) to buffet.
circumfluō, -ere, -xī *vt, vi* to flow round; (*fig*) to overflow, abound.
circumfluus *adj* flowing round; surrounded (by water).
circumforāneus *adj* itinerant; (*money*) borrowed.
circumfundō, -undere, -ūdī, -ūsum *vt* to pour round, surround; (*fig*) to crowd round, overwhelm; (*pass*) to flow round.
circumgemō, -ere *vt* to growl round.
circumgestō, -āre *vt* to carry about.
circumgredior, -dī, -ssus *vt, vi* to make an encircling move, surround.
circumiaceō, -ēre *vi* to be adjacent.
circumiciō, -icere, -iēcī, -iectum *vt* to throw round, put round; to surround.
circumiecta *ntpl* neighbourhood.
circumiectus *adj* surrounding.
circumiectus, -ūs *m* enclosure; embrace.
circumit- *etc see* **circuit-.**
circumitiō, -ōnis *f see* **circuitiō.**
circumitus, -ūs *m see* **circuitus.**
circumlātus *ppp of* **circumferō.**
circumligō, -āre, -āvī, -ātum *vt* to tie to, bind

Noun declensions and verb conjugations are shown on pp xiii to xxv. The present infinitive ending of a verb shows to which conjugation it belongs: **-āre** = 1st; **-ēre** = 2nd; **-ere** = 3rd and **-īre** = 4th. Irregular verbs are shown on p xxvi

round.

circumlinō, -ere, -tum *vt* to smear all over, bedaub.

circumluō, -ere *vt* to wash.

circumluviō, -ōnis *f* alluvial land.

circummittō, -ittere, -īsī, -issum *vt* to send round.

circummoeniō (circummūniō), -īre, -īvī, -ītum *vt* to fortify.

circummūnītiō, -ōnis *f* investing.

circumpadānus *adj* of the Po valley.

circumpendeō, -ēre *vi* to hang round.

circumplaudō, -ere *vt* to applaud on all sides.

circumplector, -ctī, -xus *vt* to embrace, surround.

circumplicō, -āre, -āvī, -ātum *vt* to wind round.

circumpōnō, -pōnere, -posuī, -positum *vt* to put round.

circumpōtātiō, -ōnis *f* passing drinks round.

circumrētiō, -īre, -īvī, -ītum *vt* to ensnare.

circumrōdō, -rosī, -rodere *vt* to nibble round about; (*fig*) to slander.

circumsaepiō, -īre, -sī, -tum *vt* to fence round.

circumscindō, -ere *vt* to strip.

circumscrībō, -bere, -psī, -ptum *vt* to draw a line round; to mark the limits of; to restrict, circumscribe; to set aside; to defraud.

circumscrīptē *adv* in periods.

circumscrīptiō, -ōnis *f* circle, contour; fraud; (*RHET*) period.

circumscrīptor, -ōris *m* defrauder.

circumscrīptus *ppp of* **circumscrībō ♦** *adj* restricted; (*RHET*) periodic.

circumsecō, -āre *vt* to cut round.

circumsedeō, -edēre, -ēdī, -essum *vt* to blockade, beset.

circumsēpiō *etc see* **circumsaepiō**.

circumsessiō, -ōnis *f* siege.

circumsessus *ppp of* **circumsedeō**.

circumsīdō, -ere *vt* to besiege.

circumsiliō, -īre *vi* to hop about; (*fig*) to be rampant.

circumsistō, -sistere, -stetī surround.

circumsonō, -āre *vi* to resound on all sides ♦ *vt* to fill with sound.

circumsonus *adj* noisy.

circumspectātrīx, -īcis *f* spy.

circumspectiō, -ōnis *f* caution.

circumspectō, -āre *vt, vi* to look all round, search anxiously, be on the lookout.

circumspectus *ppp of* **circumspiciō ♦** *adj* carefully considered, cautious.

circumspectus, -ūs *m* consideration; view.

circumspiciō, -icere, -exī, -ectum *vi* to look all round; to be careful ♦ *vt* to survey; (*fig*) to consider, search for.

circumstantēs, -antium *mpl* bystanders.

circumstetī *perf of* **circumsistō**; *perf of* **circumstō**.

circumstō, -āre, -etī *vt, vi* to stand round; to

besiege; (*fig*) to encompass.

circumstrepō, -ere *vt* to make a clamour round.

circumsurgēns, -entis *pres p* rising on all sides.

circumtentus *adj* covered tightly.

circumterō, -ere *vt* to crowd round.

circumtextus *adj* embroidered round the edge.

circumtonō, -āre, -uī *vt* to thunder about.

circumvādō, -dere, -sī *vt* to assail on all sides.

circumvagus *adj* encircling.

circumvallō, -āre, -āvī, -ātum *vt* to blockade, beset.

circumvectiō, -ōnis *f* carrying about; (*sun*) revolution.

circumvector, -ārī *vi* to travel round, cruise round; (*fig*) describe.

circumvehor, -hī, -ctus *vt, vi* to ride round, sail round; (*fig*) to describe.

circumvēlō, -āre *vt* to envelop.

circumveniō, -enīre, -ēnī, -entum *vt* to surround, beset; to oppress; to cheat.

circumvertō, circumvortō, -ere *vt* to turn round.

circumvestiō, -īre *vt* to envelop.

circumvinciō, -īre *vt* to lash about.

circumvīsō, -ere *vt* to look at all round.

circumvolitō, -āre, -āvī, -ātum *vt, vi* to fly round; to hover around.

circumvolō, -āre *vt* to fly round.

circumvolvō, -vere *vt* to roll round.

circus, -ī *m* circle; the Circus Maximus (*famous Roman racecourse*); a racecourse.

Cirrha, -ae *f* town near Delphi (*sacred to Apollo*).

Cirrhaeus *adj see n.*

cirrus, -ī *m* curl of hair; fringe.

cis *prep* (*with acc*) on this side of; (*time*) within.

Cisalpīnus *adj* on the Italian side of the Alps, Cisalpine.

cisium, -ī *and* **iī** *nt* two-wheeled carriage.

Cissēis, -dis *f* Hecuba.

cista, -ae *f* box, casket; ballot box.

cistella, -ae *f* small box.

cistellātrīx, -īcis *f* keeper of the moneybox.

cistellula, -ae *f* little box.

cisterna, -ae *f* reservoir.

cistophorus, -ī *m* an Asiatic coin.

cistula, -ae *f* little box.

citātus *adj* quick, impetuous.

citerior (*sup* **-imus**) *adj* on this side, nearer.

Cithaerōn, -ōnis *m* mountain range between Attica and Boeotia.

cithara, -ae *f* lute.

citharista, -ae *m*, **citharistria, -ae** *f* lute player.

citharizō, -āre *vi* to play the lute.

citharoedus, -ī *m* a singer who accompanies himself on the lute.

citimus *adj* nearest.

citō (*com* **-ius**, *sup* **-issimē**) *adv* quickly, soon;

nōn ~ not easily.

citō, -āre, -āvī, -ātum vt to set in motion, rouse; to call (by name), appeal to, cite, mention.

citrā adv on this side, this way, not so far ♦ prep (with acc) on this side of, short of; (time) before, since; apart from; ~ **quam** before.

citreus adj of citrus wood.

citrō adv hither, this way; **ultrō ~que** to and fro.

citrus, -ī f citrus tree; citron tree.

citus ppp of **cieō** ♦ adj quick.

cīvicus adj civic, civil; **corōna ~a** civic crown for saving a citizen's life in war.

cīvīlis adj of citizens, civil; political, civilian; courteous, democratic; **iūs ~e** civil rights; Civil Law; code of legal procedure.

cīvīlitās, -ātis f politics; politeness.

cīvīliter adv like citizens; courteously.

cīvis, -is m/f citizen, fellow citizen.

cīvitās, -ātis f citizenship; community state; city; **~āte dōnāre** naturalize.

clādēs, -is f damage, disaster, ruin; defeat; (fig) scourge; **dare ~em** make havoc.

clam adv secretly; unknown ♦ prep (with acc) unknown to; ~ **mē habēre** keep from me.

clāmātor, -ōris m bawler.

clāmitātiō, -ōnis f bawling.

clāmitō, -āre, -āvī, -ātum vt, vi to bawl, screech, cry out.

clāmō, -āre, -āvī, -ātum vt, vi to shout, cry out; to call upon, proclaim.

clāmor, -ōris m shout, cry; acclamation.

clāmōsus adj noisy.

clanculum adv secretly ♦ prep (with acc) unknown to.

clandestīnō adv see **clandestīnus**.

clandestīnus adj secret.

clangor, -ōris m clang, noise.

clārē adv brightly, loudly, clearly, with distinction.

clāreō, -ēre vi to be bright, be clear; to be evident; to be renowned.

clārēscō, -ere, clāruī vi to brighten, sound clear; to become obvious; to become famous.

clārigātiō, -ōnis f formal ultimatum to an enemy; fine for trespass.

clārigō, -āre vi to deliver a formal ultimatum.

clārisonus adj loud and clear.

clāritās, -ātis f distinctness; (RHET) lucidity; celebrity.

clāritūdō, -inis f brightness; (fig) distinction.

Clarius adj of Claros ♦ m Apollo.

clārō, -āre vt to illuminate; to explain; to make famous.

Claros, -ī f town in Ionia (famous for worship of Apollo).

clārus adj (sight) bright; (sound) loud; (mind) clear; (person) distinguished; ~ **intonāre**

thunder from a clear sky; **vir ~issimus** a courtesy title for eminent men.

classiārius adj naval ♦ mpl marines.

classicula, -ae f flotilla.

classicum, -ī nt battle-signal; trumpet.

classicus adj of the first class; naval ♦ mpl marines.

classis, -is f a political class; army; fleet.

clāthrī, -ōrum mpl cage.

clātrātus adj barred.

clātrī, -ōrum mpl see **clāthrī**.

claudeō, -ēre vi to limp; (fig) to be defective.

claudicātiō, -ōnis f limping.

claudicō, -āre vi to be lame; to waver, be defective.

Claudius, -ī m patrician family name (esp Appius Claudius Caecus, famous censor); the Emperor Claudius.

Claudius, -iānus, -iālis adj see n.

claudō, -dere, -sī, -sum vt to shut, close; to cut off, block; to conclude; to imprison, confine, blockade; **agmen ~** bring up the rear.

claudō, -ere etc see **claudeō**.

claudus adj lame, crippled; (verse) elegiac; (fig) wavering.

clausī perf of **claudō**.

claustra, -ōrum ntpl bar, bolt, lock; barrier, barricade, dam.

clausula, -ae f conclusion; (RHET) ending of a period.

clausum, -ī nt enclosure.

clausus ppp of **claudō**.

clāva, -ae f club, knotty branch; (MIL) foil.

clāvārium, -ī and **iī** nt money for buying shoe nails.

clāvātor, -ōris m cudgel-bearer.

clāvicula, -ae f vine tendril.

clāviger, -ī m (Hercules) club bearer; (Janus) key-bearer.

clāvis, -is f key.

clāvus, -ī m nail; tiller, rudder; purple stripe on the tunic (broad for senators, narrow for equites); ~**um annī movēre** reckon the beginning of the year.

Cleanthēs, -is m Stoic philosopher.

clēmēns, -entis adj mild, gentle, merciful; (weather, water) mild, calm.

clēmenter adv gently, indulgently; gradually.

clēmentia, -ae f mildness, forbearance, mercy.

Cleopatra, -ae f queen of Egypt.

clepō, -ere, -sī, -tum vt to steal.

clepsydra, -ae f waterclock (used for timing speakers); ~**am dare** give leave to speak; ~**am petere** ask leave to speak.

clepta, -ae m thief.

cliēns, -entis m client, dependant; follower; vassal-state.

clienta, -ae f client.

Noun declensions and verb conjugations are shown on pp xiii to xxv. The present infinitive ending of a verb shows to which conjugation it belongs: **-āre** = 1st; **-ēre** = 2nd; **-ere** = 3rd and **-īre** = 4th. Irregular verbs are shown on p xxvi

clientēla, -ae *f* clientship, protection; clients.
clientulus, -ī *m* insignificant client.
clīnāmen, -inis *nt* swerve.
clīnātus *adj* inclined.
Cliō, -ūs *f* Muse of history.
clipeātus *adj* armed with a shield.
clipeus, -ī *m*, **-um, -ī** *nt* round bronze shield;
  disc; medallion on a metal base.
clitellae, -ārum *fpl* packsaddle, attribute of
  an ass.
clitellārius *adj* carrying packsaddles.
Clitumnus, -ī *m* river in Umbria.
clīvōsus *adj* hilly.
clīvus, -ī *m* slope, hill; **~ sacer** part of the Via
  Sacra.
cloāca, -ae *f* sewer, drain.
Cloācina, -ae *f* Venus.
Clōdius, -ī *m* Roman plebeian name (esp the
  tribune, enemy of Cicero).
Cloelia, -ae *f* Roman girl hostage (who
  escaped by swimming the Tiber).
Clōthō (acc -ō) *f* one of the Fates.
clueō, -ēre, -eor, -ērī *vi* to be called, be
  famed.
clūnis, -is *m/f* buttock.
clūrīnus *adj* of apes.
Clūsīnus *adj* see *n.*
Clūsium, -ī *nt* old Etruscan town (now Chiusi).
Clūsius, -ī *m* Janus.
Clytaemnēstra, -ae *f* wife of Agamemnon
  (whom she murdered).
Cnidius *adj* see *n.*
Cnidus, -ī *f* town in Caria (famous for worship
  of Venus).
coacervātiō, -ōnis *f* accumulation.
coacervō, -āre *vt* to heap, accumulate.
coacēscō, -ēscere, -uī *vi* to become sour.
coāctō, -āre *vt* to force.
coāctor, -ōris *m* collector (of money).
coāctōrēs agminis rearguard.
coāctum, -ī *nt* thick coverlet.
coāctus *adj* forced.
coāctus *ppp of* **cōgō**.
coāctus, -ūs *m* compulsion.
coaedificō, -āre, -ātum *vt* to build on.
coaequō, -āre, -āvī, -ātum *vt* to make equal,
  bring down to the same level.
coagmentātiō, -ōnis *f* combination.
coagmentō, -āre, -āvī, -ātum *vt* to glue, join
  together.
coagmentum, -ī *nt* joining, joint.
coāgulum, -ī *nt* rennet.
coalēscō, -ēscere, -uī, -itum *vi* to grow
  together; (fig) to agree together; to flourish.
coangustō, -āre *vt* to restrict.
coarct- *etc see* **coart-.**
coarguō, -ere, -ī *vt* to convict, prove
  conclusively.
coartātiō, -ōnis *f* crowding together.
coartō, -āre, -āvī, -ātum *vt* to compress,
  abridge.
coccineus, coccinus *adj* scarlet.
coccum, -ī *nt* scarlet.

cochlea, coclea, -ae *f* snail.
cocleāre, -is *nt* spoon.
cocles, -itis *m* man blind in one eye; surname
  of Horatius who defended the bridge.
coctilis *adj* baked; of bricks.
coctus *ppp of* **coquō** ♦ *adj* (fig) well considered.
cocus *etc see* **coquus.**
Cōcȳtius *adj* see *n.*
Cōcȳtos, -us, -ī *m* river in the lower world.
cōda *etc see* **cauda.**
cōdex *etc see* **caudex.**
cōdicillī, -ōrum *mpl* letter, note, petition;
  codicil.
Codrus, -ī *m* last king of Athens.
coēgī *perf of* **cōgō.**
coel- *etc see* **cael-.**
coemō, -emere, -ēmī, -emptum *vt* to buy
  up.
coemptiō, -ōnis *f* a form of Roman marriage;
  mock sale of an estate.
coemptiōnālis *adj* used in a mock sale;
  worthless.
coen- *etc see* **caen-** *or* **cēn-.**
coeō, -īre, -īvī *and* **iī, -itum** *vi* to meet,
  assemble; to encounter; to combine, mate;
  (wounds) to close; to agree, conspire ♦ *vt:* **~
  societātem** make a compact.
coepiō, -ere, -ī, -tum *vt, vi* begin (esp in perf
  tenses); **rēs agī ~tae sunt** things began to be
  done; **coepisse** to have begun.
coeptō, -āre, -āvī, -ātum *vi* to begin,
  attempt.
coeptum, -ī *nt* beginning, undertaking.
coeptus *ppp of* **coepiō.**
coeptus, -ūs *m* beginning.
coepulōnus, -ī *m* fellow-banqueter.
coerātor *etc see* **cūrātor.**
coerceō, -ēre, -uī, -itum *vt* to enclose; to
  confine, repress; (fig) to control, check,
  correct.
coercitiō, -ōnis *f* coercion, punishment.
coetus, coitus, -ūs *m* meeting, joining
  together; assembly, crowd.
cōgitātē *adv* deliberately.
cōgitātiō, -ōnis *f* thought, reflection; idea,
  plan; faculty of thought, imagination.
cōgitātus *adj* deliberate ♦ *ntpl* ideas.
cōgitō, -āre, -āvī, -ātum *vt, vi* to think,
  ponder, imagine; to feel disposed; to plan,
  intend.
cognātiō, -ōnis *f* relationship (by blood); kin,
  family; (fig) affinity, resemblance.
cognātus, -ī *m*, **-a, -ae** *f* relation ♦ *adj* related;
  (fig) connected, similar.
cognitiō, -ōnis *f* acquiring of knowledge,
  knowledge; idea, notion; (law) judicial
  inquiry; (comedy) recognition.
cognitor, -ōris *m* (law) attorney; witness of a
  person's identity; (fig) defender.
cognitus *adj* acknowledged.
cognitus *ppp of* **cognōscō.**
cognōmen, -inis *nt* surname; name.
cognōmentum, -ī *nt* surname, name.

cognōminis *adj* with the same name.

cognōminō, -āre, -āvī, -ātum *vt* to give a surname to; **verba ~āta** synonyms.

cognōscō, -ōscere, -ōvī, -itum *vt* to get to know, learn, understand; to know, recognize, identify; (*law*) to investigate; (*MIL*) to reconnoitre.

cōgō, -ere, coēgī, coāctum *vt* to collect, gather together; (*liquids*) to thicken, curdle; to contract, confine; to compel, force; to infer; **agmen ~** bring up the rear; **senātum ~** call a meeting of the senate.

cohaerentia, -ae *f* coherence.

cohaereō, -rēre, -sī, -sum *vi* to stick together, cohere; to cling to; (*fig*) to be consistent, harmonize; to agree, be consistent with.

cohaerēscō, -ere *vi* to stick together.

cohaesus *ppp of* cohaereō.

cohērēs, -ēdis *m/f* co-heir.

cohibeō, -ēre, -uī, -itum *vt* to hold together, encircle; to hinder, stop; (*fig*) to restrain, repress.

cohonestō, -āre *vt* to do honour to.

cohorrēscō, -ēscere, -uī *vi* to shudder all over.

cohors, -tis *f* courtyard; (*MIL*) cohort (*about 600 men*); retinue (*esp of the praetor in a province*); (*fig*) company.

cohortātiō, -ōnis *f* encouragement.

cohorticula, -ae *f* small cohort.

cohortor, -ārī, -ātus *vt* to encourage, urge.

coitiō, -ōnis *f* encounter; conspiracy.

coitus *etc see* coetus.

colaphus, -ī *m* blow with the fist, box.

Colchis, -idis *f* Medea's country (*at the E. end of the Black Sea*).

Colchis, -us, -icus *adj* Colchian.

cōleus *etc see* culleus.

cōlis *etc see* caulis.

collabāscō, -ere *vi* to waver also.

collabefactō, -āre *vt* to shake violently.

collabefīō, -fierī, -factus *vi* to be destroyed.

collābor, -bī, -psus *vi* to fall in ruin, collapse.

collacerātus *adj* torn to pieces.

collacrimātiō, -ōnis *f* weeping.

collactea, -ae *f* foster-sister.

collāpsus *ppa of* collābor.

collāre, -is *nt* neckband.

Collātia, -iae *f* ancient town near Rome ♦ *m* husband of Lucretia.

Collātīnus *adj* of Collatia.

collātiō, -ōnis *f* bringing together, combination; (*money*) contribution; (*RHET*) comparison; (*PHILOS*) analogy.

collātor, -ōris *m* contributor.

collātus *ppp of* cōnferō.

collaudātiō, -ōnis *f* praise.

collaudō, -āre, -āvī, -ātum *vt* to praise highly.

collaxō, -āre *vt* to make porous.

collēcta, -ae *f* money contribution.

collēctīcius *adj* hastily gathered.

collēctiō, -ōnis *f* gathering up; (*RHET*) recapitulation.

collēctus *ppp of* colligō.

collēctus, -ūs *m* accumulation.

collēga, -ae *m* colleague; associate.

collēgī *perf of* colligō.

collēgium, -ī *and* iī *nt* association in office; college, guild (*of magistrates, etc*).

collībertus, -ī *m* fellow freedman.

collibet, collubet, -uit *and* itum est *vi* it pleases.

collīdō, -dere, -sī, -sum *vt* to beat together, strike, bruise; (*fig*) to bring into conflict.

colligātiō, -ōnis *f* connection.

colligō, -āre, -āvī, -ātum *vt* to fasten, tie up; (*fig*) to combine; to restrain, check.

colligō, -igere, -ēgī, -ēctum *vt* to gather, collect; to compress, draw together; to check; (*fig*) to acquire; to think about; to infer, conclude; **animum, mentem ~** recover, rally; **sē ~** crouch; recover one's courage; **vāsa ~** (*MIL*) pack up.

Collīna Porta *gate in N.E. of Rome.*

collīneō, -āre *vt, vi* to aim straight.

collinō, -inere, -ēvī, -itum *vt* to besmear; (*fig*) to deface.

colliquefactus *adj* dissolved.

collis, -is *m* hill, slope.

collīsī *perf of* collīdō.

collīsus *ppp of* collīdō.

collitus *ppp of* collinō.

collocātiō, -ōnis *f* arrangement; giving in marriage.

collocō, -āre, -āvī, -ātum *vt* to place, station, arrange; to give in marriage; (*money*) to invest; (*fig*) to establish; to occupy, employ.

collocuplētō, -āre, -āvī *vt* to enrich.

collocūtiō, -ōnis *f* conversation.

colloquium, -ī *and* iī *nt* conversation, conference.

colloquor, -quī, -cūtus *vi* to converse, hold a conference ♦ *vt* to talk to.

collubet *etc see* collibet.

collūceō, -ēre *vi* to shine brightly; (*fig*) to be resplendent.

collūdō, -dere, -sī, -sum *vi* to play together *or* with; to practise collusion.

collum, -ī *nt* neck; **~ torquēre, obtorquēre, obstringere** arrest.

colluō, -uere, -uī, -ūtum *vt* to rinse, moisten.

collus *etc see* collum.

collūsiō, -ōnis *f* secret understanding.

collūsor, -ōris *m* playmate, fellow gambler.

collūstrō, -āre, -āvī, -ātum *vt* to light up; to survey.

colluviō, -ōnis, -ēs, -em, -ē *f* sweepings, filth; (*fig*) dregs, rabble.

collybus, -ī *m* money exchange, rate of exchange.

collȳra, -ae *f* vermicelli.

collȳricus *adj see n.*

collȳrium, -ī and **iī** *nt* eye lotion.

colō, -ere, -uī, cultum *vt* (*AGR*) to cultivate, work; (*place*) to live in; (*human affairs*) to cherish, protect, adorn; (*qualities, pursuits*) to cultivate, practise; (*gods*) to worship; (*men*) to honour, court; **vītam ~ live.**

colocāsia, -ae *f*, **-a, -ōrum** *ntpl* Egyptian bean, caladium.

colōna, -ae *f* country-woman.

colōnia, -ae *f* settlement, colony; settlers.

colōnicus *adj* colonial.

colōnus, -ī *m* crofter, farmer; settler, colonist.

color (colōs), -ōris *m* colour; complexion; beauty, lustre; (*fig*) outward show; (*RHET*) style, tone; colourful excuse; **~ōrem mūtāre** blush, go pale; **homō nullīus ~ōris** an unknown person.

colōrātus *adj* healthily tanned.

colōrō, -āre, -āvī, -ātum *vt* to colour, tan; (*fig*) to give a colour to.

colossus, -ī *m* gigantic statue (*esp that of Apollo at Rhodes*).

colostra, colustra, -ae *f* beestings.

coluber, -rī *m* snake.

colubra, -ae *f* snake.

colubrifer, -ī *adj* snaky.

colubrīnus *adj* wily.

coluī *perf of* **colō.**

cōlum, -ī *nt* strainer.

columba, -ae *f* dove, pigeon.

columbar, -āris *nt* kind of collar.

columbārium, -ī and **iī** *nt* dovecote.

columbīnus *adj* pigeon's ♦ *m* little pigeon.

columbus, -ī *m* dove, cock-pigeon.

columella, -ae *f* small pillar.

columen, -inis *nt* height, summit; pillar; (*fig*) chief; prop.

columna, -ae *f* column, pillar; *a pillory in the Forum Romanum;* waterspout.

columnārium, -ī and **iī** *nt* pillar tax.

columnārius, -ī *m* criminal.

columnātus *adj* pillared.

colurnus *adj* made of hazel.

colus, -ī and **ūs** *f* (*occ m*) distaff.

cōlȳphia, -ōrum *ntpl* food of athletes.

coma, -ae *f* hair (*of the head*); foliage.

comāns, -antis *adj* hairy, plumed; leafy.

cōmarchus, -ī *m* burgomaster.

comātus *adj* long-haired; leafy; **Gallia ~** Transalpine Gaul.

combibō, -ere, -ī *vt* to drink to the full, absorb.

combibō, -ōnis *m* fellow-drinker.

combūrō, -rere, -ssī, -stum *vt* to burn up; (*fig*) to ruin.

combūstus *ppp of* **combūrō.**

comedō, -ēsse, -ēdī, -ēsum and **-ēstum** *vt* to eat up, devour; (*fig*) to waste, squander; **sē ~** pine away.

Cōmēnsis *adj see* **Cōmum.**

comes, -itis *m/f* companion, partner; attendant, follower; one of a magistrate's or emperor's retinue; (*medieval title*) count.

comēs, comēst *pres tense of* **comedō.**

comēstus, comēsus *ppp of* **comedō.**

comētēs, -ae *m* comet.

cōmicē *adv* in the manner of comedy.

cōmicus, -ī *m* comedy actor, comedy writer ♦ *adj* of comedy, comic.

cōmis *adj* courteous, friendly.

cōmissābundus *adj* carousing.

cōmissātiō, -ōnis *f* Bacchanalian revel.

cōmissātor, -ōris *m* reveller.

cōmissor, -ārī, -ātus *vi* to carouse, make merry.

cōmitās, -ātis *f* kindness, affability.

comitātus, -ūs *m* escort, retinue; company.

cōmiter *adv see* **cōmis.**

comitia, -iōrum *ntpl* assembly for the election of magistrates and other business (*esp the ~* **centuriāta**); elections.

comitiālis *adj* of the elections; **~ morbus** epilepsy.

comitiātus, -ūs *m* assembly at the elections.

comitium, -ī and **iī** *nt* place of assembly.

comitō, -āre, -āvī, -ātum *vt* to accompany.

comitor, -ārī, -ātus *vt, vi* to attend, follow.

commaculō, -āre, -āvī, -ātum *vt* to stain, defile.

commanipulāris, -is *m* soldier in the same company.

commeātus, -ūs *m* passage; leave, furlough; convoy (of troops or goods); (*MIL*) lines of communication, provisions, supplies.

commeditor, -ārī *vt* to practise.

commeminī, -isse *vt, vi* to remember perfectly.

commemorābilis *adj* memorable.

commemorātiō, -ōnis *f* recollection, recounting.

commemorō, -āre, -āvī, -ātum *vt* to recall, remind; to mention, relate.

commendābilis *adj* praiseworthy.

commendātīcius *adj* of recommendation or introduction.

commendātiō, -ōnis *f* recommendation; worth, excellence.

commendātor, -ōris *m* commender (*male*).

commendātrīx, -rīcis *f* commender (*female*).

commendātus *adj* approved, valued.

commendō, -āre, -āvī, -ātum *vt* to entrust, commit, commend (to one's care or charge); to recommend, set off to advantage.

commēnsus *ppa of* **commētior.**

commentāriolum, -ī *nt* short treatise.

commentārius, -ī and **iī** *m*, **-ium, -ī** and **iī** *nt* notebook; commentary, memoir; (*law*) brief.

commentātiō, -ōnis *f* studying, meditation.

commentīcius *adj* fictitious, imaginary; false.

commentor, -ārī, -ātus *vt, vi* to study, think

over, prepare carefully; to invent, compose, write.

commentor, -ōris *m* inventor.

commentum, -ī *nt* invention, fiction; contrivance.

commentus *ppa of* **comminīscor ♦** *adj* feigned, fictitious.

commeō, -āre *vi* to pass to and fro; to go *or* come often.

commercium, -ī *and* **iī** *nt* trade, commerce; right to trade; dealings, communication.

commercor, -ārī, -ātus *vt* to buy up.

commereō, -ēre, -uī, -itum; -eor, -ērī, -itus *vt* to deserve; to be guilty of.

commētior, -tīrī, -nsus *vt* to measure.

commētō, -āre *vi* to go often.

commictus *ppp of* **commingō**.

commigrō, -āre, -āvī, -ātum *vi* to remove, migrate.

commīlitium, -ī *and* **iī** *nt* service together.

commīlitō, -ōnis *m* fellow soldier.

comminātiō, -ōnis *f* threat.

commingō, -ingere, -īnxī, -ictum *vt* to pollute.

comminīscor, -ī, commentus *vt* to devise, contrive.

comminor, -ārī, -ātus *vt* to threaten.

comminuō, -uere, -uī, -ūtum *vt* to break up, smash; to diminish; to impair.

comminus *adv* hand to hand; near at hand.

commisceō, -scēre, -scuī, -xtum *vt* to mix together, join together.

commiserātiō, -ōnis *f* (*RHET*) *passage intended to arouse pity.*

commiserēscō, -ere *vt* to pity.

commiseror, -ārī *vt* to bewail ♦ *vi* (*RHET*) to try to excite pity.

commissiō, -ōnis *f* start (*of a contest*).

commissum, -ī *nt* enterprise; offence, crime; secret.

commissūra, -ae *f* joint, connection.

commissus *ppp of* **committō**.

committō, -ittere, -īsī, -issum *vt* to join, connect, bring together; to begin, undertake; (*battle*) to join, engage in; (*offence*) to commit, be guilty of; (*punishment*) to incur, forfeit; to entrust, trust; **sē urbī ~** venture into the city.

commixtus *ppp of* **commisceō**.

commodē *adv* properly, well; aptly, opportunely; pleasantly.

commoditās, -ātis *f* convenience, ease, fitness; advantage; (*person*) kindliness; (*RHET*) apt expression.

commodō, -āre, -āvī, -ātum *vt* to adjust, adapt; to give, lend, oblige with; (*with dat*) to oblige.

commodulē, -um *adv* conveniently.

commodum, -ī *nt* convenience; advantage, interest; pay, salary; loan; **~ō tuō** at your

leisure; **~a vītae** the good things of life.

commodum *adv* opportunely; just.

commodus *adj* proper, fit, full; suitable, easy, opportune; (*person*) pleasant, obliging.

commōlior, -īrī *vt* to set in motion.

commonefaciō, -facere, -fēcī, -factum *vt* to remind, recall.

commoneō, -ēre, -uī, -itum *vt* to remind, impress upon.

commōnstrō, -āre *vt* to point out.

commorātiō, -ōnis *f* delay, residence; (*RHET*) dwelling (on a topic).

commoror, -ārī, -ātus *vi* to sojourn, wait; (*RHET*) to dwell ♦ *vt* to detain.

commōtiō, -ōnis *f* excitement.

commōtiuncula *f* slight indisposition.

commōtus *ppp of* **commoveō ♦** *adj* excited, emotional.

commoveō, -ovēre, -ōvī, -ōtum *vt* to set in motion, move, dislodge, agitate; (*mind*) to unsettle, shake, excite, move, affect; (*emotions*) to stir up, provoke.

commūne, -is *nt* common property; state; **in ~e** for a common end; equally; in general.

commūnicātiō, -ōnis *f* imparting; (*RHET*) *making the audience appear to take part in the discussion.*

commūnicō, -āre, -āvī, -ātum *vt* to share (by giving *or* receiving); to impart, communicate; **cōnsilia ~ cum** make common cause with.

commūniō, -īre, -īvī *and* **iī, -ītum** *vt* to build (a fortification); to fortify, strengthen.

commūniō, -ōnis *f* sharing in common, communion.

commūnis *adj* common, general, universal; (*person*) affable, democratic; **~ia loca** public places; **~ēs locī** general topics; **~is sēnsus** popular sentiment; **aliquid ~e habēre** have something in common.

commūnitās, -ātis *f* fellowship; sense of fellowship; affability.

commūniter *adv* in common, jointly.

commūnītiō, -ōnis *f* preparing the way.

commurmuror, -ārī, -ātus *vi* to mutter to oneself.

commūtābilis *adj* changeable.

commūtātiō, -iōnis *f* change.

commūtātus, -ūs *m* change.

commūtō, -āre, -āvī, -ātum *vt* to change, exchange, interchange.

cōmō, -ere, -psī, -ptum *vt* to arrange, dress, adorn.

cōmoedia, -ae *f* comedy.

cōmoedicē *adv* as in comedy.

cōmoedus, -ī *m* comic actor.

comōsus *adj* shaggy.

compāctiō, -ōnis *f* joining together.

compāctus *ppp of* **compingō**.

compāgēs, -is, -ō, -inis *f* joint, structure,

framework.

compār, -aris *m/f* comrade, husband, wife ♦ *adj* equal.

comparābilis *adj* comparable.

comparātē *adv* by bringing in a comparison.

comparātiō, -ōnis *f* comparison; (*ASTRO*) relative positions; agreement; preparation, procuring.

comparātīvus *adj* based on comparison.

compāreō, -ēre *vi* to be visible; to be present, be realised.

comparō, -āre, -āvī, -ātum *vt* to couple together, match; to compare; (*POL*) to agree (about respective duties); to prepare, provide; (*custom*) to establish; to procure, purchase, get.

compāscō, -ere *vt* to put (cattle) to graze in common.

compāscuus *adj* for common pasture.

compecīscor, -īscī, -tus *vi* to come to an agreement.

compectum, -tī *nt* agreement.

compediō, -īre, -ītum *vt* to fetter.

compēgī *perf of* **compingō**.

compellātiō, -ōnis *f* reprimand.

compellō, -āre, -āvī, -ātum *vt* to call, address; to reproach; (*law*) to arraign.

compellō, -ellere, -ulī, -ulsum *vt* to drive, bring together, concentrate; to impel, compel.

compendiārius *adj* short.

compendium, -ī *and* **iī** *nt* saving; abbreviating; short cut; **~ī facere** save; abridge; **~ī fierī** be brief.

compēnsātiō, -ōnis *f* (*fig*) compromise.

compēnsō, -āre, -āvī, -ātum *vt* to balance (against), make up for.

compercō, -cere, -sī *vt, vi* to save; to refrain.

comperendinātiō, -iōnis *f* adjournment for two days.

comperendinātus, -ūs *m* adjournment for two days.

comperendinō, -āre *vt* to adjourn for two days.

comperiō, -īre, -ī, -tum (*occ* **-ior**) *vt* to find out, learn; **~tus** detected; found guilty; **~tum habēre** know for certain.

compēs, -edis *f* fetter, bond.

compēscō, -ere, -uī *vt* to check, suppress.

competītor, -ōris *m*, **-rīx, -rīcis** *f* rival candidate.

competō, -ere, -īvī *and* **iī, -ītum** *vi* to coincide, agree; to be capable.

compīlātiō, -ōnis *f* plundering; compilation.

compīlō, -āre, -āvī, -ātum *vt* to pillage.

compingō, -ingere, -ēgī, -āctum *vt* to put together, compose; to lock up, hide away.

compitālia, -ium *and* **iōrum** *ntpl* festival in honour of the Lares Compitales.

compitālicius *adj* of the Compitalia.

compitālis *adj* of crossroads.

compitum, -ī *nt* crossroads.

complaceō, -ēre, -uī *and* **itus sum** *vi* to please (someone else) as well, please very much.

complānō, -āre *vt* to level, raze to the ground.

complector, -ctī, -xus *vt* to embrace, clasp; to enclose; (*speech, writing*) to deal with, comprise; (*mind*) to grasp, comprehend; to honour, be fond of.

complēmentum, -ī *nt* complement.

compleō, -ēre, -ēvī, -ētum *vt* to fill, fill up; (*MIL*) to man, make up the complement of; (*time, promise, duty*) to complete, fulfil, finish.

complētus *adj* perfect.

complexiō, -ōnis *f* combination; (*RHET*) period; (*logic*) conclusion of an argument; dilemma.

complexus, -ūs *m* embrace; (*fig*) affection, close combat; (*speech*) connection.

complicō, -āre *vt* to fold up.

complōrātiō, -iōnis *f*, **-us, -ūs** *m* loud lamentation.

complōrō, -āre, -āvī, -ātum *vt* to mourn for.

complūrēs, -ium *adj* several, very many.

complūriēns *adv* several times.

complūsculī, -ōrum *adj* quite a few.

compluvium, -ī *and* **iī** *nt* roof opening in a Roman house.

compōnō, -ōnere, -osuī, -ositum *vt* to put together, join; to compose, construct; to compare, contrast; to match, oppose; to put away, store up, stow; (*dead*) to lay out, inter; to allay, quieten, reconcile; to adjust, settle, arrange; to devise, prepare ♦ *vi* to make peace.

comportō, -āre *vt* to collect, bring in.

compos, -tis *adj* in control, in possession; sharing; **vōtī ~** having got one's wish.

compositē *adv* properly, in a polished manner.

compositiō, -ōnis *f* compounding, system; (*words*) arrangement; reconciliation; matching (of fighters).

compositor, -ōris *m* arranger.

compositūra, -ae *f* connection.

compositus *ppp of* **compōnō** ♦ *adj* orderly, regular; adapted, assumed, ready; calm, sedate; (*words*) compound; **compositō, ex compositō** as agreed.

compōtātiō, -ōnis *f* drinking party.

compōtiō, -īre *vt* to put in possession (of).

compōtor, -ōris *m*, **-rīx, -rīcis** *f* fellow drinker.

comprānsor, -ōris *m* fellow guest.

comprecātiō, -ōnis *f* public supplication.

comprecor, -ārī, -ātus *vt, vi* to pray to; to pray for.

comprehendō (comprendō), -endere, -endī, -ēnsum *vt* to grasp, catch; to seize, arrest, catch in the act; (*words*) to comprise, recount; (*thought*) to grasp, comprehend; to hold in affection; **numerō ~** count.

comprehēnsibilis *adj* conceivable.

comprehēnsiō, -ōnis *f* grasping, seizing;

perception, idea; (*RHET*) period.

comprehēnsus, comprēnsus *ppp of*
comprehendō.

comprendō *etc see* **comprehendō.**

compressī *perf of* **comprimō.**

compressiō, -ōnis *f* embrace; (*RHET*)
compression.

compressus *ppp of* **comprimō.**

compressus, -ūs *m* compression, embrace.

comprimō, -imere, -essī, -essum *vt* to
squeeze, compress; to check, restrain; to
suppress, withhold; **animam ~** hold one's
breath; **~essīs manibus** with hands folded,
idle.

comprobātiō, -ōnis *f* approval.

comprobātor, -ōris *m* supporter.

comprobō, -āre, -āvī, -ātum *vt* to prove,
make good; to approve.

comprōmissum, -ī *nt* mutual agreement to
abide by an arbitrator's decision.

comprōmittō, -ittere, -īsī, -issum *vt* to
undertake to abide by an arbitrator's
decision.

cōmpsī *perf of* **cōmō.**

cōmptus *ppp of* **cōmō** ♦ *adj* elegant.

cōmptus, -ūs *m* coiffure; union.

compulī *perf of* **compellō.**

compulsus *ppp of* **compellō.**

compungō, -ungere, -ūnxī, -ūnctum *vt* to
prick, sting, tattoo.

computō, -āre, -āvī, -ātum *vt* to reckon,
number.

Cōmum, -ī *nt* (*also* **Novum Cōmum**) town in N.
Italy (*now* Como).

cōnāmen, -inis *nt* effort; support.

cōnāta, -ōrum *ntpl* undertaking, venture.

cōnātus, -ūs *m* effort; endeavour; inclination,
impulse.

concaedēs, -ium *fpl* barricade of felled trees.

concalefaciō, -facere, -fēcī, -factum *vt* to
warm well.

concaleō, -ēre *vi* to be hot.

concalēscō, -ēscere, -uī *vi* to become hot,
glow.

concallēscō, -ēscere, -uī *vi* to become
shrewd; to become unfeeling.

concastīgō, -āre *vt* to punish severely.

concavō, -āre *vt* to curve.

concavus *adj* hollow; vaulted, bent.

concēdō, -ēdere, -essī, -essum *vi* to
withdraw, depart; to disappear, pass away,
pass; to yield, submit, give precedence,
comply ♦ *vt* to give up, cede; to grant, allow;
to pardon, overlook.

concelebrō, -āre, -āvī, -ātum *vt* to frequent,
fill, enliven; (*study*) to pursue eagerly; to
celebrate; to make known.

concēnātiō, -ōnis *f* dining together.

concentiō, -ōnis *f* chorus.

concenturiō, -āre *vt* to marshal.

concentus, -ūs *m* chorus, concert; (*fig*)
concord, harmony.

conceptiō, -ōnis *f* conception; drawing up
legal formulae.

conceptīvus *adj* (*holidays*) movable.

conceptus *ppp of* **concipiō.**

conceptus, -ūs *m* conception.

concerpō, -ere, -sī, -tum *vt* to tear up; (*fig*) to
abuse.

concertātiō, -ōnis *f* controversy.

concertātor, -ōris *m* rival.

concertātōrius *adj* controversial.

concertō, -āre, -āvī, -ātum *vi* to fight; to
dispute.

concessiō, -ōnis *f* grant, permission; (*law*)
pleading guilty and asking indulgence.

concessō, -āre *vi* to stop, loiter.

concessus *ppp of* **concēdō.**

concessus, -ūs *m* permission.

concha, -ae *f* mussel, oyster, murex; mussel
shell, oyster shell, pearl; purple dye;
trumpet, perfume dish.

conchis, -is *f* kind of bean.

conchīta, -ae *m* catcher of shellfish.

conchȳliātus *adj* purple.

conchȳlium, -ī *and* **iī** *nt* shellfish, oyster,
murex; purple.

concidō, -ere, -ī *vi* to fall, collapse; to subside,
fail, perish.

concīdō, -dere, -dī, -sum *vt* to cut up, cut to
pieces, kill; (*fig*) to ruin, strike down; (*RHET*)
to dismember, enfeeble.

**concieō, -iēre, -īvī, -itum; conciō, -īre,
-ītum** *vt* to rouse, assemble; to stir up,
shake; (*fig*) to rouse, provoke.

conciliābulum, -ī *nt* place for public
gatherings.

conciliātiō, -ōnis *f* union; winning over
(*friends, hearers*); (*PHILOS*) inclination.

conciliātor, -ōris *m* promoter.

conciliātrīx, -īcis *m*, **-īcula, -ae** *f* promoter,
matchmaker.

conciliātus, -ūs *m* combination.

conciliātus *adj* beloved; favourable.

conciliō, -āre, -āvī, -ātum *vt* to unite; to win
over, reconcile; to procure, purchase, bring
about, promote.

concilium, -ī *and* **iī** *nt* gathering, meeting;
council; (*things*) union.

concinnē *adv see* **concinnus.**

concinnitās, -ātis, -ūdō, -ūdinis *f* (*RHET*)
rhythmical style.

concinnō, -āre, -āvī, -ātum *vt* to arrange; to
bring about, produce; (*with adj*) to make.

concinnus *adj* symmetrical, beautiful; (*style*)
polished, rhythmical; (*person*) elegant,
courteous; (*things*) suited, pleasing.

concinō, -ere, -uī *vi* to sing, play, sound
together; (*fig*) to agree, harmonize ♦ *vt* to
sing about, celebrate, prophesy.

conciō *etc see* **concieō.**

concio- *etc see* **contio-.**

concipiō, -ipere, -ēpī, -eptum *vt* to take to oneself, absorb; (*women*) to conceive; (*senses*) to perceive; (*mind*) to conceive, imagine, understand; (*feelings, acts*) to harbour, foster, commit; (*words*) to draw up, intimate formally.

concīsiō, -ōnis *f* breaking up into short clauses.

concīsus *ppp of* **concīdō** ♦ *adj* broken up, concise.

concitātē *adv see* **concitātus.**

concitātiō, -ōnis *f* acceleration; (*mind*) excitement, passion; riot.

concitātor, -ōris *m* agitator.

concitātus *ppp of* **concitō** ♦ *adj* fast; excited.

concitō, -āre, -āvī, -ātum *vt* to move rapidly, bestir, hurl; to urge, rouse, impel; to stir up, occasion.

concitor, -ōris *m* instigator.

concitus, concītus *ppp of* **concieō**; *ppp of* **conciō.**

conclāmātiō, -ōnis *f* great shout.

conclāmitō, -āre *vi* to keep on shouting.

conclāmō, -āre, -āvī, -ātum *vt, vi* to shout, cry out; to call to help; (*MIL*) to give the signal; (*dead*) to call by name in mourning; **vāsa ~** give the order to pack up; **~ātum est** it's all over.

conclāve, -is *nt* room.

conclūdō, -dere, -sī, -sum *vt* to shut up, enclose; to include, comprise; to end, conclude, round off (*esp with a rhythmical cadence*); (*PHILOS*) to infer, demonstrate.

conclūsē *adv* with rhythmical cadences.

conclūsiō, -ōnis *f* (*MIL*) blockade; end, conclusion; (*RHET*) period, peroration; (*logic*) conclusion.

conclūsiuncula, -ae *f* quibble.

conclūsum, -ī *nt* logical conclusion.

conclūsus *ppp of* **conclūdō.**

concoctus *ppp of* **concoquō.**

concolor, -ōris *adj* of the same colour.

concomitātus *adj* escorted.

concoquō, -quere, -xī, -ctum *vt* to boil down; to digest; (*fig*) to put up with, stomach; (*thought*) to consider well, concoct.

concordia, -ae *f* friendship, concord, union; *goddess of Concord.*

concorditer *adv* amicably.

concordō, -āre *vi* to agree, be in harmony.

concors, -dis *adj* concordant, united, harmonious.

concrēbrēscō, -ēscere, -uī *vi* to gather strength.

concrēdō, -ere, -idī, -itum *vt* to entrust.

concremō, -āre, -āvī, -ātum *vt* to burn.

concrepō, -āre, -uī, -itum *vi* to rattle, creak, clash, snap (fingers) ♦ *vt* to beat.

concrēscō, -scere, -vī, -tum *vi* to harden, curdle, congeal, clot; to grow, take shape.

concrētiō, -ōnis *f* condensing; matter.

concrētum, -ī *nt* solid matter, hard frost.

concrētus *ppa of* **concrēscō** ♦ *adj* hard, thick, stiff, congealed; compounded.

concrīminor, -ārī, -ātus *vi* to bring a complaint.

concruciō, -āre *vt* to torture.

concubīna, -ae *f* (female) concubine.

concubīnātus, -ūs *m* concubinage.

concubīnus, -ī *m* (male) concubine.

concubitus, -ūs *m* reclining together (at table); sexual union.

concubius *adj*: **~iā nocte** during the first sleep ♦ *nt* the time of the first sleep.

conculcō, -āre *vt* to trample under foot, treat with contempt.

concumbō, -mbere, -buī, -bitum *vi* to lie together, lie with.

concupīscō, -īscere, -īvī, -ītum *vt* to covet, long for, aspire to.

concūrō, -āre *vt* to take care of.

concurrō, -rere, -rī, -sum *vi* to flock together, rush in; (*things*) to clash, meet; (*MIL*) to join battle, charge; (*events*) to happen at the same time, concur.

concursātiō, -ōnis *f* running together, rushing about; (*MIL*) skirmishing; (*dreams*) coherent design.

concursātor, -ōris *m* skirmisher.

concursiō, -ōnis *f* meeting, concourse; (*RHET*) repetition for emphasis.

concursō, -āre *vi* to collide; to rush about, travel about; (*MIL*) to skirmish ♦ *vt* to visit, go from place to place.

concursus, -ūs *m* concourse, gathering, collision; uproar; (*fig*) combination; (*MIL*) assault, charge.

concussī *perf of* **concutiō.**

concussus *ppp of* **concutiō.**

concussus, -ūs *m* shaking.

concutiō, -tere, -ssī, -ssum *vt* to strike, shake, shatter; (*weapons*) to hurl; (*power*) to disturb, impair; (*person*) to agitate, alarm; (*self*) to search, examine; to rouse.

condalium, -ī *and* **iī** *nt* slave's ring.

condecet, -ēre *vt impers* it becomes.

condecorō, -āre *vt* to enhance.

condemnātor, -ōris *m* accuser.

condemnō, -āre, -āvī, -ātum *vt* to condemn, sentence; to urge the conviction of; to blame, censure; **ambitūs ~** convict of bribery; **capitis ~** condemn to death; **vōtī ~ātus** obliged to fulfil a vow.

condēnsō, -āre, -eō, -ēre *vt* to compress, move close together.

condēnsus *adj* very dense, close, thick.

condiciō, -ōnis *f* arrangement, condition, terms; marriage contract, match; situation, position, circumstances; manner, mode; **eā ~ōne ut** on condition that; **sub ~ōne** conditionally; **hīs ~ōnibus** on these terms; **vītae ~** way of life.

condīcō, -īcere, -īxī, -ictum *vt, vi* to talk over, agree upon, promise; **ad cēnam ~** have a dinner engagement.

condidī *perf of* **condō**.

condignē *adv see* **condignus**.

condignus *adj* very worthy.

condīmentum, -ī *nt* spice, seasoning.

condiō, -īre, -īvī, -ītum *vt* to pickle, preserve, embalm; to season; (*fig*) to give zest to, temper.

condiscipulus, -ī *m* school-fellow.

condiscō, -scere, -dicī *vt* to learn thoroughly, learn by heart.

conditiō *etc see* **condiciō**.

condītiō, -ōnis *f* preserving, seasoning.

conditor, -ōris *m* founder, author, composer.

conditōrium, -ī *and* **iī** *nt* coffin, urn, tomb.

condītus *adj* savoury; (*fig*) polished.

conditus *ppp of* **condō**.

conditus *ppp of* **condiō**.

condō, -ere, -idī, -itum *vt* **1.** (*build, found: arts*) to make, compose, write; (: *institutions*) to establish **2.** (*put away for keeping, store up: fruit*) to preserve; (: *person*) to imprison; (: *dead*) to bury; (: *memory*) to lay up; (: *time*) to pass, bring to a close **3.** (*put out of sight, conceal: eyes*) to close; (: *sword*) to sheathe, plunge; (: *troops*) to place in ambush.

condocefaciō, -ere *vt* to train.

condoceō, -ēre, -uī, -tum *vt* to train.

condolēscō, -ēscere, -uī *vi* to begin to ache, feel very sore.

condōnātiō, -ōnis *f* giving away.

condōnō, -āre, -āvī, -ātum *vt* to give, present, deliver up; (*debt*) to remit; (*offence*) to pardon, let off.

condormīscō, -īscere, -īvī *vi* to fall fast asleep.

condūcibilis *adj* expedient.

condūcō, -ūcere, -ūxī, -uctum *vt* to bring together, assemble, connect; to hire, rent, borrow; (*public work*) to undertake, get the contract for; (*taxes*) to farm ♦ *vi* to be of use, profit.

conductī, -ōrum *mpl* hirelings, mercenaries.

conductīcius *adj* hired.

conductiō, -ōnis *f* hiring, farming.

conductor, -ōris *m* hirer, tenant; contractor.

conductum, -ī *nt* anything hired *or* rented.

conductus *ppp of* **condūcō**.

conduplicō, -āre *vt* to double.

condūrō, -āre *vt* to make very hard.

condus, -ī *m* steward.

cōnectō, -ctere, -xuī, -xum *vt* to tie, fasten, link, join; (*logic*) to state a conclusion.

cōnexum, -ī *nt* logical inference.

cōnexus *ppp of* **cōnectō** ♦ *adj* connected; (*time*) following.

cōnexus, -ūs *m* combination.

cōnfābulor, -ārī, -ātus *vi* to talk (to), discuss.

cōnfarreātiō, -ōnis *f* the most solemn of Roman marriage ceremonies.

cōnfarreō, -āre, -ātum *vt* to marry by confarreatio.

cōnfātālis *adj* bound by the same destiny.

cōnfēcī *perf of* **cōnficiō**.

cōnfectiō, -ōnis *f* making, completion; (*food*) chewing.

cōnfector, -ōris *m* maker, finisher; destroyer.

cōnfectus *ppp of* **cōnficiō**.

cōnferciō, -cīre, -tum *vt* to stuff, cram, pack closely.

cōnferō, -ferre, -tulī, -lātum *vt* to gather together, collect; to contribute; to confer, talk over; (*MIL*) to oppose, engage in battle; to compare; (*words*) to condense; to direct, transfer; to transform (into), turn (to); to devote, bestow; to ascribe, assign, impute; (*time*) to postpone; **capita ~** put heads together, confer; **gradum ~ cum** walk beside; **sē ~** go, turn (to); **sermōnēs ~** converse; **signa ~** join battle.

cōnfertim *adv* in close order.

cōnfertus *ppp of* **cōnferciō** ♦ *adj* crowded, full; (*MIL*) in close order.

cōnfervēscō, -vēscere, -buī *vi* to boil up, grow hot.

cōnfessiō, -ōnis *f* acknowledgement, confession.

cōnfessus *ppa of* **cōnfiteor** ♦ *adj* acknowledged, certain; in **~ō esse/in ~um venīre** be generally admitted.

cōnfestim *adv* immediately.

cōnficiō, -icere, -ēcī, -ectum *vt* to make, effect, complete, accomplish; to get together, procure; to wear out, exhaust, consume, destroy; (*COMM*) to settle; (*space*) to travel; (*time*) to pass, complete; (*PHILOS*) to be an active cause; (*logic*) to deduce; (*pass*) it follows.

cōnfictiō, -ōnis *f* fabrication.

cōnfictus *ppp of* **cōnfingō**.

cōnfīdēns, -entis *pres p of* **cōnfīdō** ♦ *adj* self-confident, bold, presumptuous.

cōnfīdenter *adv* fearlessly, insolently.

cōnfīdentia, -ae *f* confidence, self-confidence; impudence.

cōnfīdentiloquus *adj* outspoken.

cōnfīdō, -dere, -sus sum *vi* to trust, rely, be sure; **sibi ~** be confident.

cōnfīgō, -gere, -xī, -xum *vt* to fasten together; to pierce, shoot; (*fig*) to paralyse.

cōnfingō, -ingere, -inxī, -ictum *vt* to make, invent, pretend.

cōnfīnis *adj* adjoining; (*fig*) akin.

cōnfīnium, -ī *nt* common boundary; (*pl*) neighbours; (*fig*) close connection, borderland between.

cōnfīō, -fierī *occ pass of* **cōnficiō**.

cōnfirmātiō, -ōnis *f* establishing; (*person*) encouragement; (*fact*) verifying; (*RHET*) adducing of proofs.

Noun declensions and verb conjugations are shown on pp xiii to xxv. The present infinitive ending of a verb shows to which conjugation it belongs: **-āre** = 1st; **-ēre** = 2nd; **-ere** = 3rd and **-īre** = 4th. Irregular verbs are shown on p xxvi

cōnfirmātor, -ōris m guarantor (of money).
cōnfirmātus adj resolute; proved, certain.
cōnfirmō, -āre, -āvī, -ātum vt to strengthen, reinforce; (decree) to confirm, ratify; (mind) to encourage; (fact) to corroborate, prove, assert; **sē ~** recover; take courage.
cōnfiscō, -āre vt to keep in a chest; to confiscate.
cōnfīsiō, -ōnis f assurance.
cōnfīsus ppa of **cōnfīdō**.
cōnfiteor, -itērī, -essus vt, vi to confess, acknowledge; to reveal.
cōnfīxus ppp of **cōnfigō**.
cōnflagrō, -āre, -āvī, -ātum vi to burn, be ablaze.
cōnflictiō, -ōnis f conflict.
cōnflictō, -āre, -āvī, -ātum vt to strike down, contend (with); (pass) to fight, be harassed, be afflicted.
cōnflictus, -ūs m striking together.
cōnflīgō, -gere, -xī, -ctum vt to dash together; (fig) to contrast ♦ vi to fight, come into conflict.
cōnflō, -āre, -āvī, -ātum vt to ignite; (passion) to inflame; to melt down; (fig) to produce, procure, occasion.
cōnfluēns, -entis, -entēs, -entium m confluence of two rivers.
cōnfluō, -ere, -xī vi to flow together; (fig) to flock together, pour in.
cōnfodiō, -odere, -ōdī, -ossum vt to dig; to stab.
cōnfore fut infin of **cōnsum**.
cōnfōrmātiō, -ōnis f shape, form; (words) arrangement; (voice) expression; (mind) idea; (RHET) figure.
cōnfōrmō, -āre, -āvī, -ātum vt to shape, fashion.
cōnfossus ppp of **cōnfodiō** ♦ adj full of holes.
cōnfrāctus ppp of **cōnfringō**.
cōnfragōsus adj broken, rough; (fig) hard.
cōnfrēgī pvrf of **cōnfringō**.
cōnfremō, -ere, -uī vi to murmur aloud.
cōnfricō, -āre vt to rub well.
cōnfringō, -ingere, -ēgī, -āctum vt to break in pieces, wreck; (fig) to ruin.
cōnfugiō, -ugere, -ūgī vi to flee for help (to), take refuge (with); (fig) to have recourse (to).
cōnfugium, -ī and iī nt refuge.
cōnfundō, -undere, -ūdī, -ūsum vt to mix, mingle, join; to mix up, confuse, throw into disorder; (mind) to perplex, bewilder; to diffuse, spread over.
cōnfūsē adv confusedly.
cōnfūsiō, -ōnis f combination; confusion, disorder; **ōris ~** going red in the face.
cōnfūsus ppp of **cōnfundō** ♦ adj confused, disorderly, troubled.
cōnfūtō, -āre, -āvī, -ātum vt to keep from boiling over; to repress; to silence, confute.
congelō, -āre, -āvī, -ātum vt to freeze, harden ♦ vi to freeze over, grow numb.

congeminō, -āre, -āvī, -ātum vt to double.
congemō, -ere, -uī vi to groan, sigh ♦ vt to lament.
conger, -rī m sea eel.
congeriēs, -ēi f heap, mass, accumulation.
congerō, -rere, -ssī, -stum vt to collect, accumulate, build; (missiles) to shower; (speech) to comprise; (fig) to heap (upon), ascribe.
congerō, -ōnis m thief.
congerrō, -ōnis m companion in revelry.
congesticius adj piled up.
congestus ppp of **congerō**.
congestus, -ūs m accumulating; heap, mass.
congiālis adj holding a congius.
congiārium, -ī and iī nt gift of food to the people, gratuity to the army.
congius, -ī and iī m Roman liquid measure (about 6 pints).
conglaciō, -āre vi to freeze up.
conglīscō, -ere vi to blaze up.
conglobātiō, -ōnis f mustering.
conglobō, -āre, -āvī, -ātum vt to make round; to mass together.
conglomerō, -āre vt to roll up.
conglūtinātiō, -ōnis f gluing, cementing; (fig) combination.
conglūtinō, -āre, -āvī, -ātum vt to glue, cement; (fig) to join, weld together; to contrive.
congraecō, -āre vt to squander on luxury.
congrātulor, -ārī, -ātus vi to congratulate.
congredior, -dī, -ssus vt, vi to meet, accost; to contend, fight.
congregābilis adj gregarious.
congregātiō, -ōnis f union, society.
congregō, -āre, -āvī, -ātum vt to collect, assemble, unite.
congressiō, -ōnis f meeting, conference.
congressus ppa of **congredior**.
congressus, -ūs m meeting, association, union; encounter, fight.
congruēns, -entis adj suitable, consistent, proper; harmonious.
congruenter adv in conformity.
congruō, -ere, -ī vi to coincide; to correspond, suit; to agree, sympathize.
congruus adj agreeable.
coniciō, -icere, -iēcī, -iectum vt to throw together; to throw, hurl; to put, fling, drive, direct; to infer, conjecture; (augury) to interpret; **sē ~** rush, fly; devote oneself.
coniectiō, -ōnis f throwing; conjecture, interpretation.
coniectō, -āre vt to infer, conjecture, guess.
coniector, -ōris m (male) interpreter, diviner.
coniectrīx, -rīcis f (female) interpreter, diviner.
coniectūra, -ae f inference, conjecture, guess; interpretation.
coniectūrālis adj (RHET) involving a question of fact.

coniectus *ppp of* **coniciō.**
coniectus, -ūs *m* heap, mass, concourse; throwing, throw, range; (*eyes, mind*) turning, directing.
cōnifer, cōniger, -ī *adj* cone-bearing.
cōnītor, -tī, -sus *and* **-xus** *vi* to lean on; to strive, struggle on; to labour.
coniugālis *adj* of marriage, conjugal.
coniugātiō, -ōnis *f* etymological relationship.
coniugātor, -ōris *m* uniter.
coniugiālis *adj* marriage- (*in cpds*).
coniugium, -ī *and* **iī** *nt* union, marriage; husband, wife.
coniugō, -āre *vt* to form (*a friendship*); **~āta verba** words related etymologically.
coniūnctē *adv* jointly; on familiar terms; (*logic*) hypothetically.
coniūnctim *adv* together, jointly.
coniūnctiō, -ōnis *f* union, connection, association; (*minds*) sympathy, affinity; (*GRAM*) conjunction.
coniūnctum, -ī *nt* (*RHET*) connection; (*PHILOS*) inherent property (*of a body*).
coniūnctus *ppp of* **coniungō ♦** *adj* near; connected, agreeing, conforming; related, friendly, intimate.
coniungō, -ūngere, -ūnxī, -ūnctum *vt* to yoke, join together, connect; (*war*) to join forces in; to unite in love, marriage, friendship; to continue without a break.
coniūnx, -ugis *m/f* consort, wife, husband, bride.
coniūrātī, -ōrum *mpl* conspirators.
coniūrātiō, -ōnis *f* conspiracy, plot; alliance.
coniūrātus *adj* (*MIL*) after taking the oath.
coniūrō, -āre, ~ -āvī, -ātum *vi* to take an oath; to conspire, plot.
coniux *etc see* **coniūnx.**
cōnīveō, -vēre, -vī *and* **xī** *vi* to shut the eyes, blink; (*fig*) to be asleep; to connive at.
conj- *etc see* **coni-.**
conl- *etc see* **coll-.**
conm- *etc see* **comm-.**
conn- *etc see* **cōn-.**
Conōn, -is *m* Athenian commander; Greek astronomer.
cōnōpēum (-eum), -ēī *nt* mosquito net.
cōnor, -ārī, -ātus *vt* to try, attempt, venture.
conp- *etc see* **comp-.**
conquassātiō, -ōnis *f* severe shaking.
conquassō, -āre, -ātum *vt* to shake, upset, shatter.
conqueror, -rī, -stus *vt, vi* to complain bitterly of, bewail.
conquestiō, -ōnis *f* complaining; (*RHET*) appeal to pity.
conquestus *ppa of* **conqueror.**
conquestus, -ūs *m* outcry.
conquiēscō, -scere, -vī, -tum *vi* to rest, take

a respite; (*fig*) to be at peace, find recreation; (*things*) to stop, be quiet.
conquīnīscō, -ere *vi* to cower, squat, stoop down.
conquīrō, -rere, -sīvī, -sītum *vt* to search for, collect.
conquīsītē *adv* carefully.
conquīsītiō, -ōnis *f* search; (*MIL*) levy.
conquīsītor, -ōris *m* recruiting officer; (*THEATRE*) claqueur.
conquīsītus *ppp of* **conquīrō ♦** *adj* select, costly.
conr- *etc see* **corr-.**
cōnsaepiō, -īre, -sī, -tum *vt* to enclose, fence round.
cōnsaeptum, -tī *nt* enclosure.
cōnsalūtātiō, -ōnis *f* mutual greeting.
cōnsalūtō, -āre, -āvī, -ātum *vt* to greet, hail.
cōnsānēscō, -ēscere, -uī *vi* to heal up.
cōnsanguineus *adj* brother, sister, kindred ♦ *mpl* relations.
cōnsanguinitās, -ātis *f* relationship.
cōnscelerātus *adj* wicked.
cōnscelerō, -āre, -āvī, -ātum *vt* to disgrace.
cōnscendō, -endere, -endī, -ēnsum *vt, vi* to climb, mount, embark.
cōnscēnsiō, -ōnis *f* embarkation.
cōnscēnsus *ppp of* **cōnscendō.**
cōnscientia, -ae *f* joint knowledge, being in the know; (*sense of*) consciousness; moral sense, conscience, guilty conscience.
cōnscindō, -ndere, -dī, -ssum *vt* to tear to pieces; (*fig*) to abuse.
cōnsciō, -īre *vt* to be conscious of guilt.
cōnscīscō, -scere, -vī *and* **iī, -ītum** *vt* to decide on publicly; to inflict on oneself; **mortem (sibi)** ~ commit suicide.
cōnscissus *ppp of* **cōnscindō.**
cōnscītus *ppp of* **cōnscīscō.**
cōnscius *adj* sharing knowledge, privy, in the know; aware, conscious (of); conscious of guilt ♦ *m/f* confederate, confidant.
cōnscreor, -ārī *vi* to clear the throat.
cōnscrībō, -bere, -psī, -ptum *vt* to enlist, enrol; to write, compose, draw up, prescribe.
cōnscrīptiō, -ōnis *f* document, draft.
cōnscrīptus *ppp of* **cōnscrībō; patrēs ~ī** patrician and elected plebeian members; senators.
cōnsecō, -āre, -uī, -tum *vt* to cut up.
cōnsecrātiō, -ōnis *f* consecration, deification.
cōnsecrō, -āre, -āvī, -ātum *vt* to dedicate, consecrate, deify; (*fig*) to devote; to immortalise; **caput ~** doom to death.
cōnsectārius *adj* logical, consequent ♦ *ntpl* inferences.
cōnsectātiō, -ōnis *f* pursuit.
cōnsectātrīx, -īcis *f* (*fig*) follower.

Noun declensions and verb conjugations are shown on pp xiii to xxv. The present infinitive ending of a verb shows to which conjugation it belongs: **-āre** = 1st; **-ēre** = 2nd; **-ere** = 3rd and **-īre** = 4th. Irregular verbs are shown on p xxvi

cōnsectiō, -ōnis f cutting up.
cōnsector, -ārī, -ātus vt to follow, go after, try to gain; to emulate, imitate; to pursue, chase.
cōnsecūtiō, -ōnis f (PHILOS) consequences, effect; (RHET) sequence.
cōnsēdī perf of **cōnsīdō**.
cōnsenēscō, -ēscere, -uī vi to grow old, grow old together; (fig) to fade, pine, decay, become obsolete.
cōnsēnsiō, -ōnis f agreement, accord; conspiracy, plot.
cōnsēnsū adv unanimously.
cōnsēnsus ppp of **cōnsentiō**.
cōnsēnsus, -ūs m agreement, concord; conspiracy; (PHILOS) common sensation; (fig) harmony.
cōnsentāneus adj agreeing, in keeping with; ~um est it is reasonable.
cōnsentiō, -entīre, -ēnsī, -ēnsum vi to agree, determine together; to plot, conspire; (PHILOS) to have common sensations; (fig) to harmonize, suit, be consistent (with); **bellum** ~ vote for war.
cōnsequēns, -entis pres p of **cōnsequor** ♦ adj coherent, reasonable; logical, consequent ♦ nt consequence.
cōnsequor, -quī, -cūtus vt to follow, pursue; to overtake, reach; (time) to come after; (example) to follow, copy; (effect) to result, be the consequence of; (aim) to attain, get; (mind) to grasp, learn; (events) to happen to, come to; (standard) to equal, come up to; (speech) to do justice to.
cōnserō, -erere, -ēvī, -itum vt to sow, plant; (ground) to sow with, plant with; (fig) to cover, fill.
cōnserō, -ere, -uī, -tum vt to join, string together, twine; (MIL) to join battle; **manum/ manūs** ~ engage in close combat; **ex iūre manum** ~ lay claim to (in an action for possession).
cōnsertē adv connectedly.
cōnsertus ppp of **cōnserō**.
cōnserva, -ae f fellow slave.
cōnservātiō, -ōnis f preserving.
cōnservātor, -ōris m preserver.
cōnservitium, -ī and iī nt being fellow slaves.
cōnservō, -āre, -āvī, -ātum vt to preserve, save, keep.
cōnservus, -ī m fellow slave.
cōnsessor, -ōris m companion at table, fellow spectator; (law) assessor.
cōnsessus, -ūs m assembly; (law) court.
cōnsēvī perf of **cōnserō**.
cōnsīderātē adv cautiously, deliberately.
cōnsīderātiō, -ōnis f contemplation.
cōnsīderātus adj (person) circumspect; (things) well-considered.
cōnsīderō, -āre, -āvī, -ātum vt to look at, inspect; to consider, contemplate.
cōnsīdō, -īdere, -ēdī, -essum vi to sit down, take seats; (courts) to be in session; (MIL) to take up a position; (residence) to settle; (places) to subside, sink; (fig) to sink, settle down, subside.
cōnsignō, -āre, -āvī, -ātum vt to seal, sign; to attest, vouch for; to record, register.
cōnsilēscō, -ere vi to calm down.
cōnsiliārius, -ī and iī m adviser, counsellor; spokesman ♦ adj counselling.
cōnsiliātor, -ōris m counsellor.
cōnsilior, -ārī, -ātus vi to consult; (with dat) to advise.
cōnsilium, -ī and iī nt deliberation, consultation; deliberating body, council; decision, purpose; plan, measure, stratagem; advice, counsel; judgement, insight, wisdom; ~ium capere, inīre come to a decision, resolve; ~ī esse be an open question; ~iō intentionally; eō ~iō ut with the intention of; prīvātō ~iō for one's own purposes.
cōnsimilis adj just like.
cōnsipiō, -ere vi to be in one's senses.
cōnsistō, -istere, -titī vi to stand, rest, take up a position; to consist (of), depend (on); to exist, be; (fig) to stand firm, endure; (liquid) to solidify, freeze; to stop, pause, halt, come to rest; (fig) to come to a standstill, come to an end.
cōnsitiō, -ōnis f sowing, planting.
cōnsitor, -ōris m sower, planter.
cōnsitus ppp of **cōnserō**.
cōnsōbrīnus, -ī m, **-a, -ae** f cousin.
cōnsociātiō, -ōnis f society.
cōnsociō, -āre, -āvī, -ātum vt to share, associate, unite.
cōnsōlābilis adj consolable.
cōnsōlātiō, -ōnis f comfort, encouragement, consolation.
cōnsōlātor, -ōris m comforter.
cōnsōlātōrius adj of consolation.
cōnsōlor, -ārī, -ātus vt to console, comfort, reassure; (things) to relieve, mitigate.
cōnsomniō, -āre vt to dream about.
cōnsonō, -āre, -uī vi to resound; (fig) to accord.
cōnsonus adj concordant; (fig) suitable.
cōnsōpiō, -īre, -ītum vt to put to sleep.
cōnsors, -tis adj sharing in common; (things) shared in common ♦ m/f partner, colleague.
cōnsortiō, -ōnis f partnership, fellowship.
cōnsortium, -ī and iī nt society, participation.
cōnspectus ppp of **cōnspiciō** ♦ adj visible, conspicuous.
cōnspectus, -ūs m look, view, sight; appearing on the scene; (fig) mental picture, survey; **in ~um venīre** come in sight, come near.
cōnspergō, -gere, -sī, -sum vt to besprinkle; (fig) to spangle.
cōnspiciendus adj noteworthy, distinguished.
cōnspiciō, -icere, -exī, -ectum vt to observe, catch sight of; to look at (esp with admiration),

contemplate; (*pass*) to attract attention, be conspicuous, be notorious; (*mind*) to see, perceive.

cōnspicor, -ārī, -ātus *vt* to observe, see, catch sight of.

cōnspicuus *adj* visible; conspicuous, distinguished.

cōnspīrātiō, -ōnis *f* concord, unanimity; plotting, conspiracy.

cōnspīrō, -āre, -āvī, -ātum *vi* to agree, unite; to plot, conspire; (*music*) to sound together.

cōnspōnsor, -ōris *m* co-guarantor.

cōnspuō, -ere *vt* to spit upon.

cōnspurcō, -āre *vt* to pollute.

cōnspūtō, -āre *vt* to spit upon (*with contempt*).

cōnstabiliō, -īre, -īvī, -ītum *vt* to establish.

cōnstāns, -antis *pres p of* **cōnstō ♦** *adj* steady, stable, constant; consistent; faithful, steadfast.

cōnstanter *adv* steadily, firmly, calmly; consistently.

cōnstantia, -ae *f* steadiness, firmness; consistency, harmony; self-possession, constancy.

cōnsternātiō, -ōnis *f* disorder, tumult; (*horses*) stampede; (*mind*) dismay, alarm.

cōnsternō, -ernere, -rāvī, -rātum *vt* to spread, cover, thatch, pave; **~rāta nāvis** decked ship.

cōnsternō, -āre, -āvī, -ātum *vt* to startle, stampede; to alarm, throw into confusion.

cōnstīpō, -āre *vt* to crowd together.

cōnstitī *perf of* **cōnsistō**.

cōnstituō, -uere, -uī, -ūtum *vt* to put, place, set down; (*MIL*) to station, post, halt; to establish, build, create; to settle, arrange, organize; to appoint, determine, fix; to resolve, decide; **bene ~ūtum corpus** a good constitution.

cōnstitūtiō, -ōnis *f* state, condition; regulation, decree; definition, point at issue.

cōnstitūtum, -ūtī *nt* agreement.

cōnstō, -āre, -itī, -ātum *vi* to stand together; to agree, correspond, tally; to stand firm, remain constant; to exist, be; to consist (of), be composed (of); (*facts*) to be established, be well-known; (*COMM*) to cost; **sibi ~** be consistent; **inter omnēs ~at** it is common knowledge; **mihi ~at** I am determined; **ratiō ~at** the account is correct.

cōnstrātum, -ī *nt* flooring, deck.

cōnstrātus *ppp of* **cōnsternō**.

cōnstringō, -ingere, -inxī, -ictum *vt* to tie up, bind, fetter; (*fig*) to restrain, restrict; (*speech*) to compress, condense.

cōnstructiō, -ōnis *f* building up; (*words*) arrangement, sequence.

cōnstruō, -ere, -xī, -ctum *vt* to heap up; to build, construct.

cōnstuprātor, -ōris *m* debaucher.

cōnstuprō, -āre *vt* to debauch, rape.

cōnsuādeō, -ēre *vi* to advise strongly.

Cōnsuālia, -ium *ntpl* festival of Consus.

cōnsuāsor, -ōris *m* earnest adviser.

cōnsūdō, -āre *vi* to sweat profusely.

cōnsuēfaciō, -facere, -fēcī, -factum *vt* to accustom.

cōnsuēscō, -scere, -vī, -tum *vt* to accustom, inure ♦ *vi* to get accustomed; to cohabit (with); (*perf tenses*) to be accustomed, be in the habit of.

cōnsuētūdō, -inis *f* custom, habit; familiarity, social intercourse; love affair; (*language*) usage, idiom; **~ine/ex ~ine** as usual; **epistulārum ~** correspondence.

cōnsuētus *ppp of* **cōnsuēscō ♦** *adj* customary, usual.

cōnsuēvī *perf of* **cōnsuēscō**.

cōnsul, -is *m* consul; **~ dēsignātus** consul elect; **~ ōrdinārius** regular consul; **~ suffectus** *successor to a consul who has died during his term of office*; **~ iterum/tertium** consul for the second/third time; **~em creāre, dīcere, facere** elect to the consulship; **L. Domitiō App. Claudiō ~ibus** in the year 54 B.C.

cōnsulāris *adj* consular, consul's; of consular rank ♦ *m* ex-consul.

cōnsulāriter *adv* in a manner worthy of a consul.

cōnsulātus, -ūs *m* consulship; **~um petere** stand for the consulship.

cōnsulō, -ere, -uī, -tum *vi* to deliberate, take thought; (*with dat*) to look after, consult the interests of; (*with dē or in*) to take measures against, pass sentence on ♦ *vt* to consult, ask advice of; to consider; to advise (something); to decide; **bonī/optimī ~** take in good part, be satisfied with.

cōnsultātiō, -ōnis *f* deliberation; inquiry; case.

cōnsultē *adv* deliberately.

cōnsultō *adv* deliberately.

cōnsultō, -āre, -āvī, -ātum *vt, vi* to deliberate, reflect; to consult; (*with dat*) to consult the interests of.

cōnsultor, -ōris *m* counsellor; consulter, client.

cōnsultrīx, -īcis *f* protectress.

cōnsultum, -ī *nt* decree (*esp of the Senate*); consultation; response (*from an oracle*).

cōnsultus *ppp of* **cōnsulō ♦** *adj* considered; experienced, skilled ♦ *m* lawyer; **iūris ~us** lawyer.

cōnsuluī *perf of* **cōnsulō**.

(cōnsum), futūrum, fore *vi* to be all right.

cōnsummātus *adj* perfect.

cōnsummō, -āre *vt* to sum up; to complete, perfect.

cōnsūmō, -ere, -psī, -ptum *vt* to consume,

Noun declensions and verb conjugations are shown on pp xiii to xxv. The present infinitive ending of a verb shows to which conjugation it belongs: **-āre** = 1st; **-ēre** = 2nd; **-ere** = 3rd and **-īre** = 4th. Irregular verbs are shown on p xxvi

use up, eat up; to waste, squander; to
exhaust, destroy, kill; to spend, devote.
cōnsūmptiō, -ōnis *f* wasting.
cōnsūmptor, -ōris *m* destroyer.
cōnsūmptus *ppp of* **cōnsūmō.**
cōnsuō, -uere, -uī, -ūtum *vt* to sew up; (*fig*)
to contrive.
cōnsurgō, -gere, -rēxī, -rēctum *vi* to rise,
stand up; to be roused (to); to spring up,
start.
cōnsurrēctiō, -ōnis *f* standing up.
Cōnsus, -ī *m* ancient Roman god (*connected
with harvest*).
cōnsusurrō, -āre *vi* to whisper together.
cōnsūtus *ppp of* **cōnsuō.**
contābefaciō, -ere *vt* to wear out.
contābēscō, -ēscere, -uī *vi* to waste away.
contabulātiō, -ōnis *f* flooring, storey.
contabulō, -āre, -āvī, -ātum *vt* to board
over, build in storeys.
contāctus *ppp of* **contingō.**
contāctus, -ūs *m* touch, contact; contagion,
infection.
contāgēs, -is *f* contact, touch.
contāgiō, -ōnis *f*, **contāgium, -ī** *and* **iī** *nt*
contact; contagion, infection; (*fig*)
contamination, bad example.
contāminātus *adj* impure, vicious.
contāminō, -āre, -āvī, -ātum *vt* to defile; (*fig*)
to mar, spoil.
contechnor, -ārī, -ātus *vi* to think out plots.
contegō, -egere, -ēxī, -ēctum *vt* to cover up,
cover over; to protect; to hide.
contemerō, -āre *vt* to defile.
contemnō, -nere, -psī, -ptum *vt* to think
light of, have no fear of, despise, defy; to
disparage.
contemplātiō, -ōnis *f* contemplation,
surveying.
contemplātor, -ōris *m* observer.
contemplātus, -ūs *m* contemplation.
**contemplō, -āre, -āvī, -ātum, -or, -ārī,
-ātus** *vt* to look at, observe, contemplate.
contempsī *perf of* **contemnō.**
contemptim *adv* contemptuously,
slightingly.
contemptiō, -ōnis *f* disregard, scorn,
despising.
contemptor, -ōris *m* (male) despiser, defiler.
contemptrix, -rīcis *f* (female) despiser,
defiler.
contemptus *ppp of* **contemnō** ♦ *adj*
contemptible.
contemptus, -ūs *m* despising, scorn; being
slighted; **~uī esse** be despised.
contendō, -dere, -dī, -tum *vt* to stretch,
draw, tighten; (*instrument*) to tune; (*effort*)
to strain, exert; (*argument*) to assert, maintain;
(*comparison*) to compare, contrast; (*course*)
to direct ♦ *vi* to exert oneself, strive; to
hurry; to journey, march; to contend,
compete, fight; to entreat, solicit.
contentē *adv* (*from* **contendō**) earnestly,

intensely.
contentē *adv* (*from* **contineō**) closely.
contentiō, -ōnis *f* straining, effort; striving
(after); struggle, competition, dispute;
comparison, contrast, antithesis.
contentus *ppp of* **contendō** ♦ *adj* strained,
tense; (*fig*) intent.
contentus *ppp of* **contineō** ♦ *adj* content,
satisfied.
conterminus *adj* bordering, neighbouring.
conterō, -erere, -rīvī, -rītum *vt* to grind,
crumble; to wear out, waste; (*time*) to spend,
pass; (*fig*) to obliterate.
conterreō, -ēre, -uī, -itum *vt* to terrify.
contestātus *adj* proved.
contestor, -ārī, -ātus *vt* to call to witness;
lītem ~ open a lawsuit by calling witnesses.
contexō, -ere, -uī, -tum *vt* to weave,
interweave; to devise, construct; (*recital*) to
continue.
contextē *adv* in a connected fashion.
contextus *adj* connected.
contextus, -ūs *m* connection, coherence.
conticēscō (-īscō), -ēscere, -uī *vi* to become
quiet, fall silent; (*fig*) to cease, abate.
contigī *perf of* **contingō.**
contignātiō, -ōnis *f* floor, storey.
contignō, -āre *vt* to floor.
contiguus *adj* adjoining, near; within reach.
continēns, -entis *pres p of* **contineō** ♦ *adj*
bordering, adjacent; unbroken, continuous;
(*time*) successive, continual, uninterrupted;
(*person*) temperate, continent ♦ *nt* mainland,
continent; essential point (*in an argument*).
continenter *adv* (*place*) in a row; (*time*)
continuously; (*person*) temperately.
continentia, -ae *f* moderation, self-control.
contineō, -inēre, -inuī, -entum *vt* to hold,
keep together; to confine, enclose; to
contain, include, comprise; (*pass*) to consist
of, rest on; to control, check, repress.
contingō, -ingere, -igī, -āctum *vt* to touch,
take hold of, partake of; to be near, border
on; to reach, come to; to contaminate; (*mind*)
to touch, affect, concern ♦ *vi* to happen,
succeed.
contingō, -ere *vt* to moisten, smear.
continuātiō, -ōnis *f* unbroken, succession,
series; (*RHET*) period.
continuī *perf of* **contineō.**
continuō *adv* immediately, without delay;
(*argument*) necessarily.
continuō, -āre, -āvī, -ātum *vt* to join
together, make continuous; to continue
without a break; **verba ~** form a sentence.
continuus *adj* joined (to); continuous,
successive, uninterrupted; **~ā nocte** the
following night; **triduum ~um** three days
running.
cōntiō, -ōnis *f* public meeting; speech,
address; rostrum; **~ōnem habēre** hold a
meeting; deliver an address; **prō ~ōne** in
public.

cōntiōnābundus *adj* delivering a harangue, playing the demagogue.

cōntiōnālis *adj* suitable for a public meeting, demagogic.

cōntiōnārius *adj* fond of public meetings.

cōntiōnātor, -ōris *m* demagogue.

cōntiōnor, -ārī, -ātus *vi* to address a public meeting, harangue; to declare in public; to come to a meeting.

cōntiuncula, -ae *f* short speech.

contorqueō, -quēre, -sī, -tum *vt* to twist, turn; (*weapons*) to throw, brandish; (*words*) to deliver forcibly.

contortē *adv* intricately.

contortiō, -ōnis *f* intricacy.

contortor, -ōris *m* perverter.

contortulus *adj* somewhat complicated.

contortuplicātus *adj* very complicated.

contortus *ppp of* **contorqueō ♦** *adj* vehement; intricate.

contrā *adv* (*place*) opposite, face to face; (*speech*) in reply; (*action*) to fight, in opposition, against someone; (*result, with* **esse**) adverse, unsuccessful; (*comparison*) the contrary, conversely, differently; (*argument*) on the contrary, on the other hand; ~ **atque, quam** contrary to what, otherwise than ♦ *prep* (*with acc*) facing, opposite to; against; contrary to, in violation of.

contractiō, -ōnis *f* contracting; shortening; despondency.

contractiuncula, -ae *f* slight despondency.

contractus *ppp of* **contrahō ♦** *adj* contracted, narrow; short; in seclusion.

contrādīcō, -dīcere, -dīxī, -dictum (*usu two words*) *vt, vi* to oppose, object; (*law*) to be counsel for the other side.

contrādictiō, -ōnis *f* objection.

contrahō, -here, -xī, -ctum *vt* to draw together, assemble; to bring about, achieve; (*comm*) to contract, make a bargain; to shorten, narrow; to limit, depress; (*blame*) to incur; (*brow*) to wrinkle; (*sail*) to shorten; (*sky*) to overcast.

contrāriē *adv* differently.

contrārius *adj* opposite, from opposite; contrary, hostile, harmful ♦ *nt* opposite, reverse; **ex ~ō** on the contrary.

contrectābiliter *adv* so as to be felt.

contrectātiō, -ōnis *f* touching.

contrectō, -āre, -āvī, -ātum *vt* to touch, handle; (*fig*) to consider.

contremīscō, -īscere, -uī *vi* to tremble all over; (*fig*) to waver ♦ *vt* to be afraid of.

contremō, -ere *vi* to quake.

contribuō, -uere, -uī, -ūtum *vt* to bring together, join, incorporate.

contristō, -āre, -āvī, -ātum *vt* to sadden, darken, cloud.

contrītus *ppp of* **conterō ♦** *adj* trite, well-worn.

contrōversia, -ae *f* dispute, argument, debate, controversy.

contrōversiōsus *adj* much disputed.

contrōversus *adj* disputed, questionable.

contrucīdō, -āre, -āvī, -ātum *vt* to massacre.

contrūdō, -dere, -sī, -sum *vt* to crowd together.

contruncō, -āre *vt* to hack to pieces.

contrūsus *ppp of* **contrūdō**.

contubernālis, -is *m/f* tent companion; junior officer serving with a general; (*fig*) companion, mate.

contubernium, -ī *and* **iī** *nt* service in the same tent, mess; service as junior officer with a general; common tent; slaves' home.

contueor, -ērī, -itus *vt* to look at, consider, observe.

contuitus, -ūs *m* observing, view.

contulī *perf of* **cōnferō**.

contumācia, -ae *f* obstinacy, defiance.

contumāciter *adv see* **contumāx**.

contumāx, -ācis *adj* stubborn, insolent, pig-headed.

contumēlia, -ae *f* (*verbal*) insult, libel, invective; (*physical*) assault, ill-treatment.

contumēliōsē *adv* insolently.

contumēliōsus *adj* insulting, outrageous.

contumulō, -āre *vt* to bury.

contundō, -undere, -udī, -ūsum *vt* to pound, beat, bruise; (*fig*) to suppress, destroy.

contuor *etc see* **contueor**.

conturbātiō, -ōnis *f* confusion, mental disorder.

conturbātus *adj* distracted, diseased.

conturbō, -āre, -āvī, -ātum *vt* to throw into confusion; (*mind*) to derange, disquiet; (*money*) to embarrass.

contus, -ī *m* pole.

contūsus *ppp of* **contundō**.

contūtus *see* **contuitus**.

cōnūbiālis *adj* conjugal.

cōnūbium, -ī *and* **iī** *nt* marriage; **iūs ~ī** right of intermarriage.

cōnus, -ī *m* cone; (*helmet*) apex.

convador, -ārī, -ātus *vt* (*law*) to bind over.

convalēscō, -ēscere, -uī *vi* to recover, get better; (*fig*) to grow stronger, improve.

convallis, -is *f* valley with hills on all sides.

convāsō, -āre *vt* to pack up.

convectō, -āre *vt* to bring home.

convector, -ōris *m* fellow passenger.

convehō, -here, -xī, -ctum *vt* to bring in, carry.

convellō, -ellere, -ellī, -ulsum *and* **olsum** *vt* to wrench, tear away; to break up; (*fig*) to destroy, overthrow; **signa ~** decamp.

convena, -ae *adj* meeting.

convenae, -ārum *m/f* crowd of strangers, refugees.

Noun declensions and verb conjugations are shown on pp xiii to xxv. The present infinitive ending of a verb shows to which conjugation it belongs: **-āre** = 1st; **-ēre** = 2nd; **-ere** = 3rd and **-īre** = 4th. Irregular verbs are shown on p xxvi

conveniēns, -entis *pres p of* **conveniō** ♦ *adj* harmonious, consistent; fit, appropriate.
convenienter *adv* in conformity (with), consistently; aptly.
convenientia, -ae *f* conformity, harmony.
conveniō, -enīre, -ēnī, -entum *vi* to meet, assemble; (*events*) to combine, coincide; (*person*) to agree, harmonize; (*things*) to fit, suit; (*impers*) to be suitable, be proper ♦ *vt* to speak to, interview.
conventīcium, -ī *and* **iī** *nt* payment for attendance at assemblies.
conventīcius *adj* visiting regularly.
conventiculum, -ī *nt* gathering; meeting place.
conventiō, -ōnis *f* agreement.
conventum, -ī *nt* agreement.
conventus *ppp of* **conveniō**.
conventus, -ūs *m* meeting; (*law*) local assizes; (*comm*) corporation; agreement; **~ūs agere** hold the assizes.
converrō, -rere, -rī, -sum *vt* to sweep up, brush together; (*comedy*) to give a good beating to.
conversātiō, -ōnis *f* associating (with).
conversiō, -ōnis *f* revolution, cycle; change over; (*RHET*) well-rounded period; verbal repetition at end of clauses.
conversō, -āre *vt* to turn round.
conversus *ppp of* **converrō**; *ppp of* **convertō**.
convertō, -tere, -tī, -sum *vt* to turn round, turn back; (*MIL*) to wheel; to turn, direct; to change, transform; (*writings*) to translate ♦ *vi* to return, turn, change.
convestiō, -īre, -īvī, -ītum *vt* to clothe, encompass.
convexus *adj* vaulted, rounded; hollow; sloping ♦ *nt* vault, hollow.
convīciātor, -ōris *m* slanderer.
convīcior, -ārī, -ātus *vt* to revile.
convīcium, -ī *and* **iī** *nt* loud noise, outcry; invective, abuse; reproof, protest.
convīctiō, -ōnis *f* companionship.
convīctor, -ōris *m* familiar friend.
convīctus *ppp of* **convincō**.
convīctus, -ūs *m* community life, intercourse; entertainment.
convincō, -incere, -īcī, -ictum *vt* to refute, convict, prove wrong; to prove, demonstrate.
convīsō, -ere *vt* to search, examine; to pervade.
convītium *see* **convīcium**.
convīva, -ae *m/f* guest.
convīvālis *adj* festive, convivial.
convīvātor, -ōris *m* host.
convīvium, -ī *and* **iī** *nt* banquet, entertainment; guests.
convīvor, -ārī, -ātus *vi* to feast together, carouse.
convocātiō, -ōnis *f* assembling.
convocō, -āre, -āvī, -ātum *vt* to call a meeting of, muster.

convolnerō *see* **convulnerō**.
convolō, -āre, -āvī, -ātum *vi* to flock together.
convolsus *see* **convulsus**.
convolvō, -vere, -vī, -ūtum *vt* to roll up, coil up; to intertwine.
convomō, -ere *vt* to vomit over.
convorrō *see* **converrō**.
convortō *see* **convertō**.
convulnerō, -āre *vt* to wound seriously.
convulsus *ppp of* **convellō**.
cooperiō, -īre, -uī, -tum *vt* to cover over, overwhelm.
cooptātiō, -ōnis *f* electing, nominating (of new members).
cooptō, -āre, -āvī, -ātum *vt* to elect (as a colleague).
coorior, -īrī, -tus *vi* to rise, appear; to break out, begin.
coortus, -ūs *m* originating.
cōpa, -ae *f* barmaid.
cophinus, -ī *m* basket.
cōpia, -ae *f* abundance, plenty, number; resources, wealth, prosperity; (*MIL, usu pl*) troops, force; (*words, thought*) richness, fulness, store; (*action*) opportunity, facility, means, access; **prō ~ā** according to one's resources, as good as possible considering.
cōpiolae, -ārum *fpl* small force.
cōpiōsē *adv* abundantly, fully, at great length.
cōpiōsus *adj* abounding, rich, plentiful; (*speech*) eloquent, fluent.
cōpis *adj* rich.
cōpula, -ae *f* rope, leash, grapnel; (*fig*) bond.
cōpulātiō, -ōnis *f* coupling, union.
cōpulātus *adj* connected, binding.
cōpulō, -āre, -āvī, -ātum *vt* to couple, join; (*fig*) to unite, associate.
coqua, -ae *f* cook.
coquīnō, -āre *vi* to be a cook.
coquīnus *adj* of cooking.
coquō, -quere, -xī, -ctum *vt* to cook, boil, bake; to parch, burn; (*fruit*) to ripen; (*stomach*) to digest; (*thought*) to plan, concoct; (*care*) to disquiet, disturb.
coquus (cocus), -ī *m* cook.
cor, cordis *nt* heart; (*feeling*) heart, soul; (*thought*) mind, judgement; **cordī esse** please, be agreeable.
cōram *adv* in one's presence; in person ♦ *prep* (*with abl*) in the presence of, before.
corbis, -is *m/f* basket.
corbīta, -ae *f* slow boat.
corbula, -ae *f* little basket.
corculum, -ī *nt* dear heart.
Corcȳra, -ae *f* island off W. coast of Greece (*now* Corfu).
Corcȳraeus *adj see n.*
cordātē *adv see* **cordātus**.
cordātus *adj* wise.
cordolium, -ī *and* **iī** *nt* sorrow.
Corfiniēnsis *adj see n.*
Corfinium, -ī *nt* town in central Italy.

coriandrum, -ī nt coriander.
Corinthiacus, -iēnsis, -ius adj: **~ium aes**
Corinthian brass (an alloy of gold, silver and
copper).
Corinthus, -ī f Corinth.
corium (corius m) **-ī** and **iī** nt hide, skin;
leather, strap.
Cornēlia, -iae f mother of the Gracchi.
Cornēliānus, -ius adj: **lēgēs ~iae** Sulla's laws.
Cornēlius, -ī m famous Roman family name
(esp Scipios, Gracchi, Sulla).
corneolus adj horny.
corneus adj of horn.
corneus adj of the cornel tree, of cornel wood.
cornicen, -cinis m horn-blower.
cornīcula, -ae f little crow.
corniculārius, -ī and **iī** m adjutant.
corniculum, -ī nt a horn-shaped decoration.
corniger, -ī adj horned.
cornipēs, -edis adj horn-footed.
cornīx, -īcis f crow.
cornū, -ūs, -um, -ī nt horn; anything horn-
shaped; (army) wing; (bay) arm; (book)
roller-end; (bow) tip; (helmet) crest-socket;
(land) tongue, spit; (lyre) arm; (moon) horn;
(place) side; (river) branch; (yardarm) point;
anything made of horn: bow, funnel,
lantern; (music) horn; (oil) cruet; anything
like horn; beak, hoof, wart; (fig) strength,
courage; **~ cōpiae** Amalthea's horn, symbol of
plenty.
cornum, -ī nt cornelian cherry.
cornum see **cornū.**
cornus, -ī f cornelian cherry tree; javelin.
corōlla, -ae f small garland.
corōllārium, -ī and **iī** nt garland for actors;
present, gratuity.
corōna, -ae f garland, crown; (ASTRO) Corona
Borealis; (people) gathering, bystanders;
(MIL) cordon of besiegers or defenders; **sub
~ā vēndere, vēnīre** sell, be sold as slaves.
Corōnaeus, -eus, -ēnsis adj see **Corōnēa.**
corōnārium aurum gold collected in the
provinces for a victorious general.
Corōnēa, -eae f town in central Greece.
corōnō, -āre, -āvī, -ātum vt to put a garland
on, crown; to encircle.
corporeus adj corporeal; of flesh.
corpulentus adj corpulent.
corpus, -oris nt body; substance, flesh;
corpse; trunk, torso; person, individual; (fig)
structure, corporation, body politic.
corpusculum, -ī nt particle; term of
endearment.
corrādō, -dere, -sī, -sum vt to scrape
together, procure.
correctiō, -ōnis f amending, improving.
corrēctor, -ōris m reformer, critic.
corrēctus ppp of **corrigō.**
correpō, -ere, -sī vi to creep, slink, cower.

correptē adv briefly.
correptus ppp of **corripiō.**
corrīdeō, -ēre vi to laugh aloud.
corrigia, -ae f shoelace.
corrigō, -igere, -ēxī, -ēctum vt to make
straight; to put right, improve, correct.
corripiō, -ipere, -ipuī, -eptum vt to seize,
carry off, get along quickly; (speech) to
reprove, reproach, accuse; (passion) to seize
upon, attack; (time, words) to cut short; **sē
gradum, viam ~** hasten, rush.
corrōborō, -āre, -āvī, -ātum vt to make
strong, invigorate.
corrōdō, -dere, -sī, -sum vt to nibble away.
corrogō, -āre vt to gather by requesting.
corrūgō, -āre vt to wrinkle.
corrumpō, -umpere, -ūpī, -uptum vt to
break up, ruin, waste; to mar, adulterate,
falsify; (person) to corrupt, seduce, bribe.
corruō, -ere, -ī vi to fall, collapse ♦ vt to
overthrow, heap up.
corruptē adv perversely; in a lax manner.
corruptēla, -ae f corruption, bribery;
seducer.
corruptiō, -ōnis f bribing, seducing; corrupt
state.
corruptor, -ōris m, **-rīx, -rīcis** f corrupter,
seducer.
corruptus ppp of **corrumpō** ♦ adj spoiled,
corrupt, bad.
Corsus adj Corsican.
cortex, -icis m/f bark, rind; cork.
cortīna, -ae f kettle, cauldron; tripod of
Apollo; (fig) vault, circle.
corulus, -ī f hazel.
Cōrus see **Caurus.**
coruscō, -āre vt to butt; to shake, brandish ♦
vi to flutter, flash, quiver.
coruscus adj tremulous, oscillating;
shimmering, glittering.
corvus, -ī m raven; (MIL) grapnel.
Corybantēs, -ium mpl priests of Cybele.
Corybantius adj see n.
cōrycus, -ī m punchball.
corylētum, -ī nt hazel copse.
corylus, -ī f hazel.
corymbifer m Bacchus.
corymbus, -ī m cluster (esp of ivy berries).
coryphaeus, -ī m leader.
cōrytos, -us, -ī m quiver.
cōs f hard rock, flint; grindstone.
Cōs, Coī f Aegean island (famous for wine and
weaving) ♦ nt Coan wine ♦ ntpl Coan clothes.
cosmēta, -ae m master of the wardrobe.
costa, -ae f rib; side, wall.
costum, -ī nt an aromatic plant, perfume.
cothurnātus adj buskined, tragic.
cothurnus, -ī m buskin, hunting boot;
tragedy, elevated style.
cotīd see **cottīd-.**

cōtis *f see* **cōs.**

cottabus, -ī *m* game of throwing drops of wine.

cottana, -ōrum *ntpl* Syrian figs.

cottīdiānō *adv* daily.

cottīdiānus *adj* daily; everyday, ordinary.

cottīdiē *adv* every day, daily.

coturnīx, -īcis *f* quail.

Cotyttia, -ōrum *ntpl festival of Thracian goddess Cotytto.*

Cōus *adj* Coan.

covinnārius, -ī *and* **iī** *m* chariot fighter.

covinnus, -ī *m* war chariot; coach.

coxa, -ae, coxendīx, -īcis *f* hip.

coxī *perf of* **coquō.**

crābrō, -ōnis *m* hornet.

crambē-, -ēs *f* cabbage; **~ repetīta** stale repetitions.

Crantor, -oris *m Greek Academic philosopher.*

crāpula, -ae *f* intoxication, hangover.

crāpulārius *adj* for intoxication.

crās *adv* tomorrow.

crassē *adv* grossly, dimly.

Crassiānus *adj see* **Crassus.**

crassitūdō, -inis *f* thickness, density.

crassus *adj* thick, gross, dense; (*fig*) dull, stupid.

Crassus, -ī *m famous orator; wealthy politician, triumvir with Caesar and Pompey.*

crāstinum, -ī *nt* the morrow.

crāstinus *adj* of tomorrow; **diē ~ī** tomorrow.

crātēr, -is *m*, **-a, -ae** *f* bowl (*esp for mixing wine and water*); crater; a constellation.

crātis, -is *f* wickerwork, hurdle; (*AGR*) harrow; (*MIL*) faggots for lining trenches; (*shield*) ribs; (*fig*) frame, joints.

creātiō, -ōnis *f* election.

creātor, -ōris *m*, **-rīx, -rīcis** *f* creator, father, mother.

creātus *m* (*with abl*) son of.

crēber, -rī *adj* dense, thick, crowded; numerous, frequent; (*fig*) prolific, abundant.

crēbrēscō, -ēscere, -uī *vi* to increase, become frequent.

crēbritās, -ātis *f* frequency.

crēbrō *adv* repeatedly.

crēdibilis *adj* credible.

crēdibiliter *adv see* **crēdibilis.**

crēditor, -ōris *m* creditor.

crēditum, -itī *nt* loan.

crēdō, -ere, -idī, -itum *vt, vi* to entrust, lend; to trust, have confidence in; to believe; to think, suppose; **~erēs** one would have thought.

crēdulitās, -ātis *f* credulity.

crēdulus *adj* credulous, trusting.

cremō, -āre, -āvī, -ātum *vt* to burn, cremate.

Cremōna, -ae *f town in N. Italy.*

Cremōnēnsis *adj see n.*

cremor, -ōris *m* juice, broth.

creō, -āre, -āvī, -ātum *vt* to create, produce, beget; to elect (to an office); to cause, occasion.

creper, -ī *adj* dark; doubtful.

crepida, -ae *f* sandal; **nē sūtor suprā ~am** ≈ *let the cobbler stick to his last.*

crepidātus *adj* wearing sandals.

crepīdō, -inis *f* pedestal, base; bank, pier, dam.

crepidula, -ae *f* small sandal.

crepitācillum, -ī *nt* rattle.

crepitō, -āre *vi* to rattle, chatter, rustle, creak.

crepitus, -ūs *m* rattling, chattering, rustling, creaking.

crepō, -āre, -uī, -itum *vi* to rattle, creak, snap (fingers) ♦ *vt* to make rattle, clap; to chatter about.

crepundia, -ōrum *ntpl* rattle, babies' toys.

crepusculum, -ī *nt* twilight, dusk; darkness.

Crēs, -ētis *m* Cretan.

crēscō, -scere, -vī, -tum *vi* to arise, appear, be born; to grow up, thrive, increase, multiply; to prosper, be promoted, rise in the world.

Crēsius *adj* Cretan.

Crēssa, -ae *f* Cretan.

Crēta, -ae *f* Crete.

crēta, -ae *f* chalk; good mark.

Crētaeus *and* **-icus** *and* **-is, -idis** *adj see n.*

crētātus *adj* chalked; dressed in white.

Crētē *see* **Crēta.**

crēteus *adj* of chalk, of clay.

crētiō, -ōnis *f* declaration of accepting an inheritance.

crētōsus *adj* chalky, clayey.

crētula, -ae *f* white clay for sealing.

crētus *ppp of* **cernō** ♦ *ppa of* **crēscō** ♦ *adj* descended, born.

Creūsa, -ae *f wife of Jason; wife of Aeneas.*

crēvī *perf of* **cernō**; *perf of* **crēscō.**

crībrum, -ī *nt* sieve.

crīmen, -inis *nt* accusation, charge, reproach; guilt, crime; cause of offence; **esse in ~ine** stand accused.

crīminātiō, -ōnis *f* complaint, slander.

crīminātor, -ōris *m* accuser.

crīminō, -āre *vt* to accuse.

crīminor, -ārī, -ātus *dep* to accuse, impeach; (*things*) to complain of, charge with.

crīminōsē *adv* accusingly, slanderously.

crīminōsus *adj* reproachful, slanderous.

crīnālis *adj* for the hair, hair- (*in cpds*) ♦ *nt* hairpin.

crīnis, -is *m* hair; (*comet*) tail.

crīnītus *adj* long-haired; crested; **stēlla ~a** comet.

crīspāns, -antis *adj* wrinkled.

crīspō, -āre *vt* to curl, swing, wave.

crīspus *adj* curled; curly-headed; wrinkled; tremulous.

crista, -ae *f* cockscomb, crest; plume.

cristātus *adj* crested, plumed.

criticus, -ī *m* critic.

croceus *adj* of saffron, yellow.

crocinus *adj* yellow ♦ *nt* saffron oil.

crōciō, -īre vi to croak.
crocodīlus, -ī m crocodile.
crocōtārius adj of saffron clothes.
crocōtula, -ae f saffron dress.
crocus, -ī m, -um, -ī nt saffron; yellow.
Croesus, -ī m king of Lydia (famed for wealth).
crotalistria, -ae f castanet dancer.
crotalum, -ī nt rattle, castanet.
cruciābilitās, -ātis f torment.
cruciāmentum, -ī nt torture.
cruciātus, -ūs m torture; instrument of torture; (fig) ruin, misfortune.
cruciō, -āre, -āvī, -ātum vt to torture; to torment.
crūdēlis adj hard-hearted, cruel.
crūdēlitās, -ātis f cruelty, severity.
crūdēliter adv see crūdēlis.
crūdēscō, -ēscere, -uī vi to grow violent, grow worse.
crūditās, -ātis f indigestion.
crūdus adj bleeding; (food) raw, undigested; (person) dyspeptic; (leather) rawhide; (fruit) unripe; (age) immature, fresh; (voice) hoarse; (fig) unfeeling, cruel, merciless.
cruentō, -āre vt to stain with blood, wound.
cruentus adj bloody, gory; bloodthirsty, cruel; blood-red.
crumēna, -ae f purse; money.
crumilla, -ae f purse.
cruor, -ōris m blood; bloodshed.
cruppellāriī, -ōrum mpl mail-clad fighters.
crūrifragius, -ī and iī m one whose legs have been broken.
crūs, -ūris nt leg, shin.
crūsta, -ae f hard surface, crust; stucco, embossed or inlaid work.
crūstulum, -ī nt small pastry.
crūstum, -ī nt pastry.
crux, -ucis f gallows, cross; (fig) torment; abī in malam ~cem ≈ go and be hanged!
crypta, -ae f underground passage, grotto.
cryptoporticus, -ūs f covered walk.
crystallinus adj of crystal ♦ ntpl crystal vases.
crystallum, -ī nt, -us, -ī m crystal.
cubiculāris, cubiculārius adj of the bedroom ♦ m valet de chambre.
cubiculum, -ī nt bedroom.
cubīle, -is nt bed, couch; (animals) lair, nest; (fig) den.
cubital, -ālis nt cushion.
cubitālis adj a cubit long.
cubitō, -āre vi to lie (in bed).
cubitum, -ī nt elbow; cubit.
cubitus, -ūs m lying in bed.
cubō, -āre, -uī, -itum vi to lie in bed; to recline at table; (places) to lie on a slope.
cucullus, -ī m hood, cowl.
cucūlus, -ī m cuckoo.
cucumis, -eris m cucumber.
cucurbita, -ae f gourd; cupping glass.

cucurrī perf of currō.
cūdō, -ere vt to beat, thresh; (metal) to forge; (money) to coin.
cūiās, -tis pron of what country?, of what town?
cuicuimodī (gen of quisquis and mōdus) of whatever kind, whatever like.
cūius pron (interrog) whose?; (rel) whose.
culcita, -ae f mattress, pillow; eyepatch.
cūleus see culleus.
culex, -icis m/f gnat.
culīna, -ae f kitchen; food.
culleus, cūleus, -ī m leather bag for holding liquids; a fluid measure.
culmen, -inis nt stalk; top, roof, summit; (fig) height, acme.
culmus, -ī m stalk, straw.
culpa, -ae f blame, fault; mischief; in ~ā sum, mea ~a est I am at fault or to blame.
culpātus adj blameworthy.
culpitō, -āre vt to find fault with.
culpō, -āre, -āvī, -ātum vt to blame, reproach.
cultē adv in a refined manner.
cultellus, -ī m small knife.
culter, -rī m knife, razor.
cultiō, -ōnis f cultivation.
cultor, -ōris m cultivator, planter, farmer; inhabitant; supporter, upholder; worshipper.
cultrīx, -īcis f inhabitant; (fig) nurse, fosterer.
cultūra, -ae f cultivation, agriculture; (mind) care, culture; (person) courting.
cultus ppp of colō ♦ adj cultivated; (dress) well-dressed; (mind) polished, cultured ♦ ntpl cultivated land.
cultus, -ūs m cultivation, care; (mind) training, culture; (dress) style, attire; (way of life) refinement, civilization; (gods) worship; (men) honouring.
culullus, -ī m goblet.
cūlus, -ī m buttocks.
cum prep (with abl) with; (denoting accompaniment, resulting circumstances, means, dealings, companion, possession); ~ decimō tenfold; ~ eō quod, ut with the proviso that; ~ prīmīs especially; ~ māgnā calamitāte cīvitātis to the great misfortune of the community; ~ perīculō suō at one's own peril.
cum conj (time) when, whenever, while, as, after, since; (cause) since, as, seeing that; (concession) although; (condition) if; (contrast) while, whereas; multī annī sunt ~ in aere meō est for many years now he has been in my debt; aliquot sunt annī ~ vōs dēlēgī it is now some years since I chose you; ~ māximē just when; just then, just now; ~ prīmum as soon as; ~ . . . tum not only . . . but also; both . . . and.

Noun declensions and verb conjugations are shown on pp xiii to xxv. The present infinitive ending of a verb shows to which conjugation it belongs: -āre = 1st; -ēre = 2nd; -ere = 3rd and -īre = 4th. Irregular verbs are shown on p xxvi

Cūmae, -ārum *fpl* town near Naples (*famous for its Sibyl*).

Cūmaeānum, -āni *nt* Cicero's Cumaean residence.

Cūmaeus, -ānus *adj see n.*

cumba, cymba, -ae *f* boat, skiff.

cumera, -ae *f* grain chest.

cumīnum, -ī *nt* cumin.

cumque (quomque) *adv* -ever, -soever; at any time.

cumulātē *adv* fully, abundantly.

cumulātus *adj* increased; complete.

cumulō, -āre, -āvī, -ātum *vt* to heap up; to amass, increase; to fill up, overload; (*fig*) to fill, overwhelm, crown, complete.

cumulus, -ī *m* heap, mass; crowning addition, summit.

cūnābula, -ōrum *ntpl* cradle.

cūnae, -ārum *fpl* cradle.

cunctābundus *adj* hesitant, dilatory.

cunctāns, -antis *adj* dilatory, reluctant; sluggish, tough.

cunctanter *adv* slowly.

cunctātiō, -ōnis *f* delaying, hesitation.

cunctātor, -ōris *m* loiterer; one given to cautious tactics (*esp Q Fabius Maximus*).

cunctor, -ārī, -ātus *vi* to linger, delay, hesitate; to move slowly.

cūnctus *adj* the whole of; (*pl*) all together, all.

cuneātim *adv* in the form of a wedge.

cuneātus *adj* wedge-shaped.

cuneus, -ī *m* wedge; (*MIL*) wedge-shaped formation of troops; (*THEATRE*) block of seats.

cunīculus, -ī *m* rabbit; underground passage; (*MIL*) mine.

cunque *see* **cumque.**

cūpa, -ae *f* vat, tun.

cupidē *adv* eagerly, passionately.

Cupīdineus *adj see* **Cupīdō.**

cupiditās, -ātis *f* desire, eagerness, enthusiasm; passion, lust; avarice, greed; ambition; partisanship.

cupīdō, -inis *f* desire, eagerness; passion, lust; greed.

Cupīdō, -inis *m* Cupid (*son of Venus*).

cupidus *adj* desirous, eager; fond, loving; passionate, lustful; greedy, ambitious; partial.

cupiēns, -entis *pres p of* **cupiō ♦** *adj* eager, desirous.

cupienter *adv see* **cupiēns.**

cupiō, -ere, -īvī and **iī, -ītum** *vt* to wish, desire, long for; (*with dat*) to wish well.

cupītor, -ōris *m* desirer.

cupītus *ppp of* **cupiō.**

cuppēdia, -ae *f* fondness for delicacies.

cuppēdia, -ōrum *ntpl* delicacies.

cuppēdinārius, -ī *m* confectioner.

cuppēdō, -inis *f* longing, passion.

cuppes, -dis *adj* fond of delicacies.

cupressētum, -ī *nt* cypress grove.

cupresseus *adj* of cypress wood.

cupressifer, -ī *adj* cypress-bearing.

cupressus, -ī *f* cypress.

cūr *adv* why?; (*indirect*) why, the reason for.

cūra, -ae *f* care, trouble, pains (bestowed); anxiety, concern, sorrow (felt); attention (to), charge (of), concern (for); (*MED*) treatment, cure; (*writing*) work; (*law*) trusteeship; (*poet*) love; (*person*) mistress, guardian; **~ est** I am anxious; **~ae esse** be attended to, looked after.

cūrābilis *adj* troublesome.

cūralium, -ī and **iī** *nt* red coral.

cūrātē *adv* carefully.

cūrātiō, -ōnis *f* charge, management; office; treatment, healing.

cūrātor, -ōris *m* manager, overseer; (*law*) guardian.

cūrātūra, -ae *f* dieting.

cūrātus *adj* cared for; earnest, anxious.

curculiō, -ōnis *m* weevil.

curculiunculus, -ī *m* little weevil.

Curēnsis *adj see n.*

Curēs, -ium *mpl* ancient Sabine town.

Cūrētēs, -um *mpl* attendants of Jupiter in Crete.

Cūrētis, -idis *adj* Cretan.

cūria, -ae *f* earliest division of the Roman people; meeting-place of a curia; senate house; senate.

cūriālis, -is *m* member of a curia.

cūriātim *adv* by curiae.

cūriātus *adj* of the curiae; **comitia ~a** earliest Roman assembly.

cūriō, -ōnis *m* president of a curia; **~ māximus** head of all the curiae.

cūriō, -ōnis *adj* emaciated.

cūriōsē *adv* carefully; inquisitively.

cūriōsitās, -ātis *f* curiosity.

cūriōsus *adj* careful, thoughtful, painstaking; inquiring, inquisitive, officious; careworn.

curis, -ītis *f* spear.

cūrō, -āre, -āvī, -ātum *vt* to take care of, attend to; to bother about; (*with gerundive*) to get something done; (*with inf*) to take the trouble; (*with ut*) to see to it that; (*public life*) to be in charge of, administer; (*MED*) to treat, cure; (*money*) to pay, settle up; **aliud ~ā** never mind; **corpus/cutem ~** take it easy; **prōdigia ~** avert portents.

curriculum, -ī *nt* running, race; course, lap; (*fig*) career; **~ō** at full speed.

currō, -ere, cucurrī, cursum *vi* to run; to hasten, fly ♦ *vt* to run through, traverse; **~entem incitāre** ≈ spur a willing horse.

currus, -ūs *m* car, chariot; triumph; team of horses; ploughwheels.

cursim *adv* quickly, at the double.

cursitō, -āre *vi* to run about, fly hither and thither.

cursō, -āre *vi* to run about.

cursor, -ōris *m* runner, racer; courier.

cursūra, -ae *f* running.

cursus, -ūs *m* running, speed; passage, journey; course, direction; (*things*) movement, flow; (*fig*) rapidity, flow, progress; **~ honōrum** succession of magistracies; **~ rērum** course of events; **~um tenēre** keep on one's course; **~ū** at a run; **māgnō ~ū** at full speed.

curtō, -āre vt to shorten.

curtus adj short, broken off; incomplete.

curūlis adj official, curule; **aedīlis ~** patrician, aediile; **sella ~** magistrates' chair; **equī ~** horses provided for the games by the state.

curvāmen, -inis nt bend.

curvātūra, -ae f curve.

curvō, -āre, -āvī, -ātum vt to curve, bend, arch; (fig) to move.

curvus adj bent, curved, crooked; (person) aged; (fig) wrong.

cuspis, -dis f point; spear, javelin, trident, sting.

custōdēla, -ae f care, guard.

custōdia, -ae f watch, guard, care; (person) sentry, guard; (place) sentry's post, guardhouse; custody, confinement, prison; **lībera ~** confinement in one's own house.

custōdiō, -īre, -īvī and **iī, -ītum** vt to guard, defend; to hold in custody, keep watch on; to keep, preserve, observe.

custōs, -ōdis m/f guard, bodyguard, protector, protectress; jailer, warder; (MIL) sentry, spy; container.

cutīcula, -ae f skin.

cutis, -is f skin; **~em cūrāre** ≈ take it easy.

cyathissō, -āre vi to serve wine.

cyathus, -ī m wine ladle; (measure) one-twelfth of a pint.

cybaea, -ae f kind of merchant ship.

Cybēbē, Cybelē, -ēs f Phrygian mother-goddess, Magna Mater.

Cybelēius adj see n.

Cyclades, -um fpl group of Aegean islands.

cyclas, -adis f formal dress with a border.

cyclicus adj of the traditional epic stories.

Cyclōpius adj see n.

Cyclōps, -is m one-eyed giant (esp Polyphemus).

cycnēus adj of a swan, swan's.

cycnus, -ī m swan.

Cydōnius adj Cretan ♦ ntpl quinces.

cygnus see **cycnus**.

cylindrus, -ī m cylinder; roller.

Cyllēnē, -ēs and **ae** f mountain in Arcadia.

Cyllēnēus, -is, -ius adj see n.

Cyllēnius, -ī m Mercury.

cymba see **cumba**.

cymbalum, -ī nt cymbal.

cymbium, -ī and **iī** nt cup.

Cynicē adv like the Cynics.

Cynicus, -ī m a Cynic philosopher (esp Diogenes) ♦ adj Cynic.

cynocephalus, -ī m dog-headed ape.

Cynosūra, -ae f constellation of Ursa Minor.

Cynosūris, -idis adj see n.

Cynthia, -iae f Diana.

Cynthius, -ī m Apollo.

Cynthus, -ī m hill in Delos (birthplace of Apollo and Diana).

cyparissus, -ī f cypress.

Cypris, -idis f Venus.

Cyprius adj Cyprian; copper.

Cyprus, -ī f island of Cyprus (famed for its copper and the worship of Venus).

Cyrēnaeī, -aicī mpl followers of Aristippus.

Cyrēnaeus, -aicus, -ēnsis adj see n.

Cyrēnē, -ēs f, **-ae, -ārum** fpl town and province of N. Africa.

Cyrnēus adj Corsican.

Cyrus, -ī m Persian king.

Cytaeis, -idis f Medea.

Cythēra, -ae f island S. of Greece (famed for its worship of Venus).

Cytherēa, -ēae and **-ēia, -ēiae** and **-ēis, -ēidis** f Venus.

Cytherēus, Cythēriacus adj Cytherean; of Venus.

cytisus, -ī m/f cytisus (a kind of clover).

Cyzicēnus adj see **Cyzicum**.

Cyzicum, -ī nt, **-us, -os, -ī** f town on Sea of Marmora.

D, d

Dācī, -ōrum mpl Dacians, a people on the lower Danube.

Dācia, -iae f the country of the Dācī (now Romania).

Dācicus, -icī m gold coin of Domitian's reign.

dactylicus adj dactylic.

dactylus, -ī m dactyl.

Daedalēus adj see n.

daedalus adj artistic, skilful in creating; skilfully made, variegated.

Daedalus, -ī m mythical Athenian craftsman and inventor.

Dalmatae, -ārum mpl Dalmatians (a people on the East coast of the Adriatic).

Dalmatia, -iae f Dalmatia.

Dalmaticus adj see n.

dāma, -ae f deer; venison.

Damascēnus adj see n.

Damascus, -ī f Damascus.

damma f see **dama**.

damnātiō, -ōnis f condemnation.

damnātōrius adj condemnatory.

damnātus adj criminal; miserable.

damnificus adj pernicious.

Noun declensions and verb conjugations are shown on pp xiii to xxv. The present infinitive ending of a verb shows to which conjugation it belongs: **-āre** = 1st; **-ēre** = 2nd; **-ere** = 3rd and **-īre** = 4th. Irregular verbs are shown on p xxvi

damnō, -āre, -āvī, -ātum _vt_ to condemn, sentence; to procure the conviction of; (_heirs_) to oblige; to censure; **capitis/capite ~** condemn to death; **māiestātis, dē māiestāte ~** condemn for treason; **vōtī ~** oblige to fulfil a vow.

damnōsē _adv_ ruinously.

damnōsus _adj_ harmful, ruinous; spendthrift; wronged.

damnum, -ī _nt_ loss, harm, damage; (_law_) fine, damages; **~ facere** suffer loss.

Danaē, -ēs _f_ mother of Perseus.

Danaēius _adj see n._

Danaī, -ōrum _and_ **um** _mpl_ the Greeks.

Danaidēs, -idum _fpl_ daughters of Danaus.

Danaus, -ī _m_ king of Argos and father of 50 daughters.

Danaus _adj_ Greek.

danista, -ae _m_ moneylender.

danisticus _adj_ moneylending.

danō _see_ **dō.**

Dānuvius, -ī _m_ upper Danube.

Daphnē, -ēs _f_ nymph changed into a laurel tree.

Daphnis, -idis (_acc_ -im _and_ -in) _m_ mythical Sicilian shepherd.

dapinō, -āre _vt_ to serve (food).

daps, dapis _f_ religious feast; meal, banquet.

dapsilis _adj_ sumptuous, abundant.

Dardania, -iae _f_ Troy.

Dardanidēs, -idae _m_ Trojan (_esp Aeneas_).

Dardanus, -ī _m_ son of Jupiter and ancestor of Trojan kings.

Dardanus, -ius, -is, -idis _adj_ Trojan.

Darēus, -ī _m_ Persian king.

datārius _adj_ to give away.

datātim _adv_ passing from one to the other.

datiō, -ōnis _f_ right to give away; (_laws_) making.

datō, -āre _vt_ to be in the habit of giving.

dator, -ōris _m_ giver; (_sport_) bowler.

Daulias, -adis _adj see n._

Daulis, -dis _f_ town in central Greece (_noted for the story of Procne and Philomela_).

Daunias, -iadis _f_ Apulia.

Daunius _adj_ Rutulian; Italian.

Daunus, -ī _m_ legendary king of Apulia (_ancestor of Turnus_).

dē _prep_ (_with abl: movement_) down from, from; (_origin_) from, of, out of; (_time_) immediately after, in; (_thought, talk, action_) about, concerning; (_reason_) for, because of; (_imitation_) after, in accordance with; **~ industriā** on purpose; **~ integrō** afresh; **~ nocte** during the night; **diem ~ diē** from day to day.

dea, -ae _f_ goddess.

dealbō, -āre _vt_ to whitewash, plaster.

deambulātiō, -ōnis _f_ walk.

deambulō, -āre, -āvī, -ātum _vi_ to go for a walk.

deamō, -āre, -āvī, -ātum _vt_ to be in love with; to be much obliged to.

dearmātus _adj_ disarmed.

deartuō, -āre, -āvī, -ātum _vt_ to dismember, ruin.

deasciō, -āre _vt_ to smooth with an axe; (_fig_) to cheat.

dēbacchor, -ārī, -ātus _vi_ to rage furiously.

dēbellātor, -ōris _m_ conqueror.

dēbellō, -āre, -āvī, -ātum _vi_ to bring a war to an end **♦** _vt_ to subdue; to fight out.

dēbeō, -ēre, -uī, -itum _vt_ to owe; (_with inf_) to be bound, ought, should, must; to have to thank for, be indebted for; (_pass_) to be destined.

dēbilis _adj_ frail, weak, crippled.

dēbilitās, -ātis _f_ weakness, infirmity.

dēbilitātiō, -ōnis _f_ weakening.

dēbilitō, -āre, -āvī, -ātum _vt_ to cripple, disable; (_fig_) to paralyse, unnerve.

dēbitiō, -ōnis _f_ owing.

dēbitor, -ōris _m_ debtor.

dēbitum, -ī _nt_ debt.

dēblaterō, -āre _vt_ to blab.

dēcantō, -āre, -āvī, -ātum _vt_ to keep on repeating **♦** _vi_ to stop singing.

dēcēdō, -ēdere, -essī, -essum _vi_ to withdraw, depart; to retire from a province (_after term of office_); to abate, cease, die; (_rights_) to give up, forgo; (_fig_) to go wrong, swerve (from duty); **dē viā ~** get out of the way.

decem _num_ ten.

December, -ris _adj_ of December **♦** _m_ December.

decempeda, -ae _f_ ten-foot rule.

decempedātor, -ōris _m_ surveyor.

decemplex, -icis _adj_ tenfold.

decemprīmī, -ōrum _mpl_ civic chiefs of Italian towns.

decemscalmus _adj_ ten-oared.

decemvirālis _adj_ of the decemviri.

decemvirātus, -ūs _m_ office of decemvir.

decemvirī, -ōrum _and_ **um** _mpl_ commission of ten men (_for public or religious duties_).

decennis _adj_ ten years'.

decēns, -entis _adj_ seemly, proper; comely, handsome.

decenter _adv_ with propriety.

decentia, -ae _f_ comeliness.

dēceptus _ppp of_ **dēcipiō.**

dēcernō, -ernere, -rēvī, -rētum _vt_ to decide, determine; to decree; to fight it out, decide the issue.

dēcerpō, -ere, -sī, -tum _vt_ to pluck off, gather; (_fig_) to derive, enjoy.

dēcertātiō, -ōnis _f_ deciding the issue.

dēcertō, -āre, -āvī, -ātum _vi_ to fight it out, decide the issue.

dēcessiō, -ōnis _f_ departure; retirement (from a province); deduction, disappearance.

dēcessor, -ōris _m_ retiring magistrate.

dēcessus, -ūs _m_ retirement (from a province); death; (_tide_) ebbing.

decet, -ēre, -uit _vt, vi_ it becomes, suits; it is

dēcidō—dēdoleō

right, proper.

dēcidō, -ere, -ī *vi* to fall down, fall off; to die; (*fig*) to fail, come down.

dēcīdō, -dere, -dī, -sum *vt* to cut off; to settle, put an end to.

deciēns, deciēs *adv* ten times.

decimus, decumus *adj* tenth; **cum ~ō** tenfold; **~um** for the tenth time.

dēcipiō, -ipere, -ēpī, -eptum *vt* to ensnare; to deceive, beguile, disappoint.

dēcīsiō, -ōnis *f* settlement.

dēcīsus *ppp of* **dēcīdō**.

Decius, -ī *m* Roman plebeian name (*esp P Decius Mus, father and son, who devoted their lives in battle*).

Decius, -iānus *adj see n*.

dēclāmātiō, -ōnis *f* loud talking; rhetorical exercise on a given theme.

dēclāmātor, -ōris *m* apprentice in public speaking.

dēclāmātōrius *adj* rhetorical.

dēclāmitō, -āre *vi* to practise rhetoric; to bluster ♦ *vt* to practise pleading.

dēclāmō, -āre, -āvī, -ātum *vi* to practise public speaking, declaim; to bluster.

dēclārātiō, -ōnis *f* expression, making known.

dēclārō, -āre, -āvī, -ātum *vt* to make known; to proclaim, announce, reveal, express, demonstrate.

dēclīnātiō, -ōnis *f* swerving; avoidance; (*RHET*) digression; (*GRAM*) inflection.

dēclīnō, -āre, -āvī, -ātum *vt* to turn aside, deflect; (*eyes*) to close; to evade, shun ♦ *vi* to turn aside, swerve; to digress.

declive *nt* slope, decline.

dēclīvis *adj* sloping, steep, downhill.

dēclīvitās, -ātis *f* sloping ground.

dēcocta, -ae *f* a cold drink.

dēcoctor, -ōris *m* bankrupt.

dēcoctus *ppp of* **dēcoquō** ♦ *adj* (*style*) ripe, elaborated.

dēcōlō, -āre *vi* to run out; (*fig*) to fail.

dēcolor, -ōris *adj* discoloured, faded; **~ aetās** a degenerate age.

dēcolōrātiō, -ōnis *f* discolouring.

dēcolōrō, -āre, -āvī, -ātum *vt* to discolour, deface.

dēcoquō, -quere, -xī, -ctum *vt* to boil down; to cook ♦ *vi* to go bankrupt.

decor, -ōris *m* comeliness, ornament, beauty.

decōrē *adv* becomingly, beautifully.

decorō, -āre, -āvī, -ātum *vt* to adorn, embellish; (*fig*) to distinguish, honour.

decōrum, -ī *nt* propriety.

decōrus *adj* becoming, proper; beautiful, noble; adorned.

dēcrepitus *adj* decrepit.

dēcrēscō, -scere, -vī, -tum *vi* to decrease, wane, wear away; to disappear.

dēcrētum, -ī *nt* decree, resolution; (*PHILOS*) doctrine.

dēcrētus *ppp of* **dēcernō**.

dēcrēvī *perf of* **dēcernō**; *perf of* **dēcrēscō**.

decuma, -ae *f* tithe; provincial land tax; largess.

decumāna, -ae *f* wife of a tithe-collector.

decumānus *adj* paying tithes; (*MIL*) of the 10th cohort *or* legion ♦ *m* collector of tithes; **~ī, ~ōrum** *mpl* men of the 10th legion; **porta ~a** main gate of a Roman camp.

decumātēs, -ium *adj pl* subject to tithes.

decumbō, -mbere, -buī *vi* to lie down; to recline at table; to fall (in fight).

decumus *see* **decimus**.

decuria, -ae *f* group of ten; panel of judges; social club.

decuriātiō, -ōnis *f*, **decuriātus, -ūs** *m* dividing into decuriae.

decuriō, -āre, -āvī, -ātum *vt* to divide into decuriae *or* groups.

decuriō, -ōnis *m* head of a decuria; (*MIL*) cavalry officer; senator of a provincial town *or* colony.

dēcurrō, -rrere, -currī *and* **rrī, -rsum** *vt, vi* to run down, hurry, flow, sail down; to traverse; (*MIL*) to parade, charge; (*time*) to pass through; (*fig*) to have recourse to.

dēcursiō, -ōnis *f* military manoeuvre.

dēcursus *ppp of* **dēcurrō**.

dēcursus, -ūs *m* descent, downrush; (*MIL*) manoeuvre, attack; (*time*) career.

dēcurtātus *adj* mutilated.

decus, -oris *nt* ornament, glory, beauty; honour, virtue; (*pl*) heroic deeds.

dēcussō, -āre *vt* to divide crosswise.

dēcutiō, -tere, -ssī, -ssum *vt* to strike down, shake off.

dēdecet, -ēre, -uit *vt* it is unbecoming to, is a disgrace to.

dēdecorō, -āre *vt* to disgrace.

dēdecōrus *adj* dishonourable.

dēdecus, -oris *nt* disgrace, shame; vice, crime.

dedī *perf of* **dō**.

dēdicātiō, -ōnis *f* consecration.

dēdicō, -āre, -āvī, -ātum *vt* to consecrate, dedicate; to declare (property in a census return).

dēdidī *perf of* **dēdō**.

dēdignor, -ārī, -ātus *vt* to scorn, reject.

dēdiscō, -scere, -dicī *vt* to unlearn, forget.

dēditīcius, -ī *and* **iī** *m* one who has capitulated.

dēditiō, -ōnis *f* surrender, capitulation.

dēditus *ppp of* **dēdō** ♦ *adj* addicted, devoted; **~ā operā** intentionally.

dēdō, -ere, -idī, -itum *vt* to give up, yield, surrender; to devote.

dēdoceō, -ēre *vt* to teach not to.

dēdoleō, -ēre, -uī *vi* to cease grieving.

Noun declensions and verb conjugations are shown on pp xiii to xxv. The present infinitive ending of a verb shows to which conjugation it belongs: **-āre** = 1st; **-ēre** = 2nd; **-ere** = 3rd and **-īre** = 4th. Irregular verbs are shown on p xxvi

dēdūcō, -ūcere, -ūxī, -uctum _vt_ to bring down, lead away, deflect; (_MIL_) to lead, withdraw; (_bride_) to bring home; (_colony_) to settle; (_hair_) to comb out; (_important person_) to escort; (_law_) to evict, bring to trial; (_money_) to subtract; (_sail_) to unfurl; (_ship_) to launch; (_thread_) to spin out; (_writing_) to compose; (_fig_) to bring, reduce, divert, derive.

dēductiō, -ōnis _f_ leading off; settling a colony; reduction; eviction; inference.

dēductor, -ōris _m_ escort.

dēductus _ppp of_ **dēdūcō** ♦ _adj_ finely spun.

deerrō, -āre, -āvī, -ātum _vi_ to go astray.

deesse _infin of_ **dēsum**.

dēfaecō, -āre, -āvī, -ātum _vt_ to clean; (_fig_) to make clear, set at ease.

dēfatīgātiō, -ōnis _f_ tiring out; weariness.

dēfatīgō, -āre, -āvī, -ātum _vt_ to tire out, exhaust.

dēfatīscor _etc see_ **dēfetīscor**.

dēfectiō, -ōnis _f_ desertion; failure, faintness; (_ASTRO_) eclipse.

dēfector, -ōris _m_ deserter, rebel.

dēfectus _ppp of_ **dēficiō** ♦ _adj_ weak, failing.

dēfectus, -ūs _m_ failure; eclipse.

dēfendō, -dere, -dī, -sum _vt_ to avert, repel; to defend, protect; (_law_) to speak in defence, urge, maintain; (_THEATRE_) to play (a part); **crīmen ~** answer an accusation.

dēfēnsiō, -ōnis _f_ defence, speech in defence.

dēfēnsitō, -āre _vt_ to defend often.

dēfēnsō, -āre _vt_ to defend.

dēfēnsor, -ōris _m_ averter; defender, protector, guard.

dēferō, -ferre, -tulī, -lātum _vt_ to bring down, bring, carry; to bear away; (_power, honour_) to offer, confer; (_information_) to report; (_law_) to inform against, indict; to recommend (for public services); **ad cōnsilium ~** take into consideration.

dēfervēscō, -vēscere, -vī _and_ **buī** _vi_ to cool down, calm down.

dēfessus _adj_ tired, exhausted.

dēfetīgō _etc see_ **dēfatīgō**.

dēfetīscor, -tīscī, -ssus _vi_ to grow weary.

dēficiō, -icere, -ēcī, -ectum _vt, vi_ to desert, forsake, fail; to be lacking, run short, cease; (_ASTRO_) to be eclipsed; **animō ~** lose heart.

dēfīgō, -gere, -xī, -xum _vt_ to fix firmly; to drive in, thrust; (_eyes, mind_) to concentrate; (_fig_) to stupefy, astound; (_magic_) to bewitch.

dēfingō, -ere _vt_ to make, portray.

dēfīniō, -īre, -īvī, -ītum _vt_ to mark the limit of, limit; to define, prescribe; to restrict; to terminate.

dēfīnītē _adv_ precisely.

dēfīnītiō, -ōnis _f_ limiting, prescribing, definition.

dēfīnītīvus _adj_ explanatory.

dēfīnītus _adj_ precise.

dēfīō, -ierī _vi_ to fail.

dēflagrātiō, -ōnis _f_ conflagration.

dēflagrō, -āre, -āvī, -ātum _vi_ to be burned down, perish; to cool down, abate ♦ _vt_ to burn down.

dēflectō, -ctere, -xī, -xum _vt_ to bend down, turn aside; (_fig_) to pervert ♦ _vi_ to turn aside, deviate.

dēfleō, -ēre, -ēvī, -ētum _vt_ to lament bitterly, bewail ♦ _vi_ to weep bitterly.

dēflexus _ppp of_ **dēflectō**.

dēflōrēscō, -ēscere, -uī _vi_ to shed blooms; (_fig_) to fade.

dēfluō, -ere, -xī, -xum _vi_ to flow down, float down; to fall, drop, droop; (_fig_) to come from, be derived; to flow past; (_fig_) to pass away, fail.

dēfodiō, -odere, -ōdī, -ossum _vt_ to dig, dig out; to bury; (_fig_) to hide away.

dēfore _fut infin of_ **dēsum**.

dēfōrmis _adj_ misshapen, disfigured, ugly; shapeless; (_fig_) disgraceful, disgusting.

dēfōrmitās, -ātis _f_ deformity, hideousness; baseness.

dēfōrmō, -āre, -āvī, -ātum _vt_ to form, sketch; to deform, disfigure; to describe; to mar, disgrace.

dēfossus _ppp of_ **dēfodiō**.

dēfraudō, -āre _vt_ to cheat, defraud; **genium ~** deny oneself.

dēfrēnātus _adj_ unbridled.

dēfricō, -āre, -uī, -ātum _and_ **tum** _vt_ to rub down; (_fig_) to satirize.

dēfringō, -ingere, -ēgī, -āctum _vt_ to break off, break down.

dēfrūdō _etc see_ **dēfraudō**.

dēfrutum, -ī _nt_ new wine boiled down.

dēfugiō, -ugere, -ūgī _vt_ to run away from, shirk ♦ _vi_ to flee.

dēfuī _perf of_ **dēsum**.

dēfūnctus _ppa of_ **dēfungor** ♦ _adj_ discharged; dead.

dēfundō, -undere, -ūdī, -ūsum _vt_ to pour out.

dēfungor, -ungī, -ūnctus _vi_ (_with abl_) to discharge, have done with; to die.

dēfutūrus _fut p of_ **dēsum**.

dēgener, -is _adj_ degenerate, unworthy, base.

dēgenerātum, -ātī _nt_ degenerate character.

dēgenerō, -āre, -āvī, -ātum _vi_ to degenerate, deteriorate ♦ _vt_ to disgrace.

dēgerō, -ere _vt_ to carry off.

dēgō, -ere, -ī _vt_ (_time_) to pass, spend; (_war_) wage ♦ _vi_ to live.

dēgrandinat it is hailing heavily.

dēgravō, -āre _vt_ to weigh down, overpower.

dēgredior, -dī, -ssus _vi_ to march down, descend, dismount.

dēgrunniō, -īre _vi_ to grunt hard.

dēgustō, -āre _vt_ to taste, touch; (_fig_) to try, experience.

dehinc _adv_ from here; from now, henceforth; then, next.

dehīscō, -ere _vi_ to gape, yawn.

dehonestāmentum, -ī _nt_ disfigurement.

dehonestō, -āre *vt* to disgrace.
dehortor, -ārī, -ātus *vt* to dissuade, discourage.
Dēianīra, -ae *f wife of Hercules.*
dēiciō, -icere, -iēcī, -iectum *vt* to throw down, hurl, fell; to overthrow, kill; (*eyes*) to lower, avert; (*law*) to evict; (*MIL*) to dislodge; (*ship*) to drive off its course; (*hopes, honours*) to foil, disappoint.
dēiectiō, -ōnis *f* eviction.
dēiectus *ppp of* **dēiciō** ♦ *adj* low-lying; disheartened.
dēiectus, -ūs *m* felling; steep slope.
dēierō, -āre, -āvī, -ātum *vi* to swear solemnly.
dein *etc see* **deinde.**
deinceps *adv* successively, in order.
deinde, dein *adv* from there, next; then, thereafter; next in order.
Dēiotarus, -ī *m* king of Galatia (*defended by Cicero*).
Dēiphobus, -ī *m* son of Priam (*second husband of Helen*).
dēiungō, -ere *vt* to sever.
dēiuvō, -āre *vt* to fail to help.
dej- *etc see* **dei-.**
dēlābor, -bī, -psus *vi* to fall down, fly down, sink; (*fig*) to come down, fall into.
dēlacerō, -āre *vt* to tear to pieces.
dēlāmentor, -ārī *vt* to mourn bitterly for.
dēlāpsus *ppa of* **dēlābor.**
dēlassō, -āre *vt* to tire out.
dēlātiō, -ōnis *f* accusing, informing.
dēlātor, -ōris *m* informer, denouncer.
dēlectābilis *adj* enjoyable.
dēlectāmentum, -ī *nt* amusement.
dēlectātiō, -ōnis *f* delight.
dēlectō, -āre *vt* to charm, delight, amuse.
dēlēctus *ppp of* **dēligō.**
dēlēctus, -ūs *m* choice; *see also* **dīlēctus.**
dēlēgātiō, -ōnis *f* assignment.
dēlēgī *perf of* **dēligō.**
dēlēgō, -āre, -āvī, -ātum *vt* to assign, transfer, make over; to ascribe.
dēlēnificus *adj* charming.
dēlēnīmentum, -ī *nt* solace, allurement.
dēlēniō, -īre, -īvī, -ītum *vt* to soothe, solace; to seduce, win over.
dēlēnītor, -ōris *m* cajoler.
dēleō, -ēre, -ēvī, -ētum *vt* to destroy, annihilate; to efface, blot out.
Dēlia, -ae *f* Diana.
Dēliacus *adj* of Delos.
dēlīberābundus *adj* deliberating.
dēlīberātiō, -ōnis *f* deliberating, consideration.
dēlīberātīvus *adj* deliberative.
dēlīberātor, -ōris *m* consulter.
dēlīberātus *adj* determined.
dēlīberō, -āre, -āvī, -ātum *vt, vi* to consider,

deliberate, consult; to resolve, determine; **~ārī potest** it is in doubt.
dēlībō, -āre, -āvī, -ātum *vt* to taste, sip; to pick, gather; to detract from, mar.
dēlibrō, -āre *vt* to strip the bark off.
dēlibuō, -uere, -uī, -ūtum *vt* to smear, steep.
dēlicātē *adv* luxuriously.
dēlicātus *adj* delightful; tender, soft; voluptuous, spoiled, effeminate; fastidious.
dēliciae, -ārum *fpl* delight, pleasure; whimsicalities, sport; (*person*) sweetheart, darling.
dēliciolae, -ārum *fpl* darling.
dēlicium, -ī *and* **iī** *nt* favourite.
dēlicō, -āre *vt* to explain.
dēlictum, -ī *nt* offence, wrong.
dēlicuus *adj* lacking.
dēligō, -igere, -ēgī, -ēctum *vt* to select, gather; to set aside.
dēligō, -āre, -āvī, -ātum *vt* to tie up, make fast.
dēlingō, -ere *vt* to have a lick of.
dēlīnī- *etc see* **dēlēnī-.**
dēlinquō, -inquere, -īquī, -ictum *vi* to fail, offend, do wrong.
dēliquēscō, -quēscere, -cuī *vi* to melt away; (*fig*) to pine away.
dēliquiō, -ōnis *f* lack.
dēlīrāmentum, -ī *nt* nonsense.
dēlīrātiō, -ōnis *f* dotage.
dēlīrō, -āre *vi* to be crazy, drivel.
dēlīrus *adj* crazy.
dēlitēscō, -ēscere, -uī *vi* to hide away, lurk; (*fig*) to skulk, take shelter under.
dēlītigō, -āre *vi* to scold.
Dēlius, -iacus *adj see n.*
Delmatae *see* **Dalmatae.**
Dēlos, -ī *f* sacred Aegean island (*birthplace of Apollo and Diana*).
Delphī, -ōrum *mpl* town in central Greece (*famous for its oracle of Apollo*); the Delphians.
Delphicus *adj see n.*
delphīnus, -ī *and* **delphīn, -is** *m* dolphin.
Deltōton, -ī *nt* (*constellation*) Triangulum.
dēlubrum, -ī *nt* sanctuary, temple.
dēluctō, -āre, -or, -ārī *vi* to wrestle.
dēlūdificō, -āre *vt* to make fun of.
dēlūdō, -dere, -sī, -sum *vt* to dupe, delude.
dēlumbis *adj* feeble.
dēlumbō, -āre *vt* to enervate.
dēmadēscō, -ēscere, -uī *vi* to be drenched.
dēmandō, -āre *vt* to entrust, commit.
dēmarchus, -ī *m* demarch (*chief of a village in Attica*).
dēmēns, -entis *adj* mad, foolish.
dēmēnsum, -ī *nt* ration.
dēmēnsus *ppa of* **dēmētior.**
dēmenter *adv see* **dēmēns.**
dēmentia, -ae *f* madness, folly.
dēmentiō, -īre *vi* to rave.

dēmereō, -ēre, -uī, -itum, -eor, -ērī vt to earn, deserve; to do a service to.

dēmergō, -gere, -sī, -sum vt to submerge, plunge, sink; (fig) to overwhelm.

dēmessus ppp of **dēmetō**.

dēmētior, -tīrī, -nsus vt to measure out.

dēmetō, -tere, -ssuī, -ssum vt to reap, harvest; to cut off.

dēmigrātiō, -ōnis f emigration.

dēmigrō, -āre vi to move, emigrate.

dēminuō, -uere, -uī, -ūtum vt to make smaller, lessen, detract from; **capite ~** deprive of citizenship.

dēminūtiō, -ōnis f decrease, lessening; (law) right to transfer property; **capitis ~** loss of political rights.

dēmīror, -ārī, -ātus vt to marvel at, wonder.

dēmissē adv modestly, meanly.

dēmissīcius adj flowing.

dēmissiō, -ōnis f letting down; (fig) dejection.

dēmissus ppp of **dēmittō ♦** adj low-lying; drooping; humble, unassuming; dejected; (origin) descended.

dēmītigō, -āre vt to make milder.

dēmittō, -ittere, -īsī, -issum vt to let down, lower, sink; to send down, plunge; (beard) to grow; (ship) to bring to land; (troops) to move down; (fig) to cast down, dishearten, reduce, impress; **sē ~** stoop; descend; be disheartened.

dēmiūrgus, -ī m chief magistrate in a Greek state.

dēmō, -ere, -psī, -ptum vt to take away, subtract.

Dēmocriticus, -ius, -ēus adj see n.

Dēmocritus, -ī m Greek philosopher (author of the atomic theory).

dēmōlior, -īrī vt to pull down, destroy.

dēmōlītiō, -ōnis f pulling down.

dēmōnstrātiō, -ōnis f pointing out, explanation.

dēmōnstrātīvus adj (RHET) for display.

dēmōnstrātor, -ōris m indicator.

dēmōnstrō, -āre, -āvī, -ātum vt to point out; to explain, represent, prove.

dēmorior, -ī, -tuus vi to die, pass away ♦ vt to be in love with.

dēmoror, -ārī, -ātus vi to wait ♦ vt to detain, delay.

dēmortuus ppa of **dēmorior**.

Dēmosthenēs, -is m greatest Athenian orator.

dēmoveō, -ovēre, -ōvī, -ōtum vt to remove, turn aside, dislodge.

dēmpsī perf of **dēmō**.

dēmptus ppp of **dēmō**.

dēmūgītus adj filled with lowing.

dēmulceō, -cēre, -sī vt to stroke.

dēmum adv (time) at last, not till; (emphasis) just, precisely; **ibi ~** just there; **modo ~** only now; **nunc ~** now at last; **post ~** not till after; **tum ~** only then.

dēmurmurō, -āre vt to mumble through.

dēmūtātiō, -ōnis f change.

dēmūtō, -āre vt to change, make worse ♦ vi to change one's mind.

dēnārius, -ī and iī m Roman silver coin.

dēnārrō, -āre vt to relate fully.

dēnāsō, -āre vt to take the nose off.

dēnatō, -āre vi to swim down.

dēnegō, -āre, -āvī, ātum vt to deny, refuse, reject ♦ vi to say no.

dēnī, -ōrum adj ten each, in tens; ten; tenth.

dēnicālis adj for purifying after a death.

dēnique adv at last, finally; (enumerating) lastly, next; (summing up) in short, briefly; (emphasis) just, precisely.

dēnōminō, -āre vt to designate.

dēnōrmō, -āre vt to make irregular.

dēnotō, -āre, -āvī, -ātum vt to point out, specify; to observe.

dēns, dentis m tooth; ivory; prong, fluke.

dēnsē adv repeatedly.

dēnsō, -āre, -āvī, -ātum, dēnseō, -ēre vt to thicken; (ranks) to close.

dēnsus adj thick, dense, close; frequent; (style) concise.

dentālia, -ium ntpl ploughbeam.

dentātus adj toothed; (paper) polished.

dentiō, -īre vi to cut one's teeth; (teeth) to grow.

dēnūbō, -bere, -psī, -ptum vi to marry, marry beneath one.

dēnūdō, -āre, -āvī, -ātum vt to bare, strip; (fig) to disclose.

dēnūntiātiō, -ōnis f intimation, warning.

dēnūntiō, -āre, -āvī, -ātum vt to intimate, give notice of, declare; to threaten, warn; (law) to summon as witness.

dēnuō adv afresh, again, once more.

deonerō, -āre vt to unload.

deorsum, deorsus adv downwards.

deōsculor, -ārī vt to kiss warmly.

dēpaciscor etc see **dēpeciscor**.

dēpāctus adj driven in firmly.

dēpāscō, -scere, -vī, -stum, -scor, -scī vt to feed on, eat up; (fig) to devour, destroy, prune away.

dēpeciscor, -īscī, -tus vt to bargain for, agree about.

dēpectō, -ctere, -xum vt to comb; (comedy) to flog.

dēpectus ppa of **dēpeciscor**.

dēpeculātor, -ōris m embezzler.

dēpeculor, -ārī, -ātus vt to plunder.

dēpellō, -ellere, -ulī, -ulsum vt to expel, remove, cast down; (MIL) to dislodge; (infants) to wean; (fig) to deter, avert.

dēpendeō, -ēre vi to hang down, hang from; to depend on; to be derived.

dēpendō, -endere, -endī, -ēnsum vt to weigh, pay up.

dēperdō, -ere, -idī, -itum vt to lose completely, destroy, ruin.

dēpereō, -īre, -iī vi to perish, be completely destroyed; to be undone ♦ vt to be hopelessly in love with.

dēpexus *ppp of* **dēpectō.**

dēpingō, -ingere, -inxī, -ictum *vt* to paint; (*fig*) to portray, describe.

dēplangō, -gere, -xī *vt* to bewail frantically.

dēplexus *adj* grasping.

dēplōrābundus *adj* weeping bitterly.

dēplōrō, -āre, -āvī, -ātum *vi* to weep bitterly ♦ *vt* to bewail bitterly, mourn; to despair of.

dēpluit, -ere *vi* to rain down.

dēpōnō, -ōnere, -osuī, -ositum *vt* to lay down; to set aside, put away, get rid of; to wager; to deposit, entrust, commit to the care of; (*fig*) to give up.

dēpopulātiō, -ōnis *f* ravaging.

dēpopulātor, -ōris *m* marauder.

dēpopulor, -ārī, -ātus; -ō, -āre *vt* to ravage, devastate; (*fig*) to waste, destroy.

dēportō, -āre, -āvī, -ātum *vt* to carry down, carry off; to bring home (from a province); (*law*) to banish for life; (*fig*) to win.

dēposcō, -scere, -poscī *vt* to demand, require, claim.

dēpositum, -ī *nt* trust, deposit.

dēpositus *ppp of* **dēpōnō** ♦ *adj* dying, dead, despaired of.

dēprāvātē *adv* perversely.

dēprāvātiō, -ōnis *f* distorting.

dēprāvō, -āre, -āvī, -ātum *vt* to distort; (*fig*) to pervert, corrupt.

dēprecābundus *adj* imploring.

dēprecātiō, -ōnis *f* averting by prayer; imprecation, invocation; plea for indulgence.

dēprecātor, -ōris *m* intercessor.

dēprecor, -ārī, -ātus *vt* to avert (by prayer); to deprecate, intercede for.

dēprehendō, dēprendō, -endere, -endī, -ēnsum *vt* to catch, intercept; to overtake, surprise; to catch in the act, detect; (*fig*) to perceive, discover.

dēprehēnsiō, -ōnis *f* detection.

dēprehēnsus, dēprēnsus *ppp of* **dēprehendō.**

dēpressī *perf of* **dēprimō.**

dēpressus *ppp of* **dēprimō** ♦ *adj* low.

dēprimō, -imere, -essī, -essum *vt* to press down, weigh down; to dig deep; (*ship*) to sink; (*fig*) to suppress, keep down.

dēproelior, -ārī *vi* to fight it out.

dēprōmō, -ere, psī, -ptum *vt* to fetch, bring out, produce.

dēproperō, -āre *vi* to hurry up ♦ *vt* to hurry and make.

depsō, -ere *vt* to knead.

dēpudet, -ēre, -uit *v impers* not to be ashamed.

dēpūgis *adj* thin-buttocked.

dēpugnō, -āre, -āvī, -ātum *vi* to fight it out, fight hard.

dēpulī *perf of* **dēpellō.**

dēpulsiō, -ōnis *f* averting; defence.

dēpulsō, -āre *vt* to push out of the way.

dēpulsor, -ōris *m* repeller.

dēpulsus *ppp of* **dēpellō.**

dēpūrgō, -āre *vt* to clean.

dēputō, -āre *vt* to prune; to consider, reckon.

dēpygis *etc see* **dēpūgis.**

dēque *adv* down.

dērēctā, -ē, -ō *adv* straight.

dērēctus *ppp of* **dērigō** ♦ *adj* straight, upright, at right angles; straightforward.

dērelictiō, -ōnis *f* disregarding.

dērelinquō, -inquere, -īquī, -ictum *vt* to abandon, forsake.

dērepente *adv* suddenly.

dērēpō, -ere *vi* to creep down.

dēreptus *ppp of* **dēripiō.**

dērīdeō, -dēre, -sī, -sum *vt* to laugh at, deride.

dērīdiculum, -ī *nt* mockery, absurdity; object of derision.

dērīdiculus *adj* laughable.

dērigēscō, -ēscere, -uī *vi* to stiffen, curdle.

dērigō, -igere, -ēxī, -ēctum *vt* to turn, aim, direct; (*fig*) to regulate.

dēripiō, -ipere, -ipuī, -eptum *vt* to tear off, pull down.

dērīsor, -ōris *m* scoffer.

dērīsus *ppp of* **dērīdeō.**

dērīsus, -ūs *m* scorn, derision.

dērīvātiō, -ōnis *f* diverting.

dērīvō, -āre, -āvī, -ātum *vt* to lead off, draw off.

dērogō, -āre *vt* (*law*) to propose to amend; (*fig*) to detract from.

dērōsus *adj* gnawed away.

dēruncinō, -āre *vt* to plane off; (*comedy*) to cheat.

dēruō, -ere, -ī *vt* to demolish.

dēruptus *adj* steep ♦ *ntpl* precipice.

dēsaeviō, -īre *vi* to rage furiously; to cease raging.

dēscendō, -endere, -endī, -ēnsum *vi* to come down, go down, descend, dismount; (*MIL*) to march down; (*things*) to fall, sink, penetrate; (*fig*) to stoop (to), lower oneself.

dēscēnsiō, -ōnis *f* going down.

dēscēnsus, -ūs *m* way down.

dēscīscō, -īscere, -īvī *and* **iī, -ītum** *vi* to desert, revolt; to deviate, part company.

dēscrībō, -bere, -psī, -ptum *vt* to copy out; to draw, sketch; to describe; *see also* **dīscrībō.**

dēscrīptiō, -ōnis *f* copy; drawing, diagram; description.

dēscrīptus *ppp of* **dēscrībō;** *see also* **dīscrīptus.**

dēsecō, -āre, -uī, -tum *vt* to cut off.

dēserō, -ere, -uī, -tum *vt* to desert, abandon, forsake; (*bail*) to forfeit.

dēsertor, -ōris *m* deserter.

dēsertus *ppp of* **dēserō** ♦ *adj* desert,

Noun declensions and verb conjugations are shown on pp xiii to xxv. The present infinitive ending of a verb shows to which conjugation it belongs: **-āre** = 1st; **-ēre** = 2nd; **-ere** = 3rd and **-īre** = 4th. Irregular verbs are shown on p xxvi

uninhabited ♦ *ntpl* deserts.

dēserviō, -īre *vi* to be a slave (to), serve.

dēses, -idis *adj* idle, inactive.

dēsiccō, -āre *vt* to dry, drain.

dēsideō, -idēre, -ēdī *vi* to sit idle.

dēsīderābilis *adj* desirable.

dēsīderātiō, -ōnis *f* missing.

dēsīderium, -ī *and* **iī** *nt* longing, sense of loss; want; petition; **mē ~ tenet urbis** I miss Rome.

dēsīderō, -āre, -āvī, -ātum *vt* to feel the want of, miss; to long for, desire; (*casualties*) to lose.

dēsidia, -ae *f* idleness, apathy.

dēsidiōsē *adv* idly.

dēsidiōsus *adj* lazy, idle; relaxing.

dēsīdō, -īdere, -ēdī *vi* to sink, settle down; (*fig*) to deteriorate.

dēsignātiō, -ōnis *f* specifying; election (of magistrates).

dēsignātor *etc see* **dissignātor**.

dēsignātus *adj* elect.

dēsignō, -āre, -āvī, -ātum *vt* to trace out; to indicate, define; (*POL*) to elect; (*art*) to depict.

dēsiī *perf of* **dēsinō**.

dēsiliō, -ilīre, -iluī, -ultum *vi* to jump down, alight.

dēsinō, -nere, -ī *vt* to leave off, abandon ♦ *vi* to stop, desist; to end (in).

dēsipiēns, -ientis *adj* silly.

dēsipientia, -ae *f* folly.

dēsipiō, -ere *vi* to be stupid, play the fool.

dēsistō, -istere, -titī, -titum *vi* to stop, leave off, desist.

dēsitus *ppp of* **dēsinō**.

dēsōlō, -āre, -āvī, -ātum *vt* to leave desolate, abandon.

dēspectō, -āre *vt* to look down on, command a view of; to despise.

dēspectus *ppp of* **dēspiciō** ♦ *adj* contemptible.

dēspectus, -ūs *m* view, prospect.

dēspēranter *adv* despairingly.

dēspērātiō, -ōnis *f* despair.

dēspērātus *adj* despaired of, hopeless; desperate, reckless.

dēspērō, -āre, -āvī, -ātum *vt, vi* to despair, give up hope of.

dēspexī *perf of* **dēspiciō**.

dēspicātiō, -ōnis *f* contempt.

dēspicātus *adj* despised, contemptible.

dēspicātus, -ūs *m* contempt.

dēspicientia, -ae *f* contempt.

dēspiciō, -icere, -exī, -ectum *vt* to look down on; to despise ♦ *vi* to look down.

dēspoliātor, -ōris *m* robber.

dēspoliō, -āre *vt* to rob, plunder.

dēspondeō, -ondēre, -ondī *and* **opondī, -ōnsum** *vt* to pledge, promise; to betroth; to devote; to give up, despair of; **animum ~** despair.

dēspūmō, -āre *vt* to skim off.

dēspuō, -ere *vi* to spit on the ground ♦ *vt* to reject.

dēsquāmō, -āre *vt* to scale, peel.

dēstillō, -āre *vi* to drop down ♦ *vt* to distil.

dēstimulō, -āre *vt* to run through.

dēstinātiō, -ōnis *f* resolution, appointment.

dēstinātus *adj* fixed, decided.

dēstinō, -āre, -āvī, -ātum *vt* to make fast; to appoint, determine, resolve; (*archery*) to aim at; (*fig*) to intend to buy ♦ *nt* mark; intention; **~ātum est mihi** I have decided.

dēstitī *perf of* **dēstistō**.

dēstituō, -uere, -uī, -ūtum *vt* to set apart, place; to forsake, leave in the lurch.

dēstitūtiō, -ōnis *f* defaulting.

dēstitūtus *ppp of* **dēstituō**.

dēstrictus *ppp of* **dēstringō** ♦ *adj* severe.

dēstringō, -ingere, -inxī, -ictum *vt* (*leaves*) to strip; (*body*) to rub down; (*sword*) to draw; to graze, skim; (*fig*) to censure.

dēstruō, -ere, -xī, -ctum *vt* to demolish; to destroy.

dēsubitō *adv* all of a sudden.

dēsūdāscō, -ere *vi* to sweat all over.

dēsūdō, -āre *vi* to exert oneself.

dēsuēfactus *adj* unaccustomed.

dēsuētūdō, -inis *f* disuse.

dēsuētus *adj* unaccustomed, unused.

dēsultor, -ōris *m* circus rider; (*fig*) fickle lover.

dēsultūra, -ae *f* jumping down.

dēsum, deesse, -fuī *vi* to be missing, fail, fail in one's duty.

dēsūmō, -ere, -psī, -ptum *vt* to select.

dēsuper *adv* from above.

dēsurgō, -ere *vi* to rise.

dētegō, -egere, -exī, -ectum *vt* to uncover, disclose; (*fig*) to reveal, detect.

dētendō, -endere, -ēnsum *vt* (*tent*) to strike.

dētentus *ppp of* **dētineō**.

dētergeō, -gere, -sī, -sum *vt* to wipe away, clear away; to clean; to break off.

dēterior, -ōris *adj* lower; inferior, worse.

dēterius *adv* worse.

dēterminātiō, -ōnis *f* boundary, end.

dēterminō, -āre, -āvī, -ātum *vt* to bound, limit; to settle.

dēterō, -erere, -rīvī, -rītum *vt* to rub, wear away; (*style*) to polish; (*fig*) to weaken.

dēterreō, -ēre, -uī, -itum *vt* to frighten away; to deter, discourage, prevent.

dētersus *ppp of* **dētergeō**.

dētestābilis *adj* abominable.

dētestātiō, -ōnis *f* execration, curse; averting.

dētestor, -ārī, -ātus *vt* to invoke, invoke against; to curse, execrate; to avert, deprecate.

dētexō, -ere, -uī, -tum *vt* to weave, finish weaving; (*comedy*) to steal; (*fig*) to describe.

dētineō, -inēre, -inuī, -entum *vt* to hold back, detain; to keep occupied.

dētondeō, -ondēre, -ondī, -ōnsum *vt* to shear off, strip.

dētonō, -āre, -uī *vi* to cease thundering.

dētorqueō, -quēre, -sī, -tum *vt* to turn aside,

direct; to distort, misrepresent.
dētractātiō, -ōnis f declining.
dētrectātor, -ōris m disparager.
dētractiō, -ōnis f removal, departure.
dētractō etc see **dētrectō**.
dētractus ppp of **dētrahō**.
dētrahō, -here, -xī, -ctum vt to draw off,
take away, pull down; to withdraw, force to
leave; to detract, disparage.
dētrectō, -āre, -āvī, -ātum vt to decline,
shirk; to detract from, disparage.
dētrīmentōsus adj harmful.
dētrīmentum, -ī nt loss, harm; (MIL) defeat; ~
capere suffer harm.
dētrītus ppp of **dēterō**.
dētrūdō, -dere, -sī, -sum vt to push down,
thrust away; to dislodge, evict; to postpone;
(fig) to force.
dētruncō, -āre, -āvī, -ātum vt to cut off,
behead, mutilate.
dētrūsus ppp of **dētrūdō**.
dēturbō, -āre, -āvī, -ātum vt to dash down,
pull down; (fig) to cast down, deprive.
Deucaliōn, -ōnis m son of Prometheus
(survivor of the Flood).
Deucaliōnēus adj see **Deucaliōn**.
deūnx, -cis m eleven twelfths.
deūrō, -rere, -ssī, -stum vt to burn up; to
frost.
deus, -ī (voc deus, pl dī, deos, deum, dis) m
god; **dī meliōra!** Heaven forbid!; **dī tē ament!**
bless you!
deūstus ppp of **deūrō**.
deūtor, -ī vi to maltreat.
dēvastō, -āre vt to lay waste.
dēvehō, -here, -xī, -ctum vt to carry down,
convey; (pass) to ride down, sail down.
dēvellō, -ellere, -ellī and **olsī, -ulsum** vt to
pluck, pull out.
dēvēlō, -āre vt to unveil.
dēveneror, -ārī vt to worship; to avert by
prayers.
dēveniō, -enīre, -ēnī, -entum vi to come,
reach, fall into.
dēverberō, -āre, -āvī, -ātum vt to thrash
soundly.
dēversor, -ārī vi to lodge, stay (as guest).
dēversor, -ōris m guest.
dēversōriolum, -ī nt small lodging.
dēversōrium, -ī and **iī** nt inn, lodging.
dēversōrius adj for lodging.
dēverticulum, -ī nt by-road, by-pass;
digression; lodging place; (fig) refuge.
dēvertō, -tere, -tī, -sum vi to turn aside, put
up; to have recourse to; to digress.
dēvertor, -tī, versus vi see **dēvertō**.
dēvexus adj sloping, going down, steep.
dēvinciō, -cīre, -xī, -ctum vt to tie up; (fig) to
bind, lay under an obligation.
dēvincō, -incere, -īcī, -ictum vt to defeat

completely, win the day.
dēvītātiō, -ōnis f avoiding.
dēvītō, -āre vt to avoid.
dēvius adj out of the way, devious; (person)
solitary, wandering off the beaten track;
(fig) inconstant.
dēvocō, -āre, -āvī, -ātum vt to call down,
fetch; to entice away.
dēvolō, -āre vi to fly down.
dēvolvō, -vere, -vī, -ūtum vt to roll down,
fall; (wool) to spin off.
dēvorō, -āre, -āvī, -ātum vt to swallow, gulp
down; to engulf, devour; (money) to
squander; (tears) to repress; (trouble) to
endure patiently.
dēvors-, dēvort- see **dēvers-, dēvert-**.
dēvortia, -ōrum ntpl byways.
dēvōtiō, -ōnis f devoting; (magic) spell.
dēvōtō, -āre vt to bewitch.
dēvōtus ppp of **dēvoveō** ♦ adj faithful;
accursed.
dēvoveō, -ovēre, -ōvī, -ōtum vt to devote,
vow, dedicate; to give up; to curse; to
bewitch.
dēvulsus ppp of **dēvellō**.
dextella, -ae f little right hand.
dexter, -erī and **rī** adj right, right-hand; handy,
skilful; favourable.
dexteritās, -ātis f adroitness.
dextra f right hand, right-hand side; hand;
pledge of friendship.
dextrā prep (with acc) on the right of.
dextrē (compar **-erius**) adv adroitly.
dextrōrsus, -rsus, -vorsum adv to the right.
dī pl of **deus**.
diabathrārius, -ī and **iī** m slipper maker.
diabolus, -ī m devil.
diāconus, -ī m (ECCL) deacon.
diadēma, -tis nt royal headband, diadem.
diaeta, -ae f diet; living room.
dialectica, -ae, -ē, -ēs f dialectic, logic ♦ ntpl
logical questions.
dialecticē adv dialectically.
dialecticus adj dialectical ♦ m logician.
Diālis adj of Jupiter ♦ m high priest of Jupiter.
dialogus, -ī m dialogue, conversation.
Diāna, -ae f virgin goddess of hunting (also
identified with the moon and Hecate, and
patroness of childbirth).
Diānius adj of Diana ♦ nt sanctuary of Diana.
diāria, -ōrum ntpl daily allowance of food or
pay.
dibaphus, -ī f Roman state robe.
dica, -ae f lawsuit.
dicācitās, -ātis f raillery, repartee.
dicāculus adj pert.
dicātiō, -ōnis f declaration of citizenship.
dicāx, -ācis adj witty, smart.
dichorēus, -ī m double trochee.
diciō, -ōnis f power, sway, authority.

Noun declensions and verb conjugations are shown on pp xiii to xxv. The present infinitive ending of a verb shows
to which conjugation it belongs: **-āre** = 1st; **-ēre** = 2nd; **-ere** = 3rd and **-īre** = 4th. Irregular verbs are shown on p xxvi

dicis causā for the sake of appearance.
dicō, -āre, -āvī, -ātum *vt* to dedicate, consecrate; to deify; to devote, give over.
dīcō, -cere, -xī, dictum *vt* to say, tell; to mention, mean, call, name; to pronounce; (*RHET*) to speak, deliver; (*law*) to plead; (*poetry*) to describe, celebrate; (*official*) to appoint; (*time, place*) to settle, fix ♦ *vi* to speak (in public); **causam ~** plead; **iūs ~** deliver judgment; **sententiam ~** vote; **~cō** namely; **~xī** I have finished; **dictum factum** no sooner said than done.
dicrotum, -ī *nt* bireme.
Dictaeus *adj* Cretan.
dictamnus, -ī *f* dittany (*a kind of wild marjoram*).
dictāta, -ōrum *ntpl* lessons, rules.
dictātor, -ōris *m* dictator.
dictātōrius *adj* dictator's.
dictātūra, -ae *f* dictatorship.
Dictē, -ēs *f* mountain in Crete (*where Jupiter was brought up*).
dictiō, -ōnis *f* speaking, declaring; style, expression, oratory; (*oracle*) response.
dictitō, -āre *vt* to keep saying, assert; to plead often.
dictō, -āre, -āvī, -ātum *vt* to say repeatedly; to dictate; to compose.
dictum, -ī *nt* saying, word; proverb; bon mot, witticism; command.
dictus *ppa of* dīcō.
Dictynna, -ae *f* Britomartis; Diana.
Dictynnaeus *adj see n.*
didicī *perf of* discō.
dīdō, -ere, -idī, -itum *vt* to distribute, broadcast.
Dīdō, -ūs *and* **-ōnis** (*acc* -ō) *f* Queen of Carthage.
dīdūcō, -ūcere, -ūxī, -uctum *vt* to separate, split, open up; (*MIL*) to disperse; (*fig*) to part, divide.
diēcula, -ae *f* one little day.
diērēctus *adj* crucified; **abī ~** go and be hanged.
diēs, -ēī *m/f* day; set day (*usu fem*); a day's journey; (*fig*) time; **~ meus** my birthday; **~em dīcere** impeach; **~em obīre** die; **~em dē ~ē, ~em ex ~ē** from day to day; **in ~em** to a later day; for today; **in ~ēs** daily.
Diēspiter, -ris *m* Jupiter.
diffāmō, -āre, -āvī, -ātum *vt* to divulge; to malign.
differentia, -ae *f* difference, diversity; species.
differitās, -ātis *f* difference.
differō, -erre, distulī, dīlātum *vt* to disperse; to divulge, publish; (*fig*) to distract, disquiet; (*time*) to put off, delay ♦ *vi* to differ, be distinguished.
differtus *adj* stuffed, crammed.
difficilis *adj* difficult; (*person*) awkward, surly.
difficiliter *adv* with difficulty.
difficultās, -ātis *f* difficulty, distress, hardship; surliness.

difficulter *adv* with difficulty.
diffīdēns, -entis *adj* nervous.
diffīdenter *adv* without confidence.
diffīdentia, -ae *f* mistrust, diffidence.
diffīdō, -dere, -sus *vi* to distrust, despair.
diffindō, -ndere, -dī, -ssum *vt* to split, open up; (*fig*) to break off.
diffingō, -ere *vt* to remake.
diffissus *ppp of* diffindō.
diffīsus *ppa of* diffīdō.
diffiteor, -ērī *vt* to disown.
diffluēns, -entis *adj* (*RHET*) loose.
diffluō, -ere *vi* to flow away; to melt away; (*fig*) to wallow.
diffringō, -ere *vt* to shatter.
diffugiō, -ugere, -ūgī *vi* to disperse, disappear.
diffugium, -ī *and* **iī** *nt* dispersion.
diffunditō, -āre *vt* to pour out, waste.
diffundō, -undere, -ūdī, -ūsum *vt* to pour off; to spread, diffuse; to cheer, gladden.
diffūsē *adv* expansively.
diffūsilis *adj* diffusive.
diffūsus *ppp of* diffundō ♦ *adj* spreading; (*writing*) loose.
Dīgentia, -ae *f* tributary of the Anio (*near Horace's villa*).
dīgerō, -rere, -ssī, -stum *vt* to divide, distribute; to arrange, set out; to interpret.
dīgestiō, -ōnis *f* (*RHET*) enumeration.
dīgestus *ppp of* dīgerō.
digitulus, -ī *m* little finger.
digitus, -ī *m* finger; toe; inch; (*pl*) skill in counting; **~um porrigere, prōferre** take the slightest trouble; **~um trānsversum nōn discēdere** not swerve a finger's breadth; **attingere caelum ~ō** reach the height of happiness; **licērī ~ō** bid at an auction; **mōnstrārī ~ō** be a celebrity; **extrēmī, summī ~ī** the fingertips; **concrepāre ~īs** snap the fingers.
dīgladior, -ārī *vi* to fight fiercely.
dignātiō, -ōnis *f* honour, dignity.
dignē *adv see* dignus.
dignitās, -ātis *f* worth, worthiness; dignity, rank, position; political office.
dignō, -āre *vt* to think worthy.
dignor, -ārī *vt* to think worthy; to deign.
dignōscō, -ere *vt* to distinguish.
dignus *adj* worth, worthy; (*things*) fitting, proper.
dīgredior, -dī, -ssus *vi* to separate, part; to deviate, digress.
dīgressiō, -ōnis *f* parting; deviation, digression.
dīgressus *ppa of* dīgredior.
dīgressus, -ūs *m* parting.
dīiūdicātiō, -ōnis *f* decision.
dīiūdicō, -āre *vt* to decide; to discriminate.
dīiun- *etc see* disiun-.
dīlābor, -bī, -psus *vi* to dissolve, disintegrate; to flow away; (*troops*) to disperse; (*fig*) to decay, vanish.

dīlacerō, -āre vt to tear to pieces.
dīlāminō, -āre vt to split in two.
dīlaniō, -āre, -āvī, -ātum vt to tear to shreds.
dīlapidō, -āre vt to demolish.
dīlāpsus ppa of **dīlābor.**
dīlargior, -īrī vt to give away liberally.
dīlātiō, -ōnis f putting off, adjournment.
dīlātō, -āre, -āvī, -ātum vt to expand;
   (pronunciation) to broaden.
dīlātor, -ōris m procrastinator.
dīlātus ppp of **differō.**
dīlaudō, -āre vt to praise extravagantly.
dīlēctus ppp of **dīligō** ♦ adj beloved.
dīlēctus, -ūs m selection, picking; (MIL) levy;
   ~um habēre hold a levy, recruit.
dīlēxī perf of **dīligō.**
dīligēns, -entis adj painstaking,
   conscientious, attentive (to); thrifty.
dīligenter adv see **dīligēns.**
dīligentia, -ae f carefulness, attentiveness;
   thrift.
dīligō, -igere, -ēxī, -ēctum vt to prize
   especially, esteem, love.
dīlōrīcō, -āre vt to tear open.
dīlūceō, -ēre vi to be evident.
dīlūcēscit, -cēscere, -xit vi to dawn, begin to
   grow light.
dīlūcidē adv see **dīlūcidus.**
dīlūcidus adj clear, distinct.
dīlūculum, -ī nt dawn.
dīlūdium, -ī and iī nt interval.
dīluō, -uere, -uī, -ūtum vt to wash away,
   dissolve, dilute; to explain; (fig) to weaken,
   do away with.
dīluviēs, -iēī f, **-ium, -ī and iī** nt flood, deluge.
dīluviō, -āre vt to inundate.
dīmānō, -āre vi to spread abroad.
dīmēnsiō, -ōnis f measuring.
dīmēnsus adj measured.
dīmētior, -tīrī, -nsus vt to measure out.
dīmētō, -āre, -or, -ārī vt to mark out.
dīmicātiō, -ōnis f fighting, struggle.
dīmicō, -āre, -āvī, -ātum vi to fight, struggle,
   contend.
dīmidiātus adj half, halved.
dīmidius adj half ♦ nt half.
dīmissiō, -ōnis f sending away; discharging.
dīmissus ppp of **dīmittō.**
dīmittō, -ittere, -īsī, -issum vt to send away,
   send round; to let go, lay down; (meeting) to
   dismiss; (MIL) to disband, detach; (fig) to
   abandon, forsake.
dimminuō, -ere vt to dash to pieces.
dīmoveō, -ovēre, -ōvī, -ōtum vt to part,
   separate; to disperse; to entice away.
Dindymēnē, -ēnēs f Cybele.
Dindymus, -ī m mountain in Mysia (sacred to
   Cybele).
dīnōscō see **dīgnōscō.**
dīnumerātiō, -ōnis f reckoning up.

dīnumerō, -āre vt to count, reckon up; to pay
   out.
diōbolāris adj costing two obols.
dioecēsis, -is f district; (ECCL) diocese.
dioecētēs, -ae m treasurer.
Diogenēs, -is m famous Cynic philosopher; a
   Stoic philosopher.
Diomēdēs, -is m Greek hero at the Trojan War.
Diomēdēus adj see n.
Diōnaeus adj see Diōnē.
Diōnē, -ēs and **-a, -ae** f mother of Venus; Venus.
Dionȳsius, -ī m tyrant of Syracuse.
Dionȳsus, -ī m Bacchus; **-ia, -iōrum** ntpl Greek
   festival of Bacchus.
diōta, -ae f a two-handled wine jar.
diplōma, -tis nt letter of recommendation.
Dipylon, -ī nt Athenian gate.
Dircaeus adj Boeotian.
Dircē, -ēs f famous spring in Boeotia.
dīrēctus ppp of **dīrigō** ♦ adj straight;
   straightforward, simple; see also **dērēctus.**
dīrēmī perf of **dīrimō.**
dīremptus ppp of **dīrimō.**
dīremptus, -ūs m separation.
dīreptiō, -ōnis f plundering.
dīreptor, -ōris m plunderer.
dīreptus ppp of **dīripiō.**
dīrēxī perf of **dīrigō.**
dīribeō, -ēre vt to sort out (votes taken from
   ballot-boxes).
dīribitiō, -ōnis f sorting.
dīribitor, -ōris m ballot-sorter.
dīrigō, -igere, -ēxī, -ēctum vt to put in line,
   arrange; see also **dērigō.**
dīrimō, -imere, -ēmī, -emptum vt to part,
   divide; to interrupt, break off; to put an end
   to.
dīripiō, -ipere, -ipuī, -eptum vt to tear in
   pieces; to plunder, ravage; to seize; (fig) to
   distract.
dīritās, -ātis f mischief, cruelty.
**dīrumpō, disrumpō, -umpere, -ūpī,
   -uptum** vt to burst, break in pieces; (fig) to
   break off; (pass) to burst (with passion).
dīruō, -ere, -ī, -tum vt to demolish; to scatter;
   aere ~tus having one's pay stopped.
dīruptus ppp of **dīrumpō.**
dīrus adj ominous, fearful; (pers) dread,
   terrible ♦ fpl bad luck; the Furies ♦ ntpl
   terrors.
dīrutus ppp of **dīruō** ♦ adj bankrupt.
dīs, dītis adj rich.
Dīs, Dītis m Pluto.
discēdō, -ēdere, -ēssī, -essum vi to go away,
   depart; to part, disperse; (MIL) to march
   away; (result of battle) to come off; (POL) to go
   over (to a different policy); to pass away,
   disappear; to leave out of consideration; **ab
   signīs ~** break the ranks; **victor ~** come off
   best.

Noun declensions and verb conjugations are shown on pp xiii to xxv. The present infinitive ending of a verb shows
to which conjugation it belongs: **-āre** = 1st; **-ēre** = 2nd; **-ere** = 3rd and **-īre** = 4th. Irregular verbs are shown on p xxvi

disceptātiō, -ōnis *f* discussion, debate.
disceptātor, -ōris *m*, **-rīx, -rīcis** *f* arbitrator.
disceptō, -āre *vt* to debate, discuss; (*law*) to decide.
discernō, -ernere, -rēvī, -rētum *vt* to divide, separate; to distinguish between.
discerpō, -ere, -sī, -tum *vt* to tear apart, disperse; (*fig*) to revile.
discessiō, -ōnis *f* separation, departure; (*senate*) division.
discessus, -ūs *m* parting; departure; marching away.
discidium, -i *and* **iī** *nt* disintegration; separation, divorce; discord.
discīdō, -ere *vt* to cut in pieces.
discinctus *ppp of* **discingō** ♦ *adj* ungirt; negligent; dissolute.
discindō, -ndere, -dī, -ssum *vt* to tear up, cut open.
discingō, -gere, -xī, -ctum *vt* to ungird.
disciplīna, -ae *f* teaching, instruction; learning, science, school, system; training, discipline; habits.
discipulus, -ī *m*, **-a, -ae** *f* pupil, apprentice.
discissus *ppp of* **discindō**.
disclūdō, -dere, -sī, -sum *vt* to keep apart, separate out.
discō, -ere, didicī *vt* to learn, be taught, be told.
discolor, -ōris *adj* of a different colour; variegated; different.
discondūcit it is not worthwhile.
disconveniō, -īre *vi* to disagree, be inconsistent.
discordābilis *adj* disagreeing.
discordia, -ae *f* discord, disagreement.
discordiōsus *adj* seditious.
discordō, -āre *vi* to disagree, quarrel; to be unlike.
discors, -dis *adj* discordant, at variance; inconsistent.
discrepantia, -ae *f* disagreement.
discrepātiō, -ōnis *f* dispute.
discrepitō, -āre *vi* to be quite different.
discrepō, -āre, -uī *vi* to be out of tune; to disagree, differ; to be disputed.
discrētus *ppp of* **discernō**.
discrībō, -bere, -psī, -ptum *vt* to distribute, apportion, classify.
discrīmen, -inis *nt* interval, dividing line; distinction, difference; turning point, critical moment; crisis, danger.
discrīminō, -āre *vt* to divide.
discrīptē *adv* in good order.
discrīptiō, -ōnis *f* apportioning, distributing.
discrīptus *ppp of* **discrībō** ♦ *adj* secluded; well-arranged.
discruciō, -āre *vt* to torture; (*fig*) to torment, trouble.
discumbō, -mbere, -buī, -bitum *vi* to recline at table; to go to bed.
discupiō, -ere *vi* to long.
discurrō, -rrere, -currī *and* **rrī, -rsum** *vi* to

run about, run different ways.
discursus, -ūs *m* running hither and thither.
discus, -ī *m* quoit.
discussus *ppp of* **discutiō**.
discutiō, -tere, -ssī, -ssum *vt* to dash to pieces, smash; to scatter; to dispel.
disertē, -im *adv* distinctly; eloquently.
disertus *adj* fluent, eloquent; explicit.
disiciō, -icere, -iēcī, -iectum *vt* to scatter, cast asunder; to break up, destroy; (*MIL*) to rout.
disiectō, -āre *vt* to toss about.
disiectus *ppp of* **disiciō**.
disiectus, -ūs *m* scattering.
disiūnctiō, -ōnis *f* separation, differing; (*logic*) statement of alternatives; (*RHET*) a sequence of short co-ordinate clauses.
disiūnctius *adv* rather in the manner of a dilemma.
disiūnctus *ppp of* **disiungō** ♦ *adj* distinct, distant, removed; (*speech*) disjointed; (*logic*) opposite.
disiungō, -ungere, -ūnxī, -ūnctum *vt* to unyoke; to separate, remove.
dispālēscō, -ere *vi* to be noised abroad.
dispandō, -āndere, -ānsum *and* **-essum** *vt* to spread out.
dispār, -aris *adj* unlike, unequal.
disparilis *adj* dissimilar.
disparō, -āre, -āvī, -ātum *vt* to segregate.
dispart- *etc see* **dispert-**.
dispectus *ppp of* **dispiciō**.
dispellō, -ellere, -ulī, -ulsum *vt* to scatter, dispel.
dispendium, -ī *and* **iī** *nt* expense, loss.
dispennō *etc see* **dispandō**.
dispēnsātiō, -ōnis *f* management, stewardship.
dispēnsātor, -ōris *m* steward, treasurer.
dispēnsō, -āre, -āvī, -ātum *vi* to weigh out, pay out; to manage, distribute; (*fig*) to regulate.
dispercutiō, -ere *vt* to dash out.
disperdō, -ere, -idī, -itum *vt* to ruin, squander.
dispereō, -īre, -iī *vi* to go to ruin, be undone.
dispergō, -gere, -sī, -sum *vt* to disperse, spread over, spread out.
dispersē *adv* here and there.
dispersus *ppp of* **dispergō**.
dispertiō, -īre, -īvī, -ītum; -ior, -īrī *vt* to apportion, distribute.
dispertītiō, -ōnis *f* division.
dispessus *ppp of* **dispandō**.
dispiciō, -icere, -exī, -ectum *vt* to see clearly, see through; to distinguish, discern; (*fig*) to consider.
displiceō, -ēre *vi* (*with dat*) to displease; **sibi ~** be in a bad humour.
displōdō, -dere, -sum *vt* to burst with a crash.
dispōnō, -ōnere, -osuī, -ositum *vt* to set out, arrange; (*MIL*) to station.

dispositē *adv* methodically.
dispositiō, -ōnis *f* arrangement.
dispositūra, -ae *f* arrangement.
dispositus *ppp of* **dispōnō ♦** *adj* orderly.
dispositus, -ūs *m* arranging.
dispudet, -ēre, -uit *v impers* to be very ashamed.
dispulsus *ppp of* **dispellō.**
disputātiō, -ōnis *f* argument.
disputātor, -ōris *m* debater.
disputō, -āre, -āvī, -ātum *vt* to calculate; to examine, discuss.
disquīrō, -ere *vt* to investigate.
disquīsītiō, -ōnis *f* inquiry.
disrumpō *etc see* **dīrumpō.**
dissaepiō, -īre, -sī, -tum *vt* to fence off, separate off.
dissaeptum, -ī *nt* partition.
dissāvior, -ārī *vt* to kiss passionately.
dissēdī *perf of* **dissideō.**
dissēminō, -āre *vt* to sow, broadcast.
dissēnsiō, -ōnis *f* disagreement, conflict.
dissēnsus, -ūs *m* dissension.
dissentāneus *adj* contrary.
dissentiō, -entīre, -ēnsī, -ēnsum *vi* to disagree, differ; to be unlike, be inconsistent.
dissēp- *etc see* **dissaep-.**
disserēnō, -āre *vi* to clear up.
disserō, -erere, -ēvī, -itum *vt* to sow, plant at intervals.
disserō, -ere, -uī, -tum *vt* to set out in order, arrange; to examine, discuss.
disserpō, -ere *vi* to spread imperceptibly.
dissertō, -āre *vt* to discuss, dispute.
dissideō, -idēre, -ēdī, -essum *vi* to be distant; to disagree, quarrel; to differ, be unlike, be uneven.
dissignātiō, -ōnis *f* arrangement.
dissignātor, -ōris *m* master of ceremonies; undertaker.
dissignō, -āre *vt* to arrange, regulate; *see also* **dēsignō.**
dissiliō, -īre, -uī *vi* to fly apart, break up.
dissimilis *adj* unlike, different.
dissimiliter *adv* differently.
dissimilitūdō, -inis *f* unlikeness.
dissimulanter *adv* secretly.
dissimulantia, -ae *f* dissembling.
dissimulātiō, -ōnis *f* disguising, dissembling; Socratic irony.
dissimulātor, -ōris *m* dissembler.
dissimulō, -āre, -āvī, -ātum *vt* to dissemble, conceal, pretend that . . . not, ignore.
dissipābilis *adj* diffusible.
dissipātiō, -ōnis *f* scattering, dispersing.
dissipō, dissupō, -āre, -āvī, -ātum *vt* to scatter, disperse; to spread, broadcast; to squander, destroy; (*MIL*) to put to flight.
dissitus *ppp of* **disserō.**

dissociābilis *adj* disuniting; incompatible.
dissociātiō, -ōnis *f* separation.
dissociō, -āre, -āvī, -ātum *vt* to disunite, estrange.
dissolūbilis *adj* dissoluble.
dissolūtē *adv* loosely, negligently.
dissolūtiō, -ōnis *f* breaking up, destruction; looseness; (*law*) refutation; (*person*) weakness.
dissolūtum, -ī *nt* asyndeton.
dissolūtus *ppp of* **dissolvō ♦** *adj* loose; lax, careless; licentious.
dissolvō, -vere, -vī, -ūtum *vt* to unloose, dissolve; to destroy, abolish; to refute; to pay up, discharge (debt); to free, release.
dissonus *adj* discordant, jarring, disagreeing, different.
dissors, -tis *adj* not shared.
dissuādeō, -dēre, -sī, -sum *vt* to advise against, oppose.
dissuāsiō, -ōnis *f* advising against.
dissuāsor, -ōris *m* opposer.
dissultō, -āre *vi* to fly asunder.
dissuō, -ere *vt* to undo, open up.
dissupō *etc see* **dissipō.**
distaedet, -ēre *v impers* to weary, disgust.
distantia, -ae *f* diversity.
distendō (-nō), -dere, -dī, -tum *vt* to stretch out, swell.
distentus *ppp of* **distendō ♦** *adj* full ♦ *ppp of* **distineō ♦** *adj* busy.
disterminō, -āre *vt* to divide, limit.
distichon, -ī *nt* couplet.
distinctē *adv* distinctly, lucidly.
distinctiō, -ōnis *f* differentiating, difference; (*GRAM*) punctuation; (*RHET*) distinction between words.
distinctus *ppp of* **distinguō ♦** *adj* separate, distinct; ornamented, set off; lucid.
distinctus, -ūs *m* difference.
distineō, -inēre, -inuī, -entum *vt* to keep apart, divide; to distract; to detain, occupy; to prevent.
distinguō, -guere, -xī, -ctum *vt* to divide, distinguish, discriminate; to punctuate; to adorn, set off.
distō, -āre *vi* to be apart, be distant; to be different.
distorqueō, -quēre, -sī, -tum *vt* to twist, distort.
distortiō, -ōnis *f* contortion.
distortus *ppp of* **distorqueō ♦** *adj* deformed.
distractiō, -ōnis *f* parting, variance.
distractus *ppp of* **distrahō ♦** *adj* separate.
distrahō, -here, -xī, -ctum *vt* to tear apart, separate, estrange; to sell piecemeal, retail; (*mind*) to distract, perplex; **aciem ~** break up a formation; **contrōversiās ~** end a dispute; **vōcēs ~** leave a hiatus.
distribuō, -uere, -uī, -ūtum *vt* to distribute,

divide.

distribūtē *adv* methodically.

distribūtiō, -ōnis *f* distribution, division.

districtus *ppp of* **distringō** ♦ *adj* busy, occupied; perplexed; severe.

distringō, -ngere, -nxī, -ctum *vt* to draw apart; to engage, distract; (*MIL*) to create a diversion against.

distruncō, -āre *vt* to cut in two.

distulī *perf of* **differō**.

disturbō, -āre, -āvī, -ātum *vt* to throw into confusion; to demolish; to frustrate, ruin.

dītēscō, -ere *vi* to grow rich.

dīthyrambicus *adj* dithyrambic.

dīthyrambus, -ī *m* dithyramb.

dītiae, -ārum *fpl* wealth.

dītiō *etc see* **diciō**.

dītō, -āre *vt* to enrich.

diū (*comp* **diūtius,** *sup* **diūtissimē**) *adv* long, a long time; long ago; by day.

diurnum, -ī *nt* day-book; **ācta ~a** Roman daily gazette.

diurnus *adj* daily, for a day; by day, day- (*in cpds*).

dīus *adj* divine, noble.

diūtinē *adv* long.

diūtinus *adj* long, lasting.

diūtissimē, -ius *etc see* **diū**.

diūturnitās, -ātis *f* long time, long duration.

diūturnus *adj* long, lasting.

dīva, -ae *f* goddess.

dīvāricō, -āre *vt* to spread.

dīvellō, -ellere, -ellī, -ulsum *vt* to tear apart, tear in pieces; (*fig*) to tear away, separate, estrange.

dīvēndō, -ere, -itum *vt* to sell in lots.

dīverberō, -āre *vt* to divide, cleave.

dīverbium, -ī *and* **iī** *nt* (*comedy*) passage in dialogue.

dīversē *adv* in different directions, variously.

dīversitās, -ātis *f* contradiction, disagreement, difference.

dīversus, dīvorsus *ppp of* **dīvertō** ♦ *adj* in different directions, apart; different; remote; opposite, conflicting; hostile ♦ *mpl* individuals.

dīvertō, -tere, -tī, -sum *vi* to turn away; differ.

dīves, -itis *adj* rich.

dīvexō, -āre *vt* to pillage.

dīvidia, -ae *f* worry, concern.

dīvidō, -idere, -īsī, -īsum *vt* to divide, break open; to distribute, apportion; to separate, keep apart; to distinguish; (*jewel*) to set off; **sententiam ~** *take the vote separately on the parts of a motion.*

dīviduus *adj* divisible; divided.

dīvīnātiō, -ōnis *f* foreseeing the future, divination; (*law*) inquiry to select the most suitable prosecutor.

dīvīnē *adv* by divine influence; prophetically; admirably.

dīvīnitās, -ātis *f* divinity; divination; divine

quality.

dīvīnitus *adv* from heaven, by divine influence; excellently.

dīvīnō, -āre, -āvī, -ātum *vt* to foresee, prophesy.

dīvīnus *adj* divine, of the gods; prophetic; superhuman, excellent ♦ *m* soothsayer ♦ *nt* sacrifice; oath; **rēs ~a** religious service, sacrifice; **~a hūmānaque** all things in heaven and earth; **~ī crēdere** believe on oath.

dīvīsī *perf of* **dīvidō**.

dīvīsiō, -ōnis *f* division; distribution.

dīvīsor, -ōris *m* distributor; bribery agent.

dīvīsus *ppp of* **dīvidō** ♦ *adj* separate.

dīvīsus, -ūs *m* division.

dīvitiae, -ārum *fpl* wealth; (*fig*) richness.

dīvor- *etc see* **dīver-**.

dīvortium, -ī *and* **iī** *nt* separation; divorce (by consent); road fork, watershed.

dīvulgātus *adj* widespread.

dīvulgō, -āre, -āvī, -ātum *vt* to publish, make public.

dīvulsus *ppp of* **dīvellō**.

dīvum, -ī *nt* sky; **sub ~ō** in the open air.

dīvus *adj* divine; deified ♦ *m* god.

dīxī *perf of* **dīcō**.

dō, dare, dedī, datum *vt* to give; to permit, grant; to put, bring, cause, make; to give up, devote; to tell; to impute; **fābulam ~** produce a play; **in fugam ~** put to flight; **litterās ~** post a letter; **manūs ~** surrender; **nōmen ~** enlist; **operam ~** take pains, do one's best; **poenās ~** pay the penalty; **vēla ~** set sail; **verba ~** cheat.

doceō, -ēre, -uī, -tum *vt* to teach; to inform, tell; **fābulam ~** produce a play.

dochmius, -ī *and* **iī** *m* dochmiac foot.

docilis *adj* easily trained, docile.

docilitās, -ātis *f* aptness for being taught.

doctē *adv* skilfully, cleverly.

doctor, -ōris *m* teacher, instructor.

doctrīna, -ae *f* instruction, education, learning; science.

doctus *ppp of* **doceō** ♦ *adj* learned, skilled; cunning, clever.

documentum, -ī *nt* lesson, example, proof.

Dōdōna, -ae *f* town in Epirus (*famous for its oracle of Jupiter*).

Dōdōnaeus, -is, -idis *adj see* **Dōdōna**.

dōdrāns, -antis *m* three-fourths.

dogma, -tis *nt* philosophical doctrine.

dolābra, -ae *f* pickaxe.

dolēns, -entis *pres p of* **doleō** ♦ *adj* painful.

dolenter *adv* sorrowfully.

doleō, -ēre, -uī, -itum *vt*, *vi* to be in pain, be sore; to grieve, lament, be sorry (for); to pain; **cui ~et meminit** ≈ *once bitten, twice shy.*

dōliāris *adj* tubby.

dōliolum, -ī *nt* small cask.

dōlium, -ī *and* **iī** *nt* large wine jar.

dolō, -āre, -āvī, -ātum *vt* to hew, shape with an axe.

dolō, -ōnis *m* pike; sting; fore-topsail.

Dolopes–ductitō

Dolopes, -um *mpl people of Thessaly.*

Dolopia, -iae *f the country of the people of Thessaly.*

dolor, -ōris *m* pain, pang; sorrow, trouble; indignation, resentment; (*RHET*) pathos.

dolōsē *adv see* **dolōsus.**

dolōsus *adj* deceitful, crafty.

dolus, -ī *m* deceit, guile, trick; ~ **malus** wilful fraud.

domābilis *adj* tameable.

domesticus *adj* domestic, household; personal, private; of one's own country, internal ♦ *mpl* members of a household; **bellum** ~ civil war.

domī *adv* at home.

domicilium, -ī *and* **iī** *nt* dwelling.

domina, -ae *f* mistress, lady of the house; wife, mistress; (*fig*) lady.

domināns, -antis *pres p of* **dominor** ♦ *adj* (*words*) literal ♦ *m* tyrant.

dominātiō, -ōnis *f* mastery, tyranny.

dominātor, -ōris *m* lord.

dominātrīx, -rīcis *f* queen.

dominātus, -ūs *m* mastery, sovereignty.

dominicus *adj* (*ECCL*) the Lord's.

dominium, -ī *and* **iī** *nt* absolute ownership; feast.

dominor, -ārī, -ātus *vi* to rule, be master; (*fig*) to lord it.

dominus, -ī *m* master, lord; owner; host; despot; (*ECCL*) the Lord.

Domitiānus *adj m Roman Emperor.*

Domitius, -ī *m* Roman plebeian name (*esp with surname Ahenobarbus*).

domitō, -āre *vt* to break in.

domitor, -ōris *m*, **-rīx, -rīcis** *f* tamer; conqueror.

domitus *ppp of* **domō.**

domitus, -ūs *m* taming.

domō, -āre, -uī, -itum *vt* to tame, break in; to conquer.

domus, -ūs *and* **ī** *f* house (*esp in town*); home, native place; family; (*PHILOS*) sect; **~ī** at home; in peace; **~ī habēre** have of one's own, have plenty of; **~um** home(wards); **~ō** from home.

dōnābilis *adj* deserving a present.

dōnārium, -ī *and* **iī** *nt* offering; altar, temple.

dōnātiō, -ōnis *f* presenting.

dōnātīvum, -ī *nt* largess, gratuity.

dōnec (dōnicum, dōnique) *conj* until; while, as long as.

dōnō, -āre, -āvī, -ātum *vt* to present, bestow; to remit, condone (for another's sake); (*fig*) to sacrifice.

dōnum, -ī *nt* gift; offering.

dorcas, -dis *f* gazelle.

Dōrēs, -um *mpl* Dorians (*mostly the Greeks of the Peloponnese*).

Dōricus *adj* Dorian; Greek.

Dōris, -dis *f* a sea nymph; the sea.

dormiō, -īre, -īvī, -ītum *vi* to sleep, be asleep.

dormītātor, -ōris *m* dreamer.

dormītō, -āre *vi* to be drowsy, nod.

dorsum, -ī *nt* back; mountain ridge.

dōs, dōtis *f* dowry; (*fig*) gift, talent.

Dossēnus, -ī *m* hunchback, clown.

dōtālis *adj* dowry (*in cpds*), dotal.

dōtātus *adj* richly endowed.

dōtō, -āre *vt* to endow.

drachma (drachuma), -ae *f a Greek silver coin.*

dracō, -ōnis *m* serpent, dragon; (*ASTRO*) Draco.

dracōnigena, -ae *adj* sprung from dragon's teeth.

drāpeta, -ae *m* runaway slave.

Drepanum, -ī, -a, -ōrum *nt town in W. Sicily.*

dromas, -dis *m* dromedary.

dromos, -ī *m* racecourse at Sparta.

Druidēs, -um, -ae, -ārum *mpl* Druids.

Drūsiānus *adj see* **Drūsus.**

Drūsus, -ī *m* Roman surname (*esp famous commander in Germany under Augustus*).

Dryadēs, -um *fpl* woodnymphs, Dryads.

Dryopes, -um *mpl a people of Epirus.*

dubiē *adv* doubtfully.

dubitābilis *adj* doubtful.

dubitanter *adv* doubtingly, hesitatingly.

dubitātiō, -ōnis *f* wavering, uncertainty, doubting; hesitancy, irresolution; (*RHET*) misgiving.

dubitō, -āre, -āvī, -ātum *vt, vi* to waver, be in doubt, wonder, doubt; to hesitate, stop to think.

dubium *nt* doubt.

dubius *adj* wavering, uncertain; doubtful, indecisive; precarious; irresolute ♦ *nt* doubt; **in ~um vocāre** call in question; **in ~um venīre** be called in question; **sine ~ō, haud ~ē** undoubtedly.

ducēnī, -ōrum *adj* 200 each.

ducentēsima, -ae *f* one-half per cent.

ducentī, -ōrum *num* two hundred.

ducentiēs, -iēns *adv* 200 times.

dūcō, -cere, -xī, ductum *vt* to lead, guide, bring, take; to draw, draw out; to reckon, consider; (*MIL*) to lead, march, command; (*breath*) to inhale; (*ceremony*) to conduct; (*changed aspect*) to take on, receive; (*dance*) to perform; (*drink*) to quaff; (*metal*) to shape, beat out; (*mind*) to attract, induce, deceive; (*oars*) to pull; (*origin*) to derive, trace; (*time*) to prolong, put off, pass; (*udders*) to milk; (*wool*) to spin; (*a work*) to construct, compose, make; (*COMM*) to calculate; **īlia ~** become broken-winded; **in numerō hostium ~** regard as an enemy; **ōs ~** make faces; **parvī ~** think little of; **ratiōnem ~** have regard for; **uxōrem ~** marry.

ductim *adv* in streams.

ductitō, -āre *vt* to lead on, deceive; to marry.

Noun declensions and verb conjugations are shown on pp xiii to xxv. The present infinitive ending of a verb shows to which conjugation it belongs: **-āre** = 1st; **-ēre** = 2nd; **-ere** = 3rd and **-īre** = 4th. Irregular verbs are shown on p xxvi

ductō, -āre *vt* to lead, draw; to take home; to cheat.

ductor, -ōris *m* leader, commander; guide, pilot.

ductus *ppp of* **dūcō**.

ductus, -ūs *m* drawing, drawing off; form; command, generalship.

dūdum *adv* a little while ago, just now; for long; **haud ~** not long ago; **iam ~ adsum** I have been here a long time; **quam ~** how long.

duellum *etc see* **bellum**.

Duillius, -ī *m* consul who defeated the Carthaginians at sea.

duim *pres subj of* **dō**.

dulce, -iter *adv see* **dulcis**.

dulcēdō, -inis *f* sweetness; pleasantness, charm.

dulcēscō, -ere *vi* to become sweet.

dulciculus *adj* rather sweet.

dulcifer, -ī *adj* sweet.

dulcis *adj* sweet; pleasant, lovely; kind, dear.

dulcitūdō, -inis *f* sweetness.

dūlicē *adv* like a slave.

Dūlichium, -ī *nt* island in the Ionian Sea near Ithaca.

Dūlichius *adj* of Dulichium; of Ulysses.

dum *conj* while, as long as; provided that, if only; until ♦ *adv* (*enclitic*) now, a moment; (*with neg*) yet.

dūmētum, -ī *nt* thicket, thornbushes.

dummodo *conj* provided that.

dūmōsus *adj* thorny.

dumtaxat *adv* at least; only, merely.

dūmus, -ī *m* thornbush.

duo, duae, duo *num* two.

duodeciēns, -ēs *adv* twelve times.

duodecim *num* twelve.

duodecimus *adj* twelfth.

duodēnī, -ōrum *adj* twelve each, in dozens.

duodēquadrāgēsimus *adj* thirty-eighth.

duodēquadrāgintā *num* thirty-eight.

duodēquīnquāgēsimus *adj* forty-eighth.

duodētrīciēns *adv* twenty-eight times.

duodētrīgintā *num* twenty-eight.

duodēvīcēnī *adj* eighteen each.

duodēvīgintī *num* eighteen.

duoetvīcēsimānī, -ānōrum *mpl* soldiers of the 22nd legion.

duoetvīcēsimus *adj* twenty-second.

duovirī, duumvirī, -ōrum *mpl* a board of two men; colonial magistrates; **~ nāvālēs** naval commissioners (for supply and repair); **~ sacrōrum** keepers of the Sibylline Books.

duplex, -icis *adj* double, twofold; both; (*person*) false.

duplicārius, -ī *and* **iī** *m* soldier receiving double pay.

dupliciter *adv* doubly, on two accounts.

duplicō, -āre, -āvī, -ātum *vt* to double, increase; to bend.

duplus *adj* double, twice as much ♦ *nt* double ♦ *f* double the price.

dupondius, -ī *and* **iī** *m* coin worth two asses.

dūrābilis *adj* lasting.

dūrāmen, -inis *nt* hardness.

dūrateus *adj* wooden.

dūrē, -iter *adv* stiffly; hardily; harshly, roughly.

dūrēscō, -ēscere, -uī *vi* to harden.

dūritās, -ātis *f* harshness.

dūritia, -ae, -ēs, -em *f* hardness; hardiness; severity; want of feeling.

dūrō, -āre, -āvī, -ātum *vt* to harden, stiffen; to make hardy, inure; (*mind*) to dull ♦ *vi* to harden; to be patient, endure; to hold out, last; (*mind*) to be steeled.

dūruī *perf of* **dūrēscō**.

dūrus *adj* hard, harsh, rough; hardy, tough; rude, uncultured; (*character*) severe, unfeeling, impudent, miserly; (*CIRCS*) hard, cruel.

duumvirī *etc see* **duovirī**.

dux, ducis *m* leader, guide; chief, head; (*MIL*) commander, general.

dūxī *perf of* **dūcō**.

Dymantis, -antidis *f* Hecuba.

Dymās, -antis *m* father of Hecuba.

dynamis, -is *f* plenty.

dynastēs, -ae *m* ruler, prince.

Dyrrhachīnus *adj see n*.

Dyrrhachium (Dyrrachium), -ī *nt* Adriatic port (*now* Durazzo).

E, e

ē *prep see* **ex**.

ea *f pron* she, it ♦ *adj see* **is**.

eā *adv* there, that way.

eādem *adv* the same way; at the same time.

eadem *f adj see* **idem**.

eaīdem, eapse *f of* **ipse**.

eapse *f of* **ipse**.

eātenus *adv* so far.

ebenus *etc see* **hebenus**.

ēbibō, -ere, -ī *vt* to drink up, drain; to squander; to absorb.

ēblandior, -īrī *vt* to coax out, obtain by flattery; **~ītus** obtained by flattery.

Eborācum, -ī *nt* York.

ēbrietās, ātis *f* drunkenness.

ēbriolus *adj* tipsy.

ēbriōsitās, -ātis *f* addiction to drink.

ēbriōsus *adj* drunkard; (*berry*) juicy.

ēbrius *adj* drunk; full; (*fig*) intoxicated.

ēbulliō, -īre *vi* to bubble up ♦ *vt* to brag about.

ebulus, -ī *m*, **-um, -ī** *nt* danewort, dwarf elder.

ebur, -is *nt* ivory; ivory work.

Eburācum, -ī *nt* York.
eburātus *adj* inlaid with ivory.
eburneolus *adj* of ivory.
eburneus, eburnus *adj* of ivory; ivory-white.
ēcastor *interj* by Castor!
ecce *adv* look!, here is!, there is!; lo and behold!; **~a, ~am, ~illam, ~istam** here she is!; **~um, ~illum** here he is!; **~ōs, ~ās** here they are!
eccerē *interj* there now!
eccheuma, -tis *nt* pouring out.
ecclēsia, -ae *f* a Greek assembly; (*ECCL*) congregation, church.
eccum *etc see* **ecce**.
ecdicus, -ī *m* civic lawyer.
ecf- *see* **eff-**.
echidna, -ae *f* viper; **~ Lernaea** hydra.
echīnus, -ī *m* sea-urchin; hedgehog; a rinsing bowl.
Echīōn, -onis *m* Theban hero.
Echīonidēs *m* Pentheus.
Echīonius *adj* Theban.
Ēchō, -us *f* wood nymph; echo.
ecloga, -ae *f* selection; eclogue.
ecquandō *adv* ever.
ecquī, -ae, -od *adj interrog* any.
ecquid, -ī *adv* whether.
ecquis, -id *pron interrog* anyone, anything.
ecquō *adv* anywhere.
eculeus, -ī *m* foal; rack.
edācitās, -ātis *f* gluttony.
edāx, -ācis *adj* gluttonous; (*fig*) devouring, carking.
ēdentō, -āre *vt* to knock the teeth out of.
ēdentulus *adj* toothless; old.
edepol *interj* by Pollux, indeed.
ēdī *perf of* **edō**.
ēdīcō, -īcere, -īxī, -ictum *vt* to declare; to decree, publish an edict.
ēdictiō, -ōnis *f* decree.
ēdictō, -āre *vt* to proclaim.
ēdictum, -ī *nt* proclamation, edict (*esp a praetor's*).
ēdidī *perf of* **ēdō**.
ēdiscō, -ere, ēdidicī *vt* to learn well, learn by heart.
ēdisserō, -ere, -uī, -tum *vt* to explain in detail.
ēdissertō, -āre *vt* to explain fully.
ēditīcius *adj* chosen by the plaintiff.
ēditiō, -ōnis *f* publishing, edition; statement; (*law*) designation of a suit.
ēditus *ppp of* **ēdō** ♦ *adj* high; descended ♦ *nt* height; order.
edō, edere *and* **ēsse, ēdī, ēsum** *vt* to eat; (*fig*) to devour.
ēdō, -ere, -idī, -itum *vt* to put forth, discharge; to emit; to give birth to, produce; (*speech*) to declare, relate, utter; (*action*) to cause, perform; (*book*) to publish; (*POL*) to

promulgate; **lūdōs ~** put on a show; **tribūs ~** nominate tribes of jurors.
ēdoceō, -ere, -uī, -ctum *vt* to instruct clearly, teach thoroughly.
ēdomō, -āre, -uī, -itum *vt* to conquer, overcome.
Ēdōnus *adj* Thracian.
ēdormiō, -īre *vi* to have a good sleep ♦ *vt* to sleep off.
ēdormīscō, -ere *vt* to sleep off.
ēducātiō, -ōnis *f* bringing up, rearing.
ēducātor, -ōris *m* foster father, tutor.
ēducātrix, -īcis *f* nurse.
ēducō, -āre, -āvī, -ātum *vt* to bring up, rear, train; to produce.
ēdūcō, -ūcere, -ūxī, -uctum *vt* to draw out, bring away; to raise up, erect; (*law*) to summon; (*MIL*) to lead out, march out; (*ship*) to put to sea; (*young*) to hatch, rear, train.
edūlis *adj* edible.
ēdūrō, -āre *vi* to last out.
ēdūrus *adj* very hard.
effarciō *etc see* **efferciō**.
effātus *ppa of* **effor** ♦ *adj* solemnly pronounced, declared ♦ *nt* axiom; (*pl*) predictions.
effectiō, -ōnis *f* performing; efficient cause.
effector, -ōris *m*, **-rīx, -rīcis** *f* producer, author.
effectus *ppp of* **efficiō**.
effectus, -ūs *m* completion, performance; effect.
effēminātē *adv see* **effēminātus**.
effēminātus *adj* effeminate.
effēminō, -āre, -āvī, -ātum *vt* to make a woman of; to enervate.
efferātus *adj* savage.
efferciō, -cīre, -tum *vt* to cram full.
efferitās, -ātis *f* wildness.
efferō, -āre, -āvī, -ātum *vt* to make wild; (*fig*) to exasperate.
efferō (ecferō), -re, extulī, ēlātum *vt* to bring out, carry out; to lift up, raise; (*dead*) to carry to the grave; (*emotion*) to transport; (*honour*) to exalt; (*news*) to spread abroad; (*soil*) to produce; (*trouble*) to endure to the end; **sē ~** rise; be conceited.
effertus *ppp of* **efferciō** ♦ *adj* full, bulging.
efferus *adj* savage.
effervēscō, -vēscere, -buī *vi* to boil over; (*fig*) to rage.
effervō, -ere *vi* to boil up.
effētus *adj* exhausted.
efficācitās, -ātis *f* power.
efficāciter *adv* effectually.
efficāx, -ācis *adj* capable, effective.
efficiēns, -entis *pres p of* **efficiō** ♦ *adj* effective, efficient.
efficienter *adv* efficiently.
efficientia, -ae *f* power, efficacy.
efficiō, -icere, -ēcī, -ectum *vt* to make,

Noun declensions and verb conjugations are shown on pp xiii to xxv. The present infinitive ending of a verb shows to which conjugation it belongs: **-āre** = 1st; **-ēre** = 2nd; **-ere** = 3rd and **-īre** = 4th. Irregular verbs are shown on p xxvi

accomplish; to cause, bring about; (*numbers*) to amount to; (*soil*) to yield; (*theory*) to make out, try to prove.

effictus *ppp of* **effingō**.

effigiēs, -ēī, -a, -ae *f* likeness, copy; ghost; portrait, statue; (*fig*) image, ideal.

effingō, -ngere, -nxī, -ctum *vt* to form, fashion; to portray, represent; to wipe clean; to fondle.

efflāgitātiō, -ōnis *f* urgent demand.

efflāgitātus, -ūs *m* urgent request.

efflāgitō, -āre *vt* to demand urgently.

efflīctim *adv* desperately.

efflīctō, -āre *vt* to strike dead.

efflīgō, -gere, -xī, -ctum *vt* to exterminate.

efflō, -āre, -āvī, -ātum *vt* to breathe out, blow out ♦ *vi* to billow out; **animam ~** expire.

efflōrēscō, -ēscere, -uī *vi* to blossom forth.

effluō, -ere, -xī *vi* to run out, issue, emanate; (*fig*) to pass away, vanish; (*rumour*) to get known; **ex animō ~** become forgotten.

effluvium, -ī *and* **iī** *nt* outlet.

effodiō, -odere, -ōdī, -ossum *vt* to dig up; (*eyes*) to gouge out; (*house*) to ransack.

effor, -ārī, -ātus *vt* to speak, utter; (*augury*) to ordain; (*logic*) to state a proposition.

effossus *ppp of* **effodiō**.

effrēnātē *adv see* **effrēnātus**.

effrēnātiō, -ōnis *f* impetuousness.

effrēnātus *adj* unbridled, violent, unruly.

effrēnus *adj* unbridled.

effringō, -ingere, -ēgī, -āctum *vt* to break open, smash.

effugiō, -ugere, -ūgī *vi* to run away, escape ♦ *vt* to flee from, escape; to escape the notice of.

effugium, -ī *and* **iī** *nt* flight, escape; means of escape.

effulgeō, -gēre, -sī *vi* to shine out, blaze.

effultus *adj* supported.

effundō, -undere, -ūdī, -ūsum *vt* to pour forth, pour out; (*crops*) to produce in abundance; (*missiles*) to shoot; (*rider*) to throw; (*speech*) to give vent to; (*effort*) to waste; (*money*) to squander; (*reins*) to let go; **sē ~, ~undī** rush out; indulge (in).

effūsē *adv* far and wide; lavishly, extravagantly.

effūsiō, -ōnis *f* pouring out, rushing out; profusion, extravagance; exuberance.

effūsus *ppp of* **effundō** ♦ *adj* vast, extensive; loose, straggling; lavish, extravagant.

effūtiō, -īre *vt* to blab, chatter.

ēgelidus *adj* mild, cool.

egēns, -entis *pres p of* **egeō** ♦ *adj* needy.

egēnus *adj* destitute.

egeō, -ēre, -uī *vi* to be in want; (*with abl or gen*) to need, want.

Ēgeria, -ae *f* nymph who taught Numa.

ēgerō, -rere, -ssī, -stum *vt* to carry out; to discharge, emit.

egestās, -ātis *f* want, poverty.

ēgestus *ppp of* **ēgerō**.

ēgī *perf of* **agō**.

ego *pron* I; **-met** I (*emphatic*).

ēgredior, -dī, -ssus *vi* to go out, come out; to go up, climb; (*MIL*) to march out; (*NAUT*) to disembark, put to sea; (*speech*) to digress ♦ *vt* to go beyond, quit; (*fig*) to overstep, surpass.

ēgregiē *adv* uncommonly well, singularly.

ēgregius *adj* outstanding, surpassing; distinguished, illustrious.

ēgressus *ppa of* **ēgredior**.

ēgressus, -ūs *m* departure; way out; digression; (*NAUT*) landing; (*river*) mouth.

eguī *perf of* **egeō**.

ēgurgitō, -āre *vt* to lavish.

ehem *interj* (*expressing surprise*) ha!, so!

ēheu *interj* (*expressing pain*) alas!

eho *interj* (*expressing rebuke*) look here!

eī *dat of* **is**.

ei *interj* (*expressing alarm*) oh!

eia *interj* (*expressing delight, playful remonstrance, encouragement*) aha!, come now!, come on!

ēiaculor, -ārī *vt* to shoot out.

ēiciō, -icere, -iēcī, -iectum *vt* to throw out, drive out, put out; (*joint*) to dislocate; (*mind*) to banish; (*NAUT*) to bring to land, run aground, wreck; (*rider*) to throw; (*speech*) to utter; (*THEAT*) to hiss off; **sē ~** rush out, break out.

ēiectāmenta, -ōrum *ntpl* refuse.

ēiectiō, -ōnis *f* banishment.

ēiectō, -āre *vt* to throw up.

ēiectus *ppp of* **ēiciō** ♦ *adj* shipwrecked.

ēiectus, -ūs *m* emitting.

ēierō, ēiūrō, -āre *vt* to abjure, reject on oath, forswear; (*office*) to resign; **bonam cōpiam ~** declare oneself bankrupt.

ēiulātiō, -ōnis *f*, **ēiulātus, -ūs** *m* wailing.

ēiulō, -āre *vi* to wail, lament.

ēius *pron* his, her, its; **-modī** such.

ej- *etc see* **ei-**.

ēlābor, -bī, -psus *vi* to glide away, slip off; to escape, get off; to pass away.

ēlabōrātus *adj* studied.

ēlabōrō, -āre, -āvī, -ātum *vi* to exert oneself, take great pains ♦ *vt* to work out, elaborate.

ēlāmentābilis *adj* very mournful.

ēlanguēscō, -ēscere, -ī *vi* to grow faint; to relax.

ēlāpsus *ppa of* **ēlābor**.

ēlātē *adv* proudly.

ēlātiō, -ōnis *f* ecstasy, exaltation.

ēlātrō, -āre *vt* to bark out.

ēlātus *ppp of* **efferō** ♦ *adj* high; exalted.

ēlavō, -avāre, -āvī, -autum *and* **-ōtum** *vt* to wash clean; (*comedy*) to rob.

Ēlea, -ae *f* town in S. Italy (*birthplace of Parmenides*).

Ēleātēs, -āticus *adj see n.*

ēlecebra, -ae *f* snare.

ēlēctē *adv* choicely.

ēlēctilis *adj* choice.

ēlectiō, -ōnis f choice, option.
ēlectō, -āre vt to coax out.
ēlēctō, -āre vt to select.
Ēlectra, -ae f a Pleiad (daughter of Atlas; sister of Orestes).
ēlectrum, -ī nt amber; an alloy of gold and silver.
ēlēctus ppp of **ēligō** ♦ adj select, choice.
ēlēctus, -ūs m choice.
ēlegāns, -antis adj tasteful, refined, elegant; fastidious; (things) fine, choice.
ēleganter adv with good taste.
ēlegantia, -ae f taste, finesse, elegance; fastidiousness.
ēlēgī perf of **ēligō**.
elegī, -ōrum mpl elegiac verses.
elegīa, -ae f elegy.
Eleleides, -eidum fpl Bacchantes.
Eleleus, -eī m Bacchus.
elementum, -ī nt element; (pl) first principles, rudiments; beginnings; letters (of alphabet).
elenchus, -ī m a pear-shaped pearl.
elephantomacha, -ae m fighter mounted on an elephant.
elephantus, -ī, elephās, -antis m elephant; ivory.
Ēlēus, -ius, -ias adj Elean; Olympian.
Eleusīn, -is f Eleusis (Attic town famous for its mysteries of Demeter).
Eleusīus adj see **Eleusīn**.
eleutheria, -ae f liberty.
ēlevō, -āre vt to lift, raise; to alleviate; to make light of, lessen, disparage.
ēliciō, -ere, -uī, -itum vt to lure out, draw out; (god) to call down; (spirit) to conjure up; (fig) to elicit, draw.
ēlīdō, -dere, -sī, -sum vt to dash out, squeeze out; to drive out; to crush, destroy.
ēligō, -igere, -ēgī, -ēctum vt to pick, pluck out; to choose.
ēlīminō, -āre vt to carry outside.
ēlīmō, -āre vt to file; (fig) to perfect.
ēlinguis adj speechless; not eloquent.
ēlinguō, -āre vt to tear the tongue out of.
Ēlis, -idis f district and town in W. Peloponnese (famous for Olympia).
Elissa, -ae f Dido.
ēlīsus ppp of **ēlīdō**.
ēlixus adj boiled.
elleborōsus adj quite mad.
elleborus, -ī m, **-um, -ī** nt hellebore.
ellum, ellam there he (she) is!
ēlocō, -āre vt to lease, farm out.
ēlocūtiō, -ōnis f delivery, style.
ēlocūtus ppa of **ēloquor**.
ēlogium, -ī and **iī** nt short saying; inscription; (will) clause.
ēloquēns, -entis adj eloquent.
ēloquenter adv see adj.

ēloquentia, -ae f eloquence.
ēloquium, -ī and **iī** nt eloquence.
ēloquor, -quī, -cūtus vt, vi to speak out, speak eloquently.
ēlūceō, -cēre, -xī vi to shine out, glitter.
ēluctor, -ārī, -ātus vi to struggle, force a way out ♦ vt to struggle out of, surmount.
ēlūcubrō, -āre, -or, -ārī, -ātus vt to compose by lamplight.
ēlūdificor, -ārī, -ātus vt to cheat, play up.
ēlūdō, -dere, -sī, -sum vt to parry, ward off, foil; to win off at play; to outplay, outmanoeuvre; to cheat, make fun of ♦ vi to finish one's sport.
ēlūgeō, -gēre, -xī vt to mourn for.
ēlumbis adj feeble.
ēluō, -uere, -uī, -ūtum vt to wash clean; (money) to squander; (fig) to wash away, get rid of.
ēlūsus ppp of **ēlūdō**.
ēlūtus ppp of **ēluō** ♦ adj insipid.
ēluviēs, -em -ē f discharge; overflowing.
ēluviō, -ōnis f deluge.
Ēlysium, -ī nt Elysium.
Ēlysius adj Elysian.
em interj there you are!
ēmancipātiō, -ōnis f giving a son his independence; conveyance of property.
ēmancipō, -āre vt to declare independent; to transfer, give up, sell.
ēmānō, -āre, -āvī, -ātum vi to flow out; to spring (from); (news) to leak out, become known.
Ēmathia, -ae f district of Macedonia; Macedonia, Thessaly.
Ēmathius adj Macedonian, Pharsalian; **~des, ~dum** fpl Muses.
ēmātūrēscō, -ēscere, -uī vi to soften.
emāx, -ācis adj fond of buying.
emblēma, -tis nt inlaid work, mosaic.
embolium, -ī and **iī** nt interlude.
ēmendābilis adj corrigible.
ēmendātē adv see **ēmendātor**.
ēmendātiō, -ōnis f correction.
ēmendātor, -ōris m, **-rīx, -rīcis** f corrector.
ēmendātus adj faultless.
ēmendō, -āre, -āvī, -ātum vt to correct, improve.
ēmēnsus ppa of **ēmētior** ♦ adj traversed.
ēmentior, -īrī, -ītus vi to tell lies ♦ vt to pretend, fabricate; **~ītus** pretended.
ēmercor, -ārī vt to purchase.
ēmereō, -ēre, -uī, -itum, -eor, -ērī vt to earn fully, deserve; to lay under an obligation; to complete one's term of service.
ēmergō, -gere, -sī, -sum vt to raise out; (fig) to extricate ♦ vi to rise, come up, emerge; (fig) to get clear, extricate oneself; (impers) it becomes evident.
ēmeritus ppa of **ēmereor** ♦ adj superannuated,

Noun declensions and verb conjugations are shown on pp xiii to xxv. The present infinitive ending of a verb shows to which conjugation it belongs: **-āre** = 1st; **-ēre** = 2nd; **-ere** = 3rd and **-īre** = 4th. Irregular verbs are shown on p xxvi

worn-out ♦ *m* veteran.

ēmersus *ppp of* **ēmergō**.

emetica, -ae *f* emetic.

ēmētior, -tīrī, -nsus *vt* to measure out; to traverse, pass over; (*time*) to live through; (*fig*) to impart.

ēmetō, -ere *vt* to harvest.

ēmī *perf of* **emō**.

ēmicō, -āre, -uī, -ātum *vi* to dart out, dash out, flash out; (*fig*) to shine.

ēmigrō, -āre, -āvī, -ātum *vi* to remove, depart.

ēminēns, -entis *pres p of* **ēmineō** ♦ *adj* high, projecting; (*fig*) distinguished, eminent.

ēminentia, -ae *f* prominence; (*painting*) light.

ēmineō, -ēre, -uī *vi* to stand out, project; to be prominent, be conspicuous, distinguish oneself.

ēminor, -ārī *vi* to threaten.

ēminus *adv* at *or* from a distance.

ēmīror, -ārī *vt* to marvel at.

ēmissārium, -ī *and* **iī** *nt* outlet.

ēmissārius, -ī *and* **iī** *m* scout.

ēmissīcius *adj* prying.

ēmissiō, -ōnis *f* letting go, discharge.

ēmissus *ppp of* **ēmittō**.

ēmissus, -ūs *m* emission.

ēmittō, -ittere, -īsī, -issum *vt* to send out, let out; to let go, let slip; (*missile*) to discharge; (*person*) to release, free; (*sound*) to utter; (*writing*) to publish.

emō, -ere, ēmī, emptum *vt* to buy, procure; to win over; **bene ~** buy cheap; **male ~** buy dear; **in diem ~** buy on credit.

ēmoderor, -ārī *vt* to give expression to.

ēmodulor, -ārī *vt* to sing through.

ēmōlior, -īrī *vt* to accomplish.

ēmolliō, -īre, -iī, -ītum *vt* to soften; to mollify; to enervate.

ēmolumentum, -ī *nt* profit, advantage.

ēmoneō, -ēre *vt* to strongly advise.

ēmorior, -ī, -tuus *vi* to die; (*fig*) to pass away.

ēmortuālis *adj* of death.

ēmoveō, -ovēre, -ōvī, -ōtum *vt* to remove, drive away.

Empedoclēs, -is *m* Sicilian philosopher.

Empedoclēus *adj see n.*

empīricus, -ī *m* empirical doctor.

emporium, -ī *and* **iī** *nt* market, market town.

emptiō, -ōnis *f* buying; a purchase.

emptitō, -āre *vt* to often buy.

emptor, -ōris *m* purchaser.

emptus *ppp of* **emō**.

ēmulgeō, -ēre *vt* to drain.

ēmunctus *ppp of* **ēmungō** ♦ *adj* discriminating.

ēmungō, -gere, -xī, -ctum *vt* to blow the nose of; (*comedy*) to cheat.

ēmūniō, -īre, -īvī, -ītum *vt* to strengthen, secure; to build up; to make roads through.

ēn *interj* (*drawing attention*) look!, see!; (*excited question*) really, indeed; (*command*) come now!

ēnārrābilis *adj* describable.

ēnārrō, -āre, -āvī, -ātum *vt* to describe in detail.

ēnāscor, -scī, -tus *vi* to sprout, grow.

ēnatō, -āre *vi* to swim ashore; (*fig*) to escape.

ēnātus *ppa of* **ēnāscor**.

ēnāvigō, -āre *vi* to sail clear, clear ♦ *vt* to sail over.

Enceladus, -ī *m* giant under Etna.

endromis, -dis *f* sports wrap.

Endymiōn, -ōnis *m a beautiful youth loved by the Moon, and doomed to lasting sleep.*

ēnecō, -āre, -uī *and* **-āvī, -tum** *and* **ātum** *vt* to kill; to wear out; to torment.

ēnervātus *adj* limp.

ēnervis *adj* enfeebled.

ēnervō, -āre, -āvī, -ātum *vt* to weaken, unman.

ēnicō *etc see* **ēnecō**.

enim *conj* (*affirming*) yes, truly, in fact; (*explaining*) for, for instance, of course; **at ~** but it will be objected; **quid ~** well?; **sed ~** but actually.

enimvērō *conj* certainly, yes indeed.

Enīpeus, -eī *m river in Thessaly.*

ēnīsus *ppa of* **ēnītor**.

ēniteō, -ēre, -uī *vi* to shine, brighten up; (*fig*) to be brilliant, distinguish oneself.

ēnitēscō, -ēscere, -uī *vi* to shine, be brilliant.

ēnītor, -tī, -sus *and* **xus** *vi* to struggle up, climb; to strive, make a great effort ♦ *vt* to give birth to; to climb.

ēnīxē *adv* earnestly.

ēnīxus *ppa of* **ēnītor** ♦ *adj* strenuous.

Enniānus *adj see n.*

Ennius, -ī *m greatest of the early Latin poets.*

Ennosigaeus, -ī *m* Earthshaker, Neptune.

ēnō, -āre, -āvī *vi* to swim out, swim ashore; to fly away.

ēnōdātē *adv* lucidly.

ēnōdātiō, -ōnis *f* unravelling.

ēnōdis *adj* free from knots; plain.

ēnōdō, -āre, -āvī, -ātum *vt* to elucidate.

ēnōrmis *adj* irregular; immense.

ēnōtēscō, -ēscere, -uī *vi* to get known.

ēnotō, -āre *vt* to make a note of.

ēnsiculus, -ī *m* little sword.

ēnsiger, -ī *adj* with his sword.

ēnsis, -is *m* sword.

enthȳmēma, -tis *nt* argument.

ēnūbō, -bere, -psī *vi* to marry out of one's station; to marry and go away.

ēnucleātē *adv* plainly.

ēnucleātus *adj* (*style*) straightforward; (*votes*) honest.

ēnucleō, -āre *vt* to elucidate.

ēnumerātiō, -ōnis *f* enumeration; (RHET) recapitulation.

ēnumerō, -āre *vt* to count up; to pay out; to relate.

ēnūntiātiō, -ōnis *f* proposition.

ēnūntiātum, -ī *nt* proposition.

ēnūntiō, -āre *vt* to disclose, report; to

express; to pronounce.

ēnūptiō, -ōnis f marrying out of one's station.

ēnūtriō, -īre vt to feed, bring up.

eō, īre, īvī and **iī, itum** vi to go; (*MIL*) to march; (*time*) to pass; (*event*) to proceed, turn out; **in alia omnia ~** vote against a bill; **in sententiam ~** support a motion; **sīc eat** so may he fare!; **ī** (*mocking*) go on!

eō adv (*place*) thither, there; (*purpose*) with a view to; (*degree*) so far, to such a pitch; (*time*) so long; (*cause*) on that account, for the reason; (*with compar*) the; **accēdit eō** besides; **rēs erat eō locī** such was the state of affairs; **eō magis** all the more.

eōdem adv to the same place, purpose or person; **~ locī** in the same place.

Ēōs f dawn ♦ m morning star; Oriental.

Ēous adj at dawn, eastern.

Ēpamīnōndās, -ae m *Theban general.*

ēpāstus adj eaten up.

ephēbus, -ī m youth (*18 to 20*).

ephēmeris, -idis f diary.

Ephesius adj see n.

Ephesus, -ī f *Ionian town in Asia Minor.*

ephippiātus adj riding a saddled horse.

ephippium, -ī and **iī** nt saddle.

ephorus, -ī m *a Spartan magistrate,* ephor.

Ephyra, -ae, -ē, -ēs f Corinth.

Ephyrēius adj see Ephyra.

Epicharmus, -ī m *Greek philosopher and comic poet.*

epichysis, -is f kind of jug.

epicōpus adj rowing.

Epicūrēus, epicus adj epic.

Epicūrus, -ī m *famous Greek philosopher.*

Epidaurius adj see n.

Epidaurus, -ī f *town in E. Peloponnese.*

epidīcticus adj (*RHET*) for display.

epigramma, -tis nt inscription; epigram.

epilogus, -ī m peroration.

epimēnia, -ōrum ntpl a month's rations.

Epimēthis, -dis f Pyrrha (*daughter of Epimetheus*).

epirēdium, -ī and **iī** nt trace.

Ēpīrōtēs, -ōtae m native of Epirus.

Ēpīrōticus, -ēnsis adj see n.

Ēpīrus, -os, -ī f *district of N.W. Greece.*

episcopus, -ī m bishop.

epistolium, -ī and **iī** nt short note.

epistula, -ae f letter; **ab ~īs** secretary.

epitaphium, -ī and **iī** nt funeral oration.

epithēca, -ae f addition.

epitoma, -ae, -ē, -ēs f abridgement.

epitȳrum, -ī nt olive salad.

epops, -is m hoopoe.

epos (*pl -ē*) nt epic.

ēpōtō, -āre, -āvī, -um vt to drink up, drain; to waste in drink; to absorb.

epulae, -ārum fpl dishes; feast, banquet.

epulāris adj at a banquet.

epulō, -ōnis m guest at a feast; priest in charge of religious banquets.

epulor, -ārī, -ātus vi to be at a feast ♦ vt to feast on.

epulum, -ī nt banquet.

equa, -ae f mare.

eques, -itis m horseman, trooper; (*pl*) cavalry; knight, member of the equestrian order.

equester, -ris adj equestrian; cavalry- (*in cpds*).

equidem adv (*affirming*) indeed, of course, for my part; (*concessive*) to be sure.

equīnus adj horse's.

equīria, -ōrum ntpl horseraces.

equitātus, -ūs m cavalry.

equitō, -āre vi to ride.

equuleus etc see eculeus.

equulus, -ī m colt.

equus, -ī m horse; (*ASTRO*) Pegasus; **~ bipēs** seahorse; **~ō merēre** serve in the cavalry; **~īs virīsque** with might and main.

era, -ae f mistress (of the house); (*goddess*) Lady.

ērādīcō, -āre vt to root out, destroy.

ērādō, -dere, -sī, -sum vt to erase, obliterate.

Eratō f *Muse of lyric poetry.*

Eratosthenēs, -is m *famous Alexandrian geographer.*

Erebēus adj see n.

Erebus, -ī m *god of darkness; the lower world.*

Erechtheus, -eī m *legendary king of Athens.*

Erechthēus adj see n.

Erechthīdae mpl Athenians

Erechthis, -idis f Orithyia; Procris.

ērēctus ppp of **ērigō** ♦ adj upright, lofty; noble, haughty; alert, tense; resolute.

ērēpō, -ere, -sī vi to creep out, clamber up ♦ vt to crawl over, climb.

ēreptiō, -ōnis f seizure, robbery.

ēreptor, -ōris m robber.

ēreptus ppp of **ēripiō**.

ergā prep (*with acc*) towards; against.

ergastulum, -ī nt prison (*esp for slaves*); (*pl*) convicts.

ergō adv therefore, consequently; (*questions, commands*) then so; (*resuming*) well then; (*with gen*) for the sake of, because of.

Erichthonius, -ī m *a king of Troy; a king of Athens* ♦ adj Trojan; Athenian.

ēricius, -ī and **iī** m hedgehog; (*MIL*) beam with iron spikes.

Ēridanus, -ī m *mythical name of river Po.*

erifuga, -ae m runaway slave.

ērigō, -igere, -ēxī, -ēctum vt to make upright, raise up, erect; to excite; to encourage.

Ērigonē, -ēs f (*constellation*) Virgo.

Ērigonēius adj see n.

Noun declensions and verb conjugations are shown on pp xiii to xxv. The present infinitive ending of a verb shows to which conjugation it belongs: **-āre** = 1st; **-ēre** = 2nd; **-ere** = 3rd and **-īre** = 4th. Irregular verbs are shown on p xxvi

erīlis *adj* the master's, the mistress's.
Erīnȳs, -yos *f* Fury; *(fig)* curse, frenzy.
Eriphȳla, -ae *f* mother of Alcmaeon *(who killed her).*
ēripiō, -ipere, -ipuī, -eptum *vt* to tear away, pull away, take by force; to rob; to rescue; **sē ~ escape.**
ērogātiō, -ōnis *f* paying out.
ērogitō, -āre *vt* to enquire.
ērogō, -āre, -āvī, -ātum *vt* to pay out, expend; to bequeath.
errābundus *adj* wandering.
errāticus *adj* roving, shifting.
errātiō, -ōnis *f* wandering, roving.
errātum, -ī *nt* mistake, error.
errātus, -ūs *m* wandering.
errō, -āre, -āvī, -ātum *vi* to wander, stray, lose one's way; to waver; to make a mistake, err ♦ *vt* to traverse; **stēllae ~antēs** planets.
errō, -ōnis *m* vagabond.
error, -ōris *m* wandering; meander, maze; uncertainty; error, mistake, delusion; deception.
ērubēscō, -ēscere, -uī *vi* to blush; to feel ashamed ♦ *vt* to blush for, be ashamed of; to respect.
ērūca, -ae *f* colewort.
ēructō, -āre *vt* to belch, vomit; to talk drunkenly about; to throw up.
ērudiō, -īre, -iī, -ītum *vt* to educate, instruct.
ērudītē *adv* learnedly.
ērudītiō, -ōnis *f* education, instruction; learning, knowledge.
ērudītulus *adj* somewhat skilled.
ērudītus *ppp of* **ērudiō** ♦ *adj* learned, educated, accomplished.
ērumpō, -umpere, -ūpī, -uptum *vt* to break open; to make break out ♦ *vi* to burst out, break through; to end (in).
ēruō, -ere, -ī, -tum *vt* to uproot, tear out; to demolish, destroy; to elicit, draw out; to rescue.
ēruptiō, -ōnis *f* eruption; *(MIL)* sally.
ēruptus *ppp of* **ērumpō.**
erus, -ī *m* master (of the house); owner.
ērutus *ppp of* **ēruō.**
ervum, -ī *nt* vetch.
Erycīnus *adj* of Eryx; of Venus; Sicilian ♦ *f* Venus.
Erymanthius, -is *adj see n.*
Erymanthus *and* **-ī** *m* mountain range in Arcadia, *(where Hercules killed the bear).*
Eryx, -cis *m* town and mountain in the extreme W. of Sicily.
esca, -ae *f* food, tit-bits; bait.
escārius *adj* of food; of bait ♦ *ntpl* dishes.
ēscendō, -endere, -endī, -ēnsum *vi* to climb up, go up ♦ *vt* to mount.
ēscēnsiō, -ōnis *f* raid (from the coast); disembarkation.
esculentus *adj* edible, tasty.
Esquiliae, -iārum *fpl* Esquiline hill in Rome.
Esquilīnus *adj* Esquiline ♦ *f* Esquiline gate.

essedārius, -ī *and* **iī** *m* chariot fighter.
essedum, -ī *nt* war chariot.
essitō, -āre *vt* to usually eat.
ēst *pres of* **edō.**
ēstrīx, -īcis *f* glutton.
ēsuriālis *adj* of hunger.
ēsuriō, -īre, -ītum *vi* to be hungry ♦ *vt* to hunger for.
ēsurītiō, -ōnis *f* hunger.
ēsus *ppp of* **edō.**
et *conj* and; *(repeated)* both ... and; *(adding emphasis)* in fact, yes; *(comparing)* as, than ♦ *adv* also, too; even.
etenim *conj (adding an explanation)* and as a matter of fact, in fact.
etēsiae, -ārum *fpl* Etesian winds.
etēsius *adj see n.*
ēthologus, -ī *m* mimic.
etiam *adv* also, besides; *(emphatic)* even, actually; *(affirming)* yes, certainly; *(indignant)* really!; *(time)* still, as yet; again; **~ atque ~** again and again; **~ cavēs!** do be careful!; **nihil ~** nothing at all.
etiamdum *adv* still, as yet.
etiamnum, etiamnunc *adv* still, till now, till then; besides.
etiamsī *conj* even if, although.
etiamtum, etiamtunc *adv* till then, still.
Etrūria, -ae *f* district of Italy north of Rome.
Etruscus *adj* Etruscan.
etsī *conj* even if, though; and yet.
etymologia, -ae *f* etymology.
eu *interj* well done!, bravo!
Euan *m* Bacchus.
Euander *and* **rus, -rī** *m* Evander *(ancient king on the site of Rome).*
Euandrius *adj see n.*
euax *interj* hurrah!
Euboea, -oeae *f* Greek island.
Euboicus *adj* Euboean.
euge, eugepae *interj* bravo!, cheers!
Euhan *m* Bacchus.
euhāns, -antis *adj* shouting the Bacchic cry.
Euhias *f* Bacchante.
Euhius, -ī *m* Bacchus.
euhoe *interj* ecstatic cry of Bacchic revellers.
Euius, -ī *m* Bacchus.
Eumenides, -um *fpl* Furies.
eunūchus, -ī *m* eunuch.
Euphrātēs, -is *m* river Euphrates.
Eupolis, -dis *m* Athenian comic poet.
Eurīpidēs, -is *m* Athenian tragic poet.
Eurīpidēus *adj see n.*
Eurīpus, -ī *m* strait between Euboea and mainland; a channel, conduit.
Eurōpa, -ae *and* **ē, -ēs** *f* mythical princess of Tyre *(who was carried by a bull to Crete);* continent of Europe.
Eurōpaeus *adj see n.*
Eurōtās, -ae *m* river of Sparta.
Eurōus *adj* eastern.
Eurus, -ī *m* east wind; south-east wind.
Eurydicē, -ēs *f* wife of Orpheus.

Eurystheus–exanimis

Eurystheus, -eī m king of Mycenae (who imposed the labours on Hercules).

euschēmē adv gracefully.

Euterpē, -ēs f Muse of music.

Euxīnus m the Black (Sea).

ēvādō, -dere, -sī, -sum vi to come out; to climb up; to escape; to turn out, result, come true ♦ vt to pass, mount; to escape from.

ēvagor, -ārī, -ātus vi (MIL) to manoeuvre; (fig) to spread ♦ vt to stray beyond.

ēvalēscō, -ēscere, -uī vi to grow, increase; to be able; to come into vogue.

Ēvander etc see **Euander**.

ēvānēscō, -ēscere, -uī vi to vanish, die away, lose effect.

ēvangelium, -ī and **iī** nt (ECCL) Gospel.

ēvānidus adj vanishing.

ēvāsī perf of **ēvādō**.

ēvastō, -āre vt to devastate.

ēvehō, -here, -xī, -ctum vt to carry out; to raise up, exalt; to spread abroad; (pass) to ride, sail, move out.

ēvellō, -ellere, -ellī, -ulsum vt to tear out, pull out; to eradicate.

ēveniō, -enīre, -ēnī, -entum vi to come out; to turn out, result; to come to pass, happen, befall.

ēventum, -ī nt result, issue; occurrence, event; fortune, experience.

ēventus, -ūs m result, issue; success; fortune, fate.

ēverberō, -āre vt to beat violently.

ēverriculum, -ī nt dragnet.

ēverrō, -rere, -rī, -sum vt to sweep out, clean out.

ēversiō, -ōnis f overthrow, destruction.

ēversor, -ōris m destroyer.

ēversus ppp of **ēverrō**; ppp of **ēvertō**.

ēvertō, -tere, -tī, -sum vt to turn out, eject; to turn up, overturn; to overthrow, ruin, destroy.

ēvestīgātus adj tracked down.

ēvictus ppp of **ēvincō**.

ēvidēns, -entis adj visible, plain, evident.

ēvidenter adv see **ēvidēns**.

ēvidentia, -ae f distinctness.

ēvigilō, -āre, -āvī, -ātum vi to be wide awake ♦ vt to compose carefully.

ēvīlēscō, -ere vi to become worthless.

ēvinciō, -cīre, -xī, -ctum vt to garland, crown.

ēvinco, -incere, -īcī, -ictum vt to overcome, conquer; to prevail over; to prove.

ēvirō, -āre vt to castrate.

ēviscerō, -āre vt to disembowel, tear to pieces.

ēvītābilis adj avoidable.

ēvītō, -āre, -āvī, -ātum vt to avoid, clear.

ēvocātī, -ōrum mpl veteran volunteers.

ēvocātor, -ōris m enlister.

ēvocō, -āre, -āvī, -ātum vt to call out, summon; to challenge; to call up; to call forth, evoke.

ēvolō, -āre, -āvī, -ātum vi to fly out, fly away; to rush out; (fig) to rise, soar.

ēvolūtiō, -ōnis f unrolling (a book).

ēvolvō, -vere, -vī, -ūtum vt to roll out, roll along; to unroll, unfold; (book) to open, read; (fig) to disclose, unravel, disentangle.

ēvomō, -ere, -uī, -itum vt to vomit up, disgorge.

ēvulgō, -āre, -āvī, -ātum vt to divulge, make public.

ēvulsiō, -ōnis f pulling out.

ēvulsus ppp of **ēvellō**.

ex, ē prep (with abl) (place) out of, from, down from; (person) from; (time) after, immediately after, since; (change) from being; (source, material) of; (cause) by reason of, through; (conformity) in accordance with; **ex itinere** on the march; **ex parte** in part; **ex quō** since; **ex rē, ex ūsū** for the good of; **ē rē pūblicā** constitutionally; **ex sententiā** to one's liking; **aliud ex aliō** one thing after another; **ūnus ex** one of.

exacerbō, -āre vt to exasperate.

exāctiō, -ōnis f expulsion; supervision; tax; (debts) calling in.

exāctor, -ōris m expeller; superintendent; tax collector.

exāctus ppp of **exigō** ♦ adj precise, exact.

exacuō, -uere, -uī, -ūtum vt to sharpen; (fig) to quicken, inflame.

exadversum, -us adv, prep (with acc) right opposite.

exaedificātiō, -ōnis f construction.

exaedificō, -āre vt to build up; to finish the building of.

exaequātiō, -ōnis f levelling.

exaequō, -āre, -āvī, -ātum vt to level out; to compensate; to put on an equal footing; to equal.

exaestuō, -āre vi to boil up.

exaggerātiō, -ōnis f exaltation.

exaggerō, -āre, -āvī, -ātum vt to pile up; (fig) to heighten, enhance.

exagitātor, -ōris m critic.

exagitō, -āre, -āvī, -ātum vt to disturb, harass; to scold, censure; to excite, incite.

exagōga, -ae f export.

exalbēscō, -ēscere, -uī vi to turn quite pale.

exāmen, -inis nt swarm, crowd; tongue of a balance; examining.

examinō, -āre, -āvī, -ātum vt to weigh; to consider, test.

examussim adv exactly, perfectly.

exanclō, -āre vt to drain; to endure to the end.

exanimālis adj dead; deadly.

exanimātiō, -ōnis f panic.

exanimis adj lifeless, breathless; terrified.

Noun declensions and verb conjugations are shown on pp xiii to xxv. The present infinitive ending of a verb shows to which conjugation it belongs: **-āre** = 1st; **-ēre** = 2nd; **-ere** = 3rd and **-īre** = 4th. Irregular verbs are shown on p xxvi

exanimō, -āre, -āvī, -ātum *vt* to wind; to kill; to terrify, agitate; (*pass*) to be out of breath.

exanimus *see* **exanimis**.

exārdēscō, -dēscere, -sī, -sum *vi* to catch fire, blaze up; (*fig*) to be inflamed, break out.

exārēscō, -ēscere, -uī *vi* to dry, dry up.

exarmō, -āre *vt* to disarm.

exarō, -āre, -āvi, -ātum *vt* to plough up; to cultivate, produce; (*brow*) to furrow; (*writing*) to pen.

exārsī *perf of* **exārdēscō**.

exasciātus *adj* hewn out.

exasperō, -āre, -āvī, -ātum *vt* to roughen; (*fig*) to provoke.

exauctōrō, -āre, -āvī, -ātum *vt* (*MIL*) to discharge, release; to cashier.

exaudiō, -īre, -īvī, -ītum *vt* to hear clearly; to listen to; to obey.

exaugeō, -ēre *vt* to increase.

exaugurātiō, -ōnis *f* desecrating.

exaugurō, -āre *vt* to desecrate.

exauspicō, -āre *vi* to take an omen.

exbibō *etc see* **ēbibō**.

excaecō, -āre *vt* to blind; (*river*) to block up.

excandēscentia, -ae *f* growing anger.

excandēscō, -ēscere, -uī *vi* to burn, be inflamed.

excantō, -āre *vt* to charm out, spirit away.

excarnificō, -āre *vt* to tear to pieces.

excavō, -āre *vt* to hollow out.

excēdō, -ēdere, -essī, -essum *vi* to go out, go away; to die, disappear; to advance, proceed (to); to digress ♦ *vt* to leave; to overstep, exceed.

excellēns, -entis *pres p of* **excellō** ♦ *adj* outstanding, excellent.

excellenter *adv see* **excellēns**.

excellentia, -ae *f* superiority, excellence.

excellō, -ere *vi* to be eminent, excel.

excelsē *adv* loftily.

excelsitās, -ātis *f* loftiness.

excelsum, -ī *nt* height.

excelsus *adj* high, elevated; eminent, illustrious.

exceptiō, -ōnis *f* exception, restriction; (*law*) objection.

exceptō, -āre *vt* to catch, take out.

exceptus *ppp of* **excipiō**.

excernō, -ernere, -rēvī, -rētum *vt* to sift out, separate.

excerpō, -ere, -sī, -tum *vt* to take out; to select, copy out extracts; to leave out, omit.

excessus, -ūs *m* departure, death.

excetra, -ae *f* snake.

excidiō, -ōnis *f* destruction.

excidium, -ī *and* **iī** *nt* overthrow, destruction.

excidō, -ere, -ī *vi* to fall out, fall; (*speech*) to slip out, escape; (*memory*) to get forgotten, escape; (*person*) to fail, lose; (*things*) to disappear, be lost.

excīdō, -dere, -dī, -sum *vt* to cut off, hew out, fell; to raze; (*fig*) to banish.

excieō *vt see* **exciō**.

exciō, -īre, -īvī *and* **iī, -itum** *and* **ītum** *vt* to call out, rouse, summon; to occasion, produce; to excite.

excipiō, -ipere, -ēpī, -eptum *vt* to take out, remove; to exempt, make an exception of, mention specifically; to take up, catch, intercept, overhear; to receive, welcome, entertain; to come next to, follow after, succeed.

excīsiō, -ōnis *f* destroying.

excīsus *ppp of* **excīdō**.

excitātus *adj* loud, strong.

excitō, -āre, -āvī, -ātum *vt* to rouse, wake up, summon; to raise, build; to call on (to stand up); (*fig*) to encourage, revive, excite.

excitus, excītus *ppp of* **exciō**.

exclāmātiō, -ōnis *f* exclamation.

exclāmō, -āre, -āvī, -ātum *vi* to cry out, shout ♦ *vt* to exclaim, call.

exclūdō, -dere, -sī, -sum *vt* to shut out, exclude; to shut off, keep off; (*egg*) to hatch out; (*eye*) to knock out; (*fig*) to prevent, except.

exclūsiō, -ōnis *f* shutting out.

exclūsus *ppp of* **exclūdō**.

excoctus *ppp of* **excoquō**.

excōgitātiō, -ōnis *f* thinking out, devising.

excōgitō, -āre, -āvī, -ātum *vt* to think out, contrive.

excolō, -olere, -oluī, -ultum *vt* to work carefully; to perfect, refine.

excoquō, -quere, -xī, -ctum *vt* to boil away; to remove with heat, make with heat; to dry up.

excors, -dis *adj* senseless, stupid.

excrēmentum, -ī *nt* excretion.

excreō *etc see* **exscreō**.

excrēscō, -scere, -vī, -tum *vi* to grow, rise up.

excrētus *ppp of* **excernō**.

excruciō, -āre, -āvī, -ātum *vt* to torture, torment.

excubiae, -ārum *fpl* keeping guard, watch; sentry.

excubitor, -ōris *m* sentry.

excubō, -āre, -uī, -itum *vi* to sleep out of doors; to keep watch; (*fig*) to be on the alert.

excūdō, -dere, -dī, -sum *vt* to strike out, hammer out; (*egg*) to hatch; (*fig*) to make, compose.

exculcō, -āre *vt* to beat, tramp down.

excultus *ppp of* **excolō**.

excurrō, -rrere, -currī *and* **rrī, -rsum** *vi* to run out, hurry out; to make an excursion; (*MIL*) to make a sortie; (*place*) to extend, project; (*fig*) to expand.

excursiō, -ōnis *f* raid, sortie; (*gesture*) stepping forward; (*fig*) outset.

excursor, -ōris *m* scout.

excursus, -ūs *m* excursion, raid, charge.

excūsābilis *adj* excusable.

excūsātē *adv* excusably.

excūsātiō, -ōnis *f* excuse, plea.

excūsō, -āre, -āvī, -ātum *vt* to excuse; to apologize for; to plead as an excuse.

excussus *ppp of* **excutiō**.

excūsus *ppp of* **excūdō**.

excutiō, -tere, -ssī, -ssum *vt* to shake out, shake off; to knock out, drive out, cast off; (*fig*) to discard, banish; to examine, inspect.

exdorsuō, -āre *vt* to fillet.

exec- *etc see* **exsec-**.

exedō, -ēsse, -ēdī, -ēsum *vt* to eat up; to wear away, destroy; (*feelings*) to prey on.

exedra, -ae *f* hall, lecture room.

exedrium, -ī *and* **iī** *nt* sitting room.

exēmī *perf of* **eximō**.

exemplar, -āris *nt* copy; likeness; model, ideal.

exemplārēs *mpl* copies.

exemplum, -ī *nt* copy; example, sample, precedent, pattern; purport, nature; warning, object lesson; **~ dare** set an example; **~ī causā, gratiā** for instance.

exemptus *ppp of* **eximō**.

exenterō, -āre *vt* (*comedy*) to empty, clean out; to torture.

exeō, -īre, -iī, -itum *vi* to go out, leave; to come out, issue; (*MIL*) to march out; (*time*) to expire; to spring up, rise ♦ *vt* to pass beyond; to avoid; **~ ex potestāte** lose control.

exeq- *etc see* **exseq-**.

exerceō, -ēre, -uī, -itum *vt* to keep busy, supervise; (*ground*) to work, cultivate; (*MIL*) to drill, exercise; (*mind*) to engage, employ; (*occupation*) to practise, follow, carry on; (*trouble*) to worry, harass; **sē ~** practise, exercise.

exercitātiō, -ōnis *f* practice, exercise, experience.

exercitātus *adj* practised, trained, versed; troubled.

exercitium, -ī *and* **iī** *nt* exercising.

exercitō, -āre *vt* to exercise.

exercitor, -ōris *m* trainer.

exercitus *ppp of* **exerceō** ♦ *adj* disciplined; troubled; troublesome.

exercitus, -ūs *m* army (*esp the infantry*); assembly; troop, flock; exercise.

exerō *etc see* **exserō**.

exēsor, -ōris *m* corroder.

exēsus *ppp of* **exedō**.

exhālātiō, -ōnis *f* vapour.

exhālō, -āre *vt* to exhale, breathe out ♦ *vi* to steam; to expire.

exhauriō, -rīre, -sī, -stum *vt* to drain off; to empty; to take away, remove; (*fig*) to exhaust, finish; (*trouble*) to undergo, endure to the end.

exhērēdō, -āre *vt* to disinherit.

exhērēs, -ēdis *adj* disinherited.

exhibeō, -ere, -uī, -itum *vt* to hold out, produce (in public); to display, show; to

cause, occasion.

exhilarātus *adj* delighted.

exhorrēscō, -ēscere, -uī *vi* to be terrified ♦ *vt* to be terrified at.

exhortātiō, -ōnis *f* encouragement.

exhortor -ārī, -ātus *vt* to encourage.

exigō, -igere, -ēgī, -āctum *vt* to drive out, thrust; (*payment*) to exact, enforce; to demand, claim; (*goods*) to dispose of; (*time*) to pass, complete; (*work*) to finish; (*news*) to ascertain; to test, examine, consider.

exiguē *adv* briefly, slightly, hardly.

exiguitās, -ātis *f* smallness, meagreness.

exiguus *adj* small, short, meagre ♦ *nt* a little bit.

exiliō *etc see* **exsiliō**.

exīlis *adj* thin, small, meagre; poor; (*style*) flat, insipid.

exīlitās, -ātis *f* thinness, meagreness.

exīliter *adv* feebly.

exilium *etc see* **exsilium**.

exim *see* **exinde**.

eximiē *adv* exceptionally.

eximius *adj* exempt; select; distinguished, exceptional.

eximō, -imere, -ēmī, -emptum *vt* to take out, remove; to release, free; to exempt; (*time*) to waste; (*fig*) to banish.

exin *see* **exinde**.

exināniō, -īre, -iī, -ītum *vt* to empty; to pillage.

exinde *adv* (*place*) from there, next; (*time*) then, thereafter, next; (*measure*) accordingly.

exīstimātiō, -ōnis *f* opinion, judgment; reputation, character; (*money*) credit.

exīstimātor, -ōris *m* judge, critic.

exīstimō, -āre, -āvī, -ātum *vt* to value, estimate, judge, think, consider.

existō *etc see* **exsistō**.

exīstumō *vt see* **exīstimō**.

exitiābilis *adj* deadly, fatal.

exitiālis *adj* deadly.

exitiōsus *adj* pernicious, fatal.

exitium, -ī *and* **iī** *nt* destruction, ruin.

exitus, -ūs *m* departure; way out, outlet; conclusion, end; death; outcome, result.

exlēx, -ēgis *adj* above the law, lawless.

exoculō, -āre *vt* to knock the eyes out of.

exodium, -ī *and* **iī** *nt* afterpiece.

exolēscō, -scere, -vī, -tum *vi* to decay, become obsolete.

exolētus *adj* full-grown.

exonerō, -āre, -āvī, -ātum *vt* to unload, discharge; (*fig*) to relieve, exonerate.

exoptātus *adj* welcome.

exoptō, -āre, -āvī, -ātum *vt* to long for, desire.

exōrābilis *adj* sympathetic.

exōrātor, -ōris *m* successful pleader.

exōrdior, -dīrī, -sus *vt* to lay the warp; to begin.

exōrdium, -ī *and* **i ī** *nt* beginning; (*RHET*) introductory section.

exorior, -īrī, -tus *vi* to spring up, come out, rise; to arise, appear, start.

exōrnātiō, -ōnis *f* embellishment.

exōrnātor, -ōris *m* embellisher.

exōrnō, -āre, -āvī, -ātum *vt* to equip, fit out; to embellish, adorn.

exōrō, -āre, -āvī, -ātum *vt* to prevail upon, persuade; to obtain, win by entreaty.

exōrsus *ppa of* **exōrdior ♦** *adj* begun **♦** *ntpl* preamble.

exōrsus, -ūs *m* beginning.

exortus *ppa of* **exorior**.

exortus, -ūs *m* rising; east.

exos, -ossis *adj* boneless.

exōsculor, -ārī, -ātus *vt* to kiss fondly.

exossō, -āre *vt* to bone.

exōstra, -ae *f* stage mechanism; (*fig*) public.

exōsus *adj* detesting.

exōticus *adj* foreign.

expallēscō, -ēscere, -uī *vi* to turn pale, be afraid.

expalpō, -āre *vt* to coax out.

expandō, -ere *vt* to unfold.

expatrō, -āre *vt* to squander.

expavēscō, -ere, expāvī *vi* to be terrified **♦** *vt* to dread.

expect- *etc see* **exspect-**.

expediō, -īre, -īvī *and* **i ī, -ītum** *vt* to free, extricate, disentangle; to prepare, clear (for action); to put right, settle; to explain, relate; (*impers*) it is useful, expedient.

expedītē *adv* readily, freely.

expedītiō, -ōnis *f* (*MIL*) expedition, enterprise.

expedītus *ppp of* **expediō ♦** *adj* light-armed; ready, prompt; at hand **♦** *m* light-armed soldier; **in ~ō esse, habēre** be, have in readiness.

expellō, -ellere, -ulī, -ulsum *vt* to drive away, eject, expel; to remove, repudiate.

expendō, -endere, -endī, -ēnsum *vt* to weigh out; to pay out; (*penalty*) to suffer; (*mind*) to ponder, consider, judge.

expēnsum, -ī *nt* payment, expenditure.

expergēfaciō, -facere, -fēcī, -factum *vt* to rouse, excite.

expergīscor, -gīscī, -rēctus *vi* to wake up; to bestir oneself.

expergō, -ere, -ī, -itum *vt* to awaken.

experiēns, -entis *pres p of* **experior ♦** *adj* enterprising.

experientia, -ae *f* experiment; endeavour; experience, practice.

experimentum, -ī *nt* proof, test; experience.

experior, -īrī, -tus *vt* to test, make trial of; to attempt, experience; (*law*) to go to law; (*perf tenses*) to know from experience.

experrēctus *ppa of* **expergīscor**.

expers, -tis *adj* having no part in, not sharing; free from, without.

expertus *ppa of* **experior ♦** *adj* proved, tried; experienced.

expetessō, -ere *vt* to desire.

expetō, -ere, -īvī *and* **i ī, -ītum** *vt* to aim at, tend towards; to desire, covet; to attack; to demand, require **♦** *vi* to befall, happen.

expiātiō, -ōnis *f* atonement.

expictus *ppp of* **expingō**.

expīlātiō, -ōnis *f* pillaging.

expīlātor, -ōris *m* plunderer.

expīlō, -āre, -āvī, -ātum *vt* to rob, plunder.

expingō, -ingere, -inxī, -ictum *vt* to portray.

expiō, -āre, -āvī, -ātum *vt* to purify; to atone for, make amends for; to avert (evil).

expīrō *etc see* **exspīrō**.

expiscor, -ārī, -ātus *vt* to try to find out, ferret out.

explānātē *adv see* **explānātus**.

explānātiō, -ōnis *f* explanation.

explānātor, -ōris *m* interpreter.

explānātus *adj* distinct.

explānō, -āre, -āvī, -ātum *vt* to state clearly, explain; to pronounce clearly.

explaudō *etc see* **explōdō**.

explēmentum, -ī *nt* filling.

expleō, -ēre, -ēvī, -ētum *vt* to fill up; to complete; (*desire*) to satisfy, appease; (*duty*) to perform, discharge; (*loss*) to make good; (*time*) to fulfil, complete.

explētiō, -ōnis *f* satisfying.

explētus *ppp of* **expleō ♦** *adj* complete.

explicātē *adv* plainly.

explicātiō, -ōnis *f* uncoiling; expounding, analyzing.

explicātor, -ōris *m*, **-rīx, -rīcis** *f* expounder.

explicātus *adj* spread out; plain, clear.

explicātus, -ūs *m* explanation.

explicitus *adj* easy.

explicō, -āre, -āvī *and* **uī, -ātum** *and* **itum** *vt* to unfold, undo, spread out; (*book*) to open; (*MIL*) to deploy, extend; (*difficulty*) to put in order, settle; (*speech*) to develop, explain; to set free.

explōdō, -dere, -sī, -sum *vt* to hiss off, drive away; (*fig*) to reject.

explōrātē *adv* with certainty.

explōrātiō, -ōnis *f* spying.

explōrātor, -ōris *m* spy, scout.

explōrātus *adj* certain, sure.

explōrō, -āre, -āvī, -ātum *vt* to investigate, reconnoitre; to ascertain; to put to the test.

explōsī *perf of* **explōdō**.

explōsiō, -ōnis *f* driving off (the stage).

explōsus *ppp of* **explōdō**.

expoliō, -īre, -īvī, -ītum *vt* to smooth off, polish; (*fig*) to refine, embellish.

expolītiō, -ōnis *f* smoothing off; polish, finish.

expōnō, -ōnere, -osuī, -ositum *vt* to set out, put out; (*child*) to expose; (*NAUT*) to disembark; (*money*) to offer; (*fig*) to set forth, expose, display; (*speech*) to explain, expound.

exporrigō, -igere, -ēxī, -ēctum *vt* to extend, smooth out.

exportātiō, -ōnis *f* exporting.

exportō, -āre, -āvī, -ātum *vt* to carry out, export.

exposcō, -ere, expoposcī *vt* to implore, pray for; to demand.

expositīcius *adj* foundling.

expositiō, -ōnis *f* narration, explanation.

expositus *ppp of* **expōnō** ♦ *adj* open, affable; vulgar.

expostulātiō, -ōnis *f* complaint

expostulō, -āre, -āvī, -ātum *vt* to demand urgently; to complain of, expostulate.

expōtus *ppp of* **ēpōtō**.

expressus *ppp of* **exprimō** ♦ *adj* distinct, prominent.

exprimō, -imere, -essī, -essum *vt* to squeeze out, force out; to press up; (*fig*) to extort, wrest; (*art*) to mould, model; (*words*) to imitate, portray, translate, pronounce.

exprobrātiō, -ōnis *f* reproach.

exprobrō, -āre, -āvī, -ātum *vt* to reproach, cast up.

exprōmō, -ere, -psī, -ptum *vt* to bring out, fetch out; (*acts*) to exhibit, practise; (*feelings*) to give vent to; (*speech*) to disclose, state.

expugnābilis *adj* capable of being taken by storm.

expugnācior, -ōris *adj* more effective.

expugnātiō, -ōnis *f* storming, assault.

expugnātor, -ōris *m* stormer.

expugnō, -āre, -āvī, -ātum *vt* to storm, reduce; to conquer; (*fig*) to overcome, extort.

expulī *perf of* **expellō**.

expulsiō, -ōnis *f* expulsion.

expulsor, -ōris *m* expeller.

expulsus *ppp of* **expellō**.

expultrīx, -īcis *f* expeller.

expungō, -ungere, -ūnxī, -ūnctum *vt* to prick out, cancel.

expūrgātiō, -ōnis *f* excuse.

expūrgō, -āre *vt* to purify; to justify.

exputō, -āre *vt* to consider, comprehend.

exquīrō, -rere, -sīvī, -sītum *vt* to search out, investigate; to inquire; to devise.

exquīsītē *adv* with particular care.

exquīsītus *ppp of* **exquīrō** ♦ *adj* well thought out, choice.

exsaeviō, -īre *vi* to cease raging.

exsanguis *adj* bloodless, pale; feeble.

exsarciō, -cīre, -tum *vt* to repair.

exsatiō, -āre *vt* to satiate, satisfy.

exsaturābilis *adj* appeasable.

exsaturō, -āre *vt* to satiate.

exsce- *etc see* **esce-**.

exscindō, -ndere, -dī, -ssum *vt* to extirpate.

exscreō, -āre *vt* to cough up.

exscrībō, -bere, -psī, -ptum *vt* to copy out; to note down.

exsculpō, -ere, -sī, -tum *vt* to carve out; to erase; (*fig*) to extort.

exsecō, -āre, -uī, -tum *vt* to cut out; to castrate.

exsecrābilis *adj* cursing, deadly.

exsecrātiō, -ōnis *f* curse; solemn oath.

exsecrātus *adj* accursed.

exsecror, -ārī, -ātus *vt* to curse; to take an oath.

exsectiō, -ōnis *f* cutting out.

exsecūtiō, -ōnis *f* management; discussion.

exsecūtus *ppa of* **exsequor**.

exsequiae, -ārum *fpl* funeral, funeral rites.

exsequiālis *adj* funeral.

exsequor, -quī, -cūtus *vt* to follow, pursue; to follow to the grave; (*duty*) to carry out, accomplish; (*speech*) to describe, relate; (*suffering*) to undergo; (*wrong*) to avenge, punish.

exserciō *vt see* **exsarciō**.

exserō, -ere, -uī, -tum *vt* to put out, stretch out; to reveal.

exsertō, -āre *vt* to stretch out repeatedly.

exsertus *ppp of* **exserō** ♦ *adj* protruding.

exsībilō, -āre *vt* to hiss off.

exsiccātus *adj* (*style*) uninteresting.

exsiccō, -āre, -āvī, -ātum *vt* to dry up; to drain.

exsicō *etc see* **exsecō**.

exsignō, -āre *vt* to write down in detail.

exsiliō, -īre, -uī *vi* to jump up, spring out; to start.

exsilium, -ī *and* **iī** *nt* banishment, exile; retreat.

exsistō, -istere, -titī, -titum *vi* to emerge, appear; to arise, spring (from); to be, exist.

exsolvō, -vere, -vī, -ūtum *vt* to undo, loosen, open; to release, free; to get rid of, throw off; (*debt, promise*) to discharge, fulfil, pay up; (*words*) to explain.

exsomnis *adj* sleepless, watchful.

exsorbeō, -ēre, -uī *vt* to suck, drain; to devour, endure.

exsors, -tis *adj* chosen, special; free from.

exspargō *etc see* **exspergō**.

exspatior, -ārī, -ātus *vi* to go off the course.

exspectābilis *adj* to be expected.

exspectātiō, -ōnis *f* waiting, expectation.

exspectātus *adj* looked for, welcome.

exspectō, -āre, -āvī, -ātum *vt* to wait for, till; to see; to expect; to hope for, dread; to require.

exspergō, -gere, -sum *vt* to scatter; to diffuse.

exspēs *adj* despairing.

exspīrātiō, -ōnis *f* exhalation.

exspīrō, -āre, -āvī, -ātum *vt* to breathe out, exhale; to emit ♦ *vi* to rush out; to expire, come to an end.

exsplendēscō, -ere _vi_ to shine.

exspoliō, -āre _vt_ to pillage.

exspuō, -uere, -uī, -ūtum _vt_ to spit out, eject; (_fig_) to banish.

exsternō, -āre _vt_ to terrify.

exstillō, -āre _vi_ to drip.

exstimulātor, -ōris _m_ instigator.

exstimulō, -āre _vt_ to goad on; to excite.

exstinctiō, -ōnis _f_ annihilation.

exstinctor, -ōris _m_ extinguisher; destroyer.

exstinguō, -guere, -xī, -ctum _vt_ to put out, extinguish; to kill, destroy, abolish.

exstirpō, -āre _vt_ to root out, eradicate.

exstitī _perf of_ **exsistō**.

exstō, -āre _vi_ to stand out, project; to be conspicuous, be visible; to be extant, exist, be.

exstructiō, -ōnis _f_ erection.

exstruō, -ere, -xī, -ctum _vt_ to heap up; to build up, construct.

exsūdō, -āre _vi_ to come out in sweat ♦ _vt_ (_fig_) to toil through.

exsūgō, -gere, -xī, -ctum _vt_ to suck out.

exsul, -is _m/f_ exile.

exsulō, -āre, -āvī, -ātum _vi_ to be an exile.

exsultātiō, -ōnis _f_ great rejoicing.

exsultim _adv_ friskily.

exsultō, -āre, -āvī, -ātum _vi_ to jump up, prance; (_fig_) to exult, run riot, boast; (_speech_) to range at will.

exsuperābilis _adj_ superable.

exsuperantia, -ae _f_ superiority.

exsuperō, -āre, -āvī, -ātum _vi_ to mount up; to gain the upper hand, excel ♦ _vt_ to go over; to surpass; to overpower.

exsurdō, -āre _vt_ to deafen; (_fig_) to dull.

exsurgō, -gere, -rēxī, -rēctum _vi_ to rise, stand up; to recover.

exsuscitō, -āre _vt_ to wake up; (_fire_) to fan; (_mind_) to excite.

exta, -ōrum _ntpl_ internal organs.

extābēscō, -ēscere, -uī _vi_ to waste away; to vanish.

extāris _adj_ sacrificial.

extemplō _adv_ immediately, on the spur of the moment; **quom ~** as soon as.

extemporālis _adj_ extempore.

extempulō _see_ **extemplō**.

extendō, -dere, -dī, -tum _and_ **extēnsum** _vt_ to stretch out, spread, extend; to enlarge, increase; (_time_) to prolong; **sē ~** exert oneself; **īre per ~tum fūnem** walk the tightrope.

extēnsus _ppp of_ **extendō**.

extentō, -āre _vt_ to strain, exert.

extentus _ppp of_ **extendō** ♦ _adj_ broad.

extenuātiō, -ōnis _f_ (_RHET_) diminution.

extenuō, -āre, -āvī, -ātum _vt_ to thin out, rarefy; to diminish, weaken.

exter _adj_ from outside; foreign.

exterebrō, -āre _vt_ to bore out; to extort.

extergeō, -gēre, -sī, -sum _vt_ to wipe off, clean; to plunder.

exterior, -ōris _adj_ outer, exterior.

exterius _adv_ on the outside.

exterminō, -āre _vt_ to drive out, banish; (_fig_) to put aside.

externus _adj_ outward, external; foreign, strange.

exterō, -erere, -rīvī, -rītum _vt_ to rub out, wear away.

exterreō, -ēre, -uī, -itum _vt_ to frighten.

extersus _ppp of_ **extergeō**.

exterus _see_ **exter**.

extexō, -ere _vt_ to unweave; (_fig_) to cheat.

extimēscō, -ēscere, -uī _vi_ to be very frightened ♦ _vt_ to be very afraid of.

extimus _adj_ outermost, farthest.

extin- _etc see_ **exstin-**.

extispex, -icis _m_ diviner.

extollō, -ere _vt_ to lift up, raise; (_fig_) to exalt, beautify; (_time_) to defer.

extorqueō, -quēre, -sī, -tum _vt_ to wrench out, wrest; to dislocate; (_fig_) to obtain by force, extort.

extorris _adj_ banished, in exile.

extortor, -ōris _m_ extorter.

extortus _ppp of_ **extorqueō**.

extrā _adv_ outside; **~ quam** except that, unless ♦ _prep_ (_with acc_) outside, beyond; free from; except.

extrahō, -here, -xī, -ctum _vt_ to draw out, pull out; to extricate, rescue; to remove; (_time_) to prolong, waste.

extrāneus, -ī _m_ stranger ♦ _adj_ external, foreign.

extraōrdinārius _adj_ special, unusual.

extrārius _adj_ external; unrelated ♦ _m_ stranger.

extrēmitās, -ātis _f_ extremity, end.

extrēmum, -ī _nt_ end; **ad ~** at last.

extrēmum _adv_ for the last time.

extrēmus _adj_ outermost, extreme; last; utmost, greatest, meanest.

extrīcō, -āre, -āvī, -ātum _vt_ to disentangle, extricate; to clear up.

extrīnsecus _adv_ from outside, from abroad; on the outside.

extrītus _ppp of_ **exterō**.

extrūdō, -dere, -sī, -sum _vt_ to drive out; to keep out; (_sale_) to push.

extulī _perf of_ **efferō**.

extumeō, -ēre _vi_ to swell up.

extundō, -undere, -udī, -ūsum _vt_ to beat out, hammer out; (_comedy_) to extort; (_fig_) to form, compose.

exturbō, -āre, -āvī, -ātum _vt_ to drive out, throw out, knock out; (_wife_) to put away; (_fig_) to banish, disturb.

exūberō, -āre _vi_ to abound.

exul _etc see_ **exsul**.

exulcerō, -āre, -āvī, -ātum _vt_ to aggravate.

exululō, -āre _vi_ to howl wildly ♦ _vt_ to invoke with cries.

exūnctus _ppp of_ **exungō**.

exundō, -āre *vi* to overflow; to be washed up.
exungō, -ere *vt* to anoint liberally.
exuō, -uere, -uī, -ūtum *vt* to draw out, put
off; to lay aside; to strip.
exūrō, -rere, -ssī, -stum *vt* to burn up; to dry
up; to burn out; (*fig*) to inflame.
exūstiō, -ōnis *f* conflagration.
exūtus *ppp of* **exuō**.
exuviae, -ārum *fpl* clothing, arms; hide;
spoils.

F, f

faba, -ae *f* bean.
fabālis *adj* bean- (*in cpds*).
fābella, -ae *f* short story, fable; play.
faber, -rī *m* craftsman (*in metal, stone, wood*),
tradesman, smith; (*MIL*) artisan; **~ ferrārius**
blacksmith; **~ tignārius** carpenter ♦ *adj*
skilful.
Fabius, -ī *m* Roman family name (*esp Q F
Maximus Cunctator, dictator against Hannibal*).
fabrē *adv* skilfully.
fabrēfaciō, -facere, -fēcī, -factum *vt* to
make, build, forge.
fabrica, -ae *f* art, trade; work of art;
workshop; (*comedy*) trick.
fabricātiō, -ōnis *f* structure.
fabricātor, -ōris *m* artificer.
Fabricius, -ī *m* Roman family name (*esp C F
Luscinus, incorruptible commander against
Pyrrhus*).
Fabricius, -iānus *adj see n.*
fabricō, -āre; -or, -ārī, -ātus *vt* to make,
build, forge.
fabrīlis *adj* artificer's ♦ *ntpl* tools.
fābula, -ae *f* story; common talk; play, drama;
fable; **~ae!** nonsense!; **lupus in ~ā** ≈ *talk of the
devil!*
fābulor, -ārī, -ātus *vi* to talk, converse ♦ *vt* to
say, invent.
fābulōsus *adj* legendary.
facessō, -ere, -īvī, -ītum *vt* to perform, carry
out; to cause (trouble) ♦ *vi* to go away, retire.
facētē *adv* humorously; brilliantly.
facētiae, -ārum *fpl* wit, clever talk, humour.
facētus *adj* witty, humorous; fine, genteel,
elegant.
faciēs, -ēī *f* form, shape; face, looks;
appearance, aspect, character.

facile *adv* easily; unquestionably; readily;
pleasantly.
facilis *adj* easy; well-suited; ready, quick;
(*person*) good-natured, approachable;
(*fortune*) prosperous.
facilitās, -ātis *f* ease, readiness; (*speech*)
fluency; (*person*) good nature, affability.
facinorōsus *adj* criminal.
facinus, -oris *nt* deed, action; crime.
faciō, -ere, fēcī, factum (*imp* **fac**, *pass* **fīō**) *vt*
to make, create, compose, cause; to do,
perform; (*profession*) to practise; (*property*)
to put under; (*value*) to regard, think of;
(*words*) to represent, pretend, suppose ♦ *vi*
to do, act; (*religion*) to offer sacrifice; (*with* **ad**
or dat) to be of use; **cōpiam ~** afford an
opportunity; **damnum ~** suffer loss; **metum
~** excite fear; **proelium ~** join battle; **rem ~**
make money; **verba ~** talk; **māgnī ~** think
highly of; **quid tibi faciam?** how am I to
answer you?; **quid tē faciam?** what am I to do
with you?; **fac sciam** let me know; **fac
potuisse** suppose one could have.
factiō, -ōnis *f* making, doing; group, party,
faction (*esp in politics and chariot racing*).
factiōsus *adj* factious, oligarchical.
factitō, -āre, -āvī, -ātum *vt* to keep making
or doing; to practise; to declare (to be).
factor, -ōris *m* (*sport*) batsman.
factum, -ī *nt* deed, exploit.
factus *ppp of* **faciō**.
facula, -ae *f* little torch.
facultās, -ātis *f* means, opportunity; ability;
abundance, supply, resources.
fācundē *adv see* **fācundus**.
fācundia, -ae *f* eloquence.
fācundus *adj* fluent, eloquent.
faeceus *adj* impure.
faecula, -ae *f* wine lees.
faenebris *adj* of usury.
faenerātiō, -ōnis *f* usury.
faenerātō *adv* with interest.
faenerātor, -ōris *m* moneylender.
faenerō, -āre; -or, -ārī, -ātus *vt* to lend at
interest; to ruin with usury; (*fig*) to trade in.
faenīlia, -um *ntpl* hayloft.
faenum, -ī *nt* hay; **~ habet in cornū** he is
dangerous.
faenus, -oris *nt* interest; capital lent at
interest; (*fig*) profit, advantage.
faenusculum, -ī *nt* a little interest.
Faesulae, -ārum *fpl* town in Etruria (*now
Fiesole*).
Faesulānus *adj see n.*
faex, faecis *f* sediment, lees; brine (of
pickles); (*fig*) dregs.
fāgineus, fāginus *adj* of beech.
fāgus, -ī *f* beech.
fala, -ae *f* siege tower, used in assaults;
(*Circus*) pillar.

Noun declensions and verb conjugations are shown on pp xiii to xxv. The present infinitive ending of a verb **shows**
to which conjugation it belongs: **-āre** = 1st; **-ēre** = 2nd; **-ere** = 3rd and **-īre** = 4th. Irregular verbs are shown on p xxvi

falārica, -ae *f* a missile, firebrand.
falcārius, -ī *and* **iī** *m* sicklemaker.
falcātus *adj* scythed; sickle-shaped.
falcifer, -ī *adj* scythe-carrying.
Falernus *adj* Falernian (*of a district in N. Campania famous for its wine*) ♦ *nt* Falernian wine.
Faliscī, -ōrum *mpl* a people of S.E. Etruria (*with chief town Falerii*).
Faliscus *adj see n.*
fallācia, -ae *f* trick, deception.
fallāciter *adv see* **fallāx.**
fallāx, -ācis *adj* deceitful, deceptive.
fallō, -lere, fefellī, -sum *vt* to deceive, cheat, beguile; to disappoint, fail, betray; (*promise*) to break; to escape the notice of, be unknown to; (*pass*) to be mistaken; **mē ~lit** I am mistaken; I do not know.
falsē *adv* wrongly, by mistake; fraudulently.
falsidicus *adj* lying.
falsificus *adj* deceiving.
falsiiūrius *adj* perjurious.
falsiloquus *adj* lying.
falsiparēns, -entis *adj* with a pretended father.
falsō *adv see* **falsē.**
falsus *ppa of* **fallō** ♦ *adj* false, mistaken; deceitful; forged, falsified; sham, fictitious ♦ *nt* falsehood, error.
falx, falcis *f* sickle, scythe; pruning hook; (*MIL*) siege hook.
fāma, -ae *f* talk, rumour, tradition; public opinion; reputation, fame; infamy.
famēlicus *adj* hungry.
famēs, -is *f* hunger; famine; (*fig*) greed; (*RHET*) poverty of expression.
fāmigerātiō, -ōnis *f* rumour.
fāmigerātor, -ōris *m* telltale.
familia, -ae *f* domestics, slaves of a household; family property, estate; family, house; school, sect; **pater ~ās** master of a household; **~am dūcere** be head of a sect, company *etc.*
familiāris *adj* domestic, household, family; intimate, friendly; (*entrails*) relating to the sacrificer ♦ *m* servant; friend.
familiāritās, -ātis *f* intimacy, friendship.
familiāriter *adv* on friendly terms.
fāmōsus *adj* celebrated; infamous; slanderous.
famula, -ae *f* maidservant, handmaid.
famulāris *adj* of servants.
famulātus, -ūs *m* slavery.
famulor, -ārī *vi* to serve.
famulus, -ī *m* servant, attendant ♦ *adj* serviceable.
fānāticus *adj* inspired; frantic, frenzied.
fandī *gerund of* **for.**
fandum, -ī *nt* right.
fānum, -ī *nt* sanctuary temple.
fār, farris *nt* spelt; corn; meal.
farciō, -cīre, -sī, -tum *vt* to stuff, fill full.
farīna, -ae *f* meal, flour.

farrāgō, -inis *f* mash, hotch-potch; medley.
farrātus *adj* of corn; filled with corn.
farsī *perf of* **farciō.**
fartem, -im *f acc* filling; mincemeat.
fartor, -ōris *m* fattener, poulterer.
fartus *ppp of* **farciō.**
fās *nt* divine law; right; **~ est** it is lawful, possible.
fascia, -ae *f* band, bandage; streak of cloud.
fasciculus, -ī *m* bundle, packet.
fascinō, -āre *vt* to bewitch, (*esp with the evil eye*).
fascinum, -ī *nt*, **-us, -ī** *m* charm.
fasciola, -ae *f* small bandage.
fascis, -is *m* bundle, faggot; soldier's pack, burden; (*pl*) rods and axe carried before the highest magistrates; high office (*esp the consulship*).
fassus *ppa of* **fateor.**
fāstī, -ōrum *mpl* register of days for legal and public business; calendar; registers of magistrates and other public records.
fastīdiō, -īre, -iī, -ītum *vt* to loathe, dislike, despise ♦ *vi* to feel squeamish, be disgusted; to be disdainful.
fastīdiōsē *adv* squeamishly; disdainfully.
fastīdiōsus *adj* squeamish, disgusted; fastidious, nice; disagreeable.
fastīdium, -ī *and* **iī** *nt* squeamishness, distaste; disgust, aversion; disdain, pride.
fastīgātē *adv* in a sloping position.
fastīgātus *adj* sloping up *or* down.
fastīgium, -ī *and* **iī** *nt* gable, pediment; slope; height, depth; top, summit; (*fig*) highest degree, acme, dignity; (*speech*) main headings.
fāstus *adj* lawful for public business.
fastus, -ūs *m* disdain, pride.
Fāta *ntpl* the Fates.
fātālis *adj* fateful, destined; fatal, deadly.
fātāliter *adv* by fate.
fateor, -tērī, -ssus *vt* to confess, acknowledge; to reveal, bear witness to.
fāticanus, -inus *adj* prophetic.
fātidicus *adj* prophetic ♦ *m* prophet.
fātifer, -ī *adj* deadly.
fatīgātiō, -ōnis *f* weariness.
fatīgō, -āre, -āvī, -ātum *vt* to tire, exhaust; to worry, importune; to wear down, torment.
fātiloqua, -ae *f* prophetess.
fatīscō, -ere; -or, -ī *vi* to crack, split; (*fig*) to become exhausted.
fatuitās, -ātis *f* silliness.
fātum, -ī *nt* divine word, oracle; fate, destiny; divine will; misfortune, doom, death; **~ō obīre** die a natural death.
fātur, fātus *3rd pers, ppa of* **for.**
fatuus *adj* silly; unwieldy ♦ *m* fool.
faucēs, -ium *fpl* throat; pass, narrow channel, chasm; (*fig*) jaws.
Faunus, -ī *m* father of Latinus (*god of forests and herdsmen, identified with Pan*); (*pl*) woodland spirits, Fauns.

fauste *adv see* **faustus.**
faustitās, -ātis *f* good fortune, fertility.
faustus *adj* auspicious, lucky.
fautor, -ōris *m* supporter, patron.
fautrix, -īcis *f* protectress.
favea, -ae *f* pet slave.
faveō, -ēre, fāvī, fautum *vi* (*with dat*) to favour, befriend, support; **~ linguīs** keep silence.
favilla, -ae *f* embers, ashes; (*fig*) spark.
favitor *etc see* **fautor.**
Favōnius, -ī *m* west wind, zephyr.
favor, -ōris *m* favour, support; applause.
favōrābilis *adj* in favour; pleasing.
favus, -ī *m* honeycomb.
fax, facis *f* torch, wedding torch, funeral torch; marriage, death; (*ASTRO*) meteor; (*fig*) flame, fire, instigator; guide; **facem praeferre** act as guide.
faxim, faxō *old subj and fut of* **faciō.**
febrīcula, -ae *f* slight fever.
febris, -is *f* fever.
Februārius, -ī *m* February ♦ *adj* of February.
februum, -ī *nt* purification; **Februa** *pl festival of purification in February.*
fēcī *perf of* **faciō.**
fēcunditās, -ātis *f* fertility; (*style*) exuberance.
fēcundō, -āre *vt* to fertilise.
fēcundus *adj* fertile, fruitful; fertilising; (*fig*) abundant, rich, prolific.
fefellī *perf of* **fallō.**
fel, fellis *nt* gall bladder, bile; poison; (*fig*) animosity.
fēlēs, -is *f* cat.
fēlīcitās, -ātis *f* happiness, good luck.
fēlīciter *adv* abundantly; favourably; happily.
fēlix, -īcis *adj* fruitful; auspicious, favourable; fortunate, successful.
fēmella, -ae *f* girl.
fēmina, -ae *f* female, woman.
fēmineus *adj* woman's, of women; unmanly.
femur, -oris *and* **inis** *nt* thigh.
fēn- *etc see* **faen-.**
fenestra, -ae *f* window; (*fig*) loophole.
fera, -ae *f* wild beast.
ferācius *adv* more fruitfully.
ferālis *adj* funereal; of the Feralia; deadly ♦ *ntpl festival of the dead in February.*
ferāx, -ācis *adj* fruitful, productive.
ferbuī *perf of* **ferveō.**
ferculum, -ī *nt* litter, barrow; dish, course.
ferē *adv* almost, nearly, about; quite, just; usually, generally, as a rule; (*with neg*) hardly; **nihil ~** hardly anything.
ferentārius, -ī *and* **iī** *m* a light-armed soldier.
Feretrius, -ī *m* an epithet of Jupiter.
feretrum, -ī *nt* bier.
fēriae, -ārum *fpl* festival, holidays; (*fig*) peace, rest.

fēriātus *adj* on holiday, idle.
ferīnus *adj* of wild beasts ♦ *f* game.
feriō, -īre *vt* to strike, hit; to kill, sacrifice; (*comedy*) to cheat; **foedus ~** conclude a treaty.
feritās, -ātis *f* wildness, savagery.
fermē *see* **ferē.**
fermentum, -ī *nt* yeast; beer; (*fig*) passion, vexation.
ferō, ferre, tulī, lātum *vt* to carry, bring, bear; to bring forth, produce; to move, stir, raise; to carry off, sweep away, plunder; (*pass*) to rush, hurry, fly, flow, drift; (*road*) to lead; (*trouble*) to endure, suffer, sustain; (*feelings*) to exhibit, show; (*speech*) to talk about, give out, celebrate; (*bookkeeping*) to enter; (*CIRCS*) to allow, require; **sē ~** rush, move; profess to be, boast; **condiciōnem, lēgem ~** propose terms, a law; **iūdicem ~** sue; **sententiam, suffrāgium ~** vote; **signa ~** march; attack; **aegrē, graviter ~** be annoyed at; **laudibus ~** extol; **in oculīs ~** be very fond of; **prae sē ~** show, declare; **fertur, ferunt** it is said, they say; **ut mea fert opīniō** in my opinion.
ferōcia, -ae *f* courage; spirit; pride, presumption.
ferōcitās, -ātis *f* high spirits, aggressiveness; presumption.
ferōciter *adv* bravely; insolently.
Fērōnia, -ae *f old Italian goddess.*
ferōx, -ōcis *adj* warlike, spirited, daring; proud, insolent.
ferrāmentum, -ī *nt* tool, implement.
ferrārius *adj* of iron; **faber ~** blacksmith ♦ *f* iron-mine, iron-works.
ferrātus *adj* ironclad, ironshod ♦ *mpl* men in armour.
ferreus *adj* of iron, iron; (*fig*) hard, cruel; strong, unyielding.
ferrūgineus *adj* rust-coloured, dark.
ferrūgō, -inis *f* rust; dark colour; gloom.
ferrum, -ī *nt* iron; sword; any iron implement; force of arms; **~ et ignis** devastation.
fertilis *adj* fertile, productive; fertilising.
fertilitās, -ātis *f* fertility.
ferula, -ae *f* fennel; staff, rod.
ferus *adj* wild; uncivilised, cruel ♦ *m* beast.
fervefaciō, -ere, -tum *vt* to boil.
fervēns, -entis *pres p of* **ferveō** ♦ *adj* hot; raging; (*fig*) impetuous, furious.
ferventer *adv* hotly.
ferveō, -vēre, -buī *vi* to boil, burn; (*fig*) to rage, bustle, be agitated.
fervēscō, -ere *vi* to boil up, grow hot.
fervidus *adj* hot, raging; (*fig*) fiery, violent.
fervō, -vere, -vī *vi see* **ferveō.**
fervor, -ōris *m* seething; heat; (*fig*) ardour, passion.
Fescennīnus *adj* Fescennine (*a kind of ribald*

Noun declensions and verb conjugations are shown on pp xiii to xxv. The present infinitive ending of a verb shows to which conjugation it belongs: **-āre** = 1st; **-ēre** = 2nd; **-ere** = 3rd and **-īre** = 4th. Irregular verbs are shown on p xxvi

song, perhaps from Fescennium in Etruria).
fessus _adj_ tired, worn out.
festīnanter _adv_ hastily.
festīnātiō, -ōnis _f_ haste, hurry.
festīnō, -āre _vi_ to hurry, be quick ♦ _vt_ to hasten, accelerate.
festīnus _adj_ hasty, quick.
fēstīvē _adv_ gaily; humorously.
fēstīvitās, -ātis _f_ gaiety, merriment; humour, fun.
fēstīvus _adj_ gay, jolly; delightful; _(speech)_ humorous.
festūca, -ae _f_ rod _(with which slaves were manumitted)._
fēstus _adj_ festal, on holiday ♦ _nt_ holiday; feast.
fētiālis, -is _m_ priest who carried out the ritual in making war and peace.
fētūra, -ae _f_ breeding; brood.
fētus _adj_ pregnant; newly delivered; _(fig)_ productive, full of.
fētus, -ūs _m_ breeding, bearing, producing; brood, young; fruit, produce; _(fig)_ production.
fiber, -rī _m_ beaver.
fibra, -ae _f_ fibre; section of lung _or_ liver; entrails.
fībula, -ae _f_ clasp, brooch; clamp.
ficedula, -ae _f_ fig pecker.
fictē _adv_ falsely.
fictilis _adj_ clay, earthen ♦ _nt_ jar; clay figure.
fictor, -ōris _m_ sculptor; maker, inventor.
fictrīx, -īcis _f_ maker.
fictūra, -ae _f_ shaping, invention.
fictus _ppp of_ **fingō** ♦ _adj_ false, fictitious ♦ _nt_ falsehood.
fīculnus _adj_ of the fig tree.
fīcus, -ī _and_ **ūs** _f_ fig tree; fig.
fidēle _adv_ faithfully, surely, firmly.
fidēlia, -ae _f_ pot, pail; **dē eādem ~ā duōs parietēs dealbāre** ≈ _kill two birds with one stone._
fidēlis _adj_ faithful, loyal; trustworthy, sure.
fidēlitās, -ātis _f_ faithfulness, loyalty.
fidēliter _adv_ faithfully, surely, firmly.
Fīdēnae, -ārum _fpl_ ancient Latin town.
Fīdēnās, -ātis _adj see n._
fīdēns, -entis _pres p of_ **fīdō** ♦ _adj_ bold, resolute.
fīdenter _adv see_ **fīdens.**
fīdentia, -ae _f_ self-confidence.
fidēs, -eī _f_ trust, faith, belief; trustworthiness, honour, loyalty, truth; promise, assurance, word; guarantee, safe-conduct, protection; _(COMM)_ credit; _(law)_ good faith; ~ **mala** dishonesty; **rēs ~que** entire resources; **~em facere** convince; **~em servāre ergā** keep faith with; **dī vostram ~em!** for Heaven's sake!; **ex fidē bonā** in good faith.
fidēs, -is _f (usu pl)_ stringed instrument, lyre, lute; _(ASTRO)_ Lyra.
fīdī _perf of_ **findō.**
fidicen, -inis _m_ musician; lyric poet.
fidicina, -ae _f_ music girl.
fidicula, -ae _f_ small lute.

Fidius, -ī _m_ an epithet of Jupiter.
fīdō, -dere, -sus _vi (with dat or abl)_ to trust, rely on.
fīdūcia, -ae _f_ confidence, assurance; self-confidence; _(law)_ trust, security.
fīdūciārius _adj_ to be held in trust.
fīdus _adj_ trusty, reliable; sure, safe.
fīgō, -gere, -xī, -xum _vt_ to fix, fasten, attach; to drive in, pierce; _(speech)_ to taunt.
figulāris _adj_ a potter's.
figulus, -ī _m_ potter; builder.
figūra, -ae _f_ shape, form; nature, kind; phantom; _(RHET)_ figure of speech.
figūrō, -āre _vt_ to form, shape.
fīlātim _adv_ thread by thread.
fīlia, -ae _f_ daughter.
fīlicātus _adj_ with fern patterns.
fīliola, -ae _f_ little daughter.
fīliolus, -ī _m_ little son.
fīlius, -ī _and_ **iī** _m_ son; **terrae ~** a nobody.
filix, -cis _f_ fern.
fīlum, -ī _nt_ thread; band of wool, fillet; string, shred, wick; contour, shape; _(speech)_ texture, quality.
fimbriae, -ārum _fpl_ fringe, end.
fimus, -ī _m_ dung; dirt.
findō, -ndere, -dī, -ssum _vt_ to split, divide; to burst.
fingō, -ere, finxī, fictum _vt_ to form, shape, make; to mould, model; to dress, arrange; to train; _(mind, speech)_ to imagine, suppose, represent, sketch; to invent, fabricate; **vultum ~** compose the features.
fīniō, -īre, -īvī, -ītum _vt_ to bound, limit; to restrain; to prescribe, define, determine; to end, finish, complete ♦ _vi_ to finish, die.
fīnis, -is _m (occ f)_ boundary, border; _(pl)_ territory; bound, limit; end; death; highest point, summit; aim, purpose; ~ **bonōrum** the chief good; **quem ad ~em?** how long?; **~e genūs** up to the knee.
fīnītē _adv_ within limits.
fīnitimus _adj_ neighbouring, adjoining; akin, like ♦ _mpl_ neighbours.
fīnītor, -ōris _m_ surveyor.
fīnītumus _adj see_ **fīnitimus.**
fīnītus _ppp of_ **fīniō** ♦ _adj (RHET)_ well-rounded.
finxī _perf of_ **fingō.**
fīō, fierī, factus _vi_ to become, arise; to be made, be done; to happen; **quī fit ut?** how is it that?; **ut fit** as usually happens; **quid mē fīet?** what will become of me?
firmāmen, -inis _nt_ support.
firmāmentum, -ī _nt_ support, strengthening; _(fig)_ mainstay.
firmātor, -ōris _m_ establisher.
firmē _adv_ powerfully, steadily.
firmitās, -ātis _f_ firmness, strength; steadfastness, stamina.
firmiter _adv see_ **firmē.**
firmitūdō, -inis _f_ strength, stability.
firmō, -āre, -āvī, -ātum _vt_ to strengthen, support, fortify; _(mind)_ to encourage,

firmus–flōs

steady; (*fact*) to confirm, prove, assert.
firmus *adj* strong, stable, firm; (*fig*) powerful, constant, sure, true.
fiscella, -ae *f* wicker basket.
fiscina, -ae *f* wicker basket.
fiscus, -ī *m* purse, moneybox; public exchequer; imperial treasury, the emperor's privy purse.
fissilis *adj* easy to split.
fissiō, -ōnis *f* dividing.
fissum, -ī *nt* slit, fissure.
fissus *ppp of* **findō**.
fistūca, -ae *f* rammer.
fistula, -ae *f* pipe, tube; panpipes; (*MED*) ulcer.
fistulātor, -ōris *m* panpipe player.
fīsus *ppa of* **fīdō**.
fīxī *perf of* **fīgō**.
fīxus *ppp of* **fīgō** ♦ *adj* fixed, fast, permanent.
flābellifera, -ae *f* fanbearer.
flābellum, -ī *nt* fan.
flābilis *adj* airy.
flābra, -ōrum *ntpl* blasts, gusts; wind.
flacceō, -ēre *vi* to flag, lose heart.
flaccēscō, -ere *vi* to flag, droop.
flaccidus *adj* flabby, feeble.
flaccus *adj* flap-eared.
Flaccus, -ī *m* surname of Horace.
flagellō, -āre *vt* to whip, lash.
flagellum, -ī *nt* whip, lash; strap, thong; (*vine*) shoot; (*polyp*) arm; (*feelings*) sting.
flāgitātiō, -ōnis *f* demand.
flāgitātor, -ōris *m* demander, dun.
flāgitiōsē *adv* infamously.
flāgitiōsus *adj* disgraceful, profligate.
flāgitium, -ī and iī *nt* offence, disgrace, shame; scoundrel.
flāgitō, -āre, -āvī, -ātum *vt* to demand, importune, dun; (*law*) to summon.
flagrāns, -antis *pres p of* **flagrō** ♦ *adj* hot, blazing; brilliant; passionate.
flagranter *adv* passionately.
flagrantia, -ae *f* blazing; (*fig*) shame.
flagrō, -āre *vi* to blaze, burn, be on fire; (*feelings*) to be excited, be inflamed; (*ill-will*) to be the victim of.
flagrum, -ī *nt* whip, lash.
flāmen, -inis *m* priest of a particular deity.
flāmen, -inis *nt* blast, gale, wind.
flāminica, -ae *f* wife of a priest.
Flāminīnus, -ī *m* Roman surname (*esp the conqueror of Philip V of Macedon*).
flāminium, -ī and iī *nt* priesthood.
Flāminius, -ī *m* Roman family name (*esp the consul defeated by Hannibal*).
Flāminius, -iānus *adj*: Via ~ia *road from Rome N.E. to Ariminum.*
flamma, -ae *f* flame, fire; torch, star; fiery colour; (*fig*) passion; danger, disaster.
flammeolum, -ī *nt* bridal veil.
flammēscō, -ere *vi* to become fiery.

flammeus *adj* fiery, blazing; flame-coloured ♦ *nt* bridal veil.
flammifer, -ī *adj* fiery.
flammō, -āre, -āvī, -ātum *vi* to blaze ♦ *vt* to set on fire, burn; (*fig*) to inflame, incense.
flammula, -ae *f* little flame.
flātus, -ūs *m* blowing, breath; breeze; (*fig*) arrogance.
flāvēns, -entis *adj* yellow, golden.
flāvēscō, -ere *vi* to turn yellow.
Flāviānus *adj see n.*
Flāvius, -ī *m* Roman family name (*esp the emperors Vespasian, Titus and Domitian*).
flāvus *adj* yellow, golden.
flēbilis *adj* lamentable; tearful, mournful.
flēbiliter *adv see* **flēbilis**.
flectō, -ctere, -xī, -xum *vt* to bend, turn; to turn aside, wheel; (*promontory*) to round; (*mind*) to direct, persuade, dissuade ♦ *vi* to turn, march.
fleō, -ēre, -ēvī, -ētum *vi* to weep, cry ♦ *vt* to lament, mourn for.
flētus, -ūs *m* weeping, tears.
flexanimus *adj* moving.
flexī *perf of* **flectō**.
flexibilis *adj* pliant, flexible; fickle.
flexilis *adj* pliant.
flexiloquus *adj* ambiguous.
flexiō, -ōnis *f* bending, winding, (*voice*) modulation.
flexipēs, -edis *adj* twining.
flexuōsus *adj* tortuous.
flexūra, -ae *f* bending.
flexus *ppp of* **flectō** ♦ *adj* winding.
flexus, -ūs *m* winding, bending; change.
flīctus, -ūs *m* collision.
flō, -āre, -āvī, -ātum *vt, vi* to blow; (*money*) to coin.
floccus, -ī *m* bit of wool; triviality; ~ī nōn faciō ≈ I don't care a straw for.
Flōra, -ae *f* goddess of flowers.
Flōrālis *adj see n.*
flōrēns, -entis *pres p of* **flōreō** ♦ *adj* in bloom; bright; prosperous, flourishing.
flōreō, -ēre, -uī *vi* to blossom, flower; (*age*) to be in one's prime; (*wine*) to froth; (*fig*) to flourish, prosper; (*places*) to be gay with.
flōrēscō, -ere *vi* to begin to flower; to grow prosperous.
flōreus *adj* of flowers, flowery.
flōridulus *adj* pretty, little.
flōridus *adj* of flowers, flowery; fresh, pretty; (*style*) florid, ornate.
flōrifer, -ī *adj* flowery.
flōrilegus *adj* flower-sipping.
flōrus *adj* beautiful.
flōs, -ōris *m* flower, blossom; (*wine*) bouquet; (*age*) prime, heyday; (*youth*) downy beard, youthful innocence; (*fig*) crown, glory; (*speech*) ornament.

Noun declensions and verb conjugations are shown on pp xiii to xxv. The present infinitive ending of a verb shows to which conjugation it belongs: **-āre** = 1st; **-ēre** = 2nd; **-ere** = 3rd and **-īre** = 4th. Irregular verbs are shown on p xxvi

flōsculus, -ī *m* little flower; (*fig*) pride, ornament.
flūctifragus *adj* surging.
flūctuātiō, -ōnis *f* wavering.
flūctuō, -āre *vi* to toss, wave; (*fig*) to rage, swell, waver.
flūctuōsus *adj* stormy.
flūctus, -ūs *m* wave; flowing, flood; (*fig*) disturbance; ~ūs (*pl*) **in simpulō** ≈ *a storm in a teacup.*
fluēns, -entis *pres p of* **fluō ♦** *adj* lax, loose, enervated; (*speech*) fluent.
fluenta, -ōrum *ntpl* stream, flood.
fluenter *adv* in a flowing manner.
fluentisonus *adj* wave-echoing.
fluidus *adj* flowing, fluid; lax, soft; relaxing.
fluitō, -āre *vi* to flow, float about; to wave, flap, move unsteadily; (*fig*) to waver.
flūmen, -inis *nt* stream, river; (*fig*) flood, flow, fluency; **adversō ~ine** upstream; **secundō ~ine** downstream.
flūmineus *adj* river- (*in cpds*).
fluō, -ere, -xī, -xum *vi* to flow; to overflow, drip; (*fig*) to fall in, fall away, vanish; (*speech*) to run evenly; (*CIRCS*) to proceed, tend.
flūtō *etc see* **fluitō**.
fluviālis *adj* river- (*in cpds*).
fluviātilis *adj* river- (*in cpds*).
flūvidus *etc see* **fluidus**.
fluvius, -ī *and* **iī** *m* river, stream.
fluxī *perf of* **fluō**.
fluxus *adj* flowing, loose, leaky; (*person*) lax, dissolute; (*thing*) frail, fleeting, unreliable.
fōcāle, -is *nt* scarf.
foculus, -ī *m* stove, fire.
focus, -ī *m* hearth, fireplace; pyre, altar; (*fig*) home.
fodicō, -āre *vt* to nudge, jog.
fodiō, -ere, fōdī, fossum *vt* to dig; to prick, stab; (*fig*) to goad.
foedē *adv see* **foedus**.
foederātus *adj* confederated.
foedifragus *adj* perfidious.
foeditās, -ātis *f* foulness, hideousness.
foedō, -āre, -āvī, -ātum *vt* to mar, disfigure; to disgrace, sully.
foedus *adj* foul, hideous, revolting; vile, disgraceful.
foedus, -eris *nt* treaty, league; agreement, compact; law.
foen- *etc see* **faen-**.
foeteō, -ēre *vi* to stink.
foetidus *adj* stinking.
foetor, -ōris *m* stench.
foetu- *etc see* **fētu-**.
foliātum, -ī *nt* nard oil.
folium, -ī *and* **iī** *nt* leaf.
folliculus, -ī *m* small bag; eggshell.
follis, -is *m* bellows; punchball; purse.
fōmentum, -ī *nt* poultice, bandage; (*fig*) alleviation.
fōmes, -itis *m* tinder, kindling.

fōns, fontis *m* spring, source; water; (*fig*) origin, fountainhead.
fontānus *adj* spring- (*in cpds*).
fonticulus, -ī *m* little spring.
for, fārī, fātus *vt, vi* to speak, utter.
forābilis *adj* penetrable.
forāmen, -inis *nt* hole, opening.
forās *adv* out, outside.
forceps, -ipis *m/f* tongs, forceps.
forda, -ae *f* cow in calf.
fore, forem *fut infin, imperf subj of* **sum**.
forēnsis *adj* public, forensic; of the marketplace.
foris, -is *f* (*usu pl*) door; (*fig*) opening, entrance.
forīs *adv* out of doors, outside, abroad; from outside, from abroad; ~ **cēnāre** dine out.
fōrma, -ae *f* form, shape, appearance; mould, stamp, last; (*person*) beauty; (*fig*) idea, nature, kind.
fōrmāmentum, -ī *nt* shape.
fōrmātūra, -ae *f* shaping.
Formiae, -ārum *fpl* town in S. Latium.
Formiānus *adj* of Formiae ♦ *nt* villa at Formiae.
formīca, -ae *f* ant.
formīcinus *adj* crawling.
formīdābilis *adj* terrifying.
formīdō, -āre, -āvī, -ātum *vt, vi* to fear, be terrified.
formīdō, -inis *f* terror, awe, horror; scarecrow.
formīdolōsē *adv see* **formīdolōsus**.
formīdolōsus *adj* fearful, terrifying; afraid.
fōrmō, -āre, -āvī, -ātum *vt* to shape, fashion, form.
fōrmōsitās, -ātis *f* beauty.
fōrmōsus *adj* beautiful, handsome.
fōrmula, -ae *f* rule, regulation; (*law*) procedure, formula; (*PHILOS*) principle.
fornācula, -ae *f* small oven.
fornāx, -ācis *f* furnace, oven, kiln.
fornicātus *adj* arched.
fornix, -icis *m* arch, vault; brothel.
forō, -āre *vt* to pierce.
Foroiūliēnsis *adj see* **Forum Iuli**.
fors, fortis *f* chance, luck ♦ *adv* perchance; ~**te** by chance, as it happened; perhaps; **nē ~te** in case; **sī ~te** if perhaps; in the hope that.
forsan, forsit, forsitan *adv* perhaps.
fortasse, -is *adv* perhaps, possibly; (*irony*) very likely.
forticulus *adj* quite brave.
fortis *adj* strong, sturdy; brave, manly, resolute.
fortiter *adv* vigorously; bravely.
fortitūdō, -inis *f* courage, resolution; strength.
fortuītō *adv* by chance.
fortuītus *adj* casual, accidental.
fortūna, -ae *f* chance, luck, fortune; good luck, success; misfortune; circumstances, lot; (*pl*) possessions; ~**ae fīlius** Fortune's

favourite; **~am habēre** be successful.
fortūnātē adv see **fortūnātus.**
fortūnātus adj happy, lucky; well off, rich,
blessed.
fortūnō, -āre vt to bless, prosper.
forulī, -ōrum mpl bookcase.
forum, -ī nt public place, market; market
town; Roman Forum between the Palatine and
Capitol; public affairs, law courts, business;
~ boārium cattle market; **~ olitōrium**
vegetable market; **~ piscātorium** fish
market; **~ agere** hold an assize; **~ attingere**
enter public life; **cēdere ~ō** go bankrupt; **utī
~ō** take advantage of a situation.
Forum Iūli colony in S. Gaul (now Fréjus).
forus, -ī m gangway; block of seats; (bees) cell
frame.
fossa, -ae f ditch, trench.
fossiō, -ōnis f digging.
fossor, -ōris m digger.
fossus ppp of **fodiō.**
fōtus ppp of **foveō.**
fovea, -ae f pit, pitfall.
foveō, -ēre, fōvī, fōtum vt to warm, keep
warm; (MED) to foment; to fondle, keep; (fig)
to cherish, love, foster, pamper, encourage;
castra ~ remain in camp.
frāctus ppp of **frangō** ♦ adj weak, faint.
frāga, -ōrum ntpl strawberries.
fragilis adj brittle, fragile; frail, fleeting.
fragilitās, -ātis f frailness.
fragmen, -inis nt (pl) fragments, ruins,
wreck.
fragmentum, -ī nt fragment, remnant.
fragor, -ōris m crash, din; disintegration.
fragōsus adj crashing, roaring, breakable;
rough.
frāgrāns, -antis adj fragrant.
framea, -ae f German spear.
frangō, -angere, -ēgī, -āctum vt to break,
shatter, wreck; to crush, grind; (fig) to break
down, weaken, humble; (emotion) to touch,
move; **cervīcem ~** strangle.
frāter, -ris m brother; cousin; (fig) friend, ally.
frāterculus, -ī m brother.
frāternē adv like a brother.
frāternitās, -ātis f brotherhood.
frāternus adj brotherly, a brother's, fraternal.
frātricīda, -ae m fratricide.
fraudātiō, -ōnis f deceit, fraud.
fraudātor, -ōris m swindler.
fraudō, -āre, -āvī, -ātum vt to cheat, defraud;
to steal, cancel.
fraudulentus adj deceitful, fraudulent.
fraus, -audis f deceit, fraud; delusion, error;
offence, wrong; injury, damage; **lēgī ~dem
facere** evade the law; **in ~dem incidere** be
disappointed; **sine ~de** without harm.
fraxineus, fraxinus adj of ash.
fraxinus, -ī f ash tree; ashen spear.

Fregellae, -ārum fpl town in S. Latium.
Fregellānus adj see n.
frēgī perf of **frangō.**
fremebundus adj roaring.
fremitus, -ūs m roaring, snorting, noise.
fremō, -ere, -uī, -itum vi to roar, snort,
grumble ♦ vt to shout for, complain.
fremor, -ōris m murmuring.
frendō, -ere vi to gnash the teeth.
frēnō, -āre, -āvī, -ātum vt to bridle; (fig) to
curb, restrain.
frēnum, -ī nt (pl -a, -ōrum nt, -ī, -ōrum m)
bridle, bit; (fig) curb, check; **~ōs dare** give
vent to; **~um mordēre** ≈ take the bit between
one's teeth.
frequēns, -entis adj crowded, numerous,
populous; regular, repeated, frequent; **~
senatus** a crowded meeting of the senate.
frequentātiō, -ōnis f accumulation.
frequenter adv in large numbers; repeatedly,
often.
frequentia, -ae f full attendance, throng,
crowd.
frequentō, -āre, -āvī, -ātum vt to crowd,
populate; to visit repeatedly, frequent; to
repeat; (festival) to celebrate, keep.
fretēnsis adj of the Straits of Messina.
fretum, -ī nt strait; sea; (fig) violence; **~
Siciliēnse** Straits of Messina.
fretus, -ūs m strait.
frētus adj relying, confident.
fricō, -āre, -uī, -tum vt to rub, rub down.
frictus ppp of **frigō.**
frīgefactō, -āre vt to cool.
frīgeō, -ēre vi to be cold; (fig) to be lifeless,
flag; to be coldly received, fall flat.
frīgerāns adj cooling.
frīgēscō, -ere vi to grow cold; to become
inactive.
frīgida, -ae f cold water.
frīgidē adv feebly.
frīgidulus adj rather cold, faint.
frīgidus adj cold, cool; chilling; (fig) dull,
torpid; (words) flat, uninteresting.
frīgō, -gere, -xī, -ctum vt to roast, fry.
frīgus, -oris nt cold; cold weather, winter;
death; (fig) dullness, inactivity; coldness,
indifference.
friguttiō, -īre vi to stammer.
friō, -āre vt to crumble.
fritillus, -ī m dice box.
frīvolus adj empty, paltry.
frīxī perf of **frigō.**
frondātor, -ōris m vinedresser, pruner.
frondeō, -ēre vi to be in leaf.
frondēscō, -ere vi to become leafy, shoot.
frondeus adj leafy.
frondifer, -ī adj leafy.
frondōsus adj leafy.
frōns, -ondis f leaf, foliage; garland of leaves.

Noun declensions and verb conjugations are shown on pp xiii to xxv. The present infinitive ending of a verb shows
to which conjugation it belongs: **-āre** = 1st; **-ēre** = 2nd; **-ere** = 3rd and **-īre** = 4th. Irregular verbs are shown on p xxvi

frōns, -ontis *f* forehead, brow; front, facade; (*fig*) look, appearance, exterior; **~ontem contrahere** frown; **ā ~onte** in front; **in ~onte** in breadth.

frontālia, -um *ntpl* frontlet.

frontō, -ōnis *m* a broad-browed man.

frūctuārius *adj* productive; paid for out of produce.

fructuōsus *adj* productive; profitable.

frūctus *ppa of* **fruor**.

frūctus, -ūs *m* enjoyment; revenue, income; produce, fruit; (*fig*) consequence, reward; **~uī esse** be an asset (to); **~um percipere** reap the fruits (of).

frūgālis *adj* thrifty, worthy.

frūgālitās, -ātis *f* thriftiness, restraint.

frūgāliter *adv* temperately.

frūgēs *etc see* **frūx**.

frūgī *adj* (*indecl*) frugal, temperate, honest; useful.

frūgifer, -ī *adj* fruitful, fertile.

frūgiferēns, -entis *adj* fruitful.

frūgilegus *adj* food-gatherering.

frūgiparus *adj* fruitful.

frūmentārius *adj* of corn, corn- (*in cpds*) ♦ *m* corn dealer; **lēx ~a** a law about the distribution of corn; **rēs ~a** commissariat.

frūmentātiō, -ōnis *f* foraging.

frūmentātor, -ōris *m* corn merchant, forager.

frūmentor, -ārī, -ātus *vi* to go foraging.

frūmentum, -ī *nt* corn, grain, (*pl*) crops.

frūnīscor, -ī *vt* to enjoy.

fruor, -uī, -ūctus *vt, vi* (*usu with abl*) to enjoy, enjoy the company of; (*law*) to have the use and enjoyment of.

frūstillātim *adv* in little bits.

frūstrā *adv* in vain, for nothing; groundlessly; in error; **~ esse** be deceived; **~ habēre** foil.

frūstrāmen, -inis *nt* deception.

frūstrātiō, -ōnis *f* deception, frustration.

frūstrō, -āre; -or, -ārī, -ātus *vt* to deceive, trick.

frūstulentus *adj* full of crumbs.

frūstum, -ī *nt* bit, scrap.

frutex, -icis *m* bush, shrub; (*comedy*) blockhead.

fruticētum, -ī *nt* thicket.

fruticor, -ārī *vi* to sprout.

fruticōsus *adj* bushy.

frūx, -ūgis *f*, **-ūgēs, -ūgum** fruits of the earth, produce; (*fig*) reward, success; virtue; **sē ad ~ūgem bonam recipere** reform.

fuam *old pres subj of* **sum**.

fūcātus *adj* counterfeit, artificial.

fūcō, -āre, -āvī, -ātum *vt* to paint, dye (*esp red*).

fūcōsus *adj* spurious.

fūcus, -ī *m* red dye, rouge; bee glue; (*fig*) deceit, pretence.

fūcus, -ī *m* drone.

fūdī *perf of* **fundō**.

fuga, -ae *f* flight, rout; banishment; speed, swift passing; refuge; (*fig*) avoidance, escape; **~am facere, in ~am dare** put to flight.

fugācius *adv* more timidly.

fugāx, -ācis *adj* timorous, shy, fugitive; swift, transient; (*with gen*) avoiding.

fūgī *perf of* **fugiō**.

fugiēns, -entis *pres p of* **fugiō** ♦ *adj* fleeting, dying; averse (to).

fugiō, -ere, fūgī, -itum *vi* to flee, run away, escape; to go into exile; (*fig*) to vanish, pass swiftly ♦ *vt* to flee from, escape from; to shun, avoid; (*fig*) to escape, escape notice of; **~e quaerere** do not ask; **mē ~it** I do not notice *or* know.

fugitīvus, -ī *m* runaway slave, truant, deserter ♦ *adj* fugitive.

fugitō, -āre *vt* to flee from, shun.

fugō, -āre, -āvī, -ātum *vt* to put to flight; to banish; to rebuff.

fulcīmen, -inis *nt* support.

fulciō, -cīre, -sī, -tum *vt* to prop, support; to strengthen, secure; (*fig*) to sustain, bolster up.

fulcrum, -ī *nt* bedpost; couch.

fulgeō, -gēre, -sī *vi* to flash, lighten; to shine; (*fig*) to be illustrious.

fulgidus *adj* flashing.

fulgō *etc see* **fulgeō**.

fulgor, -ōris *m* lightning; flash, brightness; (*fig*) splendour.

fulgur, -is *nt* lightning; thunderbolt; splendour.

fulgurālis *adj* on lightning as an omen.

fulgurātor, -ōris *m* interpreter of lightning.

fulgurītus *adj* struck by lightning.

fulgurō, -āre *vi* to lighten.

fulica, -ae *f* coot.

fūlīgō, -inis *f* soot; black paint.

fulix, -cis *f see* **fulica**.

fullō, -ōnis *m* fuller.

fullōnius *adj* fuller's.

fulmen, -inis *nt* thunderbolt; (*fig*) disaster.

fulmenta, -ae *f* heel of a shoe.

fulmineus *adj* of lightning; (*fig*) deadly.

fulminō, -āre *vi* to lighten; (*fig*) to threaten.

fulsī *perf of* **fulciō**; *perf of* **fulgeō**.

fultūra, -ae *f* support.

fultus *ppp of* **fulciō**.

Fulvia, -iae *f* wife of M. Antony.

Fulvius, -ī *m* Roman family name.

fulvus *adj* yellow, tawny, dun.

fūmeus *adj* smoking.

fūmidus *adj* smoky, smoking.

fūmifer, -ī *adj* smoking.

fūmificō, -āre *vi* to burn incense.

fūmificus *adj* steaming.

fūmō, -āre *vi* to smoke, steam.

fūmōsus *adj* smoky, smoked.

fūmus, -ī *m* smoke, steam.

fūnāle, -is *nt* cord; wax torch; chandelier.

fūnambulus, -ī *m* tightrope walker.

fūnctiō, -ōnis *f* performance.

fūnctus *ppa of* **fungor**.

fūnda, -ae f sling; dragnet.
fundāmen, -inis nt foundation.
fundāmentum, -ī nt foundation; **~a agere, iacere** lay the foundations.
Fundānus adj see **Fundī**.
fundātor, -ōris m founder.
Fundī, -ōrum mpl coast town in Latium.
funditō, -āre vt to sling.
funditor, -ōris m slinger.
funditus adv utterly, completely; at the bottom.
fundō, -āre, -āvī, -ātum vt to found; to secure; (fig) to establish, make secure.
fundō, -ere, fūdī, fūsum vt to pour, shed, spill; (metal) to cast; (solids) to hurl, scatter, shower; (MIL) to rout; (crops) to produce in abundance; (speech) to utter; (fig) to spread, extend.
fundus, -ī m bottom; farm, estate; (law) authorizer.
fūnebris adj funeral- (in cpds); murderous.
fūnerātus adj killed.
fūnereus adj funeral- (in cpds); fatal.
fūnestō, -āre vt to pollute with murder, desecrate.
fūnestus adj deadly, fatal; sorrowful, in mourning.
fungīnus adj of a mushroom.
fungor, -gi, fūnctus vt, vi (usu with abl) to perform, discharge, do; to be acted on.
fungus, -ī m mushroom, fungus; (candle) clot on the wick.
fūniculus, -ī m cord.
fūnis, -is m rope, rigging; **~em dūcere** be the master.
fūnus, -eris nt funeral; death; corpse; ruin, destruction.
fūr, fūris m thief; slave.
fūrācissimē adv most thievishly.
fūrāx, -ācis adj thieving.
furca, -ae f fork; fork-shaped pole; pillory.
furcifer, -ī m gallows rogue.
furcilla, -ae f little fork.
furcillō, -āre vt to prop up.
furcula, -ae f forked prop; **~ae Caudīnae** Pass of Caudium.
furenter adv furiously.
furfur, -is m bran; scurf.
Furia, -ae f Fury, avenging spirit; madness, frenzy, rage.
furiālis adj of the Furies; frantic, fearful; infuriating.
furiāliter adv madly.
furibundus adj mad, frenzied.
furiō, -āre, -āvī, -ātum vt to madden.
furiōsē adv in a frenzy.
furiōsus adj mad, frantic.
furnus, -ī m oven.
furō, -ere vi to rave, rage, be mad, be crazy.
fūror, -ārī, -ātus vt to steal; to pillage; to impersonate.
furor, -ōris m madness, frenzy, passion.
fūrtificus adj thievish.
fūrtim adv by stealth, secretly.
fūrtīvē adv secretly.
fūrtīvus adj stolen; secret, furtive.
fūrtō adv secretly.
fūrtum, -ī nt theft, robbery; (pl) stolen goods; (fig) trick, intrigue.
fūrunculus, -ī m pilferer.
furvus adj black, dark.
fuscina, -ae f trident.
fuscō, -āre vt to blacken.
fuscus adj dark, swarthy; (voice) husky, muffled.
fūsē adv diffusely.
fūsilis adj molten, softened.
fūsiō, -ōnis f outpouring.
fūstis, -is m stick, club, cudgel; (MIL) beating to death.
fūstuārium, -ī and iī nt beating to death.
fūsus ppp of **fundō** ♦ adj broad, diffuse; copious.
fūsus, -ī m spindle.
futtile adv in vain.
futtilis adj brittle; worthless.
futtilitās, -ātis f futility.
futūrum, -ī nt future.
futūrus fut p of **sum** ♦ adj future, coming.

G, g

Gabiī, -iōrum mpl ancient town in Latium.
Gabinius, -ī m Roman family name (esp Aulus, tribune 67 B.C.).
Gabinius, -iānus adj: **lēx ~ia** law giving Pompey command against the pirates.
Gabīnus adj see **Gabiī**.
Gādēs, -ium fpl town in Spain (now Cadiz).
Gāditānus adj see n.
gaesum, -ī nt Gallic javelin.
Gaetūlī, -ōrum mpl African people N of Sahara.
Gaetūlus, -icus adj Gaetulian; African.
Gāius, -ī m Roman praenomen (esp emperor Caligula).
Gāius, -ia m/f (wedding ceremony) bridegroom, bride.
Galatae, -ārum mpl Galatians of Asia Minor.
Galatia, -iae f Galatia.
Galba, -ae m Roman surname (esp emperor 68–9).
galbaneus adj of galbanum, a Syrian plant.

---

galbinus *adj* greenish-yellow ♦ *ntpl* pale green clothes.
galea, -ae *f* helmet.
galeātus *adj* helmeted.
galērītus *adj* rustic.
galērum, -ī *nt*, **-us, -ī** *m* leather hood, cap; wig.
galla, -ae *f* oak apple.
Gallī, -ōrum *mpl* Gauls (*people of what is now France and N. Italy*).
Gallia, -iae *f* Gaul.
Gallicānus *adj* of Italian Gaul.
Gallicus *adj* Gallic ♦ *f* a Gallic shoe.
gallīna, -ae *f* hen; **~ae albae fīlius** fortune's favourite.
gallīnāceus *adj* of poultry.
gallīnārius, -ī *and* **iī** *m* poultry farmer.
Gallograecī, -ōrum *mpl* Galatians.
Gallograecia, -iae *f* Galatia.
gallus, -ī *m* cock.
Gallus, -ī *m* Gaul; Roman surname (*esp the lyric poet; priest of Cybele*).
ganēa, -ae *f* low eating house.
ganeō, -ōnis *m* profligate.
ganeum, -ī *nt* low eating house.
Gangaridae, -ārum *mpl* a people on the Ganges.
Gangēs, -is *m* river Ganges.
Gangēticus *adj see n.*
ganniō, -īre *vi* to yelp; (*fig*) to grumble.
gannītus, -ūs *m* yelping.
Ganymēdēs, -is *m* Ganymede, (*cup bearer in Olympus*).
Garamantes, -um *mpl* N. African tribe.
Garamantis, -idis *adj see n.*
Gargānus, -ī *m* mountain in E. Italy.
garriō, -īre *vi* to chatter.
garrulitās, -ātis *f* chattering.
garrulus *adj* talkative, babbling.
garum, -ī *nt* fish sauce.
Garumna, -ae *f* river Garonne.
gaudeō, -ēre, gāvīsus *vt, vi* to rejoice, be pleased, delight (in); **in sē, in sinū ~** be secretly pleased.
gaudium, -ī *and* **iī** *nt* joy, delight, enjoyment.
gaulus, -ī *m* bucket.
gausape, -is *nt*, **-a, -ōrum** *pl* a woollen cloth, frieze.
gāvīsus *ppa of* **gaudeō.**
gāza, -ae *f* treasure, riches.
gelidē *adv* feebly.
gelidus *adj* cold, frosty; stiff, numb; chilling ♦ *f* cold water.
gelō, -āre *vt* to freeze.
Gelōnī, -ōrum *mpl* Scythian tribe (*now Ukraine*).
gelū, -ūs *nt* frost, cold; chill.
gemebundus *adj* groaning.
gemellipara, -ae *f* mother of twins.
gemellus *adj* twin, double; alike ♦ *m* twin.
geminātiō, -ōnis *f* doubling.
geminō, -āre, -āvī, -ātum *vt* to double, bring together; to repeat ♦ *vi* to be double.

geminus *adj* twin, double, both; similar ♦ *mpl* twins (*esp Castor and Pollux*).
gemitus, -ūs *m* groan, sigh; moaning sound.
gemma, -ae *f* bud, precious stone, jewel; jewelled cup, signet.
gemmātus *adj* bejewelled.
gemmeus *adj* jewelled; sparkling.
gemmifer, -ī *adj* gem-producing.
gemmō, -āre *vi* to bud, sprout; to sparkle.
gemō, -ere, -uī, -itum *vi* to sigh, groan, moan ♦ *vt* to bewail.
Gemōniae, -ārum *fpl* steps in Rome on which bodies of criminals were thrown.
genae, -ārum *fpl* cheeks; eyes, eye sockets.
geneālogus, -ī *m* genealogist.
gener, -ī *m* son-in-law.
generālis *adj* of the species; universal.
generāliter *adv* generally.
generāscō, -ere *vi* to be produced.
generātim *adv* by species, in classes; in general.
generātor, -ōris *m* producer.
generō, -āre, -āvī, -ātum *vt* to breed, procreate.
generōsus *adj* high-born, noble; well-stocked; generous, chivalrous; (*things*) noble, honourable.
genesis, -is *f* birth; horoscope.
genethliacon, -ī *nt* birthday poem.
genetīvus *adj* native, inborn.
genetrīx, -īcis *f* mother.
geniālis *adj* nuptial; joyful, genial.
geniāliter *adv* merrily.
geniculātus *adj* jointed.
genista, -ae *f* broom.
genitābilis *adj* productive.
genitālis *adj* fruitful, generative; of birth.
genitāliter *adv* fruitfully.
genitor, -ōris *m* father, creator.
genitus *ppp of* **gignō.**
genius, -ī *and* **iī** *m* guardian spirit; enjoyment, inclination; talent; **~iō indulgēre** enjoy oneself.
gēns, gentis *f* clan, family, stock, race; tribe, people, nation; descendant; (*pl*) foreign peoples; **minimē gentium** by no means; **ubi gentium** where in the world.
genticus *adj* national.
gentīlicius *adj* family.
gentīlis *adj* family, hereditary; national ♦ *m* kinsman.
gentīlitās, -ātis *f* clan relationship.
genū, -ūs *nt* knee.
genuālia, -um *ntpl* garters.
genuī *perf of* **gignō.**
genuīnus *adj* natural.
genuīnus *adj* of the cheek ♦ *mpl* back teeth.
genus, -eris *nt* birth, descent, noble birth, descendant, race; kind, class, species, respect, way; (*logic*) genus, general term; **id ~** of that kind; **in omnī ~ere** in all respects.
geōgraphia, -ae *f* geography.
geōmetrēs, -ae *m* geometer.

geōmetria, -ae f geometry.
geōmetricus adj geometrical ♦ ntpl geometry.
germānē adv sincerely.
Germānī, -ōrum mpl Germans.
Germānia, -iae f Germany.
Germānicus adj, m cognomen of Nero Claudius Drusus and his son.
germānitās, -ātis f brotherhood, sisterhood; relation of sister colonies.
germānus adj of the same parents, full (brother, sister); genuine, true ♦ m full brother ♦ f full sister.
germen, -inis nt bud, shoot; embryo; (fig) germ.
gerō, -rere, -ssī, -stum vt to carry, wear; to bring; (plants) to bear, produce; (feelings) to entertain, show; (activity) to conduct, manage, administer, wage; (time) spend; **mōrem ~** comply, humour; **persōnam ~** play a part; **sē ~** behave; **sē medium ~** be neutral; **prae sē ~** exhibit; **rēs ~stae** exploits.
gerō, -ōnis nt carrier.
gerrae, -ārum fpl trifles, nonsense.
gerrō, -ōnis m idler.
gerulus, -ī m carrier.
Gēryōn, -onis m mythical three-bodied king killed by Hercules.
gessī perf of **gerō**.
gestāmen, -inis nt arms, ornaments, burden; litter, carriage.
gestiō, -ōnis f performance.
gestiō, -īre vi to jump for joy, be excited; to be very eager.
gestitō, -āre vt to always wear or carry.
gestō, -āre vt to carry about, usually wear; to fondle; to blab; (pass) to go for a ride, drive, sail.
gestor, -ōris m telltale.
gestus ppp of **gerō**.
gestus, -ūs m posture, gesture; gesticulation.
Getae, -ārum mpl Thracian tribe on the lower Danube.
Geticus adj Getan, Thracian.
gibbus, -ī m hump.
Gigantes, -um mpl Giants, sons of Earth.
Gigantēus adj see n.
gignō, -ere, genuī, genitum vt to beget, bear, produce; to cause.
gilvus adj pale yellow, dun.
gingīva, -ae f gum.
glaber, -rī adj smooth, bald ♦ m favourite slave.
glaciālis adj icy.
glaciēs, -ēī f ice.
glaciō, -āre vt to freeze.
gladiātor, -ōris m gladiator; (pl) gladiatorial show.
gladiātōrius adj of gladiators ♦ nt gladiators' pay.
gladiātūra, -ae f gladiator's profession.

gladius, -ī and iī m sword; (fig) murder, death; **~ium stringere** draw the sword; **suō sibi ~iō iugulāre** ≈ beat at his own game.
glaeba, -ae f sod, clod of earth; soil; lump.
glaebula, -ae f small lump; small holding.
glaesum etc see **glēsum**.
glandifer, -ī adj acorn-bearing.
glandium, -ī and iī nt glandule (in meat).
glāns, -andis f acorn, nut; bullet.
glārea, -ae f gravel.
glāreōsus adj gravelly.
glaucūma, -ae f cataract; **~am ob oculōs obicere** ≈ throw dust in the eyes of.
glaucus adj bluish grey.
glēba etc see **glaeba**.
glēsum, -ī nt amber.
glīs, -īris m dormouse.
glīscō, -ere vi to grow, swell, blaze up.
globōsus adj spherical.
globus, -ī m ball, sphere; (MIL) troop; mass, crowd, cluster.
glomerāmen, -inis nt bell.
glomerō, -āre, -āvī, -ātum vt to form into a ball, gather, accumulate.
glomus, -eris nt ball of thread, clue.
glōria, -ae f glory, fame; ambition, pride, boasting; (pl) glorious deeds.
glōriātiō, -ōnis f boasting.
glōriola, -ae f a little glory.
glōrior, -ārī, -ātus vt, vi to boast, pride oneself.
glōriōsē adv see **glōriōsus**.
glōriōsus adj famous, glorious; boastful.
glūten, -inis nt glue.
glūtinātor, -ōris m bookbinder.
gluttiō, -īre vt to gulp down.
gnāruris, gnārus adj knowing, expert; known.
gnātus see **nātus**.
gnāvus see **nāvus**.
Gnōsius and **iacus** and **ias** adj of Cnossos, Cretan.
Gnōsis, -idis f Ariadne.
Gnōsus, -ī f Cnossos (ancient capital of Crete) ♦ f Ariadne.
gōbiō, -ōnis, gōbius, -ī and iī m gudgeon.
Gorgiās, -ae m Sicilian sophist and teacher of rhetoric.
Gorgō, -ōnis f mythical monster capable of turning men to stone, Medusa.
Gorgoneus adj: **equus ~** Pegasus; **lacus ~** Hippocrene.
Gortȳna, -ae f Cretan town.
Gortȳnius, -iacus adj Gortynian, Cretan.
gōrȳtos, -ī m quiver.
grabātus, -ī m camp bed, low couch.
Gracchānus adj see n.
Gracchus, -ī m Roman surname (esp the famous tribunes Tiberius and Gaius).
gracilis adj slender, slight, meagre, poor;

(*style*) plain.

gracilitās, -ātis *f* slimness, leanness; (*style*) simplicity.

grāculus, -ī *m* jackdaw.

gradātim *adv* step by step, gradually.

gradātiō, -ōnis *f* (*RHET*) climax.

gradior, -adī, -essus *vi* to step, walk.

Grādīvus, -ī *m* Mars.

gradus, -ūs *m* step, pace; stage, step towards; firm stand, position, standing; (*pl*) stair, steps; (*hair*) braid; (*MATH*) degree; (*fig*) degree, rank; **citātō, plēnō ~ū** at the double; **suspēnsō ~ū** on tiptoe; **dē ~ū deicī** be disconcerted.

Graecē *adv* in Greek.

Graecia, -iae *f* Greece; **Māgna ~** S. Italy.

graecissō, -āre *vi* to ape the Greeks.

graecor, -ārī *vi* to live like Greeks.

Graeculus *adj* (*contemptuous*) Greek.

Graecus *adj* Greek.

Grāiugena, -ae *m* Greek.

Grāius *adj* Greek.

grallātor, -ōris *m* stiltwalker.

grāmen, -inis *nt* grass; herb.

grāmineus *adj* grassy; of cane.

grammaticus *adj* literary, grammatical ♦ *m* teacher of literature and language ♦ *f/ntpl* grammar, literature, philology.

grānāria, -ōrum *ntpl* granary.

grandaevus *adj* aged, very old.

grandēscō, -ere *vi* to grow.

grandiculus *adj* quite big.

grandifer, -ī *adj* productive.

grandiloquus, -ī *m* grand speaker; boaster.

grandinat, -āre *vi* it hails.

grandis *adj* large, great, tall; old; strong; (*style*) grand, sublime; **~ nātū** old.

granditās, -ātis *f* grandeur.

grandō, -inis *f* hail.

grānifer, -ī *adj* grain-carrying.

grānum, -ī *nt* seed, grain.

graphicē *adv* nicely.

graphicus *adj* fine, masterly.

graphium, -ī and iī *nt* stilus, pen.

grassātor, -ōris *m* vagabond; robber, footpad.

grassor, -ārī, -ātus *vi* to walk about, prowl, loiter; (*action*) to proceed; (*fig*) to attack, rage against.

grātē *adv* with pleasure; gratefully.

grātēs *fpl* thanks.

grātia, -ae *f* charm, grace; favour, influence, regard, friendship; kindness, service; gratitude, thanks; **~am facere** excuse; **~am referre** return a favour; **in ~am redīre cum** be reconciled to; **~ās agere** thank; **~ās habēre** feel grateful; **~ā** (*with gen*) for the sake of; **eā ~ā** on that account; **~īs** for nothing.

Grātiae, -ārum *fpl* the three Graces.

grātificātiō, -ōnis *f* obligingness.

grātificor, -ārī *vi* to do a favour, oblige ♦ *vt* to make a present of.

gratiīs, grātīs *adv* for nothing.

grātiōsus *adj* in favour, popular; obliging.

grātor, -ārī, -ātus *vi* to rejoice, congratulate.

grātuītō *adv* for nothing.

grātuītus *adj* free, gratuitous.

grātulābundus *adj* congratulating.

grātulātiō, -ōnis *f* rejoicing; congratulation; public thanksgiving.

grātulor, -ārī, -ātus *vt, vi* to congratulate; to give thanks.

grātus *adj* pleasing, welcome, dear; grateful, thankful; (*acts*) deserving thanks; **~um facere** do a favour.

gravātē *adv* reluctantly, grudgingly.

gravātim *adv* unwillingly.

gravēdinōsus *adj* liable to colds.

gravēdō, -inis *f* cold in the head.

graveolēns, -entis *adj* strong-smelling.

gravēscō, -ere *vi* to become heavy; to grow worse.

graviditās, -ātis *f* pregnancy.

gravidō, -āre *vt* to impregnate.

gravidus *adj* pregnant; loaded, full.

gravis *adj* heavy; loaded, pregnant; (*smell*) strong, offensive; (*sound*) deep, bass; (*body*) sick; (*food*) indigestible; (*fig*) oppressive, painful, severe; important, influential, dignified.

gravitās, -ātis *f* weight, severity, sickness; importance, dignity, seriousness; **annōnae ~** high price of corn.

graviter *adv* heavily; strongly, deeply; severely, seriously, violently; gravely, with dignity; **~ ferre** be vexed at.

gravō, -āre *vt* to load, weigh down; to oppress, aggravate.

gravor, -ārī *vt, vi* to feel annoyed, object to, disdain.

gregālis *adj* of the herd, common ♦ *m* comrade.

gregārius *adj* common; (*MIL*) private.

gregātim *adv* in crowds.

gremium, -ī *nt* bosom, lap.

gressus *ppa of* **gradior**.

gressus, -ūs *m* step; course.

grex, -egis *m* flock, herd; company, troop.

grunniō, -īre *vi* to grunt.

grunnītus, -ūs *m* grunting.

grūs, -uis *f* crane.

grȳps, -ȳpis *m* griffin.

gubernāclum (gubernāculum), -ī *nt* rudder, tiller; helm, government.

gubernātiō, -ōnis *f* steering, management.

gubernātor, -ōris *m* steersman, pilot, governor.

gubernātrīx, -īcis *f* directress.

gubernō, -āre, -āvī, -ātum *vt* to steer, pilot; to manage, govern.

gula, -ae *f* gullet, throat; gluttony, palate.

gulōsus *adj* dainty.

gurges, -itis *m* abyss, deep water, flood; (*person*) spendthrift.

gurguliō, -ōnis *f* gullet, windpipe.

gurgustium, -ī and iī *nt* hovel, shack.

gustātus, -ūs *m* sense of taste; flavour.
gustō, -āre, -āvī, -ātum *vt* to taste; to have a snack; (*fig*) to enjoy, overhear; **prīmīs labrīs ~ have** a superficial knowledge of.
gustus, -ūs *m* tasting; preliminary dish.
gutta, -ae *f* drop; spot, speck.
guttātim *adv* drop by drop.
guttur, -is *nt* throat, gluttony.
gūtus, -ī *m* flask.
Gȳās, -ae *m* giant with a hundred arms.
Gȳgaeus *adj see n.*
Gȳgēs, -is *and* **ae** *m* king of Lydia (*famed for his magic ring*).
gymnasiarchus, -ī *m* master of a gymnasium.
gymnasium, -ī *and* **iī** *nt* sports ground, school.
gymnasticus *adj* gymnastic.
gymnicus *adj* gymnastic.
gynaecēum, -ēī *and* **ium, -iī** *nt* women's quarters.
gypsātus *adj* coated with plaster.
gypsum, -ī *nt* plaster of Paris; a plaster figure.
gȳrus, -ī *m* circle, coil, ring; course.

H, h

ha *interj* (*expressing joy or laughter*) hurrah!, ha ha!
habēna, -ae *f* strap; (*pl*) reins; (*fig*) control; **~ās dare, immittere** allow to run freely.
habeō, -ēre, -uī, -itum *vt* to have, hold; to keep, contain, possess; (*fact*) to know; (*with infin*) to be in a position to; (*person*) to treat, regard, consider; (*action*) to make, hold, carry out ♦ *vi* to have possessions; **ōrātiōnem ~** make a speech; **in animō ~** intend; **prō certō ~** be sure; **sē ~** find oneself, be; **sibi, sēcum ~** keep to oneself; (*fight*) **~et a** hit!; **bene ~et** it is well; **sīc ~et** so it is; **sīc ~ētō** be sure of this.
habilis *adj* manageable, handy; suitable, nimble, expert.
habilitās, -ātis *f* aptitude.
habitābilis *adj* habitable.
habitātiō, -ōnis *f* dwelling, house.
habitātor, -ōris *m* tenant, inhabitant.
habitō, -āre, -āvī, -ātum *vt* to inhabit ♦ *vi* to live, dwell; to remain, be always (in).
habitūdō, -inis *f* condition.
habitus *ppp of* **habeō** ♦ *adj* stout; in a humour.
habitus, -ūs *m* condition, appearance; dress;

character, quality; disposition, feeling.
hāc *adv* this way.
hāctenus *adv* thus far, so far; till now.
Hadria, -ae *f* town in N. Italy; Adriatic Sea.
Hadriānus, -ānī *m* emperor Hadrian.
Hadriāticus *and* **acus** *adj* of emperor Hadrian.
haedilia, -ae *f* little kid.
haedinus *adj* kid's.
haedulus, -ī *m* little kid.
haedus, -ī *m* kid; (*ASTRO*, *usu pl*) the Kids (*a cluster in Auriga*).
Haemonia, -ae *f* Thessaly.
Haemonius *adj* Thessalian.
Haemus, -ī *m* mountain range in Thrace.
haereō, -rēre, -sī, -sum *vi* to cling, stick, be attached; (*nearness*) to stay close, hang on; (*continuance*) to linger, remain (at); (*stoppage*) to stick fast, come to a standstill, be at a loss.
haerēscō, -ere *vi* to adhere.
haeresis, -is *f* sect.
haesī *perf of* **haereō**.
haesitantia, -ae *f* stammering.
haesitātiō, -ōnis *f* stammering; indecision.
haesitō, -āre *vi* to get stuck; to stammer; to hesitate, be uncertain.
hahae, hahahae *see* **ha**.
hālitus, -ūs *m* breath, vapour.
hallex, -icis *m* big toe.
hallūc- *see* **ālūc-**.
hālō, -āre *vi* to be fragrant ♦ *vt* to exhale.
hāluc *etc see* **ālūc**.
halyaeetos, -ī *m* osprey.
hama, -ae *f* water bucket.
Hamādryas, -adis *f* woodnymph.
hāmātilis *adj* with hooks.
hāmātus *adj* hooked.
Hamilcar, -is *m* father of Hannibal.
hāmus, -ī *m* hook; talons.
Hannibal, -is *m* famous Carthaginian general in 2nd Punic War.
hara, -ae *f* stye, pen.
harēna, -ae *f* sand; desert, seashore; arena (*in the amphitheatre*).
harēnōsus *adj* sandy.
hariola, -ae *f*, **hariolus, -ī** *m* soothsayer.
hariolor, -ārī *vi* to prophesy; to talk nonsense.
harmonia, -ae *f* concord, melody; (*fig*) harmony.
harpagō, -āre *vt* to steal.
harpagō, -ōnis *m* grappling hook; (*person*) robber.
harpē, -ēs *f* scimitar.
Harpȳiae, -ārum *fpl* Harpies (*mythical monsters, half woman, half bird*).
harundifer, -ī *adj* reed-crowned.
harundineus *adj* reedy.
harundinōsus *adj* abounding in reeds.
harundō, -inis *f* reed, cane; fishing rod; shaft, arrow; (*fowling*) limed twig; (*music*) pipe,

---

Noun declensions and verb conjugations are shown on pp xiii to xxv. The present infinitive ending of a verb shows to which conjugation it belongs: **-āre** = 1st; **-ēre** = 2nd; **-ere** = 3rd and **-īre** = 4th. Irregular verbs are shown on p xxvi

flute; (_toy_) hobbyhorse; (_weaving_) comb; (_writing_) pen.

haruspex, -icis _m_ diviner (_from entrails_); prophet.

haruspica, -ae _f_ soothsayer.

haruspicīnus _adj_ of divination by entrails ♦ _f_ art of such divination.

haruspicium, -ī _and_ **iī** _nt_ divination.

Hasdrubal, -is _m_ brother of Hannibal.

hasta, -ae _f_ spear, pike; sign of an auction sale; **sub ~ā vēndere** put up for auction.

hastātus _adj_ armed with a spear ♦ _mpl_ first line of Roman army in battle; **prīmus ~** 1st company of hastati.

hastīle, -is _nt_ shaft, spear, javelin; vine prop.

hau, haud _adv_ not, not at all.

hauddum _adv_ not yet.

haudquāquam _adv_ not at all, not by any means.

hauriō, -rīre, -sī, -stum _vt_ to draw, draw off, derive; to drain, empty, exhaust; to take in, drink, swallow, devour.

haustus _ppp of_ **hauriō**.

haustus, -ūs _m_ drawing (water); drinking; drink, draught.

haut _etc see_ **haud**.

hebdomas, -dis _f_ week.

Hēbē, -ēs _f_ goddess of youth (_cup bearer to the gods_).

hebenus, -ī _f_ ebony.

hebeō, -ēre _vi_ to be blunt, dull, sluggish.

hebes, -tis _adj_ blunt, dull, sluggish; obtuse, stupid.

hebēscō, -ere _vi_ to grow dim or dull.

hebetō, -āre _vt_ to blunt, dull, dim.

Hebrus, -ī _m_ Thracian river (_now_ Maritza).

Hecatē, -ēs _f_ goddess of magic (_and often identified with Diana_).

Hecatēius, -ēis _adj see n._

hecatombē, -ēs _f_ hecatomb.

Hector, -is _m_ son of Priam (_chief warrior of the Trojans against the Greeks_).

Hectoreus _adj_ of Hector; Trojan.

Hecuba, -ae _and_ **ē, -ēs** _f_ wife of Priam.

hedera, -ae _f_ ivy.

hederiger, -ī _adj_ wearing ivy.

hederōsus _adj_ covered with ivy.

hēdychrum, -ī _nt_ a cosmetic perfume.

hei, heia _etc see_ **ei, eia**.

Helena, -ae _and_ **ē, -ēs** _f_ Helen (_wife of Menelaus, abducted by Paris_).

Helenus, -ī _m_ son of Priam (_with prophetic powers_).

Hēliades, -um _fpl_ daughters of the Sun (_changed to poplars or alders, and their tears to amber_).

Helicē, -ēs _f_ the Great Bear.

Helicōn, -ōnis _m_ mountain in Greece sacred to Apollo and the Muses.

Helicōniades, -um _fpl_ the Muses.

Helicōnius _adj see_ **Helicōn**.

Hellas, -dis _f_ Greece.

Hellē, -ēs _f_ mythical Greek princess (_carried by the golden-fleeced ram, and drowned in the Hellespont_).

Hellēspontius, -iacus _adj see n._

Hellēspontus, -ī _m_ Hellespont (_now_ Dardanelles).

helluō, -ōnis _m_ glutton.

helluor, -ārī _vi_ to be a glutton.

helvella, -ae _f_ a savoury herb.

Helvētiī, -ōrum _mpl_ people of E. Gaul (_now_ Switzerland).

Helvētius, -cus _adj see n._

hem _interj_ (_expressing surprise_) eh?, well well!

hēmerodromus, -ī _m_ express courier.

hēmicillus, -ī _m_ mule.

hēmicyclium, -ī _and_ **iī** _nt_ semicircle with seats.

hēmīna, -ae _f_ half a pint.

hendecasyllabī, -ōrum _mpl_ hendecasyllabics, verses of eleven syllables.

heptēris, -is _f_ ship with seven banks of oars.

hera _etc see_ **era**.

Hēra, -ae _f_ Greek goddess identified with Juno.

Hēraclītus, -ī _m_ early Greek philosopher.

Hēraea, -aeōrum _ntpl_ festival of Hera.

herba, -ae _f_ blade, young plant; grass, herb, weed.

herbēscō, -ere _vi_ to grow into blades.

herbeus _adj_ grass-green.

herbidus _adj_ grassy.

herbifer, -ī _adj_ grassy.

herbōsus _adj_ grassy, made of turf; made of herbs.

herbula, -ae _f_ little herb.

hercīscō, -ere _vt_ to divide an inheritance.

hercle _interj_ by Hercules!

herctum, -ī _nt_ inheritance.

Hercule _interj_ by Hercules!

Herculēs, -is _and_ **ī** _m_ mythical Greek hero, later deified.

Herculeus _adj_: **arbor ~** poplar; **urbs ~** Herculaneum.

here _etc see_ **herī**.

hērēditārius _adj_ inherited; about an inheritance.

hērēditās, -ātis _f_ inheritance; **~ sine sacrīs** a gift without awkward obligations.

hērēdium, -ī _and_ **iī** _nt_ inherited estate.

hērēs, -ēdis _m/f_ heir, heiress; (_fig_) master, successor.

herī _adv_ yesterday.

herīlis _etc see_ **erilis**.

Hermēs, -ae _m_ Greek god identified with Mercury; Hermes pillar.

Hernicī, -ōrum _mpl_ people of central Italy.

Hernicus _adj see n._

Hērodotus, -ī _m_ first Greek historian.

hērōicus _adj_ heroic, epic.

hērōīna, -ae _f_ demigoddess.

hērōis, -dis _f_ demigoddess.

hērōs, -is _m_ demigod, hero.

hērōus _adj_ heroic, epic.

herus _etc see_ **erus**.

Hēsiodēus, -īus adj see n.
Hēsiodus, -ī m Hesiod (Greek didactic poet).
Hesperia, -iae f Italy; Spain.
Hesperides, -idum fpl keepers of a garden in the far West.
Hesperius, -is adj western.
Hesperus, -ī m evening star.
hesternus adj of yesterday.
heu interj (expressing dismay or pain) oh!, alas!
heus interj (calling attention) ho!, hallo!
hexameter, -rī m hexameter verse.
hexēris, -is f ship with six banks of oars.
hiātus, -ūs m opening, abyss; open mouth, gaping; (GRAM) hiatus.
Hibērēs, -um mpl Spaniards.
Hibēria, -iae f Spain.
hīberna, -ōrum ntpl winter quarters.
hībernācula, -ōrum ntpl winter tents.
Hibernia, -ae f Ireland.
hībernō, -āre vi to winter, remain in winter quarters.
hībernus adj winter, wintry.
Hibērus, -icus adj Spanish.
Hibērus, -ī m river Ebro.
hibīscum, -ī nt marsh mallow.
hibrida, hybrida, -ae m/f mongrel, half-breed.
hīc, haec, hōc pron, adj this; he, she, it; my, the latter, the present; **hīc homō** I; **hōc magis** the more; **hōc est** that is.
hīc adv here; herein; (time) at this point.
hīce, haece, hōce emphatic forms of **hīc, haec, hōc.**
hīcine, haecine, hōcine emphatic forms of **hīc, haec, hōc.**
hiemālis adj winter, stormy.
hiemō, -āre vi to pass the winter; to be wintry, stormy.
hiems, (hiemps), -is f winter; stormy weather, cold.
Hierōnymus, -ī m Jerome.
Hierosolyma, -ōrum ntpl Jerusalem.
Hierosolymārius adj see n.
hietō, -āre vi to yawn.
hilare adv see **hilaris.**
hilaris adj cheerful, merry.
hilaritās, -ātis f cheerfulness.
hilaritūdō, -inis f merriment.
hilarō, -āre vt to cheer, gladden.
hilarulus adj a gay little thing.
hilarus etc see **hilaris.**
hīllae, -ārum fpl smoked sausage.
Hīlōtae, -ārum mpl Helots (of Sparta).
hīlum, -ī nt something, a whit.
hinc adv from here, hence; on this side; from this source, for this reason; (time) henceforth.
hinniō, -īre vi to neigh.
hinnītus, -ūs m neighing.
hinnuleus, -ī m fawn.

hiō, -āre vi to be open, gape, yawn; (speech) to be disconnected, leave a hiatus ♦ vt to sing.
hippagōgī, -ōrum fpl cavalry transports.
hippocentaurus, -ī m centaur.
hippodromos, -ī m racecourse.
Hippolytus, -ī m son of Theseus (slandered by stepmother Phaedra).
hippomanes, -is nt mare's fluid; membrane on foal's forehead.
Hippōnactēus adj of Hipponax ♦ m iambic verse used by Hipponax.
Hippōnax, -ctis m Greek satirist.
hippotoxotae, -ārum mpl mounted archers.
hīra, -ae f the empty gut.
hircīnus adj of a goat.
hircōsus adj goatish.
hircus, -ī m he-goat; goatish smell.
hirnea, -ae f jug.
hirq- etc see **hirc-.**
hirsūtus adj shaggy, bristly; uncouth.
hirtus adj hairy, shaggy; rude.
hirūdō, -inis f leech.
hirundinīnus adj swallows'.
hirundō, -inis f swallow.
hīscō, -ere vi to gape; to open the mouth ♦ vt to utter.
Hispānia, -iae f Spain.
Hispāniēnsis, -us adj Spanish.
hispidus adj hairy, rough.
Hister, -rī m lower Danube.
historia, -ae f history, inquiry; story.
historicus adj historical ♦ m historian.
histricus adj of the stage.
histriō, -ōnis m actor.
histriōnālis adj of an actor.
histriōnia, -ae f acting.
hiulcē adv with hiatus.
hiulcō, -āre vt to split open.
hiulcus adj gaping, open; (speech) with hiatus.
hodiē adv today; nowadays, now; up to the present.
hodiernus adj today's.
holitor, -ōris m market gardener.
holitōrius adj for market gardeners.
holus, -eris nt vegetables.
holusculum, -ī nt small cabbage.
Homēricus adj see n.
Homērus, -ī m Greek epic poet, Homer.
homicīda, -ae m killer, murderer.
homicīdium, -ī and iī nt murder.
homō, -inis m/f human being, man; (pl) people, the world; (derogatory) fellow, creature; **inter ~inēs esse** be alive; see the world.
homullus, -ī, homunciō, -ōnis, homunculus, -ī m little man, poor creature, mortal.
honestās, -ātis f good character, honourable reputation; sense of honour, integrity;

Noun declensions and verb conjugations are shown on pp xiii to xxv. The present infinitive ending of a verb shows to which conjugation it belongs: **-āre** = 1st; **-ēre** = 2nd; **-ere** = 3rd and **-īre** = 4th. Irregular verbs are shown on p xxvi

(*things*) beauty.
honestē *adv* decently, virtuously.
honestō, -āre *vt* to honour, dignify, embellish.
honestus *adj* honoured, respectable; honourable, virtuous; (*appearance*) handsome ♦ *m* gentleman ♦ *nt* virtue, good; beauty.
honor, -ōris *m* honour, esteem; public office, position, preferment; award, tribute, offering; ornament, beauty; ~**ōris causā** out of respect; for the sake of; ~**ōrem praefārī** apologize for a remark.
honōrābilis *adj* a mark of respect.
honōrārius *adj* done out of respect, honorary.
honōrātē *adv* honourably.
honōrātus *adj* esteemed, distinguished; in high office; complimentary.
honōrificē *adv* in complimentary terms.
honōrificus *adj* complimentary.
honōrō, -āre, -āvī, -ātum *vt* to do honour to, embellish.
honōrus *adj* complimentary.
honōs *etc see* **honor.**
hōra, -ae *f* hour; time, season; (*pl*) clock; **in ~ās** hourly; **in ~am vīvere** ≈ *live from hand to mouth.*
hōraeum, -ī *nt* pickle.
Horātius, -ī *m* Roman family name (*esp the defender of Rome against Porsenna); the lyric poet Horace.*
Horātius *adj see n.*
hordeum, -ī *nt* barley.
horia, -ae *f* fishing smack.
hōrnō *adv* this year.
hōrnōtinus *adj* this year's.
hōrnus *adj* this year's.
hōrologium, -ī *and* **iī** *nt* clock.
horrendus *adj* fearful, terrible; awesome.
horrēns, -entis *pres p of* **horreō** ♦ *adj* bristling, shaggy.
horreō, -ēre, -uī *vi* to stand stiff, bristle; to shiver, shudder, tremble ♦ *vt* to dread; to be afraid, be amazed.
horrēscō, -ere *vi* to stand on end, become rough; to begin to quake; to start, be terrified ♦ *vt* to dread.
horreum, -ī *nt* barn, granary, store.
horribilis *adj* terrifying; amazing.
horridē *adv see* **horridus.**
horridulus *adj* protruding a little; unkempt; (*fig*) uncouth.
horridus *adj* bristling, shaggy, rough, rugged; shivering; (*manners*) rude, uncouth; frightening.
horrifer, -ī *adj* chilling; terrifying.
horrificē *adv* in awesome manner.
horrificō, -āre *vt* to ruffle; to terrify.
horrificus *adj* terrifying.
horrisonus *adj* dread-sounding.
horror, -ōris *m* bristling; shivering, ague; terror, fright, awe, a terror.
hōrsum *adv* this way.

hortāmen, -inis *nt* encouragement.
hortāmentum, -ī *nt* encouragement.
hortātiō, -ōnis *f* harangue, encouragement.
hortātor, -ōris *m* encourager.
hortātus, -ūs *m* encouragement.
Hortēnsius, -ī *m* Roman family name (*esp an orator in Cicero's time*).
hortor, -ārī, -ātus *vt* to urge, encourage, exhort, harangue.
hortulus, -ī *m* little garden.
hortus, -ī *m* garden; (*pl*) park.
hospes, -itis *m,* **hospita, -ae** *f* host, hostess; guest, friend; stranger, foreigner ♦ *adj* strange.
hospitālis *adj* host's, guest's; hospitable.
hospitālitās, -ātis *f* hospitality.
hospitāliter *adv* hospitably.
hospitium, -ī *and* **iī** *nt* hospitality, friendship; lodging, inn.
hostia, -ae *f* victim, sacrifice.
hostiātus *adj* provided with victims.
hosticus *adj* hostile; strange ♦ *nt* enemy territory.
hostīlis *adj* of the enemy, hostile.
hostīliter *adv* in hostile manner.
hostīmentum, -ī *nt* recompense.
hostiō, -īre *vt* to requite.
hostis, -is *m/f* enemy.
hūc *adv* hither, here; to this, to such a pitch; ~ **illūc** hither and thither.
hui *interj* (*expressing surprise*) ho!, my word!
hūiusmodī such.
hūmānē, -iter *adv* humanly; gently, politely.
hūmānitās, -ātis *f* human nature, mankind; humanity, kindness, courtesy; culture, refinement.
hūmānitus *adv* in accordance with human nature; kindly.
hūmānus *adj* human, humane, kind, courteous; cultured, refined, well-educated; ~**ō māior** superhuman.
humātiō, -ōnis *f* burying.
hūme-, hūmi- *see* **ūme-, ūmi-.**
humilis *adj* low, low-lying, shallow; (*condition*) lowly, humble, poor; (*language*) commonplace; (*mind*) mean, base.
humilitās, -ātis *f* low position, smallness, shallowness; lowliness, insignificance; meanness, baseness.
humiliter *adv* meanly, humbly.
humō, -āre, -āvī, -ātum *vt* to bury.
humus, -ī *f* earth, ground; land; ~**ī** on the ground.
hyacinthinus *adj* of the hyacinthus.
hyacinthus, -ī *m* iris, lily.
Hyades, -um *fpl* Hyads (*a group of stars in Taurus*).
hyaena, -ae *f* hyena.
hyalus, -ī *m* glass.
Hybla, -ae *f* mountain in Sicily (*famous for bees*).
Hyblaeus *adj see n.*
hybrida *etc see* **hibrida.**

Hydaspēs, -is *m* tributary of river Indus (*now* Jelum).

Hȳdra, -ae *f* hydra (*a mythical dragon with seven heads*).

hydraulus, -ī *m* water organ.

hydria, -ae *f* ewer.

Hydrochous, -ī *m* Aquarius.

hydrōpicus *adj* suffering from dropsy.

hydrōps, -is *m* dropsy.

hydrus, -ī *m* serpent.

Hylās, -ae *m a* youth loved by Hercules.

Hymēn, -enis, Hymenaeus, -ī *m god of marriage*; wedding song; wedding.

Hymettius *adj see n.*

Hymettus, -ī *m* mountain near Athens (*famous for honey and marble*).

Hypanis, -is *m* river of Sarmatia (*now* Bug).

Hyperboreī, -ōrum *mpl* fabulous people in the far North.

Hyperboreus *adj see n.*

Hyperīōn, -onis *m* father of the Sun; the Sun.

hypodidasculus, -ī *m* assistant teacher.

hypomnēma, -tis *nt* memorandum.

Hyrcānī, -ōrum *mpl* people on the Caspian Sea.

Hyrcānus *adj* Hyrcanian.

I, i

Iacchus, -ī *m* Bacchus; wine.

iaceō, -ēre, -uī *vi* to lie; to be ill, lie dead; (*places*) to be situated, be flat *or* low-lying, be in ruins; (*dress*) to hang loose; (*fig*) to be inactive, be downhearted; (*things*) to be dormant, neglected, despised.

iaciō, -ere, iēcī, iactum *vt* to throw; to lay, build; (*seed*) to sow; (*speech*) to cast, let fall, mention.

iactāns, -antis *pres p of* **iactō** ♦ *adj* boastful.

iactanter *adv* ostentatiously.

iactantia, -ae *f* boasting, ostentation.

iactātiō, -ōnis *f* tossing, gesticulation; boasting, ostentation; ~ **populāris** publicity.

iactātus, -ūs *m* waving.

iactitō, -āre *vt* to mention, bandy.

iactō, -āre, -āvī, -ātum *vt* to throw, scatter; to shake, toss about; (*mind*) to disquiet; (*ideas*) to consider, discuss, mention; (*speech*) to boast of; **sē** ~ waver, fluctuate; to behave ostentatiously, be officious.

iactūra, -ae *f* throwing overboard; loss, sacrifice.

iactus *ppp of* **iaciō**.

iactus, -ūs *m* throwing, throw; **intrā tēlī iactum** within spear's range.

iacuī *perf of* **iaceō**.

iaculābilis *adj* missile.

iaculātor, -ōris *m* thrower, shooter; light-armed soldier.

iaculātrīx, -īcis *f* huntress.

iaculor, -ārī, -ātus *vt* to throw, hurl, shoot; to throw the javelin; to shoot at, hit; (*fig*) to aim at, attack.

iaculum, -ī *nt* javelin; fishing net.

iāien- *etc see* **iēn-**.

iam *adv* (*past*) already, by then; (*present*) now, already; (*future*) directly, very soon; (*emphasis*) indeed, precisely; (*inference*) therefore, then surely; (*transition*) moreover, next; **iam dūdum** for a long time, long ago; immediately; **iam iam** right now, any moment now; **non** ~ no longer; **iam ... iam** at one time ... at another; **iam nunc** just now; **iam prīdem** long ago, for a long time; **iam tum** even at that time; **sī iam** supposing for the purpose of argument.

iambēus *adj* iambic.

iambus, -ī *m* iambic foot; iambic poetry.

Iānālis *adj see* **Iānus**.

Iāniculum, -ī *nt* Roman hill across the Tiber.

iānitor, -ōris *m* doorkeeper, porter.

iānua, -ae *f* door; entrance; (*fig*) key.

Iānuārius *adj* of January ♦ *m* January.

Iānus, -ī *m* god of gateways and beginnings; archway, arcade.

Iapetīonidēs, -ae *m* Atlas.

Iapetus, -ī *m a* Titan (*father of Atlas and Prometheus*).

Iāpyx, -gis *adj* Iapygian; Apulian ♦ *m* west-north-west wind from Apulia.

Iāsōn, -onis *m* Jason (*leader of Argonauts, husband of Medea*).

Iāsonius *adj see n.*

iaspis, -dis *f* jasper.

Ibēr- *etc see* **Hibēr-**.

ibi *adv* there; then; in this, at it.

ibīdem *adv* in the same place; at that very moment.

ibis, -is *and* **idis** *f* ibis.

Icarium, -ī *nt* Icarian Sea.

Icarius *adj see n.*

Icarus, -ī *m* son of Daedalus (*drowned in the Aegean*).

īcō, -ere, -ī, ictum *vt* to strike; **foedus** ~ make a treaty.

ictericus *adj* jaundiced.

ictis, -dis *f* weasel.

ictus *ppp of* **īcō**.

ictus, -ūs *m* stroke, blow; wound; (*metre*) beat.

Īda, -ae, -ē, -ēs *f* mountain in Crete; mountain near Troy.

Īdaeus *adj* Cretan; Trojan.

idcircō *adv* for that reason; for the purpose.

Noun declensions and verb conjugations are shown on pp xiii to xxv. The present infinitive ending of a verb shows to which conjugation it belongs: -**āre** = 1st; -**ēre** = 2nd; -**ere** = 3rd and -**īre** = 4th. Irregular verbs are shown on p xxvi

īdem, eadem, idem *pron* the same; also, likewise.
identidem *adv* repeatedly, again and again.
ideō *adv* therefore, for this reason, that is why.
idiōta, -ae *m* ignorant person, layman.
īdōlon, -ī *nt* apparition.
idōneē *adv see* **idōneus**.
idōneus *adj* fit, proper, suitable, sufficient.
Īdūs, -uum *fpl* Ides (*the 15th March, May, July, October, the 13th of other months*).
iēcī *perf of* **iaciō**.
iecur, -oris *and* **inoris** *nt* liver; (*fig*) passion.
iecusculum, -ī *nt* small liver.
iēiūniōsus *adj* hungry.
iēiūnitās, -ātis *f* fasting; (*fig*) meagreness.
iēiūnium, -ī *and* **iī** *nt* fast; hunger; leanness.
iēiūnus *adj* fasting, hungry; (*things*) barren, poor, meagre; (*style*) feeble.
iēntāculum, -ī *nt* breakfast.
igitur *adv* therefore, then, so.
ignārus *adj* ignorant, unaware; unknown.
ignāvē, -iter *adv* without energy.
ignāvia, -ae *f* idleness, laziness; cowardice.
ignāvus *adj* idle, lazy, listless; cowardly; relaxing.
ignēscō, -ere *vi* to take fire, burn.
igneus *adj* burning, fiery.
igniculus, -ī *m* spark; (*fig*) fire, vehemence.
ignifer, -ī *adj* fiery.
ignigena, -ae *m* the fireborn (Bacchus).
ignipēs, -edis *adj* fiery-footed.
ignipotēns, -entis *adj* fire-working (Vulcan).
ignis, -is *m* fire, a fire; firebrand, lightning; brightness, redness; (*fig*) passion, love.
ignōbilis *adj* unknown, obscure; low-born.
ignōbilitās, -ātis *f* obscurity; low birth.
ignōminia, -ae *f* dishonour, disgrace.
ignōminiōsus *adj* (*person*) degraded, disgraced; (*things*) shameful.
ignōrābilis *adj* unknown.
ignōrantia, -ae *f* ignorance.
ignōrātiō, -ōnis *f* ignorance.
ignōrō, -āre, -āvī, -ātum *vt* to not know, be unacquainted with; to disregard.
ignōscō, -scere, -vī, -tum *vt, vi* to forgive, pardon.
ignōtus *adj* unknown; low-born; ignorant.
īlex, -icis *f* holm oak.
īlia, -um *ntpl* groin; entrails; ~ dūcere become broken-winded.
Īlia, -ae *f* mother of Romulus and Remus.
Īliadēs, -adae *m* son of Ilia; Trojan.
Īlias, -dis *f* the Iliad; a Trojan woman.
īlicet *adv* it's all over, let us go; immediately.
īlicō *adv* on the spot; instantly.
īlignus *adj* of holm oak.
Īlīthyia, -ae *f* Greek goddess of childbirth.
Īlium, -on, -ī *nt*, **-os, -ī** *f* Troy.
Īlius, -acus *adj* Trojan.
illā *adv* that way.
illābefactus *adj* unbroken.
illābor, -bī, -psus *vi* to flow into, fall down.

illabōrō, -āre *vi* to work (at).
illāc *adv* that way.
illacessītus *adj* unprovoked.
illacrimābilis *adj* unwept; inexorable.
illacrimō, -āre; -or, -ārī *vi* to weep over, lament; to weep.
illaesus *adj* unhurt.
illaetābilis *adj* cheerless.
illāpsus *ppa of* **illābor**.
illaqueō, -āre *vt* to ensnare.
illātus *ppp of* **īnferō**.
illaudātus *adj* wicked.
ille, -a, -ud *pron and adj* that, that one; he, she, it; the famous; the former, the other; **ex ~ō** since then.
illecebra, -ae *f* attraction, lure, bait, decoy bird.
illecebrōsus *adj* seductive.
illectus *ppp of* **illiciō**.
illēctus *adj* unread.
illepidē *adv see* **illepidus**.
illepidus *adj* inelegant, churlish.
illex, -icis *m/f* lure.
illēx, -ēgis *adj* lawless.
illexī *perf of* **illiciō**.
illībātus *adj* unimpaired.
illīberālis *adj* ungenerous, mean, disobliging.
illīberālitās, -ātis *f* meanness.
illīberāliter *adv see* **illīberālis**.
illic, -aec, -ūc *pron* he, she, it; that.
illīc *adv* there, yonder; in that matter.
illiciō, -icere, -exī, -ectum *vt* to seduce, decoy, mislead.
illicitātor, -ōris *m* sham bidder (at an auction).
illicitus *adj* unlawful.
illīdō, -dere, -sī, -sum *vt* to strike, dash against.
illigō, -āre, -āvī, -ātum *vt* to fasten on, attach; to connect; to impede, encumber, oblige.
illim *adv* from there.
illīmis *adj* clear.
illinc *adv* from there; on that side.
illinō, -inere, -ēvī, -itum *vt* to smear over, cover, bedaub.
illiquefactus *adj* melted.
illīsī *perf of* **illīdō**.
illīsus *ppp of* **illīdō**.
illitterātus *adj* uneducated, uncultured.
illitus *ppp of* **illinō**.
illō *adv* (to) there; to that end.
illōtus *adj* dirty.
illūc *adv* (to) there; to that; to him/her.
illūceō, -ēre *vi* to blaze.
illūcēscō, -cēscere, -xī *vi* to become light, dawn.
illūdō, -dere, -sī, -sum *vt, vi* to play, amuse oneself; to abuse; to jeer at, ridicule.
illūminātē *adv* luminously.
illūminō, -āre, -āvī, -ātum *vt* to light up; to enlighten; to embellish.
illūsiō, -ōnis *f* irony.
illūstris *adj* bright, clear; distinct, manifest;

distinguished, illustrious.
illūstrō, -āre, -āvī, -ātum *vt* to illuminate; to make clear, explain; to make famous.
illūsus *ppp of* **illūdō**.
illuviēs, -ēī *f* dirt, filth; floods.
Illyria, -ae *f*, **-cum, -cī** *nt* Illyria.
Illyricus, -us *adj see* **Illyricum.**
Illyriī, -ōrum *mpl people E. of the Adriatic.*
Ilva, -ae *f* Italian island (*now* Elba).
imāginārius *adj* fancied.
imāginātiō, -ōnis *f* fancy.
imāginor, -ārī, *vt* to picture to oneself.
imāgō, -inis *f* likeness, picture, statue; portrait of ancestor; apparition, ghost; echo, mental picture, idea; (*fig*) semblance, mere shadow; (*RHET*) comparison.
imbēcillē *adv* faintly.
imbēcillitās, -ātis *f* weakness, helplessness.
imbēcillus *adj* weak, frail; helpless.
imbellis *adj* non-combatant; peaceful; cowardly.
imber, -ris *m* rain, heavy shower; water; (*fig*) stream, shower.
imberbis, imberbus *adj* beardless.
imbibō, -ere, -ī *vt* (*mind*) to conceive; to resolve.
imbrex, -icis *f* tile.
imbricus *adj* rainy.
imbrifer, -ī *adj* rainy.
imbuō, -uere, -uī, -ūtum *vt* to wet, steep, dip; (*fig*) to taint, fill; to inspire, accustom, train; to begin, be the first to explore.
imitābilis *adj* imitable.
imitāmen, -inis *nt* imitation; likeness.
imitāmenta, -ōrum *ntpl* pretence.
imitātiō, -ōnis *f* imitation.
imitātor,-ōris *m*, **-rīx,-rīcis** *f* imitator.
imitātus *adj* copied.
imitor, -ārī, -ātus *vt* to copy, portray; to imitate, act like.
immadēscō, -ēscere, -uī *vi* to become wet.
immāne *adv* savagely.
immānis *adj* enormous, vast; monstrous, savage, frightful.
immānitās, -ātis *f* vastness; savageness, barbarism.
immānsuētus *adj* wild.
immātūritās, -ātis *f* over-eagerness.
immātūrus *adj* untimely.
immedicābilis *adj* incurable.
immemor, -is *adj* unmindful, forgetful, negligent.
immemorābilis *adj* indescribable, not worth mentioning.
immemorātus *adj* hitherto untold.
immēnsitās, -ātis *f* immensity.
immēnsum, -ī *nt* infinity, vast extent ♦ *adv* exceedingly.
immēnsus *adj* immeasurable, vast, unending.
immerēns, -entis *adj* undeserving.

immergō, -gere, -sī, -sum *vt* to plunge, immerse.
immeritō *adv* unjustly.
immeritus *adj* undeserving, innocent; undeserved.
immersābilis *adj* never foundering.
immersus *ppp of* **immergō.**
immētātus *adj* unmeasured.
immigrō, -āre, -āvī, -ātum *vi* to move (into).
immineō, -ēre, -uī *vi* to overhang, project; to be near, adjoin, impend; to threaten, be a menace to; to long for, grasp at.
imminuō, -uere, -uī, -ūtum *vt* to lessen, shorten; to impair; to encroach on, ruin.
imminūtiō, -ōnis *f* mutilation; (*RHET*) understatement.
immisceō, -scēre, -scuī, -xtum *vt* to intermingle, blend; **sē ~** join, meddle with.
immiserābilis *adj* unpitied.
immisericorditer *adv* unmercifully.
immisericors, -dis *adj* pitiless.
immissiō, -ōnis *f* letting grow.
immissus *ppp of* **immittō.**
immītis *adj* unripe; severe, inexorable.
immittō, -ittere, -īsī, -issum *vt* to let in, put in; to graft on; to let go, let loose, let grow; to launch, throw; to incite, set on.
immīxtus *ppp of* **immisceō.**
immo *adv* (*correcting preceding words*) no, yes; on the contrary, or rather; **~ sī** ah, if only.
immōbilis *adj* motionless; immovable.
immoderātē *adv* extravagantly.
immoderātiō, -ōnis *f* excess.
immoderātus *adj* limitless; excessive, unbridled.
immodestē *adv* extravagantly.
immodestia, -ae *f* license.
immodestus *adj* immoderate.
immodicē *adv see* **immodicus.**
immodicus *adj* excessive, extravagant, unruly.
immodulātus *adj* unrhythmical.
immolātiō, -ōnis *f* sacrifice.
immolātor, -ōris *m* sacrificer.
immolītus *adj* erected.
immolō, -āre, -āvī, -ātum *vt* to sacrifice; to slay.
immorior, -ī, -tuus *vi* to die upon; to waste away.
immorsus *adj* bitten; (*fig*) stimulated.
immortālis *adj* immortal, everlasting.
immortālitās, -ātis *f* immortality; lasting fame.
immortāliter *adv* infinitely.
immōtus *adj* motionless, unmoved, immovable.
immūgiō, -īre, -iī *vi* to roar (in).
immulgeō, -ēre *vt* to milk.
immundus *adj* unclean, dirty.
immūniō, -īre, -īvī *vt* to strengthen.

immūnis _adj_ with no public obligations, untaxed, free from office; exempt, free (from).

immūnitās, -ātis _f_ exemption, immunity, privilege.

immūnītus _adj_ undefended; (_roads_) unmetalled.

immurmurō, -āre _vi_ to murmur (at).

immūtābilis _adj_ unalterable.

immūtābilitās, -ātis _f_ immutability.

immūtātiō, -ōnis _f_ exchange; (_RHET_) metonymy.

immūtātus _adj_ unchanged.

immūtō, -āre, -āvī, -ātum _vt_ to change; (_words_) to substitute by metonymy.

impācātus _adj_ aggressive.

impāctus _ppp of_ **impingō**.

impār, -aris _adj_ unequal, uneven, unlike; no match for, inferior; (_metre_) elegiac.

imparātus _adj_ unprepared, unprovided.

impariter _adv_ unequally.

impāstus _adj_ hungry.

impatiēns, -entis _adj_ unable to endure, impatient.

impatienter _adv_ intolerably.

impatientia, -ae _f_ want of endurance.

impavidē _adv see_ **impavidus**.

impavidus _adj_ fearless, undaunted.

impedīmentum, -ī _nt_ hindrance, obstacle; (_pl_) baggage, luggage, supply train.

impediō, -īre, -īvī and iī, -ītum _vt_ to hinder, entangle; to encircle; (_fig_) to embarrass, obstruct, prevent.

impedītiō, -ōnis _f_ obstruction.

impedītus _adj_ (_MIL_) hampered with baggage, in difficulties; (_place_) difficult, impassable; (_mind_) busy, obsessed.

impēgī _perf of_ **impingō**.

impellō, -ellere, -ulī, -ulsum _vt_ to strike, drive; to set in motion, impel, shoot; to incite, urge on; (_fig_) to overthrow, ruin.

impendeō, -ēre _vi_ to overhang; to be imminent, threaten.

impendiō _adv_ very much.

impendium, -ī and iī _nt_ expense, outlay; interest on a loan.

impendō, -endere, -endī, -ēnsum _vt_ to weigh out, pay out, spend; (_fig_) to devote.

impenetrābilis _adj_ impenetrable.

impēnsa, -ae _f_ expense, outlay.

impēnsē _adv_ very much; earnestly.

impēnsus _ppp of_ **impendō** ♦ _adj_ (_cost_) high, dear; (_fig_) great, earnest.

imperātor, -ōris _m_ commander-in-chief, general; emperor; chief, master.

imperātōrius _adj_ of a general; imperial.

imperātum, -ī _nt_ order.

imperceptus _adj_ unknown.

impercussus _adj_ noiseless.

imperditus _adj_ not slain.

imperfectus _adj_ unfinished, imperfect.

imperfossus _adj_ not stabbed.

imperiōsus _adj_ powerful, imperial; tyrannical.

imperītē _adv_ awkwardly.

imperītia, -ae _f_ inexperience.

imperitō, -āre _vt, vi_ to rule, command.

imperītus _adj_ inexperienced, ignorant.

imperium, -ī and iī _nt_ command, order; mastery, sovereignty, power; military command, supreme authority; empire; (_pl_) those in command, the authorities.

impermissus _adj_ unlawful.

imperō, -āre, -āvī, -ātum _vt, vi_ to order, command; to requisition, demand; to rule, govern, control; to be emperor.

imperterritus _adj_ undaunted.

impertiō, -īre, -īvī and iī, -ītum _vt_ to share, communicate, impart.

imperturbātus _adj_ unruffled.

impervius _adj_ impassable.

impetibilis _adj_ intolerable.

impetis (_gen_), **-e** (_abl_) _m_ force; extent.

impetrābilis _adj_ attainable; successful.

impetrātiō, -ōnis _f_ favour.

impetriō, -īre _vt_ to succeed with the auspices.

impetrō, -āre, -āvī, -ātum _vt_ to achieve; to obtain, secure (_a request_).

impetus, -ūs _m_ attack, onset; charge; rapid motion, rush; (_mind_) impulse, passion.

impexus _adj_ unkempt.

impiē _adv_ wickedly.

impietās, -ātis _f_ impiety, disloyalty, unfilial conduct.

impiger, -rī _adj_ active, energetic.

impigrē _adv see adj._

impigritās, -ātis _f_ energy.

impingō, -ingere, -ēgī, -āctum _vt_ to dash, force against; to force upon; (_fig_) to bring against, drive.

impiō, -āre _vt_ to make sinful.

impius _adj_ (_to gods_) impious; (_to parents_) undutiful; (_to country_) disloyal; wicked, unscrupulous.

implācābilis _adj_ implacable.

implācābiliter _adv see adj._

implācātus _adj_ unappeased.

implacidus _adj_ savage.

impleō, -ēre, -ēvī, -ētum _vt_ to fill; to satisfy; (_time, number_) to make up, complete; (_duty_) to discharge, fulfil.

implexus _adj_ entwined; involved.

implicātiō, -ōnis _f_ entanglement.

implicātus _adj_ complicated, confused.

implicitē _adv_ intricately.

implicō, -āre, -āvī and uī, -ātum and itum _vt_ to entwine, enfold, clasp; (_fig_) to entangle, involve; to connect closely, join.

implōrātiō, -ōnis _f_ beseeching.

implōrō, -āre, -āvī, -ātum _vt_ to invoke, entreat, appeal to.

implūmis _adj_ unfledged.

impluō, -ere _vi_ to rain upon.

impluvium, -ī and iī _nt_ roof-opening of the Roman atrium; rain basin in the atrium.

impolītē _adv_ without ornament.

impolītus *adj* unpolished, inelegant.

impollūtus *adj* unstained.

impōnō, -ōnere, -osuī, -ositum *vt* to put in, lay on, place; to embark; (*fig*) to impose, inflict, assign; to put in charge; (*tax*) to impose; (*with dat*) to impose upon, cheat.

importō, -āre, -āvī, -ātum *vt* to bring in, import; (*fig*) to bring upon, introduce.

importūnē *adv see adj.*

importūnitās, -ātis *f* insolence, ill nature.

importūnus *adj* unsuitable; troublesome; ill-natured, uncivil, bullying.

importuōsus *adj* without a harbour.

impos, -tis *adj* not master (of).

impositus, impostus *ppp of* **impōnō**.

impotēns, -entis *adj* powerless, weak; with no control over; headstrong, violent.

impotenter *adv* weakly; violently.

impotentia, -ae *f* poverty; want of self-control, violence.

impraesentiārum *adv* at present.

imprānsus *adj* fasting, without breakfast.

imprecor, -ārī *vt* to invoke.

impressiō, -ōnis *f* (MIL) thrust, raid; (*mind*) impression; (*speech*) emphasis; (*rhythm*) beat.

impressus *ppp of* **imprimō**.

imprīmīs *adv* especially.

imprimō, -imere, -essī, -essum *vt* to press upon, impress, imprint, stamp.

improbātiō, -ōnis *f* blame.

improbē *adv* badly, wrongly; persistently.

improbitās, -ātis *f* badness, dishonesty.

improbō, -āre, -āvī, -ātum *vt* to disapprove, condemn, reject.

improbulus *adj* a little presumptuous.

improbus *adj* bad, inferior (in quality); wicked, perverse, cruel; unruly, persistent, rebellious.

imprōcērus *adj* undersized.

imprōdictus *adj* not postponed.

imprōmptus *adj* unready, slow.

improperātus *adj* lingering.

improsper, -ī *adj* unsuccessful.

improsperē *adv* unfortunately.

imprōvidē *adv see adj.*

imprōvidus *adj* unforeseeing, thoughtless.

imprōvīsus *adj* unexpected; ~ō, de ~ō, ex ~ō unexpectedly.

imprūdēns, -entis *adj* unforeseeing, not expecting; ignorant, unaware.

imprūdenter *adv* thoughtlessly, unawares.

imprūdentia, -ae *f* thoughtlessness; ignorance; aimlessness.

impūbēs, -eris *and* **is** *adj* youthful; chaste.

impudēns, -entis *adj* shameless, impudent.

impudenter *adv see adj.*

impudentia, -ae *f* impudence.

impudīcitia, -ae *f* lewdness.

impudīcus *adj* shameless; immodest.

impugnātiō, -ōnis *f* assault.

impugnō, -āre, -āvī, -ātum *vt* to attack; (*fig*) to oppose, impugn.

impulī *perf of* **impellō**.

impulsiō, -ōnis *f* pressure; (*mind*) impulse.

impulsor, -ōris *m* instigator.

impulsus *ppp of* **impellō**.

impulsus, -ūs *m* push, pressure, impulse; (*fig*) instigation.

impūne *adv* safely, with impunity.

impūnitās, -ātis *f* impunity.

impūnītē *adv* with impunity.

impūnītus *adj* unpunished.

impūrātus *adj* vile.

impūrē *adv see adj.*

impūritās, -ātis *f* uncleanness.

impūrus *adj* unclean; infamous, vile.

imputātus *adj* unpruned.

imputō, -āre, -āvī, -ātum *vt* to put to one's account; to ascribe, credit, impute.

īmulus *adj* little tip of.

īmus *adj* lowest, deepest, bottom of; last.

in *prep* (*with abl*) in, on, at; among; in the case of; (*time*) during; (*with acc*) into, on to, to, towards; against; (*time*) for, till; (*purpose*) for; ~ armīs under arms; ~ equō on horseback; ~ eō esse ut be in the position of; be on the point of; ~ hōrās hourly; ~ modum in the manner of; ~ rem of use; ~ universum in general.

inaccessus *adj* unapproachable.

inacēscō, -ere *vi* to turn sour.

Īnachidēs, -idae *m* Perseus; Epaphus.

Īnachis, -idis *f* Io.

Īnachius *adj* of Inachus, Argive, Greek.

Īnachus, -ī *m* first king of Argos.

inadsuētus *adj* unaccustomed.

inadūstus *adj* unsinged.

inaedificō, -āre, -āvī, -ātum *vt* to build on, erect; to wall up, block up.

inaequābilis *adj* uneven.

inaequālis *adj* uneven; unequal; capricious.

inaequāliter *adv see adj.*

inaequātus *adj* unequal.

inaequō, -āre *vt* to level up.

inaestimābilis *adj* incalculable; invaluable; valueless.

inaestuō, -āre *vi* to rage in.

inamābilis *adj* hateful.

inamārēscō, -ere *vi* to become bitter.

inambitiōsus *adj* unambitious.

inambulātiō, -ōnis *f* walking about.

inambulō, -āre *vi* to walk up and down.

inamoenus *adj* disagreeable.

inanimus *adj* lifeless, inanimate.

ināniō, -īre *vt* to make empty.

inānis *adj* empty, void; poor, unsubstantial; useless, worthless, vain, idle ♦ *nt* (PHILOS) space; (*fig*) vanity.

inānitās, -ātis *f* empty space; inanity.

Noun declensions and verb conjugations are shown on pp xiii to xxv. The present infinitive ending of a verb shows to which conjugation it belongs: -āre = 1st; -ēre = 2nd; -ere = 3rd and -īre = 4th. Irregular verbs are shown on p xxvi

inaniter *adv* idly, vainly.

inaratus *adj* fallow.

inardescō, -dēscere, -sī *vi* to be kindled, flare up.

inass- *etc see* **inads-**.

inattenuātus *adj* undiminished.

inaudāx, -ācis *adj* timorous.

inaudiō, -īre *vt* to hear of, learn.

inaudītus *adj* unheard of, unusual; without a hearing.

inaugurātō *adv* after taking the auspices.

inaugurō, -āre *vi* to take auspices ♦ *vt* to consecrate, inaugurate.

inaurēs, -ium *fpl* earrings.

inaurō, -āre, -āvi, -ātum *vt* to gild; (*fig*) to enrich.

inauspicātō *adv* without taking the auspices.

inauspicātus *adj* done without auspices.

inausus *adj* unattempted.

incaeduus *adj* uncut.

incalēscō, -ēscere, -uī *vi* to grow hot; (*fig*) to warm, glow.

incalfaciō, -ere *vt* to heat.

incallidē *adv* unskilfully.

incallidus *adj* stupid, simple.

incandēscō, -ēscere, -uī *vi* to become hot; to turn white.

incānēscō, -ēscere, -uī *vi* to grow grey.

incantātus *adj* enchanted.

incānus *adj* grey.

incassum *adv* in vain.

incastīgātus *adj* unrebuked.

incautē *adv* negligently.

incautus *adj* careless, heedless; unforeseen, unguarded.

incēdō, -ēdere, -ēssī, -ēssum *vi* to walk, parade, march; (*MIL*) to advance; (*feelings*) to come upon.

incelebrātus *adj* not made known.

incēnātus *adj* supperless.

incendiārius, -ī *and* **iī** *m* incendiary.

incendium, -ī *and* **iī** *nt* fire, conflagration; heat; (*fig*) fire, vehemence, passion.

incendō, -ere, -ī, incēnsum *vt* to set fire to, burn; to light, brighten; (*fig*) to inflame, rouse, incense.

incēnsiō, -ōnis *f* burning.

incēnsus *ppp of* **incendō**.

incēnsus *adj* not registered.

incēpī *perf of* **incipiō**.

inceptiō, -ōnis *f* undertaking.

inceptō, -āre *vt* to begin, attempt.

inceptor, -ōris *m* originator.

inceptum, -ī *nt* beginning, undertaking, attempt.

inceptus *ppp of* **incipiō**.

incērō, -āre *vt* to cover with wax.

incertō *adv* not for certain.

incertus *adj* uncertain, doubtful, unsteady ♦ *nt* uncertainty.

incēssō, -ere, -īvī *vt* to attack; (*fig*) to assail.

incēssus, -ūs *m* gait, pace, tramp; invasion; approach.

incestē *adv see adj.*

incestō, -āre *vt* to pollute, dishonour.

incestus *adj* sinful; unchaste, incestuous ♦ *nt* incest.

incestus, -ūs *m* incest.

incho- *etc see* **incoh-**.

incidō, -idere, -idī, -āsum *vi* to fall upon, fall into; to meet, fall in with, come across; to befall, occur, happen; **in mentem** ~ occur to one.

incīdō, -dere, -dī, -sum *vt* to cut open; to cut up; to engrave, inscribe; to interrupt, cut short.

incīle, -is *nt* ditch.

incīlō, -āre *vt* to rebuke.

incingō, -gere, -xī, -ctum *vt* to gird, wreathe; to surround.

incinō, -ere *vt* to sing, play.

incipiō, -ipere, -ēpī, -eptum *vt, vi* to begin.

incipissō, -ere *vt* to begin.

incīsē *adv* in short clauses.

incīsim *adv* in short clauses.

incīsiō, -ōnis *f* clause.

incīsum, -ī *nt* clause.

incīsus *ppp of* **incīdō**.

incitāmentum, -ī *nt* incentive.

incitātē *adv* impetuously.

incitātiō, -ōnis *f* inciting; rapidity.

incitātus *ppp of* **incitō** ♦ *adj* swift, rapid; **equō ~ō** at a gallop.

incitō, -āre, -āvī, -ātum *vt* to urge on, rush; to rouse, encourage, excite; to inspire; to increase; **sē ~** rush; **currentem ~ ≈ spur a willing horse.**

incitus *adj* swift.

incitus *adj* immovable; **ad ~ās, ~a redigere** bring to a standstill.

inclāmō, -āre *vt, vi* to call out, cry out to; to scold, abuse.

inclārēscō, -ēscere, -uī *vi* to become famous.

inclēmēns, -entis *adj* severe.

inclēmenter *adv* harshly.

inclēmentia, -ae *f* severity.

inclīnātiō, -ōnis *f* leaning, slope; (*fig*) tendency, inclination, bias; (*CIRCS*) change; (*voice*) modulation.

inclīnātus *adj* inclined, prone; falling; (*voice*) deep.

inclīnō, -āre, -āvī, -ātum *vt* to bend, turn; to turn back; (*fig*) to incline, direct, transfer; to change ♦ *vi* to bend, sink; (*MIL*) to give way; (*fig*) to change, deteriorate; to incline, tend, turn in favour.

inclitus *etc see* **inclutus**.

inclūdō, -dere, -sī, -sum *vt* to shut in, keep in, enclose; to obstruct, block; (*fig*) to include; (*time*) to close, end.

inclūsiō, -ōnis *f* imprisonment.

inclūsus *ppp of* **inclūdō**.

inclutus *adj* famous, glorious.

incoctus *ppp of* **incoquō**.

incoctus *adj* uncooked, raw.

incōgitābilis *adj* thoughtless.

incōgitāns, -antis *adj* thoughtless.
incōgitantia, -ae *f* thoughtlessness.
incōgitō, -āre *vt* to contrive.
incognitus *adj* unknown, unrecognised; (*law*) untried.
incohātus *adj* unfinished.
incohō, -āre, -āvī, -ātum *vt* to begin, start.
incola, -ae *f* inhabitant, resident.
incolō, -ere, -uī *vt* to live in, inhabit ♦ *vi* to live, reside.
incolumis *adj* safe and sound, unharmed.
incolumitās, -ātis *f* safety.
incomitātus *adj* unaccompanied.
incommendātus *adj* unprotected.
incommodē *adv* inconveniently, unfortunately.
incommoditās, -ātis *f* inconvenience, disadvantage.
incommodō, -āre *vi* to be inconvenient, annoy.
incommodum, -ī *nt* inconvenience, disadvantage, misfortune.
incommodus *adj* inconvenient, troublesome.
incommūtābilis *adj* unchangeable.
incompertus *adj* unknown.
incompositē *adv see adj.*
incompositus *adj* in disorder, irregular.
incōmptus *adj* undressed, inelegant.
inconcessus *adj* forbidden.
inconciliō, -āre *vt* to win over (by guile); to trick, inveigle, embarrass.
inconcinnus *adj* inartistic, awkward.
inconcussus *adj* unshaken, stable.
inconditē *adv* confusedly.
inconditus *adj* undisciplined, not organised; (*language*) artless.
incōnsīderātē *adv see adj.*
incōnsīderātus *adj* thoughtless, ill-advised.
incōnsōlābilis *adj* incurable.
incōnstāns, -antis *adj* fickle, inconsistent.
incōnstanter *adv* inconsistently.
incōnstantia, -ae *f* fickleness, inconsistency.
incōnsultē *adv* indiscreetly.
incōnsultū without consulting.
incōnsultus *adj* indiscreet, ill-advised; unanswered; not consulted.
incōnsūmptus *adj* unconsumed.
incontāminātus *adj* untainted.
incontentus *adj* untuned.
incontinēns, -entis *adj* intemperate.
incontinenter *adv* without self-control.
incontinentia, -ae *f* lack of self-control.
inconveniēns, -entis *adj* ill-matched.
incoquō, -quere, -xī, -ctum *vt* to boil; to dye.
incorrēctus *adj* unrevised.
incorruptē *adv* justly.
incorruptus *adj* unspoiled; uncorrupted, genuine.
incrēbrēscō, incrēbēscō, -ēscere, -uī *vi* to increase, grow, spread.

incrēdibilis *adj* incredible, extraordinary.
incrēdibiliter *adv see adj.*
incrēdulus *adj* incredulous.
incrēmentum, -ī *nt* growth, increase; addition; offspring.
increpitō, -āre *vt* to rebuke; to challenge.
increpō, -āre, -uī, -itum *vi* to make a noise, sound; (*news*) to be noised abroad ♦ *vt* to cause to make a noise; to exclaim against, rebuke.
incrēscō, -scere, -vī *vi* to grow in, increase.
incrētus *adj* sifted in.
incruentātus *adj* unstained with blood.
incruentus *adj* bloodless, without bloodshed.
incrūstō, -āre *vt* to encrust.
incubō, -āre, -uī, -itum *vi* to lie in or on; (*fig*) to brood over.
incubuī *perf of* **incubō**; *perf of* **incumbō**.
inculcō, -āre, -āvī, -ātum *vt* to force in; to force upon, impress on.
inculpātus *adj* blameless.
incultē *adv* uncouthly.
incultus *adj* uncultivated; (*fig*) neglected, uneducated, rude.
incultus, -ūs *m* neglect, squalor.
incumbō, -mbere, -buī, -bitum *vi* to lean, recline on; to fall upon, throw oneself upon; to oppress, lie heavily upon; (*fig*) to devote attention to, take pains with; to incline.
incūnābula, -ōrum *ntpl* swaddling clothes; (*fig*) cradle, infancy, birthplace, origin.
incūrātus *adj* neglected.
incūria, -ae *f* negligence.
incūriōsē *adv* carelessly.
incūriōsus *adj* careless, indifferent.
incurrō, -rrere, -rrī *and* **curri, -rsum** *vi* to run into, rush, attack; to invade; to meet with, get involved in; (*events*) to occur, coincide.
incursiō, -ōnis *f* attack; invasion, raid; collision.
incursō, -āre *vt, vi* to run into, assault; to frequently invade; (*fig*) to meet, strike.
incursus, -ūs *m* assault, striking; (*mind*) impulse.
incurvō, -āre *vt* to bend, crook.
incurvus *adj* bent, crooked.
incūs, -ūdis *f* anvil.
incūsātiō, -ōnis *f* blaming.
incūsō, -āre, -āvī, -ātum *vt* to find fault with, accuse.
incussī *perf of* **incutiō**.
incussus *ppp of* **incutiō**.
incussus, -ūs *m* shock.
incustōdītus *adj* unguarded, unconcealed.
incūsus *adj* forged.
incutiō, -tere, -ssī, -ssum *vt* to strike, dash against; to throw; (*fig*) to strike into, inspire with.
indāgātiō, -ōnis *f* search.
indāgātor, -ōris *m* explorer.

indāgātrīx, -rīcis *f* female explorer.
indāgō, -āre *vt* to track down; (*fig*) to trace, investigate.
indāgō, -inis *f* (*hunt*) drive, encirclement.
indaudiō *etc see* **inaudiō.**
inde *adv* from there, from that, from them; on that side; from then, ever since; after that, then.
indēbitus *adj* not due.
indēclīnātus *adj* constant.
indecor, -is *adj* dishonourable, a disgrace.
indecōrē *adv* indecently.
indecōrō, -āre *vt* to disgrace.
indecōrus *adj* unbecoming, unsightly.
indēfēnsus *adj* undefended.
indēfessus *adj* unwearied, tireless.
indēflētus *adj* unwept.
indēiectus *adj* undemolished.
indēlēbilis *adj* imperishable.
indēlībātus *adj* unimpaired.
indemnātus *adj* unconvicted.
indēplōrātus *adj* unlamented.
indēprēnsus *adj* undetected.
indeptus *ppa of* **indipīscor.**
indēsertus *adj* unforsaken.
indēstrictus *adj* unscathed.
indētōnsus *adj* unshorn.
indēvītātus *adj* unerring.
index, -icis *m* forefinger; witness, informer; (*book, art*) title, inscription; (*stone*) touchstone; (*fig*) indication, pointer, sign.
India, -iae *f* India.
indicātiō, -ōnis *f* value.
indīcente mē without my telling.
indicium, -ī *and* **iī** *nt* information, evidence; reward for information; indication, sign, proof; ~ **profitērī, offerre** ≈ turn King's evidence; ~ **postulāre, dare** ask, grant permission to give evidence.
indicō, -āre, -āvī, -ātum *vt* to point out; to disclose, betray; to give information, give evidence; to put a price on.
indīcō, -īcere, -īxī, -ictum *vt* to declare, proclaim, appoint.
indictus *ppp of* **indīcō.**
indictus *adj* not said, unsung; **causā ~ā** without a hearing.
Indicus *adj see n.*
indidem *adv* from the same place *or* thing.
indidī *perf of* **indō.**
indifferēns, -entis *adj* neither good nor bad.
indigena, -ae *m* native ♦ *adj* native.
indigēns, -entis *adj* needy.
indigentia, -ae *f* need; craving.
indigeō, -ēre, -uī *vi* (*with abl*) to need, want, require; to crave.
indiges, -etis *m* national deity.
indīgestus *adj* confused.
indignābundus *adj* enraged.
indignāns, -antis *adj* indignant.
indignātiō, -ōnis *f* indignation.
indignē *adv* unworthily; indignantly.
indignitās, -ātis *f* unworthiness, enormity;

insulting treatment; indignation.
indignor, -ārī, -ātus *vt* to be displeased with, be angry at.
indignus *adj* unworthy, undeserving; shameful, severe; undeserved.
indigus *adj* in want.
indīligēns, -entis *adj* careless.
indīligenter *adv see adj.*
indīligentia, -ae *f* carelessness.
indipīscor, -ī, indeptus *vt* to obtain, get, reach.
indīreptus *adj* unplundered.
indiscrētus *adj* closely connected, indiscriminate, indistinguishable.
indisertē *adv* without eloquence.
indisertus *adj* not eloquent.
indispositus *adj* disorderly.
indissolūbilis *adj* imperishable.
indistinctus *adj* confused, obscure.
inditus *ppp of* **indō.**
indīviduus *adj* indivisible; inseparable ♦ *nt* atom.
indō, -ere, -idī, -itum *vt* to put in *or* on; to introduce; to impart, impose.
indocilis *adj* difficult to teach, hard to learn; untaught.
indoctē *adv* unskilfully.
indoctus *adj* untrained, illiterate, ignorant.
indolentia, -ae *f* freedom from pain.
indolēs, -is *f* nature, character, talents.
indolēscō, -ēscere, -uī *vi* to feel sorry.
indomitus *adj* untamed, wild; ungovernable.
indormiō, -īre *vi* to sleep on; to be careless.
indōtātus *adj* with no dowry; unhonoured; (*fig*) unadorned.
indubitō, -āre *vi* to begin to doubt.
indubius *adj* undoubted.
indūcō, -ūcere, -ūxī, -uctum *vt* to bring in, lead on; to introduce; to overlay, cover over; (*fig*) to move, persuade, seduce; (*book-keeping*) to enter; (*dress*) to put on; (*public show*) to exhibit; (*writing*) to erase; **animum, in animum ~** determine, imagine.
inductiō, -ōnis *f* leading, bringing on; (*mind*) purpose, intention; (*logic*) induction.
inductus *ppp of* **indūcō.**
indugredior *etc see* **ingredior.**
induī *perf of* **induō.**
indulgēns, -entis *pres p of* **indulgeō** ♦ *adj* indulgent, kind.
indulgenter *adv* indulgently.
indulgentia, -ae *f* indulgence, gentleness.
indulgeō, -gēre, -sī *vi* (*with dat*) to be kind to, indulge, give way to; to indulge in ♦ *vt* to concede; **sibi ~** take liberties.
induō, -uere, -uī, -ūtum *vt* (*dress*) to put on; (*fig*) to assume, entangle.
indup- *etc see* **imp-.**
indūrēscō, -ēscere, -uī *vi* to harden.
indūrō, -āre *vt* to harden.
Indus, -ī *m* Indian; Ethiopian; mahout.
Indus *adj see n.*
industria, -ae *f* diligence; **dē, ex ~ā** on

purpose.
industriē *adv see* **industrius**.
industrius *adj* diligent, painstaking.
indūtiae, -ārum *fpl* truce, armistice.
indūtus *ppp of* **induō**.
indūtus, -us *m* wearing.
induviae, -ārum *fpl* clothes.
indūxī *perf of* **indūcō**.
inēbriō, -āre *vt* to intoxicate; (*fig*) to saturate.
inedia, -ae *f* starvation.
inēditus *adj* unpublished.
inēlegāns, -antis *adj* tasteless.
inēleganter *adv* without taste.
inēluctābilis *adj* inescapable.
inēmorior, -ī *vi* to die in.
inemptus *adj* unpurchased.
inēnārrābilis *adj* indescribable.
inēnōdābilis *adj* inexplicable.
ineō, -īre, -īvī *and* **iī, -itum** *vi* to go in, come in;
to begin ♦ *vt* to enter; to begin, enter upon,
form, undertake; **cōnsilium ~** form a plan;
grātiam ~ win favour; **numerum ~**
enumerate; **ratiōnem ~** calculate, consider,
contrive; **suffrāgium ~** vote; **viam ~** find out a
way.
ineptē *adv see adj*.
ineptia, -ae *f* stupidity; (*pl*) nonsense.
ineptiō, -īre *vi* to play the fool.
ineptus *adj* unsuitable; silly, tactless, absurd.
inermis, inermus *adj* unarmed, defenceless;
harmless.
inerrāns, -antis *adj* fixed.
inerrō, -āre *vi* to wander about in.
iners, -tis *adj* unskilful; inactive, indolent,
timid; insipid.
inertia, -ae *f* lack of skill; idleness, laziness.
inērudītus *adj* uneducated.
inēscō, -āre *vt* to entice, deceive.
inēvectus *adj* mounted.
inēvītābilis *adj* inescapable.
inexcītus *adj* peaceful.
inexcūsābilis *adj* with no excuse.
inexercitātus *adj* untrained.
inexhaustus *adj* unexhausted.
inexōrābilis *adj* inexorable; (*things*) severe.
inexperrēctus *adj* unawakened.
inexpertus *adj* inexperienced; untried.
inexpiābilis *adj* inexpiable; implacable.
inexplēbilis *adj* insatiable.
inexplētus *adj* incessant.
inexplicābilis *adj* inexplicable; impracticable,
unending.
inexplōrātō *adv* without making a
reconnaissance.
inexplōrātus *adj* unreconnoitred.
inexpugnābilis *adj* impregnable, safe.
inexspectātus *adj* unexpected.
inexstinctus *adj* unextinguished; insatiable,
imperishable.
inexsuperābilis *adj* insurmountable.

inextrīcābilis *adj* inextricable.
īnfabrē *adv* unskilfully.
īnfabricātus *adj* unfashioned.
īnfacētus *adj* not witty, crude.
īnfācundus *adj* ineloquent.
īnfāmia, -ae *f* disgrace, scandal.
īnfāmis *adj* infamous, disreputable.
īnfāmō, -āre, -āvī, -ātum *vt* to disgrace,
bring into disrepute.
īnfandus *adj* unspeakable, atrocious.
īnfāns, -antis *adj* mute, speechless; young,
infant; tongue-tied; childish ♦ *m/f* infant,
child.
īnfantia, -ae *f* inability to speak; infancy; lack
of eloquence.
īnfatuō, -āre *vt* to make a fool of.
īnfaustus *adj* unlucky.
īnfector, -ōris *m* dyer.
īnfectus *ppp of* **īnficiō**.
īnfectus *adj* undone, unfinished; **rē ~ā** without
achieving one's purpose.
īnfēcunditās, -ātis *f* infertility.
īnfēcundus *adj* unfruitful.
īnfēlīcitās, -ātis *f* misfortune.
īnfēlīciter *adv see adj*.
īnfēlīcō, -āre *vt* to make unhappy.
īnfēlīx, -īcis *adj* unfruitful; unhappy, unlucky.
īnfēnsē *adv* aggressively.
īnfēnsō, -āre *vt* to make dangerous, make
hostile.
īnfēnsus *adj* hostile, dangerous.
īnferciō, -īre *vt* to cram in.
īnferiae, -ārum *fpl* offerings to the dead.
īnferior, -ōris *compar of* **īnferus**.
īnferius *compar of* **īnfrā**.
īnfernē *adv* below.
īnfernus *adj* beneath; of the lower world;
infernal ♦ *mpl* the shades ♦ *ntpl* the lower
world.
īnferō, -re, intulī, illātum *vt* to carry in,
bring to, put on; to move forward; (*fig*) to
introduce, cause; (*book-keeping*) to enter;
(*logic*) to infer; **bellum ~** make war (on);
pedem ~ advance; **sē ~** repair, rush, strut
about; **signa ~** attack, charge.
īnferus (*compar* **~ior**, *superl* **īnfimus**) *adj* lower,
below ♦ *mpl* the dead, the lower world ♦
compar lower; later; inferior ♦ *superl* lowest,
bottom of; meanest, humblest.
īnfervēscō, -vēscere, -buī *vi* to boil.
īnfestē *adv* aggressively.
īnfestō, -āre *vt* to attack.
īnfestus *adj* unsafe; dangerous, aggressive.
īnficet- *see* **īnfacēt-**.
īnficiō, -icere, -ēcī, -ectum *vt* to dip, dye,
discolour; to taint, infect; (*fig*) to instruct,
corrupt, poison.
īnfidēlis *adj* faithless.
īnfidēlitās, -ātis *f* disloyalty.
īnfidēliter *adv* treacherously.

Noun declensions and verb conjugations are shown on pp xiii to xxv. The present infinitive ending of a verb shows
to which conjugation it belongs: **-āre** = 1st; **-ēre** = 2nd; **-ere** = 3rd and **-īre** = 4th. Irregular verbs are shown on p xxvi

infīdus *adj* unsafe, treacherous.
īnfīgō, -gere, -xī, -xum *vt* to thrust, drive in; (*fig*) to impress, imprint.
īnfimus *superl of* **īnferus**.
īnfindō, -ere *vt* to cut into, plough.
īnfinitās, -ātis *f* boundless extent, infinity.
īnfinītē *adv* without end.
īnfinītiō, -ōnis *f* infinity.
īnfinītus *adj* boundless, endless, infinite; indefinite.
īnfirmātiō, -ōnis *f* invalidating, refuting.
īnfirmē *adv* feebly.
īnfirmitās, -ātis *f* weakness; infirmity, sickness.
īnfirmō, -āre *vt* to weaken; to invalidate, refute.
īnfirmus *adj* weak, indisposed; weak-minded; (*things*) trivial.
īnfit *vi* (*defec*) begins.
īnfitiālis *adj* negative.
īnfitiās eō deny.
īnfitiātiō, -ōnis *f* denial.
īnfitiātor, -ōris *m* denier (of a debt).
īnfitior, -ārī, -ātus *vt* to deny, repudiate.
īnfīxus *ppp of* **īnfīgō**.
īnflammātiō, -ōnis *f* (*fig*) exciting.
īnflammō, -āre, -āvī, -ātum *vt* to set on fire, light; (*fig*) to inflame, rouse.
īnflatē *adv* pompously.
īnflātiō, -ōnis *f* flatulence.
īnflātus, -ūs *m* blow; inspiration ♦ *adj* blown up, swollen; (*fig*) puffed up, conceited; (*style*) turgid.
īnflectō, -ctere, -xī, -xum *vt* to bend, curve; to change; (*voice*) to modulate; (*fig*) to affect, move.
īnflētus *adj* unwept.
īnflexiō, -ōnis *f* bending.
īnflexus *ppp of* **īnflectō**.
īnflīgō, -gere, -xī, -ctum *vt* to dash against, strike; to inflict.
īnflō, -āre, -āvī, -ātum *vt* to blow, inflate; (*fig*) to inspire, puff up.
īnfluō, -ere, -xī, -xum *vi* to flow in; (*fig*) to stream, pour in.
īnfodiō, -odere, -ōdī, -ossum *vt* to dig in, bury.
īnfōrmātiō, -ōnis *f* sketch, idea.
īnfōrmis *adj* shapeless; hideous.
īnfōrmō, -āre, -āvī, -ātum *vt* to shape, fashion; to sketch; to educate.
īnfortūnātus *adj* unfortunate.
īnfortūnium, -ī *and* **iī** *nt* misfortune.
īnfossus *ppp of* **īnfodiō**.
īnfrā (*compar* **īnferius**) *adv* underneath, below ♦ *compar* lower down ♦ *prep* (*with acc*) below, beneath, under; later than.
īnfrāctiō, -ōnis *f* weakening.
īnfrāctus *ppp of* **īnfringō**.
īnfragilis *adj* strong.
īnfremō, -ere, -uī *vi* to growl.
īnfrēnātus *ppp of* **īnfrēnō**.
īnfrēnātus *adj* without a bridle.

īnfrendō, -ere *vi* to gnash.
īnfrēnis, -us *adj* unbridled.
īnfrēnō, -āre, -āvī, -ātum *vt* to put a bridle on, harness; (*fig*) to curb.
īnfrequēns, -entis *adj* not crowded, infrequent; badly attended.
īnfrequentia, -ae *f* small number; emptiness.
īnfringō, -ingere, -ēgī, -actum *vt* to break, bruise; (*fig*) to weaken, break down, exhaust.
īnfrōns, -ondis *adj* leafless.
īnfūcātus *adj* showy.
īnfula, -ae *f* woollen band, fillet, badge of honour.
īnfumus *etc see* **infimus**.
īnfundō, -undere, -ūdī, -ūsum *vt* to pour in *or* on; to serve; (*fig*) to spread.
īnfuscō, -āre *vt* to darken; to spoil, tarnish.
īnfūsus *ppp of* **īnfundō**.
ingeminō, -āre *vt* to redouble ♦ *vi* to be redoubled.
ingemīscō, -īscere, -uī *vi* to groan, sigh ♦ *vt* to sigh over.
ingemō, -ere, -uī *vt, vi* to sigh for, mourn.
ingenerō, -āre, -āvī, -ātum *vt* to engender, produce, create.
ingeniātus *adj* with a natural talent.
ingeniōsē *adv* cleverly.
ingeniōsus *adj* talented, clever; (*things*) naturally suited.
ingenitus *ppp of* **ingignō** ♦ *adj* inborn, natural.
ingenium, -ī *and* **iī** *nt* nature; (*disposition*) bent, character; (*intellect*) ability, talent, genius; (*person*) genius.
ingēns, -entis *adj* huge, mighty, great.
ingenuē *adv* liberally, frankly.
ingenuitās, -ātis *f* noble birth, noble character.
ingenuus *adj* native, innate; free-born; noble, frank; delicate.
ingerō, -rere, -ssī, -stum *vt* to carry in; to heap on; to throw, hurl; (*fig*) to press, obtrude.
ingignō, -ignere, -enuī, -enitum *vt* to engender, implant.
inglōrius *adj* inglorious.
ingluviēs, -ēī *f* maw; gluttony.
ingrātē *adv* unwillingly; ungratefully.
ingrātiīs, ingrātīs *adv* against one's will.
ingrātus *adj* disagreeable, unwelcome; ungrateful, thankless.
ingravēscō, -ere *vi* to grow heavy, become worse, increase.
ingravō, -āre *vt* to weigh heavily on; to aggravate.
ingredior, -dī, -ssus *vt, vi* to go in, enter; to walk, march; to enter upon, engage in; to commence, begin to speak.
ingressiō, -ōnis *f* entrance; beginning; pace.
ingressus, -ūs *m* entrance; (*MIL*) inroad; beginning; walking, gait.
ingruō, -ere, -ī *vi* to fall upon, assail.
inguen, -inis *nt* groin.
ingurgitō, -āre *vt* to pour in; **sē ~** gorge

oneself; (*fig*) to be absorbed in.
ingustātus *adj* untasted.
inhabilis *adj* unwieldy, awkward; unfit.
inhabitābilis *adj* uninhabitable.
inhabitō, -āre *vt* to inhabit.
inhaereō, -rēre, -sī, -sum *vi* to stick in, cling
  to; to adhere, be closely connected with; to
  be always in.
inhaerēscō, -ere *vi* to take hold, cling fast.
inhālō, -āre *vt* to breathe on.
inhibeō, -ēre, -uī, -itum *vt* to check, restrain,
  use, practise; ~ **rēmīs/nāvem** back water.
inhibitiō, -ōnis *f* backing water.
inhiō, -āre *vi* to gape ♦ *vt* to gape at, covet.
inhonestē *adv see adj.*
inhonestō, -āre *vt* to dishonour.
inhonestus *adj* dishonourable, inglorious;
  ugly.
inhonōrātus *adj* unhonoured; unrewarded.
inhonōrus *adj* defaced.
inhorreō, -ēre, -uī *vt* to stand erect, bristle.
inhorrēscō, -ēscere, -uī *vi* to bristle up; to
  shiver, shudder, tremble.
inhospitālis *adj* inhospitable.
inhospitālitās, -ātis *f* inhospitality.
inhospitus *adj* inhospitable.
inhūmānē *adv* savagely; uncivilly.
inhūmānitās, -ātis *f* barbarity; discourtesy,
  churlishness, meanness.
inhūmāniter *adv* = **inhūmānē**.
inhūmānus *adj* savage, brutal; ill-bred,
  uncivil, uncultured.
inhumātus *adj* unburied.
inibi *adv* there, therein; about to happen.
īniciō, -icere, -iēcī, -iectum *vt* to throw into,
  put on; (*fig*) to inspire, cause; (*speech*) to
  hint, mention; **manum** ~ take possession.
iniectus, -ūs *m* putting in, throwing over.
inimīcē *adv* hostilely.
inimīcitia, -ae *f* enmity.
inimīcō, -āre *vt* to make enemies.
inimīcus *adj* unfriendly, hostile; injurious ♦
  m/f enemy; ~**issimus** greatest enemy.
inīquē *adv* unequally, unjustly.
inīquitās, -ātis *f* unevenness; difficulty;
  injustice, unfair demands.
inīquus *adj* unequal, uneven; adverse,
  unfavourable, injurious; unfair, unjust;
  excessive; impatient, discontented ♦ *m*
  enemy.
initiō, -āre *vt* to initiate.
initium, -ī *and* **iī** *nt* beginning; (*pl*) elements,
  first principles; holy rites, mysteries.
initus *ppp of* **ineō**.
initus, -ūs *m* approach; beginning.
iniūcundē *adv see adj.*
iniūcunditās, -ātis *f* unpleasantness.
iniūcundus *adj* unpleasant.
iniungō, -ungere, -ūnxī, -ūnctum *vt* to join,
  attach; (*fig*) to impose, inflict.

iniūrātus *adj* unsworn.
iniūria, -ae *f* wrong, injury, injustice; insult,
  outrage; severity, revenge; unjust
  possession; ~**ā** unjustly.
iniūriōsē *adv* wrongfully.
iniūriōsus *adj* unjust, wrongful; harmful.
iniūrius *adj* wrong, unjust.
iniūssū without orders (from).
iniūssus *adj* unbidden.
iniūstē *adv see adj.*
iniūstitia, -ae *f* injustice, severity.
iniūstus *adj* unjust, wrong; excessive, severe.
inl- *etc see* **ill-**.
inm- *etc see* **imm-**.
innābilis *adj* that none may swim.
innāscor, -scī, -tus *vi* to be born in, grow up
  in.
innatō, -āre *vt* to swim in, float on; to swim,
  flow into.
innātus *ppa of* **innāscor** ♦ *adj* innate, natural.
innāvigābilis *adj* unnavigable.
innectō, -ctere, -xuī, -xum *vt* to tie, fasten
  together, entwine; (*fig*) to connect; to
  contrive.
innītor, -tī, -xus *and* **sus** *vi* to rest, lean on; to
  depend.
innō, -āre *vi* to swim in, float on, sail on.
innocēns, -entis *adj* harmless; innocent;
  upright, unselfish.
innocenter *adv* blamelessly.
innocentia, -ae *f* innocence; integrity,
  unselfishness.
innocuē *adv* innocently.
innocuus *adj* harmless; innocent; unharmed.
innōtēscō, -ēscere, -uī *vi* to become known.
innovō, -āre *vt* to renew; **sē** ~ return.
innoxius *adj* harmless, safe; innocent;
  unharmed.
innuba, -ae *adj* unmarried.
innūbilus *adj* cloudless.
innūbō, -bere, -psī *vi* to marry into.
innumerābilis *adj* countless.
innumerābilitās, -ātis *f* countless number.
innumerābiliter *adv* innumerably.
innumerālis *adj* numberless.
innumerus *adj* countless.
innuō, -ere, -ī *vi* to give a nod.
innūpta, -ae *adj* unmarried.
Īnō, -ūs *f daughter of Cadmus.*
inoblītus *adj* unforgetful.
inobrutus *adj* not overwhelmed.
inobservābilis *adj* unnoticed.
inobservātus *adj* unobserved.
inoffēnsus *adj* without hindrance,
  uninterrupted.
inofficiōsus *adj* irresponsible; disobliging.
inolēns, -entis *adj* odourless.
inolēscō, -scere, -vī *vi* to grow in.
inōminātus *adj* inauspicious.
inopia, -ae *f* want, scarcity, poverty,

helplessness.
inopīnāns, -antis *adj* unaware.
inopīnātō *adv* unexpectedly.
inopīnātus *adj* unexpected; off one's guard.
inopīnus *adj* unexpected.
inopiōsus *adj* in want.
inops, -is *adj* destitute, poor, in need (of);
helpless, weak; (*speech*) poor in ideas.
inōrātus *adj* unpleaded.
inōrdinātus *adj* disordered, irregular.
inōrnātus *adj* unadorned, plain; uncelebrated.
Inōus *adj see* **n**.
inp - *etc see* **imp -**.
inquam *vt* (*defec*) to say; (*emphatic*) I repeat,
maintain.
inquiēs, -ētis *adj* restless.
inquiētō, -āre *vt* to unsettle, make difficult.
inquiētus *adj* restless, unsettled.
inquilīnus, -ī *m* inhabitant, tenant.
inquinātē *adv* filthily.
inquinātus *adj* filthy, impure.
inquinō, -āre, -āvī, -ātum *vt* to defile, stain,
contaminate.
inquīrō, -rere, -sīvī, -sītum *vt* to search for,
inquire into; (*law*) to collect evidence.
inquīsītiō, -ōnis *f* searching, inquiry; (*law*)
inquisition.
inquīsītor, -ōris *m* searcher, spy;
investigator.
inquīsītus *ppp of* **inquīrō**.
inquīsītus *adj* not investigated.
inr - *etc see* **irr -**.
insalūtātus *adj* ungreeted.
insānābilis *adj* incurable.
insānē *adv* madly.
insānia, -ae *f* madness; folly, mania, poetic
rapture.
insāniō, -īre, -īvī, -ītum *vi* to be mad, rave; to
rage; to be inspired.
insānitās, -ātis *f* unhealthiness.
insānum *adv* (*slang*) frightfully.
insānus *adj* mad; frantic, furious; outrageous.
insatiābilis *adj* insatiable; never cloying.
insatiābiliter *adv see adj*.
insatietās, -ātis *f* insatiateness.
insaturābilis *adj* insatiable.
insaturābiliter *adv see adj*.
inscendō, -endere, -endī, -ēnsum *vt, vi* to
climb up, mount, embark.
inscēnsiō, -ōnis *f* going on board.
inscēnsus *ppp of* **inscendō**.
insciēns, -entis *adj* unaware; stupid.
inscienter *adv* ignorantly.
inscientia, -ae *f* ignorance, inexperience;
neglect.
inscītē *adv* clumsily.
inscītia, -ae *f* ignorance, stupidity,
inattention.
inscītus *adj* ignorant, stupid.
inscius *adj* unaware, ignorant.
inscrībō, -bere, -psī, -ptum *vt* to write on,
inscribe; to ascribe, assign; (*book*) to entitle;
(*for sale*) to advertise.

inscrīptiō, -ōnis *f* inscribing, title.
inscrīptus *ppp of* **inscrībō**.
insculpō, -ere, -sī, -tum *vt* to carve in,
engrave on.
insectātiō, -ōnis *f* hot pursuit; (*words*)
abusing, persecution.
insectātor, -ōris *m* persecutor.
insector, -ārī, -ātus; -ō, -āre *vt* to pursue,
attack, criticise.
insectus *adj* notched.
insēdābiliter *adv* incessantly.
insēdī *perf of* **insīdō**.
insenēscō, -escere, -uī *vi* to grow old in.
insēnsilis *adj* imperceptible.
insepultus *adj* unburied.
insequēns, -entis *pres p of* **insequor** ♦ *adj* the
following.
insequor, -quī, -cūtus *vt* to follow, pursue
hotly; to proceed; (*time*) to come after, come
next; (*fig*) to attack, persecute.
inserō, -erere, -ēvī, -itum *vt* to graft; (*fig*) to
implant.
inserō, -ere, -uī, -tum *vt* to let in, insert; to
introduce, mingle, involve.
insertō, -āre *vt* to put in.
insertus *ppp of* **inserō**.
inserviō, -īre, -iī, -ītum *vt, vi* to be a slave (to);
to be devoted, submissive (to).
insessus *ppp of* **insīdō**.
insībilō, -āre *vi* to whistle in.
insideō, -ēre *vi* to sit on *or* in; to remain fixed
♦ *vt* to hold, occupy.
insidiae, -ārum *fpl* ambush; (*fig*) trap,
trickery.
insidiātor, -ōris *nt* soldier in ambush; (*fig*)
waylayer, plotter.
insidior, -ārī, -ātus *vi* to lie in ambush; (*with
dat*) to lie in wait for, plot against.
insidiōsē *adv* insidiously.
insidiōsus *adj* artful, treacherous.
insīdō, -īdere, -ēdī, -essum *vi* to settle on;
(*fig*) to become fixed, rooted in ♦ *vt* to
occupy.
insigne, -is *nt* distinguishing mark, badge,
decoration; (*pl*) insignia, honours; (*speech*)
purple passages.
insigniō, -īre *vt* to distinguish.
insignis *adj* distinguished, conspicuous.
insignītē *adv* remarkably.
insigniter *adv* markedly.
insilia, -um *ntpl* treadle (of a loom).
insiliō, -īre, -uī *vi* to jump into *or* onto.
insimulātiō, -ōnis *f* accusation.
insimulō, -āre, -āvī, -ātum *vt* to charge,
accuse, allege (*esp falsely*).
insincērus *adj* adulterated.
insinuātiō, -ōnis *f* ingratiating.
insinuō, -āre, -āvī, -ātum *vt* to bring in,
introduce stealthily ♦ *vi* to creep in, worm
one's way in, penetrate; **sē ~** ingratiate
oneself; to make one's way into.
insipiēns, -entis *adj* senseless, foolish.
insipienter *adv* foolishly.

īnsipientia, -ae *f* folly.

īnsistō, -istere, -titī *vi* to stand on, step on; to stand firm, halt, pause; to tread on the heels, press on, pursue; to enter upon, apply oneself to, begin; to persist, continue.

īnsitiō, -ōnis *f* grafting; grafting time.

īnsitīvus *adj* grafted; (*fig*) spurious.

īnsitor, -ōris *m* grafter.

īnsitus *ppp of* **īnserō ♦** *adj* innate; incorporated.

īnsociābilis *adj* incompatible.

īnsōlābiliter *adv* unconsolably.

īnsolēns, -entis *adj* unusual, unaccustomed; excessive, extravagant, insolent.

īnsolenter *adv* unusually; immoderately, insolently.

īnsolentia, -ae *f* inexperience, novelty, strangeness; excess, insolence.

īnsolēscō, -ere *vi* to become insolent, elated.

īnsolidus *adj* soft.

īnsolitus *adj* unaccustomed, unusual.

īnsomnia, -ae *f* sleeplessness.

īnsomnis *adj* sleepless.

īnsomnium, -ī *and* **iī** *nt* dream.

īnsonō, -āre, -uī *vi* to resound, sound; to make a noise.

īnsōns, -ontis *adj* innocent; harmless.

īnsōpītus *adj* sleepless.

īnspectō, -āre *vt* to look at.

īnspectus *ppp of* **īnspiciō**.

īnspērāns, -antis *adj* not expecting.

īnspērātus *adj* unexpected; ~ō, ex ~ō unexpectedly.

īnspergō, -gere, -sī, -sum *vt* to sprinkle on.

īnspiciō, -icere, -exī, -ectum *vt* to look into; to examine, inspect; (*MIL*) to review; (*mind*) to consider, get to know.

īnspīcō, -āre *vt* to sharpen.

īnspīrō, -āre, -āvī, -ātum *vt, vi* to blow on, breathe into.

īnspoliātus *adj* unpillaged.

īnspūtō, -āre *vt* to spit on.

īnstābilis *adj* unsteady, not firm; (*fig*) inconstant.

īnstāns, -antis *pres p of* **īnstō ♦** *adj* present; urgent, threatening.

īnstanter *adv* vehemently.

īnstantia, -ae *f* presence; vehemence.

īnstar *nt* (*indecl*) likeness, appearance; as good as, worth.

īnstaurātiō, -ōnis *f* renewal.

īnstaurātīvus *adj* renewed.

īnstaurō, -āre, -āvī, -ātum *vt* to renew, restore; to celebrate; to requite.

īnsternō, -ernere, -rāvī, -rātum *vt* to spread over, cover.

īnstīgātor, -ōris *m* instigator.

īnstīgātrīx, -rīcis *f* female instigator.

īnstīgō, -āre *vt* to goad, incite, instigate.

īnstillō, -āre *vt* to drop on, instil.

īnstimulātor, -ōris *m* instigator.

īnstimulō, -āre *vt* to urge on.

īnstinctor, -ōris *m* instigator.

īnstinctus *adj* incited, inspired.

īnstinctus, -ūs *m* impulse, inspiration.

īnstipulor, -ārī, -ātus *vi* to bargain for.

īnstita, -ae *f* flounce of a lady's tunic.

īnstitī *perf of* **īnsistō**.

īnstitiō, -ōnis *f* stopping.

īnstitor, -ōris *m* pedlar.

īnstituō, -uere, -uī, -ūtum *vt* to set, implant; to set up, establish, build, appoint; to marshal, arrange, organize; to teach, educate; to undertake, resolve on.

īnstitūtiō, -ōnis *f* custom; arrangement; education; (*pl*) principles of education.

īnstitūtum, -ī *nt* way of life, tradition, law; stipulation, agreement; purpose; (*pl*) principles.

īnstō, -āre, -itī *vi* to stand on or in; to be close, be hard on the heels of, pursue; (*events*) to approach, impend; (*fig*) to press on, work hard at; (*speech*) to insist, urge.

īnstrātus *ppp of* **īnsternō**.

īnstrēnuus *adj* languid, slow.

īnstrepō, -ere *vi* to creak.

īnstructiō, -ōnis *f* building; setting out.

īnstructius *adv* in better style.

īnstructor, -ōris *m* preparer.

īnstructus *ppp of* **īnstruō ♦** *adj* provided, equipped; prepared, versed.

īnstructus, -ūs *m* equipment.

īnstrūmentum, -ī *nt* tool, instrument; equipment, furniture, stock; (*fig*) means, provision; dress, embellishment.

īnstruō, -ere, -xī, -ctum *vt* to erect, build up; (*MIL*) to marshal, array; to equip, provide, prepare; (*fig*) to teach, train.

īnsuāsum, -ī *nt* a dark colour.

īnsuāvis *adj* disagreeable.

īnsūdō, -āre *vi* to perspire on.

īnsuēfactus *adj* accustomed.

īnsuēscō, -scere, -vī, -tum *vt* to train, accustom **♦** *vi* to become accustomed.

īnsuētus *ppp of* **īnsuēscō**.

īnsuētus *adj* unaccustomed, unused; unusual.

īnsula, -ae *f* island; block of houses.

īnsulānus, -ī *m* islander.

īnsulsē *adv see adj.*

īnsulsitās, -ātis *f* lack of taste, absurdity.

īnsulsus *adj* tasteless, absurd, dull.

īnsultō, -āre, vt, vi to jump on, leap in; (*fig*) to exult, taunt, insult.

īnsultūra, -ae *f* jumping on.

īnsum, inesse, īnfuī *vi* to be in *or* on; to belong to.

īnsūmō, -ere, -psī, -ptum *vt* to spend, devote.

īnsuō, -uere, -uī, -ūtum *vt* to sew in, sew up in.

īnsuper *adv* above, on top; besides, over and above; (*prep with abl*) besides.

īnsuperābilis *adj* unconquerable, impassable.

īnsurgō, -gere, -rēxī, -rēctum *vi* to stand up, rise to; to rise, grow, swell; to rise against.

īnsusurrō, -āre *vt, vi* to whisper.

īnsūtus *ppp of* **īnsuō**.

intābēscō, -ēscere, -uī *vi* to melt away, waste away.

intāctilis *adj* intangible.

intāctus *adj* untouched, intact; untried; undefiled, chaste.

intāminātus *adj* unsullied.

intēctus *ppp of* **integō**.

intēctus *adj* uncovered, unclad; frank.

integellus *adj* fairly whole *or* pure.

integer, -rī *adj* whole, complete, unimpaired, intact; sound, fresh, new; (*mind*) unbiassed, free; (*character*) virtuous, pure, upright; (*decision*) undecided, open; **in ~rum restituere** restore to a former state; **ab, dē, ex ~rō** afresh; **~rum est mihi** I am at liberty (to).

integō, -egere, -ēxī, -ēctum *vt* to cover over; to protect.

integrāscō, -ere *vi* to begin all over again.

integrātiō, -ōnis *f* renewing.

integrē *adv* entirely; honestly; correctly.

integritās, -ātis *f* completeness, soundness; integrity, honesty; (*language*) correctness.

integrō, -āre *vt* to renew, replenish, repair; (*mind*) to refresh.

integumentum, -ī *nt* cover, covering, shelter.

intellēctus *ppp of* **intellegō**.

intellēctus, -ūs *m* understanding; (*word*) meaning.

intellegēns, -entis *pres p of* **intellegō** ♦ *adj* intelligent, a connoisseur.

intellegenter *adv* intelligently.

intellegentia, -ae *f* discernment, understanding; taste.

intellegō, -egere, -ēxī, -ēctum *vt* to understand, perceive, realize; to be a connoisseur.

intemerātus *adj* pure, undefiled.

intemperāns, -antis *adj* immoderate, extravagant; incontinent.

intemperanter *adv* extravagantly.

intemperantia, -ae *f* excess, extravagance; arrogance.

intemperātē *adv* dissolutely.

intemperātus *adj* excessive.

intemperiae, -ārum *fpl* inclemency; madness.

intemperiēs, -ēī *f* inclemency, storm; (*fig*) fury.

intempestīvē *adv* inopportunely.

intempestīvus *adj* unseasonable, untimely.

intempestus *adj* (*night*) the dead of; unhealthy.

intemptātus *adj* untried.

intendō, -dere, -dī, -tum *vt* to stretch out,

strain, spread; (*weapon*) to aim; (*tent*) to pitch; (*attention, course*) to direct, turn; (*fact*) to increase, exaggerate; (*speech*) to maintain; (*trouble*) to threaten ♦ *vi* to make for, intend; **animō ~** purpose; **sē ~** exert oneself.

intentē *adv* strictly.

intentiō, -ōnis *f* straining, tension; (*mind*) exertion, attention; (*law*) accusation.

intentō, -āre *vt* to stretch out, aim; (*fig*) to threaten with, attack.

intentus *ppp of* **intendō** ♦ *adj* taut; attentive, intent; strict; (*speech*) vigorous.

intentus, -ūs *m* stretching out.

intepeō, -ēre *vi* to be warm.

intepēscō, -ēscere, -uī *vi* to be warmed.

inter *prep* (*with acc*) between, among, during, in the course of; in spite of; **~ haec** meanwhile; **~ manūs** within reach; **~ nōs** confidentially; **~ sē** mutually, one another; **~ sīcāriōs** in the murder court; **~ viam** on the way.

interāmenta, -ōrum *ntpl* ship's timbers.

interaptus *adj* joined together.

interārēscō, -ere *vi* to wither away.

interbibō, -ere *vi* to drink up.

interbītō, -ere *vi* to fall through.

intercalāris *adj* intercalary.

intercalārius *adj* intercalary.

intercalō, -āre *vt* to intercalate.

intercapēdō, -inis *f* interruption, respite.

intercēdō, -ēdere, -ēssī, -ēssum *vi* to come between, intervene; to occur; to become surety; to interfere, obstruct; (*tribune*) to protest, veto.

interceptiō, -ōnis *f* taking away.

interceptor, -ōris *m* embezzler.

interceptus *ppp of* **intercipiō**.

intercēssiō, -ōnis *f* (*law*) becoming surety; (*tribune*) veto.

intercēssor, -ōris *m* mediator, surety; interposer of the veto; obstructor.

intercidō, -ere, -ī *vi* to fall short; to happen in the meantime; to get lost, become obsolete, be forgotten.

intercīdō, -dere, -dī, -sum *vt* to cut through, sever.

intercinō, -ere *vt* to sing between.

intercipiō, -ipere, -ēpi, -eptum *vt* to intercept; to embezzle, steal; to cut off, obstruct.

intercīsē *adv* piecemeal.

intercīsus *ppp of* **intercīdō**.

interclūdō, -dere, -sī, -sum *vt* to cut off, block, shut off, prevent; **animam ~** suffocate.

interclūsiō, -ōnis *f* stoppage.

interclūsus *ppp of* **interclūdō**.

intercolumnium, -ī and iī *nt* space between two pillars.

intercurrō, -ere *vi* to mingle with; to intercede; to hurry in the meantime.

intercursō, -āre *vi* to crisscross; to attack

between the lines.
intercursus, -ūs *m* intervention.
intercus, -tis *adj*: **aqua ~** dropsy.
interdīcō, -īcere, -īxī, -ictum *vt, vi* to forbid,
interdict; (*praetor*) to make a provisional
order; **aquā et ignī ~** banish.
interdictiō, -ōnis *f* prohibiting, banishment.
interdictum, -ī *nt* prohibition; provisional
order (by a praetor).
interdiū *adv* by day.
interdō, -are *vt* to make at intervals; to
distribute; **nōn ~uim** I wouldn't care.
interductus, -ūs *m* punctuation.
interdum *adv* now and then, occasionally.
intereā *adv* meanwhile, in the meantime;
nevertheless.
interēmī *perf of* **interimō**.
interemptus *ppp of* **interimō**.
intereō, -īre, -iī, -itum *vi* to be lost, perish,
die.
interequitō, -āre *vt, vi* to ride between.
interesse *infin of* **intersum**.
interfātiō, -ōnis *f* interruption.
interfātur, -ārī, -ātus *vi* to interrupt.
interfectiō, -ōnis *f* killing.
interfector, -ōris *m* murderer.
interfectrīx, -rīcis *f* murderess.
interfectus *ppp of* **interficiō**.
interficiō, -icere, -ēcī, -ectum *vt* to kill,
destroy.
interfīō, -ierī *vi* to pass away.
interfluō, -ere, -xī *vt, vi* to flow between.
interfodiō, -ere *vt* to pierce.
interfugiō, -ere *vi* to flee among.
interfuī *perf of* **intersum**.
interfulgeō, -ēre *vi* to shine amongst.
interfūsus *ppp* lying between; marked here
and there.
interiaceō, -ēre *vi* to lie between.
interibi *adv* in the meantime.
intericiō, -icere, -iēcī, -iectum *vt* to put
amongst or between, interpose, mingle;
annō ~iectō after a year.
interiectus, -ūs *m* coming in between;
interval.
interiī *perf of* **intereō**.
interim *adv* meanwhile, in the meantime;
sometimes; all the same.
interimō, -imere, -ēmī, -emptum *vt* to
abolish, destroy, kill.
interior, -ōris *adj* inner, interior; nearer, on
the near side; secret, private; more
intimate, more profound.
interitiō, -ōnis *f* ruin.
interitus, -ūs *m* destruction, ruin, death.
interiūnctus *adj* joined together.
interius *adv* inwardly; too short.
interlābor, -ī *vi* to glide between.
interlegō, -ere *vt* to pick here and there.
interlinō, -inere, -ēvī, -itum *vt* to smear in

parts; to erase here and there.
interloquor, -quī, -cūtus *vi* to interrupt.
interlūceō, -cēre, -xī *vi* to shine through, be
clearly seen.
interlūnia, -ōrum *ntpl* new moon.
interluō, -ere *vt* to wash, flow between.
intermēnstruus *adj* of the new moon ♦ *nt* new
moon.
interminātus *ppa of* **interminor** ♦ *adj*
forbidden.
interminātus *adj* endless.
interminor, -ārī, -ātus *vi* to threaten; to
forbid threateningly.
intermisceō, -scēre, -scuī, -xtum *vt* to mix,
intermingle.
intermissiō, -ōnis *f* interruption.
intermittō, -ittere, -īsī, -issum *vt* to break
off; to interrupt; to omit, neglect; to allow to
elapse ♦ *vi* to cease, pause.
intermixtus *ppp of* **intermisceō**.
intermorior, -ī, -tuus *vi* to die suddenly.
intermortuus *adj* falling unconscious.
intermundia, -ōrum *ntpl* space between
worlds.
intermūrālis *adj* between two walls.
internātus *adj* growing among.
internecīnus *adj* murderous, of
extermination.
interneciō, -ōnis *f* massacre, extermination.
internecīvus *adj* = **internecīnus**.
internectō, -ere *vt* to enclasp.
internōdia, -ōrum *ntpl* space between joints.
internōscō, -scere, -vī, -tum *vt* to
distinguish between.
internūntia, -iae *f* messenger, mediator,
go-between.
internūntiō, -āre *vi* to exchange messages.
internūntius, -ī and iī *m* messenger, mediator,
go-between.
internus *adj* internal, civil ♦ *ntpl* domestic
affairs.
interō, -erere, -rīvī, -rītum *vt* to rub in; (*fig*)
to concoct.
interpellātiō, -ōnis *f* interruption.
interpellātor, -ōris *m* interrupter.
interpellō, -āre, -āvī, -ātum *vt* to interrupt;
to disturb, obstruct.
interpolis *adj* made up.
interpolō, -āre *vt* to renovate, do up; (*writing*)
to falsify.
interpōnō, -ōnere, -osuī, -ositum *vt* to put
between or amongst, insert; (*time*) to allow
to elapse; (*person*) to introduce, admit;
(*pretext etc*) to put forward, interpose; **fidem
~** pledge one's word; **sē ~** interfere, become
involved.
interpositiō, -ōnis *f* introduction.
interpositus *ppp of* **interpōnō**.
interpositus, -ūs *m* obstruction.
interpres, -tis *m/f* agent, negotiator;

interpreter, explainer, translator.
interpretātiō, -ōnis *f* interpretation,
exposition, meaning.
interpretātus *adj* translated.
interpretor, -ārī, -ātus *vt* to interpret,
explain, translate, understand.
interprimō, -imere, -essī, -essum *vt* to
squeeze.
interpūnctiō, -ōnis *f* punctuation.
interpūnctus *adj* well-divided ♦ *ntpl*
punctuation.
interquiēscō, -scere, -vī *vi* to rest awhile.
interrēgnum, -ī *nt* regency, interregnum;
interval between consuls.
interrēx, -ēgis *m* regent; deputy consul.
interritus *adj* undaunted, unafraid.
interrogātiō, -ōnis *f* question; (*law*) cross-
examination; (*logic*) syllogism.
interrogātiuncula, -ae *f* short argument.
interrogō, -āre, -āvī, -ātum *vt* to ask, put a
question; (*law*) to cross-examine, bring to
trial.
interrumpō, -umpere, -ūpī, -uptum *vt* to
break up, sever; (*fig*) to break off, interrupt.
interruptē *adv* interruptedly.
intersaepiō, -īre, -sī, -tum *vt* to shut off,
close.
interscindō, -ndere, -dī, -ssum *vt* to cut off,
break down.
interserō, -erere, -ēvī, -itum *vt* to plant at
intervals.
interserō, -ere, -uī, -tum *vt* to interpose.
intersitus *ppp of* **interserō**.
interspīrātiō, -ōnis *f* pause for breath.
interstinguō, -guere, -ctum *vt* to mark, spot;
to extinguish.
interstringō, -ere *vt* to strangle.
intersum, -esse, -fuī *vi* to be between; to be
amongst, be present at; (*time*) to elapse; ~**est**
there is a difference; it is of importance, it
concerns, it matters; **meā** ~**est** it is
important for me.
intertextus *adj* interwoven.
intertrahō, -here, -xī *vt* to take away.
intertrīmentum, -ī *nt* wastage; loss, damage.
interturbātiō, -ōnis *f* confusion.
intervallum, -ī *nt* space, distance, interval;
(*time*) pause, interval, respite; difference.
intervellō, -ere *vt* to pluck out; to tear apart.
interveniō, -enīre, -ēnī, -entum *vi* to come
on the scene, intervene; to interfere (with),
interrupt; to happen, occur.
interventor, -ōris *m* intruder.
interventus, -ūs *m* appearance, intervention;
occurrence.
intervertō, -tere, -tī, -sum *vt* to embezzle; to
rob, cheat.
intervīsō, -ere, -ī, -um *vt* to have a look at,
look and see; to visit occasionally.
intervolitō, -āre *vi* to fly about, amongst.
intervomō, -ere *vt* to throw up (amongst).
intervortō *vt see* **intervortō**.
intestābilis *adj* infamous, wicked.

intestātō *adv* without making a will.
intestātus *adj* intestate; not convicted by
witnesses.
intestīnus *adj* internal ♦ *nt and ntpl* intestines,
entrails.
intexō, -ere, -uī, -tum *vt* to inweave,
embroider, interlace.
intibum, -ī *nt* endive.
intimē *adv* most intimately, cordially.
intimus *adj* innermost; deepest, secret;
intimate ♦ *m* most intimate friend.
intingō (intinguō), -gere, -xī, -ctum *vt* to
dip in.
intolerābilis *adj* unbearable; irresistible.
intolerandus *adj* intolerable.
intolerāns, -antis *adj* impatient; unbearable.
intoleranter *adv* excessively.
intolerantia, -ae *f* insolence.
intonō, -āre, -uī, -ātum *vi* to thunder,
thunder out.
intōnsus *adj* unshorn, unshaven; long-haired,
bearded; uncouth.
intorqueō, -quēre, -sī, -tum *vt* to twist, wrap
round; to hurl at.
intortus *ppp of* **intorqueō** ♦ *adj* twisted, curled;
confused.
intrā *adv* inside, within ♦ *prep* (*with acc*) inside,
within; (*time*) within, during; (*amount*) less
than, within the limits of.
intrābilis *adj* navigable.
intractābilis *adj* formidable.
intractātus *adj* not broken in; unattempted.
intremīscō, -īscere, -uī *vi* to begin to shake.
intremō, -ere *vi* to tremble.
intrepidē *adv see adj*.
intrepidus *adj* calm, brave; undisturbed.
intricō, -āre *vt* to entangle.
intrīnsecus *adv* on the inside.
intrītus *adj* not worn out.
intrīvī *perf of* **interō**.
intrō *adv* inside, in.
intrō, -āre, -āvī, -ātum *vt, vi* to go in, enter; to
penetrate.
intrōdūcō, -ūcere, -ūxī, -uctum *vt* to bring
in, introduce, escort in; to institute.
intrōductiō, -ōnis *f* bringing in.
intrōeō, -īre, -iī, -itum *vi* to go into, enter.
intrōferō, -ferre, -tulī, -lātum *vt* to carry
inside.
intrōgredior, -dī, -ssus *vi* to step inside.
introitus, -ūs *m* entrance; beginning.
intrōlātus *ppp of* **intrōferō**.
intrōmittō, -ittere, -īsī, -issus *vt* to let in,
admit.
intrōrsum, intrōrsus *adv* inwards, inside.
intrōrumpō, -ere *vi* to break into.
intrōspectō, -āre *vt* to look in at.
intrōspiciō, -icere, -exī, -ectum *vt* to look
inside; to look at, examine.
intubum *etc see* **intibum**.
intueor, -ērī, -itus *vt* to look at, watch; to
contemplate, consider; to admire.
intumēscō, -ēscere, -uī *vi* to begin to swell,

rise; to increase; to become angry.
intumulātus *adj* unburied.
intuor *etc see* **intueor**.
inturbidus *adj* undisturbed; quiet.
intus *adv* inside, within, in; from within.
intūtus *adj* unsafe; unguarded.
inula, -ae *f* elecampane.
inultus *adj* unavenged; unpunished.
inumbrō, -āre *vt* to shade; to cover.
inundō, -āre, -āvī, -ātum *vt, vi* to overflow,
flood.
inunguō, -unguere, -ūnxī, -ūnctum *vt* to
anoint.
inurbānē *adv see adj.*
inurbānus *adj* rustic, unmannerly,
unpolished.
inurgeō, -ēre *vi* to push, butt.
inūrō, -rere, -ssī, -stum *vt* to brand; (*fig*) to
brand, inflict.
inūsitātē *adv* strangely.
inūsitātus *adj* unusual, extraordinary.
inūstus *ppp of* **inūrō**.
inūtilis *adj* useless; harmful.
inūtilitās, -ātis *f* uselessness, harmfulness.
inūtiliter *adv* unprofitably.
invādō, -dere, -sī, -sum *vt, vi* to get in, make
one's way in; to enter upon; to fall upon,
attack, invade; to seize, take possession of.
invalēscō, -ēscere, -uī *vi* to grow stronger.
invalidus *adj* weak; inadequate.
invāsī *perf of* **invādō**.
invectiō, -ōnis *f* importing; invective.
invectus *ppp of* **invehō**.
invehō, -here, -xī, -ctum *vt* to carry in, bring
in; **sē ~** attack.
invehor, -hī, -ctus *vi* to ride, drive, sail in or
into, enter; to attack; to inveigh against.
invēndibilis *adj* unsaleable.
inveniō, -enīre, -ēnī, -entum *vt* to find, come
upon; to find out, discover; to invent,
contrive; to win, get.
inventiō, -ōnis *f* invention; (*RHET*) compiling
the subject-matter.
inventor, -ōris *m* inventor, discoverer.
inventrīx, -rīcis *f* inventor, discoverer.
inventus *ppp of* **inveniō** ♦ *nt* invention,
discovery.
invenustus *adj* unattractive; unlucky in love.
inverēcundus *adj* immodest, shameless.
invergō, -ere *vt* to pour upon.
inversiō, -ōnis *f* transposition; irony.
inversus *ppp of* **invertō** ♦ *adj* upside down,
inside out; perverted.
invertō, -tere, -tī, -sum *vt* to turn over,
invert; to change, pervert.
invesperāscit, -ere *vi* it is dusk.
investīgātiō, -ōnis *f* search.
investīgātor, -ōris *m* investigator.
investīgō, -āre, -āvī, -ātum *vt* to follow the
trail of; (*fig*) to track down, find out.

inveterāscō, -scere, -vī *vi* to grow old (in); to
become established, fixed, inveterate; to
grow obsolete.
inveterātiō, -ōnis *f* chronic illness.
inveterātus *adj* of long standing, inveterate.
invexī *perf of* **invehō**.
invicem *adv* in turns, alternately; mutually,
each other.
invictus *adj* unbeaten; unconquerable.
invidentia, -ae *f* envy.
invideō, -idēre, -īdī, -īsum *vt, vi* to cast an
evil eye on; (*with dat*) to envy, grudge; to
begrudge.
invidia, -ae *f* envy, jealousy, ill-will;
unpopularity.
invidiōsē *adv* spitefully.
invidiōsus *adj* envious, spiteful; enviable;
invidious, hateful.
invidus *adj* envious, jealous, hostile.
invigilō, -āre *vi* to be awake over; to watch
over, be intent on.
inviolābilis *adj* invulnerable; inviolable.
inviolātē *adv* inviolately.
inviolātus *adj* unhurt; inviolable.
invīsitātus *adj* unseen, unknown, strange.
invīsō, -ere, -ī, -um *vt* to go and see, visit,
have a look at; to inspect.
invīsus *adj* hateful, detested; hostile.
invīsus *adj* unseen.
invītāmentum, -ī *nt* attraction, inducement.
invītātiō, -ōnis *f* invitation; entertainment.
invītātus, -ūs *m* invitation.
invītē *adv* unwillingly.
invītō, -āre, -āvī, -ātum *vt* to invite; to treat,
entertain; to summon; to attract, induce.
invītus *adj* against one's will, reluctant.
invius *adj* trackless, impassable; inaccessible.
invocātus *ppp of* **invocō**.
invocātus *adj* unbidden, uninvited.
invocō, -āre, -āvī, -ātum *vt* to call upon,
invoke; to appeal to; to call.
involātus, -ūs *m* flight.
involitō, -āre *vi* to play upon.
involō, -āre *vi* to fly at, pounce on, attack.
involūcre, -is *nt* napkin.
involūcrum, -ī *nt* covering, case.
involūtus *ppp of* **involvō** ♦ *adj* complicated.
involvō, -vere, -vī, -ūtum *vt* to roll on; to
wrap up, envelop, entangle.
involvolus, -ī *m* caterpillar.
invulnerātus *adj* unwounded.
iō *interj* (*joy*) hurrah!; (*pain*) oh!; (*calling*) ho
there!
Iōannēs, -is *m* John.
iocātiō, -ōnis *f* joke.
iocor, -ārī, -ātus *vt, vi* to joke, jest.
iocōsē *adv* jestingly.
iocōsus *adj* humorous, playful.
ioc ulāris *adj* laughable, funny ♦ *ntpl* jokes.
ioculārius *adj* ludicrous.

ioculātor, -ōris *m* jester.
ioculor, -ārī *vi* to joke.
ioculus, -ī *m* a bit of fun.
iocus, -ī *m* (*pl* **-a, -ōrum** *nt*) joke, jest; **extrā ~um** joking apart; **per ~um** for fun.
Iōnes, -um *mpl* Ionians.
Iōnia, -iae *f* Ionia, coastal district of Asia Minor.
Iōnium, -ī *nt* Ionian Sea, W. of Greece.
Iōnius, -icus *adj* Ionian.
iōta *nt* (*indecl*) Greek letter I.
Iovis *gen of* **Iuppiter**.
Iphianasse, -ae *f* Iphigenia.
Iphigenīa, -ae *f* daughter of Agamemnon (*who sacrificed her at Aulis to Diana*).
ipse, -a, -um, -īus *prep* self, himself *etc*; in person, for one's own part, of one's own accord, by oneself; just, precisely, very; the master, the host.
ipsissimus his very own self; **nunc ~um** right now.
īra, -ae *f* anger, rage; object of indignation.
īrācundē *adv* angrily.
īrācundia, -ae *f* irascibility, quick temper; rage, resentment.
īrācundus *adj* irascible, choleric; resentful.
īrāscor, -ī *vi* to be angry, get furious.
īrātē *adv see adj*.
īrātus *adj* angry, furious.
īre *infin of* **eō**.
Īris, -dis (*acc* **-m**) *f* messenger of the gods; the rainbow.
īrōnīa, -ae *f* irony.
irrāsus *adj* unshaven.
irraucēscō, -cēscere, -sī *vi* to become hoarse.
irredivīvus *adj* irreparable.
irreligātus *adj* not tied.
irreligiōsē *adv see adj*.
irreligiōsus *adj* impious.
irremeābilis *adj* from which there is no returning.
irreparābilis *adj* irretrievable.
irrepertus *adj* undiscovered.
irrēpō, -ere, -sī *vi* to steal into, insinuate oneself into.
irreprehēnsus *adj* blameless.
irrequiētus *adj* restless.
irresectus *adj* unpared.
irresolūtus *adj* not slackened.
irrētiō, -īre, -iī, -ītum *vt* to ensnare, entangle.
irretortus *adj* not turned back.
irreverentia, -ae *f* disrespect.
irrevocābilis *adj* irrevocable; implacable.
irrevocātus *adj* without an encore.
irrīdeō, -dēre, -sī, -sum *vi* to laugh, joke ♦ *vt* to laugh at, ridicule.
irrīdiculē *adv* unwittily.
irrīdiculum, -ī *nt* laughing stock.
irrigātiō, -ōnis *f* irrigation.
irrigō, -āre, -āvī, -ātum *vt* to water, irrigate; to inundate; (*fig*) to shed over, flood, refresh.
irriguus *adj* well-watered, swampy; refreshing.
irrīsiō, -ōnis *f* ridicule, mockery.

irrīsor, -ōris *m* scoffer.
irrīsus *ppp of* **irrīdeō**.
irrīsus, -ūs *m* derision.
irrītābilis *adj* excitable.
irrītāmen, -inis *nt* excitement, provocation.
irrītātiō, -ōnis *f* incitement, irritation.
irrītō, -āre, -āvī, -ātum *vt* to provoke, incite, enrage.
irritus *adj* invalid, null and void; useless, vain, ineffective; (*person*) unsuccessful; **ad ~um cadere** come to nothing.
irrogātiō, -ōnis *f* imposing.
irrogō, -āre *vt* to propose (a measure) against; to impose.
irrōrō, -āre *vt* to bedew.
irrumpō, -umpere, -ūpī, -uptum *vt, vi* to rush in, break in; to intrude, invade.
irruō, -ere, -ī *vi* to force a way in, rush in, attack; (*speech*) to make a blunder.
irruptiō, -ōnis *f* invasion, raid.
irruptus *ppp of* **irrumpō**.
irruptus *adj* unbroken.
is, ea, id *pron* he, she, it; this, that, the; such; **nōn is sum quī** I am not the man to; **id** (*with vi*) for this reason; **id quod** what; **ad id** hitherto; for the purpose; besides; **in eō est** it has come to this; one is on the point of; it depends on this.
Ismara, -ōrum *ntpl*, **-us, -ī** *m* Mt Ismarus in Thrace.
Ismarius *adj* Thracian.
Isocratēs, -is *m* Athenian orator and teacher of rhetoric.
istāc *adv* that way.
iste, -a, -ud, -īus *pron* that of yours; (*law*) your client, the plaintiff, the defendant; (*contemptuous*) the fellow; that, such.
Isthmius *adj*, *ntpl* the Isthmian Games.
Isthmus (-os), -ī *m* Isthmus of Corinth.
istic, -aec, -uc *and* **oc** *pron* that of yours, that.
istīc *adv* there; in this, on this occasion.
istinc *adv* from there; of that.
istīusmodī such, of that kind.
istō, istōc *adv* to you, there, yonder.
istōrsum *adv* in that direction.
istūc *adv* (to) there, to that.
ita *adv* thus, so; as follows; yes; accordingly; **itane?** really?; **nōn ita** not so very; **ita ut** just as; **ita ... ut** so, to such an extent that; on condition that; only in so far as that; **ita ... ut nōn** without; **ut ... ita** just as ... so; although ... nevertheless.
Italī, -ōrum *mpl* Italians.
Italia, -iae *f* Italy.
Italicus, -is, -us *adj* Italian.
itaque *conj* and so, therefore, accordingly.
item *adv* likewise, also.
iter, -ineris *nt* way, journey, march; a day's journey or march; route, road, passage; (*fig*) way, course; **~ mihi est** I have to go to; **~ dare** grant a right of way; **~ facere** to journey, march, travel; **ex, in ~inere** on the way, on the march; **māgnīs ~ineribus** by forced

marches.
iterātiō, -ōnis *f* repetition.
iterō, -āre, -āvī, -ātum *vt* to repeat, renew; to plough again.
iterum *adv* again, a second time; ~ **atque** ~ repeatedly.
Ithaca, -ae, -ē, -ēs *f* island W. of Greece (*home of Ulysses*).
Ithacēnsis, -us *adj* Ithacan.
Ithacus, -ī *m* Ulysses.
itidem *adv* in the same way, similarly.
itiō, -ōnis *f* going.
itō, -āre *vi* to go.
itus, -ūs *m* going, movement, departure.
iuba, -ae *f* mane; crest.
Iuba, -ae *m* king of Numidia (*supporter of Pompey*).
iubar, -is *nt* brightness, light.
iubātus *adj* crested.
iubeō, -ēre, -ssī, -ssum *vt* to order, command, tell; (*greeting*) to bid; (*MED*) to prescribe; (*POL*) to decree, ratify, appoint.
iūcundē *adv* agreeably.
iūcunditās, -ātis *f* delight, enjoyment.
iūcundus *adj* delightful, pleasing.
Iūdaea, -ae *f* Judaea, Palestine.
Iūdaeus, -ī *m* Jew.
Iūdaeus, Iūdaicus *adj* Jewish.
iūdex, -icis *m* judge; (*pl*) panel of jurors; (*fig*) critic.
iūdicātiō, -ōnis *f* judicial inquiry; opinion.
iūdicātum, -ī *nt* judgment, precedent.
iūdicātus, -ūs *m* office of judge.
iūdiciālis *adj* judicial, forensic.
iūdiciārius *adj* judiciary.
iūdicium, -ī and iī *nt* trial; court of justice; sentence; judgment, opinion; discernment, taste, tact; **in ~ vocāre, -ō arcessere** sue, summon.
iūdicō, -āre, -āvī, -ātum *vt* to judge, examine, sentence, condemn; to form an opinion of, decide; to declare.
iugālis *adj* yoked together; nuptial.
iugātiō, -ōnis *f* training (*of a vine*).
iūgerum, -ī *nt* a land measure (*240 x 120 feet*).
iūgis *adj* perpetual, never-failing.
iūglāns, -andis *f* walnut tree.
iugō, -āre, -āvī, -ātum *vt* to couple, marry.
iugōsus *adj* hilly.
Iugulae, -ārum *fpl* Orion's Belt.
iugulō, -āre, -āvī, -ātum *vt* to cut the throat of, kill, murder.
iugulus, -ī *m*, **-um, -ī** *nt* throat.
iugum, -ī *nt* (*animals*) yoke, collar; pair, team; (*MIL*) yoke of subjugation; (*mountain*) ridge, height, summit; (*ASTRO*) Libra; (*loom*) crossbeam; (*ship*) thwart; (*fig*) yoke, bond.
Iugurtha, -ae *m* king of Numidia (*rebel against Rome*).
Iugurthīnus *adj see n.*

Iūlēus *adj* of Iulus; of Caesar; of July.
Iūlius, -ī *m* Roman family name (*esp Caesar*); (*month*) July.
Iūlius, -iānus *adj see n.*
Iūlus, -ī *m* son of Aeneas, Ascanius.
iūmentum, -ī *nt* beast of burden, packhorse.
iunceus *adj* of rushes; slender.
iuncōsus *adj* rushy.
iūnctiō, -ōnis *f* union.
iūnctūra, -ae *f* joint; combination; relationship.
iūnctus *ppp of* **iungō** ♦ *adj* connected, attached.
iuncus, -ī *m* rush.
iungō, -gere, iūnxī, iūnctum *vt* to join together, unite; to yoke, harness; to mate; (*river*) to span, bridge; (*fig*) to bring together, connect, associate; (*agreement*) to make; (*words*) to compound.
iūnior, -ōris *adj* younger.
iūniperus, -ī *f* juniper.
Iūnius, -ī *m* Roman family name; (*month*) June.
Iūnius *adj* of June.
Iūnō, -ōnis *f* Roman goddess wife of Jupiter, patroness of women and marriage.
Iūnōnālis *adj see n.*
Iūnōnicola, -ae *m* worshipper of Juno.
Iūnōnigena, -ae *m* Vulcan.
Iūnōnius *adj* = **Iūnōnālis**.
Iuppiter, Iovis *m* Jupiter (*king of the gods, god of sky and weather*); ~ **Stygius** Pluto; **sub Iove** in the open air.
iūrātor, -ōris *m* sworn judge.
iūrecōnsultus *etc see* **iūriscōnsultus**.
iūreiūrō, -āre *vi* to swear.
iūreperītus *etc see* **iūrisperītus**.
iūrgium, -ī and iī *nt* quarrel, brawl.
iūrgō, -āre *vi* to quarrel, squabble ♦ *vt* to scold.
iūridiciālis *adj* of law, juridical.
iūriscōnsultus, -ī *m* lawyer.
iūrisdictiō, -ōnis *f* administration of justice; authority.
iūrisperītus *adj* versed in the law.
iūrō, -āre, -āvī, -ātum *vi, vt* to swear, take an oath; to conspire; **in nōmen ~** swear allegiance to; **in verba ~** take a prescribed form of oath; **~ātus** having sworn, under oath.
iūs, iūris *nt* broth, soup.
iūs, iūris *nt* law, right, justice; law court; jurisdiction, authority; ~ **gentium** international law; ~ **pūblicum** constitutional law; **summum ~** the strict letter of the law; ~ **dīcere** administer justice; **suī iūris** independent; **iūre** rightly, justly.
iūsiūrandum, iūrisiūrandī *nt* oath.
iussī *perf of* **iubeō**.
iussū *abl m* by order.
iussus *ppp of* **iubeō** ♦ *nt* order, command, prescription.

Noun declensions and verb conjugations are shown on pp xiii to xxv. The present infinitive ending of a verb shows to which conjugation it belongs: **-āre** = 1st; **-ēre** = 2nd; **-ere** = 3rd and **-īre** = 4th. Irregular verbs are shown on p xxvi

iūstē *adv* duly, rightly.
iūstificus *adj* just dealing.
iūstitia, -ae *f* justice, uprightness, fairness.
iūstitium, -ī *and* **iī** *nt* cessation of legal
  business.
iūstus *adj* just, fair; lawful, right; regular,
  proper ♦ *nt* right ♦ *ntpl* rights; formalities,
  obsequies.
iūtus *ppp of* **iuvō.**
iuvenālis *adj* youthful ♦ *ntpl* youthful games.
Iuvenālis, -is *m* Juvenal (*Roman satirist*).
iuvenāliter *adv* vigorously, impetuously.
iuvenca, -ae *f* heifer; girl.
iuvencus, -ī *m* bullock; young man ♦ *adj*
  young.
iuvenēscō, -ēscere, -uī *vi* to grow up; to grow
  young again.
iuvenīlis *adj* youthful.
iuvenīliter *adv see adj.*
iuvenis *adj* young ♦ *m/f* young man *or* woman
  (*20-45 years*), man, warrior.
iuvenor, -ārī *vi* to behave indiscreetly.
iuventa, -ae *f* youth.
iuventās, -ātis *f* youth.
iuventūs, -ūtis *f* youth, manhood; men,
  soldiers.
iuvō, -āre, iūvī, iūtum *vt* to help, be of use to;
  to please, delight; **~at mē** I am glad.
iuxtā *adv* near by, close; alike, just the same ♦
  prep (*with acc*) close to, hard by; next to; very
  like, next door to; **~ ac, cum, quam** just the
  same as.
iuxtim *adv* near; equally.
īvī *perf of* **eō.**
Ixīōn, -onis *m* Lapith king (*bound to a revolving
  wheel in Tartarus*).
Ixīoneus *adj see n.*
Ixīonidae, -ārum *mpl* Centaurs.
Ixīonidēs, -ae *m* Pirithous.

$$J, j$$

J *see* **I.**

$$K, k$$

Kalendae, -ārum *fpl* Kalends, first day of
  each month.
Karthāgō *see* **Carthāgō.**

$$L, l$$

labāscō, -ere *vi* to totter, waver.
lābēcula, -ae *f* aspersion.
labefaciō, -facere, -fēcī, -factum (*pass* **-fīō,
  -fierī**) *vt* to shake; (*fig*) to weaken, ruin.
labefactō, -āre, -āvī, -ātum *vt* to shake; (*fig*)
  to weaken, destroy.
labellum, -ī *nt* lip.
lābellum, -ī *nt* small basin.
Laberius, -ī *m* Roman family name (*esp a
  writer of mimes*).
lābēs, -is *f* sinking, fall; ruin, destruction.
lābēs, -is *f* spot, blemish; disgrace, stigma;
  (*person*) blot.
labia, -iae *f* lip.
Labiēnus, -ī *m* Roman surname (*esp Caesar's
  officer who went over to Pompey*).
labiōsus *adj* large-lipped.
labium, -ī *and* **iī** *nt* lip.
labō, -āre *vi* to totter, be unsteady, give way;
  to waver, hesitate, collapse.
lābor, -bī, -psus *vi* to slide, glide; to sink, fall;
  to slip away, pass away; (*fig*) to fade,
  decline, perish; to be disappointed, make a
  mistake.
labor (-ōs), -ōris *m* effort, exertion, labour;
  work, task; hardship, suffering, distress;
  (*ASTRO*) eclipse.
labōrifer, -ī *adj* sore afflicted.
labōriōsē *adv* laboriously, with difficulty.
labōriōsus *adj* troublesome, difficult;
  industrious.
labōrō, -āre, -āvī, -ātum *vi* to work, toil, take
  pains; to suffer, be troubled (with), be in
  distress; to be anxious, worried ♦ *vt* to work
  out, make, produce.
labōs *etc see* **labor.**
labrum, -ī *nt* lip; edge, rim; **primīs ~īs gustāre**
  acquire a smattering of.
lābrum, -ī *nt* tub, vat; bath.
lābrusca, -ae *f* wild vine.
lābruscum, -ī *nt* wild grape.

labyrintheūs *adj* labyrinthine.
labyrinthus, -ī *m* labyrinth, maze (*esp that of Cnossos in Crete*).
lac, lactis *nt* milk.
Lacaena, -ae *f* Spartan woman ♦ *adj* Spartan.
Lacedaemōn (-ō), -onis (*acc* -ona) *f* Sparta.
Lacedaemonius *adj* Spartan.
lacer, -ī *adj* torn, mangled, lacerated; tearing.
lacerātiō, -ōnis *f* tearing.
lacerna, -ae *f* cloak (*worn in cold weather*).
lacernātus *adj* cloaked.
lacerō, -āre, -āvī, -ātum *vt* to tear, lacerate, mangle; (*ship*) to wreck; (*speech*) to slander, abuse; (*feeling*) to torture, distress; (*goods, time*) to waste, destroy.
lacerta, -ae *f* lizard; a seafish.
lacertōsus *adj* brawny.
lacertus, -ī *m* upper arm, arm; (*pl*) brawn, muscle.
lacertus, -ī *m* lizard; a sea fish.
lacessō, -ere, -īvī *and* **iī, -ītum** *vt* to strike, provoke, challenge; (*fig*) to incite, exasperate.
Lachesis, -is *f* one of the Fates.
lacinia, -ae *f* flap, corner (*of dress*).
Lacīnium, -ī *nt* promontory in S. Italy, with a temple of Juno.
Lacīnius *adj see n.*
Lacō (-ōn), -ōnis *m* Spartan; Spartan dog.
Lacōnicus *adj* Spartan ♦ *nt* sweating bath.
lacrima, -ae *f* tear; (*plant*) gumdrop.
lacrimābilis *adj* mournful.
lacrimābundus *adj* bursting into tears.
lacrimō, -āre, -āvī, -ātum *vt, vi* to weep, weep for.
lacrimōsus *adj* tearful; lamentable.
lacrimula, -ae *f* tear, crocodile tear.
lacrum- *etc see* **lacrim-.**
lactāns, -antis *adj* giving milk; sucking.
lactātiō, -ōnis *f* allurement.
lactēns, -entis *adj* sucking; milky, juicy.
lacteolus *adj* milk-white.
lactēs, -ium *fpl* guts, small intestines.
lactēscō, -ere *vi* to turn to milk.
lacteus *adj* milky, milk-white.
lactō, -āre *vt* to dupe, wheedle.
lactūca, -ae *f* lettuce.
lacūna, -ae *f* hole, pit; pool, pond; (*fig*) deficiency.
lacūnar, -āris *nt* panel ceiling.
lacūnō, -āre *vt* to panel.
lacūnōsus *adj* sunken.
lacus, -ūs *m* vat, tank; lake; reservoir, cistern.
laedō, -dere, -sī, -sum *vt* to hurt, strike, wound; (*fig*) to offend, annoy, break.
Laelius, -ī *m* Roman family name (*esp the friend of Scipio*).
laena, -ae *f* a lined cloak.
Lāērtēs, -ae *m* father of Ulysses.
Lāērtiadēs *m* Ulysses.

Lāērtius *adj see n.*
laesī *perf of* **laedō.**
laesiō, -ōnis *f* attack.
Laestrygonēs, -um *mpl* fabulous cannibals of Campania, founders of Formiae.
Laestrygonius *adj see n.*
laesus *ppp of* **laedō.**
laetābilis *adj* joyful.
laetē *adv* gladly.
laetificō, -āre *vt* to gladden.
laetificus *adj* glad, joyful.
laetitia, -ae *f* joy, delight, exuberance.
laetor, -ārī, -ātus *vi* to rejoice, be glad.
laetus *adj* glad, cheerful; delighting (in); pleasing, welcome; (*growth*) fertile, rich; (*style*) exuberant.
laevē *adv* awkwardly.
laevus *adj* left; stupid; ill-omened, unfortunate; (*augury*) lucky, favourable ♦ *f* left hand.
laganum, -ī *nt* a kind of oilcake.
lagēos, -ī *f* a Greek vine.
lagoena, -ae *f* flagon.
lagōis, -idis *f* a kind of grouse.
lagōna, -ae *f* flagon.
Lāiadēs, -ae *m* Oedipus.
Lāius, -ī *m* father of Oedipus.
lallō, -āre *vi* to sing a lullaby.
lāma, -ae *f* bog.
lamberō, -āre *vt* to tear to pieces.
lambō, -ere, -ī *vt* to lick, touch; (*river*) to wash.
lāmenta, -ōrum *ntpl* lamentation.
lāmentābilis *adj* mournful, sorrowful.
lāmentārius *adj* sorrowful.
lāmentātiō, -ōnis *f* weeping, lamentation.
lāmentor, -ārī, -ātus *vi* to weep, lament ♦ *vt* to weep for, bewail.
lamia, -ae *f* witch.
lāmina (lammina, lāmna), -ae *f* plate, leaf (*of metal, wood*); blade; coin.
lampas, -dis *f* torch; brightness, day.
Lamus, -ī *m* Laestrygonian king.
lāna, -ae *f* wool.
lānārius, -ī *and* **iī** *m* wool-worker.
lānātus *adj* woolly.
lancea, -ae *f* spear, lance.
lancinō, -āre, *vt* to tear up; to squander.
lāneus *adj* woollen.
languefaciō, -ere *vt* to make weary.
langueō, -ēre *vi* to be weary, be weak, droop; to be idle, dull.
languēscō, -ēscere, -uī *vi* to grow faint, droop.
languidē *adv see adj.*
languidulus *adj* languid.
languidus *adj* faint, languid, sluggish; listless, feeble.
languor, -ōris *m* faintness, fatigue, weakness; dullness, apathy.
laniātus, -ūs *m* mangling; (*mind*) anguish.

Noun declensions and verb conjugations are shown on pp xiii to xxv. The present infinitive ending of a verb shows to which conjugation it belongs: **-āre** = 1st; **-ēre** = 2nd; **-ere** = 3rd and **-īre** = 4th. Irregular verbs are shown on p xxvi

laniēna, -ae *f* butcher's shop.
lānificium, -ī *and* **iī** *nt* wool-working.
lānificus *adj* wool-working.
lāniger, -ī *adj* fleecy ♦ *m/f* ram, sheep.
laniō, -āre, -āvī, -ātum *vt* to tear to pieces, mangle.
lanista, -ae *m* trainer of gladiators, fencing master; (*fig*) agitator.
lānitium, -ī *and* **iī** *nt* woolgrowing.
lanius, -ī *and* **iī** *m* butcher.
lanterna, -ae *f* lamp.
lanternārius, -ī *and* **iī** *m* guide.
lānūgō, -inis *f* down, woolliness.
Lānuvīnus *adj see n.*
Lānuvium, -ī *nt* Latin town on the Appian Way.
lānx, lancis *f* dish, platter; (*balance*) scale.
Lāomedōn, -ontis *m* king of Troy (*father of Priam*).
Lāomedontēus *adj and* **ontiadēs, -ae** *m* son of Lāomedōn; (*pl*) Trojans.
Lāomedontius *adj* Trojan.
lapathum, -ī *nt,* **-us, -ī** *f* sorrel.
lapicīda, -ae *m* stonecutter.
lapicīdīnae, -ārum *fpl* quarries.
lapidārius *adj* stone- (*in cpds*).
lapidātiō, -ōnis *f* throwing of stones.
lapidātor, -ōris *m* stone thrower.
lapideus *adj* of stones, stone- (*in cpds*).
lapidō, -āre *vt* to stone ♦ *vi* to rain stones.
lapidōsus *adj* stony; hard as stone.
lapillus, -ī *m* stone, pebble; precious stone, mosaic piece.
lapis, -dis *m* stone; milestone, boundary stone, tombstone; precious stone; marble; auctioneer's stand; (*abuse*) blockhead; **bis ad eundem (offendere)** ≈ *make the same mistake twice*; **Juppiter** ~ the Jupiter stone.
Lapithae, -ārum *and* **-um** *mpl* Lapiths (*mythical people of Thessaly*).
Lapithaeus, -ēius *adj see n.*
lappa, -ae *f* goosegrass.
lāpsiō, -ōnis *f* tendency.
lāpsō, -āre *vi* to slip, stumble.
lāpsus *ppa of* **lābor.**
lāpsus, -ūs *m* fall, slide, course, flight; error, failure.
laqueāria, -ium *ntpl* panelled ceiling.
laqueātus *adj* panelled, with a panelled ceiling.
laqueus, -ī *m* noose, snare, halter; (*fig*) trap.
Lār, Laris *m* tutelary deity, household god; hearth, home.
lārdum *etc see* **lāridum.**
largē *adv* plentifully, generously, very much.
largificus *adj* bountiful.
largifluus *adj* copious.
largiloquus *adj* talkative.
largior, -īrī, -ītus *vt* to give freely, lavish; to bestow, confer ♦ *vi* to give largesses.
largitās, -ātis *f* liberality, abundance.
largiter *adv* = **large.**
largītiō, -ōnis *f* giving freely, distributing; bribery.

largītor, -ōris *m* liberal giver, dispenser; spendthrift; briber.
largus *adj* copious, ample; liberal, bountiful.
lāridum, -ī *nt* bacon fat.
Lārissa (Lārīsa), -ae *f* town in Thessaly.
Lārissaeus, -ēnsis *adj see n.*
Lārius, -ī *m* lake Como.
larix, -cis *f* larch.
larva, -ae *f* ghost; mask.
larvātus *adj* bewitched.
lasanum, -ī *nt* pot.
lasārpīcifer, -ī *adj* producing asafoetida.
lascīvia, -ae *f* playfulness; impudence, lewdness.
lascīviō, -īre *vi* to frolic, frisk; to run wild, be irresponsible.
lascīvus *adj* playful, frisky; impudent, lustful.
laserpīcium, -ī *and* **iī** *nt* silphium.
lassitūdō, -inis *f* fatigue, heaviness.
lassō, -āre, *vt* to tire, fatigue.
lassulus *adj* rather weary.
lassus *adj* tired, exhausted.
lātē *adv* widely, extensively; **longē ~que** far and wide, everywhere.
latebra, -ae *f* hiding place, retreat; (*fig*) loophole, pretext.
latebricola, -ae *adj* low-living.
latebrōsē *adv* in hiding.
latebrōsus *adj* secret, full of coverts; porous.
latēns, -entis *pres p of* **lateō** ♦ *adj* hidden, secret.
latenter *adv* in secret.
lateō, -ēre, -uī *vi* to lie hid, lurk, skulk; to be in safety, live a retired life; to be unknown, escape notice.
later, -is *m* brick, tile; **~em lavāre** ≈ *waste one's time.*
laterāmen, -inis *nt* earthenware.
laterculus, -ī *m* small brick, tile; kind of cake.
latericius *adj* of bricks ♦ *nt* brickwork.
lāterna *etc see* **lanterna.**
latēscō, -ere *vi* to hide oneself.
latex, -icis *m* water; any other liquid.
Latiar, -iaris *nt* festival of Jupiter Latiaris.
Latiaris *adj* Latin.
latibulum, -ī *nt* hiding place, den, lair.
lāticlāvius *adj* with a broad purple stripe ♦ *m* senator, patrician.
lātifundium, -ī *and* **iī** *nt* large estate.
Latīnē *adv* in Latin, into Latin; ~ **loquī** speak Latin, speak plainly, speak correctly; ~ **reddere** translate into Latin.
Latīnitās, -ātis *f* good Latin, Latinity; Latin rights.
Latīnus *adj* Latin ♦ *m* legendary king of the Laurentians.
lātiō, -ōnis *f* bringing; proposing.
latitō, -āre *vi* to hide away, lurk, keep out of the way.
lātitūdō, -inis *f* breadth, width; size; broad pronunciation.
Latium, -ī *nt* district of Italy including Rome; Latin rights.

Latius = Latiaris, Latinus.
Lātōis, -idis f Diana.
Lātōis , -ius adj see n.
lātom- etc see **lautum-**.
Lātōna, -ae f mother of Apollo and Diana.
Lātōnigenae, -ārum pl Apollo and Diana.
Lātōnius adj, f Diana.
lātor, -ōris m proposer.
Lātōus adj of Latona ♦ m Apollo.
lātrātor, -ōris m barker.
lātrātus, -ūs m barking.
lātrō, -āre vi to bark; to rant, roar ♦ vt to bark at; to clamour for.
latrō, -ōnis m mercenary soldier; bandit, brigand; (chess) man.
latrōcinium, -ī and **iī** nt highway robbery, piracy.
latrōcinor, -ārī, -ātus vi to serve as a mercenary; to be a brigand or pirate.
latrunculus, -ī m brigand; (chess) man.
lātumiae etc see **lautumiae**.
lātus ppp of **ferō**.
lātus adj broad, wide; extensive; (pronunciation) broad; (style) diffuse.
latus, -eris nt side, flank; lungs; body; ~ **dare** expose oneself; ~ **tegere** walk beside; **~eris dolor** pleurisy; **ab ~ere** on the flank.
latusculum, -ī nt little side.
laudābilis adj praiseworthy.
laudābiliter adv laudably.
laudātiō, -ōnis f commendation, eulogy; panegyric, testimonial.
laudātor, -ōris m, **-rīx, -rīcis** f praiser, eulogizer; speaker of a funeral oration.
laudātus adj excellent.
laudō, -āre, -āvī, -ātum vt to praise, commend, approve; to pronounce a funeral oration over; to quote, name.
laurea, -ae f bay tree; crown of bay; triumph.
laureātus adj crowned with bay; (despatches) victorious.
Laurentēs, -um mpl Laurentians (people of ancient Latium).
Laurentius adj see n.
laureola, -ae f triumph.
laureus adj of bay.
lauricomus adj bay-covered.
lauriger, -ī adj crowned with bay.
laurus, -ī f bay tree; bay crown; victory, triumph.
laus, laudis f praise, approval; glory, fame; praiseworthy act, merit, worth.
lautē adv elegantly, splendidly; excellently.
lautia, -ōrum ntpl State banquet.
lautitia, -ae f luxury.
lautumiae, -ārum fpl stone quarry; prison.
lautus ppp of **lavō** ♦ adj neat, elegant, sumptuous; fine, grand, distinguished.
lavābrum, -ī nt bath.
lavātiō, -ōnis f washing, bath; bathing gear.

Lāvīnium, -ī nt town of ancient Latium.
Lāvīnius adj see n.
lavō, -āre, lāvī, lautum (lavātum and **lōtum)** vt to wash, bathe; to wet, soak, wash away.
laxāmentum, -ī nt respite, relaxation.
laxē adv loosely, freely.
laxitās, -ātis f roominess.
laxō, -āre, -āvī, -ātum vt to extend, open out; to undo; to slacken; (fig) to release, relieve; to relax, abate ♦ vi (price) to fall off.
laxus adj wide, loose, roomy; (time) deferred; (fig) free, easy.
lea, -ae f lioness.
leaena, -ae f lioness.
Lēander, -rī m Hero's lover (who swam the Hellespont).
lebēs, -ētis m basin, pan, cauldron.
lectīca, -ae f litter, sedan chair.
lectīcārius, -ī and **iī** m litter-bearer.
lectīcula, -ae f small litter; bier.
lēctiō, -ōnis f selecting; reading, calling the roll.
lectisterniātor, -ōris m arranger of couches.
lectisternium, -ī and **iī** nt religious feast.
lēctitō, -āre vt to read frequently.
lēctiuncula, -ae f light reading.
lēctor, -ōris m reader.
lectulus, -ī m couch, bed.
lectus, -ī m couch, bed; bier.
lēctus ppp of **legō** ♦ adj picked; choice, excellent.
Lēda, -ae and **ē, -ēs** f mother of Castor, Pollux, Helen and Clytemnestra.
Lēdaeus adj see n.
lēgātiō, -ōnis f mission, embassy; members of a mission; (MIL) staff appointment, command of a legion; **lībera ~** free commission (to visit provinces); **vōtīva ~** free commission for paying a vow in a province.
lēgātor, -ōris m testator.
lēgātum, -ī nt legacy, bequest.
lēgātus, -ī m delegate, ambassador; deputy, lieutenant; commander (of a legion).
lēgifer, -ī adj law-giving.
legiō, -ōnis f legion (up to 6000 men); (pl) troops, army.
legiōnārius adj legionary.
lēgirupa, -ae; -iō, -iōnis m lawbreaker.
lēgitimē adv lawfully, properly.
lēgitimus adj lawful, legal; right, proper.
legiuncula, -ae f small legion.
lēgō, -āre, -āvī, -ātum vt to send, charge, commission; to appoint as deputy or lieutenant; (will) to leave, bequeath.
legō, -ere, lēgī, lēctum vt to gather, pick; to choose, select; (sail) to furl; (places) to traverse, pass, coast along; (view) to scan; (writing) to read, recite; **senātum ~** call the

---

Noun declensions and verb conjugations are shown on pp xiii to xxv. The present infinitive ending of a verb shows to which conjugation it belongs: **-āre** = 1st; **-ēre** = 2nd; **-ere** = 3rd and **-īre** = 4th. Irregular verbs are shown on p xxvi

roll of the senate.

lēgulēius, -ī *and* **iī** *m* pettifogging lawyer.

legūmen, -inis *nt* pulse, bean.

lembus, -ī *m* pinnace, cutter.

Lemnias *f* Lemnian woman.

Lemnicola, -ae *m* Vulcan.

lēmniscātus *adj* beribboned.

lēmniscus, -ī *m* ribbon (*hanging from a victor's crown*).

Lēmnius *adj see n.*

Lēmnos (-us), -ī *f* Aegean island, abode of Vulcan.

Lemurēs, -um *mpl* ghosts.

lēna, -ae *f* procuress; seductress.

Lēnaeus *adj* Bacchic ♦ *m* Bacchus.

lēnīmen, -inis *nt* solace, comfort.

lēnīmentum, -ī *nt* sop.

lēniō, -īre, -īvī *and* **iī, -ītum** *vt* to soften, soothe, heal, calm.

lēnis *adj* soft, smooth, mild, gentle, calm.

lēnitās, -ātis *f* softness, smoothness, mildness, tenderness.

lēniter *adv* softly, gently; moderately, half-heartedly.

lēnitūdō, -inis *f* smoothness, mildness.

lēnō, -ōnis *m* pander, brothel keeper; go-between.

lēnōcinium, -ī *and* **iī** *nt* pandering; allurement; meretricious ornament.

lēnōcinor, -ārī, -ātus *vi* to pay court to; to promote.

lēnōnius *adj* pander's.

lēns, lentis *f* lentil.

lentē *adv* slowly; calmly, coolly.

lentēscō, -ere *vi* to become sticky, soften; to relax.

lentiscifer, -ī *adj* bearing mastic trees.

lentiscus, -ī *f* mastic tree.

lentitūdō, -inis *f* slowness, dullness, apathy.

lentō, -āre *vt* to bend.

lentulus *adj* rather slow.

lentus *adj* sticky, sluggish; pliant; slow, lasting, lingering; (*person*) calm, at ease, indifferent.

lēnunculus, -ī *m* skiff.

leō, -ōnis *m* lion.

Leōnidās, -ae *m* Spartan king who fell at Thermopylae.

leōnīnus *adj* lion's.

Leontīnī, -ōrum *mpl* town in Sicily.

Leontīnus *adj see n.*

lepas, -dis *f* limpet.

lepidē *adv* neatly, charmingly; (*reply*) very well, splendidly.

lepidus *adj* pleasant, charming, neat, witty.

lepōs (lepor), -ōris *m* pleasantness, charm; wit.

lepus, -oris *m* hare.

lepusculus, -ī *m* young hare.

Lerna, -ae *and* **ē, -ēs** *f* marsh near Argos (*where Hercules killed the Hydra*).

Lernaeus *adj* Lernaean.

Lesbias, -iadis *f* Lesbian woman.

Lesbis, Lesbius *adj see n.*

Lesbos (-us), -ī *f* Aegean island (*home of Alcaeus and Sappho*).

Lesbous *f* Lesbian woman.

lētālis *adj* deadly.

Lēthaeus *adj* of Lethe; infernal; soporific.

lēthargicus, -ī *m* lethargic person.

lēthargus, -ī *m* drowsiness.

Lēthē, -ēs *f* river in the lower world, which caused forgetfulness.

lētifer, -ī *adj* fatal.

lētō, -āre *vt* to kill.

lētum, -ī *nt* death; destruction.

Leucadius *adj see n.*

Leucas, -dis *and* **dia, -diae** *f* island off W. Greece.

Leucothea, -ae, -ē, -ēs *f* Ino (*a sea goddess*).

Leuctra, -ōrum *ntpl* battlefield in Boeotia.

Leuctricus *adj see n.*

levāmen, -inis *nt* alleviation, comfort.

levāmentum, -ī *nt* mitigation, consolation.

levātiō, -ōnis *f* relief; diminishing.

lēvī *perf of* **linō.**

leviculus *adj* rather vain.

levidēnsis *adj* slight.

levipēs, -edis *adj* light-footed.

levis *adj* (*weight*) light; (*MIL*) light-armed; (*fig*) easy, gentle; (*importance*) slight, trivial; (*motion*) nimble, fleet; (*character*) fickle, unreliable.

lēvis *adj* smooth; (*youth*) beardless, delicate.

levisomnus *adj* light-sleeping.

levitās, -ātis *f* lightness; nimbleness; fickleness, frivolity.

lēvitās, -ātis *f* smoothness; fluency.

leviter *adv* lightly; slightly; easily.

levō, -āre *vt* to lighten, ease; (*fig*) to alleviate, lessen; to comfort, relieve; to impair; (*danger*) to avert; **sē ~** rise.

lēvō, -āre *vt* to smooth, polish.

lēvor, -ōris *m* smoothness.

lēx, lēgis *f* law, statute; bill; rule, principle; contract, condition; **lēgem ferre** propose a bill; **lēgem perferre** carry a motion; **lēge agere** proceed according to law; **sine lēge** out of control.

lībāmen, -inis *nt* offering, libation.

lībāmentum, -ī *nt* offering, libation.

lībātiō, -ōnis *f* libation.

lībella, -ae *f* small coin, as; level; **ad ~am** exactly; **ex ~ā** sole heir.

libellus, -ī *m* small book; notebook, diary, letter; notice, programme, handbill; petition, complaint; lampoon.

libēns, -entis *adj* willing, glad.

libenter *adv* willingly, with pleasure.

liber, -rī *m* inner bark (of a tree); book; register.

Līber, -ī *m* Italian god of fertility (*identified with Bacchus*).

līber, -ī *adj* free, open, unrestricted, undisturbed; (*with abl*) free from; (*speech*) frank; (*POL*) free, not slave, democratic.

Lībera, -ae *f* Proserpine; Ariadne.
Līberālia, -ālium *ntpl festival of Liber in March.*
līberālis *adj* of freedom, of free citizens, gentlemanly, honourable; generous, liberal; handsome.
līberālitās, -ātis *f* courtesy, kindness; generosity; bounty.
līberāliter *adv* courteously, nobly; generously.
līberātiō, -ōnis *f* delivery, freeing; (*law*) acquittal.
līberātor, -ōris *m* liberator, deliverer.
līberē *adv* freely, frankly, boldly.
līberī, -ōrum *mpl* children.
līberō, -āre, -āvī, -ātum *vt* to free, set free, release; to exempt; (*law*) to acquit; (*slave*) to give freedom to; **fidem ~** keep one's promise; **nōmina ~** cancel debts.
līberta, -ae *f* freedwoman.
lībertās, -ātis *f* freedom, liberty; status of a freeman; (*POL*) independence; freedom of speech, outspokenness.
lībertīnus *adj* of a freedman, freed ♦ *m* freedman ♦ *f* freedwoman.
lībertus, -ī *m* freedman.
libet (lubet), -ēre, -uit *and* **itum est** *vi* (*impers*) it pleases; **mihi ~** I like; **ut ~** as you please.
libīdinōsē *adv* wilfully.
libīdinōsus *adj* wilful, arbitrary, extravagant; sensual, lustful.
libīdō (lubīdō), -inis *f* desire, passion; wilfulness, caprice; lust.
libita, -ōrum *ntpl* pleasure, fancy.
Libitīna, -ae *f* goddess of burials.
lībō, -āre, -āvī, -ātum *vt* to taste, sip, touch; to pour (*a libation*), offer; to extract, take out; to impair.
lībra, -ae *f* pound; balance, pair of scales; **ad ~am** of equal size.
lībrāmentum, -ī *nt* level surface, weight (*to give balance or movement*); (*water*) fall.
lībrāria, -ae *f* head spinner.
lībrāriolus, -ī *m* copyist.
lībrārium, -ī *and* **iī** *nt* bookcase.
lībrārius *adj* of books ♦ *m* copyist.
lībrātus *adj* level; powerful.
lībrīlis *adj* weighing a pound.
lībritor, -ōris *m* slinger.
lībrō, -āre, -āvī, -ātum *vt* to poise, hold balanced; to swing, hurl.
lībum, -ī *nt* cake.
Liburna, -ae *f* a fast galley, frigate.
Liburnī, -ōrum *mpl people of Illyria.*
Liburnus *adj* Liburnian.
Libya, -ae, -ē, -ēs *f* Africa.
Libycus *adj* African.
Libyes, -um *mpl* Libyans, *people in N. Africa.*
Libyssus, Libystinus, Libystis *adj* = **Libycus.**
licēns, -entis *adj* free, bold, unrestricted.
licenter *adv* freely, lawlessly.

licentia, -ae *f* freedom, license; lawlessness, licentiousness.
liceō, -ēre, -uī *vi* to be for sale, value at.
liceor, -ērī, -itus *vt, vi* to bid (at an auction), bid for.
licet, -ēre, -uit *and* **itum est** *vi* (*impers*) it is permitted, it is lawful; (*reply*) all right ♦ *conj* although; **mihi ~** I may.
Licinius, -ī *m* Roman family name (*esp with surname Crassus*).
Licinius *adj see n.*
licitātiō, -ōnis *f* bidding (*at a sale*).
licitor, -ārī *vi* to make a bid.
licitus *adj* lawful.
līcium, -ī *and* **iī** *nt* thread.
līctor, -ōris *m* lictor (*an attendant with fasces preceding a magistrate*).
licuī *perf of* **liceō**; *perf of* **liquēscō.**
liēn, -ēnis *m* spleen.
ligāmen, -inis *nt* band, bandage.
ligāmentum, -ī *nt* bandage.
Liger, -is *m* river Loire.
lignārius, -ī *and* **iī** *m* carpenter.
lignātiō, -ōnis *f* fetching wood.
lignātor, -ōris *m* woodcutter.
ligneolus *adj* wooden.
ligneus *adj* wooden.
lignor, -ārī *vi* to fetch wood.
lignum, -ī *nt* wood, firewood, timber; **in silvam ~a ferre** ≈ carry coals to Newcastle.
ligō, -āre, -āvī, -ātum *vt* to tie up, bandage; (*fig*) to unite.
ligō, -ōnis *m* mattock, hoe.
ligula, -ae *f* shoestrap.
Ligur, -ris *m/f* Ligurian.
Liguria, -riae *f district of N.W. Italy.*
ligūriō (ligurriō), -īre *vt* to lick; to eat daintily; (*fig*) to feast on, lust after.
ligūrītiō, -ōnis *f* daintiness.
Ligus, -ris *m/f* Ligurian.
Ligusticus, -stīnus *adj see n.*
ligustrum, -ī *nt* privet.
līlium, -ī *and* **iī** *nt* lily; (*MIL*) spiked pit.
līma, -ae *f* file; (*fig*) revision.
līmātius *adv* more elegantly.
līmātulus *adj* refined.
līmāx, -ācis *f* slug, snail.
limbus, -ī *m* fringe, hem.
līmen, -inis *nt* threshold, lintel; doorway; entrance; house, home; (*fig*) beginning.
līmes, -itis *m* path between fields, boundary; path, track, way; frontier, boundary line.
līmō, -āre, -āvī, -ātum *vt* to file; (*fig*) to polish, refine; to file down, investigate carefully; to take away from.
līmōsus *adj* muddy.
limpidus *adj* clear, limpid.
līmus *adj* sidelong, askance.
līmus, -ī *m* mud, slime, dirt.
līmus, -ī *m* ceremonial apron.

Noun declensions and verb conjugations are shown on pp xiii to xxv. The present infinitive ending of a verb shows to which conjugation it belongs: **-āre** = 1st; **-ēre** = 2nd; **-ere** = 3rd and **-īre** = 4th. Irregular verbs are shown on p xxvi

līnea, -ae *f* line, string; plumbline; boundary; **ad ~am, rectā ~ā** vertically; **extrēmā ~ā amāre** love at a distance.

līneāmentum, -ī *nt* line; feature; outline.

līneus *adj* flaxen, linen.

lingō, -ere *vt* to lick.

lingua, -ae *f* tongue; speech, language; tongue of land; **~ Latīna** Latin.

lingula, -ae *f* tongue of land.

līniger, -ī *adj* linen-clad.

linō, -ere, lēvī, litum *vt* to daub, smear; to overlay; (*writing*) to rub out; (*fig*) to befoul.

linquō, -ere, līquī *vt* to leave, quit; to give up, let alone; (*pass*) to faint, swoon; **~itur ut** it remains to.

linteātus *adj* canvas.

linteō, -ōnis *m* linen weaver.

linter, -ris *f* boat; trough.

linteum, -ī *nt* linen cloth, canvas; sail.

linteus *adj* linen.

lintriculus, -ī *m* small boat.

līnum, -ī *nt* flax; linen; thread, line, rope; net.

Lipara, -ae, -ē, -ēs *f* island N. of Sicily (*now* Lipari).

Liparaeus, -ēnsis *adj see n.*

lippiō, -īre *vi* to have sore eyes.

lippitūdō, -inis *f* inflammation of the eyes.

lippus *adj* blear-eyed, with sore eyes; (*fig*) blind.

liquefaciō, -facere, -fēcī, -factum (*pass* **-fīō**) *vt* to melt, dissolve; to decompose; (*fig*) to enervate.

liquēns, -entis *adj* fluid, clear.

liquēscō, -ere, licuī *vi* to melt; to clear; (*fig*) to grow soft, waste away.

liquet, -ēre, licuit *vi* (*impers*) it is clear, it is evident; **nōn ~** not proven.

līquī *perf of* **linquō**.

liquidō *adv* clearly.

liquidus *adj* fluid, liquid, flowing; clear, transparent, pure; (*mind*) calm, serene ♦ *nt* liquid water.

liquō, -āre *vt* to melt; to strain.

līquor, -ī *vi* to flow; (*fig*) to waste away.

liquor, -ōris *m* fluidity; liquid, the sea.

Līris, -is *m* river between Latium and Campania.

līs, lītis *f* quarrel, dispute; lawsuit; matter in dispute; **lītem aestimāre** assess damages.

litātiō, -ōnis *f* favourable sacrifice.

lītera *etc see* **littera**.

lītigātor, -ōris *m* litigant.

lītigiōsus *adj* quarrelsome, contentious; disputed.

lītigium, -ī *and* **iī** *nt* quarrel.

lītigō, -āre *vi* to quarrel; to go to law.

litō, -āre, -āvī, -ātum *vi* to offer an acceptable sacrifice, obtain favourable omens; (*with dat*) to propitiate ♦ *vt* to offer successfully.

lītorālis *adj* of the shore.

lītoreus *adj* of the shore.

littera, -ae *f* letter (of the alphabet).

litterae, -ārum *fpl* writing; letter, dispatch; document, ordinance; literature; learning, scholarship; **~ās discere** learn to read and write; **homō trium ~ārum** thief (*of fur*); **sine ~īs** uncultured.

litterārius *adj* of reading and writing.

litterātē *adv* in clear letters; literally.

litterātor, -ōris *m* grammarian.

litterātūra, -ae *f* writing, alphabet.

litterātus *adj* with letters on it, branded; educated, learned.

litterula, -ae *f* small letter; short note; (*pl*) studies.

litūra, -ae *f* correction, erasure, blot.

litus *ppp of* **linō**.

lītus, -oris *nt* shore, beach, coast; bank; **~ arāre** labour in vain.

lituus, -ī *m* augur's staff; trumpet; (*fig*) starter.

līvēns, -entis *pres p of* **līveō** ♦ *adj* bluish, black and blue.

līveō, -ēre *vi* to be black and blue; to envy.

līvēscō, -ere *vi* to turn black and blue.

Līviānus *adj* = Līvius.

līvidulus *adj* a little jealous.

līvidus *adj* bluish, black and blue; envious, malicious.

Līvius, -ī Roman family name (*esp the first Latin poet*); *the famous historian, Livy.*

Līvius *adj see n.*

līvor, -ōris *m* bluish colour; envy, malice.

lixa, -ae *m* sutler, camp-follower.

locātiō, -ōnis *f* leasing; lease, contract.

locātōrius *adj* concerned with leases.

locitō, -āre *vt* to let frequently.

locō, -āre, -āvī, -ātum *vt* to place, put; to give in marriage; to let, lease, hire out; to contract for; (*money*) to invest.

loculus, -ī *m* little place; (*pl*) satchel, purse.

locuplēs, -ētis *adj* rich, opulent; reliable, responsible.

locuplētō, -āre *vt* to enrich.

locus, -ī *m* (*pl* **-ī** *m and* **-a** *nt*) place, site, locality, region; (*MIL*) post; (*theatre*) seat; (*book*) passage; (*speech*) topic, subject, argument; (*fig*) room, occasion; situation, state; rank, position; **-ī** individual spots; **~a** regions, ground; **~ī commūnēs** general arguments; **~ō** (*with gen*) instead of; **in ~ō** opportunely; **eō ~ī** in the position; **intereā ~ī** meanwhile.

lōcusta, -ae *f* locust.

locūtiō, -ōnis *f* speech; pronunciation.

locūtus *ppa of* **loquor**.

lōdīx, -īcis *f* blanket.

logica, -ōrum *ntpl* logic.

logos (-us), -ī *m* word; idle talk; witticism.

lōlīg- *etc see* **lollīg-**.

lolium, -ī *and* **iī** *nt* darnel.

lollīgō, -inis *f* cuttlefish.

lōmentum, -ī *nt* face cream.

Londinium, -ī *nt* London.

longaevus *adj* aged.

longē *adv* far, far off; (*time*) long; (*compar*) by far, very much; **~ esse** be far away, of no

longinquitās–lūdus

avail; ~ **latēque** everywhere.
longinquitās, -ātis f length; distance;
duration.
longinquus adj distant, remote; foreign,
strange; lasting, wearisome; (hope) long
deferred.
longitūdō, -inis f length; duration; **in ~inem**
lengthwise.
longiusculus adj rather long.
longulē adv rather far.
longulus adj rather long.
longurius, -ī and **iī** m long pole.
longus adj long; vast; (time) long, protracted,
tedious; (hope) far-reaching; ~**a nāvis**
warship; ~**um est** it would be tedious; **nē**
~**um faciam** ≈ to cut a long story short.
loquācitās, -ātis f talkativeness.
loquāciter adv see adj.
loquāculus adj somewhat talkative.
loquāx, -ācis adj talkative, chattering.
loquella, -ae f language, words.
loquor, -quī, cūtus vt, vi to speak, talk, say; to
talk about, mention; (fig) to indicate; **rēs**
~**quitur ipsa** the facts speak for themselves.
lōrārius, -ī and **iī** m flogger.
lōrātus adj strapped.
lōreus adj of leather strips.
lōrīca, -ae f breastplate; parapet.
lōrīcātus adj mailed.
lōripēs, -edis adj bandylegged.
lōrum, -ī nt strap; whip, lash; leather charm;
(pl) reins.
lōtos (-us), -ī f lotus.
lōtus ppp of **lavō**.
lubēns see **libēns**.
lubentia, -ae f pleasure.
lubet, lubīdō see **libet, libīdō**.
lūbricō, -āre vt to make slippery.
lūbricus adj slippery, slimy; gliding, fleeting;
(fig) dangerous, hazardous.
Luca bōs f elephant.
Lūcānia, -iae f district of S. Italy.
Lūcanica f kind of sausage.
Lūcanus adj Lucanian ♦ m the epic poet Lucan.
lūcar, -āris nt forest tax.
lucellum, -ī nt small gain.
lūceō, -cēre, -xī vi to shine, be light; (impers)
to dawn, be daylight; (fig) to shine, be clear;
meridiē nōn ~cēre ≈ (argue) that black is white.
Lūcerēs, -um mpl a Roman patrician tribe.
Lūceria, -iae f town in Apulia.
Lūcerīnus adj see n.
lucerna, -ae f lamp; (fig) ≈ midnight oil.
lūcēscō, -ere vi to begin to shine, get light,
dawn.
lūcidē adv clearly.
lūcidus adj bright, clear; (fig) lucid.
lūcifer, -ī adj light-bringing ♦ m morning star,
Venus; day.
lūcifugus adj shunning the light.

Lūcīlius, -ī m Roman family name (esp the first
Latin satirist).
Lūcīna, -ae f goddess of childbirth.
lūcīscō etc see **lūcēscō**.
Lucmō (Lucumō), -ōnis m Etruscan prince
or priest.
Lucrētia, -iae f wife of Collatinus, ravished by
Tarquin.
Lucrētius, -ī m Roman family name (esp the
philosophic poet).
lucrifuga, -ae m non-profiteer.
Lucrīnēnsis adj see n.
Lucrīnus, -ī m lake near Baiae (famous for
oysters).
lucror, -ārī, -ātus vt to gain, win, acquire.
lucrōsus adj profitable.
lucrum, -ī nt profit, gain; greed; wealth; ~**ī**
facere gain, get the credit of; ~**ō esse** be of
advantage; **in ~īs pōnere** count as gain.
luctāmen, -inis nt struggle, exertion.
luctātiō, -ōnis f wrestling; fight, contest.
luctātor, -ōris m wrestler.
lūctificus adj baleful.
lūctisonus adj mournful.
luctor, -ārī, -ātus vi to wrestle; to struggle,
fight.
lūctuōsus adj sorrowful, lamentable.
lūctus, -ūs m mourning, lamentation;
mourning (dress).
lūcubrātiō, -ōnis f work by lamplight,
nocturnal study.
lūcubrō, -āre, -āvī, -ātum vi to work by night
♦ vt to compose by night.
lūculentē adv splendidly, right.
lūculenter adv very well.
lūculentus adj bright; (fig) brilliant, excellent,
rich, fine.
Lūcullus, -ī m Roman surname (esp the
conqueror of Mithridates).
lūcus, -ī m grove; wood.
lūdia, -ae f woman gladiator.
lūdibrium, -ī and **iī** nt mockery, derision;
laughing stock; sport, play; ~**iō habēre** make
fun of.
lūdibundus adj playful; safely, easily.
lūdicer, -rī adj playful; theatrical.
lūdicrum, -ī nt public show, play; sport.
lūdificātiō, -ōnis f ridicule; tricking.
lūdificātor, -ōris m mocker.
lūdificō, -āre, -or, -ārī, -ātus vt to make a fool
of, ridicule; to delude, thwart.
lūdiō, -ōnis m actor.
lūdius, -ī and **iī** m actor; gladiator.
lūdō, -dere, -sī, -sum vi to play; to sport,
frolic; to dally, make love ♦ vt to play at; to
amuse oneself with; to mimic, imitate; to
ridicule, mock; to delude.
lūdus, -ī m game, sport, play; (pl) public
spectacle, games; school; (fig) child's play;
fun, jest; (love) dalliance; ~**um dare** humour;

Noun declensions and verb conjugations are shown on pp xiii to xxv. The present infinitive ending of a verb shows
to which conjugation it belongs: **-āre** = 1st; **-ēre** = 2nd; **-ere** = 3rd and **-īre** = 4th. Irregular verbs are shown on p xxvi

~ōs facere put on a public show; make fun of.
luella, -ae *f* atonement.
luēs, -is *f* plague, pest; misfortune.
Lugdūnēnsis *adj see n.*
Lugdūnum, -ī *nt* town in E. Gaul (*now* Lyons).
lūgeō, -gēre, -xī *vt, vi* to mourn; to be in mourning.
lūgubris *adj* mourning; disastrous; (*sound*) plaintive ♦ *ntpl* mourning dress.
lumbī, -ōrum *mpl* loins.
lumbricus, -ī *m* worm.
lūmen, -inis *m* light; lamp, torch; day; eye; life; (*fig*) ornament, glory; clarity.
lūmināre, -is *nt* window.
lūminōsus *adj* brilliant.
lūna, -ae *f* moon; month; crescent.
lūnāris *adj* of the moon.
lūnātus *adj* crescent-shaped.
lūnō, -āre *vt* to bend into a crescent.
luō, -ere, -ī *vt* to pay; to atone for; to avert by expiation.
lupa, -ae *f* she-wolf; prostitute.
lupānar, -āris *nt* brothel.
lupātus *adj* toothed ♦ *m and ntpl* curb.
Lupercal, -ālis *nt a grotto sacred to Pan.*
Lupercālia, -ālium *ntpl festival of Pan in February.*
Lupercus, -ī *m* Pan; priest of Pan.
lupīnum, -ī *nt* lupin; sham money, counters.
lupīnus *adj* wolf's.
lupīnus, -ī *m* lupin; sham money, counters.
lupus, -ī *m* wolf; (*fish*) pike; toothed bit; grapnel; **~ in fābulā** ≈ *talk of the devil.*
lūridus *adj* pale yellow, ghastly pallid.
lūror, -ōris *m* yellowness.
lūscinia, -ae *f* nightingale.
luscitiōsus *adj* purblind.
luscus *adj* one-eyed.
lūsiō, -ōnis *f* play.
Lūsitānia, -iae *f* part of W. Spain (*including what is now Portugal*).
Lūsitānus *adj see n.*
lūsitō, -āre *vi* to play.
lūsor, -ōris *m* player; humorous writer.
lūstrālis *adj* lustral, propitiatory; quinquennial.
lūstrātiō, -ōnis *f* purification; roving.
lūstrō, -āre, -āvī, -ātum *vt* to purify; (*motion*) to go round, encircle, traverse; (*MIL*) to review; (*eyes*) to scan, survey; (*mind*) to consider; (*light*) to illuminate.
lustror, -ārī *vi* to frequent brothels.
lustrum, -ī *nt* den, lair; (*pl*) wild country; (*fig*) brothels; debauchery.
lūstrum, -ī *nt* purificatory sacrifice; (*time*) five years.
lūsus *ppp of* **lūdō.**
lūsus, -ūs *m* play, game, sport; dalliance.
lūteolus *adj* yellow.
Lutetia, -ae *f* town in N. Gaul (*now* Paris).
lūteus *adj* yellow, orange.
luteus *adj* of clay; muddy, dirty, (*fig*) vile.
lutitō, -āre *vt* to throw mud at.

lutulentus *adj* muddy, filthy; (*fig*) foul.
lūtum, -ī *nt* dyer's weed; yellow.
lutum, -ī *nt* mud, mire; clay.
lūx, lūcis *f* light; daylight; day; life; (*fig*) public view; glory, encouragement, enlightenment; **lūce** in the daytime; **prīmā lūce** at daybreak; **lūce carentēs** the dead.
lūxī *perf of* **lūceō;** *perf of* **lūgeō.**
luxor, -ārī *vi* to live riotously.
luxuria, -ae, -ēs, -ēī *f* rankness, profusion; extravagance, luxury.
luxuriō, -āre, -or, -ārī *vi* to grow to excess, be luxuriant; (*fig*) to be exuberant, run riot.
luxuriōsē *adv* voluptuously.
luxuriōsus *adj* luxuriant; excessive, extravagant; voluptuous.
luxus, -ūs *m* excess, debauchery, pomp.
Lyaeus, -ī *m* Bacchus; wine.
Lycaeus, -ī *m* mountain in Arcadia (*sacred to Pan*).
Lycāōn, -onis *m* father of Callisto, the Great Bear.
Lycāonius *adj see n.*
Lycēum (Lycīum), -ī *nt* Aristotle's school at Athens.
lychnūchus, -ī *m* lampstand.
lychnus, -ī *m* lamp.
Lycia, -ae *f* country in S.W. Asia Minor.
Lycius *adj* Lycian.
Lyctius *adj* Cretan.
Lycurgus, -ī *m* Thracian king killed by Bacchus; Spartan lawgiver; Athenian orator.
Lȳdia, -iae *f* country of Asia Minor.
Lȳdius *adj* Lydian; Etruscan.
Lȳdus, -ī *m* Lydian.
lympha, -ae *f* water.
lymphāticus *adj* crazy, frantic.
lymphātus *adj* distracted.
Lynceus, -eī *m* keen-sighted Argonaut.
lynx, lyncis *m/f* lynx.
lyra, -ae *f* lyre; lyric poetry.
lyricus *adj* of the lyre, lyrical.
Lysiās, -ae *m* Athenian orator.

M, m

Macedō, -onis *m* Macedonian.
Macedonia *f* Macedonia.
Macedonicus, -onius *adj see n.*
macellum, -ī *nt* market.
maceō, -ēre *vi* to be lean.
macer, -rī *adj* lean, meagre; poor.
māceria, -ae *f* wall.
mācerō, -āre *vt* to soften; (*body*) to enervate; (*mind*) to distress.

macēscō, -ere *vi* to grow thin.
machaera, -ae *f* sword.
machaerophorus, -ī *m* soldier armed with a sword.
Machāōn, -onis *m* legendary Greek surgeon.
Machāonius *adj see n.*
māchina, -ae *f* machine, engine; (*fig*) scheme, trick.
māchināmentum, -ī *nt* engine.
māchinātiō, -ōnis *f* mechanism, machine; (*fig*) contrivance.
māchinātor, -ōris *m* engineer; (*fig*) contriver.
māchinor, -ārī, -ātus *vt* to devise, contrive; (*fig*) to plot, scheme.
maciēs, -ēī *f* leanness, meagreness; poorness.
macilentus *adj* thin.
macrēscō, -ere *vi* to grow thin.
macritūdō, -inis *f* leanness.
macrocollum, -ī *nt* large size of paper.
mactābilis *adj* deadly.
mactātus, -ūs *m* sacrifice.
macte blessed; well done!
mactō, -āre, -āvī, -ātum *vt* to sacrifice; to punish, kill.
mactō, -āre *vt* to glorify.
macula, -ae *f* spot, stain; (*net*) mesh; (*fig*) blemish, fault.
maculō, -āre, -āvī, -ātum *vt* to stain, defile.
maculōsus *adj* dappled, mottled; stained, polluted.
madefaciō, -facere, -fēcī, -factum (*pass* **-fīō, -fierī**) *vt* to wet, soak.
madeō, -ēre *vi* to be wet, be drenched; to be boiled soft; (*comedy*) to be drunk; (*fig*) to be steeped in.
madēscō, -ere *vi* to get wet, become moist.
madidus *adj* wet, soaked; sodden; drunk.
madulsa, -ae *m* drunkard.
Maeander (-ros), -rī *m a winding river of Asia Minor*; winding, wandering.
Maecēnās, -ātis *m friend of Augustus, patron of poets.*
maena, -ae *f* sprat.
Maenala, -ōrum *ntpl mountain range in Arcadia.*
Maenalis, -ius *adj* of Maenalus; Arcadian.
Maenalus (-os), -ī *m* Maenala.
Maenas, -dis *f* Bacchante.
Maeniānum *nt* balcony.
Maenius, -ī *m Roman family name*; **~ia columna** whipping post in the Forum.
Maeonia, -ae *f* Lydia.
Maeonidēs, -dae *m* Homer.
Maeonius, -s *adj* Lydian; Homeric; Etruscan.
Maeōticus, -us *adj* Scythian, Maeotic.
Maeōtis, -dis *f* Sea of Azov.
maereō, -ēre *vi* to mourn, be sad.
maeror, -ōris *m* mourning, sorrow, sadness.
maestiter *adv see adj.*
maestitia, -ae *f* sadness, melancholy.
maestus *adj* sad, sorrowful; gloomy;

mourning.
māgālia, -um *ntpl* huts.
mage *etc see* **magis.**
magicus *adj* magical.
magis (mage) *adv* more; **eō ~** the more, all the more.
magister, -rī *m* master, chief, director; (*school*) teacher; (*fig*) instigator; **~ equitum** chief of cavalry, second in command to a dictator; **~ mōrum** censor; **~ sacrōrum** chief priest.
magisterium, -ī *and* **iī** *nt* presidency, tutorship.
magistra, -ae *f* mistress, instructress.
magistrātus, -ūs *m* magistracy, office; magistrate, official.
magnanimitās, -ātis *f* greatness.
māgnanimus *adj* great, brave.
Magnēs, -ētis *m* Magnesian; magnet.
Magnēsia *f district of Thessaly.*
Magnēsius, -essus, -ētis *adj see n.*
magnidicus *adj* boastful.
magnificē *adv* grandly; pompously.
magnificentia, -ae *f* greatness, grandeur; pomposity.
magnificō, -āre *vt* to esteem highly.
magnificus (*compar* **-entior** *superl* **-entissimus**) *adj* great, grand, splendid; pompous.
magniloquentia, -ae *f* elevated language; pomposity.
magniloquus *adj* boastful.
magnitūdō, -inis *f* greatness, size, large amount; dignity.
magnopere *adv* greatly, very much.
magnus (*compar* **māior** *superl* **māximus**) *adj* great, large, big, tall; (*voice*) loud; (*age*) advanced; (*value*) high, dear; (*fig*) grand, noble, important; **avunculus ~** great-uncle; **~a loquī** boast; **~ī aestimāre** think highly of; **~ī esse** be highly esteemed; **~ō stāre** cost dear; **~ō opere** very much.
magus, -ī *m* wise man; magician ♦ *adj* magic.
Māia, -ae *f mother of Mercury.*
māiestās, -ātis *f* greatness, dignity, majesty; treason; **~ātem laedere, minuere** offend against the sovereignty of; **lēx ~ātis** law against treason.
māior, -ōris *compar of* **magnus; ~ nātū** older, elder.
māiōrēs, -ōrum *mpl* ancestors; **in ~us crēdere/ferre** exaggerate.
Māius, -ī *m* May ♦ *adj* of May.
māiusculus *adj* somewhat greater; a little older.
māla, -ae *f* cheek, jaw.
malacia, -ae *f* dead calm.
malacus *adj* soft.
male (*compar* **pēius,** *superl* **pessimē**) *adv* badly, wrongly, unfortunately; not; (*with words having bad sense*) very much; **~ est animō** I

feel ill; ~ **sānus** insane; ~ **dīcere** abuse, curse; ~ **facere** harm.

maledicē *adv* abusively.

maledictiō, -ōnis *f* abuse.

maledictum, -ī *nt* curse.

maledicus *adj* scurrilous.

malefactum, -ī *nt* wrong.

maleficē *adv see adj.*

maleficium, -ī *and* **iī** *nt* misdeed, wrong, mischief.

maleficus *adj* wicked ♦ *m* criminal.

malesuādus *adj* seductive.

malevolēns, -entis *adj* spiteful.

malevolentia, -ae *f* ill-will.

malevolus *adj* ill-disposed, malicious.

mālifer, -ī *adj* apple-growing.

malīgnē *adv* spitefully; grudgingly.

malīgnitās, -ātis *f* malice; stinginess.

malīgnus *adj* unkind, ill-natured, spiteful; stingy; (*soil*) unfruitful; (*fig*) small, scanty.

malitia, -ae *f* badness, malice; roguishness.

malitiōsē *adv see adj.*

malitiōsus *adj* wicked, crafty.

maliv- *etc see* **malev-**.

mālle *infin of* **mālō**.

malleolus, -ī *m* hammer; (*MIL*) fire-brand.

malleus, -ī *m* hammer, mallet, maul.

mālō, -le, -uī *vt* to prefer; would rather.

malobathrum, -ī *nt* an oriental perfume.

māluī *perf of* **mālō**.

mālum, -ī *nt* apple, fruit.

malum, -ī *nt* evil, wrong, harm, misfortune; (*interj*) mischief.

mālus, -ī *f* apple tree.

mālus, -ī *m* mast, pole.

malus (*compar* **pēior** *superl* **pessimus**) *adj* bad, evil, harmful; unlucky; ugly; **ī in ~am rem** go to hell!

malva, -ae *f* mallow.

Māmers, -tis *m* Mars.

Māmertīnī, -ōrum *mpl mercenary troops who occupied Messana.*

mamma, -ae *f* breast; teat.

mammilla, -ae *f* breast.

mānābilis *adj* penetrating.

manceps, -ipis *m* purchaser; contractor.

mancipium, -ī *and* **iī** *nt* formal purchase; property; slave.

mancipō, -āre *vt* to sell, deliver up.

mancup- *etc see* **mancip-**.

mancus *adj* crippled.

mandātum, -ī *nt* commission, command; (*law*) contract.

mandātus, -ūs *m* command.

mandō, -āre, -āvī, -ātum *vt* to entrust, commit; to commission, command.

mandō, -ere, -ī, mānsum *vt* to chew, eat, devour.

mandra, -ae *f* drove of cattle.

mandūcus, -ī *m* masked figure of a glutton.

māne *nt* (*indecl*) morning ♦ *adv* in the morning, early.

maneō, -ēre, mānsī, mānsum *vi* to remain;

to stay, stop; to last, abide, continue ♦ *vt* to wait for, await; **in condiciōne** ~ abide by an agreement.

Mānēs, -ium *mpl* ghosts, shades of the dead; the lower world; bodily remains.

mangō, -ōnis *m* dealer.

manicae, -ārum *fpl* sleeves, gloves; handcuffs.

manicātus *adj* with long sleeves.

manicula, -ae *f* little hand.

manifestō, -āre *vt* to disclose.

manifestō *adv* clearly, evidently.

manifestus *adj* clear, obvious; convicted, caught.

manipl- *etc see* **manipul-**.

manipulāris *adj* of a company ♦ *m* private (in the ranks); fellow soldier.

manipulātim *adv* by companies.

manipulus, -ī *m* bundle (*esp of hay*); (*MIL*) company.

Manlius, -iānus *adj see n.*

Manlius, -ī *m* Roman family name (*esp the saviour of the Capitol from the Gauls*); a severe disciplinarian.

mannus, -ī *m* Gallic horse.

mānō, -āre, -āvī, -ātum *vi* to flow, drip, stream; (*fig*) to spread, emanate.

mānsī *perf of* **maneō**.

mānsiō, -ōnis *f* remaining, stay.

mānsitō, -āre *vi* to stay on.

mānsuēfaciō, -facere, -fēcī, -factum (*pass* **-fīō, -fierī**) *vt* to tame.

mānsuēscō, -scere, -vī, -tum *vt* to tame ♦ *vi* to grow tame, grow mild.

mānsuētē *adv see adj.*

mānsuētūdō, -inis *f* tameness; gentleness.

mānsuētus *ppp of* **mānsuēscō** ♦ *adj* tame; mild, gentle.

mānsus *ppp of* **mandō**; *ppp of* **maneō**.

mantēle, -is *nt* napkin, towel.

mantēlum, -ī *nt* cloak.

mantica, -ae *f* knapsack.

manticinor, -ārī, -ātus *vi* to be a prophet.

mantō, -āre *vi* to remain, wait.

Mantua, -ae *f* birthplace of Vergil in N. Italy.

manuālis *adj* for the hand.

manubiae, -ārum *fpl* money from sale of booty.

manūbrium, -ī *and* **iī** *nt* handle, haft.

manuleātus *adj* with long sleeves.

manūmissiō, -ōnis *f* emancipation (of a slave).

manūmittō, -ittere, -īsī, -issum *vt* to emancipate, make free.

manupretium, -ī *and* **iī** *nt* pay, wages, reward.

manus, -ūs *f* hand; corps, band, company; (*elephant*) trunk; (*art*) touch; (*work*) handiwork, handwriting; (*war*) force, valour, hand to hand fighting; (*fig*) power; ~ **extrēma** finishing touch; ~ **ferrea** grappling iron; **~um dare** give up, yield; **~ū** artificially; **~ū mittere** emancipate; **ad ~um** at hand; **in ~ū** obvious; subject; **in ~ūs venīre** come to hand; **in ~ibus** well known; at hand; **in ~ibus habēre** be engaged on; fondle; **per ~ūs** forcibly; **per ~ūs trādere** hand down.

mapālia, -um *ntpl* huts.

mappa, -ae *f* napkin, cloth.

Marathōn, -ōnis *f* Attic village famous for Persian defeat.

Marathōnius *adj see n.*

Marcellia, -iōrum *ntpl festival of the Marcelli.*

Marcellus, -ī *m* Roman surname (*esp the captor of Syracuse*).

marceō, -ēre *vi* to droop, be faint.

marcēscō, -ere *vi* to waste away, grow feeble.

Marciānus *adj see n.*

marcidus *adj* withered; enervated.

Marcius, -ī *m* Roman family name (*esp Ancus, fourth king*).

Marcius *adj see n.*

mare, -is *nt* sea; **~ nostrum** Mediterranean; **~ inferum** Tyrrhenian Sea; **~ superum** Adriatic.

Mareōticus *adj* Mareotic; Egyptian.

margarīta, -ae *f* pearl.

marginō, -āre *vt* to put a border *or* kerb on.

margō, -inis *m/f* edge, border, boundary; **~ cēnae** side dishes.

Mariānus *adj see n.*

Marīca, -ae *f* nymph of Minturnae.

marīnus *adj* of the sea.

marītālis *adj* marriage- (*in cpds*).

maritimus *adj* of the sea, maritime, coastal ♦ *ntpl* coastal area.

marītō, -āre *vt* to marry.

marītus, -i *m* husband ♦ *adj* nuptial.

Marius, -ī *m* Roman family name (*esp the victor over Jugurtha and the Teutons*).

Marius *adj see n.*

marmor, -is *nt* marble; statue, tablet; sea.

marmoreus *adj* of marble; like marble.

Marō, -ōnis *m* surname of Vergil.

marra, -ae *f* kind of hoe.

Mars, Martis *m* god of war, father of Romulus; war, conflict; planet Mars; **aequō Marte** on equal terms; **suō Marte** by one's own exertions.

Marsī, -ōrum *mpl people of central Italy, famous as fighters.*

Marsicus, -us *adj* Marsian.

marsuppium, -ī *and* **iī** *nt* purse.

Mārtiālis *adj* of Mars.

Mārticola, -ae *m* worshipper of Mars.

Mārtigena, -ae *m* son of Mars.

Mārtius *adj* of Mars; of March; warlike.

mās, maris *m* male, man ♦ *adj* male; manly.

māsculus *adj* male, masculine; manly.

Masinissa, -ae *m* king of Numidia.

massa, -ae *f* lump, mass.

Massicum, -ī *nt* Massic wine.

Massicus, -ī *m* mountain in Campania, famous for vines.

Massilia, -ae *f* Greek colony in Gaul (*now Marseilles*).

Massiliēnsis *adj see n.*

mastīgia, -ae *nt* scoundrel.

mastrūca, -ae *f* sheepskin.

mastrūcātus *adj* wearing sheepskin.

matara, -ae *and* **is, -is** *f* Celtic javelin.

matelliō, -ōnis *m* pot.

māter, -ris *f* mother; **Māgna ~** Cybele.

mātercula, -ae *f* poor mother.

māteria, -ae; -ēs, -ēī *f* matter, substance; wood, timber; (*fig*) subject matter, theme; occasion, opportunity; (*person*) ability, character.

māteriārius, -ī *and* **iī** *m* timber merchant.

māteriātus *adj* timbered.

māteriēs *etc see* **māteria.**

māterior, -ārī *vi* to fetch wood.

māternus *adj* mother's.

mātertera, -ae *f* aunt (maternal).

mathēmaticus, -ī *m* mathematician; astrologer.

mātricīda, -ae *m* matricide.

mātricīdium, -ī *and* **iī** *nt* a mother's murder.

mātrimōnium, -ī *and* **iī** *nt* marriage.

mātrimus *adj* whose mother is still alive.

mātrōna, -ae *f* married woman, matron, lady.

mātrōnālis *adj* a married woman's.

matula, -ae *f* pot.

mātūrē *adv* at the right time; early, promptly.

mātūrēscō, -ēscere, -uī *vi* to ripen.

mātūritās, -ātis *f* ripeness; (*fig*) maturity, perfection, height.

mātūrō, -āre, -āvī, -ātum *vt* to bring to maturity; to hasten, be too hasty with ♦ *vi* to make haste.

mātūrus *adj* ripe, mature; timely, seasonable; early.

Mātūta, -ae *f* goddess of dawn.

mātūtīnus *adj* morning, early.

Mauritānia, -ae *f* Mauretania (*now* Morocco).

Maurus, -ī *m* Moor ♦ *adj* Moorish, African.

Maurūsius *adj see n.*

Māvors, -tis *m* Mars.

Māvortius *adj see n.*

maxilla, -ae *f* jaw.

maximē *adv* most, very much, especially; precisely, just; certainly, yes; **cum ~** just as; **quam ~** as much as possible.

maximitās, -ātis *f* great size.

maximus *superl of* **magnus.**

māxum- *etc see* **māxim-.**

māzonomus, -ī *m* dish.

meāpte my own.

meātus, -ūs *m* movement, course.

mēcastor *interj* by Castor!

mēcum with me.

meddix tuticus *m* senior Oscan magistrate.

Mēdēa, -ae *f* Colchian wife of Jason, expert in magic.

Noun declensions and verb conjugations are shown on pp xiii to xxv. The present infinitive ending of a verb shows to which conjugation it belongs: **-āre** = 1st; **-ēre** = 2nd; **-ere** = 3rd and **-īre** = 4th. Irregular verbs are shown on p xxvi

Mēdēis *adj* magical.
medentēs, -entum *mpl* doctors.
medeor, -ērī *vi* (*with dat*) to heal, remedy.
mediastīnus, -ī *m* drudge.
mēdica, -ae *f* lucern (*kind of clover*).
medicābilis *adj* curable.
medicāmen, -inis *nt* drug, medicine;
cosmetic; (*fig*) remedy.
medicāmentum, -ī *nt* drug, medicine; potion,
poison; (*fig*) relief; embellishment.
medicātus, -ūs *m* charm.
medicīna, -ae *f* medicine; cure; (*fig*) remedy,
relief.
medicō, -āre, -āvī, -ātum *vt* to cure; to steep,
dye.
medicor, -ārī *vt*, *vi* to cure.
medicus *adj* healing ♦ *m* doctor.
medietās, -ātis *f* mean.
medimnum, -ī *nt*, **-us, -ī** *m* bushel.
mediocris *adj* middling, moderate, average.
mediocritās, -ātis *f* mean, moderation;
mediocrity.
mediocriter *adv* moderately, not particularly;
calmly.
Mediolānēnsis *adj see n.*
Mediolānum, -ī *nt* town in N. Italy (*now*
Milan).
meditāmentum, -ī *nt* preparation, drill.
meditātiō, -ōnis *f* thinking about;
preparation, practice.
meditātus *adj* studied.
mediterrāneus *adj* inland.
meditor, -ārī, -ātus *vt*, *vi* to think over,
contemplate, reflect; to practise, study.
medius *adj* middle, the middle of;
intermediate; intervening; middling,
moderate; neutral ♦ *nt* middle; public ♦ *m*
mediator; ~um complectī clasp round the
waist; ~um sē gerere be neutral; ~ō midway;
~ō temporis meanwhile; in ~um for the
common good; in ~um prōferre publish; dē
~ō tollere do away with; ē ~ō abīre die,
disappear; in ~ō esse be public; in ~ō positus
open to all; in ~ō relinquere leave undecided.
medius fidius *interj* by Heaven!
medix *etc see* **meddix.**
medulla, -ae *f* marrow, pith.
medullitus *adv* from the heart.
medullula, -ae *f* marrow.
Mēdus, -ī *m* Mede, Persian.
Mēdus *adj see n.*
Medūsa, -ae *f* Gorgon, whose look turned
everything to stone.
Medūsaeus *adj*: ~ equus Pegasus.
Megalēnsia (Megalēsia), -um *ntpl festival of
Cybele in April.*
Megara, -ae *f*, **-ōrum** *ntpl town in Greece near
the Isthmus.*
Megarēus and icus *adj* Megarean.
megistānes, -um *mpl* grandees.
mehercle, mehercule, mehercules *interj* by
Hercules!
mēiō, -ere *vi* to make water.

mel, mellis *nt* honey.
melancholicus *adj* melancholy.
melē *pl* melos.
Meleager (-ros), -rī *m* prince of Calydon.
melicus *adj* musical; lyrical.
melilōtos, -ī *f* kind of clover.
melimēla, -ōrum *ntpl* honey apples.
Mēlīnum, -ī *nt* Melian white.
melior, -ōris *adj* better.
melisphyllum, -ī *nt* balm.
Melita, -ae *f* Malta.
Melitēnsis *adj* Maltese.
melius *nt* melior ♦ *adv* better.
meliusculē *adv* fairly well.
meliusculus *adj* rather better.
mellifer, -ī *adj* honey-making.
mellītus *adj* honeyed; sweet.
melos, -ī *nt* tune, song.
Melpomenē, -ēs *f* Muse of tragedy.
membrāna, -ae *f* skin, membrane, slough;
parchment.
membrānula, -ae *f* piece of parchment.
membrātim *adv* limb by limb; piecemeal; in
short sentences.
membrum, -ī *nt* limb, member; part, division;
clause.
mēmet *emphatic form of* **mē.**
meminī, -isse *vi* (*with gen*) to remember,
think of; to mention.
Memnōn, -onis *m* Ethiopian king, killed at Troy.
Memnonius *adj see n.*
memor, -is *adj* mindful, remembering; in
memory (of).
memorābilis *adj* memorable, remarkable.
memorandus *adj* noteworthy.
memorātus, -ūs *m* mention.
memorātus *adj* famed.
memoria, -ae *f* memory, remembrance; time,
lifetime; history; **haec** ~ our day; ~ae
prōdere hand down to posterity; **post**
hominum ~am since the beginning of
history.
memoriola, -ae *f* weak memory.
memoriter *adv* from memory; accurately.
memorō, -āre, -āvī, -ātum *vt* to mention,
say, speak.
Memphis, -is and idos *f* town in middle Egypt.
Memphītēs and ītis and īticus *adj* of
Memphis; Egyptian.
Menander (-ros), -rī *m* Greek writer of comedy.
Menandrēus *adj see n.*
menda, -ae *f* fault.
mendācium, -ī and iī *nt* lie.
mendāciunculum, -ī *nt* fib.
mendāx, -ācis *adj* lying; deceptive, unreal ♦
m liar.
mendīcitās, -ātis *f* beggary.
mendīcō, -āre; -or, -ārī, *vi* to beg, go begging.
mendīcus *adj* beggarly, poor ♦ *m* beggar.
mendōsē *adv see adj.*
mendōsus *adj* faulty; wrong, mistaken.
mendum, -ī *nt* fault, blunder.
Menelāēus *adj see n.*

Menelāus, -ī m brother of Agamemnon, husband of Helen.
Menoetiadēs, -ae m Patroclus.
mēns, mentis f mind, understanding; feelings, heart; idea, plan, purpose; courage; **venit in mentem** it occurs; **mente captus** insane; **eā mente ut** with the intention of.
mēnsa, -ae f table; meal, course; counter, bank; **secunda ~** dessert.
mēnsārius, -ī and **iī** m banker.
mēnsiō, -ōnis f (metre) quantity.
mēnsis, -is m month.
mēnsor, -ōris m measurer, surveyor.
mēnstruālis adj for a month.
mēnstruus adj monthly; for a month ♦ nt a month's provisions.
mēnsula, -ae f little table.
mēnsūra, -ae f measure, measurement; standard, standing; amount, size, capacity.
mēnsus ppa of **mētior**.
menta, -ae f mint.
Menteus adj see n.
mentiēns, -ientis m fallacy.
mentiō, -ōnis f mention, hint.
mentior, -īrī, -ītus vi to lie, deceive ♦ vt to say falsely; to feign, imitate.
mentītus adj lying, false.
Mentor, -is m artist in metalwork; ornamental cup.
mentum, -ī nt chin.
meō, -āre vi to go, pass.
mephītis, -is f noxious vapour, malaria.
merācus adj pure.
mercābilis adj buyable.
mercātor, -ōris m merchant, dealer.
mercātūra, -ae f commerce; purchase; goods.
mercātus, -ūs m trade, traffic; market, fair.
mercēdula, -ae f poor wages, small rent.
mercēnārius adj hired, mercenary ♦ m servant.
mercēs, -ēdis f pay, wages, fee; bribe; rent; (fig) reward, retribution, cost.
mercimōnium, -ī and **iī** nt wares, goods.
mercor, -ārī, -ātus vt to trade in, purchase.
Mercurius, -ī m messenger of the gods, god of trade, thieves, speech and the lyre; **stēlla ~ī** planet Mercury.
Mercuriālis adj see n.
merda, -ae f dung.
merenda, -ae f lunch.
mereō, -ēre, -uī; -eor, -ērī, -itus vt, vi to deserve; to earn, win, acquire; (MIL) to serve; **bene ~ dē** do a service to, serve well; **~ equō** serve in the cavalry.
meretrīcius adj a harlot's.
meretrīcula, -ae f pretty harlot.
meretrīx, -īcis f harlot.
mergae, -ārum fpl pitchfork.
merges, -itis f sheaf.
mergō, -gere, -sī, -sum vt to dip, immerse,

sink; (fig) to bury, plunge, drown.
mergus, -ī m (bird) diver.
merīdiānus adj midday; southerly.
merīdiātiō, -ōnis f siesta.
merīdiēs, -ēī f midday, noon; south.
merīdiō, -āre, vi to take a siesta.
meritō, -āre vt to learn.
meritō adv deservedly.
meritōrius adj money-earning ♦ ntpl lodgings.
meritum, -ī nt service, kindness, merit; blame.
meritus ppp of **mereō** ♦ adj deserved, just.
merops, -is f bee-eater.
mersī perf of **mergō**.
mersō, -āre vt to immerse, plunge; to overwhelm.
mersus ppp of **mergō**.
merula, -ae f blackbird.
merum, -ī nt wine.
merus adj pure, undiluted; bare, mere.
merx, mercis f goods, wares.
Messalla, -ae m Roman surname (esp ~ Corvīnus Augustan orator, soldier and literary patron).
Messallīna, -īnae f wife of emperor Claudius; wife of Nero.
Messāna, -ae f Sicilian town (now Messina).
messis, -is f harvest.
messor, -ōris m reaper.
messōrius adj a reaper's.
messuī perf of **metō**.
messus ppp of **metō**.
mēta, -ae f pillar at each end of the Circus course; turning point, winning post; (fig) goal, end, limit.
metallum, -ī nt mine, quarry; metal.
mētātor, -ōris m surveyor.
Metaurus, -ī m river in Umbria, famous for the defeat of Hasdrubal.
Metellus, -ī m Roman surname (esp the commander against Jugurtha).
Mēthymna, -ae f town in Lesbos.
Mēthymnaeus adj see n.
mētior, -tīrī, -nsus vt to measure, measure out; to traverse; (fig) to estimate, judge.
metō, -tere, -ssuī, -ssum vt to reap, gather; to mow, cut down.
mētor, -ārī, -ātus vt to measure off, lay out.
metrēta, -ae f liquid measure (about 9 gallons).
metuculōsus adj frightful.
metuō, -uere, -uī, -ūtum vt to fear, be apprehensive.
metus, -ūs m fear, alarm, anxiety.
meus adj my, mine.
mī dat of **ego**; voc and mpl of **meus**.
mīca, -ae f crumb, grain.
micō, -āre, -uī vi to quiver, flicker, beat, flash, sparkle.
Midās, -ae m Phrygian king whose touch turned

everything to gold.
migrātiō, -ōnis f removal, change.
migrō, -āre, -āvī, -ātum vi to remove, change, pass away ♦ vt to transport, transgress.
mīles, -itis m soldier, infantryman; army troops.
Mīlēsius adj see n.
Mīlētus, -ī f town in Asia Minor.
mīlia, -um ntpl thousands; ~ **passuum** miles.
mīliārium (milliārium), -ī and **iī** nt milestone.
mīlitāris adj military, a soldier's.
mīlitāriter adv in a soldierly fashion.
mīlitia, -ae f military service, war; the army; ~**ae** on service; **domī ~aeque** at home and abroad.
mīlitō, -āre vi to serve, be a soldier.
milium, -ī and **iī** nt millet.
mīlle, (pl ~**ia**) num a thousand; ~ **passūs** a mile.
mīllensimus, -ēsimus adj thousandth.
mīllia etc see **mīlia.**
milliārium etc see **mīliārium.**
mīlliēns, -ēs adv a thousand times.
Milō, -ōnis m tribune who killed Clodius and was defended by Cicero.
Milōniānus adj see n.
Miltiadēs, -is m Athenian general, victor at Marathon.
mīluīnus adj resembling a kite; rapacious.
mīluus (mīlvus), -ī m kite; gurnard.
mīma, -ae f actress.
Mimallonis, -dis f Bacchante.
mīmicē adv see adj.
mīmicus adj farcical.
Mimnermus, -ī m Greek elegiac poet.
mīmula, -ae f actress.
mīmus, -ī m actor; mime, farce.
mina, -ae f Greek silver coin.
mināciter adv see adj.
minae, -ārum fpl threats; (wall) pinnacles.
minanter adv threateningly.
minātiō, -ōnis f threat.
mināx, -ācis adj threatening; projecting.
Minerva, -ae f goddess of wisdom and arts, esp weaving; (fig) talent, genius; working in wool; **sūs ~am** ≈ "teach your grandmother!"
miniānus adj red-leaded.
miniātulus adj painted red.
minimē adv least, very little; (reply) no, not at all.
minimus adj least, smallest, very small; youngest.
miniō, -āre, -āvī, -ātum vt to colour red.
minister, -rī m, ~**ra,** ~**rae** f attendant, servant; helper, agent, tool.
ministerium, -ī and **iī** nt service, office, duty; retinue.
ministrātor, -ōris m, ~**rīx,** ~**rīcis** f assistant, handmaid.
ministrō, -āre vt to serve, supply; to manage.
minitābundus adj threatening.
minitor, -ārī, -ō, -āre vt, vi to threaten.
minium, -ī and **iī** nt vermilion, red lead.

Mīnōis, -idis f Ariadne.
Mīnōius, -us adj see n.
minor, -ārī, -ātus vt, vi to threaten; to project.
minor, -ōris adj smaller, less, inferior; younger; (pl) descendants.
Mīnōs, -is m king of Crete, judge in the lower world.
Mīnōtaurus, -ī m monster of the Cretan labyrinth, half bull, half man.
Minturnae, -ārum fpl town in S. Latium.
Minturnēnsis adj see n.
minum- etc see **minim-.**
minuō, -uere, -uī, -ūtum vt to make smaller, lessen; to chop up; to reduce, weaken ♦ vi (tide) to ebb.
minus nt minor ♦ adv less; not, not at all; **quō ~** (prevent) from.
minusculus adj smallish.
minūtal, -ālis nt mince.
minūtātim adv bit by bit.
minūtē adv in a petty manner.
minūtus ppp of **minuō** ♦ adj small; paltry.
mīrābilis adj wonderful, extraordinary.
mīrābiliter adv see adj.
mīrābundus adj astonished.
mīrāculum, -ī nt marvel, wonder; amazement.
mīrandus adj wonderful.
mīrātiō, -ōnis f wonder.
mīrātor, -ōris m admirer.
mīrātrīx, -īcis adj admiring.
mīrē adv see adj.
mīrificē adv see adj.
mīrificus adj wonderful.
mirmillō see **murmillō.**
mīror, -ārī, -ātus vt to wonder at, be surprised at, admire ♦ vi to wonder, be surprised.
mīrus adj wonderful, strange; ~**um quam, quantum** extraordinarily.
miscellānea, -ōrum ntpl (food) hotchpotch.
misceō, -scēre, -scuī, -xtum vt to mix, mingle, blend; to join, combine; to confuse, embroil.
misellus adj poor little.
Mīsēnēnsis adj see n.
Mīsēnum, -ī nt promontory and harbour near Naples.
miser, -ī adj wretched, poor, pitiful, sorry.
miserābilis adj pitiable, sad, plaintive.
miserābiliter adv see adj.
miserandus adj deplorable.
miserātiō, -ōnis f pity, compassion, pathos.
miserē adv see adj.
misereō, -ēre, -uī, -eor, -ērī, -itus vt, vi (with gen) to pity, sympathize with; ~**et mē** I pity, I am sorry.
miserēscō, -ere vi to feel pity.
miseria, -ae f misery, trouble, distress.
misericordia, -ae f pity, sympathy, mercy.
misericors, -dis adj sympathetic, merciful.
miseriter adv sadly.
miseror, -ārī, -ātus vt to deplore; to pity.

mīsī *perf of* **mittō.**

missa, -ae *f* (*ECCL*) mass.

missilis *adj* missile.

missiō, -ōnis *f* sending; release; (*MIL*) discharge; (*gladiators*) quarter; (*events*) end; **sine ~ōne** to the death.

missitō, -āre *vt* to send repeatedly.

missus *ppp of* **mittō.**

missus, -ūs *m* sending; throwing; ~ **sagittae** bowshot.

mitella, -ae *f* turban.

mītēscō, -ere *vi* to ripen; to grow mild.

Mithridātēs, -is *m* king of Pontus, defeated by Pompey.

Mithridātēus, -icus *adj see n.*

mītigātiō, -ōnis *f* soothing.

mītigō, -āre, -āvī, -ātum *vt* to ripen, soften; to calm, pacify.

mītis *adj* ripe, mellow; soft, mild; gentle.

mitra, -ae *f* turban.

mittō, -ere, mīsī, missum *vt* to send, dispatch; to throw, hurl; to let go, dismiss; to emit, utter; (*news*) to send word; (*gift*) to bestow; (*event*) to end; (*speech*) to omit, stop; **sanguinem ~** bleed ; **ad cēnam ~** invite to dinner; **missum facere** forgo.

mītulus, -ī *m* mussel.

mixtim *adv* promiscuously.

mixtūra, -ae *f* mingling.

Mnēmosynē, -ēs *f* mother of the Muses.

mnēmosynon, -ī *nt* souvenir.

mōbilis *adj* movable; nimble, fleet; excitable, fickle.

mōbilitās, -ātis *f* agility, rapidity; fickleness.

mōbiliter *adv* rapidly.

mōbilitō, -āre *vt* to make rapid.

moderābilis *adj* moderate.

moderāmen, -inis *nt* control; government.

moderanter *adv* with control.

moderātē *adv* with restraint.

moderātim *adv* gradually.

moderātiō, -ōnis *f* control, government; moderation; rules.

moderātor, -ōris *m* controller, governor.

moderātrīx, -īcis *f* mistress, controller.

moderātus *adj* restrained, orderly.

moderor, -ārī, -ātus *vt, vi* (*with dat*) to restrain, check; (*with acc*) to manage, govern, guide.

modestē *adv* with moderation; humbly.

modestia, -ae *f* temperate behaviour, discipline; humility.

modestus *adj* sober, restrained; well-behaved, disciplined; modest, unassuming.

modiālis *adj* holding a peck.

modicē *adv* moderately; slightly.

modicus *adj* moderate; middling, small, mean.

modificātus *adj* measured.

modius, -ī *and* **iī** *m* corn measure, peck.

modo *adv* only; at all, in any way; (*with imp*) just; (*time*) just now, a moment ago, in a moment ♦ *conj* if only; **nōn ~** not only; **non ~ ... sed** not only ... but also ...; **~ nōn** all but, almost; **~ ... ~** sometimes ... sometimes; **~ ... tum** at first ... then.

modulātē *adv* melodiously.

modulātor, -ōris *m* musician.

modulātus *adj* played, measured.

modulor, -ārī, - ātus *vt* to modulate, play, sing.

modulus, -ī *m* measure.

modus, -ī *m* measure; size; metre, music; way, method; limit, end; **ēius ~ī** such; **~ō, in, ~um** like.

moecha, -ae *f* adulteress.

moechor, -ārī *vi* to commit adultery.

moechus, -ī *m* adulterer.

moenera *etc see* **mūnus.**

moenia, -um *ntpl* defences, walls; town, stronghold.

moeniō *etc see* **mūniō.**

Moesī, -ōrum *mpl* people on lower Danube (now Bulgaria).

mola, -ae *f* millstone, mill; grains of spelt.

molāris, -is *m* millstone; (*tooth*) molar.

mōlēs, -is *f* mass, bulk, pile; dam, pier, massive structure; (*fig*) greatness, weight, effort, trouble.

molestē *adv see adj.*

molestia, -ae *f* trouble, annoyance, worry; (*style*) affectation.

molestus *adj* irksome, annoying; (*style*) laboured.

mōlīmen, -inis *nt* exertion, labour; importance.

mōlīmentum, -ī *nt* great effort.

mōlior, -īrī, -ītus *vt* to labour at, work, build; to wield, move, heave; to undertake, devise, occasion ♦ *vi* to exert oneself, struggle.

mōlītiō, -ōnis *f* laborious work.

mōlītor, -ōris *m* builder.

mollēscō, -ere *vi* to soften, become effeminate.

molliculus *adj* tender.

molliō, -īre, -īvī, -ītum *vt* to soften, make supple; to mitigate, make easier; to demoralize.

mollis *adj* soft, supple; tender, gentle; (*character*) sensitive, weak, unmanly; (*poetry*) amatory; (*opinion*) changeable; (*slope*) easy.

molliter *adv* softly, gently; calmly; voluptuously.

mollitia, -ae, -ēs, -ēī *f* softness, suppleness; tenderness, weakness, effeminacy.

mollitūdō, -inis *f* softness; susceptibility.

molō, -ere *vt* to grind.

Molossī, -ōrum *mpl* Molossians, people in Epirus.

Molossicus, -us *adj see n.*

Molossis, -idis *f* country of the Molossians.

Noun declensions and verb conjugations are shown on pp xiii to xxv. The present infinitive ending of a verb shows to which conjugation it belongs: **-āre** = 1st; **-ēre** = 2nd; **-ere** = 3rd and **-īre** = 4th. Irregular verbs are shown on p xxvi

Molossus, -ī *m* Molossian hound.
mōly, -os *nt* a magic herb.
mōmen, -inis *nt* movement, momentum.
mōmentum, -ī *nt* movement; change; (*time*) short space, moment; (*fig*) cause, influence, importance; **nullīus ~ī** unimportant.
momordī *perf of* **mordeō.**
Mona, -ae *f* Isle of Man; Anglesey.
monachus, -ī *m* monk.
monēdula, -ae *f* jackdaw.
moneō, -ēre, -uī, -itum *vt* to remind, advise, warn; to instruct, foretell.
monēris, -is *f* galley with one bank of oars.
monērula *etc see* **monēdula.**
monēta, -ae *f* mint; money; stamp.
monīle, -is *nt* necklace, collar.
monim- *etc see* **monum-.**
monitiō, -ōnis *f* admonishing.
monitor, -ōris *m* admonisher; prompter; teacher.
monitum, -ī *nt* warning; prophecy.
monitus, -ūs *m* admonition; warning.
monogrammus *adj* shadowy.
monopodium, -ī *and* **iī** *nt* table with one leg.
mōns, montis *m* mountain.
mōnstrātor, -ōris *m* shower, inventor.
mōnstrātus *adj* distinguished.
mōnstrē *adv see adj.*
mōnstrō, -āre, -āvī, -ātum *vt* to point out, show; to inform, instruct; to appoint; to denounce.
mōnstrum, -ī *nt* portent, marvel; monster.
mōnstruōsus *adj* unnatural.
montānus *adj* mountainous; mountain- (*in cpds*), highland.
monticola, -ae *m* highlander.
montivagus *adj* mountain-roving.
montuōsus, montōsus *adj* mountainous.
monumentum, -ī *nt* memorial, monument; record.
Mopsopius *adj* Athenian.
mora, -ae *f* delay, pause; hindrance; space of time, sojourn; **~am facere** put off.
mora, -ae *f* division of the Spartan army.
mōrālis *adj* moral.
morātor, -ōris *m* delayer.
mōrātus *adj* mannered, of a nature; (*writing*) in character.
morbidus *adj* unwholesome.
morbus, -ī *m* illness, disease; distress.
mordāciter *adv see adj.*
mordāx, -ācis *adj* biting, sharp, pungent; (*fig*) snarling, carking.
mordeō, -dēre, momordī, -sum *vt* to bite; to bite into, grip; (*cold*) to nip; (*words*) to sting, hurt, mortify.
mordicus *adv* with a bite; (*fig*) doggedly.
mōrēs *pl of* **mōs.**
morētum, -ī *nt* salad.
moribundus *adj* dying, mortal; deadly.
mōrigeror, -ārī, -ātus *vi* (*with dat*) to gratify, humour.
mōrigerus *adj* obliging, obedient.

morior, -ī, -tuus *vi* to die; to decay, fade.
moritūrus *fut p of* **morior.**
mōrologus *adj* foolish.
moror, -ārī, -ātus *vi* to delay, stay, loiter ♦ *vt* to detain, retard; to entertain; (*with neg*) to heed, object; **nihil, nīl ~** have no objection to; to not care for; to withdraw a charge against.
mōrōsē *adv see adj.*
mōrōsitās, -ātis *f* peevishness.
mōrōsus *adj* peevish, difficult.
Morpheus, -eos *m* god of dreams.
mors, mortis *f* death; corpse; **mortem sibi cōnscīscere** commit suicide; **mortis poena** capital punishment.
morsiuncula, -ae *f* little kiss.
morsus *ppp of* **mordeō** ♦ *ntpl* little bits.
morsus, -ūs *m* bite; grip; (*fig*) sting, vexation.
mortālis *adj* mortal; transient; man-made ♦ *m* human being.
mortālitās, -ātis *f* mortality, death.
mortārium, -ī *and* **iī** *nt* mortar.
mortifer, -ī *adj* fatal.
mortuus *ppa of* **morior** ♦ *adj* dead ♦ *m* dead man.
mōrum, -ī *nt* blackberry, mulberry.
mōrus, -ī *f* black mulberry tree.
mōrus *adj* foolish ♦ *m* fool.
mōs, mōris *m* nature, manner; humour, mood; custom, practice, law; (*pl*) behaviour, character, morals; **~ māiōrum** national tradition; **mōrem gerere** oblige, humour; **mōre, in mōrem** like.
Mosa, -ae *m* river Meuse.
Mōsēs, -is *m* Moses.
mōtiō, -ōnis *f* motion.
mōtō, -āre *vt* to keep moving.
mōtus *ppp of* **moveō.**
mōtus, -ūs *m* movement; dance, gesture; (*mind*) impulse, emotion; (*POL*) rising, rebellion; **terrae ~** earthquake.
movēns, -entis *pres p of* **moveō** ♦ *adj* movable ♦ *ntpl* motives.
moveō, -ēre, mōvī, mōtum *vt* to move, set in motion; to disturb; to change; to dislodge, expel; to occasion, begin; (*opinion*) to shake; (*mind*) to affect, influence, provoke ♦ *vi* to move; **castra ~** strike camp; **sē ~** budge; to dance.
mox *adv* presently, soon, later on; next.
Mōysēs *see* **Mōsēs.**
mūcidus *adj* snivelling; mouldy.
Mūcius, -ī *m* Roman family name (*esp Scaevola, who burned his right hand before Porsena*).
mūcrō, -ōnis *m* point, edge; sword.
mūcus, -ī *m* mucus.
mūgilis, -is *m* mullet.
muginor, -ārī *vi* to hesitate.
mūgiō, -īre *vi* to bellow, groan.
mūgītus, -ūs *m* lowing, roaring.
mūla, -ae *f* she-mule.
mulceō, -cēre, -sī, -sum *vt* to stroke, caress;

to soothe, alleviate, delight.

Mulciber, -is *and* **ī** *m* Vulcan.

mulcō, -āre, -āvī, -ātum *vt* to beat, ill-treat, damage.

mulctra, -ae *f*, **-ārium, -ārī,** *and* **āriī, -um, -ī** *nt* milkpail.

mulgeō, -ēre, mulsī *vt* to milk.

muliebris *adj* woman's, feminine; effeminate.

muliebriter *adv* like a woman; effeminately.

mulier, -is *f* woman; wife.

mulierārius *adj* woman's.

muliercula, -ae *f* girl.

mulierōsitās, -ātis *f* fondness for women.

mulierōsus *adj* fond of women.

mūlīnus *adj* mulish.

mūliō, -ōnis *m* mule driver.

mūliōnius *adj* mule driver's.

mullus, -ī *m* red mullet.

mulsī *perf of* **mulceō;** *perf of* **mulgeō.**

mulsus *ppp of* **mulceō.**

mulsus *adj* honeyed, sweet ♦ *nt* honey-wine, mead.

multa, -ae *f* penalty, fine; loss.

multangulus *adj* many-angled.

multāticius *adj* fine- (*in cpds*).

multātiō, -ōnis *f* fining.

multēsimus *adj* very small.

multicavus *adj* many-holed.

multicia, -ōrum *ntpl* transparent garments.

multifāriam *adv* in many places.

multifidus *adj* divided into many parts.

multiformis *adj* of many forms.

multiforus *adj* many-holed.

multigeneris, -us *adj* of many kinds.

multiiugis, -us *adj* yoked together; complex.

multiloquium, -ī *and* **iī** *nt* talkativeness.

multiloquus *adj* talkative.

multimodīs *adv* variously.

multiplex, -icis *adj* with many folds, tortuous; many-sided, manifold, various; (*comparison*) far greater; (*character*) fickle, sly.

multiplicō, -āre, -āvī, -ātum *vt* to multiply, enlarge.

multipotēns, -entis *adj* very powerful.

multitūdō, -inis *f* great number, multitude, crowd.

multivolus *adj* longing for much.

multō *adv* much, far, by far; (*time*) long.

multō, -āre, -āvī, -ātum *vt* to punish, fine.

multum *adv* much, very, frequently.

multus (*compar* **plūs** *superl* **plūrimus**) *adj* much, many; (*speech*) lengthy, tedious; (*time*) late; **~ā nocte** late at night; **nē ~a ≈** *to cut a long story short.*

mūlus, -ī *m* mule.

Mulvius *adj* Mulvian (*a Tiber bridge above Rome*).

mundānus, -ī *m* world citizen.

munditia, -ae, -ēs, -ēī *f* cleanness; neatness; elegance.

mundus *adj* clean, neat, elegant; **in ~ō esse** be in readiness.

mundus, -ī *m* toilet gear; universe, world, heavens; mankind.

mūnerigerulus, -ī *m* bringer of presents.

mūnerō, -āre, -or, -ārī *vt* to present, reward.

mūnia, -ōrum *ntpl* official duties.

mūniceps, -ipis *m/f* citizen (*of a municipium*), fellow-citizen.

mūnicipālis *adj* provincial.

mūnicipium, -ī *and* **iī** *nt* provincial town, burgh.

mūnificē *adv see adj.*

mūnificentia, -ae *f* liberality.

mūnificō, -āre *vt* to treat generously.

mūnificus *adj* liberal.

mūnīmen, -inis *nt* defence.

mūnīmentum, -ī *nt* defencework, protection.

mūniō, -īre, -iī, -ītum *vt* to fortify, secure, strengthen; (*road*) to build; (*fig*) to protect.

mūnis *adj* ready to oblige.

mūnītiō, -ōnis *f* building; fortification; (*river*) bridging.

mūnītō, -āre *vt* (*road*) to open up.

mūnītor, -ōris *m* sapper, builder.

mūnus, -eris *nt* service, duty; gift; public show; entertainment; tax; (*funeral*) tribute; (*book*) work.

mūnusculum, -ī *nt* small present.

mūraena, -ae *f* a fish.

mūrālis *adj* wall- (*in cpds*), mural, for fighting from *or* attacking walls.

mūrex, -icis *m* purple-fish; purple dye, purple; jagged rock.

muria, -ae *f* brine.

murmillō, -ōnis *m* kind of gladiator.

murmur, -is *nt* murmur, hum, rumbling, roaring.

murmurillum, -ī *nt* low murmur.

murmurō, -āre *vi* to murmur, rumble; to grumble.

murra, -ae *f* myrrh.

murreus *adj* perfumed; made of the stone called murra.

murrina, -ae *f* myrrh wine.

murrina, -ōrum *ntpl* murrine vases.

murt- *etc see* **myrt-.**

mūrus, -ī *m* wall; dam; defence.

mūs, mūris *m/f* mouse, rat.

Mūsa, -ae *f* goddess inspiring an art; poem; (*pl*) studies.

mūsaeus *adj* poetic, musical.

musca, -ae *f* fly.

mūscipula, -ae *f*, **-um, -ī** *nt* mousetrap.

mūscōsus *adj* mossy.

mūsculus, -ī *m* mouse; muscle; (MIL) shed.

mūscus, -ī *m* moss.

mūsicē *adv* very pleasantly.

mūsicus *adj* of music, of poetry ♦ *m* musician ♦ *f* music, culture ♦ *ntpl* music.

Noun declensions and verb conjugations are shown on pp xiii to xxv. The present infinitive ending of a verb shows to which conjugation it belongs: **-āre** = 1st; **-ēre** = 2nd; **-ere** = 3rd and **-īre** = 4th. Irregular verbs are shown on p xxvi

mussitō, -āre *vi* to say nothing; to mutter ♦ *vt* to bear in silence.
mussō, -āre *vt, vi* to say nothing, brood over; to mutter, murmur.
mustāceum, -ī *nt*, **-us, -ī** *m* wedding cake.
mūstēla, -ae *f* weasel.
mustum, -ī *nt* unfermented wine, must; vintage.
mūtābilis *adj* changeable, fickle.
mūtābilitās, -ātis *f* fickleness.
mūtātiō, -ōnis *f* change, alteration; exchange.
mutilō, -āre, -āvī, -ātum *vt* to cut off, maim; to diminish.
mutilus *adj* maimed.
Mutina, -ae *f* town in N. Italy (now Modena).
Mutinēnsis *adj see n.*
mūtiō *etc see* **muttiō.**
mūtō, -āre, -āvī, -ātum *vt* to shift; to change, alter; to exchange, barter ♦ *vi* to change; **~āta verba** figurative language.
muttiō, -īre *vi* to mutter, mumble.
mūtuātiō, -ōnis *f* borrowing.
mūtuē *adv* mutually, in turns.
mūtuitō, -āre *vt* to try to borrow.
mūtuō *adv* = **mūtuē.**
mūtuor, -ārī, -ātus *vt* to borrow.
mūtus *adj* dumb, mute; silent, still.
mūtuum, -ī *nt* loan.
mūtuus *adj* borrowed, lent; mutual, reciprocal; **~um dare** lend; **~um sūmere** borrow; **~um facere** return like for like.
Mycēnae, -ārum *fpl* Agamemnon's capital in S. Greece.
Mycēnaeus, -ēnsis *adj*, **-is, -idis** *f* Iphigenia.
Mygdonius *adj* Phrygian.
myoparō, -ōnis *m* pirate galley.
myrīca, -ae *f* tamarisk.
Myrmidones, -um *mpl* followers of Achilles.
Myrōn, -ōnis *m* famous Greek sculptor.
myropōla, -ae *m* perfumer.
myropōlium, -ī *and* **iī** *nt* perfumer's shop.
myrothēcium, -ī *and* **iī** *nt* perfume-box.
myrrh- *etc see* **murr-.**
myrtētum, -ī *nt* myrtlegrove.
myrteus *adj* myrtle- (*in cpds*).
Myrtoum mare Sea N.W. of Crete.
myrtum, -ī *nt* myrtle-berry.
myrtus, -ī *and* **ūs** *f* myrtle.
Mȳsia, -iae *f* country of Asia Minor.
Mȳsius, -us *adj see n.*
mysta, -ae *m* priest of mysteries.
mystagōgus, -ī *m* initiator.
mystērium, -ī *and* **iī** *nt* secret religion, mystery; secret.
mysticus *adj* mystic.
Mytilēnae, -ārum *fpl*; **-ē, -es** *f* capital of Lesbos.
Mytilēnaeus *adj see n.*
Mytilēnēnsis *adj see n.*

N, n

nablium, -ī *and* **iī** *nt* kind of harp.
nactus *ppa of* **nancīscor.**
nae *etc see* **nē.**
naenia *etc see* **nēnia.**
Naeviānus *adj see n.*
Naevius, -ī *m* early Latin poet.
naevus, -ī *m* mole (on the body).
Nāias, -adis *and* **s, -dis** *f* water nymph, Naiad.
Nāicus *adj see n.*
nam *conj* (*explaining*) for; (*illustrating*) for example; (*transitional*) now; (*interrog*) but; (*enclitic*) an emphatic particle.
namque *conj* for, for indeed, for example.
nancīscor, -i, nactus *and* **nanctus** *vt* to obtain, get; to come upon, find.
nānus, -ī *m* dwarf.
Napaeae, -ārum *fpl* dell nymphs.
nāpus, -ī *m* turnip.
Narbō, -ōnis *m* town in S. Gaul.
Narbōnēnsis *adj see n.*
narcissus, -ī *m* narcissus.
nardus, -ī *f*, **-um, -ī** *nt* nard, nard oil.
nāris, -is *f* nostril; (*pl*) nose; (*fig*) sagacity, scorn.
nārrābilis *adj* to be told.
nārrātiō, -ōnis *f* narrative.
nārrātor, -ōris *m* storyteller, historian.
nārrātus, -ūs *m* narrative.
nārrō, -āre, -āvī, -ātum *vt* to tell, relate, say; **male ~** bring bad news.
narthēcium, -ī *and* **iī** *nt* medicine chest.
nāscor, -scī, -tus *vi* to be born; to originate, grow, be produced.
Nāsō, -ōnis *m* surname of Ovid.
nassa, -ae *f* wicker basket for catching fish; (*fig*) snare.
nasturtium, -ī *and* **iī** *nt* cress.
nāsus, -ī *m* nose.
nāsūtē *adv* sarcastically.
nāsūtus *adj* big-nosed; satirical.
nāta, -ae *f* daughter.
nātālicius *adj* of one's birthday, natal ♦ *f* birthday party.
nātālis *adj* of birth, natal ♦ *m* birthday ♦ *mpl* birth, origin.
nātātiō, -ōnis *f* swimming.
natātor, -ōris *m* swimmer.
nātiō, -ōnis *f* tribe, race; breed, class.
natis, -is *f* (*usu pl*) buttocks.
nātīvus *adj* created; inborn, native, natural.
natō, -āre *vi* to swim, float; to flow, overflow; (*eyes*) to swim, fail; (*fig*) to waver.
nātrīx, -īcis *f* watersnake.
nātū *abl m* by birth, in age; **grandis ~, māgnō ~** quite old; **māior ~** older; **māximus ~** oldest.

nātūra, -ae *f* birth; nature, quality, character; natural order of things; the physical world; (*physics*) element; **rērum ~** Nature.

nātūrālis *adj* by birth; by nature, natural.

nātūrāliter *adv* by nature.

nātus *ppa of* **nāscor ♦** *m* son ♦ *adj* born, made (for); old, of age; **prō, ē rē nātā** under the circumstances, as things are; **annōs vīgintī ~ 20** years old.

nauarchus, -ī *m* captain.

naucī: nōn esse, facere, habēre to be worthless, consider worthless.

nauclēricus *adj* skipper's.

nauclērus, -ī *m* skipper.

naufragium, -ī *and* **iī** *nt* shipwreck, wreck; **~ facere** be shipwrecked.

naufragus *adj* shipwrecked, wrecked; (*sea*) dangerous to shipping ♦ *m* shipwrecked man; (*fig*) ruined man.

naulum, -ī *nt* fare.

naumachia, -ae *f* mock sea fight.

nausea, -ae *f* seasickness.

nauseō, -āre *vi* to be sick; (*fig*) to disgust.

nauseola, -ae *f* squeamishness.

nauta, (nāvita), -ae *m* sailor, mariner.

nauticus *adj* nautical, sailors' ♦ *mpl* seamen.

nāvālis *adj* naval, of ships ♦ *nt and ntpl* dockyard; rigging.

nāvicula, -ae *f* boat.

nāviculāria, -ae *f* shipping business.

nāviculārius, -i *and* **iī** *m* ship-owner.

nāvifragus *adj* dangerous.

nāvigābilis *adj* navigable.

nāvigātiō, -ōnis *f* voyage.

nāviger, -ī *adj* ship-carrying.

nāvigium, -ī *and* **iī** *nt* vessel, ship.

nāvigō, -āre, -āvī, -ātum *vi* to sail, put to sea ♦ *vt* to sail across, navigate.

nāvis, -is *f* ship; **~ longa** warship; **~ mercātōria** merchantman; **~ onerāria** transport; **~ praetōria** flagship; **~em dēdūcere** launch; **~em solvere** set sail; **~em statuere** heave to; **~em subdūcere** beach; **~ibus atque quadrīgīs** with might and main.

nāvita *etc see* **nauta.**

nāvitās, -ātis *f* energy.

nāviter *adv* energetically; absolutely.

nāvō, -āre *vt* to perform energetically; **operam ~** be energetic; to come to the assistance (of).

nāvus *adj* energetic.

Naxos, -ī *f* Aegean island (*famous for wines and the story of Ariadne*).

nē *interj* truly, indeed.

nē *adv* not ♦ *conj* that not, lest; (*fear*) that; (*purpose*) so that ... not, to avoid, to prevent.

-ne *enclitic* (*introducing a question*).

Neāpolis, -is *f* Naples.

Neāpolītānus *adj see n.*

nebula, -ae *f* mist, vapour, cloud.

nebulō, -ōnis *m* idler, good-for-nothing.

nebulōsus *adj* misty, cloudy.

nec *etc see* **neque.**

necdum *adv* and not yet.

necessāriē, -ō *adv* of necessity, unavoidably.

necessārius *adj* necessary, inevitable; indispensable; (*kin*) related ♦ *m/f* relative ♦ *ntpl* necessities.

necesse *adj* (*indecl*) necessary, inevitable; needful.

necessitās, -ātis *f* necessity, compulsion; requirement, want; relationship, connection.

necessitūdō, -inis *f* necessity, need, want; connection; friendship (*pl*) relatives.

necessum *etc see* **necesse.**

necne *adv* or not.

necnōn *adv* also, besides.

necō, -āre, -āvī, -ātum *vt* to kill, murder.

necopīnāns, -antis *adj* unaware.

necopīnātō *adv see adj.*

necopīnātus *adj* unexpected.

necopīnus *adj* unexpected; unsuspecting.

nectar, -is *nt* nectar (*the drink of the gods*).

nectareus *adj* of nectar.

nectō, -ctere, -xī *and* **xuī, -xum** *vt* to tie, fasten, connect; to weave; (*fig*) to bind, enslave (*esp for debt*); to contrive, frame.

nēcubi *conj* so that nowhere.

nēcunde *conj* so that from nowhere.

nēdum *adv* much less, much more.

nefandus *adj* abominable, impious.

nefāriē *adv see adj.*

nefārius *adj* heinous, criminal.

nefās *nt* (*indecl*) wickedness, sin, wrong ♦ *interj* horror!, shame!

nefāstus *adj* wicked; unlucky; (*days*) closed to public business.

negātiō, -ōnis *f* denial.

negitō, -āre *vt* to deny, refuse.

neglēctiō, -ōnis *f* neglect.

neglēctus *ppp of* **neglegō.**

neglēctus, -ūs *m* neglecting.

neglegēns, -entis *pres p of* **neglegō ♦** *adj* careless, indifferent.

neglegenter *adv* carelessly.

neglegentia, -ae *f* carelessness, neglect, coldness.

neglegō, -egere, -ēxī, -ēctum *vt* to neglect, not care for; to slight, disregard; to overlook.

negō, -āre, -āvī, -ātum *vt, vi* to say no; to say not, deny; to refuse, decline.

negōtiālis *adj* business- (*in cpds*).

negōtiāns, -antis *m* businessman.

negōtiātiō, -ōnis *f* banking business.

negōtiātor, -ōris *m* businessman, banker.

negōtiolum, -ī *nt* trivial matter.

negōtior, -ārī, -ātus *vi* to do business, trade.

negōtiōsus *adj* busy.

Noun declensions and verb conjugations are shown on pp xiii to xxv. The present infinitive ending of a verb shows to which conjugation it belongs: -āre = 1st; -ēre = 2nd; -ere = 3rd and -īre = 4th. Irregular verbs are shown on p xxvi

negōtium, -ī _and_ **iī** _nt_ business, work; trouble; matter, thing; **quid est ~i?** what is the matter?
Nēlēius _adj see n._
Nēleus, -eī _m_ father of Nestor.
Nēlēus _adj see n._
Nemea, -ae _f_ town in S. Greece, where Hercules killed the lion.
Nemea, -ōrum _ntpl_ Nemean Games.
Nemeaeus _adj_ Nemean.
nēmō, -inis _m/f_ no one, nobody ♦ _adj_ no; **~ nōn** everybody; **nōn ~** many; **~ ūnus** not a soul.
nemorālis _adj_ sylvan.
nemorēnsis _adj_ of the grove.
nemoricultrīx, -īcis _f_ forest dweller.
nemorivagus _adj_ forest-roving.
nemorōsus _adj_ well-wooded; leafy.
nempe _adv_ (confirming) surely, of course, certainly; (in questions) do you mean?
nemus, -oris _nt_ wood, grove.
nēnia, -ae _f_ dirge; incantation; song, nursery rhyme.
neō, nēre, nēvī, nētum _vt_ to spin; to weave.
Neoptolemus, -ī _m_ Pyrrhus (son of Achilles).
nepa, -ae _f_ scorpion.
nepōs, -ōtis _m_ grandson; descendant; spendthrift.
nepōtīnus, -ī _m_ little grandson.
neptis, -is _f_ granddaughter.
Neptūnius _adj:_ **~ hērōs** Theseus.
Neptūnus, -ī _m_ Neptune (god of the sea); sea.
nēquam _adj_ (indecl) worthless, bad.
nēquāquam _adv_ not at all, by no means.
neque, nec _adv_ not ♦ _conj_ and not, but not; neither, nor; **~ ... et** not only not ... but also.
nequeō, -īre, -īvī, -ītum _vi_ to be unable, cannot.
nēquīquam _adv_ fruitlessly, for nothing; without good reason.
nēquior, nēquissimus _compar, superl of_ **nēquam.**
nēquiter _adv_ worthlessly, wrongly.
nēquitia, -ae, -ēs _f_ worthlessness, badness.
Nērēis, -eidis _f_ Nereid, sea nymph.
Nērēius _adj see n._
Nēreus, -eī _m_ a sea god; the sea.
Nēritius _adj_ of Neritos; Ithacan.
Nēritos, -ī _m_ island near Ithaca.
Nerō, -ōnis _m_ Roman surname (esp the emperor).
Nerōniānus _adj see n._
nervōsē _adv_ vigorously.
nervōsus _adj_ sinewy, vigorous.
nervulī, -ōrum _mpl_ energy.
nervus, -ī _m_ sinew; string; fetter, prison; (shield) leather; (pl) strength, vigour, energy.
nesciō, -īre, -īvī _and_ **iī, -ītum** _vt_ to not know, be ignorant of; to be unable; **~ quis, quid** somebody, something; **~ an** probably.
nescius _adj_ ignorant, unaware; unable; unknown.
Nestor, -oris _m_ Greek leader at Troy (famous

for his great age and wisdom).
neu _etc see_ **nēve.**
neuter, -rī _adj_ neither; neuter.
neutiquam _adv_ by no means, certainly not.
neutrō _adv_ neither way.
nēve, neu _conj_ and not; neither, nor.
nēvī _perf of_ **neō.**
nex, necis _f_ murder, death.
nexilis _adj_ tied together.
nexum, -ī _nt_ personal enslavement.
nexus _ppp of_ **nectō.**
nexus, -ūs _m_ entwining, grip; (law) bond, obligation, (esp enslavement for debt).
nī _adv_ not ♦ _conj_ if not, unless; that not; **quid nī?** why not?
nīcētērium, -ī _and_ **iī** _nt_ prize.
nictō, -āre _vi_ to wink.
nīdāmentum, -ī _nt_ nest.
nīdor, -ōris _m_ steam, smell.
nīdulus, -ī _m_ little nest.
nīdus, -ī _m_ nest; (pl) nestlings; (fig) home.
niger, -rī _adj_ black, dark; dismal, ill-omened; (character) bad.
nigrāns, -antis _adj_ black, dusky.
nigrēscō, -ere _vi_ to blacken, grow dark.
nigrō, -āre _vi_ to be black.
nigror, -ōris _m_ blackness.
nihil, nīl _nt_ (indecl) nothing ♦ _adv_ not; **~ ad nōs** it has nothing to do with us; **~ est** it's no use; **~ est quod** there is no reason why; **~ nisi** nothing but, only; **~ nōn** everything; **nōn ~** something.
nihilum, -ī _nt_ nothing; **~ī esse** be worthless; **~ō minus** none the less.
nīl, nīlum _see_ **nihil, nihilum.**
Nīliacus _adj_ of the Nile; Egyptian.
Nīlus, -ī _m_ Nile; conduit.
nimbifer, -ī _adj_ stormy.
nimbōsus _adj_ stormy.
nimbus, -ī _m_ cloud, rain, storm.
nimiō _adv_ much, far.
nimīrum _adv_ certainly, of course.
nimis _adv_ too much, very much; **nōn ~** not very.
nimium _adv_ too, too much; very, very much.
nimius _adj_ too great, excessive; very great ♦ _nt_ excess.
ningit, ninguit, -ere _vi_ it snows.
ninguēs, -ium _fpl_ snow.
Nioba, -ae, -ē, -ēs _f_ daughter of Tantalus (changed to a weeping rock).
Niobēus _adj see n._
Nīreus, -eī _and_ **eos** _m_ handsomest of the Greeks at Troy.
Nīsaeus, -eius _adj see n._
Nīsēis, -edis _f_ Scylla.
nisi _conj_ if not, unless; except, but.
nīsus _ppa of_ **nītor.**
nīsus, -ūs _m_ pressure, effort; striving, soaring.
Nīsus, -ī _m_ father of Scylla.
nītēdula, -ae _f_ dormouse.
nitēns, -entis _pres p of_ **niteō** ♦ _adj_ bright;

brilliant, beautiful.

niteō, -ēre *vi* to shine, gleam; to be sleek, be greasy; to thrive, look beautiful.

nitēscō, -ere, nituī *vi* to brighten, shine, glow.

nitidiusculē *adv* rather more finely.

nitidiusculus *adj* a little shinier.

nitidē *adv* magnificently.

nitidus *adj* bright, shining; sleek; blooming; smart, spruce; (*speech*) refined.

nitor, -ōris *m* brightness, sheen; sleekness, beauty; neatness, elegance.

nītor, -tī, -sus and **xus** *vi* to rest on, lean on; to press, stand firmly; to press forward, climb; to exert oneself, strive, labour; to depend on.

nitrum, -ī *nt* soda.

nivālis *adj* snowy.

niveus *adj* of snow, snowy, snow-white.

nivōsus *adj* snowy.

nix, nivis *f* snow.

nīxor, -ārī *vi* to rest on; to struggle.

nīxus *ppp of* **nītor.**

nīxus, -ūs *m* pressure; labour.

nō, nāre, nāvī *vi* to swim, float; to sail, fly.

nōbilis *adj* known, noted, famous, notorious; noble, high-born; excellent.

nōbilitās, -ātis *f* fame; noble birth; the nobility; excellence.

nōbilitō, -āre, -āvī, -ātum *vt* to make famous *or* notorious.

nocēns, -entis *pres p of* **noceō ♦** *adj* harmful; criminal, guilty.

noceō, -ēre, -uī, -itum *vi* (*with dat*) to harm, hurt.

nocīvus *adj* injurious.

noctifer, -ī *m* evening star.

noctilūca, -ae *f* moon.

noctivagus *adj* night-wandering.

noctū *adv* by night.

noctua, -ae *f* owl.

noctuābundus *adj* travelling by night.

nocturnus *adj* night- (*in cpds*), nocturnal.

nōdō, -āre, -āvī, -ātum *vt* to knot, tie.

nōdōsus *adj* knotty.

nōdus, -ī *m* knot; knob; girdle; (*fig*) bond, difficulty.

nōlō, -le, -uī *vt, vi* to not wish, be unwilling, refuse; ~ī, ~īte do not.

Nomas, -dis *m/f* nomad; Numidian.

nōmen, -inis *nt* name; title; (*COMM*) demand, debt; (*GRAM*) noun; (*fig*) reputation, fame; account, pretext; ~ **dare profitērī** enlist; ~ **dēferre** accuse; ~**ina facere** enter the items of a debt.

nōmenclātor, -ōris *m slave who told his master the names of people.*

nōminātim *adv* by name, one by one.

nōminātiō, -ōnis *f* nomination.

nōminitō, -āre *vt* to usually name.

nōminō, -āre, -āvī, -ātum *vt* to name, call; to mention; to make famous; to nominate; to accuse, denounce.

nomisma, -tis *nt* coin.

nōn *adv* not; no.

Nōnae, -ārum *fpl* Nones (*7th day of March, May, July, October, 5th of other months*).

nōnāgēsimus *adj* ninetieth.

nōnāgiēns, -ēs *adv* ninety times.

nōnāgintā *num* ninety.

nōnānus *adj* of the ninth legion.

nōndum *adv* not yet.

nōngentī, -ōrum *num* nine hundred.

nonna, -ae *f* nun.

nōnne *adv* do not?, is not? *etc.*; (*indirect*) whether not.

nōnnullus *adj* some.

nōnnunquam *adv* sometimes.

nōnus *adj* ninth ♦ *f* ninth hour.

nōnusdecimus *adj* nineteenth.

Nōricum, -ī *nt country between the Danube and the Alps.*

Nōricus *adj see n.*

nōrma, -ae *f* rule.

nōs *pron* we, us; I, me.

nōscitō, -āre *vt* to know, recognise; to observe, examine.

nōscō, -scere, -vī, -tum *vt* to get to know, learn; to examine; to recognise, allow; (*perf*) to know.

nōsmet *pron* (*emphatic*) *see* **nōs.**

noster, -rī *adj* our, ours; for us; my; (*with names*) my dear, good old ♦ *m* our friend ♦ *mpl* our side, our troops; ~**rī, ~rum** of us.

nostrās, -ātis *adj* of our country, native.

nota, -ae *f* mark, sign, note; (*writing*) note, letter; (*pl*) memoranda, shorthand, secret writing; (*books*) critical mark, punctuation; (*wine, etc*) brand, quality; (*gesture*) sign; (*fig*) sign, token; (*censor's*) black mark; (*fig*) stigma, disgrace.

notābilis *adj* remarkable; notorious.

notābiliter *adv* perceptibly.

notārius, -ī and **iī** *m* shorthand writer; secretary.

notātiō, -ōnis *f* marking; choice; observation; (*censor*) stigmatizing; (*words*) etymology.

nōtēscō, -ere, notuī *vi* to become known.

nothus *adj* bastard; counterfeit.

nōtiō, -ōnis *f* (*law*) cognisance, investigation; (*PHILOS*) idea.

nōtitia, -ae, -ēs, -ēī *f* fame; acquaintance; (*PHILOS*) idea, preconception.

notō, -āre, -āvī, -ātum *vt* to mark, write; to denote; to observe; to brand, stigmatize.

nōtuī *perf of* **nōtēscō.**

nōtus *ppp of* **nōscō ♦** *adj* known, familiar; notorious ♦ *mpl* acquaintances.

Notus (-os), -ī *m* south wind.

novācula, -ae *f* razor.

Noun declensions and verb conjugations are shown on pp xiii to xxv. The present infinitive ending of a verb shows to which conjugation it belongs: **-āre** = 1st; **-ēre** = 2nd; **-ere** = 3rd and **-īre** = 4th. Irregular verbs are shown on p xxvi

novālis, -is *f*, **-e, -is** *nt* fallow land; field; crops.

novātrīx, -īcis *f* renewer.

novē *adv* unusually.

novellus *adj* young, fresh, new.

novem *num* nine.

November, -ris *adj* of November ♦ *m* November.

novendecim *num* nineteen.

novendiālis *adj* nine days'; on the ninth day.

novēnī, -ōrum *adj* in nines; nine.

Novēnsilēs, -ium *mpl* new gods.

noverca, -ae *f* stepmother.

novercālis *adj* stepmother's.

nōvī *perf of* **nōscō.**

novīcius *adj* new.

noviēns, -ēs *adv* nine times.

novissimē *adv* lately; last of all.

novissimus *adj* latest, last, rear.

novitās, -ātis *f* newness, novelty; strangeness.

novō, -āre, -āvī, -ātum *vt* to renew, refresh; to change; (*words*) to coin; **rēs ~** effect a revolution.

novus *adj* new, young, fresh, recent; strange, unusual; inexperienced; **~ homō** upstart, first of his family to hold curule office; **~ae rēs** revolution; **~ae tabulae** cancellation of debts; **quid ~ī** what news?

nox, noctis *f* night; darkness, obscurity; **nocte, noctū** by night; **dē nocte** during the night.

noxa, -ae *f* hurt, harm; offence, guilt; punishment.

noxia, -ae *f* harm, damage; guilt, fault.

noxius *adj* harmful; guilty.

nūbēcula, -ae *f* cloudy look.

nūbēs, -is *f* cloud; (*fig*) gloom; veil.

nūbifer, -ī *adj* cloud-capped; cloudy.

nūbigena, -ae *m* cloudborn, Centaur.

nūbilis *adj* marriageable.

nūbilus *adj* cloudy; gloomy, sad ♦ *ntpl* clouds.

nūbō, -bere, -psī, -ptum *vi* (*women*) to be married.

nucleus, -ī *m* nut, kernel.

nūdius day since, days ago; **~ tertius** the day before yesterday.

nūdō, -āre, -āvī, -ātum *vt* to bare, strip, expose; (*MIL*) to leave exposed; to plunder; (*fig*) to disclose, betray.

nūdus *adj* naked, bare; exposed, defenceless; wearing only a tunic; (*fig*) destitute, poor; mere; unembellished, undisguised; **vestīmenta dētrahere ~ō** ≈ *draw blood from a stone.*

nūgae, -ārum *fpl* nonsense, trifles; (*person*) waster.

nūgātor, -ōris *m* silly creature, liar.

nūgātōrius *adj* futile.

nūgāx, -ācis *adj* frivolous.

nūgor, -ārī, -ātus *vi* to talk nonsense; to cheat.

nullus, -īus (*dat* **-ī**) *adj* no, none; not, not at all; non-existent, of no account ♦ *m/f* nobody.

num *interrog particle* surely not? (*indirect*) whether, if.

Numa, -ae *m* second king of Rome.

nūmen, -inis *nt* nod, will; divine will, power; divinity, god.

numerābilis *adj* easy to count.

numerātus *adj* in cash ♦ *nt* ready money.

numerō, -āre, -āvī, -ātum *vt* to count, number; (*money*) to pay out; (*fig*) to reckon, consider as.

numerō *adv* just now, quickly, too soon.

numerōsē *adv* rhythmically.

numerōsus *adj* populous; rhythmical.

numerus, -ī *m* number; many, numbers; (*MIL*) troop; (*fig*) a cipher; (*pl*) mathematics; rank, category, regard; rhythm, metre, verse; **in ~ō esse, habērī** be reckoned as; **nullō ~ō** of no account.

Numida *adj see n.*

Numidae, -ārum *mpl* Numidians (*people of N. Africa*).

Numidia, -iae *f* the country of the Numidians.

Numidicus *adj see n.*

Numitor, -ōris *m* king of Alba (*grandfather of Romulus*).

nummārius *adj* money- (*in cpds*), financial; mercenary.

nummātus *adj* moneyed.

nummulī, -ōrum *mpl* some money, cash.

nummus, -ī *m* coin, money, cash; (*Roman coin*) sestertius; (*Greek coin*) two-drachma piece.

numnam, numne *see* **num.**

numquam *adv* never; **~ nōn** always; **nōn ~** sometimes.

numquid (*question*) do you? does he? *etc*; (*indirect*) whether.

nunc *adv* now; at present, nowadays; but as it is; **~ ... ~** at one time ... at another.

nuncupātiō, -ōnis *f* pronouncing.

nuncupō, -āre, -āvī, -ātum *vt* to call, name; to pronounce formally.

nūndinae, -ārum *fpl* market day; market; trade.

nūndinātiō, -ōnis *f* trading.

nūndinor, -ārī *vi* to trade, traffic; to flock together ♦ *vt* to buy.

nūndinum, -ī *nt* market time; **trīnum ~** 17 days.

nunq- *etc see* **numq-.**

nūntiātiō, -ōnis *f* announcing.

nūntiō, -āre, -āvī, -ātum *vt* to announce, report, tell.

nūntius *adj* informative, speaking ♦ *m* messenger; message, news; injunction; notice of divorce ♦ *nt* message.

nūper *adv* recently, lately.

nūpsī *perf of* **nūbō.**

nūpta, -ae *f* bride, wife.

nūptiae, -ārum *fpl* wedding, marriage.

nūptiālis *adj* wedding- (*in cpds*), nuptial.

nurus, -ūs *f* daughter-in-law; young woman.

nūsquam *adv* nowhere; in nothing, for nothing.

nūtō, -āre *vi* to nod; to sway, totter, falter.
nūtrīcius, -ī *m* tutor.
nūtrīcō, -āre, -or, -ārī *vt* to nourish, sustain.
nūtrīcula, -ae *f* nurse.
nūtrīmen, -inis *nt* nourishment.
nūtrīmentum, -ī *nt* nourishment, support.
nūtriō, -īre, -īvī, -ītum *vt* to suckle, nourish, rear, nurse.
nūtrīx, -īcis *f* nurse, foster mother.
nūtus, -ūs *m* nod; will, command; (*physics*) gravity.
nux, nucis *f* nut; nut tree, almond tree.
Nyctēis, -idis *f* Antiopa.
nympha, -ae, -ē, -ēs *f* bride; nymph; water.
Nysa, -ae *f* birthplace of Bacchus.
Nysaeus, -ēis, -ius *adj see n.*

O, o

ō *interj* (*expressing joy, surprise, pain, etc*) oh!; (*with voc*) O!
ob *prep* (*with acc*) in front of; for, on account of, for the sake of; **quam ~ rem** accordingly.
obaerātus *adj* in debt ♦ *m* debtor.
obambulō, -āre *vi* to walk past, prowl about.
obarmō, -āre *vt* to arm (against).
obarō, -āre *vt* to plough up.
obc- *etc see* **occ-**.
obdō, -ere, -idī, -itum *vt* to shut; to expose.
obdormīscō, -īscere, -īvī *vi* to fall asleep ♦ *vt* to sleep off.
obdūcō, -ūcere, -ūxī, -uctum *vt* to draw over, cover; to bring up; (*drink*) to swallow; (*time*) to pass.
obductō, -āre *vt* to bring as a rival.
obductus *ppp of* **obdūcō**.
obdūrēscō, -ēscere, -uī *vi* to harden; to become obdurate.
obdūrō, -āre *vi* to persist, stand firm.
obduticō, -ōnis *f* veiling.
obeō, -īre, -īvī, and iī, -itum *vi* to go to, meet; to die; (*ASTRO*) to set ♦ *vt* to visit, travel over; to survey, go over; to envelop; (*duty*) to engage in, perform; (*time*) to meet; **diem ~** die; (*law*) to appear on the appointed day.
obequitō, -āre *vi* to ride up to.
oberrō, -āre *vi* to ramble about; to make a mistake.
obēsus *adj* fat, plump; coarse.
ōbex, -icis *m/f* bolt, bar, barrier.
obf- *etc see* **off-**.
obg- *etc see* **ogg-**.

obhaerēscō, -rēscere, -sī *vi* to stick fast.
obiaceō, -ēre *vi* to lie over against.
obiciō, -icere, -iēcī, -iectum *vt* to throw to, set before; (*defence*) to put up, throw against; (*fig*) to expose, give up; (*speech*) to taunt, reproach.
obiectātiō, -ōnis *f* reproach.
obiectō, -āre *vt* to throw against; to expose, sacrifice; to reproach; (*hint*) to let on.
obiectus *ppp of* **obiciō** ♦ *adj* opposite, in front of; exposed ♦ *ntpl* accusations.
obiectus, -ūs *m* putting in the way, interposing.
obīrātus *adj* angered.
obiter *adv* on the way; incidentally.
obitus *ppp of* **obeō**.
obitus, -ūs *m* death, ruin; (*ASTRO*) setting; visit.
obiūrgātiō, -ōnis *f* reprimand.
obiūrgātor, -ōris *m* reprover.
obiūrgātōrius *adj* reproachful.
obiūrgitō, -āre *vt* to keep on reproaching.
obiūrgō, -āre, -āvī, -ātum *vt* to scold, rebuke; to deter by reproof.
oblanguēscō, -ēscere, -uī *vi* to become feeble.
oblātrātrīx, -īcis *f* nagging woman.
oblātus *ppp of* **offerō**.
oblectāmentum, -ī *nt* amusement.
oblectātiō, -ōnis *f* delight.
oblectō, -āre, -āvī, -ātum *vt* to delight, amuse, entertain; to detain; (*time*) to spend pleasantly; **sē ~** enjoy oneself.
oblīdō, -dere, -sī, -sum *vt* to crush, strangle.
obligātiō, -ōnis *f* pledge.
obligō, -āre, -āvī, -ātum *vt* to tie up, bandage; to put under an obligation, embarrass; (*law*) to render liable, make guilty; to mortgage.
oblīmō, -āre *vt* to cover with mud.
oblinō, -inere, -ēvī, -itum *vt* to smear over; to defile; (*fig*) to overload.
oblīquē *adv* sideways; indirectly.
oblīquō, -āre *vt* to turn aside, veer.
oblīquus *adj* slanting, downhill; from the side, sideways; (*look*) askance, envious; (*speech*) indirect.
oblīsus *ppp of* **oblīdō**.
oblitēscō, -ere *vi* to hide away.
oblitterō, -āre, -āvī, -ātum *vt* to erase, cancel; (*fig*) to consign to oblivion.
oblitus *ppp of* **oblinō**.
oblītus *ppa of* **oblīvīscor**.
oblīviō, -ōnis *f* oblivion, forgetfulness.
oblīviōsus *adj* forgetful.
oblīvīscor, -vīscī, -tus *vt, vi* to forget.
oblīvium, -ī and iī *nt* forgetfulness, oblivion.
oblocūtor, -ōris *m* contradicter.
oblongus *adj* oblong.
oblogquor, -quī, -cūtus *vi* to contradict, interrupt; to abuse; (*music*) to accompany.

Noun declensions and verb conjugations are shown on pp xiii to xxv. The present infinitive ending of a verb shows to which conjugation it belongs: **-āre** = 1st; **-ēre** = 2nd; **-ere** = 3rd and **-īre** = 4th. Irregular verbs are shown on p xxvi

obluctor, -ārī *vi* to struggle against.
obmōlior, -īrī *vt* to throw up (*as a defence*).
obmurmurō, -āre *vi* to roar in answer.
obmūtēscō, -ēscere, -uī *vi* to become silent; to cease.
obnātus *adj* growing on.
obnītor, -tī, -xus *vi* to push against, struggle; to stand firm, resist.
obnīxē *adv* resolutely.
obnīxus *ppa of* **obnītor** ♦ *adj* steadfast.
obnoxiē *adv* slavishly.
obnoxiōsus *adj* submissive.
obnoxius *adj* liable, addicted; culpable; submissive, slavish; under obligation, indebted; exposed (to danger).
obnūbō, -bere, -psī, -ptum *vt* to veil, cover.
obnūntiātiō, -ōnis *f* announcement of an adverse omen.
obnūntiō, -āre *vt* to announce an adverse omen.
oboediēns, -entis *pres p of* **oboediō** ♦ *adj* obedient.
oboedienter *adv* readily.
oboedientia, -ae *f* obedience.
oboediō, -īre *vi* to listen; to obey, be subject to.
oboleō, -ēre, -uī *vt* to smell of.
oborior, -īrī, -tus *vi* to arise, spring up.
obp- *etc see* **opp-**.
obrēpō, -ere, -sī, -tum *vt, vi* to creep up to, steal upon, surprise; to cheat.
obrētiō, -īre *vt* to entangle.
obrigēscō, -ēscere, -uī *vi* to stiffen.
obrogō, -āre, -āvī, -ātum *vt* to invalidate (*by making a new law*).
obruō, -ere, -ī, -tum *vt* to cover over, bury, sink; to overwhelm, overpower ♦ *vi* to fall to ruin.
obrussa, -ae *f* test, touchstone.
obrutus *ppp of* **obruō**.
obsaepiō, -īre, -sī, -tum *vt* to block, close.
obsaturō, -āre *vt* to sate, glut.
obscaen- *etc see* **obscen-**.
obscēnē *adv* indecently.
obscēnitās, -ātis *f* indecency.
obscēnus *adj* filthy; indecent; ominous.
obscūrātiō, -ōnis *f* darkening, disappearance.
obscūrē *adv* secretly.
obscūritās, -ātis *f* darkness; (*fig*) uncertainty; (*rank*) lowliness.
obscūrō, -āre, -āvī, -ātum *vt* to darken; to conceal, suppress; (*speech*) to obscure; (*pass*) to become obsolete.
obscūrus *adj* dark, shady, hidden; (*fig*) obscure, indistinct; unknown, ignoble; (*character*) reserved.
obsecrātiō, -ōnis *f* entreaty; public prayer.
obsecrō, -āre *vt* to implore, appeal to.
obsecundō, -āre *vi* to comply with, back up.
obsēdī *perf of* **obsideō**.
obsēp- *etc see* **obsaep-**.
obsequēns, -entis *pres p of* **obsequor** ♦ *adj*

compliant; (*gods*) gracious.
obsequenter *adv* compliantly.
obsequentia, -ae *f* complaisance.
obsequiōsus *adj* complaisant.
obsequium, -ī *and* **iī** *nt* compliance, indulgence; obedience, allegiance.
obsequor, -quī, -cūtus *vi* to comply with, yield to, indulge.
obserō, -āre *vt* to bar, close.
obserō, -erere, -ēvī, -itum *vt* to sow, plant; to cover thickly.
observāns, -antis *pres p of* **observō** ♦ *adj* attentive, respectful.
observantia, -ae *f* respect.
observātiō, -ōnis *f* watching; caution.
observitō, -āre *vt* to observe carefully.
observō, -āre, -āvī, -ātum *vt* to watch, watch for; to guard; (*laws*) to keep, comply with; (*person*) to pay respect to.
obses, -idis *m/f* hostage; guarantee.
obsessiō, -ōnis *f* blockade.
obsessor, -ōris *m* frequenter; besieger.
obsessus *ppp of* **obsideō**.
obsideō, -idēre, -ēdī, -essum *vt* to sit at, frequent; (*MIL*) to blockade, besiege; to block, fill, take up; to guard, watch for ♦ *vi* to sit.
obsidiō, -ōnis *f* siege, blockade; (*fig*) imminent danger.
obsidium, -ī *and* **iī** *nt* siege, blockade; hostageship.
obsīdō, -ere *vt* to besiege, occupy.
obsignātor, -ōris *m* sealer; witness.
obsignō, -āre, -āvī, -ātum *vt* to seal up; to sign and seal; (*fig*) to stamp.
obsistō, -istere, -titī, -titum *vi* to put oneself in the way, resist.
obsitus *ppp of* **obserō**.
obsolefīō, -fierī *vi* to wear out, become degraded.
obsolēscō, -scere, -vī, -tum *vi* to wear out, become out of date.
obsolētius *adv* more shabbily.
obsolētus *ppa of* **obsolēscō** ♦ *adj* worn out, shabby; obsolete; (*fig*) ordinary, mean.
obsōnātor, -ōris *m* caterer.
obsōnātus, -ūs *m* marketing.
obsōnium, -ī *and* **iī** *nt* food eaten with bread, (*usu fish*).
obsōnō, -āre, -or, -ārī *vi* to cater, buy provisions; to provide a meal.
obsonō, -āre *vi* to interrupt.
obsorbeō, -ēre *vt* to swallow, bolt.
obstantia, -ium *ntpl* obstructions.
obstetrīx, -īcis *f* midwife.
obstinātiō, -ōnis *f* determination, stubbornness.
obstinātē *adv* firmly, obstinately.
obstinātus *adj* firm, resolute; stubborn.
obstinō, -āre *vi* to be determined, persist.
obstipēscō *etc see* **obstupēscō**.
obstīpus *adj* bent, bowed, drawn back.
obstitī *perf of* **obstō**.
obstō, -āre, -itī *vi* to stand in the way; to

obstruct, prevent.

obstrepō, -ere, -uī, -itum *vi* to make a noise; to shout against, cry down, molest ♦ *vt* to drown (in noise); to fill with noise.

obstrictus *ppp of* **obstringō.**

obstringō, -ingere, -īnxī, -ictum *vt* to bind up, tie round; (*fig*) to confine, hamper; to lay under an obligation.

obstructiō, -ōnis *f* barrier.

obstructus *ppp of* **obstruō.**

obstrūdō (obtrūdō), -dere, -sī, -sum *vt* to force on to; to gulp down.

obstruō, -ere, -xī, -ctum *vt* to build up against, block; to shut, hinder.

obstupefaciō, -facere, -fēcī, -factum (*pass* **-fīō, -fierī**) *vt* to astound, paralyse.

obstupēscō, -ēscere, -uī *vi* to be astounded, paralysed.

obstupidus *adj* stupefied.

obsum, -esse, -fuī *vi* to be against, harm.

obsuō, -uere, -uī, -ūtum *vt* to sew on, sew up.

obsurdēscō, -ēscere, -uī *vi* to grow deaf; to turn a deaf ear.

obsūtus *ppp of* **obsuō.**

obtegō, -egere, -ēxī, -ēctum *vt* to cover over; to conceal.

obtemperātiō, -ōnis *f* obedience.

obtemperō, -āre, -āvī, -ātum *vi* (*with dat*) to comply with, obey.

obtendō, -dere, -dī, -tum *vt* to spread over, stretch over against; to conceal; to make a pretext of.

obtentus *ppp of* **obtendō**; *ppp of* **obtineō.**

obtentus, -ūs *m* screen; pretext.

obterō, -erere, -rīvī, -rītum *vt* to trample on, crush; to disparage.

obtestātiō, -ōnis *f* adjuring; supplication.

obtestor, -ārī, -ātus *vt* to call to witness; to entreat.

obtexō, -ere, -uī *vt* to overspread.

obticeō, -ēre *vi* to be silent.

obticēscō, -ēscere, -uī *vi* to be struck dumb.

obtigī *perf of* **obtingō.**

obtigō *see* **obtegō.**

obtineō, -inēre, -inuī, -entum *vt* to hold, possess; to maintain; to gain, obtain ♦ *vi* to prevail, continue.

obtingō, -ngere, -gī *vi* to fall to one's lot; to happen.

obtorpēscō, -ēscere, -uī *vi* to become numb, lose feeling.

obtorqueō, -quēre, -sī, -tum *vt* to twist about, wrench.

obtrectātiō, -ōnis *f* disparagement.

obtrectātor, -ōris *m* disparager.

obtrectō, -āre *vt, vi* to detract, disparage.

obtrītus *ppp of* **obterō.**

obtrūdō *etc see* **obstrūdō.**

obtruncō, -āre *vt* to cut down, slaughter.

obtueor, -ērī, -or, -ī *vt* to gaze at, see clearly.

obtulī *perf of* **offerō.**

obtundō, -undere, -udī, -ūsum *and* **-ūnsum** *vt* to beat, thump; to blunt; (*speech*) to deafen, annoy.

obturbō, -āre *vt* to throw into confusion; to bother, distract.

obturgēscō, -ere *vi* to swell up.

obtūrō, -āre *vt* to stop up, close.

obtūsus, obtūnsus *ppp of* **obtundō** ♦ *adj* blunt; (*fig*) dulled, blurred, unfeeling.

obtūtus, -ūs *m* gaze.

obumbrō, -āre *vt* to shade, darken; (*fig*) to cloak, screen.

obuncus *adj* hooked.

obūstus *adj* burnt, hardened in fire.

obvallātus *adj* fortified.

obveniō, -enīre, -ēnī, -entum *vi* to come up; to fall to; to occur.

obversor, -ārī *vi* to move about before; (*visions*) to hover.

obversus *ppp of* **obvertō** ♦ *adj* turned towards ♦ *mpl* enemy.

obvertō, -tere, -tī, -sum *vt* to direct towards, turn against.

obviam *adv* to meet, against; ~ **ire** to go to meet.

obvius *adj* in the way, to meet; opposite, against; at hand, accessible; exposed.

obvolvō, -vere, -vī, -ūtum *vt* to wrap up, muffle up; (*fig*) to cloak.

occaecō, -āre, -āvī, -ātum *vt* to blind, obscure, conceal; to benumb.

occallēscō, -ēscere, -uī *vi* to grow a thick skin; to become hardened.

occanō, -ere *vi* to sound the attack.

occāsiō, -ōnis *f* opportunity, convenient time; (*MIL*) surprise.

occāsiuncula, -ae *f* opportunity.

occāsus, -ūs *m* setting; west; downfall, ruin.

occātiō, -ōnis *f* harrowing.

occātor, -ōris *m* harrower.

occēdō, -ere *vi* to go up to.

occentō, -āre *vt, vi* to serenade; to sing a lampoon.

occēpī *perf of* **occipiō.**

occepsō *archaic fut of* **occipiō.**

occeptō, -āre *vt* to begin.

occidēns, -entis *pres p of* **occidō** ♦ *m* west.

occīdiō, -ōnis *f* massacre; ~**ōne occīdere** annihilate.

occīdō, -dere, -dī, -sum *vt* to fell; to cut down, kill; to pester.

occidō, -idere, -idī, -āsum *vi* to fall; to set; to die, perish, be ruined.

occiduus *adj* setting; western; failing.

occinō, -ere, -uī *vi* to sing inauspiciously.

occipiō, -ipere, -ēpī, -eptum *vt, vi* to begin.

occipitium, -ī *and* **iī** *nt* back of the head.

occīsiō, -ōnis *f* massacre.

occīsor, -ōris *m* killer.

Noun declensions and verb conjugations are shown on pp xiii to xxv. The present infinitive ending of a verb shows to which conjugation it belongs: **-āre** = 1st; **-ēre** = 2nd; **-ere** = 3rd and **-īre** = 4th. Irregular verbs are shown on p xxvi

occīsus *ppp of* **occīdō.**
occlāmitō, -āre *vi* to bawl.
occlūdō, -dere, -sī, -sum *vt* to shut up; to stop.
occō, -āre *vt* to harrow.
occubō, -āre *vi* to lie.
occulcō, -āre *vt* to trample down.
occulō, -ere, -uī, -tum *vt* to cover over, hide.
occultātiō, -ōnis *f* concealment.
occultātor, -ōris *m* hider.
occultē *adv* secretly.
occultō, -āre, -āvī, -ātum *vt* to conceal, secrete.
occultus *ppp of* **occulō** ♦ *adj* hidden, secret; (*person*) reserved, secretive ♦ *nt* secret, hiding.
occumbō, -mbere, -buī, -bitum *vi* to fall, die.
occupātiō, -ōnis *f* taking possession; business; engagement.
occupātus *adj* occupied, busy.
occupō, -āre, -āvī, -ātum *vt* to take possession of, seize; to occupy, take up; to surprise, anticipate; (*money*) to lend, invest.
occurrō, -rere, -rī, -sum *vi* to run up to, meet; to attack; to fall in with; to hurry to; (*fig*) to obviate, counteract; (*words*) to object; (*thought*) to occur, suggest itself.
occursātiō, -ōnis *f* fussy welcome.
occursō, -āre *vi* to run to meet, meet; to oppose; (*thought*) to occur.
occursus, -ūs *m* meeting.
Ōceanītis, -ītidis *f* daughter of Ocean.
Ōceanus, -ī *m* Ocean, a stream encircling the earth; the Atlantic.
ocellus, -ī *m* eye; darling, gem.
ōcior, -ōris *adj* quicker, swifter.
ōcius *adv* more quickly; sooner, rather; quickly.
ocrea, -ae *f* greave.
ocreātus *adj* greaved.
Octāviānus *adj* of Octavius ♦ *m* Octavian (*a surname of Augustus*).
Octāvius, -ī *m* Roman family name (*esp the emperor Augustus; his father*).
octāvum *adv* for the eighth time.
octāvus *adj* eighth ♦ *f* eighth hour.
octāvusdecimus *adj* eighteenth.
octiēns, -ēs *adv* eight times.
octingentēsimus *adj* eight hundredth.
octingentī, -ōrum *num* eight hundred.
octipēs, -edis *adj* eight-footed.
octō *num* eight.
Octōber, -ris *adj* of October ♦ *m* October.
octōgēnī, -ōrum *adj* eighty each.
octōgēsimus *adj* eightieth.
octōgiēns, -ēs *adv* eighty times.
octōgintā *num* eighty.
octōiugis *adj* eight together.
octōnī, -ōrum *adj* eight at a time, eight each.
octōphoros *adj* (*litter*) carried by eight bearers.
octuplicātus *adj* multiplied by eight.

octuplus *adj* eightfold.
octussis, -is *m* eight asses.
oculātus *adj* with eyes; visible; **~ā diē vēndere** sell for cash.
oculus, -ī *m* eye; sight; (*plant*) bud; (*fig*) darling, jewel; **~ōs adicere ad** glance at, covet; **ante ~ōs pōnere** imagine; **ex ~īs** out of sight; **esse in ~īs** be in view; be a favourite.
ōdī, -isse *vt* to hate, dislike.
odiōsē *adv see adj.*
odiōsus *adj* odious, unpleasant.
odium, -ī *and* **iī** *nt* hatred, dislike, displeasure; insolence; **~iō esse** be hateful, be disliked.
odor (-ōs), -ōris *m* smell, perfume, stench; (*fig*) inkling, suggestion.
odōrātiō, -ōnis *f* smelling.
odōrātus *adj* fragrant, perfumed.
odōrātus, -ūs *m* sense of smell; smelling.
odōrifer, -ī *adj* fragrant; perfume-producing.
odōrō, -āre *vt* to perfume.
odōror, -ārī, -ātus *vt* to smell, smell out; (*fig*) to search out; to aspire to; to get a smattering of.
odōrus *adj* fragrant; keen-scented.
odōs *etc see* **odor.**
Odrysius *adj* Thracian.
Odyssēa, -ae *f* Odyssey.
Oeagrius *adj* Thracian.
Oebalia, -iae *f* Tarentum.
Oebalidēs, -idae *m* Castor, Pollux.
Oebalis, -idis *f* Helen.
Oebalius *adj* Spartan.
Oebalus, -ī *m* king of Sparta.
Oedipūs, -odis *and* **ī** *m* king of Thebes; solver of riddles.
oenophorum, -ī *nt* wine basket.
Oenopia, -ae *f* Aegina.
Oenotria, -ae *f* S.E. Italy.
Oenotrius *adj* Italian.
oestrus, -ī *m* gadfly; (*fig*) frenzy.
Oeta, -ae, -ē, -ēs *f* mountain range in Thessaly, associated with Hercules.
Oetaeus *adj see n.*
ofella, -ae *f* morsel.
offa, -ae *f* pellet, lump; swelling.
offectus *ppp of* **officiō.**
offendō, -endere, -endī, -ēnsum *vt* to hit; to hit on, come upon; to offend, blunder; to take offence; to fail, come to grief.
offēnsa, -ae *f* displeasure, enmity; offence, injury.
offēnsiō, -ōnis *f* stumbling; stumbling block; misfortune, indisposition; offence, displeasure.
offēnsiuncula, -ae *f* slight displeasure; slight check.
offēnsō, -āre *vt, vi* to dash against.
offēnsus *ppp of* **offendō** ♦ *adj* offensive; displeased ♦ *nt* offence.
offēnsus, -ūs *m* shock; offence.
offerō, -re, obtulī, oblātum *vt* to present, show; to bring forward, offer; to expose; to cause, inflict; **sē ~** encounter.

offerumenta, -ae *f* present.
officīna, -ae *f* workshop factory.
officiō, -icere, -ēcī, -ectum *vt* to obstruct; to interfere with; to hurt, prejudice.
officiōsē *adv* courteously.
officiōsus *adj* obliging; dutiful.
officium, -ī *and* **iī** *nt* service, attention; ceremonial; duty, sense of duty; official duty, function.
offīgō, -ere *vt* to fasten, drive in.
offirmātus *adj* determined.
offirmō, -āre *vt, vi* to persevere in.
offlectō, -ere *vt* to turn about.
offrēnātus *adj* checked.
offūcia, -ae *f* (*cosmetic*) paint; (*fig*) trick.
offulgeō, -gēre, -sī *vi* to shine on.
offundō, -undere, -ūdī, -ūsum *vt* to pour out to; to pour over; to spread; to cover, fill.
offūsus *ppp of* **offundō**.
ogganniō, -īre *vi* to growl at.
oggerō, -ere *vt* to bring, give.
Ōgygius *adj* Theban.
oh *interj* (*expressing surprise, joy, grief*) oh!
ohē *interj* (*expressing surfeit*) stop!, enough!
oi *interj* (*expressing complaint, weeping*) oh!, oh dear!
oiei *interj* (*lamenting*) oh dear!
Oīleus, -eī *m* father of the less famous Ajax.
olea, -ae *f* olive; olive tree.
oleāginus *adj* of the olive tree.
oleārius *adj* oil- (*in cpds*) ♦ *m* oil seller.
oleaster, -rī *m* wild olive.
olēns, -entis *pres p of* **oleō** ♦ *adj* fragrant; stinking, musty.
oleō, -ēre, -uī *vt, vi* to smell, smell of; (*fig*) to betray.
oleum, -ī *nt* olive oil, oil; wrestling school; **~ et operam perdere** waste time and trouble.
olfaciō, -facere, -fēcī, -factum *vt* to smell, scent.
olfactō, -āre *vt* to smell at.
olidus *adj* smelling, rank.
ōlim *adv* once, once upon a time; at the time, at times; for a good while; one day (*in the future*).
olit- *etc see* **holit-**.
olīva, -ae *f* olive, olive tree; olive branch, olive staff.
olīvētum, -ī *nt* olive grove.
olīvifer, -ī *adj* olive-bearing.
olīvum, -ī *nt* oil; wrestling school; perfume.
olla, -ae *f* pot, jar.
olle, ollus *etc see* **ille**.
olor, -ōris *m* swan.
olōrīnus *adj* swan's.
olus *etc see* **holus**.
Olympia, -ae *f* site of the Greek games in Elis.
Olympia, -ōrum *ntpl* Olympic Games.
Olympiacus *adj* = **Olympicus**.
Olympias, -adis *f* Olympiad, period of four

years.
Olympicus, -us *adj* Olympic.
Olympionīcēs, -ae *m* Olympic winner.
Olympus, -ī *m* mountain in N. Greece, abode of the gods; heaven.
omāsum, -ī *nt* tripe; paunch.
ōmen, -inis *nt* omen, sign; solemnity.
ōmentum, -ī *nt* bowels.
ōminor, -ārī, -ātus *vt* to forebode, prophesy.
ōmissus *ppp of* **ōmittō** ♦ *adj* remiss.
ōmittō, -ittere, -īsī, -issum *vt* to let go; to leave off, give up; to disregard, overlook; (*speech*) to pass over, omit.
omnifer, -ī *adj* all-sustaining.
omnigenus *adj* of all kinds.
omnimodīs *adv* wholly.
omnīnō *adv* entirely, altogether, at all; in general; (*concession*) to be sure, yes; (*number*) in all, just; **~ nōn** not at all.
omniparēns, -entis *adj* mother of all.
omnipotēns, -entis *adj* almighty.
omnis *adj* all, every, any; every kind of; the whole of ♦ *nt* the universe ♦ *mpl* everybody ♦ *ntpl* everything.
omnituēns, -entis *adj* all-seeing.
omnivagus *adj* roving everywhere.
omnivolus *adj* willing everything.
onager, -rī *m* wild ass.
onerārius *adj* (*beast*) of burden; (*ship*) transport.
onerō, -āre, -āvī, -ātum *vt* to load, burden; (*fig*) to overload, oppress; to aggravate.
onerōsus *adj* heavy, burdensome, irksome.
onus, -eris *nt* load, burden, cargo; (*fig*) charge, difficulty.
onustus *adj* loaded, burdened; (*fig*) filled.
onyx, -chis *m/f* onyx; onyx box.
opācitās, -ātis *f* shade.
opācō, -āre *vt* to shade.
opācus *adj* shady; dark.
ope *abl of* **ops**.
opella, -ae *f* light work, small service.
opera, -ae *f* exertion, work; service; care, attention; leisure, time; (*person*) workman, hired rough; **~am dare** pay attention; do one's best; **~ae pretium** worth while; **~ā meā** thanks to me.
operārius *adj* working ♦ *m* workman.
operculum, -ī *nt* cover, lid.
operīmentum, -ī *nt* covering.
operiō, -īre, -uī, -tum *vt* to cover; to close; (*fig*) to overwhelm, conceal.
operor, -ārī, -ātus *vi* to work, take pains, be occupied.
operōsē *adv* painstakingly.
operōsus *adj* active, industrious; laborious, elaborate.
opertus *ppp of* **operiō** ♦ *adj* covered, hidden ♦ *nt* secret.
opēs *pl of* **ops**.

Noun declensions and verb conjugations are shown on pp xiii to xxv. The present infinitive ending of a verb shows to which conjugation it belongs: **-āre** = 1st; **-ēre** = 2nd; **-ere** = 3rd and **-īre** = 4th. Irregular verbs are shown on p xxvi

opicus *adj* barbarous, boorish.
opifer, -ī *adj* helping.
opifex, -icis *m/f* maker; craftsman, artisan.
ōpiliō, -ōnis *m* shepherd.
opīmitās, -ātis *f* abundance.
opīmus *adj* rich, fruitful, fat; copious, sumptuous; (*style*) overloaded; **spolia ~a** spoils of an enemy commander killed by a Roman general.
opīnābilis *adj* conjectural.
opīnātiō, -ōnis *f* conjecture.
opīnātor, -ōris *m* conjecturer.
opīnātus, -ūs *m* supposition.
opīniō, -ōnis *f* opinion, conjecture, belief; reputation, esteem; rumour; **contrā, praeter ~ōnem** contrary to expectation.
opīniōsus *adj* dogmatic.
opīnor, -ārī, -ātus *vi* to think, suppose, imagine ♦ *adj* imagined.
opiparē *adv see adj.*
opiparus *adj* rich, sumptuous.
opitulor, -ārī, -ātus *vi* (*with dat*) to help.
oportet, -ēre, -uit *vt* (*impers*) ought, should.
oppēdō, -ere *vi* to insult.
opperior, -īrī, -tus *vt, vi* to wait, wait for.
oppetō, -ere, -īvī, -ītum *vt* to encounter; to die.
oppidānus *adj* provincial ♦ *mpl* townsfolk.
oppidō *adv* quite, completely, exactly.
oppidulum, -ī *nt* small town.
oppidum, -ī *nt* town.
oppignerō, -āre *vt* to pledge.
oppilō, -āre *vt* to stop up.
oppleō, -ēre, -ēvī, -ētum *vt* to fill, choke up.
oppōnō, -ōnere, -osuī, -ositum *vt* to put against, set before; to expose; to present; (*argument*) to adduce, reply, oppose; (*property*) to pledge, mortgage.
opportūnitās, -ātis *f* suitableness, advantage; good opportunity.
opportūnē *adv* opportunely.
opportūnus *adj* suitable, opportune; useful; exposed.
oppositiō, -ōnis *f* opposing.
oppositus *ppp of* **oppōnō** ♦ *adj* against, opposite.
oppositus, -ūs *m* opposing.
oppsuī *perf of* **oppōnō**.
oppressiō, -ōnis *f* violence; seizure; overthrow.
oppressus *ppp of* **opprimō**.
oppressus, -ūs *m* pressure.
opprimō, -imere, -essī, -essum *vt* to press down, crush; to press together, close; to suppress, overwhelm, overthrow; to surprise, seize.
opprobrium, -ī *and* **iī** *nt* reproach, disgrace, scandal.
opprobrō, -āre *vt* to taunt.
oppugnātiō, -ōnis *f* attack, assault.
oppugnātor, -ōris *m* assailant.
oppugnō, -āre, -āvī, -ātum *vt* to attack, assault.

ops, -opis *f* power, strength; help.
Ops goddess of plenty.
ops- *etc see* **obs-**.
optābilis *adj* desirable.
optātiō, -ōnis *f* wish.
optātus *adj* longed for ♦ *nt* wish; **~ātō** according to one's wish.
optimās, -ātis *adj* aristocratic ♦ *mpl* the nobility.
optimē *adv* best, very well; just in time.
optimus *adj* best, very good; excellent; **~ō iūre** deservedly.
optiō, -ōnis *f* choice ♦ *m* assistant.
optīvus *adj* chosen.
optō, -āre, -āvī, -ātum *vt* to choose; to wish for.
optum- *etc see* **optim-**.
opulēns, -entis *adj* rich.
opulentia, -ae *f* wealth; power.
opulentō, -āre *vt* to enrich.
opulentē, -er *adv* sumptuously.
opulentus *adj* rich, sumptuous, powerful.
opum *fpl* resources, wealth.
opus, -eris *nt* work, workmanship; (*art*) work, building, book; (*MIL*) siege work; (*colloq*) business; (*with* **esse**) need; **virō ~ est** a man is needed; **magnō ~ere** much, greatly.
opusculum, -ī *nt* little work.
ōra, -ae *f* edge, boundary; coast; country, region; (*NAUT*) hawser.
ōrāculum, -ī *nt* oracle, prophecy.
ōrātē *adv see adj.*
ōrātiō, -ōnis *f* speech, language; a speech, oration; eloquence; prose; emperor's message; **~ōnem habēre** deliver a speech.
ōrātiuncula, -ae *f* short speech.
ōrātor, -ōris *m* speaker, spokesman, orator.
ōrātōrius *adj* oratorical.
ōrātrīx, -īcis *f* suppliant.
ōrātus, -ūs *m* request.
orbātor, -ōris *m* bereaver.
orbiculātus *adj* round.
orbis, -is *m* circle, ring, disc, orbit; world; (*movement*) cycle, rotation; (*style*) rounding off; **~ lacteus** Milky Way; **~ signifer** Zodiac; **~ fortūnae** wheel of Fortune; **~ terrārum** the earth, world; **in ~em cōnsistere** form a circle; **in ~em īre** go the rounds.
orbita, -ae *f* rut, track, path.
orbitās, -ātis *f* childlessness, orphanhood, widowhood.
orbitōsus *adj* full of ruts.
orbō, -āre, -āvī, -ātum *vt* to bereave, orphan, make childless.
orbus *adj* bereaved, orphan, childless; destitute.
orca, -ae *f* vat.
orchas, -dis *f* kind of olive.
orchēstra, -ae *f* senatorial seats (in the theatre).
Orcus, -ī *m* Pluto; the lower world; death.
ōrdinārius *adj* regular.
ōrdinātim *adv* in order, properly.

ōrdinātiō, -ōnis *f* orderly arrangement.
ōrdinātus *adj* appointed.
ōrdinō, -āre, -āvī, -ātum *vt* to arrange, regulate, set in order.
ōrdior, -dīrī, -sus *vt, vi* to begin, undertake.
ōrdō, -inis *m* line, row, series; order, regularity, arrangement; (*MIL*) rank, line, company, (*pl*) captains; (*building*) course, layer; (*seats*) row; (*POL*) class, order, station; **ex ~ine** in order, in one's turn; one after the other; **extrā ~inem** irregularly, unusually.
Orēas, -dis *f* mountain nymph.
Orestēs, -is *and* **ae** *m* son of Agamemnon, whom he avenged by killing his mother.
Orestēus *adj see n.*
orexis, -is *f* appetite.
organum, -ī *nt* instrument, organ.
orgia, -ōrum *ntpl* Bacchic revels; orgies.
orichalcum, -ī *nt* copper ore, brass.
ōricilla, -ae *f* lobe.
oriēns, -entis *pres p of* **orior** ♦ *m* morning; east.
orīgō, -inis *f* beginning, source; ancestry, descent; founder.
Ōriōn, -onis *and* **ōnis** *m* mythical hunter and constellation.
orior, -īrī, -tus *vi* to rise; to spring, descend.
oriundus *adj* descended, sprung.
ōrnāmentum, -ī *nt* equipment, dress; ornament, decoration; distinction, pride of.
ōrnātē *adv* elegantly.
ōrnātus *ppp of* **ōrnō** ♦ *adj* equipped, furnished; embellished, excellent.
ōrnātus, -ūs *m* preparation; dress, equipment; embellishment.
ōrnō, -āre, -āvī, -ātum *vt* to fit out, equip, dress, prepare; to adorn, embellish, honour.
ornus, -ī *f* manna ash.
ōrō, -āre, -āvī, -ātum *vt* to speak, plead; to beg, entreat; to pray.
Orontēs, -is *and* **ī** *m* river of Syria.
Orontēus *adj* Syrian.
Orpheus, -eī *and* **eos** (*acc* **-ea**) *m* legendary Thracian singer, who went down to Hades for Eurydice.
Orphēus, -icus *adj see n.*
ōrsus *ppa of* **ōrdior** ♦ *ntpl* beginning; utterance.
ōrsus, -ūs *m* beginning.
ortus *ppa of* **orior** ♦ *adj* born, descended.
ortus, -ūs *m* rising; east; origin, source.
Ortygia, -ae *and* **ē, -ēs** *f* Delos.
Ortygius *adj see n.*
oryx, -gis *m* gazelle.
oryza, -ae *f* rice.
os, ossis *nt* bone; (*fig*) very soul.
ōs, -ōris *nt* mouth; face; entrance, opening; effrontery; **ūnō ōre** unanimously; **in ōre esse** be talked about; **quō ōre redībō** how shall I have the face to go back?
oscen, -inis *m* bird of omen.

ōscillum, -ī *nt* little mask.
ōscitāns, -antis *pres p of* **ōscitō** ♦ *adj* listless, drowsy.
ōscitanter *adv* half-heartedly.
ōscitō, -āre; -or, -ārī *vi* to yawn, be drowsy.
ōsculātiō, -ōnis *f* kissing.
ōsculor, -ārī, -ātus *vt* to kiss; to make a fuss of.
ōsculum, -ī *nt* sweet mouth; kiss.
Oscus *adj* Oscan.
Osīris, -is *and* **idis** *m* Egyptian god, husband of Isis.
Ossa, -ae *f* mountain in Thessaly.
osseus *adj* bony.
ossifraga, -ae *f* osprey.
ostendō, -dere, -dī, -tum *vt* to hold out, show, display; to expose; to disclose, reveal; (*speech*) to say, make known.
ostentātiō, -ōnis *f* display; showing off, ostentation; pretence.
ostentātor, -ōris *m* displayer, boaster.
ostentō, -āre *vt* to hold out, proffer, exhibit; to show off, boast of; to make known, indicate.
ostentum, -ī *nt* portent.
ostentus *ppp of* **ostendō**.
ostentus, -ūs *m* display, appearance; proof.
Ōstia, -ae *f*, **-ōrum** *ntpl* port at the Tiber mouth.
ōstiārium, -ī *and* **iī** *nt* door tax.
ōstiātim *adv* from door to door.
Ōstiēnsis *adj see n.*
ōstium, -ī *and* **iī** *nt* door; entrance, mouth.
ostrea, -ae *f* oyster.
ostreōsus *adj* rich in oysters.
ostreum, -ī *nt* oyster.
ostrifer, -ī *adj* oyster-producing.
ostrīnus *adj* purple.
ostrum, -ī *nt* purple; purple dress *or* coverings.
ōsus, ōsūrus *ppa and fut p of* **ōdī**.
Othō, -ōnis *m* author of a law giving theatre seats to Equites; Roman emperor after Galba.
Othōniānus *adj see n.*
ōtiolum, -ī *nt* bit of leisure.
ōtior, -ārī *vi* to have a holiday, be idle.
ōtiōsē *adv* leisurely; quietly; fearlessly.
ōtiōsus *adj* at leisure, free; out of public affairs; neutral, indifferent; quiet, unexcited; (*things*) free, idle ♦ *m* private citizen, civilian.
ōtium, -ī *and* **iī** *nt* leisure, time (for), idleness, retirement; peace, quiet.
ovātiō, -ōnis *f* minor triumph.
ovīle, -is *nt* sheep fold, goat fold.
ovillus *adj* of sheep.
ovis, -is *f* sheep.
ovō, -āre *vi* to rejoice; to celebrate a minor triumph.
ōvum, -ī *nt* egg.

Noun declensions and verb conjugations are shown on pp xiii to xxv. The present infinitive ending of a verb shows to which conjugation it belongs: **-āre** = 1st; **-ēre** = 2nd; **-ere** = 3rd and **-īre** = 4th. Irregular verbs are shown on p xxvi

P, p

pābulātiō, -ōnis *f* foraging.
pābulātor, -ōris *m* forager.
pābulor, -ārī *vi* to forage.
pābulum, -ī *nt* food, fodder.
pācālis *adj* of peace.
pācātus *adj* peaceful, tranquil ♦ *nt* friendly country.
Pachȳnum, -ī *nt* S.E. point of Sicily (*now* Cape Passaro).
pācifer, -ī *adj* peace-bringing.
pācificātiō, -ōnis *f* peacemaking.
pācificātor, -ōris *m* peacemaker.
pācificātōrius *adj* peacemaking.
pācificō, -āre *vi* to make a peace ♦ *vt* to appease.
pācificus *adj* peacemaking.
pacīscor, -īscī, -tus *vi* to make a bargain, agree ♦ *vt* to stipulate for; to barter.
pācō, -āre, -āvi, -ātum *vt* to pacify, subdue.
pactiō, -ōnis *f* bargain, agreement, contract; collusion; (*words*) formula.
Pactōlus, -ī *m* river of Lydia (*famous for its gold*).
pactor, -ōris *m* negotiator.
pactum, -ī *nt* agreement, contract.
pactus *ppa of* **pacīscor** ♦ *adj* agreed, settled; betrothed.
Pācuvius, -ī *m* Latin tragic poet.
Padus, -ī *m* river Po.
paeān, -ānis *m* healer, epithet of Apollo; hymn of praise, shout of joy; (*metre*) paeon.
paedagōgus, -ī *m* slave who took children to school.
paedor, -ōris *m* filth.
paelex, -icis *f* mistress, concubine.
paelicātus, -ūs *m* concubinage.
Paelignī, -ōrum *mpl* people of central Italy.
Paelignus *adj see n.*
paene *adv* almost, nearly.
paenīnsula, -ae *f* peninsula.
paenitendus *adj* regrettable.
paenitentia, -ae *f* repentance.
paenitet, -ēre, -uit *vt, vi* (*impers*) to repent, regret, be sorry; to be dissatisfied; **an ~et** is it not enough?
paenula, -ae *f* travelling cloak.
paenulātus *adj* wearing a cloak.
paeōn, -ōnis *m* metrical foot of one long and three short syllables.
paeōnius *adj* healing.
Paestānus *adj see n.*
Paestum, -ī *nt* town in S. Italy.
paetulus *adj* with a slight cast in the eye.
paetus *adj* with a cast in the eye.
pāgānus *adj* rural ♦ *m* villager, yokel.

pāgātim *adv* in every village.
pāgella, -ae *f* small page.
pāgina, -ae *f* (*book*) page, leaf.
pāginula, -ae *f* small page.
pāgus, -ī *m* village, country district; canton.
pāla, -ae *f* spade; (*ring*) bezel.
palaestra, -ae *f* wrestling school, gymnasium; exercise, wrestling; (*RHET*) exercise, training.
palaestricē *adv* in gymnastic fashion.
palaestricus *adj* of the wrestling school.
palaestrīta, -ae *m* head of a wrestling school.
palam *adv* openly, publicly, well-known ♦ *prep* (*with abl*) in the presence of.
Palātīnus *adj* Palatine; imperial.
Palātium, -ī *nt* Palatine Hill in Rome; palace.
palātum, -ī *nt* palate; taste, judgment.
palea, -ae *f* chaff.
paleāria, -ium *ntpl* dewlap.
Palēs, -is *f goddess of shepherds.*
Palīlis *adj* of Pales ♦ *ntpl festival of Pales.*
palimpsēstus, -ī *m* palimpsest.
Palinūrus, -ī *m* pilot of Aeneas; promontory in S. Italy.
paliūrus, -ī *m* Christ's thorn.
palla, -ae *f* woman's robe; tragic costume.
Palladium, -ī *nt image of Pallas.*
Palladius *adj* of Pallas.
Pallantēus *adj see n.*
Pallas, -dis *and* **dos** *f* Athene, Minerva; oil; olive tree.
Pallās, -antis *m ancestor or son of Evander.*
pallēns, -entis *pres p of* **palleō** ♦ *adj* pale; greenish.
palleō, -ēre, -uī *vi* to be pale or yellow; to fade; to be anxious.
pallēscō, -escere, -uī *vi* to turn pale, turn yellow.
palliātus *adj* wearing a Greek cloak.
pallidulus *adj* palish.
pallidus *adj* pale, pallid, greenish; in love.
palliolum, -ī *nt* small cloak, cape, hood.
pallium, -ī *and* **iī** *nt* coverlet; Greek cloak.
pallor, -ōris *m* paleness, fading; fear.
palma, -ae *f* (*hand*) palm, hand; (*oar*) blade; (*tree*) palm, date; branch; (*fig*) prize, victory, glory.
palmāris *adj* excellent.
palmārius *adj* prizewinning.
palmātus *adj* palm-embroidered.
palmes, -itis *m* pruned shoot, branch.
palmētum, -ī *nt* palm grove.
palmifer, -ī *adj* palm-bearing.
palmōsus *adj* palm-clad.
palmula, -ae *f* oar blade.
pālor, -ārī, -ātus *vi* to wander about, straggle.
palpātiō, -ōnis *f* flatteries.
palpātor, -ōris *m* flatterer.
palpebra, -ae *f* eyelid.
palpitō, -āre *vi* to throb, writhe.
palpō, -āre; -or, -ārī *vt* to stroke; to coax, flatter.
palpus, -ī *m* coaxing.

palūdāmentum, -ī *nt* military cloak.
palūdātus *adj* in a general's cloak.
palūdōsus *adj* marshy.
palumbēs, -is *m/f* wood pigeon.
pālus, -ī *m* stake, pale.
palūs, -ūdis *f* marsh, pool, lake.
palūster, -ris *adj* marshy.
pampineus *adj* of vineshoots.
pampinus, -ī *m* vineshoot.
Pān, -ānos (*acc* **-āna**) *m* Greek god of shepherds, hills and woods, esp associated with Arcadia.
panacēa, -ae *f* a herb supposed to cure all diseases.
Panaetius, -ī *m* Stoic philosopher.
Panchāeus *adj* see n.
Panchāaius *adj* see n.
Panchāia, -iae *f* part of Arabia.
panchrēstus *adj* good for everything.
pancratium, -ī and **iī** *nt* all-in boxing and wrestling match.
pandiculor, -āre *vi* to stretch oneself.
Pandīōn, -onis *m* king of Athens, father of Procne and Philomela.
Pandīonius *adj* see n.
pandō, -ere, -ī, pānsum and **passum** *vt* to spread out, stretch, extend; to open; (*fig*) to disclose, explain.
pandus *adj* curved, bent.
pangō, -ere, panxī and **pepigī, pāctum** *vt* to drive in, fasten; to make, compose; to agree, settle.
pānicula, -ae *f* tuft.
pānicum, -ī *nt* Italian millet.
pānis, -is *m* bread, loaf.
Pāniscus, -ī *m* little Pan.
panniculus, -ī *m* rag.
Pannonia, -ae *f* country on the middle Danube.
Pannonius *adj* see n.
pannōsus *adj* ragged.
pannus, -ī *m* piece of cloth, rag, patch.
Panormus, -ī *f* town in Sicily (*now* Palermo).
pānsa *adj* splayfoot.
pānsus *ppp of* **pandō.**
panthēra, -ae *f* panther.
Panthoidēs, -ae *m* Euphorbus.
Panthūs, -ī *m* priest of Apollo at Troy.
panticēs, -um *mpl* bowels; sausages.
panxī *perf of* **pangō.**
papae *interj* (expressing wonder) ooh!
pāpas, -ae *m* tutor.
papāver, -is *nt* poppy.
papāvereus *adj* see n.
Paphius *adj* see n.
Paphos, -ī *f* town in Cyprus, sacred to Venus.
pāpiliō, -ōnis *m* butterfly.
papilla, -ae *f* teat, nipple; breast.
pappus, -ī *m* woolly seed.
papula, -ae *f* pimple.
papȳrifer, -ī *adj* papyrus-bearing.
papȳrum, -ī *nt* papyrus; paper.

papȳrus, -ī *m/f* papyrus; paper.
pār, paris *adj* equal, like; a match for; proper, right ♦ *m* peer, partner, companion ♦ *nt* pair; **pār parī respondēre** return like for like; **parēs cum paribus facillimē congregantur** ≈ birds of a feather flock together; **lūdere pār impār** play at evens and odds.
parābilis *adj* easy to get.
parasīta, -ae *f* woman parasite.
parasītaster, -rī *m* sorry parasite.
parasīticus *adj* of a parasite.
parasītus, -ī *m* parasite, sponger.
parātē *adv* with preparation; carefully; promptly.
parātiō, -ōnis *f* trying to get.
paratragoedō, -āre *vi* to talk theatrically.
parātus *ppp of* **parō** ♦ *adj* ready; equipped; experienced.
parātus, -ūs *m* preparation, equipment.
Parca, -ae *f* Fate.
parcē *adv* frugally; moderately.
parcō, -cere, pepercī, -sum *vt, vi* (with dat) to spare, economize; to refrain from, forgo; (with inf) to forbear, stop.
parcus *adj* sparing, thrifty; niggardly, scanty; chary.
pardus, -ī *m* panther.
pārēns, -entis *pres p of* **pāreō** ♦ *adj* obedient ♦ *mpl* subjects.
parēns, -entis *m/f* parent, father, mother; ancestor; founder.
parentālis *adj* parental ♦ *ntpl* festival in honour of dead ancestors and relatives.
parentō, -āre *vi* to sacrifice in honour of dead parents or relatives; to avenge (with the death of another).
pāreō, -ēre, -uī, -itum *vi* to be visible, be evident; (with dat) to obey, submit to, comply with; **~et** it is proved.
pariēs, -etis *m* wall.
parietinae, -ārum *fpl* ruins.
Parīlia, -ium *ntpl* festival of Pales.
parīlis *adj* equal.
pariō, -ere, peperī, -tum *vt* to give birth to; to produce, create, cause; to procure.
Paris, -idis *m* son of Priam (abductor of Helen).
pariter *adv* equally, alike; at the same time, together.
paritō, -āre *vt* to get ready.
Parius *adj* see **Paros.**
parma, -ae *f* shield, buckler.
parmātus *adj* armed with a buckler.
parmula, -ae *f* little shield.
Parnāsis, -idis *adj* Parnassian.
Parnāsius *adj* = **Parnāsis.**
Parnāsus, -ī *m* mount Parnassus in central Greece, sacred to the Muses.
parō, -āre, -āvī, -ātum *vt* to prepare, get ready, provide; to intend, set about; to procure, get, buy; to arrange.

Noun declensions and verb conjugations are shown on pp xiii to xxv. The present infinitive ending of a verb shows to which conjugation it belongs: **-āre** = 1st; **-ēre** = 2nd; **-ere** = 3rd and **-īre** = 4th. Irregular verbs are shown on p xxvi

parocha, -ae *f* provision of necessaries (*to officials travelling*).

parochus, -ī *m* purveyor; host.

paropsis, -dis *f* dish.

Paros, -ī *f* Aegean island (*famous for white marble*).

parra, -ae *f* owl.

Parrhasis, -idis, -ius *adj* Arcadian.

parricīda, -ae *m* parricide, assassin; traitor.

parricīdium, -ī *and* **iī** parricide, murder; high treason.

pars, -tis *f* part, share, fraction; party, side; direction; respect, degree; (*with pl verb*) some; (*pl*) stage part, role; duty, function; **māgna ~** the majority; **in māgnam ~tem** largely; **in eam ~tem** in that direction, on that side, in that sense; **nullā ~te** not at all; **omnī ~te** entirely; **ex ~te** partly; **ex alterā ~te** on the other hand; **ex māgnā ~te** to a large extent; **prō ~te** to the best of one's ability; **~tēs agere** play a part; **duae ~tēs** two-thirds; **trēs ~tēs** three-fourths; **multīs ~ibus** a great deal.

parsimōnia, -ae *f* thrift, frugality.

parthenicē, -ēs *f* a plant.

Parthenopē, -ēs *f* old name of Naples.

Parthenopēius *adj see n.*

Parthī, -ōrum *mpl* Parthians (*Rome's great enemy in the East*).

Parthicus, -us *adj see n.*

particeps, -ipis *adj* sharing, partaking ♦ *m* partner.

participō, -āre *vt* to share, impart, inform.

particula, -ae *f* particle.

partim *adv* partly, in part; mostly; some ... others.

partiō, -īre, -īvī, -ītum; -ior, -īrī *vt* to share, distribute, divide.

partītē *adv* methodically.

partītiō, -ōnis *f* distribution, division.

parturiō, -īre *vi* to be in labour; (*fig*) to be anxious ♦ *vt* to teem with, be ready to produce; (*mind*) to brood over.

partus *ppp of* **pariō** ♦ *ntpl* possessions.

partus, -ūs *m* birth; young.

parum *adv* too little, not enough; not very, scarcely.

parumper *adv* for a little while.

parvitās, -ātis *f* smallness.

parvulus, parvolus *adj* very small, slight; quite young ♦ *m* child.

parvus (*comp* **minor** *super l* **minimus**) *adj* small, little, slight; (*time*) short; (*age*) young; **~ī esse** be of little value.

Pascha, -ae *f* Easter.

pāscō, -scere, -vī, -stum *vt* to feed, put to graze; to keep, foster; (*fig*) to feast, cherish ♦ *vi* to graze, browse.

pāscuus *adj* for pasture ♦ *nt* pasture.

Pāsiphaē, -ēs *f* wife of Minos (*mother of the Minotaur*).

passer, -is *m* sparrow; (*fish*) plaice; **~ marīnus** ostrich.

passerculus, -ī *m* little sparrow.

passim *adv* here and there, at random; indiscriminately.

passum, -ī *nt* raisin wine.

passus *ppp of* **pandō** ♦ *adj* spread out, dishevelled; dried.

passus *ppa of* **patior**.

passus, -ūs *m* step, pace; footstep; **mille ~ūs** mile; **mīlia ~uum** miles.

pastillus, -ī *m* lozenge.

pāstor, -ōris *m* shepherd.

pāstōrālis *adj* shepherd's, pastoral.

pāstōricius, pāstōrius *adj* shepherd's.

pāstus *ppp of* **pāscō**.

pāstus, -ūs *m* pasture, food.

Patara, -ae *f* town in Lycia (*with oracle of Apollo*).

Pataraeus *and* **eus** *adj see n.*

Patavīnus *adj see n.*

Patavium, -ī *nt* birthplace of Livy (*now Padua*).

patefaciō, -facere, -fēcī, -factum (*pass* **-fīō, -fierī**) *vt* to open, open up; to disclose.

patefactiō, -ōnis *f* disclosing.

patefīō *etc see* **patefaciō**.

patella, -ae *f* small dish, plate.

patēns, -entis *pres p of* **pateō** ♦ *adj* open, accessible, exposed; broad; evident.

patenter *adv* clearly.

pateō, -ēre, -uī *vi* to be open, accessible, exposed; to extend; to be evident, known.

pater, -ris *m* father; (*pl*) forefathers; senators.

patera, -ae *f* dish, saucer, bowl.

paterfamiliās, patrisfamiliās *m* master of the house.

paternus *adj* father's, paternal; native.

patēscō, -ere *vi* to open out; to extend; to become evident.

patibilis *adj* endurable; sensitive.

patibulātus *adj* pilloried.

patibulum, -ī *nt* fork-shaped yoke, pillory.

patiēns, -entis *pres p of* **patior** ♦ *adj* able to endure; patient; unyielding.

patienter *adv* patiently.

patientia, -ae *f* endurance, stamina; forbearance; submissiveness.

patina, -ae *f* dish, pan.

patior, -tī, -ssus *vt* to suffer, experience; to submit to; to allow, put up with; **facile ~** be well pleased with; **aegrē ~** be displeased with.

Patrae, -ārum *fpl* Greek seaport (*now* Patras).

patrātor, -ōris *m* doer.

patrātus *adj*: **pater ~** officiating priest.

Patrēnsis *adj see n.*

patria, -ae *f* native land, native town, home.

patricius *adj* patrician ♦ *m* aristocrat.

patrimōnium, -ī *and* **iī** *nt* inheritance, patrimony.

patrimus *adj* having a father living.

patrissō, -āre *vi* to take after one's father.

patrītus *adj* of one's father.

patrius *adj* father's; hereditary, native.

patrō–pelliō

patrō, -āre, -āvī, -ātum *vt* to achieve, execute, complete.
patrōcinium, -ī *and* **iī** *nt* patronage, advocacy, defence.
patrōcinor, -ārī *vi* (*with dat*) to defend, support.
patrōna, -ae *f* patron goddess; protectress, safeguard.
patrōnus, -ī *m* patron, protector; (*law*) advocate, counsel.
patruēlis *adj* cousin's ♦ *m* cousin.
patruus, -ī *m* (paternal) uncle ♦ *adj* uncle's.
patulus *adj* open; spreading, broad.
paucitās, -ātis *f* small number, scarcity.
pauculus *adj* very few.
paucus *adj* few, little ♦ *mpl* a few, the select few ♦ *ntpl* a few words.
paulātim *adv* little by little, gradually.
paulisper *adv* for a little while.
Paullus, -ī *m* = **Paulus.**
paulō *adv* a little, somewhat.
paululus *adj* very little ♦ *nt* a little bit.
paulum *adv* = **paulō.**
paulus *adj* little.
Paulus, -ī *m* Roman surname (*esp victor of Pydna*).
pauper, -is *adj* poor; meagre ♦ *mpl* the poor.
pauperculus *adj* poor.
pauperiēs, -ēī *f* poverty.
pauperō, -āre *vt* to impoverish; to rob.
paupertās, -ātis *f* poverty, moderate means.
pausa, -ae *f* stop, end.
pauxillātim *adv* bit by bit.
pauxillulus *adj* very little.
pauxillus *adj* little.
pavefactus *adj* frightened.
paveō, -ēre, pāvī *vi* to be terrified, quake ♦ *vt* to dread, be scared of.
pavēscō, -ere *vt, vi* to become alarmed (at).
pāvī *perf of* **pāscō.**
pavidē *adv* in a panic.
pavidus *adj* quaking, terrified.
pavīmentātus *adj* paved.
pavīmentum, -ī *nt* pavement, floor.
paviō, -īre *vt* to strike.
pavitō, -āre *vi* to be very frightened; to shiver.
pāvō, -ōnis *m* peacock.
pavor, -ōris *m* terror, panic.
pāx, pācis *f* peace; (*gods*) grace; (*mind*) serenity ♦ *interj* enough!; **pāce tuā** by your leave.
peccātum, -ī *nt* mistake, fault, sin.
peccō, -āre, -āvī, -ātum *vi* to make a mistake, go wrong, offend.
pecorōsus *adj* rich in cattle.
pecten, -inis *m* comb; (*fish*) scallop; (*loom*) reed; (*lyre*) plectrum.
pectō, -ctere, -xī, -xum *vt* to comb.
pectus, -oris *nt* breast; heart, feeling; mind,

thought.
pecū *nt* flock of sheep; (*pl*) pastures.
pecuārius *adj* of cattle ♦ *m* cattle breeder ♦ *ntpl* herds.
pecūlātor, -ōris *m* embezzler.
pecūlātus, -ūs *m* embezzlement.
pecūliāris *adj* one's own; special.
pecūliātus *adj* provided with money.
pecūliōsus *adj* with private property.
pecūlium, -ī *and* **iī** *nt* small savings, private property.
pecūnia, -ae *f* property; money.
pecūniārius *adj* of money.
pecūniōsus *adj* moneyed, well-off.
pecus, -oris *nt* cattle, herd, flock; animal.
pecus, -udis *f* sheep, head of cattle, beast.
pedālis *adj* a foot long.
pedārius *adj* (*senator*) without full rights.
pedes, -itis *m* foot soldier, infantry ♦ *adj* on foot.
pedester, -ris *adj* on foot, pedestrian; infantry- (*in cpds*); on land; (*writing*) in prose, prosaic.
pedetemptim *adv* step by step, cautiously.
pedica, -ae *f* fetter, snare.
pedis, -is *m* louse.
pedisequa, -ae *f* handmaid.
pedisequus, -ī *m* attendant, lackey.
peditātus, -ūs *m* infantry.
pedum, -ī *nt* crook.
Pēgaseus *and* **is, -idis** *adj* Pegasean.
Pēgasus, -ī *m* mythical winged horse (*associated with the Muses*).
pēgma, -tis *nt* bookcase; stage elevator.
pēierō, -āre *vi* to perjure oneself.
pēior, -ōris *compar of* **malus.**
pēius *adv* worse.
pelagius *adj* of the sea.
pelagus, -ī (*pl* -ē) *nt* sea, open sea.
pelamys, -dis *f* young tunny fish.
Pelasgī, -ōrum *mpl* Greeks.
Pelasgias *and* **is** *and* **us** *adj* Grecian.
Pēleus, -eī *and* **eos** (*acc* -ea) *m* king of Thessaly (*father of Achilles*).
Peliās, -ae *m* uncle of Jason.
Pēlias *and* **iacus** *and* **ius** *adj see* **Pēlion.**
Pēlīdēs, -īdae *m* Achilles; Neoptolemus.
Pēlion, -ī *nt* mountain in Thessaly.
Pella, -ae, -ē, -ēs *f* town of Macedonia (*birthplace of Alexander*).
pellācia, -ae *f* attraction.
Pellaeus *adj* of Pella; Alexandrian; Egyptian.
pellāx, -ācis *adj* seductive.
pellēctiō, -ōnis *f* reading through.
pellectus *ppp of* **pelliciō.**
pellegō *etc see* **perlegō.**
pelliciō, -icere, -exī, -ectum *vt* to entice, inveigle.
pellicula, -ae *f* skin, fleece.
pelliō, -ōnis *m* furrier.

Noun declensions and verb conjugations are shown on pp xiii to xxv. The present infinitive ending of a verb shows to which conjugation it belongs: -**āre** = 1st; -**ēre** = 2nd; -**ere** = 3rd and -**īre** = 4th. Irregular verbs are shown on p xxvi

pellis, -is *f* skin, hide; leather, felt; tent.
pellītus *adj* wearing skins, with leather coats.
pellō, -ere, pepulī, pulsum *vt* to push, knock, drive; to drive off, rout, expel; (*lyre*) to play; (*mind*) to touch, affect; (*feeling*) to banish.
pellūc- *etc see* **perlūc-**.
Pelopēis *and* **ēis** *and* **ēus** *adj see n.*
Pelopidae, -idārum *mpl* house of Pelops.
Pelopōias *adj see n.*
Peloponnēsiacus, -ius *adj see n.*
Peloponnēsus, -ī *f* Peloponnese, S. Greece.
Pelops, -is *m* son of Tantalus (*grandfather of Agamemnon*).
pelōris, -idis *f* a large mussel.
pelta, -ae *f* light shield.
peltastae, -ārum *mpl* peltasts.
peltātus *adj* armed with the pelta.
Pēlūsiacus *adj see n.*
Pēlūsium, -ī *nt* Eygptian town at the E. mouth of the Nile.
Pēlūsius *adj see n.*
pelvis, -is *f* basin.
penārius *adj* provision- (*in cpds*).
Penātēs, -ium *mpl* spirits of the larder, household gods; home.
penātiger, -ī *adj* carrying his home gods.
pendeō, -ēre, pependī *vi* to hang; to overhang, hover; to hang down, be flabby; (*fig*) to depend; to gaze, listen attentively; (*mind*) to be in suspense, be undecided.
pendō, -ere, pependī, pēnsum *vt* to weigh; to pay; (*fig*) to ponder, value ♦ *vi* to weigh.
pendulus *adj* hanging; in doubt.
Pēnēēis *and* **ēius** *and* **ēus** *adj see n.*
Pēnelopē, ēs *and* **a, -ae** *f* wife of Ulysses (*famed for her constancy*).
Pēnelopēus *adj see n.*
penes *prep* (*with acc*) in the power or possession of; in the house of, with.
penetrābilis *adj* penetrable; piercing.
penetrālis *adj* penetrating; inner, inmost ♦ *ntpl* inner room, interior, sanctuary; remote parts.
penetrō, -āre, -āvī, -ātum *vt, vi* to put into, penetrate, enter.
Pēnēus, -ī *m* chief river of Thessaly.
pēnicillus, -ī *m* painter's brush, pencil.
pēniculus, -ī *m* brush; sponge.
pēnis, -is *m* penis.
penitē *adj* inwardly.
penitus *adv* inside, deep within; deeply, from the depths; utterly, thoroughly.
penna, pinna, -ae *f* feather, wing; flight.
pennātus *adj* winged.
penniger, -ī *adj* feathered.
pennipotēns, -entis *adj* winged.
pennula, -ae *f* little wing.
pēnsilis *adj* hanging, pendent.
pēnsiō, -ōnis *f* payment, instalment.
pēnsitō, -āre *vt* to pay; to consider.
pēnsō, -āre, -āvī, -ātum *vt* to weight out; to compensate, repay; to consider, judge.
pēnsum, -ī *nt* spinner's work; task, duty;

weight, value; **~ī esse** be of importance; **~ī habēre** care at all about.
pēnsus *ppp of* **pendō.**
pentēris, -is *f* quinquereme.
Pentheus, -eī *and* **eos** *m* king of Thebes (*killed by Bacchantes*).
pēnūria, -ae *f* want, need.
penus, -ūs *and* **ī** *m/f,* **-um, -ī, -us, -oris** *nt* provisions, store of food.
pependī *perf of* **pendeō;** *perf of* **pendō.**
pepercī *perf of* **parcō.**
peperī *perf of* **pariō.**
pepigī *perf of* **pangō.**
peplum, -ī *nt,* **-us, -ī** *m* state robe of Athena.
pepulī *perf of* **pellō.**
per *prep* (*with acc: space*) through, all over; (*: time*) throughout, during; (*: means*) by, by means of; (*: cause*) by reason of, for the sake of; **~ īram** in anger; **~ manūs** from hand to hand; **~ mē** as far as I am concerned; **~ vim** forcibly; **~ ego tē deōs ōrō** in Heaven's name I beg you.
pēra, -ae *f* bag.
perabsurdus *adj* very absurd.
peraccommodātus *adj* very convenient.
perācer, -ris *adj* very sharp.
peracerbus *adj* very sour.
peracēscō, -ēscere, -uī *vi* to get vexed.
perāctiō, -ōnis *f* last act.
perāctus *ppp of* **peragō.**
peracūtē *adv* very acutely.
peracūtus *adj* very sharp, very clear.
peradulēscēns, -entis *adj* very young.
peraequē *adv* quite equally, uniformly.
peragitātus *adj* harried.
peragō, -agere, -ēgī, -āctum *vt* to carry through, complete; to pass through, pierce; to disturb; (*law*) to prosecute to a conviction; (*words*) to go over, describe.
peragrātiō, -ōnis *f* travelling.
peragrō, -āre, -āvī, -ātum *vt* to travel through, traverse.
peramāns, -antis *adj* very fond.
peramānter *adv* devotedly.
perambulō, -āre *vt* to walk through, traverse.
peramoenus *adj* very pleasant.
peramplus *adj* very large.
perangustē *adv see adj.*
perangustus *adj* very narrow.
perantīquus *adj* very old.
perappositus *adj* very suitable.
perarduus *adj* very difficult.
perargūtus *adj* very witty.
perarō, -āre *vt* to furrow; to write (on wax).
perattentē *adv see adj.*
perattentus *adj* very attentive.
peraudiendus *adj* to be heard to the end.
perbacchor, -ārī *vt* to carouse through.
perbeātus *adj* very happy.
perbellē *adv* very nicely.
perbene *adv* very well.
perbenevolus *adj* very friendly.
perbenignē *adv* very kindly.

perbibō, -ere, -ī *vt* to drink up, imbibe.
perbītō, -ere *vi* to perish.
perblandus *adj* very charming.
perbonus *adj* very good.
perbrevis *adj* very short.
perbreviter *adv* very briefly.
perca, -ae *f* perch.
percalefactus *adj* quite hot.
percalēscō, -ēscere, -uī *vi* to become quite hot.
percallēscō, -ēscere, -uī *vi* to become quite hardened ♦ *vt* to become thoroughly versed in.
percārus *adj* very dear.
percautus *adj* very cautious.
percelebrō, -āre *vt* to talk much of.
perceler, -is *adj* very quick.
perceleriter *adv see adj.*
percellō, -ellere, -ulī, -ulsum *vt* to knock down, upset; to strike; (*fig*) to ruin, overthrow; to discourage, unnerve.
percēnseō, -ēre, -uī *vt* to count over; (*place*) to travel through; (*fig*) to review.
perceptiō, -ōnis *f* harvesting; understanding, idea.
perceptus *ppp of* **percipiō**.
percieō, -iēre, -iō, -īre *vt* to rouse, excite.
percipiō, -ipere, -ēpī, -eptum *vt* to take, get hold of; to gather in; (*senses*) to feel; (*mind*) to learn, grasp, understand.
percitus *ppp of* **percieō** ♦ *adj* roused, excited; excitable.
percoctus *ppp of* **percoquō**.
percolō, -āre *vt* to filter through.
percolō, -olere, -oluī, -ultum *vt* to embellish; to honour.
percōmis *adj* very friendly.
percommodē *adv* very conveniently.
percommodus *adj* very suitable.
percontātiō, -ōnis *f* asking questions.
percontātor, -ōris *m* inquisitive person.
percontor, -ārī, -ātus *vt* to question, inquire.
percontumāx, -ācis *adj* very obstinate.
percoquō, -quere, -xī, -ctum *vt* to cook thoroughly, heat, scorch, ripen.
percrēbēscō, percrēbrēscō, -ēscere, -uī *vi* to be spread abroad.
percrepō, -āre, -uī *vi* to resound.
perculī *perf of* **percellō**.
perculsus *ppp of* **percellō**.
percultus *ppp of* **percolō**.
percunct- *etc see* **percont-**.
percupidus *adj* very fond.
percupiō, -ere *vi* to wish very much.
percūriōsus *adj* very inquisitive.
percūrō, -āre *vt* to heal completely.
percurrō, -rrere, -currī *and* **rrī, -rsum** *vt* to run through, hurry over; (*fig*) to run over, look over ♦ *vi* to run along; to pass.
percursātiō, -ōnis *f* travelling through.

percursiō, -ōnis *f* running over.
percursō, -āre *vi* to rove about.
percursus *ppp of* **percurrō**.
percussiō, -ōnis *f* beating; (*fingers*) snapping; (*music*) time.
percussor, -ōris *m* assassin.
percussus *ppp of* **percutiō**.
percussus, -ūs *m* striking.
percutiō, -tere, -ssī, -ssum *vt* to strike, beat; to strike through, kill; (*feeling*) to shock, impress, move; (*colloq*) to trick.
perdēlīrus *adj* quite crazy.
perdidī *perf of* **perdō**.
perdifficilis *adj* very difficult.
perdifficiliter *adv* with great difficulty.
perdignus *adj* most worthy.
perdīligēns, -entis *adj* very diligent.
perdīligenter *adv see adj.*
perdiscō, -scere, -dicī *vt* to learn by heart.
perdisertē *adv* very eloquently.
perditē *adv* desperately; recklessly.
perditor, -ōris *m* destroyer.
perditus *ppp of* **perdō** ♦ *adj* desperate, ruined; abandoned, profligate.
perdiū *adv* for a very long time.
perdiūturnus *adj* protracted.
perdīves, -itis *adj* very rich.
perdīx, -īcis *m/f* partridge.
perdō, -ere, -idī, -itum *vt* to destroy, ruin; to squander, waste; to lose; **dī tē ~uint** curse you!
perdoceō, -ēre, -uī, -tum *vt* to teach thoroughly.
perdolēscō, -ēscere, -uī *vi* to take it to heart.
perdomō, -āre, -uī, -itum *vt* to subjugate, tame completely.
perdormīscō, -ere *vi* to sleep on.
perdūcō, -ūcere, -ūxī, -uctum *vt* to bring, guide to; to induce, seduce; to spread over; to prolong, continue.
perductō, -āre *vt* to guide.
perductor, -ōris *m* guide; pander.
perductus *ppp of* **perdūcō**.
perduelliō, -ōnis *f* treason.
perduellis, -is *m* enemy.
perduint *archaic subj of* **perdō**.
perdūrō, -āre *vi* to endure, hold out.
peredō, -edere, -ēdī, -ēsum *vt* to consume, devour.
peregrē *adv* away from home, abroad; from abroad.
peregrīnābundus *adj* travelling.
peregrīnātiō, -ōnis *f* living abroad, travel.
peregrīnātor, -ōris *m* traveller.
peregrīnitās, -ātis *f* foreign manners.
peregrīnor, -ārī, -ātus *vi* to be abroad, travel; to be a stranger.
peregrīnus *adj* foreign, strange ♦ *m* foreigner, alien.
perēlegāns, -antis *adj* very polished.

Noun declensions and verb conjugations are shown on pp xiii to xxv. The present infinitive ending of a verb shows to which conjugation it belongs: **-āre** = 1st; **-ēre** = 2nd; **-ere** = 3rd and **-īre** = 4th. Irregular verbs are shown on p xxvi

perēleganter _adv_ in a very polished manner.
perēloquēns, -entis _adj_ very eloquent.
perēmī _perf of_ **perimō.**
peremnia, -ium _ntpl_ auspices taken on crossing a river.
peremptus _ppp of_ **perimō.**
perendiē _adv_ the day after tomorrow.
perendinus _adj_ (the day) after tomorrow.
perennis _adj_ perpetual, unfailing.
perennitās, -ātis _f_ continuance.
perennō, -āre _vi_ to last a long time.
pereō, -īre, -iī, -itum _vi_ to be lost, pass away, perish, die; (_fig_) to be wasted, be in love, be undone.
perequitō, -āre _vt, vi_ to ride up and down.
pererrō, -āre, -āvī, -ātum _vt_ to roam over, cover.
pererudītus _adj_ very learned.
perēsus _ppp of_ **peredō.**
perexcelsus _adj_ very high.
perexiguē _adv_ very meagrely.
perexiguus _adj_ very small, very short.
perfacētē _adv_ very wittily.
perfacētus _adj_ very witty.
perfacile _adv_ very easily.
perfacilis _adj_ very easy; very courteous.
perfamiliāris _adj_ very intimate ♦ _m_ very close friend.
perfectē _adv_ fully.
perfectiō, -ōnis _f_ completion, perfection.
perfector, -ōris _m_ perfecter.
perfectus _ppp of_ **perficiō** ♦ _adj_ complete, perfect.
perferō, -ferre, -tulī, -lātum _vt_ to carry through, bring, convey; to bear, endure, put up with; (_work_) to finish, bring to completion; (_law_) to get passed; (_message_) to bring news.
perficiō, -icere, -ēcī, -ectum _vt_ to carry out, finish, complete; to perfect; to cause, make.
perficus _adj_ perfecting.
perfidēlis _adj_ very loyal.
perfidia, -ae _f_ treachery, dishonesty.
perfidiōsē _adv see adj._
perfidiōsus _adj_ treacherous, dishonest.
perfidus _adj_ treacherous, faithless.
perfīgō, -gere, -xī, -xum _vt_ to pierce.
perflābilis _adj_ that can be blown through.
perflāgitiōsus _adj_ very wicked.
perflō, -āre _vt_ to blow through, blow over.
perfluctuō, -āre _vt_ to flood through.
perfluō, -ere, -xī _vi_ to run out, leak.
perfodiō, -odere, -ōdī, -ossum _vt_ to dig through, excavate, pierce.
perforō, -āre, -āvī, -ātum _vt_ to bore through, pierce.
perfortiter _adv_ very bravely.
perfossor, -ōris _m:_ ~ **parietum** burglar.
perfossus _ppp of_ **perfodiō.**
perfrāctus _ppp of_ **perfringō.**
perfrēgī _perf of_ **perfringō.**
perfremō, -ere _vi_ to snort along.
perfrequēns, -entis _adj_ much frequented.
perfricō, -āre, -uī, -tum _and_ **ātum** _vt_ to rub all

over; **ōs** ~ put on a bold face.
perfrīgefaciō, -ere _vt_ to make shudder.
perfrīgēscō, -gēscere, -xī _vi_ to catch a bad cold.
perfrīgidus _adj_ very cold.
perfringō, -ingere, -ēgī, -āctum _vt_ to break through, fracture, wreck; (_fig_) to violate; to affect powerfully.
perfrīxī _perf of_ **perfrīgēscō.**
perfrūctus _ppa of_ **perfruor.**
perfruor, -uī, -ūctus _vi_ (_with abl_) to enjoy to the full; to fulfil.
perfuga, -ae _m_ deserter.
perfugiō, -ugere, -ūgī _vi_ to flee for refuge, desert to.
perfugium, -ī _and_ **iī** _nt_ refuge, shelter.
perfūnctiō, -ōnis _f_ performing.
perfūnctus _ppa of_ **perfungor.**
perfundō, -undere, -ūdī, -ūsum _vt_ to pour over, drench, besprinkle; to dye; (_fig_) to flood, fill.
perfungor, -gī, perfūnctus _vi_ (_with abl_) to perform, discharge; to undergo.
perfurō, -ere _vi_ to rage furiously.
perfūsus _ppp of_ **perfundō.**
Pergama, -ōrum _ntpl_ Troy.
Pergamēnus _adj see n._
Pergameus _adj_ Trojan.
Pergamum, -ī _nt_ town in Mysia (_famous for its library_).
pergaudeō, -ēre _vi_ to be very glad.
pergō, -gere, -rēxī, -rēctum _vi_ to proceed, go on, continue ♦ _vt_ to go on with, continue.
pergraecor, -ārī _vi_ to have a good time.
pergrandis _adj_ very large; very old.
pergraphicus _adj_ very artful.
pergrātus _adj_ very pleasant.
pergravis _adj_ very weighty.
pergraviter _adv_ very seriously.
pergula, -ae _f_ balcony; school; brothel.
perhibeō, -ēre, -uī, -itum _vt_ to assert, call, cite.
perhīlum _adv_ very little.
perhonōrificē _adv_ very respectfully.
perhonōrificus _adj_ very complimentary.
perhorrēscō, -ēscere, -uī _vi_ to shiver, tremble violently ♦ _vt_ to have a horror of.
perhorridus _adj_ quite horrible.
perhūmāniter _adv see adj._
perhūmānus _adj_ very polite.
Periclēs, -is _and_ **ī** _m_ famous Athenian statesman and orator.
perīclitātiō, -ōnis _f_ experiment.
perīclitor, -ārī, -ātus _vt_ to test, try; to risk, endanger ♦ _vi_ to attempt, venture; to run a risk, be in danger.
perīculōsē _adv see adj._
perīculōsus _adj_ dangerous, hazardous.
perīculum (perīclum), -ī _nt_ danger, risk; trial, attempt; (_law_) lawsuit, writ.
peridōneus _adj_ very suitable.
periī _perf of_ **pereō.**
perillūstris _adj_ very notable; highly honoured.

perimbēcillus *adj* very weak.
perimō, -imere, -ēmī, -emptum *vt* to destroy, prevent, kill.
perincommodē *adv see adj.*
perincommodus *adj* very inconvenient.
perinde *adv* just as, exactly as.
perindulgēns, -entis *adj* very tender.
perinfirmus *adj* very feeble.
peringeniōsus *adj* very clever.
perinīquus *adj* very unfair; very discontented.
perinsignis *adj* very conspicuous.
perinvītus *adj* very unwilling.
periodus, -ī *f* sentence, period.
Peripatēticī, -ōrum *mpl* Peripatetics (*followers of Aristotle*).
peripetasmata, -um *ntpl* curtains.
perīrātus *adj* very angry.
periscelis, -dis *f* anklet.
peristrōma, -atis *nt* coverlet.
peristylum, -ī *nt* colonnade, peristyle.
perītē *adv* expertly.
perītia, -ae *f* practical knowledge, skill.
perītus *adj* experienced, skilled, expert.
periūcundē *adv see adj.*
periūcundus *adj* very enjoyable.
periūrium, -ī and iī *nt* perjury.
periūrō *see* **pēierō.**
periūrus *adj* perjured, lying.
perlābor, -bī, -psus *vi* to glide along *or* through, move on.
perlaetus *adj* very glad.
perlāpsus *ppa of* **perlābor.**
perlātē *adv* very extensively.
perlateō, -ēre *vi* to lie quite hidden.
perlātus *ppp of* **perferō.**
perlegō, -egere, -ēgī, -ēctum *vt* to survey; to read through.
perlevis *adj* very slight.
perleviter *adv see adj.*
perlibēns, -entis *adj* very willing.
perlibenter *adv see adj.*
perlīberālis *adj* very genteel.
perlīberāliter *adv* very liberally.
perlibet, -ēre *vi* (*impers*) (I) should very much like.
perliciō *etc see* **pelliciō.**
perlitō, -āre, -āvī, -ātum *vi* to sacrifice with auspicious results.
perlongē *adv* very far.
perlongus *adj* very long, very tedious.
perlub- *etc see* **perlib-.**
perlūceō, -cēre, -xī *vi* to shine through, be transparent; (*fig*) to be quite intelligible.
perlūcidulus *adj* transparent.
perlūcidus *adj* transparent; very bright.
perlūctuōsus *adj* very mournful.
perluō, -ere *vt* to wash thoroughly; (*pass*) to bathe.
perlūstrō, -āre *vt* to traverse; (*fig*) to survey.

permāgnus *adj* very big, very great.
permānanter *adv* by flowing through.
permānāscō, -ere *vi* to penetrate.
permaneō, -anēre, -ānsī, -ānsum *vi* to last, persist, endure to the end.
permānō, -āre, -āvī, -ātum *vi* to flow *or* ooze through, penetrate.
permānsiō, -ōnis *f* continuing, persisting.
permarīnus *adj* of seafaring.
permātūrēscō, -ēscere, -uī *vi* to ripen fully.
permediocris *adj* very moderate.
permēnsus *ppa of* **permētior.**
permeō, -āre *vt, vi* to pass through, penetrate.
permētior, -tīrī, -nsus *vt* to measure out; to traverse.
permīrus *adj* very wonderful.
permisceō, -scēre, -scuī, -xtum *vt* to mingle, intermingle; to throw into confusion.
permissiō, -ōnis *f* unconditional surrender; permission.
permissus *ppp of* **permittō.**
permissus, -ūs *m* leave, permission.
permitiālis *adj* destructive.
permitiēs, -ēī *f* ruin.
permittō, -ittere, -īsī, -issum *vt* to let go, let pass; to hurl; to give up, entrust, concede; to allow, permit.
permixtē *adv see adj.*
permixtiō, -ōnis *f* mixture; disturbance.
permixtus *ppp of* **permisceō** ♦ *adj* promiscuous, disordered.
permodestus *adj* very moderate.
permolestē *adv* with much annoyance.
permolestus *adj* very troublesome.
permōtiō, -ōnis *f* excitement; emotion.
permōtus *ppp of* **permoveō.**
permoveō, -ovēre, -ōvī, -ōtum *vt* to stir violently; (*fig*) to influence, induce; to excite, move deeply.
permulceō, -cēre, -sī, -sum *vt* to stroke, caress; (*fig*) to charm, flatter; to soothe, appease.
permulsus *ppp of* **permulceō.**
permultus *adj* very much, very many.
permūniō, -īre, -īvī, -ītum *vt* to finish fortifying; to fortify strongly.
permūtātiō, -ōnis *f* change, exchange.
permūtō, -āre, -āvī, -ātum *vt* to change completely; to exchange; (*money*) to remit by bill of exchange.
perna, -ae *f* ham.
pernecessārius *adj* very necessary; very closely related.
pernecesse *adj* indispensable.
pernegō, -āre *vi* to deny flatly.
perniciābilis *adj* ruinous.
perniciēs, -ēī *f* destruction, ruin, death.
perniciōsē *adv see adj.*
perniciōsus *adj* ruinous.

Noun declensions and verb conjugations are shown on pp xiii to xxv. The present infinitive ending of a verb shows to which conjugation it belongs: **-āre** = 1st; **-ēre** = 2nd; **-ere** = 3rd and **-īre** = 4th. Irregular verbs are shown on **p xxvi**

pernīcitās, -ātis *f* agility, swiftness.
pernīciter *adv* nimbly.
pernimius *adj* much too much.
pernīx, -īcis *adj* nimble, agile, swift.
pernōbilis *adj* very famous.
pernoctō, -āre *vi* to stay all night.
pernōscō, -scere, -vī, -tum *vt* to examine
  thoroughly; to become fully acquainted
  with, know thoroughly.
pernōtēscō, -ēscere, -uī *vi* to become
  generally known.
pernōtus *ppp of* **pernōscō**.
pernox, -octis *adj* all night long.
pernumerō, -āre *vt* to count up.
pērō, -ōnis *m* rawhide boot.
perobscūrus *adj* very obscure.
perodiōsus *adj* very troublesome.
perofficiōsē *adv* very attentively.
peroleō, -ēre *vi* to give off a strong smell.
peropportūnē *adv* very opportunely.
peropportūnus *adj* very timely.
peroptātō *adv* very much to one's wish.
peropus est it is most essential.
perōrātiō, -ōnis *f* peroration.
perōrnātus *adj* very ornate.
perōrnō, -āre *vt* to give great distinction to.
perōrō, -āre, -āvī, -ātum *vt* to plead at
  length; (*speech*) to bring to a close; to
  conclude.
perōsus *adj* detesting.
perpācō, -āre *vt* to quieten completely.
perparcē *adv* very stingily.
perparvulus *adj* very tiny.
perparvus *adj* very small.
perpāstus *adj* well fed.
perpauculus *adj* very very few.
perpaucus *adj* very little, very few.
perpaulum, -ī *nt* a very little.
perpauper, -is *adj* very poor.
perpauxillum, -ī *nt* a very little.
perpellō, -ellere, -ulī, -ulsum *vt* to urge,
  force, influence.
perpendiculum, -ī *nt* plumbline; **ad ~**
  perpendicularly.
perpendō, -endere, -endī, -ēnsum *vt* to
  weigh carefully, judge.
perperam *adv* wrongly, falsely.
perpes, -etis *adj* continuous.
perpessiō, -ōnis *f* suffering, enduring.
perpessus *ppa of* **perpetior**.
perpetior, -tī, -ssus *vt* to endure patiently,
  allow.
perpetrō, -āre, -āvī, -ātum *vt* to perform,
  carry out.
perpetuitās, -ātis *f* continuity, uninterrupted
  duration.
perpetuō *adv* without interruption, forever,
  utterly.
perpetuō, -āre *vt* to perpetuate, preserve.
perpetuus *adj* continuous, entire; universal;
  in **~um** forever.
perplaceō, -ēre *vi* to please greatly.
perplexē *adv* obscurely.

perplexor, -ārī *vi* to cause confusion.
perplexus *adj* confused, intricate, obscure.
perplicātus *adj* interlaced.
perpluō, -ere *vi* to let the rain through, leak.
perpoliō, -īre, -īvī, -ītum *vt* to polish
  thoroughly.
perpolītus *adj* finished, refined.
perpopulor, -ārī, -ātus *vt* to ravage
  completely.
perpōtātiō, -ōnis *f* drinking bout.
perpōtō, -āre *vi* to drink continuously ♦ *vt* to
  drink off.
perprimō, -ere *vt* to lie on.
perpugnāx, -ācis *adj* very pugnacious.
perpulcher, -rī *adj* very beautiful.
perpulī *perf of* **perpellō**.
perpūrgō, -āre, -āvī, -ātum *vt* to make quite
  clean; to explain.
perpusillus *adj* very little.
perquam *adv* very, extremely.
perquīrō, -rere, -sīvī, -sītum *vt* to search for,
  inquire after; to examine carefully.
perquīsītius *adv* more accurately.
perrārō *adv* very seldom.
perrārus *adj* very uncommon.
perreconditus *adj* very abstruse.
perrēpō, -ere *vt* to crawl over.
perrēptō, -āre, -āvī, -ātum *vt, vi* to creep
  about *or* through.
perrēxī *perf of* **pergō**.
perrīdiculē *adv see adj.*
perrīdiculus *adj* very laughable.
perrogātiō, -ōnis *f* passing (of a law).
perrogō, -āre *vt* to ask one after another.
perrumpō, -umpere, -ūpī, -uptum *vt, vi* to
  break through, force a way through; (*fig*) to
  break down.
perruptus *ppp of* **perrumpō**.
Persae, -ārum *mpl* Persians.
persaepe *adv* very often.
persalsē *adv see adj.*
persalsus *adj* very witty.
persalūtātiō, -ōnis *f* greeting everyone in
  turn.
persalūtō, -āre *vt* to greet in turn.
persānctē *adv* most solemnly.
persapiēns, -entis *adj* very wise.
persapienter *adv see adj.*
perscienter *adv* very discreetly.
perscindō, -ndere, -dī, -ssum *vt* to tear
  apart.
perscītus *adj* very smart.
perscrībō, -bere, -psī, -ptum *vt* to write in
  full; to describe, report; (*record*) to enter;
  (*money*) to make over in writing.
perscrīptiō, -ōnis *f* entry; assignment.
perscrīptor, -ōris *m* writer.
perscrīptus *ppp of* **perscrībō**.
perscrūtor, -ārī, -ātus *vt* to search, examine
  thoroughly.
persecō, -āre, -uī, -tum *vt* to dissect; to do
  away with.
persector, -ārī *vt* to investigate.

persecūtiō, -ōnis f (law) prosecution.
persecūtus ppa of **persequor.**
persedeō, -edēre, -ēdī, -essum vi to remain sitting.
persegnis adj very slow.
Persēius adj see **Perseus.**
persentiō, -entīre, -ēnsī vt to see clearly; to feel deeply.
persentīscō, -ere vi to begin to see; to begin to feel.
Persephonē, -ēs f Proserpine.
persequor, -quī, -cūtus vt to follow all the way; to pursue, chase, hunt after; to overtake; (pattern) to be a follower of, copy; (enemy) to proceed against, take revenge on; (action) to perform, carry out; (words) to write down, describe.
Persēs, -ae m last king of Macedonia.
Persēs, -ae m Persian.
Perseus, -eī and **eos** (acc **-ea**) m son of Danaë (killer of Medusa, rescuer of Andromeda).
Persēus adj see n.
persevērāns, -antis pres p of **persevērō ♦** adj persistent.
persevēranter adv see adj.
persevērāntia, -ae f persistence.
persevērō, -āre, -āvī, -ātum vi to persist ♦ vt to persist in.
persevērus adj very strict.
Persicus adj Persian; of Perses.
Persicum nt peach.
persīdō, -īdere, -ēdī, -essum vi to sink down into.
persignō, -āre vt to record.
persimilis adj very like.
persimplex, -icis adj very simple.
Persis, -idis f Persia.
persistō, -istere, -titī vi to persist.
persōlus adj one and only.
persolūtus ppp of **persolvō.**
persolvō, -vere, -vī, -ūtum vt to pay, pay up; to explain.
persōna, -ae f mask; character, part; person, personality.
persōnātus adj masked; in an assumed character.
personō, -āre, -uī, -itum vi to resound, ring (with); to play ♦ vt to make resound; to cry aloud.
perspectē adv intelligently.
perspectō, -āre vt to have a look through.
perspectus ppp of **perspiciō ♦** adj well-known.
perspeculor, -ārī vt to reconnoitre.
perspergō, -gere, -sī, -sum vt to besprinkle.
perspicāx, -ācis adj sharp, shrewd.
perspicientia, -ae f full understanding.
perspiciō, -icere, -exī, -ectum vt to see through; to examine, observe.
perspicuē adv clearly.
perspicuitās, -ātis f clarity.

perspicuus adj transparent; clear, evident.
persternō, -ernere, -rāvī, -rātum vt to pave all over.
perstimulō, -āre vt to rouse violently.
perstitī perf of **persistō;** perf of **perstō.**
perstō, -āre, -itī, -ātum vi to stand fast; to last; to continue, persist.
perstrātus ppp of **persternō.**
perstrepō, -ere vi to make a lot of noise.
perstrictus ppp of **perstringō.**
perstringō, -ingere, -inxī, -ictum vt to graze, touch lightly; (words) to touch on, belittle, censure; (senses) to dull, deaden.
perstudiōsē adv very eagerly.
perstudiōsus adj very fond.
persuādeō, -dēre, -sī, -sum vi (with dat) to convince, persuade; **~sum habeō, mihi ~sum est** I am convinced.
persuāsiō, -ōnis f convincing.
persuāsus, -ūs m persuasion.
persubtīlis adj very fine.
persultō, -āre vt, vi to prance about, frisk over.
pertaedet, -dēre, -sum est vt (impers) to be weary of, be sick of.
pertegō, -egere, -ēxī, -ēctum vt to cover over.
pertemptō, -āre vt to test carefully; to consider well; to pervade, seize.
pertendō, -ere, -ī vi to push on, persist ♦ vt to go on with.
pertenuis adj very small, very slight.
perterebrō, -āre vt to bore through.
pertergeō, -gēre, -sī, -sum vt to wipe over; to touch lightly.
perterrefaciō, -ere vt to scare thoroughly.
perterreō, -ēre, -uī, -itum vt to frighten thoroughly.
perterricrepus adj with a terrifying crash.
perterritus adj terrified.
pertexō, -ere, -uī, -tum vt to accomplish.
pertica, -ae f pole, staff.
pertimefactus adj very frightened.
pertimēscō, -ēscere, -uī vt, vi to be very alarmed, be very afraid of.
pertinācia, -ae f perseverance, stubbornness.
pertināciter adv see adj.
pertināx, -ācis adj very tenacious; unyielding, stubborn.
pertineō, -ēre, -uī vi to extend, reach; to tend, lead to, concern; to apply, pertain, belong; **quod ~et ad** as far as concerns.
pertingō, -ere vi to extend.
pertolerō, -āre vt to endure to the end.
pertorqueō, -ēre vt to distort.
pertractātē adv in a hackneyed fashion.
pertractātiō, -ōnis f handling.
pertractō, -āre vt to handle, feel all over; (fig) to treat, study.
pertractus ppp of **pertrahō.**

Noun declensions and verb conjugations are shown on pp xiii to xxv. The present infinitive ending of a verb shows to which conjugation it belongs: **-āre** = 1st; **-ēre** = 2nd; **-ere** = 3rd and **-īre** = 4th. Irregular verbs are shown on p xxvi

pertrahō, -here, -xī, -ctum *vt* to drag across, take forcibly; to entice.
pertrect- *etc see* **pertract-**.
pertristis *adj* very sad, very morose.
pertulī *perf of* **perferō**.
pertumultuōsē *adv* very excitedly.
pertundō, -undere, -udī, -ūsum *vt* to perforate.
perturbātē *adv* in confusion.
perturbātiō, -ōnis *f* confusion, disturbance; emotion.
perturbātrīx, -īcis *f* disturber.
perturbātus *ppp of* **perturbō ♦** *adj* troubled; alarmed.
perturbō, -āre, -āvī, -ātum *vt* to throw into disorder, upset, alarm.
perturpis *adj* scandalous.
pertūsus *ppp of* **pertundō ♦** *adj* in holes, leaky.
perungō, -ungere, -ūnxī, -ūnctum *vt* to smear all over.
perurbānus *adj* very refined; over-fine.
perūrō, -rere, -ssi, -stum *vt* to burn up, scorch; to inflame, chafe; to freeze, nip.
Perusia, -iae *f* Etruscan town (*now* Perugia).
Perusīnus *adj see n.*
perūstus *ppp of* **perūrō**.
perūtilis *adj* very useful.
pervādō, -dere, -sī, -sum *vt, vi* to pass through, spread through; to penetrate, reach.
pervagātus *adj* widespread, well-known; general.
pervagor, -ārī, -ātus *vi* to range, rove about; to extend, spread ♦ *vt* to pervade.
pervagus *adj* roving.
pervariē *adv* very diversely.
pervastō, -āre, -āvī, -ātum *vt* to devastate.
pervāsus *ppp of* **pervādō**.
pervectus *ppp of* **pervehō**.
pervehō, -here, -xī, -ctum *vt* to carry, convey, bring through; (*pass*) to ride, drive, sail through; to attain.
pervellō, -ere, -ī *vt* to pull, twitch, pinch; to stimulate; to disparage.
perveniō, -enīre, -ēnī, -entum *vi* to come to, arrive, reach; to attain to.
pervēnor, -ārī *vi* to chase through.
perversē *adv* perversely.
perversitās, -ātis *f* perverseness.
perversus (pervorsus) *ppp of* **pervertō ♦** *adj* awry, squint; wrong, perverse.
pervertō, -tere, -tī, -sum *vt* to overturn, upset; to overthrow, undo; (*speech*) to confute.
pervesperī *adv* very late.
pervestīgātiō, -ōnis *f* thorough search.
pervestīgō, -āre, -āvī, -ātum *vt* to track down; to investigate.
pervetus, -eris *adj* very old.
pervetustus *adj* antiquated.
pervicācia, -ae *f* obstinacy; firmness.
pervicāciter *adv see adj.*
pervicāx, -ācis *adj* obstinate, wilful; dogged.

pervictus *ppp of* **pervincō**.
pervideō, -idēre, -īdī, -īsum *vt* to look over, survey; to consider; to discern.
pervigeō, -ēre, -uī *vi* to continue to flourish.
pervigil, -is *adj* awake, watchful.
pervigilātiō, -ōnis *f* vigil.
pervigilium, -ī *and* **iī** *nt* vigil.
pervigilō, -āre, -āvī, -ātum *vt, vi* to stay awake all night, keep vigil.
pervīlis *adj* very cheap.
pervincō, -incere, -īcī, -ictum *vt, vi* to conquer completely; to outdo, surpass; to prevail upon, effect; (*argument*) to carry a point, maintain, prove.
pervīvō, -ere *vi* to survive.
pervius *adj* passable, accessible.
pervolgō *etc see* **pervulgō**.
pervolitō, -āre *vt, vi* to fly about.
pervolō, -āre, -āvī, -ātum *vt, vi* to fly through *or* over, fly to.
pervolō, -elle, -oluī *vi* to wish very much.
pervolūtō, -āre *vt* (*books*) to read through.
pervolvō, -vere, -vī, -ūtum *vt* to tumble about; (*book*) to read through; (*pass*) to be very busy (with).
pervor- *etc see* **perver-**.
pervulgātus *adj* very common.
pervulgō, -āre, -āvī, -ātum *vt* to make public, impart; to haunt.
pēs, pedis *m* foot; (*length*) foot; (*verse*) foot, metre; (*sailrope*) sheet; **pedem cōnferre** come to close quarters; **pedem referre** go back; **ante pedēs** self-evident; **pedibus** on foot, by land; **pedibus īre in sententiam** take sides; **pedibus aequīs** (*NAUT*) with the wind right aft; **servus ā pedibus** footman.
pessimē *superl of* **male**.
pessimus *superl of* **malus**.
pessulus, -ī *m* bolt.
pessum *adv* to the ground, to the bottom; **~ dare** put an end to, ruin, destroy; **~ īre** sink, perish.
pestifer, -ī *adj* pestilential; baleful, destructive.
pestilēns, -entis *adj* unhealthy; destructive.
pestilentia, -ae *f* plague, pest; unhealthiness.
pestilitās, -ātis *f* plague.
pestis, -is *f* plague, pest; ruin, destruction.
petasātus *adj* wearing the petasus.
petasunculus, -ī *m* small leg of pork.
petasus, -ī *m* broadbrimmed hat.
petessō, -ere *vt* to be eager for.
petītiō, -ōnis *f* thrust, attack; request, application; (*office*) candidature, standing for; (*law*) civil suit, right of claim.
petītor, -ōris *m* candidate; plaintiff.
petītūriō, -īre *vt* to long to be a candidate.
petītus *ppp of* **petō**.
petītus, -ūs *m* falling to.
petō, -ere, -īvī *and* **iī, -ītum** *vt* to aim at, attack; (*place*) to make for, go to; to seek, look for, demand, ask; to go and fetch; (*law*) to sue; (*love*) to court; (*office*) to stand for.

petorritum, -ī *nt* carriage.
petrō, -ōnis *m* yokel.
Petrōnius, -ī *m arbiter of fashion under Nero.*
petulāns, -antis *adj* pert, impudent,
  lascivious.
petulanter *adv see adj.*
petulantia, -ae *f* pertness, impudence.
petulcus *adj* butting.
pexus *ppp of* **pectō.**
Phaeāccius *and* **cus, -x** *adj* Phaeacian.
Phaeāces, -cum *mpl fabulous islanders in the
  Odyssey.*
Phaedra, -ae *f stepmother of Hippolytus.*
Phaedrus, -ī *m pupil of Socrates; writer of Latin
  fables.*
Phaethōn, -ontis *m son of the Sun (killed while
  driving his father's chariot).*
Phaethonteus *adj see n.*
Phaethontiades, -um *fpl sisters of Phaethon.*
phalangae, -ārum *fpl* wooden rollers.
phalangītae, -ārum *mpl* soldiers of a
  phalanx.
phalanx, -gis *f* phalanx; troops, battle order.
Phalaris, -dis *m tyrant of Agrigentum.*
phalerae, -ārum *fpl* medallions, badges;
  (*horse*) trappings.
phalerātus *adj* wearing medallions;
  ornamented.
Phalēreus, -icus *adj see n.*
Phalērum, -ī *nt harbour of Athens.*
pharetra, -ae *f* quiver.
pharetrātus *adj* wearing a quiver.
Pharius *adj see n.*
pharmaceutria, -ae *f* sorceress.
pharmacopōla, -ae *m* quack doctor.
Pharsālicus, -ius *adj see n.*
Pharsālus (-os), -ī *f town in Thessaly (where
  Caesar defeated Pompey).*
Pharus (-os), -ī *f island off Alexandria with a
  famous lighthouse;* lighthouse.
phasēlus, -ī *m/f* French beans; (*boat*) pinnace.
Phāsiacus *adj* Colchian.
Phāsiānus, -āna *m/f* pheasant.
Phāsis, -dis *and* **dos** *m river of Colchis.*
Phāsis *adj see n.*
phasma, -tis *nt* ghost.
Pherae, -ārum *fpl town in Thessaly (home of
  Admetus).*
Pheraeus *adj see n.*
phiala, -ae *f* saucer.
Phīdiacus *adj see n.*
Phīdiās, -ae *m famous Athenian sculptor.*
philēma, -tis *nt* kiss.
Philippī, -ōrum *mpl town in Macedonia (where
  Brutus and Cassius were defeated).*
Philippēus *adj see n.*
Philippicae *fpl Cicero's speeches against Antony.*
Philippicus *adj see n.*
Philippus, -ī *m king of Macedonia;* gold coin.
philitia, (phīditia), -ōrum *ntpl* public meals

at Sparta.
Philō (-ōn), -ōnis *m Academic philosopher
  (teacher of Cicero).*
Philoctētēs, -ae *m Greek archer who gave
  Hercules poisoned arrows.*
philologia, -ae *f* study of literature.
philologus *adj* scholarly, literary.
Philomēla, -ae *f sister of Procne;* nightingale.
philosophē *adv see adj.*
philosophia, -ae *f* philosophy.
philosophor, -ārī, -ātus *vi* to philosophize.
philosophus, -ī *m* philosopher ♦ *adj*
  philosophical.
philtrum, -ī *nt* love potion.
philyra, -ae *f* inner bark of the lime tree.
phīmus, -ī *m* dice box.
Phlegethōn, -ontis *m a river of Hades.*
Phlegethontis *adj see n.*
Phlīāsius *adj see n.*
Phlīūs, -ūntis *f town in Peloponnese.*
phōca, -ae *f* seal.
Phōcaicus *adj see n.*
Phōcēus *adj see n.*
Phōcis, -idis *f country of central Greece.*
Phōcius *adj see n.*
Phoebas, -adis *f* prophetess.
Phoebē, -ēs *f* Diana, the moon.
Phoebēius, -ēus *adj see n.*
Phoebigena, -ae *m son of Phoebus,
  Aesculapius.*
Phoebus, -ī *m* Apollo; the sun.
Phoenīcē, -cēs *f* Phoenicia.
Phoenīces, -cum *mpl* Phoenicians.
phoenīcopterus, -ī *m* flamingo.
Phoenīssus *adj* Phoenician ♦ *f* Dido.
Phoenīx, -īcis *m friend of Achilles.*
phoenīx, -īcis *m* phoenix.
Phorcis, -idos = **Phorcȳnis.**
Phorcus, -ī *m son of Neptune (father of
  Medusa).*
Phorcȳnis, -ȳnidos *f* Medusa.
Phraātēs, -ae *m king of Parthia.*
phrenēsis, -is *f* delirium.
phrenēticus *adj* mad, delirious.
Phrixēus *adj see n.*
Phrixus, -ī *m Helle's brother (who took the ram
  with the golden fleece to Colchis).*
Phryges, -um *mpl* Phrygians; Trojans.
Phrygia, -iae *f* Phrygia (*country of Asia Minor*);
  Troy.
Phrygius *adj* Phrygian, Trojan.
Phthia, -ae *f home of Achilles in Thessaly.*
Phthīōta, -ōtēs, -ōtae *m native of Phthia.*
phthisis *f* consumption.
Phthius *adj see n.*
phy *interj* bah!
phylaca, -ae *f* prison.
phylarchus, -ī *m* chieftain.
physica, -ae *and* **ē, -ēs** *f* physics.
physicē *adv* scientifically.

Noun declensions and verb conjugations are shown on pp xiii to xxv. The present infinitive ending of a verb shows
to which conjugation it belongs: **-āre** = 1st; **-ēre** = 2nd; **-ere** = 3rd and **-īre** = 4th. Irregular verbs are shown on p xxvi

physicus *adj* of physics, natural ♦ *m* natural philosopher ♦ *ntpl* physics.

physiognōmōn, -onis *m* physiognomist.

physiologia, -ae *f* natural philosophy, science.

piābilis *adj* expiable.

piāculāris *adj* atoning ♦ *ntpl* sin offerings.

piāculum, -ī *nt* sin offering; victim; atonement, punishment; sin, guilt.

piāmen, -inis *nt* atonement.

pīca, -ae *f* magpie.

picāria, -ae *f* pitch hut.

picea, -ae *f* pine.

Picēns, -entis *adj* = **Picēnus.**

Picēnum, -ēnī *nt* Picenum.

Picēnus *adj* of Picenum in E. Italy.

piceus *adj* pitch black; of pitch.

pictor, -ōris *m* painter.

pictūra, -ae *f* painting; picture.

pictūrātus *adj* painted; embroidered.

pictus *ppp of* **pingō** ♦ *adj* coloured, tattooed; (*style*) ornate; (*fear*) unreal.

pīcus, -ī *m* woodpecker.

piē *adv* religiously, dutifully.

Pīeris, -dis *f* Muse.

Pīerius *adj* of the Muses, poetic.

pietās, -ātis *f* sense of duty (*to gods, family, country*), piety, filial affection, love, patriotism.

piger, -rī *adj* reluctant, slack, slow; numbing, dull.

piget, -ēre, -uit *vt* (*impers*) to be annoyed, dislike; to regret, repent.

pigmentārius, -ī *and* **iī** *m* dealer in paints.

pigmentum, -ī *nt* paint, cosmetic; (*style*) colouring.

pignerātor, -ōris *m* mortgagee.

pignerō, -āre *vt* to pawn, mortgage.

pigneror, -ārī, -ātus *vt* to claim, accept.

pignus, -oris *and* **eris** *nt* pledge, pawn, security; wager, stake; (*fig*) assurance, token; (*pl*) children, dear ones.

pigritia, -ae, -ēs, -ēī *f* sluggishness, indolence.

pigrō, -āre, -or, -ārī *vi* to be slow, be slack.

pīla, -ae *f* mortar.

pīla, -ae *f* pillar; pier.

pila, -ae *f* ball, ball game.

pīlānus, -ī *m* soldier of the third line.

pīlātus *adj* armed with javelins.

pīlentum, -ī *nt* carriage.

pilleātus *adj* wearing the felt cap.

pilleolus, -ī *m* skullcap.

pilleum, -ī *nt*, **pilleus, -ī** *m* felt cap presented to freed slaves; (*fig*) liberty.

pilōsus *adj* hairy.

pīlum, -ī *nt* javelin.

pīlus, -ī *m* division of triarii; **prīmus ~** chief centurion.

pilus, -ī *m* hair; a whit.

Pimplēa, -ae *and* **is, -idis** *f* Muse.

Pimplēus *adj* of the Muses.

Pindaricus *adj* see n.

Pindarus, -ī *m* Pindar (*Greek lyric poet*).

Pindus, -ī *m* mountain range in Thessaly.

pīnētum, -ī *nt* pine wood.

pīneus *adj* pine- (*in cpds*).

pingō, -ere, pinxī, pictum *vt* to paint, embroider; to colour; (*fig*) to embellish, decorate.

pinguēscō, -ere *vi* to grow fat, become fertile.

pinguis *adj* fat, rich, fertile; (*mind*) gross, dull; (*ease*) comfortable, calm; (*weather*) thick ♦ *nt* grease.

pīnifer, -ī, pīniger, -ī *adj* pine-clad.

pinna, -ae *f* feather; wing, arrow; battlement; (*fish*) fin.

pinnātus *adj* feathered, winged.

pinniger, -ī *adj* winged; finny.

pinnipēs, -edis *adj* wing-footed.

pinnirapus, -ī *m* plume-snatcher.

pinnula, -ae *f* little wing.

pīnotērēs, -ae *m* hermit crab.

pīnsō, -ere *vt* to beat, pound.

pīnus, -ūs *and* **ī** *f* stone pine, Scots fir; ship, torch, wreath.

pinxī *perf of* **pingō.**

piō, -āre *vt* to propitiate, worship; to atone for, avert; to avenge.

piper, -is *nt* pepper.

pīpilō, -āre *vi* to chirp.

Pīraea, -ōrum *ntpl* Piraeus (*port of Athens*).

Pīraeeus *and* **us, -ī** *m* main port of Athens.

Pīraeus *adj* see n.

pīrāta, -ae *m* pirate.

pīrāticus *adj* pirate ♦ *f* piracy.

Pīrēnē, -ēs *f* spring in Corinth.

Pīrēnis, -idis *adj* see n.

Pīrithous, -ī *m* king of the Lapiths.

pirum, -ī *nt* pear.

pirus, -ī *f* pear tree.

Pīsa, -ae *f* Greek town near the Olympic Games site.

Pīsae, -ārum *fpl* town in Etruria (*now* Pisa).

Pīsaeus *adj* see n.

Pīsānus *adj* see n.

piscārius *adj* fish- (*in cpds*), fishing- (*in cpds*).

piscātor, -ōris *m* fisherman.

piscātōrius *adj* fishing- (*in cpds*).

piscātus, -ūs *m* fishing; fish; catch, haul.

pisciculus, -ī *m* little fish.

piscīna, -ae *f* fishpond; swimming pool.

piscīnārius, -ī *and* **iī** *m* person keen on fish ponds.

piscis -is *m* fish; (*ASTRO*) Pisces.

piscor, -ārī, -ātus *vi* to fish.

piscōsus *adj* full of fish.

pisculentus *adj* full of fish.

Pīsistratidae, -idārum *mpl* sons of Pisistratus.

Pīsistratus, -ī *m* tyrant of Athens.

pistillum, -ī *nt* pestle.

pistor, -ōris *m* miller; baker.

pistrilla, -ae *f* little mortar.

pīstrīnum, -ī *nt* mill, bakery; drudgery.

pistris, -is *and* **īx, -īcis** *f* sea monster, whale;

swift ship.

pithēcium, -ī and **iī** nt little ape.

pītuīta, -ae f phlegm; catarrh, cold in the head.

pītuītōsus adj phlegmatic.

pius adj dutiful, conscientious; godly, holy; filial, affectionate; patriotic; good, upright ♦ mpl the blessed dead.

pix, picis f pitch.

plācābilis adj easily appeased.

plācābilitās, -ātis f readiness to condone.

plācāmen, -inis, plācāmentum, -ī nt peace-offering.

plācātē adv calmly.

plācātiō, -ōnis f propitiating.

plācātus ppp of **plācō** ♦ adj calm, quiet, reconciled.

placenta, -ae f cake.

Placentia, -iae f town in N. Italy (now Piacenza).

Placentīnus adj see n.

placeō, -ēre, -uī, -itum vi (with dat) to please, satisfy; **~et** it seems good, it is agreed, resolved; **mihi ~eō** I am pleased with myself.

placidē adv peacefully, gently.

placidus adj calm, quiet, gentle.

placitum,-ī nt principle, belief.

placitus ppa of **placeō** ♦ adj pleasing; agreed on.

plācō, -āre, -āvī, -ātum vt to calm, appease, reconcile.

plāga, -ae f blow, stroke, wound.

plaga, -ae f region, zone.

plaga, -ae f hunting net, snare, trap.

plagiārius, -ī and **iī** m plunderer, kidnapper.

plāgigerulus adj much flogged.

plāgōsus adj fond of punishing.

plagula, -ae f curtain.

planctus, -ūs m beating the breast, lamentation.

plānē adv plainly, clearly; completely, quite; certainly.

plangō, -gere, -xī, -ctum vt, vi to beat noisily; to beat in grief; to lament loudly, bewail.

plangor, -ōris m beating; loud lamentation.

plānipēs, -edis m ballet dancer.

plānitās, -ātis f perspicuity.

plānitiēs, -ēī, (-a, -ae) f level ground, plain.

planta, -ae f shoot, slip; sole, foot.

plantāria, -ium ntpl slips, young trees.

plānus adj level, flat; plain, clear ♦ nt level ground; **dē ~ō** easily.

planus, -ī m impostor.

platalea, -ae f spoonbill.

platea, -ae f street.

Platō, -ōnis m Plato (founder of the Academic school of philosophy).

Platōnicus adj see n.

plaudō, -dere, -sī, -sum vt to clap, beat, stamp ♦ vi to clap, applaud; to approve, be

pleased with.

plausibilis adj praiseworthy.

plausor, -ōris m applauder.

plaustrum, -ī nt waggon, cart; (ASTRO) Great Bear; **~ percellere** upset the applecart.

plausus ppp of **plaudō**.

plausus, -ūs m flapping; clapping, applause.

Plautīnus adj see n.

Plautus, -ī m early Latin comic poet.

plēbēcula, -ae f rabble.

plēbēius adj plebeian; common, low.

plēbicola, -ae m friend of the people.

plēbiscītum, -ī nt decree of the people.

plēbs (plēbēs), -is f common people, plebeians; lower classes, masses.

plēctō, -ere vt to punish.

plēctrum, -ī nt plectrum; lyre, lyric poetry.

Plēias, -dis f Pleiad; (pl) the Seven Sisters.

plēnē adv fully, entirely.

plēnus adj full, filled; (fig) sated; (age) mature; (amount) complete; (body) stout, plump; (female) pregnant; (matter) solid; (style) copious; (voice) loud; **ad ~um** abundantly.

plērumque adv generally, mostly.

plērusque adj a large part, most; (pl) the majority, the most; very many.

plexus adj plaited, interwoven.

Plīas see **Plēias**.

plicātrīx, -īcis f clothes folder.

plicō, -āre, -āvī and **uī, -ātum** and **itum** vt to fold, coil.

Plīnius, -ī m Roman family name (esp Pliny the Elder, who died in the eruption of Vesuvius); Pliny the Younger, writer of letters).

plōrātus, -ūs m wailing.

plōrō, -āre, -āvī, -ātum vi to wail, lament ♦ vt to weep for, bewail.

plōstellum, -ī nt cart.

ploxenum, -ī nt cart box.

pluit, -ere, -it vi (impers) it is raining.

plūma, -ae f soft feather, down.

plumbeus adj of lead; (fig) heavy, dull, worthless.

plumbum, -ī nt lead; bullet, pipe, ruler; **~ album** tin.

plūmeus adj down, downy.

plūmipēs, -edis adj feather-footed.

plūmōsus adj feathered.

plūrimus superl of **multus**.

plūs, -ūris compar of **multus** ♦ adv more.

plūsculus adj a little more.

pluteus, -ī m shelter, penthouse; parapet; couch; bookcase.

Plūtō, -ōnis m king of the lower world.

Plūtōnius adj see n.

pluvia, -ae f rain.

pluviālis adj rainy.

pluvius adj rainy, rain- (in cpds).

pōcillum, -ī nt small cup.

pōculum, -ī nt cup; drink, potion.

Noun declensions and verb conjugations are shown on pp xiii to xxv. The present infinitive ending of a verb shows to which conjugation it belongs: **-āre** = 1st; **-ēre** = 2nd; **-ere** = 3rd and **-īre** = 4th. Irregular verbs are shown on p xxvi

podagra, -ae *f* gout.
podagrōsus *adj* gouty.
podium, -ī *and* **iī** *nt* balcony.
poēma, -tis *nt* poem.
poena, -ae *f* penalty, punishment; **poenas dare** to be punished.
Poenī, -ōrum *mpl* Carthaginians.
Poenus, Pūnicus *adj* Punic.
poēsis, -is *f* poetry, poem.
poēta, -ae *m* poet.
poēticē *adv* poetically.
poēticus *adj* poetic ♦ *f* poetry.
poētria, -ae *f* poetess.
pol *interj* by Pollux!, truly.
polenta, -ae *f* pearl barley.
poliō, -īre, -īvī, -ītum *vt* to polish; to improve, put in good order.
polītē *adv* elegantly.
polītīa, -ae *f* Plato's Republic.
politicus *adj* political.
polītus *adj* polished, refined, cultured.
pollen, -inis *nt* fine flour, meal.
pollēns, -entis *pres p of* **polleō** ♦ *adj* powerful, strong.
pollentia, -ae *f* power.
polleō, -ēre *vi* to be strong, be powerful.
pollex, -icis *m* thumb.
polliceor, -ērī, -itus *vt* to promise, offer.
pollicitātiō, -ōnis *f* promise.
pollicitor, -ārī, -ātus *vt* to promise.
pollicitum, -ī *nt* promise.
Polliō, -ōnis *m* Roman surname (*esp C. Asinius, soldier, statesman and literary patron under Augustus*).
pollis, -inis *m/f see* **pollen**.
pollūcibiliter *adv* sumptuously.
pollūctus *adj* offered up ♦ *nt* offering.
polluō, -uere, -uī, -ūtum *vt* to defile, pollute, dishonour.
Pollūx, -ūcis *m* twin brother of Castor (*famous as a boxer*).
polus, -ī *m* pole, North pole; sky.
Polyhymnia, -ae *f* a Muse.
Polyphēmus, -ī *m* one-eyed Cyclops.
pōlypus, -ī *m* polypus.
pōmārium, -ī *and* **iī** *nt* orchard.
pōmārius, -ī *and* **iī** *m* fruiterer.
pōmerīdiānus *adj* afternoon.
pōmērium, -ī *and* **iī** *nt* free space round the city boundary.
pōmifer, -ī *adj* fruitful.
pōmoerium *see* **pōmērium**.
pōmōsus *adj* full of fruit.
pompa, -ae *f* procession; retinue, train; ostentation.
Pompeiānus *adj see n.*
Pompeiī, -ōrum *mpl Campanian town buried by an eruption of Vesuvius.*
Pompeius, -ī *m* Roman family name (*esp Pompey the Great*).
Pompeius, -ānus *adj see n.*
Pompilius, -ī *m* Numa (*second king of Rome*).
Pompilius *adj see n.*

Pomptīnus *adj* Pomptine (*name of marshy district in S. Latium*).
pōmum, -ī *nt* fruit; fruit tree.
pōmus, -ī *f* fruit tree.
ponderō, -āre *vt* to weigh; to consider, reflect on.
ponderōsus *adj* heavy, weighty.
pondō *adv* in weight; pounds.
pondus, -eris *nt* weight; mass, burden; (*fig*) importance, authority; (*character*) firmness; (*pl*) balance.
pōne *adv* behind.
pōnō, -ere, posuī, positum *vt* to put, place, lay, set; to lay down, lay aside; (*fig*) to regard, reckon; (*art*) to make, build; (*camp*) to pitch; (*corpse*) to lay out, bury; (*example*) to take; (*food*) to serve; (*hair*) to arrange; (*hope*) to base, stake; (*hypothesis*) to suppose, assume; (*institution*) to lay down, ordain; (*money*) to invest; (*sea*) to calm; (*theme*) to propose; (*time*) to spend, devote; (*tree*) to plant; (*wager*) to put down ♦ *vi* (*wind*) to abate.
pōns, pontis *m* bridge; drawbridge; (*ship*) gangway, deck.
ponticulus, -ī *m* small bridge.
Ponticus *adj see* **Pontus**.
pontifex, -icis *m* high priest, pontiff.
pontificālis *adj* pontifical.
pontificātus, -ūs *m* high priesthood.
pontificius *adj* pontiff's.
pontō, -ōnis *m* ferryboat.
pontus, -ī *m* sea.
Pontus, -ī *m* Black Sea; *kingdom of Mithridates in Asia Minor.*
popa, -ae *m* minor priest.
popanum, -ī *nt* sacrificial cake.
popellus, -ī *m* mob.
popīna, -ae *f* eating house, restaurant.
popīnō, -ōnis *m* glutton.
popl- *etc see* **pūbl-**.
poples, -itis *m* knee.
poposcī *perf of* **poscō**.
poppysma, -tis *nt* clicking of the tongue.
populābilis *adj* destroyable.
populābundus *adj* ravaging.
populāris *adj* of, from, for the people; popular, democratic; native ♦ *m* fellow countryman ♦ *mpl* the people's party, the democrats.
populāritās, -ātis *f* courting popular favour.
populāriter *adv* vulgarly; democratically.
populātiō, -ōnis *f* plundering; plunder.
populātor, -ōris *m* ravager.
pōpuleus *adj* poplar- (*in cpds*).
pōpulifer, -ī *adj* rich in poplars.
populor, -ārī, -ātus; -ō, -āre *vt* to ravage, plunder; to destroy, ruin.
populus, -ī *m* people, nation; populace, the public; large crowds; district.
pōpulus, -ī *f* poplar tree.
porca, -ae *f* sow.
porcella, -ae *f*, **-us, -ī** *m* little pig.

porcīna, -ae *f* pork.
porcīnārius, -ī *and* **iī** *m* pork seller.
Porcius, -ī *m* family name of Cato.
Porcius *adj see n.*
porculus, -ī *m* porker.
porcus, -ī *m* pig, hog.
porgō *etc see* **porrigō.**
Porphyriōn, -ōnis *m* a Giant.
porrēctiō, -ōnis *f* extending.
porrēctus *ppp of* **porrigō** ♦ *adj* long, protracted; dead.
porrēxī *perf of* **porrigō.**
porriciō, -ere *vt* to make an offering of; **inter caesa et porrēcta** ≈ *at the eleventh hour.*
porrigō, -igere, -ēxī, -ēctum *vt* to stretch, spread out, extend; to offer, hold out.
porrīgō, -inis *f* scurf, dandruff.
porrō *adv* forward, a long way off; (*time*) in future, long ago; (*sequence*) next, moreover, in turn.
porrum, -ī *nt* leek.
Porsena, Porsenna, Porsinna, -ae *f* king of Clusium in Etruria.
porta, -ae *f* gate; entrance, outlet.
portātiō, -ōnis *f* carrying.
portendō, -dere, -dī, -tum *vt* to denote, predict.
portentificus *adj* marvellous.
portentōsus *adj* unnatural.
portentum, -ī *nt* omen, unnatural happening; monstrosity, monster; (*story*) marvel.
porthmeus, -eī *and* **eos** *m* ferryman.
porticula, -ae *f* small gallery.
porticus, -ūs *m* portico, colonnade; (MIL) gallery; (PHILOS) Stoicism.
portiō, -ōnis *f* share, instalment; **prō ~ōne** proportionally.
portitor, -ōris *m* customs officer.
portitor, -ōris *m* ferryman.
portō, -āre, -āvī, -ātum *vt* to carry, convey, bring.
portōrium, -ī *and* **iī** *nt* customs duty, tax.
portula, -ae *f* small gate.
portuōsus *adj* well-off for harbours.
portus, -ūs *m* harbour, port; (*fig*) safety, haven.
pōsca, -ae *f* a vinegar drink.
poscō, -ere, poposcī *vt* to ask, require, demand; to call on.
Posīdōnius, -ī *m* Stoic philosopher (*teacher of Cicero*).
positiō, -ōnis *f* position, climate.
positor, -ōris *m* builder.
positūra, -ae *f* position; formation.
positus *ppp of* **pōnō** ♦ *adj* situated.
posse *infin of* **possum.**
possēdī *perf of* **possideō;** *perf of* **possīdō.**
possessiō, -ōnis *f* seizing; occupation; possession, property.
possessiuncula, -ae *f* small estate.

possessor, -ōris *m* occupier, possessor.
possessus *ppp of* **possideō** *and* **possīdō.**
possideō, -idēre, -ēdī, -essum *vt* to hold, occupy; to have, possess.
possīdō, -īdere, -ēdī, -essum *vt* to take possession of.
possum, -sse, -tuī *vi* to be able, can; to have power, avail.
post *adv* (*place*) behind; (*time*) after; (*sequence*) next ♦ *prep* (*with acc*) behind; after, since; **paulō ~** soon after; **~ urbem conditam** since the foundation of the city.
posteā *adv* afterwards, thereafter; next, then; **~ quam** *conj* after.
posterior, -ōris *adj* later, next; inferior, less important.
posteritās, -ātis *f* posterity, the future.
posterius *adv* later.
posterus *adj* next, following ♦ *mpl* posterity.
postferō, -re *vt* to put after, sacrifice.
postgenitī, -ōrum *mpl* later generations.
posthabeō, -ēre, -uī, -itum *vt* to put after, neglect.
posthāc *adv* hereafter, in future.
postibi *adv* then, after that.
postīculum, -ī *nt* small back building.
postīcus *adj* back- (*in cpds*), hind- (*in cpds*) ♦ *nt* back door.
postideā *adv* after that.
postillā *adv* afterwards.
postis, -is *m* doorpost, door.
postlīminium, -ī *and* **iī** *nt* right of recovery.
postmerīdiānus *adj* in the afternoon.
postmodo, postmodum *adv* shortly, presently.
postpōnō, -ōnere, -osuī, -ositum *vt* to put after, disregard.
postputō, -āre *vt* to consider less important.
postquam *conj* after, when.
postrēmō *adv* finally.
postrēmus *adj* last, rear; lowest, worst.
postrīdiē *adv* next day, the day after.
postscaenium, -ī *and* **iī** *nt* behind the scenes.
postscrībō, -ere *vt* to write after.
postulātiō, -ōnis *f* demand, claim; complaint.
postulātum, -ī *nt* demand, claim.
postulātus, -ūs *m* claim.
postulō, -āre, -āvī, -ātum *vt* to demand, claim; (*law*) to summon, prosecute; to apply for a writ (to prosecute).
postumus *adj* last, last-born.
postus *etc see* **positus.**
posuī *perf of* **pōnō.**
pōtātiō, -ōnis *f* drinking.
pōtātor, -ōris *m* toper.
pote *etc see* **potis.**
potēns, -entis *adj* able, capable; powerful, strong, potent; master of, ruling over; successful in carrying out.
potentātus, -ūs *m* political power.

Noun declensions and verb conjugations are shown on pp xiii to xxv. The present infinitive ending of a verb shows to which conjugation it belongs: **-āre** = 1st; **-ēre** = 2nd; **-ere** = 3rd and **-īre** = 4th. Irregular verbs are shown on p xxvi

potenter *adv* powerfully; competently.
potentia, -ae *f* power, force, efficacy;
tyranny.
potērium, -ī *and* **iī** *nt* goblet.
potesse *archaic infin of* **possum.**
potestās, -ātis *f* power, ability; control,
sovereignty, authority; opportunity,
permission; (*person*) magistrate; (*things*)
property; **~ātem suī facere** allow access to
oneself.
potin can (you)?, is it possible?
pōtiō, -ōnis *f* drink, draught, philtre.
potiō, -īre *vt* to put into the power of.
potior, -īrī, -ītus *vi* (*with gen and abl*) to take
possession of, get hold of, acquire; to be
master of.
potior, -ōris *adj* better, preferable.
potis *adj* (*indecl*) able; possible.
potissimum *adv* especially.
potissimus *adj* chief, most important.
pōtitō, -āre *vt* to drink much.
potius *adv* rather, more.
pōtō, -āre, -āvī, -ātum *and* **um** *vt* to drink.
pōtor, -ōris *m* drinker.
pōtrīx, -īcis *f* woman tippler.
potuī *perf of* **possum.**
pōtulenta, -ōrum *ntpl* drinks.
pōtus *ppp of* **pōtō** ♦ *adj* drunk.
pōtus, -ūs *m* drink.
prae *adv* in front, before; in comparison ♦ *prep*
(*with abl*) in front of; compared with; (*cause*)
because of, for; **~ sē** openly; **~ sē ferre**
display; **~ manū** to hand.
praeacūtus *adj* pointed.
praealtus *adj* very high, very deep.
praebeō, -ēre, -uī, -itum *vt* to hold out,
proffer; to give, supply; to show, represent;
sē ~ behave, prove.
praebibō, -ere, -ī *vt* to toast.
praebitor, -ōris *m* purveyor.
praecalidus *adj* very hot.
praecānus *adj* prematurely grey.
praecautus *ppp of* **praecaveō.**
praecaveō, -avēre, -āvī, -autum *vt* to guard
against ♦ *vi* to beware, take precautions.
praecēdō, -dere, -ssī, -ssum *vt* to go before;
to surpass ♦ *vi* to lead the way; to excel.
praecellō, -ere *vi* to excel, be distinguished ♦
vt to surpass.
praecelsus *adj* very high.
praecentiō, -ōnis *f* prelude.
praecentō, -āre *vi* to sing an incantation for.
praeceps, -ipitis *adj* head first, headlong;
going down, precipitous; rapid, violent,
hasty; inclined (to); dangerous ♦ *nt* edge of
an abyss, precipice; danger ♦ *adv* headlong;
into danger.
praeceptiō, -ōnis *f* previous notion; precept.
praeceptor, -ōris *m* teacher.
praeceptrīx, -rīcis *f* teacher.
praeceptum, -ī *nt* maxim, precept; order.
praeceptus *ppp of* **praecipiō.**
praecerpō, -ere, -sī, -tum *vt* to gather

prematurely; to forestall.
praecīdō, -dere, -dī, -sum *vt* to cut off,
damage; (*fig*) to cut short, put an end to.
praecinctus *ppp of* **praecingō.**
praecingō, -ingere, -inxī, -inctum *vt* to gird
in front; to surround.
praecinō, -inere, -inuī, -entum *vt* to play
before; to chant a spell ♦ *vt* to predict.
praecipiō, -ipere, -ēpī, -ēptum *vt* to take
beforehand, get in advance; to anticipate; to
teach, admonish, order.
praecipitanter *adv* at full speed.
praecipitem *acc of* **praeceps.**
praecipitō, -āre, -āvī, -ātum *vt* to throw
down, throw away, hasten; (*fig*) to remove,
carry away, ruin ♦ *vi* to rush headlong, fall;
to be hasty.
praecipuē *adv* especially, chiefly.
praecipuus *adj* special; principal,
outstanding.
praecīsē *adv* briefly, absolutely.
praecīsus *ppp of* **praecīdō** ♦ *adj* steep.
praeclārē *adv* very clearly; excellently.
praeclārus *adj* very bright; beautiful,
splendid; distinguished, noble.
praeclūdō, -dere, -sī, -sum *vt* to close, shut
against; to close to, impede.
praecō, -ōnis *m* crier, herald; auctioneer.
praecōgitō, -āre *vt* to premeditate.
praecognitus *adj* foreseen.
praecolō, -olere, -oluī, -ultum *vt* to cultivate
early.
praecompositus *adj* studied.
praecōnium, -ī *and* **iī** *nt* office of a crier;
advertisement; commendation.
praecōnius *adj* of a public crier.
praecōnsūmō, -ere, -ptum *vt* to use up
beforehand.
praecontrectō, -āre *vt* to consider
beforehand.
praecordia, -ōrum *ntpl* midriff; stomach;
breast, heart; mind.
praecorrumpō, -umpere, -ūpī, -uptum *vt* to
bribe beforehand.
praecox, -cis *adj* early, premature.
praecultus *ppp of* **praecolō.**
praecurrentia, -ium *ntpl* antecedents.
praecurrō, -rrere, -currī *and* **rrī, -rsum** *vi* to
hurry on before, precede; to excel ♦ *vt* to
anticipate; to surpass.
praecursiō, -ōnis *f* previous occurrence;
(*RHET*) preparation.
praecursor, -ōris *m* advance guard; scout.
praecutiō, -ere *vt* to brandish before.
praeda, -ae *f* booty, plunder; (*animal*) prey;
(*fig*) gain.
praedābundus *adj* plundering.
praedamnō, -āre *vt* to condemn beforehand.
praedātiō, -ōnis *f* plundering.
praedātor, -ōris *m* plunderer.
praedātōrius *adj* marauding.
praedēlassō, -āre *vt* to weaken beforehand.
praedēstinō, -āre *vt* to predetermine.

praediātor, -ōris m buyer of landed estates.
praediātōrius adj relating to the sale of estates.
praedicābilis adj laudatory.
praedicātiō, -ōnis f proclamation; commendation.
praedicātor, -ōris m eulogist.
praedicō, -āre, -āvī, -ātum vt to proclaim, make public; to declare; to praise, boast.
praedīcō, -īcere, -īxī, -ictum vt to mention beforehand, prearrange; to foretell; to warn, command.
praedictiō, -ōnis f foretelling.
praedictum, -ī nt prediction; command; prearrangement.
praedictus ppp of **praedīcō**.
praediolum, -ī nt small estate.
praediscō, -ere vt to learn beforehand.
praedispositus adj arranged beforehand.
praeditus adj endowed, provided.
praedium, -ī and iī nt estate.
praedīves, -itis adj very rich.
praedō, -ōnis m robber, pirate.
praedor, -ārī, -ātus vt, vi to plunder, rob; (fig) to profit.
praedūcō, -ūcere, -ūxī, -uctum vt to draw in front.
praedulcis adj very sweet.
praedūrus adj very hard, very tough.
praeēmineō, -ēre vt to surpass.
praeeō, -īre, -īvī and iī, -itum vi to lead the way, go first; (formula) to dictate, recite first ♦ vt to precede, outstrip.
praeesse infin of **praesum**.
praefātiō, -ōnis f formula; preface.
praefātus ppa of **praefor**.
praefectūra, -ae f superintendence; governorship; Italian town governed by Roman edicts, prefecture; district, province.
praefectus ppp of **praeficiō** ♦ m overseer, director, governor, commander; ~ **classis** admiral; ~ **legiōnis** colonel; ~ **urbis** or **urbī** city prefect (of Rome).
praeferō, -ferre, -tulī, -lātum vt to carry in front, hold out; to prefer; to show, display; to anticipate; (pass) to hurry past, outflank.
praeferōx, -ōcis adj very impetuous, very insolent.
praefervidus adj very hot.
praefestīnō, -āre vi to be too hasty; to hurry past.
praefica, -ae f hired mourner.
praeficiō, -icere, -ēcī, -ectum vt to put in charge, give command over.
praefidēns, -entis adj over-confident.
praefigō, -gere, -xī, -xum vt to fasten in front, set up before; to tip, point; to transfix.
praefiniō, -īre, -īvī and iī, -ītum vt to determine, prescribe.
praefiscinē, -ī adv without offence.

praeflōrō, -āre vt to tarnish.
praefluō, -ere vt, vi to flow past.
praefocō, -āre vt to choke.
praefodiō, -odere, -ōdī vt to dig in front of; to bury beforehand.
praefor, -ārī, -ātus vt, vi to say in advance, preface; to pray beforehand; to predict.
praefractē adv resolutely.
praefrāctus ppp of **praefringō** ♦ adj abrupt; stern.
praefrīgidus adj very cold.
praefringō, -ingere, -ēgī, -āctum vt to break off, shiver.
praefuī perf of **praesum**.
praefulciō, -cīre, -sī, -tum vt to prop up; to use as a prop.
praefulgeō, -ulgēre, -ulsī vt to shine conspicuously; to outshine.
praegelidus adj very cold.
praegestiō, -īre vi to be very eager.
praegnāns, -antis adj pregnant; full.
praegracilis adj very slim.
praegrandis adj very large, very great.
praegravis adj very heavy; very wearisome.
praegravō, -āre vt to weigh down; to eclipse.
praegredior, -dī, -ssus vt, vi to go before; to go past; to surpass.
praegressiō, -ōnis f precession, precedence.
praegustātor, -ōris m taster.
praegustō, -āre vt to taste beforehand.
praehibeō, -ēre vt to offer, give.
praeiaceō, -ēre vt to lie in front of.
praeiūdicium, -ī and iī nt precedent, example; prejudgment.
praeiūdicō, -āre, -āvī, -ātum vt to prejudge, decide beforehand.
praeiuvō, -āre vt to give previous assistance to.
praelābor, -bī, -psus vt, vi to move past, move along.
praelambō, -ere vt to lick first.
praelātus ppp of **praeferō**.
praelegō, -ere vt to coast along.
praeligō, -āre vt to bind, tie up.
praelongus adj very long, very tall.
praeloquor, -quī, -cūtus vi to speak first.
praelūceō, -cēre, -xī vi to light, shine; to outshine.
praelūstris adj very magnificent.
praemandāta ntpl warrant of arrest.
praemandō, -āre, -āvī, -ātum vt to bespeak.
praemātūrē adv too soon.
praemātūrus adj too early, premature.
praemedicātus adj protected by charms.
praemeditātiō, -ōnis f thinking over the future.
praemeditātus adj premeditated.
praemeditor, -ārī, -ātus vt to think over, practise.
praemetuenter adv anxiously.

Noun declensions and verb conjugations are shown on pp xiii to xxv. The present infinitive ending of a verb shows to which conjugation it belongs: **-āre** = 1st; **-ēre** = 2nd; **-ere** = 3rd and **-īre** = 4th. Irregular verbs are shown on p xxvi

praemetuō, -ere *vi* to be anxious ♦ *vt* to fear the future.

praemissus *ppp of* **praemittō.**

praemittō, -ittere, -īsī, -issum *vt* to send in advance.

praemium, -ī *and* **iī** *nt* prize, reward.

praemolestia, -ae *f* apprehension.

praemōlior, -īrī *vt* to prepare thoroughly.

praemoneō, -ēre, -uī, -itum *vt* to forewarn, foreshadow.

praemonitus, -ūs *m* premonition.

praemōnstrātor, -ōris *m* guide.

praemōnstrō, -āre *vt* to guide; to predict.

praemordeō, -ēre *vt* to bite off; to pilfer.

praemorior, -ī, -tuus *vi* to die too soon.

praemūniō, -īre, -īvī, -ītum *vt* to fortify, strengthen, secure.

praemūnītiō, -ōnis *f* (*RHET*) preparation.

praenārrō, -āre *vt* to tell beforehand.

praenatō, -āre *vt* to flow past.

Praeneste, -is *nt/f* Latin town (*now* Palestrina).

Praenestīnus *adj see n.*

praeniteō, -ēre, -uī *vi* to seem more attractive.

praenōmen, -inis *nt* first name.

praenōscō, -ere *vt* to foreknow.

praenōtiō, -ōnis *f* preconceived idea.

praenūbilus *adj* very gloomy.

praenūntia, -iae *f* harbinger.

praenūntiō, -āre *vt* to foretell.

praenūntius, -ī *and* **iī** *m* harbinger.

praeoccupō, -āre, -āvī, -ātum *vt* to take first, anticipate.

praeolit mihi I get a hint of.

praeoptō, -āre, -āvī, -ātum *vt* to choose rather, prefer.

praepandō, -ere *vt* to spread out; to expound.

praeparātiō, -ōnis *f* preparation.

praeparō, -āre, -āvī, -ātum *vt* to prepare, prepare for; **ex ~ātō** by arrangement.

praepediō, -īre, -īvī, -ītum *vt* to shackle, tether; to hamper.

praependeō, -ēre *vi* to hang down in front.

praepes, -etis *adj* swift, winged; of good omen ♦ *f* bird.

praepilātus *adj* tipped with a ball.

praepinguis *adj* very rich.

praepolleō, -ēre *vi* to be very powerful, be superior.

praeponderō, -āre *vt* to outweigh.

praepōnō, -ōnere, -osuī, -ositum *vt* to put first, place in front; to put in charge, appoint commander; to prefer.

praeportō, -āre *vt* to carry before.

praepositiō, -ōnis *f* preference; (*GRAM*) preposition.

praepositus *ppp of* **praepōnō** ♦ *m* overseer, commander.

praepossum, -sse, -tuī *vi* to gain the upper hand.

praeposterē *adv* the wrong way round.

praeposterus *adj* inverted, perverted; absurd.

praepotēns, -entis *adj* very powerful.

praeproperanter *adv* too hastily.

praeproperē *adv* too hastily.

praeproperus *adj* overhasty, rash.

praepūtium, -ī *and* **iī** *nt* foreskin.

praequam *adv* compared with.

praequestus *adj* complaining beforehand.

praeradiō, -āre *vt* to outshine.

praerapidus *adj* very swift.

praereptus *ppp of* **praeripiō.**

praerigēscō, -ēscere, -uī *vi* to become very stiff.

praeripiō, -ipere, -ipuī, -eptum *vt* to take before, forestall; to carry off prematurely; to frustrate.

praerōdō, -dere, -sum *vt* to bite the end of, nibble off.

praerogātīva, -ae *f* tribe or century with the first vote, the first vote; previous election; omen, sure token.

praerogātīvus *adj* voting first.

praerōsus *ppp of* **praerōdō.**

praerumpō, -umpere, -ūpī, -uptum *vt* to break off.

praeruptus *ppp of* **praerumpō** ♦ *adj* steep, abrupt; headstrong.

praes, -aedis *m* surety; property of a surety.

praesaep- *etc see* **praesēp-.**

praesāgiō, -īre *vt* to have a presentiment of, forebode.

praesāgītiō, -ōnis *f* foreboding.

praesāgium, -ī *and* **iī** *nt* presentiment; prediction.

praesāgus *adj* foreboding, prophetic.

praesciō, -īre, -iī *vt* to know before.

praescīscō, -ere *vt* to find out beforehand.

praescius *adj* foreknowing.

praescrībō, -bere, -psī, -ptum *vt* to write first; to direct, command; to dictate, describe; to put forward as a pretext.

praescrīptiō, -ōnis *f* preface, heading; order, rule; pretext.

praescrīptum, -ī *nt* order, rule.

praescrīptus *ppp of* **praescrībō.**

praesecō, -āre, -uī, -tum *and* **-ātum** *vt* to cut off, pare.

praesēns, -entis *adj* present, in person; (*things*) immediate, ready, prompt; (*mind*) resolute; (*gods*) propitious ♦ *ntpl* present state of affairs; **in ~ēns** for the present; **~in rē ~entī** on the spot.

praesēnsiō, -ōnis *f* foreboding; preconception.

praesēnsus *ppp of* **praesentiō.**

praesentārius *adj* instant, ready.

praesentia, -ae *f* presence; effectiveness.

praesentiō, -entīre, -ēnsī, -ēnsum *vt* to presage, have a foreboding of.

praesēpe, -is *nt*, **-ēs, -is** *f* stable, fold, pen; hovel; hive.

praesēpiō, -īre, -sī, -tum *vt* to barricade.

praesēpis *f* = **praesēpe.**

praesertim *adv* especially.
praeserviō, -īre *vi* to serve as a slave.
praeses, -idis *m* guardian, protector; chief, ruler.
praesideō, -idēre, -ēdī *vi* to guard, defend; to preside over, direct.
praesidiārius *adj* garrison-.
praesidium, -ī *and* **iī** *nt* defence, protection; support, assistance; guard, garrison, convoy; defended position, entrenchment.
praesignificō, -āre *vt* to foreshadow.
praesignis *adj* conspicuous.
praesonō, -āre, -uī *vi* to sound before.
praespargō, -ere *vt* to strew before.
praestābilis *adj* outstanding; preferable.
praestāns, -antis *pres p of* **praestō** ♦ *adj* outstanding, pre-eminent.
praestantia, -ae *f* pre-eminence.
praestes, -itis *adj* presiding, guardian.
praestīgiae, -ārum *fpl* illusion, sleight of hand.
praestīgiātor, -ōris *m*, **-rīx, -rīcis** *f* conjurer, cheat.
praestinō, -āre *vt* to buy.
praestitī *perf of* **praestō**.
praestituō, -uere, -uī, -ūtum *vt* to prearrange, prescribe.
praestitus *ppp of* **praestō**.
praestō *adv* at hand, ready.
praestō, -āre, -itī, -itum *and* **ātum** *vi* to be outstanding, be superior; (*impers*) it is better ♦ *vt* to excel; to be responsible for, answer for; (*duty*) to discharge, perform; (*quality*) to show, prove; (*things*) to give, offer, provide; **sē ~** behave, prove.
praestōlor, -ārī, -ātus *vt, vi* to wait for, expect.
praestrictus *ppp of* **praestringō**.
praestringō, -ingere, -inxī, -ictum *vt* to squeeze; to blunt, dull; (*eyes*) to dazzle.
praestruō, -ere, -xī, -ctum *vt* to block up; to build beforehand.
praesul, -is *m/f* public dancer.
praesultātor, -ōris *m* public dancer.
praesultō, -āre *vi* to dance before.
praesum, -esse, -fuī *vi* (*with dat*) to be at the head of, be in command of; to take the lead; to protect.
praesūmō, -ere, -psī, -ptum *vt* to take first; to anticipate; to take for granted.
praesūtus *adj* sewn over at the point.
praetemptō, -āre *vt* to feel for, grope for; to test in advance.
praetendō, -dere, -dī, -tum *vt* to hold out, put before, spread in front of; to give as an excuse, allege.
praetentō *etc see* **praetemptō**.
praetentus *ppp of* **praetendō** ♦ *adj* lying over against.
praetepeō, -ēre, -uī *vi* to glow before.

praeter *adv* beyond; excepting ♦ *prep* (*with acc*) past, along; except, besides; beyond, more than, in addition to, contrary to.
praeteragō, -ere *vt* to drive past.
praeterbītō, -ere *vt, vi* to pass by.
praeterdūcō, -ere *vt* to lead past.
pra250tereā *adv* besides; moreover; henceforth.
praetereō, -īre, -iī, -itum *vi* to go past ♦ *vt* to pass, overtake; to escape, escape the notice of; to omit, leave out, forget, neglect; to reject, exclude; to surpass; to transgress.
praeterequitāns, -antis *adj* riding past.
praeterfluō, -ere *vt, vi* to flow past.
praetergredior, -dī, -ssus *vt* to pass, march past; to surpass.
praeterhāc *adv* further, more.
praeteritus *ppp of* **praetereō** ♦ *adj* past, gone by ♦ *ntpl* the past.
praeterlābor, -bī, -psus *vt* to flow past, move past ♦ *vi* to slip away.
praeterlātus *adj* driving, flying past.
praetermeō, -āre *vi* to pass by.
praetermissiō, -ōnis *f* omission, passing over.
praetermittō, -ittere, -īsī, -issum *vt* to let pass; to omit, neglect; to make no mention of; to overlook.
praeterquam *adv* except, besides.
praetervectiō, -ōnis *f* passing by.
praetervehor, -hī, -ctus *vt, vi* to ride past, sail past; to march past; to pass by, pass over.
praetervolō, -āre *vt, vi* to fly past; to escape.
praetexō, -ere, -uī, -tum *vt* to border, fringe; to adorn; to pretend, disguise.
praetextātus *adj* wearing the toga praetexta, under age.
praetextus *ppp of* **praetexō** ♦ *adj* wearing the toga praetexta ♦ *f* toga with a purple border; Roman tragedy ♦ *nt* pretext.
praetextus, -ūs *m* splendour; pretence.
praetimeō, -ēre *vi* to be afraid in advance.
praetinctus *adj* dipped beforehand.
praetor, -ōris *m* chief magistrate, commander; praetor; propraetor, governor.
praetōriānus *adj* of the emperor's bodyguard.
praetōrium, -ī *and* **iī** *nt* general's tent, camp headquarters; governor's residence; council of war; palace, grand building; emperor's bodyguard.
praetōrius *adj* praetor's, praetorian; of a propraetor; of the emperor's bodyguard ♦ *m* ex-praetor; **~ia cohors** bodyguard of general *or* emperor; **porta ~ia** camp gate facing the enemy.
praetorqueō, -ēre *vt* to strangle first.
praetrepidāns, -antis *adj* very impatient.
praetruncō, -āre *vt* to cut off.
praetulī *perf of* **praeferō**.
praetūra, -ae *f* praetorship.

Noun declensions and verb conjugations are shown on pp xiii to xxv. The present infinitive ending of a verb shows to which conjugation it belongs: **-āre** = 1st; **-ēre** = 2nd; **-ere** = 3rd and **-īre** = 4th. Irregular verbs are shown on p xxvi

praeumbrāns, -antis *adj* obscuring.
praeūstus *adj* hardened at the point; frostbitten.
praeut *adv* compared with.
praevaleō, -ēre, -uī *vi* to be very powerful, have most influence, prevail.
praevalidus *adj* very strong, very powerful; too strong.
praevāricātiō, -ōnis *f* collusion.
praevāricātor, -ōris *m* advocate guilty of collusion.
praevāricor, -ārī, -ātus *vi* (*with dat*) to favour by collusion.
praevehor, -hī, -ctus *vi* to ride, fly in front, flow past.
praeveniō, -enīre, -ēnī, -entum *vt, vi* to come before; to anticipate, prevent.
praeverrō, -ere *vt* to sweep before.
praevertō, -ere, -ī; -or, -ī *vt* to put first, prefer; to turn to first, attend first to; to oustrip; to anticipate, frustrate, prepossess.
praevideō, -idēre, -īdī, -īsum *vt* to foresee.
praevitiō, -āre *vt* to taint beforehand.
praevius *adj* leading the way.
praevolō, -āre *vi* to fly in front.
pragmaticus *adj* of affairs ♦ *m* legal expert.
prandeō, -ēre, -ī *vi* to take lunch ♦ *vt* to eat.
prandium, -ī and iī *nt* lunch.
prānsor, -ōris *m* guest at lunch.
prānsus *adj* having lunched, fed.
prasinus *adj* green.
prātēnsis *adj* meadow.
prātulum, -ī *nt* small meadow.
prātum, -ī *nt* meadow; grass.
prāvē *adv* wrongly, badly.
prāvitās, -ātis *f* irregularity; perverseness, depravity.
prāvus *adj* crooked, deformed; perverse, bad, wicked.
Prāxitelēs, -is *m* famous Greek sculptor.
Prāxitelius *adj see n.*
precāriō *adv* by request.
precārius *adj* obtained by entreaty.
precātiō, -ōnis *f* prayer.
precātor, -ōris *m* intercessor.
preces *pl of* **prex.**
preciae, -ārum *fpl* kind of vine.
precor, -ārī, -ātus *vt, vi* to pray, beg, entreat; to wish (well), curse.
prehendō, -endere, -endī, -ēnsum *vt* to take hold of, catch; to seize, detain; to surprise; (*eye*) to take in; (*mind*) to grasp.
prehēnsō *etc see* **prēnsō.**
prehēnsus *ppp of* **prehendō.**
prēlum, -ī *nt* wine press, oil press.
premō, -mere, -ssī, -ssum *vt* to press, squeeze; to press together, compress; (*eyes*) to close; (*reins*) to tighten; (*trees*) to prune; to press upon, lie, sit, stand on, cover, conceal, surpass; to press hard on, follow closely; (*coast*) to hug; to press down, lower, burden; (*fig*) to overcome, rule; (*words*) to disparage; to press in, sink, stamp, plant; to press back,

repress, check, stop.
prendō *etc see* **prehendō.**
prēnsātiō, -ōnis *f* canvassing.
prēnsō (prehēnsō), -āre, -āvī, -ātum *vt* to clutch at, take hold of, buttonhole.
prēnsus *ppp of* **prehendō.**
presbyter, -ī *m* (*ECCL*) elder.
pressē *adv* concisely, accurately, simply.
pressī *perf of* **premō.**
pressiō, -ōnis *f* fulcrum.
pressō, -āre *vt* to press.
pressus *ppp of* **premō** ♦ *adj* (*style*) concise, compressed; (*pace*) slow; (*voice*) subdued.
pressus, -ūs *m* pressure.
prēster, -ēris *m* waterspout.
pretiōsē *adv* expensively.
pretiōsus *adj* valuable, expensive; extravagant.
pretium, -ī and iī *nt* price, value; worth; money, fee, reward; **māgnī -ī, in -iō** valuable; **operae ~** worth while.
prex, -ecis *f* request, entreaty; prayer; good wish; curse.
Priamēis, -ēidis *f* Cassandra.
Priamēius *adj see* **Priamus.**
Priamidēs, -idae *m* son of Priam.
Priamus, -ī *m* king of Troy.
Priāpus, -ī *m* god of fertility and of gardens.
prīdem *adv* long ago, long.
prīdiē *adv* the day before.
prīmaevus *adj* youthful.
prīmānī, -ōrum *mpl* soldiers of the 1st legion.
prīmārius *adj* principal, first-rate.
prīmigenus *adj* original.
prīmipīlāris, -is *m* chief centurion.
prīmipīlus, -ī *m* chief centurion.
prīmitiae, -ārum *fpl* first fruits.
prīmitus *adv* originally.
prīmō *adv* at first; firstly.
prīmōrdium, -ī and iī *nt* beginning; **~ia rērum** atoms.
prīmōris *adj* first, foremost, tip of; principal ♦ *mpl* nobles; (*MIL*) front line.
prīmulum *adv* first.
prīmulus *adj* very first.
prīmum *adv* first, to begin with, in the first place; for the first time; **cum, ubi, ut ~** as soon as; **quam ~** as soon as possible; **~ dum** in the first place.
prīmus *adj* first, foremost, tip of; earliest; principal, most eminent; **~ veniō** I am the first to come; **prima lux** dawn, daylight; **~ō mēnse** at the beginning of the month; **~īs digitīs** with the fingertips; **~ās agere** play the leading part; **~ās dare** give first place to; **in ~īs** in the front line; especially.
prīnceps, -ipis *adj* first, in front, chief, most eminent ♦ *m* leader, chief; first citizen, emperor; (*MIL*) company, captain, captaincy ♦ *pl* (*MIL*) the second line.
prīncipālis *adj* original; chief; the emperor's.
prīncipātus, -ūs *m* first place; post of commander-in-chief; emperorship.

prīncipiālis *adj* from the beginning.
prīncipium, -ī *and* **iī** *nt* beginning, origin; first to vote ♦ *pl* first principles; (*MIL*) front line; camp headquarters.
prior, -ōris (*nt* **-us**) *adj* former, previous, first; better, preferable ♦ *mpl* forefathers.
prīscē *adv* strictly.
prīscus *adj* former, ancient, old-fashioned.
prīstinus *adj* former, original; of yesterday.
prius *adv* previously, before; in former times; **~ quam** before, sooner than.
prīvātim *adv* individually, privately; at home.
prīvātiō, -ōnis *f* removal.
prīvātus *adj* individual, private; not in public office ♦ *m* private citizen.
Prīvernās, -ātis *adj see n.*
Prīvernum, -ī *nt* old Latin town.
prīvigna, -ae *f* stepdaughter.
prīvignus, -ī *m* stepson; *pl* stepchildren.
prīvilēgium, -ī *and* **iī** *nt* law in favour of *or* against an individual.
prīvō, -āre, -āvī, -ātum *vt* to deprive, rob; to free.
prīvus *adj* single, one each; own, private.
prō *adv* (*with* **ut** *and* **quam**) in proportion (as) ♦ *prep* (*with abl*) in front of, on the front of; for, on behalf of, instead of, in return for; as, as good as; according to, in proportion to, by virtue of; **~ eō ac** just as; **~ eō quod** just because; **~ eō quantum, ut** in proportion as.
prō *interj* (*expressing wonder or sorrow*) O!, alas!
proāgorus, -ī *m* chief magistrate (*in Sicilian towns*).
proavītus *adj* ancestral.
proavus, -ī *m* great-grandfather, ancestor.
probābilis *adj* laudable; credible, probable.
probābilitās, -ātis *f* credibility.
probābiliter *adv* credibly.
probātiō, -ōnis *f* approval; testing.
probātor, -ōris *m* approver.
probātus *adj* tried, excellent; acceptable.
probē *adv* well, properly; thoroughly, well done!
probitās, -ātis *f* goodness, honesty.
probō, -āre, -āvī, -ātum *vt* to approve, approve of; to appraise; to recommend; to prove, show.
probrōsus *adj* abusive; disgraceful.
probrum, -ī *nt* abuse, reproach; disgrace; infamy, unchastity.
probus *adj* good, excellent; honest, upright.
procācitās, -ātis *f* impudence.
procāciter *adv* insolently.
procāx, -ācis *adj* bold, forward, insolent.
prōcēdō, -ēdere, -essī, -essum *vi* to go forward, advance; to go out, come forth; (*time*) to go on, continue; (*fig*) to make progress, get on; (*events*) to turn out, succeed.
procella, -ae *f* hurricane, storm; (*MIL*) charge.

procellōsus *adj* stormy.
procer, -is *m* chief, noble, prince.
prōcēritās, -ātis *f* height; length.
prōcērus *adj* tall; long.
prōcessiō, -ōnis *f* advance.
prōcessus, -ūs *m* advance, progress.
prōcidō, -ere, -ī *vi* to fall forwards, fall down.
prōcinctus, -ūs *m* readiness (for action).
prōclāmātor, -ōris *m* bawler.
prōclāmō, -āre *vi* to cry out.
prōclīnātus *adj* tottering.
prōclīnō, -āre *vt* to bend.
prōclīvē *adv* downwards; easily.
prōclīvis, -us *adj* downhill, steep; (*mind*) prone, willing; (*act*) easy; **in ~ī** easy.
prōclīvitās, -ātis *f* descent; tendency.
prōclīvus *etc see* **proclīvis**.
Procnē, -ēs *f* wife of Tereus (*changed to a swallow*); swallow.
prōcōnsul, -is *m* proconsul, governor.
prōcōnsulāris *adj* proconsular.
prōcōnsulātus, -ūs *m* proconsulship.
prōcrāstinātiō, -ōnis *f* procrastination.
prōcrāstinō, -āre *vt* to put off from day to day.
prōcreātiō, -ōnis *f* begetting.
prōcreātor, -ōris *m* creator, parent.
prōcreātrīx, -īcis *f* mother.
prōcreō, -āre *vt* to beget, produce.
prōcrēscō, -ere *vi* to be produced, grow up.
Procrūstēs, -ae *m* Attic highwayman (*who tortured victims on a bed*).
prōcubō, -āre *vi* to lie on the ground.
prōcūdō, -dere, -dī, -sum *vt* to forge; to produce.
procul *adv* at a distance, far, from afar.
prōculcō, -āre *vt* to trample down.
prōcumbō, -mbere, -buī, -bitum *vi* to fall forwards, bend over; to sink down, be broken down.
prōcūrātiō, -ōnis *f* management; (*religion*) expiation.
prōcūrātor, -ōris *m* administrator, financial agent; (*province*) governor.
prōcūrātrīx, -īcis *f* governess.
prōcūrō, -āre, -āvī, -ātum *vt* to take care of, manage; to expiate ♦ *vi* to be a procurator.
prōcurrō, -rrere, -currī *and* **rrī, -rsum** *vi* to rush forward; to jut out.
prōcursātiō, -ōnis *f* charge.
prōcursātor, -ōris *m* skirmisher.
prōcursō, -āre *vi* to make a sally.
prōcursus, -ūs *m* charge.
prōcurvus *adj* curving forwards.
procus, -ī *m* nobleman.
procus, -ī *m* wooer, suitor.
Procyōn, -ōnis *m* Lesser Dog Star.
prōdeambulō, -āre *vi* to go out for a walk.
prōdeō, -īre, -iī, -itum *vi* to come out, come forward, appear; to go ahead, advance; to

---

Noun declensions and verb conjugations are shown on pp xiii to xxv. The present infinitive ending of a verb shows to which conjugation it belongs: **-āre** = 1st; **-ēre** = 2nd; **-ere** = 3rd and **-īre** = 4th. Irregular verbs are shown on p xxvi

project.

prōdesse *infin of* **prōsum.**

prōdīcō, -īcere, -īxī, -ictum *vt* to appoint, adjourn.

prōdictātor, -ōris *m* vice-dictator.

prōdigē *adv* extravagantly.

prōdigentia, -ae *f* profusion.

prōdigiāliter *adv* unnaturally.

prōdigiōsus *adj* unnatural, marvellous.

prōdigium, -ī *and* **iī** *nt* portent; unnatural deed; monster.

prōdigō, -igere, -ēgī, -āctum *vt* to squander.

prōdigus *adj* wasteful; lavish, generous.

prōditiō, -ōnis *f* betrayal.

prōditor, -ōris *m* traitor.

prōditus *ppp of* **prōdō.**

prōdō, -ere, -idī, -itum *vt* to bring forth, produce; to make known, publish; to betray, give up; (*tradition*) to hand down.

prōdoceō, -ēre *vt* to preach.

prodromus, -ī *m* forerunner.

prōdūcō, -ūcere, -ūxī, -uctum *vt* to bring forward, bring out; to conduct; to drag in front; to draw out, extend; (*acting*) to perform; (*child*) to beget, bring up; (*fact*) to bring to light; (*innovation*) to introduce; (*rank*) to promote; (*slave*) to put up for sale; (*time*) to prolong, protract, put off; (*tree*) to cultivate; (*vowel*) to lengthen.

prōductē *adv* long.

prōductiō, -ōnis *f* lengthening.

prōductō, -āre *vt* to spin out.

prōductus *ppp of* **prōdūcō** ♦ *adj* lengthened, long.

proēgmenon, -ī *nt* a preferred thing.

proeliātor, -ōris *m* fighter.

proelior, -ārī, -ātus *vi* to fight, join battle.

proelium, -ī *and* **iī** *nt* battle, conflict.

profānō, -āre *vt* to desecrate.

profānus *adj* unholy, common; impious; ill-omened.

profātus *ppa of* **profor.**

profectiō, -ōnis *f* departure; source.

profectō *adv* really, certainly.

profectus *ppa of* **proficīscor.**

prōfectus *ppp of* **prōficiō.**

prōfectus, -ūs *m* growth, progress, profit.

prōferō, -ferre, -tulī, -lātum *vt* to bring forward, forth or out; to extend, enlarge; (*time*) to prolong, defer; (*instance*) to mention, quote; (*knowledge*) to publish, reveal; **pedem ~** proceed; **signa ~** advance.

professiō, -ōnis *f* declaration; public register; profession.

professor, -ōris *m* teacher.

professōrius *adj* authoritative.

professus *ppa of* **profiteor.**

profēstus *adj* not holiday, working.

prōficiō, -icere, -ēcī, -ectum *vi* to make progress, profit; to be of use.

proficīscor, -icīscī, -ectus *vi* to set out, start; to originate, proceed.

profiteor, -itērī, -essus *vt* to declare, profess; to make an official return of; to promise, volunteer.

prōflīgātor, -ōris *m* spendthrift.

prōflīgātus *adj* dissolute.

prōflīgō, -āre, -āvī, -ātum *vt* to dash to the ground; to destroy, overthrow; to bring almost to an end; to degrade.

prōflō, -āre *vt* to breathe out.

prōfluēns, -entis *pres p of* **prōfluō** ♦ *adj* flowing; fluent ♦ *f* running water.

prōfluenter *adv* easily.

prōfluentia, -ae *f* fluency.

prōfluō, -ere, -xī *vi* to flow on, flow out; (*fig*) to proceed.

prōfluvium, -ī *and* **iī** *nt* flowing.

profor, -ārī, -ātus *vi* to speak, give utterance.

profugiō, -ugere, -ūgī *vi* to flee, escape; to take refuge (with) ♦ *vt* to flee from.

profugus *adj* fugitive; exiled; nomadic.

prōfuī *perf of* **prōsum.**

profundō, -undere, -ūdī, -ūsum *vt* to pour out, shed; to bring forth, produce; to prostrate; to squander; **sē ~** burst forth, rush out.

profundus *adj* deep, vast, high; infernal; (*fig*) profound, immoderate ♦ *nt* depths, abyss.

profūsē *adv* in disorder, extravagantly.

profūsus *ppp of* **profundō** ♦ *adj* lavish; excessive.

prōgener, -ī *m* grandson-in-law.

prōgenerō, -āre *vt* to beget.

prōgeniēs, -ēī *f* descent; offspring, descendants.

prōgenitor, -ōris *m* ancestor.

prōgignō, -ignere, -enuī, -enitum *vt* to beget, produce.

prōgnātus *adj* born, descended ♦ *m* son, descendant.

Prognē *see* **Procnē.**

prōgnōstica, -ōrum *ntpl* weather signs.

prōgredior, -dī, -ssus *vi* to go forward, advance; to go out.

prōgressiō, -ōnis *f* advancing, increase; (*RHET*) climax.

prōgressus *ppa of* **prōgredior.**

prōgressus, -ūs *m* advance, progress; (*events*) march.

prōh *see* **prō** *interj.*

prohibeō, -ēre, -uī, -itum *vt* to hinder, prevent; to keep away, protect; to forbid.

prohibitiō, -ōnis *f* forbidding.

prōiciō, -icere, -iēcī, -iectum *vt* to throw down, fling forwards; to banish; (*building*) to make project; (*fig*) to discard, renounce; to forsake; (*words*) to blurt out; (*time*) to defer; **sē ~** rush forward, run into danger; to fall prostrate.

prōiectiō, -ōnis *f* forward stretch.

prōiectus *ppp of* **prōiciō** ♦ *adj* projecting, prominent; abject, useless; downcast; addicted (to).

prōiectus, -ūs *m* jutting out.

proinde, proin *adv* consequently, therefore;

just (as).

prōlābor, -bī, -psus *vi* to slide, move forward; to fall down; (*fig*) to go on, come to; to slip out; to fail, fall, sink into ruin.

prōlāpsiō, -ōnis *f* falling.

prōlāpsus *ppa of* **prōlābor.**

prōlātiō, -ōnis *f* extension; postponement; adducing.

prōlātō, -āre *vt* to extend; to postpone.

prōlātus *ppp of* **prōferō.**

prōlectō, -āre *vt* to entice.

prōlēs, -is *f* offspring; child; descendants, race.

prōlētārius, -ī *and* **iī** *m* citizen of the lowest class.

prōliciō, -cere, -xī *vt* to entice.

prōlixē *adv* fully, copiously, willingly.

prōlixus *adj* long, wide, spreading; (*person*) obliging; (*CIRCS*) favourable.

prōlogus, -ī *m* prologue.

prōloquor, -quī, -cūtus *vt* to speak out.

prōlubium, -ī *and* **iī** *nt* inclination.

prōlūdō, -dere, -sī, -sum *vi* to practise.

prōluō, -uere, -uī, -ūtum *vt* to wash out, wash away.

prōlūsiō, -ōnis *f* prelude.

prōluviēs, -ēī *f* flood; excrement.

prōmereō, -ēre, -uī; prōmereor, -ērī, -itus *vt* to deserve, earn.

prōmeritum, -ī *nt* desert, merit, guilt.

Promētheus, -eī *and* **eos** *m* demigod who stole fire from the gods.

Promētheūs *adj see n.*

prōminēns, -entis *pres p of* **prōmineō ♦** *adj* projecting ♦ *nt* headland, spur.

prōmineō, -ēre, -uī *vi* to jut out, overhang; to extend.

prōmiscam, -ē, -uē *adv* indiscriminately.

prōmiscuus (prōmiscus) *adj* indiscriminate, in common; ordinary; open to all.

prōmīsī *perf of* **prōmittō.**

prōmissiō, -ōnis *f* promise.

prōmissor, -ōris *m* promiser.

prōmissum, -ī *nt* promise.

prōmissus *ppp of* **prōmittō ♦** *adj* long.

prōmittō, -ittere, -īsī, -issum *vt* to let grow; to promise, give promise of.

prōmō, -ere, -psī, -ptum *vt* to bring out, produce; to disclose.

prōmont- *etc see* **prōmunt-.**

prōmōtus *ppp of* **prōmoveō ♦** *ntpl* preferable things.

prōmoveō, -ovēre, -ōvī, -ōtum *vt* to move forward, advance; to enlarge; to postpone; to disclose.

prōmpsī *perf of* **prōmō.**

prōmptē *adv* readily; easily.

prōmptō, -āre *vt* to distribute.

prōmptū *abl m:* in ~ at hand, in readiness; obvious, in evidence; easy.

prōmptus *ppp of* **prōmō ♦** *adj* at hand, ready; prompt, resolute; easy.

prōmulgātiō, -ōnis *f* promulgating.

prōmulgō, -āre, -āvī, -ātum *vt* to make public, publish.

prōmulsis, -idis *f* hors d'oeuvre.

prōmunturium, -ī *and* **iī** *nt* headland, promontory, ridge.

prōmus, -ī *m* cellarer, butler.

prōmūtuus *adj* as a loan in advance.

prōnepōs, -ōtis *m* great-grandson.

pronoea, -ae *f* providence.

prōnōmen, -inis *nt* pronoun.

prōnuba, -ae *f* matron attending a bride.

prōnūntiātiō, -ōnis *f* declaration; (*RHET*) delivery; (*logic*) proposition.

prōnūntiātor, -ōris *m* narrator.

prōnūntiātum, -ātī *nt* proposition.

prōnūntiō, -āre, -āvī, -ātum *vt* to declare publicly, announce; to recite, deliver; to narrate; to nominate.

prōnurus, -ūs *f* granddaughter-in-law.

prōnus *adj* leaning forward; headlong, downwards; sloping, sinking; (*fig*) inclined, disposed, favourable; easy.

prooemium, -ī *and* **iī** *nt* prelude, preface.

propāgātiō, -ōnis *f* propagating; extension.

propāgātor, -ōris *m* enlarger.

propāgō, -āre, -āvī, -ātum *vt* to propagate; to extend; to prolong.

propāgō, -inis *f* (*plant*) layer, slip; (*men*) offspring, posterity.

prōpalam *adv* openly, known.

prōpatulum, -ī *nt* open space.

prōpatulus *adj* open.

prope *adv* (*comp* **propius,** *superl* **proximē**) near; nearly ♦ *prep* (*with acc*) near, not far from.

propediem *adv* very soon.

prōpellō, -ellere, -ulī, -ulsum *vt* to drive, push forward, impel; to drive away, keep off.

propemodum, -o *adv* almost.

prōpendeō, -endēre, -endī, -ēnsum *vi* to hang down; to preponderate; to be disposed (to).

prōpēnsē *adv* willingly.

prōpēnsiō, -ōnis *f* inclination.

prōpēnsus *adj* inclining; inclined, well-disposed; important.

properanter *adv* hastily, quickly.

properantia, -ae *f* haste.

properātiō, -ōnis *f* haste.

properātō *adv* quickly.

properātus *adj* speedy.

properē *adv* quickly.

properipēs, -edis *adj* swiftfooted.

properō, -āre, -āvī, -ātum *vt* to hasten, do with haste ♦ *vi* to make haste, hurry.

Propertius, -ī *m* Latin elegiac poet.

properus *adj* quick, hurrying.

Noun declensions and verb conjugations are shown on pp xiii to xxv. The present infinitive ending of a verb shows to which conjugation it belongs: **-āre** = 1st; **-ēre** = 2nd; **-ere** = 3rd and **-īre** = 4th. Irregular verbs are shown on p xxvi

prōpexus *adj* combed forward.
propīnō, -āre *vt* to drink as a toast; to pass on (a cup).
propinquitās, -ātis *f* nearness; relationship, friendship.
propinquō, -āre *vi* to approach ♦ *vt* to hasten.
propinquus *adj* near, neighbouring; related ♦ *m/f* relation ♦ *nt* neighbourhood.
propior, -ōris *adj* nearer; more closely related, more like; (*time*) more recent.
propitiō, -āre *vt* to appease.
propitius *adj* favourable, gracious.
propius *adv* nearer, more closely.
propōla, -ae *f* retailer.
prōpolluō, -ere *vt* to defile further.
prōpōnō, -ōnere, -osuī, -ositum *vt* to set forth, display; to publish, declare; to propose, resolve; to imagine; to expose; (*logic*) to state the first premise; **ante oculōs ~** picture to oneself.
Propontiacus *adj see n.*
Propontis, -idis and **idos** *f* Sea of Marmora.
prōporrō *adv* furthermore; utterly.
prōportiō, -ōnis *f* symmetry, analogy.
prōpositiō, -ōnis *f* purpose; theme; (*logic*) first premise.
prōpositum, -ī *nt* plan, purpose; theme; (*logic*) first premise.
prōpositus *ppp of* **prōpōnō**.
prōpraetor, -ōris *m* propraetor, governor; vice-praetor.
propriē *adv* properly, strictly; particularly.
proprietās, -ātis *f* peculiarity, property.
prōpritim *adv* properly.
proprius *adj* one's own, peculiar; personal, characteristic; permanent; (*words*) literal, regular.
propter *adv* near by ♦ *prep* (*with acc*) near, beside; on account of; by means of.
proptereā *adv* therefore.
prōpudium, -ī and **iī** *nt* shameful act; villain.
prōpugnāculum, -ī *nt* bulwark, tower; defence.
prōpugnātiō, -ōnis *f* defence.
prōpugnātor, -ōris *m* defender, champion.
prōpugnō, -āre *vi* to make a sortie; to fight in defence.
prōpulsātiō, -ōnis *f* repulse.
prōpulsō, -āre, -āvī, -ātum *vt* to repel, avert.
prōpulsus *ppp of* **prōpellō**.
Propylaea, -ōrum *ntpl* gateway to the Acropolis of Athens.
prō quaestōre *m* proquaestor.
prōquam *conj* according as.
prōra, -ae *f* prow, bows; ship.
prōrēpō, -ere, -sī, -tum *vi* to crawl out.
prōrēta -ae *m* man at the prow.
prōreus, -eī *m* man at the prow.
prōripiō, -ipere, -ipuī, -eptum *vt* to drag out; to hurry away; **sē ~** rush out, run away.
prōrogātiō, -ōnis *f* extension; deferring.
prōrogō, -āre, -āvī, -ātum *vt* to extend, prolong, continue; to defer.

prōrsum *adv* forwards; absolutely.
prōrsus *adv* forwards; absolutely; in short.
prōrumpō, -umpere, -ūpī, -uptum *vt* to fling out; (*pass*) to rush forth ♦ *vi* to break out, burst forth.
prōruō, -ere, -ī, -tum *vt* to throw down, demolish ♦ *vi* to rush forth.
prōruptus *ppp of* **prōrumpō**.
prōsāpia, -ae *f* lineage.
proscaenium, -ī and **iī** *nt* stage.
proscindō, -ndere, -dī, -ssum *vt* to plough up; (*fig*) to revile.
prōscrībō, -bere, -psī, -ptum *vt* to publish in writing; to advertise; to confiscate; to proscribe, outlaw.
prōscrīptiō, -ōnis *f* advertisement; proscription.
prōscrīpturiō, -īre *vi* to want to have a proscription.
prōscrīptus *ppp of* **prōscrībō** ♦ *m* outlaw.
prōsecō, -āre, -uī, -tum *vt* to cut off (for sacrifice).
prōsēminō, -āre *vt* to scatter; to propagate.
prōsentiō, -entīre, -ēnsī *vt* to see beforehand.
prōsequor, -quī, -cūtus *vt* to attend, escort; to pursue, attack; to honour (with); (*words*) to proceed with, continue.
Proserpina, -ae *f* Proserpine (*daughter of Ceres and wife of Pluto*).
proseucha, -ae *f* place of prayer.
prōsiliō, -īre, -uī *vi* to jump up, spring forward; to burst out, spurt.
prōsocer, -ī *m* wife's grandfather.
prōspectō, -āre *vt* to look out at, view; to look forward to, await; (*place*) to look towards.
prōspectus *ppp of* **prōspiciō**.
prōspectus, -ūs *m* sight, view, prospect; gaze.
prōspeculor, -ārī *vi* to look out, reconnoitre ♦ *vt* to watch for.
prosper, prosperus *adj* favourable, successful.
prosperē *adv see adj.*
prosperitās, -ātis *f* good fortune.
prosperō, -āre *vt* to make successful, prosper.
prosperus *etc see* **prosper**.
prōspicientia, -ae *f* foresight.
prōspiciō, -icere, -exī, -ectum *vi* to look out, watch; to see to, take precautions ♦ *vt* to descry, watch for; to foresee; to provide; (*place*) to command a view of.
prōsternō, -ernere, -rāvī, -rātum *vt* to throw in front, prostrate; to overthrow, ruin; **sē ~** fall prostrate; to demean oneself.
prōstibulum, -ī *nt* prostitute.
prōstituō, -uere, -uī, -ūtum *vt* to put up for sale, prostitute.
prōstō, -āre, -itī *vi* to project; to be on sale; to prostitute oneself.
prōstrātus *ppp of* **prōsternō**.
prōsubigō, -ere *vt* to dig up.

prōsum, -desse, -fuī *vi* (*with dat*) to be useful to, benefit.

Prōtagorās, -ae *m* Greek sophist (*native of Abdera*).

prōtēctus *ppp of* **prōtegō.**

prōtegō, -egere, -ēxī, -ēctum *vt* to cover over, put a projecting roof on; (*fig*) to shield, protect.

prōtēlō, -āre *vt* to drive off.

prōtēlum, -ī *nt* team of oxen; (*fig*) succession.

prōtendō, -dere, -dī, -tum *vt* to stretch out, extend.

prōtentus *ppp of* **prōtendō.**

prōterō, -erere, -rīvī, -rītum *vt* to trample down, crush; to overthrow.

prōterreō, -ēre, -uī, -itum *vt* to scare away.

protervē *adv* insolently; boldly.

protervitās, -ātis *f* forwardness, insolence.

protervus *adj* forward, insolent, violent.

Prōtesilāēus *adj see n.*

Prōtesilāus, -ī *m* first Greek killed at Troy.

Prōteus, -eī *and* **eos** *m* seagod with power to assume many forms.

prothȳmē *adv* gladly.

prōtinam *adv* immediately.

prōtinus *adv* forward, onward; continuously; right away, forthwith.

prōtollō, -ere *vt* to stretch out; to put off.

prōtractus *ppp of* **prōtrahō.**

prōtrahō, -here, -xī, -ctum *vt* to draw on (to); to drag out; to bring to light, reveal.

prōtrītus *ppp of* **prōterō.**

prōtrūdō, -dere, -sī, -sum *vt* to thrust forward, push out; to postpone.

prōtulī *perf of* **prōferō.**

prōturbō, -āre, -āvī, -ātum *vt* to drive off; to overthrow.

prout *conj* according as.

prōvectus *ppp of* **prōvehō** ♦ *adj* advanced.

prōvehō, -here, -xī, -ctum *vt* to carry along, transport; to promote, advance, bring to; (*speech*) to prolong; (*pass*) to drive, ride, sail on.

prōveniō, -enīre, -ēnī, -entum *vi* to come out, appear; to arise, grow; to go on, prosper, succeed.

prōventus, -ūs *m* increase; result, success.

prōverbium, -ī *and* **iī** *nt* saying, proverb.

prōvidēns, -entis *pres p of* **prōvideō** ♦ *adj* prudent.

prōvidenter *adv* with foresight.

prōvidentia, -ae *f* foresight, forethought.

prōvideō, -idēre, -īdī, -īsum *vi* to see ahead; to take care, make provision ♦ *vt* to foresee; to look after, provide for; to obviate.

prōvidus *adj* foreseeing, cautious, prudent; provident.

prōvincia, -ae *f* sphere of action, duty, province.

prōvinciālis *adj* provincial ♦ *mpl* provincials.

prōvīsiō, -ōnis *f* foresight; precaution.

prōvīsō *adv* with forethought.

prōvīsō, -ere *vi* to go and see.

prōvīsor, -ōris *m* foreseer; provider.

prōvīsus *ppp of* **prōvideō.**

prōvīsus, -ūs *m* looking forward; foreseeing; providing providence.

prōvīvō, -vere, -xī *vi* to live on.

prōvocātiō, -ōnis *f* challenge; appeal.

prōvocātor, -ōris *m* kind of gladiator.

prōvocō, -āre, -āvī, -ātum *vt* to challenge, call out; to provoke; to bring about ♦ *vi* to appeal.

prōvolō, -āre *vi* to fly out, rush out.

prōvolvō, -vere, -vī, -ūtum *vt* to roll forward, tumble over; (*pass*) to fall down, humble oneself, be ruined; **sē ~** wallow.

prōvomō, -ere *vt* to belch forth.

proximē *adv* next, nearest; (*time*) just before *or* after; (*with acc*) next to, very close to, very like.

proximitās, -ātis *f* nearness; near relationship; similarity.

proximus *adj* nearest, next; (*time*) previous, last, following, next; most akin, most like ♦ *m* next of kin ♦ *nt* next door.

proxum *etc see* **proxim-.**

prūdēns, -entis *adj* foreseeing, aware; wise, prudent, circumspect; skilled, versed (in).

prūdenter *adv* prudently; skilfully.

prūdentia, -ae *f* prudence, discretion; knowledge.

pruīna, -ae *f* hoar frost.

pruīnōsus *adj* frosty.

prūna, -ae *f* live coal.

prūnitius *adj* of plum tree wood.

prūnum, -ī *nt* plum.

prūnus, -ī *f* plum tree.

prūriō, -īre *vi* to itch.

prytanēum, -ī *nt* Greek town hall.

prytanis, -is *m* Greek chief magistrate.

psallō, -ere *vi* to play the lyre *or* lute.

psaltērium, -ī *and* **iī** *nt* kind of lute.

psaltria, -ae *f* girl musician.

psecas, -adis *f* slave who perfumed the lady's hair.

psēphisma, -tis *nt* decree of the people.

Pseudocatō, -ōnis *m* sham Cato.

pseudomenos, -ī *m* sophistical argument.

pseudothyrum, -ī *nt* back door.

psithius *adj* psithian (*kind of Greek vine*).

psittacus, -ī *m* parrot.

psychomantēum (-īum), -ī *nt* place of necromancy.

-pte *enclitic* (*to pronouns*) self, own.

ptisanārium, -ī *and* **iī** *nt* gruel.

Ptolemaēus, -us *adj see n.*

Ptolemaeus, -ī *m* Ptolemy (*name of Egyptian kings*).

pūbēns, -entis *adj* full-grown; (*plant*) juicy.

pūbertās, -ātis f manhood; signs of puberty.
pūbēs (pūber), -eris adj grown up, adult; (plant) downy.
pūbēs, -is f hair at age of puberty; groin; youth, men, people.
pūbēscō, -ēscere, -uī vi to grow to manhood, become mature; to become clothed.
pūblicānus adj of public revenue ♦ m tax farmer.
pūblicātiō, -ōnis f confiscation.
pūblicē adv by or for the State, at the public expense; all together.
pūblicitus adv at the public expense; in public.
pūblicō, -āre, -āvī, -ātum vt to confiscate; to make public.
Pūblicola, -ae m P. Valerius (an early Roman consul).
pūblicum, -ī nt State revenue; State territory; public.
pūblicus adj of the State, public, common ♦ m public official; **~a causa** criminal trial; **rēs ~a** the State; **dē ~ō** at the public expense; **in ~ō** in public.
Pūblius, -ī m Roman first name.
pudendus adj shameful.
pudēns, -entis adj bashful, modest.
pudenter adv modestly.
pudet, -ēre, -uit and **itum est** vt (impers) to shame, be ashamed.
pudibundus adj modest.
pudīcē adv see adj.
pudīcitia, -ae f modesty, chastity.
pudīcus adj modest, chaste.
pudor, -ōris m shame, modesty, sense of honour; disgrace.
puella, -ae f girl; sweetheart, young wife.
puellāris adj girlish, youthful.
puellula, -ae f little girl.
puellus, -ī m little boy.
puer, -ī m boy, child; son; slave.
puerīlis adj boyish, child's; childish, trivial.
puerīliter adv like a child; childishly.
pueritia, -ae f childhood, youth.
puerperium, -ī and **iī** nt childbirth.
puerperus adj to help childbirth ♦ f woman in labour.
puertia etc see **pueritia**.
puerulus, -ī m little boy, slave.
pugil, -is m boxer.
pugilātiō, -iōnis f, **-us, -ūs** m boxing.
pugillāris adj that can be held in the hand ♦ mpl, ntpl writing tablets.
pugillātōrius adj: **follis ~** punchball.
pugiō, -ōnis m dirk, dagger.
pugiunculus, -ī m small dagger.
pugna, -ae f fight, battle.
pugnācitās, -ātis f fondness for a fight.
pugnāciter adv aggressively.
pugnāculum, -ī nt fortress.
pugnātor, -ōris m fighter.
pugnāx, -ācis adj fond of a fight, aggressive; obstinate.

pugneus adj with the fist.
pugnō, -āre, -āvī, -ātum vi to fight; to disagree; to struggle; **sēcum ~** be inconsistent; **~ātum est** the battle was fought.
pugnus, -ī m fist.
pulchellus adj pretty little.
pulcher, -rī adj beautiful, handsome; fine, glorious.
pulchrē adv excellently; well done!
pulchritūdō, -inis f beauty, excellence.
pūlēium, pūlegium, -ī and **iī** nt pennyroyal.
pūlex, -icis m flea.
pullārius, -ī and **iī** m keeper of the sacred chickens.
pullātus adj dressed in black.
pullulō, -āre vi to sprout.
pullus, -ī m young (of animals), chicken.
pullus adj dark-grey; mournful ♦ nt dark grey clothes.
pulmentārium, -ārī and **-āriī, -um, -ī** nt relish; food.
pulmō, -ōnis m lung.
pulmōneus adj of the lungs.
pulpa, -ae f fleshy part.
pulpāmentum, -ī nt tit-bits.
pulpitum, -ī nt platform, stage.
puls, pultis f porridge.
pulsātiō, -ōnis f beating.
pulsō, -āre, -āvī, -ātum vt to batter, knock, strike.
pulsus ppp of **pellō**.
pulsus, -ūs m push, beat, blow; impulse.
pultiphagus, -ī m porridge eater.
pultō, -āre vt to beat, knock at.
pulvereus adj of dust, dusty, fine as dust; raising dust.
pulverulentus adj dusty; laborious.
pulvillus, -ī m small cushion.
pulvīnar, -āris nt sacred couch; seat of honour.
pulvīnus, -ī m cushion, pillow.
pulvis, -eris m dust, powder; arena; effort.
pulvisculus, -ī m fine dust.
pūmex, -icis m pumice stone; stone, rock.
pūmiceus adj of soft stone.
pūmicō, -āre vt to smooth with pumice stone.
pūmiliō, -ōnis m/f dwarf, pygmy.
pūnctim adv with the point.
pūnctum, -ī nt point, dot; vote; (time) moment; (speech) short section.
pūnctus ppp of **pungō**.
pungō, -ere, pupugī, pūnctum vt to prick, sting, pierce; (fig) to vex.
Pūnicānus adj in the Carthaginian style.
Pūnicē adv in Punic.
pūniceus adj reddish, purple.
Pūnicum, -ī nt pomegranate.
Pūnicus adj Punic, Carthaginian; purple-red.
pūniō (poeniō), -īre; -ior, -īrī vt to punish; to avenge.
pūnītor, -ōris m avenger.
pūpa, -ae f doll.

pūpilla, -ae f ward; (eye) pupil.
pūpillāris adj of a ward, of an orphan.
pūpillus, -ī m orphan, ward.
puppis, -is f after part of a ship, stern; ship.
pupugī perf of **pungō**.
pūpula, -ae f (eye) pupil.
pūpulus, -ī m little boy.
pūrē adv cleanly, brightly; plainly, simply, purely, chastely.
pūrgāmen, -inis nt sweepings, dirt; means of expiation.
pūrgāmentum, -ī nt refuse, dirt.
pūrgātiō, -ōnis f purging; justification.
pūrgō, -āre, -āvī, -ātum vt to cleanse, purge, clear away; to exculpate, justify; to purify.
pūriter adv cleanly, purely.
purpura, -ae f purple-fish, purple; purple cloth; finery, royalty.
purpurātus adj wearing purple ♦ m courtier.
purpureus adj red, purple, black; wearing purple; bright, radiant.
purpurissum, -ī nt kind of rouge.
pūrus adj clear, unadulterated, free from obstruction or admixture; pure, clean; plain, unadorned; (moral) pure, chaste ♦ nt clear sky.
pūs, pūris nt pus; (fig) malice.
pusillus adj very little; petty, paltry.
pūsiō, -ōnis m little boy.
pūstula, -ae f pimple, blister.
putāmen, -inis nt peeling, shell, husk.
putātiō, -ōnis f pruning.
putātor, -ōris m pruner.
puteal, -ālis nt low wall round a well or sacred place.
puteālis adj well- (in cpds).
pūteō, -ēre vi to stink.
Puteolānus adj see n.
Puteolī, -ōrum mpl town on the Campanian coast.
puter, putris, -ris adj rotten, decaying; crumbling, flabby.
putēscō, -ēscere, -uī vi to become rotten.
puteus, -ī m well; pit.
pūtidē adv see **pūtidus**.
pūtidiusculus adj somewhat nauseating.
pūtidus adj rotten, stinking; (speech) affected, nauseating.
putō, -āre, -āvī, -ātum vt to think, suppose; to think over; to reckon, count; (money) to settle; (tree) to prune.
pūtor, -ōris m stench.
putrefaciō, -facere, -fēcī, -factum vt to make rotten; to make crumble.
putrēscō, -ere vi to rot, moulder.
putridus adj rotten, decayed; withered.
putris etc see **puter**.
putus adj perfectly pure.
putus, -ī m boy.
pycta, -ēs, -ae m boxer.

Pydna, -ae f town in Macedonia.
Pydnaeus adj see n.
pȳga, -ae f buttocks.
Pygmaeus adj Pygmy.
Pyladēs, -ae and is m friend of Orestes.
Pyladēus adj see n.
Pylae, -ārum fpl Thermopylae.
Pylaicus adj see n.
Pylius adj see n.
Pylos, -ī f Pylus (Peloponnesian town, home of Nestor).
pyra, -ae f funeral pyre.
Pyramaeus adj see **Pyramus**.
pyramis, -idis f pyramid.
Pyramus, -ī m lover of Thisbe.
Pyrēnē, -ēs f Pyrenees.
pyrethrum, -ī nt Spanish camomile.
Pyrgēnsis adj see **Pyrgī**.
Pyrgī, -ōrum mpl ancient town in Etruria.
pyrōpus, -ī m bronze.
Pyrrha, -ae and ē, -ēs f wife of Deucalion.
Pyrrhaeus adj see n.
Pyrrhō, -ōnis m Greek philosopher (founder of the Sceptics).
Pyrrhōnēus adj see n.
Pyrrhus, -ī m son of Achilles; king of Epirus, enemy of Rome.
Pythagorās, -ae m Greek philosopher who founded a school in S. Italy.
Pythagorēus, -icus adj Pythagorean.
Pythius, -icus adj Pythian, Delphic ♦ m Apollo ♦ f priestess of Apollo ♦ ntpl Pythian Games.
Pythō, -ūs f Delphi.
Pythōn, -ōnis m serpent killed by Apollo.
pytisma, -tis nt what is spit out.
pytissō, -āre vi to spit out wine.
pyxis, -dis f small box, toilet box.

Q, q

quā adv where, which way; whereby; as far as; partly … partly.
quācumque adv wherever; anyhow.
quādam: ~ tenus adv only so far.
quadra, -ae f square; morsel; table.
quadrāgēnī, -ōrum adj forty each.
quadrāgēsimus adj fortieth ♦ f 2 ½ per cent tax.
quadrāgiēns, -ēs adv forty times.
quadrāgintā num forty.
quadrāns, -antis m quarter; (coin) quarter as.
quadrantārius adj of a quarter.

quadrātum, -ī *nt* square; (*ASTRO*) quadrature.
quadrātus *ppp of* **quadrō ♦** *adj* square; **~ō
agmine** in battle order.
quadriduum, -ī *nt* four days.
quadriennium, -ī *and* **ī ī** *nt* four years.
quadrifāriam *adv* in four parts.
quadrifidus *adj* split in four.
quadrīgae, -ārum *fpl* team of four; chariot.
quadrīgārius, -ī *and* **ī ī** *m* chariot racer.
quadrīgātus *adj* stamped with a chariot.
quadrīgulae, -ārum *fpl* little four horse team.
quadriiugī, -ōrum *mpl* team of four.
quadriiugis, -us *adj* of a team of four.
quadrilībris *adj* weighing four pounds.
quadrīmulus *adj* four years old.
quadrīmus *adj* four years old.
quadringēnārius *adj* of four hundred each.
quadringēnī, -ōrum *adj* four hundred each.
quadringentēsimus *adj* four-hundredth.
quadringentī, -ōrum *num* four hundred.
quadringentiēns, -ēs *adv* four hundred
times.
quadripertītus *adj* fourfold.
quadrirēmis, -is *f* quadrireme.
quadrivium, -ī *and* **ī ī** *nt* crossroads.
quadrō, -āre *vt* to make square; to complete ♦
vi to square, fit, agree.
quadrum, -ī *nt* square.
quadrupedāns, -antis *adj* galloping.
quadrupēs, -edis *adj* four-footed, on all fours
♦ *m/f* quadruped.
quadruplātor, -ōris *m* informer, twister.
quadruplex, -icis *adj* four-fold.
quadruplum, -ī *nt* four times as much.
quaeritō, -āre *vt* to search diligently for; to
earn (a living); to keep on asking.
quaerō, -rere, -sīvī *and* **siī, -sītum** *vt* to look
for, search for; to seek, try to get; to
acquire, earn; (*plan*) to think out, work out;
(*question*) to make inquiries; (*law*) to
investigate; (*with infin*) to try, wish; **quid
~ris?** in short; **sī ~ris/~rimus** to tell the truth.
quaesītiō, -ōnis *f* inquisition.
quaesītor, -ōris *m* investigator, judge.
quaesītus *ppp of* **quaerō ♦** *adj* special; far-
fetched ♦ *nt* question ♦ *ntpl* gains.
quaesīvī *perf of* **quaerō.**
quaesō, -ere *vt* to ask, beg.
quaesticulus, -ī *m* slight profit.
quaestiō, -ōnis *f* seeking, questioning;
investigation, research; criminal trial;
court; **servum in ~ōnem ferre** take a slave for
questioning by torture; **~ōnēs perpetuae**
standing courts.
quaestiuncula, -ae *f* trifling question.
quaestor, -ōris *m* quaestor, treasury official.
quaestōrius *adj* of a quaestor ♦ *m* ex-quaestor
♦ *nt* quaestor's tent or residence.
quaestuōsus *adj* lucrative, productive;
money-making; wealthy.
quaestūra, -ae *f* quaestorship; public money.
quaestus, -ūs *m* profit, advantage; money-
making, occupation; **~uī habēre** make money

out of; **~um facere** make a living.
quālibet *adv* anywhere; anyhow.
quālis *adj* (*interrog*) what kind of?; (*relat*) such
as, even as.
quāliscumque *adj* of whatever kind; any,
whatever.
qualiscunque *adj* = **qualiscumque.**
quālitās, -ātis *f* quality, nature.
quāliter *adv* just as.
quālubet *adv* anywhere; anyhow.
quālus, -ī *m* wicker basket.
quam *adv* (*interrog, excl*) how?, how much?;
(*comparison*) as, than; (*with superl*) as . . . as
possible; (*emphatic*) very; **dīmidium ~ quod**
half of what; **quīntō diē ~** four days after.
quamdiū *adv* how long?; as long as.
quamlibet, quamlubet *adv* as much as you
like, however.
quamobrem *adv* (*interrog*) why?; (*relat*) why ♦
conj therefore.
quamquam *conj* although; and yet.
quamvīs *adv* however, ever so ♦ *conj* however
much, although.
quānam *adv* what way.
quandō *adv* (*interrog*) when?; (*relat*) when;
(*with sī, nē, num*) ever ♦ *conj* when; since.
quandōcumque, quandocunque *adv*
whenever, as often as; some day.
quandōque *adv* whenever; some day ♦ *conj*
seeing that.
quandō quidem *conj* seeing that, since.
quanquam *etc see* **quamquam.**
quantillus *adj* how little, how much.
quantopere *adv* how much; (*after* **tantopere**)
as.
quantulus *adj* how little, how small.
quantuluscumque *adj* however small,
however trifling.
quantum *adv* how much; as much as;
~cumque as much as ever; **~libet** however
much; **~vīs** as much as you like; although.
quantus *adj* how great; so great as, such as; **~ī**
how dear, how highly; **~ō** (*with compar*) how
much; the; **in ~um** as far as.
quantuscumque *adj* however great,
whatever size.
quantuslibet *adj* as great as you like.
quantus quantus *adj* however great.
quantusvīs *adj* however great.
quāpropter *adv* why; and therefore.
quāquā *adv* whatever way.
quārē *adv* how, why; whereby; and therefore.
quartadecumānī, -ōrum *mpl* men of the
fourteenth legion.
quartānus *adj* every four days ♦ *f* quartan
fever ♦ *mpl* men of the fourth legion.
quartārius, -ī *and* **ī ī** *m* quarter pint.
quartus *adj* fourth; **quartum/quartō** for the
fourth time.
quartusdecimus *adj* fourteenth.
quasi *adv* as if; as it were; (*numbers*) about.
quasillus, -ī *m*, **-um, -ī** *nt* wool basket.
quassātiō, -ōnis *f* shaking.

quassō, -āre, -āvī, -ātum *vt* to shake, toss; to shatter, damage.

quassus *ppp of* **quatiō ♦** *adj* broken.

quatefaciō, -facere, -fēcī *vt* to shake, give a jolt to.

quātenus *adv* (*interrog*) how far?; how long?; (*relat*) as far as; in so far as, since.

quater *adv* four times; ~ **deciēs** fourteen times.

quaternī, -ōrum *adj* four each, in fours.

quatiō, -tere, -ssum *vt* to shake, disturb, brandish; to strike, shatter; (*fig*) to agitate, harass.

quattuor *num* four.

quattuordecim *num* fourteen.

quattuorvirātus, -ūs *m* membership of quattuorviri.

quattuorvirī, -ōrum *mpl* board of four officials.

-que *conj* and; both . . . and; (*after neg*) but.

quemadmodum *adv* (*interrog*) how?; (*relat*) just as.

queō, -īre, -īvī *and* **iī, -itum** *vi* to be able, can.

quercētum, -ī *nt* oak forest.

querceus *adj* of oak.

quercus, -ūs *f* oak; garland of oak leaves; acorn.

querēla, querella, -ae *f* complaint; plaintive sound.

queribundus *adj* complaining.

querimōnia, -ae *f* complaint; elegy.

queritor, -ārī *vi* to complain much.

quernus *adj* oak- (*in cpds*).

queror, -rī, -stus *vt, vi* to complain, lament; (*birds*) to sing.

querquetulānus *adj* of oakwoods.

querulus *adj* complaining; plaintive, warbling.

questus *ppa of* **queror**.

questus, -ūs *m* complaint, lament.

quī, quae, quod *pron* (*interrog*) what?, which?; (*relat*) who, which, that; what; and this, he, etc.; (*with* **sī, nisi, nē, num**) any.

quī *adv* (*interrog*) how?; (*relat*) with which, whereby; (*indef*) somehow; (*excl*) indeed.

quia *conj* because; ~**nam** why?

quicquam *nt see* **quisquam**.

quicque *nt see* **quisque**.

quicquid *nt see* **quisquis**.

quīcum with whom, with which.

quīcumque, quīcunque *pron* whoever, whatever, all that; every possible.

quid *nt see* **quis ♦** *adv* why?

quīdam, quaedam, quoddam *pron* a certain, a sort of, a . . . .

quiddam *nt* something.

quidem *adv* (*emphatic*) in fact; (*qualifying*) at any rate; (*conceding*) it is true; (*alluding*) for instance; **nē** . . . ~ not even.

quidlibet *nt* anything.

quidnam *nt see* **quisnam**.

quidnī *adv* why not?

quidpiam *nt =* **quispiam**.

quidquam *nt =* **quisquam**.

quidquid *nt =* **quisquis**.

quiēs, -ētis *f* rest, peace, quiet; sleep, dream, death; neutrality; lair.

quiēscō, -scere, -vī, -tum *vi* to rest, keep quiet; to be at peace, keep neutral; to sleep; (*with acc and infin*) to stand by and see; (*with infin*) to cease.

quiētē *adv* peacefully, quietly.

quiētus *ppa of* **quiēscō ♦** *adj* at rest; peaceful, neutral; calm, quiet, asleep.

quīlibet, quaelibet, quodlibet *pron* any, anyone at all.

quīn *adv* (*interrog*) why not?; (*correcting*) indeed, rather ♦ *conj* who not; but that, but, without; (*preventing*) from; (*doubting*) that.

quīnam, quaenam, quodnam *pron* which?, what?

Quīnct- *etc see* **Quīnt-**.

quīncūnx, -ūncis *m* five-twelfths; number five on a dice; **in ~ūncem dispositī** arranged in oblique lines.

quīndeciēns, -ēs *adv* fifteen times.

quīndecim *num* fifteen; ~ **prīmī** fifteen chief magistrates.

quīndecimvirālis *adj* of the council of fifteen.

quīndecimvirī, -ōrum *mpl* council of fifteen.

quīngēnī, -ōrum *adj* five hundred each.

quīngentēsimus *adj* five-hundredth.

quīngentī, -ōrum *num* five hundred.

quīngentiēns, -ēs *adv* five hundred times.

quīnī, -ōrum *adj* five each; five; ~ **dēnī** fifteen each; ~ **vīcēnī** twenty-five each.

quīnquāgēnī, -ōrum *adj* fifty each.

quīnquāgēsimus *adj* fiftieth ♦ *f* 2 per cent tax.

quīnquāgintā *num* fifty.

Quīnquātria, -iōrum *and* **ium** *ntpl* festival of Minerva.

Quīnquātrūs, -uum *fpl* festival of Minerva.

quīnque *num* five.

quīnquennālis *adj* quinquennial; lasting five years.

quīnquennis *adj* five years old; quinquennial.

quīnquennium, -ī *and* **iī** *nt* five years.

quīnquepartītus *adj* fivefold.

quīnqueprīmī, -ōrum *mpl* five leading men.

quīnguerēmis *adj* five-banked ♦ *f* quinquereme.

quīnquevirātus, -ūs *m* membership of the board of five.

quīnquevirī, -ōrum *mpl* board of five.

quīnquiēns, -ēs *adv* five times.

quīnquiplicō, -āre *vt* to multiply by five.

quīntadecimānī, -ōrum *mpl* men of the fifteenth legion.

quīntānus *adj* of the fifth ♦ *f street in a camp*

Noun declensions and verb conjugations are shown on pp xiii to xxv. The present infinitive ending of a verb shows to which conjugation it belongs: **-āre** = 1st; **-ēre** = 2nd; **-ere** = 3rd and **-īre** = 4th. Irregular verbs are shown on p xxvi

between the 5th and 6th maniples ♦ *mpl* men of the fifth legion.

Quīntiliānus, -ī *m* Quintilian (*famous teacher of rhetoric in Rome*).

Quīntīlis *adj* of July.

quīntum, -ō *adv* for the fifth time.

Quīntus, -ī *m* Roman first name.

quīntus *adj* fifth.

quīntusdecimus *adj* fifteenth.

quippe *adv* (*affirming*) certainly, of course ♦ *conj* (*explaining*) for in fact, because, since; ~ **quī** since I, he *etc*.

quippiam *etc see* **quispiam**.

quippinī *adv* certainly.

Quirīnālis *adj* of Romulus; Quirinal (hill).

Quirīnus, -ī *m* Romulus ♦ *adj* of Romulus.

Quirīs, -ītis *m* inhabitant of Cures; Roman citizen; citizen.

quirītātiō, -ōnis *f* shriek.

Quirītēs *pl* inhabitants of Cures; Roman citizens.

quirītō, -āre *vi* to cry out, wail.

quis, quid *pron* who?, what?; (*indef*) anyone, anything.

quīs *poetic form of* **quibus**.

quisnam, quaenam, quidnam *pron* who?, what?

quispiam, quaepiam, quodpiam *and* **quidpiam** *pron* some, some one, something.

quisquam, quaequam, quicquam *and* **quidquam** *pron* any, anyone, anything; **nec ~** and no one.

quisque, quaeque, quodque *pron* each, every, every one; **quidque, quicque** everything; **decimus ~** every tenth; **optimus ~** all the best; **prīmus ~** the first possible.

quisquiliae, -ārum *fpl* refuse, rubbish.

quisquis, quaequae, quodquod, quidquid *and* **quicquid** *pron* whoever, whatever, all.

quīvīs, quaevīs, quodvīs, quidvīs *pron* any you please, anyone, anything.

quīvīscumque, quaevīscumque, quodvīscumque *pron* any whatsoever.

quō *adv* (*interrog*) where?; whither?; for what purpose?, what for?; (*relat*) where, to which (place), to whom; (*with compar*) the (more); (*with sī*) anywhere ♦ *conj* (*with subj*) in order that; **nōn ~** not that.

quoad *adv* how far?; how long? ♦ *conj* as far as, as long as; until.

quōcircā *conj* therefore.

quōcumque *adv* whithersoever.

quod *conj* as for, in that, that; because; why; ~ **sī** but if.

quōdam modo *adv* in a way.

quoi, quoius *old forms of* **cui, cūius**.

quōlibet *adv* anywhere, in any direction.

quom *etc see* **cum** *conj*.

quōminus *conj* that not; (*preventing*) from.

quōmodo *adv* (*interrog*) just as; (*relat*) just as; ~**cumque** howsoever; ~**nam** how?

quōnam *adv* where, where to?

quondam *adv* once, formerly; sometimes;

(*fut*) one day.

quōniam *conj* since, seeing that.

quōpiam *adv* anywhere.

quōquam *adv* anywhere.

quoque *adv* also, too.

quōquō *adv* to whatever place, wherever.

quōquō modo *adv* howsoever.

quōquō versus, -um *adv* in every direction.

quōrsus, quōrsum *adv* where to?, in what direction?; what for?, to what end?

quot *adj* how many; as many as, every.

quotannīs *adv* every year.

quotcumque *adj* however many.

quotēnī, -ōrum *adj* how many.

quotīd- *etc see* **cottīd-**.

quotiēns, -ēs *adv* how often?; (*relat*) as often as.

quotiēnscumque *adv* however often.

quotquot *adj* however many.

quotumus *adj* which number?, what date?.

quotus *adj* what number, how many; ~ **quisque** how few; ~**a hōra** what time.

quotuscumque *adj* whatever number, however big.

quōusque *adv* how long, till when; how far.

quōvīs *adv* anywhere.

quum *etc see* **cum** *conj*.

R, r

rabidē *adv* furiously.

rabidus *adj* raving, mad; impetuous.

rabiēs, -em, -ē *f* madness, rage, fury.

rabiō, -ere *vi* to rave.

rabiōsē *adv* wildly.

rabiōsulus *adj* somewhat rabid.

rabiōsus *adj* furious, mad.

rabula, -ae *m* wrangling lawyer.

racēmifer, -ī *adj* clustered.

racēmus, -ī *m* stalk of a cluster; bunch of grapes; grape.

radiātus *adj* radiant.

rādīcitus *adv* by the roots; utterly.

rādīcula, -ae *f* small root.

radiō, -āre *vt* to irradiate ♦ *vi* to radiate, shine.

radius, -ī *and* **iī** *m* stick, rod; (*light*) beam, ray; (*loom*) shuttle; (*MATH*) rod for drawing figures, radius of a circle; (*plant*) long olive; (*wheel*) spoke.

rādīx, -īcis *f* root; radish; (*hill*) foot; (*fig*) foundation, origin.

rādō, -dere, -sī, -sum *vt* to scrape, shave, scratch; to erase; to touch in passing, graze, pass along.

raeda, -ae *f* four-wheeled carriage.

raedārius, -ī and **iī** m driver.
Raetī, -ōrum mpl Alpine people between Italy and Germany.
Raetia, -iae f country of the Raetī.
Raeticus and **ius** and **us** adj see n.
rāmālia, -ium ntpl twigs, brushwood.
rāmentum, -ī nt shavings, chips.
rāmeus adj of branches.
rāmex, -icis m rupture, blood vessels of the lungs.
Ramnēnsēs, Ramnēs, -ium mpl one of the original Roman tribes; a century of equites.
rāmōsus adj branching.
rāmulus, -ī m twig, sprig.
rāmus, -ī m branch, bough.
rāna, -ae f frog; frogfish.
rancēns, -entis adj putrid.
rancidulus adj rancid.
rancidus adj rank, rancid; disgusting.
rānunculus, -ī m tadpole.
rapācida, -ae m son of a thief.
rapācitās, -ātis f greed.
rapāx, -ācis adj greedy, grasping, ravenous.
raphanus, -ī m radish.
rapidē adv swiftly, hurriedly.
rapiditās, -ātis f rapidity.
rapidus adj tearing, devouring; swift, rapid; hasty, impetuous.
rapīna, -ae f pillage, robbery; booty, prey.
rapiō, -ere, -uī, -tum vt to tear, snatch, carry off; to seize, plunder; to hurry, seize quickly.
raptim adv hastily, violently.
raptiō, -ōnis f abduction.
raptō, -āre, -āvī, -ātum vt to seize and carry off, drag away, move quickly; to plunder, lay waste; (passion) to agitate.
raptor, -ōris m plunderer, robber; ravisher.
raptus ppp of **rapiō** ♦ nt plunder.
raptus, -ūs m carrying off, abduction; plundering.
rāpulum, -ī nt small turnip.
rāpum, -ī nt turnip.
rārēfaciō, -facere, -fēcī, -factum (pass -fīō, -fierī) vt to rarefy.
rārēscō, -ere vi to become rarefied, grow thin; to open out.
rāritās, -ātis f porousness, open texture; thinness, fewness.
rārō, -ē adv seldom.
rārus adj porous, open in texture; thin, scanty; scattered, straggling, here and there; (MIL) in open order; few, infrequent; uncommon, rare.
rāsī perf of **rādō**.
rāsilis adj smooth, polished.
rāstrum, -ī nt hoe, mattock.
rāsus ppp of **rādō**.
ratiō, -ōnis f 1. (reckoning of) account, calculation; list, register; affair, business.

2. (relation) respect, consideration; procedure, method, system, way, kind.
3. (reason) reasoning, thought; cause, motive; science, knowledge, philosophy; ~ **atque ūsus** theory and practice; ~ **est** it is reasonable; **Stōicōrum** ~ Stoicism; **~ōnem dūcere, inīre** calculate; **~ōnem habēre** take account of, have to do with, consider; **~ōnem reddere** give an account of; **cum ~ōne** reasonably; **meae ~ōnēs** my interests; **ā ~ōnibus** accountant.
ratiōcinātiō, -ōnis f reasoning; syllogism.
ratiōcinātīvus adj syllogistic.
ratiōcinātor, -ōris m accountant.
ratiōcinor, -ārī, -ātus vt, vi to calculate; to consider; to argue, infer.
ratiōnālis adj rational; syllogistic.
ratis, -is f raft; boat.
ratiuncula, -ae f small calculation; slight reason; petty syllogism.
ratus ppa of **reor** ♦ adj fixed, settled, sure; valid; **prō ~ā (parte)** proportionally; **~um dūcere, facere, habēre** ratify.
raucisonus adj hoarse.
raucus adj hoarse; harsh, strident.
raudus, -eris nt copper coin.
raudusculum, -ī nt bit of money.
Ravenna, -ae f port in N.E. Italy.
Ravennās, -ātis adj see n.
rāvis, -im f hoarseness.
rāvus adj grey, tawny.
rea, -ae f defendant, culprit.
reāpse adv in fact, actually.
Reāte, -is nt ancient Sabine town.
Reātīnus adj see n.
rebellātiō, -ōnis f revolt.
rebellātrīx, -īcis f rebellious.
rebelliō, -ōnis f revolt.
rebellis adj rebellious ♦ mpl rebels.
rebellium, -ī and **iī** nt revolt.
rebellō, -āre vi to revolt.
rebītō, -ere vi to return.
reboō, -āre vi to re-echo ♦ vt to make resound.
recalcitrō, -āre vi to kick back.
recaleō, -ēre vi to be warm again.
recalēscō, -ere vi to grow warm again.
recalfaciō, -facere, -fēcī vt to warm again.
recalvus adj bald in front.
recandēscō, -ēscere, -uī vi to whiten (in response to); to glow.
recantō, -āre, -āvī, -ātum vt to recant; to charm away.
reccidī perf of **recidō**.
recēdō, -ēdere, -essī, -essum vi to move back, withdraw, depart; (place) to recede; (head) to be severed.
recellō, -ere vi to spring back.
recēns, -entis adj fresh, young, recent; (writer) modern; (with **ab**) immediately after ♦ adv newly, just.

recēnseō, -ēre, -uī, -um *vt* to count; to review.
recēnsiō, -ōnis *f* revision.
recēnsus *ppp of* **recēnseō**.
recēpī *perf of* **recipiō**.
receptāculum, -ī *nt* receptacle, reservoir; refuge, shelter.
receptō, -āre *vt* to take back; to admit, harbour; to tug hard at.
receptor, -ōris *m* (male) receiver, shelterer.
receptrīx, -īcis *f* (female) receiver, shelterer.
receptum, -ī *nt* obligation.
receptus *ppp of* **recipiō**.
receptus, -ūs *m* withdrawal; retreat; return; refuge; **~uī canere** sound the retreat.
recessī *perf of* **recēdō**.
recessim *adv* backwards.
recessus, -ūs *m* retreat, departure; recess, secluded spot; (*tide*) ebb.
recidīvus *adj* resurrected; recurring.
recidō, -idere, -cidī, -āsum *vi* to fall back; to recoil, relapse; (*fig*) to fall, descend.
recīdō, -dere, -dī, -sum *vt* to cut back, cut off.
recingō, -gere, -ctum *vt* to ungird, loose.
recinō, -ere *vt, vi* to re-echo, repeat; to sound a warning.
reciper- *etc see* **recuper-**.
recipiō, -ipere, -ēpī, -eptum *vt* to take back, retake; to get back, regain, rescue; to accept, admit; (MIL) to occupy; (*duty*) to undertake; (*promise*) to pledge, guarantee; **sē ~** withdraw, retreat; **nōmen ~** receive notice of a prosecution.
reciprocō, -āre *vt* to move to and fro; (*ship*) to bring round to another tack; (*proposition*) to reverse ♦ *vi* (*tide*) to rise and fall.
reciprocus *adj* ebbing.
recīsus *ppp of* **recīdō**.
recitātiō, -ōnis *f* reading aloud, recital.
recitātor, -ōris *m* reader, reciter.
recitō, -āre, -āvī, -ātum *vt* to read out, recite.
reclāmātiō, -ōnis *f* outcry (*of disapproval*).
reclāmitō, -āre *vi* to cry out against.
reclāmō, -āre *vi* to cry out, protest; to reverberate.
reclīnis *adj* leaning back.
reclīnō, -āre, -āvī, -ātum *vt* to lean back.
reclūdō, -dere, -sī, -sum *vt* to open up; to disclose.
reclūsus *ppp of* **reclūdō**.
recoctus *ppp of* **recoquō**.
recōgitō, -āre *vi* to think over, reflect.
recognitiō, -ōnis *f* review.
recognōscō, -ōscere, -ōvī, -itum *vt* to recollect; to examine, review.
recolligō, -igere, -ēgī, -ēctum *vt* to gather up; (*fig*) to recover, reconcile.
recolō, -olere, -oluī, -ultum *vt* to recultivate; to resume; to reflect on, contemplate; to revisit.
recommīnīscor, -ī *vi* to recollect.

recompositus *adj* rearranged.
reconciliātiō, -ōnis *f* restoration, reconciliation.
reconciliō, -āre, -āvī, -ātum *vt* to win back again, restore, reconcile.
reconcinnō, -āre *vt* to repair.
reconditus *ppp of* **recondō** ♦ *adj* hidden, secluded; abstruse, profound; (*disposition*) reserved.
recondō, -ere, -idī, -itum *vt* to store away, stow; to hide away, bury.
recōnflō, -āre *vt* to rekindle.
recoquō, -quere, -xī, -ctum *vt* to cook again, boil again; to forge again, recast; (*fig*) to rejuvenate.
recordātiō, -ōnis *f* recollection.
recordor, -ārī, -ātus *vt, vi* to recall, remember; to ponder over.
recreō, -āre, -āvī, -ātum *vt* to remake, reproduce; to revive, refresh.
recrepō, -āre *vt, vi* to ring, re-echo.
recrēscō, -scere, -vī *vi* to grow again.
recrūdēscō, -ēscere, -uī *vi* (*wound*) to open again; (*war*) to break out again.
rēctā *adv* straight forward, right on.
rēctē *adv* straight; correctly, properly, well; quite; (*inf*) good, all right, no thank you.
rēctiō, -ōnis *f* government.
rēctor, -ōris *m* guide, driver, helmsman; governor, master.
rēctum, -ī *nt* right, virtue.
rēctus *ppp of* **regō** ♦ *adj* straight; upright, steep; right, correct, proper; (*moral*) good, virtuous.
recubō, -āre *vi* to lie, recline.
recultus *ppp of* **recolō**.
recumbō, -mbere, -buī *vi* to lie down, recline; to fall, sink down.
recuperātiō, -ōnis *f* recovery.
recuperātor, -ōris *m* recapturer; (*pl*) board of justices who tried civil cases requiring a quick decision, esp cases involving foreigners.
recuperātōrius *adj* of the recuperatores.
recuperō, -āre, -āvī, -ātum *vt* to get back, recover, recapture.
recūrō, -āre *vt* to restore.
recurrō, -ere, -ī *vi* to run back; to return, recur; to revert.
recursō, -āre *vi* to keep coming back, keep recurring.
recurvō, -āre *vt* to bend back, curve.
recurvus *adj* bent, curved.
recūsātiō, -ōnis *f* refusal, declining; (*law*) objection, counterplea.
recūsō, -āre, -āvī, -ātum *vt* to refuse, decline, be reluctant; (*law*) to object, plead in defence.
recussus *adj* reverberating.
redāctus *ppp of* **redigō**.
redambulō, -āre *vi* to come back.
redamō, -āre *vt* to love in return.
redārdēscō, -ere *vi* to blaze up again.

redarguō, -ere, -ī vt to refute, contradict.
redauspicō, -āre vi to take auspices for going back.
redditus ppp of **reddō**.
reddō, -ere, -idī, -itum vt to give back, return, restore; to give in, response, repay; to give up, deliver, pay; (copy) to represent, reproduce; (speech) to report, repeat, recite, reply; to translate; (with adj) to make; **iūdicium ~** fix the date for a trial; **iūs ~** administer justice.
redēgī perf of **redigō**.
redēmī perf of **redimō**.
redemptiō, -ōnis f ransoming; bribing; (revenue) farming.
redemptō, -āre vt to ransom.
redemptor, -ōris m contractor.
redemptūra, -ae f contracting.
redemptus ppp of **redimō**.
redeō, -īre, -iī, -itum vi to go back, come back, return; (speech) to revert; (money) to come in; (CIRCS) to be reduced to, come to.
redhālō, -āre vt to exhale.
redhibeō, -ēre vt to take back.
redigō, -igere, -ēgī, -āctum vt to drive back, bring back; (money) to collect, raise; (to a condition) to reduce, bring; (number) to reduce; **ad irritum ~** make useless.
rediī perf of **redeō**.
redimīculum, -ī nt band.
redimiō, -īre, -iī, -ītum vt to bind, crown, encircle.
redimō, -imere, -ēmī, -emptum vt to buy back; to ransom, redeem; to release, rescue; (good) to procure; (evil) to avert; (fault) to make amends for; (COMM) to undertake by contract, hire.
redintegrō, -āre, -āvī, -ātum vt to restore, renew, refresh.
redipīscor, -ī vt to get back.
reditiō, -ōnis f returning.
reditus, -ūs m return, returning; (money) revenue.
redivīvus adj renovated.
redoleō, -ēre, -uī vi to give out a smell ♦ vt to smell of, smack of.
redomitus adj broken in again.
redōnō, -āre vt to restore; to give up.
redūcō, -ūcere, -ūxī, -uctum vt to draw back; to lead back, bring back; to escort home; to marry again; (troops) to withdraw; (fig) to restore; (to a condition) to make into.
reductiō, -ōnis f restoration.
reductor, -ōris m man who brings back.
reductus ppp of **redūcō** ♦ adj secluded, aloof.
reduncus adj curved back.
redundantia, -ae f extravagance.
redundō, -āre, -āvī, -ātum vi to overflow; to abound, be in excess; (fig) to stream.
reduvia, -ae f hangnail.

redux, -cis adj (gods) who brings back; (men) brought back, returned.
refectus ppp of **reficiō**.
refellō, -ere, -ī vt to disprove, rebut.
referciō, -cīre, -sī, -tum vt to stuff, cram, choke full.
referiō, -īre vt to hit back; to reflect.
referō, -ferre, -ttulī, -lātum vt to bring back, carry back; to give back, pay back, repay; to repeat, renew; (authority) to refer to, trace back to; (blame, credit) to ascribe; (likeness) to reproduce, resemble; (memory) to recall; (news) to report, mention; (opinion) to reckon amongst; (record) to enter; (senate) to lay before, move; (speech) to reply, say in answer; **grātiam ~** be grateful, requite; **pedem, gradum ~** return; retreat; **ratiōnēs ~** present an account; **sē ~** return.
refert, -ferre, -tulit vi (impers) it is of importance, it matters, it concerns; **meā ~** it matters to me.
refertus ppp of **referciō** ♦ adj crammed, full.
referveō, -ēre vi to boil over.
refervēscō, -ere vi to bubble up.
reficiō, -icere, -ēcī, -ectum vt to repair, restore; (body, mind) to refresh, revive; (money) to get back, get in return; (POL) to re-elect.
refigō, -gere, -xī, -xum vt to unfasten, take down; (fig) to annul.
refingō, -ere vt to remake.
refīxus ppp of **refigō**.
reflāgitō, -āre vt to demand back.
reflātus, -ūs m contrary wind.
reflectō, -ctere, -xī, -xum vt to bend back, turn back; (fig) to bring back ♦ vi to give way.
reflexus ppp of **reflectō**.
reflō, -āre, -āvī, -ātum vi to blow contrary ♦ vt to breathe out again.
refluō, -ere vi to flow back, overflow.
refluus adj ebbing.
reformīdō, -āre vt to dread; to shun in fear.
reformō, -āre vt to reshape.
refōtus ppp of **refoveō**.
refoveō, -ovēre, -ōvī, -ōtum vt to refresh, revive.
refrāctāriolus adj rather stubborn.
refrāctus ppp of **refringō**.
refrāgor, -ārī, -ātus vi (with dat) to oppose, thwart.
refrēgī perf of **refringō**.
refrēnō, -āre, vt to curb, restrain.
refricō, -āre, -uī, -ātum vt to scratch open; to reopen, renew ♦ vi to break out again.
refrīgerātiō, -ōnis f coolness.
refrīgerō, -āre, -āvī, -ātum vi to cool, cool off; (fig) to flag.
refrīgēscō, -gēscere, -xī vi to grow cold; (fig) to flag, grow stale.

refringō, -ingere, -ēgī, -āctum _vt_ to break open; to break off; (_fig_) to break, check.

refrīxī _perf of_ **refrīgēscō**.

refugiō, -ugere, -ūgī _vi_ to run back, flee, shrink ♦ _vt_ to run away from, shun.

refugium, -ī _and_ **iī** _nt_ refuge.

refugus _adj_ fugitive, receding.

refulgeō, -gēre, -sī _vi_ to flash back, reflect light.

refundō, -undere, -ūdī, -ūsum _vt_ to pour back, pour out; (_pass_) to overflow.

refūsus _ppp of_ **refundō**.

refūtātiō, -ōnis _f_ refutation.

refūtātus, -ūs _m_ refutation.

refūtō, -āre, -āvī, -ātum _vt_ to check, repress; to refute, disprove.

rēgālis _adj_ king's, royal, regal.

rēgāliter _adv_ magnificently; tyrannically.

regerō, -rere, -ssī, -stum _vt_ to carry back, throw back.

rēgia, -ae _f_ palace; court; (_camp_) royal tent; (_town_) capital.

rēgiē _adv_ regally; imperiously.

rēgificus _adj_ magnificent.

regignō, -ere _vt_ to reproduce.

Rēgillānus _and_ **ēnsis** _adj see_ **Rēgillus**.

Rēgillus, -ī _m Sabine town_; lake in Latium (_scene of a Roman victory over the Latins_).

regimen, -inis _nt_ guiding, steering; rudder; rule, command, government; ruler.

rēgīna, -ae _f_ queen, noblewoman.

Rēgīnus _adj see_ **Rēgium**.

regiō, -ōnis _f_ direction, line; boundary line; quarter, region; district, ward, territory; (_fig_) sphere, province; **ē ~ōne** in a straight line; (_with gen_) exactly opposite.

regiōnātim _adv_ by districts.

Rēgium, -ī _and_ **iī** _nt_ town in extreme S. of Italy, (_now_ Reggio).

rēgius _adj_ king's, kingly, royal; princely, magnificent.

reglūtinō, -āre _vt_ to unstick.

rēgnātor, -ōris _m_ ruler.

rēgnātrix, -īcis _adj_ imperial.

rēgnō, -āre, -āvī, -ātum _vi_ to be king, rule, reign; to be supreme, lord it; (_things_) to prevail, predominate ♦ _vt_ to rule over.

rēgnum, -ī _nt_ kingship, monarchy; sovereignty, supremacy; despotism; kingdom; domain.

regō, -ere, rēxī, rēctum _vt_ to keep straight, guide, steer; to manage, direct; to control, rule, govern; **~ fīnēs** (_law_) mark out the limits.

regredior, -dī, -ssus _vi_ to go back, come back, return; (_MIL_) to retire.

regressus _ppa of_ **regredior**.

regressus, -ūs _m_ return; retreat.

rēgula, -ae _f_ rule, ruler; stick, board; (_fig_) rule, pattern, standard.

rēgulus, -ī _m_ petty king, chieftain; prince.

Rēgulus, -ī _m_ Roman consul taken prisoner by the Carthaginians.

regustō, -āre _vt_ to taste again.

rēiciō, -icere, -iēcī, -iectum _vt_ to throw back, throw over the shoulder, throw off; to drive back, repel; to cast off, reject; to reject with contempt, scorn; (_jurymen_) to challenge, refuse; (_matter for discussion_) to refer; (_time_) to postpone; **sē ~** fling oneself.

rēiectāneus _adj_ to be rejected.

rēiectiō, -ōnis _f_ rejection; (_law_) challenging.

rēiectō, -āre _vt_ to throw back.

rēiectus _ppp of_ **rēiciō**.

relābor, -bī, -psus _vi_ to glide back, sink back, fall back.

relanguēscō, -ēscere, -ī _vi_ to faint; to weaken.

relātiō, -ōnis _f_ (_law_) retorting; (_pl_) magistrate's report; (_RHET_) repetition.

relātor, -ōris _m_ proposer of a motion.

relātus _ppp of_ **referō**.

relātus, -ūs _m_ official report; recital.

relaxātiō, -ōnis _f_ easing.

relaxō, -āre, -āvī, -ātum _vt_ to loosen, open out; (_fig_) to release, ease, relax, cheer.

relēctus _ppp of_ **relegō**.

relēgātiō, -ōnis _f_ banishment.

relēgō, -āre, -āvī, -ātum _vt_ to send away, send out of the way; to banish; (_fig_) to reject; to refer, ascribe.

relegō, -egere, -ēgī, -ēctum _vt_ to gather up; (_place_) to traverse, sail over again; (_speech_) to go over again, reread.

relentēscō, -ere _vi_ to slacken off.

relēvī _perf of_ **relinō**.

relevō, -āre, -āvī, -ātum _vt_ to lift up; to lighten; (_fig_) to relieve, ease, comfort.

relictiō, -ōnis _f_ abandoning.

relictus _ppp of_ **relinquō**.

rēlicuus _etc see_ **reliquus**.

religātiō, -ōnis _f_ tying up.

rēligiō, -ōnis _f_ religious scruple, reverence, awe; religion; superstition; scruples, conscientiousness; holiness, sanctity (_in anything_); object of veneration, sacred place; religious ceremony, observance.

rēligiōsē _adv_ devoutly; scrupulously, conscientiously.

rēligiōsus _adj_ devout, religious; superstitious; involving religious difficulty; scrupulous, conscientious; (_objects_) holy, sacred.

religō, -āre, -āvī, -ātum _vt_ to tie up, fasten behind; (_ship_) to make fast, moor; (_fig_) to bind.

relinō, -inere, -ēvī _vt_ to unseal.

relinquō, -inquere, -īquī, -ictum _vt_ to leave, leave behind; to bequeath; to abandon, forsake; (_argument_) to allow; (_pass_) to remain.

rēliquiae, -ārum _fpl_ leavings, remainder, relics.

reliquus _adj_ remaining, left; (_time_) subsequent, future; (_debt_) outstanding ♦ _nt_ remainder, rest; arrears ♦ _mpl_ the rest; **~um est** it remains, the next point is; **~ī facere**

leave behind, leave over, omit; **in ~um** for the future.

rell- *etc see* **rel-**.

relūceō, -cēre, -xī *vi* to blaze.

relūcēscō, -cēscere, -xī *vi* to become bright again.

reluctor, -ārī, -ātus *vi* to struggle against, resist.

remaneō, -anēre, -ānsī *vi* to remain behind; to remain, continue, endure.

remānō, -āre *vi* to flow back.

remānsiō, -ōnis *f* remaining behind.

remedium, -ī *and* **iī** *nt* cure, remedy, medicine.

remēnsus *ppa of* **remētior**.

remeō, -āre *vi* to come back, go back, return.

remētior, -tīrī, -nsus *vt* to measure again; to go back over.

rēmex, -igis *m* rower, oarsman.

Rēmī, -ōrum *mpl* people of Gaul (*in region of what is now* Rheims).

rēmigātiō, -ōnis *f* rowing.

rēmigium, -ī *and* **iī** *nt* rowing; oars; oarsmen.

rēmigō, -āre *vi* to row.

remigrō, -āre *vi* to move back, return (home).

reminīscor, -ī *vt, vi* (*usu with gen*) to remember, call to mind.

remisceō, -scēre, -xtum *vt* to mix up, mingle.

remissē *adv* mildly, gently.

remissiō, -ōnis *f* release; (*tension*) slackening, relaxing; (*payment*) remission; (*mind*) slackness, mildness, relaxation; (*illness*) abating.

remissus *ppp of* **remittō** ♦ *adj* slack; negligent; mild, indulgent, cheerful.

remittō, -ittere, -īsī, -issum *vt* to let go back, send back, release; to slacken, loosen, relax; to emit, produce; (*mind*) to relax, relieve; (*notion*) to discard, give up; (*offence, penalty*) to let off, remit; (*right*) to resign, sacrifice; (*sound*) to give back ♦ *vi* to abate.

remixtus *ppp of* **remisceō**.

remōlior, -īrī, -ītus *vt* to heave back.

remollēscō, -ere *vi* to become soft again, be softened.

remolliō, -īre *vt* to weaken.

remora, -ae *f* hindrance.

remorāmina, -um *ntpl* hindrances.

remordeō, -dēre, -sum *vt* (*fig*) to worry, torment.

remoror, -ārī, -ātus *vi* to linger, stay behind ♦ *vt* to hinder, delay, defer.

remorsus *ppp of* **remordeō**.

remōtē *adv* far.

remōtiō, -ōnis *f* removing.

remōtus *ppp of* **removeō** ♦ *adj* distant, remote; secluded; (*fig*) far removed, free from.

removeō, -ovēre, -ōvī, -ōtum *vt* to move back, withdraw, set aside; to subtract.

remūgiō, -īre *vi* to bellow in answer, re-echo.

remulceō, -cēre, -sī *vt* to stroke; (*tail*) to droop.

remulcum, -ī *nt* towrope.

remūnerātiō, -ōnis *f* recompense, reward.

remūneror, -ārī, -ātus *vt* to repay, reward.

remurmurō, -āre *vi* to murmur in answer.

rēmus, -ī *m* oar.

Remus, -ī *m* brother of Romulus.

renārrō, -āre *vt* to tell over again.

renāscor -scī, -tus *vi* to be born again; to grow, spring up again.

renātus *ppa of* **renāscor**.

renāvigō, -āre *vi* to sail back.

reneō, -ēre *vt* to unspin, undo.

rēnēs, -um *mpl* kidneys.

renīdeō, -ēre *vi* to shine back, be bright; to be cheerful, smile, laugh.

renīdēscō, -ere *vi* to reflect the gleam of.

renītor, -ī *vi* to struggle, resist.

renō, -āre *vi* to swim back.

rēnō, -ōnis *m* fur.

renōdō, -āre *vt* to tie back in a knot.

renovāmen, -inis *nt* new condition.

renovātiō, -ōnis *f* renewal; compound interest.

renovō, -āre, -āvī, -ātum *vt* to renew, restore; to repair, revive, refresh; (*speech*) to repeat; **faenus ~** take compound interest.

renumerō, -āre *vt* to pay back.

renūntiātiō, -ōnis *f* report, announcement.

renūntiō, -āre, -āvī, -ātum *vt* to report, bring back word; to announce, make an official statement; (*election*) to declare elected, return; (*duty*) to refuse, call off, renounce.

renūntius, -ī *and* **iī** *m* reporter.

renuō, -ere, -ī *vt, vi* to deny, decline, refuse.

renūtō, -āre *vi* to refuse firmly.

reor, rērī, ratus *vi* to think, suppose.

repāgula, -ōrum *ntpl* (*door*) bolts, bars.

repandus *adj* curving back, turned up.

reparābilis *adj* retrievable.

reparcō, -ere *vi* to be sparing with, refrain.

reparō, -āre, -āvī, -ātum *vt* to retrieve, recover; to restore, repair; to purchase; (*mind, body*) to refresh; (*troops*) to recruit.

repastinātiō, -ōnis *f* digging up again.

repellō, -ellere, -pulī, -ulsum *vt* to push back, drive back, repulse; to remove, reject.

rependō, -endere, -endī, -ēnsum *vt* to return by weight; to pay, repay; to requite, compensate.

repēns, -entis *adj* sudden; new.

repēnsus *ppp of* **rependō**.

repente *adv* suddenly.

repentīnō *adv* suddenly.

repentīnus *adj* sudden, hasty; upstart.

repercō *etc see* **reparcō**.

repercussus *ppp of* **repercutiō**.

repercussus, -ūs *m* reflection, echo.

Noun declensions and verb conjugations are shown on pp xiii to xxv. The present infinitive ending of a verb shows to which conjugation it belongs: **-āre** = 1st; **-ēre** = 2nd; **-ere** = 3rd and **-īre** = 4th. Irregular verbs are shown on p xxvi

repercutiō, -tere, -ssī, -ssum *vt* to make rebound, reflect, echo.

reperiō, -īre, repperī, -tum *vt* to find, find out; to get, procure; to discover, ascertain; to devise, invent.

repertor, -ōris *m* discoverer, inventor, author.

repertus *ppp of* **reperiō ♦** *ntpl* discoveries.

repetītiō, -ōnis *f* repetition; (*RHET*) anaphora.

repetītor, -ōris *m* reclaimer.

repetītus *ppp of* **repetō ♦** *adj*: **altē/longē ~** far-fetched.

repetō, -ere, -īvī and **iī, -ītum** *vt* to go back to, revisit; to fetch back, take back; (*MIL*) to attack again; (*action, speech*) to resume, repeat; (*memory*) to recall, think over; (*origin*) to trace, derive; (*right*) to claim, demand back; **rēs ~** demand satisfaction; reclaim one's property; **pecūniae ~undae** extortion.

repetundae, -ārum *fpl* extortion (*by a provincial governor*).

repexus *adj* combed.

repleō, -ēre, -ēvī, -ētum *vt* to fill up, refill; to replenish, make good, complete; to satiate, fill to overflowing.

replētus *adj* full.

replicātiō, -ōnis *f* rolling up.

replicō, -āre *vt* to roll back, unroll, unfold.

rēpō, -ere, -sī, -tum *vi* to creep, crawl.

repōnō, -ōnere, -osuī, -ositum *vt* to put back, replace, restore; to bend back; to put (in the proper place); (*performance*) to repeat; (*something received*) to repay; (*store*) to lay up, put away; (*task*) to lay aside, put down; (*hope*) to place, rest; (*with* **prō**) substitute; **in numerō, in numerum ~** count, reckon among.

reportō, -āre, -āvī, -ātum *vt* to bring back, carry back; (*prize*) to win, carry off; (*words*) to report.

reposcō, -ere *vt* to demand back; to claim, require.

repositus *ppp of* **repōnō ♦** *adj* remote.

repostor, -ōris *m* restorer.

repostus *etc see* **repositus**.

repōtia, -ōrum *ntpl* second drinking.

repperī *perf of* **reperiō**.

reppulī *perf of* **repellō**.

repraesentātiō, -ōnis *f* vivid presentation; (*COMM*) cash payment.

repraesentō, -āre, -āvī, -ātum *vt* to exhibit, reproduce; to do at once, hasten; (*COMM*) to pay cash.

reprehendō, -endere, -endī, -ēnsum *vt* to hold back, catch, restrain; to hold fast, retain; to blame, rebuke, censure; to refute.

reprehēnsiō, -ōnis *f* check; blame, reprimand, refutation.

reprehēnsō, -āre *vt* to keep holding back.

reprehēnsor, -ōris *m* censurer, critic, reviser.

reprehēnsus *ppp of* **reprehendō**.

reprendō *etc see* **reprehendō**.

repressor, -ōris *m* restrainer.

repressus *ppp of* **reprimō**.

reprimō, -imere, -essī, -essum *vt* to keep back, force back; to check, restrain, suppress.

reprōmissiō, -ōnis *f* counterpromise.

reprōmittō, -ittere, -īsī, -issum *vt* to promise in return, engage oneself.

rēptō, -āre *vi* to creep about, crawl along.

repudiātiō, -ōnis *f* rejection.

repudiō, -āre, -āvī, -ātum *vt* to reject, refuse, scorn; (*wife*) to divorce.

repudium, -ī and **iī** *nt* divorce; repudiation.

repuerāscō, -ere *vi* to become a child again; to behave like a child.

repugnanter *adv* reluctantly.

repugnantia, -ium *ntpl* contradictions.

repugnō, -āre, -āvī, -ātum *vi* to oppose, resist; to disagree, be inconsistent.

repulsa, -ae *f* refusal, denial, repulse; (*election*) rebuff.

repulsō, -āre *vi* to throb, reverberate.

repulsus *ppp of* **repellō**.

repulsus, -ūs *m* (*light*) reflection; (*sound*) echoing.

repungō, -ere *vt* to prod again.

repūrgō, -āre, -āvī, -ātum *vt* to clear again, cleanse again; to purge away.

reputātiō, -ōnis *f* pondering over.

reputō, -āre, -āvī, -ātum *vt* to count back; to think over, consider.

requiēs, -ētis *f* rest, relaxation, repose.

requiēscō, -scere, -vī, -tum *vi* to rest, find rest; to cease ♦ *vt* to stay.

requiētus *adj* rested, refreshed.

requīritō, -āre *vt* to keep asking after.

requīrō, -rere, -sīvī and **siī, -sītum** *vt* to search for, look for; to ask, inquire after; (*with* **ex** *or* **ab**) to question; to need, want, call for; to miss, look in vain for.

requisītus *ppp of* **requīrō**.

rēs, reī *f* thing, object; circumstance, case, matter, affair; business, transaction; fact, truth, reality; possessions, wealth, money; advantage, interest; (*law*) case; (*MIL*) campaign, operations; (*POL*) politics, power, the State; (*writing*) subject matter, story, history; **~ mihi est tēcum** I have to do with you; **~ dīvīna** sacrifice; **~ mīlitāris** war; **~ pūblica** public affairs, politics, the State, republic; **~ rūstica** agriculture; **rem facere** get rich; **rem gerere** wage war, fight; **ad rem** to the point, to the purpose; **in rem** usefully; **ob rem** to the purpose; **ob eam rem** therefore; **ī in malam rem** go to the devil!; **contrā rem pūblicam** unconstitutionally; **ē rē pūblicā** constitutionally; **rē vērā** in fact, actually; **eā rē** for that reason; **tuā rē, ex tuā rē** to your advantage; **ab rē** unhelpfully; **ē rē (nātā)** as things are; **prō rē** according to circumstances; **rēs adversae** failure, adversity; **rēs dubiae** danger; **rēs gestae**

achievements, career; **rēs novae** revolution; **rēs prosperae, secundae** success, prosperity; **rērum māximus** greatest in the world; **rērum scrīptor** historian.

resacrō *etc see* **resecrō**.

resaeviō, -īre *vi* to rage again.

resalūtō, -āre *vt* to greet in return.

resānēscō, -ēscere, -uī *vi* to heal up again.

resarciō, -cīre, -tum *vt* to patch up, repair.

rescindō, -ndere, -dī, -ssum *vt* to cut back, cut open, break down; to open up; (*law, agreement*) to repeal, annul.

rescīscō, -īscere, -īvī *and* **iī, -ītum** *vt* to find out, learn.

rescissus *ppp of* **rescindō**.

rescrībō, -bere, -psī, -ptum *vt* to write back, reply; to rewrite, revise; (*emperors*) to give a decision; (MIL) to transfer, re-enlist; (*money*) to place to one's credit, pay back.

rescrīptus *ppp of* **rescrībō** ♦ *nt* imperial rescript.

resecō, -āre, -uī, -tum *vt* to cut back, cut short; to curtail; **ad vīvum ~** cut to the quick.

resecrō, -āre *vt* to pray again; to free from a curse.

resectus *ppp of* **resecō**.

resecūtus *ppa of* **resequor**.

resēdī *perf of* **resideō**; *perf of* **resīdō**.

resēminō, -āre *vt* to reproduce.

resequor, -quī, -cūtus *vt* to answer.

reserō, -āre, -āvī, -ātum *vt* to unbar, unlock; to disclose.

reservō, -āre, -āvī, -ātum *vt* to keep back, reserve; to preserve, save.

reses, -idis *adj* remaining; inactive; idle; calm.

resideō, -idēre, -ēdī *vi* to remain behind; to be idle, be listless; (*fig*) to remain, rest.

resīdō, -idere, -ēdī *vi* to sit down, sink down, settle; to subside; (*fig*) to abate, calm down.

residuus *adj* remaining, left over; (*money*) outstanding.

resignō, -āre *vt* to unseal, open; (*fig*) to reveal; (COMM) to cancel, pay back.

resiliō, -īre, -uī *vi* to spring back; to recoil, rebound, shrink.

resīmus *adj* turned up.

rēsīna, -ae *f* resin.

rēsīnātus *adj* smeared with resin.

resipiō, -ere *vt* to savour of, smack of.

resipīscō, -īscere, -iī *and* **uī** *vi* to come to one's senses.

resistō, -istere, -titī *vi* to stand still, stop, halt; to resist, oppose; to rise again.

resolūtus *ppp of* **resolvō**.

resolvō, -vere, -vī, -ūtum *vt* to unfasten, loosen, open, release; to melt, dissolve; to relax; (*debt*) to pay up; (*difficulty*) to banish, dispel; (*tax*) to abolish; (*words*) to explain.

resonābilis *adj* answering.

resonō, -āre *vi* to resound, re-echo ♦ *vt* to echo the sound of; to make resound.

resonus *adj* echoing.

resorbeō, -ēre *vt* to suck back, swallow again.

respectō, -āre *vi* to look back; to gaze about, watch ♦ *vt* to look back at, look for; to have regard for.

respectus *ppp of* **respiciō**.

respectus, -ūs *m* looking back; refuge; respect, regard.

respergō, -gere, -sī, -sum *vt* to besprinkle, splash.

respersiō, -ōnis *f* sprinkling.

respersus *ppp of* **respergō**.

respiciō, -icere, -exī, -ectum *vt* to look back at, see behind; (*help*) to look to; (*care*) to have regard for, consider, respect ♦ *vi* to look back, look.

respīrāmen, -inis *nt* windpipe.

respīrātiō, -ōnis *f* breathing; exhalation; taking breath, pause.

respīrātus, -ūs *m* inhaling.

respīrō, -āre, -āvī, -ātum *vt, vi* to breathe, blow back; to breathe again, revive; (*things*) to abate.

resplendeō, -ēre *vi* to flash back, shine brightly.

respondeō, -ondēre, -ondī, -ōnsum *vt* to answer, reply; (*lawyer, priest, oracle*) to advise, give a response; (*law court*) to appear; (*pledge*) to promise in return; (*things*) to correspond, agree, match; **pār parī ~** return like for like, give tit for tat.

respōnsiō, -ōnis *f* answering; refutation.

respōnsitō, -āre *vi* to give advice.

respōnsō, -āre *vt, vi* to answer back; to defy.

respōnsor, -ōris *m* answerer.

respōnsum, -ī *nt* answer, reply; response, opinion, oracle.

rēspūblica, reīpūblicae *f* public affairs, politics, the State, republic.

respuō, -ere, -ī *vt* to spit out, eject; to reject, refuse.

restagnō, -āre *vi* to overflow; to be flooded.

restaurō, -āre *vt* to repair, rebuild.

resticula, -ae *f* rope, cord.

restinctiō, -ōnis *f* quenching.

restinctus *ppp of* **restinguō**.

restinguō, -guere, -xī, -ctum *vt* to extinguish, quench; (*fig*) to destroy.

restiō, -ōnis *m* rope maker.

restipulātiō, -ōnis *f* counterobligation.

restipulor, -ārī *vt* to stipulate in return.

restis, -is *f* rope.

restitī *perf of* **resistō**; *perf of* **restō**.

restitō, -āre *vi* to stay behind, hesitate.

restituō, -uere, -uī, -ūtum *vt* to replace, restore; to rebuild, renew; to give back, return; (*to a condition*) to reinstate; (*decision*) to quash, reverse; (*character*) to reform.

restitūtiō, -ōnis f restoration; reinstating.
restitūtor, -ōris m restorer.
restitūtus ppp of **restituō**.
restō, -āre, -itī vi to stand firm; to resist; to remain, be left; to be in store (for); **quod ~at** for the future.
restrictē adv sparingly; strictly.
restrictus ppp of **restringō** ♦ adj tight, short; niggardly; severe.
restringō, -ngere, -nxī, -ctum vt to draw back tightly, bind fast; (teeth) to bare; (fig) to check.
resultō, -āre vi to rebound; to re-echo.
resūmō, -ere, -psī, -ptum vt to take up again, get back, resume.
resupīnō, -āre vt to turn back, throw on one's back.
resupīnus adj lying back, face upwards.
resurgō, -gere, -rēxī, -rēctum vi to rise again, revive.
resuscitō, -āre vt to revive.
retardātiō, -ōnis f hindering.
retardō, -āre, -āvī, -ātum vt to retard, detain, check.
rēte, -is nt net; (fig) snare.
retēctus ppp of **retegō**.
retegō, -egere, -ēxī, -ēctum vt to uncover, open; to reveal.
retemptō, -āre vt to try again.
retendō, -endere, -endī, -entum and **ēnsum** vt to slacken, relax.
retēnsus ppp of **retendō**.
retentiō, -ōnis f holding back.
retentō etc see **retemptō**.
retentō, -āre vt to keep back, hold fast.
retentus ppp of **retendō**; ppp of **retineō**.
retēxī perf of **retegō**.
retexō, -ere, -uī, -tum vt to unravel; (fig) to break up, cancel; to renew.
rētiārius, -ī and **iī** m net-fighter.
reticentia, -ae f saying nothing; pause.
reticeō, -ēre, -uī vi to be silent, say nothing ♦ vt to keep secret.
rēticulum, -ī nt small net, hairnet; network bag.
retināculum, -ī nt tether, hawser.
retinēns, -entis pres p of **retineō** ♦ adj tenacious, observant.
retinentia, -ae f memory.
retineō, -inēre, -inuī, -entum vt to hold back, detain, restrain; to keep, retain, preserve.
retinniō, -īre vi to ring.
retonō, -āre vi to thunder in answer.
retorqueō, -quēre, -sī, -tum vt to turn back, twist.
retorridus adj dried up, wizened.
retortus ppp of **retorqueō**.
retractātiō, -ōnis f hesitation.
retractō, -āre, -āvī, -ātum vt to rehandle, take up again; to reconsider, revise; to withdraw ♦ vi to draw back, hesitate.
retractus ppp of **retrahō** ♦ adj remote.

retrahō, -here, -xī, -ctum vt to draw back, drag back; to withdraw, remove.
retrectō etc see **retractō**.
retribuō, -uere, -uī, -ūtum vt to restore, repay.
retrō adv back, backwards, behind; (time) back, past.
retrōrsum adv backwards, behind; in reverse order.
retrūdō, -dere, -sum vt to push back; to withdraw.
rettulī perf of **referō**.
retundō, -undere, -udī and **tudī, -ūsum** and **ūnsum** vt to blunt; (fig) to check, weaken.
retūnsus, retūsus ppp of **retundō** ♦ adj blunt, dull.
reus, -ī m the accused, defendant; guarantor, debtor, one responsible; culprit, criminal; **vōtī** ~ one who has had a prayer granted.
revalēscō, -ēscere, -uī vi to recover.
revehō, -here, -xī, -ctum vt to carry back, bring back; (pass) to ride, drive, sail back.
revellō, -ellere, -ellī, -ulsum (olsum) vt to pull out, tear off; to remove.
revēlō, -āre vt to unveil, uncover.
reveniō, -enīre, -ēnī, -entum vi to come back, return.
rēvērā adv in fact, actually.
reverendus adj venerable, awe-inspiring.
reverēns, -entis pres p of **revereor** ♦ adj respectful, reverent.
reverenter adv respectfully.
reverentia, -ae f respect, reverence, awe.
revereor, -ērī, -itus vt to stand in awe of; to respect, revere.
reversiō (revorsiō), -ōnis f turning back; recurrence.
reversus ppa of **revertor**.
revertō, -ere, -ī; revertor, -tī, -sus vi to turn back, return; to revert.
revexī perf of **revehō**.
revictus ppp of **revincō**.
revinciō, -cīre, -xī, -ctum vt to tie back, bind fast.
revincō, -incere, -īcī, -ictum vt to conquer, repress; (words) to refute, convict.
revinctus ppp of **revinciō**.
revirēscō, -ēscere, -uī vi to grow green again; to be rejuvenated; to grow strong again, flourish again.
revīsō, -ere vt, vi to come back to, revisit.
revīvēscō, -vīscō, -vīscere, -xī vi to come to life again, revive.
revocābilis adj revocable.
revocāmen, -inis nt recall.
revocātiō, -ōnis f recalling; (word) withdrawing.
revocō, -āre, -āvī, -ātum vt to call back, recall; (action) to revoke; (former state) to recover, regain; (growth) to check; (guest) to invite in return; (judgment) to apply, refer; (law) to summon again; (performer) to encore; (troops) to withdraw.

revolō, -āre *vi* to fly back.
revolsus *etc see* **revulsus**.
revolūbilis *adj* that may be rolled back.
revolūtus *ppp of* **revolvō**.
revolvō, -vere, -vī, -ūtum *vt* to roll back,
unroll, unwind; (*speech*) to relate, repeat;
(*thought*) to think over; (*writing*) to read over;
(*pass*) to revolve, return, come round.
revomō, -ere, -uī *vt* to disgorge.
revor- *etc see* **rever-**.
revulsus *ppp of* **revellō**.
rēx, rēgis *m* king; tyrant, despot; leader;
patron, rich man.
rēxī *perf of* **regō**.
Rhadamanthus, -ī *m judge in the lower world.*
Rhaeti *etc see* **Raetī**.
Rhamnūs, -ūntis *f town in Attica (famous for
its statue of Nemesis).*
Rhamnūsis, -ūsidis *f Nemesis.*
Rhamnūsius *adj see n.*
rhapsōdia, -ae *f a book of Homer.*
Rhea, -ae *f Cybele.*
Rhea Silvia, -ae, -ae *f mother of Romulus and
Remus.*
Rhēgium *etc see* **Rēgium**.
Rhēnānus *adj* Rhenish.
rhēnō *etc see* **rēnō**.
Rhēnus, -ī *m* Rhine.
Rhēsus, -ī *m Thracian king (killed at Troy).*
rhētor, -oris *m* teacher of rhetoric; orator.
rhētorica, -ae *and* **ē, -ēs** *f* art of oratory,
rhetoric.
rhētoricē *adv* rhetorically, in an oratorical
manner.
rhētoricī, -ōrum *mpl* teachers of rhetoric.
rhētoricus *adj* rhetorical, on rhetoric.
rhīnocerōs, -ōtis *m* rhinoceros.
rhō *nt (indecl)* Greek letter rho.
Rhodanus, -ī *m* Rhone.
Rhodius *adj see* **Rhodopē**.
Rhodopē, -ēs *f mountain range in Thrace.*
Rhodopēius *adj* Thracian.
Rhodos (Rhodus), -ī *f island of Rhodes.*
Rhoetēum, -ī *nt promontory on the Dardanelles
(near Troy).*
Rhoetēus *adj* Trojan.
rhombus, -ī *m* magician's circle; (*fish*) turbot.
rhomphaea, -ae *f long barbarian javelin.*
rhythmicus, -ī *m* teacher of prose rhythm.
rhythmos (-us), -ī *m* rhythm, symmetry.
rīca, -ae *f* sacrificial veil.
rīcinium, -ī *and* **iī** *nt small cloak with hood.*
rictum, -ī *nt*, **-us, -ūs** *m* open mouth, gaping
jaws.
rīdeō, -dēre, -sī, -sum *vi* to laugh, smile ♦ *vt*
to laugh at, smile at; to ridicule
rīdibundus *adj* laughing.
rīdiculāria, -ium *ntpl* jokes.
rīdiculē *adv* jokingly; absurdly.
rīdiculus *adj* amusing, funny; ridiculous, silly

♦ *m* jester ♦ *nt* joke.
rigēns, -entis *pres p of* **rigeō** ♦ *adj* stiff, rigid,
frozen.
rigeō, -ēre *vi* to be stiff.
rigēscō, -ēscere, -uī *vi* to stiffen, harden; to
bristle.
rigidē *adv* rigorously.
rigidus *adj* stiff, rigid, hard; (*fig*) hardy, strict,
inflexible.
rigō, -āre *vt* to water, moisten, bedew; to
convey (water).
rigor, -ōris *m* stiffness, hardness; numbness,
cold; strictness, severity.
riguī *perf of* **rigēscō**.
riguus *adj* irrigating; watered.
rīma, -ae *f* crack, chink.
rīmor, -ārī, -ātus *vt* to tear open; to search
for, probe, examine; to find out.
rīmōsus *adj* cracked, leaky.
ringor, -ī *vi* to snarl.
rīpa, -ae *f* river bank; shore.
Rīphaeī, -ōrum *mpl mountain range in N.
Scythia.*
Rīphaeus *adj see* **Rīphaeī**.
rīpula, -ae *f* riverbank.
riscus, -ī *m* trunk, chest.
rīsī *perf of* **rīdeō**.
rīsor, -ōris *m* scoffer.
rīsus, -ūs *m* laughter, laugh; laughing stock.
rīte *adv* with the proper formality or ritual;
duly, properly, rightly; in the usual manner;
fortunately.
rītus, -ūs *m* ritual, ceremony; custom, usage;
~ū after the manner of.
rīvālis, -is *m* rival in love.
rīvālitās, -ātis *f* rivalry in love.
rīvulus, -ī *m* brook.
rīvus, -ī *m* stream, brook; ē ~ō flūmina māgna
facere ≈ make a mountain of a molehill.
rixa, -ae *f* quarrel, brawl, fight.
rixor, -ārī, -ātus *vi* to quarrel, brawl,
squabble.
rōbīginōsus *adj* rusty.
rōbīgō, -inis *f* rust; blight, mould, mildew.
rōboreus *adj* of oak.
rōborō, -āre *vt* to strengthen, invigorate.
rōbur, -oris *nt* oak; hard wood; prison,
dungeon (*at Rome*); (*fig*) strength, hardness,
vigour; best part, élite, flower.
rōbustus *adj* of oak; strong, hard; robust,
mature.
rōdō, -dere, -sī, -sum *vt* to gnaw; (*rust*) to
corrode; (*words*) to slander.
rogālis *adj* of a pyre.
rogātiō, -ōnis *f* proposal, motion, bill;
request; (*RHET*) question.
rogātiuncula, -ae *f* unimportant bill;
question.
rogātor, -ōris *m* proposer; polling clerk.
rogātus, -ūs *m* request.

Noun declensions and verb conjugations are shown on pp xiii to xxv. The present infinitive ending of a verb shows
to which conjugation it belongs: **-āre** = 1st; **-ēre** = 2nd; **-ere** = 3rd and **-īre** = 4th. Irregular verbs are shown on p xxvi

rogitō, -āre *vt* to ask for, inquire eagerly.
rogō, -āre, -āvī, -ātum *vt* to ask, ask for; (*bill*) to propose, move; (*candidate*) to put up for election; **lēgem ~, populum ~** introduce a bill; **magistrātum populum ~** nominate for election to an office; **militēs sacrāmentō ~** administer the oath to the troops; **mālō emere quam rogāre** I'd rather buy it than borrow it.
rogus, -ī *m* funeral pyre.
Rōma, -ae *f* Rome.
Rōmānus *adj* Roman.
Rōmuleus, -us *adj* of Romulus; Roman.
Rōmulidae, -idārum *mpl* the Romans.
Rōmulus, -ī *m founder and first king of Rome.*
rōrāriī, -ōrum *mpl* skirmishers.
rōridus *adj* dewy.
rōrifer, -ī *adj* dew-bringing.
rōrō, -āre *vi* to distil dew; to drip, trickle ♦ *vt* to bedew, wet.
rōs, rōris *m* dew; moisture, water; (*plant*) rosemary; **~ marīnus** rosemary.
rosa, -ae *f* rose; rose bush.
rosāria, -ōrum *ntpl* rose garden.
rōscidus *adj* dewy; wet.
Roscius, -ī *m*: **L. ~ Othō** *tribune in 67 BC, whose law reserved theatre seats for the equites;* **Q. ~ Gallus** *famous actor defended by Cicero;* **Sex. ~** *of Ameria, defended by Cicero.*
Roscius, -iānus *adj see n.*
rosētum, -ī *nt* rosebed.
roseus *adj* rosy; of roses.
rōsī *perf of* **rōdō.**
rōstrātus *adj* beaked, curved; **columna ~a** *column commemorating a naval victory.*
rōstrum, -ī *nt* (*bird*) beak, bill; (*animal*) snout, muzzle; (*ship*) beak, end of prow; (*pl*) orators' platform in the Forum.
rōsus *ppp of* **rōdō.**
rota, -ae *f* wheel; potter's wheel, torture wheel; car, disc.
rotō, -āre, -āvī, -ātum *vt* to turn, whirl, roll; (*pass*) to revolve.
rotundē *adv* elegantly.
rotundō, -āre *vt* to round off.
rotundus *adj* round, circular, spherical; (*style*) well-turned, smooth.
rubefaciō, -facere, -fēcī, -factum *vt* to redden.
rubēns, -entis *pres p of* **rubeō** ♦ *adj* red; blushing.
rubeō, -ēre *vi* to be red; to blush.
ruber, -rī *adj* red; **mare ~rum** Red Sea; Persian Gulf; **ōceanus ~** Indian Ocean; **Saxa ~ra** *stone quarries between Rome and Veii.*
rubēscō, -ēscere, -uī *vi* to redden, blush.
rubēta, -ae *f* toad.
rubēta, -ōrum *ntpl* bramble bushes.
rubeus *adj* of bramble.
Rubicō, -ōnis *m stream marking the frontier between Italy and Gaul.*
rubicundulus *adj* reddish.
rubicundus *adj* red, ruddy.

rūbīg- *etc see* **rōbīg-.**
rubor, -ōris *m* redness; blush; bashfulness; shame.
rubrīca, -ae *f* red earth, red ochre.
rubuī *perf of* **rubēscō.**
rubus, -ī *m* bramble bush; bramble, blackberry.
ructō, -āre; -or, -ārī *vt, vi* to belch.
ructus, -us *m* belching.
rudēns, -entis *pres p of* **rudō** ♦ *m* rope; (*pl*) rigging.
Rudiae, -iārum *fpl* town in S. Italy (*birthplace of Ennius*).
rudiārius, -ī and iī *m* retired gladiator.
rudīmentum, -ī *nt* first attempt, beginning.
Rudīnus *adj see* **Rudiae.**
rudis *adj* unwrought, unworked, raw; coarse, rough, badly-made; (*age*) new, young; (*person*) uncultured, unskilled, clumsy; ignorant (of), inexperienced (in).
rudis, -is *f* stick, rod; foil (*for fighting practice*); (*fig*) discharge.
rudō, -ere, -īvī, -ītum *vi* to roar, bellow, bray; to creak.
rūdus, -eris *nt* rubble, rubbish; piece of copper.
rūdus, -eris *nt* copper coin.
Rūfulī, -ōrum *mpl* military tribunes (*chosen by the general*).
rūfulus *adj* red-headed.
rūfus *adj* red, red-haired.
rūga, -ae *f* wrinkle, crease.
rūgō, -āre *vi* to become creased.
rūgōsus *adj* wrinkled, shrivelled, corrugated.
ruī *perf of* **ruō.**
ruīna, -ae *f* fall, downfall; collapse, falling in; debris, ruins; destruction, disaster, ruin (*fig*).
ruīnōsus *adj* collapsing; ruined.
rumex, -icis *f* sorrel.
rūmificō, -āre *vt* to report.
Rūmīna, -ae *f goddess of nursing mothers;* **fīcus ~ālis** the fig tree of Romulus and Remus (*under which the she-wolf suckled them*).
rūminātiō, -ōnis *f* chewing the cud; (*fig*) ruminating.
rūminō, -āre *vt, vi* to chew the cud.
rūmor, -ōris *m* noise, cheering; rumour, hearsay; public opinion; reputation.
rumpia *etc see* **rhomphaea.**
rumpō, -ere, rūpī, ruptum *vt* to break, burst, tear; to break down, burst through; (*activity*) to interrupt; (*agreement*) to violate, annul; (*delay*) to put an end to; (*voice*) to give vent to; (*way*) to force through.
rūmusculī, -ōrum *mpl* gossip.
rūna, -ae *f* dart.
runcō, -āre *vt* to weed.
ruō, -ere, -ī, -tum *vi* to fall down, tumble; to rush, run, hurry; to come to ruin ♦ *vt* to dash down, hurl to the ground; to throw up, turn up.
rūpēs, -is *f* rock, cliff.

rūpī *perf of* **rumpō.**
ruptor, -ōris *m* violator.
ruptus *ppp of* **rumpō.**
rūricola, -ae *adj* rural, country- (*in cpds*).
rūrigena, -ae *m* countryman.
rūrsus, rūrsum (rūsum) *adv* back,
  backwards; on the contrary, in return;
  again.
rūs, rūris *nt* the country, countryside; estate,
  farm; **rūs** to the country; **rūrī** in the country;
  rūre from the country.
ruscum, -ī *nt* butcher's-broom.
russus *adj* red.
rūsticānus *adj* country- (*in cpds*), rustic.
rūsticātiō, -ōnis *f* country life.
rūsticē *adv* in a countrified manner,
  awkwardly.
rūsticitās, -ātis *f* country manners, rusticity.
rūsticor, -ārī *vi* to live in the country.
rūsticulus, -ī *m* yokel.
rūsticus *adj* country- (*in cpds*), rural; simple,
  rough, clownish ♦ *m* countryman.
rūsum *see* **rūrsus.**
rūta, -ae *f* (*herb*) rue; (*fig*) unpleasantness.
ruta caesa *ntpl* minerals and timber on an
  estate.
rutilō, -āre *vt* to colour red ♦ *vi* to glow red.
rutilus *adj* red, auburn.
rutrum, -ī *nt* spade, shovel, trowel.
rūtula, -ae *f* little piece of rue.
Rutulī, -ōrum *mpl* ancient Latin people.
Rutulus *adj* Rutulian.
Rutupiae, -iārum *fpl* seaport in Kent (*now
  Richborough*).
Rutupīnus *adj see n.*
rutus *ppp of* **ruō.**

S, s

Saba, -ae *f* town in Arabia Felix.
Sabaeus *adj see n.*
Sabāzia, -iōrum *ntpl* festival of Bacchus.
Sabāzius, -ī *m* Bacchus.
sabbata, -ōrum *ntpl* Sabbath, Jewish holiday.
Sabellus, -ī *m* Sabine, Samnite.
Sabellus, -icus *adj see n.*
Sabīnī, -ōrum *mpl* Sabines (*a people of central
  Italy*).
Sabīnus *adj* Sabine ♦ *f* Sabine woman ♦ *nt*
  Sabine estate; Sabine wine; **herba ~a** savin (*a
  kind of juniper*).
Sabrīna, -ae *f* river Severn.

saburra, -ae *f* sand, ballast.
Sacae, -ārum *mpl* tribe of Scythians.
saccipērium, -ī *and* **iī** *nt* purse-pocket.
saccō, -āre *vt* to strain, filter.
sacculus, -ī *m* little bag, purse.
saccus, -ī *m* bag, purse, wallet.
sacellum, -ī *nt* chapel.
sacer, -rī *adj* sacred, holy; devoted for
  sacrifice, forfeited; accursed, criminal,
  infamous; **Mōns ~** *hill to which the Roman
  plebs seceded;* **Via ~ra** *street from the Forum to
  the Capitol.*
sacerdōs, -ōtis *m/f* priest, priestess.
sacerdōtium, -ī *and* **iī** *nt* priesthood.
sacrāmentum, -ī *nt* deposit made by parties to a
  lawsuit; civil lawsuit, dispute; (*MIL*) oath of
  allegiance, engagement.
sacrārium, -ī *and* **iī** *nt* shrine, chapel.
sacrātus *adj* holy, hallowed; **~āta lēx** *a law
  whose violation was punished by devotion to the
  infernal gods.*
sacricola, -ae *m/f* sacrificing priest *or*
  priestess.
sacrifer, -ī *adj* carrying holy things.
sacrificālis *adj* sacrificial.
sacrificātiō, -ōnis *f* sacrificing.
sacrificium, -ī *and* **iī** *nt* sacrifice.
sacrificō, -āre *vt, vi* to sacrifice.
sacrificulus, -ī *m* sacrificing priest; **rēx ~** high
  priest.
sacrificus *adj* sacrificial.
sacrilegium, -ī *and* **iī** *nt* sacrilege.
sacrilegus *adj* sacrilegious; profane, wicked
  ♦ *m* templerobber.
sacrō, -āre, -āvī, -ātum *vt* to consecrate; to
  doom, curse; to devote, dedicate; to make
  inviolable; (*poetry*) to immortalize.
sacrōsanctus *adj* inviolable, sacrosanct.
sacruficō *etc see* **sacrificō.**
sacrum, -rī *nt* holy thing, sacred vessel;
  shrine; offering, victim; rite; (*pl*) sacrifice,
  worship, religion; **~ra facere** sacrifice; **inter
  ~rum saxumque** ≈ with one's back to the wall;
  hērēditās sine ~rīs *a gift with no awkward
  obligations.*
saeclum *etc see* **saeculum.**
saeculāris *adj* centenary; (*ECCL*) secular,
  pagan.
saeculum, -ī *nt* generation, lifetime, age; the
  age, the times; century; **in ~a** (*ECCL*) for ever.
saepe *adv* often, frequently.
saepe numerō *adv* very often.
saepēs, -is *f* hedge, fence.
saepīmentum, -ī *nt* enclosure.
saepiō, -īre, -sī, -tum *vt* to hedge round,
  fence in, enclose; (*fig*) to shelter, protect.
saeptus *ppp of* **saepiō** ♦ *nt* fence, wall; stake,
  pale; (*sheep*) fold; (*Rome*) voting area in the
  Campus Martius.
saeta, -ae *f* hair, bristle.

Noun declensions and verb conjugations are shown on pp xiii to xxv. The present infinitive ending of a verb shows
to which conjugation it belongs: **-āre** = 1st; **-ēre** = 2nd; **-ere** = 3rd and **-īre** = 4th. Irregular verbs are shown on p xxvi

saetiger, -ī *adj* bristly.
saetōsus *adj* bristly, hairy.
saevē, -iter *adv* fiercely, cruelly.
saevidicus *adj* furious.
saeviō, -īre, -iī, -ītum *vi* to rage, rave.
saevitia, -ae *f* rage; ferocity, cruelty.
saevus *adj* raging, fierce; cruel, barbarous.
sāga, -ae *f* fortune teller.
sagācitās, -ātis *f* (*dogs*) keen scent; (*mind*) shrewdness.
sagāciter *adv* keenly; shrewdly.
sagātus *adj* wearing a soldier's cloak.
sagāx, -ācis *adj* (*senses*) keen, keen-scented; (*mind*) quick, shrewd.
sagīna, -ae *f* stuffing, fattening; food, rich food; fatted animal.
sagīnō, -āre *vt* to cram, fatten; to feed, feast.
sāgiō, -īre *vi* to perceive keenly.
sagitta, -ae *f* arrow.
sagittārius, -ī and iī *m* archer.
sagittifer, -ī *adj* armed with arrows.
sagmen, -inis *nt* tuft of sacred herbs (*used as a mark of inviolability*).
sagulum, -ī *nt* short military cloak.
sagum, -ī *nt* military cloak; woollen mantle.
Saguntīnus *adj see* **Saguntum**.
Saguntum, -ī *nt*, **-us (os), -ī** *f town in E. Spain*.
sāgus *adj* prophetic.
sāl, salis *m* salt; brine, sea; (*fig*) shrewdness, wit, humour, witticism; good taste.
salacō, -ōnis *m* swaggerer.
Salamīnius *adj see* **Salamīs**.
Salamīs, -īnis *f Greek island near Athens; town in Cyprus*.
salapūtium, -ī and iī *nt* manikin.
salārius *adj* salt- (*in cpds*) ♦ *nt* allowance, salary.
salāx, -ācis *adj* lustful, salacious.
salebra, -ae *f* roughness, rut.
Saliāris *adj* of the Salii; sumptuous.
salictum, -ī *nt* willow plantation.
salientēs, -ium *fpl* springs.
salignus *adj* of willow.
Saliī, -ōrum *mpl* priests of Mars.
salillum, -ī *nt* little saltcellar.
salīnae, -ārum *fpl* saltworks.
salīnum, -ī *nt* saltcellar.
saliō, -īre, -uī, -tum *vi* to leap, spring; to throb.
saliunca, -ae *f* Celtic nard.
salīva, -ae *f* saliva, spittle; taste.
salix, -icis *f* willow.
Sallustiānus *adj see* **Sallustius**.
Sallustius, -ī *m* Sallust (*Roman historian*); *his wealthy grand-nephew*.
Salmōneus, -eos *m* son of Aeolus (*punished in Tartarus for imitating lightning*).
Salmōnis, -idis *f his daughter Tyro*.
salsāmentum, -ī *nt* brine, pickle; salted fish.
salsē *adv* wittily.
salsus *adj* salted; salt, briny; (*fig*) witty.
saltātiō, -ōnis *f* dancing, dance.
saltātor, -ōris *m* dancer.

saltātōrius *adj* dancing- (*in cpds*).
saltātrīx, -īcis *f* dancer.
saltātus, -ūs *m* dance.
saltem *adv* at least, at all events; **nōn ~** not even.
saltō, -āre *vt, vi* to dance.
saltuōsus *adj* wooded.
saltus, -ūs *m* leap, bound.
saltus, -ūs *m* woodland pasture, glade; pass, ravine.
salūber *adj see* **salūbris**.
salūbris *adj* health-giving, wholesome; healthy, sound.
salūbritās, -ātis *f* healthiness; health.
salūbriter *adv* wholesomely; beneficially.
saluī *perf of* **saliō**.
salum, -ī *nt* sea, high sea.
salūs, -ūtis *f* health; welfare, life; safety; good wish, greeting; **~ūtem dīcere** greet; bid farewell.
salūtāris *adj* wholesome, healthy; beneficial; **~ littera A** (*for absolvō = acquittal*).
salūtāriter *adv* beneficially.
salūtātiō, -ōnis *f* greeting; formal morning visit, levee.
salūtātor, -ōris *m* morning caller; male courtier.
salūtātrīx, -rīcis *f* morning caller; female courtier.
salūtifer, -ī *adj* health-giving.
salūtigerulus *adj* carrying greetings.
salūtō, -āre, -āvī, -ātum *vt* to greet, salute, wish well; to call on, pay respects to.
salvē *adv* well, in good health; all right.
salvē *impv of* **salveō**.
salveō, -ēre *vi* to be well, be in good health; **~ē, ~ētō, ~ēte** hail!, good day!, goodbye!; **~ēre iubeō** I bid good day.
salvus, salvos *adj* safe, alive, intact, well; without violating; all right; **~ sīs** good day to you!; **~a rēs est** all is well; **~ā lēge** without breaking the law.
Samaous *adj see* **Samē**.
Samarobrīva, -ae *f* Belgian town (*now Amiens*).
sambūca, -ae *f* harp.
sambūcistria, -ae *f* harpist.
Samē, -ēs *f* old name of the Greek island Cephallenia.
Samius *adj* Samian ♦ *ntpl* Samian pottery.
Samnīs, -ītis *adj* Samnite.
Samnium, -ī and iī *nt* district of central Italy.
Samos (-us), -ī *f* Aegean island off Asia Minor (*famous for its pottery and as the birthplace of Pythagoras*).
Samothrācēs, -um *mpl* Samothracians.
Samothrācia, -iae and a, -ae *f* Samothrace (*island in the N. Aegean*).
Samothrācius *adj see n*.
sānābilis *adj* curable.
sānātiō, -ōnis *f* healing.
sanciō, -cīre, -xī, -ctum *vt* to make sacred or inviolable; to ordain, ratify; to enact a

punishment against.

sanctimōnia, -ae f sanctity; chastity.

sanctiō, -ōnis f decree, penalty for violating a law.

sanctitās, -ātis f sacredness; integrity, chastity.

sanctitūdō, -inis f sacredness.

sanctō adv solemnly, religiously.

sanctor, -ōris m enacter.

sanctus ppp of **sanciō** ♦ adj sacred, inviolable; holy, venerable; pious, virtuous, chaste.

sandaligerula, -ae f sandalbearer.

sandalium, -ī and **iī** nt sandal, slipper.

sandapila, -ae f common bier.

sandyx, -ycis f scarlet.

sānē adv sensibly; (intensive) very, doubtless; (ironical) to be sure, of course; (concessive) of course, indeed; (in answer) certainly, surely; (with impv) then, if you please; ~ **quam** very much; **haud** ~ not so very, not quite.

sanguen etc see **sanguis**.

sanguināns, -antis adj bloodthirsty.

sanguinārius adj bloodthirsty.

sanguineus adj bloody, of blood; blood-red.

sanguinolentus adj bloody; blood-red; sanguinary.

sanguis, -inis m blood, bloodshed; descent, family; offspring; (fig) strength, life; **~inem dare** shed one's blood; **~inem mittere** let blood.

saniēs, -em, -ē f diseased blood, matter; venom.

sānitās, -ātis f (body) health, sound condition; (mind) sound sense, sanity; (style) correctness, purity.

sanna, -ae f grimace, mocking.

sanniō, -ōnis m clown.

sānō, -āre, -āvī, -ātum vt to cure, heal; (fig) to remedy, relieve.

Sanquālis avis f osprey.

sānus adj (body) sound, healthy; (mind) sane, sensible; (style) correct; **male** ~ mad, inspired; **sānun es?** are you in your senses?

sanxī perf of **sanciō**.

sapa, -ae f new wine.

sapiēns, -entis pres p of **sapiō** ♦ adj wise, discreet ♦ m wise man, philosopher; man of taste.

sapienter adv wisely, sensibly.

sapientia, -ae f wisdom, discernment; philosophy; knowledge.

sapiō, -ere, -īvī and **uī** vi to have a flavour or taste; to have sense, be wise ♦ vt to taste of, smell of, smack of; to understand.

sapor, -ōris m taste, flavour; (food) delicacy; (fig) taste, refinement.

Sapphicus adj see **Sapphō**.

Sapphō, -ūs f famous Greek lyric poetess, native of Lesbos.

sarcina, -ae f bundle, burden; (MIL) pack.

sarcinārius adj baggage- (in cpds).

sarcinātor, -ōris m patcher.

sarcinula, -ae f little pack.

sarciō, -cīre, -sī, -tum vt to patch, mend, repair.

sarcophagus, -ī m sepulchre.

sarculum, -ī nt light hoe.

Sardēs (-is), -ium fpl Sardis (capital of Lydia).

Sardiānus adj see **Sardēs**.

Sardinia, -iniae f island of Sardinia.

sardonyx, -chis f sardonyx.

Sardus, -ōus, -iniēnsis adj see **Sardinia**.

sariō, -īre, -īvī and **uī** vt to hoe, weed.

sarīsa, -ae f Macedonian lance.

sarīsophorus, -ī m Macedonian lancer.

Sarmatae, -ārum mpl Sarmatians (a people of S.E. Russia).

Sarmaticus, -is adj see **Sarmatae**.

sarmentum, -ī nt twigs, brushwood.

Sarpēdōn, -onis m king of Lycia.

Sarra, -ae f Tyre.

sarrācum, -ī nt cart.

Sarrānus adj Tyrian.

sarriō etc see **sariō**.

sarsī perf of **sarciō**.

sartāgō, -inis f frying pan.

sartor, -ōris m hoer, weeder.

sartus ppp of **sarciō**.

sat etc see **satis**.

satagō, -ere vi to have one's hands full, be in trouble; to bustle about, fuss.

satelles, -itis m/f attendant, follower; assistant, accomplice.

satiās, -ātis f sufficiency; satiety.

satietās, -ātis f sufficiency; satiety.

satin, satine see **satisne**.

satiō, -āre, -āvī, -ātum vt to satisfy, appease; to fill, saturate; to glut, cloy, disgust.

satiō, -ōnis f sowing, planting; (pl) fields.

satis, sat adj enough, sufficient ♦ adv enough, sufficiently; tolerably, fairly, quite; ~ **accipiō** take sufficient bail; ~ **agō, agitō** have one's hands full, be harassed; ~ **dō** offer sufficient bail; ~ **faciō** satisfy; give satisfaction, make amends; (creditor) pay.

satisdatiō, -ōnis f giving security.

satisdō see **satis**.

satisfaciō see **satis**.

satisfactiō, -ōnis f amends, apology.

satisne adv quite, really.

satius compar of **satis**; better, preferable.

sator, -ōris m sower, planter; father; promoter.

satrapēs, -is m satrap (Persian governor).

satur, -ī adj filled, sated; (fig) rich.

satura, -ae f mixed dish; medley; (poem) satire; **per ~am** confusingly.

satureia, -ōrum ntpl (plant) savory.

saturitās, -ātis f repletion; fulness, plenty.

Saturnālia, -ium and **iōrum** ntpl festival of

Noun declensions and verb conjugations are shown on pp xiii to xxv. The present infinitive ending of a verb shows to which conjugation it belongs: **-āre** = 1st; **-ēre** = 2nd; **-ere** = 3rd and **-īre** = 4th. Irregular verbs are shown on p xxvi

Saturn in December.

Saturnia, -iae *f* Juno.

Saturnīnus, -ī *m* revolutionary tribune in 103 and 100 B.C.

Saturnius *adj see n.*

Saturnus, -ī *m* Saturn (*god of sowing, ruler of the Golden Age*); the planet Saturn.

saturō, -āre, -āvī, -ātum *vt* to fill, glut, satisfy; to disgust.

satus *ppp of* **serō ♦** *m* son ♦ *f* daughter ♦ *ntpl* crops.

satus, -ūs *m* sowing, planting; begetting.

satyriscus, -ī *m* little satyr.

satyrus, -ī *m* satyr.

sauciātiō, -ōnis *f* wounding.

sauciō, -āre *vt* to wound, hurt.

saucius *adj* wounded, hurt; ill, stricken.

Sauromatae *etc see* **Sarmatae**.

sāviātiō, -ōnis *f* kissing.

sāviolum, -ī *nt* sweet kiss.

sāvior, -ārī *vt* to kiss.

sāvium, -ī *and* **iī** *nt* kiss.

saxātilis *adj* rock- (*in cpds*).

saxētum, -ī *nt* rocky place.

saxeus *adj* of rock, rocky.

saxificus *adj* petrifying.

saxōsus *adj* rocky, stony.

saxulum, -ī *nt* small rock.

saxum, -ī *nt* rock, boulder; the Tarpeian Rock.

scaber, -rī *adj* rough, scurfy; mangy, itchy.

scabiēs, -em, -ē *f* roughness, scurf; mange, itch.

scabillum, -ī *nt* stool; a castanet played with the foot.

scabō, -ere, scābī *vt* to scratch.

Scaea porta, -ae, -ae *f the west gate of Troy.*

scaena, -ae *f* stage, stage setting; (*fig*) limelight, public life; outward appearance, pretext.

scaenālis *adj* theatrical.

scaenicus *adj* stage- (*in cpds*), theatrical ♦ *m* actor.

Scaevola, -ae *m early Roman who burned his hand off before Porsenna; famous jurist of Cicero's day.*

scaevus *adj* on the left; perverse ♦ *f* omen.

scālae, -ārum *fpl* steps, ladder, stairs.

scalmus -ī *m* tholepin.

scalpellum, -ī *nt* scalpel, lancet.

scalpō, -ere, -sī, -tum *vt* to carve, engrave; to scratch.

scalprum, -ī *nt* knife, penknife; chisel.

scalpurriō, -īre *vi* to scratch.

Scamander, -rī *m* river of Troy (*also called Xanthus*).

scammōnea, -ae *f* (*plant*) scammony.

scamnum, -ī *nt* bench, stool; throne.

scandō, -ere *vt, vi* to climb, mount.

scapha, -ae *f* boat, skiff.

scaphium, -ī *and* **iī** *nt* a boat-shaped cup.

scapulae, -ārum *fpl* shoulder blades;

shoulders.

scāpus, -ī *m* shaft; (*loom*) yarnbeam.

scarus, -ī *m* (*fish*) scar.

scatebra, -ae *f* gushing water.

scateō, -ēre; -ō, -ere *vi* to bubble up, gush out; (*fig*) to abound, swarm.

scatūriginēs, -um *fpl* springs.

scatūriō, -īre *vi* to gush out; (*fig*) to be full of.

scaurus *adj* large-ankled.

scelerātē *adv* wickedly.

scelerātus *adj* desecrated; wicked, infamous, accursed; pernicious.

scelerō, -āre *vt* to desecrate.

scelerōsus *adj* vicious, accursed.

scelestē *adv* wickedly.

scelestus *adj* wicked, villainous, accursed; unlucky.

scelus, -eris *nt* wickedness, crime, sin; (*person*) scoundrel; (*event*) calamity.

scēn- *etc see* **scaen-**.

scēptrifer, -ī *adj* sceptered.

scēptrum, -ī *nt* staff, sceptre; kingship, power.

scēptūchus, -ī *m* sceptre-bearer.

scheda *etc see* **scida**.

schēma, -ae *f* form, figure, style.

Schoenēis, -ēidis *f* Atalanta.

Schoenēius *adj see* **Schoenēis**.

Schoeneus, -eī *m* father of Atalanta.

schoenobatēs, -ae *m* rope dancer.

schola, -ae *f* learned discussion, dissertation; school; sect, followers.

scholasticus *adj* of a school ♦ *m* rhetorician.

scida, -ae *f* sheet of paper.

sciēns, -entis *pres p of* **sciō ♦** *adj* knowing, purposely; versed in, acquainted with.

scienter *adv* expertly.

scientia, -ae *f* knowledge, skill.

scīlicet *adv* evidently, of course; (*concessive*) no doubt; (*ironical*) I suppose, of course.

scilla *etc see* **squilla**.

scindō, -ndere, -dī, -ssum *vt* to cut open, tear apart, split, break down; to divide, part.

scintilla, -ae *f* spark.

scintillō, -āre *vi* to sparkle.

scintillula, -ae *f* little spark.

sciō, -īre, -īvī, -ītum *vt* to know; to have skill in; (*with infin*) to know how to; **quod ~iam** as far as I know; **~ītō** you may be sure.

Scīpiadēs, -ae *m* Scipio.

scīpiō, -ōnis *m* staff.

Scīpiō, -ōnis *m* famous Roman family name (*esp the conqueror of Hannibal* Africanus); Aemilianus (*destroyer of Carthage and patron of literature*).

scirpeus *adj* rush (*in cpds*) ♦ *f* wickerwork frame.

scirpiculus, -ī *m* rush basket.

scirpus, -ī *m* bulrush.

scīscitor, -ārī, -ātus; -ō, -āre *vt* to inquire; to question.

scīscō, -scere, -vī, -tum *vt* to inquire, learn; (*POL*) to approve, decree, appoint.

scissus *ppp of* **scindō ♦** *adj* split; (*voice*) harsh.
scītāmenta, -ōrum *ntpl* dainties.
scītē *adv* cleverly, tastefully.
scītor, -ārī, -ātus *vt, vi* to inquire; to consult.
scītulus *adj* neat, smart.
scītum, -ī *nt* decree, statute.
scītus *ppp of* **sciō**; *ppp of* **scīscō ♦** *adj* clever, shrewd, skilled; (*words*) sensible, witty; (*appearance*) fine, smart.
scītus, -ūs *m* decree.
sciūrus, -ī *m* squirrel.
scīvī *perf of* **sciō**; *perf of* **scīscō**.
scobis, -is *f* sawdust, filings.
scomber, -rī *m* mackerel.
scōpae, -ārum *fpl* broom.
Scopās, -ae *m famous Greek sculptor*.
scopulōsus *adj* rocky.
scopulus, -ī *m* rock, crag, promontory; (*fig*) danger.
scorpiō, -ōnis, -us *and* **os, -ī** *m* scorpion; (*MIL*) a kind of catapult.
scortātor, -ōris *m* fornicator.
scorteus *adj* of leather.
scortor, -ārī *vi* to associate with harlots.
scortum, -ī *nt* harlot, prostitute.
screātor, -ōris *m* one who clears his throat noisily.
screātus, -ūs *m* clearing the throat.
scrība, -ae *m* clerk, writer.
scrībō, -bere, -psī, -ptum *vt* to write, draw; to write down, describe; (*document*) to draw up; (*law*) to designate; (*MIL*) to enlist.
scrīnium, -ī *and* **iī** *nt* book box, lettercase.
scrīptiō, -ōnis *f* writing; composition; text.
scrīptitō, -āre, -āvī, -ātum *vt* to write regularly, compose.
scrīptor, -ōris *m* writer, author; secretary; **rērum ~** historian.
scrīptula, -ōrum *ntpl* lines of a squared board.
scrīptum, -ī *nt* writing, book, work; (*law*) ordinance; **duōdecim ~a** Twelve Lines (*a game played on a squared board*).
scrīptūra, -ae *f* writing; composition; document; (*POL*) tax on public pastures; (*will*) provision.
scrīptus *ppp of* **scrībō**.
scrīptus, -ūs *m* clerkship.
scrīpulum, -ī *nt* small weight, scruple.
scrobis, -is *f* ditch, trench; grave.
scrōfa, -ae *f* breeding sow.
scrōfipāscus, -ī *m* pig breeder.
scrūpeus *adj* stony, rough.
scrūpōsus *adj* rocky, jagged.
scrūpulōsus *adj* stony, rough; (*fig*) precise.
scrūpulum *etc see* **scrīpulum**.
scrūpulus, -ī *m* small sharp stone; (*fig*) uneasiness, doubt, scruple.
scrūpus, -ī *m* sharp stone; (*fig*) uneasiness.
scrūta, -ōrum *ntpl* trash.

scrūtor, -ārī, -ātus *vt* to search, probe into, examine; to find out.
sculpō, -ere, -sī, -tum *vt* to carve, engrave.
sculpōneae, -ārum *fpl* clogs.
sculptilis *adj* carved.
sculptor, -ōris *m* sculptor.
sculptus *ppp of* **sculpō**.
scurra, -ae *m* jester; dandy.
scurrīlis *adj* jeering.
scurrīlitās, -ātis *f* scurrility.
scurror, -ārī *vi* to play the fool.
scūtāle, -is *nt* sling strap.
scūtātus *adj* carrying a shield.
scutella, -ae *f* bowl.
scutica, -ae *f* whip.
scutra, -ae *f* flat dish.
scutula, -ae *f* small dish.
scutula *f* wooden roller; secret letter.
scutulāta, -ae *f* a checked garment.
scūtulum, -ī *nt* small shield.
scūtum, -ī *nt* shield.
Scylla, -ae *f* dangerous rock *or* sea monster (*in the Straits of Messina*).
Scyllaeus *adj see* **Scylla**.
scymnus, -ī *m* cub.
scyphus, -ī *m* wine cup.
Scyrius, -ias *adj see* **Scyros**.
Scyros *and* **us, -ī** *f Aegean island near Euboea*.
scytala *see* **scutula**.
Scytha *and* **ēs, -ae** *m* Scythian.
Scythia, -iae *f* Scythia (*country N.E. of the Black Sea*).
Scythicus *adj* Scythian.
Scythis, -idis *f* Scythian woman.
sē *pron* himself, herself, itself, themselves; one another; **apud ~** at home; in his senses; **inter ~** mutually.
sēbum, -ī *nt* tallow, suet, grease.
sēcēdō, -ēdere, -essī, -essum *vi* to withdraw, retire; to revolt, secede.
sēcernō, -ernere, -rēvī, -rētum *vt* to separate, set apart; to dissociate; to distinguish.
sēcessiō, -ōnis *f* withdrawal; secession.
sēcessus, -ūs *m* retirement, solitude; retreat, recess.
sēclūdō, -dere, -sī, -sum *vt* to shut off, seclude; to separate, remove.
sēclūsus *ppp of* **sēclūdō ♦** *adj* remote.
secō, -āre, -uī, -tum *vt* to cut; to injure; to divide; (*MED*) to operate on; (*motion*) to pass through; (*dispute*) to decide.
sēcrētiō, -ōnis *f* separation.
sēcrētō *adv* apart, in private, in secret.
sēcrētum, -ī *nt* privacy, secrecy; retreat, remote place; secret, mystery.
sēcrētus *ppp of* **sēcernō ♦** *adj* separate; solitary, remote; secret, private.
secta, -ae *f* path; method, way of life; (*POL*) party; (*PHILOS*) school.

sectārius *adj* leading.
sectātor, -ōris *m* follower, adherent.
sectilis *adj* cut; for cutting.
sectiō, -ōnis *f* auctioning of confiscated goods.
sector, -ōris *m* cutter; buyer at a public sale.
sector, -ārī, -ātus *vt* to follow regularly, attend; to chase, hunt.
sectūra, -ae *f* digging.
sectus *ppp of* **secō**.
sēcubitus, -ūs *m* lying alone.
sēcubō, -āre, -uī *vi* to sleep by oneself; to live alone.
secuī *perf of* **secō**.
sēcul- *etc see* **saecul-**.
sēcum with himself *etc*.
secundānī, -ōrum *mpl* men of the second legion.
secundārius *adj* second-rate.
secundō *adv* secondly.
secundō, -āre *vt* to favour, make prosper.
secundum *prep* (*place*) behind, along; (*time*) after; (*rank*) next to; (*agreement*) according to, in favour of ♦ *adv* behind.
secundus *adj* following, next, second; inferior; favourable, propitious, fortunate ♦ *fpl* (*play*) subsidiary part; (*fig*) second fiddle ♦ *ntpl* success, good fortune; **~ō flūmine** downstream; **rēs ~ae** prosperity, success.
secūricula, -ae *f* little axe.
secūrifer, -ī *adj* armed with an axe.
secūriger, -ī *adj* armed with an axe.
secūris, -is *f* axe; (*fig*) death blow; (*POL*) authority, supreme power.
secūritās, -ātis *f* freedom from anxiety, composure; negligence; safety, feeling of security.
secūrus *adj* untroubled, unconcerned; carefree, cheerful; careless.
secus *nt* (*indecl*) sex.
secus *adv* otherwise, differently; badly; **nōn ~** even so.
secūtor, -ōris *m* pursuer.
sed *conj* but; but also, but in fact.
sēdātē *adv* calmly.
sēdātiō, -ōnis *f* calming.
sēdātus *ppp of* **sēdō** ♦ *adj* calm, quiet, composed.
sēdecim *num* sixteen.
sēdēcula, -ae *f* low stool.
sedentārius *adj* sitting.
sedeō, -ēre, sēdī, sessum *vi* to sit; (*army*) to be encamped, blockade; (*magistrates*) to be in session; (*clothes*) to suit, fit; (*places*) to be low-lying; (*heavy things*) to settle, subside; (*weapons*) to stick fast; (*inactivity*) to be idle; (*thought*) to be firmly resolved.
sēdēs, -is *f* seat, chair; abode, home; site, ground, foundation.
sēdī *perf of* **sedeō**.
sedīle, -is *nt* seat, chair.
sēditiō, -ōnis *f* insurrection, mutiny.
sēditiōsē *adv* seditiously.

sēditiōsus *adj* mutinous, factious; quarrelsome; troubled.
sēdō, -āre, -āvī, -ātum *vt* to calm, allay, lull.
sēdūcō, -ūcere, -ūxī, -uctum *vt* to take away, withdraw; to divide.
sēductiō, -ōnis *f* taking sides.
sēductus *ppp of* **sēdūcō** ♦ *adj* remote.
sēdulitās, -ātis *f* earnestness, assiduity; officiousness.
sēdulō *adv* busily, diligently; purposely.
sēdulus *adj* busy, diligent, assiduous; officious.
seges, -itis *f* cornfield; crop.
Segesta, -ae *f* town in N.W. Sicily.
Segestānus *adj see* **Segesta**.
segmentātus *adj* flounced.
segmentum, -ī *nt* brocade.
segne, -iter *adv* slowly, lazily.
segnipēs, -edis *adj* slow of foot.
segnis *adj* slow, sluggish, lazy.
segnitia, -ae *and* **ēs, -em, -ē** *f* slowness, sluggishness, sloth.
sēgregō, -āre, -āvī, -ātum *vt* to separate, put apart; to dissociate.
sēiugātus *adj* separated.
sēiugis, -is *m* chariot and six.
sēiūnctim *adv* separately.
sēiūnctiō, -ōnis *f* separation.
sēiūnctus *ppp of* **sēiungō**.
sēiungō, -gere, sēiūnxī, sēiūnctum *vt* to separate, part.
sēlēctiō, -ōnis *f* choice.
sēlēctus *ppp of* **sēligō**.
Seleucus, -ī *m* king of Syria.
sēlībra, -ae *f* half pound.
sēligō, -igere, -ēgī, -ēctum *vt* to choose, select.
sella, -ae *f* seat, chair, stool, sedan chair; **~ cūrūlis** chair of office for higher magistrates.
sellisternia, -ōrum *ntpl* sacred banquets to goddesses.
sellula, -ae *f* stool; sedan chair.
sellulārius, -ī *and* **iī** *m* mechanic.
sēmanimus *etc see* **sēmianimis**.
semel *adv* once; once for all; first; ever; **~ atque iterum** again and again; **~ aut iterum** once or twice.
Semelē, -ēs *f* mother of Bacchus.
Semelēius *adj see* **Semelē**.
sēmen, -inis *nt* seed; (*plant*) seedling, slip; (*men*) race, child; (*physics*) particle; (*fig*) origin, instigator.
sēmentifer, -ī *adj* fruitful.
sēmentis, -is *f* sowing, planting; young corn.
sēmentīvus *adj* of seed time.
sēmermis *etc see* **sēmiermis**.
sēmēstris *adj* half-yearly, for six months.
sēmēsus *adj* half-eaten.
sēmet *pron* self, selves.
sēmiadapertus *adj* half-open.
sēmianimis, -us *adj* half-dead.
sēmiapertus *adj* half-open.
sēmibōs, -ovis *adj* half-ox.

sēmicaper, -rī *adj* half-goat.
sēmicremātus, sēmicremus *adj* half-burned.
sēmicubitālis *adj* half a cubit long.
sēmideus *adj* half-divine ♦ *m* demigod.
sēmidoctus *adj* half-taught.
sēmiermis, -us *adj* half-armed.
sēmiēsus *adj* half-eaten.
sēmifactus *adj* half-finished.
sēmifer, -ī *adj* half-beast; half-savage.
sēmigermānus *adj* half-German.
sēmigravis *adj* half-overcome.
sēmigrō, -āre *vi* to go away.
sēmihiāns, -antis *adj* half-opened.
sēmihomō, -inis *m* half-man, half-human.
sēmihōra, -ae *f* half an hour.
sēmilacer, -ī *adj* half-mangled.
sēmilautus *adj* half-washed.
sēmilīber, -ī *adj* half-free.
sēmilixa, -ae *m* not much better than a camp follower.
sēmimarīnus *adj* half in the sea.
sēmimās, -āris *m* hermaphrodite ♦ *adj* castrated.
sēmimortuus *adj* half-dead.
sēminārium, -ī *and* **iī** *nt* nursery, seed plot.
sēminātor, -ōris *m* originator.
sēminecis *adj* half-dead.
sēminium, -ī *and* **iī** *nt* procreation; breed.
sēminō, -āre *vt* to sow; to produce; to beget.
sēminūdus *adj* half-naked; almost unarmed.
sēmipāgānus *adj* half-rustic.
sēmiplēnus *adj* half-full, half-manned.
sēmiputātus *adj* half-pruned.
Semīramis, -is *and* **idis** *f* queen of Assyria.
Semīramius *adj see n.*
sēmirāsus *adj* half-shaven.
sēmireductus *adj* half turned back.
sēmirefectus *adj* half-repaired.
sēmirutus *adj* half-demolished, half in ruins.
sēmis, -issis *m* (coin) half an as; (interest) ½ per cent per month (*i.e. 6 per cent per annum*); (*area*) half an acre.
sēmisepultus *adj* half-buried.
sēmisomnus *adj* half-asleep.
sēmisupīnus *adj* half lying back.
sēmita, -ae *f* path, way.
sēmitālis *adj* of byways.
sēmitārius *adj* frequenting byways.
sēmiūst- *etc see* **sēmūst-**.
sēmivir, -ī *adj* half-man; emasculated; unmanly.
sēmivīvus *adj* half-dead.
sēmodius, -ī *and* **iī** *m* half a peck.
sēmōtus *ppp of* **sēmoveō** ♦ *adj* remote; distinct.
sēmoveō, -ovēre, -ōvī, -ōtum *vt* to put aside, separate.
semper *adv* always, ever, every time.
sempiternus *adj* everlasting, lifelong.

Semprōnius, -ī *m* Roman family name (*esp the Gracchi*).
Semprōnius, -iānus *adj see n.*
sēmūncia, -ae *f* half an ounce; a twenty-fourth.
sēmūnciārius *adj* (*interest*) at the rate of one twenty-fourth.
sēmūstulātus *adj* half-burned.
sēmūstus *adj* half-burned.
senāculum, -ī *nt* open air meeting place (*of the Senate*).
sēnāriolus, -ī *m* little trimeter.
sēnārius, -ī *and* **iī** *m* (iambic) trimeter.
senātor, -ōris *m* senator.
senātōrius *adj* senatorial, in the Senate.
senātus, -ūs *m* Senate; meeting of the Senate.
senātūscōnsultum, -ī *nt* decree of the Senate.
Seneca, -ae *m* Stoic philosopher, tutor of Nero.
senecta, -ae *f* old age.
senectus *adj* old, aged.
senectūs, -ūtis *f* old age; old men.
seneō, -ēre *vi* to be old.
senēscō, -ēscere, -uī *vi* to grow old; (*fig*) to weaken, wane, pine away.
senex, -is (*compar* -**ior**) *adj* old (*over 45*) ♦ *m/f* old man, old woman.
sēnī, -ōrum *adj* six each, in sixes; six; ~ **dēnī** sixteen each.
senīlis *adj* of an old person, senile.
sēniō, -ōnis *m* number six on a dice.
senior *compar of* **senex**.
senium, -ī *and* **iī** *nt* weakness of age, decline; affliction; peevishness.
Senonēs, -um *mpl* tribe of S. Gaul.
sēnsī *perf of* **sentiō**.
sēnsifer, -ī *adj* sensory.
sēnsilis *adj* having sensation.
sēnsim *adv* tentatively, gradually.
sēnsus *ppp of* **sentiō** ♦ *ntpl* thoughts.
sēnsus, -ūs *m* (*body*) feeling, sensation, sense; (*intellect*) understanding, judgment, thought; (*emotion*) sentiment, attitude, frame of mind; (*language*) meaning, purport, sentence; **commūnis** ~ universal human feelings, human sympathy, social instinct.
sententia, -ae *f* opinion, judgment; purpose, will; (*law*) verdict, sentence; (*POL*) vote, decision; (*language*) meaning, sentence, maxim, epigram; **meā ~ā** in my opinion; **dē meā ~ā** in accordance with my wishes; **ex meā ~ā** to my liking; **ex animī meī ~ā** to the best of my knowledge and belief; **in ~am pedibus īre** support a motion.
sententiola, -ae *f* phrase.
sententiōsē *adv* pointedly.
sententiōsus *adj* pithy.
senticētum, -ī *nt* thornbrake.
sentīna, -ae *f* bilge water; (*fig*) dregs, scum.
sentiō, -īre, -sēnsī, sēnsum *vt* (*senses*) to

Noun declensions and verb conjugations are shown on pp xiii to xxv. The present infinitive ending of a verb shows to which conjugation it belongs: **-āre** = 1st; **-ēre** = 2nd; **-ere** = 3rd and **-īre** = 4th. Irregular verbs are shown on p xxvi

feel, see, perceive; (_CIRCS_) to experience, undergo; (_mind_) to observe, understand; (_opinion_) to think, judge; (_law_) to vote, decide.

sentis, -is _m_ thorn, brier.

sentīscō, -ere _vt_ to begin to perceive.

sentus _adj_ thorny; untidy.

senuī _perf of_ **senēscō**.

seorsum, seorsus _adv_ apart, differently.

sēparābilis _adj_ separable.

sēparātim _adv_ apart, separately.

sēparātiō, -ōnis _f_ separation, severing.

sēparātius _adv_ less closely.

sēparātus _adj_ separate, different.

sēparō, -āre, -āvī, -ātum _vt_ to part, separate, divide; to distinguish.

sepeliō, -elīre, -elīvī _and_ **eliī, -ultum** _vt_ to bury; (_fig_) to overwhelm, overcome.

sēpia, -ae _f_ cuttlefish.

Sēplasia, -ae _f street in Capua where perfumes were sold._

sēpōnō, -ōnere, -osuī, -ositum _vt_ to put aside, pick out; to reserve; to banish; to appropriate; to separate.

sēpositus _ppp of_ **sēpōnō** ♦ _adj_ remote; distinct, choice.

sēpse _pron_ oneself.

septem _num_ seven.

September, -ris _m_ September ♦ _adj_ of September.

septemdecim _etc see_ **septendecim**.

septemfluus _adj_ with seven streams.

septemgeminus _adj_ sevenfold.

septemplex, -icis _adj_ sevenfold.

septemtriō _etc see_ **septentriōnēs**.

septemvirālis _adj_ of the septemviri ♦ _mpl_ the septemviri.

septemvirātus, -ūs _m_ office of septemvir.

septemvirī, -ōrum _mpl_ board of seven officials.

septēnārius, -ī _and_ **iī** _m_ verse of seven feet.

septendecim _num_ seventeen.

septēnī, -ōrum _adj_ seven each, in sevens.

septentriō, -ōnis _m_, **-ōnēs, -ōnum** _mpl_ Great Bear, Little Bear; north; north wind.

septentriōnālis _adj_ northern ♦ _ntpl_ northern regions.

septiēns, -ēs _adv_ seven times.

septimānī, -ōrum _mpl_ men of the seventh legion.

septimum _adv_ for the seventh time; ~ **decimus** seventeenth.

septimus _adj_ seventh.

septingentēsimus _adj_ seven hundredth.

septingentī, -ōrum _adj_ seven hundred.

septuāgēsimus _adj_ seventieth.

septuāgintā _adj_ seventy.

septuennis _adj_ seven years old.

septumus _adj see_ **septimus**.

septūnx, -ūncis _m_ seven ounces, seven-twelfths.

sepulcrālis _adj_ funeral.

sepulcrētum, -ī _nt_ cemetery.

sepulcrum, -ī _nt_ grave, tomb.

sepultūra, -ae _f_ burial, funeral.

sepultus _ppp of_ **sepeliō**.

Sequāna, -ae _f_ river Seine.

Sequānī, -ōrum _mpl people of N. Gaul._

sequāx, -ācis _adj_ pursuing, following.

sequens, -entis _pres p of_ **sequor** ♦ _adj_ following, next.

sequester, -rī _and_ **ris** _m_ trustee; agent, mediator.

sequestrum, -rī _nt_ deposit.

sēquius _compar of_ **secus**; otherwise; **nihilō ~** nonetheless.

sequor, -quī, -cūtus _vt, vi_ to follow; to accompany, go with; (_time_) to come after, come next, ensue; (_enemy_) to pursue; (_objective_) to make for, aim at; (_pulling_) to come away easily; (_share, gift_) to go to, come to; (_words_) to come naturally.

sera, -ae _f_ door bolt, bar.

Serāpēum, -ēī _nt temple of Serapis._

Serāpis, -is _and_ **idis** _m chief Egyptian god._

serēnitās, -ātis _f_ fair weather.

serēnō, -āre _vt_ to clear up, brighten up.

serēnus _adj_ fair, clear; (_wind_) fair-weather; (_fig_) cheerful, happy ♦ _nt_ clear sky, fair weather.

Sērēs, -um _mpl_ Chinese.

serēscō, -ere _vi_ to dry off.

sēria, -ae _f_ tall jar.

sērica, -ōrum _ntpl_ silks.

Sēricus _adj_ Chinese; silk.

seriēs, -em, -ē _f_ row, sequence, succession.

sēriō _adv_ in earnest, seriously.

sēriola, -ae _f_ small jar.

Serīphius _adj see_ **Serīphus**.

Serīphus (-os), -ī _f_ Aegean island.

sērius _adj_ earnest, serious.

sērius _compar of_ **sērō**.

sermō, -ōnis _m_ conversation, talk; learned discussion, discourse; common talk, rumour; language, style; every day language, prose; (_pl_) Satires (of Horace).

sermōcinor, -ārī _vi_ to converse.

sermunculus, -ī _m_ gossip, rumour.

serō, -ere, sēvī, -satum _vt_ to sow, plant; (_fig_) to produce, sow the seeds of.

serō, -ere, -tum _vt_ to sew, join, wreathe; (_fig_) to compose, devise, engage in.

sērō (_compar_ **-ius**) _adv_ late; too late.

serpēns, -entis _m/f_ snake, serpent; (_constellation_) Draco.

serpentigena, -ae _m_ offspring of a serpent.

serpentipēs, -edis _adj_ serpent-footed.

serperastra, -ōrum _ntpl_ splints.

serpō, -ere, -sī, -tum _vi_ to creep, crawl; (_fig_) to spread slowly.

serpyllum, -ī _nt_ wild thyme.

serra, -ae _f_ saw.

serrācum _etc see_ **sarrācum**.

serrātus _adj_ serrated, notched.

serrula, -ae _f_ small saw.

Sertōriānus _adj see_ **Sertōrius**.

Sertōrius, -ī *m* commander under Marius, who held out against Sulla in Spain.

sertus *ppp of* **serō** ♦ *ntpl* garlands.

serum, -ī *nt* whey, serum.

sērum, -ī *nt* late hour.

sērus *adj* late; too late; **~ā nocte** late at night.

serva, -ae *f* maidservant, slave.

servābilis *adj* that cannot be saved.

servātor, -ōris *m* deliverer; watcher.

servātrīx, -īcis *f* deliverer.

servīlis *adj* of slaves, servile.

servīliter *adv* slavishly.

Servīlius, -ī *m* Roman family name of many consuls.

Servīlius, -ānus *adj see n.*

serviō, -īre, -īvī *and* **iī, -ītum** *vi* to be a slave; (*with dat*) to serve, be of use to, be good for; (*property*) to be mortgaged.

servitium, -ī *and* **iī** *nt* slavery, servitude; slaves.

servitūdō, -inis *f* slavery.

servitūs, -ūtis *f* slavery, service; slaves; (*property*) liability.

Servius, -ī *m* sixth king of Rome; famous jurist of Cicero's day.

servō, -āre, -āvī, -ātum *vt* to save, rescue; to keep, preserve, retain; to store, reserve; to watch, observe, guard; (*place*) to remain in.

servolus, -ī *m* young slave.

servos, -ī *m see* **servus.**

servula, -ae *f* servant girl.

servulus, -ī *m* young slave.

servus, -ī *m* slave, servant ♦ *adj* slavish, serving; (*property*) liable to a burden.

sescēnāris *adj* a year and a half old.

sescēnī, -ōrum *adj* six hundred each.

sescentēsimus *adj* six hundredth.

sescentī, -ōrum *num* six hundred; an indefinitely large number.

sescentiēns, -ēs *adv* six hundred times.

sēsē *etc see* **sē.**

seselis, -is *f* (*plant*) seseli.

sesqui *adv* one and a half times.

sesquialter, -ī *adj* one and a half.

sesquimodius, -ī *and* **iī** *m* a peck and a half.

sesquioctāvus *adj* of nine to eight.

sesquiopus, -eris *nt* a day and a half's work.

sesquipedālis *adj* a foot and a half.

sesquipēs, -edis *m* a foot and a half.

sesquiplāga, -ae *f* a blow and a half.

sesquiplex, -icis *adj* one and a half times.

sesquitertius *adj* of four to three.

sessilis *adj* for sitting on.

sessiō, -ōnis *f* sitting; seat; session; loitering.

sessitō, -āre, -āvī *vi* to sit regularly.

sessiuncula, -ae *f* small meeting.

sessor, -ōris *m* spectator; resident.

sēstertium, -ī *nt* 1000 sesterces; **dēna ~ia** 10,000 sesterces; **centēna mīlia ~ium** 100,000 sesterces; **deciēns ~ium** 1,000,000 sesterces.

sēstertius, -ī *and* **iī** *m* sesterce, a silver coin.

Sestius, -ī *m* tribune defended by Cicero.

Sestius, -iānus *adj* of a Sestius.

Sestos (-us), -ī *f* town on Dardanelles (*home of Hero*).

Sestus *adj see* **Sestos.**

sēt- *etc see* **saet-.**

Sētia, -iae *f* town in S. Latium (*famous for wine*).

Sētiānus *adj see* **Sētia.**

sētius *compar of* **secus.**

seu *etc see* **sīve.**

sevērē *adv* sternly, severely.

sevēritās, -ātis *f* strictness, austerity.

sevērus *adj* strict, stern; severe, austere; grim, terrible.

sēvī *perf of* **serō.**

sēvocō, -āre *vt* to call aside; to withdraw, remove.

sēvum *etc see* **sēbum.**

sex *num* six.

sexāgēnārius *adj* sixty years old.

sexāgēnī, -ōrum *adj* sixty each.

sexāgēsimus *adj* sixtieth.

sexāgiēns, -ēs *adv* sixty times.

sexāgintā *num* sixty.

sexangulus *adj* hexagonal.

sexcēn- *etc see* **sescēn-.**

sexcēnārius *adj* of six hundred.

sexennis *adj* six years old, after six years.

sexennium, -ī *and* **iī** *nt* six years.

sexiēns, -ēs *adv* six times.

sexprīmī, -ōrum *mpl* a provincial town, council.

sextadecimānī, -ōrum *mpl* men of the sixteenth legion.

sextāns, -antis *m* a sixth; (*coin, weight*) a sixth of an as.

sextārius, -ī *and* **iī** *m* pint.

Sextīlis, -is *m* August ♦ *adj* of August.

sextula, -ae *f* a sixth of an ounce.

sextum *adv* for the sixth time.

sextus *adj* sixth; **~ decimus** sixteenth.

sexus, -ūs *m* sex.

sī *conj* if; if only; to see if; **sī forte** in the hope that; **sī iam** assuming for the moment; **sī minus** if not; **sī quandō** whenever; **sī quidem** if indeed; since; **sī quis** if anyone, whoever; **mīrum sī** surprising that; **quod sī** and if, but if.

sībila, -ōrum *ntpl* whistle, hissing.

sībilō, -āre *vi* to hiss, whistle ♦ *vt* to hiss at.

sībilus, -ī *m* whistle, hissing.

sībilus *adj* hissing.

Sibulla, Sibylla, -ae *f* prophetess, Sibyl.

Sibyllīnus *adj see* **Sibylla.**

sīc *adv* so, thus, this way, as follows; as one is, as things are; on this condition; yes.

sīca, -ae *f* dagger.

Sicānī, -ōrum *mpl* ancient people of Italy

(later of Sicily).

Sicānia, -iae *f* Sicily.

Sicānus, -ius *adj* Sicanian, Sicilian.

sīcārius, -ī *and* **iī** *m* assassin, murderer.

siccē *adv* (*speech*) firmly.

siccitās, -ātis *f* dryness, drought; (*body*) firmness; (*style*) dullness.

siccō, -āre, -āvī, -ātum *vt* to dry; to drain, exhaust; (*sore*) to heal up.

siccoculus *adj* dry-eyed.

siccus *adj* dry; thirsty, sober; (*body*) firm, healthy; (*argument*) solid, sound; (*style*) flat, dull ♦ *nt* dry land.

Sicilia, -ae *f* Sicily.

sicilicula, -ae *f* little sickle.

Siciliēnsis, -s, -dis *adj* Sicilian.

sīcine is this how?

sīcubi *adv* if anywhere, wheresoever.

Siculus *adj* Sicilian.

sīcunde *adv* if from anywhere.

sīcut, sīcutī *adv* just as, as in fact; (*comparison*) like, as; (*example*) as for instance; (*with subj*) as if.

Sicyōn, -ōnis *f* town in N. Peloponnese.

Sicyōnius *adj see* **Sicyōn.**

sīdereus *adj* starry; (*fig*) radiant.

Sidicīnī, -ōrum *mpl* people of Campania.

Sidicīnus *adj see n.*

sīdō, -ere, -ī *vi* to sit down, settle; to sink, subside; to stick fast.

Sīdōn, -ōnis *f* famous Phoenician town.

Sīdōnis, -ōnidis *adj* Phoenician ♦ *f* Europa; Dido.

Sīdōnius *adj* Sidonian, Phoenician.

sīdus, -eris *nt* constellation; heavenly body, star; season, climate, weather; destiny; (*pl*) sky; (*fig*) fame, glory.

siem *archaic subj of* **sum.**

Sigambrī *etc see* **Sugambri.**

Sīgēum, -ī *nt* promontory near Troy.

Sīgēus, -ius *adj* Sigean.

sigilla, -ōrum *ntpl* little figures; seal.

sigillātus *adj* decorated with little figures.

signātor, -ōris *m* witness (to a document).

signifer, -ī *adj* with constellations; ~ **orbis** Zodiac ♦ *m* (MIL) standard-bearer.

significanter *adv* pointedly, tellingly.

significātiō, -ōnis *f* indication, signal, token; sign of approval; (RHET) emphasis; (*word*) meaning.

significō, -āre, -āvī, -ātum *vt* to indicate, show; to betoken, portend; (*word*) to mean.

signō, -āre, -āvī, -ātum *vt* to mark, stamp, print; (*document*) to seal; (*money*) to coin, mint; (*fig*) to impress, designate, note.

signum, -ī *nt* mark, sign, token; (MIL) standard; signal, password; (*art*) design, statue; (*document*) seal; (ASTRO) constellation; **~a cōnferre** join battle; **~a cōnstituere** halt; **~a convertere** wheel about; **~a ferre** move camp; attack; **~a inferre** attack; **~a prōferre** advance; **~a sequī** march in order; **ab ~īs discēdere** leave the ranks; **sub ~īs īre** march

in order.

Sīla, -ae *f* forest in extreme S. Italy

sīlānus, -ī *m* fountain, jet of water.

silēns, -entis *pres p of* **sileō** ♦ *adj* still, silent ♦ *mpl* the dead.

silentium, -ī *and* **iī** *nt* stillness, silence; (*fig*) standstill, inaction.

Sīlēnus, -ī *m* old and drunken companion of Bacchus.

sileō, -ēre, -uī *vi* to be still, be silent; to cease ♦ *vt* to say nothing about.

siler, -is *nt* willow.

silēscō, -ere *vi* to calm down, fall silent.

silex, -icis *m* flint, hard stone; rock.

silicernium, -ī *and* **iī** *nt* funeral feast.

silīgō, -inis *f* winter wheat; fine flour.

siliqua, -ae *f* pod, husk; (*pl*) pulse.

sillybus, -ī *m* label bearing a book's title.

Silurēs, -um *mpl* British tribe in S. Wales.

silūrus, -ī *m* sheatfish.

sīlus *adj* snub-nosed.

silva, -ae *f* wood, forest; plantation, shrubbery; (*plant*) flowering stem; (LIT) material.

Silvānus, -ī *m* god of uncultivated land.

silvēscō, -ere *vi* to run to wood.

silvestris *adj* wooded, forest- (*in cpds*); wild; pastoral.

silvicola, -ae *m/f* sylvan.

silvicultrīx, -īcis *adj* living in the woods.

silvifragus *adj* tree-breaking.

silvōsus *adj* woody.

sīmia, -ae *f* ape.

simile, -is *nt* comparison, parallel.

similis *adj* like, similar; ~ **atque** like what; **vērī ~** probable.

similiter *adv* similarly.

similitūdō, -inis *f* likeness, resemblance; imitation; analogy; monotony; (RHET) simile.

sīmiolus, -ī *m* monkey.

simītu *adv* at the same time, together.

sīmius, -ī *and* **iī** *m* ape.

Simoīs, -entis *m* river of Troy.

Simōnidēs, -is *m* Greek lyric poet of Ceos (*famous for dirges*).

Simōnidēus *adj see n.*

simplex, -icis *adj* single, simple; natural, straightforward; (*character*) frank, sincere.

simplicitās, -ātis *f* singleness; frankness, innocence.

simpliciter *adv* simply, naturally; frankly.

simplum, -ī *nt* simple sum.

simpulum, -ī *nt* small ladle; **excitāre fluctūs in ~ō** ≈ *raise a storm in a teacup.*

simpuvium, -ī *and* **iī** *nt* libation bowl.

simul *adv* at the same time, together, at once; likewise, also; both … and; ~ **ac atque, ut** as soon as ♦ *conj* as soon as.

simulācrum, -ī *nt* likeness, image, portrait, statue; phantom, ghost; (*writing*) symbol; (*fig*) semblance, shadow.

simulāmen, -inis *nt* copy.

simulāns, -antis *pres p of* **simulō** ♦ *adj*

imitative.
simulātē *adv* deceitfully.
simulātiō, -ōnis *f* pretence, shamming, hypocrisy.
simulātor, -ōris *m* imitator; pretender, hypocrite.
simulatque *conj* as soon as.
simulō, -āre, -āvī, -ātum *vt* to imitate, represent; to impersonate; to pretend, counterfeit.
simultās, -ātis *f* feud, quarrel.
sīmulus *adj* snub-nosed.
sīmus *adj* snub-nosed.
sīn *conj* but if; **~ aliter, minus** but if not.
sināpi, -is *nt*, **-is, -is** *f* mustard.
sincērē *adv* honestly.
sincēritās, -ātis *f* integrity.
sincērus *adj* clean, whole, genuine; (*fig*) pure, sound, honest.
sincipitāmentum, -ī *nt* half a head.
sinciput, -itis *nt* half a head; brain.
sine *prep* (*with abl*) without, -less (*in cpds*).
singillātim *adv* singly, one by one.
singulāris *adj* one at a time, single, sole; unique, extraordinary.
singulāriter *adv* separately; extremely.
singulārius *adj* single.
singulī, -ōrum *adj* one each, single, one.
singultim *adv* in sobs.
singultō, -āre *vi* to sob, gasp, gurgle ♦ *vt* to gasp out.
singultus, -ūs *m* sob, gasp, death rattle.
singulus *etc see* **singulī**.
sinister, -rī *adj* left; (*fig*) perverse, unfavourable; (*Roman auspices*) lucky; (*Greek auspices*) unlucky.
sinistra, -rae *f* left hand, left-hand side.
sinistrē *adv* badly.
sinistrōrsus, -um *adv* to the left.
sinō, -ere, sīvī, situm *vt* to let, allow; to let be; **nē dī sīrint** God forbid!
Sinōpē, -ēs *f* Greek colony on the Black Sea.
Sinōpēnsis, -eus *adj see* **Sinōpē**.
Sinuessa, -ae *f* town on the borders of Latium and Campania.
Sinuessānus *adj see* **Sinuessa**.
sīnum *etc see* **sīnus**.
sinuō, -āre, -āvī, -ātum *vt* to wind, curve.
sinuōsus *adj* winding, curved.
sinus, -ūs *m* curve, fold; (*fishing*) net; (GEOG) bay, gulf, valley; (*hair*) curl; (*ship*) sail; (*toga*) fold, pocket, purse; (*person*) bosom; (*fig*) protection, love, heart, hiding place; **in -ū gaudēre** be secretly glad.
sīnus, -ī *m* large cup.
sīparium, -ī *and* **iī** *nt* act curtain.
sīphō, -ōnis *m* siphon; fire engine.
sīquandō *adv* if ever.
sīquī, sīquis *pron* if any, if anyone, whoever.
sīquidem *adv* if in fact ♦ *conj* since.

sīrempse *adj* the same.
Sīrēn, -ēnis *f* Siren.
sīris, sīrit *perf subj of* **sinō**.
Sīrius, -ī *m* Dog Star ♦ *adj* of Sirius.
sirpe, -is *nt* silphium.
sīrus, -ī *m* corn pit.
sīs (*for* **sī vīs**) *adv* please.
sistō, -ere, stitī, statum *vt* to place, set, plant; (*law*) to produce in court; (*monument*) to set up; (*movement*) to stop, arrest, check ♦ *vi* to stand, rest; (*law*) to appear in court; (*movement*) to stand still, stop, stand firm; **sē ~** appear, present oneself; **tūtum ~** see safe; **vadimōnium ~** duly appear in court; **~ī nōn potest** the situation is desperate.
sistrum, -ī *nt* Egyptian rattle, cymbal.
sisymbrium, -ī *and* **iī** *nt* fragrant herb, perhaps mint.
Sīsyphius *adj*, **-idēs, -idae** *m* Ulysses.
Sīsyphus, -ī *m* criminal condemned in Hades to roll a rock repeatedly up a hill.
sitella, -ae *f* lottery urn.
Sīthonis, -idis *adj* Thracian.
Sīthonius *adj* Thracian.
sitīculōsus *adj* thirsty, dry.
sitiēns, -entis *pres p of* **sitiō** ♦ *adj* thirsty, dry; parching; (*fig*) eager.
sitienter *adv* eagerly.
sitiō, -īre *vi* to be thirsty; to be parched ♦ *vt* to thirst for, covet.
sitis, -is *f* thirst; drought.
sittybus *etc see* **sillybus**.
situla, -ae *f* bucket.
situs *ppp of* **sinō** ♦ *adj* situated, lying; founded; (*fig*) dependent.
situs, -ūs *m* situation, site; structure; neglect, squalor, mould; (*mind*) dullness.
sīve *conj* or if; or; whether ... or.
sīvī *perf of* **sinō**.
smaragdus, -ī *m/f* emerald.
smīlax, -acis *f* bindweed.
Smintheus, -eī *m* Apollo.
Smyrna, -ae *f* Ionian town in Asia Minor.
Smyrnaeus *adj see* **Smyrna**.
sobol- *etc see* **subol-**.
sobriē *adv* temperately; sensibly.
sobrīna, -ae *f* cousin (*on the mother's side*).
sobrīnus, -ī *m* cousin (*on the mother's side*).
sobrius *adj* sober; temperate, moderate; (*mind*) sane, sensible.
soccus, -ī *m* slipper (*esp the sock worn by actors in comedy*); comedy.
socer, -ī *m* father-in-law.
sociābilis *adj* compatible.
sociālis *adj* of allies, confederate; conjugal.
sociāliter *adv* sociably.
sociennus, -ī *m* friend.
societās, -ātis *f* fellowship, association; alliance.
sociō, -āre, -āvī, -ātum *vt* to unite, associate,

Noun declensions and verb conjugations are shown on pp xiii to xxv. The present infinitive ending of a verb shows to which conjugation it belongs: **-āre** = 1st; **-ēre** = 2nd; **-ere** = 3rd and **-īre** = 4th. Irregular verbs are shown on p xxvi

share.

sociofraudus, -ī *m* deceiver of friends.

socius *adj* associated, allied ♦ *m* friend, companion; partner, ally.

sōcordia, -ae *f* indolence, apathy; folly.

sōcordius *adv* more carelessly, lazily.

sōcors, -dis *adj* lazy, apathetic; stupid.

Sōcratēs, -is *m famous Athenian philosopher.*

Sōcraticus *adj* of Socrates, Socratic ♦ *mpl* the followers of Socrates.

socrus, -ūs *f* mother-in-law.

sodālicium, -ī *and* **iī** *nt* fellowship; secret society.

sodālicius *adj* of fellowship.

sodālis, -is *m/f* companion, friend; member of a society, accomplice.

sodālitās, -ātis *f* companionship, friendship; society, club; secret society.

sodālitius *etc see* **sodālicius.**

sodēs *adv* please.

sōl, sōlis *m* sun; sunlight, sun's heat; (*poetry*) day; (*myth*) Sun god; ~ **oriēns, ~is ortus** east; ~ **occidēns, ~is occāsus** west.

sōlāciolum, -ī *nt* a grain of comfort.

sōlācium, -ī *and* **iī** *nt* comfort, consolation, relief.

sōlāmen, -inis *nt* solace, relief.

sōlāris *adj* of the sun.

sōlārium, -ī *and* **iī** *nt* sundial; clock; balcony, terrace.

sōlātium *etc see* **sōlācium.**

sōlātor, -ōris *m* consoler.

soldūriī, -ōrum *mpl* retainers.

soldus *etc see* **solidus.**

solea, -ae *f* sandal, shoe; fetter; (*fish*) sole.

soleārius, -ī *and* **iī** *m* sandal maker.

soleātus *adj* wearing sandals.

soleō, -ēre, -itus *vi* to be accustomed, be in the habit, usually do; **ut ~** as usual.

solidē *adv* for certain.

soliditās, -ātis *f* solidity.

solidō, -āre *vt* to make firm, strengthen.

solidus *adj* solid, firm, dense; whole, complete; (*fig*) sound, genuine, substantial ♦ *nt* solid matter, firm ground.

sōliferreum, -ī *nt* an all-iron javelin.

sōlistimus *adj* (*AUG*) most favourable.

sōlitārius *adj* solitary, lonely.

sōlitūdō, -inis *f* solitariness, loneliness; destitution; (*place*) desert.

solitus *ppa of* **soleō** ♦ *adj* usual, customary ♦ *nt* custom; **plūs ~ō** more than usual.

solium, -ī *and* **iī** *nt* seat, throne; tub; (*fig*) rule.

sōlivagus *adj* going by oneself; single.

sollemne, -is *nt* religious rite, festival; usage, practice.

sollemnis *adj* annual, regular; religious, solemn; usual, ordinary.

sollemniter *adv* solemnly.

sollers, -tis *adj* skilled, clever, expert; ingenious.

sollerter *adv* cleverly.

sollertia, -ae *f* skill, ingenuity.

sollicitātiō, -ōnis *f* inciting.

sollicitō, -āre, -āvī, -ātum *vt* to stir up, disturb; to trouble, distress, molest; to rouse, urge, incite, tempt, tamper with.

sollicitūdō, -inis *f* uneasiness, anxiety.

sollicitus *adj* agitated, disturbed; (*mind*) troubled, worried, alarmed; (*things*) anxious, careful; (*cause*) disquieting.

solliferreum *etc see* **sōliferreum.**

sollistimus *etc see* **sōlistimus.**

soloecismus, -ī *m* grammatical mistake.

Solōn, -ōnis *m famous Athenian lawgiver.*

sōlor, -ārī, -ātus *vt* to comfort, console; to relieve, ease.

sōlstitiālis *adj* of the summer solstice; midsummer.

sōlstitium, -ī *and* **iī** *nt* summer solstice; midsummer, summer heat.

solum, -ī *nt* ground, floor, bottom; soil, land, country; (*foot*) sole; (*fig*) basis; ~**ō aequāre** raze to the ground.

sōlum *adv* only, merely.

sōlus (*gen* **-īus,** *dat* **-ī**) *see* **vicis;** *adj* only, alone; lonely, forsaken; (*place*) lonely, deserted.

solūtē *adv* loosely, freely, carelessly, weakly, fluently.

solūtiō, -ōnis *f* loosening; payment.

solūtus *ppp of* **solvō** ♦ *adj* loose, free; (*from distraction*) at ease, at leisure, merry; (*from obligation*) exempt; (*from restraint*) free, independent, unprejudiced; (*moral*) lax, weak, insolent; (*language*) prose, unrhythmical; (*speaker*) fluent; **ōrātiō ~a, verba ~a** prose.

solvō, -vere, -vī, -ūtum *vt* to loosen, undo; to free, release, acquit, exempt; to dissolve, break up, separate; to relax, slacken, weaken; to cancel, remove, destroy; to solve, explain; to pay, fulfil; (*argument*) to refute; (*discipline*) to undermine; (*feelings*) to get rid of; (*hair*) to let down; (*letter*) to open; (*sail*) to unfurl; (*siege*) to raise; (*troops*) to dismiss ♦ *vi* to set sail; to pay; **nāvem ~** set sail; **poenās ~** be punished; **praesēns ~** pay cash; **rem ~** pay; **sacrāmentō ~** discharge; **~vendō esse** be solvent.

Solyma, -ōrum *ntpl* Jerusalem.

Solymus *adj* of the Jews.

somniculōsē *adv* sleepily.

somniculōsus *adj* sleepy.

somnifer, -ī *adj* soporific; fatal.

somniō, -āre *vt* to dream, dream about; to talk nonsense.

somnium, -ī *and* **iī** *nt* dream; nonsense, fancy.

somnus, -ī *m* sleep; sloth.

sonābilis *adj* noisy.

sonipēs, -edis *m* steed.

sonitus, -ūs *m* sound, noise.

sonivius *adj* noisy.

sonō, -āre, -uī, -itum *vi* to sound, make a noise ♦ *vt* to utter, speak, celebrate; to sound like.

sonor, -ōris *m* sound, noise.

sonōrus *adj* noisy, loud.

sōns, sontis *adj* guilty.

sonticus *adj* critical; important.

sonus, -ī *m* sound, noise; (*fig*) tone.

Sophistēs, -ae *m* sophist.

Sophoclēs, -is *m* famous Greek tragic poet.

Sophoclēus *adj* of Sophocles, Sophoclean.

sophus *adj* wise.

sōpiō, -īre, -īvī, -ītum *vt* to put to sleep; (*fig*) to calm, lull.

sopor, -ōris *m* sleep; apathy.

sopōrifer, -ī *adj* soporific, drowsy.

sopōrō, -āre *vt* to lull to sleep; to make soporific.

sopōrus *adj* drowsy.

Sōracte, -is *nt* mountain in S. Etruria.

sorbeō, -ēre, -uī *vt* to suck, swallow; (*fig*) to endure.

sorbillō, -āre *vt* to sip.

sorbitiō, -ōnis *f* drink, broth.

sorbum, -ī *nt* service berry.

sorbus, -ī *f* service tree.

sordeō, -ēre *vi* to be dirty, be sordid; to seem shabby; to be of no account.

sordēs, -is *f* dirt, squalor, shabbiness; mourning; meanness; vulgarity; (*people*) rabble.

sordēscō, -ere *vi* to become dirty.

sordidātus *adj* shabbily dressed, in mourning.

sordidē *adv* meanly, vulgarly.

sordidulus *adj* soiled, shabby.

sordidus *adj* dirty, squalid, shabby; in mourning; poor, mean; base, vile.

sōrex, -icis *m* shrewmouse.

sōricīnus *adj* of the shrewmouse.

sōrītēs, -ae *m* chain syllogism.

soror, -ōris *f* sister.

sorōricīda, -ae *m* murderer of a sister.

sorōrius *adj* of a sister.

sors, sortis *f* lot; allotted duty; oracle, prophecy; fate, fortune; (*money*) capital, principal.

sōrsum *etc see* **seōrsum**.

sortilegus *adj* prophetic ♦ *m* soothsayer.

sortior, -īrī, -ītus *vi* to draw *or* cast lots ♦ *vt* to draw lots for, allot, obtain by lot; to distribute, share; to choose; to receive.

sortītiō, -ōnis *f* drawing lots, choosing by lot.

sortītus *ppa of* **sortior** ♦ *adj* assigned, allotted; **~ō** by lot.

sortītus, -ūs *m* drawing lots.

Sosius, -ī *m* Roman family name (*esp two brothers Sosii, famous booksellers in Rome*).

sōspes, -itis *adj* safe and sound, unhurt; favourable, lucky.

sōspita, -ae *f* saviour.

sōspitālis *adj* beneficial.

sōspitō, -āre *vt* to preserve, prosper.

sōtēr, -ēris *m* saviour.

spādīx, -īcis *adj* chestnut-brown.

spadō, -ōnis *m* eunuch.

spargō, -gere, -sī, -sum *vt* to throw, scatter, sprinkle; to strew, spot, moisten; to disperse, spread abroad.

sparsus *ppp of* **spargō** ♦ *adj* freckled.

Sparta, -ae, -ē, -ēs *f* famous Greek city.

Spartacus, -ī *m* gladiator who led a revolt against Rome.

Spartānus, -icus *adj* Spartan.

Spartiātēs, -iātae *m* Spartan.

spartum, -ī *nt* Spanish broom.

sparulus, -ī *m* bream.

sparus, -ī *m* hunting spear.

spatha, -ae *f* broadsword.

spatior, -ārī, -ātus *vi* to walk; to spread.

spatiōsē *adv* greatly; after a time.

spatiōsus *adj* roomy, ample, large; (*time*) prolonged.

spatium, -ī and iī *nt* space, room, extent; (*between points*) distance; (*open space*) square, walk, promenade; (*race*) lap, track, course; (*time*) period, interval; (*opportunity*) time, leisure; (*metre*) quantity.

speciēs, -ēī *f* seeing, sight; appearance, form, outline; (*thing seen*) sight; (*mind*) idea; (*in sleep*) vision, apparition; (*fair show*) beauty, splendour; (*false show*) pretence, pretext; (*classification*) species; **in ~em** for the sake of appearances; like; **per ~em** under the pretence; **sub ~ē** under the cloak.

specillum, -ī *nt* probe.

specimen, -inis *nt* sign, evidence, proof; pattern, ideal.

speciōsē *adv* handsomely.

speciōsus *adj* showy, beautiful; specious, plausible.

spectābilis *adj* visible; notable, remarkable.

spectāclum, spectāculum, -ī *nt* sight, spectacle; public show, play; theatre, seats.

spectāmen, -inis *nt* proof.

spectātiō, -ōnis *f* looking; testing.

spectātor, -ōris *m* onlooker, observer, spectator; critic.

spectātrīx, -īcis *f* observer.

spectātus *ppp of* **spectō** ♦ *adj* tried, proved; worthy, excellent.

spectiō, -ōnis *f* the right to take auspices.

spectō, -āre, -āvī, -ātum *vt* to look at, observe, watch; (*place*) to face; (*aim*) to look to, bear in mind, contemplate, tend towards; (*judging*) to examine, test.

spectrum, -ī *nt* spectre.

specula, -ae *f* watchtower, lookout; height.

spēcula, -ae *f* slight hope.

speculābundus *adj* on the lookout.

speculāris *adj* transparent ♦ *ntpl* window.

speculātor, -ōris *m* explorer, investigator; (*MIL*) spy, scout.

speculātōrius *adj* for spying, scouting ♦ *f* spy

Noun declensions and verb conjugations are shown on pp xiii to xxv. The present infinitive ending of a verb shows to which conjugation it belongs: **-āre** = 1st; **-ēre** = 2nd; **-ere** = 3rd and **-īre** = 4th. Irregular verbs are shown on p xxvi

boat.

speculātrix, -īcis f watcher.

speculor, -ārī, -ātus vt to spy out, watch for, observe.

speculum, -ī nt mirror.

specus, -ūs m, nt cave; hollow, chasm.

spēlaeum, -ī nt cave, den.

spēlunca, -ae f cave, den.

spērābilis adj to be hoped for.

spērāta, -ātae f bride.

Spercheis, -idis adj see **Spercheus**.

Spercheus (-os), -ī m river in Thessaly.

spernō, -ere, sprēvī, sprētum vt to remove, reject, scorn.

spērō, -āre, -āvī, -ātum vt to hope, hope for, expect; to trust; to look forward to.

spēs, speī f hope, expectation; **praeter spem** unexpectedly; **spē dēiectus** disappointed.

Speusippus, -ī m successor of Plato in the Academy.

sphaera, -ae f ball, globe, sphere.

Sphinx, -ingis f fabulous monster near Thebes.

spīca, -ae f (grain) ear; (plant) tuft; (ASTRO) brightest star in Virgo.

spīceus adj of ears of corn.

spīculum, -ī nt point, sting; dart, arrow.

spīna, -ae f thorn; prickle; fish bone; spine, back; (pl) difficulties, subtleties.

spīnētum, -ī nt thorn hedge.

spīneus adj of thorns.

spīnifer, -ī adj prickly.

spīnōsus adj thorny, prickly; (style) difficult.

spintēr, -ēris nt elastic bracelet.

spīnus, -ī f blackthorn, sloe.

spīra, -ae f coil; twisted band.

spīrābilis adj breathable, life-giving.

spīrāculum, -ī nt vent.

spīrāmentum, -ī nt vent, pore; breathing space.

spīritus, -ūs m breath, breathing; breeze, air; inspiration; character, spirit, courage, arrogance.

spīrō, -āre, -āvī, -ātum vi to breathe, blow; to be alive; to be inspired ♦ vt to emit, exhale; (fig) to breathe, express.

spissātus adj condensed.

spissē adv closely; slowly.

spissēscō, -ere vi to thicken.

spissus adj thick, compact, crowded; slow; (fig) difficult.

splendeō, -ēre vi to be bright, shine; to be illustrious.

splendēscō, -ere vi to become bright.

splendidē adv brilliantly, magnificently, nobly.

splendidus adj bright, brilliant, glittering; (sound) clear; (dress, house) magnificent; (person) illustrious; (appearance) showy.

splendor, -ōris m brightness, lustre; magnificence; clearness; nobility.

spoliātiō, -ōnis f plundering.

spoliātor, -ōris m robber.

spoliātrix, -īcis f robber.

spoliō, -āre, -āvī, -ātum vt to strip; to rob, plunder.

spolium, -ī and iī nt (beast) skin; (enemy) spoils, booty.

sponda, -ae f bed frame; bed, couch.

spondālium, -ī and iī nt hymn accompanied by the flute.

spondeō, -ēre, spopondī, spōnsum vt to promise, pledge, vow; (law) to go bail for; (marriage) to betroth.

spondēus, -ī m spondee.

spongia, -ae f sponge; coat of mail.

spōnsa, -ae f fiancée, bride.

spōnsālia, -ium ntpl engagement.

spōnsiō, -ōnis f promise, guarantee; (law) agreement that the loser in a suit pays the winner a sum; bet.

spōnsor, -ōris m guarantor, surety.

spōnsus ppp of **spondeō** ♦ m fiancé, bridegroom ♦ nt agreement, covenant.

spōnsus, -ūs m contract, surety.

sponte f (abl) voluntarily, of one's own accord; unaided, by oneself; spontaneously.

spopondī perf of **spondeō**.

sportella, -ae f fruit basket.

sportula, -ae f small basket; gift to clients, dole.

sprētiō, -ōnis f contempt.

sprētor, -ōris m despiser.

sprētus ppp of **spernō**.

sprēvī perf of **spernō**.

spūma, -ae f foam, froth.

spūmēscō, -ere vi to become frothy.

spūmeus adj foaming, frothy.

spūmifer, -ī adj foaming.

spūmiger, -ī adj foaming.

spūmō, -āre vi to foam, froth.

spūmōsus adj foaming.

spuō, -uere, -uī, -ūtum vi to spit ♦ vt to spit out.

spurcē adv obscenely.

spurcidicus adj obscene.

spurcificus adj obscene.

spurcitia, -ae and ēs, -ēī f filth, smut.

spurcō, -āre vt to befoul.

spurcus adj filthy, nasty, foul.

spūtātilicus adj despicable.

spūtātor, -ōris m spitter.

spūtō, -āre vt to spit out.

spūtum, -ī nt spit, spittle.

squāleō, -ēre, -uī vi to be rough, stiff, clotted; to be parched; to be neglected, squalid, filthy; to be in mourning.

squālidē adv rudely.

squālidus adj rough, scaly; neglected, squalid, filthy; (speech) unpolished.

squālor, -ōris m roughness; filth, squalor.

squāma, -ae f scale; scale armour.

squāmeus adj scaly.

squāmifer, -ī adj scaly.

squāmiger, -ī adj scaly ♦ mpl fishes.

squāmōsus adj scaly.

squilla, -ae f prawn, shrimp.

st *interj* sh!
stabilīmentum, -ī *nt* support.
stabiliō, -īre *vt* to make stable; to establish.
stabilis *adj* firm, steady; (*fig*) steadfast, unfailing.
stabilitās, -ātis *f* firmness, steadiness, reliability.
stabulō, -āre *vt* to house, stable ♦ *vi* to have a stall.
stabulum, -ī *nt* stall, stable, steading; lodging, cottage; brothel.
stacta, -ae *f* myrrh oil.
stadium, -ī *and* **iī** *nt* stade, furlong; racetrack.
Stagīra, -ōrum *ntpl* town in Macedonia (*birthplace of Aristotle*).
Stagīrītēs, -ītae *m* Aristotle.
stagnō, -āre *vi* to form pools; to be inundated ♦ *vt* to flood.
stagnum, -ī *nt* standing water, pool, swamp; waters.
stāmen, -inis *nt* warp; thread; (*instrument*) string; (*priest*) fillet.
stāmineus *adj* full of threads.
stata *adj*: **Stata māter** Vesta.
statārius *adj* standing, stationary, steady; calm ♦ *f* refined comedy ♦ *mpl* actors in this comedy.
statēra, -ae *f* scales.
statim *adv* steadily; at once, immediately; **~ ut** as soon as.
statiō, -ōnis *f* standing still; station, post, residence; (*pl*) sentries; (*NAUT*) anchorage.
Statius, -ī *m* Caecilius (*early writer of comedy*); Papinius (*epic and lyric poet of the Silver Age*).
statīvus *adj* stationary ♦ *ntpl* standing camp.
stator, -ōris *m* attendant, orderly.
Stator, -ōris *m* the Stayer (*epithet of Jupiter*).
statua, -ae *f* statue.
statūmen, -inis *nt* (*ship*) rib.
statuō, -uere, -uī, -ūtum *vt* to set up, place; to bring to a stop; to establish, constitute; to determine, appoint; to decide, settle; to decree, prescribe; (*with infin*) to resolve, propose; (*with acc and infin*) to judge, consider, conclude; (*army*) to draw up; (*monument*) to erect; (*price*) to fix; (*sentence*) to pass; (*tent*) to pitch; (*town*) to build; **condiciōnem ~** dictate (to); **finem ~** put an end (to); **iūs ~** lay down a principle; **modum ~** impose restrictions; **apud animum ~** make up one's mind; **dē sē ~** commit suicide; **gravius ~ in** deal severely with.
statūra, -ae *f* height, stature.
status *ppp of* **sistō** ♦ *adj* appointed, due.
status, -ūs *m* posture, attitude; position; (*social*) standing, status, circumstances; (*POL*) situation, state, form of government; (*nature*) condition; **reī pūblicae ~** the political situation; constitution; **dē ~ū movēre** dislodge.

statūtus *ppp of* **statuō**.
stega, -ae *f* deck.
stēliō *see* **stēlliō**.
stēlla, -ae *f* star; **~ errāns** planet.
stēllāns, -antis *adj* starry.
stēllātus *adj* starred; set in the sky.
stēllifer, -ī *adj* starry.
stēlliger, -ī *adj* starry.
stēlliō, -ōnis *m* newt.
stemma, -tis *nt* pedigree.
stercoreus *adj* filthy.
stercorō, -āre *vt* to manure.
stercus, -oris *nt* dung.
sterilis *adj* barren, sterile; bare, empty; unprofitable, fruitless.
sterilitās, -ātis *f* barrenness.
sternāx, -ācis *adj* bucking.
sternō, -ere, strāvī, strātum *vt* to spread, cover, strew; to smooth, level; to stretch out, extend; to throw to the ground, prostrate; to overthrow; (*bed*) to make; (*horse*) to saddle; (*road*) to pave.
sternūmentum, -ī *nt* sneezing.
sternuō, -ere, -ī *vt, vi* to sneeze.
Steropē, -ēs *f* a Pleiad.
sterquilīnium, -ī *and* **iī**, (**-um, -ī**) *nt* dung heap.
stertō, -ere, -uī *vi* to snore.
Stēsichorus, -ī *m* Greek lyric poet.
stetī *perf of* **stō**.
Sthenelēius *and* **eis** *and* **ēidis** *adj see n.*
Sthenelus, -ī *m* father of Eurystheus; father of Cycnus.
stigma, -tis *nt* brand.
stigmatiās, -ae *m* branded slave.
stilla, -ae *f* drop.
stillicidium, -ī *and* **iī** *nt* dripping water, rainwater from the eaves.
stillō, -āre, -āvī, -ātum *vi* to drip, trickle ♦ *vt* to let fall in drops, distil.
stilus, -ī *m* stake; pen; (*fig*) writing, composition, style; **~um vertere** erase.
stimulātiō, -ōnis *f* incentive.
stimulātrix, -īcis *f* provocative woman.
stimuleus *adj* smarting.
stimulō, -āre, -āvī, -ātum *vt* to goad; to trouble, torment; to rouse, spur on, excite.
stimulus, -ī *m* goad; (*MIL*) stake; (*pain*) sting, pang; (*incentive*) spur, stimulus.
stinguō, -ere *vt* to extinguish.
stīpātiō, -ōnis *f* crowd, retinue.
stīpātor, -ōris *m* attendant; (*pl*) retinue, bodyguard.
stīpendiārius *adj* tributary, liable to a money tax; (*MIL*) receiving pay ♦ *mpl* tributary peoples.
stīpendium, -ī *and* **iī** *nt* tax tribute; soldier's pay; military service, campaign; **~ merēre, merērī** serve; **~ ēmerērī** complete one's period of service.

stīpes, -itis *m* log, trunk; tree; (*insult*) blockhead.

stīpō, -āre, -āvī, -ātum *vt* to press, pack together; to cram, stuff full; to crowd round, accompany in a body.

stips, stipis *f* donation, contribution.

stipula, -ae *f* stalk, blade, stubble; reed.

stipulātiō, -ōnis *f* promise, bargain.

stipulātiuncula, -ae *f* slight stipulation.

stipulātus *adj* promised.

stipulor, -ārī *vt, vi* to demand a formal promise, bargain, stipulate.

stīria, -ae *f* icicle.

stirpēs *etc see* **stirps.**

stirpitus *adj* thoroughly.

stirps, -is *f* lower trunk and roots, stock; plant, shoot; family, lineage, progeny; origin; **ab ~e** utterly.

stīva, -ae *f* plough handle.

stlattārius *adj* seaborne.

stō, stāre, stetī, statum *vi* to stand; to remain in position, stand firm; to be conspicuous; (*fig*) to persist, continue; (*battle*) to go on; (*hair*) to stand on end; (*NAUT*) to ride at anchor; (*play*) to be successful; (*price*) to cost; (*with ab, cum, prō*) to be on the side of, support; (*with in*) to rest, depend on; (*with per*) to be the fault of; **stat sententia** one's mind is made up; **per Āfrānium stetit quōminus dīmicārētur** there was no battle.

Stōicē *adv* like a Stoic.

Stōicus *adj* Stoic ♦ *m* Stoic philosopher ♦ *ntpl* Stoicism.

stola, -ae *f* long robe (*esp worn by matrons*).

stolidē *adv* stupidly.

stolidus *adj* dull, stupid.

stomachor, -ārī, -ātus *vi* to be vexed, be annoyed.

stomachōsē *adv see adj.*

stomachōsus *adj* angry, irritable.

stomachus, -ī *m* gullet; stomach; taste, liking; dislike, irritation, chagrin.

stōrea (storia), -ae *f* rush mat, rope mat.

strabō, -ōnis *m* squinter.

strāgēs, -is *f* heap, confused mass; havoc, massacre.

strāgulus *adj* covering ♦ *nt* bedspread, rug.

strāmen, -inis *nt* straw, litter.

strāmentum, -ī *nt* straw, thatch; straw bed; covering, rug.

strāmineus *adj* straw-thatched.

strangulō, -āre, -āvī, -ātum *vt* to throttle, choke.

strangūria, -ae *f* difficult discharge of urine.

stratēgēma, -tis *nt* a piece of generalship, stratagem.

stratēgus, -ī *m* commander, president.

stratiōticus *adj* military.

strātum, -ī *nt* coverlet, blanket; bed, couch; horsecloth, saddle; pavement.

strātus *ppp of* **sternō** ♦ *adj* prostrate.

strāvī *perf of* **sternō.**

strēnuē *adv* energetically, quickly.

strēnuitās, -ātis *f* energy, briskness.

strēnuus *adj* brisk, energetic, busy; restless.

strepitō, -āre *vi* to make a noise, rattle, rustle.

strepitus, -ūs *m* din, clatter, crashing, rumbling; sound.

strepō, -ere, -uī *vi* to make a noise, clang, roar, rumble, rustle *etc* ♦ *vt* to bawl out.

striāta, -ae *f* scallop.

strictim *adv* superficially, cursorily.

strictūra, -ae *f* mass of metal.

strictus *ppp of* **stringō** ♦ *adj* close, tight.

strīdeō, -ēre, -ī; -ō, -ere, -ī *vi* to creak, hiss, shriek, whistle.

strīdor, -ōris *m* creaking, hissing, grating.

strīdulus *adj* creaking, hissing, whistling.

strigilis *f* scraper, strigil.

strigō, -āre *vi* to stop, jib.

strigōsus *adj* thin, scraggy; (*style*) insipid.

stringō, -ngere, -nxī, -ctum *vt* to draw together, draw tight; to touch, graze; to cut off, prune, trim; (*sword*) to draw; (*mind*) to affect, pain.

stringor, -ōris *m* twinge.

strix, -igis *f* screech owl.

stropha, -ae *f* trick.

Strophades, -um *fpl* islands off S Greece.

strophiārius, -ī *and* **iī** *m* maker of breastbands.

strophium, -ī *and* **iī** *nt* breastband; headband.

structor, -ōris *m* mason, carpenter; (*at table*) server, carver.

structūra, -ae *f* construction, structure; works.

structus *ppp of* **struō.**

struēs, -is *f* heap, pile.

struix, -icis *f* heap, pile.

strūma, -ae *f* tumour.

strūmōsus *adj* scrofulous.

struō, -ere, -xī, -ctum *vt* to pile up; to build, erect; to arrange in order; to make, prepare; to cause, contrive, plot.

strūtheus *adj* sparrow- (*in cpds*).

strūthiocamēlus, -ī *m* ostrich.

Strȳmōn, -onis *m* river between Macedonia and Thrace (*now* Struma).

Strȳmonius *adj* Strymonian, Thracian.

studeō, -ēre, -uī *vi* (*usu with dat*) to be keen, be diligent, apply oneself to; to study; (*person*) to be a supporter of.

studiōsē *adv* eagerly, diligently.

studiōsus *adj* (*usu with gen*) keen on, fond of, partial to; studious ♦ *m* student.

studium, -ī *and* **iī** *nt* enthusiasm, application, inclination; fondness, affection; party spirit, partisanship; study, literary work.

stultē *adv* foolishly.

stultiloquentia, -ae *f* foolish talk.

stultiloquium, -ī *and* **iī** *nt* foolish talk.

stultitia, -ae *f* folly, silliness.

stultividus *adj* simple-sighted.

stultus *adj* foolish, silly ♦ *m* fool.

stupefaciō, -facere, -fēcī, -factum (*pass* -fīō, -fierī) *vt* to stun, astound.

stupeō, -ēre, -uī *vi* to be stunned, be astonished; to be brought to a standstill ♦ *vt* to marvel at.

stupēscō, -ere *vi* to become amazed.

stūpeus *etc see* **stuppeus.**

stupiditās, -ātis *f* senselessness.

stupidus *adj* senseless, astounded; dull, stupid.

stupor, -ōris *m* numbness, bewilderment; dullness, stupidity.

stuppa, -ae *f* tow.

stuppeus *adj* of tow.

stuprō, -āre, -āvī, -ātum *vt* to defile; to ravish.

stuprum, -ī *nt* debauchery, unchastity.

sturnus, -ī *m* starling.

Stygius *adj* of the lower world, Stygian.

stylus *etc see* **stilus.**

Stymphalicus, (-ius, -is) *adj* Stymphalian.

Stymphalum, -ī *nt*, **Stymphalus, -ī** *m* district of Arcadia (*famous for birds of prey killed by Hercules*).

Styx, -ygis and **ygos** *f* river of Hades.

Styxius *adj see* **n.**

suādēla, -ae *f* persuasion.

suādeō, -dēre, -sī, -sum *vi* (*with dat*) to advise, urge, recommend.

suāsiō, -ōnis *f* speaking in favour (of a proposal); persuasive type of oratory.

suāsor, -ōris *m* adviser; advocate.

suāsus *ppp of* **suādeō.**

suāsus, -ūs *m* advice.

suāveolēns, -entis *adj* fragrant.

suāviātiō *etc see* **sāviātiō.**

suāvidicus *adj* charming.

suāviloquēns, -entis *adj* charming.

suāviloquentia, -ae *f* charm of speech.

suāvior *etc see* **sāvior.**

suāvis *adj* sweet, pleasant, delightful.

suāvitās, -ātis *f* sweetness, pleasantness, charm.

suāviter *adv see* **suāvis.**

suāvium *etc see* **sāvium.**

sub *prep* 1. *with abl* (*place*) under, beneath; (*hills, walls*) at the foot of, close to; (*time*) during, at; (*order*) next to; (*rule*) under, in the reign of. 2. *with acc* (*place*) under, along under; (*hills, walls*) up to, to; (*time*) up to, just before, just after; ~ **ictum venīre** come within range; ~ **manum** to hand.

subabsurdē *adv see* **adj.**

subabsurdus *adj* somewhat absurd.

subaccūsō, -āre *vt* to find some fault with.

subāctiō, -ōnis *f* working (the soil).

subāctus *ppp of* **subigō.**

subadroganter *adv* a little conceitedly.

subagrestis *adj* rather boorish.

subalāris *adj* carried under the arms.

subamārus *adj* rather bitter.

subaquilus *adj* brownish.

subauscultō, -āre *vt, vi* to listen secretly, eavesdrop.

subbasilicānus, -ī *m* lounger.

subblandior, -īrī *vi* (*with dat*) to flirt with.

subc- *etc see* **succ-.**

subdidī *perf of* **subdō.**

subdifficilis *adj* rather difficult.

subdiffīdō, -ere *vi* to be a little doubtful.

subditīcius *adj* sham.

subditīvus *adj* sham.

subditus *ppp of* **subdō** ♦ *adj* spurious.

subdō, -ere, -idī, -itum *vt* to put under, plunge into; to subdue; to substitute, forge.

subdoceō, -ēre *vt* to teach as an assistant.

subdolē *adv* slily.

subdolus *adj* sly, crafty, underhand.

subdubitō, -āre *vi* to be a little undecided.

subdūcō, -ūcere, -ūxī, -uctum *vt* to pull up, raise; to withdraw, remove; to take away secretly, steal; (*account*) to balance; (*ship*) to haul up, beach; **sē ~** steal away, disappear.

subductiō, -ōnis *f* (*ship*) hauling up; (*thought*) reckoning.

subductus *ppp of* **subdūcō.**

subedō, -ēsse, -ēdī *vt* to wear away underneath.

subēgī *perf of* **subigō.**

subeō, -īre, -iī, -itum *vi* to go under, go in; to come up to, climb, advance; to come immediately after; to come to the assistance, succeed; to come as a substitute, succeed; to come secretly, steal in; to come to mind, suggest itself ♦ *vt* to enter, plunge into; to climb; to approach, attack; to take the place of; to steal into; to submit to, undergo, suffer; (*mind*) to occur to.

sūber, -is *nt* cork tree; cork.

subesse *infin of* **subsum.**

subf- *etc see* **suff-.**

subg- *etc see* **sugg-.**

subhorridus *adj* somewhat uncouth.

subiaceō, -ēre, -uī *vi* to lie under, be close (to); to be connected (with).

subiciō, -icere, -iēcī, -iectum *vt* to put under, bring under; to bring up, throw up; to bring near; to submit, subject, expose; to subordinate, deal with under; to append, add on, answer; to adduce, suggest; to substitute; to forge; to suborn; **sē ~** grow up.

subiectē *adv* submissively.

subiectiō, -ōnis *f* laying under; forging.

subiectō, -āre *vt* to lay under, put to; to throw up.

subiector, -ōris *m* forger.

subiectus *ppp of* **subiciō** ♦ *adj* neighbouring, bordering; subject, exposed.

subigitātiō, -ōnis *f* lewdness.

subigitō, -āre *vt* to behave improperly to.

Noun declensions and verb conjugations are shown on pp xiii to xxv. The present infinitive ending of a verb shows to which conjugation it belongs: **-āre** = 1st; **-ēre** = 2nd; **-ere** = 3rd and **-īre** = 4th. Irregular verbs are shown on p xxvi

subigō, -igere, -ēgī, -āctum *vt* to bring up to; to impel, compel; to subdue, conquer; (*animal*) to tame, break in; (*blade*) to sharpen; (*boat*) to row, propel; (*cooking*) to knead; (*earth*) to turn up, dig; (*mind*) to train.

subiī *perf of* **subeō.**

subimpudēns, -entis *adj* rather impertinent.

subinānis *adj* rather empty.

subinde *adv* immediately after; repeatedly.

subīnsulsus *adj* rather insipid.

subinvideō, -ēre *vi* to be a little envious of.

subinvīsus *adj* somewhat odious.

subinvītō, -āre *vt* to invite vaguely.

subīrāscor, -scī, -tus *vi* to be rather angry.

subīrātus *adj* rather angry.

subitārius *adj* sudden, emergency (*in cpds*).

subitō *adv* suddenly.

subitus *ppp of* **subeō ♦** *adj* sudden, unexpected; (*man*) rash; (*troops*) hastily raised ♦ *nt* surprise, emergency.

subiūnctus *ppp of* **subiungō.**

subiungō, -ungere, -ūnxī, -ūnctum *vt* to harness; to add, affix; to subordinate, subdue.

sublābor, -bī, -psus *vi* to sink down; to glide away.

sublāpsus *ppa of* **sublābor.**

sublātē *adv* loftily.

sublātiō, -ōnis *f* elevation.

sublātus *ppp of* **tollō ♦** *adj* elated.

sublectō, -āre *vt* to coax.

sublēctus *ppp of* **sublegō.**

sublegō, -egere, -ēgī, -ēctum *vt* to gather up; to substitute; (*child*) to kidnap; (*talk*) to overhear.

sublestus *adj* slight.

sublevātiō, -ōnis *f* alleviation.

sublevō, -āre, -āvī, -ātum *vt* to lift up, hold up; to support, encourage; to lighten, alleviate.

sublica, -ae *f* pile, palisade.

sublicius *adj* on piles.

subligāculum, -ī, subligar, -āris *nt* loincloth.

subligō, -āre *vt* to fasten on.

sublīmē *adv* aloft, in the air.

sublīmis *adj* high, raised high, lifted up; (*character*) eminent, aspiring; (*language*) lofty, elevated.

sublīmitās, -ātis *f* loftiness.

sublīmus *etc see* **sublīmis.**

sublingiō, -ōnis *m* scullion.

sublinō, -inere, -ēvī, -itum *vt*: **ōs ~** to fool, bamboozle.

sublitus *ppp of* **sublinō.**

sublūceō, -ēre *vi* to glimmer.

sublūo, -ere *vt* (*river*) to flow past the foot of.

sublūstris *adj* faintly luminous.

sublūtus *ppp of* **sublūo.**

subm- *etc see* **summ-.**

subnātus *adj* growing up underneath.

subnectō, -ctere, -xuī, -xum *vt* to tie under, fasten to.

subnegō, -āre *vt* to half refuse.

subnexus *ppp of* **subnectō.**

subniger, -rī *adj* darkish.

subnīxus *and* **sus** *adj* supported, resting (on); relying (on).

subnuba, -ae *f* rival.

subnūbilus *adj* overcast.

subō, -āre *vi* to be in heat.

subobscēnus *adj* rather indecent.

subobscūrus *adj* somewhat obscure.

subodiōsus *adj* rather odious.

suboffendō, -ere *vi* to give some offence.

subolēs, -is *f* offspring, children.

subolēscō, -ere *vi* to grow up.

subolet, -ēre *vi* (*impers*) there is a faint scent; **~ mihi** I detect, have an inkling.

suborior, -īrī *vi* to spring up in succession.

subōrnō, -āre, -āvī, -ātum *vt* to fit out, equip; to instigate secretly, suborn.

subortus, -ūs *m* rising up repeatedly.

subp- *etc see* **supp-.**

subrancidus *adj* slightly tainted.

subraucus *adj* rather hoarse.

subrēctus *ppp of* **subrigō.**

subrēmigō, -āre *vi* to paddle under (water).

subrēpō, -ere, -sī, -tum *vi* to creep along, steal up to.

subreptus *ppp of* **subripiō.**

subrīdeō, -dēre, -sī *vi* to smile.

subrīdiculē *adv* rather funnily.

subrigō, -igere, -ēxī, -ēctum *vt* to lift, raise.

subringor, -ī *vi* to make a wry face, be rather vexed.

subripiō, -ipere, -ipuī *and* **upuī, -eptum** *vt* to take away secretly, steal.

subrogō, -āre *vt* to propose as successor.

subrōstrānī, -ōrum *mpl* idlers.

subrubeō, -ēre *vi* to blush slightly.

subrūfus *adj* ginger-haired.

subruō, -ere, -ī, -tum *vt* to undermine, demolish.

subrūsticus *adj* rather countrified.

subrutus *ppp of* **subruō.**

subscrībō, -bere, -psī, -ptum *vt* to write underneath; (*document*) to sign, subscribe; (*censor*) to set down; (*law*) to add to an indictment, prosecute; (*fig*) to record; (*with dat*) to assent to, approve.

subscrīptiō, -ōnis *f* inscription underneath; signature; (*censor*) noting down; (*law*) subscription (to an indictment); register.

subscrīptor, -ōris *m* subscriber (to an indictment).

subscrīptus *ppp of* **subscrībō.**

subsecīvus *etc see* **subsicīvus.**

subsecō, -āre, -uī, -ctum *vt* to cut off, clip.

subsēdī *perf of* **subsīdō.**

subsellium, -ī *and* **iī** *nt* bench, seat; (*law*) the bench, the court.

subsentiō, -entīre, -ēnsī *vt* to have an inkling of.

subsequor, -quī, -cūtus *vt, vi* to follow closely; to support; to imitate.

subserviō, -īre *vi* to be a slave; (*fig*) to comply

(with).

subsicīvus *adj* left over; (*time*) spare; (*work*) overtime.

subsidiārius *adj* in reserve ♦ *mpl* reserves.

subsidium, -ī *and* **iī** *nt* reserve ranks, reserve troops; relief, aid, assistance.

subsīdō, -īdere, -ēdī, -essum *vi* to sit down, crouch, squat; to sink down, settle, subside; (*ambush*) to lie in wait; (*residence*) to stay, settle ♦ *vt* to lie in wait for.

subsignānus *adj* special reserve (troops).

subsignō, -āre *vt* to register; to guarantee.

subsiliō, -īre, -uī *vi* to leap up.

subsistō, -istere, -titī *vi* to stand still, make a stand; to stop, halt; to remain, continue, hold out; (*with dat*) to resist ♦ *vt* to withstand.

subsortior, -īrī, -ītus *vt* to choose as a substitute by lot.

subsortītiō, -ōnis *f* choosing of substitutes by lot.

substantia, -ae *f* means, wealth.

substernō, -ernere, -rāvī, -rātum *vt* to scatter under, spread under; (*fig*) to put at one's service.

substitī *perf of* **subsistō**.

substituō, -uere, -uī, -ūtum *vt* to put next; to substitute; (*idea*) to present, imagine.

substitūtus *ppp of* **substituō**.

substō, -āre *vi* to hold out.

substrātus *ppp of* **substernō**.

substrictus *ppp of* **substringō** ♦ *adj* narrow, tight.

substringō, -ngere, -nxī, -ctum *vt* to bind up; to draw close; to check.

substructiō, -ōnis *f* foundation.

substruō, -ere, -xī, -ctum *vt* to lay, pave.

subsultō, -āre *vi* to jump up.

subsum, -esse *vi* to be underneath; to be close to, be at hand; (*fig*) to underlie, be latent in.

subsūtus *adj* fringed at the bottom.

subtēmen, -inis *nt* woof; thread.

subter *adv* below, underneath ♦ *prep* (*with acc and abl*) beneath; close up to.

subterdūcō, -cere, -xī *vt* to withdraw secretly.

subterfugiō, -ugere, -ūgī *vt* to escape from, evade.

subterlābor, -ī *vt, vi* to flow past under; to slip away.

subterrāneus *adj* underground.

subtexō, -ere, -uī, -tum *vt* to weave in; to veil, obscure.

subtīlis *adj* slender, fine; (*senses*) delicate, nice; (*judgment*) discriminating, precise; (*style*) plain, direct.

subtīlitās, -ātis *f* fineness; (*judgment*) acuteness, exactness; (*style*) plainness, directness.

subtīliter *adv* finely; accurately; simply.

subtimeō, -ēre *vt* to be a little afraid of.

subtractus *ppp of* **subtrahō**.

subtrahō, -here, -xī, -ctum *vt* to draw away from underneath; to take away secretly; to withdraw, remove.

subtristis *adj* rather sad.

subturpiculus *adj* a little bit mean.

subturpis *adj* rather mean.

subtus *adv* below, underneath.

subtūsus *adj* slightly bruised.

subūcula, -ae *f* shirt, vest.

sūbula, -ae *f* awl.

subulcus, -ī *m* swineherd.

Subūra, -ae *f a disreputable quarter of Rome.*

Subūrānus *adj see* **Subūra**.

suburbānitās, -ātis *f* nearness to Rome.

suburbānus *adj* near Rome ♦ *nt* villa near Rome ♦ *mpl inhabitants of the towns near Rome.*

suburbium, -ī *and* **iī** *nt* suburb.

suburgeō, -ēre *vt* to drive close (to).

subvectiō, -ōnis *f* transport.

subvectō, -āre *vt* to carry up regularly.

subvectus *ppp of* **subvehō**.

subvectus, -ūs *m* transport.

subvehō, -here, -xī, -ctum *vt* to carry up, transport upstream.

subveniō, -enīre, -ēnī, -entum *vi* (*with dat*) to come to the assistance of, relieve, reinforce.

subventō, -āre *vi* (*with dat*) to come quickly to help.

subvereor, -ērī *vi* to be a little afraid.

subversor, -ōris *m* subverter.

subversus *ppp of* **subvertō**.

subvertō, -tere, -tī, -sum *vt* to turn upside down, upset; to overthrow, subvert.

subvexī *perf of* **subvehō**.

subvexus *adj* sloping upwards.

subvolō, -āre *vi* to fly upwards.

subvolvō, -ere *vt* to roll uphill.

subvortō *etc see* **subvertō**.

succavus *adj* hollow underneath.

succēdō, -ēdere, -essī, -essum *vt, vi* (*with dat*) to go under, pass into, take on; (*with dat, acc,* **in**) to go up, climb; (*with dat, acc,* **ad, sub**) to march on, advance to; (*with dat,* **in**) to come to take the place of, relieve; (*with dat,* **in, ad**) to follow after, succeed, succeed to; (*result*) to turn out, be successful.

succendō, -endere, -endī, -ēnsum *vt* to set fire to, kindle; (*fig*) to fire, inflame.

succēnseō *etc see* **suscēnseō**.

succēnsus *ppp of* **succendō**.

succenturiātus *adj* in reserve.

succenturiō, -ōnis *m* under-centurion.

successī *perf of* **succēdō**.

successiō, -ōnis *f* succession.

successor, -ōris *m* successor.

successus *ppp of* **succēdō**.

Noun declensions and verb conjugations are shown on pp xiii to xxv. The present infinitive ending of a verb shows to which conjugation it belongs: **-āre** = 1st; **-ēre** = 2nd; **-ere** = 3rd and **-īre** = 4th. Irregular verbs are shown on p xxvi

successus, -ūs *m* advance uphill; result, success.

succīdia, -ae *f* leg *or* side of meat, flitch.

succīdō, -dere, -dī, -sum *vt* to cut off, mow down.

succidō, -ere, -ī *vi* to sink, give way.

succiduus *adj* sinking, failing.

succinctus *ppp of* **succingō**.

succingō, -gere, -xī, -ctum *vt* to gird up, tuck up; to equip, arm.

succingulum, -ī *nt* girdle.

succinō, -ere *vi* to chime in.

succīsus *ppp of* **succīdō**.

succlāmātiō, -ōnis *f* shouting, barracking.

succlāmō, -āre, -āvī, -ātum *vt* to shout after, interrupt with shouting.

succontumēliōsē *adv* somewhat insolently.

succrēscō, -ere *vi* to grow up (from *or* to).

succrispus *adj* rather curly.

succumbō, -mbere, -buī, -bitum *vi* to fall, sink under; to submit, surrender.

succurrō, -rere, -rī, -sum *vi* to come quickly up; to run to the help of, succour; (*idea*) to occur.

succus *etc see* **sūcus**.

succussus, -ūs *m* shaking.

succustōs, -ōdis *m* assistant keeper.

succutiō, -tere, -ssī, -ssum *vt* to toss up.

sūcidus *adj* juicy, fresh, plump.

sūcinum, -ī *nt* amber.

sūctus *ppp of* **sūgō**.

sucula, -ae *f* winch, windlass.

sucula, -ae *f* piglet; (*pl*) the Hyads.

sūcus, -ī *m* juice, sap; medicine, potion; taste, flavour; (*fig*) strength, vigour, life.

sūdārium, -ī *and* **iī** *nt* handkerchief.

sūdātōrius *adj* for sweating ♦ *nt* sweating bath.

sudis, -is *f* stake, pile, pike, spike.

sūdō, -āre, -āvī, -ātum *vi* to sweat, perspire; to be drenched with; to work hard ♦ *vt* to exude.

sūdor, -ōris *m* sweat, perspiration; moisture; hard work, exertion.

sudus *adj* cloudless, clear ♦ *nt* fine weather.

sueō, -ēre *vi* to be accustomed.

suēscō, -scere, -vī, -tum *vi* to be accustomed ♦ *vt* to accustom.

Suessa, -ae *f* town in *Latium*.

Suessiōnēs, -um *mpl* people of Gaul (*now* Soissons).

suētus *ppp of* **suēscō** ♦ *adj* accustomed; usual.

Suēvī, -ōrum *mpl* people of N.E. Germany.

sūfes, -etis *m* chief magistrate of Carthage.

suffarcinātus *adj* stuffed full.

suffectus *ppp of* **sufficiō** ♦ *adj* (*consul*) appointed to fill a vacancy during the regular term of office.

sufferō, -re *vt* to support, undergo, endure.

suffes *etc see* **sūfes**.

sufficiō, -icere, -ēcī, -ectum *vt* to dye, tinge; to supply, provide; to appoint in place (of another), substitute ♦ *vi* to be adequate, suffice.

suffīgō, -gere, -xī, -xum *vt* to fasten underneath, nail on.

suffīmen, -inis, suffīmentum, -ī *nt* incense.

suffiō, -īre *vt* to fumigate, perfume.

suffīxus *ppp of* **suffīgō**.

sufflāmen, -inis *nt* brake.

sufflō, -āre *vt* to blow up; to puff up.

suffocō, -āre *vt* to choke, stifle.

suffodiō, -odere, -ōdī, -ossum *vt* to stab; to dig under, undermine.

suffossus *ppp of* **suffodiō**.

suffrāgātiō, -ōnis *f* voting for, support.

suffrāgātor, -ōris *m* voter, supporter.

suffrāgātōrius *adj* supporting a candidate.

suffrāgium, -ī *and* **iī** *nt* vote, ballot; right of suffrage; (*fig*) judgment, approval; ~ **ferre** vote.

suffrāgor, -ārī, -ātus *vi* to vote for; to support, favour.

suffringō, -ere *vt* to break.

suffugiō, -ugere, -ūgī *vt* to run for shelter ♦ *vt* to elude.

suffugium, -ī *and* **iī** *nt* shelter, refuge.

suffulciō, -cīre, -sī, -tum *vt* to prop up, support.

suffundō, -undere, -ūdī, -ūsum *vt* to pour in; to suffuse, fill; to tinge, colour, blush; to overspread.

suffūror, -ārī *vi* to filch.

suffuscus *adj* darkish.

suffūsus *ppp of* **suffundō**.

Sugambrī, -ōrum *mpl* people of N.W. Germany.

suggerō, -rere, -ssī, -stum *vt* to bring up to, supply; to add on, put next.

suggestum, -ī *nt* platform.

suggestus *ppp of* **suggerō**.

suggestus, -ūs *m* platform, stage.

suggrandis *adj* rather large.

suggredior, -dī, -ssus *vi* to come up close, approach ♦ *vt* to attack.

sūgillātiō, -ōnis *f* affronting.

sūgillātus *adj* bruised; insulted.

sūgō, -gere, -xī, -ctum *vt* to suck.

suī *gen of* **sē**.

suī *perf of* **suō**.

suillus *adj* of pigs.

sulcō, -āre *vt* to furrow, plough.

sulcus, -ī *m* furrow; trench; track.

sulfur *etc see* **sulpur**.

Sulla, -ae *m* famous Roman dictator.

Sullānus *adj see n.*

sullāturiō, -īre *vi* to hanker after being a Sulla.

Sulmō, -ōnis *m* town in E. Italy (*birthplace of Ovid*).

Sulmōnēnsis *adj see n.*

sultis *adv* please.

sum, esse, fuī *vi* to be, exist; ~ **ab** belong to; ~ **ad** be designed for; ~ **ex** consist of; **est, sunt** there is, are; **est mihi** I have; **mihi tēcum nīl est** I have nothing to do with you; **est quod** something; there is a reason for; **est ubi**

          sūmen–superiniciō

sometimes; **est ut** it is possible that; **est** (*with gen*) to belong to, be the duty of, be characteristic of; (*with infin*) it is possible, it is permissible; **sunt quī** some; **fuit Ilium** Troy is no more.

sūmen, -inis *nt* udder, teat; sow.

summa, -ae *f* main part, chief point, main issue; gist, summary; sum, amount, the whole; supreme power; **~ rērum** the general interest, the whole responsibility; **~ summārum** the universe; **ad ~am** in short, in fact; in conclusion; **in ~ā** in all; after all.

Summānus, -ī *m god of nocturnal thunderbolts.*

summās, -ātis *adj* high-born, eminent.

summātim *adv* cursorily, summarily.

summātus, -ūs *m* sovereignty.

summē *adv* in the highest degree, extremely.

summergō, -gere, -sī, -sum *vt* to plunge under, sink.

summersus *ppp of* **summergō.**

sumministrō, -āre, -āvī, -ātum *vt* to provide, furnish.

summissē *adv* softly; humbly, modestly.

summissiō, -ōnis *f* lowering.

summissus *ppp of* **summittō ♦** *adj* low; (*voice*) low, calm; (*character*) mean, grovelling, submissive, humble.

summittō, -ittere, -īsī, -issum *vt* (*growth*) to send up, raise, rear; to despatch, supply; to let down, lower, reduce, moderate; to supersede; to send secretly; **animum ~** submit; **sē ~** condescend.

summolestē *adv* with some annoyance.

summolestus *adj* a little annoying.

summoneō, -ēre, -uī *vt* to drop a hint to.

summorōsus *adj* rather peevish.

summotor, -ōris *m* clearer.

summōtus *ppp of* **summoveō.**

summoveō, -ovēre, -ōvī, -ōtum *vt* to move away, drive off; to clear away (to make room); to withdraw, remove, banish; (*fig*) to dispel.

summum, -ī *nt* top, surface.

summum *adv* at the most.

summus *adj* highest, the top of, the surface of; last, the end of; (*fig*) utmost, greatest, most important; (*person*) distinguished, excellent ♦ *m* head of the table.

summūtō, -āre *vt* to substitute.

sūmō, -ere, -psī, -ptum *vt* to take, take up; to assume, arrogate; (*action*) to undertake; (*argument*) to assume, take for granted; (*dress*) to put on; (*punishment*) to exact; (*for a purpose*) to use, spend.

sūmptiō, -ōnis *f* assumption.

sūmptuārius *adj* sumptuary.

sūmptuōsē *adv see adj.*

sūmptuōsus *adj* expensive, lavish, extravagant.

sūmptus *ppp of* **sūmō.**

sūmptus, -ūs *m* expense, cost.

Sūnium, -ī *and* **iī** *nt S.E. promontory of Attica.*

suō, suere, suī, sūtum *vt* to sew, stitch, join together.

suōmet, suōpte *emphatic abl of* **suus.**

suovetaurīlia, -ium *ntpl* sacrifice of a pig, sheep and bull.

supellex, -ectilis *f* furniture, goods, outfit.

super *etc adj see* **superus.**

super *adv* above, on the top; besides, moreover; left, remaining ♦ *prep* (*with abl*) upon, above; concerning; besides; (*time*) at; (*with acc*) over, above, on; beyond; besides, over and above.

superā *etc see* **suprā.**

superābilis *adj* surmountable, conquerable.

superaddō, -ere, -itum *vt* to add over and above.

superāns, -antis *pres p of* **superō ♦** *adj* predominant.

superātor, -ōris *m* conqueror.

superbē *adv* arrogantly, despotically.

superbia, -ae *f* arrogance, insolence, tyranny; pride, lofty spirit.

superbiloquentia, -ae *f* arrogant speech.

superbiō, -īre *vi* to be arrogant, take a pride in; to be superb.

superbus *adj* arrogant, insolent, overbearing; fastidious; superb, magnificent.

supercilium, -ī *and* **iī** *nt* eyebrow; (*hill*) brow, ridge; (*fig*) arrogance.

superēmineō, -ēre *vt* to overtop.

superesse *infin of* **supersum.**

superficiēs, -ēī *f* surface; (*law*) a building (*esp on another's land*).

superfiō, -ierī *vi* to be left over.

superfīxus *adj* fixed on top.

superfluō, -ere *vi* to overflow.

superfuī *perf of* **supersum.**

superfundō, -undere, -ūdī, -ūsum *vt, vi* to pour over, shower; (*pass*) to overflow, spread out.

superfūsus *ppp of* **superfundō.**

supergredior, -dī, -ssus *vt* to surpass.

superiaciō, -iacere, -iēcī, -iectum *and* **iactum** *vt* to throw over, overspread; to overtop; (*fig*) to exaggerate.

superiectus *ppp of* **superiaciō.**

superimmineō, -ēre *vi* to overhang.

superimpendēns, -entis *adj* overhanging.

superimpōnō, -ōnere, -osuī, -ositum *vt* to place on top.

superimpositus *ppp of* **superimpōnō.**

superincidēns, -entis *adj* falling from above.

superincubāns, -antis *adj* lying upon.

superincumbō, -ere *vi* to fling oneself down upon.

superingerō, -ere *vt* to pour down.

superiniciō, -icere, -iēcī, -iectum *vt* to throw upon, put on top.

Noun declensions and verb conjugations are shown on pp xiii to xxv. The present infinitive ending of a verb shows to which conjugation it belongs: **-āre** = 1st; **-ēre** = 2nd; **-ere** = 3rd and **-īre** = 4th. Irregular verbs are shown on p xxvi

superiniectus *ppp of* **superinicō**.
superīnsternō, -ere *vt* to lay over.
superior, -ōris *adj* higher, upper; (*time, order*) preceding, former; (*age*) older; (*battle*) victorious, stronger; (*quality*) superior, greater.
superlātiō, -ōnis *f* exaggeration.
superlātus *adj* exaggerated.
supernē *adv* at the top, from above.
supernus *adj* upper; celestial.
superō, -āre, -āvī, -ātum *vi* to rise above, overtop; to have the upper hand; to be in excess, be abundant; to be left over, survive ♦ *vt* to pass over, surmount, go beyond; to surpass, outdo; (MIL) to overcome, conquer; (NAUT) to sail past, double.
superobruō, -ere *vt* to overwhelm.
superpendēns, -entis *adj* overhanging.
superpōnō, -ōnere, -osuī, -ositum *vt* to place upon; to put in charge of.
superpositus *ppp of* **superpōnō**.
superscandō, -ere *vt* to climb over.
supersedeō, -ēdēre, -ēdī, -essum *vi* to forbear, desist from.
superstes, -itis *adj* standing over; surviving.
superstitiō, -ōnis *f* awful fear, superstition.
superstitiōsē *adv* superstitiously; scrupulously.
superstitiōsus *adj* superstitious; prophetic.
superstō, -āre *vt, vi* to stand over, stand on.
superstrātus *adj* spread over.
superstruō, -ere, -xī, -ctum *vt* to build on top.
supersum, -esse, -fuī *vi* to be left, remain; to survive; to be in abundance, be sufficient; to be in excess.
supertegō, -ere *vt* to cover over.
superurgēns, -entis *adj* pressing from above.
superus (*compar* **-ior,** *superl* **suprēmus, summus**) *adj* upper, above ♦ *mpl* the gods above; the living ♦ *ntpl* the heavenly bodies; higher places; **mare ~um** Adriatic Sea.
supervacāneus *adj* extra, superfluous.
supervacuus *adj* superfluous, pointless.
supervādō, -ere *vt* to climb over, surmount.
supervehor, -hī, -ctus *vt* to ride past, sail past.
superveniō, -enīre, -ēnī, -entum *vt* to overtake, come on top of ♦ *vi* to come on the scene, arrive unexpectedly.
superventus, -ūs *m* arrival.
supervolitō, -āre *vt* to fly over.
supervolō, -āre *vt, vi* to fly over.
supīnō, -āre, -āvī, -ātum *vt* to upturn, lay on its back.
supīnus *adj* lying back, face up; sloping, on a slope; backwards; (*mind*) indolent, careless.
suppāctus *ppp of* **suppingō**.
suppaenitet, -ēre *vt impers* to be a little sorry.
suppalpor, -ārī *vi* to coax gently.
suppār, -aris *adj* nearly equal.
supparasītor, -ārī *vi* to flatter gently.

supparus, -ī *m,* **supparum, -ī** *nt* woman's linen garment; topsail.
suppeditātiō, -ōnis *f* abundance.
suppeditō, -āre, -āvī, -ātum *vi* to be at hand, be in full supply, be sufficient; to be rich in ♦ *vt* to supply, furnish.
suppēdō, -ere *vi* to break wind quietly.
suppetiae, -ārum *fpl* assistance.
suppetior, -ārī, -ātus *vi* to come to the assistance of.
suppetō, -ere, -īvī, *and* **iī, -ītum** *vi* to be available, be in store; to be equal to, suffice for.
suppīlō, -āre *vt* to steal.
suppingō, -ingere, -āctum *vt* to fasten underneath.
supplantō, -āre *vt* to trip up.
supplēmentum, -ī *nt* full complement; reinforcements.
suppleō, -ēre *vt* to fill up, make good, make up to the full complement.
supplex, -icis *adj* suppliant, in entreaty.
supplicātiō, -ōnis *f* day of prayer, public thanksgiving.
suppliciter *adv* in supplication.
supplicium, -ī *and* **iī** *nt* prayer, entreaty; sacrifice; punishment, execution, suffering; **~iō afficere** execute.
supplicō, -āre, -āvī, -ātum *vi* (*with dat*) to entreat, pray to, worship.
supplōdō, -dere, -sī *vt* to stamp.
supplōsiō, -ōnis *f* stamping.
suppōnō, -ōnere, -osuī, -ositum *vt* to put under, apply; to subject; to add on; to substitute, falsify.
supportō, -āre *vt* to bring up, transport.
supposītīcius *adj* spurious.
suppositiō, -ōnis *f* substitution.
suppositus *ppp of* **suppōnō**.
supposuī *perf of* **suppōnō**.
suppressiō, -ōnis *f* embezzlement.
suppressus *ppp of* **supprimō** ♦ *adj* (*voice*) low.
supprimō, -imere, -essī, -essum *vt* to sink; to restrain, detain, put a stop to; to keep secret, suppress.
supprōmus, -ī *m* underbutler.
suppudet, -ēre *vt* (*impers*) to be a little ashamed.
suppūrō, -āre *vi* to fester.
suppus *adj* head downwards.
supputō, -āre *vt* to count up.
suprā *adv* above, up on top; (*time*) earlier, previously; (*amount*) more; **~ quam** beyond what ♦ *prep* (*with acc*) over, above; beyond; (*time*) before; (*amount*) more than, over.
suprāscandō, -ere *vt* to surmount.
suprēmum *adv* for the last time.
suprēmus *adj* highest; last, latest; greatest; supreme ♦ *ntpl* moment of death; funeral rites; testament.
sūra, -ae *f* calf (of the leg).
sūrculus, -ī *m* twig, shoot; graft; slip.
surdaster, -rī *adj* rather deaf.

surditās, -ātis f deafness.
surdus adj deaf; silent.
surēna, -ae m grand vizier (of the Parthians).
surgō, -ere, surrēxī, surrēctum vi to rise,
get up, stand up; to arise, spring up, grow.
surpere etc = **surripere** etc.
surr- etc see **subr-**.
surrēxī perf of **surgō.**
surruptīcius adj stolen.
surrupuī perf of **subripiō.**
sūrsum, sūrsus adv upwards, up, high up; ~
deōrsum up and down.
sūs, suis m/f pig, boar, hog, sow.
Sūsa, -ōrum ntpl ancient Persian capital.
suscēnseō, -ēre, -uī vi to be angry, be
irritated.
susceptiō, -ōnis f undertaking.
susceptus ppp of **suscipiō.**
suscipiō, -ipere, -ēpī, -eptum vt to take up,
undertake; to receive, catch; (child) to
acknowledge; to beget; to take under one's
protection.
suscitō, -āre, -āvī, -ātum vt to lift, raise; to
stir, rouse, awaken; to encourage, excite.
suspectō, -āre vt, vi to look up at, watch; to
suspect, mistrust.
suspectus ppp of **suspiciō** ♦ adj suspected,
suspicious.
suspectus, -ūs m looking up; esteem.
suspendium, -ī and **iī** nt hanging.
suspendō, -endere, -endī, -ēnsum vt to
hang, hang up; (death) to hang; (building) to
support; (mind) to keep in suspense;
(movement) to check, interrupt; (pass) to
depend.
suspēnsus ppp of **suspendō** ♦ adj raised,
hanging, poised; with a light touch; (fig) in
suspense, uncertain, anxious; dependent; ~ō
gradū on tiptoe.
suspicāx, -ācis adj suspicious.
suspiciō, -icere, -exī, -ectum vt to look up at,
look up to; to admire, respect; to mistrust.
suspiciō, -ōnis f mistrust, suspicion.
suspiciōsē adv suspiciously.
suspiciōsus adj suspicious.
suspicor, -ārī, -ātus vt to suspect; to surmise,
suppose.
suspīrātus, -ūs m sigh.
suspīritus, -ūs m deep breath, difficult
breathing; sigh.
suspīrium, -ī and **iī** nt deep breath, sigh.
suspīrō, -āre, -āvī, -ātum vi to sigh ♦ vt to
sigh for; to exclaim with a sigh.
susque dēque adv up and down.
sustentāculum, -ī nt prop.
sustentātiō, -ōnis f forbearance.
sustentō, -āre, -āvī, -ātum vt to hold up,
support; (fig) to uphold, uplift; (food, means)
to sustain, support; (enemy) to check, hold;
(trouble) to suffer; (event) to hold back,
postpone.
sustineō, -inēre, -inuī, -entum vt to hold up,
support; to check, control; (fig) to uphold,
maintain; (food, means) to sustain, support;
(trouble) to bear, suffer, withstand; (event) to
put off.
sustollō, -ere vt to lift up, raise; to destroy.
sustulī perf of **tollō.**
susurrātor, -ōris m whisperer.
susurrō, -āre vt, vi to murmur, buzz, whisper.
susurrus, -ūs m murmuring, whispering.
susurrus adj whispering.
sūtēla, -ae f trick.
sūtilis adj sewn.
sūtor, -ōris m shoemaker; ~ **nē suprā**
crepidam ≈ let the cobbler stick to his last.
sūtōrius adj shoemaker's; ex-cobbler.
sūtrīnus adj shoemaker's.
sūtūra, -ae f seam.
sūtus ppp of **suō.**
suus adj his, her, its, their; one's own, proper,
due, right ♦ mpl one's own troops, friends,
followers etc ♦ nt one's own property.
Sybaris, -is f town in S. Italy (noted for its
debauchery).
Sybarīta, -ītae m Sybarite.
Sȳchaeus, -ī m husband of Dido.
sȳcophanta, -ae m slanderer, cheat,
sycophant.
sȳcophantia, -ae f deceit.
sȳcophantiōsē adv deceitfully.
sȳcophantor, -ārī, vi to cheat.
Syēnē, -ēs f town in S. Egypt (now Assuan).
syllaba, -ae f syllable.
syllabātim adv syllable by syllable.
symbola, -ae f contribution.
symbolus, -ī m token, symbol.
symphōnia, -ae f concord, harmony.
symphōniacus adj choir (in cpds).
Symplēgades, -um fpl clashing rocks in the
Black Sea.
synedrus, -ī m senator (in Macedonia).
Synephēbī, -ōrum mpl Youths Together
(comedy by Caecilius).
syngrapha, -ae f promissory note.
syngraphus, -ī m written contract; passport,
pass.
Synnada, -ōrum ntpl town in Phrygia (famous
for marble).
Synnadēnsis adj see n.
synodūs, -ontis m bream.
synthesis, -is f dinner service; suit of clothes;
dressinggown.
Syphāx, -ācis m king of Numidia.
Syrācūsae, -ārum fpl Syracuse.
Syrācūsānus, Syrācūsānius, Syrācosius
adj Syracusan.
Syria, -iae f country at the E. end of the
Mediterranean.
Syrius, -us and **iacus, -iscus** adj Syrian.

Noun declensions and verb conjugations are shown on pp xiii to xxv. The present infinitive ending of a verb shows
to which conjugation it belongs: **-āre** = 1st; **-ēre** = 2nd; **-ere** = 3rd and **-īre** = 4th. Irregular verbs are shown on p xxvi

syrma, -ae *f* robe with a train; (*fig*) tragedy.
Syrtis, -is *f* Gulf of Sidra in N. Africa; sandbank.

T, t

tabella, -ae *f* small board, sill; writing tablet,
voting tablet, votive tablet; picture; (*pl*)
writing, records, dispatches.
tabellārius *adj* about voting ♦ *m* courier.
tābeō, -ēre *vi* to waste away; to be wet.
taberna, -ae *f* cottage; shop; inn; (*circus*)
stalls.
tabernāculum, -ī *nt* tent; ~ **capere** choose a
site (for auspices).
tabernāriī, -ōrum *mpl* shopkeepers.
tābēs, -is *f* wasting away, decaying, melting;
putrefaction; plague, disease.
tābēscō, -ēscere, -uī *vi* to waste away, melt,
decay; (*fig*) to pine, languish.
tābidulus *adj* consuming.
tābidus *adj* melting, decaying; pining;
corrupting, infectious.
tābificus *adj* melting, wasting.
tabula, -ae *f* board, plank; writing tablet;
votive tablet; map; picture; auction; (*pl*)
account books, records, lists, will; ~ **Sullae**
Sulla's proscriptions; **XII ~ae** Twelve Tables
of Roman laws; **~ae novae** cancellation of
debts.
tabulārium, -ī *and* **iī** *nt* archives.
tabulātiō, -ōnis *f* flooring, storey.
tabulātum, -ī *nt* flooring, storey; (*trees*) layer,
row.
tābum, -ī *nt* decaying matter; disease, plague.
taceō, -ēre, -uī, -itum *vi* to be silent, say
nothing; to be still, be hushed ♦ *vt* to say
nothing about, not speak of.
tacitē *adv* silently; secretly.
taciturnitās, -ātis *f* silence, taciturnity.
taciturnus *adj* silent, quiet.
tacitus *ppp of* **taceō** ♦ *adj* silent, mute, quiet;
secret, unmentioned; tacit, implied; **per ~um**
quietly.
Tacitus, -ī *m* famous Roman historian.
tāctilis *adj* tangible.
tāctiō, -ōnis *f* touching; sense of touch.
tāctus *ppp of* **tangō**.
tāctus, -ūs *m* touch, handling, sense of touch;
influence.
taeda, -ae *f* pitch pine, pinewood; torch;
plank; (*fig*) wedding.
taedet, -ēre, -uit *and* **taesum est** *vt* (*impers*)
to be weary (of), loathe.
taedifer, -ī *adj* torch-bearing.
taedium, -ī *and* **iī** *nt* weariness, loathing.

Taenaridēs, -idae *m* Spartan (*esp Hyacinthus*).
Taenarius, -is *adj* of Taenarus; Spartan.
Taenarum (-on), -ī *nt*, **Taenarus (-os), -ī** *m/f*
town and promontory in S. Greece (*now*
Matapan); the lower world.
taenia, -ae *f* hairband, ribbon.
taesum est *perf of* **taedet**.
taeter, -rī *adj* foul, hideous, repulsive.
taetrē *adv* hideously.
taetricus *see* **tetricus**.
tagāx, -ācis *adj* light-fingered.
Tagus, -ī *m* river of Lusitania (*now* Tagus).
tālāris *adj* reaching to the ankles ♦ *ntpl* winged
sandals; a garment reaching to the ankles.
tālārius *adj* of dice.
Talāsius, -ī *and* **iī** *m* god of weddings; wedding
cry.
tālea, -ae *f* rod, stake.
talentum, -ī *nt* talent, *a Greek weight about
25.4kg*; a large sum of money (*esp the Attic
talent of 60 minae*).
tāliō, -ōnis *f* retaliation in kind.
tālis *adj* such; the following.
talpa, -ae *f* mole.
tālus, -ī *m* ankle; heel; (*pl*) knuckle bones,
oblong dice.
tam *adv* so, so much, so very.
tamdiū *adv* so long, as long.
tamen *adv* however, nevertheless, all the
same.
Tāmesis, -is *and* **a, -ae** *m* Thames.
tametsī *conj* although.
tamquam *adv* as, just as, just like ♦ *conj* as if.
Tanagra, -ae *f* town in Boeotia.
Tanais, -is *m* river in Sarmatia (*now* Don).
Tanaquil, -ilis *f* wife of the elder Tarquin.
tandem *adv* at last, at length, finally;
(*question*) just.
tangō, -ere, tetigī, tāctum *vt* to touch,
handle; (*food*) to taste; (*with force*) to hit,
strike; (*with liquid*) to sprinkle; (*mind*) to
affect, move; (*place*) to reach; to border on;
(*task*) to take in hand; (*by trick*) to take in,
fool; (*in words*) to touch on, mention; **dē caelō
tāctus** struck by lightning.
tanquam *see* **tamquam**.
Tantalidēs *adj*, **-idēs, -idae** *m* Pelops, Atreus,
Thyestes *or* Agamemnon.
Tantalis, -idis *f* Niobe *or* Hermione.
Tantalus, -ī *m* father of Pelops (*condemned to
hunger and thirst in Tartarus, or to the threat of
an overhanging rock*).
tantillus *adj* so little, so small.
tantisper *adv* so long, just for a moment.
tantopere *adv* so much.
tantulus *adj* so little, so small.
tantum *adv* so much, so, as; only, merely; ~
modo only; ~ **nōn** all but, almost; ~ **quod** only
just.
tantummodo *adv* only.
tantundem *adv* just as much, just so much.
tantus *adj* so great; so little ♦ *nt* so much; so
little; **~ī esse** be worth so much, be so dear,

be so important; ~ō so much, so far; (*with compar*) so much the; ~ō **opere** so much; **in** ~**um** to such an extent; **tria** ~**a** three times as much.

tantusdem *adj* just so great.

tapēta, -ae *m*, **-ia, -ium** *ntpl* carpet, tapestry, hangings.

Taprobanē, -ēs *f* Ceylon.

tardē *adv* slowly, tardily.

tardēscō, -ere *vi* to become slow, falter.

tardipēs, -edis *adj* limping.

tarditās, -ātis *f* slowness, tardiness; (*mind*) dullness.

tardiusculus *adj* rather slow.

tardō, -āre, -āvī, -ātum *vt* to retard, impede ♦ *vi* to delay, go slow.

tardus *adj* slow, tardy, late; (*mind*) dull; (*speech*) deliberate.

Tarentīnus *adj* Tarentine.

Tarentum, -ī *nt* town in S. Italy (*now* Taranto).

tarmes, -itis *m* woodworm.

Tarpēius *adj* Tarpeian; **mōns** ~ the Tarpeian *Rock on the Capitoline Hill from which criminals were thrown.*

tarpezīta, -ae *m* banker.

Tarquiniēnsis *adj* of Tarquinii.

Tarquiniī, -iōrum *mpl ancient town in Etruria.*

Tarquinius *adj* of Tarquin.

Tarquinius, -ī *m* Tarquin (*esp Priscus, the fifth king of Rome, and Superbus, the last king*).

Tarracīna, -ae *f*, **-ae, -ārum** *fpl town in Latium.*

Tarracō, -ōnis *f* town in Spain (*now* Tarragona).

Tarracōnēnsis *adj see n.*

Tarsēnsis *adj see n.*

Tarsus, -ī *f capital of Cilicia.*

Tartareus *adj* infernal.

Tartarus (-os), -ī *m*, **-a, -ōrum** *ntpl* Tartarus, the lower world (*esp the part reserved for criminals*).

tat *interj* hallo there!

Tatius, -ī *m* Sabine king (*who ruled jointly with Romulus*).

Tatius *adj see n.*

Taum, -ī *nt* Firth of Tay.

taureus *adj* bull's ♦ *f* whip of bull's hide.

Taurī, -ōrum *mpl* Thracians of the Crimea.

Tauricus *adj see n.*

tauriförmis *adj* bull-shaped.

Taurīnī, -ōrum *mpl* people of N. Italy (*now* Turin).

taurīnus *adj* bull's.

Tauromenītānus *adj see n.*

Tauromenium, -ī *and* **iī** *nt town in E. Sicily.*

taurus, -ī *m* bull.

Taurus, -ī *m* mountain range in S.E. Asia Minor.

taxātiō, -ōnis *f* valuing.

taxeus *adj* of yews.

taxillus, -ī *m* small dice.

taxō, -āre *vt* to value, estimate.

taxus, -ī *f* yew.

Tāygeta, -ōrum *ntpl*, **Tāygetus, -ī** *m* mountain *range in S. Greece.*

Tāygetē, -ēs *f* a Pleiad.

tē *acc and abl of* **tū.**

-te *suffix for* **tū.**

Teānēnsis *adj see n.*

Teānum, -ī *nt* town in Apulia; town in Campania.

techina, -ae *f* trick.

Tecmessa, -ae *f wife of Ajax.*

tēctor, -ōris *m* plasterer.

tēctōriolum, -ī *nt* a little plaster.

tēctōrium, -ī *and* **iī** *nt* plaster, stucco.

tēctōrius *adj* of a plasterer.

tēctum, -ī *nt* roof, ceiling, canopy; house, dwelling, shelter.

tēctus *ppp of* **tegō** ♦ *adj* hidden; secret, reserved, close.

tēcum with you.

Tegea, -ae *f* town in Arcadia.

Tegeaeus *adj* Arcadian ♦ *m* the god Pan ♦ *f* Atalanta.

Tegeātae, -ātārum *mpl* Tegeans.

teges, -etis *f* mat.

tegillum, -ī *nt* hood, cowl.

tegimen, -inis *nt* covering.

tegimentum, -ī *nt* covering.

tegm- *etc see* **tegim-.**

tegō, -ere, tēxī, -tēctum *vt* to cover; to hide, conceal; to protect, defend; to bury; **latus** ~ walk by the side of.

tēgula, -ae *f* tile; (*pl*) tiled roof.

tegum- *etc see* **tegim-.**

Tēius *adj* of Teos.

tēla, -ae *f* web; warp; yarnbeam, loom; (*fig*) plan.

Telamōn, -ōnis *m* father of Ajax.

Tēlegonus, -ī *m* son of Ulysses and Circe.

Tēlemachus, -ī *m* son of Ulysses and Penelope.

Tēlephus, -ī *m* king of Mysia (*wounded by Achilles' spear*).

tellūs, -ūris *f* the earth; earth, ground; land, country.

tēlum, -ī *nt* weapon, missile; javelin, sword; (*fig*) shaft, dart.

temerārius *adj* accidental; rash, thoughtless.

temerē *adv* by chance, at random; rashly, thoughtlessly; **nōn** ~ not for nothing; not easily; hardly ever.

temeritās, -ātis *f* chance; rashness, thoughtlessness.

temerō, -āre, -āvī, -ātum *vt* to desecrate, disgrace.

tēmētum, -ī *nt* wine, alcohol.

temnō, -ere *vt* to slight, despise.

tēmō, -ōnis *m* beam (of plough *or* carriage); cart; (ASTRO) the Plough.

Tempē *ntpl* famous valley in Thessaly.

temperāmentum, -ī *nt* moderation,

Noun declensions and verb conjugations are shown on pp xiii to xxv. The present infinitive ending of a verb shows to which conjugation it belongs: **-āre** = 1st; **-ēre** = 2nd; **-ere** = 3rd and **-īre** = 4th. Irregular verbs are shown on p xxvi

compromise.

temperāns, -antis *pres p of* **temperō** ♦ *adj* moderate, temperate.

temperanter *adv* with moderation.

temperantia, -ae *f* moderation, self-control.

temperātē *adv* with moderation.

temperātiō, -ōnis *f* proper mixture, composition, constitution; organizing power.

temperātor, -ōris *m* organizer.

temperātus *ppp of* **temperō** ♦ *adj* moderate, sober.

temperī *adv* in time, at the right time.

temperiēs, -ēī *f* due proportion; temperature, mildness.

temperō, -āre, -āvī, -ātum *vt* to mix in due proportion, blend, temper; to regulate, moderate, tune; to govern, rule ♦ *vi* to be moderate, forbear, abstain; (*with dat*) to spare, be lenient to.

tempestās, -ātis *f* time, season, period; weather; storm; (*fig*) storm, shower.

tempestīvē *adv* at the right time, appropriately.

tempestīvitās , -ātis *f* seasonableness.

tempestīvus *adj* timely, seasonable, appropriate; ripe, mature; early.

templum, -ī *nt* space marked off for taking auspices; open space, region, quarter; sanctuary; temple.

temporārius *adj* for the time, temporary.

temptābundus *adj* making repeated attempts.

temptāmentum, -ī *nt* trial, attempt, proof.

temptāmina, -um *ntpl* attempts, essays.

temptātiō, -ōnis *f* trial, proof; attack.

temptātor, -ōris *m* assailant.

temptō, -āre, -āvī, -ātum *vt* to feel, test by touching; to make an attempt on, attack; to try, essay, attempt; to try to influence, tamper with, tempt, incite; **vēnās ~** feel the pulse.

tempus, -oris *nt* time; right time, opportunity; danger, emergency, circumstance; (*head*) temple; (*verse*) unit of metre; (*verb*) tense; **~ore** at the right time, in time; **ad ~us** at the right time; for the moment; **ante ~us** too soon; **ex ~ore** on the spur of the moment; to suit the circumstances; **in ~ore** in time; **in ~us** temporarily; **per ~us** just in time; **prō ~ore** to suit the occasion.

tēmulentus *adj* intoxicated.

tenācitās, -ātis *f* firm grip; stinginess.

tenāciter *adv* tightly, firmly.

tenāx, -ācis *adj* gripping, tenacious; sticky; (*fig*) firm, persistent; stubborn; stingy.

tendicula, -ae *f* little snare.

tendō, -ere, tetendī, tentum *and* **tēnsum** *vt* to stretch, spread; to strain; (*arrow*) to aim, shoot; (*bow*) to bend; (*course*) to direct; (*lyre*) to tune; (*tent*) to pitch; (*time*) to prolong; (*trap*) to lay ♦ *vi* to encamp; to go, proceed; to

aim, tend; (*with infin*) to endeavour, exert oneself.

tenebrae, -ārum *fpl* darkness, night; unconsciousness, death, blindness; (*place*) dungeon, haunt, the lower world; (*fig*) ignorance, obscurity.

tenebricōsus *adj* gloomy.

tenebrōsus *adj* dark, gloomy.

Tenedius *adj see n.*

Tenedos (-us), -ī *f Aegean island near Troy.*

tenellulus *adj* dainty little.

teneō, -ēre, -uī *vt* to hold, keep; to possess, occupy, be master of; to attain, acquire; (*argument*) to maintain, insist; (*category*) to comprise; (*goal*) to make for; (*interest*) to fascinate; (*law*) to bind, be binding on; (*mind*) to grasp, understand, remember; (*movement*) to hold back, restrain ♦ *vi* to hold on, last, persist; (*rumour*) to prevail; **cursum ~** keep on one's course; **sē ~** remain; to refrain.

tener, -ī *adj* tender, delicate; young, weak; effeminate; (*poet*) erotic.

tenerāscō, -ere *vi* to grow weak.

tenerē *adv* softly.

teneritās, -ātis *f* weakness.

tenor, -ōris *m* steady course; **ūnō ~ōre** without a break, uniformly.

tēnsa, -ae *f carriage bearing the images of the gods in procession.*

tēnsus *ppp of* **tendō** ♦ *adj* strained.

tentā- *etc see* **temptā-**.

tentīgō, -inis *f* lust.

tentō *etc see* **temptō**.

tentōrium, -ī *and* **iī** *nt* tent.

tentus *ppp of* **tendō**.

tenuiculus *adj* paltry.

tenuis *adj* thin, fine; small, shallow; (*air*) rarefied; (*water*) clear; (*condition*) poor, mean, insignificant; (*style*) refined, direct, precise.

tenuitās, -ātis *f* thinness, fineness; poverty, insignificance; (*style*) precision.

tenuiter *adv* thinly; poorly; with precision; superficially.

tenuō, -āre, -āvī, -ātum *vt* to make thin, attenuate, rarefy; to lessen, reduce.

tenus *prep* (*with gen or abl*) as far as, up to, down to; **verbō ~** in name, nominally.

Teos, -ī *f town on coast of Asia Minor* (*birthplace of Anacreon*).

tepefaciō, -facere, -fēcī, -factum *vt* to warm.

tepeō, -ēre *vi* to be warm, be lukewarm; (*fig*) to be in love.

tepēscō, -ēscere, -uī *vi* to grow warm; to become lukewarm, cool off.

tepidus *adj* warm, lukewarm.

tepor, -ōris *m* warmth; coolness.

ter *adv* three times, thrice.

terdeciēns *and* **ēs** *adv* thirteen times.

terebinthus, -ī *f* turpentine tree.

terebra, -ae *f* gimlet.

terebrō, -āre vt to bore.
terēdō, -inis f grub.
Terentia, -iae f Cicero's wife.
Terentius, -ī m Roman family name (*esp the comic poet Terence*).
Terentius, -iānus adj see n.
teres, -etis adj rounded (*esp cylindrical*), smooth, shapely; (*fig*) polished, elegant.
Tēreus, -eī and **eos** m king of Thrace (*husband of Procne, father of Itys*).
tergeminus adj threefold, triple.
tergeō, -gēre, -sī, -sum vt to wipe off, scour, clean; to rub up, burnish.
terginum, -ī nt rawhide.
tergiversātiō, -ōnis f refusal, subterfuge.
tergiversor, -ārī, -ātus vi to hedge, boggle, be evasive.
tergō etc see **tergeō.**
tergum, -ī nt back; rear; (*land*) ridge; (*water*) surface; (*meat*) chine; (*skin*) hide, leather, anything made of leather; **~a vertere** take to flight; **ā ~ō** behind, in the rear.
tergus, -oris see **tergum.**
termes, -itis m branch.
Terminālia, -ium ntpl Festival of the god of Boundaries.
terminātiō, -ōnis f decision; (*words*) clausula.
terminō, -āre, -āvī, -ātum vt to set bounds to, limit; to define, determine; to end.
terminus, -ī m boundary line, limit, bound; god of boundaries.
ternī, -ōrum adj three each; three.
terō, -ere, -trīvī, trītum vt to rub, crush, grind; to smooth, sharpen; to wear away, use up; (*road*) to frequent; (*time*) to waste; (*word*) to make commonplace.
Terpsichorē, -ēs f Muse of dancing.
terra, -ae f dry land, earth, ground, soil; land, country; **orbis ~ārum** the world; **ubi ~ārum** where in the world.
terrēnus adj of earth; terrestrial, land- (*in cpds*) ♦ nt land.
terreō, -ēre, -uī, -itum vt to frighten, terrify; to scare away; to deter.
terrestris adj earthly, on earth, land- (*in cpds*).
terribilis adj terrifying, dreadful.
terricula, -ōrum ntpl scare, bogy.
terrificō, -āre vt to terrify.
terrificus adj alarming, formidable.
terrigena, -ae m earth-born.
terriloquus adj alarming.
territō, -āre vt to frighten, intimidate.
territōrium, -ī and **iī** nt territory.
territus adj terrified.
terror, -ōris m fright, alarm, terror; a terror.
tersī perf of **tergeō.**
tersus ppp of **tergeō** ♦ adj clean; neat, terse.
tertiadecimānī, -ōrum mpl men of the thirteenth legion.
tertiānus adj recurring every second day ♦ f a

fever ♦ mpl men of the third legion.
tertiō adv for the third time; thirdly.
tertium adv for the third time.
tertius adj third; **~ decimus (decumus)** thirteenth.
terūncius, -ī and **iī** m quarter-as; a fourth; (*fig*) farthing.
tesqua (tesca), -ōrum ntpl waste ground, desert.
tessella, -ae f cube of mosaic stone.
tessera, -ae f cube, dice; (*mil*) password; token (*for mutual recognition of friends*); ticket (*for doles*).
tesserārius, -ī and **iī** m officer of the watch.
testa, -ae f brick, tile; (*earthenware*) pot, jug, sherd; (*fish*) shell, shellfish.
testāmentārius adj testamentary ♦ m forger of wills.
testāmentum, -ī nt will, testament.
testātiō, -ōnis f calling to witness.
testātus ppa of **testor** ♦ adj public.
testiculus, -ī m testicle.
testificātiō, -ōnis f giving evidence, evidence.
testificor, -ārī, -ātus vt to give evidence, vouch for; to make public, bring to light; to call to witness.
testimōnium, -ī and **iī** nt evidence, testimony; proof.
testis, -is m/f witness; eyewitness.
testis, -is m testicle.
testor, -ārī, -ātus vt to give evidence, testify; to prove, vouch for; to call to witness, appeal to ♦ vi to make a will.
testū (*abl* -ū) nt earthenware lid, pot.
testūdineus adj of tortoiseshell, tortoise- (*in cpds*).
testūdō, -inis f tortoise; tortoiseshell; lyre, lute; (*mil*) shelter for besiegers, covering of shields; (*building*) vault.
testum, -i nt earthenware lid, pot.
tēte emphatic acc of **tū.**
tetendī perf of **tendō.**
tēter etc see **taeter.**
Tēthys, -os f sea goddess; the sea.
tetigī perf of **tangō.**
tetrachmum, tetradrachmum, -ī nt four drachmas.
tetraō, -ōnis m blackcock, grouse or capercailzie.
tetrarchēs, -ae m tetrarch, ruler.
tetrarchia, -ae f tetrarchy.
tetricus adj gloomy, sour.
tetulī archaic perf of **ferō.**
Teucer, -rī m son of Telamon of Salamis; son-in-law of Dardanus.
Teucrī, -rōrum mpl Trojans.
Teucria, -riae f Troy.
Teutonī, -ōrum and **es, -um** mpl Teutons (*a German people*).

Noun declensions and verb conjugations are shown on pp xiii to xxv. The present infinitive ending of a verb shows to which conjugation it belongs: **-āre** = 1st; **-ēre** = 2nd; **-ere** = 3rd and **-īre** = 4th. Irregular verbs are shown on p xxvi

Teutonicus *adj* Teutonic, German.
tēxī *perf of* **tegō**.
texō, -ere, -uī, -tum *vt* to weave; to plait; to build, make; (*fig*) to compose, contrive.
textilis *adj* woven ♦ *nt* fabric.
textor, -ōris *m* weaver.
textrīnum, -ī *nt* weaving; shipyard.
textūra, -ae *f* web, fabric.
textus *ppp of* **texō** ♦ *nt* web, fabric.
textus, -ūs *m* texture.
texuī *perf of* **texō**.
Thāis, -idis *f* an Athenian courtesan.
thalamus, -ī *m* room, bedroom; marriage bed; marriage.
thalassicus *adj* sea-green.
thalassinus *adj* sea-green.
Thalēs, -is *and* **ētis** *m* early Greek philosopher (*one of the seven wise men*).
Thalia, -ae *f* Muse of comedy.
thallus, -ī *m* green bough.
Thamyrās, -ae *m* blinded Thracian poet.
Thapsitānus *adj see* **Thapsus**.
Thapsus (-os), -ī *f* town in N. Africa (*scene of Caesar's victory*).
Thasius *adj see* **Thasus**.
Thasus (-os), -ī *f* Greek island in N. Aegean.
Thaumantias, -dis *f* Iris.
theātrālis *adj* of the theatre, in the theatre.
theātrum, -ī *nt* theatre; audience; (*fig*) theatre, stage.
Thēbae, -ārum *fpl* Thebes (*capital of Boeotia*); town in Upper Egypt.
Thēbais, -aidis *f* Theban woman; epic poem by Statius.
Thēbānus *adj* Theban.
thēca, -ae *f* case, envelope.
Themis, -dis *f* goddess of justice.
Themistoclēs, -ī *and* **is** *m* famous Athenian statesman.
Themistoclēus *adj see* **Themistoclēs**.
thēnsaurārius *adj* of treasure.
thēnsaurus *see* **thēsaurus**.
theologus, -ī *m* theologian.
Theophrastus, -ī *m* Greek philosopher (*successor to Aristotle*).
Theopompēus, -īnus *adj see n.*
Theopompus, -ī *m* Greek historian.
thermae, -ārum *fpl* warm baths.
Thermōdōn, -ontis *m* river of Pontus (*where the Amazons lived*).
Thermōdontēus, -ontiacus *adj* Amazonian.
thermopōlium *nt* restaurant serving warm drinks.
thermōpotō, -āre *vt* to refresh with warm drinks.
Thermopylae, -ārum *fpl* famous Greek pass defended by Leonidas.
thēsaurus, -ī *m* treasure, store; storehouse, treasury.
Thēseus, -eī *and* **eos** *m* Greek hero (*king of Athens*).
Thēsēus, -ēius *adj*, **-īdēs, -īdae** *m* Hippolytus; (*pl*) Athenians.

Thespiae, -ārum *fpl* Boeotian town near Helicon.
Thespiēnsis *and* **as, -adis** *adj* Thespian.
Thespis, -is *m* traditional founder of Greek tragedy.
Thessalia, -iae *f* Thessaly (*district of N. Greece*).
Thessalicus, -us *and* **is, -idis** *adj* Thessalian.
Thetis, -idis *and* **idos** *f* sea nymph (*mother of Achilles*); the sea.
thiasus, -ī *m* Bacchic dance.
Thoantēus *adj see n.*
Thoās, -antis *m* king of Crimea (*killed by Orestes*); king of Lemnos (*father of Hypsipyle*).
tholus, -ī *m* rotunda.
thōrāx, -ācis *m* breastplate.
Thrāca, -ae, (-ē, -ēs), (-ia, -iae) *f* Thrace.
Thracius, (Thrēicius) *adj* Thracian.
Thrasea, -ae *m* Stoic philosopher under Nero.
Thrasymachus, -ī *m* Greek sophist.
Thrāx, -ācis *m* Thracian; kind of gladiator.
Thrēssa, -ae, (Thrēissa, -ae) *f* Thracian woman.
Thrēx, -ēcis *m* kind of gladiator.
Thūcydidēs, -is *m* famous Greek historian.
Thūcydidius *adj* Thucydidean.
Thūlē, -ēs *f* island in the extreme N. (*perhaps Shetland*).
thunnus *see* **thynnus**.
thūr, -is *nt* = **tūs, tūris**.
Thūriī, -iōrum *mpl* town in S. Italy.
Thūrīnus *adj see n.*
thūs *see* **tūs**.
thȳa (thȳia), -ae *f* citrus tree.
Thybris, -is *and* **idis** *m* river Tiber.
Thyestēs, -ae *m* brother of Atreus (*whose son's flesh he served up to him to eat*).
Thyestēus *adj*, **-iadēs, -iadae** *m* Aegisthus.
Thyias (Thȳas), -adis *f* Bacchante.
Thȳlē *see* **Thūlē**.
thymbra, -ae *f* savory.
thymum, -ī *nt* garden thyme.
Thȳnia, -iae *f* Bithynia.
thynnus, -ī *m* tunnyfish.
Thȳnus, (-iacus), (-ias) *adj* Bithynian.
Thyōneus, -eī *m* Bacchus.
thyrsus, -ī *m* Bacchic wand.
tiāra, -ae *f*, **-ās, -ae** *m* turban.
Tiberiānus *adj see n.*
Tiberīnus, -īnis *adj*, **-īnus, -īnī** *m* Tiber.
Tiberis (Tibris), -is *m* river Tiber.
Tiberius, -ī *m* Roman praenomen (*esp the second emperor*).
tibi *dat of* **tū**.
tībia, -ae *f* shinbone; pipe, flute.
tībīcen, -inis *m* flute player; pillar.
tībīcina, -ae *f* flute player.
tībīcinium, -ī *and* **iī** *nt* flute playing.
Tibullus, -ī *m* Latin elegiac poet.
Tībur, -is *nt* town on the river Anio (*now Tivoli*).
Tīburs, -tis, (-tīnus), (-nus) *adj* Tiburtine.
Tīcīnus, -ī *m* tributary of the river Po.

Tigellīnus, -ī m favourite of Nero.
tigillum, -ī nt small log, small beam.
tignārius adj working in wood; **faber ~** carpenter.
tignum, -ī nt timber, trunk, log.
Tigrānēs, -is m king of Armenia.
tigris, -is and **idis** f tiger.
tīlia, -ae f lime tree.
Tīmaeus, -ī m Sicilian historian; Pythagorean philosopher; a dialogue of Plato.
timefactus adj frightened.
timeō, -ēre, -uī vt, vi to fear, be afraid.
timidē adv timidly.
timiditās, -ātis f timidity, cowardice.
timidus adj timid, cowardly.
timor, -ōris m fear, alarm; a terror.
tinctilis adj dipped in.
tinctus ppp of **tingō.**
tinea, -ae f moth, bookworm.
tingō, -gere, -xī, -ctum vt to dip, soak; to dye, colour; (fig) to imbue.
tinnīmentum, -ī nt ringing noise.
tinniō, -īre vt, vi to ring, tinkle.
tinnītus, -ūs m ringing, jingle.
tinnulus adj ringing, jingling.
tintinnābulum, -ī nt bell.
tintinō, -āre vi to ring.
tīnus, -ī m a shrub, laurustinus.
tinxī perf of **tingō.**
Tīphys, -os m helmsman of the Argo.
tippula, -ae f water spider.
Tīresiās, -ae m blind soothsayer of Thebes.
Tīridātēs, -ae m king of Armenia.
tīrō, -ōnis m recruit, beginner.
Tīrō, -ōnis m Cicero's freedman secretary.
tīrōcinium, -ī and **iī** nt first campaign; recruits; (fig) first attempt, inexperience.
Tīrōniānus adj see **Tīrō.**
tīrunculus, -ī m young beginner.
Tīryns, -this f ancient town in S.E. Greece (home of Hercules).
Tīrynthius adj of Tiryns, of Hercules ♦ m Hercules.
tis archaic gen of **tū.**
Tīsiphonē, -ēs f a Fury.
Tīsiphonēus adj guilty.
Tītān, -ānis, (-ānus, -ānī) m Titan (an ancient race of gods); the sun.
Tītānius, (-āniacus), (-ānis) adj see n.
Tīthōnius adj see n.
Tīthōnus, -ī m consort of Aurora (granted immortality without youth).
tītillātiō, -ōnis f tickling.
tītillō, -āre vt to tickle.
titubanter adv falteringly.
titubātiō, -ōnis f staggering.
titubō, -āre vi to stagger, totter; to stammer; to waver, falter.
titulus, -ī m inscription, label, notice; title of honour; fame; pretext.

Tityos, -ī m giant punished in Tartarus.
Tmōlus, -ī m mountain in Lydia.
toculiō, -ōnis m usurer.
tōfus, -ī m tufa.
toga, -ae f toga (dress of the Roman citizen); (fig) peace; **~ candida** dress of election candidates; **~ picta** ceremonial dress of a victor in triumph; **~ praetexta** purple-edged toga of magistrates and children; **~ pūra, virīlis** plain toga of manhood.
togātus adj wearing the toga ♦ m Roman citizen; client ♦ f drama on a Roman theme.
togula, -ae f small toga.
tolerābilis adj bearable, tolerable; patient.
tolerābiliter adv patiently.
tolerāns, -antis pres p of **tolerō** ♦ adj patient.
toleranter adv patiently.
tolerantia, -ae f endurance.
tolerātiō, -ōnis f enduring.
tolerātus adj tolerable.
tolerō, -āre, -āvī, -ātum vt to bear, endure; to support, sustain.
tollēnō, -ōnis m crane, derrick, lift.
tollō, -ere, sustulī, sublātum vt to lift, raise; to take away, remove; to do away with, abolish, destroy; (anchor) to weigh; (child) to acknowledge, bring up; (mind) to elevate, excite, cheer; (passenger) to take on board; **signa ~** decamp.
Tolōsa, -ae f Toulouse.
Tolōsānus adj see **Tolōsa.**
tolūtim adv at a trot.
tomāculum, -ī nt sausage.
tōmentum, -ī nt stuffing, padding.
Tomis, -is f town on the Black Sea (to which Ovid was exiled).
Tomītānus adj see **Tomis.**
Tonāns, -antis m Thunderer (epithet of Jupiter).
tondeō, -ēre, totondī, tōnsum vt to shear, clip, shave; to crop, reap, mow; to graze, browse on; (fig) to fleece, rob.
tonitrālis adj thunderous.
tonitrus, -ūs m, **-ua, -uōrum** ntpl thunder.
tonō, -āre, -uī vi to thunder ♦ vt to thunder out.
tōnsa, -ae f oar.
tōnsillae, -ārum fpl tonsils.
tōnsor, -ōris m barber.
tōnsōrius adj for shaving.
tōnstrīcula, -ae f barber girl.
tōnstrīna, -ae f barber's shop.
tōnstrīx, -īcis f woman barber.
tōnsūra, -ae f shearing, clipping.
tōnsus ppp of **tondeō.**
tōnsus, -ūs m coiffure.
tōphus see **tōfus.**
topiārius adj of ornamental gardening ♦ m topiarist ♦ f topiary.
topicē, -ēs f the art of finding topics.

Noun declensions and verb conjugations are shown on pp xiii to xxv. The present infinitive ending of a verb shows to which conjugation it belongs: **-āre** = 1st; **-ēre** = 2nd; **-ere** = 3rd and **-īre** = 4th. Irregular verbs are shown on p xxvi

toral, -ālis *nt* valance.
torcular, -āris *and* **um, -ī** *nt* press.
toreuma, -tis *nt* embossed work, relief.
tormentum, -ī *nt* windlass, torsion catapult, artillery; shot; rack, torture; (*fig*) torment, anguish.
tormina, -um *ntpl* colic.
torminōsus *adj* subject to colic.
tornō, -āre, -āvī, -ātum *vt* to turn (in a lathe), round off.
tornus, -ī *m* lathe.
torōsus *adj* muscular.
torpēdō, -inis *f* numbness, lethargy; (*fish*) electric ray.
torpeō, -ēre *vi* to be stiff, be numb; to be stupefied.
torpēscō, -ēscere, -uī *vi* to grow stiff, numb, listless.
torpidus *adj* benumbed.
torpor, -ōris *m* numbness, torpor, listlessness.
torquātus *adj* wearing a neckchain.
Torquātus, -ī *m* surname of Manlius.
torqueō, -quēre, -sī, -tum *vt* to turn, twist, bend, wind; (*missile*) to whirl, hurl, brandish; (*body*) to rack, torture; (*mind*) to torment.
torquēs *and* **is, -is** *m/f* neckchain, necklace, collar.
torrēns, -entis *pres p of* **torreō** ♦ *adj* scorching, hot; rushing, rapid ♦ *m* torrent.
torreō, -ēre, -uī, tostum *vt* to parch, scorch, roast.
torrēscō, -ere *vi* to become parched.
torridus *adj* parched, dried up; frostbitten.
torris, -is *m* brand, firebrand.
torsī *perf of* **torqueō**.
tortē *adv* awry.
tortilis *adj* twisted, winding.
tortor, -ārī *vi* to writhe.
tortor, -ōris *m* torturer, executioner.
tortuōsus *adj* winding; (*fig*) complicated.
tortus *ppp of* **torqueō** ♦ *adj* crooked; complicated.
tortus, -ūs *m* twisting, writhing.
torulus, -ī *m* tuft (of hair).
torus, -ī *m* knot, bulge; muscle, brawn; couch, bed; (*earth*) bank, mound; (*language*) ornament.
torvitās, -ātis *f* wildness, grimness.
torvus *adj* wild, grim, fierce.
tostus *ppp of* **torreō**.
tot *adj* (*indecl*) so many, as many.
totidem *adj* (*indecl*) just as many, the same number of.
totiēns, totiēs *adv* so often, as often.
totondī *perf of* **tondeō**.
tōtus (*gen* **-īus**, *dat* **-ī**) *adj* entire, the whole, all; entirely, completely taken up with; **ex ~ō** totally; **in ~ō** on the whole.
toxicum, -ī *nt* poison.
trabālis *adj* for beams; **clāvus ~** large nail.
trabea, -ae *f* ceremonial robe.
trabeātus *adj* wearing a ceremonial robe.

trabs, -abis *f* beam, timber; tree; ship; roof.
Trāchīn, -īnis *f* town in Thessaly (*where Hercules cremated himself*).
Trāchīnius *adj see* **Trāchīn**.
tractābilis *adj* manageable, tractable.
tractātiō, -ōnis *f* handling, treatment.
tractātus, -ūs *m* handling.
tractim *adv* slowly, little by little.
tractō, -āre, -āvī, -ātum *vt* to maul; to handle, deal with, manage; (*activity*) to conduct, perform; (*person*) to treat; (*subject*) to discuss, consider.
tractus *ppp of* **trahō** ♦ *adj* fluent.
tractus, -ūs *m* dragging, pulling, drawing; train, track; (*place*) extent, region, district; (*movement*) course; (*time*) lapse; (*word*) drawling.
trādidī *perf of* **trādō**.
trāditiō, -ōnis *f* surrender; handing down.
trāditor, -ōris *m* traitor.
trāditus *ppp of* **trādō**.
trādō, -ere, -idī, -itum *vt* to hand over, deliver, surrender; to commit, entrust; to betray; to bequeath, hand down; (*narrative*) to relate, record; (*teaching*) to propound; **sē ~** surrender, devote oneself.
trādūcō (trānsdūcō), -ūcere, -ūxī, -uctum *vt* to bring across, lead over, transport across; to transfer; to parade, make an exhibition of (in public); (*time*) to pass, spend.
trāductiō, -ōnis *f* transference; (*time*) passage; (*word*) metonymy.
trāductor, -ōris *m* transferrer.
trāductus *ppp of* **trādūcō**.
trādux, -ucis *m* vine layer.
tragicē *adv* dramatically.
tragicocōmoedia, -ae *f* tragicomedy.
tragicus *adj* of tragedy, tragic; in the tragic manner, lofty; terrible, tragic ♦ *m* writer of tragedy.
tragoedia, -ae *f* tragedy; (*fig*) bombast.
tragoedus, -ī *m* tragic actor.
trāgula, -ae *f* kind of javelin.
trahea, -ae *f* sledge.
trahō, -here, -xī, -ctum *vt* to draw, drag, pull, take with one; to pull out, lengthen; to draw together, contract; to carry off, plunder; (*liquid*) to drink, draw; (*money*) to squander; (*wool*) to spin; (*fig*) to attract; (*appearance*) to take on; (*consequence*) to derive, get; (*praise, blame*) to ascribe, refer; (*thought*) to ponder; (*time*) to spin out.
trāiciō, -icere, -iēcī, -iectum *vt* to throw across, shoot across; (*troops*) to get across, transport; (*with weapon*) to pierce, stab; (*river, etc*) to cross; (*fig*) to transfer ♦ *vi* to cross.
trāiectiō, -ōnis *f* crossing, passage; (*fig*) transferring; (*RHET*) exaggeration; (*words*) transposition.
trāiectus *ppp of* **trāiciō**.
trāiectus, -ūs *m* crossing, passage.

trālāt- *etc see* **trānslāt-**.
Trallēs, -ium *fpl town in Lydia.*
Tralliānus *adj see* n.
trālūceō *etc see* **trānslūceō**.
trāma, -ae *f* woof, web.
trāmes, -itis *m* footpath, path.
trāmittō *etc see* **trānsmittō**.
trānatō *etc see* **trānsnatō**.
trānō, -āre, -āvī, -ātum *vt, vi* to swim across;
    (*air*) to fly through.
tranquillē *adv* quietly.
tranquillitās, -ātis *f* quietness, calm; (*fig*)
    peace, quiet.
tranquillō, -āre *vt* to calm.
tranquillus *adj* quiet, calm ♦ *nt* calm sea.
trāns *prep* (*with acc*) across, over, beyond.
trānsabeō, -īre, -iī *vt* to pierce.
trānsāctor, -ōris *m* manager.
trānsāctus *ppp of* **trānsigō**.
trānsadigō, -ere *vt* to drive through, pierce.
Trānsalpīnus *adj* Transalpine.
**trānscendō (trānsscendō), -endere, -endī,
    -ēnsum** *vt, vi* to pass over, surmount; to
    overstep, surpass, transgress.
**trānscrībō (trānsscrībō), -bere, -psī,
    -ptum** *vt* to copy out; (*fig*) to make over,
    transfer.
trānscurrō, -rere, -rī, -sum *vt, vi* to run
    across, run past, traverse.
trānscursus, -ūs *m* running through; (*speech*)
    cursory remark.
trānsd- *etc see* **trād-**.
trānsēgī *perf of* **trānsigō**.
trānsenna, -ae *f* net, snare; trellis,
    latticework.
trānseō, -īre, -iī, -itum *vt, vi* to pass over,
    cross over; to pass along *or* through; to pass
    by; to outstrip, surpass, overstep; (*change*)
    to turn into; (*speech*) to mention briefly,
    leave out, pass on; (*time*) to pass, pass away.
trānsferō, -ferre, -tulī, -lātum *vt* to bring
    across, transport, transfer; (*change*) to
    transform; (*language*) to translate; (*RHET*) to
    use figuratively; (*time*) to postpone; (*writing*)
    to copy.
trānsfīgō, -gere, -xī, -xum *vt* to pierce; to
    thrust through.
trānsfīxus *ppp of* **trānsfīgō**.
trānsfodiō, -odere, -ōdī, -ossum *vt* to run
    through, stab.
trānsfōrmis *adj* changed in shape.
trānsfōrmō, -āre *vt* to change in shape.
trānsfossus *ppp of* **trānsfodiō**.
trānsfuga, -ae *m/f* deserter.
trānsfugiō, -ugere, -ūgī *vi* to desert, come
    over.
trānsfugium, -ī *and* **iī** *nt* desertion.
trānsfundō, -undere, -ūdī, -ūsum *vt* to
    decant, transfuse.
trānsfūsiō, -ōnis *f* transmigration.

trānsfūsus *ppp of* **trānsfundō**.
trānsgredior, -dī, -ssus *vt, vi* to step across,
    cross over, cross; to pass on; to exceed.
trānsgressiō, -ōnis *f* passage; (*words*)
    transposition.
trānsgressus *ppa of* **trānsgredior**.
trānsgressus, -ūs *m* crossing.
trānsiciō *etc see* **trāiciō**.
trānsigō, -igere, -ēgī, -āctum *vt* to carry
    through, complete, finish; (*difference*) to
    settle; (*time*) to pass, spend; (*with cum*) to put
    an end to; (*with weapon*) to stab.
trānsiī *perf of* **trānseō**.
trānsiliō, trānssiliō, -īre, -uī *vi* to jump
    across ♦ *vt* to leap over; (*fig*) to skip,
    disregard; to exceed.
trānsitiō, -ōnis *f* passage; desertion; (*disease*)
    infection.
trānsitō, -āre *vi* to pass through.
trānsitus *ppp of* **trānseō**.
trānsitus, -ūs *m* passing over, passage;
    desertion; passing by; transition.
trānslātīcius, trālātīcius *adj* traditional,
    customary, common.
trānslātiō, trālātiō, -ōnis *f* transporting,
    transferring; (*language*) metaphor.
trānslātīvus *adj* transferable.
trānslātor, -ōris *m* transferrer.
trānslātus *ppp of* **trānsferō**.
trānslegō, -ere *vt* to read through.
trānslūceō, -ēre *vi* to be reflected; to shine
    through.
trānsmarīnus *adj* overseas.
trānsmeō, -āre *vi* to cross.
trānsmigrō, -āre *vi* to emigrate.
trānsmissiō, -ōnis *f* crossing.
trānsmissus *ppp of* **trānsmittō**.
trānsmissus, -ūs *m* crossing.
trānsmittō, -ittere, -īsī, -issum *vt* to send
    across, put across; to let pass through; to
    transfer, entrust, devote; to give up, pass
    over; (*place*) to cross over, go through, pass
    ♦ *vi* to cross.
trānsmontānus *adj* beyond the mountains.
trānsmoveō, -ovēre, -ōvī, -ōtum *vt* to move,
    transfer.
trānsmūtō, -āre *vt* to shift.
trānsnatō, trānatō, -āre *vi* to swim across ♦
    vt to swim.
trānsnō *etc see* **trānō**.
Trānspadānus *adj* north of the Po.
trānspectus, -ūs *m* view.
trānspiciō, -ere *vt* to look through.
trānspōnō, -ōnere, -osuī, -ositum *vt* to
    transfer.
trānsportō, -āre *vt* to carry across, transport,
    remove.
trānspositus *ppp of* **trānspōnō**.
Trānsrhēnānus *adj* east of the Rhine.
trānss- *etc see* **trāns-**.

Noun declensions and verb conjugations are shown on pp xiii to xxv. The present infinitive ending of a verb shows
to which conjugation it belongs: **-āre** = 1st; **-ēre** = 2nd; **-ere** = 3rd and **-īre** = 4th. Irregular verbs are shown on p xxvi

Trānstiberīnus *adj* across the Tiber.
trānstineō, -ēre *vi* to get through.
trānstrum, -ī *nt* thwart.
trānstulī *perf of* **trānsferō**.
trānsultō, -āre *vi* to jump across.
trānsūtus *adj* pierced.
trānsvectiō, -ōnis *f* crossing.
trānsvectus *ppp of* **trānsvehō**.
trānsvehō, -here, -xi, -ctum *vt* to carry across, transport.
trānsvehor, -hī, -ctus *vi* to cross, pass over; (*parade*) to ride past; (*time*) to elapse.
trānsverberō, -āre *vt* to pierce through, wound.
trānsversus (trāversus) *adj* lying across, crosswise, transverse; **digitum ~um** a finger's breadth; **dē ~ō** unexpectedly; **ex ~ō** sideways.
trānsvolitō, -āre *vt* to fly through.
trānsvolō, -āre *vt, vi* to fly across, fly through; to move rapidly across; to fly past, disregard.
trānsvorsus *etc see* **trānsversus**.
trapētus, -ī *m* olive mill, oil mill.
trapezīta *etc see* **tarpezīta**.
Trapezūs, -ūntis *f* Black Sea town (*now* Trebizond).
Trasumennus (Trasimēnus), -ī *m* lake in Etruria (*where Hannibal defeated the Romans*).
trāv- *see* **trānsv-**.
trāvectiō *etc see* **trānsvectiō**.
traxī *perf of* **trahō**.
trecēnī, -ōrum *adj* three hundred each.
trecentēsimus *adj* three-hundredth.
trecentī, -ōrum *num* three hundred.
trecentiēns, -ēs *adv* three hundred times.
trechedīpna, -ōrum *ntpl* dinner shoes (of parasites).
tredecim *num* thirteen.
tremebundus *adj* trembling.
tremefaciō, -facere, -fēcī, -factum *vt* to shake.
tremendus *adj* formidable, terrible.
tremēscō (tremīscō), -ere *vi* to begin to shake ♦ *vt* to be afraid of.
tremō, -ere, -uī *vi* to tremble, quake, quiver ♦ *vt* to tremble at, dread.
tremor, -ōris *m* shaking, quiver, tremor; earthquake.
tremulus *adj* trembling, shivering.
trepidanter *adv* with agitation.
trepidātiō, -ōnis *f* agitation, alarm, consternation.
trepidē *adv* hastily, in confusion.
trepidō, -āre, -āvī, -ātum *vi* to be agitated, bustle about, hurry; to be alarmed; to flicker, quiver ♦ *vt* to start at.
trepidus *adj* restless, anxious, alarmed; alarming, perilous.
trēs, trium *num* three.
trēssis, -is *m* three asses.
trēsvirī, triumvirōrum *mpl* three commissioners, triumvirs.

Trēverī, -ōrum *mpl* people of E. Gaul (*about what is now* Trèves).
Trēvericus *adj see* n.
triangulum, -ī *nt* triangle.
triangulus *adj* triangular.
triāriī, -ōrum *mpl* the third line (*in Roman battle order*), the reserves.
tribuārius *adj* of the tribes.
tribūlis, -is *m* fellow tribesman.
tribulum, -ī *nt* threshing sledge.
tribulus, -ī *m* star thistle.
tribūnal, -ālis *nt* platform; judgment seat; camp platform, cenotaph.
tribūnātus, -ūs *m* tribuneship, rank of tribune.
tribūnicius *adj* of a tribune ♦ *m* ex-tribune.
tribūnus, -ī *m* tribune; ~ **plēbis** tribune of the people, a magistrate who defended the rights of the plebeians; ~ **mīlitum** *or* **mīlitāris** military tribune, an officer under the legatus; **~ī aerāriī** paymasters.
tribuō, -uere, -uī, -ūtum *vt* to assign, allot; to give, bestow, pay; to concede, allow; to ascribe, attribute; (*subject*) to divide; (*time*) to devote.
tribus, -ūs *m* tribe.
tribūtārius *adj*: **~ae tabellae** letters of credit.
tribūtim *adv* by tribes.
tribūtiō, -ōnis *f* distribution.
tribūtum, -ī *nt* contribution, tribute, tax.
tribūtus *ppp of* **tribuō**.
tribūtus *adj* arranged by tribes.
trīcae, -ārum *fpl* nonsense; tricks, vexations.
trīcēnī, -ōrum *adj* thirty each, in thirties.
triceps, -ipitis *adj* three-headed.
trīcēsimus *adj* thirtieth.
trichila, -ae *f* arbour, summerhouse.
trīciēns, -ēs *adv* thirty times.
trīclīnium, -ī and iī *nt* dining couch; dining room.
trīcō, -ōnis *m* mischief-maker.
trīcor, -ārī *vi* to make mischief, play tricks.
tricorpor, -is *adj* three-bodied.
tricuspis, -idis *adj* three-pointed.
tridēns, -entis *adj* three-pronged ♦ *m* trident.
tridentifer, -ī *adj* trident-wielding.
tridentiger, -ī *adj* trident-wielding.
trīduum, -ī *nt* three days.
triennia, -ium *ntpl* a triennial festival.
triennium, -ī and iī *nt* three years.
triēns, -entis *m* a third; (*coin*) a third of an as; (*measure*) a third of a pint.
trientābulum, -ī *nt* land given by the State as a third of a debt.
trientius *adj* sold for a third.
triērarchus, -ī *m* captain of a trireme.
triēris, -is *f* trireme.
triētēricus *adj* triennial ♦ *ntpl* festival of Bacchus.
triētēris, -idis *f* three years; a triennial festival.
trifāriam *adv* in three parts, in three places.
trifaux, -aucis *adj* three-throated.

trifidus *adj* three-forked.
trifōrmis *adj* triple.
trifūr, -ūris *m* archthief.
trifurcifer, -ī *m* hardened criminal.
trigeminus *adj* threefold, triple ♦ *mpl* triplets.
trigintā *num* thirty.
trigōn, -ōnis *m* a ball game.
trilībris *adj* three-pound.
trilinguis *adj* three-tongued.
trilīx, -īcis *adj* three-ply, three-stranded.
trimēstris *adj* of three months.
trimetrus, -ī *m* trimeter.
trīmus *adj* three years old.
Trīnacria, -iae *f* Sicily.
Trīnacrius, -is, -idis *adj* Sicilian.
trīnī, -ōrum *adj* three each, in threes; triple.
Trinobantēs, -um *mpl* British tribe in East Anglia.
trinōdis *adj* three-knotted.
triōbolus, -ī *m* half-a-drachma.
Triōnēs, -um *mpl* the Plough; the Little Bear.
tripartītō *adv* in *or* into three parts.
tripartītus, tripertītus *adj* divided into three parts.
tripectorus *adj* three-bodied.
tripedālis *adj* three-foot.
tripert- *etc see* **tripart-**.
tripēs, -edis *adj* three-legged.
triplex, -icis *adj* triple, threefold ♦ *nt* three times as much ♦ *mpl* three-leaved writing tablet.
triplus *adj* triple.
Triptolemus, -ī *m* inventor of agriculture, judge in Hades.
tripudiō, -āre *vi* to dance.
tripudium, -ī *and* **iī** *nt* ceremonial dance, dance; a favourable omen (*when the sacred chickens ate greedily*).
tripūs, -odis *f* tripod; the Delphic oracle.
triquetrus *adj* triangular; Sicilian.
trirēmis *adj* with three banks of oars ♦ *f* trireme.
trīs *etc see* **trēs**.
triscurria, -ōrum *ntpl* sheer fooling.
tristē *adv* sadly; severely.
trīstī = **trīvistī**.
tristiculus *adj* rather sad.
tristificus *adj* ominous.
tristimōnia, -ae *f* sadness.
tristis *adj* sad, glum, melancholy; gloomy, sombre, dismal; (*taste*) bitter; (*smell*) offensive; (*temper*) severe, sullen, ill-humoured.
tristitia, -ae *f* sadness, sorrow, melancholy; moroseness, severity.
tristitiēs, -ēī *f* sorrow.
trisulcus *adj* three-forked.
tritavus, -ī *m* great-great-great-grandfather.
trīticeus *adj* of wheat, wheaten.
trīticum, -ī *nt* wheat.

Trītōn, -ōnis *m* sea god (*son of Neptune*); African lake (*where Minerva was born*).
Trītōnius, -ōniacus, -ōnis *adj* of Lake Triton, of Minerva ♦ *f* Minerva.
trītūra, -ae *f* threshing.
trītus *ppp of* **terō** ♦ *adj* well-worn; (*judgment*) expert; (*language*) commonplace, trite.
trītus, -ūs *m* rubbing, friction.
triumphālis *adj* triumphal ♦ *ntpl* insignia of a triumph.
triumphō, -āre, -āvī, -ātum *vi* to celebrate a triumph; to triumph, exult ♦ *vt* to triumph over, win by conquest.
triumphus, -ī *m* triumphal procession, victory parade; triumph, victory.
triumvir, -ī *m* commissioner, triumvir; mayor (*of a provincial town*).
triumvirālis *adj* triumviral.
triumvirātus, -ūs *m* office of triumvir, triumvirate.
triumvirī, -ōrum *mpl* three commissioners, triumvirs.
trivenēfica, -ae *f* old witch.
trīvī *perf of* **terō**.
Trivia, -ae *f* Diana.
triviālis *adj* common, popular.
trivium, -ī *and* **iī** *nt* crossroads; public street.
trivius *adj* of the crossroads.
Trōas, -adis *f* the district of Troy, Troad; Trojan woman ♦ *adj* Trojan.
trochaeus, -ī *m* trochee; tribrach.
trochlea, -ae *f* block and tackle.
trochus, -ī *m* hoop.
Trōglodytae, -ārum *mpl* cave dwellers of Ethiopia.
Trōia, -ae *f* Troy.
Trōilus, -ī *m* son of Priam.
Trōiugena, -ae *m/f* Trojan; Roman.
Trōius *and* **ānus** *and* **cus** *adj* Trojan.
tropaeum, -ī *nt* victory memorial, trophy; victory; memorial, token.
Trōs, -ōis *m* king of Phrygia; Trojan.
trucīdātiō, -ōnis *f* butchery.
trucīdō, -āre, -āvī, -ātum *vt* to slaughter, massacre.
truculentē *adv see* **truculentus**.
truculentia, -ae *f* ferocity, inclemency.
truculentus *adj* ferocious, grim, wild.
trudis, -is *f* pike.
trūdō, -dere, -sī, -sum *vt* to push, thrust, drive; (*buds*) to put forth.
trulla, -ae *f* ladle, scoop; washbasin.
truncō, -āre, -āvī, -ātum *vt* to lop off, maim, mutilate.
truncus, -ī *m* (*tree*) trunk, bole; (*human*) trunk, body; (*abuse*) blockhead ♦ *adj* maimed, broken, stripped (of); defective.
trūsī *perf of* **trūdō**.
trūsitō, -āre *vi* to keep pushing.
trūsus *ppp of* **trūdō**.

Noun declensions and verb conjugations are shown on pp xiii to xxv. The present infinitive ending of a verb shows to which conjugation it belongs: **-āre** = 1st; **-ēre** = 2nd; **-ere** = 3rd and **-īre** = 4th. Irregular verbs are shown on p xxvi

trutina, -ae f balance, scales.
trux, -ucis adj savage, grim, wild.
trȳgōnus, -ī m stingray.
tū pron you, thou.
tuātim adv in your usual fashion.
tuba, -ae f trumpet, war trumpet.
tūber, -is nt swelling, lump; (food) truffle.
tuber, -is f kind of apple tree.
tubicen, -inis m trumpeter.
tubilūstria, -ōrum ntpl festival of trumpets.
tuburcinor, -ārī vi to gobble up, guzzle.
tubus, -ī m pipe.
tuditō, -āre vt to strike repeatedly.
tueor, -ērī, -itus and **tūtus** vt to see, watch,
   look; to guard, protect, keep.
tugurium, -ī and **iī** nt hut, cottage.
tuitiō, -ōnis f defence.
tuitus ppa of **tueor.**
tulī perf of **ferō.**
Tulliānum, -ī nt State dungeon of Rome.
Tulliānus adj see **Tullius.**
Tulliola, -ae f little Tullia (_Cicero's daughter_).
Tullius, -ī and **iī** m Roman family name (_esp the
   sixth king_); _the orator Cicero._
Tullus, -ī m third king of Rome.
tum adv (time) then, at that time; (sequence)
   then, next ♦ conj moreover, besides; ~ ... ~ at
   one time ... at another; ~ ... **cum** at the time
   when, whenever; **cum** ... ~ not only ... but; ~
   dēmum only then; ~ **ipsum** even then; ~
   māximē just then; ~ **vērō** then more than
   ever.
tumefaciō, -facere, -fēcī, -factum vt to
   make swell; (fig) to puff up.
tumeō, -ēre vi to swell, be swollen; (emotion)
   to be excited; (pride) to be puffed up;
   (language) to be turgid.
tumēscō, -ēscere, -uī vi to begin to swell,
   swell up.
tumidus adj swollen, swelling; (emotion)
   excited, enraged; (pride) puffed up;
   (language) bombastic.
tumor, -ōris m swelling, bulge; hillock; (fig)
   commotion, excitement.
tumulō, -āre vt to bury.
tumulōsus adj hilly.
tumultuārius adj hasty; (troops) emergency.
tumultuātiō, -ōnis f commotion.
tumultuō, -āre; -or, -ārī vi to make a
   commotion, be in an uproar.
tumultuōsē adv see **tumultuōsus.**
tumultuōsus adj uproarious, excited,
   turbulent.
tumultus, -ūs m commotion, uproar,
   disturbance; (MIL) rising, revolt, civil war;
   (weather) storm; (mind) disorder.
tumulus, -ī m mound, hill; burial mound,
   barrow.
tunc adv (time) then, at that time; (sequence)
   then, next; ~ **dēmum** only then; ~ **quoque**
   then too; even so.
tundō, -ere, tutudī, tūnsum and **tūsum** vt to
   beat, thump, hammer; (grain) to pound;

(speech) to din, importune.
Tūnēs, -ētis m Tunis.
tunica, -ae f tunic; (fig) skin, husk.
tunicātus adj wearing a tunic.
tunicula, -ae f little tunic.
tūnsus ppp of **tundō.**
tuor etc see **tueor.**
turba, -ae f disorder, riot, disturbance; brawl,
   quarrel; crowd, mob, troop, number.
turbāmenta, -ōrum ntpl propaganda.
turbātē adv in confusion.
turbātiō, -ōnis f confusion.
turbātor, -ōris m agitator.
turbātus ppp of **turbō** ♦ adj troubled,
   disorderly.
turbellae, -ārum fpl stir, row.
turben etc see **turbō.**
turbidē adv in disorder.
turbidus adj confused, wild, boisterous;
   (water) troubled, muddy; (fig) disorderly,
   troubled, alarmed, dangerous.
turbineus adj conical.
turbō, -āre, -āvī, -ātum vt to disturb, throw
   into confusion; (water) to trouble, make
   muddy.
turbō, -inis m whirl, spiral, rotation; reel,
   whorl, spindle; (toy) top; (wind) tornado,
   whirlwind; (fig) storm.
turbulentē and **er** adv wildly.
turbulentus adj agitated, confused,
   boisterous, stormy; troublemaking,
   seditious.
turdus, -ī m thrush.
tūreus adj of incense.
turgeō, -gēre, -sī vi to swell, be swollen;
   (speech) to be bombastic.
turgēscō, -ere vi to swell up, begin to swell;
   (fig) to become enraged.
turgidulus adj poor swollen.
turgidus adj swollen, distended; bombastic.
tūribulum, -ī nt censer.
tūricremus adj incense-burning.
tūrifer, -ī adj incense-producing.
tūrilegus adj incense-gathering.
turma, -ae f troop, squadron (of cavalry);
   crowd.
turmālis adj of a troop; equestrian.
turmātim adv troop by troop.
Turnus, -ī m Rutulian king (chief opponent of
   Aeneas).
turpiculus adj ugly little; slightly indecent.
turpificātus adj debased.
turpilucricupidus adj fond of filthy lucre.
turpis adj ugly, deformed, unsightly; base,
   disgraceful ♦ nt disgrace.
turpiter adv repulsively; shamefully.
turpitūdō, -inis f deformity; disgrace,
   infamy.
turpō, -āre vt to disfigure, soil.
turriger, -ī adj turreted.
turris, -is f tower, turret; siege tower;
   (elephant) howdah; (fig) mansion.
turrītus adj turreted; castellated; towering.

U, u

tursī *perf of* **turgeō.**
turtur, -is *m* turtledove.
tūs, tūris *nt* incense, frankincense.
Tusculānēnsis *adj* at Tusculum.
Tusculānum, -ānī *nt* villa at Tusculum (*esp Cicero's*).
Tusculānus *adj* Tusculan.
tūsculum, -ī *nt* a little incense.
Tusculum, -ī *nt* Latin town near Rome.
Tusculus *adj* Tusculan.
Tuscus *adj* Etruscan.
tussiō, -īre *vi* to cough, have a cough.
tussis, -is *f* cough.
tūsus *ppp of* **tundō.**
tūtāmen, -inis *nt* defence.
tūtāmentum, -ī *nt* protection.
tūte *emphatic form of* **tū.**
tūtē *adv* safely, in safety.
tūtēla, -ae *f* keeping, charge, protection; (*of minors*) guardianship, wardship; (*person*) watcher, guardian; ward, charge.
tūtemet *emphatic form of* **tū.**
tūtor, -ārī, -ātus, -ō, -āre *vt* to watch, guard, protect; to guard against.
tūtor, -ōris *m* protector; (*law*) guardian.
tutudī *perf of* **tundō.**
tūtus *ppp of* **tueō** ♦ *adj* safe, secure; cautious ♦ *nt* safety.
tuus *adj* your, yours, thy, thine; your own, your proper; of you.
Tȳdeus, -eī *and* **eos** *m* father of Diomede.
Tȳdīdēs, -īdae *m* Diomede.
tympanotrība, -ae *m* timbrel player.
tympanum (typanum), -ī *nt* drum, timbrel (*esp of the priests of Cybele*); (*mechanism*) wheel.
Tyndareus, -eī *m* king of Sparta (*husband of Leda*).
Tyndaridae, -idārum *mpl* Castor and Pollux.
Tyndaris, -idis *f* Helen; Clytemnestra.
Typhōeus, -eos *m* giant under Etna.
Typhōius, -is *adj see n.*
typus, -ī *m* figure.
tyrannicē *adv see* **tyrannicus.**
tyrannicīda, -ae *m* tyrannicide.
tyrannicus *adj* tyrannical.
tyrannis, -idis *f* despotism, tyranny.
tyrannoctonus, -ī *m* tyrannicide.
tyrannus, -ī *m* ruler, king; despot, tyrant.
Tyrās, -ae *m* river Dniester.
Tyrius *adj* Tyrian, Phoenician, Carthaginian; purple.
tȳrotarīchos, -ī *m* dish of salt fish and cheese.
Tyrrhēnia, -iae *f* Etruria.
Tyrrhēnus *adj* Etruscan, Tyrrhenian.
Tyrtaeus, -ī *m* Spartan war poet.
Tyrus (-os), -ī *f* Tyre (*famous Phoenician seaport*).

ūber, -is *nt* breast, teat; (*fig*) richness.
ūber, -is *adj* fertile, plentiful, rich (in); (*language*) full, copious.
ūberius (*superl* **-rime**) *compar adj* more fully, more copiously.
ūbertās, -ātis *f* richness, plenty, fertility.
ūbertim *adv* copiously.
ubī *adv* (*interrog*) where; (*relat*) where, in which, with whom; when
ubīcumque *adv* wherever; everywhere.
Ubiī, -ōrum *mpl* German tribe on the lower Rhine.
ubīnam *adv* where (in fact)?
ubīquāque *adv* everywhere.
ubīque *adv* everywhere, anywhere.
ubiubī *adv* wherever.
ubīvīs *adv* anywhere.
ūdus *adj* wet, damp.
ulcerō, -āre *vt* to make sore, wound.
ulcerōsus *adj* full of sores; wounded.
ulcīscor, -ī, ultus *vt* to take vengeance on, punish; to take vengeance for, avenge.
ulcus, -eris *nt* sore, ulcer; **~ tangere** touch on a delicate subject.
ūlīgō, -inis *f* moisture, marshiness.
Ulixēs, -is *m* Ulysses, Odysseus (*king of Ithaca, hero of Homer's Odyssey*).
ullus (*gen* **-īus,** *dat* **-ī**) *adj* any.
ulmeus *adj* of elm.
ulmus, -ī *f* elm; (*pl*) elm rods.
ulna, -ae *f* elbow; arm; (*measure*) ell.
ulterior, -ōris *compar adj* farther, beyond, more remote.
ulterius *compar of* **ultrā.**
ultimus *superl adj* farthest, most remote, the end of; (*time*) earliest, latest, last; (*degree*) extreme, greatest, lowest ♦ *ntpl* the end; **~um** for the last time; **ad ~um** finally.
ultiō, -ōnis *f* vengeance, revenge.
ultor, -ōris *m* avenger, punisher.
ultrā *adv* beyond, farther, besides ♦ *prep* (*with acc*) beyond, on the far side of; (*time*) past; (*degree*) over and above.
ultrīx, -īcis *adj* avenging.
ultrō *adv* on the other side, away; besides; of one's own accord, unasked, voluntarily.
ultrō tribūta *ntpl* State expenditure for public works.
ultus *ppa of* **ulcīscor.**
ulula, -ae *f* screech owl.
ululātus, -ūs *m* wailing, shrieking, yells, whoops.

Noun declensions and verb conjugations are shown on pp xiii to xxv. The present infinitive ending of a verb shows to which conjugation it belongs: **-āre** = 1st; **-ēre** = 2nd; **-ere** = 3rd and **-īre** = 4th. Irregular verbs are shown on p xxvi

ululō, -āre, -āvī, -ātum *vi* to shriek, yell, howl
♦ *vt* to cry out to.
ulva, -ae *f* sedge.
umbella, -ae *f* parasol.
Umber, -rī *adj* Umbrian ♦ *m* Umbrian dog.
umbilīcus, -ī *m* navel; (*fig*) centre; (*book*)
roller end; (*sea*) cockle *or* pebble.
umbō, -ōnis *m* boss (*of a shield*); shield; elbow.
umbra, -ae *f* shadow, shade; (*dead*) ghost;
(*diner*) uninvited guest; (*fish*) grayling;
(*painting*) shade; (*place*) shelter, school,
study; (*unreality*) semblance, mere shadow.
umbrāculum, -ī *nt* arbour; school; parasol.
umbrāticola, -ae *m* lounger.
umbrāticus *adj* fond of idling; in retirement.
umbrātilis *adj* in retirement, private,
academic.
Umbria, -riae *f* Umbria (*district of central Italy*).
umbrifer, -ī *adj* shady.
umbrō, -āre *vt* to shade.
umbrōsus *adj* shady.
ūmectō, -āre *vt* to wet, water.
ūmectus *adj* damp, wet.
ūmeō, -ēre *vi* to be damp, be wet.
umerus, -ī *m* upper arm, shoulder.
ūmēscō, -ere *vi* to become damp, get wet.
ūmidē *adv* with damp.
ūmidulus *adj* dampish.
ūmidus *adj* wet, damp, dank, moist.
ūmor, -ōris *m* liquid, fluid, moisture.
umquam, unquam *adv* ever, at any time.
ūnā *adv* together.
ūnanimāns, -antis *adj* in full agreement.
ūnanimitās, -ātis *f* concord.
ūnanimus *adj* of one accord, harmonious.
ūncia, -ae *f* a twelfth; (*weight*) ounce; (*length*)
inch.
ūnciārius *adj* of a twelfth; (*interest*) 8⅓ per
cent.
ūnciātim *adv* little by little.
uncīnātus *adj* barbed.
ūnciola, -ae *f* a mere twelfth.
ūnctiō, -ōnis *f* anointing.
ūnctitō, -āre *vt* to anoint regularly.
ūnctiusculus *adj* rather too unctuous.
ūnctor, -ōris *m* anointer.
ūnctūra, -ae *f* anointing (*of the dead*).
ūnctus *ppp of* **ungō** ♦ *adj* oiled; greasy,
resinous; (*fig*) rich, sumptuous ♦ *nt*
sumptuous dinner.
uncus, -ī *m* hook, grappling-iron.
uncus *adj* hooked, crooked, barbed.
unda, -ae *f* wave, water; (*fig*) stream, surge.
unde *adv* from where, whence; from whom,
from which; **~ petitur** the defendant; **~ unde**
from wherever; somehow or other.
ūndeciēns *and* **ēs** *adv* eleven times.
ūndecim *num* eleven.
ūndecimus *adj* eleventh.
undecumque *adv* from wherever.
ūndēnī, -ōrum *adj* eleven each, eleven.
ūndēnōnāgintā *num* eighty-nine.
ūndeoctōgintā *num* seventy-nine.

ūndēquadrāgintā *num* thirty-nine.
ūndēquīnquāgēsimus *adj* forty-ninth.
ūndēquīnquāgintā *num* forty-nine.
ūndēsexāgintā *num* fifty-nine.
ūndētrīcēsimus *adj* twenty-ninth.
ūndēvīcēsimānī, -ōrum *mpl* men of the
nineteenth legion.
ūndēvīcēsimus *adj* nineteenth.
ūndēvīgintī *num* nineteen.
undique *adv* from every side, on all sides,
everywhere; completely.
undisonus *adj* sea-roaring.
undō, -āre *vi* to surge; (*fig*) to roll, undulate.
undōsus *adj* billowy.
ūnetvīcēsimānī, -ōrum *mpl* men of the *twenty-
first legion.*
ūnetvīcēsimus *adj* twenty-first.
ungō (unguō), -gere, ūnxī, ūnctum *vt* to
anoint, smear, grease.
unguen, -inis *nt* fat, grease, ointment.
unguentārius, -ī *and* **iī** *m* perfumer.
unguentātus *adj* perfumed.
unguentum, -ī *nt* ointment, perfume.
unguiculus, -ī *m* fingernail.
unguis, -is *m* nail (*of finger or toe*); claw, talon,
hoof; **ad ~em** with perfect finish;
trānsversum ~em a hair's breadth; **dē tenerō
~ī** from earliest childhood.
ungula, -ae *f* hoof, talon, claw.
unguō *etc see* **ungō**.
ūnicē *adv* solely, extraordinarily.
ūnicolor, -ōris *adj* all one colour.
ūnicus *adj* one and only, sole; unparalleled,
unique.
ūnifōrmis *adj* simple.
ūnigena, -ae *adj* only-begotten; of the same
parentage.
ūnimanus *adj* with only one hand.
ūniō, -ōnis *m* a single large pearl.
ūniter *adv* together in one.
ūniversālis *adj* general.
ūniversē *adv* in general.
ūniversitās, -ātis *f* the whole; the universe.
ūniversus *adj* all taken together, entire,
general ♦ *mpl* the community as a whole ♦ *nt*
the universe; **in ~um** in general.
unquam *etc see* **umquam**.
ūnus *num* one ♦ *adj* sole, single, only; one and
the same; the outstanding one; an
individual; **~ et alter** one or two; **~ quisque**
every single one; **nēmō ~** not a single one; **ad
~um** to a man.
ūnxī *perf of* **ungō**.
ūpiliō, -ōnis *m* shepherd.
upupa, -ae *f* hoopoe; crowbar.
Urania, -ae *and* **ē, -ēs** *f* Muse of astronomy.
urbānē *adv* politely; wittily, elegantly.
urbānitās, -ātis *f* city life; refinement,
politeness; wit.
urbānus *adj* town (*in cpds*), city (*in cpds*);
refined, polite; witty, humorous;
impertinent ♦ *m* townsman.
urbicapus, -ī *m* taker of cities.

urbs, urbis *f* city; Rome.
urceolus, -ī *m* jug.
urceus, -ī *m* pitcher, ewer.
ūrēdō, -inis *f* blight.
urgeō, -gēre, -sī *vt, vi* to force on, push
   forward; to press hard on, pursue closely; to
   crowd, hem in; to burden, oppress;
   (*argument*) to press, urge; (*work, etc*) to urge
   on, ply hard, follow up.
ūrīna, -ae *f* urine.
ūrīnātor, -ōris *m* diver.
urna, -ae *f* water jar, urn; voting urn, lottery
   urn, cinerary urn, money jar.
urnula, -ae *f* small urn.
ūrō, -ere, ūssī, ūstum *vt* to burn; to scorch,
   parch; (*cold*) to nip; (*MED*) to cauterize;
   (*rubbing*) to chafe, hurt; (*passion*) to fire,
   inflame; (*vexation*) to annoy, oppress.
ursa, -ae *f* she-bear, bear; (*ASTRO*) Great Bear,
   Lesser Bear.
ursī *perf of* **urgeō**.
ursīnus *adj* bear's.
ursus, -ī *m* bear.
urtīca, -ae *f* nettle.
ūrus, -ī *m* wild ox.
Usipetēs, -etum, (-iī, -iōrum) *mpl* German
   tribe on the Rhine.
ūsitātē *adv* in the usual manner.
ūsitātus *adj* usual, familiar.
uspiam *adv* anywhere, somewhere.
usquam *adv* anywhere; in any way, at all.
usque *adv* all the way (to, from), right on,
   right up to; (*time*) all the time, as long as,
   continuously; (*degree*) even, as much as; ~
   quāque everywhere; every moment, on
   every occasion.
ūssī *perf of* **ūrō**.
ūstor, -ōris *m* cremator.
ūstulō, -āre *vt* to burn.
ūstus *ppp of* **ūrō**.
ūsūcapiō, -apere, -ēpī, -aptum *vt* to acquire
   ownership of, take over.
ūsūcapiō, -ōnis *f* ownership by use *or*
   possession.
ūsūra, -ae *f* use, enjoyment; interest, usury.
ūsūrārius *adj* for use and enjoyment; paying
   interest.
ūsurpātiō, -ōnis *f* making use (of).
ūsurpō, -āre, -āvī, -ātum *vt* to make use of,
   employ, exercise; (*law*) to take possession
   of, enter upon; (*senses*) to perceive, make
   contact with; (*word*) to call by, speak of.
ūsus *ppa of* **ūtor**.
ūsus, -ūs *m* use, enjoyment, practice;
   experience, skill; usage, custom;
   intercourse, familiarity; usefulness, benefit,
   advantage; need, necessity; ~ **est, venit**
   there is need (of); ~ **uī esse, ex ~ū esse** be of
   use, be of service; ~**ū venīre** happen; ~ **et
   frūctus** use and enjoyment, usufruct.

ut, utī *adv* how; (*relat*) as; (*explaining*)
   considering how, according as; (*place*)
   where; ~ **in ōrātōre** for an orator ♦ *conj* **1.** *with*
   indic: (*manner*) as; (*concessive*) while, though;
   (*time*) when, as soon as. **2.** *with subj:*
   (*expressing the idea of a verb*) that, to;
   (*purpose*) so that, to; (*causal*) seeing that;
   (*concessive*) granted that, although; (*result*)
   that, so that; (*fear*) that not; ~ ... **ita** while ...
   nevertheless; ~ **nōn** without; ~ **quī** seeing
   that I, he, *etc*; ~ **quisque māximē** the more.
utcumque (utcunque) *adv* however;
   whenever; one way or another.
ūtēnsilis *adj* of use ♦ *ntpl* necessaries.
ūter, -ris *m* bag, skin, bottle.
uter (*gen* **-rīus,** *dat* **-rī**), **-ra, -rum** *pron* which (of
   two), the one that; one or the other.
utercumque, utracumque, utrumcumque
   pron whichever (of two).
uterlibet, utralibet, utrumlibet *pron*
   whichever (of the two) you please, either
   one.
uterque, utraque, utrumque *pron* each (of
   two), either, both.
uterum, -ī *nt*, **uterus, -ī** *m* womb; child; belly.
utervīs, utravīs, utrumvīs *pron* whichever
   (of two) you please; either.
ūtī *infin of* **ūtor**.
utī *etc see* **ut**.
ūtibilis *adj* useful, serviceable.
Utica, -ae *f* town near Carthage (*where Cato*
   committed suicide).
Uticēnsis *adj see n*.
ūtilis *adj* useful, expedient, profitable; fit (for).
ūtilitās, -ātis *f* usefulness, expediency,
   advantage.
ūtiliter *adv* usefully, advantageously.
utinam *adv* I wish!, would that!, if only!
utique *adv* at least, by all means, especially.
ūtor, ūtī, ūsus *vi* (*with abl*) to use, employ; to
   possess, enjoy; to practise, experience;
   (*person*) to be on intimate terms with, find;
   ūtendum rogāre borrow.
utpote *adv* inasmuch as, as being.
ūtrārius, -ī *and* **iī** *m* watercarrier.
ūtriculārius, -ī *and* **iī** *m* bagpiper.
utrimque (utrinque) *adv* on both sides, on
   either side.
utrō *adv* in which direction.
utrobīque *see* **utrubīque**.
utrōque *adv* in both directions, both ways.
utrubī *adv* on which side.
utrubīque *adv* on both sides, on either side.
utrum *adv* whether.
utut *adv* however.
ūva, -ae *f* grape, bunch of grapes; vine;
   cluster.
ūvēscō, -ere *vi* to become wet.
ūvidulus *adj* moist.
ūvidus *adj* wet, damp; drunken.

Noun declensions and verb conjugations are shown on pp xiii to xxv. The present infinitive ending of a verb shows
to which conjugation it belongs: **-āre** = 1st; **-ēre** = 2nd; **-ere** = 3rd and **-īre** = 4th. Irregular verbs are shown on p xxvi

uxor, -ōris *f* wife.
uxorcula, -ae *f* little wife.
uxōrius *adj* of a wife; fond of his wife.

V, v

vacāns, -antis *pres p of* **vacō ♦** *adj* unoccupied; (*woman*) single.
vacātiō, -ōnis *f* freedom, exemption; exemption from military service; payment for exemption from service.
vacca, -ae *f* cow.
vaccīnium, -ī *and* **iī** *nt* hyacinth.
vaccula, -ae *f* heifer.
vacēfiō, -ierī *vi* to become empty.
vacillō, -āre *vi* to stagger, totter; to waver, be unreliable.
vacīvē *adv* at leisure.
vacīvitās, -ātis *f* want.
vacīvus *adj* empty, free.
vacō, -āre, -āvī, -ātum *vi* to be empty, vacant, unoccupied; to be free, aloof (from); to have time for, devote one's time to; **~at** there is time.
vacuātus *adj* empty.
vacuēfaciō, -facere, -fēcī, -factum *vt* to empty, clear.
vacuitās, -ātis *f* freedom, exemption; vacancy.
vacuus *adj* empty, void, wanting; vacant; free (from), clear; disengaged, at leisure; (*value*) worthless; (*woman*) single **♦** *nt* void, space.
vadimōnium, -ī *and* **iī** *nt* bail, security; **~ sistere** appear in court; **~ dēserere** default.
vādō, -ere *vi* to go, go on, make one's way.
vador, -ārī, -ātus *vt* to bind over by bail.
vadōsus *adj* shallow.
vadum, -ī *nt* shoal, shallow, ford; water, sea; bottom.
vae *interj* woe!, alas!
vafer, -rī *adj* crafty, subtle.
vafrē *adv* artfully.
vagē *adv* far afield.
vāgīna, -ae *f* sheath, scabbard; (*grain*) husk.
vāgiō, -īre *vi* to cry.
vāgītus, -ūs *m* crying, bleating.
vagor, -ārī, -ātus *vi* to wander, rove, go far afield; (*fig*) to spread.
vāgor, -ōris *m* cry.
vagus *adj* wandering, unsettled; (*fig*) fickle, wavering, vague.
vah *interj* (*expressing surprise, joy, anger*) oh!, ah!
valdē *adv* greatly, intensely; very.
valē, valēte *interj* goodbye, farewell.

valēns, -entis *pres p of* **valeō ♦** *adj* strong, powerful, vigorous; well, healthy.
valenter *adv* strongly.
valentulus *adj* strong.
valeō, -ēre, -uī, -itum *vi* to be strong; to be able, have the power (to); to be well, fit, healthy; (*fig*) to be powerful, effective, valid; (*force*) to prevail; (*money*) to be worth; (*word*) to mean; **~ apud** have influence over, carry weight with; **~ēre iubeō** say goodbye to; **~ē dīcō** say goodbye; **~eās** away with you!
valēscō, -ere *vi* to grow strong, thrive.
valētūdinārium, -ī *and* **iī** *nt* hospital.
valētūdō, -inis *f* state of health, health; illness.
valgus *adj* bow-legged.
validē *adv* powerfully, very.
validus *adj* strong, powerful, able; sound, healthy; effective.
vallāris *adj* (*decoration*) for scaling a rampart.
vallēs, vallis, -is *f* valley.
vallō, -āre, -āvī, -ātum *vt* to palisade, entrench, fortify.
vallum, -ī *nt* rampart, palisade, entrenchment.
vallus, -ī *m* stake; palisade, rampart; (*comb*) tooth.
valvae, -ārum *fpl* folding door.
vānēscō, -ere *vi* to disappear, pass away.
vānidicus, -ī *m* liar.
vāniloquentia, -ae *f* idle talk.
vāniloquus *adj* untruthful; boastful.
vānitās, -ātis *f* emptiness; falsehood, worthlessness, fickleness; vanity.
vānitūdō, -inis *f* falsehood.
vannus, -ī *f* winnowing fan.
vānus *adj* empty; idle, useless, groundless; false, untruthful, unreliable; conceited.
vapidus *adj* spoilt, corrupt.
vapor, -ōris *m* steam, vapour; heat.
vapōrārium, -ī *and* **iī** *nt* steam pipe.
vapōrō, -āre *vt* to steam, fumigate, heat **♦** *vi* to burn.
vappa, -ae *f* wine that has gone flat; (*person*) good-for-nothing.
vāpulō, -āre *vi* to be flogged, beaten; to be defeated.
variantia, -ae *f* diversity.
variātiō, -ōnis *f* difference.
vāricō, -āre *vi* to straddle.
vāricōsus *adj* varicose.
vāricus *adj* with feet wide apart.
variē *adv* diversely, with varying success.
varietās, -ātis *f* difference, diversity.
variō, -āre, -āvī, -ātum *vt* to diversify, variegate; to make different, change, vary **♦** *vi* to change colour; to differ, vary.
varius *adj* coloured, spotted, variegated; diverse, changeable, various; (*ability*) versatile; (*character*) fickle.
Varius, -ī *m* epic poet (*friend of Vergil and Horace*).
varix, -icis *f* varicose vein.

Varrō, -ōnis *m consul defeated at Cannae; antiquarian writer of Cicero's day.*
Varrōniānus *adj see* **Varrō.**
vārus *adj* knock-kneed; crooked; contrary.
vas, vadis *m* surety, bail.
vās, vāsis (*pl* **vāsa, -ōrum**) *nt* vessel, dish; utensil, implement; (*MIL*) baggage.
vāsārium, -ī *and* **iī** *nt* furnishing allowance (of a governor).
vāsculārius, -ī *and* **iī** *m* metalworker.
vāsculum, -ī *nt* small dish.
vastātiō, -ōnis *f* ravaging.
vastātor, -ōris *m* ravager.
vastē *adv* (*size*) enormously; (*speech*) coarsely.
vastificus *adj* ravaging.
vastitās, -ātis *f* desolation, desert; devastation, destruction.
vastitiēs, -ēī *f* ruin.
vastō, -āre, -āvī, -ātum *vt* to make desolate, denude; to lay waste, ravage.
vastus *adj* empty, desolate, uncultivated; ravaged, devastated; (*appearance*) uncouth, rude; (*size*) enormous, vast.
vāsum *etc see* **vās.**
vātēs, -is *m/f* prophet, prophetess; poet, bard.
Vāticānus *adj* Vatican (*hill on right bank of Tiber*).
vāticinātiō, -ōnis *f* prophesying, prediction.
vāticinātor, -ōris *m* prophet.
vāticinor, -ārī, -ātus *vt, vi* to prophesy; to celebrate in verse; to rave, rant.
vāticinus *adj* prophetic.
-ve *conj* or; either ... or.
vēcordia, -ae *f* senselessness; insanity.
vēcors, -dis *adj* senseless, foolish, mad.
vectīgal, -ālis *nt* tax; honorarium (to a magistrate); income.
vectiō, -ōnis *f* transport.
vectis, -is *m* lever, crowbar; (*door*) bolt, bar.
Vectis, -is *f* Isle of Wight.
vectō, -āre *vt* to carry; (*pass*) to ride.
vector, -ōris *m* carrier; passenger, rider.
vectōrius *adj* transport (*in cpds*).
vectūra, -ae *f* transport; (*payment*) carriage, fare.
vectus *ppp of* **vehō.**
Vediovis, -is = **Vēiovis.**
vegetus *adj* lively, sprightly.
vēgrandis *adj* small.
vehemēns, -entis *adj* impetuous, violent; powerful, strong.
vehementer *adv* violently, eagerly; powerfully, very much.
vehementia, -ae *f* vehemence.
vehiculum, -ī *nt* carriage, cart; (*sea*) vessel.
vehō, -here, -xī, -ctum *vt* to carry, convey; (*pass*) to ride, sail, drive.
Vēiēns, -entis, (-entānus), (**-us**) *adj see* **Vēiī.**
Vēiī, -ōrum *mpl* ancient town in S. Etruria.
Vēiovis, -is *m* ancient Roman god (*anti-Jupiter*).

vel *conj* or, or perhaps; or rather; or else; either ... or ♦ *adv* even, if you like; perhaps; for instance; ~ **māximus** the very greatest.
Vēlābrum, -ī *nt* low ground between Capitol and Palatine hills.
vēlāmen, -inis *nt* covering, garment.
vēlāmentum, -ī *nt* curtain; (*pl*) draped olive branches carried by suppliants.
vēlārium, -ī *and* **iī** *nt* awning.
vēlātī, -ōrum *mpl* supernumerary troops.
vēles, -itis *m* light-armed soldier, skirmisher.
vēlifer, -ī *adj* carrying sail.
vēlificātiō, -ōnis *f* sailing.
vēlificō, -āre *vi* to sail ♦ *vt* to sail through.
vēlificor, -ārī *vi* to sail; (*with dat*) to make an effort to obtain.
Velīnus, -ī *m* a Sabine lake.
vēlitāris *adj* of the light-armed troops.
vēlitātiō, -ōnis *f* skirmishing.
vēlitēs *pl of* **vēles.**
vēlitor, -ārī *vi* to skirmish.
vēlivolus *adj* sail-winged.
velle *infin of* **volō.**
vellicō, -āre *vt* to pinch, pluck, twitch; (*speech*) to taunt, disparage.
vellō, -ere, vellī *and* **vulsī, vulsum** *vt* to pluck, pull, pick; to pluck out, tear up.
vellus, -eris *nt* fleece, pelt; wool; fleecy clouds.
vēlō, -āre, -āvī, -ātum *vt* to cover up, clothe, veil; (*fig*) to conceal.
vēlōcitās, -ātis *f* speed, rapidity.
vēlōciter *adv* rapidly.
vēlōx, -ōcis *adj* fast, quick, rapid.
vēlum, -ī *nt* sail; curtain, awning; **rēmis ~isque** with might and main; ~**a dare** set sail.
velut, velutī *adv* as, just as; for instance; just as if.
vēmēns *etc see* **vehemēns.**
vēna, -ae *f* vein, artery; vein of metal; water course; (*fig*) innermost nature of feelings, talent, strength; ~**ās temptāre** feel the pulse; ~**ās tenēre** have one's finger on the pulse (of).
vēnābulum, -ī *nt* hunting spear.
Venāfrānus *adj see* *n.*
Venāfrum, -ī *nt* Samnite town famous for olive oil.
vēnālicius *adj* for sale ♦ *m* slave dealer.
vēnālis *adj* for sale; bribable ♦ *m* slave offered for sale.
vēnāticus *adj* hunting (*in cpds*).
vēnātiō, -ōnis *f* hunting; a hunt; public show of fighting wild beasts; game.
vēnātor, -ōris *m* hunter.
vēnātōrius *adj* hunter's.
vēnātrīx, -īcis *f* huntress.
vēnātūra, -ae *f* hunting.
vēnātus, -ūs *m* hunting.
vēndibilis *adj* saleable; (*fig*) popular.

Noun declensions and verb conjugations are shown on pp xiii to xxv. The present infinitive ending of a verb shows to which conjugation it belongs: **-āre** = 1st; **-ēre** = 2nd; **-ere** = 3rd and **-īre** = 4th. Irregular verbs are shown on p xxvi

vēnditātiō, -ōnis *f* showing off, advertising.
vēnditātor, -ōris *m* braggart.
vēnditiō, -ōnis *f* sale.
vēnditō, -āre *vt* to try to sell; to praise up,
advertise; **sē ~ ingratiate** oneself (with).
vēnditor, -ōris *m* seller.
vēndō (*pass* **vēneō**), **-ere, -idī, -itum** *vt* to sell;
to betray; to praise up.
venēficium, -ī *and* **iī** *nt* poisoning; sorcery.
venēficus *adj* poisonous; magic ♦ *m* sorcerer
♦ *f* sorceress.
venēnātus *adj* poisonous; magic.
venēnifer, -ī *adj* poisonous.
venēnō, -āre *vt* to poison.
venēnum, -ī *nt* drug, potion; dye; poison;
magic charm; (*fig*) mischief; charm.
vēneō, -īre, -iī, -itum *vi* to be sold.
venerābilis *adj* honoured, venerable.
venerābundus *adj* reverent.
venerātiō, -ōnis *f* respect, reverence.
venerātor, -ōris *m* reverencer.
Venereus, Venerius *adj* of Venus ♦ *m* highest
throw at dice.
veneror, -ārī, -ātus *vt* to worship, revere,
pray to; to honour, respect; to ask for,
entreat.
Venetia, -iae *f* district of the Veneti.
Veneticus *adj see n.*
Venetus *adj* Venetian; (*colour*) blue.
vēnī *perf of* **veniō**.
venia, -ae *f* indulgence, favour, kindness;
permission, leave; pardon, forgiveness;
bonā tuā ~ā by your leave; **bonā ~ā audīre**
give a fair hearing.
vēniī *perf of* **vēneō**.
veniō, -īre, vēnī, ventum *vi* to come; (*fig*) to
fall into, incur, go as far as; **in amīcitiam ~**
make friends (with); **in spem ~** entertain
hopes.
vēnor, -ārī, -ātus *vt, vi* to hunt, chase.
venter, -ris *m* stomach, belly; womb, unborn
child.
ventilātor, -ōris *m* juggler.
ventilō, -āre *vt* to fan, wave, agitate.
ventiō, -ōnis *f* coming.
ventitō, -āre *vi* to keep coming, come
regularly.
ventōsus *adj* windy; like the wind; fickle;
conceited.
ventriculus, -ī *m* belly; (*heart*) ventricle.
ventriōsus *adj* pot-bellied.
ventulus, -ī *m* breeze.
ventus, -ī *m* wind.
vēnūcula, -ae *f* kind of grape.
vēnum, vēnō *for sale.*
vēnumdō (vēnundō), -āre, -edī, -atum *vt* to
sell, put up for sale.
venus, -eris *f* charm, beauty; love, mating.
Venus, -eris *f* goddess of love; planet Venus;
highest throw at dice.
Venusia, -iae *f* town in Apulia (*birthplace of
Horace*).
Venusīnus *adj see* **Venusia.**

venustās, -ātis *f* charm, beauty.
venustē *adv* charmingly.
venustulus *adj* charming little.
venustus *adj* charming, attractive, beautiful.
vēpallidus *adj* very pale.
veprēcula, -ae *f* little brier bush.
veprēs, -is *m* thornbush, bramblebush.
vēr, vēris *nt* spring; **~ sacrum** offerings of
firstlings.
vērātrum, -ī *nt* hellebore.
vērāx, -ācis *adj* truthful.
verbēna, -ae *f* vervain; (*pl*) *sacred boughs
carried by heralds or priests.*
verber, -is *nt* lash, scourge; (*missile*) strap; (*pl*)
flogging, strokes.
verberābilis *adj* deserving a flogging.
verberātiō, -ōnis *f* punishment.
verbereus *adj* deserving a flogging.
verberō, -āre, -āvī, -ātum *vt* to flog, beat,
lash.
verberō, -ōnis *m* scoundrel.
verbōsē *adv* verbosely.
verbōsus *adj* wordy.
verbum, -ī *nt* word; saying, expression; (*GRAM*)
verb; (*pl*) language, talk; **~ ē (dē, prō) ~ō**
literally; **ad ~um** word for word; **~ī causa
(grātiā)** for instance; **~ō** orally; briefly; **~a
dare** cheat, fool; **~a facere** talk; **meīs ~īs** in
my name.
vērē *adv* really, truly, correctly.
verēcundē *adv see adj.*
verēcundia, -ae *f* modesty, shyness;
reverence, dread; shame.
verēcundor, -ārī *vi* to be bashful, feel shy.
verēcundus *adj* modest, shy, bashful.
verendus *adj* venerable.
vereor, -ērī, -itus *vt, vi* to fear, be afraid; to
revere, respect.
verētrum, -ī *nt* the private parts.
Vergiliae, -ārum *fpl* the Pleiads.
Vergilius, -ī *m* Vergil, Virgil (*famous epic
poet*).
vergō, -ere *vt* to turn, incline ♦ *vi* to turn,
incline, decline; (*place*) to face.
vēridicus *adj* truthful.
vērī similis *adj* probable.
vērī similitūdō, -inis *f* probability.
vēritās, -ātis *f* truth, truthfulness; reality,
real life; (*character*) integrity; (*language*)
etymology.
veritus *ppa of* **vereor.**
vermiculātus *adj* inlaid with wavy lines,
mosaic.
vermiculus, -ī *m* grub.
vermina, -um *ntpl* stomach pains.
vermis, -is *m* worm.
verna, -ae *f* slave born in his master's home.
vernāculus *adj* of home-born slaves; native.
vernīlis *adj* slavish; (*remark*) smart.
vernīliter *adv* slavishly.
vernō, -āre *vi* to bloom, be spring-like; to be
young.
vernula, -ae *f* young home-born slave; native.

vērnus–vetustās

vērnus *adj* of spring.

vērō *adv* in fact, assuredly; (*confirming*) certainly, yes; (*climax*) indeed; (*adversative*) but in fact; **minimē ~** certainly not.

Vērōna, -ae *f* town in N. Italy (*birthplace of Catullus*).

Vērōnēnsis *adj see* **Vērōna**.

verpus, -ī *m* circumcised man.

verrēs, -is *m* boar.

Verrēs, -is *m* praetor prosecuted by Cicero.

Verrīnus *adj* boar's, pork (*in cpds*).

Verrius *and* **īnus** *adj see n*.

verrō, -rere, -rī, -sum *vt* to sweep, scour; to sweep away, carry off.

verrūca, -ae *f* wart; (*fig*) slight blemish.

verrūcōsus *adj* warty.

verruncō, -āre *vi* to turn out successfully.

versābundus *adj* rotating.

versātilis *adj* revolving; versatile.

versicolor, -ōris *adj* of changing *or* various colours.

versiculus, -ī *m* short line; (*pl*) unpretentious verses.

versificātor, -ōris *m* versifier.

versipellis *adj* of changed appearance; crafty ♦ *m* werewolf.

versō, -āre, -āvī, -ātum *vt* to keep turning, wind, twist; (*fig*) to upset, disturb, ruin; (*mind*) to ponder, consider.

versor, -ārī, -ātus *vi* to live, be, be situated; to be engaged (in), be busy (with).

versum *adv* turned, in the direction.

versūra, -ae *f* borrowing to pay a debt; loan.

versus *ppp of* **vertō** ♦ *adv* turned, in the direction.

versus, -ūs *m* line, row; verse; (*dance*) step.

versūtē *adv* craftily.

versūtiae, -ārum *fpl* tricks.

versūtiloquus *adj* sly.

versūtus *adj* clever; crafty, deceitful.

vertex, -icis *m* whirlpool, eddy; whirlwind; crown of the head, head; top, summit; (*sky*) pole.

verticōsus *adj* eddying, swirling.

vertīgō, -inis *f* turning round; dizziness.

vertō, -tere, -tī, -sum *vt* to turn; to turn over, invert; to turn round; to turn into, change, exchange; (*cause*) to ascribe, impute; (*language*) to translate; (*war*) to overthrow, destroy; (*pass*) to be (in), be engaged (in) ♦ *vi* to turn; to change; to turn out; **in fugam ~** put to flight; **terga ~** flee; **solum ~** emigrate; **vitiō ~** blame; **annō ~tente** in the course of a year.

Vertumnus, -ī *m* god of seasons.

verū, -ūs *nt* spit; javelin.

vērum *adv* truly, yes; but actually; but, yet; **~ tamen** nevertheless.

vērum, -ī *nt* truth, reality; right; **~ī similis** probable.

vērus *adj* true, real, actual; truthful; right,

reasonable.

verūtum, -ī *nt* javelin.

verūtus *adj* armed with the javelin.

vervēx, -ēcis *m* wether.

vēsānia, -ae *f* madness.

vēsāniēns, -entis *adj* raging.

vēsānus *adj* mad, insane; furious, raging.

vescor, -ī *vi* (*with abl*) to feed, eat; to enjoy.

vescus *adj* little, feeble; corroding.

vēsīca, -ae *f* bladder; purse; football.

vēsīcula, -ae *f* small bladder, blister.

vespa, -ae *f* wasp.

Vespasiānus, -ī *m* Roman emperor.

vesper, -is *and* **ī** *m* evening; supper; evening star; west; **~e, ~ī** in the evening.

vespera, -ae *f* evening.

vesperāscō, -ere *vi* to become evening, get late.

vespertīliō, -ōnis *m* bat.

vespertīnus *adj* evening (*in cpds*), in the evening; western.

vesperūgō, -inis *f* evening star.

Vesta, -ae *f* Roman goddess of the hearth.

Vestālis *adj* Vestal ♦ *f* virgin priestess of Vesta.

vester, -rī *adj* your, yours.

vestibulum, -ī *nt* forecourt, entrance.

vestīgium, -ī *and* **iī** *nt* footstep, footprint, track; (*fig*) trace, sign, vestige; (*time*) moment, instant; **ē ~ī** instantly.

vestīgō, -āre, -āvī, -ātum *vt* to track, trace, search for, discover.

vestīmentum, -ī *nt* clothes.

vestiō, -īre, -iī, -ītum *vt* to clothe, dress; to cover, adorn.

vestipica, -ae *f* wardrobe woman.

vestis, -is *f* clothes, dress; coverlet, tapestry, blanket; (*snake*) slough; **~em mūtāre** change one's clothes; go into mourning.

vestispica *etc see* **vestipica**.

vestītus, -ūs *m* clothes, dress; covering; **mūtāre ~um** go into mourning; **redīre ad suum ~um** come out of mourning.

Vesuvius, -ī *m* the volcano Vesuvius.

veterānus *adj* veteran.

veterāscō, -scere, -vī *vi* to grow old.

veterātor, -ōris *m* expert, old hand; sly fox.

veterātōriē *adv see* **veterātōrius**.

veterātōrius *adj* crafty.

veterīnus *adj* of burden ♦ *f and* *ntpl* beasts of burden.

veternōsus *adj* lethargic, drowsy.

veternus, -ī *m* lethargy, drowsiness.

vetitus *ppp of* **vetō** ♦ *nt* prohibition.

vetō, -āre, -uī, -itum *vt* to forbid, prohibit, oppose; (*tribune*) to protest.

vetulus *adj* little old, poor old.

vetus, -eris *adj* old, former ♦ *mpl* the ancients ♦ *fpl* the old shops (*in the Forum*) ♦ *ntpl* antiquity, tradition.

vetustās, -ātis *f* age, long standing; antiquity;

great age, future age.
vetustus *adj* old, ancient; old-fashioned.
vexāmen, -inis *nt* shaking.
vexātiō, -ōnis *f* shaking; trouble, distress.
vexātor, -ōris *m* troubler, opponent.
vexī *perf of* **vehō**.
vexillārius, -ī *and* **iī** *m* standard-bearer,
     ensign; (*pl*) special reserve of veterans.
vexillum, -ī *nt* standard, flag; company, troop;
     ~ **prōpōnere** hoist the signal for battle.
vexō, -āre, -āvī, -ātum *vt* to shake, toss,
     trouble, distress, injure, attack.
via, -ae *f* road, street, way; journey, march;
     passage; (*fig*) way, method, fashion; the
     right way; ~**ā** properly; **inter ~ās** on the way.
viālis *adj* of the highways.
viārius *adj* for the upkeep of roads.
viāticātus *adj* provided with travelling
     money.
viāticus *adj* for a journey ♦ *nt* travelling
     allowance; (*MIL*) prizemoney, savings.
viātor, -ōris *m* traveller; (*law*) summoner.
vībīx, -īcis *f* weal.
vibrō, -āre, -āvī, -ātum *vt* to wave, shake,
     brandish, hurl, launch ♦ *vi* to shake, quiver,
     vibrate; to shimmer, sparkle.
vīburnum, -ī *nt* wayfaring-tree *or* guelder
     rose.
vīcānus *adj* village (*in cpds*) ♦ *mpl* villagers.
Vica Pota, -ae, -ae *f* goddess of victory.
vicārius *adj* substituted ♦ *m* substitute, proxy;
     underslave.
vīcātim *adv* from street to street; in villages.
vice (*with gen*) on account of; like.
vicem in turn; (*with gen*) instead of; on
     account of; like; **tuam** ~ on your account.
vīcēnārius *adj* of twenty.
vīcēnī, -ōrum *adj* twenty each, in twenties.
vicēs *pl of* **vicis**.
vīcēsimānī, -ōrum *mpl* men of the twentieth
     legion.
vīcēsimārius *adj* derived from the 5 per cent tax.
vīcēsimus *adj* twentieth ♦ *f* a 5 per cent tax.
vīcī *perf of* **vincō**.
vicia, -ae *f* vetch.
vīciēns *and* **ēs** *adv* twenty times.
vīcīnālis *adj* neighbouring.
vīcīnia, -ae *f* neighbourhood, nearness.
vīcīnitās, -ātis *f* neighbourhood, nearness.
vīcīnus *adj* neighbouring, nearby; similar,
     kindred ♦ *m/f* neighbour ♦ *nt* neighbour-
     hood.
vicis *gen* (*acc* **-em**, *abl* **-e**) *f* interchange,
     alternation, succession; recompense,
     retaliation; fortune, changing conditions;
     duty, function, place; **in ~em** in turn,
     mutually.
vicissim *adv* in turn, again.
vicissitūdō, -inis *f* interchange, alternation.
victima, -ae *f* victim, sacrifice.
victimārius, -ī *and* **iī** *m* assistant at sacrifices.
victitō, -āre *vi* to live, subsist.
victor, -ōris *m* conqueror, victor, winner ♦ *adj*

victorious.
victōria, -ae *f* victory.
victōriātus, -ūs *m* silver coin stamped with
     Victory.
Victōriola, -ae *f* little statue of Victory.
victrīx, -īcis *f* conqueror ♦ *adj* victorious.
victus *ppp of* **vincō**.
vīctus, -ūs *m* sustenance, livelihood; way of
     life.
vīculus, -ī *m* hamlet.
vīcus, -ī *m* (*city*) quarter, street; (*country*)
     village, estate.
vidēlicet *adv* clearly, evidently; (*ironical*) of
     course; (*explaining*) namely.
videō, -ēre, vīdī, vīsum *vt* to see, look at;
     (*mind*) to observe, be aware, know; to
     consider, think over; to see to, look out for;
     to live to see; (*pass*) to seem, appear; to seem
     right, be thought proper; **mē ~ē** rely on me;
     vīderit let him see to it; **mihi ~eor esse** I think
     I am; **sī (tibi) vidētur** if you like.
viduāta *adj* widowed.
viduitās, -ātis *f* bereavement, want;
     widowhood.
vīdulus, -ī *m* trunk, box.
viduō, -āre *vt* to bereave.
viduus *adj* bereft, bereaved; unmarried; (*with*
     abl) without ♦ *f* widow; spinster.
Vienna, -ae *f* town in Gaul on the Rhone.
viētus *adj* shrivelled.
vigeō, -ēre, -uī *vi* to thrive, flourish.
vigēscō, -ere *vi* to begin to flourish, become
     lively.
vīgēsimus *etc see* **vīcēsimus**.
vigil, -is *adj* awake, watching, alert ♦ *m*
     watchman, sentinel; (*pl*) the watch, police.
vigilāns, -antis *pres p of* **vigilō** ♦ *adj* watchful.
vigilanter *adv* vigilantly.
vigilantia, -ae *f* wakefulness; vigilance.
vigilāx, -ācis *adj* watchful.
vigilia, -ae *f* lying awake, sleeplessness;
     keeping watch, guard; a watch; the watch,
     sentries; vigil; vigilance.
vigilō, -āre, -āvī, -ātum *vi* to remain awake;
     to keep watch; to be vigilant ♦ *vt* to spend
     awake, make while awake at night.
vīgintī *num* twenty.
vīgintīvirātus, -ūs *m* membership of a board of
     twenty.
vīgintīvirī, -ōrum *mpl* a board *or* commission
     of twenty men.
vigor, -ōris *m* energy, vigour.
vīlica, -ae *f* wife of a steward.
vīlicō, -āre *vi* to be an overseer.
vīlicus, -ī *m* overseer, manager of an estate,
     steward.
vīlis *adj* cheap; worthless, poor, mean,
     common.
vīlitās, -ātis *f* cheapness, low price;
     worthlessness.
vīliter *adv* cheaply.
vīlla, -ae *f* country house, villa.
vīllic- *etc see* **vīlic-**.

villōsus *adj* hairy, shaggy.

vīllula, -ae *f* small villa.

vīllum, -ī *nt* a drop of wine.

villus, -ī *m* hair, fleece; (*cloth*) nap.

vīmen, -inis *nt* osier; basket.

vīmentum, -ī *nt* osier.

Vīminālis *adj* Viminal (*hill of Rome*).

vīmineus *adj* of osiers, wicker.

vīnāceus *adj* grape (*in cpds*).

Vīnālia, -ium *ntpl* Wine festival.

vīnārius *adj* of wine, wine (*in cpds*) ♦ *m* vintner ♦ *nt* wine flask.

vincibilis *adj* easily won.

vinciō, -cīre, -xī, -ctum *vt* to bind, fetter; to encircle; (*fig*) to confine, restrain, envelop, attach.

vinclum *nt see* **vinculum**.

vincō, -ere, vīcī, victum *vt* to conquer, defeat, subdue; to win, prevail, be successful; (*fig*) to surpass, excel; (*argument*) to convince, refute, prove conclusively; (*life*) to outlive.

vinctus *ppp of* **vinciō**.

vinculum, -ī *nt* bond, fetter, chain; (*pl*) prison.

vīndēmia, -ae *f* vintage grape harvest.

vīndēmiātor, -ōris *m* vintager.

vīndēmiola, -ae *f* small vintage.

Vīndēmitor, -ōris *m* the Vintager (*a star in Virgo*).

vindex, -icis *m* champion, protector; liberator; avenger ♦ *adj* avenging.

vindicātiō, -ōnis *f* punishment of offences.

vindiciae, -ārum *fpl* legal claim; ~**ās ab lībertāte in servitūtem dare** condemn a free person to slavery.

vindicō, -āre, -āvī, -ātum *vt* to lay claim to; to claim, appropriate; to liberate, protect, champion; to avenge, punish; **in lībertātem ~** emancipate.

vindicta, -ae *f* rod used in manumitting a slave; defence, deliverance; revenge, punishment.

vīnea, -ae *f* vineyard; vine; (*MIL*) penthouse (for besiegers).

vīnētum, -ī *nt* vineyard.

vīnitor, -ōris *m* vine-dresser.

vinnulus *adj* delightful.

vīnolentia, -ae *f* wine drinking.

vīnolentus *adj* drunk.

vīnōsus *adj* fond of wine, drunken.

vīnum, -ī *nt* wine.

vinxī *perf of* **vinciō**.

viola, -ae *f* violet; stock.

violābilis *adj* vulnerable.

violāceus *adj* violet.

violārium, -ī *and* **iī** *nt* violet bed.

violārius, -ī *and* **iī** *m* dyer of violet.

violātiō, -ōnis *f* desecration.

violātor, -ōris *m* violator, desecrator.

violēns, -entis *adj* raging, vehement.

violenter *adv* violently, furiously.

violentia, -ae *f* violence, impetuosity.

violentus *adj* violent, impetuous, boisterous.

violō, -āre, -āvī, -ātum *vt* to do violence to, outrage, violate; (*agreement*) to break.

vīpera, -ae *f* viper, adder, snake.

vīpereus *adj* snake's, serpent's.

vīperīnus *adj* snake's, serpent's.

vir, virī *m* man; grown man; brave man, hero; husband; (*MIL*) footsoldier.

virāgō, -inis *f* heroine, warrior maid.

virecta, -ōrum *ntpl* grassy sward.

vireō, -ēre, -uī *vi* to be green; (*fig*) to be fresh, flourish.

vīrēs *pl of* **vīs**.

virēscō, -ere *vi* to grow green.

virga, -ae *f* twig; graft; rod, staff, walking stick, wand; (*colour*) stripe.

virgātor, -ōris *m* flogger.

virgātus *adj* made of osiers; striped.

virgētum, -ī *nt* thicket of osiers.

virgeus *adj* of brushwood.

virgidēmia, -ae *f* crop of flogging.

virginālis *adj* maidenly, of maids.

virginārius *adj* of maids.

virgineus *adj* maidenly, virgin, of virgins.

virginitās, -ātis *f* maidenhood.

virgō, -inis *f* maid, virgin; young woman, girl; constellation Virgo; a Roman aqueduct.

virgula, -ae *f* wand.

virgulta, -ōrum *ntpl* thicket, shrubbery; cuttings, slips.

virguncula, -ae *f* little girl.

viridāns, -antis *adj* green.

viridārium, -ī *and* **iī** *nt* plantation, garden.

viridis *adj* green; fresh, young, youthful ♦ *ntpl* greenery.

viriditās, -ātis *f* verdure, greenness; freshness.

viridor, -ārī *vi* to become green.

virīlis *adj* male, masculine; man's, adult; manly, brave, bold; ~ **pars** one's individual part or duty; **prō ~ī parte, portiōne** to the best of one's ability.

virīlitās, -ātis *f* manhood.

virīliter *adv* manfully.

virītim *adv* individually, separately.

vīrōsus *adj* slimy; rank.

virtūs, -ūtis *f* manhood, full powers; strength, courage, ability, worth; (*MIL*) valour, prowess, heroism; (*moral*) virtue; (*things*) excellence, worth.

vīrus, -ī *nt* slime; poison; offensive smell; salt taste.

vīs (*acc* **vim**, *abl* **vī**, *pl* **vīrēs**) *f* power, force, strength; violence, assault; quantity, amount; (*mind*) energy, vigour; (*word*) meaning, import; (*pl*) strength; (*MIL*) troops; **per vim** forcibly; **dē vī damnārī** be convicted of assault; **prō vīribus** with all one's might.

vīs 2nd pers of **volō**.

viscātus adj limed.

viscerātiō, -ōnis f public distribution of meat.

viscō, -āre vt to make sticky.

viscum, -ī nt mistletoe; bird lime.

viscus, -eris (usu pl **-era, -erum**) nt internal organs; flesh; womb, child; (fig) heart, bowels.

vīsendus adj worth seeing.

vīsiō, -ōnis f apparition; idea.

vīsitō, -āre vt to see often; to visit.

vīsō, -ere, -ī, -um vt to look at, survey; to see to; to go and see, visit.

Visurgis, -is m river Weser.

vīsus ppp of **video** ♦ nt vision.

vīsus, -ūs m sight, the faculty of seeing; a sight, vision.

vīta, -ae f life, livelihood; way of life; career, biography.

vītābilis adj undesirable.

vītābundus adj avoiding, taking evasive action.

vītālis adj of life, vital ♦ nt subsistence ♦ ntpl vitals.

vītāliter adv with life.

vītātiō, -ōnis f avoidance.

Vitellius, -ī m Roman emperor in AD 69.

Vitellius, -iānus adj see n.

vitellus, -ī m little calf; (egg) yolk.

vīteus adj of the vine.

vīticula, -ae f little vine.

vītigenus adj produced from the vine.

vitilēna, -ae f procuress.

vitiō, -āre, -āvī, -ātum vt to spoil, corrupt, violate; to falsify.

vitiōsē adv badly, defectively.

vitiōsitās, -ātis f vice.

vitiōsus adj faulty, corrupt; wicked, depraved; ~ **cōnsul** a consul whose election had a religious flaw in it.

vītis, -is f vine; vine branch; centurion's staff, centurionship.

vītisator, -ōris m vine planter.

vitium, -ī and **iī** nt fault, flaw, defect; (moral) failing, offence, vice; (religion) flaw in the auspices.

vītō, -āre, -āvī, -ātum vt to avoid, evade, shun.

vītor, -ōris m basket maker, cooper.

vitreus adj of glass; glassy ♦ ntpl glassware.

vitricus, -ī m stepfather.

vitrum, -ī nt glass; woad.

vitta, -ae f headband, sacrificial fillet.

vittātus adj wearing a fillet.

vitula, -ae f (of cow) calf.

vitulīnus adj of veal ♦ f veal.

vītulor, -ārī vi to hold a celebration.

vitulus, -ī m calf; foal; ~ **marīnus** seal.

vituperābilis adj blameworthy.

vituperātiō, -ōnis f blame, censure; scandalous conduct.

vituperātor, -ōris m critic.

vituperō, -āre vt to find fault with, disparage; (omen) to spoil.

vīvārium, -ī and **iī** nt fishpond, game preserve.

vīvātus adj animated.

vīvāx, -ācis adj long-lived; lasting; (sulphur) inflammable.

vīvēscō, -ere vi to grow, become active.

vīvidus adj full of life; (art) true to life, vivid; (mind) lively.

vīvirādīx, -īcis f a rooted cutting, layer.

vīvīscō etc see **vīvēscō**.

vīvō, -vere, -xī, -ctum vi to live, be alive; to enjoy life; (fame) to last, to be remembered; (with abl) to live on; ~**ve** farewell!; ~**xērunt** they are dead.

vīvus adj alive, living; (light) burning; (rock) natural; (water) running; ~**ō videntīque** before his very eyes; **mē** ~**ō** as long as I live, in my lifetime; **ad** ~**um resecāre** cut to the quick; **dē** ~**ō dētrahere** take out of capital.

vix adv with difficulty, hardly, scarcely.

vixdum adv hardly, as yet.

vīxī perf of **vīvō**.

vocābulum, -ī nt name, designation; (GRAM) noun.

vōcālis adj speaking, singing, tuneful ♦ f vowel.

vōcāmen, -inis nt name.

vocātiō, -ōnis f invitation; (law) summons.

vocātus, -ūs m summons, call.

vōciferātiō, -ōnis f loud cry, outcry.

vōciferor, -ārī vt to cry out loud, shout.

vocitō, -āre, -āvī, -ātum vt to usually call; to shout.

vocīvus etc see **vacīvus**.

vocō, -āre, -āvī, -ātum vt to call, summon; to call, name; (gods) to call upon; (guest) to invite; (MIL) to challenge; (fig) to bring (into some condition or plight); ~ **dē** name after; ~**in dubium** ~ call in question; **in iūdicium** ~ call to account.

vōcula, -ae f weak voice; soft tone; gossip.

volaema ntpl kind of large pear.

Volaterrae, -ārum fpl old Etruscan town (now Volterra).

Volaterrānus adj see n.

volāticus adj winged; fleeting, inconstant.

volātilis adj winged; swift; fleeting.

volātus, -ūs m flight.

Volcānius adj see n.

Volcānus, -ī m Vulcan (god of fire); fire.

volēns, -entis pres p of **volō** ♦ adj willing, glad, favourable; **mihi** ~**entī est** it is acceptable to me.

volg- etc see **vulg-**.

volitō, -āre vi to fly about, flutter; to hurry, move quickly; (fig) to hover, soar; to get excited.

voln- etc see **vuln-**.

volō, -āre, -āvī, -ātum vi to fly; to speed.

volō, velle, voluī vt to wish, want; to be

willing; to will, purpose, determine; (*opinion*) to hold, maintain; (*word, action*) to mean; ~ **dīcere** I mean; **bene** ~ like; **male** ~ dislike; **ōrātum tē** ~ I beg you; **paucīs tē** ~ a word with you!; **numquid vīs?** (*before leaving*) is there anything else?; **quid sibi vult?** what does he mean?; what is he driving at?; **velim faciās** please do it; **vellem fēcissēs** I wish you had done it.

volōnēs, -um *mpl* volunteers.

volpēs *etc see* **vulpēs**.

Volscī, -ōrum *mpl people in S. Latium.*

Volscus *adj* Volscian.

volsella, -ae *f* tweezers.

volsus *ppp of* **vellō**.

volt, voltis *older forms of* **vult, vultis**.

Voltumna, -ae *f patron goddess of Etruria.*

voltus *etc see* **vultus**.

volūbilis *adj* spinning, revolving; (*fortune*) fickle; (*speech*) fluent.

volubilitās, -ātis *f* whirling motion; roundness; fluency; inconstancy.

volūbiliter *adv* fluently.

volucer, -ris *adj* winged; flying, swift; fleeting.

volucris, -is *f* bird; insect.

volūmen, -inis *nt* roll, book; coil, eddy, fold.

voluntārius *adj* voluntary ♦ *mpl* volunteers.

voluntās, -ātis *f* will, wish, inclination; attitude, goodwill; last will, testament; **suā ~āte** of one's own accord; **ad ~ātem** with the consent (of).

volup *adv* agreeably, to one's satisfaction.

voluptābilis *adj* agreeable.

voluptās, -ātis *f* pleasure, enjoyment; (*pl*) entertainments, sports.

voluptuārius *adj* pleasureable, agreeable; voluptuous.

volūtābrum, -ī *nt* wallowing place.

volūtātiō, -ōnis *f* wallowing.

volūtō, -āre *vt* to roll about, turn over; (*mind*) to occupy, engross; (*thought*) to ponder, think over; (*pass*) to wallow, flounder.

volūtus *ppp of* **volvō**.

volva, -ae *f* womb; (*dish*) sow's womb.

volvō, -vere, -vī, -ūtum *vt* to roll, turn round; to roll along; (*air*) to breathe; (*book*) to open; (*circle*) to form; (*thought*) to ponder, reflect on; (*time*) to roll on; (*trouble*) to undergo; (*pass*) to roll, revolve ♦ *vi* to revolve, elapse.

vōmer, -eris *m* ploughshare.

vomica, -ae *f* sore, ulcer, abscess, boil.

vōmis *etc see* **vōmer**.

vomitiō, -ōnis *f* vomiting.

vomitus, -ūs *m* vomiting, vomit.

vomō, -ere, -uī, -itum *vt* to vomit, throw up;

to emit, discharge.

vorāgō, -inis *f* abyss, chasm, depth.

vorāx, -ācis *adj* greedy, ravenous; consuming.

vorō, -āre, -āvī, -ātum *vt* to swallow, devour; (*sea*) to swallow up; (*reading*) to devour.

vors-, vort- *etc see* **vers-, vert-** *etc.*

vōs *pron* you.

Vosegus, -ī *m* Vosges mountains.

voster *etc see* **vester**.

vōtīvus *adj* votive, promised in a vow.

votō *etc see* **vetō**.

vōtum, -ī *nt* vow, prayer; votive offering; wish, longing; **~ī damnārī** have one's prayer granted.

vōtus *ppp of* **voveō**.

voveō, -ēre, vōvī, vōtum *vt* to vow, promise solemnly; to dedicate; to wish.

vōx, vōcis *f* voice; sound, cry, call; word, saying, expression; accent; **unā vōce** unanimously.

Vulcānus *see* **Volcānus**.

vulgāris *adj* common, general.

vulgāriter *adv* in the common fashion.

vulgātor, -ōris *m* betrayer.

vulgātus *adj* common; generally known, notorious.

vulgivagus *adj* roving; inconstant.

vulgō *adv* publicly, commonly, usually, everywhere.

vulgō, -āre, -āvī, -ātum *vt* to make common, spread; to publish, divulge, broadcast; to prostitute; to level down.

vulgus, -ī *nt* (*occ m*) the mass of the people, the public; crowd, herd; rabble, populace.

vulnerātiō, -ōnis *f* wounding, injury.

vulnerō, -āre, -āvī, -ātum *vt* to wound, hurt; to damage.

vulnificus *adj* wounding, dangerous.

vulnus, -eris *nt* wound, injury; (*things*) damage, hole; (*fig*) blow, misfortune, pain.

vulpēcula, -ae *f* little fox.

vulpēs, -is *f* fox; (*fig*) cunning.

vulsī *perf of* **vellō**.

vulsus *ppp of* **vellō**.

vulticulus, -ī *m* a mere look (from).

vultum *etc see* **vultus**.

vultuōsus *adj* affected.

vultur, -is *m* vulture.

vulturius, -ī and iī *m* vulture, bird of prey; (*dice*) an unlucky throw.

Vulturnus, -ī *m* river in Campania.

vultus, -ūs *m* look, expression (*esp in* the eyes); face; (*things*) appearance.

vulva *etc see* **volva**.

Noun declensions and verb conjugations are shown on pp xiii to xxv. The present infinitive ending of a verb shows to which conjugation it belongs: **-āre** = 1st; **-ēre** = 2nd; **-ere** = 3rd and **-īre** = 4th. Irregular verbs are shown on p xxvi

X, x

Xanthippē, -ēs *f wife of Socrates.*
Xanthus, -ī *m river of Troy (identified with Scamander); river of Lycia.*
xenium, -ī *and* **iī** *nt present.*

Xenocratēs, -is *m disciple of Plato.*
Xenophanēs, -is *m early Greek philosopher.*
Xenophōn, -ontis *m famous Greek historian.*
Xenophontēus *adj see n.*
xērampelinae, -ārum *fpl* dark-coloured clothes.
Xerxēs, -is *m Persian king defeated at Salamis.*
xiphiās, -ae *m* swordfish.
xystum, -ī *nt,* **xystus, -ī** *m* open colonnade, walk, avenue.

Z, z

Zacynthius *adj see n.*
Zacynthus (-os), -ī *f* island off W. Greece (*now* Zante).
Zama, -ae *f* town in Numidia (*where Scipio defeated Hannibal*).
Zamēnsis *adj see n.*
zāmia, -ae *f* harm.
Zanclaeus *and* **ēius** *adj see n.*
Zanclē, -ēs *f old name of Messana.*
zēlotypus *adj* jealous.

Zēnō *and* **ōn, -ōnis** *m founder of Stoicism; a philosopher of Elea; an Epicurean teacher of Cicero.*
Zephyrītis, -idis *f* Arsinoe (*queen of Egypt*).
Zephyrus, -ī *m* west wind, zephyr; wind.
Zēthus, -ī *m brother of Amphion.*
Zeuxis, -is *and* **idis** *m famous Greek painter.*
zmaragdus *etc see* **smaragdus.**
Zmyrna *etc see* **Smyrna.**
zōdiacus, -ī *m* zodiac.
zōna, -ae *f* belt, girdle; (*GEOG*) zone; (*ASTRO*) Orion's Belt.
zōnārius *adj* of belts; **sector ~** cutpurse ♦ *m* belt maker.
zōnula, -ae *f* little belt.
zōthēca, -ae *f* private room.
zōthēcula, -ae *f* cubicle.

ROMAN LIFE AND CULTURE

KEY EVENTS IN ROMAN HISTORY

B.C.

753	Foundation of Rome. Romulus became first king.
600-510	Rome ruled by Etruscan kings.
510	Expulsion of Tarquin and republic established.
507	Consecration of Temple of Jupiter on Capitol.
451	Code of Twelve Tables laid basis of Roman law.
390	Gauls sacked Rome.
367	Lex Liciniae Sextiae; plebeians allowed to be consul.
354	Treaty with Samnites.
343-341	First Samnite war; Romans occupied northern Campania.
340-338	Latin War; separate treaties made with Latins.
327-304	Second Samnite war; Rome increased influence in southern Italy.
321	Samnites defeated Romans at Caudine Forks; truce.
312	Appian Way, first Roman road, built.
298-290	Third Samnite war; Rome now all-powerful in southern Italy.
287	Hortensian Law; People's Assembly became a law-making body.
282-272	Wars with Tarentum and King Pyrrhus of Epirus.
270	Whole peninsula under Roman power.
264-241	First Punic war; Rome defended Greek cities in Sicily.
260	Fleet built; first naval victory at Mylae against Carthaginians.
241	Roman victory over Carthage secured Sicily, source of corn supply.
226	River Ebro treaty; Carthage should not cross into northern Spain.
218-201	Second Punic war against Hannibal.
216	Rome defeated at Battle of Cannae.
214-205	First Macedonian war with Philip V.
202	Scipio defeated Hannibal at Zama.
201	Peace concluded with Carthage; Rome now controlled the western Mediterranean.
200-196	Second Macedonian war; freedom of Greece proclaimed.
172-168	Third Macedonian war; Perseus crushed at Pydna.
148	Macedonia became a Roman province.
146	Carthage destroyed; Corinth destroyed.
133	Tiberius Gracchus became tribune; his assassination caused class conflict.
123-122	Gaius Gracchus carried out political/economic reforms.
121	Gaius was killed.
111-105	Marius and Sulla conducted war against Jugurtha of Numidia.
91-89	Social war between Rome and allies.
89-85	War with Mithridates VI of Pontus.
83-82	Civil war between Sulla and Marius; Sulla captured Rome.
81-79	Sulla, dictator, restored constitution, introduced reforms.
78	Death of Sulla.

77-72	Pompey fought Sertorius in Spain.
73-71	Spartacus' slave revolt.
70	Pompey and Crassus joint consuls; tribunes restored.
67	End of war against Mithridates; pirates controlled by Pompey.
63	Cicero suppressed Catiline's conspiracy.
60	First Triumvirate (Caesar, Pompey, Crassus) was formed.
58-51	Caesar conquered Gaul.
53	Battle of Carrhae; Rome defeated by Parthians; Crassus killed.
49	Caesar crossed Rubicon; civil war with Pompey began.
48	Pompey defeated by Caesar at Pharsalus; Caesar became dictator.
44	Caesar assassinated; Antony sought revenge against conspirators.
43	Second Triumvirate (Antony, Octavian, Lepidus).
42	Battle of Philippi; Triumvirate defeated Brutus and Cassius.
41-40	Antony and Octavian divided territory.
33-32	Rupture between Antony and Octavian.
31	Battle of Actium; Octavian defeated Antony and Cleopatra at sea.
27	Octavian returned powers to Senate; received name Augustus.
18	Julian laws promoted morality, condemned adultery, regulated divorce.
12	Augustus became Pontifex Maximus, head of state religion.
2	Augustus became 'pater patriae', father of his country; apex of his power.

A.D.

4	Tiberius adopted as Augustus' heir.
6	Annexation of Judaea.
9	Varus' three legions destroyed in Germany.
14	Death of Augustus.
14-37	Tiberius emperor; efficient administrator but unpopular.
14-16	Germanicus' successful campaign in Germany.
19	Germanicus died mysteriously; funeral at Antioch.
21-22	Sefanus organized Praetorian Guard.
26-31	Sefanus powerful in Rome; executed in 31.
37-41	Caligula emperor; cruel and tyrannical, was murdered by a tribune.
41-54	Claudius emperor; conquered Britain; showed political judgement.
57-68	Nero emperor; great fire (64); Christians persecuted.
68-69	Year of four emperors - Galba, Otho, Vitellius, Vespasian.
69-79	Vespasian began Flavian dynasty. Colosseum built.
70	Titus, Vespasian's son, captured Jerusalem, destroyed the Temple.
79-81	Titus emperor. Vesuvius erupted (79), Pompeii destroyed.
81-96	Domitian emperor. Border built in Germany; period ended in terror.
96-98	Nerva emperor after Domitian's assassination.
98-117	Trajan emperor - conqueror of Dacia and Parthian empire.
117-138	Hadrian, cultured traveller, soldier and administrator of empire.
122	Hadrian's Wall built between Solway and Tyne.
138-161	Antoninus Pius emperor; orderly, peaceful rule.
141-143	Antonine's Wall built between Forth and Clyde.
161-180	Marcus Aurelius emperor; Commodus, his son, shared power (177-180).

162	War with Parthia.
175-180	War against Germans on the Danube.
180-192	Commodus emperor.
193-211	Septimius Severus became emperor after crisis; died in Britain. Authorized special benefits for army.
211-217	Deterioration under criminal rule of Caracalla.
212	All free men of the empire became citizens.
284-305	Diocletian and Maximian co-emperors, empire divided into 12 dioceses. Prices imposed throughout empire.
303	Christians persecuted by Diocletian.
312	Constantine's victory at Milvian Bridge gave him Rome.
313	Edict of Milan ended persecution of Christians.
324	Constantine became sole emperor.
325	Council of Nicaea made Christianity religion of the empire.
330	Constantine made Byzantium seat of government; renamed it Constantinople.
337	Constantine died a Christian, trying to reorganize the empire.
379-395	Emperor Theodosius kept empire formally intact.
410	Alaric and Goths captured and destroyed Rome.

GOVERNMENT AND ADMINISTRATION

Republic

There was no written constitution. The Republic evolved from the struggle between the Senate and the People - Senatus Populusque Romanus - SPQR.

The Senate (Senatus)
This was the governing body, largely in the hands of the nobles (nobiles) or patricians (patricii).

- it prepared proposals to bring before the people
- it passed decrees (senatus consulta)
- it dealt with emergencies
- it controlled finances and building contracts
- it appointed magistrates to provinces
- it directed foreign relations
- it supervised state religion

The People (Populus)
The resolutions of the people, plebiscita, could have the force of law, but the Senate was allowed greater control. There were four assemblies:

- comitia curiata   formal duties
- comitia centuriata   elected magistrates
- comitia tributa   elected lesser magistrates
- concilium plebis   passed plebiscita

The Knights (Equites)
A third element, or class, emerged (originally from Rome's cavalry) to engage in trade and finance. These businessmen acquired more political influence and became wealthy. By the time of Cicero, they could enter the Senate. Cicero tried to reconcile the three classes, **senatores**, **equites** and **plebs** by his **concordia ordinum** (harmony of the classes).

Magistrates (Magistratus)
A magistrate was an official elected annually by the people. Offices were held in a strict order - **cursus honorum**. After ten years' military service, a young man could begin on the lowest rung of the ladder as follows:

Age	Office	Number	Duties
28	**Quaestor**	(8)	• administered finance maintained public records
30	**Aedile**	(4)	• maintained roads, water supply organized games and festivals
33(39)	**Praetor**	(6)	• civil judge could introduce laws

39(43)	**Consul**	(2)	• commanded army
			  conducted elections
			  presided over Senate
			  carried out its decrees

Other magistrates:

Tribune (10) (tribunus plebis)	•	defended plebs' rights had right of veto
Censor (2)	•	conducted census (every 5 years) conducted purification revised roll of senators
Dictator (1)	•	ruled in crisis (maximum of 6 months) conducted military and domestic matters

Imperium (supreme power) was held by consuls and praetors and dictators.
Potestas (power to enforce laws) was held by all magistrates.
Lictores (lictors *or* officials) carried **fasces** (bundles of rods) in front of consuls, praetors and dictators as a sign of their authority.

ORGANIZATION OF THE ARMY

Empire

At the time of Augustus there were 28 **legions** (later 25), each legion consisting of approximately 5000 infantrymen, trained for close combat. It was organized as follows:

Legio	Legion	5000 men
10 Cohortes	Cohorts	500 men
6 Centuriae	Centuries	80/100 men

Officers

Legatus	legionary commander
6 **Tribuni Militum**	tribunes
60 **Centuriones**	centurions (from ranks), in charge of centuries

Recruitment	Citizens
Length of service	20/25 years
Duties	Offensive in important battles, repelling invasion *etc*
Pay	250/300 denarii per day
On retirement	Land or cash bounty

Additional **auxiliary forces** were recruited to help the legions. Particularly necessary were cavalry, drawn from all parts of the Empire, slingers, bowmen, etc. Infantrymen were often recruited locally and formed cohorts of about 500 men.

Auxilia	Auxiliaries	
Ala	Cavalry unit	500 men approx.
16 Turmae	turmae	32 men
Cohors	Infantry unit	500 men

Officers

Decurio	Decurion (cavalry officer)

Recruitment	Non-citizens
Length of service	25 years
Duties	Frontier skirmishes, occupation, assisting legions

Pay	100 denarii per day
On retirement	Citizenship for self/family

The **Praetorian Guard** was the Emperor's special bodyguard. Three cohorts were based in Rome, six more in nearby towns.

Praetorium	Praetorian Guard	4500 men
9 Cohortes	cohorts	500 men

Officers		
2 **Praefecti Praetorio**	praetorian prefects	
Recruitment	Citizens (Italy)	
Length of service	16 years	
Duties	Preserving emperor's power and safety	
Pay	1000 denarii per day	
On retirement	5000 denarii	

FAMILY TREE

tritavus *m* tritavia
(great-great-great-great-grandfather) (great-great-great-great-grandmother)

atavus *m* atavia
(great-great-great-grandfather) (great-great-great-grandmother)

abavus *m* abavia
(great-great-grandfather) (great-great-grandmother)

proavus *m* proavia
(great-grandfather) (great-grandmother)

avus *m* avia
(grandfather) (grandmother)

noverca *m* pater *m* māter *m* vītricus
(step-mother) (father) (mother) (step-father)

amita māxima (great-great-grandaunt)
mātertera māxima (great-great-grandaunt)

patruus māximus (great-great-granduncle)
avunculus māximus (great-great-granduncle)

amita māior (great-grandaunt)
mātertera māior (great-grandaunt)

patruus māior (great-granduncle)
avunculus māior (great-granduncle)

amita māgna (grandaunt)
mātertera māgna (grandaunt)

patruus māgnus (granduncle)
avunculus māgnus (granduncle)

amita (aunt)
mātertera (aunt)

patruus (uncle)
avunculus (uncle)

prōsocer *m* prōsocrus
(grandfather-in-law) (grandmother-in-law)

socer *m* socrus
(father-in-law) (mother-in-law)

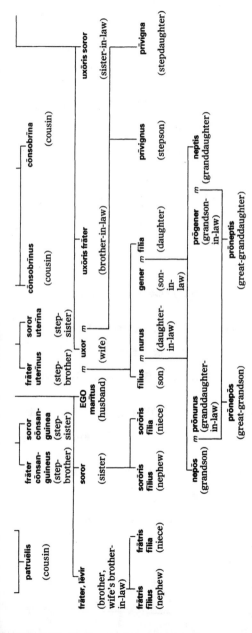

Note: *This is the Family Tree of the man designated **EGO** in the fourth generation from the end.*

MAJOR WRITERS

ENNIUS (Quintus Ennius: b 239 B.C.) **Annales**.

PLAUTUS (Titus Maccus _or_ Maccius Plautus: b 254 B.C.) **Amphitruo**; the **Aulularia**; the **Menaechmi** and **Miles Gloriosus**.

TERENCE (Publius Terentius Afer) **Andria**; **Mother-in-law**; **Phormio**.

LUCRETIUS (Titus Lucretius Carus: 94 - 55 B.C.) **De Rerum Natura**.

CATULLUS (Gaius Valerius Catullus: c.84 - c.54 B.C.) Lyric poetry; **Ave atque vale**.

CICERO (Marcus Tullius Cicero: b 106 B.C.) **Pro Caelio**; **De Legibus**; the **Tusculan Disputations**; **De Officiis**; **Philippics**.

JULIUS CAESAR (Gaius Iulius Caesar: b c.102 B.C. and assassinated in 44 B.C.) **Bellum Gallicum**; **Bellum Civile**.

SALLUST (Gaius Sallustius Crispus: 86 - 35 B.C.) **Bellum Catilinae**; **Bellum Iugurthinum**.

VIRGIL (Publius Vergilius Maro: 70 - 19 B.C.) **Eclogues**; **Georgics**; the **Aeneid**.

HORACE (Quintus Horatius Flaccus: b 65 A.D.) **Satires**; **Odes**; **Epistles**.

LIVY (Titus Livius: 59 B.C. - 17 A.D.) **Ab Urbe Condita**.

OVID (Publius Ovidius Naso: 43 B.C. - 17 A.D.) the **Heroides, Ars Amatoria**; the **Metamorphoses**; **Tristia**.

SENECA (Lucius Annaeus Seneca: 4 B.C. - 65 A.D.) **Dialogi**; **Epistolae Morales**.

QUINTILIAN (Marcus Fabius Quintilianus: c.35 - c.95 A.D.) **Institutio Oratorio**.

MARTIAL (Marcus Valerius Martialis: 40 - 104 A.D.) the **Epigrams**.

JUVENAL (Decimus Iunius Iuvenalis) **Satires**.

TACITUS (Cornelius Tacitus) **Agricola**; **Germania**; **Histories**; the **Annals**.

PLINY (Gaius Plinius Secundus: b 61 _or_ 62 A.D.) **Letters**.

GEOGRAPHICAL NAMES

The following list of geographical names and their adjectives includes both ancient and medieval Latin forms. The former are printed in Roman type, the latter in Italics. Medieval place names tend to have a variety of Latin forms, but only one has been selected in each case; occasionally both the ancient and the medieval forms have been given. Modern names which have a ready-made Latin form (*e.g.* America) have been omitted, and many names not included in this selection can be easily Latinized on the analogy of those which do appear.

Aachen	*Aquīsgrānum nt*	*adj Aquīsgrānēnsis*
Aberdeen	*Aberdōnia f*	*adj Aberdōnēnsis*
Abergavenny	Gobannium nt	
Aberystwith	*Aberistyvium nt*	
Adige, *River*	Athesis m	
Adriatic	Mare superum nt	*adj* Hadriāticus
Aegean	Mare Aegaeum nt	*adj* Aegaeus
Afghanistan	Ariāna f	*adj* Ariānus
Africa	Libya f,	*adj* Libycus,
	Africa f	Africānus
Agrigento	Agrigentum nt	*adj* Agrigentīnus
Aisne, *River*	Axona m	
Aix-en-Provence	Aquae Sextiae *fpl*	*adj Aquēnsis*
Aix-la-Chapelle	*Aquīsgrānum nt*	*adj Aquisgrānēnsis*
Aix-Les-Bains	Aquae Grātiānae *fpl*	
Ajaccio	*Adiacium nt*	*adj Adiacēnsis*
Aldborough	Isurium (*nt*)	
	Brigantum	
Alexandria	Alexandrēa,	
	Alexandrīa f	*adj* Alexandrīnus
Algiers	*Algerium nt*	*adj Algerīnus*
Alps	Alpēs *fpl*	*adj* Alpīnus
Alsace	*Alsatia f*	
Amalfi	*Amalphis f*	*adj* Amalphītānus
Ambleside	Galava f	
Amiens	*Ambiānum nt*	*adj Ambiānēnsis*
Amsterdam	*Amstelodamum nt*	*adj Amstelodamēnsis*
Ancaster	Causennae *fpl*	
Angers	*Andegāvum nt*	*adj* Andegāvēnsis
Anglesey	Mona f	
Aniene, *River*	Aniō m	*adj* Aniēnus
Anjou	Andegāvēnsis ager m	
Ankara	Ancyra f	*adj* Ancyrānus
Antibes	Antipolis f	*adj* Antipolītānus
Antioch	Antiochīa f	*adj* Antiochēnus
Antwerp	*Antwerpium nt*	*adj Antwerpiēnsis*
Anzio	Antium nt	*adj* Antiās, Antiānus
Aosta	Augusta Praetōria f	
Apennines	Mōns Apennīnus m	

Aragon	*Aragōnia f*	
Archangel	*Archangelopolis f*	
Ardennes	Arduenna *f*	
Arezzo	Ārētium *nt*	*adj* Ārētīnus
Argenteuil	*Argentōlium nt*	
Argyll	*Argadia f*	
Arles	Arelās *f*	*adj* Arelātēnsis
Armagh	Armācha *f*	*adj* Armāchānus
Arno, *River*	Arnus *m*	*adj* Arniēnsis
Arras	Atrebatēs *mpl*	*adj* Atrebatēnsis
Artois	Atrebatēs *mpl*	
Assisi	Assīsium *nt*	*adj* Assīsiēnsis
Athens	Athēnae *fpl*	*adj* Athēniēnsis
Atlantic	Mare Atlanticum *nt*	
Augsburg	Augusta (*f*) Vindelicōrum	*adj* Augustānus
Autun	Augustodūnum *nt*	*adj* Augustodūnēnsis
Auvergne	Arvernī *mpl*	*adj* Arvernus
Aventine	Aventīnus *m*	
Avignon	Aveniō *f*	*adj* Aveniōnēnsis
Avon, *River*	Auvona *m*	
Babylon	Babylōn *f*	*adj* Babylōnius
Baden-Baden	Aquae Aurēliae *fpl*	
Balearic Islands	Baliārēs Insulae *fpl*	*adj* Baliāricus
Balkh	Bactra *ntpl*	*adj* Bactriānus
Baltic	*Balticum Mare nt*	
Bangor	*Bangertium nt*	*adj* *Bangertiēnsis*
Barcelona	Barcinō *f*	*adj* Barcinōnēnsis
Bari	Bārium *nt*	*adj* *Bārēnsis*
Basle	Basilēa *f*	*adj* Basilēēnsis
Basques	Vasconēs *mpl*	*adj* Vasconicus
Bath	Aquae (*fpl*) Sulis	
Bayeux	*Augustodūrum nt*	
Bayreuth	*Barūthum nt*	
Beauvais	Bellovacī *mpl*	*adj* *Bellovacēnsis*
Beirut	Bērȳtus *f*	*adj* Bērȳtius
Belgium	Belgae *mpl*	*adj* Belgicus
Bergen	*Bergae fpl*	
Berlin	*Berolīnum nt*	*adj* *Berolīnēnsis*
Berne	Vērona *f*	
Berwick	*Barvīcum nt*	
Besançon	Vesontiō *m*	*adj* *Bisuntīnus*
Black Sea	Pontus (Euxīnus) *m*	*adj* Ponticus
Bobbio	*Bobbium nt*	*adj* *Bobbiēnsis*
Bohemia	Boiohaemī *mpl*	
Bologna	Bonōnia *f*	*adj* Bonōniēnsis
Bonn	*Bonna f*	
Bordeaux	*Burdigala f*	*adj* *Burdigalēnsis*
Boulogne	Bonōnia *f*	*adj* Bononiēnsis
Bourges	Avāricum *nt*	*adj* Avāricēnsis
Brabant	*Brabantia f*	
Braganza	Brigantia *f*	*adj* Brigantiēnsis

Brancaster	Branodūnum *nt*	
Brandenburg	*Brandenburgia f*	*adj Brandenburgēnsis*
Bremen	*Brēma f*	*adj Brēmēnsis*
Breslau	*Bratislavia f*	*adj Bratislaviēnsis*
Brindisi	Brundisium *nt*	*adj* Brundisīnus
Bristol	*Bristolium nt*	*adj Bristoliēnsis*
Britain	Britannia *f*	*adj* Britannicus
Brittany	Armoricae *fpl*	
Bruges	*Brugae fpl*	*adj Brugēnsis*
Brunswick	*Brunsvīcum nt*	*adj Brunsvīcēnsis*
Brussels	*Bruxellae fpl*	*adj Bruxellēnsis*
Bucharest	*Bucarestum nt*	*adj Bucarestiēnsis*
Burgos	*Burgī mpl*	*adj Burgitānus*
Burgundy	Burgundiōnēs *mpl*	
Cadiz	Gādēs *fpl*	*adj* Gāditānus
Caen	*Cadomum nt*	*adj Cadomēnsis*
Caerleon	Isca *f*	
Caermarthen	Maridūnum *nt*	
Caernarvon	Segontium *nt*	
Caerwent	Venta *(f)* Silurum	
Cagliari	Caralis *f*	*adj* Caralītānus
Cairo	*Cairus f*	
Calais	*Calētum nt*	*adj* Calētanus
Cambrai	*Camerācum nt*	*adj Camerācēnsis*
Cambridge	*Cantabrigia f*	*adj Cantabrigiēnsis*
Campagna	Campānia *f*	*adj* Campānus
Cannes	*Canoē f*	
Canterbury	Durovernum *nt*,	*adj Cantuāriēnsis*
	Cantuāria f	
Capri	Capreae *fpl*	*adj* Capreēnsis
Cardigan	Ceretica *f*	
Carlisle	Luguvallium *nt*	
Cartagena	Carthāgō Nova *f*	
Carthage	Carthāgō *f*	*adj* Carthāginiēnsis
Caspian Sea	Mare Caspium *nt*	
Cevennes	Gebenna *f*	*adj* Gebennicus
Ceylon	Tāprobanē *f*	
Champagne	*Campānia f*	*adj Campānicus*
Chartres	Carnūtēs *mpl*	*adj* Carnōtēnus
Chelmsford	Caesaromagus *m*	
Cherbourg	*Caesaris burgus m*	
Chester	Deva *f*	
Chichester	Rēgnum *nt*	
China	Sēres *mpl*	*adj* Sēricus
Cirencester	Corinium (*nt*)	
	Dobunōrum	
Clairvaux	*Clāra Vallis f*	*adj Clāravallēnsis*
Clermont	Nemossus *f*	
Cluny	*Clīniacum nt*	*adj Clīniacēnsis*
Clyde, *River*	Clōta *f*	
Colchester	Camulodūnum *nt*	
Cologne	Colōnia Agrippīna *f*	*adj Colōniēnsis*

Como, _Lake_	Lārius _m_	_adj_ Lārius
Constance, _Lake_	Lacus Brigantīnus _m_	
Copenhagen	_Hafnia f_	
Corbridge	Corstopitum _nt_	
Cordoba	Corduba _f_	_adj_ Cordubēnsis
Corfu	Corcȳra _f_	_adj_ Corcȳraeus
Corinth	Corinthus _f_	_adj_ Corinthius
Cork	Corcagia _f_	_adj_ Corcagiēnsis
Cornwall	_Cornubia f_	
Cracow	_Cracovia f_	_adj_ Cracoviēnsis
Crete	Crēta _f_	_adj_ Crētēnsis, Crēticus
Cumberland	_Cumbria f_	
Cyprus	Cyprus _f_	_adj_ Cyprius
Cyrene	Cȳrēnae _fpl_	_adj_ Cȳrēnaicus
Damascus	Damascus _f_	_adj_ Damascēnus
Danube, _River_	_(lower)_ Ister _m_, _(upper)_ Dānuvius _m_	
Dardanelles	Hellēspontus _m_	_adj_ Hellēspontius
Dee, _River_	Deva _f_	
Denmark	Dānia _f_	_adj_ Dānicus
Derby	_Derventiō m_	
Devon	_Devōnia f_	
Dijon	_Diviō f_	_adj_ Diviōnēnsis
Dneiper, _River_	Borysthenēs _m_	
Dneister, _River_	Danaster _m_	
Don, _River_ (Russian)	Tanais _m_	
Doncaster	Dānum _nt_	
Dorchester	Durnovāria _f_	
Douro, _River_	Durius _m_	
Dover	Dubrī _mpl_	
Dover, _Straits of_	Fretum Gallicum _nt_	
Dresden	_Dresda f_	_adj_ Dresdēnsis
Dublin	_Dublīnum nt_	_adj_ Dublīnēnsis
Dumbarton	_Britannodūnum nt_	
Dundee	_Taodūnum nt_	
Dunstable	Durocobrīvae _fpl_	
Durham	_Dunelmum nt_	_adj_ Dunelmēnsis
Ebro, _River_	Hibērus _m_	
Eden, _River_	Itūna _f_	
Edinburgh	_Edinburgum nt_	_adj_ Edinburgēnsis
Egypt	Aegyptus _f_	_adj_ Aegyptius
Elba	Ilva _f_	
Elbe, _River_	Albis _m_	
England	Anglia _f_	_adj_ Anglicus
Etna	Aetna _f_	_adj_ Aetnaeus
Europe	Eurōpa	_adj_ Eurōpaeus
Exeter	Isca (_f_) Dumnoniōrum	
Fiesole	Faesulae _fpl_	_adj_ Faesulānus
Flanders	Menapiī _mpl_	
Florence	Flōrentia _f_	_adj_ Flōrentīnus
Fontainebleau	_Bellofontānum nt_	
Forth, _River_	Bodotria _f_	

France	Gallia *f*	*adj* Gallicus
Frankfurt	*Francofurtum nt*	
Frejus	Forum (*nt*) Iūliī	*adj* Foroiūliēnsis
Friesland	Frīsiī *mpl*	*adj* Frīsius
Gallipoli	*Callipolis f*	*adj* Callipolitānus
Galloway	*Gallovidia f*	
Ganges	Gangēs *m*	*adj* Gangēticus
Garda, *Lake*	Bēnācus *m*	
Garonne, *River*	Garumna *f*	
Gaul	Gallia *f*	*adj* Gallicus
Gdansk	*Gedānum m*	
Geneva	Genāva *f*	*adj* Genāvēnsis
Geneva, *Lake*	Lemannus lacus *m*	
Genoa	Genua *f*	*adj* Genuēnsis
Germany	Germānia *f*	*adj* Germānicus
Ghent	*Gandavum nt*	*adj* Gandavēnsis
Gibraltar	Calpē *f*	*adj* Calpētānus
Gibraltar, *Straits of*	Fretum Gāditānum *nt*	
Glasgow	*Glasgua f*	*adj* Glasguēnsis
Gloucester	Glēvum *nt*	
Gothenburg	*Gothoburgum nt*	
Graz	*Graecium nt*	
Greece	Graecia *f*	*adj* Graecus
Greenwich	*Grenovīcum nt*	
Grenoble	Grātiānopolis *f*	
Groningen	*Groninga f*	
Guadalquivir, *River*	Baetis *m*	
Guadiana, *River*	Anas *m*	
Guernsey	*Sarnia f*	
Hague, *The*	Haga (*f*) Comitis	
Halle	*Halla f*	*adj* Hallēnsis
Hamadān	Ecbatana *ntpl*	
Hamburg	*Hamburgum nt*	*adj·*Hamburgēnsis
Hanover	*Hannovera f*	
Harwich	*Harvīcum nt*	
Havre	Grātiae Portus *m*	
Hebrides	Ebūdae Insulae *fpl*	
Hexham	Axelodūnum *nt*	
Holland	Batāvī *mpl*	*adj* Batāvus
Ibiza	Ebusus *f*	*adj* Ebusitānus
Ilkley	Olicāna *f*	
Inn, *River*	Aenus *m*	
Ipswich	*Gippevīcum nt*	
Ireland	Hibernia *f*	*adj* Hibernicus
Isar, *River*	Isara *f*	
Istanbul	Bȳzantium *nt*	*adj* Bȳzantīnus
Italy	Italia *f*	*adj* Italicus
Jersey	Caesarea *f*	
Jerusalem	Hierosolyma *ntpl*	*adj* Hierosolymītānus
Jutland	Chersonnēsus Cimbrica *f*	
Karlsbad	*Aquae Carolīnae fpl*	

Kent	Cantium *nt*	
Kiel	*Chilonium nt*	
Koblenz	Cōnfluentēs *mpl*	
Lancaster	*Lancastria f*	
Lanchester	Longovicium *nt*	
Land's End	Bolerium Prōmunturium *nt*	
Lausanne	Lausōnium *nt*	*adj* Lausōniēnsis
Lebanon	Libanus *m*	
Leeds	*Ledesia f*	
Leicester	Ratae (*fpl*) Coritānōrum	
Leiden	Lugdūnum (*nt*) Batāvōrum	
Leipsig	*Lipsia f*	*adj* Lipsiēnsis
Lērida	Ilerda *f*	*adj* Ilerdēnsis
Lichfield	*Etocētum nt*	
Limoges	Augustorītum *nt*	
Lincoln	Lindum *nt*	
Lisbon	Olisīpō *m*	*adj* Olisīpōnēnsis
Lizard Point	Damnonium Prōmunturium *nt*	
Loire, *River*	Liger *m*	*adj* Ligericus
Lombardy	*Langobardia f*	
London	Londinium *nt*	*adj* Londiniēnsis
Lorraine	*Lōthāringia f*	
Lucerne	*Lūceria f*	*adj* Lūcernēnsis
Lund	Londinium (*nt*) Gothōrum	
Lyons	Lugdūnum *nt*	*adj* Lugdūnēnsis
Madrid	*Matrītum nt*	*adj* Matrītēnsis
Maggiore, *Lake*	Verbannus *m*	
Main, *River*	Moenus *m*	
Mainz	Mogontiacum *nt*	
Majorca	Baliāris Māior *f*	
Malta	Melita *f*	
Man, *Isle of*	Monapia *f*	
Manchester	*Mancunium nt*	
Marmara, *Sea of*	Propontis *f*	
Marne, *River*	*Māterna f*	
Marseilles	Massilia *f*	*adj* Massiliēnsis
Matapan	Taenarum *nt*	*adj* Taenarius
Mediterranean	Mare internum *nt*	
Melun	Melodūnum *nt*	
Mērida	Ēmerita *f*	*adj* Ēmeritēnsis
Messina	Messāna *f*	*adj* Messānius
Metz	Dīvodūrum *nt*	
Meuse, *River*	Mosa *f*	
Milan	Mediōlānum *nt*	*adj* Mediōlānēnsis
Minorca	Baliāris Minor *f*	
Modena	Mutina *f*	*adj* Mutinēnsis
Mons	Montēs *mpl*	
Monte Cassino	Casīnum *nt*	*adj* Casīnās
Moray	*Moravia f*	

Morocco	Maurētānia *f*	*adj* Maurus
Moscow	*Moscovia f*	
Moselle, *River*	Mosella *f*	
Munich	*Monacum nt*	*adj Monacēnsis*
Nantes	Namnētēs *mpl*	
Naples	Neāpolis *f*	*adj* Neāpolītānus
Neckar, *River*	Nīcer *m*	
Newcastle	Pōns (*m*) Aeliī,	*adj Novocastrēnsis*
	Novum Castrum nt	
Nice	Nīcaea *f*	*adj* Nicaeēnsis
Nile, *River*	Nīlus *m*	*adj* Nīlōticus
Nîmes	Nemausus *f*	*adj* Nemausēnsis
Norway	*Norvēgia f*	*adj Norvēgiānus*
Norwich	*Nordovīcum nt*	
Oder, *River*	Viadrus *m*	
Oporto	Portus Calēnsis *m*	
Orange	Arausiō *f*	
Orkneys	Orcades *fpl*	
Orléans	*Aurēliānum nt*	*adj Aurēliānēnsis*
Oudenarde	*Aldenarda f*	
Oxford	*Oxonia f*	*adj Oxoniēnsis*
Padua	Patavium *nt*	*adj* Patavīnus
Palermo	Panormus *m*	*adj* Panormitānus
Paris	Lutetia *f*, Parīsiī *mpl*	*adj* Parīsiēnsis
Patras	Patrae *fpl*	*adj* Patrēnsis
Persian Gulf	Mare Rubrum *nt*	
Piacenza	Placentia *f*	*adj* Placentīnus
Po, *River*	Padus	*adj* Padānus
Poitiers	Limōnum *nt*	
Poland	*Polōnia f*	
Portsmouth	Māgnus Portus *m*	
Portugal	Lūsitānia *f*	
Pozzuoli	Puteolī *mpl*	*adj* Puteolānus
Prague	*Prāga f*	*adj Prāgēnsis*
Provence	Prōvincia *f*	
Pyrenees	Pӯrēnaeī montēs *mpl*	
Red Sea	Sinus Arābicus *m*	
Rheims	Dūrocortorum *nt*	
Rhine, *River*	Rhēnus *m*	*adj* Rhēnānus
Rhodes	Rhodos *f*	*adj* Rhodius
Rhône, *River*	Rhodanus *m*	
Richborough	Rutupiae *fpl*	*adj* Rutupīnus
Rimini	Arīminum	*adj* Arīminēnsis
Rochester	Dūrobrīvae *fpl*	
Rome	Rōma *f*	*adj* Rōmānus
Rotterdam	*Roterodamum nt*	*adj Roterodamēnsis*
Rouen	*Rothomagus f*	*adj Rothomagēnsis*
Saar, *River*	*Sangona f*	
Salisbury	Sarisberia *f*	
Salzburg	*Iuvāvum nt*	*adj Salisburgēnsis*
Saône, *River*	Arar *m*	

Savoy	*Sabaudia f*	
Scheldt, *River*	Scaldis *m*	
Schleswig	*Slesvīcum nt*	
Scilly Isles	Cassiterides *fpl*	
Scotland	Calēdonia *f*	*adj* Calēdonius
Seine, *River*	Sēquana *f*	
Severn, *River*	Sabrīna *f*	
Seville	Hīspalis *f*	*adj* Hispalēnsis
Shrewsbury	*Salōpia f*	
Sicily	Sicilia *f*	*adj* Siculus
Sidra, *Gulf of*	Syrtis (māior) *f*	
Silchester	Callēva (*f*) Atrebatum	
Soissons	Augusta (*f*) Suessiōnum	
Solway Firth	Itūna (*f*) aestuārium	
Somme, *River*	Samara *f*	
Spain	Hispānia *f*	*adj* Hispānus
St. Albans	Verulamium *nt*	
St. Andrews	*Andreopolis f*	
St. Bernard	(*Great*) Mōns Pennīnus *m*, (*Little*) Alpis Grāia *f*	
St. Gallen	*Sangallēnse coenobium nt*	*adj Sangallēnsis*
St. Gotthard	Alpēs summae *fpl*	
St. Moritz	*Agaunum nt*	*adj* Agaunēnsis
Strasbourg	Argentorātus *f*	*adj* Argentorātēnsis
Swabia	Suēvia *f*	*adj* Suēvicus
Sweden	*Suēcia f*	*adj* Suēcicus
Switzerland	Helvētia *f*	*adj* Helvēticus
Syracuse	Syrācūsae *fpl*	*adj* Syrācūsānus
Tangier	Tingī *f*	*adj* Tingitānus
Taranto	Tarentum *nt*	*adj* Tarentīnus
Tarragona	Tarracō *f*	*adj* Tarracōnēnsis
Tay, *River*	Taus *m*	
Thames, *River*	Tamesis *m*	
Thebes	Thēbae *fpl*	*adj* Thēbānus
Tiber, *River*	Tiberis *m*	*adj* Tiberīnus
Tivoli	Tībur *nt*	*adj* Tīburtīnus
Toledo	Tolētum *nt*	*adj* Tolētānus
Toulon	*Tolōna f*	*adj Tolōnēnsis*
Toulouse	Tolōsa *f*	*adj* Tolōsānus
Tours	Caesarodūnum *nt*	
Trèves, Trier	Augusta (*f*) Treverōrum	
Trieste	Tergeste *nt*	*adj* Tergestīnus
Tripoli	Tripolis *f*	*adj* Tripolitānus
Tunis	Tūnēs *f*	*adj* Tūnētānus
Turin	Augusta (*f*) Taurīnōrum	*adj* Taurīnus
Tuscany	Etrūria *f*	*adj* Etrūscus
Tyrrhenian Sea	Mare īnferum *nt*	
Utrecht	*Ultrāiectum nt*	*adj Ultrāiectēnsis*
Vardar, *River*	Axius *m*	
Venice	Venetī *mpl*, *Venetiae fpl*	*adj* Venetus
Verdun	*Virodūnum nt*	*adj Virodūnēnsis*

Versailles	*Versāliae fpl*	*adj Versāliēnsis*
Vichy	Aquae *(fpl)* Sōlis	
Vienna	*Vindobona f*	*adj Vindobenēnsis*
Vosges	Vosegus *m*	
Wales	*Cambria f*	
Wallsend	Segedūnum *nt*	
Warsaw	*Varsavia f*	*adj Varsaviēnsis*
Wash, *The*	Metaris *(m)* aestuārium	
Wear, *River*	Vedra *f*	
Weser, *River*	Visurgis *m*	
Westminster	*Westmonastērium nt*	*adj Westmonastēriēnsis*
Wiesbaden	Mattiacum *nt*	*adj* Mattiacus
Wight, *Isle of*	Vectis *f*	
Winchester	Venta *(f)* Belgārum	
Worcester	Vigornia *f*	
Worms	*Vormatia f*	
Wroxeter	Viroconium *nt*	
York	Eburācum *nt*	*adj* Eburācēnsis
Zuider Zee	Flēvō *m*	
Zurich	*Turicum nt*	*adj* Tigurīnus

NUMERALS

	Cardinal		Ordinal	
1	ūnus	I	prīmus	1st
2	duo	II	secundus, alter	2nd
3	trēs	III	tertius	3rd
4	quattuor	IV	quārtus	4th
5	quīnque	V	quīntus	5th
6	sex	VI	sextus	6th
7	septem	VII	septimus	7th
8	octō	VIII	octāvus	8th
9	novem	IX	nōnus	9th
10	decem	X	decimus	10th
11	undecim	XI	undecimus	11th
12	duodecim	XII	duodecimus	12th
13	tredecim	XIII	tertius decimus	13th
14	quattuordecim	XIV	quārtus decimus	14th
15	quīndecim	XV	quīntus decimus	15th
16	sēdecim	XVI	sextus decimus	16th
17	septendecim	XVII	septimus decimus	17th
18	duodēvīgintī	XVIII	duodēvīcēsimus	18th
19	ūndēvīgintī	XIX	ūndēvīcēsimus	19th
20	vīgintī	XX	vīcēsimus	20th
21	vīgintī ūnus	XXI	vīcēsimus prīmus	21st
28	duodētrīgintā	XXVIII	duodētrīcēsimus	28th
29	ūndētrīgintā	XXIX	ūndētrīcēsimus	29th
30	trīgintā	XXX	trīcēsimus	30th
40	quadrāgintā	XL	quadrāgēsimus	40th
50	quīnquāgintā	L	quīnquāgēsimus	50th
60	sexāgintā	LX	sexāgēsimus	60th
70	septuāgintā	LXX	septuāgēsimus	70th
80	octōgintā	LXXX	octōgēsimus	80th
90	nōnāgintā	XC	nōnāgēsimus	90th
100	centum	C	centēsimus	100th
101	centum et ūnus	CI	centēsimus prīmus	101st
122	centum vīgintī duo	CXXII	centēsimus vīcēsimus alter	122nd
200	ducentī	CC	ducentēsimus	200th
300	trecentī	CCC	trecentēsimus	300th
400	quadringentī	CCCC	quadringentēsimus	400th
500	quīngentī	D	quīngentēsimus	500th
600	sēscentī	DC	sēscentēsimus	600th
700	septingentī	DCC	septingentēsimus	700th
800	octingentī	DCCC	octingentēsimus	800th
900	nōngentī	DCCCC	nōngentēsimus	900th
1000	mīlle	M	mīllēsimus	1000th
1001	mīlle et ūnus	MI	mīllēsimus prīmus	1001st
1102	mīlle centum duo	MCII	mīllēsimus centēsimus alter	1102nd
3000	tria mīlia	MMM	ter mīllēsimus	3000th
5000	quīnque mīlia	IƆƆ	quīnquiēs mīllēsimus	5000th
10,000	decem mīlia	CCIƆƆ	deciēs mīllēsimus	10,000th
100,000	centum mīlia	CCCIƆƆƆ	centiēs mīllēsimus	100,000th
1,000,000	deciēs centēna mīlia	CCCCIƆƆƆƆ	deciēs centiēs mīllēsimus	1,000,000th

NUMERALS

	Distributive		Adverb	
1	singulī	I	semel	1st
2	bīnī	II	bis	2nd
3	ternī (trīnī)	III	ter	3rd
4	quaternī	IV	quater	4th
5	quīnī	V	quīnquiēs	5th
6	sēnī	VI	sexiēs	6th
7	septēnī	VII	septiēs	7th
8	octōnī	VIII	octiēs	8th
9	novēnī	IX	noviēs	9th
10	dēnī	X	deciēs	10th
11	undēnī	XI	undeciēs	11th
12	duodēnī	XII	duodeciēs	12th
13	ternī dēnī	XIII	ter deciēs	13th
14	quaternī dēnī	XIV	quattuordeciēs	14th
15	quīnī dēnī	XV	quīndeciēs	15th
16	sēnī dēnī	XVI	sēdeciēs	16th
17	septēnī dēnī	XVII	septiēs deciēs	17th
18	duodēvīcēnī	XVIII	duodēvīciēs	18th
19	ūndēvīcēnī	XIX	ūndēvīciēs	19th
20	vīcēnī	XX	vīciēs	20th
21	vīcēnī singulī	XXI	semel et vīciēs	21st
28	duodētrīcēnī	XXVIII	duodētrīciēs	28th
29	ūndētrīcēnī	XXIX	ūndētrīciēs	29th
30	trīcēnī	XXX	trīciēs	30th
40	quadrāgēnī	XL	quadrāgiēs	40th
50	quīnquāgēnī	L	quīnquāgiēs	50th
60	sexāgēnī	LX	sexāgiēs	60th
70	septuāgēnī	LXX	septuāgiēs	70th
80	octōgēnī	LXXX	octōgiēs	80th
90	nōnagēnī	XC	nōnāgiēs	90th
100	centēnī	C	centiēs	100th
101	centēnī singulī	CI	semel et centiēs	101st
122	centēnī vīcēnī bīnī	CXXII	centiēs vīciēs bis	122nd
200	ducēnī	CC	ducentiēs	200th
300	trecēnī	CCC	trecentiēs	300th
400	quadringēnī	CCCC	quadringentiēs	400th
500	quīngēnī	D	quīngentiēs	500th
600	sexcēnī	DC	sexcentiēs	600th
700	septingēnī	DCC	septingentiēs	700th
800	octingēnī	DCCC	octingentiēs	800th
900	nōngēnī	DCCCC	nōngentiēs	900th
1000	singula mīlia	M	mīlliēs	1000th
1001	singula mīlia singulī	MI	semel et mīlliēs	1001st
1102	singula mīlia centēnī bīnī	MCII	mīlliēs centiēs bis	1102nd
3000	trīna mīlia	MMM	ter mīlliēs	3000th
5000	quīna mīlia	IↃↃ	quīnquiēs mīlliēs	5000th
10,000	dēna mīlia	CCIↃↃ	deciēs mīlliēs	10,000th
100,000	centēna mīlia	CCCIↃↃↃ	centiēs mīlliēs	100,000th
1,000,000	deciēs centēna mīlia	CCCCIↃↃↃↃ	mīlliēs mīlliēs	1,000,000th

DATES

MONTHS

Three days of the month have special names:

Kalendae the 1st.

Nōnae the 5th of most months, but the 7th of March, May, July and October.

> "In March, July, October, May,
> The Nones are on the 7th day."

Idūs the 13th of most months, but the 15th of March, May, July and October.

If the date is one of these three days, it is expressed in the ablative, with the adjective of the month in agreement, *e.g.*

1st January, **Kalendīs Iānuāriīs**, usually abbreviated **Kal. Ian.**

The day immediately before any of these three is expressed by **prīdiē** with the accusative, *e.g.*

4th February, **prīdiē Nōnās Februāriās**, usually abbreviated **prid. Non. Feb.**

All other dates are expressed as so many days before the next named day, and in reckoning the interval both the date and the named day are counted, *e.g.* the 11th is the 5th day before the 15th.

The formula is all in the accusative, begining with the words **ante diem**, *e.g.* 11th March, **ante diem quīntum Idūs Martiās**, usually abbreviated **a.d. V Id. Mar.**

The following selection of dates for April and May should be a sufficient guide to the dates of any month in the year:—

APRIL		MAY
Kal. Apr.	1	Kal. Mai.
a.d IV Non. Apr.	2	a.d. VI Non. Mai.
a.d. III Non. Apr.	3	a.d. V Non. Mai.
prid. Non. Apr.	4	a.d. IV Non. Mai.
Non. Apr.	5	a.d. III Non. Mai.
a.d. VIII Id. Apr.	6	prid. Non. Mai.
a.d. VII Id. Apr.	7	Non. Mai.
a.d. VI Id. Apr.	8	a.d. VIII Id. Mai.
a.d. V Id. Apr.	9	a.d. VII Id. Mai.
a.d. IV Id. Apr.	10	a.d. VI Id. Mai.
a.d. III Id. Apr.	11	a.d. V Id. Mai.
prid. Id. Apr.	12	a.d. IV Id. Mai.
Id. Apr.	13	a.d. III Id. Mai.
a.d. XVIII Kal. Mai.	14	prid. Id. Mai.
a.d. XVII Kal. Mai.	15	Id. Mai.
a.d. XVI Kal. Mai.	16	a.d. XVII Kal. Iun.

a.d. XV Kal. Mai.	17	a.d. XVI Kal. Iun.
a.d. XII Kal. Mai.	20	a.d. XIII Kal. Iun.
a.d. VII Kal. Mai.	25	a.d. VIII Kal. Iun.
prid. Kal. Mai.	30	a.d. III Kal. Iun.
—	31	prid. Kal. Iun.

YEARS

A year is denoted either by giving the names of the consuls or by reckoning the number of years from the traditional date of the foundation of Rome, 753 B.C. (A date B.C. should be subtracted from 754, a date A.D. should be added to 753.)

E.g. "In the year 218 B.C.," *either* P. Cornelio Scipione Ti. Sempronio Longo coss. *or* a. u. c. DXXXVI.

MEASURES

Length

12 ūnciae = 1 pēs
5 pedēs = 1 passus
125 passūs = 1 stadium
8 stadia = mīlle passūs

The Roman mile was about 1.48 km.

Area

100 pedēs quadrātī = 1 scrīpulum
144 scrīpula = 1 āctus quadrātus
2 āctūs quadrātī = 1 iugerum
2 iugera = 1 hērēdium
100 hērēdia = 1 centuria

The **iugerum** was about 2529.28 square metres.

Capacity

	4 cochleāria	= 1 cyathus
	12 cyathī	= 1 sextārius
(liquid)	6 sextāriī	= 1 congius
	8 congiī	= 1 amphora
	20 amphorae	= 1 culleus
(dry)	8 sextāriī	= 1 sēmodius
	2 sēmodiī	= 1 modius

The **sextārius** was about half a litre, the **modius** about 9 litres.

Weight

4 scrīpula = 1 sextula
6 sextulae = 1 ūncia
12 ūnciae = 1 lībra

The Roman lb. was about 326 gr, and the **ūncia** was therefore about 27 gr. The twelfths of the **lībra** have the following names, which are also used to denote fractions generally, *e.g.* **hērēs ex triente**, heir to a third of an estate.

¹⁄₁₂ ūncia	⁵⁄₁₂ quīncūnx	¾ dōdrāns
⅙ sextāns	½ sēmis	⅚ dextāns
¼ quadrāns	⁷⁄₁₂ septūnx	¹¹⁄₁₂ deūnx
⅓ triēns	⅔ bēs	

MONEY

Roman

2½ assēs	=	1 sēstertius (*or* nummus)
4 sēstertii	=	1 dēnārius
25 dēnārii	=	1 aureus

The sesterce is represented by a symbol for 2½, properly **II S(ēmis)**, usually standardized in the form HS. The *ntpl* **sēstertia** with the distributive numeral denotes thousands of sesterces, and the numeral adverb with the *gen pl* **sēstertium** (understanding **centēna milia**) means hundred thousands, *e.g.*

10,000 sesterces	= dēna sēstertia	= HS X̄
1,000,000 "	= deciēs sēstertium	= HS IX̄I

Greek

100 drachumae	=	1 mina
60 minae	=	1 talentum

LATIN VERSE

QUANTITY

Both vowels and syllables in Latin may be described as long or short. A long vowel or syllable is one on which the voice dwells for a longer time than on a short one, in much the same way as a minim is long compared with a crotchet in musical notation.

A syllable is long if the vowel in it is either long in itself or followed by two or more consonants. The letter **x** counts as a double consonant, the letter **h** not at all, and the following pairs of consonants occurring in the same word after a short vowel do not necessarily make the syllable long:

br, cr, dr, fr, gr, pr, tr; fl, gl, pl.

A syllable is short if its vowel is a short one and not followed by two or more consonants (except for the groups noted in the preceding paragraph).

Examples: In **dūcō** both the vowels are long ("by nature") and therefore the two syllables are long.

In **deus** both the vowels are short, neither is followed by more than one consonant, and therefore the two syllables are short; but if a word beginning with a consonant follows, then the syllable **-us** will become long.

In **adsunt** both the vowels are short, but they are both followed by two consonants, and the two syllables are therefore "long by position".

This long or short characteristic of Latin vowels and syllables is called "quantity." To determine the quantities of vowels no general rules can be given, and some of them are now not known for certain. The vowel quantities of words will have to be learned when the words are learned, or else looked up when the need arises. In final syllables, however, there is a certain regularity to be found, and the following table shows the commonest of these:

ENDING

	Long	Short
-a	1st decl abl sing 1st conj impv sing numerals and most adverbs	1st decl nom and voc sing all nom and acc ntpl **ita, quia**
-e	5th decl abl sing 2nd conj impv sing most adverbs Greek nouns	all other noun and verb endings **bene, male** enclitics

-i	*all endings, except*	**quasi, nisi:** *and sometimes* **mihi, tibi, sibi, ibi, ubi**
-o	*all endings, except*	*sometimes iambic words, esp* **cito, duo, ego, homo, modo, puto, rogo, scio**
-u	*all endings*	
-as	*all endings, except*	*Greek nouns*
-es	*all endings, except*	*3rd decl nom sing with short* **-e-** *in stem* **es** (be) *and compounds* **penes**
-is	*1st and 2nd decl dat and abl pl* *3rd decl acc pl* *4th conj 2nd pers sing* **vīs, sīs, velīs**	*all others*
-os	*all endings, except*	*2nd decl nom sing* **os** (bone) **compos, impos**
-us	*3rd decl nom sing with long* **-u-** *in stem* *4th decl gen sing and nom and acc pl*	*all others*

METRES

Latin Verse is a pattern of long and short syllables, grouped together in "feet" or in lyric lines.

FEET

The commonest Feet employed in Latin metres are:

Anapaest	(short—short—long)	˘ ˘ –
Dactyl	(long—short—short)	– ˘ ˘
Iambus	(short—long)	˘ –
Proceleusmatic	(short—short—short—short)	˘ ˘ ˘ ˘
Spondee	(long—long)	– –
Tribrach	(short—short—short)	˘ ˘ ˘
Trochee	(long—short)	– ˘

CAESURA AND DIAERESIS

The longer lines usually have a regular break near the middle, occurring either in the middle of a foot (**Caesura**) or at the end of a foot (**Diaeresis**). This break need not imply a pause in the sense of the words, but merely the end of a word, provided that it does not go too closely with the word following, as in the case of a preposition before a noun. See examples on pages 4–9 where the caesura is marked †, and the diaeresis //.

ELISION

A vowel or a vowel followed by **m** at the end of a word ("open vowel") is regularly elided before a vowel at the beginning of the next word in the same line. In reciting, the elided syllable should not be dropped entirely, but slurred into the following vowel. An open vowel at the end of a line does not elide before a vowel at the beginning of the next line.

FINAL SYLLABLES

Where the metre requires the final syllable in a line to be long, this syllable may in fact be a short one. This position in the line is commonly called a **syllaba anceps**, and marked down as being either long or short. It is perhaps better to regard this syllable, when the vowel is short, as long by position, since metrical length is a matter of duration, and the end of a line calls naturally for a slight pause in reading, even if the sense runs on to the next line. In the metrical schemes which follow, a long final syllable should be understood in this sense: it may in itself be a short one.

Latin metres fall into three fairly distinct categories, associated with three different genres of verse: 1. *Dactylic*
                                  2. *Iambic and Trochaic*
                                  3. *Lyric*

DACTYLIC VERSE

The Dactylic metres are the **Hexameter** and the **Pentameter**. The Hexameter is the medium of epic, didactic and pastoral poetry, of satires and epistles, and other examples of occasional verse. In conjunction with the Pentameter it forms the **Elegiac Couplet**, the metre most commonly used for love poetry, occasional pieces, and the epigram.

Dactylic Hexameter

The first four feet may be either **dactyls** or **spondees**, the 5th is regularly a dactyl, the 6th always a spondee. In Virgil and later poets the last word is either disyllabic or trisyllabic. A **Caesura** normally occurs in either the 3rd or the 4th foot, and pastoral poetry often has the "**Bucolic Diaeresis**" at the end of the 4th foot. In Virgilian and later usage there is a tendency for words and feet to overlap in the first four feet and to coincide in the last two. Similarly in the first part of the line the metrical ictus and the normal accent of the spoken word tend to fall on different syllables, whereas they regularly coincide in the last two feet.

Example:

Clāss(em) āp|teñt tăcĭ|tī' sŏcĭ|ōsqu(e) ād | lĭtŏră| tōrquēnt

(*Virgil, Aen.* 4, 289)

Occasional lines will be found in the poets, which deliberately violate the above rules for the sake of obtaining some special effect,

pēr cō|nūbĭă| nōstrā,' pēr| īncēp|tōs hўmĕ|nāeōs

(*Aen.* 4, 316)

The above echoes Greek hexameter, where the final word is Greek and has four syllables, and the caesura comes between the two short syllables of the dactyl in the 3rd foot:

cūm sŏcĭ|īs nā|tōquĕ' pĕ|nātĭbŭs| ēt māg|nīs dīs

(*Aen.* 3, 12)

Note the solemn, archaic touch, suggesting a line of Ennius, where the 5th foot is a spondee, and the last word is monosyllabic.

pār̆tŭr̆ĭ|ent mōn|tēs,⁺ nā|scētūr| r̆ĭd̆ĭcŭ|lūs mūs

(Hor, A. P. 139)

The monosyllabic ending, above, creates a comic effect.

Dactylic Pentameter

This line has two equal parts of 2½ feet each. The two feet in the first part may be either **dactyls** or **spondees**, those in the second part are always dactylic. The two half-feet are long (though the final syllable may be a short one), and there is always a diaeresis between the two parts of the line. In Ovid and later poets the last word in the line is regularly disyllabic.

Example:

Aēnē|ān ăn̆ĭ|mō // nōxqŭe d̆ĭ|ēsqŭe r̆ĕ|fērt

(Ovid, Her. 7, 26)

SCANSION

The following procedure may assist beginners to scan a normal hexameter or pentameter correctly:—

1. Mark off elisions.
2. Mark the first syllable long, and (Hexameter) the last five dactyl and spondee, or (Pentameter) the last seven syllables, two dactyls and a long syllable.
3. Mark all diphthongs long.
4. Mark all syllables that are long by position, omitting any doubtful cases.
5. Mark any other syllables known to be long.
6. Mark any syllables known to be short.
7. Fill in the few (if any) remaining syllables, and identify the principal caesura.
8. Read the line aloud.

IAMBIC AND TROCHAIC VERSE

The Iambic and Trochaic metres occur mainly in dramatic verse, but some are found elsewhere, as in the lyrics of Catullus and Horace. The principal Iambic metres are the **Senarius**, the **Septenarius**, and the **Octonarius**; the principal Trochaic metres are the Septenarius and Octonarius.

Iambic Senarius

Basically this line consists of six iambic feet, but in practice such a line is very rare.

Example:

Phăsēl‖lŭs īl‖lĕ quēm| vĭ dē|tĭs, hōs|pĭ tēs

(*Cat.* 4, 1)

In drama the last foot is always iambic, and the 5th regularly a spondee. The **spondee** is also very common in the first four feet, the **dactyl** and the **tribrach** are frequent, occasionally the **anapaest** is found, and, more rarely, the **proceleusmatic**. There is usually a **caesura** in either the third or the fourth foot.

Example:

Ĭn hāc| hă bĭ tās|sĕ plātĕ|ā dĭc|tūmst Chrȳ|sĭ dēm

(*Ter, And.* 796)

Iambic Septenarius

This line consists of seven and a half feet, basically iambic, but allowing the same variations as in the Senarius. The 4th foot is regularly an Iambus, and is usually followed by a diaeresis: this is an aid to identifying the line.

Example:

N(am) ĭdcĭr|c(o) āccēr|sōr nūp|tĭ ās| quōd m(i) ād|pără|rī sēn|sĭt

(*Ter, And.* 690)

Iambic Octonarius

This line has eight iambic feet, with the same variations as in the other iambic lines. The 4th and 8th feet are regularly iambic, and a diaeresis follows the 4th foot.

Example:

Cūrā|bĭ tūr.| sēd pătĕr| ă dēst.| că vĕt(e) ēs|sĕ trĭs|tēm sēn|tĭ āt

(*Ter, And.* 403)

Trochaic Septenarius

Apart from drama, this line is common in popular verses, and comes into its own in later Latin poetry. It consists of seven and a half **trochees**, but in practice only the seventh foot is regularly trochaic, while the others may be **spondee, dactyl, tribrach,** or (more rarely) **anapaest.** There is usually a **diaeresis** after the 4th foot.

Example:

Crās ă|mēt quī| nūnqu(am) ă|māvĭt,| quĭqu(e) ă| māvĭt| crās ă|mēt

(*Pervigilium Veneris*)

Trochaic Octonarius

This is a line of eight trochees, allowing the same variations as above. There is a diaeresis after the 4th foot.

Example:

Prōin tū| sōllĭcĭ|tūdĭn|(em) īstām| fālsām| quāe t(e) ēx|crŭcĭăt| mīttās

(*Ter, Heaut.* 177)

LYRIC VERSE

In most lyric metres the line is not to be subdivided into feet, but is itself the unit of scansion, and has a fixed number of syllables. The commonest, which are those used by Catullus and Horace, are the **Hendecasyllabic**, the **Asclepiads**, the **Glyconic** and the **Pherecratic**, which occur either singly or in combinations to form either couplets or stanzas of four lines. Beside these groupings there are the **Alcaic** and **Sapphic** stanzas. Elisions occur much more rarely than in the other metres.

Hendecasyllabic

This is Catullus's favourite line. It consists of eleven syllables in the following pattern:

— — — ˘— ˘— ˘——

Either the first or the second syllable may occasionally be short, and there is usually a caesura after the 5th syllable.

Example:

Vīvāmūs, mĕā Lēsbĭ(a), ātqu(e) ămēmūs

(*Cat.* 5, 1)

Asclepiads

There are two Asclepiad lines, of which the **Lesser** is by far the commoner. It has twelve syllables, in the following pattern with a caesura after the 6th syllable:

$$-\ -\ -\ \smile\ \smile\ -\ \| \ -\ \smile\ \smile\ -\ \smile\ \smile$$

Māecēnās, ătăvīs⁺ ēdĭtē rēgĭbūs

(*Hor, Od. I*, 1, 1)

The **Greater Asclepiad** is formed by adding a **choriambus** $-\ \smile\ \smile\ -$ after the 6th syllable with a **diaeresis** both before and after it.

Example:

Nūllām, Vārē, săcrā vītē prĭūs sēvĕrĭs ārbŏrēm

(*Hor, Od. I*, 18, 1)

Glyconic

The **Glyconic** occurs by itself in Catullus, but more usually it is found in combination with the **Lesser Asclepiad** or the **Pherecratic**. It consists of eight syllables ($-\ -\ -\ \smile\ \smile\ -\ \smile\ -$), so that it is like a Lesser Asclepiad minus the **choriambus**. It has no regular caesura.

Example:

Dōnēc grātŭs ĕrām tĭbī

(*Hor. Od. III*, 9, 1)

Pherecratic

The **Pherecratic** is a Glyconic minus the second last (short) syllable. It is found only in combination with other lines.

Example:

Sūspēndĭssĕ pŏtēntī

(*Hor, Od. I*, 5, 11)

Alcaic Stanza

The **Alcaic stanza** has four lines, of which the first two have the same pattern
– – ˘ – – – ˘ ˘ – ˘ –. In these there is a regular **caesura** after the 5th syllable. The
third line is – – ˘ – – – ˘ – – and the 4th – ˘ ˘ – ˘ ˘ – ˘ – –. Neither of the last two
lines has a regular break in it.

Example:

> Nūnc ēst bĭbēndūm,† nūnc pĕdĕ lībĕrō
> pūlsāndă tēllūs,† nūnc Sălĭărĭbūs
>   ōrnārĕ pūlvīnār dĕōrūm
>   tēmpŭs ĕrāt dăpĭbūs, sŏdālēs.

> (*Hor, Od. I.* 37, 1-4)

Sapphic Stanza

The **Sapphic stanza** also has four lines, of which the first three are the same:
– ˘ – – – ˘ ˘ – ˘ – –. As in the Alcaic there is a **caesura** after the 5th syllable. The
last line is a short **Adonic** – ˘ ˘ – –

Example:

> Īntĕgēr vītāe† scĕlĕrīsquĕ pūrūs
> nōn ēgēt Māurĭs† iăcŭlīs nĕqu(e) ārcū
> nēc vĕnēnātīs† grăvĭdā săgīttīs,
>   Fūscĕ, phărētrā.

> (*Hor, Od. I.* 22, 1-4)

LATIN PHRASES USED IN ENGLISH

What follows is a list of some of the Latin phrases used in English today.

ab initio from the beginning.

ab ovo (lit: from the egg) from the beginning.

absit omen (lit: may the (evil) omen be absent) may the presentiment not become real or take place.

ab urbe condita (used in dates) from the foundation of the city (*i.e. from the foundation of Rome in 753 B.C.*).

A.D. abbr for **anno Domini**.

ad hoc (lit: for this) for a particular purpose only: **an ad hoc committee; an ad hoc decision.**

ad hominem (lit: according to the person) 1 directed against a person rather than against his or her arguments. 2 based on or appealing to emotion rather than reason.

ad infinitum without end; endlessly; to infinity.

ad interim for the meantime; for the present: **ad interim measures.**

ad-lib (abbr for **ad libitum**) ♦ *adj* improvised; impromptu ♦ *adv* without restraint; freely; as one pleases ♦ *vb* to improvise and deliver without preparation.

ad libitum (lit: according to pleasure) as one pleases.

ad majorem Dei gloriam for the greater glory of God (*the Jesuit motto*).

ad nauseam (lit: to (the point of) nausea) to a disgusting extent.

ad rem (lit: to the matter) to the point; without digression: **to reply ad rem; an ad rem discussion.**

advocatus diaboli devil's advocate.

ad valorem (lit: according to value) in proportion to the estimated value of the goods taxed.

aet. (abbr for **aetatis**) at the age of.

Agnus Dei Lamb of God.

alma mater (lit: nurturing mother) one's former university, college or school.

alter ego (lit: other self) 1 a second self. 2 a very close and intimate friend.

a.m. abbr for **ante meridiem**.

AMDG abbr for **ad majorem Dei gloriam**.

amor patriae love of one's country; patriotism.

an. (abbr for **anno**) in the year.

anno Domini in the year of our Lord.

anno urbis conditae in the year of the foundation of the city (*i.e. of Rome in 753 B.C., used in dates*)

anno regni in the year of the reign (of).

annus mirabilis	(lit: wonderful year) a year of wonders.
antebellum	(lit: before the war) of or during the period before a war, especially the American Civil War.
ante meridiem	before noon.
ante-mortem	before death (*esp in legal or medical contexts*).
a.p.	(abbr for **ante prandium**) before a meal (*in prescriptions*).
apparatus criticus	(lit: critical apparatus) textual notes (*list of variant readings, etc., relating to a document, especially in a scholarly edition of a text*).
aq.	abbr for **aqua**.
aqua vitae	(lit: water of life) brandy.
a.r.	abbr for **anno regni**.
arbiter elegantiae *or* **elegantiarum**	judge in a matter of taste.
arcus senilis	(lit: senile bow) opaque circle around the cornea of the eye (*often seen in elderly people*).
argumentum ad hominem	(lit: argument according to the person: Logic) **1** fallacious argument that attacks not an opponent's beliefs but his motives or character. **2** argument that shows an opponent's statement to be inconsistent with his other beliefs.
ars longa vita brevis	art is long, life is short.
AUC	abbr for: **1 ab urbe condita. 2 anno urbis conditae**.
aut vincere aut mori	death or victory.
aurora australis	the southern lights.
aurora borealis	the northern lights.
ave	**1** hail! **2** farewell!
ave atque vale	hail and farewell!
Ave Maria	Hail Mary.
beatae memoriae	of blessed memory.
Beata Virgo	the Blessed Virgin.
Beata Virgo Maria	the Blessed Virgin Mary.
b.i.d	(abbr for **bis in die**) twice a day (*in prescriptions*).
bis dat, qui cito dat	the person who gives promptly gives twice.
BV	abbr for **Beata Virgo**.
c, ca	abbr for **circa**.
camera obscura	(lit: dark chamber) camera obscura.
carpe diem	(lit: seize the day) enjoy the pleasures of the moment without concern for the future.
casus belli	(lit: occasion of war) **1** an event or act used to justify war. **2** the immediate cause of a quarrel.
caveat emptor	let the buyer beware.
cetera desunt	the rest is missing.

eteris paribus	other things being equal.
irca	around.
:odex Juris Canonici	(lit: book of canon law) the official code of canon law (*in the Roman Catholic Church*).
:ogito, ergo sum	I think, therefore I am (*the basis of Descartes' philosophy*).
ompos mentis	of sound mind; sane.
'oram populo	in the presence of the people; openly.
orpus delicti	(lit: the body of the crime: LAW) the body of facts that constitute an offence.
:orpus Juris Canonici	(lit: body of canon law) the official compilation of canon law (*in the Roman Catholic Church*).
:orpus Juris Civilis	(lit: body of civil law) the body of Roman or civil law.
orrigenda	things to be corrected.
orpus vile	(lit: worthless body) person or thing fit only to be the object of an experiment.
ulpa	1 (*LAW*) an act of neglect. 2 (*gen*) a fault; sin; guilt.
um grano salis	with a grain of salt; not too literally.
um laude	(*chiefly US*) with praise (*the lowest of three designations for above-average achievement in examinations*).
urriculum vitae	(lit: the course of one's life) curriculum vitae.
le facto	*adv* in fact ♦ *adj* existing in fact.
le gustibus non est disputandum	there is no arguing about tastes.
le jure	according to law; by right; legally.
le mortuis nil nisi bonum	say nothing but good of the dead.
le novo	anew.
)eo gratias	thanks be to God.
)eo Optimo Maximo	to God, the best, the Greatest.
)eo volente	God willing.
e profundis	out of the depths of misery or dejection.
eus ex machina	(lit: the god from the machine) 1 (*in ancient Greek and Roman drama*) a god introduced into a play to resolve the plot. 2 any unlikely or artificial device serving this purpose.
)ies Irae	(lit: the day of wrath) 1 a famous Latin hymn of the 13th century, describing the Last Judgment. It is used in the Mass for the dead. 2 a musical setting of this hymn, usually part of a setting of the Requiem.
isjecta membra	the scattered remains.
)OM	abbr for **Deo Optimo Maximo**.
ramatis personae	(lit: the persons of the drama) the list of characters in a drama.

Ecce Homo	behold the man (*the words of Pontius Pilate to Christ's accusers* [*John 19:5*]).
editio princeps	(lit: the first edition) the first printed edition of a work
e.g., eg	abbr for **exempli gratia**.
emeritus	retired from office.
e pluribus unum	one out of many (*motto of USA*).
ER	1 (abbr for **Elizabeth Regina**) Queen Elizabeth; 2 (abb for **Eduardus Rex**) King Edward.
errare est humanum	to err is human.
erratum (*pl* **errata**)	error.
et seq.	(abbr for **et sequens**) and the following.
et seqq.	(abbr for **et sequentia**) and those that follow.
ex	(lit: out of, from) 1 (*FINANCE*) not participating in; excluding; without: **ex bonus; ex dividend; ex rights.** 2 (*COMMERCE*) without charge to the buyer until removed from: **ex quay; ex ship; ex works.**
ex cathedra	(lit: from the chair) 1 with authority. 2 defined by the pope as infallibly true, to be accepted by all Roman Catholics.
exeat	(lit: let him or her go out) formal leave of absence.
exempli gratia	for example.
exeunt	they go out (*used as a stage direction*).
exeunt omnes	they all go out (*used as a stage direction*).
exit	he or she goes out (*used as a stage direction*).
ex libris	(lit: from the books (of)) from the collection or library of.
ex officio	by right of position or office.
ex parte	(*LAW*) on behalf of one side or party only (*of an application in a judicial proceeding*): **an ex parte injunction.**
ex post facto	having retrospective effect: **an ex post facto law.**
ex silentio	(lit: from silence) based on a lack of evidence to the contrary (*of a theory, assumption etc*).
extempore	(lit: instantaneously) without planning or preparation impromptu.
ex voto	*adv, adj* in accordance with a vow ♦ *n* offering made fulfilment of a vow.
facile princeps	(lit: easily first) an obvious leader.
fecit (*abbr* **fec**)	(he or she) made it (*used formerly on works of art next to the artist's name*).
felo de se	suicide.
festina lente	more haste, less speed.
fiat lux	let there be light.
Fidei Defensor	defender of the faith.

dus Achates	(lit: faithful Achates) faithful friend or companion (*the name of the faithful companion of Aeneas in Virgil's Aeneid*).
oruit	(he or she) flourished (*used to indicate the period when a historical figure, whose birth and death dates are unknown, was most active*).
ons et origo	the source and origin.
enius loci	(lit: genius of the place) 1 the guardian spirit of a place. 2 the special atmosphere of a particular place.
Gloria in Excelsis Deo	(lit: glory to God in the highest) 1 the Greater Doxology, beginning in Latin with these words. 2 a musical setting of this.
Gloria Patri	(lit: glory to the father) 1 the Lesser Doxology, beginning in Latin with these words. 2 a musical setting of this.
inc illae lacrimae	hence those tears.
IJ	(abbr for **hic jacet**) here lies (*on gravestones*).
IJS	(abbr for **hic jacet sepultus**) here lies buried (*on gravestones*).
orrible dictu	horrible to relate.
oid.	abbr for **ibidem**.
oidem	in the same place (*in annotations, bibliographies, etc., when referring to a book, article, chapter, or page previously cited*).
d est	that is (to say); in other words.
dem	the same (*used to refer to an article, chapter, etc., previously cited*).
e.	abbr for **id est**.
gn.	abbr for **ignotus**.
gnoratio elenchi	(lit: an ignorance of proof: *Logic*) 1 a purported refutation of a proposition that does not in fact prove it false but merely establishes a related but strictly irrelevant proposition. 2 the fallacy of arguing in this way.
gnotum per ignotius	(lit: the unknown by means of the more unknown) an explanation that is obscurer than the thing to be explained.
gnotus	unknown.
gnis fatuus	will o' the wisp.
mp.	1 (abbr for **Imperator**) Emperor; 2 (abbr for **Imperatrix**) Empress.
a absentia	in one's absence; in the absence of: **he was condemned in absentia.**
a aeternum	forever; eternally.
a articulo mortis	at the point of death.

in camera	(lit: in the chamber) in private.
in extenso	at full length.
in extremis	(lit: in the furthest reaches) **1** in extremity; in dire straits. **2** at the point of death.
infra	below.
infra dig	(abbr for **infra dignitatem**) beneath one's dignity.
in loco parentis	in place of a parent (*said of a person acting in a parenta capacity*).
in medias res	(lit: into the midst of things) in or into the middle of events or a narrative.
in memoriam	in memory of; as a memorial to (*used in obituaries, epitaphs etc*).
in perpetuum	for ever.
in personam	(lit: against the person) directed against a specific person or persons (*LAW: of a judicial act*).
in propria persona	in person; personally.
in rem	(lit: against the matter) directed against property rather than against a specific person (*LAW: of a judicia act*).
in rerum natura	in the nature of things.
INRI	(lit: Jesus of Nazareth, King of the Jews) abbr for **Iesu Nazarenus Rex Iudaeorum** (*the inscription placed ove Christ's head during the Crucifixion*).
in situ	(lit: in position) in the natural, original, or appropriate position.
inter alia	among other things.
inter alios	among other people.
inter vivos	(*LAW*) between living people: **an inter vivos gift**.
in toto	totally; entirely; completely.
in utero	within the womb.
in vacuo	in a vacuum.
in vino veritas	in wine there is truth.
in vitro	(lit: in glass) made to occur outside the body of the organism in an artificial environment (*of biological processes or reactions*): **in vitro fertilization**.
in vivo	(lit: in a living (thing)) occurring or carried out in the living organism (*of biological processes or experiments*).
ipse dixit	(lit: he himself said it) an arbitrary and unsupported assertion.
ipsissima verba	the very words.
ipso facto	by the fact itself.
i.q.	(lit: the same as) abbr for **idem quod**.
lapsus linguae	a slip of the tongue.
lc	(abbr for **(in) loco citato**) in the place cited.

ex loci	the law of the place.
ex non scripta	the unwritten law; common law.
ex scripta	the written law; statute law.
ex talionis	the law of revenge or retaliation.
oc. cit.	(abbr for (**in**) **loco citato**) in the place cited (*in textual annotation*).
magna cum laude	(chiefly US) with great praise (*the second of three designations for above-average achievement in examinations*).
magnum opus	a great work of art or literature (*especially the greatest single work of an artist*).
mala fide	undertaken in bad faith.
mare clausum	(lit: closed sea: LAW) a sea coming under the jurisdiction of one nation and closed to all others.
mare liberum	(lit: free sea: LAW) a sea open to navigation by shipping of all nations.
mare nostrum	(lit: our sea) the Mediterranean.
mater	mother (*often used facetiously*).
mater dolorosa	(lit: sorrowful mother) the Virgin Mary sorrowing for the dead Christ (*especially as depicted in art*).
materfamilias	(lit: mother of family) the mother of a family or the female head of a family.
materia medica	(lit: medical matter) **1** the branch of medical science concerned with the study of drugs used in the treatment of disease. **2** the drugs used in the treatment of disease.
mea culpa	(lit: my fault) an acknowledgement of guilt.
memento mori	(lit: remember you must die) an object, such as a skull, intended to remind people of the inevitability of death.
mens sana in corpore sano	a healthy mind in a healthy body.
mens rea	(lit: guilty mind: LAW) a criminal intention or knowledge that an act is wrong.
miles gloriosus	a braggart soldier (*especially as a stock figure in comedy*).
mirabile dictu	wonderful to relate.
mittimus	(lit: we send) a warrant of commitment to prison or a command to a jailer directing him to hold someone in prison.
modus operandi	procedure; method of operating; manner of working.
modus ponens	(lit: mood that affirms) the principle that whenever a conditional statement and its antecedent are given to be true its consequent may be validly inferred.

modus tollens	(lit: mood that denies) the principle that whenever a conditional statement and the negation of its consequent are given to be true, the negation of its antecedent may be validly inferred.
modus vivendi	(lit: way of living) a working arrangement between conflicting interests; practical compromise.
motu proprio	(lit: of his own accord) an administrative papal bull.
multum in parvo	much in a small space.
mutatis mutandis	with the necessary changes.
NB, N.B., nb, n.b.	(abbr for **nota bene**) note well.
nem. con.	(abbr for **nemine contradicente**) no-one contradicting; unanimously.
nemo me impune lacessit	no-one provokes me with impunity.
ne plus ultra	(lit: not more beyond) the extreme or perfect point or state.
nihil	nil; nothing.
nihil obstat	there is no obstacle.
nil desperandum	(lit: nothing to be despaired of) never despair.
nisi prius	(lit: unless previously) 1 _in England_ (a) a direction that a case be brought up to Westminster for trial before a single judge and jury. (b) the writ giving this direction 2 _in the US_ a court where civil actions are tried by a single judge sitting with a jury as distinguished from an appellate court.
nolens volens	whether willing or unwilling.
noli me tangere	(lit: do not touch me) a warning against interfering with or against touching a person or thing.
nolle prosequi	(lit: do not pursue) an entry made on the court record when the plaintiff in a civil suit or prosecutor in a criminal prosecution undertakes not to continue the action or prosecution.
nolo contendere	(lit: I do not wish to contend) a plea made by a defendant to a criminal charge having the same effect in those proceedings as a plea of guilty but not precluding him from denying the charge in a subsequent action.
non compos mentis	(lit: not in control of one's mind) mentally incapable of managing one's own affairs; of unsound mind; insane.
non prosequitur	(lit: he does not proceed) a judgment in favour of a defendant when the plaintiff failed to take the necessary steps in an action within the time allowed.
non sequitur	(lit: it does not follow) 1 (_gen_) a statement having little or no relevance to what preceded it. 2 (_Logic_) a conclusion that does not follow from the premises.
nulli secundus	second to none.

umen	(lit: divine power) **1** (*especially in ancient Roman religion*) a deity or spirit presiding over a thing or place. **2** a guiding principle, force, or spirit.
unc Dimittis	(lit: now let depart) **1** the Canticle of Simeon (*Luke 2:29-32*). **2** a musical setting of this.
b.	**1** abbr for **obiit**. **2** (abbr for **obiter**) incidentally; in passing.
biit	he or she died (*on gravestones*).
biter dictum	(lit: something said in passing) **1** (*LAW*) an observation by a judge on some point of law not directly in issue in the case before him and thus neither requiring his decision nor serving as a precedent, but nevertheless of persuasive authority. **2** any comment, remark, or observation made in passing.
bscurum per obscurius	(lit: the obscure by means of the more obscure) an explanation that is obscurer than the thing to be explained.
mnium-gatherum	(*often facetious*) a miscellaneous collection; assortment.
nus probandi	(*LAW*) the burden of proof.
p. cit.	(abbr of **opere citato**) in the work cited.
pus anglicanum	(lit: English work) fine embroidery (*especially of church vestments*).
ra pro nobis	pray for us.
tempora! O mores!	oh the times! oh the customs!
.a.	abbr of **per annum**.
ace	by leave of; with due deference to (*used to acknowledge politely someone who disagrees with the speaker or writer*).
ari passu	with equal speed or progress; equably (*often used to refer to the right of creditors to receive assets from the same source without one taking precedence*).
assim	here and there; throughout (*used to indicate that what is referred to occurs frequently in the work cited*).
aterfamilias	(lit: father of the family) **1** the male head of a household. **2** the head of a household having authority over its members.
ax vobiscum	peace be with you.
eccavi	(lit: I have sinned) a confession of guilt.
eculium	(lit: property) property that a father or master allowed his child or slave to hold as his own.
er annum	every year; year by year.
er ardua ad astra	through difficulties to the stars (*motto of the RAF*).
er capita	(lit: according to heads) of or for each person.
er contra	on the contrary.

per diem	(lit: for the day) **1** every day; by the day. **2** an allowance for daily expenses, usually those incurred while working.
per mensem	every month; by the month.
per pro	(abbr for **per procurationem**) by delegation to; through the agency of (*used when signing documents on behalf of someone else*).
persona grata	an acceptable person (*especially a diplomat acceptable to the government of the country to which he is sent*).
persona non grata	unacceptable or unwelcome person.
petitio principii	(lit: an assumption at the beginning: *Logic*) a form of fallacious reasoning in which the conclusion has been assumed in the premises; begging the question.
pia mater	(lit: pious mother) the innermost of the three membranes that cover the brain and spinal cord.
pinxit	(he or she) painted this (*used formerly on works of art next to the artist's name*).
p.m., P.M., pm, PM	abbr. for **1** post meridiem **2** postmortem.
post-bellum	(lit: after war) of or during the period after a war, especially the American Civil War.
post hoc	(lit: after this: *Logic*) the fallacy of assuming that temporal succession is evidence of causal relation.
post hoc, ergo propter hoc	after this, therefore because of this (*a fallacy of reasoning*).
post meridiem	after noon.
postmortem	(lit: after death) *n* **1** dissection and examination of a dead body to determine the cause of death. **2** analysis or study of a recently completed event ♦ *adj* occurring after death.
pp	abbr for **1** per pro. **2** post prandium after a meal (*in prescriptions*).
PPS	(lit: after postscript; abbr for **post postscriptum**) additional postscript.
pr	(abbr for: **per rectum**) through the rectum (*in prescriptions*).
prima facie	at a first view.
primum mobile	(lit: first moving (thing)) prime mover.
primus inter pares	first among equals.
prn	(abbr for **pro re nata**) as the situation demands, as needed (*in prescriptions*).
pro forma	(lit: for form's sake) **1** prescribing a set form or procedure. **2** performed in a set manner.
pro patria	for one's country.
pro rata	in proportion.
pro tempore	for the time being.
proxime accessit	(lit: he or she came next) the runner-up.

q.e.	(abbr for **quod est**) which is.
QED	abbr for **quod erat demonstrandum**.
QEF	abbr for **quod erat faciendum**.
quid pro quo	(lit: something for something) **1** a reciprocal exchange. **2** something given in compensation, especially an advantage or object given in exchange for another.
quis custodiet ipsos custodes?	who will guard the guards?
q.l.	(abbr for **quantum libet**) as much as you please (*in prescriptions*).
qm	(abbr for **quaque mane**) every morning (*in prescriptions*).
qn	(abbr for **quaque nocte**) every night (*in prescriptions*).
quod erat demonstrandum	which was to be proved.
quod erat faciendum	which was to be done.
quot homines, tot sententiæ	there are as many opinions as there are people.
quo vadis?	whither goest thou?
qqv	(abbr for **quae vide**) which (*words, items etc*) see (*denoting a cross reference to more than one item*).
qs	(abbr for **quantum sufficit**) as much as will suffice (*in prescriptions*).
qv	(abbr for **quod vide**) which (word, item etc) see (*denoting a cross reference*).
rara avis	(lit: rare bird) an unusual, uncommon or exceptional person or thing.
reductio ad absurdum	(lit: reduction to the absurd) **1** a method of disproving a proposition by showing that its inevitable consequences would be absurd. **2** a method of indirectly proving a proposition by assuming its negation to be true and showing that this leads to an absurdity. **3** application of a principle or a proposed principle to an instance in which it is absurd.
requiescat	(lit: may he or she rest) a prayer for the repose of the souls of the dead.
requiescat in pace	may he or she rest in peace.
res gestae	(lit: things done) **1** things done or accomplished; achievements. **2** (*LAW*) incidental facts and circumstances that are admissible in evidence because they introduce or explain the matter in issue.
res ipsa loquitur	(*LAW*) the thing or matter speaks for itself.
res judicata	(*LAW*) a matter already adjudicated upon that cannot be raised again.
res publica	(lit: the public thing) the state, republic, or commonwealth.

resurgam	I shall rise again.
RI	1 (abbr for **Regina et Imperatrix**) Queen and Empress 2 (abbr for **Rex et Imperator**) King and Emperor.
rigor mortis	(lit: rigidity of death) the stiffness of joints and muscular rigidity of a dead body.
RIP	abbr for **requiescat** or **requiescant in pace**.
risus sardonicus	(lit: sardonic laugh) fixed contraction of the facial muscles resulting in a peculiar distorted grin, caused especially by tetanus.
sanctum sanctorum	(lit: holy of holies) 1 (*Bible*) the holy of holies. 2 (*often facetious*) an especially private place.
sartor resartus	the tailor patched.
schola cantorum	(lit: school of singers) a choir or choir school maintained by a church.
scire facias	(lit: cause (him) to know) 1 (*LAW, rare*) a judicial writ founded upon some record, such as a judgement, letters patent, etc., requiring the person against whom it is brought to show cause why the record should not be enforced or annulled. 2 a proceeding begun by the issue of such a writ.
semper fidelis	always faithful.
semper idem	always the same.
seq.	(abbr for **sequens**) the following (one).
seqq.	(abbr for **sequentia**) the following (ones).
seriatim	in order.
sic	thus (*often used to call attention to some quoted mistake*).
sic itur ad astra	such is the way to the stars.
sic transit gloria mundi	so passes the glory of the world.
si monumentum requiris, circumspice	if you seek (his) monument, look around you (*inscription on the architect Sir Christopher Wren's tomb in St Paul's Cathedral*).
sine die	without a day.
sine prole	(*LAW*) without issue.
sine qua non	(lit: without which not) an indispensable condition or requirement.
sl	(abbr for **sine loco**) without place (*of publication*).
sp	abbr for **sine prole**.
spiritus asper	rough breathing.
spiritus lenis	smooth breathing.
SPQR	(abbr for **Senatus Populusque Romanus**) the Senate and People of Rome.
sq.	(abbr for **sequens**) the following (one).
sqq.	(abbr for **sequentia**) the following (ones).

Stabat Mater	(lit: the mother was standing) 1 a Latin hymn, probably of the 13th century, commemorating the sorrows of the Virgin Mary at the crucifixion and used in the Mass and various other services. 2 a musical setting of this hymn.
status quo	(lit: the state in which) the existing state of affairs.
stet	let it stand.
sub judice	before a court of law or a judge; under judicial consideration.
sub rosa	(lit: under the rose) secretly.
sub voce	under the word.
sui generis	(lit: of its own kind) unique.
sui juris	(lit: of one's own right) (_LAW_) of full age and not under disability; legally competent to manage one's own affairs; independent.
summa cum laude	(_chiefly u.s._) with the utmost praise (_the highest of three designations for above-average achievement in examinations. In Britain it is sometimes used to designate a first-class honours degree_).
summum bonum	the principle of goodness in which all moral values are included or from which they are derived; highest or supreme good.
suo jure	(_chiefly LAW_) in one's own right.
suo loco	(_chiefly LAW_) in a person or thing's own or rightful place.
supra	above.
sursum corda	lift up your hearts (to God).
SV	abbr for **sub voce**.
tabula rasa	(lit: a scraped tablet) 1 the mind in its uninformed original state. 2 an opportunity for a fresh start; clean slate.
taedium vitae	(lit: weariness of life) the feeling that life is boring and dull.
Te Deum	(lit: Thee, God) 1 an ancient Latin hymn in rhythmic prose, sung or recited at matins in the Roman Catholic Church and in English translation at morning prayer in the Church of England and used by both churches as an expression of thanksgiving on special occasions. 2 a musical setting of this hymn. 3 a service of thanksgiving in which the recital of this hymn forms a central part.
te igitur	(lit: Thee, therefore: _Roman Catholic Church_) the first prayer of the canon of the Mass.
tempore	in the time of.
tempus fugit	time flies.
terminus ad quem	(lit: the end to which) the aim or terminal point.
terminus a quo	(lit: the end from which) the starting point; beginning.

terra firma	the solid earth; firm ground.
terra incognita	an unexplored or unknown land, region or area for study.
tertium quid	a third something.
t.i.d.	(abbr for **ter in die**) three times a day (_in prescriptions_
tu quoque	you likewise (_a retort made by a person accused of a crime implying that the accuser is also guilty of the sam crime_).
uberrima fides	utmost good faith.
ubique	everywhere.
ubi supra	where (mentioned or cited) above.
ultima Thule	(lit: the most distant Thule) **1** the utmost boundary or limit. **2** a remote goal or aim.
ultra vires	beyond one's powers.
una voce	with one voice.
urbi et orbi	(_Roman Catholic Church_) to the city and the world (_a phrase qualifying the solemn papal blessing_).
ut dict.	(abbr for **ut dictum**) as directed.
ut infra	as below.
ut supra	as above.
v.	abbr for **1 verso**. **2 versus**. **3 vide**.
vade in pace	go in peace.
vade mecum	(lit: go with me) a handbook or other aid carried on th person for immediate use when needed.
væe victis	woe to the conquered!
vale	farewell!
veni, vidi, vici	I came, I saw, I conquered.
venire facias	(lit: you must make come: _LAW_) a writ directing a sheriff to summon suitable persons to form a jury.
verbatim et litteratim	word for word and letter for letter.
verb. sap.	(abbr for **verbum sapienti sat est**) a word is enough to the wise.
verso	**1** the back of a sheet of printed paper. **2** the side of a coin opposite to the obverse; reverse.
versus	**1** against; in opposition to. **2** as opposed to; in contrast with.
via	by way of.
via media	a middle course.
vice	in the place of; instead of; as a substitute for.
vice versa	the other way round.
vide	see.
videlicet	namely; to wit.

vi et armis	(lit: by force and arms) a kind of trespass accompanied by force and violence.
VIR	(abbr for **Victoria Imperatrix Regina**) Victoria, Empress and Queen.
virginibus puerisque	for maidens and youths.
vis inertiæ	the power of inertia.
viva voce	(lit: with living voice) *adv, adj* by word of mouth ♦ *n* an oral examination.
viz.	abbr for **videlicet**.
vl	(abbr for **varia lecto**) variant reading.
vollente Deo	God willing.
vox populi	the voice of the people; popular or public opinion.
vox populi, vox Dei	the voice of the people is the voice of God.
VR	(abbr for **Victoria Regina**) Queen Queen Victoria.
VRI	(abbr for **Victoria Regina et Imperatrix**) Victoria, Queen and Empress.

English-Latin

A, a

a, an *art not translated*; (*a certain*) quīdam; **twice a day** bis in diē; **four acres a man** quaterna in singulōs iūgera.

aback *adv*: **taken ~** dēprehēnsus.

abaft *adv* in puppī ♦ *prep* post, pōne.

abandon *vt* relinquere; (*wilfully*) dērelinquere, dēserere; (*to danger*) ōbicere; (*to pleasure*) dēdere; (*plan*) abicere; **~ hope** spem abicere.

abandoned *adj* perditus.

abase *vt* dēprimere; **~ oneself** sē prōsternere.

abash *vt* perturbāre; rubōrem incutere (*dat*).

abate *vt* minuere, imminuere; (*a portion*) remittere ♦ *vi* (*fever*) dēcēdere; (*passion*) dēfervēscere; (*price*) laxāre; (*storm*) cadere.

abatement *n* remissiō *f*, dēminūtiō *f*.

abbess *n* abbātissa *f*.

abbey *n* abbātia *f*.

abbot *n* abbās *m*.

abbreviate *vt* imminuere.

abbreviation *n* (*writing*) nota *f*.

abdicate *vt* sē abdicāre (*abl*).

abdication *n* abdicātiō *f*.

abduct *vt* abripere.

abduction *n* raptus *m*.

aberration *n* error *m*.

abet *vt* adiuvāre, adesse (*dat*), favēre (*dat*).

abettor *n* adiūtor *m*, minister *m*, fautor *m*, socius *m*.

abeyance *n*: **in ~** intermissus; **be in ~** iacēre.

abhor *vt* ōdisse, invīsum habēre.

abhorrence *n* odium *nt*.

abhorrent *adj*: **~ to** aliēnus ab.

abide *vi* (*dwell*) habitāre; (*tarry*) commorārī; (*last*) dūrāre; **~ by** *vt fus* stāre (*abl*), perstāre in (*abl*).

abiding *adj* perpetuus, diūturnus.

ability *n* (*to do*) facultās *f*, potestās *f*; (*physical*) vīrēs *fpl*; (*mental*) ingenium *nt*; **to the best of my ~** prō meā parte, prō virīlī parte.

abject *adj* abiectus, contemptus; (*downcast*) dēmissus.

abjectly *adv* humiliter, dēmissē.

abjure *vt* ēiūrāre.

ablative *n* ablātīvus *m*.

ablaze *adj* flāgrāns, ardēns.

able *adj* perītus, doctus; **be ~** posse, valēre.

able-bodied *adj* rōbustus.

ablution *n* lavātiō *f*.

ably *adv* perītē, doctē.

abnegation *n* abstinentia *f*.

abnormal *adj* inūsitātus; (*excess*) immodicus.

abnormally *adv* inūsitātē, praeter mōrem.

aboard *adv* in nāvī; **go ~** nāvem cōnscendere; **put ~** impōnere.

abode *n* domicilium *nt*, sēdes *f*.

abolish *vt* tollere, ē mediō tollere, abolēre; (*law*) abrogāre.

abolition *n* dissolūtiō *f*; (*law*) abrogātiō *f*.

abominable *adj* dētestābilis, nefārius.

abominably *adv* nefāriē, foedē.

abominate *vt* dētestārī.

abomination *n* odium *nt*; (*thing*) nefas *nt*.

aboriginal *adj* prīscus.

aborigines *n* aborīginēs *mpl*.

abortion *n* abortus *m*.

abortive *adj* abortīvus; (*fig*) inritus; **be ~** ad inritum redigī.

abound *vi* abundāre, superesse; **~ in** abundāre (*abl*), adfluere (*abl*).

abounding *adj* abundāns, adfluēns; cōpiōsus ab.

about *adv* (*place*) usu expressed by cpd verbs; (*number*) circiter, ferē, fermē ♦ *prep* (*place*) circā, circum (*acc*); (*number*) circā, ad (*acc*); (*time*) sub (*acc*); (*concerning*) dē (*abl*); **~ to die** moritūrus; **I am ~ to go** in eō est ut eam.

above *adv* suprā; **from ~** dēsuper; **over and ~** īnsuper ♦ *prep* suprā (*acc*); (*motion*) super (*acc*); (*rest*) super (*abl*); **be ~** (*conduct*) indignārī.

abreast *adv* (*ships*) aequātīs prōrīs; **walk ~ of** latus tegere (*dat*).

abridge *vt* contrahere, compendī facere.

abridgement *n* epitomē *f*.

abroad *adv* peregrē; (*out of doors*) forīs; **be ~** peregrīnārī; **from ~** peregrē.

abrogate *vt* dissolvere; (*law*) abrogāre.

abrupt *adj* subitus, repentīnus; (*speech*) concīsus.

abscess *n* vomica *f*.

abscond *vi* aufugere.

absence *n* absentia *f*; **in my ~** mē absente; **leave of ~** commeātus *m*.

absent *adj* absēns; **be ~** abesse; **~ oneself** *vi* deesse, nōn adesse.

absent-minded *adj* immemor, parum attentus.

absolute *adj* absolūtus, perfectus; (*not limited*) īnfīnītus; (*not relative*) simplex; **~ power** rēgnum *nt*, dominātus *m*; **~ ruler** rēx.

absolutely *adv* absolūtē, omnīnō.

absolution *n* venia *f*.

absolve vt absolvere, exsolvere; (from punishment) condōnāre.

absorb vt bibere, absorbēre; (fig) distringere; **I am ~ed in** tōtus sum in (abl).

absorbent adj bibulus.

abstain vi abstinēre, sē abstinēre; (from violence) temperāre.

abstemious adj sobrius.

abstinence n abstinentia f, continentia f.

abstinent adj abstinēns, sobrius.

abstract adj mente perceptus, cōgitātiōne comprehēnsus ♦ n epitomē f ♦ vt abstrahere, dēmere.

abstraction n (idea) nōtiō f; (inattention) animus parum attentus.

abstruse adj reconditus, obscūrus, abstrūsus.

absurd adj ineptus, absurdus.

absurdity n ineptiae fpl, insulsitās f.

absurdly adv ineptē, absurdē.

abundance n cōpia f, abundantia f; **there is ~ of** abundē est (gen).

abundant adj cōpiōsus, abundāns, largus; **be ~** abundāre.

abundantly adv abundē, abundanter, adfātim.

abuse vt abūtī (abl); (words) maledīcere (dat) ♦ n probra ntpl, maledicta ntpl, convīcium nt, contumēlia f.

abusive adj maledicus, contumēliōsus.

abut vi adiacēre; **~ting on** cōnfīnis (dat), fīnitimus (dat).

abysmal adj profundus.

abyss n profundum nt, vorāgō f; (water) gurges m; (fig) barathrum nt.

academic adj scholasticus; (style) umbrātilis; (sect) Acadēmicus.

academy n schola f; (Plato's) Acadēmīa f.

accede vi adsentīrī; **~ to** accipere.

accelerate vt, vi adcelerāre, festīnāre; (process) mātūrāre.

accent n vōx f; (intonation) sonus m; (mark) apex m ♦ vt (syllable) acuere; (word) sonum admovēre (dat).

accentuate vt exprimere.

accept vt accipere.

acceptable adj acceptus, grātus, probābilis; **be ~** placēre.

acceptation n significātiō f.

access n aditus m; (addition) accessiō f; (illness) impetus m.

accessary n socius m, particeps m.

accessible adj (person) adfābilis, facilis; **be ~** (place) patēre; (person) facilem sē praebēre.

accession n (addition) accessiō f; (king's) initium rēgnī.

accident n cāsus m, calamitās f.

accidental adj fortuītus.

accidentally adv cāsū, fortuītō.

acclaim vt adclāmāre.

acclamation n clāmor m, studium nt.

acclimatize vt aliēnō caelō adsuēfacere.

accommodate vt accommodāre, aptāre; (lodging) hospitium parāre (dat); **~ oneself to** mōrigerārī (dat).

accommodating adj facilis.

accommodation n hospitium nt.

accompany vt comitārī; (courtesy) prōsequī; (to Forum) dēdūcere; (music) concinere (dat).

accomplice n socius m, particeps m, cōnscius m.

accomplish vt efficere, perficere, patrāre.

accomplished adj doctus, perītus.

accomplishment n effectus m, perfectiō f, fīnis m; **~s** pl artēs fpl.

accord vi inter sē congruere, cōnsentīre ♦ vt dare, praebēre, praestāre ♦ n cōnsēnsus m, concordia f; (music) concentus m; **of one's own ~** suā sponte, ultrō; **with one ~** unā vōce.

accordance n: **in ~ with** ex, ē (abl), secundum (acc).

according adv: **~ to** ex, ē (abl), secundum (acc); (proportion) prō (abl); **~ as** prōut.

accordingly adv itaque, igitur, ergō.

accost vt appellāre, adloquī, compellāre.

account n ratiō f; (story) nārrātiō f, expositiō f; **on ~ of** ob (acc); propter (acc), causā (gen); **be of no ~** (person) nihilī aestimārī, nēquam esse; **on that ~** idcircō ideō; **on your ~** tuā grātiā, tuō nōmine; **give an ~** ratiōnem reddere; **present an ~** ratiōnem referre; **take ~ of** ratiōnem habēre (gen); **put down to my ~** mihī expēnsum ferre; **the ~s balance** ratiō cōnstat/convenit.

account vi: **~ for** ratiōnēs reddere, adferre (cūr); **that ~s for it** haec causa est; (PROV) hinc illae lacrimae.

accountant n ā ratiōnibus, ratiōcinātor m.

accountable adj reus; **I am ~ for** mihi ratiō reddenda est (gen).

account book n tabulae fpl; cōdex acceptī et expēnsī.

accoutred adj īnstructus, ōrnātus.

accoutrements n ōrnāmenta ntpl, arma ntpl.

accredited adj pūblicā auctōritate missus.

accretion n accessiō f.

accrue vi (addition) cēdere; (advantage) redundāre.

accumulate vt cumulāre, congerere, coacervāre ♦ vi crēscere, cumulārī.

accumulation n cumulus m, acervus m.

accuracy n cūra f; (writing) subtīlitās f.

accurate adj (work) exāctus, subtīlis; (worker) dīligēns.

accurately adv subtīliter, ad amussim, dīligenter.

accursed adj sacer; (fig) exsecrātus, scelestus.

accusation n (act) accūsātiō f; (charge) crīmen nt; (unfair) īnsimulātiō f; (false) calumnia f; **bring an ~ against** accūsāre; (to a magistrate) nōmen dēferre (gen).

accusative n (case) accūsātīvus m.

accuse vt accūsāre, crīminārī, reum facere; (falsely) īnsimulāre; **the ~d** reus; (said by prosecutor) iste.

accuser n accūsātor m; (civil suit) petītor m; (informer) dēlātor m.

accustom vt adsuēfacere; ~ **oneself**
adsuēscere, consuēscere.

accustomed adj adsuētus; **be ~** solēre;
become ~ adsuēscere, consuēscere.

ace n ūniō f; **I was within an ~ of going**
minimum āfuit quin īrem.

acerbity n acerbitās f.

ache n dolor m ♦ vi dolēre.

achieve vt cōnficere, patrāre; (win) cōnsequī,
adsequī.

achievement n factum nt, rēs gesta.

acid adj acidus.

acknowledge vt (fact) agnōscere; (fault)
fatērī, cōnfitērī; (child) tollere; (service)
grātiās agere prō (abl); **I have to ~ your letter
of 1st March** accēpī litterās tuās Kal. Mart.
datās.

acknowledgement n cōnfessiō f; grātia f.

acme n fastīgium nt, flōs m.

aconite n aconītum nt.

acorn n glāns f.

acoustics n rēs audītōria f.

acquaint vt certiōrem facere, docēre; ~
oneself with cognōscere; **~ed with** gnārus
(gen), perītus (gen).

acquaintance n (with fact) cognitiō f, scientia
f; (with person) familiāritās f, ūsus m; (person)
nōtus m, familiāris m.

acquiesce vi (assent) adquiēscere; (submit)
aequō animō patī.

acquiescence n: **with your ~** tē nōn
adversante, pāce tuā.

acquire vt adquīrere, adipīscī, cōnsequī;
nancīscī.

acquirements n artēs fpl.

acquisition n (act) comparātiō f, quaestus m;
(thing) quaesītum nt.

acquisitive adj quaestuōsus.

acquit vt absolvere; ~ **oneself** sē praestāre,
officiō fungī.

acquittal n absolūtiō f.

acre n iūgerum nt.

acrid adj asper, ācer.

acrimonious adj acerbus, truculentus.

acrimony n acerbitās f.

acrobat n fūnambulus m.

acropolis n arx f.

across adv trānsversus ♦ prep trāns (acc).

act n factum nt, facinus nt; (play) āctus m; (POL)
āctum nt, senātūs cōnsultum nt, dēcrētum nt;
I was in the ~ of saying in eō erat ut dīcerem;
caught in the ~ dēprehēnsus ♦ vi facere,
agere; (conduct) sē gerere; (stage)
histriōnem esse, partēs agere; (pretence)
simulāre ♦ vt: **a part** partēs agere,
persōnam sustinēre; ~ **the part of** agere; ~ **as**
esse, munere fungī (gen); ~ **upon**
(instructions) exsequī.

action n (doing) āctiō f; (deed) factum nt,
facinus nt; (legal) āctiō f, līs f; (MIL) proelium
nt; (of play) āctiō f; (of speaker) gestus m; **bring
an ~ against** lītem intendere, āctiōnem
īnstituere (dat); **be in ~** agere, rem gerere;

(MIL) pugnāre, in aciē dīmicāre; **man of ~** vir
strēnuus.

active adj impiger, strēnuus, sēdulus, nāvus.

actively adv impigrē, strēnuē, nāviter.

activity n (motion) mōtus m; (energy) industria
f, sēdulitās f.

actor n histriō m; (in comedy) cōmoedus m; (in
tragedy) tragoedus m.

actress n mīma f.

actual adj vērus, ipse.

actually adv rē vērā.

actuate vt movēre, incitāre.

acumen n acūmen nt, ingenī aciēs, argūtiae
fpl.

acute adj acūtus, ācer; (pain) ācer; (speech)
argūtus, subtīlis.

acutely adv acūtē, ācriter, argūtē.

acuteness n (mind) acūmen nt, aciēs f,
subtīlitas f.

adage n prōverbium nt.

adamant n adamās m ♦ adj obstinātus.

adamantine adj adamantinus.

adapt vt accommodāre.

adaptable adj flexibilis, facile
accommodandus.

adaptation n accommodātiō f.

add vt addere, adicere, adiungere; **be ~ed**
accēdere.

adder n vīpera f.

addicted adj dēditus.

addition n adiūnctiō f, accessiō f,
additāmentum nt, incrēmentum nt; **in ~**
īnsuper, praetereā; **in ~ to** praeter (acc).

additional adj novus, adiūnctus.

addled adj (egg) inritus; (brain) inānis.

address vt compellāre, alloquī; (crowd)
cōntiōnem habēre apud (acc); (letter)
īnscrībere; ~ **oneself** (to action) accingī ♦ n
adloquium nt; (public) cōntiō f, ōratiō f; (letter)
īnscrīptiō f.

adduce vt (argument) adferre; (witness)
prōdūcere.

adept adj perītus.

adequate adj idōneus, dignus, pār; **be ~**
sufficere.

adequately adv satis, ut pār est.

adhere vi haerēre, adhaerēre; ~ **to** inhaerēre
(dat), inhaerēscere in (abl); (agreement)
manēre, stāre in (abl).

adherent n adsectātor m; (of party) fautor m;
(of person) cliēns m.

adhesive adj tenax.

adieu interj valē, valēte; **bid ~ to** valēre iubēre.

adjacent adj fīnitimus, vīcīnus; **be ~ to**
adiacēre (dat).

adjoin vi adiacēre (dat).

adjoining adj fīnitimus, adiūnctus; proximus.

adjourn vt (short time) differre; (longer time)
prōferre; (case) ampliāre ♦ vi rem differre,
prōferre.

adjournment n dīlātiō f, prōlātiō f.

adjudge vt addīcere, adiūdicāre.

adjudicate vi dēcernere.

adjudicator n arbiter m.
adjunct n appendix f, accessiō f.
adjure vt obtestārī, obsecrāre.
adjust vt (adapt) accommodāre; (put in order) compōnere.
adjutant n (MIL) optiō m; (civil) adiūtor m.
administer vt administrāre, gerere; (justice) reddere; (oath to) iūreiūrandō adigere; (medicine) dare, adhibēre.
administration n administrātiō f.
administrator n administrātor m, prōcūrātor m.
admirable adj admīrābilis, ēgregius.
admirably adv ēgregiē.
admiral n praefectus classis; ~'s ship nāvis praetōria.
admiralty n praefectī classium.
admiration n admīrātiō f, laus f.
admire vt admīrārī; mīrārī.
admirer n laudātor m; amātor m.
admissible adj aequus.
admission n (entrance) aditus m; (of guilt etc) cōnfessiō f.
admit vt (let in) admittere, recipere, accipere; (to membership) adscīscere; (argument) concēdere; (fault) fatērī; ~ of patī, recipere.
admittedly adv sānē.
admonish vt admonēre, commonēre, hortārī.
admonition n admonitiō f.
ado n negōtium nt; make much ~ about nothing fluctūs in simpulō excitāre; without more ~ prōtinus, sine morā.
adolescence n prīma adulēscentia f.
adolescent adj adulēscēns ♦ n adulēscentulus m.
adopt vt (person) adoptāre; (custom) adscīscere; ~ a plan consilium capere.
adoption n (person) adoptiō f; (custom) adsūmptiō f; by ~ adoptīvus.
adoptive adj adoptīvus.
adorable adj amābilis, venustus.
adorably adv venustē.
adoration n (of gods) cultus m; (of kings) venerātiō f; (love) amor m.
adore vt (worship) venerārī; (love) adamāre.
adorn vt ōrnāre, exōrnāre, decorāre.
adornment n ōrnāmentum nt, decus nt; ōrnātus m.
adrift adj fluctuāns; be ~ fluctuāre.
adroit adj sollers, callidus.
adroitly adv callidē, scītē.
adroitness n sollertia f, calliditās f.
adulation n adūlātiō f, adsentātiō f.
adulatory adj blandus.
adult adj adultus.
adulterate vt corrumpere, adulterāre.
adulterer n adulter m.
adulteress n adultera f.
adulterous adj incestus.
adultery n adulterium nt; commit ~ adulterāre.
adults npl pūberēs mpl.
adumbrate vt adumbrāre.
advance vt prōmovēre; (a cause) fovēre;

(money) crēdere; (opinion) dīcere; (to honours) prōvehere; (time) mātūrāre ♦ vi prōcēdere, prōgredī, adventāre; (MIL) signa prōferre, pedem īnferre; (progress) prōficere; (walk) incēdere; ~ to the attack signa īnferre ♦ n prōgressus m, prōcessus m; (attack) impetus m; (money) mūtuae pecūniae; in ~ mātūrius; fix in ~ praefīnīre; get in ~ praecipere.
advanced adj prōvectus; well ~ (task) adfectus.
advancement n (POL) honōs m.
advantage n (benefit) commodum nt, bonum nt, ūsus m; (of place or time) opportūnitās f; (profit) fructus m; (superiority) praestantia f; it is an ~ bono est; be of ~ to prōdesse (dat), ūsuī esse (dat); to your ~ in rem tuam; it is to your ~ tibi expedit, tuā interest; take ~ of (CIRCS) ūtī; (person) dēcipere, fallere; have an ~ over praestāre (dat); be seen to ~ māximē placēre.
advantageous adj ūtilis, opportūnus.
advantageously adv ūtiliter, opportūnē.
advent n adventus m.
adventitious adj fortuītus.
adventure n (exploit) facinus memorābile nt; (hazard) perīculum nt.
adventurer n vir audāx m; (social) parasītus m.
adventurous adj audāx.
adversary n adversārius m, hostis m.
adverse adj adversus, contrārius, inimīcus.
adversely adv contrāriē, inimīcē, male.
adversity n rēs adversae fpl, calamitās f.
advert vi: ~ to attingere.
advertise vt prōscrībere; vēnditāre.
advertisement n prōscrīptiō f, libellus m.
advice n cōnsilium nt; (POL) auctōritās f; (legal) respōnsum nt; ask ~ of cōnsulere; on the ~ of Sulla auctōre Sullā.
advisable adj ūtilis, operae pretium.
advise vt monēre, suādēre (dat), cēnsēre (dat); ~ against dissuādēre.
advisedly adv cōnsultō.
adviser n auctor m, suāsor m.
advocacy n patrōcinium nt.
advocate n patrōnus m, causidicus m; (supporter) auctor m; be an ~ causam dīcere ♦ vt suādēre, cēnsēre.
adze n ascia f.
aedile n aedīlis m.
aedile's adj aedīlicius.
aedileship n aedīlitās f.
aegis n aegis f; (fig) praesidium nt.
Aeneid n Aenēis f.
aerial adj āerius.
aesthetic adj pulchritūdinis amāns, artificiōsus.
afar adv procul; from ~ procul.
affability n cōmitās f, facilitās f, bonitās f.
affable adj cōmis, facilis, commodus.
affably adv cōmiter.
affair n negōtium nt, rēs f.
affect vt afficere, movēre, commovēre;

(*concern*) attingere; (*pretence*) simulāre.
affectation *n* simulātiō *f*; (*RHET*) adfectātiō *f*; (*in diction*) īnsolentia *f*; quaesīta *ntpl*.
affected *adj* (*style*) molestus, pūtidus.
affectedly *adv* pūtidē.
affecting *adj* miserābilis.
affection *n* amor *m*, cāritās *f*, studium *nt*; (*family*) pietās *f*.
affectionate *adj* amāns, pius.
affectionately *adv* amanter, piē.
affiance *vt* spondēre.
affidavit *n* testimōnium *nt*.
affinity *n* affīnitās *f*, cognātiō *f*.
affirm *vt* adfirmāre, adsevērāre.
affirmation *n* adfirmātiō *f*.
affirmative *adj*: **I reply in the ~** āiō.
affix *vt* adfīgere, adiungere.
afflict *vt* adflīctāre, angere, vexāre; affligere.
affliction *n* miseria *f*, dolor *m*, rēs adversae *fpl*.
affluence *n* cōpia *f*, opēs *fpl*.
affluent *adj* dīves, opulentus, locuplēs.
afford *vt* praebēre, dare; **I cannot ~** rēs mihi nōn suppetit ad.
affray *n* rixa *f*, pugna *f*.
affright *vt* terrēre ♦ *n* terror *m*, pavor *m*.
affront *vt* offendere, contumēliam dīcere (*dat*) ♦ *n* iniūria *f*, contumēlia *f*.
afield *adv* forīs; **far ~** peregrē.
afloat *adj* natāns; **be ~** natāre.
afoot *adv* pedibus; **be ~** gerī.
aforesaid *adj* suprā dictus.
afraid *adj* timidus; **be ~ of** timēre, metuere; verērī.
afresh *adv* dēnuō, dē integrō.
Africa *n* Africa *f*.
aft *adv* in puppī, puppim versus.
after *adj* posterior ♦ *adv* post (*acc*), posteā; **the day ~** postrīdiē ♦ *conj* postquam; **the day ~** postrīdiē quam ♦ *prep* post (*acc*); (*in rank*) secundum (*acc*); (*in imitation*) ad (*acc*), dē (*abl*); **~ all** tamen, dēnique; **~ reading the book** librō lēctō; **one thing ~ another** aliud ex aliō; **immediately ~** statim ab.
aftermath *n* ēventus *m*.
afternoon *n*: **in the ~** post merīdiem ♦ *adj* postmerīdiānus.
afterthought *n* posterior cōgitātiō *f*.
afterwards *adv* post, posteā, deinde.
again *adv* rūrsus, iterum; **~ and ~** etiam atque etiam, identidem; **once ~** dēnuō; (*new point in a speech*) quid?
against *prep* contrā (*acc*), adversus (*acc*), in (*acc*); **~ the stream** adversō flūmine; **~ one's will** invitus.
agape *adj* hiāns.
age *n* (*life*) aetās *f*; (*epoch*) aetās *f*, saeculum *nt*; **old ~** senectūs *f*; **he is of ~** suī iūris est; **he is eight years of ~** octō annōs nātus est, nōnum annum agit; **of the same ~** aequālis.
aged *adj* senex, aetāte prōvectus; (*things*) antīquus.
agency *n* opera *f*; **through the ~ of** per (*acc*).
agent *n* āctor *m*, prōcūrātor *m*; (*in crime*)

minister *m*.
aggrandize *vt* augēre, amplificāre.
aggrandizement *n* amplificātiō *f*.
aggravate *vt* (*wound*) exulcerāre; (*distress*) augēre; **become ~d** ingravēscere.
aggravating *adj* molestus.
aggregate *n* summa *f*.
aggression *n* incursiō *f*, iniūria *f*.
aggressive *adj* ferōx.
aggressiveness *n* ferōcitās *f*.
aggressor *n* oppugnātor *m*.
aggrieved *adj* īrātus; **be ~** indignārī.
aghast *adj* attonitus, stupefactus; **stand ~** obstupēscere.
agile *adj* pernix, vēlōx.
agility *n* pernīcitās *f*.
agitate *vt* agitāre; (*mind*) commovēre, perturbāre.
agitation *n* commōtiō *f*, perturbātiō *f*, trepidātiō *f*; (*POL*) tumultus *m*.
agitator *n* turbātor *m*, concitātor *m*.
aglow *adj* fervidus ♦ *adv*: **be ~** fervēre.
ago *adv* abhinc (*acc*); **three days ~** abhinc trēs diēs; **long ~** antīquitus, iamprīdem, iamdūdum; **a short time ~** dūdum.
agog *adj* sollicitus, ērēctus.
agonize *vt* cruciāre, torquēre.
agonizing *adj* horribilis.
agony *n* cruciātus *m*, dolor *m*.
agrarian *adj* agrārius; **~ party** agrāriī *mpl*.
agree *vi* (*together*) cōnsentīre, congruere; (*with*) adsentīrī (*dat*), sentīre cum; (*bargain*) pacīscī; (*facts*) cōnstāre, convenīre; (*food*) facilem esse ad concoquendum; **~ upon** cōnstituere, compōnere; **it is agreed** constat (inter omnes).
agreeable *adj* grātus, commodus, acceptus.
agreeableness *n* dulcēdō *f*, iūcunditās *f*.
agreeably *adv* iūcundē.
agreement *n* (*together*) cōnsēnsus *m*, concordia *f*; (*with*) cōnsēnsiō *f*; (*pact*) pactiō *f*, conventum *nt*, foedus *nt*; **according to ~** compāctō, ex compositō; **be in ~** cōnsentīre, congruere.
agricultural *adj* rūsticus, agrestis.
agriculture *n* rēs rūstica *f*, agrī cultūra *f*.
aground *adv*: **be ~** sīdere; **run ~** in lītus ēicī, offendere.
ague *n* horror *m*, febris *f*.
ahead *adv* ante; **go ~** anteīre, praeīre; **go-~** *adj* impiger; **ships in line ~** agmen nāvium.
aid *vt* adiuvāre, succurrere (*dat*), subvenīre (*dat*) ♦ *n* auxilium *nt*, subsidium *nt*.
aide-de-camp *n* optiō *m*.
ail *vt* dolēre ♦ *vi* aegrōtāre, labōrāre, languēre.
ailing *adj* aeger, īnfīrmus.
ailment *n* morbus *m*, valētūdō *f*.
aim *vt* intendere; **~ at** petere; (*fig*) adfectāre, spectāre, sequī; (*with verb*) id agere ut ♦ *n* fīnis *m*, prōpositum *nt*.
aimless *adj* inānis, vānus.
aimlessly *adv* sine ratiōne.
aimlessness *n* vānitās *f*.

air *n* āēr *m*; (*breeze*) aura *f*; (*look*) vultus *m*, speciēs *f*; (*tune*) modus *m*; **in the open** ~ sub dīvō; **~s** fastus *m*; **give oneself ~s** sē iactāre.

airily *adv* hilarē.

airy *adj* (*of air*) āerius; (*light*) tenuis; (*place*) apertus; (*manner*) hilaris.

aisle *n* āla *f*.

ajar *adj* sēmiapertus.

akin *adj* cōnsanguineus, cognātus.

alacrity *n* alacritās *f*.

alarm *n* terror *m*, formīdō *f*, trepidātiō *f*; (*sound*) clāmor *m*; **sound an** ~ ad arma conclāmāre; **give the** ~ increpāre; **be in a state of** ~ trepidāre ♦ *vt* terrēre, perterrēre, perturbāre.

alarming *adj* formīdolōsus.

alas *interj* heu.

albeit *conj* etsī, etiamsī.

alcove *n* zōthēca *f*.

alder *n* alnus *f*.

alderman *n* decuriō *m*.

ale *n* cervīsia *f*.

alehouse *n* caupōna *f*, taberna *f*.

alert *adj* prōmptus, alacer, vegetus.

alertness *n* alacritās *f*.

alien *adj* externus; ~ **to** abhorrēns ab ♦ *n* peregrīnus *m*.

alienate *vt* aliēnāre, abaliēnāre, āvertere, āvocāre.

alienation *n* aliēnātiō *f*.

alight *vi* (*from horse*) dēscendere, dēsilīre; (*bird*) īnsīdere.

alight *adj*: **be** ~ ārdēre; **set** ~ accendere.

alike *adj* pār, similis ♦ *adv* aequē, pariter.

alive *adj* vīvus; **be** ~ vīvere.

all *adj* omnis; (*together*) ūniversus, cūnctus; (*whole*) tōtus; ~ **but** paene; ~ **for** studiōsus (*gen*); ~ **in** cōnfectus; ~ **of** tōtus; ~ **over with** āctum dē (*abl*); ~ **the best men** optimus quisque; ~ **the more** eō plūs, tantō plūs; **at** ~ ullō modō, quid; **it is** ~ **up with** actum est de (*abl*); **not at** ~ haudquāquam ♦ *n* fortūnae *fpl*.

allay *vt* sēdāre, mītigāre, lēnīre.

allegation *n* adfirmātiō *f*; (*charge*) īnsimulātiō *f*.

allege *vt* adfirmāre, praetendere; (*in excuse*) excūsāre.

allegiance *n* fidēs *f*; **owe** ~ **to** in fidē esse (*gen*); **swear** ~ **to** in verba iūrāre (*gen*).

allegory *n* allēgoria *f*, immūtāta ōrātiō *f*.

alleviate *vt* mītigāre, adlevāre, sublevāre.

alleviation *n* levātiō *f*, levāmentum *nt*.

alley *n* (*garden*) xystus *m*; (*town*) angiportus *m*.

alliance *n* societās *f*, foedus *nt*.

allied *adj* foederātus, socius; (*friends*) coniūnctus.

alligator *n* crocodīlus *m*.

allocate *vt* adsignāre, impertīre.

allot *vt* adsignāre, distribuere; **be ~ted** obtingere.

allotment *n* (*land*) adsignātiō *f*.

allow *vt* sinere, permittere (*dat*), concēdere (*dat*), patī; (*admit*) fatērī, concēdere;

(*approve*) comprobāre; **it is ~ed** licet (*dat* + *infin*); ~ **for** *vt fus* ratiōnem habēre (*gen*).

allowance *n* venia *f*, indulgentia *f*; (*pay*) stīpendium *nt*; (*food*) cibāria *ntpl*; (*for travel*) viāticum *nt*; **make** ~ **for** indulgēre (*dat*), ignōscere (*dat*), excūsāre.

alloy *n* admixtum *nt*.

all right *adj* rēctē; **it is** ~ bene est.

allude *vi*: ~ **to** dēsignāre, attingere, significāre.

allure *vt* adlicere, pellicere.

allurement *n* blanditia *f*, blandīmentum *nt*, illecebra *f*.

alluring *adj* blandus.

alluringly *adv* blandē.

allusion *n* mentiō *f*, indicium *nt*.

alluvial *adj*: ~ **land** adluviō *f*.

ally *n* socius *m* ♦ *vt* sociāre, coniungere.

almanac *n* fāstī *mpl*.

almighty *adj* omnipotēns.

almond *n* (*nut*) amygdalum *nt*; (*tree*) amygdala *f*.

almost *adv* paene, ferē, fermē, propemodum.

alms *n* stipem (*no nom*) *f*.

aloe *n* aloē *f*.

aloft *adj* sublīmis ♦ *adv* sublīmē.

alone *adj* sōlus, sōlitārius, ūnus ♦ *adv* sōlum.

along *prep* secundum (*acc*), praeter (*acc*) ♦ *adv* porrō; **all** ~ iamdūdum, ab initiō; ~ **with** unā cum (*abl*).

alongside *adv*: **bring** ~ adpellere; **come** ~ ad crepīdinem accēdere.

aloof *adv* procul; **stand** ~ sē removēre ♦ *adj* sēmōtus.

aloofness *n* sōlitūdō *f*, sēcessus *m*.

aloud *adv* clārē, māgnā vōce.

alphabet *n* elementa *ntpl*.

Alps *n* Alpēs *fpl*.

already *adv* iam.

also *adv* etiam, et, quoque; īdem.

altar *n* āra *f*.

alter *vt* mūtāre, commūtāre; (*order*) invertere.

alteration *n* mūtātiō *f*, commūtātiō *f*.

altercation *n* altercātiō *f*, iūrgium *nt*.

alternate *adj* alternus ♦ *vt* variāre.

alternately *adv* invicem.

alternation *n* vicem (*no nom*) *f*, vicissitūdō *f*.

alternative *adj* alter, alius ♦ *n* optiō *f*.

although *conj* quamquam (*indic*), etsī/etiamsī (+ *cond clause*); quamvīs (+ *subj*).

altitude *n* altitūdō *f*.

altogether *adv* omnīnō; (*emphasis*) plānē, prōrsus.

altruism *n* beneficentia *f*.

alum *n* alūmen *nt*.

always *adv* semper.

amalgamate *vt* miscēre, coniungere.

amalgamation *n* coniūnctiō *f*, temperātiō *f*.

amanuensis *n* librārius *m*.

amass *vt* cumulāre, coacervāre.

amateur *n* idiōta *m*.

amatory *adj* amātōrius.

amaze *vt* obstupefacere; attonāre; **be ~d**

obstupēscere.
amazement n stupor m; **in ~** attonitus, stupefactus.
ambassador n lēgātus m.
amber n sūcinum nt.
ambidextrous adj utrīusque manūs compos.
ambiguity n ambiguitās f; (RHET) amphibolia f.
ambiguous adj ambiguus, anceps, dubius.
ambiguously adv ambiguē.
ambition n glōria f, laudis studium.
ambitious adj glōriae cupidus, laudis avidus.
amble vi ambulāre.
ambrosia n ambrosia f.
ambrosial adj ambrosius.
ambuscade n īnsidiae fpl.
ambush n īnsidiae fpl ♦ vt īnsidiārī (dat).
ameliorate vt corrigere, meliōrem reddere.
amelioration n prōfectus m.
amenable adj facilis, docilis.
amend vt corrigere, ēmendāre.
amendment n ēmendātiō f.
amends n (apology) satisfactiō f; **make ~ for** expiāre; **make ~ to** satisfacere (dat).
amenity n (scenery) amoenitās f; (comfort) commodum nt.
amethyst n amethystus f.
amiability n benignitās f, suāvitās f.
amiable adj benignus, suāvis.
amiably adv benignē, suāviter.
amicable adj amīcus, cōmis.
amicably adv amīcē, cōmiter.
amid, amidst prep inter (acc).
amiss adv perperam, secus, incommodē; **take ~** aegrē ferre.
amity n amīcitia f.
ammunition n tēla ntpl.
amnesty n venia f.
among, amongst prep inter (acc), apud (acc).
amorous adj amātōrius, amāns.
amorously adv cum amōre.
amount vi: **~ to** efficere; (fig) esse ♦ n summa f.
amours n amōrēs mpl.
amphibious adj anceps.
amphitheatre n amphitheātrum nt.
ample adj amplus, satis.
amplification n amplificātiō f.
amplify vt amplificāre.
amplitude n amplitūdō f, cōpia f.
amputate vt secāre, amputāre.
amuck adv: **run ~** bacchārī.
amulet n amulētum nt.
amuse vt dēlectāre, oblectāre.
amusement n oblectāmentum nt, dēlectātiō f; **for ~** animī causā.
amusing adj rīdiculus, facētus.
an indef art see **a**.
anaemic adj exsanguis.
analogous adj similis.
analogy n prōportiō f, comparātiō f.
analyse vt excutere, perscrūtārī.
analysis n explicātiō f.
anapaest n anapaestus m.

anarchical adj sēditiōsus.
anarchy n reī pūblicae perturbātiō, lēgēs nullae fpl, licentia f.
anathema n exsecrātiō f; (object) pestis f.
ancestor n proavus m; **~s** pl māiōrēs mpl.
ancestral adj patrius.
ancestry n genus nt, orīgō f.
anchor n ancora f; **lie at ~** in ancorīs stāre; **weigh ~** ancoram tollere ♦ vi ancoram iacere.
anchorage n statiō f.
ancient adj antīquus, prīscus, vetustus; **~ history, ~ world** antīquitās f; **from/in ~ times** antīquitus; **the ~s** veterēs.
and conj et, atque, ac, -que; **~ ...** not nec, neque; **~ so** itaque.
anecdote n fābella f.
anent prep dē (abl).
anew adv dēnuō, ab integrō.
angel n angelus m.
angelic adj angelicus; (fig) dīvīnus, eximius.
anger n īra f ♦ vt inrītāre.
angle n angulus m ♦ vi hāmō piscārī.
angler n piscātor m.
Anglesey n Mona f.
angrily adv īrātē.
angry adj īrātus; **be ~** īrāscī (dat).
anguish n cruciātus m, dolor m; (mind) angor m.
angular adj angulātus.
animal n animal nt; (domestic) pecus f; (wild) fera f.
animate vt animāre.
animated adj excitātus, vegetus.
animation n ārdor m, alacritās f.
animosity n invidia f, inimīcitia f.
ankle n tālus m.
annalist n annālium scrīptor.
annals n annālēs mpl.
annex vt addere.
annexation n adiectiō f.
annihilate vt dēlēre, exstinguere, perimere.
annihilation n exstinctiō f, interneciō f.
anniversary n diēs anniversārius; (public) sollemne nt.
annotate vt adnotāre.
annotation n adnotātiō f.
announce vt nūntiāre; (officially) dēnūntiāre, prōnūntiāre; (election result) renūntiāre.
announcement n (official) dēnūntiātiō f; (news) nūntius m.
announcer n nūntius m.
annoy vt inrītāre, vexāre; **be ~ed with** aegrē ferre.
annoyance n molestia f, vexātiō f; (felt) dolor m.
annoying adj molestus.
annual adj annuus, anniversārius.
annually adv quotannīs.
annuity n annua ntpl.
annul vt abrogāre, dissolvere, tollere.
annulment n abrogātiō f.
anoint vt ungere, illinere.

anomalous *adj* novus.
anomaly *n* novitās *f*.
anon *adv* mox.
anonymous *adj* incertī auctōris.
anonymously *adv* sine nōmine.
another *adj* alius; (*second*) alter; **of ~** aliēnus; **one after ~** alius ex aliō; **one ~ inter sē**, alius alium; **in ~ place** alibī; **to ~ place** aliō; **in ~ way** aliter; **at ~ time** aliās.
answer *vt* respondēre (*dat*); (*by letter*) rescrībere (*dat*); (*agree*) respondēre, congruere; **~ a charge** crīmen dēfendere; **~ for** *vt fus* (*surety*) praestāre; (*account*) ratiōnem referre; (*substitute*) īnstar esse (*gen*); ♦ *n* respōnsum *nt*; (*to a charge*) dēfēnsiō *f*; **~ to the name of** vocārī; **give an ~** respondēre.
answerable *adj* reus; **I am ~ for** ... ratiō mihī reddenda est ... (*gen*).
ant *n* formīca *f*.
antagonism *n* simultās *f*, inimīcitia *f*.
antagonist *n* adversārius *m*, hostis *m*.
antarctic *adj* antarcticus.
antecedent *adj* antecēdēns, prior.
antediluvian *adj* prīscus, horridus, Deucaliōnēus.
antelope *n* dorcas *f*.
anterior *adj* prior.
anteroom *n* vestibulum *nt*.
anthology *n* excerpta *ntpl*; **make an ~** excerpere.
anthropology *n* rēs hūmānae *fpl*.
anticipate *vt* (*expect*) exspectāre; (*forestall*) antevenīre, occupāre, (*in thought*) animō praecipere.
anticipation *n* exspectātiō *f*, spēs *f*; praesūmptiō *f*.
antics *n* gestus *m*, ineptiae *fpl*.
anticyclo..e *n* serēnitās *f*.
antidote *n* remedium *nt*, medicāmen *nt*.
antipathy *n* fastīdium *nt*, odium *nt*; (*things*) repugnantia *f*.
antiphonal *adj* alternus.
antiphony *n* alterna *ntpl*.
antipodes *n* contrāria pars terrae.
antiquarian *adj* historicus.
antiquary *n* antīquārius *m*.
antiquated *adj* prīscus, obsolētus.
antique *adj* antīquus, prīscus.
antiquity *n* antīquitās *f*, vetustas *f*, veterēs *mpl*.
antithesis *n* contentiō *f*, contrārium *nt*.
antlers *n* cornua *ntpl*.
anvil *n* incūs *f*.
anxiety *n* sollicitūdō *f*, metus *m*, cūra *f*; anxietās *f*.
anxious *adj* sollicitus, anxius; avidus; cupidus.
any *adj* ullus; (*interrog*) ecquī; (*after* sī, nisī, num, nē) quī; (*indef*) quīvīs, quīlibet; **hardly ~** nullus ferē; **~ further** longius; **~ longer** (*of time*) diutius.
anybody *pron* aliquis; (*indef*) quīvīs, quīlibet;

(*after* sī, nisī, num, nē) quis; (*interrog*) ecquis, numquis; (*after neg*) quisquam; **hardly ~** nēmō ferē.
anyhow *adv* ullō modō, quōquō modō.
anyone *pron see* **anybody.**
anything *pron* aliquid; quidvīs, quidlibet; (*interrog*) ecquid, numquid; (*after neg*) quicquam; (*after* sī, nisī, num, nē) quid; **hardly ~** nihil ferē.
anywhere *adv* usquam, ubīvīs.
apace *adv* citō, celeriter.
apart *adv* seōrsum, sēparātim ♦ *adj* dīversus; **be six feet ~** sex pedēs distāre; **set ~** sēpōnere; **stand ~** distāre; **joking ~** remōtō iocō; **~ from** praeter (*acc*).
apartment *n* cubiculum *nt*, conclāve *nt*.
apathetic *adj* lentus, languidus, ignāvus.
apathy *n* lentitūdō *f*, languor *m*, ignāvia *f*.
ape *n* sīmia *f* ♦ *vt* imitārī.
aperture *n* hiātus *m*, forāmen *nt*, rīma *f*.
apex *n* fastīgium *nt*.
aphorism *n* sententia *f*.
apiary *n* alveārium *nt*.
apiece *adv* in singulōs; **two ~** bīnī.
aplomb *n* cōnfīdentia *f*.
apocryphal *adj* commentīcius.
apologetic *adj* cōnfitēns, veniam petēns.
apologize *vi* veniam petere, sē excūsāre.
apology *n* excūsātiō *f*.
apoplectic *adj* apoplēcticus.
apoplexy *n* apoplēxis *f*.
apostle *n* apostolus *m*.
apothecary *n* medicāmentārius *m*.
appal *vt* perterrēre, cōnsternere.
appalling *adj* dīrus.
apparatus *n* īnstrūmenta *ntpl*, ōrnāmenta *ntpl*.
apparel *n* vestis *f*, vestīmenta *ntpl*.
apparent *adj* manifestus, apertus, ēvidēns.
apparently *adv* speciē, ut vidētur.
apparition *n* vīsum *nt*, speciēs *f*.
appeal *vi* (*to magistrate*) appellāre; (*to people*) prōvocāre ad; (*to gods*) invocāre, testārī; (*to senses*) placēre (*dat*) ♦ *n* appellātiō *f*, prōvocātiō *f*, testātiō *f*.
appear *vi* (*in sight*) apparēre; (*in court*) sistī; (*in public*) prōdīre; (*at a place*) adesse, advenīre; (*seem*) vidērī.
appearance *n* (*coming*) adventus *m*; (*look*) aspectus *m*, faciēs *f*; (*semblance*) speciēs *f*; (*thing*) vīsum *nt*; **for the sake of ~s** in speciem; (*formula*) dicis causā; **make one's ~** prōcēdere, prōdīre.
appeasable *adj* plācābilis.
appease *vt* plācāre, lēnīre, mītigāre, sēdāre.
appeasement *n* plācātiō *f*; (*of enemy*) pācificātiō *f*.
appellant *n* appellātor *m*.
appellation *n* nōmen *nt*.
append *vt* adiungere, subicere.
appendage *n* appendix *f*, adiūnctum *nt*.
appertain *vi* pertinēre.
appetite *n* adpetītus *m*; (*for food*) fāmēs *f*.
applaud *vt* plaudere; (*fig*) laudāre.

applause n plausus m; (fig) adsēnsiō f, adprobātiō f.

apple n pōmum nt; mālum nt; ~ **tree** mālus f; ~ **of my eye** ocellus meus; **upset the ~ cart** plaustrum percellere.

appliance n māchina f, īnstrūmentum nt.

applicable adj aptus, commodus; **be ~** pertinēre.

applicant n petītor m.

application n (work) industria f; (mental) intentiō f; (asking) petītiō f; (MED) fōmentum nt.

apply vt adhibēre, admovēre; (use) ūtī (abl); ~ **oneself to** sē adplicāre, incumbere in (acc) ♦ vi pertinēre; (to a person) adīre (acc); (for office) petere.

appoint vt (magistrate) creāre, facere, cōnstituere; (commander) praeficere; (guardian, heir) īnstituere; (time) dīcere, statuere; (for a purpose) dēstināre; (to office) creāre.

appointment n cōnstitūtum nt; (duty) mandātum nt; (office) magistrātus m; **have an ~ with** cōnstitūtum habēre cum; **keep an ~** ad cōnstitūtum venīre.

apportion vt dispertīre, dīvīdere; (land) adsignāre.

apposite adj aptus, appositus.

appraisal n aestimātiō f.

appraise vt aestimāre.

appreciable adj haud exiguus.

appreciate vt aestimāre.

appreciation n aestimātiō f.

apprehend vt (person) comprehendere; (idea) intellegere, mente comprehendere; (fear) metuere, timēre.

apprehension n comprehēnsiō f; metus m, formīdō f.

apprehensive adj anxius, sollicitus; **be ~ of** metuere.

apprentice n discipulus m, tīrō m.

apprenticeship n tīrōcinium nt.

apprise vt docēre, certiōrem facere.

approach vt appropinquāre ad (acc), accēdere ad; (person) adīre ♦ vi (time) adpropinquāre; (season) appetere ♦ n (act) accessus m, aditus m; (time) adpropinquātiō f; (way) aditus m; **make ~es to** adīre ad, ambīre, petere.

approachable adj (place) patēns; (person) facilis.

approbation n adprobātiō f, adsēnsiō f.

appropriate adj aptus, idōneus, proprius ♦ vt adscīscere, adsūmere.

appropriately adv aptē, commodē.

approval n adprobātiō f, adsēnsus m, favor m.

approve vt, vi adprobāre, comprobāre, adsentīrī (dat); (law) scīscere.

approved adj probātus, spectātus.

approximate adj propinquus ♦ vi: ~ **to** accēdere ad.

approximately adv prope, propemodum; (number) ad (acc).

appurtenances n īnstrūmenta ntpl, apparātus m.

apricot n armēniacum nt; ~ **tree** n armēniaca f.

April n mēnsis Aprīlis m; **of ~** Aprīlis.

apron n operīmentum nt.

apropos of prep quod attinet ad.

apse n apsis f.

apt adj aptus, idōneus; (pupil) docilis, prōmptus; ~ **to** prōnus, prōclīvis ad; **be ~ to** solēre.

aptitude n ingenium nt, facultās f.

aptly adv aptē.

aquarium n piscīna f.

aquatic adj aquātilis.

aqueduct n aquae ductus m.

aquiline adj (nose) aduncus.

arable land n arvum nt.

arbiter n arbiter m.

arbitrarily adv ad libīdinem, licenter.

arbitrary adj libīdinōsus (act); (ruler) superbus.

arbitrate vi dīiūdicāre, disceptāre.

arbitration n arbitrium nt, dīiūdicātiō f.

arbitrator n arbiter m, disceptātor m.

arbour n umbrāculum nt.

arbutus n arbutus f.

arc n arcus m.

arcade n porticus f.

arch n fornix m, arcus m ♦ vt arcuāre ♦ adj lascīvus, vafer.

archaeologist n antīquitātis investīgātor m.

archaeology n antīquitātis investīgātiō f.

archaic adj prīscus.

archaism n verbum obsolētum nt.

archbishop n archiepiscopus m.

arched adj fornicātus.

archer n sagittārius m.

archery n sagittāriōrum ars f.

architect n architectus m.

architecture n architectūra f.

architrave n epistylium nt.

archives n tabulae (pūblicae) fpl.

arctic adj arcticus, septentriōnālis ♦ n septentriōnēs mpl.

ardent adj ārdēns, fervidus, vehemēns.

ardently adv ārdenter, ācriter, vehementer.

ardour n ārdor m, fervor m.

arduous adj difficilis, arduus.

area n regiō f; (MATH) superficiēs f.

arena n harēna f.

argonaut n argonauta m.

argosy n onerāria f.

argue vi (discuss) disserere, disceptāre; (dispute) ambigere; disputāre; (reason) argūmentārī ♦ vt (prove) arguere.

argument n (discussion) contrōversia f, disputātiō f; (reason) ratiō f; (proof, theme) argūmentum nt.

argumentation n argūmentātiō f.

argumentative adj lītigiōsus.

aria n canticum nt.

arid adj āridus, siccus.

aright adv rectē, vērē.

arise vi orīrī, coorīrī, exsistere; ~ **from** nāscī ex, proficīscī ab.

aristocracy *n* optimātēs *mpl*, nōbilēs *mpl*;
(*govt*) optimātium dominātus *m*.
aristocrat *n* optimās *m*.
aristocratic *adj* patricius, generōsus.
arithmetic *n* numerī *mpl*, arithmētica *ntpl*.
ark *n* arca *f*.
arm *n* bracchium *nt*; (*upper*) lacertus *m*; (*sea*)
sinus *m*; (*weapon*) tēlum *nt* ♦ *vt* armāre ♦ *vi*
arma capere.
armament *n* bellī apparātus *m*; cōpiae *fpl*.
armed *adj* (*men*) armātus; **light-~ troops** levis
armātūra *f*, vēlitēs *mpl*.
armistice *n* indutiae *fpl*.
armlet *n* armilla *f*.
armour *n* arma *ntpl*; (*kind of*) armātūra *f*.
armourer *n* (armōrum) faber *m*.
armoury *n* armāmentārium *nt*.
armpit *n* āla *f*.
arms *npl* (MIL) arma *ntpl*; **by force of ~** vī et
armīs; **under ~** in armīs.
army *n* exercitus *m*; (*in battle*) aciēs *f*; (*on
march*) agmen *nt*.
aroma *n* odor *m*.
aromatic *adj* frāgrāns.
around *adv* circum (*acc*), circā (*acc*) ♦ *prep*
circum (*acc*).
arouse *vt* suscitāre, ērigere, excitāre.
arraign *vt* accūsāre.
arrange *vt* (*in order*) compōnere, ōrdināre,
dīgerere, dispōnere; (*agree*) pacīscī; **~ a
truce** indūtias compōnere.
arrangement *n* ōrdō *m*, collocātiō *f*, dispositiō
f; pactum *nt*, cōnstitūtum *nt*.
arrant *adj* summus.
array *n* vestis *f*, habitus *m*; (MIL) aciēs *f* ♦ *vt*
vestīre, exōrnāre; (MIL) īnstruere.
arrears *n* residuae pecūniae *fpl*, reliqua *ntpl*.
arrest *vt* comprehendere, adripere; (*attention*)
in sē convertere; (*movement*) morārī,
tardāre ♦ *n* comprehēnsiō *f*.
arrival *n* adventus *m*.
arrive *vi* advenīre (ad + *acc*), pervenīre (ad +
acc).
arrogance *n* superbia *f*, adrogantia *f*, fastus *m*.
arrogant *adj* superbus, adrogāns.
arrogantly *adv* superbē, adroganter.
arrogate *vt* adrogāre.
arrow *n* sagitta *f*.
arsenal *n* armāmentārium *nt*.
arson *n* incēnsiōnis crīmen *nt*.
art *n* ars *f*, artificium *nt*; **fine ~s** ingenuae artēs.
artery *n* artēria *f*.
artful *adj* callidus, vafer, astūtus.
artfully *adv* callidē, astūtē.
artfulness *n* astūtia *f*, dolus *m*.
artichoke *n* cinara *f*.
article *n* rēs *f*, merx *f*; (*clause*) caput *nt*; (*term*)
condiciō *f*.
articulate *adj* explānātus, distinctus ♦ *vi*
explānāre, exprimere.
articulately *adv* explānātē, clārē.
articulation *n* prōnūntiātiō *f*.
artifice *n* ars *f*, artificium *nt*, dolus *m*.

artificer *n* artifex *m*, opifex *m*, faber *m*.
artificial *adj* (*work*) artificiōsus; (*appearance*)
fūcātus.
artificially *adv* arte, manū.
artillery *n* tormenta *ntpl*.
artisan *n* faber *m*, opifex *m*.
artist *n* artifex *m*; pictor *m*.
artistic *adj* artificiōsus, ēlegāns.
artistically *adv* artificiōsē, ēleganter.
artless *adj* (*work*) inconditus; (*person*) simplex.
artlessly *adv* inconditē; simpliciter, sine dolō.
artlessness *n* simplicitās *f*.
as *adv* (*before adj, adv*) tam; (*after* **aequus, īdem,
similis**) ac, atque; (*correlative*) quam, quālis,
quantus ♦ *conj* (*compar*) ut (+ *indic*), sīcut,
velut, quemadmodum; (*cause*) cum (+ *indic*),
quoniam, quippe quī; (*time*) dum, ut ♦ *relat
pron* quī, quae, quod (+ *subj*); **~ being** utpote; **~
follows** ita; **~ for** quod attinet ad; **~ if** quasi,
tamquam si, velut; (= *while*) ūsū expressed by
pres part; **~ it were** ut ita dīcam; **~ yet** adhūc;
~ soon ~ simul ac/atque (+ *perf indic*); **~ . . . as
possible** quam (+ *superl*).
as *n* (*coin*) as *m*.
ascend *vt*, *vi* ascendere.
ascendancy *n* praestantia *f*, auctōritās *f*.
ascendant *adj* surgēns, potēns; **be in the ~**
praestāre.
ascent *n* ascēnsus *m*; (*slope*) clīvus *m*.
ascertain *vt* comperīre, cognōscere.
ascetic *adj* nimis abstinēns, austērus.
asceticism *n* dūritia *f*.
ascribe *vt* adscrībere, attribuere, adsignāre.
ash *n* (*tree*) fraxinus *f* ♦ *adj* fraxineus.
ashamed *adj*: **I am ~** pudet mē; **~ of** pudet (+
acc of person, + *gen of thing*).
ashen *adj* pallidus.
ashes *n* cinis *m*.
ashore *adv* (*motion*) in lītus; (*rest*) in lītore; **go
~** ēgredī.
Asia *n* Asia *f*.
aside *adv* sēparatim, sē- (*in cpd*).
ask *vt* (*question*) rogāre, quaerere; (*request*)
petere, poscere; (*beg, entreat*) ōrāre; **~ for** *vt
fus* petere; rogāre; scīscitārī; percontārī.
askance *adv* oblīquē; **look ~ at** līmīs oculīs
aspicere, invidēre (*dat*).
askew *adv* prāvē.
aslant *adv* oblīquē.
asleep *adj* sōpītus; **be ~** dormīre; **fall ~**
obdormīre, somnum inīre.
asp *n* aspis *f*.
asparagus *n* asparagus *m*.
aspect *n* (*place*) aspectus *m*; (*person*) vultus *m*;
(CIRCS) status *m*; **have a southern ~** ad
merīdiem spectāre; **there is another ~ to the
matter** aliter sē rēs habet.
aspen *n* pōpulus *f*.
asperity *n* acerbitās *f*.
asperse *vt* maledīcere (*dat*), calumniārī.
aspersion *n* calumnia *f*, **cast ~s on** calumniārī,
īnfāmiā aspergere.
asphalt *n* bitūmen *nt*.

asphyxia n strangulātiō f.
asphyxiate vt strangulāre.
aspirant n petītor m.
aspirate n (GRAM) aspīrātiō f.
aspiration n spēs f; (POL) ambitiō f.
aspire vi: ~ **to** adfectāre, petere, spērāre.
ass n asinus m, asellus m; (fig) stultus.
assail vt oppugnāre, adorīrī, aggredī.
assailable adj expugnābilis.
assailant n oppugnātor m.
assassin n sīcārius m, percussor m.
assassinate vt interficere, occīdere, iugulāre.
assassination n caedēs f, parricidium nt.
assault vt oppugnāre, adorīrī, aggredī;
  (speech) invehī in (acc) ♦ n impetus m,
  oppugnātiō f; (personal) vīs f.
assay vt (metal) spectāre; temptāre, cōnārī.
assemble vt convocāre, congregāre, cōgere ♦
  vi convenīre, congregārī.
assembly n coetus m, conventus m; (plebs)
  concilium nt; (Roman people) comitia ntpl;
  (troops) cōntiō f; (things) congeriēs f.
assent vi adsentīrī, adnuere ♦ n adsēnsus m.
assert vt adfirmāre, adsevērāre, dīcere.
assertion n adfirmātiō f, adsevērātiō f, dictum
  nt, sententia f.
assess vt cēnsēre, aestimāre; ~ **damages**
  lītem aestimāre.
assessment n cēnsus m, aestimātiō f.
assessor n cēnsor m; (assistant) cōnsessor m.
assets n bona ntpl.
assiduity n dīligentia f, sēdulitās f, industria f.
assiduous adj dīligēns, sēdulus, industrius.
assign vt tribuere, attribuere; (land)
  adsignāre; (in writing) perscrībere; (task)
  dēlēgāre; (reason) adferre.
assignation n cōnstitūtum nt.
assignment n adsignātiō f, perscrīptiō f; (task)
  mūnus nt, pēnsum nt.
assimilate vt aequāre; (food) concoquere;
  (knowledge) concipere.
assist vt adiuvāre, succurrere (dat), adesse
  (dat).
assistance n auxilium nt, opem (no nom) f;
  come to the ~ **of** subvenīre (dat); **be of** ~ **to**
  auxiliō esse (dat).
assistant n adiūtor m, minister m.
assize n conventus m; **hold** ~**s** conventūs
  agere.
associate vt cōnsociāre, coniungere ♦ vi rem
  inter sē cōnsociāre; ~ **with** familiāriter ūtī
  (abl) ♦ n socius m, sodālis m.
association n societās f; (club) sodālitās f.
assort vt dīgerere, dispōnere ♦ vi congruere.
assortment n (of goods) variae mercēs fpl.
assuage vt lēnīre, mītigāre, sēdāre.
assume vt (for oneself) adsūmere, adrogāre;
  (hypothesis) pōnere; (office) inīre.
assumption n (hypothesis) sūmptiō f, positum
  nt.
assurance n (given) fidēs f, pignus nt; (felt)
  fīdūcia f; (boldness) cōnfīdentia f.
assure vt cōnfirmāre, prōmittere (dat).

assured adj (person) fīdēns; (fact) explōrātus,
  certus.
assuredly adv certō, certē, profectō, sānē.
astern adv ā puppī; (movement) retrō; ~ **of**
  post.
asthma n anhēlitus m.
astonish vt obstupefacere; attonāre.
astonished adj attonitus, stupefactus; **be** ~**ed**
  at admīrārī.
astonishing adj mīrificus, mīrus.
astonishment n stupor m, admīrātiō f.
astound vt obstupefacere.
astray adj vagus; **go** ~ errāre, aberrāre,
  deerrāre.
astride adj vāricus.
astrologer n Chaldaeus m, mathēmaticus m.
astrology n Chaldaeōrum dīvīnātiō f.
astronomer n astrologus m.
astronomy n astrologia f.
astute adj callidus, vafer.
astuteness n calliditās f.
asunder adv sēparātim, dis- (in cpd).
asylum n asȳlum nt.
at prep in (abl), ad (acc); (time) usu expressed by
  abl; (towns, small islands) loc; ~ **the house of**
  apud (acc); ~ **all events** saltem; see also **dawn,
  hand, house** etc.
atheism n deōs esse negāre.
atheist n atheos m; **be an** ~ deōs esse negāre.
Athenian adj Atheniensis.
Athens n Athenae fpl; **at/from** ~ Athenis; **to** ~
  Athenas.
athirst adj sitiens; (fig) avidus.
athlete n athlēta m.
athletic adj rōbustus, lacertōsus.
athletics n athlētica ntpl.
athwart prep trāns (acc).
atlas n orbis terrārum dēscrīptiō f.
atmosphere n āēr m.
atom n atomus f, corpus indīviduum nt.
atone vi: ~ **for** expiāre.
atonement n expiātiō f, piāculum nt.
atrocious adj immānis, nefārius, scelestus.
atrociously adv nefāriē, scelestē.
atrociousness n immānitās f.
atrocity n nefas nt, scelus nt, flāgitium nt.
atrophy vi marcēscere.
attach vt adiungere, adfīgere, illigāre; (word)
  subicere; ~**ed to** amāns (gen).
attachment n vinculum nt; amor m, studium
  nt.
attack vt oppugnāre, adorīrī, aggredī;
  impetum facere in (acc); (speech) īnsequī,
  invehī in (acc); (disease) ingruere in (acc) ♦ n
  impetus m, oppugnātiō f, incursus m.
attacker n oppugnātor m.
attain vt adsequī, adipīscī, cōnsequī; ~ **to**
  pervenīre ad.
attainable adj impetrābilis, in prōmptū.
attainder n: **bill of** ~ prīvilēgium nt.
attainment n adeptiō f.
attainments npl doctrīna f, ērudītiō f.
attaint vt māiestātis condemnāre.

attempt _vt_ cōnārī, temptāre; (_with effort_)
mōlīrī ♦ _n_ cōnātus _m_, inceptum _nt_; (_risk_)
perīculum _nt_; **first ~s** rudīmenta _ntpl_.

attend _vt_ (_meeting_) adesse (_dat_), interesse
(_dat_); (_person_) prōsequī, comitārī; (_master_)
appārēre (_dat_); (_invalid_) cūrāre ♦ _vi_ animum
advertere, animum attendere; **~ to** (_task_)
adcūrāre; **~ upon** prōsequī, adsectārī; **~ the
lectures of** audīre; **not ~** aliud agere; **~ first to**
praevertere (_dat_); **well ~ed** frequēns; **thinly
~ed** īnfrequēns.

attendance _n_ (_courtesy_) adsectātiō _f_; (_MED_)
cūrātiō _f_; (_service_) apparitiō _f_; **constant ~**
adsiduitās _f_; **full ~** frequentia _f_; **poor ~**
īnfrequentia _f_; **dance ~ on** haerēre (_dat_).

attendant _n_ famulus _m_, minister _m_; (_on
candidate_) sectātor _m_; (_on nobleman_)
adsectātor _m_; (_on magistrate_) apparitor _m_.

attention _n_ animadversiō _f_, animī attentiō _f_;
(_to work_) cūra _f_; (_respect_) observantia _f_;
attract ~ digitō mōnstrarī; **call ~ to** indicāre;
pay ~ to animadvertere, observāre;
ratiōnem habēre (_gen_); **~ !** hōc age!

attentive _adj_ intentus; (_to work_) dīligēns.

attentively _adv_ intentē, dīligenter.

attenuate _vt_ attenuāre.

attest _vt_ cōnfirmāre, testārī.

attestation _n_ testificātiō _f_.

attestor _n_ testis _m_.

attic _n_ cēnāculum _nt_.

attire _vt_ vestīre ♦ _n_ vestis _f_, habitus _m_.

attitude _n_ (_body_) gestus _m_, status _m_, habitus
_m_; (_mind_) ratiō _f_.

attorney _n_ āctor _m_; advocātus _m_.

attract _vt_ trahere, attrahere, adlicere.

attraction _n_ vīs attrahendī; illecebra _f_,
invītāmentum _nt_.

attractive _adj_ suāvis, venustus, lepidus.

attractively _adv_ suāviter, venustē, lepidē.

attractiveness _n_ venustās _f_, lepōs _m_.

attribute _vt_ tribuere, attribuere, adsignāre ♦
_n_ proprium _nt_.

attrition _n_ attrītus _m_.

attune _vt_ modulārī.

auburn _adj_ flāvus.

auction _n_ auctiō _f_; (_public_) hasta _f_; **hold an ~**
auctiōnem facere; **sell by ~** sub hastā
vēndere.

auctioneer _n_ praecō _m_.

audacious _adj_ audāx; protervus.

audaciously _adv_ audācter, protervē.

audacity _n_ audācia _f_, temeritās _f_.

audible _adj_: **be ~** exaudīrī posse.

audibly _adv_ clārā vōce.

audience _n_ audītōrēs _mpl_; (_interview_) aditus _m_;
give an ~ to admittere.

audit _vt_ īnspicere ♦ _n_ ratiōnum īnspectiō _f_.

auditorium _n_ cavea _f_.

auditory _adj_ audītōrius.

auger _n_ terebra _f_.

augment _vt_ augēre, adaugēre ♦ _vi_ crēscere,
augērī.

augmentation _n_ incrēmentum _nt_.

augur _n_ augur _m_; **~'s staff** lituus _m_ ♦ _vi_
augurārī; (_fig_) portendere.

augural _adj_ augurālis.

augurship _n_ augurātus _m_.

augury _n_ augurium _nt_, auspicium _nt_; ōmen _nt_;
take ~ies augurārī; **after taking ~ies**
augurātō.

august _adj_ augustus.

August _n_ mēnsis Augustus, Sextīlis; **of ~**
Sextīlis.

aunt _n_ (_paternal_) amita _f_; (_maternal_) mātertera
_f_.

auspices _n_ auspicium _nt_; **take ~** auspicārī;
after taking ~ auspicātō; **without taking ~**
inauspicātō.

auspicious _adj_ faustus, fēlīx.

auspiciously _adv_ fēlīciter, prosperē.

austere _adj_ austērus, sevērus, dūrus.

austerely _adv_ sevērē.

austerity _n_ sevēritās _f_, dūritia _f_.

authentic _adj_ vērus, certus.

authenticate _vt_ recognōscere.

authenticity _n_ auctōritās _f_, fidēs _f_.

author _n_ auctor _m_, inventor _m_; scrīptor _m_.

authoress _n_ auctor _f_.

authoritative _adj_ fīdus; imperiōsus.

authority _n_ auctōritās _f_, potestās _f_, iūs _nt_; (_MIL_)
imperium _nt_; (_LIT_) auctor _m_, scrīptor _m_;
enforce ~ iūs suum exsequī; **have great ~**
multum pollēre; **on Caesar's ~** auctōre
Caesare; **an ~ on** perītus (_gen_).

authorize _vt_ potestātem facere (_dat_),
mandāre; (_law_) sancīre.

autobiography _n_ dē vītā suā scrīptus liber _m_.

autocracy _n_ imperium singulāre _nt_, tyrannis _f_.

autocrat _n_ tyrannus _m_, dominus _m_.

autocratic _adj_ imperiōsus.

autograph _n_ manus _f_, chīrographum _nt_.

automatic _adj_ necessārius.

automatically _adv_ necessāriō.

autonomous _adj_ līber.

autonomy _n_ lībertās _f_.

Autumn _n_ auctumnus _m_.

autumnal _adj_ auctumnālis.

auxiliaries _npl_ auxilia _ntpl_, auxiliāriī _mpl_.

auxiliary _adj_ auxiliāris ♦ _n_ adiūtor _m_; **~ forces**
auxilia _ntpl_; novae copiae _fpl_.

avail _vi_ valēre ♦ _vt_ prōdesse (_dat_); **~ oneself of**
ūtī (_abl_) ♦ _n_ ūsus _m_; **of no ~** frustrā.

available _adj_ ad manum, in prōmptū.

avalanche _n_ montis ruīna _f_.

avarice _n_ avāritia _f_, cupīditās _f_.

avaricious _adj_ avārus, cupidus.

avariciously _adv_ avārē.

avenge _vt_ ulcīscī (+ _abl_), vindicāre.

avenger _n_ ultor _m_, vindex _m_.

avenue _n_ xystus _m_; (_fig_) aditus _m_, iānua _f_.

aver _vt_ adfirmāre, adsevērāre.

average _n_ medium _nt_; **on the ~** ferē.

averse _adj_ āversus (ab); **be ~ to** abhorrēre ab.

aversion _n_ odium _nt_, fastīdium _nt_.

avert _vt_ arcēre, dēpellere; (_by prayer_)
dēprecārī.

aviary *n* aviārium *nt*.
avid *adj* avidus.
avidity *n* aviditās *f*.
avidly *adv* avidē.
avoid *vt* vītāre, fugere, dēclīnāre; (*battle*) dētrectāre.
avoidance *n* fuga *f*, dēclīnātiō *f*.
avow *vt* fatērī, cōnfitērī.
avowal *n* cōnfessiō *f*.
avowed *adj* apertus.
avowedly *adv* apertē, palam.
await *vt* exspectāre; (*future*) manēre.
awake *vt* suscitāre, exsuscitāre ♦ *vi* expergīscī ♦ *adj* vigil.
awaken *vt* exsuscitāre.
award *vt* tribuere; (*law*) adiūdicāre ♦ *n* (*decision*) arbitrium *nt*, iūdicium *nt*; (*thing*) praemium *nt*.
aware *adj* gnārus ♦ *adj* conscius (*gen*); **be ~** scīre; **become ~ of** percipere.
away *adv* ā-, ab- (*in cpd*); **be ~** abesse ab (*abl*); **far ~** procul, longē; **make ~ with** dē mediō tollere.
awe *n* formīdō *f*, reverentia *f*, rēligiō *f*; **stand in ~ of** verērī; (*gods*) venerārī.
awe-struck *adj* stupidus.
awful *adj* terribilis, formīdolōsus, dīrus.
awfully *adv* formīdolōsē.
awhile *adv* aliquamdiū, aliquantisper, parumper.
awkward *adj* incallidus, inconcinnus; (*to handle*) inhabilis; (*fig*) molestus.
awkwardly *adv* incallidē, imperītē.
awkwardness *n* imperītia *f*, īnscītia *f*.
awl *n* sūbula *f*.
awning *n* vēlum *nt*.
awry *adj* prāvus, dissidēns.
axe *n* secūris *f*.
axiom *n* prōnūntiātum *nt*, sententia *f*.
axiomatic *adj* ēvidēns, manifestus.
axis *n* axis *m*.
axle *n* axis *m*.
aye *adv* semper; **for ~** in aeternum.
azure *adj* caeruleus.

B, b

baa *vi* bālāre ♦ *n* bālātus *m*.
babble *vi* garrīre, blaterāre.
babbler *n* garrulus *m*.
babbling *adj* garrulus.
babe *n* īnfāns *m/f*.
babel *n* dissonae vōcēs *fpl*.
baboon *n* sīmia *f*.
baby *n* īnfāns *m/f*.
Bacchanalian *adj* Bacchicus.
Bacchante *n* Baccha *f*.

bachelor *n* caelebs *m*; (*degree*) baccalaureus *m*.
back *n* tergum *nt*; (*animal*) dorsum *nt*; (*head*) occipitium *nt*; **at one's ~ ā tergō; behind one's ~** (*fig*) clam (*acc*); **put one's ~ up** stomachum movēre (*dat*); **turn one's ~ on** sē āvertere ab ♦ *adj* āversus, postīcus ♦ *adv* retrō, retrōrsum, re- (*in cpds*) ♦ *vt* obsecundāre (*dat*), adesse (*dat*); **~ water** inhibēre rēmīs, inhibēre nāvem ♦ *vi*: **~ out of** dētrectāre, dēfugere.
backbite *vt* obtrectāre (*dat*), maledīcere (*dat*).
backbone *n* spīna *f*.
backdoor *n* postīcum *nt*.
backer *n* fautor *m*.
background *n* recessus *m*, umbra *f*.
backing *n* fidēs *f*, favor *m*.
backslide *vi* dēscīscere.
backward *adj* āversus; (*slow*) tardus; (*late*) sērus.
backwardness *n* tardītās *f*, pigritia *f*.
backwards *adv* retrō, retrōrsum.
bacon *n* lārdum *nt*.
bad *adj* malus, prāvus, improbus, turpis; **go ~** corrumpī; **be ~ for** obesse (*dat*), nocēre (*dat*).
badge *n* īnsigne *nt*, īnfula *f*.
badger *n* mēles *f* ♦ *vt* sollicitāre
badly *adv* male, prāvē, improbē, turpiter.
badness *n* prāvitās *f*, nēquitia *f*, improbitās *f*.
baffle *vt* ēlūdere, fallere, frustrārī.
bag *n* saccus *m*, folliculus *m*; **hand~** mantica *f*.
bagatelle *n* nūgae *fpl*, floccus *m*.
baggage *n* impedīmenta *ntpl*, vāsa *ntpl*, sarcinae *fpl*; **~ train** impedīmenta *ntpl*; **without ~** expedītus.
bail *n* vadimōnium *nt*; (*person*) vas *m*; **become ~ for** spondēre prō (*abl*); **accept ~ for** vadārī; **keep one's ~** vadimōnium obīre ♦ *vt* spondēre prō (*abl*).
bailiff *n* (*POL*) apparitor *m*; (*private*) vīlicus *m*.
bait *n* esca *f*, illecebra *f* ♦ *vt* lacessere.
bake *vt* coquere, torrēre.
bakehouse *n* pistrīna *f*.
baker *n* pistor *m*.
bakery *n* pistrīna *f*.
balance *n* (*scales*) lībra *f*, trutina *f*; (*equilibrium*) lībrāmentum *nt*; (*money*) reliqua *ntpl* ♦ *vt* lībrāre; (*fig*) compēnsāre; **the account ~s** ratiō cōnstat.
balance sheet *n* ratiō acceptī et expēnsī.
balcony *n* podium *nt*, Maeniānum *nt*.
bald *adj* calvus; (*style*) āridus, iēiūnus.
baldness *n* calvitium *nt*; (*style*) iēiūnitās *f*.
bale *n* fascis *m*; **~ out** *vt* exhaurīre.
baleful *adj* fūnestus, perniciōsus, tristis.
balk *n* tignum *nt* ♦ *vt* frustrārī, dēcipere.
ball *n* globus *m*; (*play*) pila *f*; (*wool*) glomus *nt*; (*dance*) saltātiō *f*.
ballad *n* carmen *nt*.
ballast *n* saburra *f*.
ballet *n* saltātiō *f*.
ballot *n* suffrāgium *nt*.
ballot box urna *f*.
balm *n* unguentum *nt*; (*fig*) sōlātium *nt*.
balmy *adj* lēnis, suāvis.

balsam n balsamum nt.
balustrade n cancellī mpl.
bamboozle vt cōnfundere.
ban vt interdīcere (dat), vetāre ♦ n interdictum nt.
banal adj trītus.
banana n ariēna f; (tree) pāla f.
band n vinculum nt, redimīculum nt; (head) īnfula f; (men) caterva f, manus f, grex f ♦ vi: ~ **together** cōnsociārī.
bandage n fascia f, īnfula f ♦ vt obligāre, adligāre.
bandbox n: **out of a** ~ (fig) dē capsulā.
bandeau n redimīculum nt.
bandit n latrō m.
bandy vt iactāre; ~ **words** altercārī ♦ adj vārus.
bane n venēnum nt, pestis f, perniciēs f.
baneful adj perniciōsus, pestifer.
bang vt pulsāre ♦ n fragor m.
bangle n armilla f.
banish vt pellere, expellere, ēicere; (law) aquā et ignī interdīcere (dat); (temporarily) relēgāre; (feeling) abstergēre.
banishment n (act) aquae et ignis interdictiō f; relēgātiō f; (state) exsilium nt, fuga f.
bank n (earth) agger m; (river) rīpa f; (money) argentāria f.
banker n argentārius m; (public) mēnsārius m.
bankrupt adj: **be** ~ solvendō nōn esse; **declare oneself** ~ bonam cōpiam ēiūrāre; **go** ~ dēcoquere ♦ n dēcoctor m.
banner n vexillum nt.
banquet n cēna f, epulae fpl; convīvium nt; (religious) daps f ♦ vi epulārī.
banter n cavillātiō f ♦ vi cavillārī.
baptism n baptisma nt.
baptize vt baptizāre.
bar n (door) sera f; (gate) claustrum nt; (metal) later m; (wood) asser m; (lever) vectis m; (obstacle) impedīmentum nt; (law-court) cancellī mpl; (barristers) advocātī mpl; (profession) forum nt; **of the** ~ forēnsis; **practise at the** ~ causās agere.
bar vt (door) obserāre; (way) obstāre (dat), interclūdere, prohibēre; (exception) excipere, exclūdere.
barb n acūleus m, dēns m, hāmus m.
barbarian n barbarus m ♦ adj barbarus.
barbarism n barbaria f.
barbarity n saevitia f, ferōcia f, immānitās f, inhūmānitās f.
barbarous adj barbarus, saevus, immānis, inhūmānus.
barbarously adv barbarē, inhūmānē.
barbed adj hāmātus.
barber n tōnsor m; ~**'s shop** tōnstrīna f.
bard n vātēs m/f; (Gallic) bardus m.
bare adj nūdus; (mere) merus; **lay** ~ nūdāre, aperīre, dētegere ♦ vt nūdāre.
barefaced adj impudēns.
barefoot adj nūdis pedibus.
bare-headed adj capite aperto.
barely adv vix.

bargain n pactum nt, foedus nt; **make a** ~ pacīscī; **make a bad** ~ male emere; **into the** ~ grātiīs ♦ vi pacīscī.
barge n linter f.
bark n cortex m; (dog) lātrātus m; (ship) nāvis f, ratis f ♦ vi lātrāre.
barking n latratus m.
barley n hordeum nt; **of** ~ hordeāceus.
barn n horreum nt.
barrack vt obstrepere (dat).
barracks n castra ntpl.
barrel n cūpa f; ligneum vās nt.
barren adj sterilis.
barrenness n sterilitās f.
barricade n claustrum nt, mūnīmentum nt ♦ vt obsaepīre, obstruere; ~ **off** intersaepīre.
barrier n impedīmentum nt; (racecourse) carcer nt.
barrister n advocātus m, patrōnus m, causidicus m.
barrow n ferculum nt; (mound) tumulus m.
barter vt mūtāre ♦ vi mercēs mūtāre ♦ n mūtātiō f, commercium nt.
base adj turpis, vīlis; (birth) humilis, ignōbilis; (coin) adulterīnus.
base n fundāmentum nt; (statue) basis f; (hill) rādīcēs fpl; (MIL) castra ntpl.
baseless adj falsus, inānis.
basely adv turpiter.
basement n basis f; (storey) īmum tabulātum nt.
baseness n turpitūdō f.
bashful adj pudīcus, verēcundus.
bashfulness n pudor m, verēcundia f.
basic adj prīmus.
basin n alveolus m, pelvis f; **wash**~ aquālis m.
basis n fundāmentum nt.
bask vi aprīcārī.
basket n corbis f, fiscus m; (for bread) canistrum nt; (for wool) quasillum nt.
basking n aprīcātiō f.
bas-relief n toreuma nt.
bass adj (voice) gravis.
bastard adj nothus.
bastion n prōpugnāculum nt.
bat n vespertīliō m; (games) clāva f.
batch n numerus m.
Bath n Aquae Sulis fpl.
bath n balneum nt; (utensil) lābrum nt, lavātiō f; **Turkish** ~ Lacōnicum nt; **cold** ~ frīgidārium nt; **hot** ~ calidārium nt; ~ **superintendent** balneātor m ♦ vt lavāre.
bathe vt lavāre ♦ vi lavārī, perluī.
bathroom n balneāria ntpl.
baths n (public ~) balneae fpl.
batman n cālō m.
baton n virga f, scīpiō m.
battalion n cohors f.
batter vt quassāre, pulsāre, verberāre.
battering ram n ariēs m.
battery n (assault) vīs f.
battle n pugna f, proelium nt, certāmen nt; **a** ~ **was fought** pugnatum est; **pitched** ~ iūstum

proelium; line of ~ aciēs *f*; **drawn ~** anceps proelium ♦ *vi* pugnāre, contendere; **~ order** aciēs *f*.
battle-axe *n* bipennis *f*.
battlefield, battle-line *n* aciēs *f*.
battlement *n* pinna *f*.
bawl *vt* vōciferārī, clāmitāre.
bay *n* (*sea*) sinus *m*; (*tree*) laurus *f*, laurea *f*; **of ~** laureus; **at ~** interclūsus ♦ *adj* (*colour*) spādīx ♦ *vi* (*dog*) lātrāre.
be *vi* esse; (*circs*) versārī; (*condition*) sē habēre; **~ at** adesse (*dat*); **~ amongst** interesse (*dat*); **~ in** inesse (*dat*); **consul-to-~** cōnsul dēsignātus; **how are you?** quid agis?; **so ~ it** estō; *see also* **absent, here** *etc*.
beach *n* lītus *nt*, acta *f* ♦ *vt* (*ship*) subdūcere.
beacon *n* ignis *m*.
bead *n* pilula *f*.
beadle *n* apparitor *m*.
beak *n* rōstrum *nt*.
beaked *adj* rōstrātus.
beaker *n* cantharus *m*, scyphus *m*.
beam *n* (*wood*) trabs *f*, tignum *nt*; (*balance*) iugum *nt*; (*light*) radius *m*; (*ship*) latus *nt*; **on the ~** ā latere ♦ *vi* fulgēre; (*person*) adrīdēre.
beaming *adj* hilaris.
bean *n* faba *f*.
bear *n* ursus *m*, ursa *f*; **Great B~** septentriōnēs *mpl*, Arctos *f*; **Little B~** septentriō minor *m*, Cynosūra *f*; **~'s** ursīnus ♦ *vt* (*carry*) ferre, portāre; (*endure*) ferre, tolerāre, patī; (*produce*) ferre, fundere; (*child*) parere; **~ down upon** appropinquāre; **~ off** ferre; **~ out** *vt* arguere; **~ up** *vi*: **~ up under** obsistere (*dat*), sustinēre; **~ upon** innītī (*dat*); (*refer*) pertinēre ad; **~ with** *vt fus* indulgēre (*dat*); **~ oneself** sē gerere; **I cannot ~ to** addūcī nōn possum ut.
bearable *adj* tolerābilis.
beard *n* barba *f* ♦ *vt* ultrō lacessere.
bearded *adj* barbātus.
beardless *adj* imberbis.
bearer *n* bāiulus *m*; (*letter*) tabellārius *m*; (*litter*) lectīcārius *m*; (*news*) nūntius *m*.
bearing *n* (*person*) gestus *m*, vultus *m*; (*direction*) regiō *f*; **have no ~ on** nihil pertinēre ad; **I have lost my ~s** ubi sim nesciō.
beast *n* bestia *f*; (*large*) bēlua *f*; (*wild*) fera *f*; (*domestic*) pecus *f*.
beastliness *n* foedītās *f*, stuprum *nt*.
beastly *adj* foedus.
beast of burden *n* iūmentum *nt*.
beat *n* ictus *m*; (*heart*) palpitātiō *f*; (*music*) percussiō *f*; (*oars, pulse*) pulsus *m*.
beat *vt* ferīre, percutere, pulsāre; (*the body in grief*) plangere; (*punish*) caedere; (*whip*) verberāre; (*conquer*) vincere, superāre ♦ *vi* palpitāre, micāre; **~ back** repellere; **~ in** perfringere; **~ out** excutere; (*metal*) extundere; **~ a retreat** receptui canere; **~ about the bush** circuitiōne ūtī; **be ~en** vāpulāre; **dead ~** cōnfectus.

beating *n* verbera *ntpl*; (*defeat*) clādēs *f*; (*time*) percussiō *f*; **get a ~** vāpulāre.
beatitude *n* beātitūdō *f*, fēlīcitās *f*.
beau *n* nitidus homō *m*; (*lover*) amāns *m*.
beauteous *adj* pulcher, fōrmōsus.
beautiful *adj* pulcher, formōsus; (*looks*) decōrus; (*scenery*) amoenus.
beautifully *adv* pulchrē.
beautify *vt* exōrnāre, decorāre.
beauty *n* fōrma *f*, pulchritūdō *f*, amoenitās *f*.
beaver *n* castor *m*, fiber *m*; (*helmet*) buccula *f*.
becalmed *adj* ventō dēstitūtus.
because *conj* quod, quia, quoniam (+ *indic*), quippe quī; **~ of** propter (*acc*).
beck *n* nūtus *m*.
beckon *vt* innuere, vocāre.
become *vi* fierī; **what will ~ of me?** quid me fīet? ♦ *vt* decēre, convenīre in (*acc*).
becoming *adj* decēns, decōrus.
becomingly *adv* decōrē, convenienter.
bed *n* cubīle *nt*, lectus *m*, lectulus *m*; **go to ~** cubitum īre; **make a ~** lectum sternere; **be ~ridden** lectō tenērī; **camp ~** grabātus *m*; **flower~** pulvīnus *m*; **marriage ~** lectus geniālis *m*; **river~** alveus *m*.
bedaub *vt* illinere, oblinere.
bedclothes *n* strāgula *ntpl*.
bedding *n* strāgula *ntpl*.
bedeck *vt* ōrnāre, exōrnāre.
bedew *vt* inrōrāre.
bedim *vt* obscūrāre.
bedpost *n* fulcrum *nt*.
bedraggled *adj* sordidus, madidus.
bedroom *n* cubiculum *nt*.
bedstead *n* sponda *f*.
bee *n* apis *f*; **queen ~** rēx *m*.
beech *n* fāgus *f* ♦ *adj* fāginus.
beef *n* būbula *f*.
beehive *n* alvus *f*.
beekeeper *n* apiārius *m*.
beer *n* cervīsia *f*, fermentum *nt*.
beet *n* bēta *f*.
beetle *n* (*insect*) scarabaeus *m*; (*implement*) fistūca *f*.
beetling *adj* imminēns, mināx.
befall *vi, vt* accidere, ēvenīre (*dat*); (*good*) contingere (*dat*).
befit *vt* decēre, convenīre in (*acc*).
before *adv* ante, anteā, antehāc ♦ *prep* ante (*acc*); (*place*) prō (*abl*); (*presence*) apud (*acc*), cōram (*abl*) ♦ *conj* antequam, priusquam.
beforehand *adv* ante, anteā; prae (*in cpd*).
befoul *vt* inquināre, foedāre.
befriend *vt* favēre (*dat*), adiuvāre; (*in trouble*) adesse (*dat*).
beg *vt* ōrāre, obsecrāre, precārī, poscere ab, petere ab; **~ for** petere ♦ *vi* mendīcāre.
beget *vt* gignere, prōcreāre, generāre.
begetter *n* generātor *m*, creātor *m*.
beggar *n* mendīcus *m*.
beggarly *adj* mendīcus, indigēns.
beggary *n* mendīcitās *f*, indigentia *f*.
begin *vi, vt* incipere, coepisse; (*speech*)

exōrdīrī; (_plan_) īnstituere, incohāre; (_time_) inīre; ~ **with** incipere ab.

beginning _n_ initium _nt_, prīncipium _nt_, exōrdium _nt_, inceptiō _f_; (_learning_) rudīmenta _ntpl_, elementa _ntpl_; (_origin_) orīgō _f_, fōns _m_; **at the ~ of spring** ineunte vēre.

begone _interj_ apage, tē āmovē.

begotten _adj_ genitus, nātus.

begrudge _vt_ invidēre (_dat_).

beguile _vt_ dēcipere, fallere.

behalf _n_: **on ~ of** prō (_abl_); **on my ~** meō nōmine.

behave _vi_ sē gerere, sē praebēre (_with adj_); **well ~d** bene mōrātus.

behaviour _n_ mōrēs _mpl_.

behead _vt_ dētruncāre, secūrī percutere.

behest _n_ iūssum _nt_.

behind _adv_ pōne, post, ā tergō ♦ _prep_ post (_acc_), pōne (_acc_).

behindhand _adv_ sērō; **be ~** parum prōficere.

behold _vt_ aspicere, cōnspicere, intuērī ♦ _interj_ ecce, ēn.

beholden _adj_ obnoxius, obstrictus, obligātus.

behoof _n_ ūsus _m_.

behove _vt_ oportēre.

being _n_ (_life_) animātiō _f_; (_nature_) nātūra _f_; (_person_) homō _m/f_.

bejewelled _adj_ gemmeus, gemmātus.

belabour _vt_ verberāre, caedere.

belated _adj_ sērus.

belch _vi_ ructāre, ēructāre.

beldam _n_ anus _f_.

beleaguer _vt_ obsidēre, circumsedēre.

belie _vt_ abhorrēre ab, repugnāre.

belief _n_ fidēs _f_, opīniō _f_; (_opinion_) sententia _f_; **to the best of my ~** ex animī meī sententiā; **past ~** incrēdibilis.

believe _vt_, _vi_ (_thing_) crēdere; (_person_) crēdere (_dat_); (_suppose_) crēdere, putāre, arbitrārī, opīnārī; **~ in gods** deōs esse crēdere; **make ~** simulāre.

believer _n_ deōrum cultor _m_; Christiānus _m_.

belike _adv_ fortasse.

belittle _vt_ obtrectāre.

bell _n_ tintinnābulum _nt_; (_public_) campāna _f_.

belle _n_ fōrmōsa _f_, pulchra _f_.

belles-lettres _n_ litterae _fpl_.

bellicose _adj_ ferōx.

belligerent _adj_ bellī particeps.

bellow _vi_ rūdere, mūgīre ♦ _n_ mūgītus _m_.

bellows _n_ follis _m_.

belly _n_ abdōmen _nt_, venter _m_; (_sail_) sinus _m_ ♦ _vi_ tumēre.

belong _vi_ esse (_gen_), proprium esse (_gen_), inesse (_dat_); (_concern_) attinēre, pertinēre.

belongings _n_ bona _ntpl_.

beloved _adj_ cārus, dīlectus, grātus.

below _adv_ īnfrā, subter ♦ _adj_ īnferus ♦ _prep_ īnfrā (_acc_), sub (_abl, acc_).

belt _n_ zōna _f_; (_sword_) balteus _m_.

bemoan _vt_ dēplōrāre, lāmentārī.

bemused _adj_ stupefactus, stupidus.

bench _n_ subsellium _nt_; (_rowing_) trānstrum _nt_;

(_law_) iūdicēs _mpl_; **seat on the ~** iūdicātus _m_.

bend _vt_ flectere, curvāre, inclīnāre; (_bow_) intendere; (_course_) tendere, flectere; (_mind_) intendere ♦ _vi_ sē īnflectere; (_person_) sē dēmittere; **~ back** reflectere; **~ down** _vi_ dēflectere; sē dēmittere ♦ _n_ flexus _m_, ānfrāctus _m_.

beneath _adv_ subter ♦ _prep_ sub (_acc or abl_).

benediction _n_ bonae precēs _fpl_.

benedictory _adj_ faustus.

benefaction _n_ beneficium _nt_, dōnum _nt_.

benefactor _n_ patrōnus _m_; **be a ~** bene merērī (_dē_).

beneficence _n_ beneficentia _f_, līberālitās _f_.

beneficent _adj_ beneficus.

beneficial _adj_ ūtilis, salūbris.

benefit _n_ beneficium _nt_; (_derived_) fructus _m_; **have the ~ of** fruī (_abl_) ♦ _vt_ prōdesse (_dat_), usuī esse (_dat_).

benevolence _n_ benevolentia _f_, benignitās _f_.

benevolent _adj_ benevolus, benignus.

benevolently _adv_ benevolē, benignē.

benighted _adj_ nocte oppressus; (_fig_) ignārus, indoctus.

benign _adj_ benignus, cōmis.

bent _n_ (_mind_) inclīnātiō _f_, ingenium _nt_ ♦ _adj_ curvus, flexus; (_mind_) attentus; **be ~ on** studēre (_dat_).

benumb _vt_ stupefacere.

benumbed _adj_ stupefactus, torpidus; **be ~** torpēre.

bequeath _vt_ lēgāre.

bequest _n_ lēgātum _nt_.

bereave _vt_ orbāre, prīvāre.

bereavement _n_ damnum _nt_.

bereft _adj_ orbus, orbātus, prīvātus.

berry _n_ bāca _f_.

berth _n_ statiō _f_; **give a wide ~ to** dēvītāre.

beryl _n_ bēryllus _m_.

beseech _vt_ implōrāre, ōrāre, obsecrāre.

beset _vt_ obsidēre, circumsedēre.

beside _prep_ ad (_acc_), apud (_acc_); (_close_) iuxtā (_acc_); **~ the point** nihil ad rem; **be ~ oneself** nōn esse apud sē.

besides _adv_ praetereā, accēdit quod; (_in addition_) īnsuper ♦ _prep_ praeter (_acc_).

besiege _vt_ obsidēre, circumsedēre.

besieger _n_ obsessor _m_.

besmear _vt_ illinere.

besmirch _vt_ maculāre.

besom _n_ scōpae _fpl_.

besotted _adj_ stupidus.

bespatter _vt_ aspergere.

bespeak _vt_ (_order_) imperāre; (_denote_) significāre.

besprinkle _vt_ aspergere.

best _adj_ optimus; **the ~ part** māior pars ♦ _n_ flōs _m_, rōbur _nt_; **do one's ~** prō virīlī parte agere; **do one's ~ to** operam dare ut; **have the ~ of it** vincere; **make the ~ of (a situation)** aequō animō accipere; **to the ~ of one's ability** prō virīlī parte; **to the ~ of my knowledge** quod sciam ♦ _adv_ optimē.

bestial *adj* foedus.
bestir *vt* movēre; ~ **oneself** expergīscī.
bestow *vt* dōnāre, tribuere, dare, cōnferre.
bestride *vt* (*horse*) sedēre in (*abl*).
bet *n* pignus *nt* ♦ *vt* oppōnere ♦ *vi* pignore
  contendere.
betake *vt* cōnferre, recipere; ~ **o.s.** sē
  cōnferre.
bethink *vt*: ~ **oneself** sē colligere; ~ **oneself of**
  respicere.
betide *vi* accidere, ēvenīre.
betoken *vt* significāre; (*foretell*) portendere.
betray *vt* prōdere, trādere; (*feelings*) arguere;
  without ~ing one's trust salvā fidē.
betrayal *n* prōditiō *f*.
betrayer *n* prōditor *m*; (*informer*) index *m*.
betroth *vt* spondēre, dēspondēre.
betrothal *n* spōnsālia *ntpl*.
better *adj* melior; **it is ~ to** praestat (*infin*); **get**
  the ~ of vincere, superāre; **I am ~** (*in health*)
  melius est mihī; **I had ~ go** praestat īre; **get ~**
  convalēscere; **think ~ of** sententiam mūtāre
  dē ♦ *adv* melius ♦ *vt* corrigere; ~ **oneself**
  prōficere.
betterment *n* prōfectus *m*.
between *prep* inter (*acc*).
beverage *n* pōtiō *f*.
bevy *n* manus *f*, grex *f*.
bewail *vt* dēflēre, lāmentārī, dēplōrāre.
beware *vt* cavēre.
bewilder *vt* cōnfundere, perturbāre.
bewildered *adj* attonitus.
bewilderment *n* perturbātiō *f*, admīrātiō *f*.
bewitch *vt* fascināre; (*fig*) dēlēnīre.
beyond *adv* ultrā, suprā ♦ *prep* ultrā (*acc*),
  extrā (*acc*); (*motion*) trāns (*acc*); (*amount*)
  ultrā, suprā (*acc*); **go/pass ~** excēdere,
  ēgredī.
bezel *n* pāla *f*.
bias *n* inclīnātiō *f*; (*party*) favor *m* ♦ *vt*
  inclīnāre.
biassed *adj* prōpēnsior.
bibber *n* pōtor *m*, pōtātor *m*.
Bible *n* litterae sacrae *fpl*.
bibulous *adj* bibulus.
bicephalous *adj* biceps.
bicker *vi* altercārī, iūrgāre.
bid *vt* iubēre; (*guest*) vocāre, invītāre ♦ *vi* (*at*
  auction) licērī; ~ **for** licērī; ~ **good day**
  salvēre iubēre; **he ~s fair to make progress**
  spēs est eum prōfectūrum esse.
biddable *adj* docilis.
bidding *n* iussum *nt*; (*auction*) licitātiō *f*.
bide *vt* manēre, opperīrī.
biennial *adj* biennālis.
bier *n* ferculum *nt*.
bifurcate *vi* sē scindere.
bifurcation *n* (*road*) trivium *nt*.
big *adj* māgnus, grandis, amplus; (*with child*)
  gravida; **very ~** permāgnus; **talk ~** glōriārī.
bight *n* sinus *m*.
bigness *n* māgnitūdō *f*, amplitūdō *f*.
bigot *n* nimis obstinātus fautor *m*.

bigoted *adj* contumāx.
bigotry *n* contumācia *f*, nimia obstinātiō *f*.
bile *n* bīlis *f*, fel *nt*.
bilgewater *n* sentīna *f*.
bilk *vt* fraudāre.
bill *n* (*bird*) rōstrum *nt*; (*implement*) falx *f*; (*law*)
  rogātiō *f*, lēx *f*; (*money*) syngrapha *f*; (*notice*)
  libellus *m*, titulus *m*; **introduce a ~** populum
  rogāre, lēgem ferre; **carry a ~** lēgem
  perferre.
billet *n* hospitium *nt* ♦ *vt* in hospitia dīvidere.
billhook *n* falx *f*.
billow *n* flūctus *m*.
billowy *adj* undōsus.
billy goat *n* caper *m*.
bin *n* lacus *m*.
bind *vt* adligāre, dēligāre, vincīre; (*by oath*)
  adigere; (*by obligation*) obligāre,
  obstringere; (*wound*) obligāre; ~ **fast**
  dēvincīre; ~ **together** conligāre; ~ **over** *vt*
  vadārī.
binding *n* compāgēs *f* ♦ *adj* (*law*) ratus; **it is ~**
  on oportet.
bindweed *n* convolvulus *m*.
biographer *n* vītae nārrātor *m*.
biography *n* vīta *f*.
bipartite *adj* bipartītus.
biped *n* bipēs *m*.
birch *n* bētula *f*; (*flogging*) virgae ulmeae *fpl*.
bird *n* avis *f*; ~**s of a feather** parēs cum paribus
  facillimē congregantur; **kill two ~s with one**
  stone ūnō saltū duōs aprōs capere, dē eādem
  fidēliā duōs parietēs dealbāre; ~**'s-eye view**
  of dēspectus in (*acc*).
birdcatcher *n* auceps *m*.
birdlime *n* viscum *nt*.
birth *n* (*act*) partus *m*; (*origin*) genus *nt*; **low ~**
  ignōbilitās *f*; **high ~** nōbilitās *f*; **by ~** nātū,
  ortū.
birthday *n* nātālis *m*.
birthday party *n* nātālicia *ntpl*.
birthplace *n* locus nātālis *m*; (*fig*) incūnābula
  ntpl.
birthright *n* patrimōnium *nt*.
bisect *vt* dīvidere.
bishop *n* epīscopus *m*.
bison *n* ūrus *m*.
bit *n* pars *f*; (*food*) frustum *nt*; (*broken off*)
  fragmentum *nt*; (*horse*) frēnum *nt*; ~ **by ~**
  minūtātim; **a ~** *adv* aliquantulum; **a ~ sad**
  tristior.
bitch *n* canis *f*.
bite *vt* mordēre; (*frost*) ūrere ♦ *n* morsus *m*;
  with a ~ mordicus.
biting *adj* mordāx.
bitter *adj* (*taste*) acerbus, amārus; (*words*)
  asper.
bitterly *adv* acerbē, asperē.
bittern *n* būtiō *m*, ardea *f*.
bitterness *n* acerbitās *f*.
bitumen *n* bitūmen *nt*.
bivouac *n* excubiae *fpl* ♦ *vi* excubāre.
bizarre *adj* īnsolēns.

blab *vt, vi* garrīre, effūtīre.

black *adj* (*dull*) āter; (*glossy*) niger; (*dirt*)
sordidus; (*eye*) līvidus; (*looks*) trux; **~ and
blue** līvidus; ♦ *n* ātrum *nt*, nigrum *nt*; **dressed
in ~** ātrātus; (*in mourning*) sordidātus.

blackberry *n* mōrum *nt*.

blackbird *n* merula *f*.

blacken *vt* nigrāre, nigrum reddere;
(*character*) īnfāmāre, obtrectāre (*dat*).

blackguard *n* scelestus, scelerātus *m*.

blacking *n* ātrāmentum *nt*.

blacklist *n* prōscrīptiō *f*.

black magic *n* magicae artēs *fpl*.

blackmail *n* minae *fpl* ♦ *vt* minīs cōgere.

black mark *n* nota *f*.

blacksmith *n* faber *m*.

bladder *n* vēsīca *f*.

blade *n* (*grass*) herba *f*; (*oar*) palma *f*; (*sword*)
lāmina *f*.

blame *vt* reprehendere, culpāre; **I am to ~**
reus sum ♦ *n* reprehēnsiō *f*, culpa *f*.

blameless *adj* innocēns.

blamelessly *adv* innocenter.

blamelessness *n* innocentia *f*, integritās *f*.

blameworthy *adj* accūsābilis, nocēns.

blanch *vi* exalbēscere, pallēscere.

bland *adj* mītis, lēnis.

blandishment *n* blanditiae *fpl*.

blank *adj* vacuus, pūrus; (*look*) stolidus.

blanket *n* lōdīx *f*; **wet ~** nimium sevērus.

blare *vi* canere, strīdere ♦ *n* clangor *m*, strīdor
m.

blarney *n* lēnōcinium *nt*.

blaspheme *vi* maledīcere.

blasphemous *adj* maledicus, impius.

blasphemy *n* maledicta *ntpl*, impietās *f*.

blast *n* flātus *m*, īnflātus *m* ♦ *vt* discidere,
discutere; (*crops*) rōbīgine adficere.

blatant *adj* raucus.

blaze *n* flamma *f*, ignis *m*, fulgor *m* ♦ *vi*
flāgrāre, ārdēre, fulgēre; **~ up** exārdēscere
♦ *vt*: **~ abroad** pervulgāre.

blazon *vt* promulgāre.

bleach *vt* candidum reddere.

bleak *adj* dēsertus, tristis, inamoenus.

bleary-eyed *adj* lippus.

bleat *vi* bālāre ♦ *n* bālātus *m*.

bleed *vi* sanguinem fundere ♦ *vt* sanguinem
mittere (*dat*); **my heart ~s** animus mihī dolet.

bleeding *adj* crūdus, sanguineus ♦ *n* sanguinis
missiō *f*.

blemish *n* macula *f*, vitium *nt* ♦ *vt* maculāre,
foedāre.

blend *vt* miscēre, immiscēre, admiscēre ♦ *n*
coniūnctiō *f*.

bless *vt* beāre; laudāre; (*ECCL*) benedīcere; **~
with** augēre (*abl*); **~ my soul!** ita mē dī ament!

blessed *adj* beātus, fortūnātus; (*emperors*)
dīvus.

blessing *n* (*thing*) commodum *nt*, bonum *nt*;
(*ECCL*) benedictiō *f*.

blight *n* rōbīgō *f*, ūrēdō *f* ♦ *vt* rōbīgine adficere;
(*fig*) nocēre (*dat*).

blind *adj* caecus; (*in one eye*) luscus; (*fig*)
ignārus, stultus; (*alley*) nōn pervius; (*forces*)
necessārius; **turn a ~ eye to** cōnīvēre in (*abl*)
♦ *vt* excaecāre, caecāre; (*fig*) occaecāre;
(*with light*) praestringere.

blindfold *adj* capite obvolūtō.

blindly *adv* temerē.

blindness *n* caecitās *f*; (*fig*) temeritās *f*,
īnsipientia *f*.

blink *vi* nictāre.

bliss *n* fēlīcitās *f*, laetitia *f*.

blissful *adj* fēlīx, beātus, laetus.

blissfully *adv* fēlīciter, beātē.

blister *n* pustula *f*.

blithe *adj* hilaris, laetus.

blithely *adv* hilare, laetē.

blizzard *n* hiems *f*.

bloated *adj* tumidus, turgidus.

blob *n* gutta *f*, particula *f*.

block *n* (*wood*) stīpes *m*, caudex *m*; (*stone*)
massa *f*; (*houses*) īnsula *f*; **~ letter** quadrāta
littera; **stumbling ~** offēnsiō *f*.

block *vt* claudere, obstruere, interclūdere; **~
the way** obstāre.

blockade *n* obsidiō *f*; **raise a ~** obsidiōnem
solvere ♦ *vt* obsidēre, interclūdere.

blockhead *n* caudex *m*, bārō *m*, truncus *m*.

blockhouse *n* castellum *nt*.

blond *adj* flāvus.

blood *n* sanguis *m*; (*shed*) cruor *m*; (*murder*)
caedēs *f*; (*kin*) genus *nt*; **let ~** sanguinem
mittere; **staunch ~** sanguinem supprimere;
bad ~ simultās *f*; **in cold ~** cōnsultō; **own flesh
and ~** cōnsanguineus.

bloodless *adj* exsanguis; (*victory*) incruentus.

bloodshed *n* caedēs *f*.

bloodshot *adj* sanguineus.

bloodstained *adj* cruentus.

bloodsucker *n* hirūdō *f*.

bloodthirsty *adj* sanguinārius.

blood vessel *n* vēna *f*.

bloody *adj* cruentus.

bloom *n* flōs *m*; **in ~** flōrēns ♦ *vi* flōrēre,
flōrēscere, vigēre.

blossom *n* flōs *m* ♦ *vi* efflōrēscere, flōrēre.

blot *n* macula *f*; (*erasure*) litūra *f* ♦ *vt* maculāre;
~ out dēlēre, oblitterāre.

blotch *n* macula *f*.

blotched *adj* maculōsus.

blow *vt, vi* (*wind*) flāre; (*breath*) adflāre,
anhēlāre; (*instrument*) canere; (*flower*)
efflōrēscere; (*nose*) ēmungere; **~ out** *vi*
exstinguere; **~ over** *vi* (*storm*) cadere; (*fig*)
abīre; **~ up** *vt* īnflāre; (*destroy*) discutere,
disturbāre ♦ *n* ictus *m*; (*on the cheek*) alapa *f*;
(*fig*) plāga *f*; (*misfortune*) calamitās *f*; **aim a ~
at** petere; **come to ~s** ad manūs venīre.

blowy *adj* ventōsus.

bludgeon *n* fustis *m*.

blue *adj* caeruleus; **black and ~** līvidus; **true ~**
fīdissimus; **~ blood** nōbilitās *f*.

bluff *n* rūpēs *f*, prōmunturium *nt* ♦ *adj*

blunder–border

inurbānus ♦ *vt* fallere, dēcipere, verba dare (*dat*), impōnere (*dat*).

blunder *vi* errāre, offendere ♦ *n* error *m*, errātum *nt*; (*in writing*) mendum *nt*.

blunt *adj* hebes; (*manners*) horridus, rūsticus, inurbānus; **be ~** hebēre ♦ *vt* hebetāre, obtundere, retundere.

bluntly *adv* līberius, plānē et apertē.

blur *n* macula *f* ♦ *vt* obscūrāre.

blurt *vt*: **~ out** ēmittere.

blush *vi* rubēre, ērubēscere ♦ *n* rubor *m*.

bluster *vi* dēclāmitāre, lātrāre.

boa *n* boa *f*.

Boadicea *n* Boudicca *f*.

boar *n* verrēs *m*; (*wild*) aper *m*.

board *n* tabula *f*; (*table*) mēnsa *f*; (*food*) vīctus *m*; (*committee*) concilium *nt*; (*judicial*) quaestiō *f*; (*of ten men*) decemvirī *mpl*; (*gaming*) abacus *m*, alveus *m*; **on ~** in nāvī; **go on ~** in nāvem cōnscendere; **go by the ~** intercidere, perīre; **above ~** sine fraude ♦ *vt* (*building*) contabulāre; (*ship*) cōnscendere; (*person*) vīctum praebēre (*dat*) ♦ *vi*: **~ with** dēvertere ad.

boarder *n* hospes *m*.

boast *vi* glōriārī, sē iactāre; **~ of** glōriārī dē (*abl*) ♦ *n* glōria *f*, glōriātiō *f*, iactātiō *f*.

boastful *adj* glōriōsus.

boastfully *adv* glōriōsē.

boasting *n* glōriātiō *f* ♦ *adj* glōriōsus.

boat *n* linter *f*, scapha *f*, cymba *f*; (*ship*) nāvis *f*; **be in the same ~** (*fig*) in eādem nāvī esse.

boatman *n* nauta *m*.

boatswain *n* hortātor *m*.

bobbin *n* fūsus *m*.

bode *vt* portendere, praesāgīre.

bodiless *adj* sine corpore.

bodily *adj* corporeus.

bodkin *n* acus *f*.

body *n* corpus *nt*; (*dead*) cadāver *nt*; (*small*) corpusculum *nt*; (*person*) homō *m/f*; (*of people*) globus *m*, numerus *m*; (*of troops*) manus *f*, caterva *f*; (*of cavalry*) turma *f*; (*of officials*) collēgium *nt*; (*heavenly*) astrum *nt*; **in a ~** ūniversī, frequentēs.

bodyguard *n* custōs *m*, stīpātōrēs *mpl*; (*emperor's*) praetōriānī *mpl*.

bog *n* palūs *f*.

bogey *n* mōnstrum *nt*.

boggle *vi* tergiversārī, haesitāre.

boggy *adj* palūster.

bogus *adj* falsus, fictus.

Bohemian *adj* līberior, solūtior, libīdinōsus.

boil *vt* coquere; (*liquid*) fervefacere; **~ down** dēcoquere ♦ *vi* fervēre, effervēscere; (*sea*) exaestuāre; (*passion*) exārdēscere, aestuāre; **~ over** effervēscere ♦ *n* (*MED*) fūrunculus *m*.

boiler *n* cortīna *f*.

boiling *adj* (*hot*) fervēns.

boisterous *adj* (*person*) turbulentus, vehemēns; (*sea*) turbidus, agitātus; (*weather*) procellōsus, violentus.

boisterously *adv* turbidē, turbulentē.

boisterousness *n* tumultus *m*, violentia *f*.

bold *adj* audāx, fortis, intrepidus; (*impudent*) impudēns, protervus; (*language*) līber; (*headland*) prōminēns; **make ~** audēre.

boldly *adv* audācter, fortiter, intrepidē; impudenter.

boldness *n* audācia *f*, cōnfīdentia *f*; impudentia *f*, petulantia *f*; (*speech*) lībertās *f*.

bolster *n* pulvīnus *m* ♦ *vt*: **~ up** sustinēre, cōnfirmāre.

bolt *n* (*door*) claustrum *nt*, pessulus *m*, sera *f*; (*missile*) tēlum *nt*, sagitta *f*; (*lightning*) fulmen *nt*; **make a ~ for it** sē prōripere, aufugere; **a ~ from the blue** rēs subita, rēs inopīnāta ♦ *vi* (*door*) obserāre, obdere.

bombard *vt* tormentīs verberāre; (*fig*) lacessere.

bombast *n* ampullae *fpl*.

bombastic *adj* tumidus, īnflātus; **be ~** ampullārī.

bond *n* vinculum *nt*, catēna *f*, compes *f*; (*of union*) cōpula *f*, iugum *nt*, nōdus *m*; (*document*) syngrapha *f*; (*agreement*) foedus *nt* ♦ *adj* servus, addictus.

bondage *n* servitūs *f*, famulātus *m*.

bone *n* os *nt*; (*fish*) spīna *f* ♦ *vt* exossāre.

boneless *adj* exos.

bonfire *n* ignis festus *m*.

bonhomie *n* festīvitās *f*.

bon mot *n* dictum *nt*, sententia *f*.

bonny *adj* pulcher, bellus.

bony *adj* osseus.

boo *vt* explōdere.

book *n* liber *m*; (*small*) libellus *m*; (*scroll*) volūmen *nt*; (*modern form*) cōdex *m*; **~s** (*COMM*) rationēs *fpl*, tabulae *fpl*; **bring to ~** in iūdicium vocāre.

bookbinder *n* glūtinātor *m*.

bookcase *n* librārium *nt*, pēgma *nt*.

bookish *adj* litterārum studiōsus.

book-keeper *n* āctuārius *m*.

bookseller *n* librārius *m*, bibliopōla *m*.

bookshop *n* bibliothēca *f*, librāria taberna *f*.

bookworm *n* tinea *f*.

boom *n* (*spar*) longurius *m*; (*harbour*) ōbex *m/f* ♦ *vi* resonāre.

boon *n* bonum *nt*, beneficium *nt*, dōnum *nt* ♦ *adj* festīvus; **~ companion** sodālis *m*, compōtor *m*.

boor *n* agrestis *m*, rūsticus *m*.

boorish *adj* agrestis, rūsticus, inurbānus.

boorishly *adv* rūsticē.

boost *vt* efferre; (*wares*) vēnditāre.

boot *n* calceus *m*; (*MIL*) caliga *f*; (*rustic*) pērō *m*; (*tragic*) cothurnus *m* ♦ *vi* prōdesse; **to ~** īnsuper, praetereā.

booted *adj* calceātus, caligātus.

booth *n* taberna *f*.

bootless *adj* inūtilis, vānus.

bootlessly *adv* frustrā.

booty *n* praeda *f*, spolia *ntpl*.

border *n* ōra *f*, margō *f*; (*country*) fīnis *m*; (*dress*) limbus *m* ♦ *vt* praetexere, margināre;

fīnīre ♦ *vi*: ~ **on** adiacēre (*dat*), imminēre (*dat*), attingere; (*fig*) fīnitimum esse (*dat*).
bordering *adj* fīnitimus.
bore *vt* perforāre, perterebrāre; (*person*) obtundere, fatīgāre; ~ **out** exterebrāre ♦ *n* terebra *f*; (*hole*) forāmen *nt*; (*person*) homō importūnus *m*, ineptus *m*.
boredom *n* lassitūdō *f*.
borer *n* terebra *f*.
born *adj* nātus; **be** ~ nāscī.
borough *n* mūnicipium *nt*.
borrow *vt* mūtuārī.
borrowed *adj* mūtuus; (*fig*) aliēnus.
borrowing *n* mūtuātiō *f*; (*to pay a debt*) versūra *f*.
bosky *adj* nemorōsus.
bosom *n* sinus *m*; (*fig*) gremium *nt*; ~ **friend** familiāris *m/f*, sodālis *m*; **be a** ~ **friend of** ab latere esse (*gen*).
boss *n* bulla *f*; (*shield*) umbō *m*.
botanist *n* herbārius *m*.
botany *n* herbāria *f*.
botch *vt* male sarcīre, male gerere.
both *pron* ambō, uterque (*gen* **utriusque**, *each of two*) ♦ *adv*: ~ ... **and** et ... et, cum ... tum.
bother *n* negōtium *nt* ♦ *vt* vexāre, molestus esse (*dat*) ♦ *vi* operam dare.
bothersome *adj* molestus.
bottle *n* lagoena *f*, amphora *f* ♦ *vt* (*wine*) diffundere.
bottom *n* fundus *m*; (*ground*) solum *nt*; (*ship*) carīna *f*; **the** ~ **of** īmus; **be at the** ~ **of** (*cause*) auctōrem esse; **go to the** ~ pessum īre, perīre; **send to the** ~ pessum dare; **from the** ~ funditus, ab īnfimō.
bottomless *adj* profundus, fundō carēns.
bottommost *adj* īnfimus.
bough *n* rāmus *m*.
boulder *n* saxum *nt*.
boulevard *n* platea *f*.
bounce *vi* salīre, resultāre.
bound *n* fīnis *m*, modus *m*, terminus *m*; (*leap*) saltus *m*; **set ~s to** modum facere (*dat*) ♦ *vt* fīnīre, dēfīnīre, termināre ♦ *vi* salīre, saltāre ♦ *adj* adligātus, obligātus, obstrictus; **be** ~ **to** (*duty*) dēbēre; **it is** ~ **to happen** necesse est ēveniat; **be** ~ **for** tendere in (*acc*); **be storm**~ tempestāte tenērī.
boundaries *npl* fīnes *mpl*.
boundary *n* fīnis *m*; (*of fields*) terminus *m*; (*fortified*) līmes *m*; ~ **stone** terminus *m*.
boundless *adj* immēnsus, īnfīnītus.
boundlessness *n* īnfīnitās *f*, immēnsum *nt*.
bounteous *adj see* **bountiful**.
bounteously *adv* largē, līberāliter, cōpiōsē.
bountiful *adj* largus, benignus.
bounty *n* largitās *f*, līberālitās *f*; (*store*) cōpia *f*.
bouquet *n* corollārium *nt*; (*of wine*) flōs *m*.
bourn *n* fīnis *m*.
bout *n* certāmen *nt*; (*drinking*) cōmissātiō *f*.
bovine *adj* būbulus; (*fig*) stolidus.
bow *n* arcus *m*; (*ship*) prōra *f*; (*courtesy*) salūtātiō *f*; **have two strings to one's** ~

duplicī spē ūtī; **rain**~ arcus *m* ♦ *vi* flectere, inclīnāre ♦ *vi* caput dēmittere.
bowels *n* alvus *f*; (*fig*) viscera *ntpl*.
bower *n* umbrāculum *nt*, trichila *f*.
bowl *n* (*cooking*) catīnus *m*; (*drinking*) calix *m*; (*mixing wine*) crātēra *f*; (*ball*) pila *f* ♦ *vt* volvere; ~ **over** prōruere.
bow-legged *adj* valgus.
bowler *n* (*game*) dator *m*.
bowstring *n* nervus *m*.
box *n* arca *f*, capsa *f*; (*for clothes*) cista *f*; (*for medicine*) pyxis *f*; (*for perfume*) alabaster *m*; (*tree*) buxus *f*; (*wood*) buxum *nt*; (*blow on ears*) alapa *f* ♦ *vt* inclūdere; ~ **the ears of** alapam dūcere (*dat*), colaphōs īnfringere (*dat*) ♦ *vi* (*fight*) pugnīs certāre.
boxer *n* pugil *m*.
boxing *n* pugilātiō *f*.
boxing glove *n* caestus *m*.
boy *n* puer *m*; **become a** ~ **again** repuerāscere.
boycott *vt* repudiāre.
boyhood *n* pueritia *f*; **from** ~ ā puerō.
boyish *adj* puerīlis.
boyishly *adv* puerīliter.
brace *n* (*building*) fībula *f*; (*strap*) fascia *f*; (*pair*) pār *nt* ♦ *vt* adligāre; (*strengthen*) firmāre.
bracelet *n* armilla *f*.
bracing *adj* (*air*) salūbris.
bracken *n* filix *f*.
bracket *n* uncus *m*.
brackish *adj* amārus.
bradawl *n* terebra *f*.
brag *vi* glōriārī, sē iactāre.
braggart *n* glōriōsus *m*.
braid *vt* nectere.
brain *n* cerebrum *nt*; ingenium *nt*.
brainless *adj* sōcors, stultus.
brainy *adj* ingeniōsus.
brake *n* (*wood*) dūmētum *nt*; (*on wheel*) sufflāmen *nt*.
bramble *n* rubus *m*.
bran *n* furfur *nt*.
branch *n* rāmus *m*; (*kind*) genus *nt* ♦ *vi*: ~ **out** rāmōs porrigere.
branching *adj* rāmōsus.
brand *n* (*fire*) torris *m*, fax *f*; (*mark*) nota *f*; (*sword*) ēnsis *m*; (*variety*) genus *nt* ♦ *vt* (*mark*) inūrere; (*stigma*) notāre; ~ **new** recēns.
brandish *vt* vibrāre.
brass *n* orichalcum *nt*.
bravado *n* ferōcitās *f*; **out of** ~ per speciem ferōcitātis.
brave *adj* fortis, ācer ♦ *vt* adīre, patī.
bravely *adv* fortiter, ācriter.
bravery *n* fortitūdō *f*, virtūs *f*.
bravo *interj* bene, euge, macte.
brawl *n* rixa *f*, iūrgium *nt* ♦ *vi* rixārī.
brawn *n* lacertī *mpl*.
brawny *adj* lacertōsus, rōbūstus.
bray *vi* rūdere.
brazen *adj* aēneus; (*fig*) impudēns.
brazier *n* foculus *m*.
breach *n* (*in wall*) ruīna *f*; (*of friendship*)

dissēnsiō *f* ♦ *vt* perfringere; ~ **of trust** mala fidēs; **commit a ~ of promise** prōmissīs nōn stāre.

breach of the peace *n* iūrgium *nt*, tumultus *m*.

bread *n* pānis *m*.

breadth *n* lātitūdō *f*; **in ~ in** lātitūdinem (*acc*).

break *vt* frangere, perfringere; ~ **down** *vt* īnfringere, dīruere; ~ **in** *vt* (*animal*) domāre; ~ **into pieces** dīrumpere; ~ **off** *vt* abrumpere, dēfringere; (*action*) dīrimere; ~ **open** effringere, solvere; ~ **through** *vt fus* interrumpere; ~ **up** *vt* dissolvere, interrumpere; ~ **one's word** fidem fallere, violāre; **without ~ing the law** salvīs lēgibus ♦ *vi* rumpī, frangī; (*day*) illūcēscere; (*strength*) dēficere; ~ **off** *vi* dēsinere; ~ **into** intrāre; ~ **out** *vi* ērumpere; (*sore*) recrūdēscere; (*trouble*) exārdēscere; ~ **up** *vi* dīlābī, dissolvī; (*meeting*) dīmittī; ~ **through** *vi* inrumpere; ~ **with** dissidēre ab ♦ *n* intermissiō *f*, intervallum *nt*.

breakable *adj* fragilis.

breakage *n* frāctum *nt*.

breakdown *n* (*activity*) mora *f*; (*health*) dēbilitās *f*.

breaker *n* fluctus *m*.

breakfast *n* iēntāculum *nt*, prandium *nt* ♦ *vi* ientāre, prandēre.

breakwater *n* mōlēs *f*.

bream *n* sparulus *m*.

breast *n* pectus *nt*; (*woman's*) mamma *f*; **make a clean ~ of** cōnfitērī.

breastplate *n* lōrīca *f*.

breastwork *n* lōrīca *f*, pluteus *m*.

breath *n* spīritus *m*, anima *f*; (*bad*) hālitus *m*; (*quick*) anhēlitus *m*; (*of wind*) aura *f*, adflātus *m*; **below one's ~** mussitāns; **catch one's ~** obstipēscere; **hold one's ~** animam comprimere, continēre; **take a ~** spīritum dūcere; **take one's ~ away** exanimāre; **waste one's ~** operam perdere; **out of ~** exanimātus.

breathable *adj* spīrābilis.

breathe *vt, vi* spīrāre, respīrāre; (*quickly*) anhēlāre; ~ **again** respīrāre; ~ **in** *vt, vi* spīritum dūcere; ~ **out** *vt, vi* exspīrāre, exhālāre; ~ **upon** īnspīrāre (*dat*), adflāre (*dat*); ~ **one's last** animam agere, efflāre.

breathing *n* hālitus *m*, respīrātiō *f*.

breathing space *n* respīrātiō *f*.

breathless *adj* exanimātus.

breeches *n* brācae *fpl*.

breed *n* genus *nt* ♦ *vt* generāre, prōcreāre; (*raise*) ēducāre, alere; (*fig*) adferre, efficere; **well-bred** generōsus.

breeder *n* (*animal*) mātrix *f*; (*man*) generātor *m*; (*fig*) nūtrix *f*.

breeding *n* (*act*) fētūra *f*; (*manners*) mōrēs *mpl*; **good ~** hūmānitās *f*.

breeze *n* aura *f*, flātus *m*.

breezy *adj* ventōsus; (*manner*) hilaris.

brevity *n* brevitās *f*.

brew *vt* coquere ♦ *vi* (*fig*) parārī, imminēre.

bribe *vt* corrumpere ♦ *vi* largīrī ♦ *n* pecūnia *f*, mercēs *f*.

briber *n* corruptor *m*, largītor *m*.

bribery *n* ambitus *m*, largītiō *f*.

brick *n* later *m* ♦ *adj* latericius.

brickwork *n* latericium *nt*.

bridal *adj* nūptiālis; (*bed*) geniālis ♦ *n* nūptiae *fpl*.

bride *n* nūpta *f*.

bridegroom *m* marītus *m*.

bridge *n* pōns *m* ♦ *vt* pontem impōnere (*dat*).

bridle *n* frēnum *nt* ♦ *vt* frēnāre, īnfrēnāre.

brief *adj* brevis; **to be ~** nē longum sit, nē multa.

briefly *adv* breviter, paucīs verbīs.

briefness *n* brevitās *f*.

brier *n* veprēs *m*, sentis *m*.

brig *n* liburna *f*.

brigade *n* legiō *f*; (*cavalry*) turma *f*.

brigadier *n* lēgātus *m*.

brigand *n* latrō *m*, praedō *m*.

brigandage *n* latrōcinium *nt*.

bright *adj* clārus, lūculentus; (*sky*) serēnus; (*intellect*) ingeniōsus; (*manner*) hilaris, laetus; **be ~** lūcēre, splendēre.

brighten *vt* illūstrāre; laetificāre ♦ *vi* lūcēscere; (*person*) hilarem fierī.

brightly *adv* clārē.

brightness *n* fulgor *m*, candor *m*; (*sky*) serēnitās *f*.

brilliance *n* splendor *m*, fulgor *m*; (*style*) nitor *m*, lūmen *nt*, īnsignia *ntpl*.

brilliant *adj* clārus, illūstris, splendidus; (*fig*) īnsignis, praeclārus, lūculentus.

brilliantly *adv* splendidē, praeclārē, lūculentē.

brim *n* lābrum *nt*, margō *f*; **fill to the ~** explēre.

brimstone *n* sulfur *nt*.

brindled *adj* varius.

brine *n* salsāmentum *nt*.

bring *vt* ferre; (*person*) dūcere; (*charge*) intendere; (*to a place*) adferre, addūcere, advehere, dēferre; (*to a destination*) perdūcere; (*to a worse state*) redigere; ~ **about** *vt* efficere; ~ **before** dēferre ad, referre ad; ~ **back** *vt* (*thing*) referre; (*person*) redūcere; ~ **down** *vt* dēdūcere, dēferre; ~ **forth** (*from store*) dēprōmere; (*child*) parere; (*crops*) ferre, ēdere; ~ **forward** *vt* (*for discussion*) iactāre, iacere; (*reason*) adferre; ~ **home** (*bride*) dēdūcere; (*in triumph*) dēportāre; ~ **home to** pervincere; ~ **in** *vt* invehere, indūcere, intrōdūcere; (*import*) importāre; (*revenue*) reddere; ~ **off** *vt* (*success*) reportāre; ~ **on** īnferre, importāre; (*stage*) indūcere; ~ **out** *vt* efferre; (*book*) ēdere; (*play*) dare; (*talent*) ēlicere; ~ **over** perdūcere, trādūcere; ~ **to bear** adferre; ~ **to light** nūdāre, dētegere; ~ **to pass** perficere, peragere; ~ **to shore** ad litus appellere; ~ **together** contrahere, cōgere; (*enemies*) conciliāre; ~ **up** *vt* (*child*) ēducāre, tollere; (*troops*) admovēre; (*topic*) prōferre; ~ **upon oneself** sibī cōnscīscere, sibī contrahere.

brink n ōra f, margō f.
briny adj salsus.
brisk adj alacer, vegetus, ācer.
briskly adv ācriter.
briskness n alacritās f.
bristle n sēta f ♦ vi horrēre, horrēscere.
bristly adj horridus, hirsūtus.
Britain n Brittania f.
Britons n Brittani mpl.
brittle adj fragilis.
broach vt (topic) in medium prōferre.
broad adj lātus; (accent) lātus; (joke)
    inurbānus; (daylight) multus.
broadcast vt dissēmināre.
broaden vt dīlātāre.
broadly adv lātē.
broadsword n gladius m.
brocade n Attalica ntpl.
brochure n libellus m.
brogue n pērō m.
broil n rixa f, iūrgium nt ♦ vt torrēre.
broiling adj torridus.
broken adj frāctus; (fig) cōnfectus; (speech)
    īnfrāctus.
broken-hearted adj dolōre cōnfectus.
broker n īnstitor m.
bronze n aes nt ♦ adj aēneus, aerātus.
brooch n fībula f.
brood n fētus m; (fig) gēns f ♦ vi incubāre (dat);
    (fig) incubāre (dat), fovēre; ~ **over** meditārī.
brook n rīvus m ♦ vt ferre, patī.
brooklet n rīvulus m.
broom n (plant) genista f; (brush) scōpae fpl.
broth n iūs nt.
brother n frāter m; (full) germānus m; ~ **and
    sister** marītus mpl.
brotherhood n frāternitās f.
brother-in-law n lēvir m, uxōris frāter m,
    sorōris marītus m.
brotherly adj frāternus.
brow n frōns f; (eye) supercilium nt; (hill)
    dorsum nt.
browbeat vt obiūrgāre, exagitāre.
brown adj fulvus, spādīx; (skin) adūstus.
browse vi pāscī, dēpāscī.
bruise vt atterere, frangere, contundere ♦ n
    vulnus nt.
bruit vt pervulgāre.
brunt n vīs f; **bear the ~ of** exhaurīre.
brush n pēniculus m; (artist's) pēnicillus m;
    (quarrel) rixa f ♦ vt verrere, dētergēre; (teeth)
    dēfricāre; ~ **aside** vt aspernārī, neglegere; ~
    up vt (fig) excolere.
brushwood n virgulta ntpl; (for cutting)
    sarmenta ntpl.
brusque adj parum cōmis.
brutal adj atrōx, saevus, inhūmānus.
brutality n atrōcitās f, saevitia f.
brutally adv atrōciter, inhūmānē.
brute n bēlua f, bestia f.
brutish adj stolidus.
bubble n bulla f ♦ vi bullāre; ~ **over**
    effervēscere; ~ **up** scatēre.

buccaneer n praedō m, pīrāta m.
buck n cervus m ♦ vi exsultāre.
bucket n situla f, fidēlia f.
buckle n fībula f ♦ vt fībulā nectere; ~ **to**
    accingī.
buckler n parma f.
buckram n carbasus m.
bucolic adj agrestis.
bucolics n būcolica ntpl.
bud n gemma f, flōsculus m ♦ vi gemmāre.
budge vi movērī, cēdere.
budget n pūblicae pecūniae ratiō f ♦ vi: ~ **for**
    prōvidēre (dat).
buff adj lūteus.
buffalo n ūrus m.
buffet n (blow) alapa f; (fig) plāga f; (sideboard)
    abacus m ♦ vt iactāre, tundere.
buffoon n scurra m, balatrō m.
buffoonery n scurrilitās f.
bug n cīmex m.
bugbear n terricula ntpl, terror m.
bugle n būcina f.
bugler n būcinātor m.
build vt aedificāre, struere; (bridge) facere;
    (road) mūnīre; ~ **on** vt (add) adstruere;
    (hopes) pōnere; ~ **on sand** in aquā
    fundamenta pōnere; ~ **up** vt exstruere; (to
    block) inaedificāre; (knowledge) īnstruere; ~
    castles in the air spem inānem pāscere ♦ n
    statūra f.
builder n aedificātor m, structor m.
building n (act) aedificātiō f; (structure)
    aedificium nt.
bulb n bulbus m.
bulge vi tumēre, tumēscere, prōminēre ♦ vi
    tuberculum nt; (of land) locus prōminēns m.
bulk n māgnitūdō f, amplitūdō f; (mass) mōlēs
    f; (most) plērīque, māior pars.
bulky adj amplus, grandis.
bull n taurus m; ~'**s** taurīnus; **take the ~ by the
    horns** rem fortiter adgredī.
bulldog n Molossus m.
bullet n glāns f.
bulletin n libellus m.
bullion n aurum īnfectum nt, argentum
    īnfectum nt.
bullock n iuvencus m.
bully n obiūrgātor m, patruus m ♦ vt obiūrgāre,
    exagitāre.
bulrush n scirpus m.
bulwark n prōpugnāculum nt; (fig) arx f.
bump n (swelling) tuber nt, tuberculum nt;
    (knock) ictus m ♦ vi: ~ **against** offendere.
bumper n plēnum pōculum nt ♦ adj plēnus,
    māximus.
bumpkin n rūsticus m.
bumptious adj adrogāns.
bunch n fasciculus m; (of berries) racēmus m.
bundle n fascis m; (of hay) manipulus m ♦ vt
    obligāre.
bung n obtūrāmentum nt ♦ vt obtūrāre.
bungle vt male gerere.
bunk n lectus m, lectulus m.

buoy n cortex m ♦ vt sublevāre.
buoyancy n levitās f.
buoyant adj levis; (fig) hilaris.
bur n lappa f.
burden n onus nt; **beast of ~** iūmentum nt ♦ vt onerāre; **be a ~** oneri esse.
burdensome adj gravis, molestus.
bureau n scrīnium nt.
burgeon vi gemmāre.
burgess n mūniceps m.
burgh n mūnicipium nt.
burgher n mūniceps m.
burglar n fūr m.
burglary n fūrtum nt.
burial n fūnes nt, humātiō f, sepultūra f.
burin n caelum nt.
burlesque n imitātiō f ♦ vt per iocum imitārī.
burly adj crassus.
burn vt incendere, ūrere; (to ashes) cremāre ♦ vi ārdēre, flāgrāre; **~ up** ambūrere, combūrere, exūrere; **be ~ed down** dēflāgrāre; **~ out** vi exstinguī; **~ the midnight oil** lūcubrāre ♦ n (MED) ambūstum nt.
burning adj igneus.
burnish vt polīre.
burrow n cunīculus m ♦ vi dēfodere.
burst vt rumpere, dīrumpere ♦ vi rumpī, dīrumpī; **~ in** inrumpere; **~ into tears** in lacrimās effundī; **~ open** refringere; **~ out** ērumpere, prōrumpere; **~ out laughing** cachinnum tollere; **~ through** perrumpere per (acc); **~ upon** offerrī (dat), invādere ♦ n ēruptiō f; (noise) fragor m; **~ of applause** clāmōrēs mpl; **with a ~ of speed** citātō gradū, citātō equō.
bury vt sepelīre, humāre; (ceremony) efferre; (hiding) condere; (things) dēfodere; (fig) obruere; **~ the hatchet** amīcitiam reconciliāre.
bush n frutex m; dūmus m; **beat about the ~** circuitiōne ūtī.
bushel n medimnus m.
bushy adj fruticōsus; (thick) dēnsus; (hair) hirsūtus.
busily adv strēnuē, impigrē.
business n negōtium nt; (occupation) ars f, quaestus m; (public life) forum nt; (matter) rēs f; **it is your ~** tuum est; **make it one's ~ to** id agere ut; **you have no ~ to** nōn tē decet (infin); **mind one's own ~** suum negōtium agere; **~ days** diēs fāstī mpl.
businessman n negōtiātor m.
buskin n cothurnus m.
bust n imāgō f.
bustle vi trepidāre, festīnāre; **~ about** discurrere.
busy adj negōtiōsus, occupātus; (active) operōsus, impiger, strēnuus; **~ in** occupātus (abl); **~ on intentus** (dat); **keep ~** vt exercēre; **~ oneself with** pertractāre, studēre (dat).
busybody n: **be a ~** aliēnīs negōtīs sē immiscēre.
but conj sed, at; (2nd place) autem, tamen ♦ adv

modo ♦ prep praeter (acc); **nothing ~** nihil nisī; **~ that, ~ what** quīn; **not ~ what** nihilōminus.
butcher n lanius m ♦ vt trucīdāre.
butcher's shop n laniēna f.
butchery n strāgēs f, occīdiō f.
butler n prōmus m.
butt n (cask) cadus m; (of ridicule) lūdibrium nt ♦ vi arietāre; **~ in** interpellāre.
butter n būtyrum nt.
butterfly n pāpiliō m.
buttock n clūnis m/f.
button n bulla f.
buttonhole vt (fig) dētinēre, prēnsāre.
buttress n antēridēs fpl ♦ vt fulcīre.
buxom adj nitidus.
buy vt emere; **~ provisions** obsōnāre; **~ back** vt redimere; **~ off** vt redimere; **~ up** vt coemere.
buyer n emptor m; (at auctions) manceps m.
buzz n strīdor m, susurrus m ♦ vi strīdere, susurrāre.
buzzard n būteō m.
by prep (near) ad (acc), apud (acc); prope (acc); (along) secundum (acc); (past) praeter (acc); (agent) a, ab (abl); (instrument) abl; (time) ante (acc); (oath) per (acc) ♦ adv prope, iuxtā; **~ and ~** mox; **be ~** adesse, adstāre; **~ force of arms** vī et armās; **~ land and sea** terrī marique.
bygone adj praeteritus.
bystander n arbiter m; pl circumstantēs mpl.
byway n dēverticulum nt, trāmes m, sēmita f.
byword n prōverbium nt.

C, c

cabal n factiō f.
cabbage n brassica f, caulis m.
cabin n casa f; (ship) cubiculum nt.
cabinet n armārium nt.
cable n fūnis m; (anchor) ancorāle nt.
cache n thēsaurus m.
cachet n nota f.
cackle vi strepere n ♦ strepitus m, clangor m.
cacophonous adj dissonus.
cacophony n vōcēs dissonae fpl.
cadaverous adj cadāverōsus.
cadence n clausula numerōsa f, numerus m.
cadet n (son) nātū minor; (MIL) contubernālis m.
cage n cavea f ♦ vt inclūdere.
caitiff n ignāvus m.
cajole vt blandīrī, dēlēnīre.
cake n placenta f.
calamitous adj exitiōsus, calamitōsus.

calamity *n* calamitās *f*, malum *nt*; (*MIL*) clādēs *f*.
calculate *vt* ratiōnem dūcere, inīre.
calculation *n* ratiō *f*.
calculator *n* ratiōcinātor *m*.
calendar *n* fāstī *mpl*.
calends *n* Kalendae *fpl*.
calf *n* (*animal*) vitulus *m*, vitula *f*; (*leg*) sūra *f*.
calibre *n* (*fig*) ingenium *nt*, auctōritās *f*.
call *vt* vocāre; (*name*) appellāre, nōmināre; (*aloud*) clāmāre; (*to a place*) advocāre, convocāre; ~ **aside** sēvocāre; ~ **down** (*curse*) dētestārī; ~ **for** *vt fus* postulāre, requīrere; ~ **forth** ēvocāre, excīre, ēlicere; ~ **in** *vt* advocāre; ~ **together** convocāre; ~ **on** *vt fus* (*for help*) implōrāre; (*visit*) salūtāre; ~ **off** *vt* āvocāre, revocāre; ~ **out** *vi* exclāmāre; ~ **up** *vt* (*dead*) excitāre, ēlicere; (*MIL*) ēvocāre ♦ *n* vōx *f*, clāmor *m*; (*summons*) invītātiō *f*; (*visit*) salūtātiō *f*.
caller *n* salūtātor *m*.
calling *n* ars *f*, quaestus *m*.
callous *adj* dūrus; **become** ~ obdūrēscere.
callow *adj* rudis.
calm *adj* tranquillus, placidus; (*mind*) aequus ♦ *vi*: ~ **down** (*fig*) dēfervēscere ♦ *vt* sēdāre, tranquillāre ♦ *n* tranquillitās *f*; **dead** ~ (*at sea*) malacia *f*.
calmly *adv* tranquillē, placidē; aequō animō.
calumniate *vt* obtrectāre, crīminārī; (*falsely*) calumniārī.
calumniator *n* obtrectātor *m*.
calumny *n* opprobria *ntpl*, obtrectātiō *f*.
calve *vi* parere.
cambric *n* linteum *nt*.
camel *n* camēlus *m*.
camouflage *n* dissimulātiō *f* ♦ *vt* dissimulāre.
camp *n* castra *ntpl*; **summer** ~ aestīva *ntpl*; **winter** ~ hīberna *ntpl*; **in** ~ sub pellibus; **pitch** ~ castra pōnere; **strike** ~ castra movēre ♦ *adj* castrēnsis ♦ *vi* tendere.
campaign *n* stīpendium *nt*, bellum *nt*; (*rapid*) expedītiō *f* ♦ *vi* bellum gerere, stīpendium merēre.
campaigner *n* mīles *m*; **old** ~ veterānus *m*; (*fig*) veterātor *m*.
campbed *n* grabātus *m*.
camp followers *n* lixae *mpl*.
can *n* hirnea *f*.
can *vi* posse (+ *infin*); (*know how*) scīre.
canaille *n* vulgus *nt*, plebs *f*.
canal *n* fossa nāvigābilis *f*, eurīpus *m*.
cancel *vt* indūcere, abrogāre.
cancellation *n* (*writing*) litūra *f*; (*law*) abrogātiō *f*.
cancer *n* cancer *m*; (*fig*) carcinōma *nt*, ulcus *nt*.
cancerous *adj* (*fig*) ulcerōsus.
candelabrum *n* candēlābrum *nt*.
candid *adj* ingenuus, apertus, līber, simplex.
candidate *n* petītor *m*; **be a ~ for** petere.
candidature *n* petītiō *f*.
candidly *adv* ingenuē.
candle *n* candēla *f*.
candlestick *n* candēlābrum *nt*.

candour *n* ingenuitās *f*, simplicitās *f*, lībertās *f*.
cane *n* (*reed*) harundō *f*; (*for walking, punishing*) virga *f* ♦ *vt* verberāre.
canine *adj* canīnus.
canister *n* capsula *f*.
canker *n* (*plants*) rōbigō *f*; (*fig*) aerūgō *f*, carcinōma *nt* ♦ *vt* corrumpere.
Cannae *n* Cannae *fpl*.
cannibal *n* anthrōpophagus *m*.
cannon *n* tormentum *nt*.
cannot nōn posse, nequīre; **I ~ help but** ... facere nōn possum quīn ... (*subj*), nōn possum nōn ... (*infin*).
canny *adj* prūdens, prōvidus, cautus, circumspectus.
canoe *n* linter *f*.
canon *n* nōrma *f*, rēgula *f*; (*ECCL*) canonicus *m*.
canopy *n* aulaeum *nt*.
cant *n* fūcus *m*, fūcāta verba *ntpl* ♦ *vt* oblīquāre.
cantankerous *adj* importūnus.
cantankerousness *n* importūnitās *f*.
canter *n* lēnis cursus *m* ♦ *vi* lēniter currere.
canticle *n* canticum *nt*.
canto *n* carmen *nt*.
canton *n* pāgus *m*.
canvas *n* carbasus *m*, linteum *nt* ♦ *adj* carbaseus; **under** ~ sub pellibus.
canvass *vi* ambīre ♦ *vt* prēnsāre, circumīre.
canvassing *n* ambitus *m*, ambitiō *f*.
cap *n* pilleus *m*; (*priest's*) galērus *m*, apex *m*.
capability *n* facultās *f*, potestās *f*.
capable *adj* capāx, doctus, perītus.
capably *adv* bene, doctē.
capacious *adj* capāx, amplus.
capacity *n* capācitās *f*, amplitūdō *f*; (*mind*) ingenium *nt*.
caparison *n* ephippium *nt*.
cape *n* (*GEOG*) prōmunturium *nt*; (*dress*) chlamys *f*.
caper *vi* saltāre; (*animal*) lascīvīre ♦ *n* saltus *m*.
capering *n* lascivia *f*.
capital *adj* (*chief*) praecipuus, prīnceps; (*excellent*) ēgregius; (*law*) capitālis; **convict of a ~ offence** capitis damnāre ♦ *n* (*town*) caput *nt*; (*money*) sors *f*; (*class*) negōtiātōrēs *mpl*; **make** ~ **out of** ūtī (*abl*).
capitalist *n* faenerātor *m*.
capital punishment *n* capitis supplicum *nt*.
capitation tax *n* capitum exāctiō *f*.
Capitol *n* Capitolium *nt*.
capitulate *vi* sē dēdere; **troops who have ~d** dēditīciī *mpl*.
capitulation *n* dēditiō *f*.
capon *n* capō *m*.
caprice *n* libīdō *f*, incōnstantia *f*.
capricious *adj* incōnstāns, levis.
capriciously *adv* incōnstanter, leviter.
capriciousness *n* incōnstantia *f*, libīdō *f*.
capsize *vt* ēvertere ♦ *vi* ēvertī.
captain *m* dux *m*, praefectus *m*, prīnceps *m*;

(*MIL*) centuriō *m*; (*naval*) nāvarchus *m*; (*of merchant ship*) magister *m* ♦ *vt* praeesse (*dat*), dūcere.

captaincy *n* centuriātus *m*.

caption *n* caput *nt*.

captious *adj* mōrōsus; (*question*) captiōsus.

captiously *adv* mōrōsē.

captiousness *n* mōrōsitās *f*.

captivate *vt* capere, dēlēnīre, adlicere.

captive *n* captīvus *m*.

captivity *n* captīvitās *f*, vincula *ntpl*.

captor *n* (*by storm*) expugnātor *m*; victor *m*.

capture *n* (*by storm*) expugnātiō *f* ♦ *vt* capere.

car *n* currus *m*.

caravan *n* commeātus *m*.

carbuncle *n* (*MED*) fūrunculus *m*; (*stone*) acaustus *m*.

carcass *n* cadāver *nt*.

card *n* charta *f*; (*ticket*) tessera *f*; (*wool*) pecten *nt* ♦ *vt* pectere.

cardamom *n* amōmum *nt*.

cardinal *adj* praecipuus; ~ **point** cardō *m* ♦ *n* (*ECCL*) cardinālis.

care *n* cūra *f*; (*anxiety*) sollicitūdō *f*; (*attention*) dīligentia *f*; (*charge*) custōdia *f*; **take ~** cavēre; **take ~ of** cūrāre ♦ *vi* cūrāre; ~ **for** *vt fus* (*look after*) cūrāre; (*like*) amāre; **I don't ~** nīl moror; **I couldn't care less about** ... floccī nōn faciō ..., pendō; **I don't ~ about** mittō, nihil moror; **for all I ~** per mē.

career *n* curriculum *nt*; (*POL*) cursus honōrum; (*completed*) rēs gestae *fpl* ♦ *vi* ruere, volāre.

carefree *adj* sēcūrus.

careful *adj* (*cautious*) cautus; (*attentive*) dīligēns, attentus; (*work*) accūrātus.

carefully *adv* cautē, dīligenter, attentē, accūrātē.

careless *adj* incautus, neglegēns.

carelessly *adv* incautē, neglegenter.

carelessness *n* incūria *f*, neglegentia *f*.

caress *vt* fovēre, blandīrī ♦ *n* blandīmentum *nt*, amplexus *m*.

cargo *n* onus *nt*.

caricature *n* (*picture*) gryllus *m*; (*fig*) imāgō dētorta *f* ♦ *vt* dētorquēre.

carmine *n* coccum *nt* ♦ *adj* coccineus.

carnage *n* strāgēs *f*, caedēs *f*.

carnal *adj* corporeus; (*pleasure*) libīdinōsus.

carnival *n* fēriae *fpl*.

carol *n* carmen *nt* ♦ *vi* cantāre.

carouse *vi* perpōtāre, cōmissārī ♦ *n* cōmissātiō *f*.

carp *vi* obtrectāre; ~ **at** carpere, rōdere.

carpenter *n* faber *m*, lignārius *m*.

carpet *n* tapēte *nt*.

carriage *n* (*conveying*) vectūra *f*; (*vehicle*) vehiculum *nt*; (*for journeys*) raeda *f*, petorritum *nt*; (*for town*) carpentum *nt*, pīlentum *nt*; (*deportment*) gestus *m*, incessus *m*; ~ **and pair** bīgae *fpl*; ~ **and four** quadrīgae *fpl*.

carrier *n* vector *m*; (*porter*) bāiulus *m*; **letter ~** tabellārius *m*.

carrion *n* cadāver *nt*.

carrot *n* carōta *f*.

carry *vt* portāre, vehere, ferre, gerere; (*law*) perferre; (*by assault*) expugnāre; ~ **away** auferre, āvehere; (*by force*) rapere; (*with emotion*) efferre; ~ **all before one** ēvincere; ~ **along** (*building*) dūcere; ~ **back** reportāre; revehere, referre; ~ **down** dēportāre, dēvehere; ~ **in** invehere, intrōferre; ~ **off** auferre, asportāre, āvehere; (*by force*) abripere, ēripere; (*prize*) ferre, reportāre; (*success*) bene gerere; ~ **on** *vt* gerere; (*profession*) exercēre; ~ **out** *vi* efferre, ēgerere, ēvehere; (*task*) exsequī; ~ **out an undertaking** rem suscipere; ~ **over** trānsportāre, trānsferre; ~ **the day** vincere; ~ **one's point** pervincere; ~ **through** perferre; ~ **to** adferre, advehere; ~ **up** subvehere ♦ *vi* (*sound*) audīrī; ~ **on** *vi* pergere; (*flirt*) lascīvīre.

cart *n* plaustrum *nt*; carrus *nt*; **put the ~ before the horse** praeposterum dīcere ♦ *vt* plaustrō vehere.

Carthage *n* Carthāgō, Carthāginis *f*.

Carthaginian *adj* Carthāginiēnsis; Pūnicus; **the ~s** Poenī *mpl*.

carthorse *n* iūmentum *nt*.

carve *vt* sculpere; (*on surface*) caelāre; (*meat*) secāre; ~ **out** exsculpere.

carver *n* caelātor *m*.

carving *n* caelātūra *f*.

cascade *n* cataracta *m*.

case *n* (*instance*) exemplum *nt*, rēs *f*; (*legal*) āctiō *f*, līs *f*, causa *f*; (*plight*) tempus *nt*; (*GRAM*) cāsus *m*; (*receptacle*) thēca *f*, involucrum *nt*; **in ~ sī**; (*to prevent*) nē; **in any ~** utut est rēs; **in that ~** ergō; **such is the ~** sic sē rēs habet; **civil ~** causa prīvāta; **criminal ~** causa pūblica; **win a ~** causam, lītem obtinēre; **lose a ~** causam, lītem āmittere.

casement *n* fenestra *f*.

cash *n* nummī *mpl*; (*ready*) numerātum *nt*, praesēns pecūnia *f*; **pay ~** ex arcā absolvere, repraesentāre.

cash box *n* arca *f*.

cashier *n* dispēnsātor *m* ♦ *vt* (*MIL*) exauctōrāre.

cash payment *n* repraesentātiō *f*.

cask *n* cūpa *f*.

casket *n* arcula *f*, pyxis *f*.

casque *n* galea *f*, cassis *f*.

cast *vt* iacere; (*account*) inīre; (*eyes*) conicere; (*lots*) conicere; (*covering*) exuere; (*metal*) fundere; ~ **ashore** ēicere; ~ **away** prōicere; ~ **down** dēicere; (*humble*) abicere; ~ **in one's teeth** exprobrāre; ~ **lots** sortīrī; ~ **off** *vi* abicere, exuere; ~ **out** prōicere, ēicere, pellere ♦ *n* iactus *m*; (*moulding*) typus *m*, fōrma *f*; **with a ~ in the eye** paetus *m*.

castanet *n* crotalum *nt*.

castaway *n* ēiectus *m*.

caste *n* ōrdō *m*.

castigate *vt* animadvertere, castīgāre.

castigation *n* animadversiō *f*, castīgātiō *f*.

castle *n* arx *f*, castellum *nt*.
castrate *vt* castrāre.
casual *adj* fortuītus; (*person*) neglegēns.
casually *adv* temerē.
casualty *n* īnfortūnium *nt*; *pl*: **casualties** occīsī *mpl*.
casuist *n* sophistēs *m*.
cat *n* fēlēs *f*.
cataclysm *n* dīluvium *nt*, ruīna *f*.
catalogue *n* index *m*.
catapult *n* catapulta *f*, ballista *f*.
cataract *n* cataracta *f*.
catarrh *n* gravēdō *f*; **liable to** ~ gravēdinōsus.
catastrophe *n* calamitās *f*, ruīna *f*.
catastrophic *adj* calamitōsus, exitiōsus.
catch *vt* capere, dēprehendere, excipere; (*disease*) contrahere, nancīscī; (*fire*) concipere, comprehendere; (*meaning*) intellegere; ~ **at** captāre; ~ **out** *vi* dēprehendere; ~ **up with** adsequī; ~ **birds** aucupārī; ~ **fish** piscārī ♦ *n* bolus *m*.
categorical *adj* (*statement*) plānus.
categorically *adv* sine exceptiōne.
category *n* numerus *m*, genus *nt*.
cater *vi* obsōnāre.
cateran *n* praedātor *m*.
caterer *n* obsōnātor *m*.
caterpillar *n* ērūca *f*.
caterwaul *vi* ululāre.
catgut *n* chorda *f*.
catharsis *n* pūrgātiō *f*.
cathedral *n* aedēs *f*.
catholic *adj* generālis.
catkin *n* iūlus *m*.
cattle *n* (*collectively*) pecus *nt*; (*singly*) pecus *f*; (*for plough*) armenta *ntpl*.
cattle breeder *n* pecuārius *m*.
cattle market *n* forum boārium *nt*.
cattle thief *n* abāctor *m*.
cauldron *n* cortīna *f*.
cause *n* causa *f*; (*person*) auctor *m*; (*law*) causa *f*; (*party*) partēs *fpl*; **give** ~ **for** māteriam dare (*gen*); **make common** ~ **with** facere cum, stāre ab; **plead a** ~ causam dīcere; **in the** ~ **of** prō (*abl*); **without** ~ iniūriā ♦ *vt* efficere ut (+ *subj*), facere, facessere (*with* ut); cūrāre (*with gerundive*); (*feelings*) movēre, inicere, ciēre.
causeless *adj* vānus, sine causā.
causeway *n* agger *m*.
caustic *adj* (*fig*) mordāx.
cauterize *vt* adūrere.
caution *n* (*wariness*) cautiō *f*, prūdentia *f*; (*warning*) monitum *nt* ♦ *vt* monēre, admonēre.
cautious *adj* cautus, prōvidus, prūdens.
cautiously *adv* cautē, prūdenter.
cavalcade *n* pompa *f*.
cavalier *n* eques *m* ♦ *adj* adrogāns.
cavalierly *adv* adroganter.
cavalry *n* equitēs *mpl*, equitātus *m* ♦ *adj* equester; **troop of** ~ turma *f*.
cavalryman *n* eques *m*.

cave *n* spēlunca *f*, caverna *f*; antrum *nt*; ~ **in** *vi* concidere, conlābī.
cavern *n* spēlunca *f*, caverna *f*.
cavil *vi* cavillārī; ~ **at** carpere, cavillārī ♦ *n* captiō *f*, cavillātiō *f*.
cavity *n* caverna *f*, cavum *nt*.
cavort *vi* saltāre.
caw *vi* cornīcārī.
cease *vi* dēsinere, dēsistere.
ceaseless *adj* adsiduus, perpetuus.
ceaselessly *adv* adsiduē, perpetuō.
cedar *n* cedrus *f* ♦ *adj* cedrinus.
cede *vt* cēdere, concēdere.
ceiling *n* tēctum *nt*; (*panelled*) lacūnar *nt*, laqueārium *nt*.
celebrate *vt* (*rite*) celebrāre, agitāre; (*in crowds*) frequentāre; (*person, theme*) laudāre, celebrāre, dīcere.
celebrated *adj* praeclārus, illūstris, nōtus; **the** ~ **ille.**
celebration *n* celebrātiō *f*; (*rite*) sollemne *nt*.
celebrity *n* celebritās *f*, fāma *f*; (*person*) vir illūstris.
celerity *n* celeritās *f*, vēlōcitās *f*.
celery *n* apium *nt*.
celestial *adj* caelestis; dīvīnus.
celibacy *n* caelibātus *m*.
celibate *n* caelebs *m*.
cell *n* cella *f*.
cellar *n* cella *f*.
cement *n* ferrūmen *nt* ♦ *vt* coagmentāre.
cemetery *n* sepulchrētum *nt*.
cenotaph *n* tumulus honōrārius, tumulus inānis *m*.
censer *n* tūribulum *nt*, acerra *f*.
censor *n* cēnsor *m* ♦ *vt* cēnsēre.
censorious *adj* cēnsōrius, obtrectātor.
censorship *n* cēnsūra *f*.
censure *n* reprehēnsiō *f*, animadversiō *f*; (*censor's*) nota *f* ♦ *vt* reprehendere, animadvertere, increpāre; notāre.
census *n* cēnsus *m*.
cent *n*: **one per** ~ centēsima *f*; **12 per** ~ **per annum** centēsima *f* (*ie monthly*).
centaur *n* centaurus *m*.
centaury *n* (*plant*) centaurēum *nt*.
centenarian *n* centum annōs nātus *m*, nāta *f*.
centenary *n* centēsimus annus *m*.
centesimal *adj* centēsimus.
central *adj* medius.
centralize *vt* in ūnum locum cōnferre; (*power*) ad ūnum dēferre.
centre *n* centrum *nt*, media pars *f*; **the** ~ **of** medius.
centuple *adj* centuplex.
centurion *n* centuriō *m*.
century *n* (*MIL*) centuria *f*; (*time*) saeculum *nt*.
ceramic *adj* fictilis.
cereal *n* frūmentum *nt*.
ceremonial *adj* sollemnis ♦ *n* rītus *m*.
ceremonious *adj* (*rite*) sollemnis; (*person*) officiōsus.
ceremoniously *adv* sollemniter; officiōsē.

ceremony n caerimōnia f, rītus m; (politeness) officium nt; (pomp) apparātus m; **master of ceremonies** dēsignātor m.

cerise n coccum nt ♦ adj coccineus.

certain adj (sure) certus; (future) explōrātus; **a ~** quīdam, quaedam, quoddam; **be ~** (know) prō certō scīre/habēre.

certainly adv certē, certō, sine dubiō; (yes) ita, māximē; (concessive) quidem.

certainty n (thing) certum nt; (belief) fidēs f; **for a ~** prō certō, explōrātē; **regard as a ~** prō explōrātō habēre.

certificate n testimōnium nt.

certify vt (writing) recognōscere; (fact) adfirmāre, testificārī.

cessation n fīnis m; (from labour) quiēs f; (temporary) intermissiō f; (of hostilities) indutiae fpl.

chafe vt ūrere; (fig) inrītāre ♦ vi stomachārī.

chaff n palea f ♦ vt lūdere.

chaffinch n fringilla f.

chagrin n dolor m, stomachus m ♦ vt stomachum facere (dat), sollicitāre.

chain n catēna f; (for neck) torquis m; (sequence) seriēs f; **~s** pl vincula ntpl ♦ vt vincīre.

chair n sella f; (of office) sella curūlis f; (sedan) sella gestātōria f, lectīca f; (teacher's) cathedra f.

chairman n (at meeting) magister m; (of debate) disceptātor m.

chalet n casa f.

chalice n calix m.

chalk n crēta f.

chalky adj crētōsus.

challenge n prōvocātiō f ♦ vt prōvocāre, lacessere; (statement) in dubium vocāre; (fig) invītāre, dēposcere.

challenger n prōvocātor m.

chamber n conclāve nt; (bed) cubiculum nt; (bridal) thalamus m; (parliament) cūria f.

chamberlain n cubiculārius m.

chambermaid n serva f, ancilla f.

chameleon n chamaeleōn f.

chamois n rūpicapra f.

champ vt mandere.

champion n prōpugnātor m, patrōnus m; (winner) victor m ♦ vt favēre (dat), adesse (dat).

chance n fors f, fortūna f, cāsus m; (opportunity) occāsiō f; potestās f, facultās f; (prospect) spēs f; **game of ~** ālea f; **by ~** cāsū, fortuītō; **have an eye to the main ~** forō ūtī; **on the ~ of** sī forte ♦ adj fortuītus ♦ vi accidere, ēvenīre; **it chanced that** ... accidit ut ... (+ subj); **~ upon** vt fus incidere in, invenīre ♦ vt periclitārī.

chancel n absis f.

chancellor n cancellārius m.

chancy adj dubius, perīculōsus.

chandelier n candēlābrum nt.

chandler n candēlārum prōpōla m.

change n mūtātiō f, commūtātiō f, permūtātiō f; (POL) rēs novae fpl; (alternation) vicēs fpl, vicissitūdō f; (money) nummī minōrēs mpl ♦ vt mūtāre, commūtāre, permūtāre ♦ vi mūtārī; **~ hands** abaliēnarī; **~ places** ōrdinem permūtāre, inter sē loca permūtāre.

changeable adj incōnstāns, mūtābilis.

changeableness n incōnstantia f, mūtābilitās f.

changeful adj varius.

changeless adj cōnstāns, immūtābilis.

changeling adj subditus m.

channel n canālis m; (sea) fretum nt; (irrigation) rīvus m; (groove) sulcus m.

chant vt cantāre, canere ♦ n cantus m.

chaos n chaos nt; (fig) perturbātiō f.

chaotic adj perturbātus.

chap n rīma f; (man) homō m.

chapel n sacellum nt, aedicula f.

chaplain n diāconus m.

chaplet n corōna f, sertum nt.

chaps n (animal) mālae fpl.

chapter n caput nt.

char vt ambūrere.

character n (inborn) indolēs f, ingenium nt, nātūra f; (moral) mōrēs mpl; (reputation) existimātiō f; (kind) genus nt; (mark) signum nt, littera f; (THEAT) persōna f, partēs fpl; **sustain a ~** persōnam gerere; **I know his ~** sciō quālis sit.

characteristic adj proprius ♦ n proprium nt.

characteristically adv suō mōre.

characterize vt dēscrībere; proprium esse (gen).

charcoal n carbō m.

charge n (law) accūsātiō f, crīmen nt; (MIL) impetus m, dēcursus m; (cost) impēnsa f; (task) mandātum nt, onus nt; (trust) cūra f, tūtēla f; **bring a ~ against** lītem intendere (dat); **entertain a ~ against** nōmen recipere (gen); **give in ~** in custōdiam trādere; **put in ~ of** praeficere (acc, dat); **be in ~ of** praeesse (dat) ♦ vt (law) accūsāre; (falsely) īnsimulāre; (MIL) incurrere in (acc), signa īnferre in (acc), impetum facere in (acc); (duty) mandāre; (cost) ferre, īnferre; (empty space) complēre; (trust) committere; (speech) hortārī; **~ to the account of** expēnsum ferre (dat).

chargeable adj obnoxius.

charger n (dish) lānx f; (horse) equus m.

charily adv cautē, parcē.

chariot n currus m; (races) quadrīgae fpl; (war) essedum nt.

charioteer n aurīga m; (war) essedārius m.

charitable adj benevolus, benignus.

charitably adv benevolē, benignē.

charity n amor m, benignitās f, līberālitās f.

charlatan n planus m.

charm n (spell) carmen nt; (amulet) bulla f; (fig) blanditiae fpl, dulcēdō f, illecebra f; (beauty) venus f, lepōs m ♦ vt (magic) fascināre; (delight) dēlectāre, dēlēnīre.

charming adj venustus, lepidus; (speech) blandus; (scenery) amoenus.

charmingly *adv* venustē, blandē.
chart *n* tabula *f.*
charter *n* diplōma *nt* ♦ *vt* condūcere.
chary *adj* (*cautious*) cautus; (*sparing*) parcus.
chase *vt* fugāre; (*hunt*) vēnārī; (*pursue*)
   persequī, īnsequī; (*engrave*) caelāre; ~ **away**
   pellere, abigere ♦ *n* vēnātus *m*, vēnātiō *f;*
   (*pursuit*) īnsectātiō *f.*
chaser *n* (*in metal*) caelātor *m.*
chasm *n* hiātus *m.*
chaste *adj* castus, pudīcus; (*style*) pūrus.
chasten *vt* castīgāre, corrigere.
chastener *n* castīgātor *m*, corrēctor *m.*
chastise *vt* castīgāre, animadvertere.
chastisement *n* castīgātiō *f*, poena *f.*
chastity *n* castitās *f*, pudīcitia *f.*
chat *vi* colloquī, sermōcinārī ♦ *n* sermō *m*,
   colloquium *nt.*
chatelaine *n* domina *f.*
chattels *n* bona *ntpl*, rēs mancipī.
chatter *vi* garrīre; (*teeth*) crepitāre ♦ *n*
   garrulitās *f*, loquācitās *f.*
chatterbox *n* lingulāca *m/f.*
chatterer *n* garrulus *m*, loquāx *m.*
chattering *adj* garrulus, loquāx ♦ *n* garrulitās
   f, loquācitās *f*; (*teeth*) crepitus *m.*
cheap *adj* vīlis; **hold ~** parvī aestimāre; **buy ~**
   bene emere.
cheapen *vt* pretium minuere (*gen*).
cheaply *adv* vīliter, parvō pretiō.
cheapness *n* vīlitās *f.*
cheat *vt* dēcipere, fraudāre, dēfraudāre,
   frustrārī ♦ *n* fraudātor *m.*
check *vt* cohibēre, coercēre; (*movement*)
   impedīre, inhibēre; (*rebuke*) reprehendere;
   (*test*) probāre ♦ *n* impedīmentum *nt*, mora *f*;
   (*MIL*) offēnsiō *f*; (*rebuke*) reprehēnsiō *f*; (*test*)
   probātiō *f*; (*ticket*) tessera *f.*
checkmate *n* incitae calcēs *fpl* ♦ *vt* ad incitās
   redigere.
cheek *n* gena *f*; (*impudence*) ōs *nt*; ~ **s** *pl* mālae
   fpl; **how have you the ~ to say?** quō ōre dīcis?
cheekbone *n* maxilla *f.*
cheeky *adj* impudēns.
cheep *vi* pīpilāre.
cheer *vt* hilarāre, exhilarāre; hortārī; (*in
   sorrow*) cōnsōlārī ♦ *vi* clāmāre, adclāmāre; ~
   up! bonō animō es! ♦ *n* (*shout*) clāmor *m*,
   plausus *m*; (*food*) hospitium *nt*; (*mind*) animus
   m.
cheerful *adj* alacer, hilaris, laetus.
cheerfully *adv* hilare, laetē.
cheerfulness *n* hilaritās *f.*
cheerily *adv* hilare.
cheerless *adj* tristis, maestus.
cheerlessly *adv* triste.
cheery *adj* hilaris.
cheese *n* cāseus *m.*
chef *n* coquus *m.*
cheque *n* perscrīptiō *f*, syngrapha *f.*
chequer *vt* variāre.
chequered *adj* varius; (*mosaic*) tessellātus.
cherish *vt* fovēre, colere.

cherry *n* (*fruit*) cerasum *nt*; (*tree*) cerasus *f.*
chess *n* latrunculī *mpl.*
chessboard *n* abacus *m.*
chest *n* (*box*) arca *f*, arcula *f*; (*body*) pectus *nt*; ~
   of drawers armārium *nt.*
chestnut *n* castanea *f* ♦ *adj* (*colour*) spādīx.
chevalier *n* eques *m.*
chevaux-de-frise *n* ēricius *m.*
chew *vt* mandere.
chic *adj* expolītus, concinnus.
chicanery *n* (*law*) calumnia *f*; (*fig*) dolus *m.*
chick *n* pullus *m.*
chicken *n* pullus *m*; **don't count your ~s before
   they're hatched** adhūc tua messis in herbā
   est.
chicken-hearted *adj* timidus, ignāvus.
chick-pea *n* cicer *nt.*
chide *vt* reprehendere, increpāre, obiūrgāre.
chief *n* prīnceps *m*, dux *m* ♦ *adj* praecipuus,
   prīmus; ~ **point** caput *nt.*
chief command *n* summa imperiī.
chiefly *adv* in prīmīs, praesertim, potissimum.
chieftain *n* prīnceps *m*, rēgulus *m.*
chilblain *n* perniō *m.*
child *n* īnfāns *m/f*; puer *m*, puerulus *m*, puella *f*;
   fīlius *m*, fīlia *f*; ~**'s play** lūdus *m.*
childbed *n* puerperium *nt.*
childbirth *n* partus *m.*
childhood *n* pueritia *f*; **from ~** ā puerō.
childish *adj* puerīlis.
childishly *adv* puerīliter.
childless *adj* orbus.
childlessness *n* orbitās *f.*
childlike *adj* puerīlis.
children *npl* līberī *mpl.*
chill *n* frīgus *nt* ♦ *adj* frīgidus ♦ *vt* refrīgerāre.
chilly *adj* frīgidus, frīgidior.
chime *vi* sonāre, canere; ~ **in** interpellāre; (*fig*)
   cōnsonāre ♦ *n* sonus *m.*
chimera *n* chimaera *f*; (*fig*) somnium *nt.*
chimerical *adj* commentīcius.
chimney *n* camīnus *m.*
chin *n* mentum *nt.*
china *n* fictilia *ntpl.*
chink *n* rīma *f*; (*sound*) tinnītus *m* ♦ *vi* crepāre,
   tinnīre.
chip *n* assula *f*, fragmentum *nt* ♦ *vt* dolāre.
chirp *vi* pīpilāre.
chirpy *adj* hilaris.
chisel *n* scalprum *nt*, scalpellum *nt* ♦ *vt*
   sculpere.
chit *n* (*child*) pūsiō *m*, puerulus *m.*
chitchat *n* sermunculī *mpl.*
chitterlings *n* hillae *fpl.*
chivalrous *adj* generōsus.
chivalry *n* virtūs *f*; (*men*) iuventūs *f*; (*class*)
   equitēs *mpl.*
chive *n* caepe *nt.*
chock *n* cuneus *m.*
chock-full *adj* refertus.
choice *n* dēlēctus *m*, ēlēctiō *f*; (*of alternatives*)
   optiō *f* ♦ *adj* lēctus, eximius, exquīsītus.
choiceness *n* ēlegantia *f*, praestantia *f.*

choir n chorus m.
choke vt suffocāre; (*emotion*) reprimere; (*passage*) obstruere.
choler n bīlis f; (*anger*) īra f, stomachus m.
choleric adj īrācundus.
choose vt legere, ēligere, dēligere; (*alternative*) optāre; (*for office*) dēsignāre; (*with infin*) velle, mālle.
chop vt concīdere; ~ **off** praecīdere ♦ n (*meat*) offa f.
chopper n secūris f.
choppy adj (*sea*) asper.
choral adj symphōniacus.
chord n (*string*) nervus m, chorda f.
chortle vi cachinnāre.
chorus n (*singers*) chorus m; (*song*) concentus m, symphōnia f; **in ~** unā vōce.
christen vt baptizāre.
Christian adj Christiānus.
Christianity n Christiānismus m.
chronic adj inveterātus; **become ~** inveterāscere.
chronicle n annālēs mpl, ācta pūblica ntpl ♦ vt in annālēs referre.
chronicler n annālium scrīptor m.
chronological adj: **in ~ order** servātō temporum ōrdine; **make a ~ error** temporibus errāre.
chronology n temporum ratiō f, temporum ōrdō m.
chronometer n hōrologium nt.
chubby adj pinguis.
chuck vt conicere; ~ **out** extrūdere.
chuckle vi rīdēre ♦ n rīsus m.
chum n sodālis m.
church n ecclēsia f.
churl n rūsticus m.
churlish adj difficilis, importūnus; avārus.
churlishly adv rūsticē, avārē.
churlishness n mōrōsitās f, avāritia f.
chute n (*motion*) lāpsus m; (*place*) dēclīve nt.
cicada n cicāda f.
cincture n cingulum nt.
cinder n cinis m.
cipher n numerus m, nihil nt; (*code*) notae fpl; **in ~** per notās.
circle n orbis m, circulus m, gȳrus m; **form a ~** in orbem cōnsistere ♦ vi sē circumagere, circumīre.
circlet n īnfula f.
circuit n ambitus m, circuitus m; (*assizes*) conventus m.
circuitous adj longus; **a ~ route** circuitus m; (*speech*) ambāgēs fpl.
circular adj rotundus.
circulate vt (*news*) pervulgāre ♦ vi circumagī; (*news*) circumferrī, percrēbrēscere.
circulation n ambitus m; **be in ~** in manibus esse; **go out of ~** obsolēscere.
circumcise vt circumcīdere.
circumference n ambitus m.
circumlocution n ambāgēs fpl, circuitiō f.
circumnavigate vt circumvehī.

circumscribe vt circumscrībere; (*restrict*) coercēre, fīnīre.
circumspect adj cautus, prūdēns.
circumspection n cautiō f, prūdentia f, circumspectiō f.
circumspectly adv cautē, prūdenter.
circumstance n rēs f; **~s** rērum status m; (*wealth*) rēs f; **as ~s arise** ē rē nātā; **under the ~s** cum haec ita sint, essent; **under no ~s** nēquāquam.
circumstantial adj adventīcius; (*detailed*) accūrātus; **~ evidence** coniectūra f.
circumstantially adv accūrātē, subtīliter.
circumvallation n circummūnītiō f.
circumvent vt circumvenīre, fallere.
circus n circus m.
cistern n lacus m, cisterna f.
citadel n arx f.
citation n (*law*) vocātiō f; (*mention*) commemorātiō f.
cite vt in iūs vocāre; (*quote*) commemorāre, prōferre.
citizen n cīvis m/f; (*of provincial town*) mūniceps m; **fellow ~** cīvis m/f; **Roman ~s** Quirītēs mpl ♦ adj cīvīlis, cīvicus.
citizenship n cīvitās f; **deprived of ~** capite dēminūtus; **loss of ~** capitis dēminūtiō f.
citron n (*fruit*) citrum nt; (*tree*) citrus f.
city n urbs f, oppidum nt.
civic adj cīvīlis, cīvicus.
civil adj (*of citizens*) cīvīlis; (*war*) cīvilis, intestīnus, domesticus; (*manners*) urbānus, cōmis, officiōsus; (*lawsuit*) prīvātus.
civilian n togātus m.
civility n urbānitās f, cōmitās f; (*act*) officium nt.
civilization n exculta hominum vīta f, cultus atque hūmānitās.
civilize vt excolere, expolīre, ad hūmānum cultum dēdūcere.
civil war n bellum cīvīle, bellum domesticum, bellum intestīnum.
clad adj vestītus.
claim vt (*for oneself*) adrogāre, adserere; (*something due*) poscere, postulāre, vindicāre; (*at law*) petere; (*statement*) adfirmāre ♦ n postulātiō f, postulātum nt; (*at law*) petītiō f, vindiciae fpl.
claimant n petītor m.
clam n chāma f.
clamber vi scandere.
clammy adj ūmidus, lentus.
clamorous adj vōciferāns.
clamour n strepitus m, clāmōrēs mpl ♦ vi: **~ against** obstrepere (*dat*).
clamp n cōnfībula f.
clan n gēns f.
clandestine adj fūrtīvus.
clandestinely adv clam, fūrtim.
clang n clangor m, crepitus m ♦ vi increpāre.
clangour n clangor m.
clank n crepitus m ♦ vi crepitāre.
clansman n gentīlis m.

clap *vi* plaudere, applaudere; **~ eyes on**
cōnspicere; **~ in prison** in vincula conicere
♦ *n* plausus *m*; (*thunder*) fragor *m*.

clapper *n* plausor *m*.

claptrap *n* iactātiō *f*.

claque *n* plausōrēs *mpl*, operae *fpl*.

clarify *vt* pūrgāre; (*knowledge*) illūstrāre ♦ *vi*
liquēre.

clarinet *n* tībia *f*.

clarion *n* lituus *m*, cornū *nt*.

clarity *n* perspicuitās *f*.

clash *n* concursus *m*; (*sound*) strepitus *m*,
crepitus *m*; (*fig*) discrepantia *f* ♦ *vi*
concurrere; (*sound*) increpāre; (*fig*)
discrepāre ♦ *vt* conflīgere.

clasp *n* fībula *f*; (*embrace*) amplexus *m* ♦ *vt*
implicāre; amplectī, complectī; **~ together**
interiungere.

class *n* (*POL*) ōrdō *m*, classis *f*; (*kind*) genus *nt*;
(*school*) classis *f* ♦ *vt* dēscrībere; **~ as in**
numerō (*gen pl*) referre, repōnere, habēre.

classic *n* scrīptor classicus *m*.

classical *adj* classicus; **~ literature** litterae
Graecae et Rōmānae.

classics *npl* scrīptōrēs Graecī et Rōmānī.

classify *vt* dēscrībere, in ōrdinem redigere.

class-mate *n* condiscipulus *m*.

clatter *n* crepitus *m* ♦ *vi* increpāre.

clause *n* (*GRAM*) incīsum *nt*, membrum *nt*; (*law*)
caput *nt*; (*will*) ēlogium *nt*; **in short ~s** incīsim.

claw *n* unguis *m*, ungula *f* ♦ *vt* (*unguibus*)
lacerāre.

clay *n* argilla *f*; **made of ~** fictilis.

clayey *adj* argillāceus.

claymore *n* gladius *m*.

clean *adj* mundus; (*fig*) pūrus, castus; **~ slate**
novae tabulae *fpl*; **make a ~ sweep of** omnia
tollere; **show a ~ pair of heels** sē in pedēs
conicere; **my hands are ~** innocēns sum ♦ *adv*
prōrsus, tōtus ♦ *vt* pūrgāre.

cleanliness *n* munditia *f*.

cleanly *adj* mundus, nitidus ♦ *adv* mundē,
pūrē.

cleanse *vt* pūrgāre, abluere, dētergēre.

clear *adj* clārus; (*liquid*) limpidus; (*space*)
apertus, pūrus; (*sound*) clārus; (*weather*)
serēnus; (*fact*) manifestus, perspicuus;
(*language*) illūstris, dīlūcidus; (*conscience*)
rēctus, innocēns; **it is ~** liquet; **~ of** līber (*abl*),
expers (*gen*); **be ~ about** rēctē intellegere;
keep ~ of ēvītāre; **the coast is ~** arbitrī
absunt ♦ *vt* (*of obstacles*) expedīre, pūrgāre;
(*of a charge*) absolvere; (*self*) pūrgāre; (*profit*)
lucrārī; **~ away** āmovēre, tollere; **~ off** *vt*
(*debt*) solvere, exsolvere ♦ *vi* facessere; **~
out** ēluere, dētergēre; **~ up** *vt* (*difficulty*)
illūstrāre, ēnōdāre, explicāre ♦ *vi* (*weather*)
disserēnāscere.

clearance *n* pūrgātiō *f*; (*space*) intervallum *nt*.

clearing *n* (*in forest*) lūcus *m*.

clearly *adv* clārē; manifestē, apertē,
perspicuē; (*with clause*) vidēlicet.

clearness *n* clāritās *f*; (*weather*) serēnitās *f*;

(*mind*) acūmen *nt*; (*style*) perspicuitās *f*.

clear-sighted *adj* sagāx, perspicāx.

cleavage *n* discidium *nt*.

cleave *vt* (*out*) findere, discindere ♦ *vi* (*cling*): **~
to** haerēre (*dat*), adhaerēre (*dat*).

cleaver *n* dolabra *f*.

cleft *n* rīma *f*, hiātus *m* ♦ *adj* fissus, discissus.

clemency *n* clēmentia *f*, indulgentia *f*; **with ~**
clēmenter.

clement *adj* clēmēns, misericors.

clench *vt* (*nail*) retundere; (*hand*) comprimere.

clerk *n* scrība *m*; (*of court*) lēctor *m*.

clever *adj* callidus, ingeniōsus, doctus, astūtus.

cleverly *adv* doctē, callidē, ingeniōsē.

cleverness *n* calliditās *f*, sollertia *f*.

clew *n* glomus *nt*.

cliché *n* verbum trītum *nt*.

client *n* cliēns *m/f*; (*lawyer's*) cōnsultor *m*; **body
of ~s** clientēla *f*.

clientele *n* clientēla *f*.

cliff *n* rūpēs *f*, scopulus *m*.

climate *n* caelum *nt*.

climax *n* (*RHET*) gradātiō *f*; (*fig*) culmen *nt*.

climb *vt*, *vi* scandere, ascendere; **~ down**
dēscendere ♦ *n* ascēnsus *m*.

climber *n* scandēns *m*.

clime *n* caelum *nt*, plāga *f*.

clinch *vt* cōnfirmāre.

cling *vi* adhaerēre; **~ together** cohaerere.

clink *vi* tinnīre ♦ *n* tinnītus *m*.

clip *vt* tondēre; praecīdere.

clippers *n* forfex *f*.

clique *n* factiō *f*.

cloak *n* (*rain*) lacerna *f*; (*travel*) paenula *f*; (*MIL*)
sagum *nt*; palūdāmentum *nt*; (*Greek*) pallium
nt; (*fig*) involūcrum *nt*; (*pretext*) speciēs *f* ♦ *vt*
tegere, dissimulāre.

clock *n* hōrologium *nt*; (*sun*) sōlārium *nt*;
(*water*) clepsydra *f*; **ten o'~** quarta hōra.

clockwise *adv* dextrōvorsum, dextrōrsum.

clod *n* glaeba *f*.

clog *n* (*shoe*) sculpōnea *f*; (*fig*) impedīmentum
nt ♦ *vt* impedīre.

cloister *n* porticus *f*.

cloistered *adj* (*fig*) umbrātilis.

close *adj* (*shut*) clausus; (*tight*) artus; (*narrow*)
angustus; (*near*) propinquus; (*compact*)
refertus, dēnsus; (*stingy*) parcus; (*secret*)
obscūrus; (*weather*) crassus; **~ together**
dēnsus, refertus; **at ~ quarters** comminus; **be
~ at hand** īnstāre; **keep ~ to** adhaerēre; **~ to**
prope (*acc*), iuxtā (*acc*) ♦ *adv* prope, iuxtā ♦ *n*
angiportus *m*.

close *vt* claudere, operīre; (*finish*) perficere,
fīnīre, conclūdere, termināre; (*ranks*)
dēnsāre ♦ *vi* claudī; conclūdī, terminārī;
(*time*) exīre; (*wound*) coīre; (*speech*)
perōrāre; **~ with** (*fight*) manum cōnserere,
signa cōnferre; (*deal*) pacīscī; (*offer*)
accipere ♦ *n* fīnis *m*, terminus *m*; (*action*)
exitus *m*; (*sentence*) conclūsiō *f*; **at the ~ of
summer** aestāte exeunte.

closely *adv* prope; (*attending*) attentē;

(associating) coniūnctē; **follow ~** īnstāre *(dat)*.
closeness n propinquitās f; *(weather)* gravitās
   f, crassitūdō f; *(with money)* parsimōnia f;
   (friends) coniūnctiō f; *(manner)* cautiō f.
closet n cubiculum nt, cella f ♦ vt inclūdere.
clot n *(blood)* concrētus sanguis m ♦ vi
   concrēscere.
cloth n textile nt; *(piece)* pannus m; *(linen)*
   linteum nt; *(covering)* strāgulum nt.
clothe vt vestīre.
clothes n vestis f, vestītus m, vestīmenta ntpl.
clothier n vestiārius m.
clothing n vestis f, vestītus m, vestīmenta ntpl.
clotted adj concrētus.
cloud n nūbēs f, *(storm)* nimbus m; *(dust)*
   globus m; *(disfavour)* invidia f ♦ vt nūbibus
   obdūcere; *(fig)* obscūrāre.
clouded adj obnūbilus.
cloudiness n nūbilum nt.
cloudless adj pūrus, serēnus.
cloudy adj obnūbilus.
clout n pannus m.
clover n trifolium nt.
cloven adj *(hoof)* bifidus.
clown n *(boor)* rūsticus m; *(comic)* scurra m.
clownish adj rūsticus, inurbānus.
clownishness n rūsticitās f.
cloy vt satiāre.
cloying adj pūtidus.
club n *(stick)* fustis m, clāva f; *(society)*
   sodālitās f; **~ together** vi in commūne
   cōnsulere, pecūniās cōnferre.
club-footed adj scaurus.
cluck vi singultīre ♦ n singultus m.
clue n indicium nt, vestīgium nt.
clump n massa f; *(earth)* glaeba f; *(trees)*
   arbustum nt; *(willows)* salictum nt.
clumsily adv ineptē, inēleganter; inconditē,
   īnfabrē.
clumsiness n īnscītia f.
clumsy adj *(person)* inconcinnus, ineptus;
   (thing) inhabilis; *(work)* inconditus.
cluster n cumulus m; *(grapes)* racēmus m;
   (people) corōna f ♦ vi congregārī.
clutch vt prehendere, adripere; **~ at** captāre
   nt, comprehēnsiō f; **from one's ~es ē**
   manibus; **in one's ~es** in potestāte.
clutter n turba f ♦ vt impedīre, obstruere.
coach n currus m, raeda f, pīlentum nt; *(trainer)*
   magister m ♦ vt ēdocēre, praecipere *(dat)*.
coachman n aurīga m, raedārius m.
coagulate vt cōgere ♦ vi concrēscere.
coagulation n concrētiō f.
coal n carbō m; **carry ~s to Newcastle** in silvam
   ligna ferre.
coalesce vi coīre, coalēscere.
coalition n coitiō f, cōnspīrātiō f.
coarse adj *(quality)* crassus; *(manners)*
   rūsticus, inurbānus; *(speech)* īnfacētus.
coarsely adv inurbānē, inēleganter.
coarseness n crassitūdō f; rūsticitās f.
coast n lītus nt, ōra maritima f ♦ vi: **~ along**
   legere, praetervehī.

coastal adj lītorālis, maritimus.
coastline n lītus nt.
coat n pallium nt; *(animals)* pellis f ♦ vt
   indūcere, inlinere.
coating n corium nt.
coax vt blandīrī, dēlēnīre.
coaxing adj blandus ♦ n blanditiae fpl.
cob n *(horse)* mannus m; *(swan)* cygnus m.
cobble n lapis m ♦ vt sarcīre.
cobbler n sūtor m.
cobweb n arāneum nt.
cock n gallus m, gallus gallīnāceus m; *(other
   birds)* mās m; *(tap)* epitonium nt; *(hay)*
   acervus m.
cockatrice n basiliscus m.
cockchafer n scarabaeus m.
cockcrow n gallī cantus m ♦ vt ērigere.
cockerel n pullus m.
cockroach n blatta f.
cocksure adj cōnfīdēns.
cod n callarias m.
coddle vt indulgēre *(dat)*, permulcēre.
code n fōrmula f; *(secret)* notae fpl.
codicil n cōdicillī mpl.
codify vt in ōrdinem redigere.
coequal adj aequālis.
coerce vt cōgere.
coercion n vīs f.
coffer n arca f, cista f; *(public)* fiscus m.
coffin n arca f.
cog n dēns m.
cogency n vīs f, pondus nt.
cogent adj gravis, validus.
cogitate vi cōgitāre, meditārī.
cogitation n cōgitātiō f; meditātiō f.
cognate adj cognātus.
cognition n cognitiō f.
cognizance n cognitiō f; **take ~ of** cognōscere.
cognizant adj gnārus.
cohabit vi cōnsuēscere.
cohabitation n cōnsuētūdō f.
coheir n cohērēs m/f.
cohere vi cohaerēre; *(statement)* congruere.
coherence n coniūnctiō f; *(fig)* convenientia f.
coherent adj congruēns.
cohesion n coagmentātiō f.
cohesive adj tenāx.
cohort n cohors f.
coil n spīra f ♦ vt glomerāre.
coin n nummus m ♦ vt cūdere; *(fig)* fingere.
coinage n monēta f; *(fig)* fictum nt.
coincide vi concurrere; *(opinion)* cōnsentīre.
coincidence n concursus m; cōnsēnsus m; **by a
   ~** cāsū.
coincidental adj fortuītus.
coiner n *(of money)* signātor m.
col n iugum nt.
colander n cōlum nt.
cold adj frīgidus; *(icy)* gelidus; **very ~**
   perfrīgidus; **be, feel ~** algēre, frīgēre; **get ~**
   algēscere, frīgēscere ♦ n frīgus nt; *(felt)*
   algor m; *(malady)* gravēdō f; **catch ~**
   algēscere, frīgus colligere; **catch a ~**

gravēdinem contrahere; **have a ~** gravēdine labōrāre.
coldish *adj* frīgidulus, frīgidior.
coldly *adv* (*manner*) sine studiō.
coldness *n* frīgus *nt*, algor *m*.
cold water *n* frīgida *f*.
colic *n* tormina *ntpl*.
collar *n* collāre *nt*.
collarbone *n* iugulum *nt*.
collate *vt* cōnferre, comparāre.
collateral *adj* adiūnctus; (*evidence*) cōnsentāneus.
collation *n* collātiō *f*; (*meal*) prandium *nt*, merenda *f*.
colleague *n* collēga *m*.
collect *vt* colligere, cōgere, congerere; (*persons*) congregāre, convocāre; (*taxes*) exigere; (*something due*) recipere; **~ oneself** animum colligere; **cool and ~ed** aequō animō ♦ *vi* convenīre, congregārī.
collection *n* (*persons*) coetus *m*, conventus *m*; (*things*) congeriēs *f*; (*money*) exāctiō *f*.
collective *adj* commūnis.
collectively *adv* commūniter.
collector *n* (*of taxes*) exāctor *m*.
college *n* collēgium *nt*.
collide *vi* concurrere, cōnflīctārī.
collier *n* carbōnārius *m*.
collision *n* concursus *m*.
collocation *n* collocātiō *f*.
collop *n* offa *f*.
colloquial *adj* cottīdiānus.
colloquy *n* sermō *m*, colloquium *nt*.
collude *vi* praevāricārī.
collusion *n* praevāricātiō *f*.
collusive *adj* praevāricātor.
colonel *n* lēgātus *m*.
colonial *adj* colōnicus ♦ *n* colōnus *m*.
colonist *n* colōnus *m*.
colonization *n* dēductiō *f*.
colonize *vt* colōniam dēdūcere, cōnstituere in (*acc*).
colonnade *n* porticus *f*.
colony *n* colōnia *f*.
colossal *adj* ingēns, vastus.
colossus *n* colossus *m*.
colour *n* color *m*; (*paint*) pigmentum *nt*; (*artificial*) fūcus *m*; (*complexion*) color *m*; (*pretext*) speciēs *f*; **take on a ~** colōrem dūcere; **under ~ of** per speciem (*gen*); **local ~** māteria dē regiōne sūmpta ♦ *vt* colōrāre; (*dye*) īnficere, fūcāre; (*fig*) praetendere (*dat*) ♦ *vi* rubēre, ērubēscere.
colourable *adj* speciōsus.
coloured *adj* (*naturally*) colōrātus; (*artificially*) fūcātus.
colourful *adj* fūcōsus, varius.
colouring *n* pigmentum *nt*; (*dye*) fūcus *m*.
colourless *adj* perlūcidus; (*person*) pallidus; (*fig*) īnsulsus.
colours *n* (MIL) signum *nt*, vexillum *nt*; (POL) partēs *fpl*; **sail under false ~** aliēnō nōmine ūtī; **with flying ~** māximā cum glōriā.
colour sergeant *n* signifer *m*.

colt *n* equuleus *m*, equullus *m*.
coltsfoot *n* farfarus *m*.
column *n* columna *f*; (MIL) agmen *nt*.
coma *n* sopor *m*.
comb *n* pecten *m*; (*bird*) crista *f*; (*loom*) pecten *m*; (*honey*) favus *m* ♦ *vt* pectere.
combat *n* pugna *f*, proelium *nt*, certāmen *nt* ♦ *vi* pugnāre, dīmicāre, certāre ♦ *vt* pugnāre cum (*abl*), obsistere (*dat*).
combatant *n* pugnātor *m* ♦ *adj* pugnāns; **non ~** imbellis.
combative *adj* ferōx, pugnāx.
combination *n* coniūnctiō *f*, cōnfūsiō *f*; (*persons*) cōnspīrātiō *f*; (*illegal*) coniūrātiō *f*.
combine *vt* coniungere, iungere ♦ *vi* coīre, coniungī ♦ *n* societās *f*.
combustible *adj* ignī obnoxius.
combustion *n* dēflāgrātiō *f*, incendium *nt*.
come *vi* venīre, advenīre; (*after a journey*) dēvenīre; (*interj*) age!; **how ~s it that ...?**; quī fit ut ...?; **~ across** *vi* invenīre, offendere; **~ after** sequī, excipere, succēdere (*dat*); **~ again** revenīre, redīre; **~ away** *vi* abscēdere; (*when pulled*) sequī; **~ back** *vi* revenīre, redīre; regredī; **~ between** intervenīre, intercēdere; **~ down** *vi* dēvenīre, dēscendere; (*from the past*) trādī, prōdī; **~ forward** *vi* prōcēdere, prōdīre; **~ from** *vi* (*origin*) dēfluere; **~ in** *vi* inīre, introīre; ingredī; (*revenue*) redīre; **~ near** accēdere ad (*acc*), appropinquāre (*dat*); **~ nearer and nearer** adventāre; **~ of** *vi* (*family*) ortum esse ab, ex (*abl*); **~ off** *vi* ēvādere, discēdere; **~ on** *vi* prōcēdere; (*progress*) prōficere; (*interj*) age, agite; **~ on the scene** intervenīre, supervenīre, adesse; **~ out** *vi* exīre, ēgredī; (*hair, teeth*) cadere; (*flower*) flōrēscere; (*book*) ēdī; **~ over** *vi* trānsīre; (*feeling*) subīre, occupāre; **~ to** *vi* advenīre ad, in (*acc*); (*person*) adīre; (*amount*) efficere; **~ to the help of** subvenīre (*dat*); succurrere (*dat*); **~ to nought** ad nihilum recidere; **~ to pass** ēvenīre, fierī; **~ together** convenīre, coīre; **~ up** *vi* subīre, succēdere; (*growth*) prōvenīre; **~ upon** *vt fus* invenīre; **he is coming to** animus eī redit.
comedian *n* (*actor*) cōmoedus *m*; (*writer*) cōmicus *m*.
comedienne *n* mīma *f*.
comedy *n* cōmoedia *f*.
comeliness *n* decor *m*, decōrum *nt*.
comely *adj* decōrus, pulcher.
comestibles *n* vīctus *m*.
comet *n* comētēs *m*.
comfort *vt* sōlārī, cōnsōlārī, adlevāre ♦ *n* sōlācium *nt*, cōnsōlātiō *f*.
comfortable *adj* commodus; **make oneself ~** corpus cūrāre.
comfortably *adv* commodē.
comforter *n* cōnsōlātor *m*.
comfortless *adj* incommodus; **be ~** sōlātiō carēre.
comforts *npl* commoda *ntpl*.
comic *adj* cōmicus; facētus ♦ *n* scurra *m*.

comical *adj* facētus, rīdiculus.
coming *adj* futūrus ♦ *n* adventus *m.*
comity *n* cōmitās *f.*
command *vt* iubēre (+ *acc and infin*), imperāre
(*dat and* **ut** +*subj*); dūcere; (*feelings*) regere;
(*resources*) fruī (*abl*); (*view*) prōspectāre ♦ *n*
(*MIL*) imperium *nt*; (*sphere*) prōvincia *f*; (*order*)
imperium *nt*, iussum *nt*, mandātum *nt*; **be in ~**
(**of**) praeesse (*dat*); **put in ~ of** praeficere
(*dat*); **~ of language** fācundia *f.*
commandant *n* praefectus *m.*
commandeer *vt* pūblicāre.
commander *n* dux *m*, praefectus *m.*
commander in chief *n* imperātor *m.*
commandment *n* mandātum *nt.*
commemorate *vt* celebrāre, memoriae
trādere.
commemoration *n* celebrātiō *f.*
commence *vt* incipere, exōrdīrī, initium
facere (*gen*).
commencement *n* initium *nt*, exōrdium *nt*,
prīncipium *nt.*
commend *vt* laudāre; (*recommend*)
commendāre; (*entrust*) mandāre; **~ oneself** sē
probāre.
commendable *adj* laudābilis, probābilis.
commendation *n* laus *f*, commendātiō *f.*
commendatory *adj* commendātīcius.
commensurable *adj* pār.
commensurate *adj* congruēns, conveniēns.
comment *vi* dīcere, scrībere; **~ on**
interpretārī; (*with notes*) adnotāre ♦ *n*
dictum *nt*, sententia *f.*
commentary *n* commentāriī *mpl.*
commentator *n* interpres *m.*
commerce *n* mercātūra *f*, commercium *nt*;
engage in ~ mercātūrās facere, negōtiārī.
commercial dealings *n* commercium *nt.*
commercial traveller *n* īnstitor *m.*
commination *n* minae *fpl.*
comminatory *adj* mināx.
commingle *vt* intermiscēre.
commiserate *vt* miserērī (*gen*).
commiseration *n* misericordia *f*; (*RHET*)
commiserātiō *f.*
commissariat *n* rēs frūmentāria *f*,
commeātus *m*; (*staff*) frūmentāriī *mpl.*
commissary *n* lēgātus *m*; reī frūmentāriae
praefectus *m.*
commission *n* (*charge*) mandātum *nt*;
(*persons*) triumvirī *mpl*, decemvirī *mpl*, etc;
(*abroad*) lēgātiō *f*; **get a ~** (*MIL*) tribūnum fierī;
standing ~ (*law*) quaestiō perpetua *f* ♦ *vt*
mandāre, adlēgāre.
commissioner *n* lēgātus *m*; **three ~s** triumvirī
mpl; **ten ~s** decemvirī *mpl.*
commit *vt* (*charge*) committere, mandāre;
(*crime*) admittere; (*to prison*) conicere; (*to an
undertaking*) obligāre, obstringere; **~ to
memory** memoriae trādere; **~ to writing**
litterīs mandāre; **~ an error** errāre; **~ a theft**
fūrtum facere; *see also* **suicide**.
commitment *n* mūnus *nt*, officium *nt.*

committee *n* dēlēctī *mpl.*
commodious *adj* capāx.
commodity *n* merx *f*, rēs *f.*
commodore *n* praefectus classis *m.*
common *adj* (*for all*) commūnis; (*ordinary*)
vulgāris, cottīdiānus; (*repeated*) frequēns,
crēber; (*inferior*) nēquam ♦ *n* compāscuus
ager *m*, prātum *nt*; **~ man** homō plēbēius *m*; **~
soldier** gregārius mīles *m.*
commonalty *n* plēbs *f.*
commoner *n* homō plēbēius *m.*
common law *n* mōs māiōrum *m.*
commonly *adv* ferē, vulgō.
common people *n* plēbs *f*, vulgus *nt.*
commonplace *n* trītum prōverbium *nt*; (*RHET*)
locus commūnis *m* ♦ *adj* vulgāris, trītus.
commons *n* plēbs *f*; (*food*) diāria *ntpl.*
common sense *n* prūdentia *f.*
commonwealth *n* cīvitās *f*, rēs pūblica *f.*
commotion *n* perturbātiō *f*, tumultus *m*;
cause a ~ tumultuārī.
communal *adj* commūnis.
commune *n* pāgus *m* ♦ *vi* colloquī, sermōnēs
cōnferre.
communicate *vt* commūnicāre; (*information*)
nūntiāre, patefacere ♦ *vi*: **~ with**
commūnicāre (*dat*); commercium habēre
(*gen*), agere cum (*abl*).
communication *n* (*dealings*) commercium *nt*;
(*information*) litterae *fpl*, nūntius *m*; (*passage*)
commeātus *m*; **cut off the ~s of** interclūdere.
communicative *adj* loquāx.
communion *n* societās *f.*
communiqué *n* litterae *fpl*, praedicātiō *f.*
communism *n* bonōrum aequātiō *f.*
community *n* cīvitās *f*, commūne *nt*;
(*participation*) commūniō *f.*
commutation *n* mūtātiō *f.*
commute *vt* mūtāre, commūtāre.
compact *n* foedus *nt*, conventum *nt* ♦ *adj*
dēnsus ♦ *vt* dēnsāre.
companion *n* socius *m*, comes *m/f*; (*intimate*)
sodālis *m*; (*at school*) condiscipulus *m*; (*in
army*) commīlitō *m*, contubernālis *m.*
companionable *adj* facilis, commodus.
companionship *n* sodālitās *f*, cōnsuētūdō *f*;
(*MIL*) contubernium *nt.*
company *n* societās *f*, cōnsuētūdō *f*;
(*gathering*) coetus *m*, conventus *m*; (*guests*)
cēnantēs *mpl*; (*commercial*) societās *f*;
(*magistrates*) collēgium *nt*; (*MIL*) manipulus *m*;
(*THEAT*) grex *m*, caterva *f*; **~ of ten** decuria *f.*
comparable *adj* comparābilis, similis.
comparative *adj* māgnus, sī cum aliīs
cōnfertur.
comparatively *adv* ut in tālī tempore, ut in eā
regiōne, ut est captus hominum; **~ few**
perpaucī, nūllus ferē.
compare *vt* comparāre, cōnferre; **~d with** ad
(*acc*).
comparison *n* comparātiō *f*, collātiō *f*; (*RHET*)
similitūdō *f*; **in ~ with** prō (*abl*).
compartment *n* cella *f*, pars *f.*

compass *n* ambitus *m*, spatium *nt*, modus *m*; **pair of ~es** circinus *m* ♦ *vt* circumdare, cingere; (*attain*) cōnsequī.

compassion *n* misericordia *f*.

compassionate *adj* misericors, clēmēns.

compassionately *adv* clēmenter.

compatibility *n* convenientia *f*.

compatible *adj* congruēns, conveniēns; **be ~** congruere.

compatibly *adv* congruenter, convenienter.

compatriot *n* cīvis *m*, populāris *m*.

compeer *n* pār *m*; aequālis *m*.

compel *vt* cōgere.

compendious *adj* brevis.

compendiously *adv* summātim.

compendium *n* epitomē *f*.

compensate *vt* compēnsāre, satisfacere (*dat*).

compensation *n* compēnsātiō *f*; pretium *nt*, poena *f*.

compete *vi* certāre, contendere.

competence *n* facultās *f*; (*law*) iūs *nt*; (*money*) quod sufficit.

competent *adj* perītus, satis doctus, capāx; (*witness*) locuplēs; **it is ~** licet.

competition *n* certāmen *nt*, contentiō *f*.

competitor *n* competītor *m*, aemulus *m*.

compilation *n* collectānea *ntpl*, liber *m*.

compile *vt* compōnere.

compiler *n* scrīptor *m*.

complacency *n* amor suī *m*.

complacent *adj* suī contentus.

complain *vi* querī, conquerī; **~ of** (*person*) nōmen dēferre (*gen*).

complainant *n* accūsātor *m*, petītor *m*.

complaint *n* questus *m*, querimōnia *f*; (*law*) crīmen *nt*; (*MED*) morbus *m*, valētūdō *f*.

complaisance *n* cōmitās *f*, obsequium *nt*, indulgentia *f*.

complaisant *adj* cōmis, officiōsus, facilis.

complement *n* complēmentum *nt*; numerus suus *m*; **make up the ~ of** complēre.

complete *vt* (*amount, time*) complēre, explēre; (*work*) cōnficere, perficere, absolvere, peragere ♦ *adj* perfectus, absolūtus, integer; (*victory*) iūstus; (*amount*) explētus.

completely *adv* funditus, omnīnō, absolūtē, plānē; penitus.

completeness *n* integritās *f*; (*perfection*) perfectiō *f*.

completion *n* (*process*) absolūtiō *f*, cōnfectiō *f*; (*end*) fīnis *m*; **bring to ~** absolvere.

complex *adj* implicātus, multiplex.

complexion *n* color *m*.

complexity *n* implicātiō *f*.

compliance *n* accommodātiō *f*, obsequium *nt*, obtemperātiō *f*.

compliant *adj* obsequēns, facilis.

complicate *vt* implicāre, impedīre.

complicated *adj* implicātus, involūtus, impedītus.

complication *n* implicātiō *f*.

complicity *n* cōnscientia *f*.

compliment *n* blandīmentum *nt*, honōs *m* ♦ *vt* blandīrī, laudāre; **~ on** grātulārī (*dat*) dē (*abl*).

complimentary *adj* honōrificus, blandus.

compliments *npl* (*as greeting*) salūs *f*.

comply *vi* obsequī (*dat*), obtemperāre (*dat*); mōrem gerere (*dat*), mōrigerārī (*dat*).

component *n* elementum *nt*, pars *f*.

comport *vt* gerere.

compose *vt* (*art*) compōnere, condere, pangere; (*whole*) efficere, cōnflāre; (*quarrel*) compōnere, dīrimere; (*disturbance*) sēdāre; **be ~d of** cōnsistere ex (*abl*), cōnstāre ex (*abl*).

composed *adj* tranquillus, placidus.

composer *n* auctor *m*, scrīptor *m*.

composite *adj* multiplex.

composition *n* (*process*) compositiō *f*, scrīptūra *f*; (*product*) opus *nt*, poēma *nt*, carmen *nt*; (*quality*) structūra *f*.

composure *n* sēcūritās *f*, aequus animus *m*; (*face*) tranquillitās *f*.

compound *vt* miscēre; (*words*) duplicāre, iungere ♦ *vi* (*agree*) pacīscī ♦ *adj* compositus ♦ *n* (*word*) iūnctum verbum *nt*; (*area*) saeptum *nt*.

compound interest *n* anatocismus *m*.

comprehend *vt* intellegere, comprehendere; (*include*) continēre, complectī.

comprehensible *adj* perspicuus.

comprehension *n* intellegentia *f*, comprehēnsiō *f*.

comprehensive *adj* capāx; **be ~** lātē patēre, multa complectī.

compress *vt* comprimere, coartāre ♦ *n* fōmentum *nt*.

compression *n* compressus *m*.

comprise *vt* continēre, complectī, comprehendere.

compromise *n* (*by one side*) accommodātiō *f*; (*by both sides*) comprōmissum *nt* ♦ *vi* comprōmittere ♦ *vt* implicāre, in suspiciōnem vocāre; **be ~d** in suspiciōnem venīre.

comptroller *n* moderātor *m*.

compulsion *n* necessitās *f*, vīs *f*; **under ~** coāctus.

compulsory *adj* necesse, lēge imperātus; **use ~ measures** vim adhibēre.

compunction *n* paenitentia *f*.

computation *n* ratiō *f*.

compute *vt* computāre, ratiōnem dūcere.

comrade *n* socius *m*, contubernālis *m*.

comradeship *n* contubernium *nt*.

concatenation *n* seriēs *f*.

concave *adj* concavus.

conceal *vt* cēlāre, abdere, abscondere; (*fact*) dissimulāre.

concealment *n* occultātiō *f*; (*place*) latebrae *fpl*; (*of facts*) dissimulātiō *f*; **in ~** abditus, occultus; **be in ~** latēre, latitāre; **go into ~** dēlitēscere.

concede *vt* concēdere.

conceit *n* (*idea*) nōtiō *f*; (*wit*) facētiae *fpl*; (*pride*)

superbia *f*, adrogantia *f*, vānitās *f*.
conceited *adj* glōriōsus, adrogāns.
conceitedness *n* adrogantia *f*, vānitās *f*.
conceive *vt* concipere, comprehendere,
intellegere.
concentrate *vt* (*in one place*) cōgere,
congregāre; (*attention*) intendere, dēfīgere.
concentrated *adj* dēnsus.
concentration *n* animī intentiō *f*.
concept *n* nōtiō *f*.
conception *n* conceptus *m*; (*mind*)
intellegentia *f*, īnfōrmātiō *f*; (*idea*) nōtiō *f*,
cōgitātiō *f*, cōnsilium *nt*.
concern *vt* (*refer*) attinēre ad (*acc*), interesse
(*gen*); (*worry*) sollicitāre; **it ~s me** meā rēfert,
meā interest; **as far as I am ~ed** per mē ♦ *n*
rēs *f*, negōtium *nt*; (*importance*) mōmentum
nt; (*worry*) sollicitūdō *f*, cūra *f*; (*regret*) dolor
m.
concerned *adj* sollicitus, anxius; **be ~** dolēre;
be ~ about molestē ferre.
concerning *prep* dē (*abl*).
concernment *n* sollicitūdō *f*.
concert *n* (*music*) concentus *m*; (*agreement*)
cōnsēnsus *m*; **in ~** ex compositō, ūnō animō ♦
vt compōnere; (*plan*) inīre.
concession *n* concessiō *f*; **by the ~ of** concessū
(*gen*); **make a ~** concēdere, tribuere.
conciliate *vt* conciliāre.
conciliation *n* conciliātiō *f*.
conciliator *n* arbiter *m*.
conciliatory *adj* pācificus.
concise *adj* brevis; (*style*) dēnsus.
concisely *adv* breviter.
conciseness *n* brevitās *f*.
conclave *n* sēcrētus cōnsessus *m*.
conclude *vt* (*end*) termināre, fīnīre, cōnficere;
(*settle*) facere, compōnere, pangere; (*infer*)
īnferre, colligere.
conclusion *n* (*end*) fīnis *m*; (*of action*) exitus *m*;
(*of speech*) perōrātiō *f*; (*inference*) coniectūra
f; (*decision*) placitum *nt*, sententia *f*; **in ~**
dēnique; **try ~s with** contendere cum.
conclusive *adj* certus, manifestus, gravis.
conclusively *adv* sine dubiō.
concoct *vt* coquere; (*fig*) cōnflāre.
concoction *n* (*fig*) māchinātiō *f*.
concomitant *adj* adiūnctus.
concord *n* concordia *f*; (*music*) harmonia *f*.
concordant *adj* concors.
concordat *n* pactum *nt*, foedus *nt*.
concourse *n* frequentia *f*, celebrātiō *f*;
(*moving*) concursus *m*.
concrete *adj* concrētus; **in the ~** rē.
concretion *n* concrētiō *f*.
concubine *n* concubīna *f*.
concupiscence *n* libīdō *f*.
concur *vi* (*time*) concurrere; (*opinion*)
cōnsentīre, adsentīre.
concurrence *n* (*time*) concursus *m*; (*opinion*)
cōnsēnsus *m*.
concurrent *adj* (*time*) aequālis; (*opinion*)
cōnsentāneus; **be ~** concurrere, cōnsentīre.

concurrently *adv* simul, ūnā.
concussion *n* ictus *m*.
condemn *vt* damnāre, condemnāre;
(*disapprove*) improbāre; **~ to death** capitis
damnāre; **~ for treason** dē māiestāte
damnāre.
condemnation *n* damnātiō *f*; condemnātiō *f*.
condemnatory *adj* damnātōrius.
condense *vt* dēnsāre; (*words*) premere.
condescend *vi* dēscendere, sē submittere.
condescending *adj* cōmis.
condescension *n* cōmitās *f*.
condiment *n* condīmentum *nt*.
condition *n* (*of body*) habitus *m*; (*external*)
status *m*, condiciō *f*, rēs *f*; (*in society*) locus *m*,
fortūna *f*; (*of agreement*) condiciō *f*, lēx *f*; **~s of
sale** mancipī lēx *f*; **on ~ that** eā condicione ut
(*subj*); **in ~** (*animals*) nitidus ♦ *vt* fōrmāre,
regere.
conditional *adj*: **the assistance is ~ on** eā
condiciōne succurritur ut (*subj*).
conditionally *adv* sub condiciōne.
conditioned *adj* (*character*) mōrātus.
condole *vi*: **~ with** cōnsōlārī.
condolence *n* cōnsōlātiō *f*.
condonation *n* venia *f*.
condone *vt* condōnāre, ignōscere (*dat*).
conduce *vi* condūcere (ad), prōficere (ad).
conducive *adj* ūtilis, accommodātus.
conduct *vt* dūcere; (*escort*) dēdūcere; (*to a
place*) addūcere, perdūcere; (*business*)
gerere, administrāre; (*self*) gerere ♦ *n*
mōrēs *mpl*; (*past*) vīta *f*, facta *ntpl*; (*business*)
administrātiō *f*; **safe ~** praesidium *nt*.
conductor *m* dux *m*, ductor *m*.
conduit *n* canālis *m*, aquae ductus *m*.
cone *n* cōnus *m*.
coney *n* cunīculus *m*.
confabulate *vi* colloquī.
confection *n* cuppēdō *f*.
confectioner *n* cuppēdinārius *m*.
confectionery *n* dulcia *ntpl*.
confederacy *n* foederātae cīvitātēs *fpl*,
societās *f*.
confederate *adj* foederātus ♦ *n* socius *m* ♦ *vi*
coniūrāre, foedus facere.
confederation *n* societās *f*.
confer *vt* cōnferre, tribuere ♦ *vi* colloquī,
sermōnem cōnferre; **~ about** agere dē (*abl*).
conference *n* colloquium *nt*, congressus *m*.
conferment *n* dōnātiō *f*.
confess *vt* fatērī, cōnfitērī.
confessedly *adv* manifestō.
confession *n* cōnfessiō *f*.
confidant *n* cōnscius *m*.
confide *vi* fīdere (*dat*), cōnfīdere (*dat*) ♦ *vt*
crēdere, committere.
confidence *n* fidēs *f*, fīdūcia *f*; **have ~ in** fīdere
(*dat*), cōnfīdere (*dat*); **inspire ~ in** fidem
facere (*dat*); **tell in ~** tūtīs auribus dēpōnere.
confident *adj* fīdēns; **~ in** frētus (*abl*); **be ~ that**
certō scīre, prō certō habēre.
confidential *adj* arcānus, intimus.

confidentially *adv* inter nōs.
confidently *adv* fīdenter.
confiding *adj* crēdulus.
configuration *n* figūra *f*, fōrma *f*.
confine *vt* (*prison*) inclūdere, in vincula conicere; (*limit*) termināre, circumscrībere; (*restrain*) coercēre, cohibēre; (*to bed*) dētinēre; **be ~d** (*women*) parturīre.
confinement *n* custōdia *f*, vincula *ntpl*, inclūsiō *f*; (*women*) puerperium *nt*.
confines *n* fīnēs *mpl*.
confirm *vt* (*strength*) corrōborāre, firmāre; (*decision*) sancīre, ratum facere; (*fact*) adfirmāre, comprobāre.
confirmation *n* cōnfirmātiō *f*, adfirmātiō *f*.
confirmed *adj* ratus.
confiscate *vt* pūblicāre.
confiscation *n* pūblicātiō *f*.
conflagration *n* incendium *nt*, dēflāgrātiō *f*.
conflict *n* (*physical*) concursus *m*; (*hostile*) certāmen *nt*, proelium *nt*; (*verbal*) contentiō *f*, contrōversia *f*; (*contradiction*) repugnantia *f*, discrepantia *f* ♦ *vi* inter sē repugnāre.
conflicting *adj* contrārius.
confluence *n* cōnfluēns *m*.
confluent *adj* cōnfluēns.
conform *vt* accommodāre ♦ *vi* sē cōnfōrmāre (ad), obsequī (*dat*), mōrem gerere (*dat*).
conformable *adj* accommodātus, conveniēns.
conformably *adv* convenienter.
conformation *n* structūra *f*, cōnfōrmātiō *f*.
conformity *n* convenientia *f*, cōnsēnsus *m*.
confound *vt* (*mix*) cōnfundere, permiscēre; (*amaze*) obstupefacere; (*thwart*) frustrārī; (*suppress*) opprimere, obruere; **~ you!** dī tē perduint.
confounded *adj* miser, sacer, nefandus.
confoundedly *adv* mīrum quantum nefāriē.
confraternity *n* frāternitās *f*.
confront *vt* sē oppōnere (*dat*), obviam īre (*dat*), sē cōram offerre.
confuse *vt* permiscēre, perturbāre.
confused *adj* perturbātus.
confusedly *adv* perturbātē, prōmiscuē.
confusion *n* perturbātiō *f*; (*shame*) rubor *m*.
confutation *n* refūtātiō *f*.
confute *vt* refūtāre, redarguere, convincere.
congé *n* commeātus *m*.
congeal *vt* congelāre, dūrāre ♦ *vi* concrēscere.
congealed *adj* concrētus.
congenial *adj* concors, congruēns, iūcundus.
congeniality *n* concordia *f*, mōrum similitūdō *f*.
congenital *adj* nātīvus.
conger *n* conger *m*.
congested *adj* refertus, dēnsus; (*with people*) frequentissimus.
congestion *n* congeriēs *f*; frequentia *f*.
conglomerate *vt* glomerāre.
conglomeration *n* congeriēs *f*, cumulus *m*.
congratulate *vt* grātulārī (*dat*).
congratulation *n* grātulātiō *f*.

congratulatory *adj* grātulābundus.
congregate *vt* congregāre, cōgere ♦ *vi* convenīre, congregārī.
congregation *n* conventus *m*, coetus *m*.
congress *n* conventus *m*, cōnsessus *m*, concilium *nt*; senātus *m*.
congruence *n* convenientia *f*.
congruent *adj* conveniēns, congruēns.
congruently *adv* convenienter, congruenter.
congruous *adj see* **congruent**.
conical *adj* turbinātus.
coniferous *adj* cōnifer.
conjectural *adj* opīnābilis.
conjecturally *adv* coniectūrā.
conjecture *n* coniectūra *f* ♦ *vt* conicere, augurārī.
conjoin *vt* coniungere.
conjoint *adj* coniūnctus.
conjointly *adv* coniūnctē, ūnā.
conjugal *adj* coniugālis.
conjugate *vt* dēclīnāre.
conjugation *n* (*GRAM*) dēclīnātiō *f*.
conjunct *adj* coniūnctus.
conjunction *n* coniūnctiō *f*, concursus *m*.
conjure *vt* (*entreat*) obtestārī, obsecrāre; (*spirits*) ēlicere, ciēre ♦ *vi* praestigiīs ūtī.
conjurer *n* praestigiātor *m*.
conjuring *n* praestigiae *fpl*.
connate *adj* innātus, nātūrā īnsitus.
connect *vt* iungere, coniungere, cōpulāre, connectere.
connected *adj* coniūnctus; (*unbroken*) continēns; (*by marriage*) adfīnis; **be ~ed with** contingere; **be closely ~ed with** inhaerēre (*dat*), cohaerēre cum (*abl*).
connectedly *adv* coniūnctē, continenter.
connection *n* coniūnctiō *f*, contextus *m*, seriēs *f*; (*kin*) necessitūdō *f*; (*by marriage*) adfīnitās *f*; **~ between ... and ...** ratiō (*gen*) ... cum ... (*abl*); **I have no ~ with you** nīl mihī tēcum est.
connivance *n* venia *f*, dissimulātiō *f*.
connive *vi* connīvēre in (*abl*), dissimulāre.
connoisseur *n* intellegēns *m*.
connotation *n* vīs *f*, significātiō *f*.
connote *vt* significāre.
connubial *adj* coniugālis.
conquer *vt* vincere, superāre.
conquerable *adj* superābilis, expugnābilis.
conqueror *n* victor *m*.
conquest *n* victōria *f*; (*town*) expugnātiō *f*; (*prize*) praemium *nt*, praeda *f*; **the ~ of Greece** Graecia capta.
conscience *n* cōnscientia *f*; **guilty ~** mala cōnscientia; **have a clear ~** nūllīus culpae sibi cōnscium esse; **have no ~** nullam rēligiōnem habēre.
conscientious *adj* probus, rēligiōsus.
conscientiously *adv* bonā fidē, rēligiōsē.
conscientiousness *n* fidēs *f*, rēligiō *f*.
conscious *adj* sibī cōnscius; (*aware*) gnārus; (*physically*) mentis compos; **be ~** sentīre.
consciously *adv* sciēns.
consciousness *n* animus *m*; (*of action*)

cōnscientia *f*; **he lost ~** animus eum relīquit.
conscript *n* tīrō *m* ♦ *vt* cōnscrībere.
conscription *n* dēlēctus *m*; (*of wealth*) pūblicātiō *f*.
consecrate *vt* dēdicāre, cōnsecrāre; (*self*) dēvovēre.
consecrated *adj* sacer.
consecration *n* dēdicātiō *f*, cōnsecrātiō *f*; (*self*) dēvōtiō *f*.
consecutive *adj* dēinceps, continuus.
consecutively *adv* dēinceps, ōrdine.
consensus *n* cōnsēnsus *m*.
consent *vi* adsentīre (*dat*), adnuere (*infin*); (*together*) cōnsentīre ♦ *n* (*one side*) adsēnsus *m*; (*all*) cōnsēnsus *m*; **by common ~** omnium cōnsēnsū.
consequence *n* ēventus *m*, exitus *m*; (*logic*) conclūsiō *f*; (*importance*) mōmentum *nt*, auctōritās *f*; **it is of ~ interest; what will be the ~ of?** quō ēvādet?
consequent *adj* cōnsequēns.
consequential *adj* cōnsentāneus; (*person*) adrogāns.
consequently *adv* itaque, igitur, proptereā.
conservation *n* cōnservātiō *f*.
conservative *adj* reī pūblicae cōnservandae studiōsus; (*estimate*) mediōcris; **~ party** optimātēs *mpl*.
conservator *n* custōs *m*, cōnservātor *m*.
conserve *vt* cōnservāre, servāre.
consider *vt* cōnsīderāre, contemplārī; (*reflect*) sēcum volūtāre, meditari, dēlīberāre, cōgitāre; (*deem*) habēre, dūcere; (*respect*) respicere, observāre.
considerable *adj* aliquantus, nōnnullus; (*person*) illūstris.
considerably *adv* aliquantum; (*with compar*) aliquantō, multō.
considerate *adj* hūmānus, benignus.
considerately *adv* hūmānē, benignē.
consideration *n* cōnsīderātiō *f*, contemplātiō *f*, dēlīberātiō *f*; (*respect*) respectus *m*, ratiō *f*; (*importance*) mōmentum *nt*; (*reason*) ratiō *f*; (*pay*) pretium *nt*; **for a ~** mercēde, datā mercēde; **in ~ of** propter (*acc*), prō (*abl*); **on no ~** nēquāquam; **with ~** cōnsultō; **without ~** temerē; **take into ~** ad cōnsilium dēferre; **show ~ for** respectum habēre (*gen*).
considered *adj* (*reasons*) exquīsītus.
considering *prep* prō (*abl*), propter (*acc*) ♦ *conj* ut, quōniam.
consign *vt* mandāre, committere.
consist *vi* cōnstāre; **~ in** cōnstāre ex (*abl*), continērī (*abl*), positum esse in (*abl*); **~ with** congruere (*dat*), convenīre (*dat*).
consistence *n* firmitās *f*.
consistency *n* cōnstantia *f*.
consistent *adj* cōnstāns; (*with*) cōnsentāneus, congruens; (*of movement*) aequābilis; **be ~** cohaerēre.
consistently *adv* constanter.
consolable *adj* cōnsōlābilis.
consolation *n* cōnsōlātiō *f*; (*thing*) sōlācium *nt*.

consolatory *adj* cōnsōlātōrius.
console *vt* cōnsōlārī.
consoler *n* cōnsōlātor *m*.
consolidate *vt* (*liquid*) cōgere; (*strength*) corrōborāre; (*gains*) obtinēre ♦ *vi* concrēscere.
consolidation *n* concrētiō *f*; cōnfirmātiō *f*.
consonance *n* concentus *m*.
consonant *adj* cōnsonus, haud absonus ♦ *n* cōnsonāns *f*.
consort *n* cōnsors *m/f*, socius *m*; (*married*) coniunx *m/f* ♦ *vi*: **~ with** familiāriter ūtī (*abl*), coniūnctissimē vīvere cum (*abl*).
conspectus *n* summārium *nt*.
conspicuous *adj* ēminēns, īnsignis, manifestus; **be ~** ēminēre.
conspicuously *adv* manifestō, palam, ante oculōs.
conspiracy *n* coniūrātiō *f*.
conspirator *n* coniūrātus *m*.
conspire *vi* coniūrāre; (*for good*) cōnspīrāre.
constable *n* lictor *m*.
constancy *n* cōnstantia *f*, firmitās *f*; **with ~** cōnstanter.
constant *adj* cōnstāns; (*faithful*) fīdus, fidēlis; (*continuous*) adsiduus.
constantly *adv* adsiduē, saepe, crēbrō.
constellation *n* sīdus *nt*.
consternation *n* trepidātiō *f*, pavor *m*; **throw into ~** perterrēre, cōnsternere.
constituency *n* suffrāgātōrēs *mpl*.
constituent *adj*: **~ part** elementum *nt* ♦ *n* (*voter*) suffrāgātor *m*.
constitute *vt* creāre, cōnstituere; esse.
constitution *n* nātūra *f*, status *m*; (*body*) habitus *m*; (*POL*) cīvitātis fōrma *f*, reī pūblicae status *m*, lēgēs *fpl*.
constitutional *adj* lēgitimus, iūstus.
constitutionally *adv* ē rē pūblicā.
constrain *vt* cōgere.
constraint *n* vīs *f*; **under ~** coāctus; **without ~** suā sponte.
constrict *vt* comprimere, cōnstringere.
constriction *n* contractiō *f*.
construct *vt* aedificāre, exstruere.
construction *n* aedificātiō *f*; (*method*) structūra *f*; (*meaning*) interpretātiō *f*; **put a wrong ~ on** in malam partem interpretārī.
construe *vt* interpretārī.
consul *n* cōnsul *m*; **~ elect** cōnsul dēsignātus; **ex ~** cōnsulāris *m*.
consular *adj* cōnsulāris.
consulship *n* cōnsulātus *m*; **stand for the ~** cōnsulātum petere; **hold the ~** cōnsulātum gerere; **in my ~** mē cōnsule.
consult *vt* cōnsulere; **~ the interests of** cōnsulere (*dat*) ♦ *vi* dēlīberāre, cōnsiliārī.
consultation *n* (*asking*) cōnsultātiō *f*; (*discussion*) dēlīberātiō *f*.
consume *vt* cōnsūmere, absūmere; (*food*) edere.
consumer *n* cōnsūmptor *m*.
consummate *adj* summus, perfectus ♦ *vt*

perficere, absolvere.

consummation *n* absolūtiō *f*; fīnis *m*, ēventus *m*.

consumption *n* cōnsūmptiō *f*; (*disease*) tābēs *f*, phthisis *f*.

consumptive *adj* pulmōnārius.

contact *n* tāctus *m*, contāgiō *f*; **come in ~ with** contingere.

contagion *n* contāgiō *f*.

contagious *adj* tābificus; **be ~** contāgiīs vulgārī.

contain *vt* capere, continēre; (*self*) cohibēre.

container *n* vās *nt*.

contaminate *vt* contāmināre, īnficere.

contamination *n* contāgiō *f*, lābēs *f*.

contemplate *vt* contemplārī, intuērī; (*action*) in animō habēre; (*prospect*) spectāre.

contemplation *n* contemplātiō *f*; (*thought*) cōgitātiō *f*.

contemplative *adj* cōgitāns, meditāns; **in a ~ mood** cōgitātiōnī dēditus.

contemporaneous *adj* aequālis.

contemporaneously *adv* simul.

contemporary *adj* aequālis.

contempt *n* contemptiō *f*; **be an object of ~** contemptuī esse; **treat with ~** contemptum habēre, conculcāre.

contemptible *adj* contemnendus, abiectus, vīlis.

contemptuous *adj* fastīdiōsus.

contemptuously *adv* contemptim, fastīdiōsē.

contend *vi* certāre, contendere; (*in battle*) dīmicāre, pugnāre; (*in words*) adfirmāre, adsevērāre.

contending *adj* contrārius.

content *adj* contentus ♦ *n* aequus animus *m* ♦ *vt* placēre (*dat*), satisfacere (*dat*); **be ~ed** satis habēre.

contentedly *adv* aequō animō.

contention *n* certāmen *nt*; contrōversia *f*; (*opinion*) sententia *f*.

contentious *adj* pugnāx, lītigiōsus.

contentiously *adv* pugnāciter.

contentiousness *n* contrōversiae studium *nt*.

contentment *n* aequus animus *m*.

contents *n* quod inest, quae insunt; (*of speech*) argūmentum *nt*.

conterminous *adj* adfīnis.

contest *n* certāmen *nt*, contentiō *f* ♦ *vt* (*law*) lēge agere dē (*abl*); (*office*) petere; (*dispute*) repugnāre (*dat*), resistere (*dat*).

contestable *adj* contrōversus.

contestant *n* petītor *m*, aemulus *m*.

context *n* contextus *m*.

contiguity *n* vīcīnia *f*, propinquitās *f*.

contiguous *adj* vīcīnus, adiacēns; **be ~ to** adiacēre (*dat*), contingere.

continence *n* continentia *f*, abstinentia *f*.

continent *adj* continēns, abstinēns ♦ *n* continēns *f*.

continently *adv* continenter, abstinenter.

contingency *n* cāsus *m*, rēs *f*.

contingent *adj* fortuītus ♦ *n* (*MIL*) numerus *m*.

continual *adj* adsiduus, perpetuus.

continually *adv* adsiduē, semper.

continuance *n* perpetuitās *f*, adsiduitās *f*.

continuation *n* continuātiō *f*; (*of a command*) prōrogātiō *f*; (*of a story*) reliqua pars *f*.

continue *vt* continuāre; (*time*) prōdūcere; (*command*) prōrogāre ♦ *vi* (*action*) pergere; (*time*) manēre; (*endurance*) perstāre, dūrāre; **~ to** *imperf indic*.

continuity *n* continuātiō *f*; (*of speech*) perpetuitās *f*.

continuous *adj* continuus, continēns, perpetuus.

continuously *adv* perpetuō, continenter.

contort *vt* contorquēre, dētorquēre.

contortion *n* distortiō *f*.

contour *n* fōrma *f*.

contraband *adj* interdictus, vetitus.

contract *n* pactum *nt*, mandātum *nt*, conventum *nt*; (*POL*) foedus *nt*; **trial for a breach of ~** mandātī iūdicium *nt* ♦ *vt* (*narrow*) contrahere, addūcere; (*short*) dēminuere; (*illness*) contrahere; (*agreement*) pacīscī; (*for work*) locāre; (*to do work*) condūcere ♦ *vi* pacīscī.

contraction *n* contractiō *f*; (*word*) compendium *nt*.

contractor *n* redemptor *m*, conductor *m*.

contradict *vt* (*person*) contrādīcere (*dat*), refrāgārī (*dat*); (*statement*) īnfitiās īre (*dat*); (*self*) repugnāre (*dat*).

contradiction *n* repugnantia *f*, īnfitiae *fpl*.

contradictory *adj* repugnāns, contrārius; **be ~** inter sē repugnāre.

contradistinction *n* oppositiō *f*.

contraption *n* māchina *f*.

contrariety *n* repugnantia *f*.

contrariwise *adv* ē contrāriō.

contrary *adj* contrārius, adversus; (*person*) difficilis, mōrōsus; **~ to** contrā (*acc*), praeter (*acc*); **~ to expectations** praeter opīniōnem ♦ *n* contrārium *nt*; **on the ~** ē contrāriō, contrā; (*retort*) immo.

contrast *n* discrepantia *f* ♦ *vt* comparāre, oppōnere ♦ *vi* discrepāre.

contravene *vt* (*law*) violāre; (*statement*) contrādīcere (*dat*).

contravention *n* violātiō *f*.

contribute *vt* cōnferre, adferre, contribuere. ♦ *vi*: **~ towards** cōnferre ad (*acc*), adiuvāre; **~ to the cost** impēnsās cōnferre.

contribution *n* conlātiō *f*; (*money*) stipem (*no nom*) *f*.

contributor *n* quī cōnfert.

contributory *adj* adiūnctus.

contrite *adj* paenitēns.

contrition *n* paenitentia *f*.

contrivance *n* māchinātiō *f*, excōgitātiō *f*; (*thing*) māchina *f*; (*idea*) cōnsilium *nt*; (*deceit*) dolus *m*.

contrive *vt* māchinārī, excōgitāre, struere; (*to do*) efficere ut.

contriver *n* māchinātor *m*, artifex *m*, auctor *m*.

control n (*restraint*) frēnum nt; (*power*) moderātiō f, potestās f, imperium nt; **have ~ of** praeesse (*dat*); **out of ~** impotēns ♦ vt moderārī (*dat*), imperāre (*dat*).

controller n moderātor m.

controversial adj concertātōrius.

controversy n contrōversia f, disceptātiō f.

controvert vt redarguere, impugnāre, in dubium vocāre.

contumacious adj contumāx, pervicāx.

contumaciously adv contumāciter, pervicāciter.

contumacy n contumācia f, pervicācia f.

contusion n sūgillātiō f.

conundrum n aenigma nt.

convalesce vi convalēscere.

convalescence n melior valētūdō f.

convalescent adj convalēscēns.

convene vt convocāre.

convenience n opportūnitās f, commoditās f; (*thing*) commodum nt; **at your ~** commodō tuō.

convenient adj idōneus, commodus, opportūnus; **be ~** convenīre; **very ~** percommodus.

conveniently adv opportūnē, commodē.

convention n (*meeting*) conventus m; (*agreement*) conventum nt; (*custom*) mōs m, iūsta ntpl.

conventional adj iūstus, solitus.

conventionality n mōs m, cōnsuētūdō f.

converge vi in medium vergere, in eundem locum tendere.

conversant adj perītus, doctus, exercitātus; **be ~ with** versārī in (*abl*).

conversation n sermō m, colloquium nt.

converse n sermō m, colloquium nt; (*opposite*) contrārium nt ♦ vi colloquī, sermōnem cōnferre ♦ adj contrārius.

conversely adv ē contrāriō, contrā.

conversion n mūtātiō f; (*moral*) mōrum ēmendātiō f.

convert vt mūtāre, convertere; (*to an opinion*) dēdūcere ♦ n discipulus m.

convertible adj commūtābilis.

convex adj convexus.

convexity n convexum nt.

convey vt vehere, portāre, convehere; (*property*) abaliēnāre; (*knowledge*) commūnicāre; (*meaning*) significāre; **~ across** trānsmittere, trādūcere, trānsvehere; **~ away** auferre, āvehere; **~ down** dēvehere, dēportāre; **~ into** importāre, invehere; **~ to** advehere, adferre; **~ up** subvehere.

conveyance n vehiculum nt; (*property*) abaliēnātiō f.

convict vt (*prove guilty*) convincere; (*sentence*) damnāre ♦ n reus m.

conviction n (*law*) damnātiō f; (*argument*) persuāsiō f; (*belief*) fidēs f; **carry ~** fidem facere; **have a ~** persuāsum habēre.

convince vt persuādēre (*dat*); **I am firmly ~d**

mihi persuāsum habeō.

convincing adj (*argument*) gravis; (*evidence*) manifestus.

convincingly adv manifestō.

convivial adj convīvalis, festīvus.

conviviality n festīvitās f.

convocation n conventus m.

convoke vt convocāre.

convolution n spīra f.

convoy n praesidium nt ♦ vt prōsequī.

convulse vt agitāre; **be ~d with laughter** sē in cachinnōs effundere.

convulsion n (*MED*) convulsiō f; (*POL*) tumultus m.

convulsive adj spasticus.

coo vi gemere.

cook vt coquere ♦ n coquus m.

cookery n ars coquīnāria f.

cool adj frīgidus; (*conduct*) impudens; (*mind*) impavidus, lentus ♦ n frīgus nt ♦ vt refrīgerāre; (*passion*) restinguere, sēdāre ♦ vi refrīgēscere, refrīgerārī, dēfervēscere.

coolly adv aequō animō; impudenter.

coolness n frīgus nt; (*mind*) aequus animus m; impudentia f.

coop n hara f; (*barrel*) cūpa f ♦ vt inclūdere.

co-operate vi operam cōnferre; **~ with** adiuvāre, socius esse (*gen*).

co-operation n cōnsociātiō f; auxilium nt, opera f.

co-operative adj (*person*) officiōsus.

co-operator n socius m.

co-opt vt cooptāre.

coot n fulica f.

copartner n socius m.

copartnership n societās f.

cope vi: **~ with** contendere cum (*abl*); **able to ~ with** pār (*dat*); **unable to ~ with** impār (*dat*).

copier n librārius m.

coping n fastīgium nt.

copious adj cōpiōsus, largus, plēnus, abundāns.

copiously adv cōpiōsē, abundanter.

copiousness n cōpia f, ūbertās f.

copper n aes nt ♦ adj aēneus.

coppersmith n faber aerārius m.

coppice, copse n dūmētum nt, virgultum nt.

copy n exemplar nt ♦ vt imitārī; (*writing*) exscrībere, trānscrībere.

copyist n librārius m.

coracle n linter f.

coral n cūrālium nt.

cord n fūniculus m.

cordage n fūnēs mpl.

cordial adj cōmis, festīvus, amīcus; (*greetings*) multus.

cordiality n cōmitās f, studium nt.

cordially adv cōmiter, libenter, ex animō.

cordon n corōna f.

core n (*fig*) nucleus m.

cork n sūber nt; (*bark*) cortex m.

corn n frūmentum nt ♦ adj frūmentārius; (*on*

the foot) clāvus *m*; **price of ~** annōna *f*.
corndealer *n* frūmentārius *m*.
cornfield *n* seges *f*.
cornel *n* (*tree*) cornus *f*.
corner *n* angulus *m*.
cornet *n* cornū *nt*.
cornice *n* corōna *f*.
coronet *n* diadēma *nt*.
corporal *adj* corporeus.
corporal punishment *n* verbera *ntpl*.
corporation *n* collēgium *nt*; (*civic*)
   magistrātūs *mpl*.
corporeal *adj* corporeus.
corps *n* manus *f*.
corpse *n* cadāver *nt*.
corpulence *n* obēsum corpus *nt*.
corpulent *adj* obēsus, pinguis.
corpuscle *n* corpusculum *nt*.
corral *n* praesēpe *nt*.
correct *vt* corrigere, ēmendāre; (*person*)
   castīgāre ♦ *adj* vērus; (*language*) integer;
   (*style*) ēmendātus.
correction *n* ēmendātiō *f*; (*moral*) correctiō *f*;
   (*punishment*) castīgātiō *f*.
correctly *adv* bene, vērē.
correctness *n* (*fact*) vēritās *f*; (*language*)
   integritās *f*; (*moral*) probitās *f*.
corrector *n* ēmendātor *m*, corrēctor *m*.
correspond *vi* (*agree*) respondēre (*dat*),
   congruere (*dat*); (*by letter*) inter sē scrībere.
correspondence *n* similitūdō *f*; epistulae *fpl*.
correspondent *n* epistulārum scrīptor *m*.
corresponding *adj* pār.
correspondingly *adv* pariter.
corridor *n* porticus *f*.
corrigible *adj* ēmendābilis.
corroborate *vt* cōnfirmāre.
corroboration *n* cōnfirmātiō *f*.
corrode *vt* ērōdere, edere.
corrosive *adj* edāx.
corrugate *vt* rūgāre.
corrugated *adj* rūgōsus.
corrupt *vt* corrumpere, dēprāvāre; (*text*)
   vitiāre ♦ *adj* corruptus, vitiātus; (*person*)
   prāvus, vēnālis; (*text*) vitiātus.
corrupter *n* corruptor *m*.
corruptible *adj* (*matter*) dissolūbilis; (*person*)
   vēnālis.
corruption *n* (*of matter*) corruptiō *f*; (*moral*)
   corruptēla *f*, dēprāvātiō *f*; (*bribery*) ambitus
   m.
corsair *n* pīrāta *m*.
cortège *n* pompa *f*.
coruscate *vi* fulgēre.
coruscation *n* fulgor *m*.
Corybant *n* Corybas *m*.
Corybantic *adj* Corybantius.
cosmetic *n* medicāmen *nt*.
cosmic *adj* mundānus.
cosmopolitan *adj* mundānus.
cosmos *n* mundus *m*.
cost *vt* emī, stāre (*dat*); **it ~ me dear** māgnō
   mihi stetit, male ēmī; **it ~ me a talent** talentō

mihi stetit, talentō ēmī; **it ~ me my freedom**
   lībertātem perdidi ♦ *n* pretium *nt*, impēnsa *f*;
   ~ of living annōna *f*; **to your ~** incommodō tuō,
   dētrīmentō tuō; **at the ~ of one's reputation**
   violātā fāmā, nōn salvā existimātiōne; **I sell**
   at ~ price quantī ēmī vēndō.
costliness *n* sūmptus *m*; cāritās *f*.
costly *adj* cārus; (*furnishings*) lautus,
   sūmptuōsus.
costume *n* habitus *m*.
cosy *adj* commodus.
cot *n* lectulus *m*.
cote *n* columbārium *nt*.
cottage *n* casa *f*, tugurium *nt*.
cottager *n* rūsticus *m*.
cotton *n* (*tree*) gossympinus *f*; (*cloth*) xylinum
   nt.
couch *n* lectus *m* ♦ *vi* recumbere ♦ *vt* (*lance*)
   intendere; (*words*) exprimere, reddere.
cough *n* tussis *f* ♦ *vi* tussīre.
council *n* concilium *nt*; (*small*) cōnsilium *nt*.
councillor *n* (*town*) dēcuriō *m*.
counsel *n* (*debate*) cōnsultātiō *f*; (*advice*)
   cōnsilium *nt*; (*law*) advocātus *m*, patrōnus *m*;
   take ~ cōnsiliārī, dēlīberāre; **take ~ of**
   cōnsulere ♦ *vt* suādēre (*dat*), monēre.
counsellor *n* cōnsiliārius *m*.
count *vt* numerāre, computāre; **~ as** dūcere,
   habēre; **~ amongst** pōnere in (*abl*); **~ up** *vt*
   ēnumerāre; **~ upon** cōnfīdere (*dat*); **be ~ed**
   among in numerō esse (*gen*) ♦ *vi* aestimārī,
   habērī ♦ *n* ratiō *f*; (*in indictment*) caput *nt*;
   (*title*) comes *m*.
countenance *n* faciēs *f*, vultus *m*, ōs *nt*; (*fig*)
   favor *m*; **put out of ~** conturbāre ♦ *vt* favēre
   (*dat*), indulgēre (*dat*).
counter *n* (*for counting*) calculus *m*; (*for play*)
   tessera *f*; (*shop*) mēnsa *f* ♦ *adj* contrārius ♦
   adv contrā, obviam ♦ *vt* obsistere (*dat*),
   respondēre (*dat*).
counteract *vt* obsistere (*dat*), adversārī (*dat*);
   (*malady*) medērī (*dat*).
counterattack *vt* in vicem oppugnāre,
   adgredī.
counterattraction *n* altera illecebra *f*.
counterbalance *vt* compēnsāre, exaequāre.
counterclockwise *adv* sinistrōrsus.
counterfeit *adj* falsus, fūcātus, adsimulātus,
   fictus ♦ *vt* fingere, simulāre, imitārī.
countermand *vt* renūntiāre.
counterpane *n* lōdīx *f*, strāgulum *nt*.
counterpart *n* pār *m/f/nt*.
counterpoise *n* aequum pondus *nt* ♦ *vt*
   compēnsāre, exaequāre.
countersign *n* (*MIL*) tessera *f*.
counting table *n* abacus *m*.
countless *adj* innumerābilis.
countrified *adj* agrestis, rūsticus.
country *n* (*region*) regiō *f*, terra *f*; (*territory*)
   fīnēs *mpl*; (*native*) patria *f*; (*not town*) rūs *nt*;
   (*open*) agrī *mpl*; **of our ~** nostrās; **live in the ~**
   rūsticārī; **living in the ~** rūsticātiō *f*.

country house n vīlla f.
countryman n agricola m; **fellow ~** populāris m, cīvis m.
countryside n agrī mpl, rus nt.
couple n pār nt; **a ~ of** duo ♦ vt cōpulare, coniungere.
couplet n distichon nt.
courage n fortitūdō f, animus m; (MIL) virtūs f; **have the ~ to** audēre; **lose ~** animōs dēmittere; **take ~** bonō animō esse.
courageous adj fortis, ācer; audāx.
courageously adv fortiter, ācriter.
courier n tabellārius m.
course n (movement) cursus m; (route) iter nt; (sequence) seriēs f; (career) dēcursus; (for races) stadium nt, circus m; (of dinner) ferculum nt; (of stones) ōrdō m; (of water) lāpsus m; **of ~** certē, sānē, scīlicet; **as a matter of ~** continuō; **in due ~** mox; **in the ~ of** inter (acc), in (abl); **keep on one's ~** cursum tenēre; **be driven off one's ~** dēicī; **second ~** secunda mēnsa.
court n (space) ārea f; (of house) ātrium nt; (of king) aula f, (suite) cohors f, comitēs mpl; (law) iūdicium nt, iūdicēs mpl; **pay ~ to** ambīre, īnservīre (dat); **hold a ~** forum agere; **bring into ~** in iūs vocāre ♦ vt colere, ambīre; (danger) sē offerre (dat); (woman) petere.
courteous adj cōmis, urbānus, hūmānus.
courteously adv cōmiter, urbānē.
courtesan n meretrīx f.
courtesy n (quality) cōmitās f, hūmānitās f; (act) officium nt.
courtier n aulicus m; **~s** pl aula f.
courtly adj officiōsus.
cousin n cōnsobrīnus m, cōnsobrīna f.
cove n sinus m.
covenant n foedus nt, pactum nt ♦ vi pacīscī.
cover vt tegere, operīre; (hide) vēlāre; (march) claudere; **~ over** obdūcere; **~ up** vi obtegere ♦ n integumentum nt, operculum nt; (shelter) latebrae fpl, suffugium nt; (pretence) speciēs f; **under ~ of** sub (abl), sub speciē (gen); **take ~** dēlitēscere.
covering n integumentum nt, involucrum nt, operculum nt; (of couch) strāgulum nt.
coverlet n lōdīx f.
covert adj occultus; (language) oblīquus ♦ n latebra f, perfugium nt; (thicket) dūmētum nt.
covertly adv occultē, sēcrētō.
covet vt concupīscere, expetere.
covetous adj avidus, cupidus.
covetously adv avidē, cupidē.
covetousness n avidītās f, cupiditās f.
covey n grex f.
cow n vacca f ♦ vt terrēre.
coward n ignāvus m.
cowardice n ignāvia f.
cowardly adj ignāvus.
cower vi subsīdere.
cowherd m bubulcus m.
cowl n cucullus m.
coxswain n rēctor m.

coy adj pudens, verēcundus.
coyly adv pudenter, modestē.
coyness n pudor m, verēcundia f.
cozen vt fallere, dēcipere.
crab n cancer m.
crabbed adj mōrōsus, difficilis.
crack n (chink) rīma f; (sound) crepitus m ♦ vt findere, frangere; (whip) crepitāre (abl) ♦ vi (open) fatīscere; (sound) crepāre, crepitāre.
crackle vi crepitāre.
crackling n crepitus m.
cradle n cūnae fpl; (fig) incūnābula ntpl.
craft n ars f, (deceit) dolus m; (boat) nāvigium nt.
craftily adv callidē, sollerter; dolōsē.
craftsman n artifex m, faber m.
craftsmanship n ars f, artificium nt.
crafty adj callidus, sollers; dolōsus.
crag n rūpēs f, scopulus m.
cram vt farcīre, refercīre; (with food) sagīnāre.
cramp n convulsiō f; (tool) cōnfībula f ♦ vt coercēre, coartāre.
crane n (bird) grus f, (machine) māchina f, trochlea f.
crank n uncus m; (person) ineptus m.
crannied adj rīmōsus.
cranny n rīma f.
crash n (fall) ruīna f; (noise) fragor m ♦ vi ruere; strepere.
crass adj crassus; **~ stupidity** mera stultitia.
crate n crātēs fpl.
crater n crātēr m.
cravat n fōcāle nt.
crave vt (desire) concupīscere, adpetere, exoptāre; (request) ōrāre, obsecrāre.
craven adj ignāvus.
craving n cupīdō f, dēsīderium nt, adpetītiō f.
crawl vi (animal) serpere; (person) rēpere.
crayfish n commarus m.
craze n libīdō f ♦ vt mentem aliēnāre.
craziness n dēmentia f.
crazy adj dēmēns, fatuus.
creak vi crepāre.
creaking n crepitus m.
cream n spūma lactis f; (fig) flōs m.
crease n rūga f ♦ vt rūgāre.
create vt creāre, facere, gignere.
creation n (process) fabricātiō f; (result) opus nt; (human) hominēs mpl.
creative adj (nature) creātrīx; (mind) inventor, inventrīx.
creator n creātor m, auctor m, opifex m.
creature n animal nt; (person) homō m/f.
credence n fidēs f.
credentials n litterae commendātīciae fpl; (fig) auctōritās f.
credibility n fidēs f; (source) auctōritās f.
credible adj crēdibilis; (witness) locuplēs.
credit n (belief) fidēs f; (repute) existimātiō f; (character) auctōritās f, grātia f, (COMM) fidēs f; **be a ~ to** decus esse (gen); **it is to your ~** tibī laudī est; **give ~ for** laudem tribuere (gen);

have ~ fidē stāre ♦ _vt_ crēdere (_dat_); (_with money_) acceptum referre (_dat_).
creditable _adj_ honestus, laudābilis.
creditably _adv_ honestē, cum laude.
creditor _n_ crēditor _m_.
credulity _n_ crēdulitās _f_.
credulous _adj_ crēdulus.
creed _n_ dogma _nt_.
creek _n_ sinus _m_.
creel _n_ vīdulus _m_.
creep _vi_ (_animal_) serpere; (_person_) rēpere; (_flesh_) horrēre.
cremate _vt_ cremāre.
crescent _n_ lūna _f_.
crescent-shaped _adj_ lūnātus.
cress _n_ nasturtium _nt_.
crest _n_ crista _f_.
crested _adj_ cristātus.
crestfallen _adj_ dēmissus.
crevasse _n_ hiātus _m_.
crevice _n_ rīma _f_.
crew _n_ nautae _mpl_, rēmigēs _mpl_, grex _f_, turba _f_.
crib _n_ (_cot_) lectulus _m_; (_manger_) praesēpe _nt_.
cricket _n_ gryllus _m_.
crier _n_ praecō _m_.
crime _n_ scelus _nt_, facinus _nt_, flāgitium _nt_.
criminal _adj_ scelestus, facinorōsus, flāgitiōsus ♦ _n_ reus _m_.
criminality _n_ scelus _nt_.
criminally _adv_ scelestē, flāgitiōsē.
crimson _n_ coccum _m_ ♦ _adj_ coccineus.
cringe _vi_ adūlārī, adsentārī.
crinkle _n_ rūga _f_.
cripple _vt_ dēbilitāre, mūtilāre; (_fig_) frangere ♦ _adj_ claudus.
crisis _n_ discrīmen _nt_.
crisp _adj_ fragilis; (_manner_) alacer; (_hair_) crispus.
crisscross _adj_ in quīncūncem dispositus.
criterion _n_ index _m_, indicium _nt_; **take as a ~** referre ad (_acc_).
critic _n_ iūdex _m_; (_literary_) criticus, grammaticus _m_; (_adverse_) castīgātor _m_.
critical _adj_ (_mind_) accūrātus, ēlegāns; (_blame_) cēnsōrius, sevērus; (_danger_) perīculōsus, dubius; **~ moment** discrīmen _nt_.
critically _adv_ accūrātē, ēleganter; sevērē; cum perīculō.
criticism _n_ iūdicium _nt_; (_adverse_) reprehēnsiō _f_.
criticize _vt_ iūdicāre; reprehendere, castīgāre.
croak _vi_ (_raven_) crōcīre; (_frog_) coaxāre.
croaking _n_ cantus _m_ ♦ _adj_ raucus.
crock _n_ olla _f_.
crockery _n_ fictilia _ntpl_.
crocodile _n_ crocodīlus _m_; **weep ~ tears** lacrimās cōnfingere.
crocus _n_ crocus _m_.
croft _n_ agellus _m_.
crone _n_ anus _f_.
crony _n_ sodālis _m_.
crook _n_ pedum _nt_ ♦ _vt_ incurvāre.
crooked _adj_ incurvus, aduncus; (_deformed_)

prāvus; (_winding_) flexuōsus; (_morally_) perversus.
crookedly _adv_ perversē, prāvē.
crookedness _n_ prāvitās _f_.
croon _vt_, _vi_ cantāre.
crop _n_ (_grain_) seges _f_, messis _f_; (_tree_) fructus _m_; (_bird_) ingluviēs _f_ ♦ _vt_ (_reap_) metere; (_graze_) carpere, tondēre; ~ **up** _vi_ intervenīre.
cross _n_ (_mark_) decussis _m_; (_torture_) crux _f_ ♦ _adj_ trānsversus, oblīquus; (_person_) acerbus, īrātus ♦ _vt_ trānsīre; (_water_) trāicere; (_mountain_) trānscendere; superāre; (_enemy_) obstāre (_dat_), frustrārī; ~ **out** _vt_ (_writing_) expungere ♦ _vi_ trānsīre; ~ **over** (_on foot_) trānsgredī; (_by sea_) trānsmittere.
crossbar _n_ iugum _nt_.
crossbow _n_ scorpiō _m_.
cross-examination _n_ interrogātiō _f_.
cross-examine _vt_ interrogāre, percontārī.
cross-grained _adj_ (_fig_) mōrōsus.
crossing _n_ trānsitus _m_; (_on water_) trāiectus _m_.
cross purpose _n_: **be at ~s** dīversa spectāre.
cross-question _vt_ interrogāre.
crossroads _n_ quadrivium _nt_.
crosswise _adv_ ex trānsversō; **divide ~** decussāre.
crotchety _adj_ mōrōsus, difficilis.
crouch _vi_ subsīdere, sē submittere.
crow _n_ cornīx _f_; **as the ~ flies** rēctā regiōne ♦ _vi_ cantāre; (_fig_) exsultāre, gestīre.
crowbar _n_ vectis _m_.
crowd _n_ turba _f_, concursus _m_, frequentia _f_; (_small_) grex _m_; multitūdō _f_; **in ~s** gregātim ♦ _vi_ frequentāre, celebrāre ♦ _vt_ (_place_) complēre; (_person_) stīpāre.
crowded _adj_ frequēns.
crown _n_ corōna _f_; (_royal_) diadēma _nt_; (_of head_) vertex _m_; (_fig_) apex _m_, flōs _m_; **the ~ of** summus ♦ _vt_ corōnāre; (_fig_) cumulāre, fastīgium impōnere (_dat_).
crucial _adj_ gravissimus, māximī mōmentī; ~ **moment** discrīmen _nt_.
crucifixion _n_ crucis supplicium _nt_.
crucify _vt_ crucī suffīgere.
crude _adj_ crūdus; (_style_) dūrus, inconcinnus.
crudely _adv_ dūrē, asperē.
crudity _n_ asperitās _f_.
cruel _adj_ crūdēlis, saevus, atrōx.
cruelly _adv_ crūdēliter, atrōciter.
cruelty _n_ crūdēlitās _f_, saevitia _f_, atrōcitās _f_.
cruise _n_ nāvigātiō _f_ ♦ _vi_ nāvigāre.
cruiser _n_ speculātōria nāvis _f_.
crumb _n_ mīca _f_.
crumble _vi_ corruere, putrem fierī ♦ _vt_ putrefacere, friāre.
crumbling _adj_ putris.
crumple _vt_ rūgāre.
crunch _vt_ dentibus frangere.
crupper _n_ postilēna _f_.
crush _vt_ frangere, contundere, obterere; (_fig_) adflīgere, opprimere, obruere ♦ _n_ turba _f_, frequentia _f_.
crust _n_ crusta _f_; (_bread_) frustum _nt_.

crusty adj (fig) stomachōsus.
crutch n baculum nt.
cry vt, vi clāmāre, clāmitāre; (weep) flēre; (infant) vāgīre; ~ **down** dētrectāre; ~ **out** exclāmāre, vōciferārī; ~ **out against** adclāmāre, reclāmāre; ~ **up** laudāre, vēnditāre ♦ n clāmor m, vōx f; (child's) vāgītus m; (of grief) plōrātus m.
cryptic adj arcānus.
crystal n crystallum nt ♦ adj crystallinus.
cub n catulus m.
cube n cubus m.
cubit n cubitum nt.
cuckoo n coccyx m.
cucumber n cucumis m.
cud n: **chew the** ~ rūminārī.
cudgel n fustis m ♦ vt verberāre.
cue n signum nt, indicium nt.
cuff n (blow) alapa f.
cuirass n lōrīca f.
culinary adj coquīnārius.
cull vt legere, carpere, dēlībāre.
culminate vi ad summum fastīgium venīre.
culmination n fastīgium nt.
culpability n culpa f, noxa f.
culpable adj nocēns.
culprit n reus m.
cultivate vt (land) colere, subigere; (mind) excolere; (interest) fovēre, studēre (dat).
cultivation n cultus m, cultūra f.
cultivator n cultor m, agricola m.
cultural adj hūmānior.
culture n hūmānitās f, bonae artēs fpl.
cultured adj doctus, litterātus.
culvert n cloāca f.
cumber vt impedīre, obesse (dat); (load) onerāre.
cumbersome adj molestus, gravis.
cumulative adj alius ex aliō; **be** ~ cumulārī.
cuneiform adj cuneātus.
cunning adj callidus, astūtus ♦ n ars f, astūtia f, calliditās f.
cunningly adv callidē, astūtē.
cup n pōculum nt; **drink the** ~ **of** (fig) exanclāre, exhaurīre; **in one's** ~**s** ēbrius, pōtus.
cupboard n armārium nt.
Cupid n Cupīdō m, Amor m.
cupidity n avāritia f.
cupola n tholus m.
cupping glass n cucurbita f.
cur n canis m.
curable adj sānābilis.
curative adj salūbris.
curator n custōs m.
curb vt frēnāre, īnfrēnāre; (fig) coercēre, cohibēre ♦ n frēnum nt.
curdle vt cōgere ♦ vi concrēscere.
curds n concrētum lac nt.
cure vt sānāre, medērī (dat) ♦ n remedium nt; (process) sānātiō f.
curio n dēliciae fpl.
curiosity n studium nt; (thing) mīrāculum nt.
curious adj (inquisitive) cūriōsus, cupidus;

(artistic) ēlābōrātus; (strange) mīrus, novus.
curiously adv cūriōsē; summā arte; mīrum in modum.
curl n (natural) cirrus m; (artificial) cincinnus m ♦ vt (hair) crispāre ♦ vi (smoke) volvī.
curling irons n calamistrī mpl.
curly adj crispus.
currency n (coin) monēta f; (use) ūsus m; **gain** ~ (rumour) percrēbrēscere.
current adj vulgātus, ūsitātus; (time) hīc ♦ n flūmen nt; **with the** ~ secundō flūmine; **against the** ~ adversō flūmine.
currently adv vulgō.
curriculum n īnstitūtiō f.
curry vt (favour) aucupārī.
curse n exsecrātiō f, maledictum nt; (formula) exsecrābile carmen nt; (fig) pestis f; ~**s** (interj) malum! ♦ vt exsecrārī, maledīcere (dat).
cursed adj exsecrātus, sacer; scelestus.
cursorily adv breviter, strictim.
cursory adj brevis.
curt adj brevis.
curtail vt minuere, contrahere.
curtailment n dēminūtiō f, contractiō f.
curtain n aulaeum nt ♦ vt vēlāre.
curule adj curūlis.
curve n flexus m, arcus m ♦ vt flectere, incurvāre, arcuāre.
cushion n pulvīnus m.
custodian n custōs m.
custody n custōdia f, tūtēla f; (prison) carcer m; **hold in** ~ custōdīre.
custom n mōs m, cōnsuētūdō f; (national) īnstitūtum nt; ~**s** pl portōria ntpl.
customarily adv plērumque, dē mōre, vulgō.
customary adj solitus, ūsitātus; (rite) sollemnis; **it is** ~ mōs est.
customer n emptor m.
customs officer n portitor m.
cut vt secāre, caedere, scindere; (corn) metere; (branch) amputāre; (acquaintance) āversārī; (hair) dētondēre; ~ **away** abscindere, resecāre; ~ **down** rescindere, caedere, succīdere; ~ **into** incīdere; ~ **off** vt abscīdere, praecīdere; (exclude) exclūdere; (intercept) interclūdere, intercipere; (head) abscindere; ~ **out** vt excīdere, exsecāre; (omit) ōmittere; ~ **out for** aptus ad, nātus ad (acc); ~ **round** circumcīdere; ~ **short** praecīdere; (speech) incīdere, interrumpere; ~ **through** intercīdere; ~ **up** vt concīdere ♦ n vulnus nt.
cutlass n gladius m.
cutlery n cultrī mpl.
cutter n sector m; (boat) lembus m.
cutthroat n sīcārius m.
cutting n (plant) propāgō f ♦ adj acūtus; (fig) acerbus, mordāx.
cuttlefish n sēpia f.
cyclamen n baccar nt.
cycle n orbis m.
cyclone n turbō f.

cylinder n cylindrus m.
cymbal n cymbalum nt.
cynic n (*PHILOS*) cynicus m.
cynical adj mordāx, acerbus.
cynically adv mordāciter, acerbē.
cynicism n acerbitās f.
cynosure n cynosūra f.
cypress n cypressus f.

D, d

dabble vi: ~ **in** gustāre, leviter attingere.
dactyl n dactylus m.
dactylic adj dactylicus.
dagger n sīca f, pugiō f.
daily adj diūrnus, cottīdiānus ♦ adv cottīdiē, in diēs.
daintily adv molliter, concinnē; fastīdiōsē.
daintiness n munditia f, concinnitās f; (*squeamish*) fastīdium nt.
dainty adj mundus, concinnus, mollis; fastīdiōsus ♦ npl: **dainties** cuppēdia ntpl.
dais n suggestus m.
daisy n bellis f.
dale n vallis f.
dalliance n lascīvia f.
dally vi lūdere; morārī.
dam n mōlēs f, agger m; (*animal*) māter f ♦ vt obstruere, exaggerāre.
damage n damnum nt, dētrīmentum nt, malum nt; (*inflicted*) iniūria f; (*law*) damnum nt; **assess ~s** lītem aestimāre ♦ vt laedere, nocēre (*dat*); (*by evidence*) laedere; (*reputation*) violāre.
damageable adj fragilis.
dame n mātrōna f, domina f.
damn vt damnāre, exsecrārī.
damnable adj dētestābilis, improbus.
damnably adv improbē.
damnation n malum nt.
damp adj ūmidus ♦ n ūmor m ♦ vt madefacere; (*enthusiasm*) restinguere, dēmittere.
damsel n puella f, virgō f.
damson n Damascēnum nt.
dance vi saltāre ♦ n saltātiō f; (*religious*) tripudium nt.
dancer n saltātor m, saltātrīx f.
dandruff n porrīgō f.
dandy n dēlicātus m.
danger n perīculum nt, discrīmen nt.
dangerous adj perīculōsus, dubius; (*in attack*) īnfestus.
dangerously adv perīculōsē.
dangle vt suspendere ♦ vi pendēre.

dank adj ūmidus.
dapper adj concinnus, nitidus.
dapple vt variāre, distinguere.
dappled adj maculōsus, distinctus.
dare vt audēre; (*challenge*) prōvocāre; **I ~ say** haud sciō an.
daring n audācia f ♦ adj audāx.
daringly adv audācter.
dark adj obscūrus, opācus; (*colour*) fuscus, āter; (*fig*) obscūrus; **it is getting ~** advesperāscit; **keep ~** silēre ♦ n tenebrae fpl; (*mist*) cālīgō f; **keep in the ~** cēlāre.
darken vt obscūrāre, occaecāre.
darkish adj subobscūrus.
darkling adj obscūrus.
darkness n tenebrae fpl; (*mist*) cālīgō f.
darksome adj obscūrus.
darling adj cārus, dīlēctus ♦ n dēliciae fpl, voluptās f.
darn vt resarcīre.
darnel n lolium nt.
dart n tēlum nt; iaculum nt ♦ vi ēmicāre, sē conicere ♦ vt iaculārī, iacere.
dash vt adflīgere; (*hope*) frangere; **~ against** illīdere, incutere; **~ down** dēturbāre; **~ out** ēlīdere; **~ to pieces** discutere; **~ to the ground** prōsternere ♦ vi currere, sē incitāre, ruere ♦ n impetus m; (*quality*) ferōcia f.
dashing adj ferōx, animōsus.
dastardly adj ignāvus.
date n (*fruit*) palmula f; (*time*) tempus nt, diēs m; **out of ~** obsolētus; **become out of ~** exolēscere; **to ~** adhūc; **be up to ~** praesentī mōre ūtī ♦ vt (*letter*) diem adscrībere; (*past event*) repetere ♦ vi initium capere.
dative n datīvus m.
daub vt inlinere.
daughter n fīlia f; (*little*) fīliola f.
daughter-in-law n nurus f.
daunt vt terrēre, perterrēre.
dauntless adj impavidus, intrepidus.
dauntlessly adv impavidē, intrepidē.
dawdle vi cessāre, cunctārī.
dawdler n cunctātor m.
dawn n aurōra f, dīlūculum nt; (*fig*) orīgō f; prima lux f; **at ~** prīmā lūce ♦ vi dīlūcēscere; **day ~s** diēs illūcēscit; **it ~s upon me** mente concipiō.
day n diēs m/f; (*period*) aetās f; **~ about** alternīs diēbus; **~ by ~** in diēs; cotīdiē; **by ~** adj diūrnus ♦ adv interdiū; **during the ~** interdiū; **every ~** cotīdiē; **from ~ to ~** in diēs, diem dē diē; **late in the ~** multō diē; **next ~** postrīdiē; **one ~/some ~** ōlim; **the ~ after** adv postrīdiē ♦ conj postrīdiē quam; **the ~ after tomorrow** perendiē; **the ~ before** adv prīdiē ♦ conj prīdiē quam; **the ~ before yesterday** nūdius tertius; **the present ~** haec aetās; **time of ~** hōra; **twice a ~** bis (in) diē; **~s of old** praeteritum tempus; **~s to come** posterītās; **better ~s** rēs prosperae; **evil ~s** rēs adversae; **three ~s** trīduum nt; **two ~s** biduum nt; **win**

the ~ vincere.
daybook n adversāria ntpl.
daybreak n aurōra f, prīma lūx f.
daylight n diēs m; **(become)** ~ illūcēscere.
daystar n lūcifer m.
daytime n diēs m; **in the** ~ interdiū.
daze vt obstupefacere ♦ n stupor m.
dazzle vt praestringere.
dazzling adj splendidus, nitēns.
deacon n diāconus m.
deaconess n diāconissa f.
dead adj mortuus; (in battle) occīsus; (LIT)
  frīgidus; (place) iners, sōlitarius; (senses)
  hebes; ~ **of night** nox intempesta f; **be** ~ **to**
  nōn sentīre; **in** ~ **earnest** sēriō ac vērō; **rise
  from the** ~ revīvīscere ♦ adv prōrsus,
  omnīnō.
dead beat adj cōnfectus.
dead body n cadāver m.
dead calm n malacia f.
dead certainty n rēs certissima.
deaden vt (senses) hebetāre, obtundere; (pain)
  restinguere.
deadlock n incitae fpl; **reach a** ~ ad incitās
  redigī.
dead loss n mera iactūra.
deadly adj fūnestus, exitiōsus, exitiābilis;
  (enmity) implācābilis; (pain) acerbissimus.
dead weight n mōlēs f.
deaf adj surdus; **become** ~ obsurdēscere; **be** ~
  to nōn audīre, obdūrēscere contrā.
deafen vt (with noise) obtundere.
deafness n surditās f.
deal n (amount) cōpia f; **a good** ~ aliquantum nt,
  bona pars f; (wood) abiēs f ♦ adj abiēgnus ♦ vt
  (blow) dare, īnflīgere; (share) dīvidere,
  partīrī ♦ vi agere, negōtiārī; ~ **with** vt fus
  (person) agere cum (abl); (matter) tractāre.
dealer n (wholesale) negōtiātor m, mercātor m;
  (retail) caupō m.
dealings n commercium nt, negōtium nt, rēs f.
dean n decānus m.
dear adj (love) cārus, grātus; (cost) cārus,
  pretiōsus; **my** ~ **Quintus** mī Quīnte; (beginning
  of letter from Marcus) Marcus
  Quīntō salūtem; ~ **me!** (sorrow) hei!;
  (surprise) ehem!; **buy** ~ male emere; **sell** ~
  bene vēndere.
dearly adv (love) valdē, ārdenter; (value)
  magnī.
dearness n cāritās f.
dearth n inopia f, pēnūria f.
death n mors f; (natural) obitus m; (violent) nex
  f, interitus m; **condemn to** ~ capitis damnāre;
  put to ~ interficere; **give the** ~ **blow to**
  interimere.
deathbed n: **on one's** ~ moriēns, moribundus.
deathless adj immortālis.
deathly adj pallidus.
debar vt prohibēre, exclūdere.
debase vt dēprāvāre, corrumpere; (coin)
  adulterāre; (self) prōsternere, dēmittere.
debasement n dēdecus nt; (coin) adulterium

nt.
debatable adj ambiguus, dubius.
debate vt disputāre, disceptāre ♦ n
  contrōversia f, disceptātiō f, altercātiō f.
debater n disputātor m.
debauch vt corrumpere, pellicere ♦ n
  cōmissātiō f.
debauched adj perditus, prāvus.
debauchee n cōmissātor m.
debaucher n corruptor m.
debauchery n luxuria f, stuprum nt.
debilitate vt dēbilitāre.
debility n īnfirmitās f.
debit n expēnsum nt ♦ vt in expēnsum referre.
debonair adj urbānus, cōmis.
debouch vi exīre.
debris n rūdus nt.
debt n aes aliēnum nt; (booked) nōmen nt; (fig)
  dēbitum nt; **be in** ~ in aere aliēnō esse; **pay off**
  ~ aes aliēnum persolvere; **run up** ~ aes
  aliēnum contrahere; **collect** ~s nōmina
  exigere; **abolition of** ~s novae tabulae fpl.
debtor n dēbitor m.
decade n decem annī mpl.
decadence n occāsus m.
decadent adj dēgener, dēterior.
decamp vi (MIL) castra movēre; (fig)
  discēdere, aufugere.
decant vt dēfundere, diffundere.
decanter n lagoena f.
decapitate vt dētruncāre.
decay vi dīlābī, perīre, putrēscere; (fig)
  tābēscere, senēscere ♦ n ruīna f, lāpsus m;
  (fig) occāsus m, dēfectiō f.
deceased adj mortuus.
deceit n fraus f, fallācia f, dolus m.
deceitful adj fallāx, fraudulentus, dolōsus.
deceitfully adv fallāciter, dolōsē.
deceive vt dēcipere, fallere, circumvenīre,
  fraudāre.
deceiver n fraudātor m.
December n mēnsis December m; **of** ~
  December.
decemvir n decemvir m; **of the** ~s
  decemvirālis.
decemvirate n decemvirātus m.
decency n honestum nt, decōrum nt, pudor m.
decent adj honestus, pudēns.
decently adv honestē, pudenter.
deception n fraus f, fallācia f.
deceptive adj fallāx, fraudulentus.
decide vt, vi (dispute) dīiūdicāre, dēcernere,
  dīrimere; ~ **to do** statuere, cōnstituere
  (infin); **I have** ~**d** mihi certum est; ~ **the issue**
  dēcernere.
decided adj certus, firmus.
decidedly adv certē, plānē.
deciduous adj cadūcus.
decimate vt decimum quemque occīdere.
decipher vt expedīre, ēnōdāre.
decision n (of judge) iūdicium nt; (of council)
  dēcrētum nt; (of senate) auctōritās f; (of
  referee) arbitrium nt; (personal) sententia f;

(quality) cōnstantia *f.*
decisive *adj* certus; ~ **moment** discrīmen *nt.*
decisively *adv* sine dubiō.
deck *vt* ōrnāre, exōrnāre ♦ *n*
(ship) pōns *m*; **with a ~** cōnstrātus.
decked *adj* ōrnātus; *(ship)* cōnstrātus.
declaim *vt, vi* dēclāmāre, prōnūntiāre.
declamation *n* dēclāmātiō *f.*
declamatory *adj* dēclāmātōrius.
declaration *n* adfirmātiō *f*, adsevērātiō *f*;
(formal) prōfessiō *f*; *(of war)* dēnūntiātiō *f.*
declare *vt* affirmāre, adsevērāre; *(secret)*
aperīre, expōnere; *(proclamation)*
dēnūntiāre, ēdīcere; *(property in census)*
dēdicāre; *(war)* indīcere.
declension *n* dēclīnātiō *f.*
declination *n* dēclīnātiō *f.*
decline *n (slope)* dēclīve *nt*, dēiectus *m*; *(of age)*
senium *nt*; *(of power)* dēfectiō *f*; *(of nation)*
occāsus *m* ♦ *vi* inclīnāre, occidere; *(fig)*
ruere, dēlābī, dēgenerāre ♦ *vt* dētrectāre,
recūsare; *(GRAM)* dēclīnāre.
decode *vt* expedīre, ēnōdāre.
decompose *vt* dissolvere ♦ *vi* putrēscere.
decomposed *adj* putridus.
decomposition *n* dissolūtiō *f.*
decorate *vt* ōrnāre, decorāre.
decoration *n* ōrnāmentum *nt*; *(medal)* īnsigne
nt.
decorous *adj* pudēns, modestus, decōrus.
decorously *adv* pudenter, modestē.
decorum *n* pudor *m*, honestum *nt.*
decoy *n* illecebra *f* ♦ *vt* adlicere, inescāre.
decrease *n* dēminūtiō *f*, dēcessiō *f* ♦ *vt*
dēminuere, extenuāre ♦ *vi* dēcrēscere.
decree *n (of magistrate)* dēcrētum *nt*, ēdictum
nt; *(of senate)* cōnsultum *nt*, auctōritās *f*; *(of
people)* scītum *nt* ♦ *vt* ēdīcere, dēcernere;
(people) scīscere, iubēre; **the senate ~s**
placet senātuī.
decrepit *adj* īnfirmus, dēbilis, dēcrepitus.
decrepitude *n* īnfirmitās *f*, dēbilitās *f.*
decry *vt* obtrectāre, reprehendere.
decurion *n* decuriō *m.*
dedicate *vt* dēdicāre, cōnsecrāre; *(life)*
dēvovēre.
dedication *n* dēdicātiō *f*; dēvōtiō *f.*
dedicatory *adj* commendātīcius.
deduce *vt* colligere, conclūdere.
deduct *vt* dēmere, dētrahere.
deduction *n (inference)* conclūsiō *f*,
cōnsequēns *nt*; *(subtraction)* dēductiō *f*,
dēminūtiō *f.*
deed *n*, factum *nt*, facinus *nt*; gestum *nt*; *(legal)*
tabulae *fpl*; **~s** *pl* rēs gestae *fpl.*
deem *vt* dūcere, cēnsēre, habēre.
deep *adj* altus, profundus; *(discussion)*
abstrūsus; *(sleep)* artus; *(sound)* gravis;
(width) lātus; **three ~** *(MIL)* ternī in
lātitūdinem ♦ *n* altum *nt.*
deepen *vt* dēfodere, altiōrem reddere; *(fig)*
augēre ♦ *vi* altiōrem fierī; *(fig)* crēscere.
deepest *adj* īmus.

deeply *adv* altē, graviter; *(inside)* penitus; **very**
~ valdē, vehementer.
deep-seated *adj (fig)* inveterātus.
deer *n* cervus *m*, cerva *f*; *(fallow)* dāma *f.*
deface *vt* dēfōrmāre, foedāre.
defaced *adj* dēfōrmis.
defacement *n* dēfōrmitās *f.*
defalcation *n* peculātus *m.*
defamation *n* calumnia *f*, opprobrium *nt.*
defamatory *adj* contumēliōsus, probrōsus.
defame *vt* īnfāmāre, obtrectāre, calumniārī.
default *vi* dēesse; *(money)* nōn solvere ♦ *n*
dēfectiō *f*, culpa *f*; **let judgment go by ~**
vadimōnium dēserere, nōn respondēre.
defaulter *n* reus *m.*
defeat *vt* vincere, superāre; *(completely)*
dēvincere; *(plan)* frustrārī, disicere ♦ *n*
clādēs *f*; *(at election)* repulsa *f*, offēnsiō *f*; *(of
plan)* frustrātiō *f.*
defeatism *n* patientia *f.*
defeatist *n* imbellis *m.*
defect *n* vitium *nt.*
defection *n* dēfectiō *f*, sēditiō *f.*
defective *adj* mancus, vitiōsus.
defence *n* praesidium *nt*, tūtēla *f*; patrōcinium
nt; *(speech)* dēfēnsiō *f*; **speak in ~** dēfendere.
defenceless *adj* inermis, indēfēnsus; **leave ~**
nūdāre.
defences *npl* mūnīmenta *ntpl*, mūnītiōnēs *fpl.*
defend *vt* dēfendere, tuērī, custōdīre.
defendant *n* reus *m.*
defender *n* dēfēnsor *m*, prōpugnātor *m*; *(law)*
patrōnus *m.*
defensible *adj* iūstus.
defensive *adj* dēfēnsiōnis causā; **be on the ~**
sē dēfendere.
defensively *adv* dēfendendō.
defer *vt* differre, prōlātāre ♦ *vi* mōrem gerere
(dat); **I ~ to you in this** hōc tibī tribuō.
deference *n* obsequium *nt*, observantia *f*;
show ~ to observāre, īnservīre *(dat).*
deferential *adj* observāns, officiōsus.
deferment *n* dīlātiō *f*, prōlātiō *f.*
defiance *n* ferōcia *f*, minae *fpl.*
defiant *adj* ferōx, mināx.
defiantly *adv* ferōciter, mināciter.
deficiency *n* vitium *nt*; *(lack)* pēnūria *f*, inopia
f.
deficient *adj* vitiōsus, inops; **be ~** dēesse,
dēficere.
deficit *n* lacūna *f.*
defile *n* faucēs *fpl*, angustiae *fpl* ♦ *vt* inquināre,
contāmināre.
defilement *n* sordēs *f*, foedītās *f.*
define *vt (limits)* fīnīre, dēfīnīre, termināre;
(meaning) explicāre.
definite *adj* certus, dēfīnītus.
definitely *adv* dēfīnītē; prōrsus.
definition *n* dēfīnītiō *f*, explicātiō *f.*
definitive *adj* dēfīnītīvus.
deflate *vt* laxāre.
deflect *vt* dēdūcere, dēclīnāre ♦ *vi* dēflectere,
dēgredī.

deflection n dēclīnātiō f, flexus m.
deform vt dēfōrmāre.
deformed adj dēfōrmis, distortus.
deformity n dēfōrmitās f, prāvitās f.
defraud vt fraudāre, dēfraudāre.
defrauder n fraudātor m.
defray vt solvere, suppeditāre.
deft adj habilis.
deftly adv habiliter.
defunct adj mortuus.
defy vt contemnere, spernere, adversārī (dat); (challenge) prōvocāre, lacessere.
degeneracy n dēprāvātiō f.
degenerate adj dēgener ♦ vi dēgenerāre, dēscīscere.
degradation n īnfāmia f, ignōminia f, nota f.
degrade vt notāre, abicere; (from office) movēre.
degrading adj turpis, indignus.
degree n gradus; (social) locus m; **in some ~** aliquā ex parte; **by ~s** gradātim, sēnsim.
deification n apotheōsis f.
deified adj (emperor) dīvus.
deify vt cōnsecrāre, inter deōs referre.
deign vi dignārī.
deity n deus m.
dejected adj adflīctus, dēmissus.
dejectedly adv animō dēmissō.
dejection n maestitia f.
delay vt dēmorārī, dētinēre, retardāre ♦ vi cunctārī, cessāre ♦ n mora f, cunctātiō f.
delayer n morātor m, cunctātor m.
delectable adj iūcundus, amoenus.
delegate vt lēgāre, mandāre, committere ♦ n lēgātus m.
delegation n lēgātiō f, lēgātī mpl.
delete vt dēlēre.
deleterious adj perniciōsus, noxius.
deletion n (writing) litūra f.
deliberate vi dēlīberāre, cōnsulere ♦ adj (act) cōnsīderātus; (intention) certus; (manner) cōnsīderātus; (speech) lentus.
deliberately adv dē industriā.
deliberation n dēlīberātiō f.
deliberative adj dēlīberātīvus.
delicacy n (judgment) subtīlitās f, ēlegantia f; (manners) mollitia f, luxus m; (health) valētūdō f; (food) cuppēdia ntpl.
delicate adj mollis; (health) īnfirmus; (shape) gracilis; (feelings) hūmānus.
delicately adv molliter; hūmānē.
delicious adj suāvis, lautus.
delight n voluptās f, gaudium nt, dēlectātiō f ♦ vt dēlectāre, oblectāre, iuvāre ♦ vi gaudēre, dēlectārī.
delightful adj iūcundus, dulcis, festīvus; (scenery) amoenus.
delightfully adv iūcundē, suāviter.
delimitation n dēfīnītiō f.
delineate vt dēscrībere, dēpingere.
delineation n dēscrīptiō f.
delinquency n culpa f, dēlictum nt, noxa f.
delinquent n nocēns m/f, reus m.

delirious adj dēlīrus, āmēns, furiōsus; **be ~** furere, dēlīrāre.
delirium n furor m, āmentia f.
deliver vt (from) līberāre, exsolvere, ēripere; (blow) intendere; (message) referre; (speech) habēre; **~ to** dēferre, trādere, dare; **~ up** dēdere, trādere; **be ~ed of** parere.
deliverance n līberātiō f.
deliverer n līberātor m.
delivery n (of things due) trāditiō f; (of speech) āctiō f, prōnūntiātiō f; (of child) partus m.
dell n convallis f.
Delphi n Delphī mpl.
delude vt dēcipere, frustrārī, dēlūdere.
deluge n ēluviō f ♦ vt inundāre.
delusion n error m, fraus f.
delusive adj fallāx, inānis.
delve vt fodere.
demagogue n plēbicola m.
demand vt poscere, postulāre, imperāre; (urgently) flāgitāre, poscere; (thing due) exigere; (answer) quaerere; **~ back** repetere ♦ n postulātiō f, postulātum nt.
demarcation n līmes m.
demean vt (self) dēmittere.
demeanour n gestus m, mōs m, habitus m.
demented adj dēmēns, furiōsus.
demerit n culpa f, vitium nt.
demesne n fundus m.
demigod n hērōs m.
demise n obitus m ♦ vt lēgāre.
democracy n cīvitās populāris f.
democrat n homō populāris m/f.
democratic adj populāris.
demolish vt dēmōlīrī, dīruere, dēstruere; (argument) discutere.
demolition n ruīna f, ēversiō f.
demon n daemōn m.
demonstrate vt (show) mōnstrāre, ostendere, indicāre; (prove) dēmōnstrāre.
demonstration n exemplum nt; (proof) dēmōnstrātiō f.
demonstrative adj (manner) vehemēns; (RHET) dēmōnstrātīvus.
demoralization n corruptiō f, dēprāvātiō f.
demoralize vt corrumpere, dēprāvāre, labefactāre.
demote vt locō movēre.
demur vi gravārī, recūsāre ♦ n mora f, dubitātiō f.
demure adj modestus, verēcundus.
demurely adv modestē, verēcundē.
demureness n modestia f, verēcundia f, pudor m.
demurrer n (law) exceptiō f.
den n latibulum nt, latebra f; (of vice) lustrum nt.
denarius n dēnārius m.
denial n īnfitiātiō f, negātiō f.
denigrate vt obtrectāre, calumniārī.
denizen n incola m/f.
denominate vt nōmināre, appellāre.
denomination n nōmen nt; (religious) secta f.

denote *vt* notāre, significāre.
denouement *n* exitus *m*.
denounce *vt* dēferre, incūsāre.
denouncer *n* dēlātor *m*.
dense *adj* dēnsus; (*crowd*) frequēns; (*person*) stolidus.
density *n* crassitūdō *f*; (*crowd*) frequentia *f*.
dent *n* nota *f*.
dentate *adj* dentātus.
denture *n* dentēs *mpl*.
denudation *n* spoliātiō *f*.
denude *vt* spoliāre, nūdāre.
denunciation *n* (*report*) indicium *nt*, dēlātiō *f*; (*threat*) minae *fpl*.
deny *vt* īnfitiārī, īnfitiās īre, negāre, abnuere; (*on oath*) abiūrāre; ~ **oneself** genium dēfraudāre.
depart *vi* discēdere (*abl*), abīre, exīre, ēgredī.
department *n* (*district*) regiō *f*, pars *f*; (*duty*) prōvincia *f*, mūnus *nt*.
departure *n* discessus *m*, abitus *m*, dīgressus *m*, exitus *m*; (*change*) mūtātiō *f*; (*death*) obitus *m*.
depend *vi* pendēre; (*be dependent*) pendēre ex (*abl*), nītī (*abl*); (*rely*) fīdere, cōnfīdere; ~**ing on** frētus (*abl*).
dependable *adj* fīdus.
dependant *n* cliēns *m/f*.
dependence *n* clientēla *f*; (*reliance*) fīdūcia *f*.
dependency *n* prōvincia *f*.
dependent *adj* subiectus, obnoxius.
depict *vt* dēscrībere, dēpingere; (*to the life*) expingere.
deplete *vt* dēminuere.
depletion *n* dēminūtiō *f*.
deplorable *adj* turpis, nefandus, pessimus.
deplorably *adv* turpiter, pessimē, miserē.
deplore *vt* dēplōrāre, dēfiēre, conquerī.
deploy *vt* explicāre; instruere, dispōnere.
depopulate *vt* vastāre, nūdāre.
depopulation *n* vastātiō *f*, sōlitūdō *f*.
deport *vt* (*banish*) dēportāre; (*self*) gerere.
deportation *n* exsilium *nt*.
deportment *n* gestus *m*, habitus *m*.
depose *vt* dēmovēre, dēpellere; (*evidence*) testārī.
deposit *n* fīdūcia *f*, dēpositum *nt* ♦ *vt* dēpōnere, mandāre.
depositary *n* sequester *m*.
deposition *n* (*law*) testimōnium *nt*, indicium *nt*.
depository *n* apothēca *f*.
depot *n* (*for arms*) armāmentārium *nt*; (*for trade*) emporium *nt*.
deprave *vt* dēprāvāre, corrumpere.
depraved *adj* prāvus.
depravity *n* dēprāvātiō *f*, turpitūdō *f*.
deprecate *vt* abōminārī, dēprecārī.
deprecation *n* dēprecātiō *f*.
depreciate *vt* obtrectāre, dētrectāre.
depreciation *n* obtrectātiō *f*; (*price*) vīlitās *f*.
depredation *n* praedātiō *f*, dīreptiō *f*.
depress *vt* dēprimere; (*mind*) adflīgere,

frangere; **be ~ed** iacēre, animum dēspondēre.
depressing *adj* maestus, tristis.
depression *n* (*place*) cavum *nt*; (*mind*) tristitia *f*, sollicitūdō *f*.
deprivation *n* prīvātiō *f*, spoliātiō *f*.
deprive *vt* prīvāre, spoliāre.
depth *n* altitūdō *f*; (*place*) profundum *nt*, gurges *m*.
deputation *n* lēgātiō *f*, lēgātī *mpl*.
depute *vt* lēgāre, mandāre.
deputy *n* lēgātus *m*; (*substitute*) vicārius *m*.
derange *vt* conturbāre.
deranged *adj* īnsānus, mente captus.
derangement *n* perturbātiō *f*; (*mind*) īnsānia *f*, dēmentia *f*.
derelict *adj* dēsertus.
dereliction *n* (*of duty*) neglegentia *f*.
deride *vt* dērīdēre, inlūdere.
derision *n* rīsus *m*, irrīsiō *f*.
derisive *adj* mordāx.
derivation *n* orīgō *f*.
derive *vt* dūcere, trahere; (*advantage*) capere, parāre; (*pleasure*) dēcerpere, percipere; **be ~d** dēfluere.
derogate *vi* dērogāre, dētrahere; ~ **from** imminuere, obtrectāre.
derogation *n* imminūtiō *f*, obtrectātiō *f*.
derogatory *adj* indignus; ~ **remarks** obtrectātiō *f*.
derrick *n* trochlea *f*.
descant *vt* disserere ♦ *n* cantus *m*.
descend *vi* dēscendere; (*water*) dēlābī; (*from heaven*) dēlābī; (*by inheritance*) pervenīre, prōdī; (*morally*) dēlābī, sē dēmittere; **be ~ed from** orīrī ex (*abl*).
descendant *n* prōgeniēs *f*; ~**s** *pl* minōrēs *mpl*, posterī *mpl*.
descent *n* dēscensus *m*; (*slope*) clīvus *m*, dēiectus *m*; (*birth*) genus *nt*; (*hostile*) dēcursus *m*, incursiō *f*; **make a ~ upon** inrumpere in (*acc*), incursāre in (*acc*).
describe *vt* dēscrībere; (*tell*) nārrāre; (*portray*) dēpingere, exprimere.
description *n* dēscrīptiō *f*; (*tale*) nārrātiō *f*; (*kind*) genus *nt*.
descry *vt* cernere, cōnspicere, prōspectāre.
desecrate *vt* prōfānāre, exaugurāre.
desecration *n* exaugurātiō *f*, violātiō *f*.
desert *vt* dēserere, dērelinquere, dēstituere ♦ *vi* dēscīscere, dēficere ♦ *adj* dēsertus, sōlitārius ♦ *n* (*place*) sōlitūdō *f*, loca dēserta *ntpl*; (*merit*) meritum *nt*.
deserted *adj* dēsertus.
deserter *n* dēsertor *m*; (MIL) trānsfuga *m*.
desertion *n* dēfectiō *f*, trānsfugium *nt*.
deserve *vt* merērī; dignus esse quī (+ *subj*); ~ **well of** bene merērī dē (*abl*).
deserved *adj* meritus.
deservedly *adv* meritō.
deserving *adj* dignus.
desiccate *vt* siccāre.
design *n* (*drawing*) adumbrātiō *f*; (*plan*)

cōnsilium *nt*, prōpositum *nt*; **by ~** cōnsultō ♦
vt adumbrāre; **in animō habēre.**
designate *vt* dēsignāre, mōnstrāre; (*as heir*)
scrībere; (*as official*) dēsignāre ♦ *adj*
dēsignātus.
designation *n* nōmen *nt*, titulus *m*.
designedly *adv* dē industriā, cōnsultō.
designer *n* auctor *m*, inventor *m*.
designing *adj* vafer, dolōsus.
desirable *adj* optābilis, expetendus, grātus.
desire *n* cupīditās *f*; studium *nt*; (*uncontrolled*)
libīdō *f*; (*natural*) adpetītiō *f* ♦ *vt* cupere;
(*much*) exoptāre, expetere; (*command*)
iubēre.
desirous *adj* cupidus, avidus, studiōsus.
desist *vi* dēsistere.
desk *n* scrīnium *nt*.
desolate *adj* dēsertus, sōlitārius; (*place*)
vastus ♦ *vt* vastāre.
desolation *n* sōlitūdō *f*, vastitās *f*; (*process*)
vastātiō *f*.
despair *vi* dēspērāre dē (*abl*), animum
dēspondēre ♦ *n* dēspērātiō *f*.
despairingly *adv* dēspēranter.
despatch *see* **dispatch.**
desperado *n* homō dēspērātus *m*.
desperate *adj* (*hopeless*) dēspērātus; (*wicked*)
perditus; (*dangerous*) perīculōsus.
desperately *adv* dēspēranter.
desperation *n* dēspērātiō *f*.
despicable *adj* dēspectus, abiectus, turpis.
despicably *adv* turpiter.
despise *vt* contemnere, dēspicere, spernere.
despiser *n* contemptor *m*.
despite *n* malevolentia *f*, odium *nt*.
despoil *vt* spoliāre, nūdāre.
despoiler *n* spoliātor *m*, praedātor *m*.
despond *vi* animum dēspondēre, dēspērāre.
despondency *n* dēspērātiō *f*.
despondent *adj* abiectus, adflīctus, dēmissus;
be ~ animum dēspondēre.
despondently *adv* animō dēmissō.
despot *n* dominus *m*, rēx *m*.
despotic *adj* imperiōsus, superbus.
despotically *adv* superbē.
despotism *n* dominātiō *f*, superbia *f*, rēgnum
nt.
dessert *n* secunda mēnsa *f*.
destination *n* fīnis *m*.
destine *vt* dēstināre, dēsignāre; **~d to be**
futūrus.
destiny *n* fātum *nt*; **of ~** fātālis.
destitute *adj* inops, pauper, prīvātus; **~ of**
expers (*gen*).
destitution *n* inopia *f*, egestās *f*.
destroy *vt* dēlēre, ēvertere, dīrimere,
perdere.
destroyer *n* ēversor *m*.
destructible *adj* fragilis.
destruction *n* exitium *nt*, ēversiō *f*, excidium
nt.
destructive *adj* exitiābilis, perniciōsus.
destructively *adv* perniciōsē.

desuetude *n* dēsuētūdō *f*.
desultorily *adv* carptim.
desultory *adj* varius, incōnstāns.
detach *vt* abiungere, sēiungere, āmovēre,
sēparāre.
detachment *n* (*MIL*) manus *f*, cohors *f*; (*mind*)
integer animus *m*, līber animus.
detail *n*: **~s** *pl* singula *ntpl*; **in ~** singillātim ♦ *vt*
exsequī.
detain *vt* dēmorārī, dētinēre, distinēre,
morārī.
detect *vt* dēprehendere, patefacere.
detection *n* dēprehēnsiō *f*.
detective *n* inquīsītor *m*.
detention *n* retentiō *f*; (*prison*) vincula *ntpl*.
deter *vt* dēterrēre, absterrēre, impedīre.
deteriorate *vi* dēgenerāre.
deterioration *n* dēprāvātiō *f*, lāpsus *m*.
determinate *adj* certus, fīnītus.
determination *n* obstinātiō *f*, cōnstantia *f*;
(*intention*) prōpositum *nt*, sententia *f*.
determine *vt* (*fix*) fīnīre; (*decide*) statuere,
cōnstituere.
determined *adj* obstinātus; (*thing*) certus; **I
am ~ to** mihī certum est (*infin*).
determinedly *adv* cōnstanter.
deterrent *n*: **act as a ~ to** dēterrēre.
detest *vt* ōdisse, dētestārī.
detestable *adj* dētestābilis, odiōsus.
detestation *n* odium *nt*, invidia *f*.
dethrone *vt* rēgnō dēpellere.
detour *n* circuitus *m*; **make a ~** iter flectere;
(*MIL*) agmen circumdūcere.
detract *vi*: **~ from** dērogāre, dētrahere.
detraction *n* obtrectātiō *f*.
detractor *n* obtrectātor *m*, invidus *m*.
detriment *n* damnum *nt*, dētrīmentum *nt*.
detrimental *adj* damnōsus; **be ~ to** dētrīmentō
esse (*dat*).
devastate *vt* vastāre, populārī.
devastation *n* vastātiō *f*, populātiō *f*; (*state*)
vastitās *f*.
develop *vt* ēvolvere, explicāre; (*person*)
ēducāre, alere ♦ *vi* crēscere; **~ into** ēvādere
in (*acc*).
development *n* explicātiō *f*; (*of men*) ēducātiō
f; (*of resources*) cultus *m*; (*of events*) exitus *m*.
deviate *vi* dēcēdere dē viā, aberrāre,
dēclīnāre; (*speech*) dēgredī.
deviation *n* dēclīnātiō *f*; (*from truth*) error *m*;
(*in speech*) dīgressus *m*.
device *n* (*plan*) cōnsilium *nt*; (*machine*)
māchina *f*; (*emblem*) īnsigne *nt*.
devil *n* diabolus *m*; **go to the ~** abī in malam
crucem!; **talk of the ~** lupus in fābulā!
devilish *adj* scelestus, impius.
devil-may-care *adj* praeceps, lascīvus.
devilment *n* malitia *f*.
devilry *n* magicae artēs *fpl*.
devious *adj* dēvius, errābundus.
devise *vt* excōgitāre, commentārī, fingere.
devoid *adj* vacuus, expers; **be ~ of** carēre (*abl*).
devolve *vi* obtingere, obvenīre ♦ *vt* dēferre,

committere.
devote vt dēdicāre; (*attention*) dēdere,
trādere; (*life*) dēvovēre.
devoted adj dēditus, studiōsus; (*victim*)
dēvōtus, sacer; **be ~ to** studēre (*dat*),
incumbere (*dat*).
devotee n cultor m.
devotion n amor m, studium nt; rēligiō f.
devour vt dēvorāre, cōnsūmere; (*fig*) haurīre.
devout adj pius, rēligiōsus.
devoutly adv piē, rēligiōsē.
dew n rōs m.
dewy adj rōscidus.
dexterity n ars f, sollertia f.
dexterous adj sollers, habilis.
dexterously adv sollerter, habiliter.
diabolical adj scelestus, nefārius.
diadem n diadēma nt.
diagnose vt discernere, diiūdicāre.
diagnosis n iūdicium nt.
diagonal adj oblīquus.
diagram n fōrma f.
dial n sōlārium nt.
dialect n dialectus f, sermō m.
dialectic n ars disserendī f, dialecticē f ♦ adj
dialecticus.
dialectician n dialecticus m.
dialogue n dialogus m, colloquium nt.
diameter n diametros f.
diamond n adamās m.
diaphanous adj perlūcidus.
diaphragm n praecordia ntpl.
diary n ephēmeris f.
diatribe n convīcium nt.
dice n tālus m, tessera f; **game of ~** ālea f.
dictate vt dictāre ♦ n praeceptum nt; **~s of
nature** nātūrae iūdicia ntpl.
dictation n dictāta ntpl; (*fig*) arbitrium nt.
dictator n dictātor m; **~'s** dictātōrius.
dictatorial adj imperiōsus, superbus.
dictatorship n dictātūra f.
diction n (*enunciation*) ēlocūtiō f; (*words*) ōrātiō
f.
dictionary n verbōrum thēsaurus m.
die n signum nt; **the ~ is cast** iacta ālea est ♦ vi
morī, perīre, obīre; (*in battle*) cadere,
occumbere; **~ off** dēmorī; **~ out** ēmorī; **be
dying to** exoptāre.
diet n (*food*) diaeta f; (*meeting*) conventus m.
differ vi differe, discrepāre, dissentīre.
difference n discrepantia f, dissimilitūdō f; (*of
opinion*) dissēnsiō f; **there is a ~** interest.
different adj dīversus, varius, dissimilis; **~
from** alius ... ac; **in ~ directions** dīversī; **they
say ~ things** alius aliud dīcit.
differentiate vt discernere.
differently adv dīversē, variē, alius aliter; **~
from** aliter ... ac.
difficult adj difficilis, arduus; **very ~**
perdifficilis, perarduus.
difficulty n difficultās f, labor m, negōtium nt;
with ~ difficulter, aegrē, vix; **be in ~**
labōrāre.

diffidence n diffīdentia f; (*shyness*) pudor m;
with ~ modestē.
diffident adj diffīdēns; (*shy*) modestus,
verēcundus.
diffidently adv modestē.
diffuse vt diffundere, dispergere; **be ~d**
diffluere ♦ adj fūsus, diffūsus, cōpiōsus.
diffusely adv diffūsē, cōpiōsē.
diffuseness n cōpia f.
dig vt fodere; dūcere; (*nudge*) fodicāre; **~ up** vt
effodere, ēruere.
digest vt coquere, concoquere ♦ n
summārium nt.
digestion n concoctiō f; **with a bad ~** crūdus.
digger n fossor m.
dignified adj gravis, augustus.
dignify vt honōrāre, honestāre.
dignity n gravitās f, māiestās f, amplitūdō f.
digress vi dēvertere, dīgredī, dēclīnāre.
digression n dēclīnātiō f, dīgressus m.
dike n (*ditch*) fossa f; (*mound*) agger m.
dilapidated adj ruīnōsus.
dilapidation n ruīna f.
dilate vt dīlātāre; (*speech*) plūra dīcere.
dilatorily adv tardē, cunctanter.
dilatoriness n mora f, cunctātiō f.
dilatory adj tardus, lentus, segnis.
dilemma n nōdus m, angustiae fpl; **be in a ~**
haerēre; **be on the horns of a ~** auribus
tenēre lupum.
diligence n dīligentia f, industria f, cūra f.
diligent adj dīligēns, industrius, sēdulus.
diligently adv dīligenter, sēdulō.
dill n anēthum nt.
dilly-dally vi cessāre.
dilute vt dīluere, temperāre.
dim adj obscūrus; (*fig*) hebes ♦ vt obscūrāre;
hebetāre.
dimension n modus m; **~s** pl amplitūdō f,
māgnitūdō f.
diminish vt minuere, imminuere, extenuāre,
īnfringere ♦ vi dēcrēscere.
diminution n imminūtiō f, dēminūtiō f.
diminutive adj parvulus, exiguus ♦ n (*word*)
dēminūtum nt.
diminutiveness n exiguitās f.
dimly adv obscūrē.
dimness n tenebrae fpl, cālīgō f.
dimple n gelasīnus m.
din n fragor m, strepitus m; **make a ~** strepere
♦ vt obtundere.
dine vi cēnāre.
diner n convīva m.
dinghy n scapha f.
dingy adj sordidus; (*colour*) fuscus.
dining room n cēnātiō f.
dinner n cēna f.
dinner party convīvium nt.
dint n ictus m; **by ~ of** per (*acc*).
dip vt imbuere, mergere ♦ vi mergī; **~ into**
(*study*) perstringere.
diploma n diplōma nt.
diplomacy n (*embassy*) lēgātiō f; (*tact*)

iūdicium nt, sagācitās f.
diplomat n lēgātus m.
diplomatic adj sagāx, circumspectus.
diptych n tabellae fpl.
dire adj dīrus, horridus.
direct vt regere, dīrigere; (attention)
attendere, admovēre, advertere; (course)
tendere; (business) administrāre, moderārī;
(letter) īnscrībere; (order) imperāre (dat),
iubēre; (to a place) viam mōnstrāre (dat);
(weapon) intendere ♦ adj rēctus, dīrēctus;
(person) simplex; (language) apertus ♦ adv
rēctā.
direction n (of going) cursus m, iter nt; (of
looking) pars f, regiō f; (control) administrātiō
f, regimen nt; (order) praeceptum nt, iussum
nt; in the ~ of Rome Rōmam versus; in all ~s
passim, undique; in both ~s utrōque.
directly adv (place) rēctā; (time) prōtinus,
continuō, statim; (language) apertē ♦ conj
simulac.
directness n (fig) simplicitās f.
director n dux m, gubernātor m, moderātor m.
dirge n nēnia f.
dirk n pūgiō m.
dirt n sordēs f; (mud) lūtum nt.
dirty adj sordidus, foedus; (speech) inquinātus
♦ vt foedāre, inquināre.
disability n vitium nt.
disable vt dēbilitāre, imminuere.
disabled adj mutilus, dēbilis.
disabuse vt errōrem dēmere (dat).
disaccustom vt dēsuēfacere.
disadvantage n incommodum nt,
dētrīmentum nt; it is a ~ dētrīmentō est.
disadvantageous adj incommodus, inīquus.
disadvantageously adv incommodē.
disaffected adj aliēnātus, sēditiōsus.
disaffection n aliēnātiō f, sēditiō f.
disagree vi discrepāre, dissentīre, dissidēre.
disagreeable adj molestus, incommodus,
iniūcundus.
disagreeably adv molestē, incommodē.
disagreement n discordia f, dissēnsiō f,
discrepantia f.
disallow vt improbāre, abnuere, vetāre.
disappear vi dēperīre, perīre, abīre,
diffugere, ēvānēscere.
disappearance n dēcessiō f, fuga f.
disappoint vt dēcipere, spē dēicere, frustrārī;
be ~ed in a hope ā spē dēcidere, dē spē dēicī.
disappointment n frustrātiō f, malum nt.
disapprobation n reprehēnsiō f, improbātiō f.
disapproval n improbātiō f.
disapprove vt, vi improbāre, reprehendere.
disarm vt exarmāre, dearmāre; (fig) mītigāre.
disarrange vt turbāre, cōnfundere.
disarranged adj incompositus.
disarrangement n turbātiō f.
disarray n perturbātiō f ♦ vt perturbāre.
disaster n calamitās f, cāsus m; (MIL) clādēs f.
disastrous adj īnfēlīx, exitiōsus, calamitōsus.
disavow vt diffitērī, īnfitiārī.

disavowal n īnfitiātiō f.
disband vt dīmittere.
disbelief n diffīdentia f, suspiciō f.
disbelieve vt diffīdere (dat).
disburden vt exonerāre.
disburse vt ērogāre, expendere.
disbursement n impēnsa f.
disc n orbis m.
discard vt mittere, pōnere, prōicere.
discern vt cōnspicere, dīspicere, cernere; (fig)
intellegere.
discernment n iūdicium nt, intellegentia f,
sagācitās f.
discharge vt (load) exonerāre; (debt)
exsolvere; (duty) fungī (abl), exsequī;
(officer) exauctōrāre; (troops) missōs facere,
dīmittere; (weapon) iacere, iaculārī;
(prisoner) absolvere; (from body) ēdere,
reddere ♦ vi (river) effundī, īnfluere ♦ n
(bodily) dēfluxiō f; (MIL) missiō f, dīmissiō f; (of
a duty) perfūnctiō f.
disciple n discipulus m.
discipline n (MIL) modestia f; (punishment)
castīgātiō f; (study) disciplīna f ♦ vt coercēre,
castīgāre.
disciplined adj modestus.
disclaim vt renūntiāre, repudiāre, rēicere.
disclaimer n repudiātiō f.
disclose vt aperīre, patefacere, indicāre.
disclosure n indicium nt.
discoloration n dēcolōrātiō f.
discolour vt dēcolōrāre.
discoloured adj dēcolor.
discomfit vt vincere, conturbāre,
dēprehendere.
discomfiture n clādēs f; (POL) repulsa f.
discomfort n molestia f, incommodum nt.
disconcert vt conturbāre, percellere.
disconcerting adj molestus.
disconnect vt abiungere, sēiungere.
disconnected adj dissolūtus, abruptus.
disconnectedly adv dissolūtē.
disconsolate adj maestus, dēmissus.
disconsolately adv animō dēmissō.
discontent n offēnsiō f, fastīdium nt, taedium
nt.
discontented adj invidus, fastīdiōsus, parum
contentus.
discontentedly adv invītus, inīquō animō.
discontinuance n intermissiō f.
discontinue vt intermittere ♦ vi dēsistere,
dēsinere.
discord n discordia f; (music) dissonum nt.
discordance n discrepantia f, dissēnsiō f.
discordant adj discors, discrepāns; (music)
dissonus, absonus.
discount vt dētrahere; (fig) praetermittere ♦
n dēcessiō f; be at a ~ iacēre.
discountenance vt improbāre.
discourage vt dēhortārī, dēterrēre; be ~d
animum dēmittere, animō dēficere.
discouragement n animī abiectiō f; (cause)
incommodum nt.

discourse *n* sermō *m*; (*lecture*) ōrātiō *f* ♦ *vi* conloquī, disserere, disputāre.
discourteous *adj* inurbānus, asper, inhūmānus.
discourteously *adv* inhūmānē, rūsticē.
discourtesy *n* inhūmānitās *f*, acerbitās *f*.
discover *vt* (*find*) invenīre, reperīre; (*detect*) dēprehendere; (*reveal*) aperīre, patefacere; (*learn*) cognōscere.
discoverer *n* inventor *m*.
discovery *n* inventum *nt*.
discredit *vt* notāre, fidem imminuere (*gen*) ♦ *n* invidia *f*, lābēs *f*; **be in ~** iacēre.
discreditable *adj* inhonestus, turpis.
discreditably *adv* inhonestē, turpiter.
discreet *adj* prūdēns, sagāx, cautus.
discreetly *adv* prūdenter, sagāciter, cautē.
discrepancy *n* discrepantia *f*, dissēnsiō *f*.
discretion *n* prūdentia *f*; (*tact*) iūdicium *nt*; (*power*) arbitrium *nt*, arbitrātus *m*; **at your ~** arbitrātū tuō; **surrender at ~** in dēditiōnem venīre, sine ullā pactiōne sē tradere; **years of ~** adulta aetās *f*.
discretionary *adj* līber.
discriminate *vt*, *vi* discernere, internōscere, distinguere.
discriminating *adj* perspicāx, sagāx.
discrimination *n* discrīmen *nt*, iūdicium *nt*.
discursive *adj* vagus, loquāx; **be ~** excurrere.
discuss *vt* agere, disputāre, disceptāre dē (*abl*); **~ terms of peace** dē pāce agere.
discussion *n* disceptātiō *f*, disputātiō *f*.
disdain *vt* contemnere, aspernārī, fastīdīre ♦ *n* contemptiō *f*, fastīdium *nt*.
disdainful *adj* fastīdiōsus, superbus.
disdainfully *adv* fastīdiōsē, superbē.
disease *n* morbus *m*; pestilentia *f*.
diseased *adj* aeger, aegrōtus.
disembark *vi* ē nave ēgredī ♦ *vt* mīlitēs ē nāve expōnere.
disembarkation *n* ēgressus *m*.
disembodied *adj* sine corpore.
disembowel *vt* exenterāre.
disencumber *vt* exonerāre.
disengage *vt* expedīre, līberāre; (*mind*) abstrahere, abdūcere.
disengaged *adj* vacuus, ōtiōsus.
disentangle *vt* expedīre, explicāre, exsolvere.
disfavour *n* invidia *f*.
disfigure *vt* dēfōrmāre, foedāre.
disfigured *adj* dēfōrmis.
disfigurement *n* dēfōrmātiō *f*.
disfranchise *vt* cīvitātem adimere (*dat*).
disfranchised *adj* capite dēminūtus.
disfranchisement *n* capitis dēminūtiō *f*.
disgorge *vt* ēvomere.
disgrace *n* dēdecus *nt*, ignōminia *f*, īnfāmia *f* ♦ *vt* dēdecorāre, dēdecorī esse (*dat*).
disgraceful *adj* ignōminiōsus, flāgitiōsus, turpis; **~ thing** flāgitium *nt*.
disgracefully *adv* turpiter, flāgitiōsē.
disgruntled *adj* mōrōsus, invidus.

disguise *n* integumentum *nt*; (*fig*) speciēs *f*, simulātiō *f*; **in ~** mūtātā veste ♦ *vt* obtegere, involvere; (*fact*) dissimulāre; **~ oneself** vestem mūtāre.
disgust *vt* displicēre (*dat*), fastīdium movēre (*dat*); **be ~ed** stomachārī; **I am ~ed** mē taedet, mē piget ♦ *n* fastīdium *nt*, taedium *nt*.
disgusting *adj* taeter, foedus, dēfōrmis.
disgustingly *adv* foedē.
dish *n* lanx *f*; (*course*) ferculum *nt*.
dishearten *vt* percellere; **be ~ed** animō dēficere, animum dēmittere.
dishevelled *adj* solūtus, passus.
dishonest *adj* perfidus, inīquus, improbus.
dishonestly *adv* improbē, dolō malō.
dishonesty *n* mala fidēs *f*, perfidia *f*, fraus *f*.
dishonour *n* dēdecus *nt*, ignōminia *f*, turpitūdō *f* ♦ *vt* dēdecorāre.
dishonourable *adj* ignōminiōsus, indecōrus, turpis.
dishonourably *adv* turpiter, inhonestē.
disillusion *vt* errōrem adimere (*dat*).
disinclination *n* odium *nt*.
disinclined *adj* invītus, āversus.
disinfect *vt* pūrgāre.
disingenuous *adj* dolōsus, fallāx.
disingenuously *adv* dolōsē.
disinherit *vt* abdicāre, exhērēdāre.
disinherited *adj* exhērēs.
disintegrate *vt* dissolvere ♦ *vi* dīlābī, dissolvī.
disinter *vt* effodere, ēruere.
disinterested *adj* grātuītus, favōris expers.
disinterestedly *adv* sine favōre.
disinterestedness *n* innocentia *f*, integritās *f*.
disjoin *vt* sēiungere.
disjointed *adj* parum cohaerēns.
disk *n* orbis *m*.
dislike *n* odium *nt*, offēnsiō *f*, invidia *f* ♦ *vt* ōdisse; **I ~** mihī displicet, mē piget (*gen*).
dislocate *vt* extorquēre.
dislocated *adj* luxus.
dislodge *vt* dēmovēre, dēicere, dēpellere, dētrūdere.
disloyal *adj* īnfīdus, īnfidēlis; (*to gods, kin, country*) impius.
disloyally *adv* īnfidēliter.
disloyalty *n* perfidia *f*, īnfidēlitās *f*; impietās *f*.
dismal *adj* fūnestus, maestus.
dismally *adv* miserē.
dismantle *vt* nūdāre; (*building*) dīruere.
dismay *n* pavor *m*, formīdō *f* ♦ *vt* terrēre, perturbāre.
dismember *vt* discerpere.
dismiss *vt* dīmittere; (*troops*) missōs facere; (*from service*) exauctōrāre; (*fear*) mittere, pōnere.
dismissal *n* missiō *f*, dīmissiō *f*.
dismount *vi* dēgredī, (ex equō) dēscendere.
disobedience *n* contumācia *f*.
disobedient *adj* contumāx.
disobediently *adv* contrā iūssa.
disobey *vt* nōn pārēre (*dat*), aspernārī.

disoblige *vt* displicēre (*dat*), offendere.
disobliging *adj* inofficiōsus, difficilis.
disobligingly *adv* contrā officium.
disorder *n* turba *f*, cōnfūsiō *f*; (*MED*) morbus *m*; (*POL*) mōtus *m*, tumultus *m* ♦ *vt* turbāre, miscēre, sollicitāre.
disorderly *adj* immodestus, inōrdinātus, incompositus; (*POL*) turbulentus, sēditiōsus; **in a ~ manner** nullō ōrdine, temerē.
disorganize *vt* dissolvere, perturbāre.
disown *vt* (*statement*) īnfitiārī; (*thing*) abnuere, repudiāre; (*heir*) abdicāre.
disparage *vt* obtrectāre, dētrectāre.
disparagement *n* obtrectātiō *f*, probrum *nt*.
disparager *n* obtrectātor *m*, dētrectātor *m*.
disparate *adj* dispār.
disparity *n* discrepantia *f*, dissimilitūdō *f*.
dispassionate *adj* studiī expers.
dispassionately *adv* sine īrā et studiō.
dispatch *vt* mittere, dīmittere; (*finish*) absolvere, perficere; (*kill*) interficere ♦ *n* (*letter*) litterae *fpl*; (*speed*) celeritās *f*.
dispel *vt* dispellere, discutere.
dispensation *n* (*distribution*) partītiō *f*; (*exemption*) venia *f*; (*of heaven*) sors *f*; **by divine ~** dīvīnitus.
dispense *vt* dispertīrī, dīvidere ♦ *vi*: **~ with** ōmittere, praetermittere, repudiāre.
dispersal *n* dīmissiō *f*, diffugium *nt*.
disperse *vt* dispergere, dissipāre, dīsicere ♦ *vi* diffugere, dīlābī.
dispirited *adj* dēmissō animō; **be ~** animō dēficere, animum dēmittere.
displace *vt* locō movēre.
display *n* ostentātiō *f*, iactātiō *f*; **for ~** per speciem ♦ *vt* exhibēre, ostendere, praestāre, sē ferre.
displease *vt* displicēre (*dat*), offendere; **be ~d** aegrē ferre, stomachārī, indignārī.
displeasing *adj* ingrātus, odiōsus.
displeasure *n* invidia *f*, offēnsiō *f*, odium *nt*.
disport *vt*: **~ oneself** lūdere.
disposal *n* (*sale*) vēnditiō *f*; (*power*) arbitrium *nt*.
dispose *vt* (*troops*) dispōnere; (*mind*) inclīnāre, addūcere ♦ *vi*: **~ of** abaliēnāre, vēndere; (*get rid*) tollere; (*argument*) refellere.
disposed *adj* adfectus, inclīnātus, prōnus; **well ~** benevolus, bonō animō.
disposition *n* animus *m*, adfectiō *f*, ingenium *nt*, nātūra *f*; (*of troops*) dispositiō *f*.
dispossess *vt* dētrūdere, spoliāre.
disproportion *n* inconcinnitās *f*.
disproportionate *adj* impār, inconcinnus.
disproportionately *adv* inaequāliter.
disprove *vt* refūtāre, redarguere, refellere.
disputable *adj* dubius, ambiguus.
disputation *n* disputātiō *f*.
dispute *n* altercātiō *f*, contrōversia *f*; (*violent*) iūrgium *nt*; **beyond ~** certissimus ♦ *vi* altercārī, certāre, rixārī ♦ *vt* negāre, in

dubium vocāre.
disqualification *n* impedīmentum *nt*.
disqualify *vt* impedīre.
disquiet *n* sollicitūdō *f* ♦ *vt* sollicitāre.
disquisition *n* disputātiō *f*.
disregard *n* neglegentia *f*, contemptiō *f* ♦ *vt* neglegere, contemnere, ōmittere.
disrepair *n* vitium *nt*; **in ~** male sartus.
disreputable *adj* inhonestus, īnfāmis.
disrepute *n* īnfāmia *f*.
disrespect *n* neglegentia *f*, contumācia *f*.
disrespectful *adj* contumāx, īnsolēns.
disrespectfully *adv* īnsolenter.
disrobe *vt* nūdāre, vestem exuere (*dat*) ♦ *vi* vestem exuere.
disrupt *vt* dīrumpere, dīvellere.
disruption *n* discidium *nt*.
dissatisfaction *n* molestia *f*, aegritūdō *f*, dolor *m*.
dissatisfied *adj* parum contentus; **I am ~ with ... mē taedet** (*gen*) ....
dissect *vt* incīdere; (*fig*) investīgāre.
dissemble *vt*, *vi* dissimulāre; mentīrī.
dissembler *n* simulātor *m*.
disseminate *vt* dīvulgāre, dissēmināre.
dissension *n* discordia *f*, dissēnsiō *f*; (*violent*) iūrgium *nt*.
dissent *vi* dissentīre, dissidēre ♦ *n* dissēnsiō *f*.
dissertation *n* disputātiō *f*.
disservice *n* iniūria *f*, incommodum *nt*.
dissimilar *adj* dispār, dissimilis.
dissimilarity *n* discrepantia *f*, dissimilitūdō *f*.
dissident *adj* discors.
dissimulation *n* dissimulātiō *f*.
dissipate *vt* dissipāre, diffundere, disperdere.
dissipated *adj* dissolūtus, lascīvus, luxuriōsus.
dissipation *n* dissipātiō *f*; (*vice*) luxuria *f*, licentia *f*.
dissociate *vt* dissociāre, sēiungere.
dissociation *n* sēparātiō *f*, discidium *nt*.
dissoluble *adj* dissolūbilis.
dissolute *adj* dissolūtus, perditus, libīdinōsus.
dissolutely *adv* libīdinōsē, luxuriōsē.
dissoluteness *n* luxuria *f*.
dissolution *n* dissolūtiō *f*, discidium *nt*.
dissolve *vt* dissolvere; (*ice*) liquefacere; (*meeting*) dīmittere; (*contract*) dīrimere ♦ *vi* liquēscere; (*fig*) solvī.
dissonance *n* dissonum *nt*.
dissonant *adj* dissonus.
dissuade *vt* dissuādēre (*dat*), dēhortārī.
dissuasion *n* dissuāsiō *f*.
distaff *n* colus *f*.
distance *n* intervallum *nt*, spatium *nt*; (*long way*) longinquitās *f*; **at a ~** (*far*) longē; (*within sight*) procul; (*fight*) ēminus; **at a ~ of ...** spatiō (*gen*) ...; **within striking ~** intrā iactum tēlī.
distant *adj* longinquus; (*measure*) distāns; (*person*) parum familiāris; **be ~** abesse (*abl*).

distaste n fastīdium nt.
distasteful adj molestus, iniūcundus.
distemper n morbus m.
distend vt distendere.
distil vt, vi stillāre.
distinct adj (different) dīversus; (separate) distinctus; (clear) clārus, argūtus; (marked) distinctus; (sure) certus; (well-drawn) expressus.
distinction n discrīmen nt; (dissimilarity) discrepantia f; (public status) amplitūdō f; (honour) honōs m, decus nt; (mark) īnsigne nt; **there is a ~** interest; **without ~** prōmiscuē.
distinctive adj proprius, īnsignītus.
distinctively adv propriē, īnsignītē.
distinctly adv clārē, distinctē, certē, expressē.
distinguish vt distinguere, internōscere, dīiūdicāre, discernere; (honour) decorāre, ōrnāre; **~ oneself** ēminēre.
distinguished adj īnsignis, praeclārus, ēgregius, amplissimus.
distort vt dētorquēre; (fig) dēprāvāre.
distorted adj distortus.
distortion n distortiō f; dēprāvātiō f.
distract vt distrahere, distinēre, āvocāre; (mind) aliēnāre.
distracted adj āmēns, īnsānus.
distraction n (state) indīligentia f; (cause) invītāmentum nt; (madness) furor m, dēmentia f; **to ~** efflīctim.
distraught adj āmēns, dēmēns.
distress n labor m, dolor m, aegrimōnia f, aerumna f; **be in ~** labōrāre ♦ vt adflīgere, sollicitāre.
distressed adj adflīctus, sollicitus; **be ~ at rem** aegrē ferre.
distressing adj tristis, miser, acerbus.
distribute vt distribuere, dīvidere, dispertīre.
distribution n partītiō f, distribūtiō f.
district n regiō f, pars f.
distrust n diffīdentia f ♦ vt diffīdere (dat), nōn crēdere (dat).
distrustful adj diffīdēns.
distrustfully adv diffīdenter.
disturb vt perturbāre, conturbāre; commovēre; (mind) sollicitāre.
disturbance n turba f, perturbātiō f; (POL) mōtus m, tumultus m.
disturber n turbātor m.
disunion n discordia f, discidium nt.
disunite vt dissociāre, sēiungere.
disuse n dēsuētūdō f; **fall into ~** obsolēscere.
disused adj dēsuētus, obsolētus.
disyllabic adj disyllabus.
ditch n fossa f, scrobis m.
dithyrambic adj dithyrambicus.
dittany n dictamnum nt.
ditty n carmen nt, cantilēna f.
diurnal adj diūrnus.
divan n lectus m, lectulus m.
dive vi dēmergī.
diver n ūrīnātor m.

diverge vi dēvertere, dīgredī; (road) sē scindere; (opinions) discrepāre.
divergence n dīgressiō f; discrepantia f.
divers adj complūrēs.
diverse adj varius, dīversus.
diversify vt variāre.
diversion n (of water) dērīvātiō f; (of thought) āvocātiō f; (to amuse) oblectāmentum nt; **create a ~** (MIL) hostēs dīstringere; **for a ~** animī causā.
diversity n varietās f, discrepantia f.
divert vt dēflectere, āvertere; (attention) āvocāre, abstrahere; (water) dērīvāre; (to amuse) oblectāre, placēre (dat).
diverting adj iūcundus; (remark) facētus.
divest vt exuere, nūdāre; **~ oneself of** (fig) pōnere, mittere.
divide vt dīvidere; (troops) dīdūcere; **~ among** partīrī, distribuere; **~ from** sēparāre ab, sēiungere ab; **~ out** dispertīrī, dīvidere ♦ vi discēdere, sē scindere; (senate) in sententiam īre; **be ~d** (opinions) discrepāre.
divination n dīvīnātiō f; (from birds) augurium nt; (from entrails) haruspicium nt.
divine adj dīvīnus ♦ vt dīvīnāre, augurārī, hariolārī; **by ~ intervention** dīvīnitus.
divinely adv dīvīnē.
diviner n dīvīnus m, augur m, haruspex m.
divinity n (status) dīvīnitās f; (god) deus m, dea f.
divisible adj dīviduus.
division n (process) dīvīsiō f, partītiō f; (variance) discordia f, dissēnsiō f; (section) pars f; (grade) classis f; (of army) legiō f; (of time) discrīmen nt; (in senate) discessiō f.
divorce n dīvortium nt, repudium nt ♦ vt (wife) nūntium mittere (dat); (things) dīvellere, sēparāre.
divulge vt aperīre, patefacere, ēvulgāre, ēdere.
dizziness n vertīgō f.
dizzy adj vertīginōsus; (fig) attonitus.
do vt facere, agere; (duty) fungī (abl); (wrong) admittere; **~ away with** vt fus tollere; (kill) interimere; **~ one's best to** id agere ut (subj); **~ without** repudiāre; **~ not** . . . nolī/nolīte (+ infin); **how ~ you** ~? quid agis?; **I have nothing to ~ with you** mihī tēcum nihil est commercī; **it has nothing to ~ with me** nihil est ad mē; **that will ~** iam satis est; **be done** fierī; **have done with** dēfungī (abl).
docile adj docilis.
docility n docilitās f.
dock n (ships) nāvāle nt; (law) cancellī mpl ♦ vt praecīdere.
dockyard n nāvālia ntpl.
doctor n medicus m; (UNIV) doctor m ♦ vt cūrāre.
doctrine n dogma nt, dēcrētum nt; (system) ratiō f.
document n litterae fpl, tabula f.
dodge vt dēclīnāre, ēvādere ♦ n dolus m.
doe n cerva f.

doer n āctor m, auctor m.
doff vt exuere.
dog n canis m/f; ~ **star** Canīcula f; ~'**s** canīnus ♦ vt īnsequī, īnstāre (dat).
dogged adj pertināx.
doggedly adv pertināciter.
dogma n dogma nt, praeceptum nt.
dogmatic adj adrogāns.
dogmatically adv adroganter.
doing n factum nt.
dole n sportula f ♦ vt: ~ **out** dispertīrī, dīvidere.
doleful adj lūgubris, flēbilis, maestus.
dolefully adv flēbiliter.
dolefulness n maestitia f, miseria f.
doll n pūpa f.
dolorous adj lūgubris, maestus.
dolour n maestitia f, dolor m.
dolphin n delphīnus m.
dolt n stīpes m, caudex m.
domain n ager m; (king's) rēgnum nt.
dome n tholus m, testūdō f.
domestic adj domesticus, familiāris; (animal) mānsuētus ♦ n famulus m, servus m, famula f, ancilla f; ~**s** pl familia f.
domesticate vt mānsuēfacere.
domesticated adj mānsuētus.
domesticity n larēs suī mpl.
domicile n domicilium nt, domus f.
dominant adj superior, praepotēns.
dominate vt dominārī in (acc), imperāre (dat); (view) dēspectāre.
domination n dominātiō f, dominātus m.
domineer vi dominārī, rēgnāre.
dominion n imperium nt, rēgnum nt.
don vt induere ♦ n scholasticus m.
donate vt dōnāre.
donation n dōnum nt.
donkey n asellus m.
donor n dōnātor m.
doom n fātum nt ♦ vt damnāre.
door n (front) iānua f; (back) postīcum nt; (double) forēs fpl; **folding ~s** valvae fpl; **out of ~s** forīs; (to) forās; **next ~ to** iuxtā (acc).
doorkeeper n iānitor m.
doorpost n postis m.
doorway n ōstium nt.
dormant adj sōpītus; **lie ~** iacēre.
dormitory n cubiculum nt.
dormouse n glīs m.
dose n pōculum nt.
dot n pūnctum nt.
dotage n senium nt.
dotard n senex dēlīrus m.
dote vi dēsipere; ~ **upon** dēamāre.
doting adj dēsipiēns, peramāns.
dotingly adv perditē.
double adj duplex; (amount) duplus; (meaning) ambiguus ♦ n duplum nt ♦ vt duplicāre; (promontory) superāre; (fold) complicāre ♦ vi duplicārī; (MIL) currere.
double-dealer n fraudātor m.
double-dealing adj fallāx, dolōsus ♦ n fraus

f, dolus m.
doublet n tunica f.
doubly adv bis, dupliciter.
doubt n dubium nt; (hesitancy) dubitātiō f; (distrust) suspiciō f; **give one the benefit of the ~** innocentem habēre; **no ~** sānē; **I do not ~ that** ... non dubito quīn ... (+ subj); **there is no ~ that** nōn dubium est quīn (subj) ♦ vt dubitāre; (distrust) diffīdere (dat), suspicārī.
doubtful adj dubius, incertus; (result) anceps; (word) ambiguus.
doubtfully adv dubiē; (hesitation) dubitanter.
doubtless adv scīlicet, nīmīrum.
doughty adj fortis, strēnuus.
dove n columba f.
dovecote n columbārium nt.
dowdy adj inconcinnus.
dower n dōs f ♦ vt dōtāre.
dowerless adj indōtātus.
down n plūmae fpl, lānūgō f; (thistle) pappus m.
down adv deōrsum; **be ~** iacēre; ~ **with!** perea(n)t; **up and ~** sūrsum deōrsum ♦ prep dē (abl); ~ **from** dē (abl).
downcast adj dēmissus, maestus.
downfall n ruīna f; (fig) occāsus m.
downhearted adj dēmissus, frāctus animī.
downhill adj dēclīvis; (fig) prōclīvis ♦ adv in praeceps.
downpour n imber m.
downright adj dīrēctus; (intensive) merus.
downstream adv secundō flūmine.
downtrodden adj subiectus, oppressus.
downward adj dēclīvis, prōclīvis.
downwards adv deōrsum.
downy adj plūmeus.
dowry n dōs f.
doyen n pater m.
doze vi dormītāre.
dozen n duodecim.
drab adj sordidior.
drachma n drachma f.
draft n (writing) exemplum nt; (MIL) dīlēctus m; (money) syngrapha f; (literary) silva f ♦ vt scrībere; (MIL) mittere.
drag vt trahere ♦ vi (time) trahī; ~ **on** vi (war) prōdūcere ♦ n harpagō m; (fig) impedīmentum nt.
dragnet n ēverriculum nt.
dragon n dracō m.
dragoon n eques m.
drain n cloāca f ♦ vt (water) dērīvāre; (land) siccāre; (drink) exhaurīre; (resources) exhaurīre.
drainage n dērīvātiō f.
drake n anas m.
drama n fābula f; **the ~** scaena f.
dramatic adj scaenicus.
dramatist n fābulārum scrīptor m.
dramatize vt ad scaenam compōnere.
drape vt vēlāre.
drapery n vestīmenta ntpl.
drastic adj vehemēns, efficāx.
draught n (air) aura f; (drink) haustus m; (net)

bolus *m*.

draughts *n* latrunculī *mpl*.

draw *vt* dūcere, trahere; (*bow*) addūcere; (*inference*) colligere; (*picture*) scrībere, pingere; (*sword*) stringere, dēstringere; (*tooth*) eximere; (*water*) haurīre; ~ **aside** sēdūcere; ~ **away** āvocāre; ~ **back** *vt* retrahere ♦ *vi* recēdere; ~ **near** adpropinquāre; ~ **off** dētrahere; (*water*) dērīvāre; ~ **out** *vi* ēdūcere; (*lengthen*) prōdūcere; ~ **over** obdūcere; ~ **taut** addūcere; ~ **together** contrahere; ~ **up** *vt* (*MIL*) īnstruere; (*document*) scrībere.

drawback *n* scrūpulus *m*; **this was the only** ~ hōc ūnum dēfuit.

drawing *n* dēscrīptiō *f*; (*art*) graphicē *f*.

drawing room *n* sellāria *f*.

drawings *npl* līneāmenta *ntpl*.

drawl *vi* lentē dīcere.

drawling *adj* lentus in dīcendō.

dray *n* plaustrum *nt*.

dread *n* formīdō *f*, pavor *m*, horror *m* ♦ *adj* dīrus ♦ *vt* expavēscere, extimēscere, formīdāre.

dreadful *adj* terribilis, horribilis, formīdolōsus, dīrus.

dreadfully *adv* vehementer, atrōciter.

dream *n* somnium *nt* ♦ *vt*, *vi* somniāre.

dreamy *adj* somniculōsus.

dreariness *n* (*place*) vastitās *f*; (*mind*) tristitia *f*.

dreary *adj* (*place*) vastus; (*person*) tristis.

dregs *n* faex *f*; (*of oil*) amurca *f*; **drain to the** ~ exhaurīre.

drench *vt* perfundere.

dress *n* vestis *f*, vestītus *m*, vestīmenta *ntpl*; (*style*) habitus *m* ♦ *vt* vestīre; (*wound*) cūrāre; (*tree*) amputāre ♦ *vi* induī; ~ **up** *vi* vestum induere.

dressing *n* (*MED*) fōmentum *nt*.

drift *n* (*motion*) mōtus *m*; (*snow*) agger *m*; (*language*) vīs *f*; **I see the** ~ **of your speech** videō quōrsum ōrātiō tua tendat ♦ *vi* fluitāre; (*fig*) lābī, ferrī.

drill *n* terebra *f*; (*MIL*) exercitātiō *f* ♦ *vt* (*hole*) terebrāre; (*MIL*) exercēre; (*pupil*) īnstruere.

drink *vt*, *vi* bibere, pōtāre; ~ **a health** propīnāre, Graecō mōre bibere; ~ **deep of** exhaurīre; ~ **in** haurīre; ~ **up** ēpōtāre ♦ *n* pōtiō *f*.

drinkable *adj* pōtulentus.

drinker *n* pōtor *m*.

drinking bout *n* pōtātiō *f*.

drip *vi* stillāre, dēstillāre.

drive *vt* agere; (*force*) cōgere; ~ **away** abigere; (*fig*) pellere, prōpulsāre; ~ **back** repellere; ~ **home** dēfīgere; ~ **in/into** īnfīgere in (*acc*); (*flock*) cōgere in (*acc*); ~ **off** dēpellere; ~ **out** exigere, expellere, exturbāre; ~ **through** trānsfīgere ♦ *vi* vehī; ~ **away** āvehī; ~ **back** revehī; ~ **in** invehī; ~ **on** *vt* impellere; ~ **round** circumvehī; ~ **past** praetervehī; **what are you driving at?** quōrsum tua spectat ōrātiō?

♦ *n* gestātiō *f*.

drivel *vi* dēlīrāre.

drivelling *adj* dēlīrus, ineptus ♦ *n* ineptiae *fpl*.

driver *n* aurīga *m*; rēctor *m*.

drizzle *vi* rōrāre.

droll *adj* facētus, ioculāris.

drollery *n* facētiae *fpl*.

dromedary *n* dromas *m*.

drone *n* (*bee*) fūcus *m*; (*sound*) bombus *m* ♦ *vi* fremere.

droop *vi* dēmittī; (*flower*) languēscere; (*mind*) animum dēmittere.

drooping *adj* languidus.

drop *n* gutta *f* ♦ *vi* cadere; (*liquid*) stillāre ♦ *vt* mittere; (*anchor*) iacere; (*hint*) ēmittere; (*liquid*) īnstillāre; (*work*) dēsistere ab (*abl*) ♦ *vi*: ~ **behind** cessāre; ~ **in** *vi* vīsere, supervenīre; ~ **out** excidere.

dross *n* scōria *f*; (*fig*) faex *f*.

drought *n* siccitās *f*.

drouth *n* sitis *f*.

drove *n* grex *f*.

drover *n* bubulcus *m*.

drown *vt* mergere, obruere; (*noise*) obscūrāre ♦ *vi* aquā perīre.

drowse *vi* dormītāre.

drowsily *adv* somniculōsē.

drowsiness *n* sopor *m*.

drowsy *adj* sēmisomnus, somniculōsus.

drub *vt* pulsāre, verberāre.

drudge *n* mediastīnus *m* ♦ *vi* labōrāre.

drudgery *n* labor *m*.

drug *n* medicāmentum *nt* ♦ *vt* medicāre.

Druids *n* Druidae, Druidēs *mpl*.

drum *n* tympanum *nt*; (*container*) urna *f*.

drummer *n* tympanista *m*.

drunk *adj* pōtus, ēbrius, tēmulentus.

drunkard *n* ēbriōsus *m*.

drunken *adj* ēbriōsus, tēmulentus.

drunkenness *n* ēbrietās *f*.

dry *adj* siccus, āridus; (*thirst*) sitiēns; (*speech*) āridus, frīgidus; (*joke*) facētus; **be** ~ **ārēre** ♦ *vt* siccāre ♦ *vi* ārēscere; ~ **up** exārēscere.

dryad *n* dryas *f*.

dry rot *n* rōbīgō *f*.

dual *adj* duplex.

duality *n* duplex nātūra *f*.

dubiety *n* dubium *nt*.

dubious *adj* dubius, incertus; (*meaning*) ambiguus.

dubiously *adv* dubiē; ambiguē.

duck *n* anas *f* ♦ *vt* dēmergere ♦ *vi* dēmergī, sē dēmittere.

duckling *n* anaticula *f*.

duct *n* ductus *m*.

dudgeon *n* dolor *m*, stomachus *m*.

due *adj* dēbitus, meritus, iūstus; **be** ~ **dēbērī; it is** ~ **to me that . . . not** per mē stat quōminus (+ *subj*); **be** ~ **to** orīrī ex, fierī (*abl*) ♦ *n* iūs *nt*, dēbitum *nt*; (*tax*) vectīgal *nt*; (*harbour*) portōrium *nt*; **give every man his** ~ suum cuīque tribuere ♦ *adv* rēctā; ~ **to** ob (+ *acc*); propter (+ *acc*).

duel n certāmen nt.
dug n ūber nt.
duke n dux m.
dulcet adj dulcis.
dull adj hebes; (weather) subnūbilus; (language) frīgidus; (mind) tardus; **be ~** hebēre; **become ~** hebēscere ♦ vt hebetāre, obtundere, retundere.
dullard n stolidus m.
dulness n (mind) tarditās f, stultitia f.
duly adv rītē, ut pār est.
dumb adj mūtus; **be struck ~** obmūtēscere.
dun n flāgitātor m ♦ vt flāgitāre ♦ adj fuscus.
dunce n bārō m.
dune n tumulus m.
dung n fimus m.
dungeon n carcer m, rōbur nt.
dupe vt dēlūdere, fallere ♦ n crēdulus m.
duplicate n exemplar nt ♦ vt duplicāre.
duplicity n fraus f, perfidia f.
durability n firmitās f, firmitūdō f.
durable adj firmus, perpetuus.
durably adv firmē.
duration n spatium nt; (long) diūturnitās f.
duresse n vīs f.
during prep inter (acc), per (acc).
dusk n crepusculum nt, vesper m; **at ~** prīmā nocte, prīmīs tenebrīs.
dusky adj fuscus.
dust n pulvis m; **throw ~ in the eyes of** tenebrās offundere (dat) ♦ vt dētergēre.
dusty adj pulverulentus.
dutiful adj pius, officiōsus.
dutifully adv piē, officiōsē.
dutifulness n pietās f.
duty n (moral) officium nt; (task) mūnus nt; (tax) vectīgal nt; **be on ~** (MIL) statiōnem agere, excubāre; **do one's ~** officiō fungī; **do ~ for** (pers) in locum sufficī (gen); (thing) adhibērī prō (abl); **it is my ~** dēbeō, mē oportet, meum est; **it is the ~ of a commander** ducis est; **sense of ~** pietās f.
duty call n salūtātiō f.
duty-free adj immūnis.
dwarf n nānus m.
dwell vi habitāre; **~ in** incolere; **~ upon** (theme) commorārī in (abl).
dweller n incola m.
dwelling n domus f, domicilium nt; (place) sēdēs f.
dwindle vi dēcrēscere, extenuārī.
dye n fūcus m, color m ♦ vt īnficere, fūcāre.
dyer n īnfector m.
dying adj moribundus, moriēns.
dynasty n domus (rēgia) f.
dyspepsia n crūditās f.

E, e

each adj & pron quisque; (of two) uterque; **~ other** inter sē; **one ~** singulī; **~ year** quotannīs.
eager adj avidus, cupidus, alācer; **~ for** avidus (+ gen).
eagerly adv avidē, cupidē, ācriter.
eagerness n cupīdō f, ārdor m, studium nt; alacritās f.
eagle n aquila f.
ear n auris f; (of corn) spīca f; **give ~** aurem praebēre, auscultāre; **go in at one ~ and out at the other** surdīs auribus nārrārī; **prick up one's ~s** aurēs ērigere; **with long ~s** aurītus.
earl n comes m.
earlier adv ante; anteā.
early adj (in season) mātūrus; (in day) mātūtīnus; (at beginning) prīmus; (in history) antīquus ♦ adv (in day) māne; (before time) mātūrē, temperī; **~ in life** ab ineunte aetāte.
earn vt merērī, cōnsequī; **~ a living** vīctum quaerere, quaestum facere.
earnest adj (serious) sērius; (eager) ācer, sēdulus ♦ n pignus nt; (money) arrabō m; **in ~** sēdulō, ēnīxē.
earnestly adv sēriō, graviter, sēdulō.
earnestness n gravitās f, studium nt.
earnings n quaestus m.
earring n elenchus m.
earth n (planet) tellūs f; (inhabited) orbis terrārum m; (land) terra f; (soil) solum nt, humus f; (fox's) latibulum nt; **where on ~?** ubī gentium?; **of the ~** terrestris.
earthen adj (ware) fictilis; (mound) terrēnus.
earthenware n fictilia ntpl ♦ adj fictilis.
earthly adj terrestris.
earthquake n terrae mōtus m.
earthwork n agger m.
earthy adj terrēnus.
ease n facilitās f; (leisure) ōtium nt; **at ~** ōtiōsus; (in mind) sēcūrus; **ill at ~** sollicitus ♦ vt laxāre, relevāre; (pain) mītigāre.
easily adv facile; (gladly) libenter; (at leisure) ōtiōsē; **not ~** nōn temerē.
easiness n facilitās f.
east n Oriēns m, sōlis ortus m; **~ wind** eurus m.
Easter n Pascha f.
easterly, eastern adj orientālis.
eastward adv ad orientem.
easy adj facilis; (manner) adfābilis, facilis; (mind) sēcūrus; (speech) expedītus; (discipline) remissus; **~ circumstances** dīvitiae fpl, abundantia f.
eat vt edere; cōnsūmere; vescī (abl); **~ away** rōdere; **~ up** exedere.
eatable adj esculentus.
eating n cibus m.

eaves *n* suggrunda *f.*
eavesdropper *n* sermōnis auceps *m.*
ebb *n* dēcessus *m*, recessus *m*; **at ~tide**
minuente aestū; **be at a low ~** (*fig*) iacēre ♦ *vi*
recēdere.
ebony *n* ebenus *f.*
ebullient *adj* fervēns.
ebullition *n* fervor *m.*
eccentric *adj* īnsolēns.
eccentricity *n* īnsolentia *f.*
echo *n* imāgō *f* ♦ *vt, vi* resonāre.
eclipse *n* dēfectus *m*, dēfectiō *f* ♦ *vt* obscūrāre;
be ~d dēficere, labōrāre.
eclogue *n* ecloga *f.*
economic *adj* quaestuōsus, sine iactūrā.
economical *adj* (*person*) frūgī, parcus.
economically *adv* nullā iactūrā factā.
economics *n* reī familiāris dispēnsātiō *f.*
economize *vi* parcere.
economy *n* frūgālitās *f.*
ecstasy *n* alacritās *f*, furor *m.*
ecstatic *adj* gaudiō ēlātus.
eddy *n* vertex *m* ♦ *vi* volūtārī.
edge *n* ōra *f*, margō *f*; (*of dish*) labrum *nt*; (*of
blade*) aciēs *f*; **take the ~ off** obtundere; **on ~**
(*fig*) suspēnsō animō ♦ *vt* (*garment*)
praetexere; (*blade*) acuere ♦ *vi:* **~ in sē**
īnsinuāre.
edging *n* limbus *m.*
edible *adj* esculentus.
edict *n* ēdictum *nt*, dēcrētum *nt.*
edification *n* ērudītiō *f.*
edifice *n* aedificium *nt.*
edify *vt* ērudīre.
edit *vt* recognōscere, recēnsēre.
edition *n* ēditiō *f.*
educate *vt* ērudīre, īnfōrmāre; **~ in** īnstituere
ad (*acc*).
education *n* doctrīna *f*; (*process*) īnstitūtiō *f.*
eel *n* anguilla *f.*
eerie *adj* mōnstruōsus.
efface *vt* dēlēre, tollere.
effect *n* (*result*) ēventus *m*; (*impression*) vīs *f*,
effectus *m*; (*show*) iactātiō *f*; **~s** *pl* bona *ntpl*;
for ~ iactātiōnis causā; **in ~** rē vērā; **to this ~**
in hanc sententiam; **without ~** inritus ♦ *vt*
efficere, facere, patrāre.
effective *adj* valēns, validus; (*RHET*) gravis,
ōrnātus.
effectively *adv* validē, graviter, ōrnātē.
effectiveness *n* vīs *f.*
effectual *adj* efficāx, idōneus.
effectually *adv* efficāciter.
effectuate *vt* efficere, cōnsequī.
effeminacy *n* mollitiēs *f.*
effeminate *adj* mollis, effēminātus.
effeminately *adv* molliter, effēminātē.
effervesce *vi* effervēscere.
effete *adj* effētus.
efficacious *adj* efficāx.
efficaciously *adv* efficāciter.
efficacy *n* vīs *f.*
efficiency *n* virtūs *f*, perītia *f.*

efficient *adj* capāx, perītus; (*logic*) efficiēns.
efficiently *adv* perītē, bene.
effigy *n* simulācrum *nt*, effigiēs *f.*
effloresce *vi* flōrēscere.
efflorescence *n* (*fig*) flōs *m.*
effluvium *n* hālitus *m.*
effort *n* opera *f*, cōnātus *m*; (*of mind*) intentiō *f*;
make an ~ ēnītī.
effrontery *n* audācia *f*, impudentia *f.*
effusive *adj* officiōsus.
egg *n* ōvum *nt*; **lay an ~** ōvum parere ♦ *vt*
impellere, īnstīgāre.
egoism *n* amor suī *m.*
egoist *n* suī amāns *m.*
egotism *n* iactātiō *f.*
egotist *n* glōriōsus *m.*
egregious *adj* singulāris.
egress *n* exitus *m.*
eight *num* octō; **~ each** octōnī; **~ times** octiēns.
eighteen *num* duodēvīgintī.
eighteenth *adj* duodēvīcēsimus.
eighth *adj* octāvus.
eight hundred *num* octingentī.
eight hundredth *adj* octingentēsimus.
eightieth *adj* octōgēsimus.
eighty *num* octōgintā; **~ each** octōgēnī; **~ times**
octōgiēns.
either *pron* alteruter, uterlibet, utervīs ♦ *conj*
aut, vel; **~ ... or** aut ... aut; vel ... vel.
ejaculation *n* clāmor *m.*
eject *vt* ēicere, expellere.
ejection *n* expulsiō *f.*
eke *vt:* **eke out** parcendō prōdūcere.
elaborate *vt* ēlabōrāre ♦ *adj* ēlabōrātus,
exquīsītus.
elaborately *adv* summō labōre, exquīsītē.
elan *n* ferōcia *f.*
elapse *vi* abīre, intercēdere; **allow to ~**
intermittere; **a year has ~d since** annus est
cum (*indic*).
elated *adj* ēlātus; **be ~** efferrī.
elation *n* laetitia *f.*
elbow *n* cubitum *nt.*
elder *adj* nātū māior, senior ♦ *n* (*tree*)
sambūcus *f.*
elderly *adj* aetāte prōvectus.
elders *npl* patrēs *mpl.*
eldest *adj* nātū māximus.
elecampane *n* inula *f.*
elect *vt* ēligere, dēligere; (*magistrate*) creāre;
(*colleague*) cooptāre ♦ *adj* dēsignātus;
(*special*) lēctus.
election *n* (*POL*) comitia *ntpl.*
electioneering *n* ambitiō *f.*
elector *n* suffrāgātor *m.*
elegance *n* ēlegantia *f*, lepōs *m*, munditia *f*,
concinnitās *f.*
elegant *adj* ēlegāns, concinnus, nitidus.
elegantly *adv* ēleganter, concinnē.
elegiac *adj:* **~ verse** elegī *mpl*, versūs alternī
mpl.
elegy *n* elegīa *f.*
element *n* elementum *nt*; **~s** *pl* initia *ntpl*,

prīncipia *ntpl*; **out of one's ~** peregrīnus.
elementary *adj* prīmus.
elephant *n* elephantus *m*, elephas *m*.
elevate *vt* efferre, ērigere.
elevated *adj* ēditus, altus.
elevation *n* altitūdō *f*; (*style*) ēlātiō *f*.
eleven *num* ūndecim; **~ each** ūndēnī; **~ times** ūndeciēns.
eleventh *adj* ūndecimus.
elf *n* deus *m*.
elicit *vt* ēlicere; (*with effort*) ēruere.
elide *vt* ēlīdere.
eligible *adj* idōneus, aptus.
eliminate *vt* tollere, āmovēre.
elite *n* flōs *m*, rōbur *nt*.
elk *n* alcēs *f*.
ell *n* ulna *f*.
ellipse *n* (*RHET*) dētractiō *f*; (*oval*) ōvum *nt*.
elm *n* ulmus *f* ♦ *adj* ulmeus.
elocution *n* prōnūntiātiō *f*.
elongate *vt* prōdūcere.
elope *vi* aufugere.
eloquence *n* ēloquentia *f*; (*natural*) fācundia *f*, dīcendī vīs *f*.
eloquent *adj* ēloquēns; (*natural*) fācundus; (*fluent*) disertus.
eloquently *adv* fācundē, disertē.
else *adv* aliōquī, aliter ♦ *adj* alius; **or ~** aliōquī; **who ~** quis alius.
elsewhere *adv* alibī; **~ to** aliō.
elucidate *vt* ēnōdāre, illūstrāre.
elucidation *n* ēnōdātiō *f*, explicātiō *f*.
elude *vt* ēvītāre, frustrārī, fallere.
elusive *adj* fallāx.
emaciated *adj* macer.
emaciation *n* maciēs *f*.
emanate *vi* mānāre; (*fig*) ēmānāre, orīrī.
emanation *n* exhālātiō *f*.
emancipate *vt* ēmancipāre, manū mittere, līberāre.
emancipation *n* lībertās *f*.
emasculate *vt* ēnervāre, dēlumbāre.
embalm *vt* condīre.
embankment *n* agger *m*, mōlēs *f*.
embargo *n* interdictum *nt*.
embark *vi* cōnscendere, nāvem cōnscendere; **~ upon** (*fig*) ingredī ♦ *vt* impōnere.
embarkation *n* cōnscēnsiō *f*.
embarrass *vt* (*by confusing*) perturbāre; (*by obstructing*) impedīre; (*by revealing*) dēprehendere; **be ~ed** haerēre.
embarrassing *adj* incommodus, intempestīvus.
embarrassment *n* (*in speech*) haesitātiō *f*; (*in mind*) sollicitūdō *f*; (*in business*) angustiae *fpl*, difficultās *f*; (*cause*) molestia *f*, impedīmentum *nt*.
embassy *n* lēgātiō *f*.
embedded *adj* dēfixus.
embellish *vt* adōrnāre, exōrnāre, decorāre.
embellishment *n* decus *nt*, exōrnātiō *f*, ōrnāmentum *nt*.
embers *n* cinis *m*, favilla *f*.

embezzle *vt* peculārī, dēpeculārī.
embezzlement *n* peculātus *m*.
embezzler *n* peculātor *m*.
embitter *vt* exacerbāre.
emblazon *vt* īnsignīre.
emblem *n* īnsigne *nt*.
embodiment *n* exemplar *nt*.
embody *vt* repraesentāre; (*MIL*) cōnscrībere.
embolden *vt* cōnfirmāre; **~ the hearts of** animōs cōnfirmāre.
emboss *vt* imprimere, caelāre.
embrace *vt* amplectī, complectī; (*items*) continēre, comprehendere; (*party*) sequī; (*opportunity*) adripere ♦ *nt* amplexus *m*, complexus *m*.
embroider *vt* acū pingere.
embroidery *n* vestis picta *f*.
embroil *vt* miscēre, implicāre.
emend *vt* ēmendāre, corrigere.
emendation *n* ēmendātiō *f*, corrēctiō *f*.
emerald *n* smaragdus *m*.
emerge *vi* ēmergere, exsistere; ēgredī.
emergency *n* tempus *nt*, discrīmen *nt* ♦ *adj* subitārius.
emigrate *vi* migrāre, ēmigrāre.
emigration *n* migrātiō *f*.
eminence *n* (*ground*) tumulus *m*, locus ēditus *m*; (*rank*) praestantia *f*, amplitūdō *f*.
eminent *adj* ēgregius, ēminēns, īnsignis, amplus.
eminently *adv* ēgregiē, prae cēterīs, in prīmīs.
emissary *n* lēgātus *m*.
emit *vt* ēmittere.
emolument *n* lucrum *nt*, ēmolumentum *nt*.
emotion *n* animī mōtus *m*, commōtiō *f*, adfectus *m*.
emotional *adj* (*person*) mōbilis; (*speech*) flexanimus.
emperor *n* prīnceps *m*, imperātor *m*.
emphasis *n* pondus *nt*; (*words*) impressiō *f*.
emphasize *vt* exprimere.
emphatic *adj* gravis.
emphatically *adv* adsevēranter, vehementer.
empire *n* imperium *nt*.
employ *vt* ūtī (*abl*); (*for purpose*) adhibēre; (*person*) exercēre.
employed *adj* occupātus.
employees *npl* operae *fpl*.
employer *n* redemptor *m*.
employment *n* (*act*) ūsus *m*; (*work*) quaestus *m*.
empower *vt* permittere (*dat*), potestātem facere (*dat*).
emptiness *n* inānitās *f*.
empty *adj* inānis, vacuus; (*fig*) vānus, inritus ♦ *vt* exhaurīre, exinānīre ♦ *vi* (*river*) īnfluere.
emulate *vt* aemulārī.
emulation *n* aemulātiō *f*.
emulous *adj* aemulus.
emulously *adv* certātim.
enable *vt* potestātem facere (*dat*); efficere ut (*subj*).

enact *vt* dēcernere, ēdīcere, scīscere; (*part*) agere.

enactment *n* dēcrētum *nt*, lēx *f*.

enamoured *adj* amāns; **be ~ of** dēamāre.

encamp *vi* castra pōnere, tendere.

encampment *n* castra *ntpl*.

encase *vt* inclūdere.

enchant *vt* fascināre; (*fig*) dēlectāre.

enchantment *n* fascinātiō *f*; blandīmentum *nt*.

enchantress *n* sāga *f*.

encircle *vt* cingere, circumdare, amplectī.

enclose *vt* inclūdere, saepīre.

enclosure *n* saeptum *nt*, māceria *f*.

encompass *vt* cingere, circumdare, amplectī.

encounter *vt* obviam īre (*dat*), occurrere (*dat*); (*in battle*) concurrere cum (*abl*), congredī cum ♦ *n* occursus *m*, concursus *m*.

encourage *vt* cōnfirmāre, (co)hortārī, sublevāre, favēre (*dat*).

encouragement *n* hortātiō *f*, favor *m*, auxilium *nt*.

encroach *vi* invādere; **~ upon** occupāre; (*fig*) imminuere.

encrust *vt* incrustāre.

encumber *vt* impedīre, onerāre.

encumbrance *n* impedīmentum *nt*, onus *nt*.

end *n* fīnis *m*; (*aim*) prōpositum *nt*; (*of action*) ēventus *m*, exitus *m*; (*of speech*) perōrātiō *f*; **~ to ~** continuī; **at a loose ~** vacuus, ōtiōsus; **for two days on ~** biduum continenter; **in the ~** dēnique; **the ~ of** extrēmus; (*time*) exāctus; **put an ~ to** fīnem facere (*dat*), fīnem impōnere (*dat*); **to the ~ that** eō cōnsiliō ut (*subj*); **to what ~?** quō?, quōrsum? ♦ *vt* fīnīre, cōnficere; (*mutual dealings*) dīrimere ♦ *vi* dēsinere; (*event*) ēvādere; (*sentence*) cadere; (*speech*) perōrāre; (*time*) exīre; **~ up as** ēvādere; **~ with** dēsinere in (*acc*).

endanger *vt* perīclitārī, in discrīmen addūcere.

endear *vt* dēvincīre.

endearing *adj* blandus.

endearment *n* blanditiae *fpl*.

endeavour *vt* cōnārī, ēnītī ♦ *n* cōnātus *m*.

ending *n* fīnis *m*, exitus *m*.

endive *n* intubum *nt*.

endless *adj* īnfīnītus; (*time*) aeternus, perpetuus.

endlessly *adv* sine fīne, īnfīnītē.

endorse *vt* ratum facere.

endow *vt* dōnāre, īnstruere.

endowed *adj* praeditus (+ *abl*).

endowment *n* dōnum *nt*.

endurance *n* patientia *f*.

endure *vi* dūrāre, permanēre ♦ *vt* ferre, tolerāre, patī.

enemy *n* (*public*) hostis *m*, hostēs *mpl*; (*private*) inimīcus *m*; **greatest ~** inimīcissimus *m*; **~ territory** hosticum *nt*.

energetic *adj* impiger, nāvus, strēnuus; (*style*) nervōsus.

energetically *adv* impigrē, nāviter, strēnuē.

energy *n* impigritās *f*, vigor *m*, incitātiō *f*; (*mind*) contentiō *f*; (*style*) nervī *mpl*.

enervate *vt* ēnervāre, ēmollīre.

enervation *n* languor *m*.

enfeeble *vt* īnfirmāre, dēbilitāre.

enfold *vt* involvere, complectī.

enforce *vt* (*law*) exsequī; (*argument*) cōnfirmāre.

enfranchise *vt* cīvitāte dōnāre; (*slave*) manū mittere.

engage *vt* (*affection*) dēvincīre; (*attention*) distinēre, occupāre; (*enemy*) manum cōnserere cum (*abl*); (*hire*) condūcere; (*promise*) spondēre, recipere; **~ the enemy** proelium cum hostibus committere; **be ~d in** versārī in (*abl*) ♦ *vi*: **~ in** ingredī, suscipere.

engagement *n* (*comm*) occupātiō *f*; (*mil*) pugna *f*, certāmen *nt*; (*agreement*) spōnsiō *f*; **keep an ~** fidem praestāre; **break an ~** fidem fallere; **I have an ~ at your house** prōmīsī ad tē.

engaging *adj* blandus.

engender *vt* ingenerāre, ingignere.

engine *n* māchina *f*.

engineer *n* māchinātor *m* ♦ *vt* mōlīrī.

engraft *vt* īnserere.

engrave *vt* īnsculpere, incīdere, caelāre.

engraver *n* sculptor *m*, caelātor *m*.

engraving *n* sculptūra *f*, caelātūra *f*.

engross *vt* dīstringere, occupāre; **~ed in** tōtus in (*abl*).

engulf *vt* dēvorāre, obruere.

enhance *vt* amplificāre, augēre, exaggerāre.

enigma *n* aenigma *nt*, ambāgēs *fpl*.

enigmatic *adj* ambiguus, obscūrus.

enigmatically *adv* per ambāgēs, ambiguē.

enjoin *vt* imperāre (*dat*), iniungere (*dat*).

enjoy *vt* fruī (*abl*); (*advantage*) ūtī (*abl*); (*pleasure*) percipere, dēcerpere; **~ oneself** dēlectārī, geniō indulgēre.

enjoyable *adj* iūcundus.

enjoyment *n* fructus *m*; dēlectātiō *f*, voluptās *f*.

enlarge *vt* augēre, amplificāre, dīlātāre; (*territory*) prōpāgāre; **~ upon** amplificāre.

enlargement *n* amplificātiō *f*, prōlātiō *f*.

enlighten *vt* inlūstrāre; docēre, ērudīre.

enlightenment *n* ērudītiō *f*, hūmānitās *f*.

enlist *vt* scrībere, cōnscrībere; (*sympathy*) conciliāre ♦ *vi* nōmen dare.

enliven *vt* excitāre.

enmesh *vt* impedīre, implicāre.

enmity *n* inimīcitia *f*, simultās *f*.

ennoble *vt* honestāre, excolere.

ennui *n* taedium *nt*.

enormity *n* immānitās *f*; (*deed*) scelus *nt*, nefās *nt*.

enormous *adj* immānis, ingēns.

enormously *adv* immēnsum.

enough *adj* satis (*indecl gen*) ♦ *adv* satis; **more than ~** satis superque; **I have had ~ of . . .** mē taedet (*gen*) . . . .

enquire *vi* quaerere, percontārī; **~ into**

cognōscere, inquīrere in (*acc*).
enquiry *n* percontātiō *f*; (*legal*) quaestiō *f*.
enrage *vt* inrītāre, incendere.
enrapture *vt* dēlectāre.
enrich *vt* dītāre, locuplētāre; ~ **with** augēre (*abl*).
enrol *vt* adscrībere, conscrībere ♦ *vi* nōmen dare.
enshrine *vt* dēdicāre; (*fig*) sacrāre.
enshroud *vt* involvere.
ensign *n* signum *nt*, īnsigne *nt*; (*officer*) signifer *m*.
enslave *vt* in servitūtem redigere.
enslavement *n* servitūs *f*.
ensnare *vt* dēcipere, inlaqueāre, inrētīre.
ensue *vi* īnsequī.
ensure *vt* praestāre; ~ **that** efficere ut (*subj*).
entail *vt* adferre.
entangle *vt* impedīre, implicāre, inrētīre.
entanglement *n* implicātiō *f*.
enter *vi* inīre, ingredī, intrāre; (*riding*) invehī; ~ **into** introīre in (*acc*); ~ **upon** inīre, ingredī ♦ *vt* (*place*) intrare; (*account*) ferre, indūcere; (*mind*) subīre.
enterprise *n* inceptum *nt*; (*character*) prōmptus animus *m*.
enterprising *adj* prōmptus, strēnuus.
entertain *vt* (*guest*) invītāre, excipere; (*state of mind*) habēre, concipere; (*to amuse*) oblectāre.
entertainer *n* acroāma *nt*.
entertainment *n* hospitium *nt*; oblectāmentum *nt*; acroāma *nt*.
enthral *vt* capere.
enthusiasm *n* studium *nt*, fervor *m*; ~ **for** studium *nt* (+ *gen*).
enthusiastic *adj* studiōsus, fervidus.
enthusiastically *adv* summō studiō.
entice *vt* inlicere, ēlicere, invītāre.
enticement *n* illecebra *f*, lēnōcinium *nt*.
entire *adj* integer, tōtus, ūniversus.
entirely *adv* omnīnō, funditus, penitus.
entitle *vt* (*book*) īnscrībere; **be ~d** to merērī, dignum esse quī (*subj*), iūs habēre (*gen*).
entity *n* rēs *f*.
entomb *vt* humāre, sepelīre.
entrails *n* intestīna *ntpl*, exta *ntpl*.
entrance *n* aditus *m*, introitus *m*; (*act*) ingressiō *f*; (*of house*) vestibulum *nt*; (*of harbour*) ōstium *nt*.
entrance *vt* fascināre, cōnsōpīre, capere.
entreat *vt* implōrāre, obsecrāre; (*successfully*) exōrāre.
entreaty *n* precēs *fpl*.
entrenchment *n* mūnītiō *f*.
entrust *vt* committere, crēdere, mandāre; (*for keeping*) dēpōnere.
entry *n* introitus *m*, aditus *m*; **make an ~** (*book*) in tabulās referre.
entwine *vt* implicāre, involvere.
enumerate *vt* numerāre, dīnumerāre.
enunciate *vt* ēdīcere; (*word*) exprimere.
envelop *vt* implicāre, involvere.

envelope *n* involucrum *nt*.
enviable *adj* beātus.
envious *adj* invidus, invidiōsus.
enviously *adv* invidiōsē.
environment *n* vīcīnia *f*; **our** ~ ea in quibus versāmur.
envoy *n* lēgātus *m*.
envy *n* invidia *f* ♦ *vt* invidēre (*dat*).
enwrap *vt* involvere.
ephemeral *adj* brevis.
ephor *n* ephorus *m*.
epic *adj* epicus ♦ *n* epos *nt*.
epicure *n* dēlicātus *m*.
epigram *n* sententia *f*; (*poem*) epigramma *nt*.
epilepsy *n* morbus comitiālis *m*.
epilogue *n* epilogus *m*.
episode *n* ēventum *nt*.
epistle *n* epistula *f*, litterae *fpl*.
epitaph *n* epigramma *nt*, titulus *m*.
epithet *n* adsūmptum *nt*.
epitome *n* epitomē *f*.
epoch *n* saeculum *nt*.
equable *adj* aequālis; (*temper*) aequus.
equal *adj* aequus, pār; **be ~ to** aequāre; (*task*) sufficere (*dat*) ♦ *n* pār *m/f* ♦ *vt* aequāre, adaequāre.
equality *n* aequālitās *f*.
equalize *vt* adaequāre, exaequāre.
equally *adv* aequē, pariter.
equanimity *n* aequus animus *m*.
equate *vt* aequāre.
equator *n* aequinoctiālis circulus *m*.
equestrian *adj* equester.
equidistant *adj*: **be ~** aequō spatiō abesse, idem distāre.
equilibrium *n* lībrāmentum *nt*.
equine *adj* equīnus.
equinoctial *adj* aequinoctiālis.
equinox *n* aequinoctium *nt*.
equip *vt* armāre, īnstruere, ōrnāre.
equipment *n* arma *ntpl*, īnstrūmenta *ntpl*, adparātus *m*.
equipoise *n* lībrāmentum *nt*.
equitable *adj* aequus, iūstus.
equitably *adv* iūstē, aequē.
equity *n* aequum *nt*, aequitās *f*.
equivalent *adj* pār, īdem īnstar (*gen*).
equivocal *adj* anceps, ambiguus.
equivocally *adv* ambiguē.
equivocate *vi* tergiversārī.
era *n* saeculum *nt*.
eradicate *vt* ēvellere, exstirpāre.
erase *vt* dēlēre, indūcere.
erasure *n* litūra *f*.
ere *conj* priusquam.
erect *vt* ērigere; (*building*) exstruere; (*statute*) pōnere ♦ *adj* ērēctus.
erection *n* (*process*) exstructiō *f*; (*product*) aedificium *nt*.
erode *vt* rōdere.
erotic *adj* amātōrius.
err *vi* errāre, peccāre.
errand *n* mandātum *nt*.

errant *adj* vagus.
erratic *adj* incōnstāns.
erroneous *adj* falsus.
erroneously *adv* falsō, perperam.
error *n* error *m*; (*moral*) peccātum *nt*; (*writing*)
    mendum *nt*.
erudite *adj* doctus.
erudition *n* doctrīna *f*, ērudītiō *f*.
erupt *vi* ērumpere.
eruption *n* ēruptiō *f*.
escapade *n* ausum *nt*.
escape *vi* effugere, ēvādere ♦ *vt* fugere,
    ēvītāre; (*memory*) excidere ex (*abl*); ~ **the
    notice of** fallere, praeterīre ♦ *n* effugium *nt*,
    fuga *f*; **way of** ~ effugium *nt*.
eschew *vt* vītāre.
escort *n* praesidium *nt*; (*private*) dēductor *m* ♦
    vt comitārī, prōsequī; (*out of respect*)
    dēdūcere.
especial *adj* praecipuus.
especially *adv* praecipuē, praesertim,
    māximē, in prīmīs.
espionage *n* inquīsītiō *f*.
espouse *vt* (*wife*) dūcere; (*cause*) fovēre.
espy *vt* cōnspicere, cōnspicārī.
essay *n* cōnātus *m*; (*test*) perīculum *nt*; (*literary*)
    libellus *m* ♦ *vt* cōnārī, incipere.
essence *n* vīs *f*, nātūra *f*.
essential *adj* necesse, necessārius.
essentially *adv* necessāriō.
establish *vt* īnstituere, condere; (*firmly*)
    stabilīre.
established *adj* firmus, certus; **be** ~ cōnstāre;
    become ~ (*custom*) inveterāscere.
establishment *n* (*act*) cōnstitūtiō *f*; (*domestic*)
    familia *f*.
estate *n* fundus *m*, rūs *nt*; (*in money*) rēs *f*;
    (*rank*) ōrdō *m*.
esteem *vt* aestimāre, respicere ♦ *n* grātia *f*,
    opīniō *f*.
estimable *adj* optimus.
estimate *vt* aestimāre, ratiōnem inīre (*gen*) ♦
    n aestimātiō *f*, iūdicium *nt*.
estimation *n* opīniō *f*, sententia *f*.
estrange *vt* aliēnāre, abaliēnāre.
estrangement *n* aliēnātiō *f*, discidium *nt*.
estuary *n* aestuārium *nt*.
eternal *adj* aeternus, perennis.
eternally *adv* semper, aeternum.
eternity *n* aeternitās *f*.
etesian winds *n* etēsiae *fpl*.
ether *n* (*sky*) aethēr *m*.
ethereal *adj* aetherius, caelestis.
ethic, ethical *adj* mōrālis.
ethics *n* mōrēs *mpl*, officia *ntpl*.
Etruscan *n* Etruscus *m* ♦ *adj like* **bonus**.
etymology *n* verbōrum notātiō *f*.
eulogist *n* laudātor *m*.
eulogize *vt* laudāre, conlaudāre.
eulogy *n* laudātiō *f*.
eunuch *n* eunūchus *m*.
euphony *n* sonus *m*.
evacuate *vt* (*place*) exinānīre; (*people*)
    dēdūcere.
evacuation *n* discessiō *f*.
evade *vt* dēclīnāre, dēvītāre, ēlūdere.
evaporate *vt* exhālāre ♦ *vi* exhālārī.
evaporation *n* exhālātiō *f*.
evasion *n* tergiversātiō *f*.
evasive *adj* ambiguus.
eve *n* vesper *m*; (*before festival*) pervigilium *nt*;
    on the ~ **of** prīdiē (*gen*).
even *adj* aequus, aequālis; (*number*) pār ♦ *adv*
    et, etiam; (*tentative*) vel; ~ **if** etsī, etiamsī;
    tametsī; ~ **more** etiam magis; ~ **so**
    nihilōminus; ~ **yet** etiamnum; **not** ~ . . . nē
    quidem ♦ *vt* aequāre.
evening *n* vesper *m* ♦ *adj* vespertīnus; ~ **is
    drawing on** invesperāscit; **in the** ~ vesperī.
evening star *n* Vesper *m*, Hesperus *m*.
evenly *adv* aequāliter, aequābiliter.
evenness *n* aequālitās *f*, aequābilitās *f*.
event *n* ēventum *nt*; (*outcome*) ēventus *m*.
eventide *n* vespertīnum tempus *nt*.
eventuality *n* cāsus *m*.
eventually *adv* mox, aliquandō, tandem.
ever *adv* unquam; (*after* **sī, nisī, num, nē**)
    quandō; (*always*) semper; (*after interrog*)
    -nam, tandem; ~ **so** nimium, nimium
    quantum; **best** ~ omnium optimus; **for** ~ in
    aeternum.
everlasting *adj* aeternus, perpetuus,
    immortālis.
evermore *adv* semper, in aeternum.
every *adj* quisque, omnis; ~ **four years** quīntō
    quōque annō; ~ **now and then** interdum; **in** ~
    direction passim; undique; ~ **other day**
    alternīs diēbus; ~ **day** cottīdiē ♦ *adj*
    cottīdiānus.
everybody *pron* quisque, omnēs *mpl*; ~ **agrees**
    inter omnēs cōnstat; ~ **knows** nēmō est quīn
    sciat.
everyday *adj* cottīdiānus.
everyone *pron see* **everybody**.
everything omnia *ntpl*; **your health is** ~ **to me**
    meā māximē interest tē valēre.
everywhere *adv* ubīque, passim.
evict *vt* dēicere, dētrūdere.
eviction *n* dēiectiō *f*.
evidence *n* testimōnium *nt*, indicium *nt*;
    (*person*) testis *m/f*; (*proof*) argūmentum *nt*; **on
    the** ~ **of** fidē (*gen*); **collect** ~ **against** inquīrere
    in (*acc*); **turn King's** ~ indicium profitērī.
evident *adj* manifestus, ēvidēns, clārus; **it is** ~
    appāret.
evidently *adv* manifestō, clārē.
evil *adj* malus, improbus, scelerātus.
evildoer *n* scelerātus *m*, maleficus *m*.
evil eye *n* fascinum *nt*, malum *nt*, improbitās *f*.
evil-minded *adj* malevolus.
evince *vt* praestāre.
evoke *vt* ēvocāre, ēlicere.
evolution *n* seriēs *f*, prōgressus *m*; (*MIL*)
    dēcursus *m*, dēcursiō *f*.
evolve *vt* explicāre, ēvolvere ♦ *vi* crēscere.
ewe *n* ovis *f*.
ewer *n* hydria *f*.
exacerbate *vt* exacerbāre, exasperāre.

exact vt exigere ♦ adj accūrātus; (person) dīligēns; (number) exāctus.
exaction n exāctiō f.
exactly adv accūrātē; (reply) ita prōrsus; ~ **as** perinde que.
exactness n cūra f, dīligentia f.
exaggerate vt augēre, in māius extollere.
exalt vt efferre, extollere; laudāre.
exaltation n ēlātiō f.
examination n inquīsītiō f, scrūtātiō f; (of witness) interrogātiō f; (test) probātiō f.
examine vt investīgāre, scrūtārī; īnspicere; (witness) interrogāre; (case) quaerere dē (abl); (candidate) probāre.
examiner n scrūtātor m.
example n exemplum nt, documentum nt; **for** ~ exemplī grātiā; **make an** ~ **of** animadvertere in (acc); **I am an** ~ exemplō sum.
exasperate vt exacerbāre, inrītāre.
exasperation n inrītātiō f.
excavate vt fodere.
excavation n fossiō f.
excavator n fossor m.
exceed vt excēdere, superāre.
exceedingly adv nimis, valdē, nimium quantum.
excel vt praestāre (dat), exsuperāre ♦ vi excellere.
excellence n praestantia f, virtūs f.
excellent adj ēgregius, praestāns, optimus.
excellently adv ēgregiē, praeclārē.
except vt excipere ♦ prep praeter (acc) ♦ adv nisī ♦ conj praeterquam, nisī quod.
exception n exceptiō f; **make an** ~ **of** excipere; **take** ~ **to** gravārī quod; **with the** ~ **of** praeter (acc).
exceptional adj ēgregius, eximius.
exceptionally adv ēgregiē, eximiē.
excerpt vt excerpere ♦ n excerptum nt.
excess n immoderātiō f, intemperantia f ♦ adj supervacāneus; **be in** ~ superesse.
excessive adj immoderātus, immodestus, nimius.
excessively adv immodicē, nimis.
exchange vt mūtāre, permūtāre ♦ n permūtātiō f; (of currencies) collybus m.
exchequer n aerārium nt; (emperor's) fiscus m.
excise n vectīgālia ntpl ♦ vt excīdere.
excision n excīsiō f.
excitable adj mōbilis.
excite vt excitāre, concitāre; (to action) incitāre, incendere; (to hope) ērigere, exacuere; (emotion) movēre, commovēre.
excitement n commōtiō f.
exclaim vt exclāmāre; ~ **against** adclāmāre (dat).
exclamation n clāmor m, exclāmātiō f.
exclude vt exclūdere.
exclusion n exclūsiō f.
exclusive adj proprius.
exclusively adv sōlum.
excogitate vt excōgitāre.
excrescence n tūber nt.

excruciating adj acerbissimus.
exculpate vt pūrgāre, absolvere.
excursion n iter nt; (MIL) excursiō f.
excuse n excūsātiō f; (false) speciēs f ♦ vt excūsāre, ignōscere (dat); (something due) remittere; **plead in** ~ excūsāre; **put forward as an** ~ praetendere.
execrable adj dētestābilis, sacer, nefārius.
execrate vt dētestārī, exsecrārī.
execration n dētestātiō f, exsecrātiō f.
execute vt efficere, patrāre, exsequī; suppliciō afficere; (behead) secūrī percutere.
execution n effectus m; (penalty) supplicium nt, mors f.
executioner n carnifex m.
exemplar n exemplum nt.
exempt adj immūnis, līber ♦ vt līberāre.
exemption n (from tax) immūnitās f; (from service) vacātiō f.
exercise n exercitātiō f, ūsus m; (school) dictāta ntpl ♦ vt exercēre, ūtī (abl); (mind) acuere.
exert vt extendere, intendere, ūtī (abl); ~ **oneself** mōlīrī, ēnītī, sē intendere.
exertion n mōlīmentum nt; (mind) intentiō f.
exhalation n exhālātiō f, vapor m.
exhale vt exhālāre, exspīrāre.
exhaust vt exhaurīre; (tire) dēfatīgāre, cōnficere.
exhaustion n dēfatīgātiō f.
exhaustive adj plēnus.
exhibit vt exhibēre, ostendere, expōnere; (on stage) ēdere.
exhibition n expositiō f, ostentātiō f.
exhilarate vt exhilarāre.
exhort vt hortārī, cohortārī.
exhortation n hortātiō f, hortāmen nt.
exhume vt ēruere.
exigency n necessitās f.
exile n exsilium nt, fuga f; (temporary) relēgātiō f; (person) exsul m; **live in** ~ exsulāre ♦ vt in exsilium pellere, dēportāre; (temporarily) relēgāre.
exist vi esse.
existence n vīta f.
exit n exitus m, ēgressus m.
exodus n discessus m.
exonerate vt absolvere.
exorbitant adj nimius, immoderātus.
exotic adj peregrīnus.
expand vt extendere, dīlātāre.
expanse n spatium nt, lātitūdō f.
expatiate vi: ~ **upon** amplificāre.
expatriate vt extermināre ♦ n extorris m.
expect vt exspectāre, spērāre.
expectancy, expectation n spēs f, exspectātiō f, opīniō f.
expediency n ūtile nt, ūtilitās f.
expedient adj ūtilis, commodus; **it is** ~ expedit ♦ n modus m, ratiō f.
expediently adv commodē.
expedite vt mātūrāre.

expedition n (_MIL_) expedītiō f.
expeditious adj prōmptus, celer.
expeditiously adv celeriter.
expel vt pellere, expellere, ēicere.
expend vt impendere, expendere.
expenditure n impēnsae fpl, sūmptus m.
expense n impēnsae fpl, impendia ntpl; **at my ~** meō sūmptū; **at the public ~** dē pūblicō.
expensive adj cārus, pretiōsus; (_furnishings_) lautus.
expensively adv sūmptuōsē, māgnō pretiō.
experience n ūsus m, experientia f ♦ vt experīrī, patī.
experienced adj perītus, expertus (+ gen).
experiment n experīmentum nt ♦ vi: **~ with** experīrī.
expert adj perītus, sciēns.
expertly adv perītē, scienter.
expertness n perītia f.
expiate vt expiāre, lūere.
expiatio n (_act_) expiātiō f; (_penalty_) piāculum nt.
expiatory adj piāculāris.
expiration n (_breath_) exspīrātiō f; (_time_) exitus m.
expire vi exspīrāre; (_die_) animam agere, animam efflāre; (_time_) exīre.
expiry n exitus m, fīnis m.
explain vt explicāre, expōnere, explānāre, interpretārī; (_lucidly_) ēnōdāre; (_in detail_) ēdisserere.
explanation n explicātiō f, ēnōdātiō f, interpretātiō f.
explicit adj expressus, apertus.
explicitly adv apertē.
explode vt discutere ♦ vi dīrumpī.
exploit n factum nt, ausum nt; **~s** pl rēs gestae fpl ♦ vt ūtī (abl), fruī (abl).
explore vt, vi explōrāre, scrūtārī.
explorer n explōrātor m.
explosion n fragor m.
exponent n interpres m, auctor m.
export vt exportāre ♦ n exportātiō f.
exportation n exportātiō f.
expose vt dētegere, dēnūdāre, patefacere; (_child_) expōnere; (_to danger_) obicere; (_MIL_) nūdāre; (_for sale_) prōpōnere; **~ o.s.** se obicere.
exposed adj apertus, obnoxius.
exposition n explicātiō f, interpretātiō f.
expostulate vi expostulāre, conquerī.
expostulation n expostulātiō f.
exposure n (_of child_) expositiō f; (_of guilt_) dēprehēnsiō f; (_to hardship_) patientia f.
expound vt expōnere, interpretārī.
expounder n interpres m.
express vt (_in words_) exprimere, dēclārāre, ēloquī; (_in art_) effingere ♦ adj expressus; (_speed_) celerrimus.
expression n significātiō f; (_word_) vōx f, verbum nt; (_face_) vultus m.
expressive adj significāns; **~ of** index (gen); **be very ~** māximam vim habēre.

expressively adv significanter.
expressiveness n vīs f.
expressly adv plānē.
expulsion n expulsiō f, ēiectiō f.
expurgate vt pūrgāre.
exquisite adj ēlegāns, exquīsītus, eximius; (_judgment_) subtīlis.
exquisitely adv ēleganter, exquīsītē.
ex-service adj ēmeritus.
extant adj superstes; **be ~** exstāre.
extempore adv ex tempore, subitō ♦ adj extemporālis.
extemporize vi subita dīcere.
extend vt extendere, dīlātāre; (_hand_) porrigere; (_line_) dūcere; (_office_) prōrogāre; (_territory_) propāgāre ♦ vi patēre, porrigī; **~ into** incurrere in (acc).
extension n prōductiō f, prōlātiō f; (_of office_) prōrogātiō f; (_of territory_) propāgātiō f; (_extra_) incrēmentum nt.
extensive adj effūsus, amplus, lātus.
extensively adv lātē.
extent n spatium nt, amplitūdō f; **to a large ~** māgnā ex parte; **to some ~** aliquā ex parte; **to this ~** hāctenus; **to such an ~** adeō.
extenuate vt levāre, mītigāre.
exterior adj externus, exterior ♦ n speciēs f.
exterminate vt occīdiōne occīdere, interimere.
extermination n occīdiō f, interneciō f.
external adj externus.
externally adv extrīnsecus.
extinct adj mortuus; (_custom_) obsolētus.
extinction n exstinctiō f, interitus m.
extinguish vt exstinguere, restinguere.
extinguisher n exstinctor m.
extirpate vt exstirpāre, excīdere.
extol vt laudāre, laudibus efferre.
extort vt extorquēre, exprimere.
extortion n (_offence_) rēs repetundae fpl.
extortionate adj inīquus, rapāx.
extra adv īnsuper, praetereā ♦ adj additus.
extract vt excerpere, extrahere ♦ n: **make ~s** excerpere.
extraction n ēvulsiō f; (_descent_) genus nt.
extraneous adj adventīcius, aliēnus.
extraordinarily adv mīrificē, eximiē.
extraordinary adj extraōrdinārius; (_strange_) mīrus, novus; (_outstanding_) eximius, īnsignis.
extravagance n intemperantia f; (_language_) immoderātiō f, luxuria f; (_spending_) sūmptus m.
extravagant adj immoderātus, immodestus; (_spending_) sūmptuōsus, prōdigus.
extreme adj extrēmus, ultimus.
extremely adv valdē, vehementer.
extremity n extrēmum nt, fīnis m; (_distress_) angustiae fpl; **the ~ of** extrēmus.
extricate vt expedīre, absolvere; **~ oneself** ēmergere.
exuberance n ūbertās f, luxuria f.
exuberant adj ūber, laetus, luxuriōsus.

exuberantly *adv* ūbertim.
exude *vt* exsūdāre ♦ *vi* mānāre.
exult *vi* exsultārī, laetārī, gestīre.
exultant *adj* laetus.
exultantly *adv* laetē.
exultation *n* laetitia *f*.
eye *n* oculus *m*; (*needle*) forāmen *nt*; **cast ~s on**
oculōs conicere in (*acc*); **have an ~ to**
spectāre; **in your ~s** iūdice tē; **keep one's ~s**
on oculōs dēfigere in (*abl*); **lose an ~** alterō
oculō capī; **see ~ to ~** cōnsentīre; **set ~s on**
cōnspicere; **shut one's ~s to** cōnīvēre in
(*abl*); **take one's ~s off** oculōs dēicere ab
(*abl*); **up to the ~s in** tōtus in (*abl*); **with a cast**
in the ~ paetus; **with sore ~s** lippus; **sore ~s**
lippitūdō *f*; **with one's own ~s** cōram; **with**
one's ~s open sciēns ♦ *vt* intuērī, aspicere.
eyeball *n* pūpula *f*.
eyebrow *n* supercilium *nt*.
eyelash *n* palpebrae pilus *m*.
eyelid *n* palpebra *f*.
eyeshot *n* oculōrum coniectus *m*.
eyesight *n* aciēs *f*, oculī *mpl*.
eyesore *n* turpe *nt*; **it is an ~ to me** oculī meī
dolent.
eye tooth *n* dēns canīnus *m*.
eyewash *n* sycophantia *f*.
eyewitness *n* arbiter *m*; **be an ~ of** interesse
(*dat*).

$$ F, f $$

fable *n* fābula *f*, apologus *m*.
fabled *adj* fābulōsus.
fabric *n* (*built*) structūra *f*, (*woven*) textile *nt*.
fabricate *vt* fabricārī; (*fig*) comminīscī,
fingere.
fabricated *adj* commentīcius.
fabrication *n* (*process*) fabricātiō *f*; (*thing*)
commentum *nt*.
fabricator *n* auctor *m*.
fabulous *adj* commentīcius, fictus.
fabulously *adv* incrēdibiliter.
facade *n* frōns *f*.
face *n* faciēs *f*, ōs *nt*; (*aspect*) aspectus *m*;
(*impudence*) ōs *nt*; **~ to ~** cōram; **how shall**
I have the ~ to go back? quō ōre redībō?; **on**
the ~ of it ad speciem, prīmō aspectū; **put**
a bold ~ on fortem sē praebēre; **save ~**
factum pūrgāre; **set one's ~ against**
adversārī (*dat*) ♦ *vt* spectāre ad (*acc*);
(*danger*) obviam īre (*dat*), sē oppōnere
(*dat*) ♦ *vi* (*place*) spectāre, vergere; **~**
about (*MIL*) signa convertere.
facetious *adj* facētus, salsus.

facetiously *adv* facētē, salsē.
facetiousness *n* facētiae *fpl*, salēs *mpl*.
facile *adj* facilis.
facilitate *vt* expedīre.
facilities *npl* opportūnitās *f*.
facility *n* facilitās *f*.
facing *adj* adversus ♦ *prep* exadversus (*acc*).
facsimile *n* exemplār *nt*.
fact *n* rēs *f*, vērum *nt*; **as a matter of ~**
enimvērō; **the ~ that** quod; **in ~** rē vērā ♦ *conj*
etenim; (*climax*) dēnique.
faction *n* factiō *f*.
factious *adj* factiōsus, sēditiōsus.
factiously *adv* sēditiōsē.
factor *n* prōcūrātor *m*.
factory *n* officīna *f*.
faculty *n* facultās *f*, vīs *f*.
fad *n* libīdō *f*.
fade *vi* dēflōrēscere, marcēscere.
faded *adj* marcidus.
faggot *n* sarmentum *nt*.
fail *vi* dēficere, dēesse; (*fig*) cadere, dēcidere;
(*in business*) forō cēdere; **~ to** nōn posse; **~ to**
come nōn venīre ♦ *vt* dēficere, dēstituere.
failing *n* culpa *f*, vitium *nt*.
failure *n* (*of supply*) dēfectiō *f*; (*in action*)
offēnsiō *f*; (*at election*) repulsa *f*.
fain *adv* libenter.
faint *adj* (*body*) languidus, dēfessus;
(*impression*) hebes, levis; (*courage*) timidus;
(*colour*) pallidus; **be ~** languēre; hebēre ♦ *vi*
intermorī, animō linquī; **I feel ~** animō male
est.
faint-hearted *adj* animo dēmissus; timidus.
faintly *adv* languidē; leviter.
faintness *n* dēfectiō *f*, languor *m*; levitās *f*.
fair *adj* (*appearance*) pulcher, fōrmōsus; (*hair*)
flāvus; (*skin*) candidus; (*weather*) serēnus;
(*wind*) secundus; (*copy*) pūrus; (*dealings*)
aequus; (*speech*) speciōsus, blandus; (*ability*)
mediocris; (*reputation*) bonus ♦ *n* nūndinae
fpl; **~ and square** sine fūcō ac fallāciīs.
fairly *adv* iūre, iūstē; mediocriter.
fairness *n* aequitās *f*.
fair play *n* aequum et bonum *nt*.
fairy *n* nympha *f*.
faith *n* fidēs *f*; **in good ~** bonā fidē.
faithful *adj* fidēlis, fīdus.
faithfully *adv* fidēliter.
faithfulness *n* fidēlitās *f*.
faithless *adj* īnfidēlis, īnfīdus, perfidus.
faithlessly *adv* īnfidēliter.
faithlessness *n* īnfidēlitās *f*.
fake *vt* simulāre.
falchion *n* falx *f*.
falcon *n* falcō *m*.
fall *vi* cadere; (*gently*) lābī; (*morally*) prōlābī;
(*dead*) concidere, occidere; (*fortress*)
expugnārī, capī; **~ at** accidere; **~ away**
dēficere, dēscīscere; **~ back** recidere; (*MIL*)
pedem referre; **~ between** intercidere; **~**
behind cessāre; **~ by the way** intercidere; **~**
down dēcidere, dēlābī; (*building*) ruere,

corruere; ~ **due** cadere; ~ **flat** sē
prōsternere; (*speech*) frīgēre; ~ **forward**
prōlābī; ~ **foul of** incurrere in (*acc*); ~
headlong sē praecipitāre; ~ **in, into** incidere;
~ **in with** occurrere (*dat*); ~ **off** dēcidere; (*fig*)
dēscīscere; ~ **on** incumbere in (*acc*), incidere
in (*acc*); ~ **out** excidere; (*event*) ēvenīre;
(*hair*) dēfluere; ~ **short of** deesse ad; ~ **to** (*by
lot*) obtingere, obvenīre (*dat*); ~ **to the
ground** (*case*) iacēre; ~ **upon** invādere,
ingruere in (*acc*); (*one's neck*) in collum
invādere ♦ *n* cāsus *m*; (*building*) ruīna *f*;
(*moral*) lāpsus *m*; (*season*) autumnus *m*; **the ~
of Capua** Capua capta.
fallacious *adj* captiōsus, fallāx.
fallaciously *adv* fallāciter.
fallacy *n* captiō *f*.
fallible *adj*: **be ~** errāre solēre.
fallow *adj* (*land*) novālis ♦ *n* novāle *nt*; **lie ~**
cessāre.
false *adj* falsus, fictus.
falsehood *n* falsum *nt*, mendācium *nt*; **tell a ~**
mentīrī.
falsely *adv* falsō.
falsify *vt* vitiāre, interlinere.
falter *vi* (*speech*) haesitāre; (*gait*) titubāre.
faltering *adj* (*speech*) īnfrāctus; (*gait*) titubāns
♦ *n* haesitātiō *f*.
fame *n* fāma *f*, glōria *f*, nōmen *nt*.
famed *adj* illūstris, praeclārus.
familiar *adj* (*friend*) intimus; (*fact*) nōtus;
(*manner*) cōmis; ~ **spirit** genius *m*; **be ~ with**
nōvisse; **be on ~ terms with** familiāriter ūtī
(*abl*).
familiarity *n* ūsus *m*, cōnsuētūdō *f*.
familiarize *vt* adsuēfacere.
familiarly *adv* familiāriter.
family *n* domus *f*, gēns *f* ♦ *adj* domesticus,
familiāris; ~ **property** rēs familiāris *f*.
famine *n* famēs *f*.
famished *adj* famēlicus.
famous *adj* illūstris, praeclārus, nōbilis; **make
~** nōbilitāre; **the ~** ille.
fan *n* flābellum *nt*; (*winnowing*) vannus *f* ♦ *vt*
ventilāre; ~ **the flames of** (*fig*) īnflammāre.
fanatic *n* (*religious*) fānāticus *m*.
fanciful *adj* (*person*) incōnstāns; (*idea*)
commentīcius.
fancy *n* (*faculty*) mēns *f*; (*idea*) opīnātiō *f*;
(*caprice*) libīdō *f*; **take a ~ to** amāre incipere;
~ **oneself** sē amāre ♦ *vt* animō fingere,
imāginārī, sibi prōpōnere; ~ **you thinking ...!**
tē crēdere ...! ♦ *adj* dēlicātus.
fancy-free *adj* sēcūrus, vacuus.
fang *n* dēns *m*.
fantastic *adj* commentīcius, mōnstruōsus.
fantasy *n* imāginātiō *f*; (*contemptuous*)
somnium *nt*.
far *adj* longinquus ♦ *adv* longē, procul; (*with
compar*) multō; **be ~ from** longē abesse ab; **be
not ~ from doing** haud multum abest quin
(+*subj*); **by ~** longē; **how ~?** quātenus?,
quoūsque?; **so ~** hāctenus, eātenus; (*limited*)

quādam tenus; **thus ~** hāctenus; ~ **and wide**
lātē; ~ **be it from me to say** equidem dīcere
nōlim; ~ **from thinking ... I** adeō nōn crēdō ...
ut; **as ~ as** *prep* tenus (*abl*) ♦ *adv* ūsque ♦ *conj*
quātenus; (*know*) quod.
farce *n* mīmus *m*.
farcical *adj* rīdiculus.
fare *vi* sē habēre, agere ♦ *n* vectūra *f*; (*boat*)
naulum *nt*; (*food*) cibus *m*.
farewell *interj* valē, valēte; **say ~ to** valēre
iubēre.
far-fetched *adj* quaesītus, arcessītus, altē
repetītus.
farm *n* fundus *m*, praedium *nt* ♦ *vt* (*soil*) colere;
(*taxes*) redimere; ~ **out** locāre.
farmer *n* agricola *m*; (*of taxes*) pūblicānus *m*.
farming *n* agrīcultūra *f*.
farrow *vt* parere ♦ *n* fētus *m*.
far-sighted *adj* prōvidus, prūdēns.
farther *adv* longius, ultrā ♦ *adj* ulterior.
farthest *adj* ultimus, extrēmus ♦ *adv*
longissimē.
fasces *n* fascēs *mpl*.
fascinate *vt* dēlēnīre, capere.
fascination *n* dulcēdō *f*, dēlēnīmenta *ntpl*,
lēnōcinia *ntpl*.
fashion *n* mōs *m*, ūsus *m*; (*manner*) modus *m*,
ratiō *f*; (*shape*) fōrma *f* ♦ *vt* fingere, fōrmāre;
after the ~ of rītū (*gen*); **come into ~** in
mōrem venīre; **go out of ~** obsolēscere.
fashionable *adj* ēlegāns; **it is ~** mōris est.
fashionably *adv* ēleganter.
fast *adj* (*firm*) firmus; (*quick*) celer; **make ~**
dēligāre ♦ *adv* firmē; celeriter; **be ~ asleep**
artē dormīre ♦ *vi* iēiūnus esse, cibō
abstinēre ♦ *n* iēiūnium *nt*.
fasten *vt* fīgere, ligāre; ~ **down** dēfīgere; ~ **on**
inligāre; ~ **to** adligāre; ~ **together** conligāre,
cōnfīgere.
fastening *n* iūnctūra *f*.
fastidious *adj* dēlicātus, ēlegāns.
fastidiously *adv* fastīdiōsē.
fastidiousness *n* fastīdium *nt*.
fasting *n* iēiūnium *nt*, inedia *f* ♦ *adj* iēiūnus.
fastness *n* arx *f*, castellum *nt*.
fat *adj* pinguis, opīmus, obēsus; **grow ~**
pinguēscere ♦ *n* adeps *m/f*.
fatal *adj* (*deadly*) fūnestus, exitiābilis; (*fated*)
fātālis.
fatality *n* fātum *nt*, cāsus *m*.
fatally *adv*: **be ~ wounded** vulnere perīre.
fate *n* fātum *nt*, fortūna *f*, sors *f*.
fated *adj* fātālis.
fateful *adj* fātālis; fūnestus.
Fates *npl* (*goddesses*) Parcae *fpl*.
father *n* pater *m*; (*fig*) auctor *m* ♦ *vt* gignere; ~
upon addīcere, tribuere.
father-in-law *n* socer *m*.
fatherland *n* patria *f*.
fatherless *adj* orbus.
fatherly *adj* paternus.
fathom *n* sex pedēs *mpl* ♦ *vt* (*fig*) exputāre.
fathomless *adj* profundus.

fatigue n fatīgātiō f, dēfatīgātiō f ♦ vt fatīgāre, dēfatīgāre.
fatness n pinguitūdō f.
fatten vt sagīnāre.
fatty adj pinguis.
fatuity n īnsulsitās f, ineptiae fpl.
fatuous adj fatuus, īnsulsus, ineptus.
fault n culpa f, vitium nt; (written) mendum nt; **count as a ~** vitiō vertere; **find ~ with** incūsāre; **it is not your ~ that** . . . nōn per tē stat quōminus (subj).
faultily adv vitiōsē, mendōsē.
faultiness n vitium nt.
faultless adj ēmendātus, integer.
faultlessly adv ēmendātē.
faulty adj vitiōsus, mendōsus.
faun n faunus m.
fauna n animālia ntpl.
favour n grātia f, favor m; (done) beneficium nt; **win ~ with** grātiam inīre apud; **by your ~** bonā veniā tuā ♦ vt favēre (dat), indulgēre (dat).
favourable adj faustus, prosperus, secundus.
favourably adv faustē, fēlīciter, benignē.
favourite adj dīlectus, grātissimus ♦ n dēliciae fpl.
favouritism n indulgentia f, studium nt.
fawn n hinnuleus m ♦ adj (colour) gilvus ♦ vi: **~ upon** adūlārī.
fawning adj blandus ♦ n adūlātiō f.
fear n timor m, metus m, formīdō f ♦ vt timēre, metuere, formīdāre, verērī; **fearing that** veritus ne (+ imperf subj).
fearful adj timidus; horrendus, terribilis, formīdolōsus.
fearfully adv timidē; formīdolōsē.
fearless adj impavidus, intrepidus.
fearlessly adv impavidē, intrepidē.
fearlessness n fīdentia f, audācia f.
fearsome adj formīdolōsus.
feasible adj: **it is ~** fierī potest.
feast n epulae fpl; (private) convīvium nt; (public) epulum nt; (religious) daps f; (festival) festus diēs m ♦ vi epulārī, convīvārī; (fig) pāscī ♦ vt: **~ one's eyes on** oculōs pāscere (abl).
feat n factum nt, facinus nt.
feather n penna f; (downy) plūma f; **birds of a ~ flock together** parēs cum paribus facillimē congregantur.
feathered adj pennātus.
feathery adj plūmeus.
feature n līneāmentum nt; (fig) proprium nt.
February n mēnsis Februārius m; **of ~** Februārius.
federal adj sociālis, foederātus.
federate vi societātem facere.
federated adj foederātus.
federation n societās f, foederātae cīvitātēs fpl.
fee n honōs m, mercēs f.
feeble adj imbēcillus, īnfirmus, dēbilis.
feebleness n imbēcillitās f, īnfirmitās f.
feebly adv infirmē.

feed vt alere, pāscere ♦ vi pāscī; **~ on** vescī (abl) ♦ n pābulum nt.
feel vt sentīre; (with hand) tractāre, tangere; (emotion) capere, adficī (abl); (opinion) cēnsēre, sentīre; **~ one's way** pedetemptim prōgredī ♦ vi sentīre; **I ~ glad** gaudeō; **~ sure** prō certō habēre.
feeling n sēnsus m, tāctus m; (mind) animus m, adfectus m; (pity) misericordia f; **good ~** voluntās f; **bad ~** invidia f.
feign vt simulāre, fingere.
feignedly adv simulātē, fictē.
feint n simulātiō f.
felicitate vt grātulārī (dat).
felicitation n grātulātiō f.
felicitous adj fēlīx, aptus.
felicity n fēlīcitās f.
feline adj fēlīnus.
fell vt (tree) succīdere; (enemy) sternere, caedere ♦ adj dīrus, crūdēlis, atrōx ♦ n mōns m; (skin) pellis f.
fellow n socius m, aequālis m; (contemptuous) homō m.
fellow citizen n cīvis m/f.
fellow countryman n cīvis m/f, populāris m/f.
fellow feeling n misericordia f.
fellowship n societās f, sodālitās f.
fellow slave n cōnservus m;
fellow soldier n commīlitō m.
fellow student n condiscipulus m.
felon n nocēns m.
felonious adj scelestus, scelerātus.
felony n scelus nt, noxa f.
felt n coāctum nt.
female adj muliebris ♦ n fēmina f.
feminine adj muliebris.
fen n palūs f.
fence n saepēs f; **sit on the ~** quiēscere, medium sē gerere ♦ vt saepīre; **~ off** intersaepīre ♦ vi bātuere, rudibus lūdere.
fencing n rudium lūdus m; **~ master** lānista m.
fend vt arcēre ♦ vi prōvidēre.
fennel n ferula f.
fenny adj palūster.
ferment n fermentum nt; (fig) aestus m ♦ vt fermentāre; (fig) excitāre, accendere ♦ vi fervēre.
fermentation n fervor m.
fern n filix f.
ferocious adj ferōx, saevus, truculentus.
ferociously adv truculentē.
ferocity n ferōcitās f, saevitia f.
ferret n viverra f ♦ vt: **~ out** rīmārī, ēruere.
ferry n trāiectus m; (boat) cymba f, pontō m ♦ vt trānsvehere.
ferryman n portitor m.
fertile adj fertīlis, fēcundus.
fertility n fertīlitās f, fēcunditās f.
fertilize vt fēcundāre, laetificāre.
fervent adj fervidus, ārdēns.
fervently adv ārdenter.
fervid adj fervidus.
fervour n ārdor m, fervor m.

festal *adj* festus.
fester *vi* exulcerārī.
festival *n* diēs festus *m*, sollemne *nt*.
festive *adj* (*time*) festus; (*person*) festīvus.
festivity *n* hilaritās *f*; (*event*) sollemne *nt*.
festoon *n* sertum *nt* ♦ *vt* corōnāre.
fetch *vt* arcessere, addūcere; (*price*) vēnīre (*gen*); ~ **out** dēprōmere; ~ **water** aquārī.
fetching *adj* lepidus, blandus.
fetid *adj* foetidus, pūtidus.
fetter *n* compēs *f*, vinculum *nt* ♦ *vt* compedēs inicere (*dat*), vincīre; (*fig*) impedīre.
fettle *n* habitus *m*, animus *m*.
feud *n* simultās *f*, inimīcitia *f*.
fever *n* febris *f*.
feverish *adj* febrīculōsus; (*fig*) sollicitus.
few *adj* paucī; **very** ~ perpaucī; **how** ~? quotus quisque?
fewness *n* paucitās *f*.
fiancé *n* spōnsus *m*.
fiasco *n* calamitās *f*; **be a** ~ frīgēre.
fiat *n* ēdictum *nt*.
fibre *n* fibra *f*.
fickle *adj* incōnstāns, levis, mōbilis.
fickleness *n* incōnstantia *f*, levitās *f*, mōbilitās *f*.
fiction *n* fābula *f*, commentum *nt*.
fictitious *adj* fictus, falsus, commentīcius; (*character*) persōnātus.
fictitiously *adv* fictē.
fidelity *n* fidēlitās *f*, fidēs *f*.
fidget *vi* sollicitārī.
field *n* ager *m*; (*ploughed*) arvum *nt*; (*of grain*) segesf, (*MIL*) campus *m*, aciēs *f*; (*scope*) campus *m*, locus *m*; **in the** ~ (*MIL*) mīlitiae; **hold the** ~ vincere, praevalēre; ~ **of vision** cōnspectus *m*.
fiend *n* diabolus *m*.
fiendish *adj* nefārius, improbus.
fierce *adj* saevus, ācer, atrōx; (*look*) torvus.
fiercely *adv* ācriter, atrōciter, saevē.
fierceness *n* saevitia *f*, atrōcitās *f*.
fieriness *n* ārdor *m*, fervor *m*.
fiery *adj* igneus, flammeus; (*fig*) ārdēns, fervidus.
fife *n* tībia *f*.
fifteen *num* quīndecim; ~ **each** quīndēnī; ~ **times** quīndeciēns.
fifteenth *adj* quīntus decimus.
fifth *adj* quīntus ♦ *n* quīnta pars *f*.
fiftieth *adj* quīnquāgēsimus.
fifty *num* quīnquāgintā.
fig *n* fīcus *f*; (*tree*) fīcus *f*; **of** ~ fīculnus; **not care a** ~ **for** floccī nōn facere.
fight *n* pugna *f*, proelium *nt* ♦ *vi* pugnāre, dīmicāre; ~ **it out** dēcernere, dēcertāre; ~ **to the end** dēpugnāre ♦ *vt* (*battle*) committere; (*enemy*) pugnāre cum (*abl*).
fighter *n* pugnātor *m*.
fighting *n* dīmicātiō *f*.
figment *n* commentum *nt*.
figurative *adj* trānslātus; **in** ~ **language** trānslātīs per similitūdinem verbīs; **use** ~**ly** trānsferre.

figure *n* figūra *f*, fōrma *f*; (*in art*) signum *nt*; (*of speech*) figūra *f*, trānslātiō *f*; (*pl, on pottery*) sigilla *ntpl* ♦ *vt* figūrāre, fōrmāre; (*art*) fingere, effingere; ~ **to oneself** sibi prōpōnere.
figured *adj* sigillātus.
figurehead *n* (*of ship*) īnsigne *nt*.
filament *n* fibra *f*.
filch *vt* fūrārī, surripere.
file *n* (*tool*) līma *f*; (*line*) ōrdō *m*, agmen *nt*; (*of papers*) fasciculus *m*; ~**s** *pl* tabulae *fpl*; **in single** ~ simplicī ōrdine; **the rank and** ~ gregāriī mīlitēs ♦ *vt* līmāre.
filial *adj* pius.
filigree *n* diatrēta *ntpl*.
fill *vt* implēre, explēre, complēre; (*office*) fungī (*abl*); ~ **up** supplēre.
fillet *n* īnfula *f*, vitta *f* ♦ *vt* (*fish*) exossāre.
fillip *n* stimulus *m*.
filly *n* equula *f*.
film *n* membrāna *f*.
filter *n* cōlum *nt* ♦ *vt* dēliquāre ♦ *vi* percōlārī.
filth *n* sordēs *f*, caenum *nt*.
filthily *adv* foedē, inquinātē.
filthiness *n* foeditās *f*, impūritās *f*.
filthy *adj* foedus, impūrus; (*speech*) inquinātus.
fin *n* pinna *f*.
final *adj* ultimus, postrēmus, extrēmus.
finally *adv* dēnique, tandem, postrēmō.
finance *n* rēs nummāria *f*; (*state*) vectīgālia *ntpl*.
financial *adj* aerārius.
financier *n* faenerātor *m*.
finch *n* fringilla *f*.
find *vt* invenīre, reperīre; (*supplies*) parāre; (*verdict*) iūdicāre; (*pleasure*) capere; ~ **fault with** incūsāre; ~ **guilty** damnāre; ~ **out** comperīre, cognōscere.
finder *n* inventor *m*.
finding *n* iūdicium *nt*, sententia *f*.
fine *n* (*law*) multa *f*, damnum *nt*; **in** ~ dēnique ♦ *vt* multāre ♦ *adj* (*thin*) tenuis, subtīlis; (*refined*) ēlegāns, mundus, decōrus; (*beautiful*) pulcher, venustus; (*showy*) speciōsus; (*of weather*) serēnus.
finely *adv* pulchrē, ēleganter, subtīliter.
fineness *n* tenuitās *f*; ēlegantia *f*; pulchritūdō *f*; speciēs *f*; serēnitās *f*.
finery *n* ōrnātus *m*, munditiae *fpl*.
finesse *n* astūtia *f*, ars *f*, argūtiae *fpl*.
finger *n* digitus *m*; **a** ~**'s breadth** trānsversus digitus; **not lift a** ~ (*in effort*) nē manum quidem vertere ♦ *vt* pertractāre.
fingertips *npl* extrēmī digitī.
finish *n* fīnis *m*; (*art*) perfectiō *f* ♦ *vt* fīnīre, perficere; cōnficere; (*with art*) perficere, expolīre ♦ *vi* dēsinere; ~ **off** transigere, peragere, absolvere.
finishing post *n* mēta *f*.
finishing touch *n* manus extrēma.
finite *adj* circumscrīptus.

fir n abiēs f; **of ~** abiēgnus.

fire n ignis m; (conflagration) incendium nt; (in hearth) focus m; (fig) ārdor m, calor m, impetus m; **be on ~** ārdēre, flagrāre; **catch ~** flammam concipere, ignem comprehendere; **set on ~** accendere, incendere ♦ vt incendere; (fig) īnflammāre; (missile) iaculārī.

firebrand n fax f.

fire brigade n vigilēs mpl.

fireplace n focus m.

fireside n focus m.

firewood n lignum nt.

firm n societās f ♦ adj firmus, stabilis; (mind) cōnstāns; **stand ~** perstāre.

firmament n caelum nt.

firmly adv firmē, cōnstanter.

firmness n firmitās f, firmitūdō f; cōnstantia f.

first adj prīmus, prīnceps; (of two) prior ♦ adv prīmum; **at ~** prīmō, prīncipiō; **at ~ hand** ipse, ab ipsō; **come in ~** vincere; **give ~ aid to** ad tempus medērī (dat); **I was the ~ to see** prīmus vīdī.

first-class adj classicus.

first fruits npl prīmitiae fpl.

firstly adv prīmum.

first-rate adj eximius, lūculentus.

firth n aestuārium nt, fretum nt.

fiscal adj vectīgālis, aerārius.

fish n piscis m ♦ vi piscārī; (fig) expiscārī.

fisher, fisherman n piscātor m.

fishing n piscātus m ♦ adj piscātōrius.

fishing-rod n harundō f.

fish market n forum piscārium nt.

fishmonger n piscārius m.

fish pond n piscīna f.

fissile adj fissilis.

fissure n rīma f.

fist n pugnus m.

fit n (MED) convulsiō f; (of anger, illness) impetus m; **by ~s and starts** temerē, carptim ♦ vt aptāre, accommodāre; (dress) sedēre (dat); **~ out** armāre, īnstruere ♦ adj aptus, idōneus, dignus; **I see ~ to** mihi vidētur; **~ for** aptus ad (+ acc).

fitful adj dubius, incōnstāns.

fitfully adv incōnstanter.

fitly adv dignē, aptē.

fitness n convenientia f.

fitting n adparātus m, īnstrūmentum nt ♦ adj idōneus, dignus; **it is ~** convenit, decet.

fittingly adv dignē, convenienter.

five num quīnque; **~ each** quīnī; **~ times** quīnquiēns; **~ years** quīnquennium nt, lūstrum nt; **~ sixths** quīnque partēs.

five hundred num quīngentī; **~ each** quīngēnī; **~ times** quīngentiēns.

five hundredth adj quīngentēsimus.

fix vt fīgere; (time) dīcere, cōnstituere; (decision) statuere ♦ n angustiae fpl; **put in a ~** dēprehendere.

fixed adj fixus; (attention) intentus; (decision) certus; (star) inerrāns; **be firmly ~ in** īnsidēre (dat).

fixedly adv intentē.

fixity n stabilitās f; (of purpose) cōnstantia f.

fixtures npl adfīxa ntpl.

flabbergast vt obstupefacere.

flabbiness n mollitia f.

flabby adj flaccidus, mollis.

flag n vexillum nt; **~ officer** praefectus classis m ♦ vi flaccēre, flaccēscere, languēscere.

flagellate vt verberāre.

flagon n lagoena f.

flagrant adj manifestus; flāgitiōsus.

flagrantly adv flāgitiōsē.

flagship n nāvis imperātōria f.

flail n fūstis m.

flair n iūdicium nt.

flake n squāma f; **~s** pl (snow) nix f.

flame n flamma f ♦ vi flagrāre, exārdēscere.

flaming adj flammeus.

flamingo n phoenīcopterus m.

flank n latus nt; cornū m; **on the ~** ab latere, ad latus ♦ vt latus tegere (gen).

flap n flābellum nt; (dress) lacinia f ♦ vt plaudere (abl).

flare n flamma f, fulgor m ♦ vi exārdēscere, flagrāre.

flash n fulgor m; (lightning) fulgur nt; (time) mōmentum nt ♦ vi fulgēre; (motion) micāre.

flashy adj speciōsus.

flask n ampulla f.

flat adj plānus; (ground) aequus; (on back) supīnus; (on face) prōnus; (music) gravis; (style) āridus, frīgidus; **fall ~** (fig) frīgēre ♦ n (land) plānitiēs f; (sea) vadum nt; (house) tabulātum nt.

flatly adv prōrsus.

flatness n plānitiēs f.

flatten vt aequāre, complānāre.

flatter vt adūlārī (dat), adsentārī (dat), blandīrī (dat).

flatterer n adsentātor m.

flattering adj blandus.

flatteringly adv blandē.

flattery n adūlātiō f, adsentātiō f, blanditiae fpl.

flatulence n īnflātiō f.

flatulent adj īnflātus.

flaunt vt iactāre ♦ vi iactāre, glōriārī.

flaunting n iactātiō f ♦ adj glōriōsus.

flauntingly adv glōriōsē.

flautist n tībīcen m.

flavour n gustātus m, sapor m ♦ vt imbuere, condīre.

flavouring n condītiō f.

flavourless adj īnsulsus.

flaw n vitium nt.

flawless adj ēmendātus.

flax n līnum nt.

flaxen adj flāvus.

flay vt dēglūbere.

flea n pūlex m.

fleck n macula f ♦ vt variāre.

fledged adj pennātus.

flee vi fugere, effugere; (for refuge) cōnfugere.

fleece n vellus nt ♦ vt tondēre; (fig) spoliāre.
fleecy adj lāneus.
fleet n classis f ♦ adj vēlōx, celer.
fleeting adj fugāx.
fleetness n vēlōcitās f, celeritās f.
flesh n cārō f; (fig) corpus nt; **in the ~** vīvus;
  one's own ~ and blood cōnsanguineus; **put
  on ~** pinguēscere.
fleshiness n corpus nt.
fleshliness n libīdō f.
fleshly adj libīdinōsus.
fleshy adj pinguis.
flexibility n lentitia f.
flexible adj flexibilis, lentus.
flicker vi coruscāre.
flickering adj tremulus.
flight n (flying) volātus m; (fleeing) fuga f;
  (steps) scāla f; **put to ~** fugāre, in fugam
  conicere; **take to ~** sē in fugam dare, terga
  vertere.
flightiness n mōbilitās f.
flighty adj mōbilis, incōnstāns.
flimsy adj tenuis, pertenuis.
flinch vi recēdere.
fling vt iacere, conicere; (missile) intorquēre; ~
  away abicere, prōicere; ~ **open** patefacere; ~
  in one's teeth obicere (dat); ~ **to the ground**
  prōsternere ♦ vi sē incitāre ♦ n iactus m.
flint n silex m.
flinty adj siliceus.
flippancy n lascīvia f.
flippant adj lascīvus, protervus.
flippantly adv petulanter.
flirt vi lūdere, lascīvīre ♦ n lascīvus m, lascīva
  f.
flit vi volitāre.
flitch n succīdia f.
float vi innāre, fluitāre; (in air) volitāre; ~
  down dēfluere.
flock n grex m; (wool) floccus m ♦ vi
  concurrere, congregārī, cōnfluere; ~ **in**
  adfluere.
flog vt verberāre, virgīs caedere.
flogging n verbera ntpl.
flood n (deluge) ēluviō f; (river) torrēns m; (tide)
  accessus m; (fig) flūmen nt ♦ vt inundāre.
floodgate n cataracta f.
floor n solum nt; (paved) pavīmentum nt;
  (storey) tabulātum nt; (threshing) ārea f ♦ vt
  contabulāre; **be ~ed** (in argument) iacēre.
flora n herbae fpl.
floral adj flōreus.
florid adj flōridus.
flotilla n classicula f.
flounce vi sē conicere ♦ n īnstita f.
flounder vi volutāre; (in speech) haesitāre.
flour n fārīna f.
flourish vi flōrēre, vigēre ♦ vt vibrāre,
  iactāre ♦ n (RHET) calamistrī mpl; (music)
  clangor m.
flout vt aspernārī, inlūdere (dat).
flow vi fluere, mānāre; (tide) accēdere; ~ **back**
  recēdere; ~ **between** interfluere; ~ **down**

dēfluere; ~ **into** īnfluere in (acc); ~ **out**
  prōfluere, ēmānāre; ~ **past** praeterfluere; ~
  through permānāre; ~ **together** cōnfluere; ~
  towards adfluere ♦ n flūmen nt, cursus m;
  (tide) accessus m; (words) flūmen nt.
flower n flōs m, flōsculus m ♦ vi flōrēre,
  flōrēscere.
floweret n flōsculus m.
flowery adj flōridus.
flowing adj prōfluēns; ~ **with** abundāns (abl).
flowingly adv prōfluenter.
flown adj īnflātus.
fluctuate vi aestuāre, fluctuāre.
fluctuating adj incōnstāns, incertus.
fluctuation n aestus m, dubitātiō f.
fluency n fācundia f, verbōrum cōpia f.
fluent adj disertus, prōfluēns.
fluently adv disertē, prōfluenter.
fluid adj liquidus ♦ n liquor m.
fluidity n liquor m.
fluke n (anchor) dēns m; (luck) fortuītum nt.
flurry n trepidātiō f ♦ vt sollicitāre, turbāre.
flush n rubor m; **in the first ~ of victory** victōriā
  ēlātus ♦ vi ērubēscere ♦ adj (full) abundāns;
  (level) aequus.
fluster n trepidātiō f ♦ vt turbāre, sollicitāre.
flute n tībia f; **play the ~** tībiā canere.
fluted adj striātus.
flutter n tremor m; (fig) trepidātiō f ♦ vi (heart)
  palpitāre; (mind) trepidāre; (bird) volitāre.
fluvial adj fluviātilis.
flux n fluxus m; **be in a state of ~** fluere.
fly n musca f ♦ vi volāre; (flee) fugere; ~ **apart**
  dissilīre; ~ **at** involāre in (acc); ~ **away**
  āvolāre; ~ **from** fugere; ~ **in the face of**
  obviam īre (dat); ~ **out** ēvolāre; ~ **to** advolāre
  ad (acc); ~ **up** ēvolāre, subvolāre; **let ~ at**
  immittere in (acc).
flying adj volucer, volātilis; (time) fugāx.
foal n equuleus m, equulus m ♦ vt parere.
foam n spūma f ♦ vi spūmāre; (with rage)
  saevīre.
foaming adj spūmeus.
focus vt (mind) intendere.
fodder n pābulum n.
foe n hostis m; (private) inimīcus m.
fog n cālīgō f, nebula f.
foggy adj cālīginōsus, nebulōsus.
foible n vitium nt.
foil n (metal) lāmina f; (sword) rudis f ♦ vt
  ēlūdere, ad inritum redigere.
foist vt inculcāre, interpōnere.
fold n sinus m; (sheep) ovīle nt ♦ vt plicāre,
  complicāre; (hands) comprimere; (sheep)
  inclūdere; ~ **back** replicāre; ~ **over** plicāre; ~
  together complicāre; ~ **up in** involvere in
  (abl).
folding doors npl valvae fpl.
foliage n frondēs fpl.
folk n hominēs mpl ♦ adj patrius.
follow vt sequī; (calling) facere; (candidate)
  adsectārī; (enemy) īnsequī; (example)
  imitārī; (instructions) pārēre (dat);

(*predecessor*) succēdere (*dat*); (*road*)
pergere; (*speaker*) intellegere; ~ **closely**
īnsequī; ~ **hard on the heels of** īnsequī,
īnsistere (*dat*), īnstāre (*dat*); ~ **out** exsequī; ~
to the grave exsequī; ~ **up** subsequī,
īnsistere (*dat*) ♦ *vi* (*time*) īnsequī; (*inference*)
sequī; **as ~s** ita, in hunc modum.

follower *n* comes *m*; (*of candidate*) adsectātor
m; (*of model*) imitātor *m*; (*of teacher*) audītor
m.

following *adj* tālis; īnsequēns, proximus,
posterus; **on the ~ day** postrīdiē, postero diē,
proximo diē ♦ *n* adsectātōrēs *mpl*.

folly *n* stultitia *f*, dēmentia *f*, īnsipientia *f*.

foment *vt* fovēre; (*fig*) augēre.

fond *adj* amāns, studiōsus; ineptus; **be ~ of**
amāre.

fondle *vt* fovēre, mulcēre.

fondly *adv* amanter; ineptē.

food *n* cibus *m*; (*fig*) pābulum *nt*.

fool *n* stultus *m*, ineptus *m*; (*jester*) scurra *m*;
make a ~ of ludibriō habēre; **play the ~**
dēsipere ♦ *vt* dēcipere, lūdere; ~ **away**
disperdere ♦ *vi* dēsipere.

foolery *n* ineptiae *fpl*, nūgae *fpl*.

foolhardy *adj* temerārius.

foolish *adj* stultus, ineptus, īnsipiēns.

foolishly *adv* stultē, ineptē.

foolishness *n* stultitia *f*, īnsipientia *f*.

foot *n* pēs *m*; (*MIL*) peditātus *m*; **a ~ long** pedālis;
on ~ pedes; **set ~ on** īnsistere (*dat*); **set on ~**
īnstituere; **the ~ of** īmus ♦ *vt* (*bill*) solvere.

football *n* follis *m*.

footing *n* locus *m*, status *m*; **keep one's ~**
īnsistere; **on an equal ~** ex aequō.

footman *n* pedisequus *m*.

footpad *n* grassātor *m*.

footpath *n* sēmita *f*, trāmes *m*.

footprint *n* vestīgium *nt*.

foot soldier *n* pedes *m*.

footstep *n* vestīgium *nt*; **follow in the ~s of**
vestīgiīs ingredī (*gen*).

foppish *adj* dēlicātus.

for *prep* (*advantage*) *dat*; (*duration*) *acc*; (*after
noun*) *gen*; (*price*) *abl*; (*behalf*) prō (*abl*); (*cause*)
propter (*acc*), causā (*gen*); (*after neg*) prae
(*abl*); (*feelings*) erga (*acc*); (*lieu*) prō (*abl*);
(*purpose*) ad, in (*acc*); (*time fixed*) in (*acc*) ♦
conj namque; nam (*1st word*), enim (*2nd
word*); (*with pron*) quippe quī; ~ **a long time**
diū; ~ **some time** aliquamdiū.

forage *n* pābulum *nt* ♦ *vi* pābulārī, frūmentārī.

forager *n* pābulātor *m*, frūmentātor *m*.

foraging *n* pābulātiō *f*, frūmentātiō *f*.

forasmuch as *conj* quōniam.

foray *n* incursiō *f*.

forbear *vi* parcere (*dat*), supersedēre (*infin*).

forbearance *n* venia *f*, indulgentia *f*.

forbears *n* māiōrēs *mpl*.

forbid *vt* vetāre (*+ acc and infin*), interdīcere
(*dat and quominus and subj*); **Heaven ~!** dī
meliōra!

forbidding *adj* tristis.

force *n* vīs *f*; (*band of men*) manus *m*; **by ~ of
arms** vī et armis ♦ *vt* cōgere, impellere;
(*way*) rumpere, mōlīrī; (*growth*) festīnāre; ~
an engagement hostes proeliārī cogere; ~
down dētrūdere; ~ **out** extrūdere, expellere,
exturbāre; ~ **upon** inculcāre; ~ **a way in**
intrōrumpere, inrumpere.

forced *adj* (*march*) māgnus; (*style*) quaesītus; ~
march māgnum iter.

forceful *adj* validus.

forceps *n* forceps *m/f*.

forces *npl* (*MIL*) cōpiae *fpl*.

forcible *adj* validus; (*fig*) gravis.

forcibly *adv* vī, violenter; (*fig*) graviter.

ford *n* vadum *nt* ♦ *vt* vadō trānsīre.

fore *adj* prior; **to the ~** praestō ♦ *adv*: ~ **and aft**
in longitūdinem.

forearm *n* bracchium *nt* ♦ *vt*: **be ~ed**
praecavēre.

forebode *vt* ōminārī, portendere; prasentīre.

foreboding *n* praesēnsiō *f*; ōmen *nt*.

forecast *n* praedictiō *f* ♦ *vt* praedīcere,
prōvidēre.

forecourt *n* vestibulum *nt*.

forefathers *n* māiōrēs *mpl*.

forefinger *n* index *m*.

foreground *n* ēminentia *ntpl*.

forehead *n* frōns *f*.

foreign *adj* peregrīnus, externus; (*goods*)
adventīcius; ~ **to** aliēnus ab; ~ **ways**
peregrīnitās *f*.

foreigner *n* peregrīnus *m*, advena *m*.

foreknow *vt* praenōscere.

foreknowledge *n* prōvidentia *f*.

foreland *n* prōmunturium *nt*.

foremost *adj* prīmus, prīnceps.

forenoon *n* antemerīdiānum tempus *nt*.

forensic *adj* forēnsis.

forerunner *n* praenūntius *m*.

foresee *vt* praevidēre.

foreshadow *vt* praemonēre.

foresight *n* prōvidentia *f*.

forest *n* silva *f*.

forestall *vt* occupāre, antevenīre.

forester *n* silvicola *m*.

foretaste *vt* praegustāre.

foretell *vt* praedīcere, vāticinārī.

forethought *n* prōvidentia *f*.

forewarn *vt* praemonēre.

foreword *n* praefātiō *f*.

forfeit *n* multa *f*, damnum *nt* ♦ *vt* āmittere,
perdere, multārī (*abl*); (*bail*) dēserere.

forfeiture *n* damnum *nt*.

forgather *vi* congregārī, convenīre.

forge *n* fornāx *f* ♦ *vt* fabricārī, excūdere;
(*document*) subicere; (*will*) suppōnere;
(*signature*) imitārī; (*money*) adulterīnōs
nummōs percutere.

forged *adj* falsus, adulterīnus, commentīcius.

forger *n* (*of will*) subiector *m*.

forgery *n* falsum *nt*, commentum *nt*.

forget *vt* oblīvīscī (*gen*); (*thing learnt*)
dēdiscere; **be forgotten** memoriā cadere, ex

animō effluere.
forgetful *adj* immemor; (*by habit*) oblīviōsus.
forgetfulness *n* oblīviō *f*.
forgive *vt* ignōscere (*dat*), veniam dare (*dat*).
forgiveness *n* venia *f*.
forgo *vt* dīmittere, renūntiāre; (*rights*) dēcēdere dē iūre.
fork *n* furca *f*; (*small*) furcula *f*; (*road*) trivium *nt*.
forlorn *adj* inops, dēstitūtus, exspēs.
form *n* fōrma *f*, figūra *f*; (*of procedure*) fōrmula *f*; (*condition*) vigor *m*; (*etiquette*) mōs *m*; (*seat*) scamnum *nt*; (*school*) schola *f*; (*hare's*) latibulum *nt* ♦ *vt* fōrmāre, fingere, efficere; (MIL) īnstruere; (*plan*) inīre, capere.
formal *adj* iūstus; (*rite*) sollemnis.
formality *n* iūsta *ntpl*, rītus *m*; **as a** ~ dicis causā; **with due** ~ rītē.
formally *adv* rītē.
formation *n* fōrma *f*, figūra *f*; (*process*) cōnfōrmātiō *f*; **in** ~ (MIL) īnstructus.
former *adj* prior, prīstinus, vetus; **the** ~ ille.
formerly *adv* anteā, ōlim, quondam.
formidable *adj* formīdolōsus.
formidably *adv* formīdolōsē.
formula *n* fōrmula *f*; (*dictated*) praefātiō *f*.
formulate *vt* compōnere.
forsake *vt* dērelinquere, dēstituere, dēserere.
forswear *vt* pēierāre, abiūrāre.
fort *n* castellum *nt*.
forth *adv* forās; (*time*) posthāc.
forthwith *adv* extemplō, statim, prōtinus.
fortieth *adj* quadragēsimus.
fortification *n* (*process*) mūnītiō *f*; (*place*) mūnīmentum *nt*, arx *f*.
fortify *vt* mūnīre, ēmūnīre, commūnīre; (*fig*) cōnfirmāre.
fortitude *n* fortitūdō *f*.
fortnight *n* quīndecim diēs *mpl*.
fortnightly *adv* quīntō decimō quōque diē.
fortress *n* arx *f*, castellum *nt*.
fortuitous *adj* fortuītus.
fortuitously *adv* fortuītō, cāsū.
fortunate *adj* fēlīx, fortūnātus.
fortunately *adv* fēlīciter, bene.
fortune *n* fortūna *f*, fors *f*; (*wealth*) rēs *f*, dīvitiae *fpl*; **good** ~ fēlīcitās *f*, secundae rēs *fpl*; **bad** ~ adversae rēs *fpl*; **make one's** ~ rem facere, rem quaerere; **tell ~s** hariolārī.
fortune-hunter *n* captātor *m*.
fortune-teller *n* hariolus *m*, sāga *f*.
forty *num* quadrāgintā; ~ **each** quadrāgēnī; ~ **times** quadrāgiēns.
forum *n* forum *nt*.
forward *adj* (*person*) protervus, audāx; (*fruit*) praecox ♦ *adv* porrō, ante; **bring** ~ prōferre; **come** ~ prōdīre ♦ *vt* (*letter*) perferre; (*cause*) adiuvāre, favēre (*dat*).
forwardness *n* audācia *f*, alacritās *f*.
forwards *adv* porrō, prōrsus; **backwards and** ~ rursum prōrsum, hūc illūc.
fosse *n* fossa *f*.
foster *vt* alere, nūtrīre; (*fig*) fovēre.

foster child *n* alumnus *m*, alumna *f*.
foster father *n* altor *m*, ēducātor *m*.
foster mother *n* altrīx *f*, nūtrīx *f*.
foul *adj* foedus; (*speech*) inquinātus; **fall** ~ **of** inruere in (*acc*).
foully *adv* foedē, inquinātē.
foul-mouthed *adj* maledicus.
foulness *n* foeditās *f*.
found *vt* condere, fundāre, īnstituere; (*metal*) fundere.
foundation *n* fundāmenta *ntpl*.
founder *n* fundātor *m*, conditor *m* ♦ *vi* submergī, naufragium facere.
foundling *n* expositīcia *f*.
fount *n* fōns *m*.
fountain *n* fōns *m*.
fountainhead *n* fōns *m*, orīgō *f*.
four *num* quattuor (*indecl*); ~ **each** quaternī; ~ **times** quater; ~ **days** quadriduum *nt*; ~ **years** quadriennium *nt*.
fourfold *adj* quadruplex ♦ *adv* quadrifāriam.
four hundred *num* quadringentī; ~ **each** quadringēnī; ~ **times** quadringentiēns.
four hundredth *adj* quadringentēsimus.
fourteen *num* quattuordecim; ~ **each** quaternī dēnī; ~ **times** quater deciēns.
fourteenth *adj* quartus decimus.
fourth *adj* quartus ♦ *n* quadrāns *m*; **three ~s** dōdrāns *m*, trēs partēs *fpl*.
fowl *n* avis *f*; gallīna *f*.
fowler *n* auceps *m*.
fox *n* vulpes *f*; ~**'s** vulpīnus.
foxy *adj* astūtus, vafer.
fracas *n* rīxa *f*.
fraction *n* pars *f*.
fractious *adj* difficilis.
fracture *n* frāctum os *nt* ♦ *vt* frangere.
fragile *adj* fragilis.
fragility *n* fragilitās *f*.
fragment *n* fragmentum *nt*.
fragrance *n* odor *m*.
fragrant *adj* suāvis.
fragrantly *adv* suāviter.
frail *adj* fragilis, īnfirmus, dēbilis.
frailty *n* dēbilitās *f*; (*moral*) error *m*.
frame *vt* fabricārī, fingere, effingere; (*document*) compōnere ♦ *n* fōrma *f*; (*of mind*) adfectiō *f*, habitus *m*; **in a** ~ **of mind** animātus.
framer *n* fabricātor *m*, opifex *m*; (*of law*) lātor *m*.
framework *n* compāgēs *f*.
franchise *n* suffrāgium *nt*, cīvitās *f*.
frank *adj* ingenuus, apertus; (*speech*) līber.
frankincense *n* tūs *nt*.
frankly *adv* ingenuē, apertē; līberē.
frankness *n* ingenuitās *f*; (*speech*) lībertās *f*.
frantic *adj* furēns, furiōsus, dēlīrus.
frantically *adv* furenter.
fraternal *adj* frāternus.
fraternally *adv* frāternē.
fraternity *n* frāternitās *f*; (*society*) sodālitās *f*; (*guild*) collēgium *nt*.
fraternize *vi* amīcitiam iungere.
fratricide *n* frātricīda *m*; (*act*) frātris

parricīdium *nt.*
fraud *n* fraus *f*, dolus *m*, falsum *nt*; (*criminal*) dolus malus *m*.
fraudulence *n* fraus *f*.
fraudulent *adj* fraudulentus, dolōsus.
fraudulently *adv* dolōsē, dolō malō.
fraught *adj* plēnus.
fray *n* pugna *f*, rīxa *f* ♦ *vt* terere.
freak *n* mōnstrum *nt*; (*caprice*) libīdō *f*.
freckle *n* lentīgō *f*.
freckly *adj* lentīginōsus.
free *adj* līber; (*disengaged*) vacuus; (*generous*) līberālis; (*from cost*) grātuītus; (*from duty*) immūnis; (*from encumbrance*) expedītus; **be ~ from** vacāre (*abl*); **I am still ~ to** integrum est mihī (*infin*); **set ~** absolvere, līberāre; (*slave*) manū mittere ♦ *adv* grātīs, grātuītō ♦ *vt* līberāre, expedīre, exsolvere.
freebooter *n* praedō *m*.
freeborn *adj* ingenuus.
freedman *n* lībertus *m*.
freedom *n* lībertās *f*; (*from duty*) immūnitās *f*.
freehold *n* praedium līberum *nt* ♦ *adj* immūnis.
freely *adv* līberē; (*lavishly*) cōpiōsē, largē; (*frankly*) apertē; (*voluntarily*) ultrō, suā sponte.
freeman *n* cīvis *m*.
free will *n* voluntās *f*; **of one's own ~** suā sponte.
freeze *vt* gelāre, glaciāre ♦ *vi* concrēscere.
freezing *adj* gelidus; **it is ~** gelat.
freight *n* vectūra *f*; (*cargo*) onus *nt* ♦ *vt* onerāre.
freighter *n* nāvis onerāria *f*.
frenzied *adj* furēns, furiōsus, fānāticus.
frenzy *n* furor *m*, īnsania *f*.
frequency *n* adsiduitās *f*.
frequent *adj* frequēns, crēber ♦ *vt* frequentāre, commeāre in (*acc*).
frequently *adv* saepe, saepenumerō, frequenter.
fresh *adj* (*new*) recēns, novus; (*vigorous*) integer; (*water*) dulcis; (*wind*) ācer.
freshen *vt* renovāre ♦ *vi* (*wind*) incrēbrēscere.
freshly *adv* recenter.
freshman *n* tīrō *m*.
freshness *n* novitās *f*, viriditās *f*.
fret *vi* maerēre, angī ♦ *vt* sollicitāre.
fretful *adj* mōrōsus, querulus.
fretfulness *n* mōrōsitās *f*.
fretted *adj* laqueātus.
friable *adj* puter.
friction *n* trītus *m*.
friend *n* amīcus *m*, familiāris *m/f*, hospes *m*, sodālis *m*; **make ~s with** sē cōnferre ad amīcitiam (*gen*).
friendless *adj* sine amīcīs.
friendliness *n* cōmitās *f*, officium *nt*.
friendly *adj* cōmis, facilis, benīgnus; **on ~ terms** familiāriter.
friendship *n* amīcitia *f*, familiāritās *f*.

frigate *n* liburna *f*.
fright *n* horror *m*, pavor *m*, terror *m*; **take ~** extimēscere, expavēscere.
frighten *vt* terrēre, exterrēre, perterrēre; **~ away** absterrēre; **~ off** dēterrēre; **~ the life out of** exanimāre.
frightful *adj* horribilis, immānis; (*look*) taeter.
frightfully *adv* foedē.
frigid *adj* frīgidus.
frigidity *n* frīgus *nt.*
frill *n* fimbriae *fpl*; (*RHET*) calamistrī *mpl.*
fringe *n* fimbriae *fpl.*
frisk *vi* lascīvīre, exsultāre.
frisky *adj* lascīvus.
fritter *vt*: **~ away** dissipāre; (*time*) extrahere.
frivolity *n* levitās *f.*
frivolous *adj* levis, inānis.
frivolously *adv* ināniter.
fro *adv*: **to and ~** hūc illūc.
frock *n* stola *f.*
frog *n* rāna *f.*
frolic *n* lūdus *m* ♦ *vi* lūdere, lascīvīre.
frolicsome *adj* lascīvus, hilaris.
from *prep* ab (*abl*), ā (*before consonants*); (*out*) ē, ex (*abl*); (*cause*) propter (*acc*); (*prevention*) quōminus, quīn; **~ all directions** undique.
front *n* frōns *f*; **in ~** ā fronte, adversus; **in ~ of** prō (+ *abl*).
frontier *n* līmes *m*, cōnfīnia *ntpl*; **~s** fīnēs *mpl.*
front line *n* prīma aciēs.
frost *n* gelū *nt.*
frostbitten *adj*: **be ~** vī frīgoris ambūrī.
frosty *adj* gelidus, glaciālis.
froth *n* spūma *f* ♦ *vi* spūmās agere.
frothy *adj* spūmeus.
froward *adj* contumāx.
frown *n* frontis contractiō *f* ♦ *vi* frontem contrahere.
frozen *adj* glaciālis.
fructify *vt* fēcundāre.
frugal *adj* parcus, frūgī.
frugality *n* frūgālitās *f*, parsimōnia *f.*
frugally *adv* parcē, frūgāliter.
fruit *n* fructus *m*; (*tree*) māla *ntpl*; (*berry*) bāca *f*; (*fig*) fructus *m*; **~s** *pl* (*of earth*) frūgēs *fpl.*
fruiterer *n* pōmārius *m.*
fruitful *adj* fēcundus, fructuōsus.
fruitfully *adv* ferāciter.
fruitfulness *n* fēcunditās *f*, ūbertās *f.*
fruition *n* frūctus *m.*
fruitless *adj* inūtilis, vānus.
fruitlessly *adv* nēquīquam, frustrā.
fruit tree *n* pōmum *nt.*
frustrate *vt* frustrārī, ad inritum redigere.
frustration *n* frustrātiō *f.*
fry *vt* frīgere.
frying pan *n* sartāgō *f*; **out of the ~ into the fire** incidit in Scyllam quī vult vītāre Charybdim.
fuel *n* fōmes *m.*
fugitive *adj* fugitīvus ♦ *n* fugitīvus *m*, trānsfuga *m*; (*from abroad*) extorris *m.*
fulfil *vt* (*duty*) explēre, implēre; (*promise*)

praestāre; (*order*) exsequī, perficere.
fulfilment *n* absolūtiō *f.*
full *adj* plēnus (+ *abl*), refertus, explētus;
(*entire*) integer; (*amount*) solidus; (*brother*)
germānus; (*measure*) iūstus; (*meeting*)
frequēns; (*style*) cōpiōsus; **at ~ length**
porrēctus; **at ~ speed** citātō gradū, citātō
equō.
fuller *n* fullō *m.*
full-grown *adj* adultus.
full moon *n* lūna plēna.
fullness *n* (*style*) cōpia *f;* (*time*) mātūritās *f.*
fully *adv* plēnē, penitus, funditus.
fulminate *vi* intonāre.
fulsome *adj* fastīdiōsus, pūtidus.
fumble *vi* haesitāre.
fume *n* fūmus *m*, hālitus *m* ♦ *vi* stomachārī.
fumigate *vt* suffīre.
fun *n* iocus *m*, lūdus *m*; **for ~** animī causā; **make
~ of** inlūdere, dēlūdere, lūdibriō habēre.
function *n* officium *nt*, mūnus *nt.*
fund *n* cōpia *f.*
fundamental *adj* prīmus ♦ *n* prīncipium *nt*,
elementum *nt.*
funds *npl* sors *f*, pecūniae *fpl.*
funeral *n* fūnus *nt*, exsequiae *fpl* ♦ *adj* fūnebris.
funeral pile *n* rogus *m.*
funeral pyre *n* rogus *m.*
funeral rites *npl* exsequiae *fpl*, īnferiae *fpl.*
funereal *adj* fūnebria, lūgubris.
funnel *n* īnfundibulum *nt.*
funny *adj* ioculāris, rīdiculus.
fur *n* pellis *m.*
furbelow *n* īnstita *f.*
furbish *vt* expolīre; **~ up** interpolāre.
Furies *npl* Furiae *fpl.*
furious *adj* saevus, vehemēns, perīrātus.
furiously *adv* furenter, saevē, vehementer.
furl *vt* (*sail*) legere.
furlong *n* stadium *nt.*
furlough *n* commeātus *m.*
furnace *n* fornāx *f.*
furnish *vt* praebēre, suppeditāre; (*equip*)
īnstruere, ōrnāre.
furniture *n* supellex *f.*
furrow *n* sulcus *m* ♦ *vt* sulcāre.
furry *adj* villōsus.
further *adj* ulterior ♦ *adv* ultrā, porrō; amplius
♦ *vt* adiuvāre, cōnsulere (*dat*).
furtherance *n* prōgressus *m*; (*means*)
īnstrūmentum *nt.*.
furthermore *adv* praetereā, porrō.
furthest *adj* ultimus ♦ *adv* longissimē.
furtive *adj* fūrtīvus, clandestīnus.
furtively *adv* clam, fūrtim.
fury *n* furor *m*, saevitia *f*; īra *f.*
fuse *vt* fundere; (*together*) coniungere.
fusion *n* coniūnctiō *f.*
fuss *n* importūnitās *f*, querimōnia *f* ♦ *vi*
conquerī, sollicitārī.
fussy *adj* importūnus, incommodus.
fusty *adj* mūcidus.
futile *adj* inānis, inūtilis, futtilis.

futility *n* vānitās *f*, futtilitās *f.*
future *adj* futūrus, posterus ♦ *n* posterum *nt*,
reliquum *nt*; **in ~** posthāc; **for the ~** in
posterum.
futurity *n* posterum tempus *nt*, posteritās *f.*

G, g

gabble *vi* garrīre.
gable *n* fastīgium *nt.*
gadfly *n* tabānus *m.*
gag *vt* ōs praeligāre (*dat*), ōs obvolvere (*dat*).
gage *n* pignus *nt.*
gaiety *n* laetitia *f*, hilaritās *f*, festīvitās *f.*
gaily *adv* hilare, festīve.
gain *n* lucrum *nt*, quaestus *m* ♦ *vt* comparāre;
adipīscī; (*profit*) lucrārī; (*thing*) parāre,
cōnsequī, capere; (*case*) vincere; (*place*)
pervenīre ad; (*possession of*) potīrī (*gen*);
(*victory*) reportāre; **~ over** conciliāre; **~
ground** incrēbrēscere; **~ possession of**
potior (+ *abl*); **~ the upper hand** rem obtinēre.
gainful *adj* quaestuōsus.
gainsay *vt* contrādīcere (*dat*).
gait *n* incessus *m*, ingressiō *f.*
gaiters *n* ocreae *fpl.*
gala *n* diēs festus *m.*
galaxy *n* circulus lacteus *m.*
gale *n* ventus *m.*
gall *n* fel *nt*, bīlis *m* ♦ *vt* ūrere.
gallant *adj* fortis, audāx; (*courteous*)
officiōsus.
gallantly *adv* fortiter; officiōsē.
gallantry *n* virtūs *f*; urbānitās *f.*
gall bladder *n* fel *nt.*
gallery *n* porticus *f.*
galley *n* nāvis āctuāria *f*; (*cook's*) culīna *f.*
galling *adj* amārus, mordāx.
gallon *n* congius *m.*
gallop *n* cursus *m*; **at the ~** citātō equō,
admissō equō ♦ *vi* admissō equō currere.
gallows *n* īnfēlīx arbor *f*, furca *f.*
gallows bird *n* furcifer *m.*
galore *adv* adfatim.
gamble *n* ālea *f* ♦ *vi* āleā lūdere.
gambler *n* āleātor *m.*
gambling *n* ālea *f.*
gambol *n* lūsus *m* ♦ *vi* lūdere, lascīvīre,
exsultāre.
game *n* lūdus *m*; (*with dice*) ālea *f*; (*hunt*)
praeda *f*; **play the ~** rēctē facere; **public ~s**
lūdī *mpl*; **Olympic ~s** Olympia *npl*; **the ~'s up**
āctum est ♦ *adj* animōsus.
gamester *n* āleātor *m.*
gammon *n* perna *f.*
gander *n* ānser *m.*

gang n grex m, caterva f.
gangster n grassātor m.
gangway n forus m.
gaol n carcer m.
gaoler n custōs m.
gap n hiātus m, lacūna f.
gape vi hiāre, inhiāre; (opening) dēhiscere.
garb n habitus m, amictus m ♦ vt amicīre.
garbage n quisquiliae fpl.
garden n hortus m; (public) hortī mpl.
gardener n hortulānus m; (ornamental)
  topiārius m.
gardening n hortī cultūra f; (ornamental)
  topiāria f.
gargle vi gargarissāre.
garish adj speciōsus, fūcātus.
garland n sertum nt, corōna f ♦ vt corōnāre.
garlic n ālium nt.
garment n vestis f, vestīmentum nt.
garnish vt ōrnāre, decorāre.
garret n cēnāculum nt.
garrison n praesidium nt, dēfēnsōrēs mpl ♦ vt
  praesidiō mūnīre, praesidium collocāre in
  (abl).
garrotte vt laqueō gulam frangere (dat).
garrulity n garrulitās f.
garrulous adj garrulus, loquāx.
gas n vapor m.
gash n vulnus nt ♦ vt caedere, lacerāre.
gasp n anhēlitus m, singultus m ♦ vi anhēlāre.
gastronomy n gula f.
gate n porta f.
gather vt colligere, cōgere; (fruit) legere;
  (inference) colligere, conicere ♦ vi
  congregārī.
gathering n conventus m, coetus m.
gauche adj inconcinnus, illepidus.
gaudily adv splendidē, speciōsē.
gaudy adj speciōsus, fūcātus, lautus.
gauge n modulus m ♦ vt mētīrī.
Gaul n Gallia f; (person) Gallus m.
gaunt adj macer.
gauntlet n manica f.
gauze n Coa ntpl.
gay adj hilaris, festīvus, laetus.
gaze vi intuērī; ~ at intuērī, adspectāre,
  contemplārī.
gazelle n oryx m.
gazette n ācta diūrna ntpl, ācta pūblica ntpl.
gear n īnstrūmenta ntpl; (ship's) armāmenta
  ntpl.
gelding n cantērius m.
gelid adj gelidus.
gem n gemma f.
gender n genus nt.
genealogical adj dē stirpe.
genealogical table n stemma nt.
genealogist n geneālogus m.
genealogy n geneālogia f.
general adj generālis, ūniversus; (usual)
  vulgāris, commūnis; **in** ~ omnīnō ♦ n dux m,
  imperātor m; ~'**s tent** praetōrium nt.
generalissimo n imperātor m.

generality n vulgus nt; plērīque mpl.
generalize vi ūnīversē loquī.
generally adv ferē, plērumque; (discuss)
  īnfīnītē.
generalship n ductus m.
generate vt gignere, generāre.
generation n aetās f, saeculum nt.
generic adj generālis.
generically adv genere.
generosity n līberālitās f, largitās f.
generous adj līberālis, largus, benīgnus.
generously adv līberāliter, largē, benīgnē.
genesis n orīgō f, prīncipium nt.
genial adj cōmis, hilaris.
geniality n cōmitās f, hilaritās f.
genially adv cōmiter, hilare.
genitive n genitīvus m.
genius n (deity) genius m; (talent) ingenium nt,
  indolēs f; **of** ~ ingeniōsus.
genre n genus nt.
genteel adj urbānus, polītus.
gentility n urbānitās f, ēlegantia f.
gentle adj (birth) ingenuus; (manner) hūmānus,
  indulgēns, mītis; (slope) lēnis, mollis; (thing)
  placidus, lēnis.
gentleman n vir m, ingenuus m, vir honestus
  m.
gentlemanly adj ingenuus, līberālis,
  honestus.
gentleness n hūmānitās f, indulgentia f,
  lēnitās f.
gentlewoman n ingenua f, mulier honesta f.
gently adv lēniter, molliter, placidē.
gentry n ingenuī mpl, optimātēs mpl;
  (contempt) hominēs mpl.
genuine adj vērus, germānus, sincērus.
genuinely adv germānē, sincērē.
genuineness n fidēs f.
geographical adj geōgraphicus; ~ **position**
  situs m.
geography n geōgraphia f.
geometrical adj geōmetricus.
geometry n geōmetria f.
Georgics n Geōrgica ntpl.
germ n germen nt, sēmen nt.
germane adj adfīnis.
germinate vi gemmāre.
gesticulate vi sē iactāre, gestū ūtī.
gesticulation n gestus m.
gesture n gestus m, mōtus m.
get vt adipīscī, nancīscī, parāre; (malady)
  contrahere; (request) impetrāre; (return)
  capere; (reward) ferre; ~ **sth done** cūrāre
  (with gerundive); ~ **sb to do** persuādēre (dat),
  addūcere; ~ **by heart** ēdiscere; ~ **in** repōnere;
  ~ **the better of** superāre; **go and** ~ arcessere
  ♦ vi fierī; ~ **about** (rumour) palam fierī,
  percrēbrēscere; ~ **away** effugere; ~ **at**
  (intent) spectāre; ~ **behind** cessāre; ~ **off**
  absolvī; ~ **on** prōficere; ~ **out** effugere,
  ēvādere; ~ **out of hand** lascīvīre; ~ **out of the
  way** dē viā dēcēdere; ~ **ready** parāre; ~ **rid of**
  abicere, tollere; ~ **to** pervenīre ad;

~ to know cognōscere; ~ **together**
congregārī; ~ **up** exsurgere.
get-up n ōrnātus m.
ghastliness n pallor m.
ghastly adj pallidus; (sight) taeter.
ghost n larva f, īdōlon nt; ~**s** pl mānēs mpl; **give
up the** ~ animam agere, efflāre.
giant n Gigas m.
gibberish n barbaricus sermō m.
gibbet n furca f.
gibe vi inrīdēre.
giddiness n vertīgō f.
giddy adj vertīginōsus; (fig) levis.
gift n dōnum nt; (small) mūnusculum nt; ~**s** pl
(mind) ingenium nt.
gifted adj ingeniōsus.
gig n cisium nt.
gigantic adj ingēns, immānis.
gild vt inaurāre.
gill n (measure) quartārius m; (fish) branchia f.
gilt adj aurātus.
gimlet n terebra f.
gin n pedica f, laqueus m.
ginger n zingiberī nt.
gingerly adv pedetemptim.
giraffe n camēlopardālis f.
gird vt circumdāre; ~ **on** accingere; ~ **oneself**
cingī; ~ **up** succingere.
girder n tignum nt.
girdle n cingulus m ♦ vt cingere.
girl n puella f, virgō f.
girlhood n aetās puellāris f.
girlish adj puellāris.
girth n ambitus m, amplitūdō f.
gist n firmāmentum nt.
give vt dare, dōnāre, tribuere; (thing due)
reddere; ~ **away** largīrī; (bride) in
matrimōnium collocāre; (secret) prōdere; ~
back reddere, restituere; ~ **birth (to)** pārere;
~ **in** (name) profitērī; ~ **off** ēmittere; ~ **out**
(orders) ēdere; (sound) ēmittere; ~ **thanks**
gratias agere; ~ **up** dēdere, trādere; (hope of)
dēspērāre; (rights) dēcēdere dē, renūntiāre;
~ **way** cēdere; (MIL) inclīnāre ♦ vi labāre; ~ **in**
sē victum fatērī; (MIL) manūs dare; ~ **out** (fail)
dēficere; (pretend) ferre; ~ **up** dēsistere; ~
way cēdere.
giver n dator m.
glacial adj glaciālis.
glad adj laetus, alacer, hilaris; **be** ~ gaudēre.
gladden vt exhilarāre, oblectāre.
glade n saltus m.
gladiator n gladiātor m.
gladiatorial adj gladiātōrius; **present a** ~ **show**
gladiātōrēs dare.
gladly adv laetē, libenter.
gladness n laetitia f, alacritās f, gaudium nt.
glamorous adj venustus.
glamour n venustās f.
glance n aspectus m ♦ vi oculōs conicere; ~ **at**
aspicere; (fig) attingere, perstringere; ~ **off**
stringere.

glare n fulgor m ♦ vi fulgēre; ~ **at** torvīs oculīs
intuērī.
glaring adj (look) torvus; (fault) manifestus; **be**
~ ante pedēs positum esse.
glass n vitrum nt; (mirror) speculum nt.
glassy adj vitreus.
glaze vt vitrō obdūcere.
gleam n fulgor m, lūx f ♦ vi fulgēre, lūcēre.
gleaming adj splendidus, nitidus.
glean vi spīcās legere.
gleaning n spīcilegium nt.
glebe n fundus m.
glee n hilaritās f, gaudium nt.
gleeful adj hilaris, festīvus, laetus.
gleefully adv hilare, laetē.
glen n vallis f.
glib adj prōfluēns, fācundus.
glibly adv prōfluenter.
glide n lāpsus m ♦ vi lābī; ~ **away** ēlābī.
glimmer vi sublūcēre ♦ n: **a** ~ **of hope** spēcula
f.
glimpse n aspectus m ♦ vt cōnspicārī.
glint vi renīdēre.
glisten vi fulgēre, nitēre.
glitter vi micāre.
gloaming n crepusculum nt.
gloat vi: ~ **over** inhiāre, animō haurīre, oculōs
pāscere (abl).
globe n globus m, sphaera f; (inhabited) orbis
terrārum m.
globular adj globōsus.
globule n globulus m, pilula f.
gloom n tenebrae fpl; tristitia f.
gloomy adj tenebricōsus; tristis, dēmissus.
glorify vt illūstrāre, extollere, laudāre.
glorious adj illūstris, praeclārus, splendidus.
gloriously adv praeclārē, splendidē.
glory n laus f, glōria f, decus nt ♦ vi glōriārī, sē
iactāre.
gloss n nitor m ♦ vt: ~ **over** (fig) dissimulāre.
glossy adj nitidus.
glove n manica f.
glow n (light) lūmen nt; (heat) ārdor m;
(passion) calor m ♦ vi lūcēre, ārdēre, calēre,
candēre.
glowing adj candēns, ārdēns, calidus.
glue n glūten nt ♦ vt glūtināre.
glum adj tristis, maestus.
glut vt explēre, saturāre ♦ n satietās f,
abundantia f.
glutton n gāneō m, helluō m.
gluttonous adj edāx, vorāx, avidus.
gluttony n gula f, edācitās f.
gnarled adj nōdōsus.
gnash vt, vi frendere; ~ **one's teeth** dentibus
frendere.
gnat n culex m.
gnaw vt rōdere; ~ **away** ērōdere.
gnawing adj mordāx.
go vi īre, vādere; (depart) abīre, discēdere;
(event) ēvādere; (mechanism) movērī; ~
about incipere, adgredī; ~ **after** īnsequī; ~
away abīre, discēdere; ~ **back** redīre,

regredī; ~ **before** anteīre, praeīre; ~ **by**
praeterīre; (*rule*) sequī, ūtī (*abl*); ~ **down**
dēscendere; (*storm*) cadere; (*star*) occidere;
~ **for** petere; ~ **forward** prōgredī; ~ **in** intrāre,
ingredī; ~ **in for** (*profession*) facere,
exercēre; ~ **off** abīre; ~ **on** pergere; (*event*)
agī; ~ **out** exīre, ēgredī; (*fire*) extinguī; ~ **over**
trānsīre; (*to enemy*) dēscīscere; (*preparation*)
meditarī; (*reading*) legere; (*work done*)
retractāre; ~ **round** circumīre, ambīre; ~
through percurrere; penetrāre; (*suffer*)
perferre; ~ **to** adīre, petere; ~ **up** ascendere;
~ **to the help of** subvenīre (+ *dat*); ~ **to meet**
obviam īre; ~ **with** comitārī; ~ **without**
carēre (*abl*), sē abstinēre (*abl*) ♦ *n* vīs *f*,
ācrimōnia *f*.
goad *n* stimulus *m* ♦ *vt* irrītāre; pungere; (*fig*)
stimulāre.
go-ahead *adj* impiger.
goal *n* fīnis *m*, mēta *f*.
goat *n* caper *m*, capra *f*.
gobble *vt* dēvorāre.
go-between *n* internūntius *m*, internūntia *f*;
(*bribery*) sequester *m*.
goblet *n* pōculum *nt*, scyphus *m*.
god *n* deus *m*.
goddess *n* dea *f*.
godhead *n* dīvīnitās *f*, nūmen *nt*.
godless *adj* impius.
godlike *adj* dīvīnus.
godliness *n* pietās *f*, rēligiō *f*.
godly *adj* pius.
godsend *n* quasi caelō dēmissus.
going *n* itiō *f*; (*way*) iter *nt*; (*departure*)
profectiō *f*, discessus *m*.
goitre *n* strūma *nt*.
gold *n* aurum *nt* ♦ *adj* aureus.
golden *adj* aureus; (*hair*) flāvus.
gold leaf *n* bractea *f*.
goldmine *n* aurāria *f*.
goldsmith *n* aurārius *m*, aurifex *m*.
good *adj* bonus, probus; (*fit*) idōneus, aptus;
(*considerable*) magnus; ~ **day**! salvē, salvēte!;
~ **looks** fōrma *f*, pulchritūdō *f*; ~ **nature**
facilitās *f*, cōmitās *f* ♦ *n* bonum *nt*,
commodum *nt*; **do** ~ **to** prōdesse (*dat*); **make** ~
supplēre, praestāre; **seem** ~ vidērī; ♦ *interj*
bene.
goodbye *interj* valē, valēte; **say** ~ **to** valēre
iubēre.
good-for-nothing *adj* nēquam.
good-humoured *adj* cōmis.
good-looking *adj* pulcher.
goodly *adj* pulcher; (*size*) amplus.
good nature *n* facilitās *f*, cōmitās *f*.
good-natured *adj* facilis, benīgnus,
benevolus.
goodness *n* bonitās *f*; (*character*) virtūs *f*,
probitās *f*, pietās *f*.
goods *npl* bona *ntpl*, rēs *f*; (*for sale*) merx *f*.
good-tempered *adj* mītis, lēnis.
goodwill *n* benevolentia *f*, favor *m*, grātia *f*.
goose *n* ānser *m/f*.

goose flesh *n* horror *m*.
gore *n* cruor *m* ♦ *vt* cornibus cōnfodere.
gorge *n* faucēs *fpl*, gula *f*; (GEOG) angustiae *fpl* ♦
vt: ~ **oneself** sē ingurgitāre.
gorgeous *adj* lautus, splendidus.
gorgeously *adv* lautē, splendidē.
gorgeousness *n* lautitia *f*.
gormandize *vi* helluārī.
gory *adj* cruentus.
gospel *n* ēvangelium *nt*.
gossip *n* (*talk*) sermunculus *m*, rūmusculus *m*,
fāma *f*; (*person*) lingulāca *f* ♦ *vi* garrīre.
gouge *vt* ēruere.
gourd *n* cucurbita *f*.
gourmand *n* helluō *m*, gāneō *m*.
gout *n* podagra *f*, articulāris morbus *m*.
gouty *adj* arthrīticus.
govern *vt* (*subjects*) regere; (*state*)
administrāre, gubernāre; (*emotion*)
moderārī (*dat*), cohibēre.
governess *n* ēducātrīx *f*.
government *n* gubernātiō *f*, administrātiō *f*;
(*men*) magistrātūs *mpl*.
governor *n* gubernātor *m*, moderātor *m*;
(*province*) prōcōnsul *m*, prōcūrātor *m*.
gown *n* (*men*) toga *f*; (*women*) stola *f*.
grab *vt* adripere, corripere.
grace *n* grātia *f*, lepōs *m*, decor *m*; (*favour*)
grātia *f*, venia *f*; (*of gods*) pāx *f*; **be in the good**
~**s of** in grātiā esse apud (*acc*); **with a bad** ~
invītus ♦ *vt* decorāre, ōrnāre.
graceful *adj* decōrus, venustus, lepidus.
gracefully *adv* venustē, lepidē.
graceless *adj* illepidus, impudēns.
gracious *adj* benīgnus, prōpitius, misericors.
graciously *adv* benīgnē, līberāliter.
graciousness *n* benīgnitās *f*, līberālitās *f*.
gradation *n* gradus *m*.
grade *n* gradus *m*.
gradient *n* clīvus *m*.
gradual *adj* lēnis.
gradually *adv* gradātim, sēnsim, paulātim.
graft *n* surculus *m*; (POL) ambitus *m* ♦ *vt*
īnserere.
grafting *n* īnsitiō *f*.
grain *n* frūmentum *nt*; (*seed*) grānum *nt*;
against the ~ invītā Minervā.
grammar *n* grammatica *f*.
grammarian *n* grammaticus *m*.
granary *n* horreum *nt*.
grand *adj* (*person*) amplus, illūstris, ēgregius;
(*way of life*) lautus, māgnificus; (*language*)
grandis, sublīmis.
granddaughter *n* neptis *f*; **great** ~ prōneptis *f*.
grandeur *n* māiestās *f*, māgnificentia *f*; (*style*)
granditās *f*.
grandfather *n* avus *m*; **great** ~ proavus *m*;
great-great-~ abavus *m*; **of a** ~ avītus.
grandiloquence *n* māgniloquentia *f*.
grandiloquent *adj* grandiloquus, tumidus.
grandiose *adj* māgnificus.
grandmother *n* avia *f*; **great** ~ proavia *f*.
grandson *n* nepōs *m*; **great** ~ prōnepōs *m*.

grant *vt* dare, concēdere, tribuere; (*admit*) fatērī ♦ *n* concessiō *f*.

grape *n* ūva *f*.

graphic *adj* expressus; **give a ~ account of** ante oculōs ponere, oculīs subicere.

grapnel *n* manus ferrea *f*, harpagō *f*.

grapple *vi* luctārī.⁷

grappling iron *n* manus ferrea *f*.

grasp *vt* prēnsāre, comprehendere; (*with mind*) complectī, adsequī, percipere, intellegere; **~ at** captāre, adpetere ♦ *n* manus *f*, comprehēnsiō *f*; (*mind*) captus *m*.

grasping *adj* avārus, rapāx.

grass *n* herba *f*.

grasshopper *n* gryllus *m*.

grassy *adj* herbōsus; herbidus.

grate *n* focus *m* ♦ *vt* atterere; **~ upon** offendere.

grateful *adj* grātus; **feel ~** grātiam habēre.

gratefully *adv* grātē.

gratification *n* voluptās *f*.

gratify *vt* mōrem gerere (*dat*), mōrigerārī (*dat*), grātificārī (*dat*).

gratifying *adj* iūcundus.

gratis *adv* grātuītō, grātīs.

gratitude *n* grātia *f*; **show ~** grātiam referre.

gratuitous *adj* grātuītus.

gratuitously *adv* grātuītō.

gratuity *n* stips *f*; (*MIL*) dōnātīvum *nt*.

grave *n* sepulchrum *nt* ♦ *adj* gravis, austērus ♦ *vt* scalpere.

gravel *n* glārea *f*.

gravely *adv* graviter, sevērē.

gravitate *vi* vergere.

gravity *n* (*person*) sevēritās *f*, tristitia *f*; (*CIRCS*) gravitās *f*, mōmentum *nt*; (*physics*) nūtus *m*; **by force of ~** nūtū suō.

gray *adj* rāvus; (*hair*) cānus.

graze *vi* pāscī ♦ *vt* (*cattle*) pāscere; (*by touch*) stringere.

grazing *n* pāstus *m*.

grease *n* arvīna *f* ♦ *vt* ungere.

greasy *adj* pinguis, ūnctus.

great *adj* māgnus, grandis, ingēns, amplus; (*fame*) īnsignis, praeclārus; **as ~ as** ... tantus ... quantus; **~ deal** plūrimum; **~ many** plūrimī; **how ~** quantus; **very ~** permāgnus.

greatcoat *n* lacerna *f*.

greatest *adj* māximus.

greatly *adv* multum, māgnopere.

greave *n* ocrea *f*.

greed *n* avāritia *f*.

greedily *adv* avārē, cupidē.

greedy *adj* avārus, cupidus; avidus.

Greek *adj* Graecus.

green *adj* viridis; (*unripe*) crūdus; **be ~** virēre.

greenness *n* viriditās *f*.

greens *n* olus *nt*.

greet *vt* salūtāre.

greeting *n* salūs *f*, salūtātiō *f*.

grey *adj* rāvus; (*hair*) cānus.

greyhound *n* vertagus *m*.

grief *n* dolor *m*, maeror *m*, lūctus *m*; **come to ~** perīre.

grievance *n* querimōnia *f*; iniūria *f*.

grieve *vi* dolēre, maerēre, lūgēre.

grievous *adj* tristis, lūctuōsus; molestus, gravis, acerbus.

grievously *adv* graviter, valdē.

grim *adj* trux, truculentus; atrōx.

grimace *n* ōris dēprāvātiō *f*; **make a ~** ōs dūcere.

grime *n* sordēs *f*, lutum *nt*.

grimy *adj* sordidus, lutulentus.

grin *n* rīsus *m* ♦ *vi* adrīdēre.

grind *vt* contundere; (*corn*) molere; (*blade*) acuere; **~ down** (*fig*) opprimere.

grindstone *n* cōs *f*.

grip *vt* comprehendere, arripere ♦ *n* comprehēnsiō *f*; **come to ~s with** in complexum venīre (*gen*).

gripe *n* tormina *ntpl*.

grisly *adj* horridus, dīrus.

grist *n* (*fig*) ēmolumentum *nt*.

grit *n* harēna *f*.

groan *n* gemitus *m* ♦ *vi* gemere, ingemere.

groin *n* inguen *nt*.

groom *n* agāsō *m*.

groove *n* canālis *m*, stria *f*.

grope *vi* praetentāre.

gross *adj* crassus, pinguis; (*morally*) turpis, foedus.

grossly *adv* foedē, turpiter; (*very*) valdē.

grossness *n* crassitūdō *f*; turpitūdō *f*.

grotto *n* spēlunca *f*, antrum *nt*.

ground *n* (*bottom*) solum *nt*; (*earth*) terra *f*, humus *f*; (*cause*) ratiō *f*, causa *f*; (*sediment*) faex *f*; **on the ~** humī; **on the ~s that** quod (+ *subj*); **to the ~** humum; **gain ~** prōficere; (*rumour*) incrēbrēscere; **lose ~** cēdere; (*MIL*) inclīnāre ♦ *vt* īnstituere ♦ *vi* (*ship*) sīdere.

grounding *n* īnstitūtiō *f*.

groundless *adj* vānus, inānis.

groundlessly *adv* frustrā, temerē.

grounds *n* faex *f*; (*property*) praedium *nt*; (*reason*) causa *f*; **I have good ~ for doing** nōn sine causā faciō, iūstīs dē causīs faciō.

groundwork *n* fundāmentum *nt*.

group *n* globus *m*, circulus *m* ♦ *vt* dispōnere.

grouse *n* (*bird*) tetraō *m*; (*complaint*) querēla *f* ♦ *vi* querī.

grove *n* nemus *nt*, lūcus *m*.

grovel *vi* serpere, sē prōsternere, sē advolvere.

grovelling *adj* humilis, abiectus.

grow *vi* crēscere, glīscere; (*spread*) percrēbrēscere; (*become*) fierī; **~ old** (con)senēscere; **~ up** adolēscere, pūbēscere; **let ~** (*hair*) prōmittere ♦ *vt* (*crops*) colere; (*beard*) dēmittere.

growl *n* fremitus *m* ♦ *vi* fremere.

grown-up *adj* adultus, grandis.

growth *n* incrēmentum *nt*, auctus *m*.

grub *n* vermiculus *m*.

grudge *n* invidia *f* ♦ *vt* invidēre (*dat*); (*thing*) gravārī.

grudgingly *adv* invītus, gravātē.

H, h

gruesome *adj* taeter.
gruff *adj* acerbus, asper.
grumble *vi* querī, mussāre ♦ *n* querēla *f*.
grumpy *adj* mōrōsus, querulus.
grunt *n* grunnītus *m* ♦ *vi* grunnīre.
guarantee *n* (*money*) spōnsiō *f*; (*promise*) fidēs *f*; (*person*) praes *m* ♦ *vt* spondēre, praestāre.
guarantor *n* spōnsor *m*.
guard *n* custōdia *f*, praesidium *nt*; (*person*) custōs *m*; **on ~** in statiōne; **be on one's ~** cavēre; **keep ~** statiōnem agere; **off one's ~** imprūdēns, inopīnāns; **be taken off one's ~** dē gradū dēicī ♦ *vt* custōdīre, dēfendere; (*keep*) cōnservāre; **~ against** cavēre.
guarded *adj* cautus.
guardedly *adv* cautē.
guardhouse *n* custōdia *f*.
guardian *n* custōs *m*; (*of minors*) tūtor *m*.
guardianship *n* custōdia *f*, tūtēla *f*.
guardian spirit *n* genius *m*.
gudgeon *n* gōbius *m*.
guerdon *n* praemium *nt*, mercēs *f*.
guess *n* coniectūra *f* ♦ *vt* dīvīnāre, conicere.
guest *n* hospes *m*, hospita *f*; (*at dinner*) convīva *m*; **uninvited ~** umbra *f*; **~'s** hospitālis.
guffaw *n* cachinnus *m* ♦ *vi* cachinnāre.
guidance *n* moderātiō *f*; **under the ~ of God** dūcente deō.
guide *n* dux *m*, ductor *m*; (*in policy*) auctor *m* ♦ *vt* dūcere; (*steer*) regere; (*control*) moderārī.
guild *n* collēgium *nt*.
guile *n* dolus *m*, fraus *f*.
guileful *adj* dolōsus, fraudulentus.
guilefully *adv* dolosē.
guileless *adj* simplex, innocēns.
guilelessly *adv* sine fraude.
guilt *n* culpa *f*, scelus *nt*.
guiltless *adj* innocēns, īnsōns.
guiltlessly *adv* integrē.
guilty *adj* nocēns, sōns; **find ~** damnāre.
guise *n* speciēs *f*.
guitar *n* fidēs *fpl*; **play the ~** fidibus canere.
gulf *n* sinus *m*; (*chasm*) hiātus *m*.
gull *n* mergus *m* ♦ *vt* dēcipere.
gullet *n* gula *f*, guttur *nt*.
gullible *adj* crēdulus.
gulp *vt* dēvorāre, haurīre.
gum *n* gummī *nt*; (*mouth*) gingīva *f*.
gumption *n* prūdentia *f*.
gurgle *vi* singultāre.
gush *vi* sē prōfundere, ēmicāre ♦ *n* scatūrīginēs *fpl*.
gust *n* flāmen *nt*, impetus *m*.
gusto *n* studium *nt*.
gusty *adj* ventōsus.
gut *n* intestīnum *nt* ♦ *vt* exenterāre; (*fig*) extergēre.
gutter *n* canālis *m*.
guzzle *vi* sē ingurgitāre.
gymnasium *n* gymnasium *nt*, palaestra *f*; **head of a ~** gymnasiarchus *m*.
gymnastic *adj* gymnicus; **~s** *pl* palaestra *f*.
gyrate *vi* volvī.

habit *n* mōs *m*, cōnsuētūdō *f*; (*dress*) habitus *m*, vestītus *m*; **be in the ~ of** solēre.
habitable *adj* habitābilis.
habitation *n* domus *f*, domicilium *nt*; (*place*) sēdēs *f*.
habitual *adj* ūsitātus.
habitually *adv* ex mōre, persaepe.
habituate *vt* adsuēfacere, īnsuēscere.
hack *vt* caedere, concīdere ♦ *n* (*horse*) caballus *m*.
hackneyed *adj* trītus.
Hades *n* īnferī *mpl*.
haft *n* manubrium *nt*.
hag *n* anus *f*.
haggard *adj* ferus.
haggle *vi* altercārī.
hail *n* grandō *f* ♦ *vi*: **it ~s** grandinat ♦ *vt* salūtāre, adclāmāre ♦ *interj* avē, avēte; salvē, salvēte; **I ~ from Rome** Rōma mihi patria est.
hair *n* capillus *m*; crīnis *m*; (*single*) pīlus *m*; (*animals*) sēta *f*, villus *nt*; **deviate a ~'s breadth from** trānsversum digitum discēdere ab; **split ~s** cavillārī.
hairdresser *n* tōnsor *m*.
hairless *adj* (*head*) calvus; (*body*) glaber.
hairpin *n* crīnāle *nt*.
hairsplitting *adj* captiōsus ♦ *n* cavillātiō *f*.
hairy *adj* pīlōsus.
halberd *n* bipennis *f*.
halcyon *n* alcēdō *f*; **~ days** alcēdōnia *ntpl*.
hale *adj* validus, rōbustus ♦ *vt* trahere, rapere.
half *n* dīmidium *nt*, dīmidia pars *f* ♦ *adj* dīmidius, dīmidiātus; **~ as much again** sesquī; **well begun is ~ done** dīmidium factī quī coepit habet.
half-asleep *adj* sēmisomnus.
half-baked *adj* (*fig*) rudis.
half-dead *adj* sēmianimis, sēmivīvus.
half-full *adj* sēmiplēnus.
half-hearted *adj* incūriōsus, sōcors.
half-heartedly *adv* sine studiō.
half-hour *n* sēmihōra *f*.
half-moon *n* lūna dīmidiāta *f*.
half-open *adj* sēmiapertus.
half pound *n* sēlībra *f*.
half-way *adj* medius; **~ up the hill** in mediō colle.
half-yearly *adj* sēmestris.
hall *n* ātrium *nt*; (*public*) exedra *f*.
hallo *interj* heus.

hallow vt sacrāre.
hallucination n error m, somnium nt.
halo n corōna f.
halt vi īnsistere, cōnsistere ♦ vt sistere ♦ n:
come to a ~ cōnsistere, agmen cōnstituere ♦
adj claudus.
halter n capistrum nt; (fig) laqueus m.
halve vt bipartīre.
ham n perna f.
hamlet n vīcus m.
hammer n malleus m ♦ vt tundere; ~ out
excūdere.
hamper n corbis f ♦ vt impedīre; (with debt)
obstringere.
hamstring vt poplitem succīdere (dat).
hand n manus f; **left** ~ laeva f, sinistra f; **right** ~
dextra f; **an old** ~ veterātor m; **at** ~ praestō,
ad manum; **be at** ~ adesse; **at first** ~ ipse; **at**
second ~ ab aliō; **on the one** ~ ... **on the other**
et ... et, quidem ... at; **near at** ~ in expedītō,
inibī; **the matter in** ~ quod nunc īnstat, quae
in manibus sunt; **get out of** ~ lascīvīre; **have**
a ~ **in** interesse (dat); **have one's** ~**s full** satis
agere; **lay** ~**s on** manum adferre, inicere
(dat); **live from** ~ **to mouth** ad hōram vīvere;
pass from ~ **to** ~ per manūs trādere; **take in** ~
suscipere; ~**s** pl (workmen) operae fpl ♦ vt
trādere, porrigere; ~ **down** trādere,
prōdere; ~ **over** dēferre, reddere.
handbill n libellus m.
handbook n ars f.
handcuffs n manicae fpl.
handful n manipulus m.
handicap n impedīmentum nt.
handicraft n artificium nt, ars operōsa f.
handily adv habiliter.
handiness n habilitās f, commoditās f.
handiwork n opus nt, manus f.
handkerchief n sūdārium nt.
handle n (cup) ānsa f; (knife) manubrium nt;
(fig) ānsa f, occāsiō f ♦ vt tractāre.
handling n tractātiō f.
handmaid n famula f.
handsome adj fōrmōsus, pulcher; (gift)
līberālis.
handsomely adv pulchrē; līberāliter.
handsomeness n pulchritūdō f, fōrma f.
hand-to-hand adv: **fight** ~ manum cōnserere,
comminus pugnāre.
handwriting n manus f.
handy adj (to use) habilis; (near) praestō.
hang vt suspendere; (head) dēmittere; (wall)
vestīre ♦ vi pendēre; ~ **back** gravārī,
dubitāre; ~ **down** dēpendēre; ~ **on to** haerēre
(dat); ~ **over** imminēre (dat), impendēre (dat);
go and be ~**ed** abī in malam crucem!
hanger-on n cliēns m/f, assecla m/f.
hanging n (death) suspendium nt; ~**s** pl aulaea
ntpl ♦ adj pendulus.
hangman n carnifex m.
hanker vi: ~ **after** appetere, exoptāre.
hap n fors f.
haphazard adj fortuītus.

hapless adj miser, īnfēlīx.
haply adv fortasse.
happen vi accidere, ēvenīre, contingere;
(become) fierī; **as usually** ~**s** ut fit; ~ **upon**
incidere in (acc); **it** ~**s that** accidit ut
(+subj).
happily adv fēlīciter, beātē, bene.
happiness n fēlīcitās f.
happy adj fēlīx, beātus; laetus; (in some
respect) fortūnātus.
harangue n cōntiō f ♦ vt cōntiōnārī apud (+
acc), hortārī.
harass vt vexāre, lacessere, exagitāre,
sollicitāre.
harassing adj molestus.
harbinger n praenūntius m.
harbour n portus m ♦ vt recipere.
harbour dues n portōria ntpl.
hard adj dūrus; (circs) asper, inīquus; (task)
difficilis, arduus; ~ **of hearing** surdaster;
grow ~ dūrēscere ♦ adv sēdulō, valdē; ~ **by**
prope, iuxtā; **I am** ~ **put to it to do** aegerrimē
faciō.
hard cash n praesēns pecūnia f.
harden vt dūrāre ♦ vi dūrēscere; (fig)
obdūrēscere; **become** ~**ed** obdūrēscere.
hard-fought adj atrōx.
hard-hearted adj crūdēlis, dūrus, inhūmānus.
hardihood n audācia f.
hardily adv sevērē.
hardiness n rōbur nt; dūritia f.
hardly adv vix, aegrē; (severely) dūriter,
acerbē; ~ **any** nullus ferē.
hardness n dūritia f; (fig) asperitās f, inīquitās
f; (difficulty) difficultās f; ~ **of hearing** surditās
f.
hard-pressed adj: **be** ~ labōrāre.
hardship n labor m, malum nt, iniūria f.
hard-working adj industrius, nāvus, sēdulus.
hardy adj dūrus, rōbustus, sevērus.
hare n lepus m.
hark interj auscultā, auscultāte ♦ vi: ~ **back to**
repetere.
harm n iniūria f, damnum nt, malum nt,
dētrīmentum nt; **come to** ~ dētrīmentum
capere, accipere ♦ vt laedere, nocēre (dat).
harmful adj damnōsus, noxius.
harmfully adv male.
harmless adj innocēns.
harmlessly adv innocenter; (escape) salvus,
incolumis, inviolātus.
harmonious adj cōnsonus, canōrus; (fig)
concors; (things) congruēns.
harmoniously adv modulātē; concorditer;
convenienter.
harmonize vi concinere, cōnsentīre,
congruere.
harmony n concentus m; (fig) concordia f,
cōnsēnsus m.
harness n arma ntpl ♦ vt īnfrēnāre, iungere.
harp n fidēs fpl; **play the** ~ fidibus canere ♦ vi: ~
on (fig) cantāre, dictitāre; **be always** ~**ing on**
the same thing cantilēnam eandem canere.

harpist n fidicen m, fidicina f.
harpoon n iaculum nt.
harpy n Harpyia f.
harrow n rāstrum nt ♦ vt occāre.
harrower n occātor m.
harrowing adj horrendus.
harry vt vexāre, dīripere.
harsh adj dūrus, acerbus, asper; (person) inclēmēns, sevērus.
harshly adv acerbē, asperē; sevērē.
harshness n acerbitās f, asperitās f; crūdēlitās f.
hart n cervus m.
harvest n messis f ♦ vt metere, dēmetere.
harvester n messor m.
hash n farrāgō f ♦ vt comminuere.
haste n festīnātiō f, properātiō f; **in ~** festīnanter; **in hot ~** incitātus; **make ~** festīnāre.
hasten vt mātūrāre, adcelerāre ♦ vi festīnāre, properāre, mātūrāre.
hastily adv properē, raptim; temerē, incōnsultē; īrācundē.
hastiness n temeritās f; (temper) īrācundia f.
hasty adj properus, celer; (action) incōnsultus, temerārius; (temper) īrācundus, ācer; **over ~** praeproperus.
hat n petasus m.
hatch vt exclūdere, parere.
hatchet n dolābra f.
hate n odium nt, invidia f ♦ vt ōdisse.
hated adj: **to be ~ (by sb)** odiō esse (+ dat).
hateful adj odiōsus, invīsus.
hatefully adv odiōsē.
hatred n odium nt.
haughtily adv adroganter, superbē, insolenter.
haughtiness n fastus m, adrogantia f, superbia f.
haughty adj adrogāns, superbus, īnsolēns.
haul vt trahere ♦ n bolus m.
haulage n vectūra f.
haulm n culmus m.
haunch n femur nt.
haunt vt frequentāre ♦ n locus m; (animals) lustrum nt.
have vt habēre, tenēre; (get done) cūrāre (gerundive); **I ~ a house** est mihī domus; **I ~ to go** mihī abeundum est; **~ it out with rem** dēcernere cum; **~ on** gerere, gestāre, indui; **I had better go** melius est īre, praestat īre; **I had rather** mālim, māllem.
haven n portus m; (fig) perfugium nt.
havoc n exitium nt, vastātiō f, ruīna f.
hawk n accipiter m ♦ vt (wares) circumferre.
hawker n īnstitor m.
hay n faenum nt; **make ~ while the sun shines** forō ūtī.
hazard n perīculum nt, discrīmen nt, ālea f ♦ vt perīclitārī, in āleam dare.
hazardous adj perīculōsus.
haze n nebula f.
hazel n corylus f.
hazy adj nebulōsus; (fig) incertus.

he pron hic, ille, is.
head n caput nt; (person) dux m, prīnceps m; (composition) caput nt; (mind) animus m, ingenium nt; **~ over heels** cernuus; **off one's ~** dēmēns; **be at the ~ of** dūcere, praeesse (dat); **come to a ~** caput facere; (fig) in discrīmen addūcī; **give one his ~** indulgēre (dat), habēnās immittere (dat); **keep one's ~** praesentī animō ūtī; **lose one's ~** suī compotem nōn esse; **shake one's ~** abnuere ♦ vt dūcere, praeesse (dat); **~ off** intercipere ♦ vi (in a direction) tendere.
headache n capitis dolor m.
headfirst adj praeceps.
heading n caput nt.
headland n prōmunturium nt.
headlong adj praeceps ♦ adv in praeceps; **rush ~** sē praecipitāre.
headquarters n (MIL) praetōrium nt.
headship n prīncipātus m.
headsman n carnifex m.
headstrong adj impotēns, pervicāx.
headway n prōfectus m.
heady adj incōnsultus; (wine) vehemēns.
heal vt sānāre, medērī (dat) ♦ vi sānēscere; **~ over** obdūcī.
healer n medicus m.
healing adj salūbris.
health n valētūdō f, salūs f; **state of ~** valētūdō f; **ill ~** valētūdō f; **be in good ~** valēre; **drink the ~ of** propīnāre (dat).
healthful adj salūbris.
healthiness n sānitās f.
healthy adj sānus, integer; (conditions) salūber.
heap n acervus m, cumulus m; **in ~s** acervātim ♦ vt acervāre; **~ together** congerere; **~ up** adcumulāre, coacervāre, congerere.
hear vt audīre; (case) cognōscere; **~ clearly** exaudīre; **~ in secret** inaudīre.
hearer n audītor m.
hearing n (sense) audītus m; (act) audītiō f; (of case) cognitiō f; **get a ~** sibī audientiam facere; **hard of ~** surdaster; **without a ~** indictā causā.
hearken vi auscultāre.
hearsay n fāma f, rūmor m.
heart n cor nt; (emotion) animus m, pectus nt; (courage) animus m; (interior) viscera ntpl; **by ~** memoriā, memoriter; **learn by ~** ēdiscere; **the ~ of the matter** rēs ipsa; **lose ~** animum dēspondēre; **take to ~** graviter ferre.
heartache n dolor m, angor m.
heartbroken adj animī frāctus, aeger; **be ~** animō labōrāre.
heartburning n invidia f.
heartfelt adj sincērus.
hearth n focus m; **~ and home** ārae et focī.
heartily adv vehementer, valdē.
heartiness n studium nt, vigor m.
heartless adj dūrus, inhūmānus, crūdēlis.
heartlessly adv inhūmānē.
heartlessness n inhūmānitās f, crūdēlitās f.
hearty adj studiōsus, vehemēns; (health)

rōbustus; (*feeling*) sincērus.

heat *n* ārdor *m*, calor *m*; (*emotion*) ārdor *m*, aestus *m*; (*race*) missus *m* ♦ *vt* calefacere, fervefacere; (*fig*) accendere; **become ~ed** incalēscere.

heatedly *adv* ferventer, ārdenter.

heath *n* inculta loca *ntpl*.

heathcock *n* attagēn *m*.

heathen *n* pāgānus *m*.

heather *n* erīcē *f*.

heave *vt* tollere; (*missile*) conicere; (*sigh*) dūcere ♦ *vi* tumēre, fluctuāre.

heaven *n* caelum *nt*, dī *mpl*; **~ forbid!** dī meliōra; **from ~** dīvīnitus; **in ~'s name** prō deum fidem!; **be in seventh ~** digitō caelum attingere.

heavenly *adj* caelestis, dīvīnus.

heavily *adv* graviter.

heaviness *n* gravitās *f*, pondus *nt*; (*of spirit*) maestitia *f*.

heavy *adj* gravis; (*air*) crassus; (*spirit*) maestus; (*shower*) māgnus, dēnsus.

heckle *vt* interpellāre.

heckler *n* interpellātor *m*.

hectic *adj* violēns, ācer, fervidus.

hector *vt* obstrepere (*dat*).

hedge *n* saepēs *f* ♦ *vt* saepīre; **~ off** intersaepīre ♦ *vi* tergiversārī.

hedgehog *n* echīnus *m*, ēricius *m*.

heed *vt* cūrāre, respicere ♦ *n* cūra *f*, opera *f*; **pay ~** animum attendere; **take ~** cavēre.

heedful *adj* attentus, cautus, dīligēns.

heedfully *adv* attentē, cautē.

heedfulness *n* cūra *f*, dīligentia *f*.

heedless *adj* incautus, immemor, neglegēns.

heedlessly *adv* incautē, neglegenter, temerē.

heedlessness *n* neglegentia *f*.

heel *n* calx *f*; **take to one's ~s** sē in pedēs conicere ♦ *vi* sē inclīnāre.

hegemony *n* prīncipātus *m*.

heifer *n* būcula *f*.

height *n* altitūdō *f*; (*person*) prōcēritās *f*; (*hill*) collis *m*, iugum *nt*; (*fig*) fastīgium *nt*; **the ~ of** summus.

heighten *vt* augēre, exaggerāre.

heinous *adj* atrōx, nefārius.

heinously *adv* atrōciter, nefāriē.

heinousness *n* atrōcitās *f*.

heir *n* hērēs *m*; **sole ~** hērēs ex asse.

heiress *n* hērēs *f*.

heirship *n* hērēditās *f*.

hell *n* Tartarus *m*, Īnfernī *mpl*.

hellish *adj* īnfernus, scelestus.

helm *n* gubernāculum *nt*, clāvus *m*.

helmet *n* galea *f*.

helmsman *n* gubernātor *m*.

helots *n* Hīlōtae *mpl*.

help *n* auxilium *nt*, subsidium *nt*; **I am a ~** auxiliō sum ♦ *vt* iuvāre (+ *acc*), auxiliārī, subvenīre (*dat*), succurrere (*dat*) ♦ *vi* prōdesse; **I cannot ~** facere nōn possum quīn (*subj*); **it can't be ~ed** fierī nōn potest aliter; **so ~ me God** ita me dī ament.

helper *n* adiūtor *m*, adiūtrix *f*.

helpful *adj* ūtilis; **be ~ to** auxiliō esse (*dat*).

helpless *adj* inops.

helplessness *n* inopia *f*.

hem *n* ōra *f*, limbus *m* ♦ *vt*: **~ in** interclūdere, circumsedēre.

hemlock *n* cicūta *f*.

hemp *n* cannabis *f*.

hen *n* gallīna *f*.

hence *adv* hinc; (*consequence*) igitur, ideō.

henceforth, henceforward *adv* dehinc, posthāc, ex hōc tempore.

her *adj* suus, ēius.

herald *n* praecō *m*; (*POL*) fētiālis *m* ♦ *vt* praenuntiāre.

herb *n* herba *f*, olus *nt*.

herbage *n* herbae *fpl*.

herd *n* pecus *nt*; grex *f*, armentum *nt* ♦ *vi* congregārī.

herdsman *n* pāstor *m*.

here *adv* hīc; **be ~** adesse; **~ and there** passim; **here ... there** alibī ... alibī; **from ~** hinc; **~ is ... ecce** (*acc*) ....

hereabouts *adv* hīc ferē.

hereafter *adv* posthāc, posteā.

hereat *adv* hīc.

hereby *adv* ex hōc, hinc.

hereditary *adj* hērēditārius, patrius.

heredity *n* genus *nt*.

herein *adv* hīc.

hereinafter *adv* īnfrā.

hereof *adv* ēius reī.

hereupon *adv* hīc, quō factō.

herewith *adv* cum hōc, ūnā.

heritable *adj* hērēditārius.

heritage *n* hērēditās *f*.

hermaphrodite *n* androgynus *m*.

hermit *n* homō sōlitārius *m*.

hero *n* vir fortissimus *m*; (*demigod*) hērōs *m*.

heroic *adj* fortissimus, māgnanimus; (*epic*) hērōicus; (*verse*) hērōus.

heroically *adv* fortissimē, audācissimē.

heroism *n* virtūs *f*, fortitūdō *f*.

heron *n* ardea *f*.

hers *pron* suus, ēius.

herself *pron* ipsa *f*; (*reflexive*) sē.

hesitancy *n* dubitātiō *f*.

hesitant *adj* incertus, dubius.

hesitate *vi* dubitāre, haesitāre.

hesitating *adj* dubius.

hesitatingly *adv* cunctanter.

hesitation *n* dubitātiō *f*; **with ~** dubitanter.

heterogeneous *adj* dīversus, aliēnigenus.

hew *vt* dolāre, caedere; **~ down** excīdere, interscindere.

hexameter *n* hexameter *m*.

heyday *n* flōs *m*.

hiatus *n* hiātus *m*.

hiccup *n* singultus *m* ♦ *vi* singultīre.

hide *vt* cēlāre, abdere, abscondere, occultāre; **~ away** abstrūdere; **~ from** cēlāre (*acc*) ♦ *vi* sē abdere, latēre; **~ away** dēlitēscere ♦ *n* pellis *f*, corium *nt*.

hideous adj foedus, dēfōrmis, turpis.
hideously adv foedē.
hideousness n foeditās f, dēfōrmitās f.
hiding n (place) latebra f.
hierarchy n ōrdinēs mpl.
high adj altus, excelsus; (ground) ēditus; (pitch) acūtus; (rank) amplus; (price) cārus; (tide) māximus; (wind) māgnus; ~ **living** luxuria f; ~ **treason** māiestās f; ~ **and mighty** superbus; **on** ~ sublīmis ♦ adv altē.
highborn adj nōbilis, generōsus.
high-class adj (goods) lautus.
high-flown adj īnflātus, tumidus.
high-handed adj superbus, īnsolēns.
high-handedly adv superbē, licenter.
high-handedness n licentia f, superbia f.
highland adj montānus.
highlander n montānus m.
highlands npl montāna ntpl.
highly adv (value) māgnī; (intensity) valdē.
highly-strung adj trepidus.
high-minded adj generōsus.
high-spirited adj ferōx, animōsus.
highway n via f.
highwayman n grassātor m, latrō m.
hilarious adj festīvus, hilaris.
hilariously adv festīvē, hilare.
hilarity n festīvitās f, hilaritās f.
hill n collis m, mōns m; (slope) clīvus m.
hillock n tumulus m.
hilly adj montuōsus, clīvōsus.
hilt n manubrium nt, capulus m.
himself pron ipse; (reflexive) sē.
hind n cerva f.
hinder vt impedīre, obstāre (dat), morārī.
hindmost adj postrēmus; (in column) novissimus.
hindrance n impedīmentum nt, mora f.
hinge n cardō f.
hint n indicium nt, suspiciō f; **throw out a** ~ inicere ♦ vt subicere, significāre.
hip n coxendīx f.
hippodrome n spatium nt.
hire vt condūcere; ~ **out** locāre ♦ n conductiō f, locātiō f; (wages) mercēs f.
hired adj mercennārius, conductus.
hireling n mercennārius m.
hirsute adj hirsūtus.
his adj suus, ēius.
hiss vi sībilāre ♦ vt: ~ **off stage** explōdere, exsībilāre ♦ n sībilus m.
historian n historicus m, rērum scrīptor m.
historical adj historicus.
history n historia f; **the** ~ **of Rome** rēs Rōmānae fpl; **since the beginning of** ~ post hominum memoriam; **ancient** ~ antīquitās f.
histrionic adj scaenicus.
hit n ictus m, plāga f; **a** ~! (in duel) habet! ♦ vt ferīre, icere, percutere; ~ **against** offendere; ~ **upon** invenīre.
hitch n mora f ♦ vt implicāre; ~ **up** succingere.
hither adv hūc; ~ **and thither** hūc illūc ♦ adj citerior.

hitherto adv adhūc, hāctenus, hūcusque.
hive n alveārium nt.
hoar adj cānus ♦ n pruīna f.
hoard n thēsaurus m, acervus m ♦ vt condere, recondere.
hoarfrost n pruīna f.
hoarse adj raucus, fuscus.
hoarsely adv raucā vōce.
hoary adj cānus.
hoax n fraus f, fallācia f, lūdus m ♦ vt dēcipere, fallere.
hobble vi claudicāre.
hobby n studium nt.
hob-nob vi familiāriter ūtī (abl).
hocus-pocus n trīcae fpl.
hoe n sarculum nt ♦ vt sarrīre.
hog n sūs m, porcus m; ~'**s** porcīnus.
hogshead n dōlium nt.
hoist vt tollere; (sail) vēla dare.
hold n (grasp) comprehēnsiō f; (power) potestās f; (ship) alveus m; **gain a** ~ **over** obstringere, sibi dēvincīre; **get** ~ **of** potīrī (abl); **keep** ~ **of** retinēre; **lose** ~ **of** ōmittere; **take** ~ **of** prehendere, comprehendere ♦ vt tenēre, habēre; (possession) obtinēre, possidēre; (office) gerere, fungī (abl); (capacity) capere; (meeting) habēre; ~ **a meeting** concilium habēre; ~ **one's own with** parem esse (dat); ~ **over** differre, prōlātāre; ~ **water** (fig) stāre ♦ vi manēre, dūrāre; (opinion) dūcere, existimāre, adfirmāre; ~ **back** vt retinēre, inhibēre ♦ vi gravārī, dubitāre; ~ **cheap** parvī facere; ~ **fast** vt retinere, amplectī ♦ vi haerēre; ~ **good** valēre; ~ **out** vt porrigere, extendere; (hope) ostendere ♦ vi dūrāre, perstāre; ~ **together** cohaerēre; ~ **up** tollere; (falling) sustinēre; (movement) obstāre (dat), morārī; ~ **with** adsentīre (dat).
holdfast n fībula f.
holding n (land) agellus m.
hole n forāmen nt, cavum nt; **make a** ~ **in** pertundere, perforāre.
holiday n ōtium nt; festus diēs m; **on** ~ fēriātus; ~**s** pl fēriae fpl.
holily adv sānctē.
holiness n sānctitās f.
hollow adj cavus, concavus; (fig) inānis, vānus ♦ n cavum nt, caverna f ♦ vt excavāre.
hollowness n (fig) vānitās f.
holly n aquifolium nt.
holy adj sānctus.
homage n observantia f, venerātiō f; **pay** ~ **to** venerārī, colere.
home n domus f; (town, country) patria f; **at** ~ domī; **from** ~ domō ♦ adj domesticus ♦ adv domum.
homeless adj profugus.
homely adj simplex, rūsticus; (speech) plēbēius.
homestead n fundus m.
homewards adv domum.
homicide n (act) homicīdium nt, caedēs f;

(*person*) homicīda *m*.
homily *n* sermō *m*.
homogeneous *adj* aequābilis.
homologous *adj* cōnsimilis.
hone *n* cōs *f* ♦ *vt* acuere.
honest *adj* probus, frūgī, integer.
honestly *adv* probē, integrē.
honesty *n* probitās *f*, fidēs *f*.
honey *n* mel *nt*.
honeycomb *n* favus *m*.
honeyed *adj* mellītus, mulsus.
honorarium *n* stips *f*.
honorary *adj* honōrārius.
honour *n* honōs *m*; (*repute*) honestās *f*;
existimātiō *f*; (*chastity*) pudor *m*; (*trust*) fidēs *f*;
(*rank*) dignitās *f*; (*award*) decus *nt*, īnsigne *nt*;
(*respect*) observantia *f* ♦ *vt* honōrāre,
decorāre; (*respect*) observāre, colere; **do ~ to**
honestāre.
honourable *adj* honestus, probus; (*rank*)
illūstris, praeclārus.
honourably *adv* honestē.
hood *n* cucullus *m*.
hoodwink *vt* verba dare (*dat*).
hoof *n* ungula *f*.
hook *n* uncus *m*, hāmus *m* ♦ *vt* hāmō capere.
hooked *adj* aduncus, hāmātus.
hoop *n* circulus *m*; (*toy*) trochus *m*.
hoot *vi* obstrepere; **~ off** (*stage*) explōdere.
hop *n* saltus *m*; **catch on the ~** in ipsō articulō
opprimere ♦ *vi* salīre.
hope *n* spēs *f*; **in the ~ that** sī forte; **give up ~**
spem dēpōnere, dēspērāre; **past ~**
dēspērātus; **entertain ~s** spem habēre ♦ *vt*
spērāre.
hopeful *adj* bonae speī; **be ~** aliquam spem
habēre.
hopefully *adv* nōn sine spē.
hopeless *adj* dēspērātus.
hopelessly *adv* dēspēranter.
hopelessness *n* dēspērātiō *f*.
horde *n* multitūdō *f*.
horizon *n* fīniēns *m*.
horizontal *adj* aequus, lībrātus.
horizontally *adv* ad lībram.
horn *n* cornū *nt*; (*shepherd's*) būcina *f*.
horned *adj* corniger.
hornet *n* crabrō *m*; **stir up a ~'s nest** crabrōnēs
inrītāre.
horny *adj* corneus.
horoscope *n* sīdus nātālicium *nt*.
horrible *adj* horrendus, horribilis, dīrus,
foedus.
horribly *adv* foedē.
horrid *adj* horribilis.
horrify *vt* terrēre, perterrēre.
horror *n* horror *m*, terror *m*; odium *nt*.
horse *n* equus *m*; (*cavalry*) equitēs *mpl*; **flog a
dead ~** asellum currere docēre; **spur a
willing ~** currentem incitāre; **~'s** equīnus.
horseback *n*: **ride on ~back** in equō vehī; **fight
on ~back** ex equō pugnāre.
horseman *n* eques *m*.

horseradish *n* armoracia *f*.
horse soldier *n* eques *m*.
horticulture *n* hortōrum cultus *m*.
hospitable *adj* hospitālis.
hospitably *adv* hospitāliter.
hospital *n* valētūdinārium *nt*.
hospitality *n* hospitālitās *f*, hospitium *nt*.
host *n* hospes *m*; (*inn*) caupō *m*; (*number*)
multitūdō *f*; (*MIL*) exercitus *m*.
hostage *n* obses *m/f*.
hostelry *n* taberna *f*, dēversōrium *nt*.
hostile *adj* hostīlis, īnfēnsus, inimīcus;
īnfestus; **in a ~ manner** īnfēnsē, hostīliter,
inimīcē.
hostility *n* inimīcitia *f*; **hostilities** *pl* bellum *nt*.
hot *adj* calidus, fervidus, aestuōsus; (*boiling*)
fervēns; (*fig*) ārdēns; **be ~** calēre, fervēre,
ārdēre; **get ~** calēscere.
hotch-potch *n* farrāgō *f*.
hotel *n* dēversōrium *nt*.
hot-headed *adj* ārdēns, temerārius, praeceps.
hotly *adv* ārdenter, ācriter.
hot-tempered *adj* īrācundus.
hot water *n* calida *f*.
hound *n* canis *m* ♦ *vt* īnstāre (*dat*).
hour *n* hōra *f*.
hourly *adv* in hōrās.
house *n* domus *f*, aedēs *fpl*; (*country*) vīlla *f*;
(*family*) domus *f*, gēns *f*; **at the ~ of** apud (*acc*);
full ~ frequēns senātus, frequēns theātrum
♦ *vt* hospitiō accipere, recipere; (*things*)
condere.
household *n* familia *f*, domus *f* ♦ *adj*
familiāris, domesticus.
householder *n* paterfamiliās *m*, dominus *m*.
housekeeping *n* reī familiāris cūra *f*.
housemaid *n* ancilla *f*.
housetop *n* fastīgium *nt*.
housewife *n* māterfamiliās *f*, domina *f*.
housing *n* hospitium *nt*; (*horse*) ōrnāmenta
ntpl.
hovel *n* gurgustium *nt*.
hover *vi* pendēre; (*fig*) impendēre.
how *adv* (*interrog*) quemadmodum; quōmodō,
quō pactō; (*excl*) quam; **~ great/big/large**
quantus; **~ long** (*time*) quamdiū; **~ many** quot;
~ much quantum; **~ often** quotiēns.
howbeit *adv* tamen.
however *adv* tamen; autem, nihilōminus;
utcumque, quōquō modō; **~ much** quamvīs,
quantumvīs; **~ great** quantuscumque.
howl *n* ululātus *m* ♦ *vi* ululāre; (*wind*) fremere.
howsoever *adv* utcumque.
hub *n* axis *m*.
hubbub *n* tumultus *m*.
huckster *n* īnstitor *m*, propōla *m*.
huddle *n* turba *f* ♦ *vi* congregārī.
hue *n* color *m*; **~ and cry** clāmor *m*.
huff *n* offēnsiō *f* ♦ *vt* offendere.
hug *n* complexus *m* ♦ *vt* complectī.
huge *adj* ingēns, immānis, immēnsus, vastus.
hugely *adv* vehementer.
hugeness *n* immānitās *f*.

hulk *n* alveus *m.*
hull *n* alveus *m.*
hum *n* murmur *nt,* fremitus *m* ♦ *vi* murmurāre, fremere.
human *adj* hūmānus.
human being *n* homō *m/f.*
humane *adj* hūmānus, misericors.
humanely *adv* hūmānē, hūmāniter.
humanism *n* litterae *fpl.*
humanist *n* homō litterātus *m.*
humanity *n* hūmānitās *f;* misericordia *f.*
humanize *vt* excolere.
humanly *adv* hūmānitus.
human nature *n* hūmānitās *f.*
humble *adj* humilis, modestus ♦ *vt* dēprimere; (*oneself*) summittere.
humbleness *n* humilitās *f.*
humbly *adv* summissē, modestē.
humbug *n* trīcae *fpl.*
humdrum *adj* vulgāris; (*style*) pedester.
humid *adj* ūmidus, madidus; **be ~** madēre.
humidity *n* ūmor *m.*
humiliate *vt* dēprimere, dēdecorāre.
humiliation *n* dēdecus *nt.*
humility *n* modestia *f,* animus summissus *m.*
humorist *n* homō facētus *m.*
humorous *adj* facētus, ioculāris, rīdiculus.
humorously *adv* facētē.
humour *n* facētiae *fpl;* (*disposition*) ingenium *nt;* (*mood*) libīdō *f;* **be in a bad ~** sibī displicēre ♦ *vt* indulgēre (*dat*), mōrem gerere (*dat*), mōrigerārī (*dat*).
hump *n* gibbus *m.*
hunchback *n* gibber *m.*
hundred *num* centum; **~ each** centēnī; **~ times** centiēns.
hundredth *adj* centēsimus.
hundredweight *n* centumpondium *nt.*
hunger *n* famēs *f* ♦ *vi* ēsurīre.
hungrily *adv* avidē.
hungry *adj* ēsuriēns, iēiūnus, avidus; **be ~** ēsurīre.
hunt *n* vēnātiō *f,* vēnātus *m* ♦ *vt* vēnārī, indāgāre, exagitāre.
hunter *n* vēnātor *m.*
hunting *n* vēnātiō *f;* (*fig*) aucupium *nt.*
hunting spear *n* vēnābulum *nt.*
huntress *n* vēnātrix *f.*
huntsman *n* vēnātor *m.*
hurdle *n* crātēs *f;* (*obstacle*) obex *m/f.*
hurl *vt* conicere, ingerere, iaculārī, iācere.
hurly-burly *n* turba *f,* tumultus *m.*
hurrah *interj* euax, iō.
hurricane *n* procella *f.*
hurried *adj* praeproperus, praeceps, trepidus.
hurriedly *adv* properātō, cursim, festīnanter.
hurry *vt* adcelerāre, mātūrāre ♦ *vi* festīnāre, properāre; **~ along** *vt* rapere; **~ away** *vi* discēdere, properāre; **~ about** *vi* discurrere; **~ on** *vt* mātūrāre; **~ up** *vi* properāre ♦ *n* festīnātiō *f;* **in a ~** festīnanter, raptim.
hurt *n* iniūria *f,* damnum *nt;* vulnus *nt* ♦ *vt* laedere, nocēre (*dat*); **it ~s** dolet.

hurtful *adj* nocēns, damnōsus.
hurtfully *adv* nocenter, damnōsē.
hurtle *vi* volāre; sē praecipitāre.
husband *n* vir *m,* marītus *m* ♦ *vt* parcere (*dat*).
husbandry *n* agrī cultūra *f;* (*economy*) parsimōnia *f.*
hush *n* silentium *nt* ♦ *vt* silentium facere (*dat*), lēnīre ♦ *vi* tacēre, silēre; **~ up** comprimere, cēlāre ♦ *interj* st!
hushed *adj* tacitus.
husk *n* folliculus *m,* siliqua *f* ♦ *vt* dēglūbāre.
husky *adj* fuscus, raucus.
hustle *vt* trūdere, īnstāre (*dat*).
hut *n* casa *f,* tugurium *nt.*
hutch *n* cavea *f.*
hyacinth *n* hyacinthus *m.*
hybrid *n* hibrida *m/f.*
hydra *n* hydra *f.*
hyena *n* hyaena *f.*
hygiene *n* salūbritās *f.*
hygienic *adj* salūbris.
hymeneal *adj* nūptiālis.
hymn *n* carmen *nt* ♦ *vt* canere.
hyperbole *n* superlātiō *f.*
hypercritical *adj* Aristarchus *m.*
hypocaust *n* hypocaustum *nt.*
hypocrisy *n* simulātiō *f,* dissimulātiō *f.*
hypocrite *n* simulātor *m,* dissimulātor *m.*
hypocritical *adj* simulātus, fictus.
hypothesis *n* positum *nt,* sūmptiō *f,* coniectūra *f.*
hypothetical *adj* sūmptus.

I, i

I *pron* ego.
iambic *adj* iambēus.
iambus *n* iambus *m.*
ice *n* glaciēs *f.*
icicle *n* stīria *f.*
icon *n* simulacrum *nt.*
icy *adj* glaciālis, gelidus.
idea *n* nōtiō *f,* nōtitia *f,* imāgō *f;* (*Platonic*) fōrma *f;* (*expressed*) sententia *f;* **conceive the ~ of** īnfōrmāre; **with the ~ that** eō cōnsiliō ut (+ *subj*).
ideal *adj* animō comprehēnsus; (*perfect*) perfectus, optimus ♦ *n* specimen *nt,* speciēs *f,* exemplar *nt.*
identical *adj* īdem, cōnsimilis.
identify *vt* agnōscere.
identity *n:* **establish the ~ of** cognōscere quis sit.
Ides *n* Idūs *fpl.*
idiocy *n* animī imbēcillitās *f.*

idiom *n* proprium *nt*, sermō *m*.
idiomatic *adj* proprius.
idiomatically *adv* sermōne suō, sermōne propriō.
idiosyncrasy *n* proprium *nt*, libīdō *f*.
idiot *n* excors *m*.
idiotic *adj* fatuus, stultus.
idiotically *adv* stultē, ineptē.
idle *adj* ignāvus, dēses, iners; (*unoccupied*) ōtiōsus, vacuus; (*useless*) inānis, vānus; **be ~** cessāre, dēsidēre; **lie ~** (*money*) iacēre ♦ *vi* cessāre.
idleness *n* ignāvia *f*, dēsidia *f*, inertia *f*; ōtium *nt*.
idler *n* cessātor *m*.
idly *adv* ignāvē; ōtiōsē; frustrā, nēquīquam.
idol *n* simulacrum *nt*; (*person*) dēliciae *fpl*.
idolater *n* falsōrum deōrum cultor *m*.
idolatry *n* falsōrum deōrum cultus *m*.
idolize *vt* venerārī.
idyll *n* carmen Theocritēum *nt*.
if *conj* sī; (*interrog*) num, utrum; **~ anyone** sī quis; **~ ever** sī quandō; **~ not** nisī; **~ only** dum, dummodo; **~ ... or** sīve ... sīve; **as ~** quasi, velut; **but ~** sīn, quodsī; **even ~** etiamsī.
igneous *adj* igneus.
ignite *vt* accendere, incendere ♦ *vi* ignem concipere.
ignoble *adj* (*birth*) ignōbilis; (*repute*) illīberālis, turpis.
ignominious *adj* ignōminiōsus, īnfāmis, turpis.
ignominiously *adv* turpiter.
ignominy *n* ignōminia *f*, īnfāmia *f*, dēdecus *nt*.
ignoramus *n* idiōta *m*, indoctus *m*.
ignorance *n* īnscītia *f*, ignōrātiō *f*.
ignorant *adj* ignārus, indoctus; (*of something*) īnscītus, rudis; (*unaware*) īnscius; **be ~ of** nescīre, ignōrāre.
ignorantly *adv* īnscienter, īnscītē, indoctē.
ignore *vt* praetermittere.
ilex *n* īlex *f*.
Iliad *n* Ilias *f*.
ill *adj* aeger, aegrōtus, invalidus; (*evil*) malus; **be ~** aegrōtāre; **fall ~** in morbum incidere; **~ at ease** sollicitus ♦ *adv* male, improbē ♦ *n* malum *nt*, incommodum *nt*, aerumna *f*, damnum *nt*.
ill-advised *adj* incōnsultus.
ill-bred *adj* agrestis, inurbānus.
ill-disposed *adj* malevolus, invidus.
illegal *adj* illicitus, vetitus.
illegally *adv* contrā lēgēs.
ill-fated *adj* īnfēlīx.
ill-favoured *adj* turpis.
ill-gotten *adj* male partus.
ill-health *n* valētūdō *f*.
illicit *adj* vetitus.
illimitable *adj* īnfīnītus.
illiteracy *n* litterārum īnscītia *f*.
illiterate *adj* illitterātus, inērudītus.
ill-natured *adj* malevolus, malignus.
illness *n* morbus *m*, valētūdō *f*.

illogical *adj* absurdus.
ill-omened *adj* dīrus, īnfaustus.
ill-starred *adj* īnfēlīx.
ill-tempered *adj* īrācundus, amārus, stomachōsus.
ill-timed *adj* immātūrus, intempestīvus.
ill-treat *vt* malefacere (*dat*).
illuminate *vt* illūmināre, illūstrāre.
illumination *n* lūmina *ntpl*.
illusion *n* error *m*, somnium *nt*.
illusive, illusory *adj* fallāx.
illustrate *vt* illūstrāre; (*with instances*) exemplō cōnfirmāre.
illustration *n* exemplum *nt*.
illustrious *adj* illūstris, īnsignis, praeclārus.
illustriously *adv* praeclārē.
ill will *n* invidia *f*.
image *n* imāgō *f*, effigiēs *f*; (*idol*) simulacrum *nt*; (*verbal*) figūra *f*, similitūdō *f*.
imagery *n* figūrae *fpl*.
imaginary *adj* commentīcius, fictus.
imagination *n* cōgitātiō *f*, opīnātiō *f*.
imaginative *adj* ingeniōsus.
imagine *vt* animō fingere, animum indūcere, ante oculōs pōnere; (*think*) opīnārī, arbitrārī.
imbecile *adj* animō imbēcillus, fatuus, mente captus.
imbecility *n* animī imbēcillitās *f*.
imbibe *vt* adbibere; (*fig*) imbuī (*abl*).
imbrue *vt* īnficere.
imbue *vt* imbuere, īnficere, tingere.
imitable *adj* imitābilis.
imitate *vt* imitārī.
imitation *n* imitātiō *f*; (*copy*) imāgō *f*.
imitator *n* imitātor *m*, imitātrix *f*, aemulātor *m*.
immaculate *adj* integer, ēmendātus.
immaculately *adv* integrē, sine vitiō.
immaterial *adj* indifferēns.
immature *adj* immātūrus.
immeasurable *adj* immēnsus, īnfīnītus.
immediate *adj* īnstāns, praesēns; (*neighbour*) proximus.
immediately *adv* statim, extemplō, cōnfestim.
immemorial *adj* antīquissimus; **from time ~** post hominum memoriam.
immense *adj* immēnsus, immānis, ingēns, vastus.
immensely *adv* vehementer.
immensity *n* immēnsum *nt*, māgnitūdō *f*.
immerse *vt* immergere, mergere.
immigrant *n* advena *m*.
immigrate *vi* migrāre.
imminent *adj* īnstāns, praesēns; **be ~** imminēre, impendēre.
immobile *adj* fīxus, immōbilis.
immoderate *adj* immoderātus, immodestus.
immoderately *adv* immoderātē, immodestē.
immodest *adj* impudīcus, inverēcundus.
immolate *vt* immolāre.
immoral *adj* prāvus, corruptus, turpis.
immorality *n* corruptī mōrēs *mpl*, turpitūdō *f*.

immorally *adv* prāvē, turpiter.
immortal *adj* immortālis, aeternus.
immortality *n* immortālitās *f*.
immortalize *vt* in astra tollere.
immortally *adv* aeternum.
immovable *adj* fīxus, immōbilis.
immune *adj* immūnis, vacuus.
immunity *n* immūnitās *f*, vacātiō *f*.
immure *vt* inclūdere.
immutability *n* immūtābilitās *f*.
immutable *adj* immūtābilis.
imp *n* puer improbus *m*.
impact *n* ictus *m*, incussus *m*.
impair *vt* imminuere, corrumpere.
impale *vt* induere, īnfīgere.
impalpable *adj* tenuissimus.
impart *vt* impertīre, commūnicāre; (*courage*)
   addere.
impartial *adj* aequus, medius.
impartiality *n* aequābilitās *f*.
impartially *adv* sine favōre.
impassable *adj* invius; (*mountains*)
   inexsuperābilis; (*fig*) inexplicābilis.
impasse *n* mora *f*, incitae *fpl*.
impassioned *adj* ārdēns, fervidus.
impassive *adj* rigidus, sēnsū carēns.
impatience *n* aviditās *f*; (*of anything*)
   impatientia *f*.
impatient *adj* trepidus, avidus; impatiēns.
impatiently *adv* aegrē.
impeach *vt* diem dīcere (*dat*), accūsāre.
impeachment *n* accūsātiō *f*, crīmen *nt*.
impeccable *adj* ēmendātus.
impecunious *adj* pauper.
impede *vt* impedīre, obstāre (*dat*).
impediment *n* impedīmentum *nt*.
impel *vt* impellere, incitāre.
impend *vi* impendēre, imminēre, īnstāre.
impenetrable *adj* impenetrābilis; (*country*)
   invius, impervius.
impenitent *adj*: **I am ~** nīl mē paenitet.
imperative *adj* necessārius.
imperceptible *adj* tenuissimus, obscurus.
imperceptibly *adv* sēnsim.
imperfect *adj* imperfectus, vitiōsus.
imperfection *n* vitium *nt*.
imperfectly *adv* vitiōsē.
imperial *adj* imperātōrius, rēgius.
imperil *vt* in discrīmen addūcere, labefactāre.
imperious *adj* imperiōsus, superbus.
imperiously *adv* superbē.
imperishable *adj* immortālis, aeternus.
impersonate *vt* partēs agere (*gen*).
impertinence *n* importūnitās *f*, protervitās *f*.
impertinent *adj* importūnus, protervus,
   ineptus.
impertinently *adv* importūnē, ineptē,
   protervē.
imperturbable *adj* immōtus, gravis.
impervious *adj* impervius, impenetrābilis.
impetuosity *n* ārdor *m*, violentia *f*, vīs *f*.
impetuous *adj* violēns, fervidus, effrēnātus.
impetuously *adv* effrēnātē.

impetus *n* impetus *m*.
impiety *n* impietās *f*.
impinge *vi* incidere.
impious *adj* impius, profānus; **it is ~** nefas est.
impiously *adv* impiē.
impish *adj* improbus.
implacable *adj* implācābilis, inexōrābilis,
   dūrus.
implacably *adv* dūrē.
implant *vt* īnserere, ingignere.
implement *n* īnstrūmentum *nt* ♦ *vt* implēre,
   exsequī.
implicate *vt* implicāre, impedīre.
implication *n* indicium *nt*.
implicit *adj* tacitus; absolūtus.
implicitly *adv* abscond�tē; (*trust*) omnīnō,
   summā fidē.
implore *vt* implōrāre, obsecrāre.
imply *vt* significāre, continēre; **be ~ied** inesse.
impolite *adj* inurbānus, illepidus.
impolitely *adv* inurbānē.
impolitic *adj* incōnsultus, imprūdēns.
imponderable *adj* levissimus.
import *vt* importāre, invehere; (*mean*) velle ♦
   n significātiō *f*.
importance *n* gravitās *f*, mōmentum *nt*; (*rank*)
   dignitās *f*, amplitūdō *f*, auctōritās *f*; **it is of**
   great ~ to me meā māgnī rēfert.
important *adj* gravis, magnī mōmentī; **it is ~**
   interest (*+ gen*) rēfert; **more ~, most ~**
   antīquior, antīquissimus.
importation *n* invectiō *f*.
imports *npl* importātīcia *ntpl*.
importunate *adj* molestus.
importune *vt* flāgitāre, īnstāre (*dat*).
impose *vt* impōnere; (*by order*) indīcere,
   iniungere; **~ upon** illūdere, fraudāre, abūtī
   (*abl*).
imposing *adj* māgnificus, lautus.
imposition *n* fraus *f*; (*tax*) tribūtum *nt*.
impossible *adj*: **it is ~** fierī nōn potest.
impost *n* tribūtum *nt*, vectīgal *nt*.
impostor *n* planus *m*, fraudātor *m*.
imposture *n* fraus *f*, fallācia *f*.
impotence *n* īnfirmitās *f*.
impotent *adj* īnfirmus, dēbilis; (*with rage*)
   impotēns.
impotently *adv* frustrā; (*rage*) impotenter.
impound *vt* inclūdere; (*confiscate*) pūblicāre.
impoverish *vt* in inopiam redigere.
impracticable *adj*: **be ~** fierī nōn posse.
imprecate *vt* exsecrārī.
imprecation *n* exsecrātiō *f*.
impregnable *adj* inexpugnābilis.
impregnate *vt* imbuere, īnficere.
impress *vt* imprimere; (*on mind*) īnfīgere;
   (*person*) permovēre; (*MIL*) invītum scrībere.
impression *n* (*copy*) exemplar *nt*; (*mark*)
   signum *nt*; (*feeling*) impulsiō *f*; (*belief*)
   opīnātiō *f*; **make an ~ of** exprimere; **make an**
   ~ on commovēre; **have the ~** opīnārī.
impressionable *adj* crēdulus.
impressive *adj* gravis.

impressively *adv* graviter.
impressiveness *n* gravitās *f.*
imprint *n* impressiō *f*, signum *nt* ♦ *vt* imprimere; (*on mind*) īnfīgere, inūrere.
imprison *vt* inclūdere, in vincula conicere.
imprisonment *n* custōdia *f*, vincula *ntpl.*
improbable *adj* incrēdibilis, haud vērīsimilis.
impromptu *adv* ex tempore.
improper *adj* indecōrus, ineptus.
improperly *adv* prāvē, perperam.
impropriety *n* culpa *f*, offēnsa *f.*
improve *vt* ēmendāre, corrigere; (*mind*) excolere ♦ *vi* prōficere, meliōrem fierī.
improvement *n* ēmendātiō *f*, prōfectus *m.*
improvident *adj* imprōvidus; (*with money*) prōdigus.
improvidently *adv* imprōvidē; prōdigē.
improvise *vt* ex tempore compōnere, excōgitāre.
imprudence *n* imprūdentia *f.*
imprudent *adj* imprūdēns.
imprudently *adv* imprūdenter.
impudence *n* impudentia *f*, audācia *f.*
impudent *adj* impudēns, audāx.
impudently *adv* impudenter, protervē.
impugn *vt* impugnāre, in dubium vocāre.
impulse *n* impetus *m*, impulsus *m.*
impulsive *adj* praeceps, violentus.
impulsively *adv* impetū quōdam animī.
impulsiveness *n* impetus *m*, violentia *f.*
impunity *n* impūnitās *f*; **with ~** impūne.
impure *adj* impūrus, incestus, inquinātus.
impurely *adv* impūrē, incestē, inquinātē.
impurity *n* impūritās *f*, sordēs *fpl.*
imputation *n* crīmen *nt.*
impute *vt* attribuere, adsignāre; **~ as a fault** vitiō vertere.
in *prep* in (*abl*); (*with motion*) in (*acc*); (*authors*) apud (*acc*); (*time*) *abl*; **~ doing this** dum hoc faciō; **~ my youth** adulēscēns; **~ that** quod ♦ *adv* (*rest*) intrā; (*motion*) intrō.
inaccessible *adj* inaccessus.
inaccuracy *n* neglegentia *f*, incūria *f*; (*error*) mendum *nt.*
inaccurate *adj* parum dīligēns, neglegēns.
inaccurately *adv* neglegenter.
inaction *n* inertia *f.*
inactive *adj* iners, quiētus; **be ~** cessāre.
inactivity *n* inertia *f*, ōtium *nt.*
inadequate *adj* impār, parum idōneus.
inadequately *adv* parum.
inadvertency *n* imprūdentia *f.*
inadvertent *adj* imprūdēns.
inadvertently *adv* imprūdenter.
inane *adj* inānis, vānus; ineptus, stultus.
inanely *adv* ineptē.
inanimate *adj* inanimus.
inanity *n* ineptiae *fpl*, stultitia *f.*
inapplicable *adj*: **be ~** nōn valēre.
inappropriate *adj* aliēnus, parum aptus.
inarticulate *adj* īnfāns.
inartistic *adj* sine arte, dūrus, inēlegāns.
inasmuch as *conj* quōniam, cum (*subj*).

inattention *n* incūria *f*, neglegentia *f.*
inattentive *adj* neglegēns.
inattentively *adv* neglegenter.
inaudible *adj*: **be ~** audīrī nōn posse.
inaugurate *vt* inaugurāre, cōnsecrāre.
inauguration *n* cōnsecrātiō *f.*
inauspicious *adj* īnfaustus, īnfēlix.
inauspiciously *adv* malīs ōminibus.
inborn *adj* innātus.
incalculable *adj* inaestimābilis.
incantation *n* carmen *nt.*
incapable *adj* inhabilis, indocilis; **be ~** nōn posse.
incapacitate *vt* dēbilitāre.
incapacity *n* inertia *f*, īnscītia *f.*
incarcerate *vt* inclūdere, in vincula conicere.
incarnate *adj* hūmānā speciē indūtus.
incautious *adj* incautus, temerārius.
incautiously *adv* incautē.
incendiary *adj* incendiārius.
incense *n* tūs *nt* ♦ *vt* inrītāre, stomachum movēre (*dat*); **be ~d** stomachārī.
incentive *n* incitāmentum *nt*, stimulus *m.*
inception *n* initium *nt*, exōrdium *nt.*
incessant *adj* adsiduus.
incessantly *adv* adsiduē.
incest *n* incestus *m.*
inch *n* digitus *m*, ūncia *f.*
incident *n* ēventum *nt*, cāsus *m*, rēs *f.*
incidental *adj* fortuītus.
incidentally *adv* cāsū.
incipient *adj* prīmus.
incisive *adj* ācer.
incite *vt* īnstīgāre, impellere, hortārī, incitāre.
incitement *n* invītāmentum *nt*, stimulus *m.*
inciter *n* īnstimulātor *m.*
incivility *n* importūnitās *f*, inhūmānitās *f.*
inclemency *n* (*weather*) intemperiēs *f.*
inclement *adj* asper, tristis.
inclination *n* inclīnātiō *f*, animus *m*, libīdō *f*; (*slope*) clīvus *m.*
incline *vt* inclīnāre; (*person*) indūcere ♦ *vi* inclīnāre, incumbere; **~ towards sē** adclīnāre ♦ *n* adclīvitās *f*, clīvus *m.*
inclined *adj* inclīnātus, prōpēnsus; **I am ~ to think** haud sciō an.
include *vt* inclūdere, continēre, complectī.
incognito *adv* clam.
incoherent *adj* interruptus; **be ~** non cohaerēre.
income *n* fructus *m*, mercēs *f.*
incommensurate *adj* dispār.
incommode *vt* molestiam adferre (*dat*).
incomparable *adj* singulāris, eximius.
incompatibility *n* discrepantia *f*, repugnantia *f.*
incompatible *adj* īnsociābilis, repugnāns; **be ~ with** dissidēre ab, repugnāre (*dat*).
incompetence *n* inertia *f*, īnscītia *f.*
incompetent *adj* iners, īnscītus.
incomplete *adj* imperfectus.
incomprehensible *adj* incrēdibilis.

inconceivable *adj* incrēdibilis.
inconclusive *adj* inānis.
incongruous *adj* absonus, aliēnus.
inconsiderable *adj* exiguus.
inconsiderate *adj* imprōvidus, incōnsultus.
inconsistency *n* discrepantia *f*, incōnstantia *f*.
inconsistent *adj* incōnstāns; **be ~** discrepāre;
  be ~ with abhorrēre ab, repugnāre (*dat*).
inconsistently *adv* incōnstanter.
inconsolable *adj* nōn cōnsōlābilis.
inconspicuous *adj* obscūrus; **be ~** latēre.
inconstancy *n* incōnstantia *f*, levitās *f*.
inconstant *adj* incōnstāns, levis, mōbilis.
inconstantly *adv* incōnstanter.
incontestable *adj* certus.
incontinence *n* incontinentia *f*.
incontinent *adj* intemperāns.
inconvenience *n* incommodum *nt* ♦ *vt*
  incommodāre.
inconvenient *adj* incommodus.
inconveniently *adv* incommodē.
incorporate *vt* īnserere, adiungere.
incorrect *adj* falsus; **be ~** nōn cōnstāre.
incorrectly *adv* falsō, perperam.
incorrigible *adj* improbus, perditus.
incorruptibility *n* integritās *f*.
incorruptible *adj* incorruptus.
increase *n* incrēmentum *nt*, additāmentum *nt*,
  auctus *m* ♦ *vt* augēre, amplificāre ♦ *vi*
  crēscere, incrēscere.
increasingly *adv* magis magisque.
incredible *adj* incrēdibilis.
incredibly *adv* incrēdibiliter.
incredulous *adj* incrēdulus.
increment *n* incrēmentum *nt*.
incriminate *vt* crīminārī.
inculcate *vt* inculcāre, īnfīgere.
incumbent *adj*: **it is ~ on** oportet.
incur *vt* subīre; (*guilt*) admittere.
incurable *adj* īnsānābilis.
incursion *n* incursiō *f*.
indebted *adj* obnoxius; **be ~** dēbēre.
indecency *n* obscēnitās *f*.
indecent *adj* obscēnus, impudīcus.
indecently *adv* obscēnē.
indecision *n* dubitātiō *f*.
indecisive *adj* anceps, dubius; **the battle is ~**
  ancipitī Marte pugnātur.
indecisively *adv* incertō ēventū.
indecorous *adj* indecōrus.
indeed *adv* profectō, sānē; (*concessive*)
  quidem; (*interrog*) itane vērō?; (*reply*) certē,
  vērō; (*with pron*) dēmum; (*with adj, adv, conj*)
  adeō.
indefatigable *adj* impiger.
indefensible *adj*: **be ~** dēfendī nōn posse;
  (*belief*) tenērī nōn posse; (*offence*) excūsārī
  nōn posse.
indefinite *adj* incertus, ambiguus, īnfīnītus.
indefinitely *adv* ambiguē; (*time*) in incertum.
indelicate *adj* pūtidus, indecōrus.
independence *n* lībertās *f*.
independent *adj* līber, suī iūris.

indescribable *adj* inēnārrābilis.
indestructible *adj* perennis.
indeterminate *adj* incertus.
index *n* index *m*.
indicate *vt* indicāre, significāre.
indication *n* indicium *nt*, signum *nt*.
indict *vt* diem dīcere (*dat*), accūsāre, nōmen
  dēferre (*gen*).
indictment *n* accūsātiō *f*.
indifference *n* neglegentia *f*, languor *m*.
indifferent *adj* (*manner*) neglegēns, frīgidus,
  sēcūrus; (*quality*) mediocris.
indifferently *adv* neglegenter; mediocriter;
  (*without distinction*) promiscuē, sine
  discrīmine.
indigence *n* indigentia *f*, egestās *f*.
indigenous *adj* indigena.
indigent *adj* indigēns, egēnus.
indigestible *adj* crūdus.
indigestion *n* crūditās *f*.
indignant *adj* indignābundus, īrātus; **be ~**
  indignārī.
indignantly *adv* īrātē.
indignation *n* indignātiō *f*, dolor *m*.
indignity *n* contumēlia *f*, indignitās *f*.
indigo *n* Indicum *nt*.
indirect *adj* oblīquus.
indirectly *adv* oblīquē, per ambāgēs.
indirectness *n* ambāgēs *fpl*.
indiscipline *n* lascīvia *f*, licentia *f*.
indiscreet *adj* incōnsultus, imprūdēns.
indiscreetly *adv* incōnsultē, imprūdenter.
indiscretion *n* imprūdentia *f*; (*act*) culpa *f*.
indiscriminate *adj* prōmiscuus.
indiscriminately *adv* prōmiscuē, sine
  discrīmine.
indispensable *adj* necesse, necessārius.
indisposed *adj* īnfirmus, aegrōtus, (*will*)
  āversus, aliēnātus; **be ~** aegrōtāre;
  abhorrēre, aliēnārī.
indisposition *n* īnfirmitās *f*, valētūdō *f*.
indisputable *adj* certus, manifestus.
indisputably *adv* certē, sine dubiō.
indissoluble *adj* indissolūbilis.
indistinct *adj* obscūrus, obtūsus; (*speaker*)
  balbus.
indistinctly *adv* obscūrē; **pronounce ~**
  opprimere; **speak ~** balbutīre.
individual *adj* proprius ♦ *n* homō *m/f*, prīvātus
  m; **~s** *pl* singulī *mpl*.
individuality *n* proprium *nt*.
individually *adv* singulātim, prīvātim.
indivisible *adj* indīviduus.
indolence *n* dēsidia *f*, ignāvia *f*, inertia *f*.
indolent *adj* dēses, ignāvus, iners.
indolently *adv* ignāvē.
indomitable *adj* indomitus.
indoor *adj* umbrātilis.
indoors *adv* intus; (*motion*) intrā.
indubitable *adj* certus.
indubitably *adv* sine dubiō.
induce *vt* indūcere, addūcere, persuādēre
  (*dat*).

inducement n illecebra f, praemium nt.
induction n (_logic_) inductiō f.
indulge vt indulgēre (_dat_).
indulgence n indulgentia f, venia f; (_favour_)
grātia f.
indulgent adj indulgēns, lēnis.
indulgently adv indulgenter.
industrious adj industrius, impiger, dīligēns.
industriously adv industriē.
industry n industria f, dīligentia f, labor m.
inebriated adj ēbrius.
inebriation n ēbrietās f.
ineffable adj eximius.
ineffective adj inūtilis, invalidus.
ineffectively adv ināniter.
ineffectual adj inritus.
inefficient adj īnscītus, parum strēnuus.
inelegant adj inēlegāns, inconcinnus.
inelegantly adv inēleganter.
inept adj ineptus.
ineptly adv ineptē.
inequality n dissimilitūdō f, inīquitās f.
inert adj iners, sōcors, immōbilis.
inertia n inertia f.
inertly adv tardē, lentē.
inestimable adj inaestimābilis.
inevitable adj necessārius.
inevitably adv necessāriō.
inexact adj parum subtīlis.
inexhaustible adj perennis.
inexorable adj inexōrābilis.
inexpediency n inūtilitās f, incommodum nt.
inexpedient adj inūtilis; **it is ~** nōn expedit.
inexpensive adj vīlis.
inexperience n imperītia f, īnscītia f.
inexperienced adj imperītus, rudis, īnscītus.
inexpert adj imperītus.
inexpiable adj inexpiābilis.
inexplicable adj inexplicābilis, inēnōdābilis.
inexpressible adj inēnārrābilis.
inextricable adj inexplicābilis.
infallible adj certus, errōris expers.
infamous adj īnfāmis, flāgitiōsus.
infamously adv flāgitiōsē.
infamy n īnfāmia f, flāgitium nt, dēdecus nt.
infancy n īnfantia f; (_fig_) incūnābula ntpl.
infant n īnfāns m/f.
infantile adj puerīlis.
infantry n peditēs mpl, peditātus m.
infantryman n pedes m.
infatuate vt īnfatuāre.
infatuated adj dēmēns.
infatuation n dēmentia f.
infect vt īnficere.
infection n contāgiō f.
infer vt īnferre, colligere.
inference n conclūsiō f.
inferior adj (_position_) īnferior; (_quality_)
dēterior.
infernal adj īnfernus.
infest vt frequentāre.
infidel adj impius.
infidelity n perfidia f, īnfidēlitās f.

infiltrate vi sē īnsinuāre.
infinite adj īnfīnītus, immēnsus.
infinitely adv longē, immēnsum.
infinitesimal adj minimus.
infinity n īnfīnitās f.
infirm adj īnfirmus, invalidus.
infirmary n valētūdinārium nt.
infirmity n morbus m.
inflame vt accendere, incendere, īnflammāre.
be ~d exārdēscere.
inflammation n (_MED_) īnflātiō f.
inflate vt īnflāre.
inflated adj (_fig_) īnflātus, tumidus.
inflexible adj rigidus.
inflexion n (_GRAM_) flexūra f; (_voice_) flexiō f.
inflict vt īnflīgere, incutere; (_burden_)
impōnere; (_penalty_) sūmere; **be ~ed with**
labōrāre ex.
infliction n poena f; malum nt.
influence n (_physical_) impulsiō f, mōmentum
nt; (_moral_) auctōritās f; (_partial_) grātia f; **have**
~ valēre; **have great ~ with** plūrimum posse
apud; **under the ~ of** īnstinctus (_abl_) ♦ vt
impellere, movēre, addūcere.
influential adj gravis, potēns; grātiōsus.
influenza n gravēdō f.
inform vt docēre, certiōrem facere; **~ against**
nōmen dēferre (_gen_).
informant n index m, auctor m.
information n indicium nt, nūntius m.
informer n index m, dēlātor m; **turn ~** indicium
profitērī.
infrequent adj rārus.
infrequently adv rārō.
infringe vt violāre, imminuere.
infringement n violātiō f.
infuriate vt efferāre.
infuriated adj furibundus.
infuse vt īnfundere; (_fig_) inicere.
ingenious adj ingeniōsus, callidus; (_thing_)
artificiōsus.
ingeniously adv callidē, summā arte.
ingenuity n ars f, artificium nt, acūmen nt.
ingenuous adj ingenuus, simplex.
ingenuously adv ingenuē, simpliciter.
ingenuousness n ingenuitās f.
ingle n focus m.
inglorious adj inglōrius, ignōbilis, inhonestus.
ingloriously adv sine glōriā, inhonestē.
ingot n later m.
ingrained adj īnsitus.
ingratiate vt: **~ oneself with** grātiam inīre ab,
sē īnsinuāre in familiāritātem (_gen_); **~**
oneself into sē īnsinuāre in (_acc_).
ingratitude n ingrātus animus m.
ingredient n pars f.
inhabit vt incolere, habitāre in (_abl_).
inhabitable adj habitābilis.
inhabitant n incola m/f.
inhale vt haurīre.
inharmonious adj dissonus.
inherent adj īnsitus; **be ~ in** inhaerēre (_dat_),
inesse (_dat_).

inherently *adv* nātūrā.
inherit *vt* excipere.
inheritance *n* hērēditās *f*, patrimōnium *nt*; **divide an ~** herctum ciēre; **come into an ~** hērēditātem adīre.
inheritor *n* hērēs *m/f*.
inhibit *vt* prohibēre, inhibēre.
inhospitable *adj* inhospitālis.
inhuman *adj* inhūmānus, immānis, crūdēlis.
inhumanity *n* inhūmānitās *f*, crūdēlitās *f*.
inhumanly *adv* inhūmānē, crūdēliter.
inimical *adj* inimīcus.
inimitable *adj* singulāris, eximius.
iniquitous *adj* inīquus, improbus, nefārius.
iniquity *n* scelus *nt*, flāgitium *nt*.
initial *adj* prīmus.
initiate *vt* initiāre; (*with knowledge*) imbuere.
initiative *n* initium *nt*; **take the ~** initium capere, facere; occupāre (*inf*).
inject *vt* inicere.
injudicious *adj* incōnsultus, imprūdēns.
injunction *n* iussum *nt*, praeceptum *nt*.
injure *vt* laedere, nocēre (*dat*).
injurious *adj* damnōsus, nocēns.
injury *n* iniūria *f*, damnum *nt*; (*bodily*) vulnus *nt*.
injustice *n* iniūria *f*, inīquitās *f*.
ink *n* ātrāmentum *nt*.
inkling *n* audītiō *f*, suspiciō *f*.
inland *adj* mediterrāneus; **further ~** interior.
inlay *vt* īnserere.
inlet *n* sinus *m*, aestuārium *nt*.
inly *adv* penitus.
inmate *n* inquilīnus *m*.
inmost *adj* intimus.
inn *n* dēversōrium *nt*; caupōna *f*, taberna *f*.
innate *adj* innātus, īnsitus.
inner *adj* interior.
innermost *adj* intimus.
innkeeper *n* caupō *m*.
innocence *n* innocentia *f*.
innocent *adj* innocēns, īnsōns; (*character*) integer, castus.
innocently *adv* innocenter, integrē, castē.
innocuous *adj* innoxius.
innovate *vt* novāre.
innovation *n* novum *nt*, nova rēs *f*.
innovator *n* novārum rērum auctor *m*.
innuendo *n* verbum inversum *nt*.
innumerable *adj* innumerābilis.
inoffensive *adj* innocēns.
inoffensively *adv* innocenter.
inopportune *adj* intempestīvus.
inopportunely *adv* intempestīvē.
inordinate *adj* immodicus, immoderātus.
inordinately *adv* immoderātē.
inquest *n* quaestiō *f*; **hold an ~ on** quaerere dē.
inquire *vi* exquīrere, rogāre; **~ into** inquīrere in (*acc*), investigāre.
inquiry *n* quaestiō *f*, investīgātiō *f*; (*asking*) interrogātiō *f*; **make ~** exquīrere; **make ~ies about** inquīrere in (*acc*); **hold an ~ on** quaerere dē, quaestiōnem īnstituere dē.

inquisition *n* inquīsītiō *f*.
inquisitive *adj* cūriōsus.
inquisitiveness *n* cūriōsitās *f*.
inquisitor *n* inquīsītor *m*.
inroad *n* incursiō *f*, impressiō *f*; **make an ~** incursāre.
insane *adj* īnsānus, mente captus; **be ~** īnsānīre.
insanity *n* īnsānia *f*, dēmentia *f*.
insatiable *adj* īnsatiābilis, inexplēbilis, īnsaturābilis.
insatiably *adv* īnsaturābiliter.
inscribe *vt* īnscrībere.
inscription *n* epigramma *nt*; (*written*) īnscrīptiō *f*.
inscrutable *adj* obscūrus.
insect *n* bestiola *f*.
insecure *adj* īnstabilis, intūtus.
insecurity *n* perīcula *ntpl*.
insensate *adj* ineptus, stultus.
insensible *adj* torpidus; (*fig*) dūrus.
insensitive *adj* dūrus.
inseparable *adj* coniūnctus; **be the ~ companion of** ab latere esse (*gen*).
inseparably *adv* coniūnctē.
insert *vt* īnserere, immittere, interpōnere.
insertion *n* interpositiō *f*.
inshore *adv* prope lītus.
inside *adv* intus; (*motion*) intrō ♦ *adj* interior ♦ *n* pars *f* interior ♦ *prep* intrā (*acc*); **get right ~** sē īnsinuāre in (*acc*); **turn ~ out** excutere; **on the ~** interior.
insidious *adj* īnsidiōsus, subdolus.
insidiously *adv* īnsidiōsē.
insight *n* intellegentia *f*, cognitiō *f*.
insignia *n* īnsignia *ntpl*.
insignificance *n* levitās *f*.
insignificant *adj* levis, exiguus, nullīus mōmentī; (*position*) humilis.
insincere *adj* simulātus, fūcōsus.
insincerely *adv* simulātē.
insincerity *n* simulātiō *f*, fraus *f*.
insinuate *vt* īnsinuāre; (*hint*) significāre ♦ *vi* sē īnsinuāre.
insinuating *adj* blandus.
insinuation *n* ambigua verba *ntpl*.
insipid *adj* īnsulsus, frīgidus.
insipidity *n* īnsulsitās *f*.
insist *vi* īnstāre; **~ on** postulāre.
insistence *n* pertinācia *f*.
insistent *adj* pertināx.
insolence *n* īnsolentia *f*, contumācia *f*, superbia *f*.
insolent *adj* īnsolēns, contumāx, superbus.
insolently *adv* īnsolenter.
insoluble *adj* inexplicābilis.
insolvency *n* reī familiāris naufragium *nt*.
insolvent *adj*: **be ~** solvendō nōn esse.
inspect *vt* īnspicere; (*MIL*) recēnsēre.
inspection *n* cognitiō *f*; (*MIL*) recēnsiō *f*.
inspector *n* cūrātor *m*.
inspiration *n* adflātus *m*, īnstinctus *m*.
inspire *vt* īnstinguere, incendere.

instability *n* mōbilitās *f*.
install *vt* inaugurāre.
instalment *n* pēnsiō *f*.
instance *n* exemplum *nt*; **for ~** exemplī causā, grātiā; **at the ~** admonitū; **at my ~** mē auctōre ♦ *vt* memorāre.
instant *adj* īnstāns, praesēns ♦ *n* temporis pūnctum *nt*, mōmentum *nt*.
instantaneous *adj* praesēns.
instantaneously *adv* continuō, īlicō.
instantly *adv* īlicō, extemplō.
instead of *prep* prō (*abl*), locō (*gen*); (*with verb*) nōn ... sed.
instigate *vt* īnstigāre, impellere.
instigation *n* impulsus *m*, stimulus *m*; auctōritās *f*; **at my ~** mē auctōre.
instigator *n* īnstimulātor *m*, auctor *m*.
instil *vt* imbuere, adspīrāre, inicere.
instinct *n* nātūra *f*, ingenium *nt*, sēnsus *m*.
instinctive *adj* nātūrālis.
instinctively *adv* nātūrā, ingeniō suō.
institute *vt* īnstituere, inaugurāre.
institution *n* īnstitūtum *nt*; societās *f*.
instruct *vt* docēre, īnstituere, īnstruere; ērudīre; (*order*) praecipere (*dat*).
instruction *n* doctrīna *f*, disciplīna *f*; praeceptum *nt*; **give ~s** dēnūntiāre, praecipere.
instructor *n* doctor *m*, praeceptor *m*.
instructress *n* magistra *f*.
instrument *n* īnstrūmentum *nt*; (*music*) fidēs *fpl*; (*legal*) tabulae *fpl*.
instrumental *adj* ūtilis.
instrumentalist *n* fidicen *m*, fidicina *f*.
instrumentality *n* opera *f*.
insubordinate *adj* turbulentus, sēditiōsus.
insubordination *n* intemperantia *f*, licentia *f*.
insufferable *adj* intolerandus, intolerābilis.
insufficiency *n* inopia *f*.
insufficient *adj* minor; **be ~** nōn sufficere.
insufficiently *adv* parum.
insulate *vt* sēgregāre.
insult *n* iniūria *f*, contumēlia *f*, probrum *nt* ♦ *vt* maledīcere (*dat*), contumēliam impōnere (*dat*).
insulting *adj* contumēliōsus.
insultingly *adv* contumēliōsē.
insuperable *adj* inexsuperābilis.
insupportable *adj* intolerandus, intolerābilis.
insurance *n* cautiō *f*.
insure *vi* cavēre.
insurgent *n* rebellis *m*.
insurmountable *adj* inexsuperābilis.
insurrection *n* mōtus *m*, sēditiō *f*.
intact *adj* integer, intāctus, incolumis.
integrity *n* integritās *f*, innocentia *f*, fidēs *f*.
intellect *n* ingenium *nt*, mēns *f*, animus *m*.
intellectual *adj* ingeniōsus.
intelligence *n* intellegentia *f*, acūmen *nt*; (*MIL*) nūntius *m*.
intelligent *adj* ingeniōsus, sapiēns, argūtus.
intelligently *adv* ingeniōsē, sapienter, satis acūtē.

intelligible *adj* perspicuus, apertus.
intemperance *n* intemperantia *f*, licentia *f*.
intemperate *adj* intemperāns, intemperātus.
intemperately *adv* intemperanter.
intend *vt* (*with inf*) in animō habēre, velle; (*with object*) dēstināre.
intense *adj* ācer, nimius.
intensely *adv* valdē, nimium.
intensify *vt* augēre, amplificāre; **be ~ied** ingravēscere.
intensity *n* vīs *f*.
intensive *adj* ācer, multus, adsiduus.
intensively *adv* summō studiō.
intent *adj* ērēctus, intentus; **be ~ on** animum intendere in (*acc*) ♦ *n* cōnsilium *nt*; **with ~** cōnsultō.
intention *n* cōnsilium *nt*, prōpositum *nt*; **it is my ~** mihī in animō est; **with the ~ of** eā mente, eō cōnsiliō ut (*subj*).
intentionally *adv* cōnsultō, dē industriā.
inter *vt* humāre.
intercalary *adj* intercalāris.
intercalate *vt* intercalāre.
intercede *vi* intercēdere, dēprecārī.
intercept *vt* excipere, intercipere; (*cut off*) interclūdere.
intercession *n* dēprecātiō *f*; (*tribune's*) intercessiō *f*.
intercessor *n* dēprecātor *m*.
interchange *vt* permūtāre ♦ *n* permūtātiō *f*, vicissitūdō *f*.
intercourse *n* commercium *nt*, ūsus *m*, cōnsuētūdō *f*.
interdict *n* interdictum *nt* ♦ *vt* interdīcere (*dat*), vetāre.
interest *n* (*advantage*) commodum *nt*; (*study*) studium *nt*; (*money*) faenus *nt*, ūsūra *f*; **compound ~** anatocismus *m*; **rate of ~** faenus *nt*; **~ at 12 per cent (per annum)** centēsimae *fpl*; **it is of ~ interest**; **it is in my ~s** meā interest; **consult the ~s of** cōnsulere (*dat*); **take an ~ in** animum intendere (*dat*) ♦ *vt* dēlectāre, capere; (*audience*) tenēre; **~ oneself in** studēre (*dat*).
interested *adj* attentus; (*for gain*) ambitiōsus.
interesting *adj* iūcundus, novus.
interfere *vi* intervenīre; (*with*) sē interpōnere (*dat*), sē admiscēre ad; (*hinder*) officere (*dat*).
interference *n* interventus *m*, intercessiō *f*.
interim *n*: **in the ~** interim, intereā.
interior *adj* interior ♦ *n* pars interior *f*; (*country*) interiōra *ntpl*.
interject *vt* exclāmāre.
interjection *n* interiectiō *f*.
interlace *vt* intexere.
interlard *vt* variāre.
interlock *vt* implicāre.
interloper *n* interpellātor *m*.
interlude *n* embolium *nt*.
intermarriage *n* cōnūbium *nt*.
intermediary *adj* medius ♦ *n* internūntius *m*.
intermediate *adj* medius.
interment *n* humātiō *f*.

interminable *adj* sempiternus, longus.
intermingle *vt* intermiscēre ♦ *vi* sē
immiscēre.
intermission *n* intercapēdō *f*, intermissiō *f*.
intermittent *adj* interruptus.
intermittently *adv* interdum.
intern *vt* inclūdere.
internal *adj* internus; (*POL*) domesticus.
internally *adv* intus, domī.
international *adj*: ~ law iūs gentium.
internecine *adj* internecīvus.
interplay *n* vicēs *fpl*.
interpolate *vt* interpolāre.
interpose *vt* interpōnere ♦ *vi* intercēdere.
interposition *n* intercessiō *f*.
interpret *vt* interpretārī.
interpretation *n* interpretātiō *f*.
interpreter *n* interpres *m/f*.
interrogate *vt* interrogāre, percontārī.
interrogation *n* interrogātiō *f*, percontātiō *f*.
interrupt *vt* (*action*) intercipere; (*speaker*)
interpellāre; (*talk*) dirimere; (*continuity*)
intermittere.
interrupter *n* interpellātor *m*.
interruption *n* interpellātiō *f*; intermissiō *f*.
intersect *vt* dīvidere, secāre.
intersperse *vt* distinguere.
interstice *n* rīma *f*.
intertwine *vt* intexere, implicāre.
interval *n* intervallum *nt*, spatium *nt*; **after an ~**
spatiō interpositō; **after an ~ of a year** annō
interiectō; **at ~s** interdum; **at frequent ~s**
identidem; **leave an ~** intermittere.
intervene *vt* intercēdere, intervenīre.
intervention *n* intercessiō *f*, interventus *m*; **by
the ~ of** intercursū (*gen*).
interview *n* colloquium *nt*, aditus *m* ♦ *vt*
convenīre.
interweave *vt* implicāre, intexere.
intestate *adj* intestātus ♦ *adv* intestātō.
intestine *adj* intestīnus; (*POL*) domesticus ♦ *npl*
intestīna *ntpl*; (*victim's*) exta *ntpl*.
intimacy *n* familiāritās *f*.
intimate *adj* familiāris; **be an ~ friend of** ab
latere esse (*gen*); **a very ~ friend**
perfamiliāris *m/f* ♦ *vt* dēnūntiāre.
intimately *adv* familiāriter.
intimation *n* dēnūntiātiō *f*; (*hint*) indicium *nt*.
intimidate *vt* minārī (*dat*), terrōrem inicere
(*dat*).
intimidation *n* metus *m*, minae *fpl*.
into *prep* in (*acc*), intrā (*acc*).
intolerable *adj* intolerandus, intolerābilis.
intolerably *adv* intoleranter.
intolerance *n* impatientia *f*.
intolerant *adj* impatiēns, intolerāns.
intonation *n* sonus *m*, flexiō *f*.
intone *vt* cantāre.
intoxicate *vt* ēbrium reddere.
intoxicated *adj* ēbrius.
intoxication *n* ēbrietās *f*.
intractable *adj* indocilis, difficilis.
intransigent *adj* obstinātus.

intrepid *adj* intrepidus, impavidus.
intrepidity *n* audācia *f*, fortitūdō *f*.
intricacy *n* implicātiō *f*.
intricate *adj* implicātus, involūtus.
intricately *adv* implicitē.
intrigue *n* factiō *f*, artēs *fpl*, fallācia *f* ♦ *vi*
māchinārī, fallāciīs ūtī.
intriguing *adj* factiōsus; blandus.
intrinsic *adj* vērus, innātus.
intrinsically *adv* per sē.
introduce *vt* indūcere, īnferre, importāre;
(*acquaintance*) commendāre; (*custom*)
īnstituere.
introduction *n* exōrdium *nt*, prooemium *nt*; (*of
person*) commendātiō *f*; **letter of ~** litterae
commendātīciae *fpl*.
intrude *vi* sē interpōnere, intervenīre.
intruder *n* interpellātor *m*, advena *m*; (*fig*)
aliēnus *m*.
intrusion *n* interpellātiō *f*.
intuition *n* sēnsus *m*, cognitiō *f*.
inundate *vt* inundāre.
inundation *n* ēluviō *f*.
inure *vt* dūrāre, adsuēfacere.
invade *vt* invādere.
invalid *adj* aeger, dēbilis; (*null*) inritus.
invalidate *vt* īnfirmāre.
invaluable *adj* inaestimābilis.
invariable *adj* cōnstāns, immūtābilis.
invariably *adv* semper.
invasion *n* incursiō *f*.
invective *n* convīcium *nt*.
inveigh *vi*: ~ **against** invehī in (*acc*), īnsectārī.
inveigle *vt* illicere, pellicere.
invent *vt* fingere, comminīscī, invenīre.
invention *n* inventum *nt*; (*faculty*) inventiō *f*.
inventor *n* inventor *m*, auctor *m*.
inverse *adj* inversus.
inversely *adv* inversō ōrdine.
invert *vt* invertere.
invest *vt* (*in office*) inaugurāre; (*MIL*) obsidēre,
circumsedēre; (*money*) locāre.
investigate *vt* investīgāre, indāgāre; (*case*)
cognōscere.
investigation *n* investīgātiō *f*, indāgātiō *f*;
(*case*) cognitiō *f*.
investment *n* (*MIL*) obsessiō *f*; (*money*) locāta
pecūnia *f*.
inveterate *adj* inveterātus, vetus; **become ~**
inveterāscere.
invidious *adj* invidiōsus.
invidiously *adv* invidiōsē.
invigorate *vt* recreāre, reficere.
invincible *adj* invictus.
inviolable *adj* inviolātus; (*person*)
sacrōsanctus.
inviolably *adv* inviolātē.
inviolate *adj* integer.
invisible *adj* caecus; **be ~** vidērī nōn posse.
invitation *n* invītātiō *f*; **at the ~ of** invītātū
(*gen*).
invite *vt* invītāre, vocāre.
inviting *adj* suāvis, blandus.

invitingly *adv* blandē, suāviter.
invocation *n* testātiō *f*.
invoke *vt* invocāre, testārī.
involuntarily *adv* īnscienter, invītus.
involuntary *adj* coāctus.
involve *vt* implicāre, involvere; **be ~d in** inligārī (*abl*).
invulnerable *adj* inviolābilis; **be ~ vulnerārī nōn posse.**
inward *adj* interior.
inwardly *adv* intus.
inwards *adv* intrōrsus.
inweave *vt* intexere.
inwrought *adj* intextus.
irascibility *n* īrācundia *f*.
irascible *adj* īrācundus.
irate *adj* īrātus.
ire *n* īra *f*.
iris *n* hyacinthus *m*.
irk *vt* incommodāre; **I am ~ed** mē piget.
irksome *adj* molestus.
irksomeness *n* molestia *f*.
iron *n* ferrum *nt*; **of ~ ferreus ♦** *adj* ferreus.
ironical *adj* inversus.
ironically *adv* inversīs verbīs.
iron mine *n* ferrāria *f*.
ironmonger *n* negōtiātor ferrārius *m*.
ironmongery *n* ferrāmenta *ntpl*.
iron ore *n* ferrum īnfectum *nt*.
iron-tipped *adj* ferrātus.
irony *n* illūsiō *f*, verbōrum inversiō *f*, dissimulātiō *f*.
irradiate *vt* illūstrāre.
irrational *adj* absurdus, ratiōnis expers; (*animal*) brūtus.
irrationally *adv* absurdē, sine ratiōne.
irreconcilable *adj* repugnāns, īnsociābilis.
irrefutable *adj* certus, invictus.
irregular *adj* incompositus; (*ground*) inaequālis; (*meeting*) extraōrdinārius; (*troops*) tumultuārius.
irregularity *n* inaequālitās *f*; (*conduct*) prāvitās *f*, licentia *f*; (*election*) vitium *nt*.
irregularly *adv* nullō ōrdine; (*elected*) vitiō.
irrelevant *adj* aliēnus.
irreligion *n* impietās *f*.
irreligious *adj* impius.
irremediable *adj* īnsānābilis.
irreparable *adj* irrevocābilis.
irreproachable *adj* integer, innocēns.
irresistible *adj* invictus.
irresolute *adj* dubius, anceps.
irresolutely *adv* dubitanter.
irresolution *n* dubitātiō *f*.
irresponsibility *n* licentia *f*.
irresponsible *adj* lascīvus, levis.
irretrievable *adj* irrevocābilis.
irreverence *n* impietās *f*.
irreverent *adj* impius.
irreverently *adv* impiē.
irrevocable *adj* irrevocābilis.
irrigate *vt* inrigāre.
irrigation *n* inrigātiō *f*.

irritability *n* īrācundia *f*.
irritable *adj* īrācundus.
irritate *vt* inrītāre, stomachum movēre (*dat*).
irritation *n* īrācundia *f*, stomachus *m*.
island *n* īnsula *f*.
islander *n* īnsulānus *m*.
isle *n* īnsula *f*.
isolate *vt* sēgregāre, sēparāre.
isolation *n* sōlitūdō *f*.
issue *n* (*result*) ēventus *m*, exitus *m*; (*children*) prōlēs *f*; (*question*) rēs *f*; (*book*) ēditiō *f*; **decide the ~ dēcernere, dēcertāre; the point at ~ quā dē rē agitur ♦** *vt* distribuere; (*book*) ēdere; (*announcement*) prōmulgāre; (*coin*) ērogāre ♦ *vi* ēgredī, ēmānāre; (*result*) ēvādere, ēvenīre.
isthmus *n* isthmus *m*.
it *pron* hōc, id.
itch *n* (*disease*) scabiēs *f*; (*fig*) cacoēthes *nt* ♦ *vi* prūrīre.
item *n* nōmen *nt*, rēs *f*.
iterate *vt* iterāre.
itinerant *adj* vāgus, circumforāneus.
itinerary *n* iter *nt*.
its *adj* suus, ēius.
itself *pron* ipse, ipsa, ipsum.
ivory *n* ebur *nt* ♦ *adj* eburneus.
ivy *n* hedera *f*.

J, j

jabber *vi* blaterāre.
jackdaw *n* grāculus *m*.
jaded *adj* dēfessus, fatīgātus.
jagged *adj* serrātus.
jail *n* carcer *m*.
jailer *n* custōs *m*, carcerārius *m*.
jam *vt* comprimere; (*way*) obstruere.
jamb *n* postis *m*.
jangle *vi* crepitāre; rixārī.
janitor *n* iānitor *m*.
January *n* mēnsis Iānuārius *m*; **of ~ Iānuārius.**
jar *n* urna *f*; (*for wine*) amphora *f*; (*for water*) hydria *f*; (*sound*) offēnsa *f*; (*quarrel*) rixa *f* ♦ *vi* offendere.
jasper *n* iaspis *f*.
jaundice *n* morbus arquātus.
jaundiced *adj* ictericus.
jaunt *n*: **take a ~ excurrere.**
jauntily *adv* hilare, festīvē.
jauntiness *n* hilaritās *f*.
jaunty *adj* hilaris, festīvus.
javelin *n* iaculum *nt*, pīlum *nt*; **throw the ~ iaculārī.**
jaw *n* māla *f*; **~s** *pl* faucēs *fpl*.

jay n grāculus m.
jealous adj invidus; **be ~ of** invidēre (dat).
jealousy n invidia f.
jeer n irrīsiō f ♦ vi irrīdēre; **~ at** illūdere.
jejune adj iēiūnus, exīlis.
jeopardize vt in perīculum addūcere.
jeopardy n perīculum nt.
jerk n subitus mōtus m.
jest n iocus m.
jester n scurra m.
jet n (mineral) gagātēs m; (of water) saltus m ♦ vi salīre.
jetsam n ēiectāmenta ntpl.
jettison vt ēicere.
jetty n mōlēs f.
Jew n Iūdaeus.
jewel n gemma f.
Jewish adj Iūdaicus.
jig n tripudium nt.
jilt vt repudiāre.
jingle n nēnia f ♦ vi crepitāre, tinnīre.
job n opus nt.
jocose adj see **jocular**.
jocular adj facētus, ioculāris.
jocularity n facētiae fpl.
jocularly adv facētē, per iocum.
jocund adj hilaris, festīvus.
jog vt fodicāre; (fig) stimulāre ♦ vi ambulāre.
join vt iungere, coniungere, cōpulāre ♦ vi coniungī, sē coniungere; **~ in** interesse (dat), sē immiscēre (dat); **~ battle with** proelium committere (+ abl).
joiner n faber m.
joint adj commūnis ♦ n commissūra f; (of body) articulus m, nōdus m; **~ by ~** articulātim.
jointed adj geniculātus.
joint-heir n cohērēs m/f.
jointly adv ūnā, coniūnctē.
joist n tignum nt.
joke n iocus m ♦ vi iocārī, lūdere.
joking n iocus m; **~ apart** remōtō iocō.
jokingly adv per iocum.
jollity n hilaritās f, festīvitās f.
jolly adj hilaris, festīvus.
jolt vt iactāre.
jolting n iactātiō f.
jostle vt agitāre, offendere.
jot n minimum nt; **not a ~** nihil; **not care a ~** nōn floccī facere.
journal n ācta diūrna ntpl.
journey n iter nt.
journeyman n opifex m.
Jove n Iuppiter m.
jovial adj hilaris.
joviality n hilaritās f.
jovially adv hilare.
jowl n māla f; **cheek by ~** iuxtā.
joy n gaudium nt, laetitia f, alacritās f.
joyful adj laetus, hilaris.
joyfully adv laetē, hilare.
joyfulness n gaudium nt, laetitia f.
joyless adj tristis, maestus.

joyous adj see **joyful**.
joyously adv see **joyfully**.
jubilant adj laetus, gaudiō exsultāns.
judge n iūdex m, arbiter m ♦ vt iūdicāre; (think) exīstimāre, cēnsēre; **~ between** diiūdicāre.
judgeship n iūdicātus m.
judgment n iūdicium nt, arbitrium nt; (opinion) sententia f; (punishment) poena f; (wisdom) iūdicium nt; **in my ~** meō animō, meō arbitrātū; **pass ~ on** statuere dē; **sit in ~** iūdicium exercēre.
judgment seat n tribūnal nt.
judicature n iūrisdictiō f; (men) iūdicēs mpl.
judicial adj iūdiciālis; (law) iūdiciārius.
judiciary n iūdicēs mpl.
judicious adj prūdēns, cōnsīderātus.
judiciously adv prūdenter.
jug n hydria f, urceus m.
juggler n praestīgiātor m.
juggling n praestīgiae fpl.
juice n liquor m, sūcus m.
juicy adj sūcī plēnus.
July n mēnsis Quīnctīlis, Iūlius m; **of ~** Quīnctīlis, Iūlius.
jumble n congeriēs f ♦ vt cōnfundere.
jump n saltus m ♦ vi salīre; **~ across** transilīre; **~ at** (opportunity) captāre, adripere, amplectī; **~ down** dēsilīre; **~ on to** īnsilīre in (acc).
junction n coniūnctiō f.
juncture n tempus nt.
June n mēnsis Iūnius; **of ~** Iūnius.
junior adj iūnior, nātū minor.
juniper n iūniperus f.
Juno n Iūnō, Iūnōnis f.
Jupiter n Iuppiter, Iovis m.
juridical adj iūdiciārius.
jurisconsult n iūriscōnsultus m.
jurisdiction n iūrisdictiō f, diciō f; **exercise ~** iūs dīcere.
jurisprudence n iūrisprūdentia f.
jurist n iūriscōnsultus m.
juror n iūdex m.
jury n iūdicēs mpl.
just adj iūstus, aequus ♦ adv (exactly) prōrsus; (only) modo; (time) commodum, modo; (with adv) dēmum, dēnique; (with pron) adeō dēmum, ipse; **~ as** (comparison) aequē ac, perinde ac, quemadmodum; sīcut; **~ before** (time) cum māximē, sub (acc); **~ now** modo, nunc; **~ so** ita prōrsus, sānē; **only ~** vix.
justice n iūstitia f, aequitās f, iūs nt; (person) praetor m; **administer ~** iūs reddere.
justiciary n praetor m.
justifiable adj iūstus.
justifiably adv iūre.
justification n pūrgātiō f, excūsātiō f.
justify vt excūsāre, pūrgāre.
justly adv iūstē, aequē; iūre, meritō.
jut vi prōminēre, excurrere.
jutting adj prōiectus.
juvenile adj iuvenīlis, puerīlis.

K, k

keel n carīna f.
keen adj ācer; (mind) acūtus, argūtus; (sense) sagāx; (pain) acerbus; **I am ~ on** studeō.
keenly adv ācriter, sagāciter, acūtē, acerbē.
keenness n (scent) sagācitās f; (sight) aciēs f; (pain) acerbitās f; (eagerness) studium nt, ārdor m.
keep vt servāre, tenēre, habēre; (celebrate) agere, celebrāre; (guard) custōdīre; (obey) observāre; (preserve) cōnservāre; (rear) alere, pāscere; (store) condere; **~ apart** distinēre; **~ away** arcēre; **~ back** dētinēre, reservāre; **~ down** comprimere; (exuberance) dēpāscere; **~ in** cohibēre, claudere; **~ in with** grātiam sequī (gen); **~ off** arcēre, dēfendere; **~ one's word** fidem praestāre; **~ one's hands off** manūs abstinēre; **~ house** domī sē retinēre; **~ secret** cēlāre; **~ together** continēre; **~ up** sustinēre, cōnservāre; **~ up with** subsequī; **~ waiting** dēmorārī ♦ vi dūrāre, manēre ♦ n arx f.
keeper n custōs m.
keeping n custōdia f; **in ~ with** prō (abl); **be in ~ with** convenīre (dat).
keg n cadus m.
ken n cōnspectus m.
kennel n stabulum nt.
kerb n crepīdō f.
kernel n grānum nt, nucleus m.
kettle n lebēs f.
key n clāvis f; (fig) claustra ntpl, iānua f; **~ position** cardō m.
kick vi calcitrāre ♦ vt calce ferīre.
kid n haedus m.
kidnap vt surripere.
kidnapper n plagiārius m.
kidney n rēn m.
kidney bean n phasēlus m.
kid's adj haedīnus.
kill vt interficere, interimere; (in battle) occīdere; (murder) necāre, iugulāre; (time) perdere.
killer n interfector m.
kiln n fornāx f.
kin n cognātī mpl, propinquī mpl; **next of ~** proximī mpl.
kind adj bonus, benīgnus, benevolus ♦ n genus nt; **of such a ~** tālis; **what ~ of** quālis ♦ adj cōmis.
kindle vt incendere, succendere, īnflammāre.
kindliness n cōmitās f, hūmānitās f.
kindling n (fuel) fōmes m.
kindly adv benīgnē.
kindness n benīgnitās f, benevolentia f; (act) beneficium nt, officium nt, grātia f.

kindred n necessitūdō f, cognātiō f; propinquī mpl, cognātī mpl ♦ adj cognātus, adfīnis.
king n rēx m.
kingdom n rēgnum nt.
kingfisher n alcēdō f.
kingly adj rēgius, rēgālis.
kingship n rēgnum nt.
kink n vitium nt.
kinsfolk n cognātī mpl, necessāriī mpl.
kinsman n cognātus m, propinquus m, necessārius m.
kinswoman n cognāta f, propinqua f, necessāria f.
kismet n fātum nt.
kiss n ōsculum nt ♦ vt ōsculārī.
kit n (MIL) sarcina f.
kitchen n culīna f.
kitchen garden n hortus m.
kite n mīluus m.
kite's adj mīluīnus.
knack n callidītās f, artificium nt; **have the ~ of** callēre.
knapsack n sarcina f.
knave n veterātor m.
knavish adj improbus.
knavishly adv improbē.
knead vt depsere, subigere.
knee n genū nt.
kneel vi genibus nītī.
knife n culter m; (surgeon's) scalprum nt.
knight n eques m ♦ vt in ōrdinem equestrem recipere.
knighthood n ōrdō equester m.
knightly adj equester.
knit vt texere; (brow) contrahere.
knob n bulla f.
knock vt ferīre, percutere; **~ at** pulsāre; **~ against** offendere; **~ down** dēicere, adflīgere; (at auction) addīcere; **~ off** dēcutere; (work) dēsistere ab; **~ out** ēlīdere, excutere; (unconscious) exanimāre; (fig) dēvincere; **~ up** suscitāre ♦ n pulsus m, ictus m.
knock-kneed adj vārus.
knoll n tumulus m.
knot n nōdus m ♦ vt nectere.
knotty adj nōdōsus; **~ point** nōdus m.
know vt scīre; (person) nōvisse; **~ all about** explōrātum habēre; **~ again** agnōscere; **~ how to** scīre; **not ~** ignōrāre, nescīre; **let me ~** fac sciam, fac mē certiōrem; **get to ~** cognōscere ♦ n **in the ~** cōnscius.
knowing adj prūdēns, callidus.
knowingly adv cōnsultō, sciēns.
knowledge n scientia f, doctrīna f; (practical) experientia f; (of something) cognitiō f.
knowledgeable adj gnārus, doctus.
known adj nōtus; **make ~** dēclārāre.
knuckle n articulus m.
knuckle bone n tālus m.
kotow vi adulārī.
kudos n glōria f, laus f.

L, l

label n titulus m ♦ vt titulō īnscrībere.
laboratory n officīna f.
laborious adj labōriōsus, operōsus.
laboriously adv operōsē.
laboriousness n labor m.
labour n labor m, opera f; (work done) opus nt; (work allotted) pēnsum nt; (workmen) operae fpl; **be in ~** parturīre ♦ vi labōrāre, ēnītī; **~ at** ēlabōrāre; **~ under a delusion** errōre fallī.
laboured adj adfectātus.
labourer n operārius m; **~s** pl operae fpl.
labyrinth n labyrinthus m.
lace n texta rēticulāta ntpl; (shoe) ligula f ♦ vt nectere.
lacerate vt lacerāre.
laceration n lacerātiō f.
lack n inopia f, dēfectiō f ♦ vt egēre (abl), carēre (abl).
lackey n pedisequus m.
laconic adj brevis.
laconically adv ūnō verbō, paucīs verbīs.
lacuna n lacūna f.
lad n puer m.
ladder n scāla f.
lade vt onerāre.
laden adj onustus, onerātus.
lading n onus nt.
ladle n trulla f.
lady n domina f, mātrōna f, mulier f.
ladylike adj līberālis, honestus.
lag vi cessāre.
lagoon n stagnum nt.
lair n latibulum nt.
lake n lacus m.
lamb n agnus m; (flesh) agnīna f; **ewe ~** agna f.
lame adj claudus; (argument) inānis; **be ~** claudicāre.
lameness n claudicātiō f.
lament n lāmentātiō f, lāmentum nt ♦ vt lūgēre, lāmentārī; (regret) dēplōrāre.
lamentable adj lāmentābilis, miserābilis.
lamentably adv miserābiliter.
lamentation n lāmentātiō f.
lamp n lucerna f, lychnus m.
lampoon n satura f ♦ vt carmine dēstringere.
lance n hasta f, lancea f.
lancer n hastātus m.
lancet n scalpellum nt.
land n terra f; (country) terra f, regiō f; (territory) fīnēs mpl; (native) patria f; (property) praedium nt, ager m; (soil) solum nt ♦ vt expōnere ♦ vi ē nāve ēgredī ♦ adj terrēnus, terrestris.
landfall n adpulsus m.
landing place n ēgressus m.

landlady n caupōna f.
landlord n dominus m; (inn) caupō m.
landmark n lapis m; **be a ~** ēminēre.
landscape n agrōrum prōspectus m.
landslide n terrae lābēs f, lāpsus m.
landwards adv terram versus.
lane n (country) sēmita f; (town) angiportus m.
language n lingua f; (style) ōrātiō f, sermō m; (diction) verba ntpl; **bad ~** maledicta ntpl.
languid adj languidus, remissus.
languidly adv languidē.
languish vi languēre, languēscere; (with disease) tābēscere.
languor n languor m.
lank, lanky adj exīlis, gracilis.
lantern n lanterna f, lucerna f.
lap n gremium nt, sinus m ♦ vt lambere; (cover) involvere.
lapse n (time) lāpsus m; (mistake) errātum nt; **after the ~ of a year** interiectō annō ♦ vi lābī; (agreement) inritum fierī; (property) revertī.
larceny n fūrtum nt.
larch n larix f ♦ adj larignus.
lard n adeps m/f.
larder n cella penāria f.
large adj māgnus, grandis, amplus; **at ~** solūtus; **very ~** permāgnus; **as ~ as …** tantus … quantus.
largely adv plērumque.
largesse n largitiō f; (MIL) dōnātivum nt; (civil) congiārium nt; **give ~** largīrī.
lark n alauda f.
lascivious adj libīdinōsus.
lasciviously adv libīdinōsē.
lasciviousness n libīdō f.
lash n flagellum nt, lōrum nt; (eye) cilium nt ♦ vt verberāre; (tie) adligāre; (with words) castīgāre.
lashing n verbera ntpl.
lass n puella f.
lassitude n languor m.
last adj ultimus, postrēmus, suprēmus; (in line) novissimus; (preceding) proximus; **at ~** tandem, dēmum, dēnique; **for the ~ time** postrēmum ♦ n fōrma f; **let the cobbler stick to his ~** nē sūtor suprā crepidam ♦ vi dūrāre, permanēre.
lasting adj diūtinus, diūturnus.
lastly adv postrēmō, dēnique.
latch n pessulus m.
latchet n corrigia f.
late adj sērus; (date) recēns; (dead) dēmortuus; (emperor) dīvus; **~ at night** multā nocte; **till ~ in the day** ad multum diem ♦ adv sērō; **too ~** sērō; **too ~ to** sērius quam quī (subj); **of ~** nūper.
lately adv nūper.
latent adj occultus, latitāns.
later adj posterior ♦ adv posteā, posthāc, mox.
latest adj novissimus.
lath n tigillum nt.
lathe n tornus m.
lather n spūma f.

Latin *adj* Latīnus; **speak** ~ Latīnē loquī;
understand ~ Latīnē scīre; **translate into** ~
Latīnē reddere; **in Latin** latinē.
Latinity *n* Latīnitās *f*.
latitude *n* (*GEOG*) caelum *nt*; (*scope*) lībertās *f*.
latter *adj* posterior; **the** ~ hīc.
latterly *adv* nūper.
lattice *n* trānsenna *f*.
laud *n* laus *f* ♦ *vt* laudāre.
laudable *adj* laudābilis, laude dignus.
laudatory *adj* honōrificus.
laugh *n* rīsus *m*; (*loud*) cachinnus *m* ♦ *vi* rīdēre,
cachinnāre; ~ **at** (*joke*) rīdēre; (*person*)
dērīdēre; ~ **up one's sleeve** in sinū gaudēre.
laughable *adj* rīdiculus.
laughing stock *n* lūdibrium *nt*.
laughter *n* rīsus *m*.
launch *vt* (*missile*) contorquēre; (*ship*)
dēdūcere; ~ **an attack impetum dare** ♦ *vi*: ~
out into ingredī in (*acc*) ♦ *n* celōx *f*, lembus
m.
laureate *adj* laureātus.
laurel *n* laurus *m* ♦ *adj* laureus.
lave *vt* lavāre.
lavish *adj* prōdigus, largus ♦ *vt* largīrī,
profundere.
lavishly *adv* prōdigē, effūsē.
lavishness *n* largitās *f*.
law *n* lēx *f*; (*system*) iūs *nt*; (*divine*) fās *nt*; **civil** ~
iūs cīvīle; **constitutional** ~ iūs pūblicum;
international ~ iūs gentium; **go to** ~ lēge
agere, lītigāre; **break the** ~ lēges violāre;
pass a ~ (*magistrate*) lēgem perferre; (*people*)
lēgem iubēre.
law-abiding *adj* bene mōrātus.
law court *n* iūdicium *nt*; (*building*) basilica *f*.
lawful *adj* lēgitimus; (*morally*) fās.
lawfully *adv* lēgitimē, lēge.
lawgiver *n* lēgum scrīptor *m*.
lawless *adj* exlēx.
lawlessly *adv* licenter.
lawlessness *n* licentia *f*.
lawn *n* prātulum *nt*.
law-suit *n* līs *f*, āctiō *f*.
lawyer *n* iūriscōnsultus *m*, causidicus *m*.
lax *adj* dissolūtus, remissus.
laxity *n* dissolūtiō *f*.
lay *vt* pōnere, locāre; (*ambush*) collocāre,
tendere; (*disorder*) sēdāre; (*egg*) parere;
(*foundation*) iacere; (*hands*) inicere; (*plan*)
capere, inīre; (*trap*) tendere; (*wager*) facere;
~ **aside** pōnere; (*in store*) repōnere; ~ **by**
repōnere; ~ **down** dēpōnere; (*rule*) statuere;
~ **hold of** prehendere, adripere; ~ **in** condere;
~ **a motion before** referre ad; ~ **on** impōnere;
~ **open** patefacere; (*to attack*) nūdāre; ~ **out**
(*money*) impendere, ērogāre; (*camp*) mētārī;
~ **siege to** obsidēre; ~ **to heart** in pectus
dēmittere; ~ **up** recondere; ~ **upon**
iniungere, impōnere; **violent hands on** vim
adferre, adhibēre (*dat*); **whatever they could**
~ **hands on** quod cuīque in manum vēnisset;
~ **waste** vastāre ♦ *n* carmen *nt*, melos *nt*.

lay *adj* (*ECCL*) lāicus.
layer *n* corium *nt*; (*stones*) ōrdō *m*; (*plant*)
propāgō *f*.
layout *n* dēsignātiō *f*.
laze *vi* ōtiārī.
lazily *adv* ignāvē, ōtiōsē.
laziness *n* ignāvia *f*, dēsidia *f*, pigritia *f*.
lazy *adj* ignāvus, dēsidiōsus, piger.
lea *n* prātum *nt*.
lead *vt* dūcere; (*life*) agere; (*wall*) perdūcere;
(*water*) dērīvāre; ~ **across** trādūcere; ~
around circumdūcere; ~ **astray** in errōrem
indūcere; ~ **away** abdūcere; ~ **back**
redūcere; ~ **down** dēdūcere; ~ **in**
intrōdūcere; ~ **on** addūcere; ~ **out** ēdūcere; ~
over trādūcere; ~ **the way** dūcere, praeīre; ~
up to tendere ad, spectare ad; **the road ~s . . .**
via fert . . . .
lead *n* plumbum *nt* ♦ *adj* plumbeus.
leaden *adj* (*colour*) līvidus.
leader *n* dux *m*, ductor *m*.
leadership *n* ductus *m*.
leading *adj* prīmus, prīnceps, praecipuus.
leaf, *pl* **leaves** *n* folium *nt*, frōns *f*; (*paper*)
scheda *f*; **put forth leaves** frondēscere.
leaflet *n* libellus *m*.
leafy *adj* frondōsus.
league *n* foedus *nt*, societās *f*; (*distance*) tria
mīlia passuum ♦ *vi* coniūrāre, foedus
facere.
leagued *adj* foederātus.
leak *n* rīma *f* ♦ *vi* mānāre, rimās agere.
leaky *adj* rīmōsus.
lean *adj* macer, exīlis, gracilis ♦ *vi* nītī; ~ **back**
sē reclīnāre; ~ **on** innītī in (*abl*), incumbere
(*dat*); ~ **over** inclīnāre.
leaning *n* prōpēnsiō *f* ♦ *adj* inclīnātus.
leanness *n* gracilitās *f*, maciēs *f*.
leap *n* saltus *m* ♦ *vi* salīre; (*for joy*) exsultāre; ~
down dēsilīre; ~ **on to** īnsilīre in (*acc*).
leap year *n* annus bissextilis *m*.
learn *vt* discere; (*news*) accipere, audīre; (*by
heart*) ēdiscere; (*discover*) cognōscēre.
learned *adj* doctus, ērudītus, litterātus.
learnedly *adv* doctē.
learner *n* tīrō *m*, discipulus *m*.
learning *n* doctrīna *f*, ērudītiō *f*, litterae *fpl*.
lease *n* (*taken*) conductiō *f*; (*given*) locātiō *f* ♦ *vt*
condūcere; locāre.
leash *n* cōpula *f*.
least *adj* minimus ♦ *adv* minimē; **at** ~ saltem; **to
say the** ~ ut levissimē dīcam; **not in the** ~
haudquāquam.
leather *n* corium *nt*, alūta *f*.
leathery *adj* lentus.
leave *n* (*of absence*) commeātus *m*; (*permission*)
potestās *f*, venia *f*; **ask** ~ veniam petere; **give**
~ potestātem facere; **obtain** ~ impetrāre; **by
your** ~ pace tuā, bonā tuā veniā ♦ *vt*
relinquere, dēserere; (*legacy*) lēgāre; ~ **alone**
nōn tangere, manum abstinēre ab; ~ **behind**
relinquere; ~ **in the lurch** dēstituere,
dērelinquere; ~ **off** dēsinere, dēsistere ab;

(*temporarily*) intermittere; (*garment*) pōnere;
~ **out** praetermittere, ōmittere ♦ *vi*
discēdere ab (+ *abl*), abīre.
leaven *n* fermentum *nt*.
leavings *n* rēliquiae *fpl*.
lecherous *adj* salāx.
lecture *n* acroāsis *f*, audītiō *f* ♦ *vi* docēre,
scholam habēre.
lecturer *n* doctor *m*.
lecture room *n* audītōrium *nt*.
ledge *n* līmen *nt*.
ledger *n* cōdex acceptī et expēnsī.
lee *n* pars ā ventō tūta.
leech *n* hirūdō *f*.
leek *n* porrum *nt*.
leer *vi* līmīs oculīs intuērī.
lees *n* faex *f*; (*of oil*) amurca *f*.
left *adj* sinister, laevus ♦ *n* sinistra *f*, laeva *f*; **on
the** ~ ā laevā, ad laevam, ā sinistrā.
leg *n* crūs *nt*; (*of table*) pēs *m*.
legacy *n* lēgātum *nt*; ~ **hunter** captātor *m*.
legal *adj* lēgitimus.
legalize *vt* sancīre.
legally *adv* secundum lēgēs, lēge.
legate *n* lēgātus *m*.
legation *n* lēgātiō *f*.
legend *n* fābula *f*; (*inscription*) titulus *m*.
legendary *adj* fābulōsus.
legerdemain *n* praestīgiae *fpl*.
legging *n* ocrea *f*.
legible *adj* clārus.
legion *n* legiō *f*; **men of the 10th** ~ decumānī
mpl.
legionary *n* legiōnārius *m*.
legislate *vi* lēgēs scrībere, lēgēs facere.
legislation *n* lēgēs *fpl*, lēgēs scrībendae.
legislator *n* lēgum scrīptor *m*.
legitimate *adj* lēgitimus.
legitimately *adv* lēgitimē.
leisure *n* ōtium *nt*; **at** ~ ōtiōsus, vacuus; **have** ~
for vacāre (*dat*).
leisured *adj* ōtiōsus.
leisurely *adj* lentus.
lend *vt* commodāre, mūtuum dare; (*at interest*)
faenerārī; (*ear*) aurēs praebēre, admovēre; ~
a ready ear aurēs patefacere; ~ **assistance**
opem ferre.
length *n* longitūdō *f*; (*time*) diūturnitās *f*; **at** ~
tandem, dēmum, dēnique; (*speech*) cōpiōsē.
lengthen *vt* extendere; (*time*) prōtrahere;
(*sound*) prōdūcere.
lengthwise *adv* in longitūdinem.
lengthy *adj* longus, prōlixus.
leniency *n* clēmentia *f*.
lenient *adj* clēmēns, mītis.
leniently *adv* clēmenter.
lentil *n* lēns *f*.
leonine *adj* leōnīnus.
leopard *n* pardus *m*.
less *adj* minor ♦ *adv* minus; ~ **than** (*num*) intrā
(*acc*); **much** ~, **still** ~ nēdum.
lessee *n* conductor *m*.
lessen *vt* minuere, imminuere, dēminuere ♦

vi dēcrēscere.
lesson *n* documentum *nt*; **be a** ~ **to** documentō
esse (*dat*); ~**s** *pl* dictāta *ntpl*; **give** ~**s** scholās
habēre; **give** ~**s in** docēre.
lessor *n* locātor *m*.
lest *conj* nē (+ *subj*).
let *vt* (*allow*) sinere; (*lease*) locāre; (*imper*) fac;
~ **alone** ōmittere; (*mention*) nē dīcam; ~
blood sanguinem mittere; ~ **down**
dēmittere; ~ **fall** ā manibus mittere; (*word*)
ēmittere; ~ **fly** ēmittere; ~ **go** mittere,
āmittere; (*ship*) solvere; ~ **in** admittere; ~
loose solvere; ~ **off** absolvere, ignōscere
(*dat*); ~ **oneself go** geniō indulgēre; ~ **out**
ēmittere; ~ **slip** āmittere, ōmittere.
lethal *adj* mortifer.
lethargic *adj* veternōsus.
lethargy *n* veternus *m*.
letter *n* epistula *f*, litterae *fpl*; (*of alphabet*)
littera *f*; **the** ~ **of the law** scrīptum *nt*; **to the** ~
ad praescrīptum; **by** ~ per litterās; ~**s**
(*learning*) litterae *fpl*; **man of** ~**s** scrīptor *m*.
lettered *adj* litterātus.
lettuce *n* lactūca *f*.
levee *n* salūtātiō *f*.
level *adj* aequus, plānus ♦ *n* plānitiēs *f*;
(*instrument*) lībra *f*; **do one's** ~ **best** prō virīlī
parte agere; **put on a** ~ **with** exaequāre cum
♦ *vt* aequāre, adaequāre, inaequāre; (*to the
ground*) solō aequāre, sternere; (*weapon*)
intendere.
level-headed *adj* prūdēns.
levelled *adj* (*weapon*) īnfestus.
lever *n* vectis *m*.
levity *n* levitās *f*; (*fun*) iocī *mpl*, facētiae *fpl*.
levy *vt* (*troops*) scrībere; (*tax*) exigere ♦ *n*
dīlectus *m*.
lewd *adj* impudīcus.
lewdness *n* impudīcitia *f*.
liable *adj* obnoxius; **render** ~ obligāre.
liaison *n* cōnsuētūdō *f*.
liar *n* mendāx *m*.
libel *n* probrum *nt*, calumnia *f* ♦ *vt* calumniārī.
libellous *adj* probrōsus, fāmōsus.
liberal *adj* līberālis; (*in giving*) largus,
benīgnus; ~ **education** bonae artēs *fpl*.
liberality *n* līberālitās *f*, largitās *f*.
liberally *adv* līberāliter, largē, benīgnē.
liberate *vt* līberāre; (*slave*) manū mittere.
liberation *n* līberātiō *f*.
liberator *n* līberātor *m*.
libertine *n* libīdinōsus *m*.
liberty *n* lībertās *f*; (*excess*) licentia *f*; **I am at** ~
to mihī licet (*inf*); **I am still at** ~ **to** integrum
est mihī (*inf*); **take a** ~ **with** licentius ūtī (*abl*),
familiārius sē gerere in (*acc*).
libidinous *adj* libīdinōsus.
librarian *n* librārius *m*.
library *n* bibliothēca *f*.
licence *n* (*permission*) potestās *f*; (*excess*)
licentia *f*.
license *vt* potestātem dare (*dat*).
licentious *adj* dissolūtus.

licentiousness n libīdō f, licentia f.
lick vt lambere; mulcēre.
lictor n lictor m.
lid n operculum nt.
lie n mendācium nt; **give the ~ to** redarguere;
tell a ~ mentīrī ♦ vi mentīrī; (*lie down*) iacēre;
(*place*) situm esse; (*consist*) continērī; **as far**
as in me ~s quantum in mē est; **~ at anchor**
stāre; **~ between** interiacēre; **~ down**
cubāre, discumbere; **~ heavy on** premere; **~**
hid latēre; **~ in wait** īnsidiārī; **~ low**
dissimulāre; **~ on** incumbere (*dat*); **~ open**
patēre; hiāre.
lien n nexus m.
lieu n: **in ~ of** locō (*gen*).
lieutenant n decuriō m; legātus m.
life n vīta f; (*in danger*) salūs f, caput nt;
(*biography*) vīta f; (*breath*) anima f; (*RHET*)
sanguis m; (*time*) aetās f; **come to ~ again**
revīvīscere; **draw to the ~** exprimere; **for ~**
aetātem; **matter of ~ and death** capitāle nt;
prime of ~ flōs aetātis; **way of ~** mōrēs mpl.
lifeblood n sanguis m.
life-giving adj almus, vītālis.
lifeguard n custōs m; (*emperor's*) praetōriānus
m.
lifeless adj exanimis; (*style*) exsanguis.
lifelike adj expressus.
lifelong adj perpetuus.
lifetime n aetās f.
lift vt tollere, sublevāre; **~ up** efferre,
attollere.
light n lūx f, lūmen nt; (*painting*) lūmen nt; **bring**
to ~ in lūcem prōferre; **see in a favourable ~**
in meliōrem partem interpretārī; **throw ~ on**
lūmen adhibēre (*dat*) ♦ vt accendere,
incendere; (*illuminate*) illūstrāre, illūmināre;
be lit up collūcēre ♦ vi: **~ upon** invenīre,
offendere ♦ adj illūstris; (*movement*) agilis;
(*weight*) levis; **grow ~** illūcēscere,
dīlūcēscere; **make ~ of** parvī pendere.
light-armed adj expedītus.
lighten vi fulgurāre ♦ vt levāre.
lighter n linter f.
light-fingered adj tagāx.
light-footed adj celer, pernīx.
light-headed adj levis, volāticus.
light-hearted adj hilaris, laetus.
lightly adv leviter; pernīciter.
lightness n levitās f.
lightning n fulgur nt; (*striking*) fulmen nt; **be**
hit by ~ dē caelō percutī; **of ~** fulgurālis.
like adj similis, pār; **~ this** ad hunc modum ♦
adv similiter, sīcut, rītū (*gen*) ♦ vt amāre; **I ~**
mihī placet, mē iuvat; **I ~ to** libet (*inf*); **I don't**
~ nīl moror, mihī displicet; **look ~** similem
esse, referre.
likelihood n vērī similitūdō f.
likely adj vērī similis ♦ adv sānē.
liken vt comparāre, aequiperāre.
likeness n imāgō f, īnstar nt, similitūdō f.
likewise adv item; (*also*) etiam.
liking n libīdō f, grātia f; **to one's ~** ex

sententiā.
lily n līlium nt.
limb n membrum nt, artus m.
lime n calx f; (*tree*) tilia f.
limelight n celebritās f; **enjoy the ~** mōnstrārī
digitō.
limestone n calx f.
limit n fīnis m, terminus m, modus m; **mark the**
~s of dētermināre ♦ vt fīnīre, dēfinīre,
termināre; (*restrict*) circumscrībere.
limitation n modus m.
limp adj mollis, flaccidus ♦ vi claudicāre.
limpid adj limpidus.
linden n tilia f.
line n līnea f; (*battle*) aciēs f; (*limit*) modus m;
(*outline*) līneāmentum nt; (*writing*) versus m;
in a straight ~ ē regiōne; **~ of march** agmen nt;
read between the ~s dissimulātā dispicere;
ship of the ~ nāvis longa; **write a ~** pauca
scrībere ♦ vt (*street*) saepīre.
lineage n genus nt, stirps f.
lineal adj (*descent*) gentīlis.
lineaments n līneāmenta ntpl, ōris ductūs mpl.
linen n linteum nt ♦ adj linteus.
liner n nāvis f.
linger vi cunctārī, cessāre, dēmorārī.
lingering adj tardus ♦ n cunctātiō f.
linguist n: **be a ~** complūrēs linguās callēre.
link n ānulus m; (*fig*) nexus m, vinculum nt ♦ vt
coniungere.
lintel n līmen superum nt.
lion n leō m; **~'s** leōnīnus; **~'s share** māior pars.
lioness n leaena f.
lip n lābrum nt; **be on everyone's ~s in** ōre
omnium hominum esse, per omnium ōra
ferrī.
lip service n: **pay ~ to** verbō tenus obsequī
(*dat*).
liquefy vt liquefacere.
liquid adj liquidus ♦ n liquor m.
liquidate vt persolvere.
liquor n liquor m; vīnum nt.
lisp vi balbūtīre.
lisping adj blaesus.
lissom adj agilis.
list n index m, tabula f; (*ship*) inclīnātiō f ♦ vt
scrībere ♦ vi (*lean*) sē inclīnāre; (*listen*)
auscultāre; (*wish*) cupere.
listen vi auscultāre; **~ to** auscultāre, audīre.
listener n audītor m, auscultātor m.
listless adj languidus.
listlessness n languor m.
literally adv ad verbum.
literary adj (*man*) litterātus; **~ pursuits** litterae
fpl, studia ntpl.
literature n litterae fpl.
lithe adj mollis, agilis.
litigant n lītigātor m.
litigate vi lītigāre.
litigation n līs f.
litigious adj lītigiōsus.
litter n (*carriage*) lectīca f; (*brood*) fētus m;
(*straw*) strāmentum nt; (*mess*) strāgēs f ♦ vt

sternere; (*young*) parere.

little *adj* parvus, exiguus; (*time*) brevis; **very ~** perexiguus, minimus; **~ boy** puerulus *m* ♦ *n* paulum *nt*, aliquantulum *nt*; **for a ~** paulisper, parumper; **~ or nothing** vix quicquam ♦ *adv* paulum, nōnnihil; (*with comp*) paulō; **~ by ~** paulātim, sēnsim, gradātim; **think ~ of** parvī aestimāre; **too ~** parum (+ *gen*).

littleness *n* exiguitās *f*.

littoral *n* lītus *nt*.

live *vi* vīvere, vītam agere; (*dwell*) habitāre; **~ down** (*reproach*) ēluere; **~ on** (*food*) vescī (*abl*) ♦ *adj* vīvus.

livelihood *n* vīctus *m*.

liveliness *n* alacritās *f*, hilaritās *f*.

livelong *adj* tōtus.

lively *adj* alacer, hilaris.

liven *vt* exhilarāre.

liver *n* iecur *nt*.

livery *n* vestis famulāris *f*.

livid *adj* līvidus; **be ~** līvēre.

living *adj* vīvus ♦ *n* vīctus *m*; (*earning*) quaestus *m*.

lizard *n* lacerta *f*.

lo *interj* ecce.

load *n* onus *nt* ♦ *vt* onerāre.

loaf *n* pānis *m* ♦ *vi* grassārī.

loafer *n* grassātor *m*.

loam *n* lutum *nt*.

loan *n* mūtuum *nt*, mūtua pecūnia *f*.

loathe *vt* fastīdīre, ōdisse.

loathing *n* fastīdium *nt*.

loathsome *adj* odiōsus, taeter.

lobby *n* vestibulum *nt*.

lobe *n* fibra *f*.

lobster *n* astacus *m*.

local *adj* indigena, locī.

locality *n* locus *m*.

locate *vt* reperīre; **be ~d** situm esse.

location *n* situs *m*.

loch *n* lacus *m*.

lock *n* (*door*) sera *f*; (*hair*) coma *f* ♦ *vt* obserāre.

locomotion *n* mōtus *m*.

locust *n* locusta *f*.

lodge *n* casa *f* ♦ *vi* dēversārī ♦ *vt* īnfīgere; (*complaint*) dēferre.

lodger *n* inquilīnus *m*.

lodging *n* hospitium *nt*, dēversōrium *nt*.

loft *n* cēnāculum *nt*.

loftiness *n* altitūdō *f*, sublīmitās *f*.

lofty *adj* excelsus, sublīmis.

log *n* stīpes *m*; (*fuel*) lignum *nt*.

loggerhead *n*: **be at ~s** rixārī.

logic *n* dialecticē *f*.

logical *adj* dialecticus, ratiōne frētus.

logically *adv* ex ratiōne.

logician *n* dialecticus *m*.

loin *n* lumbus *m*.

loiter *vi* grassārī, cessāre.

loiterer *n* grassātor *m*, cessātor *m*.

loll *vi* recumbere.

lone *adj* sōlus, sōlitārius.

loneliness *n* sōlitūdō *f*.

lonely, lonesome *adj* sōlitārius.

long *adj* longus; (*hair*) prōmissus; (*syllable*) prōductus; (*time*) longus, diūturnus; **in the ~ run** aliquandō; **for a ~ time** diū; **to make a ~ story short** nē longum sit, nē longum faciam ♦ *adv* diū; **~ ago** iamprīdem, iamdūdum; **as ~ as** *conj* dum; **before ~** mox; **for ~** diū; **how ~** quamdiū, quōusque; **I have ~ been wishing** iam prīdem cupiō; **not ~ after** haud multō post; **any ~er** (*time*) diūtius; (*distance*) longius; **no ~er** nōn iam ♦ *vi*: **~ for** dēsīderāre, exoptāre, expetere; **~ to** gestīre.

longevity *n* vīvācitās *f*.

longing *n* dēsīderium *nt*, cupīdō *f* ♦ *adj* avidus.

longingly *adv* avidē.

longitudinally *adv* in longitūdinem.

long-lived *adj* vīvāx.

long-suffering *adj* patiēns.

long-winded *adj* verbōsus, longus.

longwise *adv* in longitūdinem.

look *n* aspectus *m*; (*expression*) vultus *m* ♦ *vi* aspicere; (*seem*) vidērī, speciem praebēre; **~ about** circumspicere; **~ after** prōvidēre (*dat*), cūrāre; **~ at** spectāre ad (+ *acc*), aspicere, intuērī; (*with mind*) contemplārī; **~ back** respicere; **~ down on** dēspectāre; (*fig*) dēspicere; **~ for** quaerere, petere; **~ forward to** exspectāre; **~ here** heus tu, ehodum; **~ into** īnspicere, intrōspicere; **~ out** prōspicere; (*beware*) cavēre; **~ round** circumspicere; **~ through** perspicere; **~ to** ratiōnem habēre (*gen*); (*leader*) spem pōnere in (*abl*); **~ towards** spectāre ad; **~ up** suspicere; **~ up to** suspicere; **~ upon** habēre.

looker-on *n* arbiter *m*.

lookout *n* (*place*) specula *f*; (*man*) vigil *m*, excubiae *fpl*.

looks *npl* speciēs *f*; **good ~** fōrma *f*, pulchritūdō *f*.

loom *n* tēla *f* ♦ *vi* in cōnspectum sē dare.

loop *n* orbis *m*, sinus *m*.

loophole *n* fenestra *f*.

loose *adj* laxus, solūtus, remissus; (*morally*) dissolūtus; **let ~ on** immittere in (*acc*) ♦ *vt* (*undo*) solvere; (*slacken*) laxāre.

loosely *adv* solūtē, remissē.

loosen *vt* (re)solvere; (*structure*) labefacere.

looseness *n* dissolūtiō *f*, dissolūtī mōrēs *mpl*.

loot *n* praeda *f*, rapīna *f*.

lop *vt* amputāre.

lopsided *adj* inaequālis.

loquacious *adj* loquāx.

loquacity *n* loquācitās *f*.

lord *n* dominus *m* ♦ *vi*: **~ it** dominārī.

lordliness *n* superbia *f*.

lordly *adj* superbus; (*rank*) nōbilis.

lordship *n* dominātiō *f*, imperium *nt*.

lore *n* litterae *fpl*, doctrīna *f*.

lose *vt* āmittere, perdere; **~ an eye** alterō oculō capī; **~ heart** animum dēspondēre; **~ one's way** deerrāre ♦ *vi* (*in contest*) vincī.

loss *n* damnum *nt*, dētrīmentum *nt*; **be at a ~** haerēre, haesitāre; **suffer ~** damnum

accipere, facere; **~es** (*in battle*) caesī *mpl.*
lost *adj* āmissus, absēns; **be ~** perīre, interīre;
  give up for ~ dēplōrāre.
lot *n* sors *f*; **be assigned by ~** sorte obvenīre;
  draw a ~ sortem dūcere; **draw ~s for** sortīrī;
  a ~ of multus, plūrimus.
loth *adj* invītus.
lottery *n* sortēs *fpl*; (*fig*) ālea *f*.
lotus *n* lōtos *f*.
loud *adj* clārus, māgnus.
loudly *adv* māgnā vōce.
loudness *n* māgna vōx *f*.
lounge *vi* ōtiārī.
louse *n* pedis *m/f*.
lout *n* agrestis *m*.
lovable *adj* amābilis.
love *n* amor *m*; **be hopelessly in ~** dēperīre; **fall
  in ~ with** adamāre ♦ *vt* amāre, dīligere; **I ~ to**
  mē iuvat (*inf*).
love affair *n* amor *m*.
loveless *adj* amōre carēns.
loveliness *n* grātia *f*, venustās *f*.
lovely *adj* pulcher, amābilis, venustus.
love poem *n* carmen amātōrium *nt*.
lover *n* amāns *m*, amātor *m*.
lovesick *adj* amōre aeger.
loving *adj* amāns.
lovingly *adv* amanter.
low *adj* humilis; (*birth*) ignōbilis; (*price*) vīlis;
  (*sound*) gravis; (*spirits*) dēmissus; (*voice*)
  dēmissus; **at ~ water** aestūs dēcessū; **be ~**
  iacēre; **lay ~** interficere ♦ *vi* mūgīre.
lower *adj* īnferior; **the ~ world** īnferī *mpl*; **of
  the ~ world** īnfernus ♦ *adv* īnferius ♦ *vt*
  dēmittere, dēprimere ♦ *vi* (*cloud*) obscūrārī,
  minārī.
lowering *adj* mināx.
lowest *adj* īnfimus, īmus.
lowing *n* mūgītus *m*.
lowland *adj* campestris.
lowlands *n* campī *mpl.*
lowliness *n* humilitās *f*.
lowly *adj* humilis, obscūrus.
low-lying *adj* dēmisssus; **be ~** sedēre.
lowness *n* humilitās *f*; (*spirit*) tristitia *f*.
loyal *adj* fidēlis, fīdus; (*citizen*) bonus.
loyally *adv* fidēliter.
loyalty *n* fidēs *f*, fidēlitās *f*.
lubricate *vt* ungere.
lucid *adj* clārus, perspicuus.
lucidity *n* perspicuitās *f*.
lucidly *adv* clārē, perspicuē.
luck *n* fortūna *f*, fors *f*; **good ~** fēlicitās *f*; **bad ~**
  īnfortūnium *nt*.
luckily *adv* fēlīciter, faustē, prosperē.
luckless *adj* īnfēlīx.
lucky *adj* fēlīx, fortūnātus; (*omen*) faustus.
lucrative *adj* quaestuōsus.
lucre *n* lucrum *nt*, quaestus *m*. ·
lucubration *n* lūcubrātiō *f*.
ludicrous *adj* rīdiculus.
ludicrously *adv* rīdiculē.
lug *vt* trahere.

luggage *n* impedīmenta *ntpl*, sarcina *f*.
lugubrious *adj* lūgubris, maestus.
lukewarm *adj* tepidus; (*fig*) segnis, neglegēns;
  be ~ tepēre.
lukewarmly *adv* segniter, neglegenter.
lukewarmness *n* tepor *m*; (*fig*) neglegentia *f*,
  incūria *f*.
lull *vt* sōpīre; (*storm*) sēdāre ♦ *n* intermissiō *f*.
lumber *n* scrūta *ntpl.*
luminary *n* lūmen *nt*, astrum *nt*.
luminous *adj* lūcidus, illūstris.
lump *n* massa *f*; (*on body*) tuber *nt*.
lumpish *adj* hebes, crassus, stolidus.
lunacy *n* īnsānia *f*.
lunar *adj* lūnāris.
lunatic *n* īnsānus *m*.
lunch *n* prandium *nt* ♦ *vi* prandēre.
lung *n* pulmō *m*; *pl* (*RHET*) latera *ntpl.*
lunge *n* ictus *m* ♦ *vi* prōsilīre.
lurch *n*: **leave in the ~** dērelinquere, dēstituere
  ♦ *vi* titubāre.
lure *n* esca *f* ♦ *vt* allicere, illicere, ēlicere.
lurid *adj* lūridus.
lurk *vi* latēre, latitāre, dēlitēscere.
luscious *adj* praedulcis.
lush *adj* luxuriōsus.
lust *n* libīdō *f* ♦ *vi* libīdine flagrāre,
  concupīscere.
lustful *adj* libīdinōsus.
lustily *adv* validē, strēnuē.
lustiness *n* vigor *m*, nervī *mpl.*
lustration *n* lūstrum *nt*.
lustre *n* fulgor *m*, splendor *m*.
lustrous *adj* illūstris.
lusty *adj* validus, lacertōsus.
lute *n* cithara *f*, fidēs *fpl.*
lute player *n* citharista *m*, citharistria *f*,
  fidicen *m*, fidicina *f*.
luxuriance *n* luxuria *f*.
luxuriant *adj* luxuriōsus.
luxuriate *vi* luxuriārī.
luxuries *pl* lautitiae *fpl.*
luxurious *adj* luxuriōsus, sūmptuōsus, lautus.
luxuriously *adv* sūmptuōsē, lautē.
luxury *n* luxuria *f*, luxus *m*.
lynx *n* lynx *m/f*; **~-eyed** lyncēus.
lyre *n* lyra *f*, fidēs *fpl*; **play the ~** fidibus canere.
lyric *adj* lyricus ♦ *n* carmen *nt*.
lyrist *n* fidicen *m*, fidicina *f*.

M, m

mace *n* scīpiō *m*.
machination *n* dolus *m*.
machine *n* māchina *f*.

mackerel *n* scomber *m.*
mad *adj* īnsānus, furiōsus, vēcors, dēmēns; **be
~** īnsānīre, furere.
madam *n* domina *f.*
madden *vt* furiāre, mentem aliēnāre (*dat*).
madly *adv* insānē, furiōsē, dēmenter.
madness *n* īnsānia *f*, furor *m*, dēmentia *f*;
(*animals*) rabiēs *f.*
maelstrom *n* vertex *m.*
magazine *n* horreum *nt*, apothēca *f.*
maggot *n* vermiculus *m.*
magic *adj* magicus ♦ *n* magicae artēs *fpl.*
magician *n* magus *m*, veneficus *m.*
magistracy *n* magistrātus *m.*
magistrate *n* magistrātus *m.*
magnanimity *n* māgnanimitās *f*, līberalitās *f.*
magnanimous *adj* generōsus, līberālis,
māgnanimus.
magnet *n* magnēs *m.*
magnificence *n* māgnificentia *f*, adparātus *m.*
magnificent *adj* māgnificus, amplus,
splendidus.
magnificently *adv* māgnificē, amplē,
splendidē.
magnify *vt* amplificāre, exaggerāre.
magnitude *n* māgnitūdō *f.*
magpie *n* pīca *f.*
maid *n* virgō *f*; (*servant*) ancilla *f.*
maiden *n* virgō *f.*
maidenhood *n* virginitās *f.*
maidenly *adj* virginālis.
mail *n* (*armour*) lōrīca *f*; (*letters*) epistulae *fpl.*
maim *vt* mutilāre.
maimed *adj* mancus.
main *adj* prīnceps, prīmus; **~ point** caput *nt*
♦ *n* (*sea*) altum *nt*, pelagus *nt*; **with might and
~** manibus pedibusque, omnibus nervīs.
mainland *n* continēns *f.*
mainly *adv* praecipuē, plērumque.
maintain *vt* (*keep*) tenēre, servāre; (*keep up*)
sustinēre; (*keep alive*) alere, sustentāre;
(*argue*) adfirmāre, dēfendere.
maintenance *n* (*food*) alimentum *nt.*
majestic *adj* augustus, māgnificus.
majestically *adv* augustē.
majesty *n* māiestās *f.*
major *adj* māior.
majority *n* māior pars *f*, plērīque; **have
attained one's ~** suī iūris esse.
make *vt* facere, fingere; (*appointment*) creāre;
(*bed*) sternere; (*cope*) superāre; (*compulsion*)
cōgere; (*consequence*) efficere; (*craft*)
fabricārī; (*harbour*) capere; (*living*) quaerere;
(*sum*) efficere; (*with adj*) reddere; (*with verb*)
cōgere; **~ away with** tollere, interimere; **~
good** supplēre, resarcīre; **~ light of** parvī
facere; **~ one's way** iter facere; **~ much of**
māgnī aestimāre, multum tribuere (*dat*); **~
for** petere; **~ out** arguere; **~ over** dēlegāre,
trānsferre; **~ ready** parāre; **~ a speech**
orātiōnem habēre; **~ a truce** indutias
compōnere; **war on** bellum inferre; **~ up**
(*loss*) supplēre; (*total*) efficere; (*story*)

fingere; **be made** fierī.
make-believe *n* simulātiō *f.*
maker *n* fabricātor *m*, auctor *m.*
make-up *n* medicāmina *ntpl.*
maladministration *n* (*charge*) repetundae *fpl.*
malady *n* morbus *m.*
malcontent *adj* novārum rērum cupidus.
male *adj* mās, māsculus.
malefactor *n* nocēns *m*, reus *m.*
malevolence *n* malevolentia *f.*
malevolent *adj* malevolus, malignus.
malevolently *adv* malignē.
malformation *n* dēprāvātiō *f.*
malice *n* invidia *f*, malevolentia *f*; **bear ~
towards** invidēre (*dat*).
malicious *adj* invidiōsus, malevolus,
malignus.
maliciously *adv* malignē.
malign *adj* malignus, invidiōsus ♦ *vt*
obtrectāre.
malignant *adj* malevolus.
maligner *n* obtrectātor *m.*
malignity *n* malevolentia *f.*
malleable *adj* ductilis.
mallet *n* malleus *m.*
mallow *n* malva *f.*
malpractices *n* dēlicta *ntpl.*
maltreat *vt* laedere, vexāre.
malversation *n* pecūlātus *m.*
man *n* (*human being*) homō *m/f*; (*male*) vir *m*;
(*MIL*) mīles *m*; (*chess*) latrunculus *m*; **to a ~**
omnēs ad ūnum; **~ who** is qui; **old ~** senex *m*;
young ~ adulēscēns *m*; **~ of war** nāvis longa *f*
♦ *vt* (*ship*) complēre; (*walls*) praesidiō
firmāre.
manacle *n* manicae *fpl* ♦ *vt* manicās inicere
(*dat*).
manage *vt* efficere, gerere, gubernāre,
administrāre; (*horse*) moderārī; (*with verb*)
posse.
manageable *adj* tractābilis, habilis.
management *n* administrātiō *f*, cūra *f*;
(*finance*) dispēnsātiō *f.*
manager *n* administrātor *m*, moderātor *m*;
dispēnsātor *m.*
mandate *n* mandātum *nt.*
mane *n* iuba *f.*
manful *adj* virīlis, fortis.
manfully *adv* virīliter, fortiter.
manger *n* praesēpe *nt.*
mangle *vt* dīlaniāre, lacerāre.
mangy *adj* scaber.
manhood *n* pūbertās *f*, toga virīlis *f.*
mania *n* īnsānia *f.*
maniac *n* furiōsus *m.*
manifest *adj* manifestus, apertus, clārus ♦ *vt*
dēclārāre, aperīre.
manifestation *n* speciēs *f.*
manifestly *adv* manifestō, apertē.
manifesto *n* ēdictum *nt.*
manifold *adj* multiplex, varius.
manikin *n* homunciō *m*, homunculus *m.*
manipulate *vt* tractāre.

manipulation *n* tractātiō *f*.
mankind *n* hominēs *mpl*, genus hūmānum *nt*.
manliness *n* virtūs *f*.
manly *adj* fortis, virīlis.
manner *n* modus *m*, ratiō *f*; (*custom*) mōs *m*,
ūsus *m*; ~s *pl* mōrēs *mpl*; **after the ~ of** rītū,
mōre (*gen*); **good ~s** hūmānitās *f*, modestia *f*.
mannered *adj* mōrātus.
mannerism *n* mōs *m*.
mannerly *adj* bene mōrātus, urbānus.
manoeuvre *n* (*MIL*) dēcursus *m*, dēcursiō *f*; (*fig*)
dolus *m* ♦ *vi* dēcurrere; (*fig*) māchinārī.
manor *n* praedium *nt*.
mansion *n* domus *f*.
manslaughter *n* homicīdium *nt*.
mantle *n* pallium *nt*; (*women's*) palla *f*.
manual *adj*: ~ **labour** opera *f* ♦ *n* libellus *m*, ars
f.
manufacture *n* fabrica *f* ♦ *vt* fabricārī.
manumission *n* manūmissiō *f*.
manumit *vt* manū mittere, ēmancipāre.
manure *n* fimus *m*, stercus *nt* ♦ *vt* stercorāre.
manuscript *n* liber *m*, cōdex *m*.
many *adj* multī; **as ~ as** tot … quot; **how ~?**
quot?; **so ~** tot; **in ~ places** multifāriam; **a**
good ~ complūrēs; **too ~** nimis multī; **the ~**
vulgus *nt*; **very ~** permultī, plūrimī.
map *n* tabula *f* ♦ *vt*: ~ **out** dēscrībere,
dēsignāre.
maple *n* acer *nt* ♦ *adj* acernus.
mar *vt* corrumpere, dēfōrmāre.
marauder *n* praedātor *m*, dēpopulātor *m*.
marble *n* marmor *nt* ♦ *adj* marmoreus.
March *n* mēnsis Martius *m*; **of ~** Martius.
march *n* iter *nt*; **line of ~** agmen *nt*; **by forced**
~es māgnīs itineribus; **on the ~** ex itinere, in
itinere; **quick ~** plēnō gradū; **a regular day's ~**
iter iūstum *nt* ♦ *vi* contendere, iter facere,
incēdere, īre; ~ **out** exīre; ~ **on** signa
prōferre, prōgredī ♦ *vt* dūcere; ~ **out**
ēdūcere; ~ **in** intrōdūcere.
mare *n* equa *f*.
margin *n* margō *f*; (*fig*) discrīmen *nt*.
marigold *n* caltha *f*.
marine *adj* marīnus ♦ *n* mīles classicus *m*.
mariner *n* nauta *m*.
marital *adj* marītus.
maritime *adj* maritimus.
marjoram *n* amāracus *m*.
mark *n* nota *f*; (*of distinction*) īnsigne *nt*; (*target*)
scopos *m*; (*trace*) vestīgium *nt*; **beside the ~**
nihil ad rem; **it is the ~ of a wise man to**
sapientis est (*inf*); **be wide of the ~** errāre ♦
vt notāre, dēsignāre; (*observe*)
animadvertere, animum attendere; ~ **out**
(*site*) mētārī, dēsignāre; (*for purpose*)
dēnotāre.
marked *adj* īnsignis, manifestus.
markedly *adv* manifestō.
marker *n* index *m*.
market *n* macellum *nt*; ~ **day** nūndinae *fpl*; ~
town emporium *nt*; **cattle ~** forum boārium
nt; **fish ~** forum piscārium *nt*.

marketable *adj* vēndibilis.
marketplace *n* forum *nt*.
market prices *npl* annōna *f*.
market town *n* emporium *nt*.
marking *n* macula *f*.
maroon *vt* dērelinquere.
marriage *n* mātrimōnium *nt*, coniugium *nt*;
(*ceremony*) nūptiae *fpl*; **give in ~** collocāre; ~
bed lectus geniālis *m*.
marriageable *adj* nūbilis.
marrow *n* medulla *f*.
marry *vt* (*a wife*) dūcere, in mātrimōnium
dūcere; (*a husband*) nūbere (*dat*).
marsh *n* palūs *f*.
marshal *n* imperātor *m* ♦ *vt* īnstruere.
marshy *adj* palūster.
mart *n* forum *nt*.
marten *n* mēlēs *f*.
martial *adj* bellicōsus, ferōx.
martyr *n* dēvōtus *m*; (*ECCL*) martyr *m/f*.
marvel *n* mīrāculum *nt*, portentum *nt* ♦ *vi*
mīrārī; ~ **at** admīrārī.
marvellous *adj* mīrus, mīrificus, mīrābilis.
marvellously *adv* mīrē, mīrum quantum.
masculine *adj* mās, virīlis.
mash *n* farrāgō *f* ♦ *vt* commiscēre,
contundere.
mask *n* persōna *f* ♦ *vt* persōnam induere (*dat*);
(*fig*) dissimulāre.
mason *n* structor *m*.
masonry *n* lapidēs *mpl*, caementum *nt*.
masquerade *n* simulātiō *f* ♦ *vi* vestem
mūtāre; ~ **as** speciem sibi induere (*gen*),
persōnam ferre (*gen*).
mass *n* mōlēs *f*; (*of small things*) congeriēs *f*; (*of*
people) multitūdō *f*; (*ECCL*) missa *f*; **the ~es**
vulgus *nt*, plēbs *f* ♦ *vt* congerere, coacervāre.
massacre *n* strāgēs *f*, caedēs *f*, interneciō *f* ♦
vt trucīdāre.
massive *adj* ingēns, solidus.
massiveness *n* mōlēs *f*, soliditās *f*.
mast *n* mālus *m*.
master *n* dominus *m*; (*school*) magister *m*; **be ~**
of dominārī in (*abl*); (*skill*) perītum esse
(*gen*); **become ~ of** potīrī (*abl*); **be one's own**
~ suī iūris esse; **not ~ of** impotēns (*gen*); **a**
past ~ veterātor *m* ♦ *vt* dēvincere; (*skill*)
ēdiscere; (*passion*) continēre.
masterful *adj* imperiōsus.
masterly *adj* doctus, perītus.
masterpiece *n* praeclārum opus *nt*.
mastery *n* dominātiō *f*, imperium *nt*,
arbitrium *nt*.
masticate *vt* mandere.
mastiff *n* Molossus *m*.
mat *n* storea *f*.
match *n* (*person*) pār *m/f*; (*marriage*) nūptiae *fpl*;
(*contest*) certāmen *nt*; **a ~ for** pār (*dat*); **no ~**
for impār (*dat*) ♦ *vt* exaequāre, adaequāre ♦
vi congruere.
matchless *adj* singulāris, ūnicus.
mate *n* socius *m*; (*married*) coniunx *m/f* ♦ *vi*
coniungī.

material adj corporeus; (significant) haud levis ◆ n māteriēs f; (literary) silva f.
materialize vi ēvenīre.
materially adv māgnopere.
maternal adj māternus.
mathematical adj mathēmaticus.
mathematician n mathēmaticus m, geōmetrēs m.
mathematics n ars mathēmatica f, numerī mpl.
matin adj mātūtīnus.
matricide n (act) mātricīdium nt; (person) mātricīda m.
matrimony n mātrimōnium nt.
matrix n fōrma f.
matron n mātrōna f.
matter n māteria f, corpus nt; (affair) rēs f; (MED) pūs nt; **what is the ~ with you?** quid tibī est? vi: **it ~s** interest, rēfert.
matting n storea f.
mattock n dolābra f.
mattress n culcita f.
mature adj mātūrus; (age) adultus ◆ vi mātūrēscere.
maturity n mātūritās f; (age) adulta aetās f.
maul n fistūca f ◆ vt contundere, dīlaniāre.
maw n ingluviēs f.
mawkish adj pūtidus.
mawkishly adv pūtidē.
maxim n dictum nt, praeceptum nt, sententia f.
maximum adj quam māximus, quam plūrimus.
May n mēnsis Māius m; **of ~** Māius.
may vi posse; **I ~** licet mihī.
mayor n praefectus m.
maze n labyrinthus m.
mead n (drink) mulsum nt; (land) prātum nt.
meagre adj exīlis, ieiūnus.
meagrely adv exīliter, ieiūnē.
meagreness n exīlitās f.
meal n (flour) farīna f; (repast) cibus m.
mealy-mouthed adj blandiloquus.
mean adj humilis, abiectus; (birth) ignōbilis; (average) medius, mediocris ◆ n modus m, mediocritās f ◆ vt dīcere, significāre; (word) valēre; (intent) velle, in animō habēre.
meander vi sinuōsō cursū fluere.
meaning n significātiō f, vīs f, sententia f; **what is the ~ of?** quid sibī vult?, quōrsum spectat?.
meanly adv abiectē, humiliter.
meanness n humilitās f; (conduct) illīberālitās f, avāritia f.
means n īnstrūmentum nt; (of doing) facultās f; (wealth) opēs fpl; **by ~ of** per (acc); **by all ~** māximē; **by no ~** nūllō modō, haudquāquam; **of small ~** pauper.
meantime, meanwhile adv intereā, interim.
measles n boa f.
measure n modus m, mēnsūra f; (rhythm) numerī mpl; (plan) cōnsilium nt; (law) rogātiō f, lēx f; **beyond ~** nimium; **in some ~** aliquā ex parte; **take ~s** cōnsulere; **take the ~ of** quālis

sit cognōscere; **without ~** immoderātē ◆ vt mētīrī; **~ out** dīmētīrī; (land) mētārī.
measured adj moderātus.
measureless adj īnfīnītus, immēnsus.
measurement n mēnsūra f.
meat n carō f.
mechanic n opifex m, faber m.
mechanical adj mēchanicus.
mechanical device māchinātiō f.
mechanics n māchinālis scientia f.
mechanism n māchinātiō f.
medal n īnsigne nt.
meddle vi sē interpōnere.
meddlesome adj cūriōsus.
Medes n Mīdi mpl.
mediate vi intercēdere; **~ between** compōnere, conciliāre.
mediator n intercessor m, dēprecātor m.
medical adj medicus.
medicate vt medicāre.
medicinal adj medicus, salūbris.
medicine n (art) medicīna f; (drug) medicāmentum nt.
medicine chest n narthēcium nt.
mediocre adj mediocris.
mediocrity n mediocritās f.
meditate vi meditārī, cōgitāre, sēcum volūtāre.
meditation n cōgitātiō f, meditātiō f.
medium n internūntius m; (means) modus m ◆ adj mediocris.
medley n farrāgō f.
meek adj mītis, placidus.
meekly adv summissō animō.
meet adj idōneus, aptus ◆ n conventus m ◆ vi convenīre ◆ vt obviam īre (dat), occurrere (dat); (fig) obīre; **~ with** invenīre, excipere.
meeting n cōnsilium nt, conventus m.
melancholic adj melancholicus.
melancholy n ātra bīlis f; tristitia f, maestitia f ◆ adj tristis, maestus.
mêlée n turba f, concursus m.
mellow adj mītis; (wine) lēnis; **become ~** mītēscere; **make ~** mītigāre.
mellowness n mātūritās f.
melodious adj canōrus, numerōsus.
melodiously adv numerōsē.
melody n melos nt, modī mpl.
melt vt liquefacere, dissolvere; (fig) movēre ◆ vi liquēscere, dissolvī; (fig) commovērī; **~ away** dēliquēscere.
member n membrum nt; (person) socius m.
membrane n membrāna f.
memento n monumentum nt.
memoir n commentārius m.
memorable adj memorābilis, commemorābilis.
memorandum n hypomnēma nt.
memorial n monumentum nt.
memorize vt ēdiscere.
memory n memoria f; **from ~** memoriter.
menace n minae fpl ◆ vt minārī, minitārī; (things) imminēre (dat).

menacing *adj* mināx.
menacingly *adv* mināciter.
menage *n* familia *f*.
mend *vt* sarcīre, reficere ♦ *vi* meliōrem fierī;
(*health*) convalēscere.
mendacious *adj* mendāx.
mendacity *n* mendācium *nt*.
mendicant *n* mendīcus *m*.
mendicity *n* mendīcitās *f*.
menial *adj* servīlis, famulāris ♦ *n* servus *m*,
famulus *m*.
menstrual *adj* mēnstruus.
mensuration *n* mētiendī ratiō *f*.
mental *adj* cōgitātiōnis, mentis.
mentality *n* animī adfectus *m*, mēns *f*.
mentally *adv* cōgitātiōne, mente.
mention *n* mentiō *f* ♦ *vt* memorāre,
mentiōnem facere (*gen*); (*casually*) inicere;
(*briefly*) attingere; **omit to ~** praetermittere.
mentor *n* auctor *m*, praeceptor *m*.
mercantile *adj* mercātōrius.
mercenary *adj* mercennārius, vēnālis ♦ *n*
mercennārius mīles *m*.
merchandise *n* mercēs *fpl*.
merchant *n* mercātor *m*.
merchantman *n* nāvis onerāria *f*.
merchant ship *n* nāvis onerāria *f*.
merciful *adj* misericors, clēmens.
mercifully *adv* clēmenter.
merciless *adj* immisericors, inclēmens,
inhūmānus.
mercilessly *adv* inhūmānē.
mercurial *adj* hilaris.
mercy *n* misericordia *f*, clēmentia *f*, venia *f*; **at
the ~ of** obnoxius (*dat*), in manū (*gen*).
mere *n* lacus *m* ♦ *adj* merus, ipse.
merely *adv* sōlum, tantum, dumtaxat.
meretricious *adj* meretricius; **~ attractions**
lēnōcinia *ntpl*.
merge *vt* cōnfundere ♦ *vi* cōnfundī.
meridian *n* merīdiēs *m* ♦ *adj* merīdiānus.
merit *n* meritum *nt*, virtūs *f* ♦ *vt* merērī.
meritorious *adj* laudābilis.
meritoriously *adv* optimē.
mermaid *n* nympha *f*.
merrily *adv* hilare, festīvē.
merriment *n* hilaritās *f*, festīvitās *f*.
merry *adj* hilaris, festīvus; **make ~** lūdere.
merrymaking *n* lūdus *m*, festīvitās *f*.
mesh *n* macula *f*.
mess *n* (*dirt*) sordēs *f*, squālor *m*; (*trouble*)
turba *f*; (*food*) cibus *m*; (MIL) contubernālēs
mpl.
message *n* nūntius *m*.
messenger *n* nūntius *m*.
messmate *n* contubernālis *m*.
metal *n* metallum *nt* ♦ *adj* ferreus, aereus.
metamorphose *vt* mūtāre, trānsfōrmāre.
metamorphosis *n* mūtātiō *f*.
metaphor *n* trānslātiō *f*.
metaphorical *adj* trānslātus.
metaphorically *adv* per trānslātiōnem.
metaphysics *n* dialectica *ntpl*.

mete *vt* mētīrī.
meteor *n* fax caelestis *f*.
meteorology *n* prognōstica *ntpl*.
methinks *vi*: **~ I am** mihī videor esse.
method *n* ratiō *f*, modus *m*.
methodical *adj* dispositus; (*person*) dīligēns.
methodically *adv* dispositē.
meticulous *adj* accūrātus.
meticulously *adv* accūrātē.
meticulousness *n* cūra *f*.
metonymy *n* immūtātiō *f*.
metre *n* numerī *mpl*, modī *mpl*.
metropolis *n* urbs *f*.
mettle *n* ferōcitās *f*, virtūs *f*.
mettlesome *adj* ferōx, animōsus.
mew *n* (*bird*) larus *m*; **~s** *pl* stabula *ntpl* ♦ *vi*
vāgīre.
miasma *n* hālitus *m*.
mid *adj* medius ♦ *prep* inter (*acc*).
midday *n* merīdiēs *m* ♦ *adj* merīdiānus.
middle *adj* medius ♦ *n* medium *nt*; **in the ~**
medius, in mediō; **~ of** medius.
middling *adj* mediocris.
midge *n* culex *m*.
midget *n* pūmiliō *m/f*.
midland *adj* mediterrāneus.
midnight *n* media nox *f*.
midriff *n* praecordia *ntpl*.
midst *n* medium *nt*; **in the ~** medius; **in the ~ of**
inter (*acc*); **through the ~ of** per medium.
midsummer *n* sōlstitium *nt* ♦ *adj* sōlstitiālis.
midway *adv* medius.
midwife *n* obstetrix *f*.
midwinter *n* brūma *f* ♦ *adj* brūmālis.
mien *n* aspectus *m*, vultus *m*.
might *n* vīs *f*, potentia *f*; **with ~ and main**
omnibus nervīs, manibus pedibusque.
mightily *adv* valdē, magnopere.
mighty *adj* ingēns, validus.
migrate *vi* abīre, migrāre.
migration *n* peregrīnātiō *f*.
migratory *adj* advena.
mild *adj* mītis, lēnis, clēmēns.
mildew *n* rōbīgō *f*.
mildly *adv* lēniter, clēmenter.
mildness *n* clēmentia *f*, mānsuētūdō *f*;
(*weather*) caelī indulgentia *f*.
mile *n* mīlle passūs *mpl*; **~s** *pl* mīlia passuum.
milestone *n* lapis *m*, mīliārium *nt*.
militant *adj* ferōx.
military *adj* mīlitāris ♦ *n* mīlitēs *mpl*.
military service *n* mīlitia *f*.
militate *vi*: **~ against** repugnāre (*dat*), facere
contrā (*acc*).
militia *n* mīlitēs *mpl*.
milk *n* lac *nt* ♦ *vt* mulgēre.
milk pail *n* mulctra *f*.
milky *adj* lacteus.
mill *n* pistrīnum *nt*.
milled *adj* (*coin*) serrātus.
millennium *n* mīlle annī *mpl*.
miller *n* pistor *m*.
millet *n* mīlium *nt*.

million *num* deciēs centēna mīlia *ntpl*.
millionaire *n* rēx *m*.
millstone *n* mola *f*, molāris *m*.
mime *n* mīmus *m*.
mimic *n* imitātor *m*, imitātrīx *f* ♦ *vt* imitārī.
mimicry *n* imitātiō *f*.
minatory *adj* mināx.
mince *vt* concīdere; **not ~ words** plānē apertēque dīcere ♦ *n* minūtal *nt*.
mind *n* mēns *f*, animus *m*, ingenium *nt*; (*opinion*) sententia *f*; (*memory*) memoria *f*; **be in one's right ~** mentis suae esse; **be of the same ~** eadem sentīre; **be out of one's ~** īnsānīre; **bear in ~** meminisse (*gen*), memorem esse (*gen*); **call to ~** memoriā repetere, recordārī; **have a ~ to** libet; **have in ~** in animō habēre; **put one's ~ to** animum applicāre ad (+ *acc*); **make up one's ~** animum indūcere, animō obstināre, statuere; **put in ~ of** admonēre (*gen*); **speak one's ~** sententiam suam aperīre; **to one's ~** ex sententiā ♦ *vt* cūrāre, attendere; **~ one's own business** suum negōtium agere ♦ *vi* gravārī; **I don't ~** nīl moror; **never ~** mitte.
minded *adj* animātus.
mindful *adj* memor.
mine *n* metallum *nt*; (*MIL*) cuniculus *m*; (*fig*) thēsaurus *m* ♦ *vi* fodere; (*MIL*) cuniculum agere ♦ *pron* meus.
miner *n* fossor *m*.
mineral *n* metallum *nt*.
mingle *vt* miscēre, commiscēre ♦ *vi* sē immiscēre.
miniature *n* minima pictūra *f*.
minimize *vt* dētrectāre.
minimum *n* minimum *nt* ♦ *adj* quam minimus.
minion *n* cliēns *mf*; dēlicātus *m*.
minister *n* administer *m* ♦ *vi* ministrāre, servīre.
ministry *n* mūnus *nt*, officium *nt*.
minor *adj* minor ♦ *n* pupillus *m*, pupilla *f*.
minority *n* minor pars *f*; **in one's ~** nōndum suī iūris.
Minotaur *n* Mīnōtaurus *m*.
minstrel *n* fidicen *m*.
minstrelsy *n* cantus *m*.
mint *n* (*plant*) menta *f*; (*money*) Monēta *f* ♦ *vt* cūdere.
minute *n* temporis mōmentum *nt*.
minute *adj* minūtus, exiguus, subtīlis.
minutely *adv* subtīliter.
minuteness *n* exiguitās *f*, subtīlitas *f*.
minutiae *n* singula *ntpl*.
minx *n* lascīva *f*.
miracle *n* mīrāculum *nt*, mōnstrum *nt*.
miraculous *adj* mīrus, mīrābilis.
miraculously *adv* dīvīnitus.
mirage *n* falsa speciēs *f*.
mire *n* lutum *nt*.
mirror *n* speculum *nt* ♦ *vt* reddere.
mirth *n* hilaritās *f*, laetitia *f*.
mirthful *adj* hilaris, laetus.
mirthfully *adv* hilare, laetē.

miry *adj* lutulentus.
misadventure *n* īnfortūnium *nt*, cāsus *m*.
misapply *vt* abūtī (*abl*); (*words*) invertere.
misapprehend *vt* male intellegere.
misapprehension *n* error *m*.
misappropriate *vt* intervertere.
misbegotten *adj* nothus.
misbehave *vi* male sē gerere.
miscalculate *vi* errāre, fallī.
miscalculation *n* error *m*.
miscall *vt* maledīcere (*dat*).
miscarriage *n* abortus *m*; (*fig*) error *m*.
miscarry *vi* aborīrī; (*fig*) cadere, inritum esse.
miscellaneous *adj* prōmiscuus, varius.
miscellany *n* farrāgō *f*.
mischance *n* īnfortūnium *nt*.
mischief *n* malum *nt*, facinus *nt*, maleficium *nt*; (*children*) lascīvia *f*.
mischievous *adj* improbus, maleficus; lascīvus.
misconceive *vt* male intellegere.
misconception *n* error *m*.
misconduct *n* dēlictum *nt*, culpa *f*.
misconstruction *n* prāva interpretātiō *f*.
misconstrue *vt* male interpretārī.
miscreant *n* scelerātus *m*.
misdeed *n* maleficium *nt*, dēlictum *nt*.
misdemeanour *n* peccātum *nt*, culpa *f*.
miser *n* avārus *m*.
miserable *adj* miser, infēlīx; **make oneself ~** sē cruciāre.
miserably *adv* miserē.
miserliness *n* avāritia *f*.
miserly *adj* avārus.
misery *n* miseria *f*, aerumna *f*.
misfortune *n* malum *nt*, īnfortūnium *nt*, incommodum *nt*, rēs adversae *fpl*.
misgiving *n* suspiciō *f*, cūra *f*; **have ~s parum** cōnfīdere.
misgovern *vt* male regere.
misgovernment *n* prāva administrātiō *f*.
misguide *vt* fallere, dēcipere.
misguided *adj* dēmēns.
mishap *n* īnfortūnium *nt*.
misinform *vt* falsa docēre.
misinterpret *vt* male interpretārī.
misinterpretation *n* prāva interpretātiō *f*.
misjudge *vt* male iūdicāre.
mislay *vt* āmittere.
mislead *vt* dēcipere, indūcere, auferre.
mismanage *vt* male gerere.
misnomer *n* falsum nōmen *nt*.
misogyny *n* mulierum odium *nt*.
misplace *vt* in aliēnō locō collocāre.
misplaced *adj* (*fig*) vānus.
misprint *n* mendum *nt*.
mispronounce *vt* prāvē appellāre.
misquote *vt* perperam prōferre.
misrepresent *vt* dētorquēre, invertere; (*person*) calumniārī.
misrepresentation *n* calumnia *f*.
misrule *n* prāva administrātiō *f*.
miss *vt* (*aim*) aberrāre (*abl*); (*loss*) requīrere,

dēsīderāre; (*notice*) praetermittere ♦ *n* error *m*; (*girl*) virgō *f*.
misshapen *adj* distortus, dēfōrmis.
missile *n* tēlum *nt*.
missing *adj* absēns; **be ~** dēesse, dēsīderārī.
mission *n* lēgātiō *f*.
missive *n* litterae *fpl*.
misspend *vt* perdere, dissipāre.
misstatement *n* falsum *nt*, mendācium *nt*.
mist *n* nebula *f*, cālīgō *f*.
mistake *n* error *m*; (*writing*) mendum *nt*; **full of ~s** mendōsus ♦ *vt*: **~ for** habēre prō (*abl*); **be ~n** errāre, fallī.
mistletoe *n* viscum *nt*.
mistranslate *vt* prāvē reddere.
mistress *n* domina *f*; (*school*) magistra *f*; (*lover*) amīca *f*.
mistrust *n* diffīdentia *f*, suspiciō *f* ♦ *vt* diffīdere (*dat*).
mistrustful *adj* diffīdēns.
mistrustfully *adv* diffīdenter.
misty *adj* nebulōsus.
misunderstand *vt* male intellegere ♦ *vi* errāre.
misunderstanding *n* error *m*; (*quarrel*) discidium *nt*.
misuse *n* malus ūsus *m* ♦ *vt* abūtī (*abl*).
mite *n* parvulus *m*; (*insect*) vermiculus *m*.
mitigate *vt* mītigāre, lēnīre.
mitigation *n* mītigātiō *f*.
mix *vt* miscēre; **~ in** admiscēre; **~ together** commiscēre; **get ~ed up with** admiscērī cum, sē interpōnere (*dat*).
mixed *adj* prōmiscuus.
mixture *n* (*act*) temperātiō *f*; (*state*) dīversitās *f*.
mnemonic *n* artificium memoriae *nt*.
moan *n* gemitus *m* ♦ *vi* gemere.
moat *n* fossa *f*.
mob *n* vulgus *nt*, turba *f* ♦ *vt* circumfundī in (*acc*).
mobile *adj* mōbilis, agilis.
mobility *n* mōbilitās *f*, agilitās *f*.
mobilize *vt* (*MIL*) ēvocāre.
mock *vt* irrīdēre, lūdibriō habēre, lūdificārī; (*ape*) imitārī; **~ at** inlūdere ♦ *n* lūdibrium *nt* ♦ *adj* simulātus, fictus.
mocker *n* dērīsor *m*.
mockery *n* lūdibrium *nt*, irrīsus *m*.
mode *n* modus *m*, ratiō *f*.
model *n* exemplar *nt*, exemplum *nt* ♦ *vt* fingere.
modeller *n* fictor *m*.
moderate *adj* (*size*) modicus; (*conduct*) moderātus ♦ *vt* temperāre; (*emotion*) temperāre (*dat*) ♦ *vi* mītigārī.
moderately *adv* modicē, moderātē, mediocriter.
moderation *n* moderātiō *f*, modus *m*; (*mean*) mediocritās *f*.
moderator *n* praefectus *m*.
modern *adj* recēns.
modernity *n* haec aetās *f*.

modest *adj* pudīcus, verēcundus.
modestly *adv* verēcundē, pudenter.
modesty *n* pudor *m*, verēcundia *f*.
modicum *n* paullulum *nt*, aliquantulum *nt*.
modification *n* mūtātiō *f*.
modify *vt* immūtāre; (*law*) derogāre aliquid dē.
modulate *vt* (*voice*) īnflectere.
modulation *n* flexiō *f*, inclīnātiō *f*.
moiety *n* dīmidia pars *f*.
moist *adj* ūmidus.
moisten *vt* ūmectāre, rigāre.
moisture *n* ūmor *m*.
molar *n* genuīnus *m*.
mole *n* (*animal*) talpa *f*; (*on skin*) naevus *m*; (*pier*) mōlēs *f*.
molecule *n* corpusculum *nt*.
molehill *n*: **make a mountain out of a ~** ē rīvō flūmina māgna facere, arcem facere ē cloācā.
molest *vt* sollicitāre, vexāre.
molestation *n* vexātiō *f*.
mollify *vt* mollīre, lēnīre.
molten *adj* liquefactus.
moment *n* temporis mōmentum *nt*, temporis pūnctum *nt*; **for a ~** parumper; **in a ~** iam; **without a ~'s delay** nullā interpositā morā; **be of great ~** māgnō mōmentō esse; **it is of ~** interest.
momentary *adj* brevis.
momentous *adj* gravis, māgnī mōmentī.
momentum *n* impetus *m*.
monarch *n* rēx *m*, tyrannus *m*.
monarchical *adj* rēgius.
monarchy *n* rēgnum *nt*.
monastery *n* monastērium *nt*.
monetary *adj* pecūniārius.
money *n* pecūnia *f*; (*cash*) nummī *mpl*; **for ~** mercēde; **ready ~** nummī, praesēns pecūnia; **make ~** rem facere, quaestum facere.
moneybag *n* fiscus *m*.
moneyed *adj* nummātus, pecūniōsus.
moneylender *n* faenerātor *m*.
moneymaking *n* quaestus *m*.
mongoose *n* ichneumōn *m*.
mongrel *n* hibrida *m*.
monitor *n* admonitor *m*.
monk *n* monachus *m*.
monkey *n* sīmia *f*.
monograph *n* libellus *m*.
monologue *n* ōrātiō *f*.
monopolize *vt* absorbēre, sibī vindicāre.
monopoly *n* arbitrium *nt*.
monosyllabic *adj* monosyllabus.
monosyllable *n* monosyllabum *nt*.
monotonous *adj* aequābilis.
monotony *n* taedium *nt*.
monster *n* mōnstrum *nt*, portentum *nt*, bēlua *f*.
monstrosity *n* mōnstrum *nt*.
monstrous *adj* immānis, mōnstruōsus; improbus.
month *n* mēnsis *m*.
monthly *adj* mēnstruus.

monument n monumentum nt.
monumental adj ingēns.
mood n adfectiō f, adfectus m, animus m; (*GRAM*) modus m; **I am in the ~ for** libet (*inf*).
moody adj mōrōsus, tristis.
moon n lūna f; **new ~** interlūnium nt.
moonlight n: **by ~** ad lūnam.
moonshine n somnia ntpl.
moonstruck adj lūnāticus.
moor vt religāre ♦ n tesqua ntpl.
moorings n ancorae fpl.
moot n conventus m; **it is a ~ point** discrepat ♦ vt iactāre.
mop n pēniculus m ♦ vt dētergēre.
mope vi maerēre.
moral adj honestus, probus; (*opposed to physical*) animī; (*PHILOS*) mōrālis ♦ n documentum nt.
morale n animus m; **~ is low** iacet animus.
morality n bonī mōrēs mpl, virtūs f.
moralize vi dē officiīs disserere.
morally adv honestē.
morals npl mōrēs mpl.
morass n palūs f.
moratorium n mora f.
morbid adj aeger.
mordant adj mordāx.
more adj plūs, pluris (*in sg + gen, in pl + adj*) ♦ adv plūs, magis, amplius; (*extra*) ultrā; **~ than** amplius quam; **~ than three feet** amplius trēs pedēs; **~ and ~** magis magisque; **never ~** immo; **~ or less** ferē; **no ~** (*time*) nōn diūtius, nunquam posteā.
moreover adv tamen, autem, praetereā.
moribund adj moribundus.
morning n māne nt; **early in the ~** bene māne; **this ~** hodiē māne; **good ~** salvē ♦ adj mātūtīnus.
morning call n salūtātiō f.
morning watch n (*NAUT*) tertia vigilia f.
moron n sōcors m.
morose adj acerbus, tristis.
moroseness n acerbitās f, tristitia f.
morrow n posterus diēs m; **on the ~** posterō diē, postrīdiē.
morsel n offa f.
mortal adj mortālis, hūmānus; (*wound*) mortifer ♦ n mortālis m/f, homō m/f; **poor ~** homunculus m.
mortality n mortālitās f; (*death*) mors f; **the ~ was high** plūrimī periērunt.
mortally adv: **be ~ wounded** mortiferum vulnus accipere.
mortar n mortārium nt.
mortgage n pignus nt, fīdūcia f ♦ vt obligāre.
mortification n dolor m, angor m.
mortified adj: **be ~ at** aegrē ferre.
mortify vt mordēre, vexāre; (*lust*) coercēre ♦ vi putrēscere.
mortise vt immittere.
mosaic n emblēma nt, lapillī mpl ♦ adj tessellātus.
mosquito n culex m.

mosquito net n cōnōpēum nt.
moss n muscus m.
mossy adj muscōsus.
most adj plūrimus, plērusque; **for the ~ part** māximam partem ♦ adv māximē, plūrimum.
mostly adv plērumque, ferē.
mote n corpusculum nt.
moth n tinea f.
mother n māter f; **of a ~** māternus.
mother-in-law n socrus f.
motherless adj mātre orbus.
motherly adj māternus.
mother tongue n patrius sermō m.
mother wit n Minerva f.
motif n argūmentum nt.
motion n mōtus m; (*for law*) rogātiō f; (*in debate*) sententia f; **propose a ~** ferre; **set in ~** movēre ♦ vt innuere.
motionless adj immōbilis.
motive n causa f, ratiō f; **I know your ~ in asking** sciō cūr rogēs.
motley adj versicolor, varius.
mottled adj maculōsus.
motto n sententia f.
mould n fōrma f; (*soil*) humus f; (*fungus*) mūcor m ♦ vt fingere, fōrmāre.
moulder vi putrēscere ♦ n fictor m.
mouldering adj puter.
mouldiness n situs m.
mouldy adj mūcidus.
moult vi pennas exuere.
mound n agger m, tumulus m.
mount n mōns m; (*horse*) equus m ♦ vt scandere, cōnscendere, ascendere ♦ vi ascendere; **~ up** ēscendere.
mountain n mōns m.
mountaineer n montānus m.
mountainous adj montuōsus.
mourn vi maerēre, lūgēre ♦ vt dēflēre, lūgēre.
mourner n plōrātor m; (*hired*) praefica f.
mournful adj (*cause*) lūctuōsus, acerbus; (*sound*) lūgubris, maestus.
mournfully adv maestē.
mourning n maeror nt, lūctus m; (*dress*) sordēs fpl; **in ~** fūnestus; **be in ~** lūgere; **put on ~** vestem mūtāre, sordēs suscipere; **wearing ~** ātrātus.
mouse n mūs m.
mousetrap n mūscipulum nt.
mouth n ōs nt; (*river*) ōstium nt.
mouthful n bucca f.
mouthpiece n interpres m.
movable adj mōbilis ♦ npl: **~s** rēs fpl, supellex f.
move vt movēre; (*emotion*) commovēre; **~ backwards and forwards** reciprocāre; **~ out of the way** dēmovēre; **~ up** admovēre ♦ vi movērī; (*residence*) dēmigrāre; (*proposal*) ferre, cēnsēre; **~ into** immigrāre in (*acc*); **~ on** prōgredī.
movement n mōtus m; (*process*) cursus m; (*society*) societās f.

mover *n* auctor *m*.
moving *adj* flēbilis, flexanimus.
mow *vt* secāre, dēmetere.
mower *n* faenisex *m*.
much *adj* multus ♦ *adv* multum; (*with compar*) multō; **as ~ as** tantum quantum; **so ~** tantum; (*with verbs*) adeo; **~ less** nēdum; **too ~** nimis ♦ *n* multum *nt*.
muck *n* stercus *nt*.
mud *n* lutum *nt*.
muddle *n* turba *f* ♦ *vt* turbāre.
muffle *vt* involvere; **~ up** obvolvere.
muffled *adj* surdus.
mug *n* pōculum *nt*.
mulberry *n* mōrum *nt*; (*tree*) mōrus *f*.
mule *n* mūlus *m*.
muleteer *n* mūliō *m*.
mulish *adj* obstinātus.
mullet *n* mullus *m*.
multifarious *adj* multiplex, varius.
multiform *adj* multifōrmis.
multiply *vt* multiplicāre ♦ *vi* crēscere.
multitude *n* multitūdō *f*.
multitudinous *adj* crēberrimus.
mumble *vt* (*words*) opprimere ♦ *vi* murmurāre.
munch *vt* mandūcāre.
mundane *adj* terrestris.
municipal *adj* mūnicipālis.
municipality *n* mūnicipium *nt*.
munificence *n* largitās *f*.
munificent *adj* largus, mūnificus.
munificently *adv* mūnificē.
munitions *n* bellī adparātus *m*.
mural *adj* mūrālis.
murder *n* parricīdium *nt*, caedēs *f*; **charge with ~** inter sīcāriōs accūsāre; **trial for ~** quaestiō inter sīcāriōs ♦ *vt* interficere, iŭgulāre, necāre.
murderer *n* sīcārius *m*, homicīda *m*, parricīda *m*, percussor *m*.
murderess *n* interfectrīx *f*.
murderous *adj* cruentus.
murky *adj* tenebrōsus.
murmur *n* murmur *nt*; (*angry*) fremitus *m* ♦ *vi* murmurāre; fremere.
murmuring *n* admurmurātiō *f*.
muscle *n* torus *m*.
muscular *adj* lacertōsus.
muse *vi* meditārī ♦ *n* Mūsa *f*.
mushroom *n* fungus *m*, bōlētus *m*.
music *n* (*art*) mūsica *f*; (*sound*) cantus *m*, modī *mpl*.
musical *adj* (*person*) mūsicus; (*sound*) canōrus.
musician *n* mūsicus *m*; (*strings*) fidicen *m*; (*wind*) tībīcen *m*.
muslin *n* sindōn *f*.
must *n* (*wine*) mustum *nt* ♦ *vi* dēbēre; **I ~ go** mē oportet īre, mihī eundum est.
mustard *n* sināpi *nt*.
muster *vt* convocāre, cōgere; (*review*) recēnsēre ♦ *vi* convenīre, coīre ♦ *n* conventus *m*; (*review*) recēnsiō *f*.
muster roll *n* album *nt*.
mustiness *n* situs *m*.
musty *adj* mūcidus.
mutability *n* incōnstantia *f*.
mutable *adj* incōnstāns, mūtābilis.
mute *adj* mūtus.
mutilate *vt* mūtilāre, truncāre.
mutilated *adj* mūtilus, truncus.
mutilation *n* lacerātiō *f*.
mutineer *n* sēditiōsus *m*.
mutinous *adj* sēditiōsus.
mutiny *n* sēditiō *f* ♦ *vi* sēditiōnem facere.
mutter *vi* mussitāre.
mutton *n* carō ovilla *f*.
mutual *adj* mūtuus.
mutually *adv* mūtuō, inter sē.
muzzle *n* ōs *nt*, rōstrum *nt*; (*guard*) fiscella *f* ♦ *vt* fiscellā capistrāre.
my *adj* meus.
myriad *n* decem mīlia; (*any large no.*) sēscentī.
myrmidon *n* satelles *m*.
myrrh *n* murra *f*.
myrtle *n* myrtus *f* ♦ *adj* myrteus.
myrtle grove *n* myrtētum *nt*.
myself *pron* ipse, egomet; (*reflexive*) mē.
mysterious *adj* arcānus, occultus.
mysteriously *adv* occultē.
mystery *n* arcānum *nt*; (*rites*) mystēria *ntpl*; (*fig*) latebra *f*.
mystic *adj* mysticus.
mystical *adj* mysticus.
mystification *n* fraus *f*, ambāgēs *fpl*.
mystify *vt* fraudāre, cōnfundere.
myth *n* fābula *f*.
mythical *adj* fābulōsus.
mythology *n* fābulae *fpl*.

N, n

nabob *n* rēx *m*.
nadir *n* fundus *m*.
nag *n* caballus *m* ♦ *vt* obiūrgitāre.
naiad *n* nāias *f*.
nail *n* clāvus *m*; (*finger*) unguis *m*; **hit the ~ on the head** rem acū tangere ♦ *vt* clāvīs adfīgere.
naive *adj* simplex.
naively *adv* simpliciter.
naiveté *n* simplicitās *f*.
naked *adj* nūdus.
nakedly *adv* apertē.
name *n* nōmen *nt*; (*repute*) existimātiō *f*; (*term*) vocābulum *nt*; **by ~** nōmine; **have a bad ~** male audīre; **have a good ~** bene audīre; **in**

the ~ of verbīs (*gen*); (*oath*) per ♦ *vt* appellāre, vocāre, nōmināre; (*appoint*) dīcere.

nameless *adj* nōminis expers, sine nōmine.

namely *adv* nempe, dīcō.

namesake *n* gentīlis *m/f.*

nanny goat *n* capra *f.*

nap *n* brevis somnus *m*; (*cloth*) villus *nt.*

napkin *n* linteum *nt.*

narcissus *n* narcissus *m.*

narcotic *adj* somnifer.

nard *n* nardus *f.*

narrate *vt* nārrāre, ēnārrāre.

narration *n* nārrātiō *f.*

narrative *n* fābula *f.*

narrator *n* nārrātor *m.*

narrow *adj* angustus ♦ *vt* coartāre ♦ *vi* coartārī.

narrowly *adv* aegrē, vix.

narrowness *n* angustiae *fpl.*

narrows *n* angustiae *fpl.*

nasal *adj* nārium.

nascent *adj* nāscēns.

nastily *adv* foedē.

nastiness *n* foeditās *f.*

nasty *adj* foedus, taeter, impūrus.

natal *adj* nātālis.

nation *n* populus *m*; (*foreign*) gēns *f.*

national *adj* pūblicus, cīvīlis; (*affairs*) domesticus.

nationality *n* cīvitās *f.*

native *adj* indigena; (*speech*) patrius ♦ *n* incola *m*, indigena *m/f.*

native land *n* patria *f.*

nativity *n* ortus *m.*

natural *adj* nātūrālis; (*innate*) nātīvus, genuīnus, īnsitus.

naturalization *n* cīvitās *f.*

naturalize *vt* cīvitāte dōnāre.

naturalized *adj* (*person*) cīvitāte dōnātus; (*thing*) īnsitus.

naturally *adv* nātūrāliter, secundum nātūram; (*of course*) scīlicet, certē.

nature *n* nātūra *f*; rērum nātūra *f*; (*character*) indolēs *f*, ingenium *nt*; (*species*) genus *nt*; **course of ~** nātūra *f*; **I know the ~ of** sciō quālis sit.

naught *n* nihil *nt*; **set at ~** parvī facere.

naughty *adj* improbus.

nausea *n* nausea *f*; (*fig*) fastīdium *nt.*

nauseate *vt* fastīdium movēre (*dat*); **be ~d with** fastīdīre.

nauseous *adj* taeter.

nautical *adj* nauticus, maritimus.

naval *adj* nāvālis.

navel *n* umbilīcus *m.*

navigable *adj* nāvigābilis.

navigate *vt, vi* nāvigāre.

navigation *n* rēs nautica *f*; (*sailing*) nāvigātiō *f.*

navigator *n* nauta *m*, gubernātor *m.*

navy *n* classis *f*, cōpiae nāvālēs *fpl.*

nay *adv* nōn; **~ more** immo.

near *adv* prope ♦ *adj* propinquus ♦ *prep* prope

(*acc*), ad (*acc*); **lie ~** adiacēre (*dat*) ♦ *vt* adpropinquāre (*dat*).

nearby *adj* iuxtā.

nearer *adj* propior.

nearest *adj* proximus.

nearly *adv* paene, prope, fermē.

neat *adj* nitidus, mundus, concinnus; (*wine*) pūrus.

neatly *adv* mundē, concinnē.

neatness *n* munditia *f.*

nebulous *adj* nebulōsus; (*fig*) incertus.

necessaries *n* rēs ad vīvendum necessāriae *fpl.*

necessarily *adv* necessāriō, necesse.

necessary *adj* necessārius, necesse; **it is ~** oportet (*+ acc and infin or gerundive of vt*).

necessitate *vt* cōgere (*inf*), efficere ut (*subj*).

necessitous *adj* egēnus, pauper.

necessity *n* necessitās *f*; (*thing*) rēs necessāria *f*; (*want*) paupertās *f*, egestās *f.*

neck *n* collum *nt.*

neckcloth *n* fōcāle *nt.*

necklace *n* monīle *nt*, torquis *m.*

nectar *n* nectar *nt.*

need *n* (*necessity*) necessitās *f*; (*want*) egestās *f*, inopia *f*, indigentia *f*; **there is ~ of** opus est (*abl*); **there is no ~ to** nihil est quod, cūr (*subj*) ♦ *vt* egēre (*abl*), carēre, indigēre (*abl*); **I ~** opus est mihī (*abl*).

needful *adj* necessārius.

needle *n* acus *f.*

needless *adj* vānus, inūtilis.

needlessly *adv* frustrā, sine causā.

needs *adv* necesse ♦ *npl* necessitātēs *fpl.*

needy *adj* egēns, inops, pauper.

nefarious *adj* nefārius, scelestus.

negation *n* negātiō *f*, īnfitiātiō *f.*

negative *adj* negāns ♦ *n* negātiō *f*; **answer in the ~** negāre ♦ *vt* vetāre, contrādīcere (*dat*).

neglect *n* neglegentia *f*, incūria *f*; (*of duty*) dērelictiō *f* ♦ *vt* neglegere, ōmittere.

neglectful *adj* neglegēns, immemor.

negligence *n* neglegentia *f*, incūria *f.*

negligent *adj* neglegēns, indīligēns.

negligently *adv* neglegenter, indīligenter.

negligible *adj* levissimus, minimī mōmentī.

negotiate *vi* agere dē ♦ *vt* (*deal*) peragere; (*difficulty*) superāre.

negotiation *n* āctiō *f*, pactum *nt.*

negotiator *n* lēgātus *m*, conciliātor *m.*

negro *n* Aethiops *m.*

neigh *vi* hinnīre.

neighbour *n* vīcīnus *m*, fīnitimus *m.*

neighbourhood *n* vīcīnia *f*, vīcīnitās *f.*

neighbouring *adj* vīcīnus, fīnitimus, propinquus.

neighbourly *adj* hūmānus, amīcus.

neighing *n* hinnītus *m.*

neither *adv* neque, nec; nēve, neu ♦ *pron* neuter ♦ *adj* neuter, neutra, neutrum (*like* alter); **~ ... nor** nec/neque ... nec/neque.

neophyte *n* tīrō *m.*

nephew *n* frātris fīlius *m*, sorōris fīlius *m.*

Nereid n Nēréis f.
nerve n nervus m; (fig) audācia f; ~**s** pl pavor m, trepidātiō f; **have the ~ to** audēre ♦ vt cōnfirmāre.
nervous adj diffīdēns, sollicitus, trepidus.
nervously adv trepidē.
nervousness n sollicitūdō f, diffīdentia f.
nest n nīdus m ♦ vi nīdificāre.
nestle vi recubāre.
nestling n pullus m.
net n rēte nt ♦ vt inrētīre.
nether adj īnferior.
nethermost adj īnfimus, īmus.
netting n rēticulum nt.
nettle n urtīca f ♦ vt inrītāre, ūrere.
neuter adj neuter.
neutral adj medius; **be ~** neutrī partī sē adiungere, medium sē gerere.
neutralize vt compēnsāre.
never adv nunquam.
nevertheless adv nihilōminus, at tamen.
new adj novus, integer, recēns.
newcomer n advena m/f.
newfangled adj novus, inaudītus.
newly adv nūper, modo.
newness n novitās f.
news n nūntius m; **what ~?** quid novī?; ~ **was brought that** nūntiātum est (+ acc and infin).
newspaper n ācta diūrna/pūblica ntpl.
newt n lacerta f.
next adj proximus; (time) īnsequēns ♦ adv dēinde, dēinceps; ~ **day** postrīdiē; ~ **to** iuxtā; **come ~ to** excipere.
nibble vi rōdere.
nice adj bellus, dulcis; (exact) accūrātus; (particular) fastīdiōsus.
nicely adv bellē, probē.
nicety n subtīlitās f.
niche n aedicula f.
nick n: **in the ~ of time** in ipsō articulō temporis.
nickname n cognōmen nt.
niece n frātris fīlia f, sorōris fīlia f.
niggardliness n illīberālitās f, avāritia f.
niggardly adj illīberālis, parcus, avārus.
nigh adv prope.
night n nox f; **by ~** noctū; **all ~** pernox; **spend the ~** pernoctāre; **be awake all ~** pervigilāre ♦ adj nocturnus.
night bird n noctua f.
nightfall n prīmae tenebrae fpl; **at ~** sub noctem.
nightingale n luscinia f.
nightly adj nocturnus ♦ adv noctū.
nightmare n incubus m.
night work n lūcubrātiō f.
nimble adj agilis, pernīx.
nimbleness n agilitās f, pernīcitās f; (mind) argūtiae fpl.
nimbly adv pernīciter.
nine num novem; ~ **each** novēnī; ~ **times** noviēns; ~ **days'** novendiālis.
nine hundred num nōngentī.
nine hundredth adj nōngentēsimus.

nineteen num ūndēvigintī; ~ **each** ūndēvīcēnī; ~ **times** deciēns et noviēns.
nineteenth adj ūndēvīcēsimus.
ninetieth adj nōnāgēsimus.
ninety num nōnāgintā; ~ **each** nōnāgēnī; ~ **times** nōnāgiēns.
ninth adj nōnus.
nip vt vellicāre; (frost) ūrere.
nippers n forceps m.
nipple n papilla f.
no adv nōn; (correcting) immo; **say ~** negāre ♦ adj nullus.
nobility n nōbilitās f; (persons) optimātēs mpl, nōbilēs mpl.
noble adj nōbilis; (birth) generōsus; (appearance) decōrus.
nobleman n prīnceps m, optimās m.
nobly adv nōbiliter, praeclārē.
nobody n nēmō m.
nocturnal adj nocturnus.
nod n nūtus m ♦ vi nūtāre; (sign) adnuere; (sleep) dormītāre.
noddle n caput nt.
node n nōdus m.
noise n strepitus m, sonitus m; (loud) fragor m; **make a ~** increpāre, strepere ♦ vt: ~ **abroad** ēvulgāre; **be ~d abroad** percrēbrēscere.
noiseless adj tacitus.
noiselessly adv tacitē.
noisily adv cum strepitū.
noisome adj taeter, gravis.
noisy adj clāmōsus.
nomadic adj vagus.
nomenclature n vocābula ntpl.
nominally adv nōmine, verbō.
nominate vt nōmināre, dīcere; (in writing) scrībere.
nomination n nōminātiō f.
nominative adj nōminātīvus.
nominee n nōminātus m.
nonappearance n absentia f.
nonce n: **for the ~** semel.
nonchalance n aequus animus m.
nonchalantly adv aequō animō.
noncombatant adj imbellis.
noncommittal adj circumspectus.
nondescript adj īnsolitus.
none adj nullus ♦ pron nēmō m.
nonentity n nihil nt, nullus m.
nones n Nōnae fpl.
nonexistent adj quī nōn est.
nonplus vt ad incitās redigere.
nonresistance n patientia f.
nonsense n nūgae fpl, ineptiae fpl.
nonsensical adj ineptus, absurdus.
nook n angulus m.
noon n merīdiēs m ♦ adj merīdiānus.
no one pron nēmō m (for gen/abl use **nullus**).
noose n laqueus m.
nor adv neque, nec; nēve, neu.
norm n nōrma f.
normal adj solitus.
normally adv plērumque.

north *n* septentriōnēs *mpl* ♦ *adj*
septentriōnālis.
northeast *adv* inter septentriōnēs et
orientem.
northerly *adj* septentriōnālis.
northern *adj* septentriōnālis.
North Pole *n* arctos *f.*
northwards *adv* ad septentriōnēs versus.
northwest *adv* inter septentriōnēs et
occidentem ♦ *adj:* ~ **wind** Cōrus *m.*
north wind *n* aquilō *m.*
nose *n* nāsus *m*, nārēs *fpl*; **blow the ~**
ēmungere; **lead by the ~** labiīs ductāre ♦ *vi*
scrūtārī.
nostril *n* nāris *f.*
not *adv* nōn, haud; ~ **at all** haudquāquam; ~ **as if**
nōn quod, nōn quō; ~ **but what** nōn quīn; ~
even nē ... quidem; ~ **so very** nōn ita; ~ **that**
nōn quō; **and** ~ neque; **does** ~, **did** ~ (*interrog*)
nonne; **if** ... ~ nisi; **that** ~ (*purpose*) nē; (*fear*)
nē nōn; ~ **long after** haud multō post; ~ **only**
... **but also** non modo/solum ... sed etiam; ~
yet nōndum.
notability *n* vir praeclārus *m.*
notable *adj* īnsignis, īnsignītus, memorābilis.
notably *adv* īnsignītē.
notary *n* scrība *m.*
notation *n* notae *fpl.*
notch *n* incīsūra *f* ♦ *vt* incīdere.
note *n* (*mark*) nota *f*; (*comment*) adnotātiō *f*;
(*letter*) litterulae *fpl*; (*sound*) vōx *f*; **make a ~ of**
in commentāriōs referre ♦ *vt* notāre;
(*observe*) animadvertere.
notebook *n* pugillārēs *mpl.*
noted *adj* īnsignis, praeclārus, nōtus.
noteworthy *adj* memorābilis.
nothing *n* nihil, nīl *nt*; ~ **but** merus, nīl nisi;
come to ~ in inritum cadere; **for ~** frustrā;
(*gift*) grātīs, grātuītō; **good for ~** nēquam;
think ~ of nihilī facere.
notice *n* (*official*) prōscrīptiō *f*; (*private*) libellus
m; **attract ~** cōnspicī; **escape ~** latēre; **escape
the ~ of** fallere; **give ~ of** dēnūntiāre; **take ~
of** animadvertere ♦ *vt* animadvertere,
cōnspicere.
noticeable *adj* cōnspicuus, īnsignis.
noticeably *adv* īnsignītē.
notification *n* dēnūntiātiō *f.*
notify *vt* (*event*) dēnūntiāre, indicāre; (*person*)
renūntiāre (*dat*), certiōrem facere.
notion *n* nōtiō *f*, īnfōrmātiō *f*; suspiciō *f.*
notoriety *n* īnfāmia *f.*
notorious *adj* fāmōsus, īnfāmis; (*thing*)
manifestus.
notoriously *adv* manifestō.
notwithstanding *adv* nihilōminus, tamen
♦ *prep:* ~ **the danger** in tantō discrīmine.
nought *n* nihil, nīl *nt.*
noun *n* nōmen *nt.*
nourish *vt* alere, nūtrīre.
nourisher *n* altor *m*, altrīx *f.*
nourishment *n* cibus *m*, alimenta *ntpl.*
novel *adj* novus, inaudītus ♦ *n* fābella *f.*
novelty *n* rēs nova *f*; novitās *f*, īnsolentia *f.*

November *n* mēnsis November *m*; **of ~**
November.
novice *n* tīrō *m.*
now *adv* nunc; (*past*) iam; ~ **and then**
interdum; **just ~** nunc; (*lately*) dūdum, modo;
~ ... ~ modo ... modo ♦ *conj* at, autem.
nowadays *adv* nunc, hodiē.
nowhere *adv* nusquam.
nowise *adv* nullō modō, haudquāquam.
noxious *adj* nocēns, noxius.
nuance *n* color *m.*
nucleus *n* sēmen *nt.*
nude *adj* nūdus.
nudge *vt* fodicāre.
nudity *n* nūdātum corpus *nt.*
nugget *n* massa *f.*
nuisance *n* malum *nt*, incommodum *nt.*
null *adj* inritus.
nullify *vt* inritum facere; (*law*) abrogāre.
numb *adj* torpēns, torpidus; **be ~** torpēre;
become ~ torpēscere.
number *n* numerus *m*; **a ~ of** complūrēs,
aliquot; **a great ~** multitūdō *f*, frequentia *f*; **a
small ~** īnfrequentia *f*; **in large ~s** frequentēs
♦ *vt* numerāre, ēnumerāre.
numberless *adj* innumerābilis.
numbness *n* torpor *m.*
numerous *adj* frequēns, crēber, plūrimī.
nun *n* monacha *f.*
nuptial *adj* nūptiālis.
nuptials *n* nūptiae *fpl.*
nurse *n* nūtrix *f* ♦ *vt* (*child*) nūtrīre; (*sick*)
cūrāre; (*fig*) fovēre.
nursery *n* (*children*) cubiculum *nt*; (*plants*)
sēminārium *nt.*
nursling *n* alumnus *m*, alumna *f.*
nurture *n* ēducātiō *f.*
nut *n* nux *f.*
nutrition *n* alimenta *ntpl.*
nutritious *adj* salūbris.
nutshell *n* putāmen *nt.*
nut tree *n* nux *f.*
nymph *n* nympha *f.*

O, o

O *interj* ō!
oaf *n* agrestis *m.*
oak *n* quercus *f*; (*evergreen*) īlex *f*; (*timber*)
rōbur *nt* ♦ *adj* quernus, īlignus, rōboreus; ~
forest quercētum *nt.*
oakum *n* stuppa *f.*
oar *n* rēmus *m.*
oarsman *n* rēmex *m.*
oaten *adj* avēnāceus.
oath *n* iūsiūrandum *nt*; (*MIL*) sacrāmentum *nt*;

(*imprecation*) exsecrātiō *f*; **false** ~ periūrium *nt*; **take an** ~ iūrāre; **take an** ~ **of allegiance to** in verba iūrāre (*gen*).

oats *n* avēna *f*.

obduracy *n* obstinātus animus *m*.

obdurate *adj* obstinātus, pervicāx.

obdurately *adv* obstinātē.

obedience *n* oboedientia *f*, obsequium *nt*.

obedient *adj* oboediēns, obsequēns; **be** ~ **to** pārēre (*dat*), obtemperāre (*dat*), obsequī (*dat*).

obediently *adv* oboedienter.

obeisance *n* obsequium *nt*; **make** ~ **to** adōrāre.

obelisk *n* obeliscus *m*.

obese *adj* obēsus, pinguis.

obesity *n* obēsitās *f*, pinguitūdō *f*.

obey *vt* pārēre (*dat*), obtemperāre (*dat*), oboedīre (*dat*); ~ **orders** dictō pārēre.

obituary *n* mortēs *fpl*.

object *n* rēs *f*; (*aim*) fīnis *m*, prōpositum *nt*; **be an** ~ **of hate** odiō esse; **with what** ~ quō cōnsiliō ♦ *vi* recūsāre, gravārī; **but, it is ~ed at enim;** ~ **to** improbāre.

objection *n* recūsātiō *f*, mora *f*; **I have no** ~ nīl moror.

objectionable *adj* invīsus, iniūcundus.

objective *adj* externus ♦ *n* prōpositum *nt*, fīnis *m*.

objurgate *vt* obiūrgāre, culpāre.

oblation *n* dōnum *nt*.

obligation *n* (*legal*) dēbitum *nt*; (*moral*) officium *nt*; **lay under an** ~ obligāre, obstringere.

obligatory *adj* dēbitus, necessārius.

oblige *vt* (*force*) cōgere; (*contract*) obligāre, obstringere; (*compliance*) mōrem gerere (*dat*), mōrigerārī (*dat*); **I am ~d to** (*action*) dēbeō (*inf*); (*person*) amāre, grātiam habēre (*dat*).

obliging *adj* cōmis, officiōsus.

obligingly *adv* cōmiter, officiōsē.

oblique *adj* oblīquus.

obliquely *adv* oblīquē.

obliquity *n* (*moral*) prāvitās *f*.

obliterate *vt* dēlēre, oblitterāre.

obliteration *n* litūra *f*.

oblivion *n* oblīviō *f*.

oblivious *adj* oblīviōsus, immemor.

oblong *adj* oblongus.

obloquy *n* vītuperātiō *f*, opprobrium *nt*.

obnoxious *adj* invīsus.

obscene *adj* obscaenus, impūrus.

obscenity *n* obscaenitās *f*, impūritās *f*.

obscure *adj* obscūrus, caecus ♦ *vt* obscūrāre, officere (*dat*).

obscurely *adv* obscūrē; (*speech*) per ambāgēs.

obscurity *n* obscūritās *f*; (*speech*) ambāgēs *fpl*.

obsequies *n* exsequiae *fpl*.

obsequious *adj* officiōsus, ambitiōsus.

obsequiously *adv* officiōsē.

obsequiousness *n* adsentātiō *f*.

observance *n* observantia *f*; (*rite*) rītus *m*.

observant *adj* attentus, dīligēns.

observation *n* observātiō *f*, animadversiō *f*; (*remark*) dictum *nt*.

observe *vt* animadvertere, contemplārī; (*see*) cernere, cōnspicere; (*remark*) dīcere; (*adhere to*) cōnservāre, observāre.

observer *n* spectātor *m*, contemplātor *m*.

obsess *vt* occupāre; **I am ~ed by** tōtus sum in (*abl*).

obsession *n* studium *nt*.

obsolescent *adj*: **be** ~ obsolēscere.

obsolete *adj* obsolētus; **become** ~ exolēscere.

obstacle *n* impedīmentum *nt*, mora *f*.

obstinacy *n* pertinācia *f*, obstinātus animus *m*.

obstinate *adj* pertināx, obstinātus.

obstinately *adv* obstinātō animō.

obstreperous *adj* clāmōsus, ferus.

obstruct *vt* impedīre, obstruere, obstāre (*dat*); (*POL*) intercēdere (*dat*); (*fig*) officere (*dat*).

obstruction *n* impedīmentum *nt*; (*POL*) intercessiō *f*.

obstructionist *n* intercessor *m*.

obtain *vt* adipīscī, nancīscī, cōnsequī; comparāre; (*by request*) impetrāre ♦ *vi* tenēre, obtinēre.

obtrude *vi* sē inculcāre ♦ *vt* ingerere.

obtrusive *adj* importūnus, molestus.

obtuse *adj* hebes, stolidus.

obtusely *adv* stolidē.

obtuseness *n* stupor *m*.

obverse *adj* obversus.

obviate *vt* tollere, praevertere.

obvious *adj* ēvidēns, manifestus, apertus; **it is** ~ appāret.

obviously *adv* ēvidenter, apertē, manifestō.

occasion *n* occāsiō *f*, locus *m*; (*reason*) causa *f* ♦ *vt* movēre, facessere, auctōrem esse (*gen*).

occasional *adj* fortuītus.

occasionally *adv* interdum, nōnnunquam.

occidental *adj* occidentālis.

occult *adj* arcānus.

occupancy *n* possessiō *f*.

occupant *n* habitātor *m*, possessor *m*.

occupation *n* quaestus *m*, occupātiō *f*.

occupier *n* possessor *m*.

occupy *vt* possidēre; (*MIL*) occupāre; (*space*) complēre; (*attention*) distinēre, occupāre.

occur *vi* ēvenīre, accidere; (*to mind*) occurrere, in mentem venīre.

occurrence *n* ēventum *nt*; rēs *f*.

ocean *n* mare *nt*, ōceanus *m*.

October *n* mēnsis Octōber *m*; **of** ~ Octōber.

ocular *adj* oculōrum; **give** ~ **proof of** ante oculōs pōnere, videntī dēmōnstrāre.

odd *adj* (*number*) impār; (*moment*) subsecīvus; (*appearance*) novus, īnsolitus.

oddity *n* novitās *f*; (*person*) homō rīdiculus *m*.

oddly *adv* mīrum in modum.

odds *n* praestantia *f*; **be at** ~ **with** dissidēre cum; **the** ~ **are against us** imparēs sumus; **the** ~ **are in our favour** superiōrēs sumus.

ode *n* carmen *nt*.

odious *adj* invīsus, odiōsus.

odium *n* invidia *f*.

odorous *adj* odōrātus.
odour *n* odor *m.*
of *prep gen;* (*origin*) ex, dē; (*cause*) *abl;* **all ~ us**
nōs omnēs; **the city ~ Rome** urbs Rōma.
off *adv* procul; (*prefix*) ab-; **~ and on** interdum;
~ with you aufer tē; **come ~** ēvādere; **well ~**
beātus; **well ~ for** abundāns (*abl*).
offal *n* quisquiliae *fpl.*
offence *n* offēnsiō *f;* (*legal*) dēlictum *nt;*
commit an ~ dēlinquere.
offend *vt* laedere, offendere; **be ~ed** aegrē
ferre ♦ *vi* delinquere; **~ against** peccāre in
(*acc*), violāre.
offender *n* reus *m.*
offensive *adj* odiōsus; (*smell*) gravis;
(*language*) contumēliōsus; **take the ~** bellum
înferre.
offensively *adv* odiōsē; graviter.
offer *vt* offerre, dare, praebēre; (*hand*)
porrigere; (*violence*) adferre; (*honour*)
dēferre; (*with verb*) profitērī, pollicērī ♦ *n*
condiciō *f;* **~ for sale** venditāre.
offering *n* dōnum *nt;* (*to the dead*) înferiae *fpl.*
off-hand *adj* neglegēns, incūriōsus.
office *n* (*POL*) magistrātus *m,* mūnus *nt,* honōs
m; (*kindness*) officium *nt;* (*place*) mēnsa *f.*
officer *n* praefectus *m;* lēgātus *m.*
official *adj* pūblicus ♦ *n* adiūtor *m,* minister *m.*
officially *adv* pūblicē.
officiate *vi* operārī, officiō fungī.
officious *adj* molestus.
officiously *adv* molestē.
officiousness *n* occursātiō *f.*
offing *n:* **in the ~** procul.
offset *vt* compēnsāre.
offspring *n* prōgeniēs *f,* līberī *mpl;* (*animal*)
fētus *m.*
often *adv* saepe, saepenumerō; **as ~ as**
quotiēns; totiēs … quotiēns; **how ~?**
quotiēns?; **so ~** totiēns; **very ~** persaepe.
ogle *vi:* **~ at** līmīs oculīs intuērī.
ogre *n* mōnstrum *nt.*
oh *interj* (*joy, surprise*) ōh!; (*sorrow*) prō!
oil *n* oleum *nt* ♦ *vt* ungere.
oily *adj* oleōsus.
ointment *n* unguentum *nt.*
old *adj* (*person*) senex; (*thing*) vetus; (*ancient*)
antīquus, prīscus; **~ age** senectūs *f;* **be ten
years ~** decem annōs habēre; **ten years ~**
decem annōs nātus; **two years ~** bīmus; **good
~** antīquus; **good ~ days** antīquitās *f;* **grow ~**
senēscere; **of ~** quondam.
olden *adj* prīscus, prīstinus.
older *adj* nātū māior, senior.
oldest *adj* nātū māximus.
old-fashioned *adj* antīquus, obsolētus.
old man *n* senex *m.*
oldness *n* vetustās *f.*
old woman *n* anus *f.*
oligarchy *n* paucōrum dominātiō *f,*
optimātium factiō *f.*
olive *n* olea *f;* **~ orchard** olīvētum *nt.*

Olympiad *n* Olympias *f.*
Olympic *adj* Olympicus; **win an ~ victory**
Olympia vincere.
Olympic Games *n* Olympia *ntpl.*
omen *n* ōmen *nt,* auspicium *nt;* **announce a bad
~** obnūntiāre; **obtain favourable ~s** litāre.
ominous *adj* înfaustus, mināx.
omission *n* praetermissiō *f,* neglegentia *f.*
omit *vt* ōmittere, praetermittere.
omnipotence *n* înfīnīta potestās *f.*
omnipotent *adj* omnipotēns.
on *prep* (*place*) in (*abl*), in- (*prefix*); (*time*) *abl;*
(*coast of*) ad (*acc*); (*subject*) dē (*abl*); (*side*) ab
(*abl*) ♦ *adv* porrō, usque; **and so ~** ac
deinceps; **~ hearing the news** nūntiō acceptō;
~ equal terms (*in battle*) aequō Marte; **~ the
following day** posterō/proximō diē; **~**
postrīdiē; **~ this side of** citrā (+ *acc*).
once *adv* semel; (*past*) ōlim, quondam; **at ~**
extemplō, statim; (*together*) simul; **for ~**
aliquandō; **~ and for all** semel; **~ more** dēnuō,
iterum; **~ upon a time** ōlim, quondam.
one *num* ūnus ♦ *pron* quīdam; (*of two*) alter,
altera, alterum; **~ and the same** ūnus; **~
another** inter sē, alius alium; **~ or the other**
alteruter; **~ day** ōlim; **~ each** singulī; **~ would
have thought** crēderēs; **be ~ of** in numerō
esse (*gen*); **be at ~** idem sentīre; **it is all ~**
nihil interest; **the ~** alter, hic; **this is the ~**
hōc illud est.
one-eyed *adj* luscus.
oneness *n* ūnitās *f.*
onerous *adj* gravis.
oneself *pron* ipse; (*reflexive*) sē.
one-sided *adj* inaequālis, inīquus.
onion *n* caepe *nt.*
onlooker *n* spectātor *m.*
only *adj* ūnus, sōlus; (*son*) ūnicus ♦ *adv* sōlum,
tantum, modo; (*with clause*) nōn nisi, nīl nisi,
nihil aliud quam; (*time*) dēmum; **if ~** sī modo;
(*wish*) utinam.
onrush *n* incursus *m.*
onset *n* impetus *m.*
onslaught *n* incursus *m;* **make an ~ on** (*words*)
invehī in (*acc*).
onto *prep* in (+ *acc*).
onus *n* officium *nt.*
onward, onwards *adv* porrō.
onyx *n* onyx *m.*
ooze *vi* mānāre, stillāre.
opaque *adj* haud perlūcidus.
open *adj* apertus; (*wide*) patēns, hiāns;
(*ground*) pūrus, apertus; (*question*) integer;
lie ~ patēre; **stand ~** hiāre; **throw ~**
adaperīre, patefacere; **it is ~ to me to** mihī
integrum est (*inf*); **while the question is still ~**
rē integrā ♦ *vt* aperīre, patefacere; (*book*)
ēvolvere; (*letter*) resolvere; (*speech*)
exōrdīrī; (*with ceremony*) inaugurāre; (*will*)
resignāre ♦ *vi* aperīrī, hiscere; (*sore*)
recrūdēscere; **~ out** extendere, pandere; **~
up** (*country*) aperīre.
open air *n:* **in the ~** sub dīvō.

open-handed _adj_ largus, mūnificus.
open-handedness _n_ largitās _f._
open-hearted _adj_ ingenuus.
opening _n_ forāmen _nt_, hiātus _m_; (_ceremony_) cōnsecrātiō _f_; (_opportunity_) occāsiō _f_, ānsa _f_ ♦ _adj_ prīmus.
openly _adv_ palam, apertē.
open-mouthed _adj_: **stand ~ at** inhiāre.
operate _vi_ rem gerere ♦ _vt_ movēre.
operation _n_ opus _nt_, āctiō _f_; (_MED_) sectiō _f._
operative _adj_ efficāx.
ophthalmia _n_ lippitūdō _f._
opiate _adj_ somnifer.
opine _vi_ opīnārī, existimāre.
opinion _n_ sententia _f_; (_of person_) existimātiō _f_; **public ~** fāma _f_; **in my ~** meō iūdiciō, meō animō.
opponent _n_ adversārius _m_, hostis _m._
opportune _adj_ opportūnus, tempestīvus.
opportunely _adv_ opportūnē.
opportunity _n_ occāsiō _f_; (_to act_) facultās _f_, potestās _f._
oppose _vt_ (_barrier_) obicere; (_contrast_) oppōnere ♦ _vi_ adversārī (_dat_), resistere (_dat_), obstāre (_dat_); **be ~d to** adversārī (_dat_); (_opinion_) dīversum esse ab.
opposite _adj_ (_facing_) adversus; (_contrary_) contrārius, dīversus ♦ _prep_ contrā (_acc_), adversus (_acc_); **directly ~ ē** regiōne (_gen_) ♦ _adv_ ex adversō.
opposition _n_ repugnantia _f_; (_party_) factiō adversa _f._
oppress _vt_ opprimere, adflīgere; (_burden_) premere, onerāre.
oppression _n_ iniūria _f_, servitūs _f._
oppressive _adj_ gravis, inīquus; **become more ~** ingravēscere.
oppressor _n_ tyrannus _m._
opprobrious _adj_ turpis.
opprobriously _adv_ turpiter.
opprobrium _n_ dēdecus _nt_, ignōminia _f._
optical _adj_ oculōrum.
optical illusion _n_ oculōrum lūdibrium _nt._
optimism _n_ spēs _f._
option _n_ optiō _f_, arbitrium _nt_; **I have no ~** nōn est arbitriī meī.
optional _adj_: **it is ~ for you** optiō tua est.
opulence _n_ opēs _fpl_, cōpia _f._
opulent _adj_ dīves, cōpiōsus.
or _conj_ aut, vel, -ve; (_after_ **utrum**) an; **~ else** aliōquīn; **~ not** (_direct_) annōn; (_indirect_) necne.
oracle _n_ ōrāculum _nt._
oracular _adj_ fātidicus; (_fig_) obscūrus.
oral _adj_: **give an ~ message** vōce nūntiāre.
orally _adv_ vōce, verbīs.
oration _n_ ōrātiō _f._
orator _n_ ōrātor _m._
oratorical _adj_ ōrātōrius.
oratory _n_ ēloquentia _f_, rhētoricē _f_; (_for prayer_) sacellum _nt_; **of ~** dīcendī, ōrātōrius.
orb _n_ orbis _m._
orbit _n_ orbis _m_, ambitus _m._
orchard _n_ pōmārium _nt._

ordain _vt_ ēdīcere, sancīre.
ordeal _n_ labor _m._
order _n_ (_arrangement_) ōrdō _m_; (_class_) ōrdō _m_; (_battle_) aciēs _f_; (_command_) iussum _nt_, imperium _nt_; (_money_) perscrīptiō _f_; **in ~** dispositus; (_succession_) deinceps; **in ~ that/to** ut (+ _subj_); **in ~ that not nē** (+ _subj_); **put in ~** dispōnere, ōrdināre; **by ~ of** iussū (_gen_); **out of ~** incompositus; **without ~s from** iniussū (_gen_) ♦ _vt_ (_arrange_) dispōnere, ōrdināre; (_command_) iubēre (+ _acc and infin_), imperāre (_dat and ut/nē_ +_subj_).
orderly _adj_ ōrdinātus; (_conduct_) modestus ♦ _n_ accēnsus _m._
ordinance _n_ ēdictum _nt_, institūtum _nt._
ordinarily _adv_ plērumque, ferē.
ordinary _adj_ ūsitātus, solitus, cottīdiānus.
ordnance _n_ tormenta _ntpl._
ordure _n_ stercus _m._
ore _n_ aes _nt_; **iron ~** ferrum īnfectum _nt._
Oread _n_ (_MYTH_) Oreas _f._
organ _n_ (_bodily_) membrum _nt_; (_musical_) organum _nt_, hydraulus _m._
organic _adj_ nātūrālis.
organically _adv_ nātūrā.
organization _n_ ōrdinātiō _f_, structūra _f._
organize _vt_ ōrdināre, īnstituere, adparāre.
orgies _n_ orgia _ntpl._
orgy _n_ cōmissātiō _f._
orient _n_ oriēns _m._
oriental _adj_ Asiāticus.
orifice _n_ ōstium _nt._
origin _n_ orīgō _f_, prīncipium _nt_; (_source_) fōns _m_; (_birth_) genus _nt._
original _adj_ prīmus, prīstinus; (_LIT_) proprius ♦ _n_ exemplar _nt._
originally _adv_ prīncipiō, antīquitus.
originate _vt_ īnstituere, auctōrem esse (_gen_) ♦ _vi_ exorīrī; **~ in** innāscī in (_abl_), initium dūcere ab.
originator _n_ auctor _m._
orisons _n_ precēs _fpl._
ornament _n_ ōrnāmentum _nt_; (_fig_) decus _nt_ ♦ _vt_ ōrnāre, decorāre; **I am ~** ōrnamentō sum.
ornamental _adj_ decōrus; **be ~** decorī esse.
ornamentally _adv_ ōrnātē.
ornate _adj_ ōrnātus.
ornately _adv_ ōrnātē.
orphan _n_ orbus _m_, orba _f._
orphaned _adj_ orbātus.
orthodox _adj_ antīquus.
orthography _n_ orthographia _f._
oscillate _vi_ reciprocāre.
osculate _vt_ ōsculārī.
osier _n_ vīmen _nt_ ♦ _adj_ vīmineus.
osprey _n_ haliaeetos _m._
ostensible _adj_ speciōsus.
ostensibly _adv_ per speciem.
ostentation _n_ iactātiō _f_, ostentātiō _f._
ostentatious _adj_ glōriōsus, ambitiōsus.
ostentatiously _adv_ glōriōsē.
ostler _n_ agāsō _m._
ostrich _n_ strūthiocamēlus _m._

other *adj* alius; (*of two*) alter; **one or the ~** alteruter; **every ~ year** tertiō quōque annō; **on the ~ side of** ultrā (*+ acc*); **of ~s** aliēnus.
otherwise *adv* aliter; (*if not*) aliōquī.
otter *n* lutra *f*.
ought *vi* dēbēre (*+ infin or gerundive of vt*); **I ~ mē** oportet; **I ~ to have said** dēbuī dīcere.
ounce *n* ūncia *f*; **two ~s** sextāns *m*; **three ~s** quadrāns *m*; **four ~s** triēns *m*; **five ~s** quīncūnx *m*; **six ~s** sēmis *m*; **seven ~s** septūnx *m*; **eight ~s** bēs *m*; **nine ~s** dōdrāns *m*; **ten ~s** dextāns *m*; **eleven ~s** deūnx *m*.
our *adj* noster.
ourselves *pron* ipsī; (*reflexive*) nōs.
oust *vt* extrūdere, ēicere.
out *adv* (*rest*) forīs; (*motion*) forās; **~ of** dē, ē/ex (*abl*); (*cause*) propter (*acc*); (*beyond*) extrā, ultrā (*acc*); **be ~** (*book*) in manibus esse; (*calculation*) errāre; (*fire*) exstinctum esse; (*secret*) palam esse.
outbreak *n* initium *nt*, ēruptiō *f*.
outburst *n* ēruptiō *f*.
outcast *n* profugus *m*.
outcome *n* ēventus *m*, exitus *m*.
outcry *n* clāmor *m*, adclāmātiō *f*; **raise an ~ against** obstrepere (*dat*).
outdistance *vt* praevertere.
outdo *vt* superāre.
outdoor *adj* sub dīvō.
outer *adj* exterior.
outermost *adj* extrēmus.
outfit *n* īnstrūmenta *ntpl*; vestīmenta *ntpl*.
outflank *vt* circumīre.
outgrow *vt* excēdere ex.
outing *n* excursiō *f*.
outlandish *adj* barbarus.
outlaw *n* prōscrīptus *m* ♦ *vt* prōscrībere, aquā et ignī interdīcere (*dat*).
outlawry *n* aquae et ignis interdictiō *f*.
outlay *n* impēnsa *f*, sūmptus *m*.
outlet *n* ēmissārium *nt*, exitus *m*.
outline *n* ductus *m*, adumbrātiō *f* ♦ *vt* adumbrāre.
outlive *vt* superesse (*dat*).
outlook *n* prōspectus *m*.
outlying *adj* longinquus, exterior.
outnumber *vt* numerō superiōrēs esse, multitūdine superāre.
out-of-doors *adv* forīs.
outpost *n* statiō *f*.
outpouring *n* effūsiō *f*.
output *n* fructus *m*.
outrage *n* flāgitium *nt*, iniūria *f* ♦ *vt* laedere, violāre.
outrageous *adj* flāgitiōsus, indignus.
outrageously *adv* flāgitiōsē.
outrider *n* praecursor *m*.
outright *adv* penitus, prōrsus; semel.
outrun *vt* praevertere.
outset *n* initium *nt*.
outshine *vt* praelūcēre (*dat*).
outside *adj* externus ♦ *adv* extrā, forīs; (*motion to*) forās; **~ in** inversus; **from ~**

extrīnsecus ♦ *n* exterior pars *f*; (*show*) speciēs *f*; **at the ~** summum, ad summum; **on the ~** extrīnsecus ♦ *prep* extrā (*acc*).
outsider *n* aliēnus *m*; (*POL*) novus homō *m*.
outskirts *n* suburbānus ager *m*; **on the ~** suburbānus.
outspoken *adj* līber.
outspokenness *n* lībertās *f*.
outspread *adj* patulus.
outstanding *adj* ēgregius, īnsignis, singulāris; (*debt*) residuus.
outstep *vt* excēdere.
outstretched *adj* passus, porrēctus, extentus.
outstrip *vt* praevertere.
outvote *vt* suffrāgiīs superāre.
outward *adj* externus; **~ form** speciēs *f* ♦ *adv* domō, forās.
outweigh *vt* praeponderāre.
outwit *vt* dēcipere, circumvenīre.
outwork *n* prōpugnāculum *nt*, bracchium *nt*.
outworn *adj* exolētus.
oval *adj* ōvātus ♦ *n* ōvum *nt*.
ovation *n* (*triumph*) ovātiō *f*; **receive an ~** cum laudibus excipī.
oven *n* furnus *m*, fornāx *f*.
over *prep* (*above*) super (*abl*), suprā (*acc*); (*across*) super (*acc*); (*extent*) per (*acc*); (*time*) inter (*acc*); **~ and above** super (*acc*), praeter (*acc*); **all ~** per; **~ against** adversus (*acc*) ♦ *adv* suprā; (*excess*) nimis; (*done*) cōnfectus; **~ again** dēnuō; **~ and above** īnsuper; **~ and ~** identidem; **be left ~** superesse, restāre; **it is all ~ with** āctum est dē.
overall *adj* tōtus ♦ *adv* ubīque, passim.
overawe *vt* formīdinem inicere (*dat*).
overbalance *vi* titubāre.
overbearing *adj* superbus.
overboard *adv* ē nāvī, in mare; **throw ~** excutere, iactāre.
overbold *adj* importūnus.
overburden *vt* praegravāre.
overcast *adj* nūbilus.
overcoat *n* paenula *f*, lacerna *f*.
overcome *vt* superāre, vincere.
overconfidence *n* cōnfīdentia *f*.
overconfident *adj* cōnfīdēns.
overdo *vt* modum excēdere in (*abl*).
overdone *adj* (*style*) pūtidus.
overdraw *vt* (*style*) exaggerāre.
overdue *adj* (*money*) residuus.
overestimate *vt* māiōris aestimāre.
overflow *n* ēluviō *f* ♦ *vi* abundāre, redundāre ♦ *vt* inundāre.
overgrown *adj* obsitus; **be ~** luxuriāre.
overhang *vt*, *vi* impendēre, imminēre (*dat*).
overhaul *vt* reficere.
overhead *adv* īnsuper.
overhear *vt* excipere, auscultāre.
overjoyed *adj* nimiō gaudiō ēlātus.
overladen *adj* praegravātus.
overland *adv* terrā.
overlap *vt* implicāre.
overlay *vt* indūcere.

overload *vt* (*fig*) obruere.
overlook *vt* (*place*) dēspectāre, imminēre (*dat*); (*knowledge*) ignōrāre; (*notice*) neglegere, praetermittere; (*fault*) ignōscere (*dat*).
overlord *n* dominus *m*.
overmaster *vt* dēvincere.
overmuch *adv* nimis, plūs aequō.
overnight *adj* nocturnus ♦ *adv* noctū.
overpower *vt* superāre, domāre, obruere, opprimere.
overpraise *vt* in māius extollere.
overrate *vt* māiōris aestimāre.
overreach *vt* circumvenīre.
overriding *adj* praecipuus.
overrule *vt* rescindere.
overrun *vt* pervagārī; (*fig*) obsidēre.
oversea *adj* trānsmarīnus.
oversee *vt* praeesse (*dat*).
overseer *n* cūrātor *m*, custōs *m*.
overset *vt* ēvertere.
overshadow *vt* officere (*dat*).
overshoot *vt* excēdere.
oversight *n* neglegentia *f*.
overspread *vt* offendere (*dat*), obdūcere.
overstep *vt* excēdere.
overt *adj* apertus.
overtake *vt* cōnsequī; (*surprise*) opprimere, dēprehendere.
overtax *vt* (*fig*) abūtī (*abl*).
overthrow *vt* ēvertere; (*destroy*) prōflīgāre, dēbellāre ♦ *n* ēversiō *f*, ruīna *f*.
overtly *adv* palam.
overtop *vt* superāre.
overture *n* exōrdium *nt*; **make ~s to** temptāre, agere cum, lēgātōs mittere ad.
overturn *vt* ēvertere.
overweening *adj* superbus, adrogāns, īnsolēns.
overwhelm *vt* obruere, dēmergere, opprimere.
overwhelming *adj* īnsignis, vehementissimus.
overwhelmingly *adv* mīrum quantum.
overwork *vi* plūs aequō labōrāre ♦ *vt* cōnficere ♦ *n* immodicus labor *m*.
overwrought *adj* (*emotion*) ēlātus; (*style*) ēlabōrātus.
owe *vt* dēbēre.
owing *adj*: **be ~** dēbērī; **~ to** (*person*) per; (*cause*) ob/propter (*acc*).
owl *n* būbō *m*; ulula *f*.
own *adj* proprius; **my ~** meus; **have of one's ~** domī habēre; **hold one's ~** parem esse ♦ *vt* possidēre, habēre; (*admit*) fatērī, cōnfitērī.
owner *n* dominus *m*, possessor *m*.
ownership *n* possessiō *f*, mancipium *nt*.
ox *n* bōs *m*.
ox herd *n* bubulcus *m*.
oyster *n* ostrea *f*.

P, p

pace *n* passus *m*; (*speed*) gradus *m*; **keep ~ gradum cōnferre** ♦ *vi* incēdere; **~ up and down** spatiārī, inambulāre.
pacific *adj* pācificus; (*quiet*) placidus.
pacification *n* pācificātiō *f*.
pacifist *n* imbellis *m*.
pacify *vt* (*anger*) plācāre; (*rising*) sēdāre.
pack *n* (*MIL*) sarcina *f*; (*animals*) grex *m*; (*people*) turba *f* ♦ *vt* (*kit*) colligere; (*crowd*) stīpāre; **~ together** coartāre; **~ up** colligere, compōnere ♦ *vi* vāsa colligere; **send ~ing** missum facere ♦ *adj* (*animal*) clītellārius.
package *n* fasciculus *m*, sarcina *f*.
packet *n* fasciculus *m*; (*ship*) nāvis āctuāria *f*.
packhorse *n* iūmentum *nt*.
packsaddle *n* clītellae *fpl*.
pact *n* foedus *nt*, pactum *nt*.
pad *n* pulvillus *m*.
padding *n* tōmentum *nt*.
paddle *n* rēmus *m* ♦ *vi* rēmigāre.
paddock *n* saeptum *nt*.
paean *n* paeān *m*.
pagan *adj* pāgānus.
page *n* (*book*) pāgina *f*; (*boy*) puer *m*.
pageant *n* pompa *f*, spectāculum *nt*.
pageantry *n* adparātus *m*.
pail *n* situla *f*.
pain *n* dolor *m*; **be in ~** dolēre ♦ *vt* dolōre adficere.
painful *adj* acerbus; (*work*) labōriōsus.
painfully *adv* acerbē, labōriōsē.
painless *adj* dolōris expers.
painlessly *adv* sine dolōre.
painlessness *n* indolentia *f*.
pains *npl* opera *f*; **take ~** operam dare; **take ~ with** (*art*) ēlabōrāre.
painstaking *adj* dīligēns, operōsus.
painstakingly *adv* dīligenter, summā cūrā.
paint *n* pigmentum *nt*; (*cosmetic*) fūcus *m* ♦ *vt* pingere; (*red*) fūcāre; (*in words*) dēpingere; (*portrait*) dēpingere.
paintbrush *n* pēnicillus *m*.
painter *n* pictor *m*.
painting *n* pictūra *f*.
pair *n* pār *nt* ♦ *vt* coniungere, compōnere.
palace *n* rēgia *f*.
palatable *adj* suāvis, iūcundus.
palate *n* palātum *nt*.
palatial *adj* rēgius.
palaver *n* colloquium *nt*, sermunculī *mpl*.
pale *n* pālus *m*, vallus *m*; **beyond the ~** extrāneus ♦ *adj* pallidus; **look ~** pallēre; **grow ~** pallēscere; **~ brown** subfuscus; **~ green** subviridis ♦ *vi* pallēscere.
paleness *n* pallor *m*.

palimpsest *n* palimpsēstus *m*.
paling *n* saepēs *f*.
palisade *n* (*MIL*) vallum *nt*.
palish *adj* pallidulus.
pall *n* (*funeral*) pallium *nt* ♦ *vi* taedēre.
pallet *n* grabātus *m*.
palliasse *n* strāmentum *nt*.
palliate *vt* extenuāre, excūsāre.
palliation *n* excūsātiō *f*.
palliative *n* lēnīmentum *nt*.
pallid *adj* pallidus.
pallor *n* pallor *m*.
palm *n* (*hand*) palma *f*; (*tree*) palma *f* ♦ *vt*: ~ **off** impōnere.
palmy *adj* flōrēns.
palpable *adj* tractābilis; (*fig*) manifestus.
palpably *adv* manifestō, propalam.
palpitate *vi* palpitāre, micāre.
palpitation *n* palpitātiō *f*.
palsied *adj* membrīs captus.
palsy *n* paralysis *f*.
paltry *adj* vīlis, frīvolus.
pamper *vt* indulgēre (*dat*).
pampered *adj* dēlicātus.
pamphlet *n* libellus *m*.
pan *n* patina *f*, patella *f*; (*frying*) sartāgō *f*; (*of balance*) lanx *f*.
pancake *n* laganum *nt*.
pander *n* lēnō *m* ♦ *vi*: ~ **to** lēnōcinārī (*dat*).
panegyric *n* laudātiō *f*.
panegyrist *n* laudātor *m*.
panel *n* (*wall*) abacus *m*; (*ceiling*) lacūnār *nt*; (*judges*) decuria *f*.
panelled *adj* laqueātus.
pang *n* dolor *m*.
panic *n* pavor *m* ♦ *vi* trepidāre.
panic-stricken *adj* pavidus.
panniers *n* clītellae *fpl*.
panoply *n* arma *ntpl*.
panorama *n* prōspectus *m*.
panpipe *n* fistula *f*.
pant *vi* anhēlāre.
panther *n* panthēra *f*.
panting *n* anhēlitus *m*.
pantomime *n* mīmus *m*.
pantry *n* cella pēnāria *f*.
pap *n* mamma *f*.
paper *n* charta *f*.
papyrus *n* papyrus *f*.
par *n*: **on a** ~ **with** pār (*dat*).
parable *n* parabolē *f*.
parade *n* pompa *f*; (*show*) adparātus *m* ♦ *vt* trādūcere, iactāre ♦ *vi* pompam dūcere, incēdere.
paradox *n* verba sēcum repugnantia; ~**es** *pl* paradoxa *ntpl*.
paragon *n* exemplar *nt*, specimen *nt*.
paragraph *n* caput *nt*.
parallel *adj* parallēlus; (*fig*) cōnsimilis.
paralyse *vt* dēbilitāre; (*with fear*) percellere; **be** ~**d** torpēre.
paralysis *n* dēbilitās *f*; (*fig*) torpēdō *f*.
paramount *adj* prīnceps, summus.

paramour *n* adulter *m*.
parapet *n* lōrīca *f*.
paraphernalia *n* adparātus *m*.
paraphrase *vt* vertere.
parasite *n* parasītus *m*.
parasol *n* umbella *f*.
parboiled *adj* subcrūdus.
parcel *n* fasciculus *m* ♦ *vt*: ~ **out** distribuere, dispertīre.
parch *vt* torrēre.
parched *adj* torridus, āridus; **be** ~ ārēre.
parchment *n* membrāna *f*.
pardon *n* venia *f* ♦ *vt* ignōscere (*dat*); (*offence*) condōnāre.
pardonable *adj* ignōscendus.
pare *vt* dēglūbere; (*nails*) resecāre.
parent *n* parēns *m/f*, genitor *m*, genetrīx *f*.
parentage *n* stirps *f*, genus *nt*.
parental *adj* patrius.
parenthesis *n* interclūsiō *f*.
parings *n* praesegmina *ntpl*.
parish *n* (*ECCL*) paroecia *f*.
parity *n* aequālitās *f*.
park *n* hortī *mpl*.
parlance *n* sermō *m*.
parley *n* colloquium *nt* ♦ *vi* colloquī, agere.
parliament *n* senātus *m*; **house of** ~ cūria *f*.
parliamentary *adj* senātōrius.
parlour *n* exedrium *nt*.
parlous *adj* difficilis, perīculōsus.
parochial *adj* mūnicipālis.
parody *n* carmen ioculāre *nt* ♦ *vt* calumniārī.
parole *n* fidēs *f*.
paronomasia *n* agnōminātiō *f*.
paroxysm *n* accessus *m*.
parricide *n* (*doer*) parricīda *m*; (*deed*) parricīdium *nt*.
parrot *n* psittacus *m*.
parry *vt* ēlūdere, prōpulsāre.
parsimonious *adj* parcus.
parsimoniously *adv* parcē.
parsimony *n* parsimōnia *f*, frūgālitās *f*.
part *n* pars *f*; (*play*) partēs *fpl*, persōna *f*; (*duty*) officium *nt*; ~**s** loca *ntpl*; (*ability*) ingenium *nt*; **for my** ~ equidem; **for the most** ~ māximam partem; **on the** ~ **of** ab; **act the** ~ **of** persōnam sustinēre, partēs agere; **have no** ~ **in** expers esse (*gen*); **in** ~ partim; **it is the** ~ **of a wise man** sapientis est; **play one's** ~ officiō satisfacere; **take** ~ **in** interesse (*dat*), particeps esse (*gen*); **take in good** ~ in bonam partem accipere; **take someone's** ~ adesse alicuī, dēfendere aliquem; **from all** ~**s** undique; **in foreign** ~**s** peregrē; **in two** ~**s** bifāriam; (*MIL*) bipartītō; **in three** ~**s** trifāriam; (*MIL*) tripartītō; **of** ~**s ingeniōsus** ♦ *vt* dīvidere, sēparāre, dirimere; ~ **company** dīversōs discēdere ♦ *vi* dīgredī, discēdere; (*things*) dissilīre; ~ **with** renūntiāre.
partake *vi* interesse, particeps esse; ~ **of** gustāre.
partial *adj* (*biased*) inīquus, studiōsus; (*incomplete*) mancus; **be** ~ **to** favēre (*dat*),

studēre (*dat*); **win a ~ victory** aliquā ex parte
vincere.
partiality *n* favor *m*, studium *nt*.
partially *adv* partim, aliquā ex parte.
participant *n* particeps *m/f*.
participate *vi* interesse, particeps esse.
participation *n* societās *f*.
particle *n* particula *f*.
parti-coloured *adj* versicolor, varius.
particular *adj* (*own*) proprius; (*special*)
praecipuus; (*exact*) dīligēns, accūrātus;
(*fastidious*) fastīdiōsus; **a ~ person** quīdam ♦
n rēs *f*; **with full ~s** subtīliter; **give all the ~s**
omnia exsequī; **in ~** praesertim.
particularity *n* subtīlitās *f*.
particularize *vt* singula exsequī.
particularly *adv* praecipuē, praesertim, in
prīmīs, māximē.
parting *n* dīgressus *m*, discessus *m* ♦ *adj*
ultimus.
partisan *n* fautor *m*, studiōsus *m*.
partisanship *n* studium *nt*.
partition *n* (*act*) partītiō *f*; (*wall*) pariēs *m*;
(*compartment*) loculāmentum *nt* ♦ *vt*
dīvidere.
partly *adv* partim, ex parte.
partner *n* socius *m*; (*in office*) collēga *f*.
partnership *n* societās *f*; **form a ~** societātem
inīre.
partridge *n* perdīx *m/f*.
parturition *n* partus *m*.
party *n* (POL) factiō *f*, partēs *fpl*; (*entertainment*)
convīvium *nt*; (MIL) manus *f*; (*individual*) homō
m/f; (*associate*) socius *m*, cōnscius *m*.
party spirit *n* studium *nt*.
parvenu *n* novus homō *m*.
pass *n* (*hill*) saltus *m*; (*narrow*) angustiae *fpl*,
faucēs *fpl*; (*crisis*) discrīmen *nt*; (*document*)
diplōma *nt*; (*fighting*) petītiō *f*; **things have
come to such a ~** in eum locum ventum est,
adeō rēs rediit ♦ *vi* īre, praeterīre; (*time*)
trānsīre; (*property*) pervenīre; **~ away** abīre;
(*die*) morī, perīre; (*fig*) dēfluere; **~ by**
praeterīre; **~ for** habērī prō (*abl*); **~ off** abīre;
~ on pergere; **~ over** trānsīre; **come to ~** fierī,
ēvenīre; **let ~** intermittere, praetermittere ♦
vt praeterīre; (*riding*) praetervehī; (*by hand*)
trādere; (*law*) iubēre; (*limit*) excēdere;
(*sentence*) interpōnere, dīcere; (*test*)
satisfacere (*dat*); (*time*) dēgere, agere; **~
accounts** ratiōnēs ratās habēre; **~ the day**
diem cōnsūmere; **~ a law** lēgem ferre; **~ a
decree** dēcernere; **~ off** ferre; **~ over**
praeterīre, mittere; (*fault*) ignōscere (*dat*); **~
round** trādere; **~ through** trānsīre.
passable *adj* (*place*) pervius; (*standard*)
mediocris.
passably *adv* mediocriter.
passage *n* iter *nt*, cursus *m*; (*land*) trānsitus *m*;
(*sea*) trānsmissiō *f*; (*book*) locus *m*; **of ~** (*bird*)
advena.
passenger *n* vector *m*.
passer-by *n* praeteriēns *m*.

passing *n* obitus *m* ♦ *adj* admodum.
passion *n* animī mōtus *m*, permōtiō *f*, ārdor *m*;
(*anger*) īra *f*; (*lust*) libīdō *f*.
passionate *adj* ārdēns, impotēns, ācer;
īrācundus.
passionately *adv* vehementer, ārdenter;
īrācundē; **be ~ in love** amōre ārdēre.
passive *adj* iners.
passiveness *n* inertia *f*, patientia *f*.
passport *n* diplōma *nt*.
password *n* tessera *f*.
past *adj* praeteritus; (*recent*) proximus ♦ *n*
praeterita *ntpl* ♦ *prep* praeter (*acc*); (*beyond*)
ultrā (*acc*).
paste *n* glūten *nt* ♦ *vt* glūtināre.
pastime *n* lūdus *m*, oblectāmentum *nt*.
pastoral *adj* pastōrālis; (*poem*) būcolicus.
pastry *n* crustum *nt*.
pasture *n* pāstus *m*, pāscuum *nt* ♦ *vt* pāscere.
pat *vt* dēmulcēre ♦ *adj* opportūnus.
patch *n* pannus *m* ♦ *vt* resarcīre.
patchwork *n* centō *m*.
pate *n* caput *nt*.
patent *adj* apertus, manifestus ♦ *n*
prīvilēgium *nt*.
patently *adv* manifestō.
paternal *adj* paternus.
path *n* sēmita *f*, trāmes *m*.
pathetic *adj* miserābilis.
pathetically *adv* miserābiliter.
pathfinder *n* explōrātor *m*.
pathless *adj* āvius.
pathos *n* misericordia *f*; (RHET) dolor *m*.
pathway *n* sēmita *f*.
patience *n* patientia *f*.
patient *adj* patiēns ♦ *n* aeger *m*.
patiently *adv* patienter, aequō animō.
patois *n* sermō *m*.
patrician *adj* patricius ♦ *n* patricius *m*.
patrimony *n* patrimōnium *nt*.
patriot *n* amāns patriae *m*.
patriotic *adj* pius, amāns patriae.
patriotically *adv* prō patriā.
patriotism *n* amor patriae *m*.
patrol *n* excubiae *fpl* ♦ *vi* circumīre.
patron *n* patrōnus *m*, fautor *m*.
patronage *n* patrōcinium *nt*.
patroness *n* patrōna *f*, fautrīx *f*.
patronize *vt* favēre (*dat*), fovēre.
patronymic *n* nōmen *nt*.
patter *vi* crepitāre ♦ *n* crepitus *m*.
pattern *n* exemplar *nt*, exemplum *nt*, nōrma *f*;
(*ideal*) specimen *nt*; (*design*) figūra *f*.
paucity *n* paucitās *f*.
paunch *n* abdōmen *nt*, venter *m*.
pauper *n* pauper *m*.
pause *n* mora *f*, intervallum *nt* ♦ *vi* īnsistere,
intermittere.
pave *vt* sternere; **~ the way** (*fig*) viam mūnīre.
pavement *n* pavīmentum *nt*.
pavilion *n* tentōrium *nt*.
paw *n* pēs *m* ♦ *vt* pede pulsāre.
pawn *n* (*chess*) latrunculus *m*; (COMM) pignus *nt*,

pawnbroker–perfect

fīdūcia *f* ♦ *vt* oppignerāre.
pawnbroker *n* pignerātor *m*.
pay *n* mercēs *f*; (*MIL*) stīpendium *nt*; (*workman*)
manupretium *nt* ♦ *vt* solvere, pendere; (*debt*)
exsolvere; (*in full*) persolvere; (*honour*)
persolvere; (*MIL*) stīpendium numerāre (*dat*);
(*penalty*) dare, luere; ~ **down** numerāre; ~ **for**
condūcere; ~ **off** dissolvere, exsolvere; ~ **out**
expendere; (*publicly*) ērogāre; ~ **up**
dēpendere; ~ **a compliment to** laudāre; ~
respects to salūtāre ♦ *vi* respondēre; **it ~s**
expedit.
payable *adj* solvendus.
paymaster *n* (*MIL*) tribūnus aerārius *m*.
payment *n* solūtiō *f*; (*money*) pēnsiō *f*.
pea *n* pīsum *nt*; **like as two ~s** tam similis quam
lac lactī est.
peace *n* pāx *f*; ~ **and quiet** ōtium *nt*; **breach of
the** ~ vīs *f*; **establish** ~ pācem conciliāre; **hold
one's** ~ reticēre; **sue for** ~ pācem petere.
peaceable *adj* imbellis, placidus.
peaceably *adv* placidē.
peaceful *adj* tranquillus, placidus, pācātus.
peacefully *adv* tranquillē.
peacemaker *n* pācificus *m*.
peace-offering *n* piāculum *nt*.
peach *n* Persicum *nt*.
peacock *n* pāvō *m*.
peak *n* apex *m*, vertex *m*.
peal *n* (*bell*) sonitus *m*; (*thunder*) fragor *m* ♦ *vi*
sonāre.
pear *n* pirum *nt*; (*tree*) pirus *f*.
pearl *n* margarīta *f*.
pearly *adj* gemmeus; (*colour*) candidus.
peasant *n* agricola *m*, colōnus *m*.
peasantry *n* agricolae *mpl*.
pebble *n* calculus *m*.
pebbly *adj* lapidōsus.
peccadillo *n* culpa *f*.
peck *n* (*measure*) modius *m* ♦ *vt* vellicāre.
peculate *vi* pecūlārī.
peculation *n* pecūlātus *m*.
peculiar *adj* (*to one*) proprius; (*strange*)
singulāris.
peculiarity *n* proprietās *f*, nota *f*.
peculiarly *adv* praecipuē, praesertim.
pecuniary *adj* pecūniārius.
pedagogue *n* magister *m*.
pedant *n* scholasticus *m*.
pedantic *adj* nimis dīligenter.
pedantically *adv* dīligentior.
pedantry *n* nimia dīligentia *f*.
peddle *vt* circumferre.
pedestal *n* basis *f*.
pedestrian *adj* pedester ♦ *n* pedes *m*.
pedigree *n* stirps *f*, stemma *nt* ♦ *adj* generōsus.
pediment *n* fastīgium *nt*.
pedlar *n* īnstitor *m*, circumforāneus *m*.
peel *n* cortex *m* ♦ *vt* glūbere.
peep *vi* dīspicere ♦ *n* aspectus *m*; **at ~ of day**
prīmā lūce.
peer *vi*: ~ **at** intuērī ♦ *n* pār *m*; (*rank*) patricius
m.

peerless *adj* ūnicus, ēgregius.
peevish *adj* stomachōsus, mōrōsus.
peevishly *adv* stomachōsē, mōrōsē.
peevishness *n* stomachus *m*, mōrōsitās *f*.
peg *n* clāvus *m*; **put a round ~ in a square hole**
bovī clītellās impōnere ♦ *vt* clāvīs dēfīgere.
pelf *n* lucrum *nt*.
pellet *n* globulus *m*.
pell-mell *adv* prōmiscuē, turbātē.
pellucid *adj* perlūcidus.
pelt *n* pellis *f* ♦ *vt* petere ♦ *vi* violenter cadere.
pen *n* calamus *m*, stilus *m*; (*cattle*) saeptum *nt* ♦
vt scrībere.
penal *adj* poenālis.
penalize *vt* poenā adficere, multāre.
penalty *n* poena *f*, damnum *nt*; (*fine*) multa *f*;
pay the ~ poenās dare.
penance *n* supplicium *nt*.
pencil *n* graphis *f*.
pending *adj* sub iūdice ♦ *prep* inter (*acc*).
penetrable *adj* pervius.
penetrate *vt* penetrāre.
penetrating *adj* ācer, acūtus; (*mind*)
perspicāx.
penetration *n* (*mind*) acūmen *nt*.
peninsula *n* paenīnsula *f*.
penitence *n* paenitentia *f*.
penitent *adj*: **I am** ~ mē paenitet.
penknife *n* scalpellum *nt*.
penmanship *n* scrīptiō *f*, manus *f*.
pennant *n* vexillum *nt*.
penny *n* dēnārius *m*.
pension *n* annua *ntpl*.
pensioner *n* ēmeritus *m*.
pensive *adj* attentus.
pensiveness *n* cōgitātiō *f*.
pent *adj* inclūsus.
penthouse *n* (*MIL*) vīnea *f*.
penurious *adj* parcus, avārus, tenāx.
penuriousness *n* parsimōnia *f*, tenācitās *f*.
penury *n* egestās *f*, inopia *f*.
people *n* hominēs *mpl*; (*nation*) populus *m*, gēns
f; **common** ~ plēbs *f* ♦ *vt* frequentāre.
peopled *adj* frequēns.
pepper *n* piper *nt*.
peradventure *adv* fortasse.
perambulate *vi* spatiārī, inambulāre.
perceive *vt* sentīre, percipere, intellegere.
perceptible *adj*: **be** ~ sentīrī posse, audīrī
posse.
perception *n* sēnsus *m*.
perch *n* (*bird's*) pertica *f*; (*fish*) perca *f* ♦ *vi*
īnsīdere.
perchance *adv* fortasse, forsitan (*subj*).
percolate *vi* permānāre.
percussion *n* ictus *m*.
perdition *n* exitium *nt*.
peregrinate *vi* peregrīnārī.
peregrination *n* peregrīnātiō *f*.
peremptorily *adv* praecīsē, prō imperiō.
peremptory *adj* imperiōsus.
perennial *adj* perennis.
perfect *adj* perfectus, absolūtus; (*entire*)

integer; (_faultless_) ēmendātus ♦ _vt_ perficere, absolvere.
perfection _n_ perfectiō _f_, absolūtiō _f_.
perfectly _adv_ perfectē, ēmendātē; (_quite_) plānē.
perfidious _adj_ perfidus, perfidiōsus.
perfidiously _adv_ perfidiōsē.
perfidy _n_ perfidia _f_.
perforate _vt_ perforāre, terebrāre.
perforation _n_ forāmen _nt_.
perforce _adv_ per vim, necessāriō.
perform _vt_ perficere, peragere; (_duty_) exsequī, fungī (_abl_); (_play_) agere.
performance _n_ (_process_) exsecūtiō _f_, fūnctiō _f_; (_deed_) factum _nt_; (_stage_) fābula _f_.
performer _n_ āctor _m_; (_music_) tībīcen _m_, fidicen _m_; (_stage_) histriō _m_.
perfume _n_ odor _m_, unguentum _nt_ ♦ _vt_ odōrāre.
perfumer _n_ unguentārius _m_.
perfumery _n_ unguenta _ntpl_.
perfunctorily _adv_ neglegenter.
perfunctory _adj_ neglegēns.
perhaps _adv_ fortasse, forsitan (_subj_), nesciō an (_subj_); (_tentative_) vel; (_interrog_) an.
peril _n_ perīculum _m_, discrīmen _nt_.
perilous _adj_ perīculōsus.
perilously _adv_ perīculōsē.
perimeter _n_ ambitus _m_.
period _n_ tempus _nt_, spatium _nt_; (_history_) aetās _f_; (_end_) terminus _m_; (_sentence_) complexiō _f_, ambitus _m_.
periodic _adj_ (_style_) circumscrīptus.
periodical _adj_ status.
periodically _adv_ certīs temporibus, identidem.
peripatetic _adj_ vagus; (_sect_) peripatēticus.
periphery _n_ ambitus _m_.
periphrasis _n_ circuitus _m_.
perish _vi_ perīre, interīre.
perishable _adj_ cadūcus, fragilis, mortālis.
peristyle _n_ peristȳlium _nt_.
perjure _vi_: ~ o.s. pēierāre.
perjured _adj_ periūrus.
perjurer _n_ periūrus _m_.
perjury _n_ periūrium _nt_; **commit** ~ pēierāre.
permanence _n_ cōnstantia _f_, stabilitās _f_.
permanent _adj_ stabilis, diūturnus, perpetuus.
permanently _adv_ perpetuō.
permeable _adj_ penetrābilis.
permeate _vt_ penetrāre ♦ _vi_ permānāre.
permissible _adj_ licitus, concessus; **it is** ~ licet.
permission _n_ potestās _f_; **ask** ~ veniam petere; **give** ~ veniam dare, potestātem facere; **by** ~ **of** permissū (_gen_); **with your kind** ~ bonā tuā veniā; **without your** ~ tē invītō.
permit _vt_ sinere, permittere (_dat_); **I am ~ted** licet mihī.
pernicious _adj_ perniciōsus, exitiōsus.
perorate _vi_ perōrāre.
peroration _n_ perōrātiō _f_, epilogus _m_.
perpendicular _adj_ dīrēctus.
perpendicularly _adv_ ad perpendiculum, ad līneam.

perpetrate _vt_ facere, admittere.
perpetual _adj_ perpetuus, perennis, sempiternus.
perpetually _adv_ perpetuō.
perpetuate _vt_ continuāre, perpetuāre.
perpetuity _n_ perpetuitās _f_.
perplex _vt_ sollicitāre, cōnfundere.
perplexing _adj_ ambiguus, perplexus.
perplexity _n_ haesitātiō _f_.
perquisite _n_ pecūlium _nt_.
persecute _vt_ īnsectārī, exagitāre; persequī.
persecution _n_ īnsectātiō _f_.
persecutor _n_ īnsectātor _m_.
perseverance _n_ pesevērantia _f_, cōnstantia _f_.
persevere _vi_ persevērāre, perstāre; ~ **in** tenēre.
Persian _n_ Persa _m_.
persist _vt_ īnstāre, perstāre, persevērāre.
persistence, persistency _n_ pertinācia _f_, persevērantia _f_.
persistent _adj_ pertināx.
persistently _adv_ pertināciter, persevēranter.
person _n_ homō _m/f_; (_counted_) caput _nt_; (_character_) persōna _f_; (_body_) corpus _nt_; **in** ~ ipse praesēns.
personage _n_ vir _m_.
personal _adj_ prīvātus, suus.
personality _n_ nātūra _f_; (_person_) vir ēgregius _m_.
personally _adv_ ipse, cōram.
personal property _n_ pecūlium _nt_.
personate _vt_ persōnam gerere (_gen_).
personification _n_ prosōpopoeia _f_.
personify _vt_ hūmānam nātūram tribuere (_dat_).
personnel _n_ membra _ntpl_, sociī _mpl_.
perspective _n_ scaenographia _f_.
perspicacious _adj_ perspicāx, acūtus.
perspicacity _n_ perspicācitās _f_, acūmen _nt_.
perspicuity _n_ perspicuitās _f_.
perspicuous _adj_ perspicuus.
perspiration _n_ sūdor _m_.
perspire _vi_ sūdāre.
persuade _vt_ persuādēre (_dat_); (_by entreaty_) exōrāre.
persuasion _n_ persuāsiō _f_.
persuasive _adj_ blandus.
persuasively _adv_ blandē.
pert _adj_ procāx, protervus.
pertain _vi_ pertinēre, attinēre.
pertinacious _adj_ pertināx.
pertinaciously _adv_ pertināciter.
pertinacity _n_ pertinācia _f_.
pertinent _adj_ appositus; **be** ~ ad rem pertinēre.
pertinently _adv_ appositē.
pertly _adv_ procāciter, protervē.
perturb _vt_ perturbāre.
perturbation _n_ animī perturbātiō _f_, trepidātiō _f_.
peruke _n_ capillāmentum _nt_.
perusal _n_ perlēctiō _f_.
peruse _vt_ perlegere; (_book_) ēvolvere.

pervade *vt* permānāre per, complēre; (*emotion*) perfundere.
pervasive *adj* crēber.
perverse *adj* perversus, prāvus.
perversely *adv* perversē.
perversion *n* dēprāvātiō *f*.
perversity *n* perversitās *f*.
pervert *vt* dēprāvāre; (*words*) dētorquēre; (*person*) corrumpere.
perverter *n* corruptor *m*.
pessimism *n* dēspērātiō *f*.
pest *n* pestis *f*.
pester *vt* sollicitāre.
pestilence *n* pestilentia *f*, pestis *f*.
pestilential *adj* pestilēns, nocēns.
pestle *n* pistillum *nt*.
pet *n* dēliciae *fpl* ♦ *vt* in dēliciīs habēre, dēlēnīre.
petard *n*: **be hoist with his own ~** suō sibī gladiō iugulārī.
petition *n* precēs *fpl*; (*POL*) libellus *m* ♦ *vt* ōrāre.
petrify *vt* (*fig*) dēfīgere; **be petrified** stupēre, obstupēscere.
pettifogger *n* lēguleius *m*.
pettiness *n* levitās *f*.
pettish *adj* stomachōsus.
petty *adj* levis, minūtus.
petulance *n* protervitās *f*.
petulant *adj* protervus, petulāns.
petulantly *adv* petulanter.
pew *n* subsellium *nt*.
phalanx *n* phalanx *f*.
phantasy *n* commentīcia *ntpl*.
phantom *n* simulacrum *nt*, īdōlon *nt*.
phases *npl* vicēs *fpl*.
pheasant *n* phāsiānus *m*.
phenomenal *adj* eximius, singulāris.
phenomenon *n* rēs *f*, novum *nt*, spectāculum *nt*.
philander *vi* lascīvīre.
philanthropic *adj* hūmānus, beneficus.
philanthropically *adv* hūmānē.
philanthropy *n* hūmānitās *f*, beneficia *ntpl*.
Philippic *n* Philippica *f*.
philologist *n* grammaticus *m*.
philology *n* grammatica *ntpl*.
philosopher *n* philosophus *m*, sapiēns *m*.
philosophical *adj* philosophus; (*temperament*) aequābilis.
philosophize *vi* philosophārī.
philosophy *n* philosophia *f*, sapientia *f*.
philtre *n* philtrum *nt*.
phlegm *n* pituīta *f*; (*temper*) lentitūdō *f*.
phlegmatic *adj* lentus.
phoenix *n* phoenīx *m*.
phrase *n* locūtiō *f*; (*GRAM*) incīsum *nt*.
phraseology *n* verba *ntpl*, ōrātiō *f*.
physic *n* medicāmentum *nt*; **~s** *pl* physica *ntpl*.
physical *adj* physicus; (*of body*) corporis.
physician *n* medicus *m*.
physicist *n* physicus *m*.
physique *n* corpus *nt*, vīrēs *fpl*.

piazza *n* forum *nt*.
pick *n* (*tool*) dolabra *f*; (*best part*) lēctī *mpl*, flōs *m* ♦ *vt* (*choose*) legere, dēligere; (*pluck*) carpere; **~ out** ēligere, excerpere; **~ up** colligere.
pickaxe *n* dolabra *f*.
picked *adj* ēlēctus, dēlēctus.
picket *n* (*MIL*) statiō *f*.
pickle *n* muria *f* ♦ *vt* condīre.
picture *n* pictūra *f*, tabula *f* ♦ *vt* dēpingere; (*to oneself*) ante oculōs pōnere.
picturesque *adj* (*scenery*) amoenus.
pie *n* crustum *nt*.
piebald *adj* bicolor, varius.
piece *n* pars *f*; (*broken off*) fragmentum *nt*; (*food*) frustum *nt*; (*coin*) nummus *m*; (*play*) fābula *f*; **break in ~s** comminuere; **fall to ~s** dīlābī; **take to ~s** dissolvere; **tear in ~s** dīlaniāre.
piecemeal *adv* membrātim, minūtātim.
pied *adj* maculōsus.
pier *n* mōlēs *f*.
pierce *vt* perfodere, trānsfīgere; (*bore*) perforāre; (*fig*) pungere.
piercing *adj* acūtus.
piety *n* pietās *f*, religiō *f*.
pig *n* porcus *m*, sūs *m/f*; **buy a ~ in a poke** spem pretiō emere; **~'s** suillus.
pigeon *n* columba *f*; **wood ~** palumbēs *f*.
pig-headed *adj* pervicāx.
pigment *n* pigmentum *nt*.
pigsty *n* hara *f*.
pike *n* dolō *m*, hasta *f*.
pikeman *n* hastātus *m*.
pile *n* acervus *m*, cumulus *m*; (*funeral*) rogus *m*; (*building*) mōlēs *f*; (*post*) sublica *f* ♦ *vt* cumulāre, congerere; **~ up** exstruere, adcumulāre, coacervāre.
pile-driver *n* fistūca *f*.
pilfer *vt* fūrārī, surripere.
pilferer *n* fūr *m*, fūrunculus *m*.
pilgrim *n* peregrīnātor *m*.
pilgrimage *n* peregrīnātiō *f*.
pill *n* pilula *f*.
pillage *n* rapīna *f*, dēpopulātiō *f*, expīlātiō *f* ♦ *vt* dīripere, dēpopulārī, expīlāre.
pillager *n* expīlātor *m*, praedātor *m*.
pillar *n* columen *nt*, columna *f*.
pillory *n* furca *f*.
pillow *n* pulvīnus *nt*, culcita *f*.
pilot *n* gubernātor *m*, ductor *m* ♦ *vt* regere, gubernāre.
pimp *n* lēnō *m*.
pimple *n* pustula *f*.
pin *n* acus *f* ♦ *vt* adfīgere.
pincers *n* forceps *m/f*.
pinch *vt* pervellere, vellicāre; (*shoe*) ūrere; (*for room*) coartāre.
pine *n* pīnus *f* ♦ *vi* tābēscere; **~ away** intābēscere; **~ for** dēsīderāre.
pinion *n* penna *f*.
pink *adj* rubicundus.
pinnace *n* lembus *m*.

pinnacle n fastīgium nt.
pint n sextārius m.
pioneer n antecursor m.
pious adj pius, religiōsus.
piously adv piē, religiōsē.
pip n grānum nt.
pipe n (music) fistula f, tībia f; (water) canālis m
♦ vi fistulā canere.
piper n tībīcen m.
pipkin n olla f.
piquancy n sāl m, vīs f.
piquant adj salsus, argūtus.
pique n offēnsio f, dolor m ♦ vt offendere.
piracy n latrōcinium nt.
pirate n pīrāta m praedō m.
piratical adj pīrāticus.
piscatorial adj piscātōrius.
piston n embolus m.
pit n fovea f, fossa f; (THEAT) cavea f.
pitch n pix f; (sound) sonus m ♦ vt (camp)
pōnere; (tent) tendere; (missile) conicere.
pitch-black adj piceus.
pitched battle n proelium iustum nt.
pitcher n hydria f.
pitchfork n furca f.
pitch pine n picea f.
piteous adj miserābilis, flēbilis.
piteously adv miserābiliter.
pitfall n fovea f.
pith n medulla f.
pithy adj (style) dēnsus; ~ **saying** sententia f.
pitiable adj miserandus.
pitiful adj miser, miserābilis; misericors.
pitifully adv miserē, miserābiliter.
pitiless adj immisericors, immītis.
pitilessly adv crūdēliter.
pittance n (food) dēmēnsum nt; (money) stips
f.
pity n misericordia f; **take ~ on** miserērī (+acc
of person, gen of things); **it is a ~ that** male
accidit quod ♦ vt miserērī (gen); **I ~ mē**
miseret (gen).
pivot n cardō m.
placability n plācābilitās f.
placable adj plācābilis.
placard n libellus m.
placate vt plācāre.
place n locus m; **in another ~** alibī; **in the first ~**
prīmum; **in ~ of** locō (gen), pro (+ abl); **to this**
~ hūc; **out of ~** intempestīvus; **give ~ to**
cēdere (dat); **take ~** fierī, accidere; **take the ~**
of in locum (gen) succēdere ♦ vt pōnere,
locāre, collocāre; **~ beside** adpōnere; **~ over**
(in charge) praepōnere; **~ round** circumdare;
~ upon impōnere.
placid adj placidus, tranquillus, quiētus.
placidity n tranquillitās f, sedātus animus m.
placidly adv placidē, quiētē.
plagiarism n fūrtum nt.
plagiarize vt fūrārī.
plague n pestilentia f, pestis f.
plain adj (lucid) clārus, perspicuus;
(unadorned) subtīlis, simplex; (frank)
sincērus; (ugly) invenustus ♦ n campus m,

plānitiēs f; **of the ~** campester.
plainly adv perspicuē; simpliciter, sincērē.
plainness n perspicuitās f; simplicitās f.
plaint n querella f.
plaintiff n petītor m.
plaintive adj flēbilis, queribundus.
plaintively adv flēbiliter.
plait vt implicāre, nectere.
plan n cōnsilium nt; (of a work) fōrma f,
dēsignātiō f; (of living) ratiō f; (intent)
prōpositum nt; (drawing) dēscrīptiō f ♦ vt (a
work) dēsignāre, dēscrībere; (intent)
cōgitāre, meditārī; cōnsilium capere or
inīre; (with verb) in animō habēre (inf).
plane n (surface) plānitiēs f; (tree) platanus f;
(tool) runcīna f ♦ adj aequus, plānus ♦ vt
runcīnāre.
planet n stēlla errāns f.
plank n tabula f.
plant n herba f, planta f ♦ vt (tree) serere; (field)
cōnserere; (colony) dēdūcere; (feet) pōnere;
~ firmly īnfīgere.
plantation n arbustum nt.
planter n sator m, colōnus m.
plaque n tabula f.
plaster n albārium nt, tectōrium nt; (MED)
emplastrum nt; **~ of Paris** gypsum nt ♦ vt
dealbāre.
plasterer n albārius m.
plastic adj ductilis, fūsilis.
plate n (dish) catillus m; (silver) argentum nt;
(layer) lāmina f ♦ vt indūcere.
platform n suggestus m; rōstrum nt, tribūnal
nt.
platitude n trīta sententia f.
platter n patella f, lanx f.
plaudit n plausus m.
plausibility n vērīsimilitūdō f.
plausible adj speciōsus, vērī similis.
play n lūdus m; (THEAT) fābula f; (voice)
inclīnātiō f; (scope) campus m; (hands) gestus
m; **~ on words** agnōminātiō f; **fair ~** aequum et
bonum ♦ vi lūdere; (fountain) scatēre ♦ vt
(music) canere; (instrument) canere (abl);
(game) lūdere (abl); (part) agere; **~ the part of**
agere; **~ a trick on** lūdificārī, impōnere (dat).
playbill n ēdictum nt.
player n lūsor m; (at dice) āleātor m; (on flute)
tībīcen m; (on lyre) fidicen m; (on stage)
histriō m.
playful adj lascīvus; (words) facētus.
playfully adv per lūdum, per iocum.
playfulness n lascīvia f; facētiae fpl.
playground n ārea f.
playmate n collūsor m.
playwright n fābulārum scrīptor m.
plea n causa f; (in defence) dēfēnsiō f, excūsātiō
f.
plead vi causam agere, causam ōrāre, causam
dīcere; (in excuse) dēprecārī, excūsāre; **~**
with obsecrāre.
pleader n āctor m, causidicus m.
pleasant adj iūcundus, dulcis, grātus; (place)

amoenus.
pleasantly *adv* iūcundē, suāviter.
pleasantry *n* facētiae *fpl*, iocus *m*.
please *vt* placēre (*dat*), dēlectāre; **try to ~**
īnservīre (*dat*); **just as you ~** quod
commodum est; **if you ~** sīs; **~d with**
contentus (*abl*); **be ~d with oneself** sibī
placēre ♦ *adv* amābō.
pleasing *adj* grātus, iūcundus, amoenus; **be ~**
to cordī esse (*dat*).
pleasurable *adj* iūcundus.
pleasure *n* voluptās *f*; (*decision*) arbitrium *nt*; **it**
is my ~ libet; **derive ~** voluptātem capere
♦ *vt* grātificārī (*dat*).
pleasure grounds *n* hortī *mpl*.
pleasure-loving *adj* dēlicātus.
plebeian *adj* plēbēius ♦ *n*: **the ~s** plēbs *f*.
plebiscite *n* suffrāgium *nt*.
plectrum *n* plēctrum *nt*.
pledge *n* pignus *nt* ♦ *vt* obligāre; **~ oneself**
prōmittere, spondēre; **~ one's word** fidem
obligāre, fidem interpōnere.
Pleiads *n* Plēiadēs *fpl*.
plenary *adj* īnfīnītus.
plenipotentiary *n* lēgātus *m*.
plenitude *n* cōpia *f*, mātūritās *f*.
plentiful *adj* cōpiōsus, largus.
plentifully *adv* cōpiōsē, largē.
plenty *n* cōpia *f*, abundantia *f*; (*enough*) satis.
pleonasm *n* redundantia *f*.
pleurisy *n* lateris dolor *m*.
pliable *adj* flexibilis, mollis, lentus.
pliant *adj* flexibilis, mollis, lentus.
pliers *n* forceps *m/f*.
plight *n* habitus *m*, discrīmen *nt* ♦ *vt* spondēre.
plod *vi* labōrāre, operam īnsūmere.
plot *n* coniūrātiō *f*, īnsidiae *fpl*; (*land*) agellus *m*;
(*play*) argūmentum *nt* ♦ *vi* coniūrāre, mōlīrī.
plotter *n* coniūrātus *m*.
plough *n* arātrum *nt* ♦ *vt* arāre; (*sea*) sulcāre; **~**
up exarāre.
ploughing *n* arātiō *f*.
ploughman *n* arātor *m*.
ploughshare *n* vōmer *m*.
pluck *n* fortitūdō *f* ♦ *vt* carpere, legere; **~ out**
ēvellere; **~ up courage** animum recipere,
animō adesse.
plucky *adj* fortis.
plug *n* obtūrāmentum *nt* ♦ *vt* obtūrāre.
plum *n* prūnum *nt*; (*tree*) prūnus *f*.
plumage *n* plūmae *fpl*.
plumb *n* perpendiculum *nt* ♦ *adj* dīrēctus ♦ *adv*
ad perpendiculum ♦ *vt* (*building*) ad
perpendiculum exigere; (*depth*) scrūtārī.
plumber *n* artifex plumbārius *m*.
plumb line *n* līnea *f*, perpendiculum *nt*.
plume *n* crista *f* ♦ *vt*: **~ oneself on** iactāre, prae
sē ferre.
plummet *n* perpendiculum *nt*.
plump *adj* pinguis.
plumpness *n* nitor *m*.
plunder *n* (*act*) rapīna *f*; (*booty*) praeda *f* ♦ *vi*
praedārī ♦ *vt* dīripere, expīlāre.

plunderer *n* praedātor *m*, spoliātor *m*.
plundering *n* rapīna *f* ♦ *adj* praedābundus.
plunge *vt* mergere, dēmergere; (*weapon*)
dēmittere ♦ *vi* mergī, sē dēmergere.
plural *adj* plūrālis.
plurality *n* multitūdō *f*, plūrēs *pl*.
ply *vt* exercēre.
poach *vt* surripere.
pocket *n* sinus *m*.
pocket money *n* pecūlium *nt*.
pod *n* siliqua *f*.
poem *n* poēma *nt*, carmen *nt*.
poesy *n* poēsis *f*.
poet *n* poēta *m*.
poetess *n* poētria *f*.
poetic *adj* poēticus.
poetical *adj* = **poetic**.
poetically *adv* poēticē.
poetry *n* (*art*) poētica *f*; (*poems*) poēmata *ntpl*,
carmina *ntpl*.
poignancy *n* acerbitās *f*.
poignant *adj* acerbus, acūtus.
poignantly *adv* acerbē, acūtē.
point *n* (*dot*) pūnctum *nt*; (*place*) locus *m*;
(*item*) caput *nt*; (*sharp end*) aciēs *f*; (*of sword*)
mucrō *m*; (*of epigram*) aculeī *mpl*; **~ of honour**
officium *nt*; **beside the ~** ab rē; **to the ~** ad
rem; **from this ~** hinc; **to that ~** eō; **up to this**
~ hāctenus, adhūc; **without ~** īnsulsus; **in ~ of**
fact nempe; **make a ~ of doing** consultō
facere; **on the ~ of death** moritūrus; **on**
the ~ of happening inibī; **I was on the ~ of**
saying in eō erat ut dīcerem; **matters have**
reached such a ~ eō rēs recidit; **come to the**
~ ad rem redīre; **the ~ at issue is** illud
quaeritur; **the main ~** cardō *m*, caput *nt*;
turning ~ articulus temporis *m* ♦ *vt* acuere,
exacuere; (*aim*) intendere; (*punctuate*)
distinguere; **~ out** indicāre, dēmōnstrāre;
ostendere.
point-blank *adj* simplex ♦ *adv* praecīsē.
pointed *adj* acūtus; (*criticism*) aculeātus; (*wit*)
salsus.
pointedly *adv* apertē, dīlūcidē.
pointer *n* index *m*.
pointless *adj* īnsulsus, frīgidus.
pointlessly *adv* īnsulsē.
point of view *n* iūdicium *nt*, sententia *f*.
poise *n* lībrāmen *nt*; (*fig*) urbānitās *f* ♦ *vt*
lībrāre.
poison *n* venēnum *nt* ♦ *vt* venēnō necāre; (*fig*)
īnficere.
poisoned *adj* venēnātus.
poisoner *n* venēficus *m*.
poisoning *n* venēficium *nt*.
poisonous *adj* noxius.
poke *vt* trūdere, fodicāre.
polar *adj* septentriōnālis.
pole *n* asser *m*, contus *m*; (ASTRO) polus *m*.
poleaxe *n* bipennis *f*.
polemic *n* contrōversia *f*.
police *n* lictōrēs *mpl*; (*night*) vigilēs *mpl*.
policy *n* ratiō *f*, cōnsilium *nt*; **honesty is the**

best ~ ea māximē condūcunt quae sunt rēctissima.

polish n (*appearance*) nitor m; (*character*) urbānitās f; (*LIT*) līma f ♦ vt polīre; (*fig*) expolīre.

polished adj polītus, mundus; (*person*) excultus, urbānus; (*style*) līmātus.

polite adj urbānus, hūmānus, cōmis.

politely adv urbānē, cōmiter.

politeness n urbānitās f, hūmānitās f, cōmitās f.

politic adj prūdēns, circumspectus.

political adj cīvīlis, pūblicus; ~ **life** rēs pūblica f.

politician n magistrātus m.

politics n rēs pūblica f; **take up** ~ ad rem pūblicam accēdere.

polity n reī pūblicae fōrma f.

poll n caput nt; (*voting*) comitia ntpl ♦ vi suffrāgia inīre.

poll tax n tribūtum nt in singula capita impositum.

pollute vt inquināre, contāmināre.

pollution n corruptēla f.

poltroon n ignāvus m.

pomegranate n mālum Pūnicum nt.

pomp n adparātus m.

pomposity n māgnificentia f, glōria f.

pompous adj māgnificus, glōriōsus.

pompously adv māgnificē, glōriōsē.

pompousness n māgnificentia f.

pond n stagnum nt, lacūna f.

ponder vi sēcum reputāre ♦ vt animō volūtāre, in mente agitāre.

ponderous adj gravis, ponderōsus.

ponderously adv graviter.

poniard n pugiō m.

pontiff n pontifex m.

pontifical adj pontificālis, pontificius.

pontoon n pontō m.

pony n mannus m.

pooh-pooh vt dērīdēre.

pool n lacūna f, stagnum nt ♦ vt cōnferre.

poop n puppis f.

poor adj pauper, inops; (*meagre*) exīlis; (*inferior*) improbus; (*pitiable*) miser; ~ **little** misellus.

poorly adj aeger, aegrōtus ♦ adv parum, tenuiter.

pop n crepitus m ♦ vi ēmicāre.

pope n pāpa m.

poplar n pōpulus f.

poppy n papāver nt.

populace n vulgus nt, plēbs f.

popular adj grātus, grātiōsus; (*party*) populāris.

popularity n populī favor m, studium nt.

popularly adv vulgō.

populate vt frequentāre.

population n populus m, cīvēs mpl.

populous adj frequēns.

porcelain n fictilia ntpl.

porch n vestibulum nt.

porcupine n hystrīx f.

pore n forāmen nt ♦ vi: ~ **over** scrūtārī, incumbere in (*acc*).

pork n porcīna f.

porous adj rārus.

porridge n puls f.

port n portus m ♦ adj (*side*) laevus, sinister.

portage n vectūra f.

portal n porta f.

portcullis n cataracta f.

portend vt portendere.

portent n mōnstrum nt, portentum nt.

portentous adj mōnstruōsus.

porter n iānitor m; (*carrier*) bāiulus m.

portico n porticus f.

portion n pars f; (*marriage*) dōs f; (*lot*) sors f.

portliness n amplitūdō f.

portly adj amplus, opīmus.

portrait n imāgō f, effigiēs f.

portray vt dēpingere, exprimere, effingere.

pose n status m, habitus m ♦ vt pōnere ♦ vi habitum sūmere.

poser n nōdus m.

posit vt pōnere.

position n (*GEOG*) situs m (*body*) status m, gestus m; (*rank*) dignitās f; (*office*) honōs m; (*MIL*) locus m; **be in a** ~ **to** habēre (*inf*); **take up a** ~ (*MIL*) locum capere.

positive adj certus; **be** ~ **about** adfirmāre.

positively adv certō, adfirmātē, rē vērā.

posse n manus f.

possess vt possidēre, habēre; (*take*) occupāre, potīrī (*abl*).

possession n possessiō f; ~**s** pl bona ntpl, fortūnae fpl; **take** ~ **of** potīrī (*abl*), occupāre, manum inicere (*dat*); (*inheritance*) obīre; (*emotion*) invādere, incēdere (*dat*); **gain** ~ **of** potior (+ *abl*).

possessor n possessor m, dominus m.

possibility n facultās f; **there is a** ~ fierī potest.

possible adj: **it is** ~ fierī potest; **as big as** ~ quam māximus.

possibly adv fortasse.

post n pālus m; (*MIL*) statiō f; (*office*) mūnus nt; (*courier*) tabellārius m; **leave one's** ~ locō cēdere, signa relinquere ♦ vt (*troops*) locāre, collocāre; (*at intervals*) dispōnere; (*letter*) dare, tabellāriō dare; (*entry*) in cōdicem referre; **be** ~**ed** (*MIL*) in statiōne esse.

postage n vectūra f.

poster n libellus m.

posterior adj posterior.

posterity n posterī mpl; (*time*) posteritās f.

postern n postīcum nt.

posthaste adv summā celeritāte.

posthumous adj postumus.

posthumously adv (*born*) patre mortuō; (*published*) auctōre mortuō.

postpone vt differre, prōferre.

postponement n dīlātiō f.

postscript n: **add a** ~ adscrībere, subicere.

postulate vt sūmere ♦ n sūmptiō f.

posture n gestus m, status m.

pot n olla f, matella f.
pot-bellied adj ventriōsus.
potency n vīs f.
potent adj efficāx, valēns.
potentate n dynastēs m, tyrannus m.
potential adj futūrus.
potentiality n facultās f.
potentially adv ut fierī posse videtur; ~ **an emperor** capāx imperiī.
potently adv efficienter.
potion n pōtiō f.
pot-pourri n farrāgō f.
potsherd n testa f.
pottage n iūs nt.
potter n figulus m; ~'s figulāris.
pottery n fictilia ntpl.
pouch n pēra f, sacculus m.
poultice n fōmentum nt, emplastrum nt.
poultry n gallīnae fpl.
pounce vi involāre, īnsilīre.
pound n lībra f; **five ~s** (weight) **of gold** aurī quīnque pondo ♦ vt conterere; pulsāre.
pour vt fundere; ~ **forth** effundere; ~ **in** īnfundere; ~ **on** superfundere; ~ **out** effundere ♦ vi fundī, fluere; ~ **down** ruere, sē praecipitāre.
pouring adj (rain) effūsus.
poverty n paupertās f, egestās f, inopia f; (style) iēiūnitās f.
powder n pulvis m.
powdery adj pulvereus.
power n potestās f; (strength) vīrēs fpl; (excessive) potentia f; (supreme) imperium nt; (divine) nūmen nt; (legal) auctōritās f; (of father) manus f; **as far as is in my ~** quantum in mē est; **have great ~** multum valēre, posse; **have of ~ attorney** cognitōrem esse; **it is still in my ~ to** integrum est mihī (inf).
powerful adj validus, potēns.
powerfully adv valdē.
powerless adj impotēns, imbēcillus; **be ~** nihil valēre.
powerlessness n imbēcillitas f.
practicable adj in apertō; **be ~** fierī posse.
practical adj (person) habilis.
practical joke n lūdus m.
practical knowledge n ūsus m.
practically adv ferē, paene.
practice n ūsus m, exercitātiō f; (RHET) meditātiō f; (habit) consuētūdō f, mōs m; **corrupt ~s** malae artēs.
practise vt (occupation) exercēre, facere; (custom) factitāre; (RHET) meditārī ♦ vi (MED) medicīnam exercēre; (law) causās agere.
practised adj exercitātus, perītus.
practitioner n (MED) medicus m.
praetor n praetor nt; ~'s praetōrius.
praetorian adj praetōrius.
praetorian guards npl praetōriānī mpl.
praetorship n praetūra f.
praise n laus f ♦ vt laudāre.
praiser n laudātor m.
praiseworthy adj laudābilis, laude dignus.

prance vi exsultāre.
prank n lūdus m.
prate vi garrīre.
prating adj garrulus.
pray vi deōs precārī, deōs venerārī ♦ vt precārī, ōrāre; ~ **for** petere, precārī; ~ **to** adōrāre.
prayer(s) n precēs fpl.
prayerful adj supplex.
preach vt, vi docēre, praedicāre.
preacher n ōrātor m.
preamble n exōrdium nt.
prearranged adj cōnstitūtus.
precarious adj dubius, perīculōsus.
precariousness n discrīmen nt.
precaution n cautiō f, prōvidentia f; **take ~s** cavēre, praecavēre.
precede vt praeīre (dat), anteīre (dat), antecēdere.
precedence n prīmārius locus m; **give ~ to** cēdere (dat); **take ~** (thing) antīquius esse; (person) prīmās agere.
precedent n exemplum nt; (law) praeiūdicium nt; **breach of ~** īnsolentia f; **in defiance of ~** īnsolenter.
preceding adj prior, superior.
precept n praeceptum nt.
preceptor n doctor m, magister m.
precinct n terminus m, templum nt.
precious adj cārus; pretiōsus; (style) pūtidus.
precious stone n gemma f.
precipice n locus praeceps m, rūpēs f.
precipitancy n festīnātiō f.
precipitate vt praecipitāre ♦ adj praeceps; praeproperus.
precipitation n festīnātiō f.
precipitous adj dēruptus, praeceps, praeruptus.
precise adj certus, subtīlis; (person) accūrātus.
precisely adv dēmum.
precision n cūra f.
preclude vt exclūdere, prohibēre.
precocious adj praecox.
precocity n festīnāta mātūritās f.
preconceive vt praecipere; ~**d idea** praeiūdicāta opīniō f.
preconception n praeceptiō f.
preconcerted adj ex compositō factus.
precursor n praenūntius m.
predatory adj praedātōrius.
predecessor n dēcessor m; **my ~** cuī succēdō.
predestination n fātum nt, necessitās f.
predestine vt dēvovēre.
predetermine vt praefīnīre.
predicament n angustiae fpl, discrīmen nt.
predicate n attribūtum nt.
predict vt praedīcere, augurārī.
prediction n praedictiō f.
predilection n amor m, studium nt.
predispose vt inclīnāre, praeparāre.
predisposition n inclīnātiō f.
predominance n potentia f, praestantia f.

predominant *adj* praepotēns, praecipuus.
predominantly *adv* plērumque.
predominate *vi* pollēre, dominārī.
pre-eminence *n* praestantia *f*.
pre-eminent *adj* ēgregius, praecipuus, excellēns.
pre-eminently *adv* ēgregiē, praecipuē, excellenter.
preface *n* prooemium *nt*, praefātiō *f* ♦ *vi* praefārī.
prefect *n* praefectus *m*.
prefecture *n* praefectūra *f*.
prefer *vt* (*charge*) dēferre; (*to office*) anteferre; (*choice*) antepōnere (*acc and dat*), posthabēre (*dat and acc*); (*with verb*) mālle.
preferable *adj* potior.
preferably *adv* potius.
preference *n* favor *m*; **give ~ to** antepōnere, praeoptāre; **in ~ to** potius quam.
preferment *n* honōs *m*, dignitās *f*.
prefix *vt* praetendere ♦ *n* praepositiō *f*.
pregnancy *n* graviditās *f*.
pregnant *adj* gravida.
prejudge *vt* praeiūdicāre.
prejudice *n* praeiūdicāta opīniō *f*; (*harmful*) invidia *f*, incommodum *nt*; **without ~** cum bonā veniā ♦ *vt* obesse (*dat*); **be ~d against** invidēre (*dat*), male opīnārī dē (*abl*).
prejudicial *adj* damnōsus; **be ~ to** obesse (*dat*), nocēre (*dat*), officere (*dat*), dētrīmentō esse (*dat*).
preliminaries *npl* praecurrentia *ntpl*.
preliminary *adj* prīmus ♦ *n* prōlūsiō *f*.
prelude *n* prooemium *nt*.
premature *adj* immātūrus; (*birth*) abortīvus.
prematurely *adv* ante tempus.
premeditate *vt* praecōgitāre, praemeditārī.
premeditated *adj* praemeditātus.
premier *adj* prīnceps, praecipuus.
premise *n* (*major*) prōpositiō *f*; (*minor*) adsūmptiō *f*; **~s** *pl* aedēs *fpl*, domus *f*.
premium *n* praemium *nt*; **be at a ~** male emī.
premonition *n* monitus *m*.
preoccupation *n* sollicitūdō *f*.
preoccupied *adj* sollicitus, districtus.
preordain *vt* praefīnīre.
preparation *n* (*process*) adparātiō *f*, comparātiō *f*; (*product*) adparātus *m*; (*of speech*) meditātiō *f*; **make ~s for** īnstruere, exōrnāre, comparāre.
prepare *vt* parāre, adparāre, comparāre; (*speech*) meditārī; (*with verb*) parāre; **~d for** parātus ad (*+ acc*).
preponderance *n* praestantia *f*.
preponderate *vi* praepollēre, vincere.
preposition *n* praepositiō *f*.
prepossess *vt* commendāre (*dat and acc*), praeoccupāre.
prepossessing *adj* suāvis, iūcundus.
prepossession *n* favor *m*.
preposterous *adj* absurdus.
prerogative *n* iūs *nt*.
presage *n* ōmen *nt* ♦ *vt* ōminārī,

portendere.
prescience *n* prōvidentia *f*.
prescient *adj* prōvidus.
prescribe *vt* imperāre; (*MED*) praescrībere; (*limit*) fīnīre.
prescription *n* (*MED*) compositiō *f*; (*right*) ūsus *m*.
presence *n* praesentia *f*; (*appearance*) aspectus *m*; **~ of mind** praesēns animus *m*; **in the ~ of** cōram (*abl*); apud (*abl*); **in my ~** mē praesente.
present *adj* praesēns, īnstāns; **be ~** adesse; **be ~ at** interesse (*dat*) ♦ *n* praesēns tempus *nt*; (*gift*) dōnum *nt*; **at ~** in praesentī, nunc; **for the ~** in praesēns ♦ *vt* dōnāre, offerre; (*on stage*) indūcere; (*in court*) sistere; **~ itself** occurrere.
presentable *adj* spectābilis.
presentation *n* dōnātiō *f*.
presentiment *n* augurium *nt*.
presently *adv* mox.
preservation *n* cōnservātiō *f*.
preserve *vt* cōnservāre, tuērī; (*food*) condīre.
preside *vi* praesidēre (*dat*).
presidency *n* praefectūra *f*.
president *n* praefectus *m*.
press *n* prēlum *nt* ♦ *vt* premere; (*crowd*) stīpāre; (*urge*) īnstāre (*dat*); **~ for** flāgitāre; **~ hard** (*pursuit*) īnsequī, īnstāre (*dat*), īnsistere (*dat*); **~ out** exprimere; **~ together** comprimere.
pressing *adj* īnstāns, gravis.
pressure *n* pressiō *f*, nīsus *m*.
prestige *n* auctōritās *f*, opīniō *f*.
presumably *adv* sānē.
presume *vt* sūmere, conicere ♦ *vi* audēre, cōnfīdere; **I ~** opīnor, crēdō.
presuming *adj* adrogāns.
presumption *n* coniectūra *f*; (*arrogance*) adrogantia *f*, licentia *f*.
presumptuous *adj* adrogāns, audāx.
presumptuously *adv* adroganter, audacter.
presuppose *vt* praesūmere.
pretence *n* simulātiō *f*, speciēs *f*; **under ~ of** per speciem (*gen*); **under false ~s** dolō malō.
pretend *vt* simulāre, fingere; **~ that ... not** dissimulāre.
pretender *n* captātor *m*.
pretension *n* postulātum *nt*; **make ~s to** adfectāre, sibī adrogāre.
pretentious *adj* adrogāns, glōriōsus.
pretext *n* speciēs *f*; **under ~ of** per speciem (*gen*); **on the ~ that** quod (*+ subj*).
prettily *adv* pulchrē, bellē.
prettiness *n* pulchritūdō *f*, lepōs *m*.
pretty *adj* formōsus, pulcher, bellus ♦ *adv* admodum, satis.
prevail *vi* vincere; (*custom*) tenēre, obtinēre; **~ upon** persuādēre (*dat*); (*by entreaty*) exōrāre.
prevailing *adj* vulgātus.
prevalent *adj* vulgātus; **be ~** obtinēre; **become ~** incrēbrēscere.
prevaricate *vi* tergiversārī.

prevarication n tergiversātiō f.
prevaricator n veterātor m.
prevent vt impedīre (+ **quōminus/quīn** and subj), prohibēre (+ acc and infin).
prevention n impedītiō f.
previous adj prior, superior.
previously adv anteā, antehāc.
prevision n prōvidentia f.
prey n praeda f ♦ vi: ~ **upon** īnsectārī; (fig) vexāre, carpere.
price n pretium nt; (of corn) annōna f; **at a high** ~ māgnī; **at a low** ~ parvī ♦ vt pretium cōnstituere (gen).
priceless adj inaestimābilis.
prick vt pungere; (goad) stimulāre; ~ **up the ears** aurēs adrigere.
prickle n acūleus m.
prickly adj aculeātus, horridus.
pride n superbia f, fastus m; (boasting) glōria f; (object) decus nt; (best part) flōs m ♦ vt: ~ **oneself on** iactāre, prae sē ferre.
priest n sacerdōs m; (especial) flāmen m; **high** ~ pontifex m, antistēs m.
priestess n sacerdōs f; **high** ~ antistita f.
priesthood n sacerdōtium nt, flāminium nt.
prig n homō fastīdiōsus m.
priggish adj fastīdiōsus.
prim adj modestior.
primarily adv prīncipiō, praecipuē.
primary adj prīmus, praecipuus.
prime adj prīmus, ēgregius; ~ **mover** auctor m ♦ n flōs m; **in one's** ~ flōrēns ♦ vt īnstruere, ērudīre.
primeval adj prīscus.
primitive adj prīstinus, incultus.
primordial adj prīscus.
prince n rēgulus m; rēgis fīlius m; prīnceps m.
princely adj rēgālis.
princess n rēgis fīlia f.
principal adj praecipuus, prīnceps, māximus ♦ n (person) prīnceps m/f; (money) sors f.
principally adv in prīmīs, māximē, māximam partem.
principle n prīncipium nt; (rule) fōrmula f, ratiō f; (character) fidēs f; ~**s** pl īnstitūta ntpl, disciplīna f; **first** ~**s** elementa ntpl, initia ntpl.
print n nota f, signum nt; (foot) vestīgium nt ♦ vt imprimere.
prior adj prior, potior.
priority n: **give** ~ **to** praevertere (dat).
prise vt sublevāre; ~ **open** vectī refringere.
prison n carcer m, vincula ntpl; **put in** ~ in vincula conicere.
prisoner n reus m; (for debt) nexus m; (of war) captīvus m; ~ **at the bar** reus m, rea f; **take** ~ capere.
pristine adj prīscus, prīstinus, vetus.
privacy n sēcrētum nt.
private adj (individual) prīvātus; (home) domesticus; (secluded) sēcrētus ♦ n (MIL) gregārius mīles m.
privately adv clam, sēcrētō.
private property n res familiāris f.
privation n inopia f, egestās f.

privet n ligustrum nt.
privilege n iūs nt, immūnitās f.
privileged adj immūnis.
privy adj sēcrētus; ~ **to** cōnscius (gen).
prize n praemium nt; (captured) praeda f; ~ **money** manubiae fpl ♦ vt māgnī aestimāre.
pro-Athenian adj rērum Athēniēnsium studiōsus.
probability n vērī similitūdō f.
probable adj vērī similis; **more** ~ vērō propior.
probably adv fortasse.
probation n probātiō f.
probationer n tīrō m.
probe vt īnspicere, scrūtārī.
probity n honestās f, integritās f.
problem n quaestiō f; **the** ~ **is** illud quaeritur.
problematical adj dubius, anceps.
procedure n ratiō f, modus m; (law) fōrmula f.
proceed vi pergere, prōcēdere, prōgredī; (narrative) īnsequī; ~ **against** persequī, lītem intendere (dat); ~ **from** orīrī, proficīscī ex.
proceedings n ācta ntpl.
proceeds n fructus m, reditus m.
process n ratiō f; (law) āctiō f; **in the** ~ **of time** post aliquod tempus.
procession n pompa f; (fig) agmen nt.
proclaim vt ēdīcere, prōnūntiāre, praedicāre, dēclārāre; ~ **war upon** bellum indīcere + dat.
proclamation n ēdictum nt.
proclivity n prōpēnsiō f.
proconsul n prōcōnsul m.
proconsular adj prōcōnsulāris.
proconsulship n prōcōnsulātus m.
procrastinate vt differre, prōferre ♦ vi cunctārī.
procrastination n prōcrāstinātiō f, mora f.
procreate vt generāre, prōcreāre.
procreation n prōcreātiō f.
procreator n generātor m.
procumbent adj prōnus.
procurator n prōcūrātor m.
procure vt parāre, adipīscī, adquīrere; (by request) impetrāre.
procurer n lēnō m.
prod vt stimulāre.
prodigal adj prōdigus ♦ n nepōs m.
prodigality n effūsiō f.
prodigally adv effūsē.
prodigious adj ingēns, immānis.
prodigy n prōdigium nt, portentum nt; (fig) mīrāculum nt.
produce vt ēdere; (young) parere; (crops) ferre; (play) dare, docēre; (line) prōdūcere; (in court) sistere; (into view) prōferre; (from store) prōmere, dēprōmere ♦ n fructus m; (of earth) frūgēs fpl; (in money) reditus m.
product n opus nt; ~ **of** fructus (gen).
production n opus nt.
productive adj fēcundus, ferāx, fructuōsus.
productivity n fēcunditās f, ūbertās f.
profanation n violātiō f.
profane adj profānus, impius ♦ vt violāre, polluere.

profanely *adv* impiē.
profanity *n* impietās *f*.
profess *vt* profitērī, prae sē ferre; ~ **to be** profitērī sē.
profession *n* professiō *f*; (*occupation*) ars *f*, haeresis *f*.
professor *n* doctor *m*.
proffer *vt* offerre, pollicērī.
proficiency *n* prōgressus *m*, perītia *f*; **attain** ~ prōficere.
proficient *adj* perītus.
profile *n* ōris līneāmenta *ntpl*; (*portrait*) oblīqua imāgō *f*.
profit *n* lucrum *nt*, ēmolumentum *nt*, fructus *m*; **make a** ~ **out of** quaestuī habēre ♦ *vt* prōdesse (*dat*) ♦ *vi*: ~ **by** fruī (*abl*), ūtī (*abl*); (*opportunity*) arripere.
profitable *adj* fructuōsus, ūtilis.
profitably *adv* ūtiliter.
profligacy *n* flāgitium *nt*, perditī mōrēs *mpl*.
profligate *adj* perditus, dissolūtus ♦ *n* nepōs *m*.
profound *adj* altus; (*discussion*) abstrūsus.
profoundly *adv* penitus.
profundity *n* altitūdō *f*.
profuse *adj* prōdigus, effūsus.
profusely *adv* effūsē.
profusion *n* abundantia *f*, adfluentia *f*; **in** ~ abundē.
progenitor *n* auctor *m*.
progeny *n* prōgeniēs *f*, prōlēs *f*.
prognostic *n* signum *nt*.
prognosticate *vt* ōminārī, augurārī, praedīcere.
prognostication *n* ōmen *nt*, praedictiō *f*.
programme *n* libellus *m*.
progress *n* prōgressus *m*; **make** ~ prōficere ♦ *vi* prōgredī.
progression *n* prōgressus *m*.
progressively *adv* gradātim.
prohibit *vt* vetāre, interdīcere (*dat*).
prohibition *n* interdictum *nt*.
project *n* prōpositum *nt* ♦ *vi* ēminēre, exstāre; (*land*) excurrere ♦ *vt* prōicere.
projectile *n* tēlum *nt*.
projecting *adj* ēminēns.
projection *n* ēminentia *f*.
proletarian *adj* plēbēius.
proletariat *n* plēbs *f*.
prolific *adj* fēcundus.
prolix *adj* verbōsus, longus.
prolixity *n* redundantia *f*.
prologue *n* prologus *m*.
prolong *vt* dūcere, prōdūcere; (*office*) prōrogāre.
prolongation *n* (*time*) propāgātiō *f*; (*office*) prōrogātiō *f*.
promenade *n* ambulātiō *f* ♦ *vi* inambulāre, spatiārī.
prominence *n* ēminentia *f*.
prominent *adj* ēminēns, īnsignis; **be** ~ ēminēre.
promiscuous *adj* prōmiscuus.

promiscuously *adv* prōmiscuē.
promise *n* prōmissum *nt*; **break a** ~ fidem fallere; **keep a** ~ fidem praestāre; **make a** ~ fidem dare; **a youth of great** ~ summae speī adulēscēns ♦ *vt* prōmittere, pollicērī; (*in marriage*) dēspondēre; ~ **in return** reprōmittere ♦ *vi*: ~ **well** bonam spem ostendere.
promising *adj* bonae speī.
promissory note *n* syngrapha *f*.
promontory *n* prōmunturium *nt*.
promote *vt* favēre (*dat*); (*growth*) alere; (*in rank*) prōdūcere.
promoter *n* auctor *m*, fautor *m*.
promotion *n* dignitās *f*.
prompt *adj* alacer, prōmptus ♦ *vt* incitāre, commovēre; (*speaker*) subicere.
prompter *n* monitor *m*.
promptitude *n* alacritās *f*, celeritās *f*.
promptly *adv* extemplō, citō.
promulgate *vt* prōmulgāre, palam facere.
promulgation *n* prōmulgātiō *f*.
prone *adj* prōnus; (*mind*) inclīnātus.
prong *n* dēns *m*.
pronounce *vt* ēloquī, appellāre; (*oath*) interpōnere; (*sentence*) dīcere, prōnūntiāre.
pronounced *adj* manifestus, īnsignis.
pronouncement *n* ōrātiō *f*, adfirmātiō *f*.
pronunciation *n* appellātiō *f*.
proof *n* documentum *nt*, argūmentum *nt*; (*test*) probātiō *f* ♦ *adj* immōtus, impenetrābilis.
prop *n* adminiculum *nt*, firmāmentum *nt* ♦ *vt* fulcīre.
propaganda *n* documenta *ntpl*.
propagate *vt* propāgāre.
propagation *n* propāgātiō *f*.
propel *vt* incitāre, prōpellere.
propensity *n* inclīnātiō *f*.
proper *adj* idōneus, decēns, decōrus; rēctus; **it is** ~ decet.
properly *adv* decōrē; rēctē.
property *n* rēs *f*, rēs mancipī, bona *ntpl*; (*estate*) praedium *nt*; (*attribute*) proprium *nt*; (*slave's*) pecūlium *nt*.
prophecy *n* vāticinium *nt*, praedictiō *f*.
prophesy *vt* vāticinārī, praedīcere.
prophet *n* vātēs *m*, fātidicus *m*.
prophetess *n* vātēs *f*.
prophetic *adj* dīvīnus, fātidicus.
prophetically *adv* dīvīnitus.
propinquity *n* (*place*) vīcīnitās *f*; (*kin*) propinquitās *f*.
propitiate *vt* plācāre.
propitiation *n* plācātiō *f*, litātiō *f*.
propitious *adj* fēlīx, faustus; (*god*) praesēns.
proportion *n* mēnsūra *f*; **in** ~ prō portiōne, prō ratā parte; **in** ~ **to** prō (*abl*).
proportionately *adv* prō portiōne, prō ratā parte.
proposal *n* condiciō *f*.
propose *vt* prōpōnere; (*motion*) ferre, rogāre; (*penalty*) inrogāre; (*candidate*) rogāre

magistrātum.
proposer n auctor m, lātor m.
proposition n (offer) condiciō f; (plan) cōnsilium nt, prōpositum nt; (logic) prōnūntiātum nt.
propound vt expōnere, in medium prōferre.
propraetor n prōpraetor m.
proprietor n dominus m.
propriety n decōrum nt; (conduct) modestia f; **with ~** decenter.
propulsion n impulsus m.
prorogation n prōrogātiō f.
prorogue vt prōrogāre.
prosaic adj pedester.
proscribe vt prōscrībere.
proscription n prōscrīptiō f.
prose n ōrātiō f, ōrātiō solūta f.
prosecute vt (task) exsequī, gerere; (at law) accūsāre, lītem intendere (dat).
prosecution n exsecūtiō f; (at law) accūsātiō f; (party) accūsātor m.
prosecutor n accūsātor m.
prosody n numerī mpl.
prospect n prōspectus m; (fig) spēs f ♦ vi explōrāre.
prospective adj futūrus, spērātus.
prosper vi flōrēre, bonā fortūnā ūtī ♦ vt fortūnāre.
prosperity n fortuna f, rēs secundae fpl, fēlīcitās f.
prosperous adj fēlix, fortūnātus, secundus.
prosperously adv prosperē.
prostrate adj prōstrātus, adflīctus; **lie ~** iacēre ♦ vt prōsternere, dēicere; **~ oneself** prōcumbere, sē prōicere.
prostration n fractus animus m.
prosy adj longus.
protagonist n prīmārum partium āctor m.
protect vt tuērī, dēfendere, custōdīre, prōtegere.
protection n tūtēla f, praesidium nt; (law) patrōcinium nt; (POL) fidēs f; **put oneself under the ~ of** in fidem venīre (gen); **take under one's ~** in fidem recipere.
protector n patrōnus m, dēfēnsor m, custōs m.
protectress n patrōna f.
protégé n cliēns m.
protest n obtestātiō f; (POL) intercessiō f ♦ vi obtestārī, reclāmāre; (POL) intercēdere.
protestation n adsevērātiō f.
prototype n archetypum nt.
protract vt dūcere, prōdūcere.
protrude vi prōminēre.
protruding adj exsertus.
protuberance n ēminentia f, tūber nt.
protuberant adj ēminēns, turgidus.
proud adj superbus, adrogāns, īnsolēns; **be ~** superbīre; **be ~ of** iactāre.
proudly adv superbē.
prove vt dēmōnstrāre, arguere, probāre; (test) experīrī ♦ vi (person) se praebēre; (event) ēvādere; **~ oneself** sē praebēre, sē praestāre; **not ~n** nōn liquet.

proved adj expertus.
provenance n orīgō f.
provender n pābulum nt.
proverb n prōverbium nt.
proverbial adj trītus; **become ~** in prōverbium venīre.
provide vt parāre, praebēre; **~ for** prōvidēre (dat); **the law ~s** lēx iubet; **~ against** praecavēre.
provided that conj dum, dummodo (+ subj).
providence n prōvidentia f; Deus m.
provident adj prōvidus, cautus.
providential adj dīvīnus; secundus.
providentially adv dīvīnitus.
providently adv cautē.
providing conj dum, dummodo.
province n prōvincia f.
provincial adj prōvinciālis; (contemptuous) oppidānus, mūnicipālis.
provision n parātus m; **make ~ for** prōvidēre (dat); **make ~** cavēre.
provisionally adv ad tempus.
provisions n cibus m, commeātus m, rēs frūmentāria f.
proviso n condiciō f; **with this ~** hāc lēge.
provocation n inrītāmentum nt, offēnsiō f.
provocative adj (language) molestus, invidiōsus.
provoke vt inrītāre, lacessere; (to action) excitāre.
provoking adj odiōsus, molestus.
provost n praefectus m.
prow n prōra f.
prowess n virtūs f.
prowl vi grassārī, vagārī.
proximate adj proximus.
proximity n propinquitās f, vīcīnia f.
proxy n vicārius m.
prude n fastīdiōsa f.
prudence n prūdentia f.
prudent adj prūdēns, cautus, sagāx.
prudently adv prūdenter, cautē.
prudery n fastīdiōsa quaedam pudīcitia f.
prudish adj fastīdiōsus.
prune vt amputāre.
pruner n putātor m.
pruning hook n falx f.
pry vi inquīrere; **~ into** scrūtārī.
pseudonym n falsum nōmen nt.
psychology n animī ratiō f.
Ptolemy n Ptolemaeus m.
puberty n pūbertās f.
public adj pūblicus; (speech) forēnsis; **~ life** rēs pūblica f, forum nt; **in ~** forīs; **appear in ~** in medium prōdīre; **make ~** in mediō pōnere, forās perferre; **make a ~ case of** in medium vocāre; **act for the ~ good** in medium cōnsulere; **be a ~ figure** in lūce versārī, digitō mōnstrārī ♦ n vulgus nt, hominēs mpl.
publican n (taxes) pūblicānus m; (inn) caupō m.
publication n ēditiō f, prōmulgātiō f; (book) liber m.
publicity n lūx f, celebritās f.

publicly *adv* palam; (*by the state*) pūblicē.
public opinion *n* fāma *f*.
publish *vt* vulgāre, dīvulgāre; (*book*) ēdere.
pucker *vt* corrūgāre.
puerile *adj* puerīlis.
puerility *n* ineptiae *fpl*.
puff *n* aura *f* ♦ *vt* īnflāre ♦ *vi* anhēlāre.
puffed up *adj* īnflātus, tumidus.
pugilism *n* pugilātus *m*.
pugilist *n* pugil *m*.
pugnacious *adj* pugnāx.
pugnacity *n* ferōcitās *f*.
puissance *n* potentia *f*, vīrēs *fpl*.
puissant *adj* potēns.
pull *n* tractus *m*; (*of gravity*) contentiō *f* ♦ *vt*
trahere, tractāre; ~ **apart** distrahere; ~ **at**
vellicāre; ~ **away** āvellere; ~ **back** retrahere;
~ **down** dēripere, dētrahere; (*building*)
dēmōlīrī; ~ **off** āvellere; ~ **out** ēvellere,
extrahere; ~ **through** *vi* pervincere; (*illness*)
convalēscere; ~ **up** (*plant*) ēruere;
(*movement*) coercēre; ~ **to pieces** dīlaniāre.
pullet *n* pullus gallīnāceus *m*.
pulley *n* trochlea *f*.
pulmonary *adj* pulmōneus.
pulp *n* carō *f*.
pulpit *n* suggestus *m*.
pulsate *vi* palpitāre, micāre.
pulse *n* (*plant*) legūmen *nt*; (*of blood*) vēnae *fpl*;
feel the ~ vēnās temptāre.
pulverize *vt* contundere.
pumice stone *n* pūmex *m*.
pummel *vt* verberāre.
pump *n* antlia *f* ♦ *vt* haurīre; ~ **out** exhaurīre.
pumpkin *n* cucurbita *f*.
pun *n* agnōminātiō *f*.
punch *n* ictus *m* ♦ *vt* pertundere, percutere.
punctilious *adj* riligiōsus.
punctiliousness *n* riligiō *f*.
punctual *adj* accūrātus, dīligēns.
punctuality *n* dīligentia *f*.
punctually *adv* ad hōram, ad tempus.
punctuate *vt* distinguere.
punctuation *n* interpūnctiō *f*.
puncture *n* pūnctiō *f* ♦ *vt* pungere.
pundit *n* scholasticus *m*.
pungency *n* ācrimōnia *f*; (*in debate*) aculeī *mpl*.
pungent *adj* ācer, mordāx.
punish *vt* pūnīre, animadvertere in (*acc*);
poenam sūmere dē (+ *abl*); **be ~ed** poenās
dare.
punishable *adj* poenā dignus.
punisher *n* vindex *m*, ultor *m*.
punishment *n* poena *f*, supplicium *nt*;
(*censors'*) animadversiō *f*; **capital** ~ capitis
supplicium *nt*; **corporal** ~ verbera *ntpl*; **inflict**
~ **on** poenā adficere, poenam capere dē (*abl*),
supplicium sūmere dē (*abl*); **submit to** ~
poenam subīre; **undergo** ~ poenās dare,
pendere, solvere.
punitive *adj* ulcīscendī causā.
punt *n* pontō *m*.
puny *adj* pusillus.

pup *n* catulus *m* ♦ *vi* parere.
pupil *n* discipulus *m*, discipula *f*; (*eye*) aciēs *f*,
pūpula *f*.
pupillage *n* tūtēla *f*.
puppet *n* pūpa *f*.
puppy *n* catulus *m*.
purblind *adj* luscus.
purchase *n* emptiō *f*; (*formal*) mancipium *nt* ♦
vt emere.
purchaser *n* emptor *m*; (*at auction*) manceps *m*.
pure *adj* pūrus, integer; (*morally*) castus;
(*mere*) merus.
purely *adv* pūrē, integrē; (*solely*) sōlum, nīl
nisi; (*quite*) omnīnō, plānē.
purgation *n* pūrgātiō *f*.
purge *vt* pūrgāre, expūrgāre.
purification *n* lūstrātiō *f*, pūrgātiō *f*.
purify *vt* pūrgāre, expūrgāre.
purist *n* fastīdiōsus *m*.
purity *n* integritās *f*, castitās *f*.
purloin *vt* surripere, fūrārī.
purple *n* purpura *f* ♦ *adj* purpureus.
purport *n* sententia *f*; (*of words*) vīs *f*; **what is**
the ~ **of?** quō spectat?, quid vult? ♦ *vt* velle
spectāre ad.
purpose *n* prōpositum *nt*, cōnsilium *nt*, mēns *f*;
for that ~ eō; **for the** ~ **of** ad (*acc*), ut (*subj*), eā
mente ut, eō cōnsiliō ut (*subj*); **on** ~ cōnsultō,
dē industriā; **to the** ~ ad rem; **to what** ~?
quō?, quōrsum?; **to no** ~ frustrā, nēquīquam;
without achieving one's ~ rē īnfectā ♦ *vt* in
animō habēre, velle.
purposeful *adj* intentus.
purposeless *adj* inānis.
purposely *adv* cōnsultō, dē industriā.
purr *n* murmur *nt* ♦ *vi* murmurāre.
purse *n* marsupium *nt*, crumēna *f*; **privy** ~
fiscus *m* ♦ *vt* adstringere.
pursuance *n* exsecūtiō *f*; **in** ~ **of** secundum
(*acc*).
pursue *vt* īnsequī, īnsectārī, persequī;
(*closely*) īnstāre (*dat*), īnsistere (*dat*); (*aim*)
petere; (*course*) īnsistere.
pursuer *n* īnsequēns *m*; (*law*) accūsātor *m*.
pursuit *n* īnsectātiō *f*; (*hunt*) vēnātiō *f*;
(*ambition*) studium *nt*.
purvey *vt* parāre; (*food*) obsōnāre.
purveyance *n* prōcūrātiō *f*.
purveyor *n* obsōnātor *m*.
purview *n* prōvincia *f*.
pus *n* pūs *nt*.
push *n* pulsus *m*, impetus *m* ♦ *vt* impellere,
trūdere, urgēre; ~ **away** āmovēre; ~ **back**
repellere; ~ **down** dēprimere, dētrūdere; ~
forward prōpellere; ~ **in** intrūdere; ~ **on**
incitāre; ~ **through** perrumpere.
pushing *adj* cōnfīdēns.
pusillanimity *n* ignāvia *f*, timor *m*.
pusillanimous *adj* ignāvus, timidus.
pustule *n* pustula *f*.
put *vt* (*in a state*) dare; (*in a position*) pōnere; (*in*
words) reddere; (*argument*) pōnere; (*spur*)
subdere; (*to some use*) adhibēre; ~ **an end to**

fīnem facere (*dat*); ~ **a question to**
interrogāre; ~ **against** adpōnere; ~ **among**
intericere; ~ **aside** sēpōnere; ~ **away** pōnere,
dēmovēre; (*store*) repōnere; ~ **back**
repōnere; repellere; ~ **beside** adpōnere; ~
between interpōnere; ~ **by** condere; ~ **down**
dēpōnere; (*revolt*) opprimere; ~ **forth**
extendere; (*growth*) mittere; ~ **forward**
ostentāre; (*plea*) adferre; ~ **in** immittere,
īnserere; (*ship*) adpellere; ~ **off** differre; ~ **on**
impōnere; (*clothes*) induere; (*play*) dare; ~
out ēicere; (*eye*) effodere; (*fire*) exstinguere;
(*money*) pōnere; (*tongue*) exserere; ~ **out of**
the way dēmovēre; ~ **out to sea** in altum
ēvehi, solvere; ~ **over** superimpōnere; ~ **to**
adpōnere; (*flight*) dare in (*acc*), fugāre,
prōfligāre; in fugam conicere; (*sea*) solvere;
~ **together** cōnferre; ~ **under** subicere; ~ **up**
(*for sale*) prōpōnere; (*lodge*) dēvertere,
dēversārī apud; ~ **up with** ferre, patī; ~ **upon**
impōnere.
putrefaction *n* pūtor *m*.
putrefy *vi* putrēscere.
putrid *adj* putridus.
puzzle *n* nōdus *m* ♦ *vt* impedīre, sollicitāre; **be**
~d haerēre.
puzzling *adj* ambiguus, perplexus.
pygmy *n* pygmaeus *m*.
pyramid *n* pȳramis *f*.
pyramidal *adj* pȳramidātus.
pyre *n* rogus *m*.
Pyrenees *npl* Pyrenaeī (montēs) *mpl*.
python *n* pȳthōn *m*.

Q, q

quack *n* (*doctor*) circulātor *m* ♦ *vi* tetrinnīre.
quadrangle *n* ārea *f*.
quadruped *n* quadrupēs *m/f*.
quadruple *adj* quadruplex.
quaestor *n* quaestor *m*; ~**'s** quaestōrius.
quaestorship *n* quaestūra *f*.
quaff *vt* ēpōtāre, haurīre.
quagmire *n* palūs *f*.
quail *n* (*bird*) coturnīx *f* ♦ *vi* pāvēscere,
trepidāre.
quaint *adj* novus, īnsolitus.
quaintness *n* īnsolentia *f*.
quake *vi* horrēre, horrēscere ♦ *n* (*earth*) mōtus
m.
quaking *n* horror *m*, tremor *m* ♦ *adj* tremulus.
qualification *n* condiciō *f*; (*limitation*) exceptiō
f.
qualified *adj* (*for*) aptus, idōneus, dignus; (*in*)
perītus, doctus.

qualify *vi* prōficere ♦ *vt* temperāre, mītigāre.
qualities *npl* ingenium *nt*.
quality *n* nātūra *f*, vīs *f*; indolēs *f*; (*rank*) locus
m, genus *nt*; **I know the ~ of** sciō quālis sit.
qualm *n* riligiō *f*, scrūpulus *m*.
quandary *n* angustiae *fpl*; **be in a ~** haerēre.
quantity *n* cōpia *f*, numerus *m*; (*metre*) vōcum
mēnsiō *f*; **a large ~** multum *nt*, plūrimum *nt*; **a**
small ~ aliquantulum *nt*.
quarrel *n* dissēnsiō *f*, contrōversia *f*; (*violent*)
rixa *f*, iūrgium *nt* ♦ *vi* rixārī, altercārī.
quarrelsome *adj* pugnāx, lītigiōsus.
quarry *n* lapicīdinae *fpl*, metallum *nt*; (*prey*)
praeda *f* ♦ *vt* excīdere.
quart *n* duō sextāriī *mpl*.
quartan *n* (*fever*) quartāna *f*.
quarter *n* quarta pars *f*, quadrāns *m*; (*sector*)
regiō *f*; (*direction*) pars *f*, regiō *f*; (*respite*)
missiō *f*; ~**s** castra *ntpl*; (*billet*) hospitium *nt*;
come to close ~s manum cōnserere; (*armies*)
signa cōnferre; **winter ~s** hīberna *ntpl* ♦ *vt*
quadrifidam dīvidere; (*troops*) in hospitia
dīvidere.
quarterdeck *n* puppis *f*.
quarterly *adj* trimestris ♦ *adv* quartō quōque
mēnse.
quartermaster *n* (*navy*) gubernātor *m*; (*army*)
castrōrum praefectus *m*.
quarterstaff *n* rudis *f*.
quash *vt* comprimere; (*decision*) rescindere.
quatrain *n* tetrastichon *nt*.
quaver *n* tremor *m* ♦ *vi* tremere.
quavering *adj* tremebundus.
quay *n* crepīdō *f*.
queasy *adj* fastīdiōsus.
queen *n* rēgīna *f*; (*bee*) rēx *m*.
queer *adj* īnsolēns, rīdiculus.
quell *vt* opprimere, domāre, dēbellāre.
quench *vt* exstinguere, restinguere; (*thirst*)
sēdāre, explēre.
querulous *adj* querulus, queribundus.
query *n* interrogātiō *f* ♦ *vt* in dubium vocāre ♦
vi rogāre.
quest *n* investīgātiō *f*; **go in ~ of** investīgāre,
anquīrere.
question *n* interrogātiō *f*; (*at issue*) quaestiō *f*,
rēs *f*; (*in doubt*) dubium *nt*; **ask a ~** rogāre,
quaerere, scīscitārī, percontārī; **call in ~** in
dubium vocāre, addubitāre; **out of the ~**
indignus; **be out of the ~** improbārī, fierī nōn
posse; **the ~ is** illud quaeritur; **there is no ~**
that nōn dubium est quīn (*subj*); **without ~**
sine dubiō ♦ *vt* interrogāre; (*closely*)
percontārī; (*doubt*) in dubium vocāre ♦ *vi*
dubitāre.
questionable *adj* incertus, dubius.
questioner *n* percontātor *m*.
questioning *n* interrogātiō *f*.
queue *n* agmen *nt*.
quibble *n* captiō *f* ♦ *vi* cavillārī.
quibbler *n* cavillātor *m*.
quibbling *adj* captiōsus.
quick *adj* (*speed*) celer, vēlōx, citus; (*to act*)

alacer, impiger; (*to perceive*) sagāx; (*with hands*) facilis; (*living*) vīvus; **be ~** properāre, festīnāre; **cut to the ~** ad vīvum resecāre; (*fig*) mordēre.

quicken *vt* adcelerāre; (*with life*) animāre.

quickening *adj* vītālis.

quickly *adv* celeriter, citō; (*haste*) properē; (*mind*) acūtē; **as ~ as possible** quam celerrimē.

quickness *n* celeritās *f*, vēlōcitās *f*; (*to act*) alacritās *f*; (*to perceive*) sagācitās *f*, sollertia *f*.

quicksand *n* syrtis *f*.

quick-tempered *adj* īrācundus.

quick-witted *adj* acūtus, sagāx, perspicāx.

quiescence *n* inertia *f*, ōtium *nt*.

quiescent *adj* iners, ōtiōsus.

quiet *adj* tranquillus, quiētus, placidus; (*silent*) tacitus; **be ~** quiēscere; silēre ♦ *n* quiēs *f*, tranquillitās *f*; silentium *nt*; (*peace*) pāx *f* ♦ *vt* pācāre, compōnere.

quietly *adv* tranquillē, quiētē; tacitē, per silentium; aequō animō.

quietness *n* tranquillitās *f*; silentium *nt*.

quill *n* penna *f*.

quince *n* cydōnium *nt*.

quinquennial *adj* quinquennālis.

quinquereme *n* quinquerēmis *f*.

quintessence *n* flōs *m*, vīs *f*.

quip *n* sāl *m*, facētiae *fpl*.

quirk *n* captiuncula *f*; **~s** *pl* trīcae *fpl*.

quit *vt* relinquere ♦ *adj* līber, solūtus.

quite *adv* admodum, plānē, prōrsus; **not ~** minus, parum; (*time*) nōndum.

quits *n* parēs *mpl*.

quiver *n* pharetra *f* ♦ *vi* tremere, contremere.

quivering *adj* tremebundus, tremulus.

quoit *n* discus *m*.

quota *n* pars *f*, rata pars *f*.

quotation *n* (*act*) commemorātiō *f*; (*passage*) locus *m*.

quote *vt* prōferre, commemorāre.

quoth *vt* inquit.

R, r

rabbit *n* cunīculus *m*.

rabble *n* turba *f*; (*class*) vulgus *nt*, plēbēcula *f*.

rabid *adj* rabidus.

rabidly *adv* rabidē.

race *n* (*descent*) genus *nt*, stirps *f*; (*people*) gēns *f*, nōmen *nt*; (*contest*) certāmen *nt*; (*fig*) cursus *m*, curriculum *nt*; (*water*) flūmen *nt*; **run a ~** cursū certāre; **run the ~** (*fig*) spatium dēcurrere ♦ *vi* certāre, contendere.

racecourse *n* (*foot*) stadium *nt*; (*horse*)

spatium *nt*.

racer *n* cursor *m*.

racial *adj* gentīlis.

rack *n* (*torture*) tormentum *nt*; (*shelf*) pluteus *m*; **be on the ~** (*fig*) cruciārī ♦ *vt* torquēre, cruciāre; **~ off** (*wine*) diffundere.

racket *n* (*noise*) strepitus *m*.

racy *adj* (*style*) salsus.

radiance *n* splendor *m*, fulgor *m*.

radiant *adj* splendidus, nitidus.

radiantly *adv* splendidē.

radiate *vi* fulgēre; (*direction*) dīversōs tendere ♦ *vt* ēmittere.

radical *adj* īnsitus, innātus; (*thorough*) tōtus ♦ *n* novārum rērum cupidus *m*.

radically *adv* omnīnō, penitus, funditus.

radish *n* rādīx *f*.

radius *n* radius *m*.

raffish *adj* dissolūtus.

raffle *n* ālea *f* ♦ *vt* āleā vēndere.

raft *n* ratis *f*.

rafter *n* trabs *f*, tignum *nt*.

rag *n* pannus *m*.

rage *n* īra *f*, furor *m*; **be all the ~** in ōre omnium esse; **spend one's ~** exsaevīre ♦ *vi* furere, saevīre; (*furiously*) dēbacchārī.

ragged *adj* pannōsus.

raid *n* excursiō *f*, incursiō *f*, impressiō *f*; **make a ~** excurrere ♦ *vt* incursiōnem facere in (*acc*).

rail *n* longurius *m* ♦ *vt* saepīre ♦ *vi*: **~ at** maledīcere (*dat*), convīcia facere (*dat*).

railing *n* saepēs *f*, cancellī *mpl*.

raillery *n* cavillātiō *f*.

raiment *n* vestis *f*.

rain *n* pluvia *f*, imber *m* ♦ *vi* pluere; **it is raining** pluit.

rainbow *n* arcus *m*.

rainstorm *n* imber *m*.

rainy *adj* pluvius.

raise *vt* tollere, ēlevāre; (*army*) cōgere, cōnscrībere; (*children*) ēducāre; (*cry*) tollere; (*from dead*) excitāre; (*laugh*) movēre; (*money*) cōnflāre; (*price*) augēre; (*siege*) exsolvere; (*structure*) exstruere; (*to higher rank*) ēvehere; **~ up** ērigere, sublevāre.

raisin *n* astaphis *f*.

rajah *n* dynastēs *m*.

rake *n* rastrum *nt*; (*person*) nepōs *m* ♦ *vt* rādere; **~ in** conrādere; **~ up** (*fig*) ēruere.

rakish *adj* dissolūtus.

rally *n* conventus *m* ♦ *vt* (*troops*) in ōrdinem revocāre; (*with words*) hortārī; (*banter*) cavillārī ♦ *vi* sē colligere.

ram *n* ariēs *m*; (*battering*) ariēs *m* ♦ *vt*: **~ down** fistūcāre; **~ home** (*fact*) inculcāre.

ramble *n* errātiō *f* ♦ *vi* vagārī, errāre.

rambling *adj* vagus; (*plant*) errāticus; (*speech*) fluēns.

ramification *n* rāmus *m*.

rammer *n* fistūca *f*.

rampage *vi* saevīre.

rampant *adj* ferōx.

rampart n agger m, vallum nt.
ranch n lātifundium nt.
rancid adj pūtidus.
rancour n odium nt, acerbitās f, invidia f.
random adj fortuītus; **at ~** temerē.
range n ōrdō m, seriēs f; (mountain) iugum nt;
  (of weapon) iactus m; **within ~** intrā tēlī
  iactum; **come within ~** sub ictum venīre ♦ vt
  ōrdināre ♦ vi ēvagārī, pervagārī; (in speech)
  excurrere.
rank n (line) ōrdō m; (class) ōrdō m; (position)
  locus m, dignitās f; **~ and file** gregāriī mīlitēs
  mpl; **keep the ~s** ōrdinēs observāre; **the ~s**
  (MIL) aciēs, aciēī f; **leave the ~s** ōrdine ēgredī,
  ab signīs discēdere; **reduce to the ~s** in
  ōrdinem redigere ♦ vt numerāre ♦ vi in
  numerō habērī.
rank adj luxuriōsus; (smell) gravis, foetidus.
rankle vi exulcerāre.
rankness n luxuriēs f.
ransack vt dīripere, spoliāre.
ransom n redemptiō f, pretium nt ♦ vt
  redimere.
rant vi latrāre.
ranter n rabula m, latrātor m.
rap n ictus m ♦ vt ferīre.
rapacious adj rapāx, avidus.
rapaciously adv avidē.
rapacity n rapācitās f, aviditās f.
rape n raptus m.
rapid adj rapidus, vēlōx, citus, incitātus.
rapidity n celeritās f, vēlōcitās f, incitātiō f.
rapidly adv rapidē, vēlōciter, citō.
rapine n rapīna f.
rapt adj intentus.
rapture n laetitia f, alacritās f.
rare adj rārus; (occurrence) īnfrequēns;
  (quality) singulāris.
rarefy vt extenuāre.
rarely adv rārō.
rarity n rāritās f, (thing) rēs īnsolita f.
rascal n furcifer m, scelestus m.
rascally adj improbus.
rash adj temerārius, audāx, incōnsultus;
  praeceps.
rashly adv temerē, incōnsultē.
rashness n temeritās f, audācia f.
rat n mūs m/f.
rate n (cost) pretium nt; (standard) nōrma f;
  (tax) vectīgal nt; (speed) celeritās f; **at any ~**
  (concessive) utique, saltem; (adversative)
  quamquam, tamen ♦ vt (value) aestimāre;
  (scold) increpāre, obiūrgāre.
rather adv potius, satius; (somewhat)
  aliquantum; (with comp) aliquantō; (with
  verbs) mālō; (correcting) immo; **~ sad** tristior;
  I would ~ mālō; **I ~ think** haud sciō an; **~ than**
  magis quam, potius quam.
ratification n (formal) sanctiō f.
ratify vt ratum facere, sancīre; (law) iubēre.
rating n taxātiō f, aestimātiō f; (navy) nauta m;
  (scolding) obiūrgātiō f.
ratiocinate vi ratiōcinārī.

ratiocination n ratiōcinātiō f.
ration n dēmēnsum nt.
rational adj animō praeditus; **be ~** sapere.
rationality n ratiō f.
rationally adv ratiōne.
rations npl cibāria ntpl, diāria ntpl.
rattle n crepitus m; (toy) crotalum nt ♦ vi
  crepitāre, increpāre.
raucous adj raucus.
ravage vt dēpopulārī, vastāre, dīripere.
rave vi furere, īnsānīre; (fig) bacchārī,
  saevīre.
raven n cornīx f.
ravenous adj rapāx, vorāx.
ravenously adv avidē.
ravine n faucēs fpl, hiātus m.
raving adj furiōsus, īnsānus ♦ n furor m.
ravish vt rapere; (joy) efferre.
raw adj crūdus; (person) rudis, agrestis.
ray n radius m; **the first ~ of hope appeared**
  prīma spēs adfulsit.
raze vt excīdere, solō aequāre.
razor n novācula f.
reach n (space) spatium nt; (mind) captus m;
  (weapon) ictus m; **out of ~ of** extrā (acc);
  within ~ ad manum ♦ vt advenīre ad (+ acc);
  attingere; (space) pertinēre ad; (journey)
  pervenīre ad.
react vi adficī; **~ to** ferre.
reaction n: **what was his ~ to?** quō animō
  tulit?
read vt legere; (a book) ēvolvere; (aloud)
  recitāre; **~ over** perlegere.
reader n lēctor m.
readily adv facile, libenter, ultrō.
readiness n facilitās f; **in ~** ad manum, in
  prōmptū, in expedītō.
reading n lēctiō f.
readjust vt dēnuō accommodāre.
ready adj parātus, prōmptus; (manner) facilis;
  (money) praesēns; **get, make ~** parāre,
  expedīre, adōrnāre.
reaffirm vt iterum adfirmāre.
real adj vērus, germānus.
real estate n fundus m, solum nt.
realism n vēritās f.
realistic adj vērī similis.
reality n rēs f, rēs ipsa f, vērum nt; **in ~** rēvērā.
realize vt intellegere, animadvertere; (aim)
  efficere, peragere; (money) redigere.
really adv vērē, rēvērā, profectō; **~?** itane
  vērō?
realm n rēgnum nt.
reap vt metere; **~ the reward of** frūctum
  percipere ex.
reaper n messor m.
reappear vi revenīre.
rear vt alere, ēducāre; (structure) exstruere ♦
  vi sē ērigere ♦ n tergum nt; (MIL) novissima
  aciēs f, novissimum agmen nt; **in the ~** ā
  tergō; **bring up the ~** agmen claudere, agmen
  cōgere ♦ adj postrēmus, novissimus.
rearguard n novissimum agmen nt.

novissimī *mpl.*

rearrange *vt* ōrdinem mūtāre (*gen*).

reason *n* (*faculty*) mēns *f*, animus *m*, ratiō *f*; (*sanity*) sānitās *f*; (*argument*) ratiō *f*; (*cause*) causa *f*; (*moderation*) modus *m*; **by ~ of** propter (*acc*); **for this ~** idcircō, ideō, proptereā; **in ~** aequus, modicus; **with good ~** iūre; **without ~** temerē, sine causā; **without good ~** frustrā, iniūriā; **give a ~ for** ratiōnem adferre (*gen*); **I know the ~ for** sciō cūr, quamobrem (*subj*); **there is no ~ for** nōn est cūr, nihil est quod (*subj*); **lose one's ~** īnsānīre ♦ *vi* ratiōcinārī, disserere.

reasonable *adj* aequus, iūstus; (*person*) modestus; (*amount*) modicus.

reasonably *adv* ratiōne, iūstē; modicē.

reasoning *n* ratiō *f*, ratiōcinātiō *f*.

reassemble *vt* colligere, cōgere.

reassert *vt* iterāre.

reassume *vt* recipere.

reassure *vt* firmāre, cōnfirmāre.

rebate *vt* dēdūcere.

rebel *n* rebellis *m* ♦ *adj* sēditiōsus ♦ *vi* rebelliōnem facere, rebellāre, dēscīscere.

rebellion *n* sēditiō *f*, mōtus *m*.

rebellious *adj* sēditiōsus.

rebound *vi* resilīre.

rebuff *n* repulsa *f* ♦ *vt* repellere, āversārī.

rebuild *vt* renovāre, restaurāre.

rebuke *n* reprehēnsiō *f*, obiūrgātiō *f* ♦ *vt* reprehendere, obiūrgāre, increpāre.

rebut *vt* refūtāre, redarguere.

recalcitrant *adj* invītus.

recall *n* revocātiō *f*, reditus *m* ♦ *vt* revocāre; (*from exile*) redūcere; (*to mind*) reminīscī (*gen*), recordārī (*gen*).

recant *vt* retractāre.

recantation *n* receptus *m*.

recapitulate *vt* repetere, summātim dīcere.

recapitulation *n* ēnumerātiō *f*.

recapture *vt* recipere.

recast *vt* reficere, retractāre.

recede *vi* recēdere.

receipt *n* (*act*) acceptiō *f*; (*money*) acceptum *nt*; (*written*) apocha *f*.

receive *vt* accipere, capere; (*in turn*) excipere.

receiver *n* receptor *m*.

recent *adj* recēns.

recently *adv* nūper, recēns.

receptacle *n* receptāculum *nt*.

reception *n* aditus *m*, hospitium *nt*.

receptive *adj* docilis.

recess *n* recessus *m*, angulus *m*; (*holiday*) fēriae *fpl.*

recharge *vt* replēre.

recipe *n* compositiō *f*.

recipient *n* quī accipit.

reciprocal *adj* mūtuus.

reciprocally *adv* mūtuō, inter sē.

reciprocate *vt* referre, reddere.

reciprocity *n* mūtuum *nt.*

recital *n* nārrātiō *f*, ēnumerātiō *f*; (*LIT*) recitātiō *f.*

recitation *n* recitātiō *f.*

recite *vt* recitāre; (*details*) ēnumerāre.

reciter *n* recitātor *m.*

reck *vt* ratiōnem habēre (*gen*).

reckless *adj* temerārius, incautus, praeceps.

recklessly *adv* incautē, temerē.

recklessness *n* temeritās *f*, neglegentia *f.*

reckon *vt* (*count*) computāre, numerāre; (*think*) cēnsēre, dūcere; (*estimate*) aestimāre; **~ on** cōnfīdere (*dat*); **~ up** dīnumerāre; (*cost*) aestimāre; **~ with** contendere cum.

reckoning *n* ratiō *f.*

reclaim *vt* repetere; (*from error*) revocāre.

recline *vi* recumbere; (*at table*) accumbere; (*plur*) discumbere.

recluse *n* homō sōlitārius *m.*

recognition *n* cognitiō *f.*

recognizance *n* vadimōnium *nt.*

recognize *vt* agnōscere; (*approve*) accipere; (*admit*) fatērī.

recoil *vi* resilīre; **~ from** refugere; **~ upon** recidere in (*acc*).

recollect *vt* reminīscī (*gen*).

recollection *n* memoria *f*, recordātiō *f.*

recommence *vt* renovāre, redintegrāre.

recommend *vt* commendāre; (*advise*) suādēre (*dat*).

recommendation *n* commendātiō *f*; (*advice*) cōnsilium *nt*; **letter of ~** litterae commendātīciae.

recompense *vt* remūnerārī, grātiam referre (*dat*) ♦ *n* praemium *nt*, remūnerātiō *f.*

reconcile *vt* compōnere, reconciliāre; **be ~d in** grātiam redīre.

reconciliation *n* reconciliātiō *f*, grātia *f.*

recondite *adj* reconditus, abstrūsus.

recondition *vt* reficere.

reconnaissance *n* explōrātiō *f.*

reconnoitre *vt, vi* explōrāre; **without reconnoitring** inexplōrātō.

reconquer *vt* recipere.

reconsider *vt* reputāre, retractāre.

reconstruct *vt* restituere, renovāre.

reconstruction *n* renovātiō *f.*

record *n* monumentum *nt*; (*LIT*) commentārius *m*; **~s** *pl* tabulae *fpl*, fāstī *mpl*, ācta *ntpl*; **break the ~** priōrēs omnēs superāre ♦ *vt* in commentārium referre; (*history*) perscrībere, nārrāre.

recount *vt* nārrāre, commemorāre.

recourse *n*: **have ~ to** (*for safety*) cōnfugere ad; (*as expedient*) dēcurrere ad.

recover *vt* recipere, recuperāre; (*loss*) reparāre; **~ oneself** sē colligere; **~ one's senses** ad sānitātem revertī ♦ *vi* convalēscere.

recovery *n* recuperātiō *f*; (*from illness*) salūs *f.*

recreate *vt* recreāre.

recreation *n* requiēs *f*, remissiō *f*, lūdus *m.*

recriminate *vi* in vicem accūsāre.

recrimination *n* mūtua accūsātiō *f.*

recruit *n* tīrō *m* ♦ *vt* (*MIL*) cōnscrībere; (*strength*) reficere.

recruiting officer n conquīsītor m.
rectify vt corrigere, ēmendāre.
rectitude n probitās f.
recumbent adj supīnus.
recuperate vi convalēscere.
recur vi recurrere, redīre.
recurrence n reditus m, reversiō f.
recurrent adj adsiduus.
red adj ruber.
redden vi ērubēscere ♦ vt rutilāre.
reddish adj subrūfus.
redeem vt redimere, līberāre.
redeemer n līberātor m.
redemption n redemptiō f.
red-haired adj rūfus.
red-handed adj: **catch ~ in** manifestō scelere dēprehendere.
red-hot adj fervēns.
red lead n minium nt.
redness n rubor m.
redolent adj: **be ~ of** redolēre.
redouble vt ingemināre.
redoubt n prōpugnāculum nt.
redoubtable adj īnfestus, formīdolōsus.
redound vi redundāre; **it ~s to my credit** mihī honōrī est.
redress n remedium nt; **demand ~ rēs** repetere ♦ vt restituere.
reduce vt minuere, attenuāre; (to a condition) redigere, dēdūcere; (MIL) expugnāre; **~ to the ranks** in ōrdinem cōgere.
reduction n imminūtiō f; (MIL) expugnātiō f.
redundancy n redundantia f.
redundant adj redundāns; **be ~** redundāre.
reduplication n gemīnātiō f.
re-echo vt reddere, referre ♦ vi resonāre.
reed n harundō f.
reedy adj harundineus.
reef n saxa ntpl ♦ vt (sail) subnectere.
reek n fūmus m ♦ vi fūmāre.
reel vi vacillāre, titubāre.
re-enlist vt rescrībere.
re-establish vt restituere.
refashion vt reficere.
refer vt (person) dēlēgāre; (matter) rēicere, remittere ♦ vi: **~ to** spectāre ad; (in speech) attingere, perstringere.
referee n arbiter m.
reference n ratiō f; (in book) locus m.
refine vt excolere, expolīre; (metal) excoquere.
refined adj hūmānus, urbānus, polītus.
refinement n hūmānitās f, cultus m, ēlegantia f.
refit vt reficere.
reflect vt reddere, repercutere ♦ vi meditārī; **~ upon** cōnsīderāre, sēcum reputāre; (blame) reprehendere.
reflection n (of light) repercussus m; (image) imāgō f; (thought) meditātiō f, cōgitātiō f; (blame) reprehēnsiō f; **cast ~s on** maculīs aspergere, vitiō vertere; **with due ~** cōnsīderātē; **without ~** incōnsultē.

reflux n recessus m.
reform n ēmendātiō f ♦ vt (lines) restituere; (error) corrigere, ēmendāre, meliōrem facere ♦ vi sē corrigere.
reformation n corrēctiō f.
reformer n corrēctor m, ēmendātor m.
refract vt īnfringere.
refractory adj contumāx.
refrain vi temperāre, abstinēre (dat), supersedēre (inf).
refresh vt recreāre, renovāre, reficere; (mind) integrāre.
refreshed adj requiētus.
refreshing adj dulcis, iūcundus.
refreshment n cibus m.
refuge n perfugium nt; (secret) latebra f; **take ~ with** perfugere ad (acc); **take ~ in** confugere.
refugee n profugus m.
refulgence n splendor m.
refulgent adj splendidus.
refund vt reddere.
refusal n recūsātiō f, dētrectātiō f.
refuse n pūrgāmenta ntpl; (fig) faex f ♦ vt (request) dēnegāre; (offer) dētrectāre, recūsāre; (with verb) nōlle.
refutation n refūtātiō f, reprehēnsiō f.
refute vt refellere, redarguere, revincere.
regain vt recipere.
regal adj rēgius, rēgālis.
regale vt excipere, dēlectāre; **~ oneself** epulārī.
regalia n īnsignia ntpl.
regally adv rēgāliter.
regard n respectus m, ratiō f; (esteem) grātia f; **with ~ to** ad (acc), quod attinet ad ♦ vt (look) intuērī, spectāre; (deem) habēre, dūcere; **send ~s to** salūtem dīcere (dat).
regarding prep dē (abl).
regardless adj neglegēns, immemor.
regency n interrēgnum nt.
regent n interrēx m.
regicide n (person) rēgis interfector m; (act) rēgis caedēs f.
regime n administrātiō f.
regimen n vīctus m.
regiment n legiō f.
region n regiō f, tractus m.
register n tabulae fpl, album nt ♦ vt in tabulās referre, perscrībere; (emotion) ostendere, sūmere.
registrar n tabulārius m.
registry n tabulārium nt.
regret n dolor m; (for past) dēsīderium nt; (for fault) paenitentia f ♦ vt dolēre; **I ~ mē** paenitet, mē piget (gen).
regretful adj maestus.
regretfully adv dolenter.
regrettable adj īnfēlīx, īnfortūnātus.
regular adj (consistent) cōnstāns; (orderly) ōrdinātus; (habitual) solitus, adsiduus; (proper) iūstus, rēctus.
regularity n moderātiō f, ōrdō m; (consistency) cōnstantia f.

regularly *adv* ōrdine; cōnstanter; iūstē, rēctē.
regulate *vt* ōrdināre, dīrigere; (*control*)
moderārī.
regulation *n* lēx *f*, dēcrētum *nt*.
rehabilitate *vt* restituere.
rehearsal *n* meditātiō *f*.
rehearse *vt* meditārī.
reign *n* rēgnum *nt*; (*emperor's*) prīncipātus *m*;
in the ~ of Numa rēgnante Numā ♦ *vi*
rēgnāre; (*fig*) dominārī.
reimburse *vt* rependere.
rein *n* habēna *f*; **give full ~ to** habēnās
immittere ♦ *vt* īnfrēnāre.
reindeer *n* rēnō *m*.
reinforce *vt* firmāre, cōnfirmāre.
reinforcement *n* subsidium *nt*; **~s** *pl* novae
cōpiae *fpl*.
reinstate *vt* restituere, redūcere.
reinstatement *n* restitūtiō *f*, reductiō *f*; (*to
legal privileges*) postlīminium *nt*.
reinvigorate *vt* recreāre.
reiterate *vt* dictitāre, iterāre.
reiteration *n* iterātiō *f*.
reject *vt* rēicere; (*with scorn*) respuere,
aspernārī, repudiāre.
rejection *n* rēiectiō *f*, repulsa *f*.
rejoice *vi* gaudēre, laetārī ♦ *vt* dēlectāre.
rejoicing *n* gaudium *nt*.
rejoin *vt* redīre ad ♦ *vi* respondēre.
rejoinder *n* respōnsum *nt*.
rejuvenate *vt*: **be ~d** repuerāscere.
rekindle *vt* suscitāre.
relapse *vi* recidere.
relate *vt* (*tell*) nārrāre, commemorāre,
expōnere; (*compare*) cōnferre ♦ *vi*
pertinēre.
related *adj* propinquus; (*by birth*) cognātus; (*by
marriage*) adfīnis; (*fig*) fīnitimus.
relation *n* (*tale*) nārrātiō *f*; (*connection*) ratiō *f*;
(*kin*) necessārius *m*, cognātus *m*, adfīnis *m*.
relationship *n* necessitūdō *f*; (*by birth*)
cognātiō *f*; (*by marriage*) adfīnitās *f*;
(*connection*) vīcīnitās *f*.
relative *adj* cum cēterīs comparātus ♦ *n*
propinquus *m*, cognātus *m*, adfīnis *m*,
necessārius *m*.
relatively *adv* ex comparātiōne.
relax *vt* laxāre, remittere ♦ *vi* languēscere.
relaxation *n* remissiō *f*, requiēs *f*, lūdus *m*.
relay *n*: **~s of horses** dispositī equī *mpl*.
release *vt* solvere, exsolvere, līberāre,
expedīre; (*law*) absolvere ♦ *n* missiō *f*,
līberātiō *f*.
relegate *vt* relēgāre.
relent *vi* concēdere, plācārī, flectī.
relentless *adj* immisericors, inexōrābilis;
(*things*) improbus.
relevant *adj* ad rem.
reliability *n* fīdūcia *f*.
reliable *adj* fīdus.
reliance *n* fīdūcia *f*, fidēs *f*.
reliant *adj* frētus.
relic *n* rēliquiae *fpl*.

relief *n* levātiō *f*, levāmen *nt*, adlevāmentum *nt*;
(*aid*) subsidium *nt*; (*turn of duty*) vicēs *fpl*; (*art*)
ēminentia *f*; (*sculpture*) toreuma *nt*; **bas ~**
anaglypta *ntpl*; **in ~** ēminēns, expressus;
throw into ~ exprimere, distinguere.
relieve *vt* levāre, sublevāre; (*aid*) subvenīre
(*dat*); (*duty*) succēdere (*dat*), excipere; (*art*)
distinguere.
religion *n* religiō *f*, deōrum cultus *m*.
religious *adj* religiōsus, pius; **~ feeling** religiō
f.
religiously *adv* religiōsē.
relinquish *vt* relinquere; (*office*) sē abdicāre
(*abl*).
relish *n* sapor *m*; (*sauce*) condīmentum *nt*; (*zest*)
studium *nt* ♦ *vt* dēlectārī (*abl*).
reluctance *n*: **with ~** invītus.
reluctant *adj* invītus.
reluctantly *adv* invītus, gravātē.
rely *vi* fīdere (*dat*), cōnfīdere (*dat*).
relying *adj* frētus (*abl*).
remain *vi* manēre, morārī; (*left over*) restāre,
superesse.
remainder *n* reliquum *nt*.
remaining *adj* reliquus; **the ~** cēterī *pl*.
remains *n* rēliquiae *fpl*.
remand *vt* (*law*) ampliāre.
remark *n* dictum *nt* ♦ *vt* dīcere; (*note*)
observāre.
remarkable *adj* īnsignis, ēgregius,
memorābilis.
remarkably *adv* īnsignītē, ēgregiē.
remediable *adj* sānābilis.
remedy *n* remedium *nt* ♦ *vt* medērī (*dat*),
sānāre.
remember *vt* meminisse (*gen*); (*recall*)
recordārī (*gen*), reminīscī (*gen*).
remembrance *n* memoria *f*, recordātiō *f*.
remind *vt* admonēre, commonefacere.
reminder *n* admonitiō *f*, admonitum *nt*.
reminiscence *n* recordātiō *f*.
remiss *adj* dissolūtus, neglegēns.
remission *n* venia *f*.
remissness *n* neglegentia *f*.
remit *vt* remittere; (*fault*) ignōscere (*dat*);
(*debt*) dōnāre; (*punishment*) condōnāre;
(*question*) referre.
remittance *n* pecūnia *f*.
remnant *n* fragmentum *nt*; **~s** *pl* rēliquiae *fpl*.
remonstrance *n* obtestātiō *f*, obiūrgātiō *f*.
remonstrate *vi* reclāmāre; **~ with** obiūrgāre;
~ about expostulāre.
remorse *n* paenitentia *f*, cōnscientia *f*.
remorseless *adj* immisericors.
remote *adj* remōtus, recōnditus.
remotely *adv* procul.
remoteness *n* longinquitās *f*.
removal *n* āmōtiō *f*; (*going*) migrātiō *f*.
remove *vt* āmovēre, dēmere, eximere,
removēre; (*out of the way*) dēmovēre ♦ *vi*
migrāre, dēmigrāre.
remunerate *vt* remūnerārī.
remuneration *n* mercēs *f*, praemium *nt*.

rend *vt* scindere, dīvellere.
render *vt* reddere; (*music*) interpretārī;
(*translation*) vertere; (*thanks*) referre.
rendering *n* interpretātiō *f*.
rendez-vous *n* cōnstitūtum *nt*.
renegade *n* dēsertor *m*.
renew *vt* renovāre, integrāre, īnstaurāre,
redintegrāre.
renewal *n* renovātiō *f*; (*ceremony*) īnstaurātiō
f.
renounce *vt* renūntiāre, mittere, repudiāre.
renovate *vt* renovāre, reficere.
renown *n* fāma *f*, glōria *f*.
renowned *adj* praeclārus, īnsignis, nōtus.
rent *n* (*tear*) fissum *nt*; (*pay*) mercēs *f* ♦ *vt* (*hire*)
condūcere; (*lease*) locāre.
renunciation *n* cessiō *f*, repudiātiō *f*.
repair *vt* reficere, sarcīre ♦ *vi* sē recipere ♦ *n*:
keep in good ~ tuērī; **in bad ~** ruīnōsus.
reparable *adj* ēmendābilis.
reparation *n* satisfactiō *f*.
repartee *n* facētiae *fpl*, salēs *mpl*.
repast *n* cēna *f*, cibus *m*.
repay *vt* remūnerārī, grātiam referre (*dat*);
(*money*) repōnere.
repayment *n* solūtiō *f*.
repeal *vt* abrogāre ♦ *n* abrogātiō *f*.
repeat *vt* iterāre; (*lesson*) reddere; (*ceremony*)
īnstaurāre; (*performance*) referre.
repeatedly *adv* identidem, etiam atque etiam.
repel *vt* repellere, dēfendere.
repellent *adj* iniūcundus.
repent *vi*: **I ~** mē paenitet (+ *gen of thing*).
repentance *n* paenitentia *f*.
repentant *adj* paenitēns.
repercussion *n* ēventus *m*.
repertory *n* thēsaurus *m*.
repetition *n* iterātiō *f*.
repine *vi* conquerī.
replace *vt* repōnere, restituere; **~ by**
substituere.
replacement *n* supplēmentum *nt*.
replenish *vt* replēre, supplēre.
replete *adj* plēnus.
repletion *n* satietās *f*.
replica *n* apographon *nt*.
reply *vi* respondēre ♦ *n* respōnsum *nt*.
report *n* (*talk*) fāma *f*, rūmor *m*; (*repute*) opīniō
f; (*account*) renūntiātiō *f*; litterae *fpl*; (*noise*)
fragor *m*; **make a ~** renūntiāre ♦ *vt* referre,
dēferre, renūntiāre.
repose *n* quiēs *f*, requiēs *f* ♦ *vt* repōnere,
pōnere ♦ *vi* quiēscere.
repository *n* horreum *nt*.
reprehend *vt* reprehendere, culpāre.
reprehensible *adj* accūsābilis, improbus.
reprehension *n* reprehēnsiō *f*, culpa *f*.
represent *vt* dēscrībere, effingere, exprimere,
imitārī; (*character*) partēs agere (*gen*),
persōnam gerere (*gen*); (*case*) prōpōnere;
(*substitute for*) vicārium esse (*gen*).
representation *n* imāgō *f*, imitātiō *f*; **make ~s
to** admonēre.

representative *n* lēgātus *m*.
repress *vt* reprimere, cohibēre.
repression *n* coercitiō *f*.
reprieve *n* mora *f*, venia *f* ♦ *vt* veniam dare
(*dat*).
reprimand *vt* reprehendere, increpāre ♦ *n*
reprehēnsiō *f*.
reprisals *n* ultiō *f*.
reproach *vt* exprobāre, obicere (*dat*) ♦ *n*
exprobrātiō *f*, probrum *nt*; (*cause*)
opprobrium *nt*.
reproachful *adj* contumēliōsus.
reprobate *adj* perditus.
reproduce *vt* propāgāre; (*likeness*) referre.
reproduction *n* prōcreātiō *f*; (*likeness*) imāgō
f.
reproductive *adj* genitālis.
reproof *n* reprehēnsiō *f*, obiūrgātiō *f*.
reprove *vt* reprehendere, increpāre,
obiūrgāre.
reptile *n* serpēns *f*.
republic *n* lībera rēspūblica *f*, cīvitās
populāris *f*.
republican *adj* populāris.
repudiate *vt* repudiāre.
repudiation *n* repudiātiō *f*.
repugnance *n* fastīdium *nt*, odium *nt*.
repugnant *adj* invīsus, adversus.
repulse *n* dēpulsiō *f*; (*at election*) repulsa *f* ♦ *vt*
repellere, āversārī, prōpulsāre.
repulsion *n* repugnantia *f*.
repulsive *adj* odiōsus, foedus.
reputable *adj* honestus.
reputation *n* fāma *f*, existimātiō *f*; (*for
something*) opīniō *f* (*gen*); **have a ~** nōmen
habēre.
repute *n* fāma *f*, existimātiō *f*; **bad ~** īnfāmia *f*.
reputed *adj*: **I am ~ to be** dīcor esse.
request *n* rogātiō *f*, postulātum *nt*; **obtain a ~**
impetrāre ♦ *vt* rogāre, petere; (*urgently*)
dēposcere.
require *vt* (*demand*) imperāre, postulāre;
(*need*) egēre (*abl*); (*call for*) requīrere.
requirement *n* postulātum *nt*, necessārium *nt*.
requisite *adj* necessārius.
requisition *n* postulātiō *f* ♦ *vt* imperāre.
requital *n* grātia *f*, vicēs *fpl*.
requite *vt* grātiam referre (*dat*), remūnerārī.
rescind *vt* rescindere, abrogāre.
rescript *n* rescrīptum *nt*.
rescue *vt* ēripere, expedīre, servāre ♦ *n* salūs
f; **come to the ~ of** subvenīre (*dat*).
research *n* investīgātiō *f*.
resemblance *n* similitūdō *f*, imāgō *f*, īnstar *nt*.
resemble *vt* similem esse (*dat*), referre.
resent *vt* aegrē ferre, indignārī.
resentful *adj* īrācundus.
resentment *n* dolor *m*, indignātiō *f*.
reservation *n* (*proviso*) exceptiō *f*.
reserve *vt* servāre; (*store*) recondere; (*in a
deal*) excipere ♦ *nt* (*MIL*) subsidium *nt*;
(*disposition*) pudor *m*, reticentia *f*; (*caution*)
cautiō *f*; **in ~** in succenturiātus; **without ~**

palam.
reserved *adj* (*place*) adsignātus; (*disposition*)
taciturnus, tēctus.
reservedly *adv* circumspectē.
reserves *npl* subsidia *ntpl*.
reservoir *n* lacus *m*.
reside *vi* habitāre; ~ **in** incolere.
residence *n* domicilium *nt*, domus *f.*
resident *n* incola *m/f.*
residual *adj* reliquus.
residue, residuum *n* reliqua pars *f.*
resign *vt* cēdere; (*office*) abdicāre mē, tē *etc* dē
(+ *abl*); ~ **oneself** acquiēscere ♦ *vi* sē
abdicāre.
resignation *n* abdicātiō *f*; (*state of mind*)
patientia *f*, aequus animus *m.*
resigned *adj* patiēns; **be ~ to** aequō animō
ferre.
resilience *n* mollitia *f.*
resilient *adj* mollis.
resist *vt* resistere (*dat*), adversārī (*dat*),
repugnāre (*dat*).
resistance *n* repugnantia *f*; **offer ~** obsistere
(*dat*).
resistless *adj* invictus.
resolute *adj* fortis, cōnstāns.
resolutely *adv* fortiter, cōnstanter.
resolution *n* (*conduct*) fortitūdō *f*, cōnstantia *f*;
(*decision*) dēcrētum *nt*, sententia *f*; (*into parts*)
sēcrētiō *f.*
resolve *n* fortitūdō *f*, cōnstantia *f* ♦ *vt*
dēcernere, cōnstituere; (*into parts*)
dissolvere; **the senate ~s** placet senātuī.
resonance *n* sonus *m.*
resonant *adj* canōrus.
resort *n* locus celeber *m*; **last ~** ultimum
auxilium *nt* ♦ *vi* frequentāre, ventitāre; (*have
recourse*) dēcurrere, dēscendere, cōnfugere.
resound *vi* resonāre, personāre.
resource *n* subsidium *nt*; (*means*) modus *m*; **~s**
pl opēs *fpl*, cōpiae *fpl.*
resourceful *adj* versūtus, callidus.
resourcefulness *n* calliditās *f*, versūtus
animus *m.*
respect *n* (*esteem*) honōs *m*, observantia *f*;
(*reference*) ratiō *f*; **out of ~** honōris causā; **pay
one's ~s to** salūtāre; **show ~ for** observāre; **in
every ~** ex omnī parte, in omnī genere; **in ~ of**
ad (*acc*), ab (*abl*) ♦ *vt* honōrāre, observāre,
verērī.
respectability *n* honestās *f.*
respectable *adj* honestus, līberālis, frūgī.
respectably *adv* honēstē.
respectful *adj* observāns.
respectfully *adv* reverenter.
respectfulness *n* observantia *f.*
respective *adj* suus (*with* quisque).
respectively *adv* alius . . . alius.
respiration *n* respīrātiō *f*, spīritus *m.*
respire *vi* respīrāre.
respite *n* requiēs *f*, intercapēdō *f*, intermissiō
f.
resplendence *n* splendor *m.*

resplendent *adj* splendidus, illūstris.
resplendently *adv* splendidē.
respond *vi* respondēre.
response *n* respōnsum *nt.*
responsibility *n* auctōritās *f*, cūra *f.*
responsible *adj* reus; (*witness*) locuplēs; **be ~
for** praestāre.
responsive *adj* (*pupil*) docilis; (*character*)
facilis.
rest *n* quiēs *f*, ōtium *nt*; (*after toil*) requiēs *f*;
(*remainder*) reliqua pars *f*; **be at ~**
requiēscere; **set at ~** tranquillāre; **the ~ of**
reliquī ♦ *vi* requiēscere, acquiēscere; ~ **on**
nītī (*abl*), innītī in (*abl*) ♦ *vt* (*hope*) pōnere in
(*abl*).
rest *n* cēterī *mpl.*
resting place *n* cubīle *nt*, sēdēs *f.*
restitution *n* satisfactiō *f*; **make ~** restituere;
demand ~ rēs repetere.
restive *adj* contumāx.
restless *adj* inquiētus, sollicitus; **be ~**
fluctuārī.
restlessness *n* sollicitūdō *f.*
restoration *n* renovātiō *f*; (*of king*) reductiō *f.*
restore *vt* reddere, restituere; (*to health*)
recreāre; (*to power*) redūcere; (*damage*)
reficere, redintegrāre.
restorer *n* restitūtor *m.*
restrain *vt* coercēre, comprimere, cohibēre.
restraint *n* moderātiō *f*, temperantia *f*, frēnī
mpl; **with ~** abstinenter.
restrict *vt* continēre, circumscrībere.
restricted *adj* artus; ~ **to** proprius (*gen*).
restriction *n* modus *m*, fīnis *m*; (*limitation*)
exceptiō *f.*
result *n* ēventus *m*, ēventum *nt*, exitus *m*; **the ~
is that** quō fit ut ♦ *vi* ēvenīre, ēvādere.
resultant *adj* cōnsequēns.
resume *vt* repetere.
resuscitate *vt* excitāre, suscitāre.
retail *vt* dīvēndere, vēndere.
retailer *n* caupō *m.*
retain *vt* retinēre, tenēre, cōnservāre.
retainer *n* satelles *m.*
retake *vt* recipere.
retaliate *vi* ulcīscī.
retaliation *n* ultiō *f.*
retard *vt* retardāre, remorārī.
retention *n* cōnservātiō *f.*
retentive *adj* tenāx.
reticence *n* taciturnitās *f.*
reticent *adj* taciturnus.
reticulated *adj* rēticulātus.
retinue *n* satellitēs *mpl*, comitātus *m.*
retire *vi* recēdere, abscēdere; (*from office*)
abīre; (*from province*) dēcēdere; (*MIL*) pedem
referre, sē recipere.
retired *adj* ēmeritus; (*place*) remōtus.
retirement *n* (*act*) recessus *m*, dēcessus *m*;
(*state*) sōlitūdō *f*, ōtium *nt*; **life of ~** vīta
prīvāta.
retiring *adj* modestus, verēcundus.
retort *vt* respondēre, referre ♦ *n*

respōnsum *nt.*
retouch *vt* retractāre.
retrace *vt* repetere, iterāre.
retract *vt* revocāre, renūntiāre.
retreat *n* (MIL) receptus *m;* (*place*) recessus *m,*
   sēcessus *m;* **sound the ~** receptuī canere ♦ *vi*
   sē recipere, pedem referre; regredī.
retrench *vt* minuere, recīdere.
retrenchment *n* parsimōnia *f.*
retribution *n* poena *f.*
retributive *adj* ultor, ultrīx.
retrieve *vt* reparāre, recipere.
retrograde *adj* (*fig*) dēterior.
retrogression *n* regressus *m.*
retrospect *n:* **in ~** respicientī.
retrospective *adj:* **be ~** retrōrsum sē referre.
retrospectively *adv* retrō.
return *n* reditus *m;* (*pay*) remūnerātiō *f;* (*profit*)
   fructus *m,* pretium *nt;* (*statement*) professiō *f;*
   make a ~ of profitērī; **in ~ for** prō (+ *abl*); **in ~**
   in vicem, vicissim ♦ *vt* reddere, restituere,
   referre ♦ *vi* redīre, revenīre, revertī; (*from*
   province) dēcēdere.
reunion *n* convīvium *nt.*
reunite *vt* reconciliāre.
reveal *vt* aperīre, patefacere.
revel *n* cōmissātiō *f,* bacchātiō *f;* **~s** *pl* orgia *ntpl*
   ♦ *vi* cōmissārī, bacchārī; **~ in** luxuriārī.
revelation *n* patefactiō *f.*
reveller *n* cōmissātor *m.*
revelry *n* cōmissātiō *f.*
revenge *n* ultiō *f;* **take ~ on** vindicāre in (*acc*) ♦
   vt ulcīscī.
revengeful *adj* ulcīscendī cupidus.
revenue *n* fructus *m,* reditus *m,* vectīgālia *ntpl.*
reverberate *vi* resonāre.
reverberation *n* repercussus *m.*
revere *vt* venerārī, colere.
reverence *n* venerātiō *f;* (*feeling*) religiō *f;*
   reverentia *f.*
reverent *adj* religiōsus, pius.
reverently *adv* religiōsē.
reverie *n* meditātiō *f,* somnium *nt.*
reversal *n* abrogātiō *f.*
reverse *adj* contrārius ♦ *n* contrārium *nt;* (MIL)
   clādēs *f* ♦ *vt* invertere; (*decision*) rescindere.
reversion *n* reditus *m.*
revert *vi* redīre, revertī.
review *n* recognitiō *f,* recēnsiō *f* ♦ *vt* (MIL)
   recēnsēre.
revile *vt* maledīcere (*dat*).
revise *vt* recognōscere, corrigere; (LIT) līmāre.
revision *n* ēmendātiō *f;* (LIT) līma *f.*
revisit *vt* revīsere.
revival *n* renovātiō *f.*
revive *vt* recreāre, excitāre ♦ *vi* revīvīscere,
   renāscī.
revocation *n* revocātiō *f.*
revoke *vt* renūntiāre, īnfectum reddere.
revolt *n* sēditiō *f,* dēfectiō *f* ♦ *vi* dēficere,
   rebellāre.
revolting *adj* taeter, obscēnus.
revolution *n* (*movement*) conversiō *f;* (*change*)

rēs novae *fpl;* (*revolt*) mōtus *m;* **effect a ~** rēs
   novāre.
revolutionary *adj* sēditiōsus, novārum rērum
   cupidus.
revolve *vi* volvī, versārī, convertī ♦ *vt* (*in*
   mind) volūtāre.
revulsion *n* mūtātiō *f.*
reward *n* praemium *nt,* mercēs *f* ♦ *vt*
   remūnerārī, compēnsāre.
rhapsody *n* carmen *nt;* (*epic*) rhapsōdia *f.*
rhetoric *n* rhētorica *f;* **of ~** rhētoricus; **exercise**
   in ~ dēclāmātiō *f;* **practise ~** dēclāmāre;
   teacher of ~ rhētōr *m.*
rhetorical *adj* rhētoricus, dēclāmātōrius.
rhetorically *adv* rhētoricē.
rhetorician *n* rhētōr *m,* dēclāmātor *m.*
rhinoceros *n* rhīnocerōs *m.*
rhyme *n* homoeoteleuton *nt;* **without ~ or**
   reason temerē.
rhythm *n* numerus *m,* modus *m.*
rhythmical *adj* numerōsus.
rib *n* costa *f.*
ribald *adj* obscēnus.
ribaldry *n* obscēnitās *f.*
ribbon *n* īnfula *f.*
rice *n* oryza *f.*
rich *adj* dīves, locuplēs; opulentus; (*fertile*)
   ūber, opīmus; (*food*) pinguis.
riches *n* dīvitiae *fpl,* opēs *fpl.*
richly *adv* opulentē, largē, lautē.
richness *n* ūbertās *f,* cōpia *f.*
rid *vt* līberāre; **get ~ of** dēpōnere, dēmovēre,
   exuere.
riddle *n* aenigma *nt;* (*sieve*) cribrum *nt* ♦ *vt*
   (*with wounds*) cōnfodere.
ride *vi* equitāre, vehī; **~ a horse** in equō vehī; **~**
   at anchor stāre; **~ away** abequitāre, āvehī; **~**
   back revehī; **~ between** interequitāre; **~**
   down dēvehī; **~ into** invehī; **~ off** āvehī; **~ out**
   ēvehī; **~ past** praetervehī; **~ round**
   circumvehī (*dat*), circumequitāre; **~ up and**
   down perequitāre; **~ up to** adequitāre ad,
   advehī ad.
rider *n* eques *m.*
ridge *n* iugum *nt.*
ridicule *n* lūdibrium *nt,* irrīsus *m* ♦ *vt* irrīdēre,
   illūdere, lūdibriō habēre.
ridiculous *adj* rīdiculus, dērīdiculus.
ridiculously *adv* rīdiculē.
riding *n* equitātiō *f.*
rife *adj* frequēns.
riff-raff *n* faex populī *f.*
rifle *vt* expīlāre, spoliāre.
rift *n* rīma *f.*
rig *vt* (*ship*) armāre, ōrnāre ♦ *n* habitus *m.*
rigging *n* rudentēs *mpl.*
right *adj* rēctus; (*just*) aequus, iūstus; (*true*)
   rēctus, vērus; (*proper*) lēgitimus, fās; (*hand*)
   dexter; **it is ~** decet (+ *acc and infin*); **it is not ~**
   dēdecet (+ *acc and infin*); **you are ~** vēra dīcis;
   if I am ~ nisi fallor; **in the ~ place** in locō; **at**
   the ~ time ad tempus; **at ~ angles** ad parēs
   angulōs; **on the ~** ā dextrā ♦ *adv* rēctē, bene,

probē; (*justifiably*) iūre; ~ **up to** usque ad (*+ acc*); ~ **on** rēctā ♦ *n* (*legal*) iūs *nt*; (*moral*) fās *nt* ♦ *vt* (*replace*) restituere; (*correct*) corrigere; (*avenge*) ulcīscī.

righteous *adj* iūstus, sanctus, pius.

righteously *adv* iūstē, sanctē, piē.

righteousness *n* sanctitās *f*, pietās *f*.

rightful *adj* iūstus, lēgitimus.

rightfully *adv* iūstē, lēgitimē.

right hand *n* dextra *f*.

right-hand *adj* dexter; ~ **man** comes *m*.

rightly *adv* rēctē, bene; iūre.

right-minded *adj* sānus.

rigid *adj* rigidus.

rigidity *n* rigor *m*; (*strictness*) sevēritās *f*.

rigidly *adv* rigidē, sevērē.

rigmarole *n* ambāgēs *fpl*.

rigorous *adj* dūrus; (*strict*) sevērus.

rigorously *adv* dūriter, sevērē.

rigour *n* dūritia *f*; sevēritās *f*.

rile *vt* inrītāre, stomachum movēre (*dat*).

rill *n* rīvulus *m*.

rim *n* labrum *nt*.

rime *n* pruīna *f*.

rind *n* cortex *m*.

ring *n* ānulus *m*; (*circle*) orbis *m*; (*of people*) corōna *f*; (*motion*) gŷrus *m* ♦ *vt* circumdare; (*bell*) movēre ♦ *vi* tinnīre, sonāre.

ringing *n* tinnītus *m* ♦ *adj* canōrus.

ringleader *n* caput *nt*, dux *m*.

ringlet *n* cincinnus *m*.

rinse *vt* colluere.

riot *n* tumultus *m*, rixa *f*; **run ~** exsultāre, luxuriārī, tumultuārī, turbās efficere; (*revel*) bacchārī.

rioter *n* cōmissātor *m*.

riotous *adj* tumultuōsus, sēditiōsus; (*debauched*) dissolūtus; ~ **living** cōmissātiō *f*, luxuria *f*.

riotously *adv* tumultuōsē; luxuriōsē.

rip *vt* scindere.

ripe *adj* mātūrus; **of ~ judgment** animī mātūrus.

ripen *vt* mātūrāre ♦ *vi* mātūrēscere.

ripeness *n* mātūritās *f*.

ripple *n* unda *f* ♦ *vi* trepidāre.

rise *vi* orīrī, surgere; (*hill*) ascendere; (*wind*) cōnsurgere; (*passion*) tumēscere; (*voice*) tollī; (*in size*) crēscere; (*in rank*) ascendere; (*in revolt*) coorīrī, arma capere; ~ **and fall** (*tide*) reciprocāre; ~ **above** superāre; ~ **again** resurgere; ~ **in** (*river*) orīrī ex (*abl*); ~ **out** ēmergere; ~ **up** exsurgere ♦ *n* ascēnsus *m*; (*slope*) clīvus *m*; (*increase*) incrēmentum *nt*; (*start*) ortus *m*; **give ~ to** parere.

rising *n* (*sun*) ortus *m*; (*revolt*) mōtus *m* ♦ *adj* (*ground*) ēditus.

risk *n* perīculum *nt*; **run a ~** perīculum subīre, ingredī ♦ *vt* perīclitārī, in āleam dare.

risky *adj* perīculōsus.

rite *n* rītus *m*.

ritual *n* caerimōnia *f*.

rival *adj* aemulus ♦ *n* aemulus *m*, rīvālis *m* ♦ *vt*

aemulārī.

rivalry *n* aemulātiō *f*.

river *n* flūmen *nt*, fluvius *m* ♦ *adj* fluviātilis.

riverbed *n* alveus *m*.

riverside *n* rīpa *f*.

rivet *n* clāvus *m* ♦ *vt* (*attention*) dēfīgere.

rivulet *n* rīvulus *m*, rīvus *m*.

road *n* via *f*, iter *nt*; **on the ~** in itinere, ex itinere; **off the ~** dēvius; **make a ~** viam mūnīre.

roadstead *n* statiō *f*.

roam *vi* errāre, vagārī; ~ **at large** ēvagārī.

roar *n* fremitus *m* ♦ *vi* fremere.

roast *vt* torrēre ♦ *adj* āssus ♦ *n* āssum *nt*.

rob *vt* spoliāre, exspoliāre, expīlāre; (*of hope*) dēicere dē.

robber *n* latrō *m*, fūr *m*; (*highway*) grassātor *m*.

robbery *n* latrōcinium *nt*.

robe *n* vestis *f*; (*woman's*) stola *f*; (*of state*) trabea *f* ♦ *vt* vestīre.

robust *adj* rōbustus, fortis.

robustness *n* rōbur *nt*, firmitās *f*.

rock *n* saxum *nt*; (*steep*) rūpēs *f*, scopulus *m* ♦ *vt* agitāre ♦ *vi* agitārī, vacillāre.

rocky *adj* saxōsus, scopulōsus.

rod *n* virga *f*; (*fishing*) harundō *f*.

roe *n* (*deer*) capreolus *m*, caprea *f*; (*fish*) ōva *ntpl*.

rogue *n* veterātor *m*.

roguery *n* nēquitia *f*, scelus *nt*.

roguish *adj* improbus, malus.

role *n* partēs *fpl*.

roll *n* (*book*) volūmen *nt*; (*movement*) gŷrus *m*; (*register*) album *nt*; **call the ~ of** legere; **answer the ~-call** ad nōmen respondēre ♦ *vt* volvere ♦ *vi* volvī, volūtārī; ~ **down** *vt* dēvolvere ♦ *vi* dēfluere; ~ **over** *vt* prōvolvere ♦ *vi* prōlābī; ~ **up** *vt* convolvere.

roller *n* (*AGR*) cylindrus *m*; (*for moving*) phalangae *fpl*; (*in book*) umbilīcus *m*.

rollicking *adj* hilaris.

rolling *adj* volūbilis.

Roman *adj* Rōmānus ♦ *n*: **the ~s** Rōmānī *mpl*.

romance *n* fābula *f*; amor *m*.

romantic *adj* fābulōsus; amātōrius.

Rome *n* Rōma *f*; **at ~** Rōmae; **from ~** Rōmā; **to ~** Rōmam.

romp *vi* lūdere.

roof *n* tēctum *nt*; (*of mouth*) palātum *nt* ♦ *vt* tegere, integere.

rook *n* corvus *m*.

room *n* conclāve *nt*; camera *f*; (*small*) cella *f*; (*bed*) cubiculum *nt*; (*dining*) cēnāculum *nt*; (*dressing*) apodytērium *nt*; (*space*) locus *m*; **make ~ for** locum dare (*dat*), cēdere (*dat*).

roominess *n* laxitās *f*.

roomy *adj* capāx.

roost *vi* stabulārī.

rooster *n* gallus gallīnāceus *m*.

root *n* rādīx *f*; **take ~** coalēscere ♦ *vt*: ~ **out** ērādīcāre.

rooted *adj* (*fig*) dēfīxus; **deeply ~** (*custom*) inveterātus; **be ~ in** īnsidēre (*dat*); **become deeply ~** inveterāscere.

rope n fūnis m; (*thin*) restis f; (*ship's*) rudēns m; **know the ~s** perītum esse.
rose n rosa f.
rosemary n rōs marīnus m.
rostrum n rōstra ntpl, suggestus m.
rosy adj roseus, purpureus.
rot n tābēs f ♦ vi putrēscere, pūtēscere ♦ vt putrefacere.
rotate vi volvī, sē convertere.
rotation n conversiō f; (*succession*) ōrdō m, vicissitūdō f; **in ~** ōrdine; **move in ~** in orbem īre.
rote n: **by ~** memoriter.
rotten adj putridus.
rotund adj rotundus.
rotundity n rotunditās f.
rouge n fūcus m ♦ vt fūcāre.
rough adj asper; (*art*) incultus, rudis; (*manners*) agrestis, inurbānus; (*stone*) impolītus; (*treatment*) dūrus, sevērus; (*weather*) atrōx, procellōsus ♦ vi: **~ it** dūram vītam vīvere.
rough-and-ready adj fortuītus.
rough draft n (LIT) silva f.
roughen vt asperāre, exasperāre.
rough-hew vt dolāre.
roughly adv asperē, dūriter; (*with numbers*) circiter.
roughness n asperitās f.
round adj rotundus; (*spherical*) globōsus; (*cylindrical*) teres ♦ n (*circle*) orbis m; (*motion*) gȳrus m; (*series*) ambitus m; **go the ~s** (MIL) vigiliās circumīre ♦ vt (*cape*) superāre; **~ off** rotundāre; (*sentence*) conclūdere; **~ up** compellere ♦ adv circum, circā; **go ~** ambīre ♦ prep circum (acc), circā (acc).
roundabout adj: **~ story** ambāgēs fpl; **~ route** circuitus m, ānfrāctus m.
roundly adv (*speak*) apertē, līberē.
rouse vt excīre, excitāre; (*courage*) adrigere.
rousing adj vehemēns.
rout n fuga f; (*crowd*) turba f ♦ vt fugāre, fundere; in fugam conicere; prōflīgāre.
route n cursus m, iter nt.
routine n ūsus m, ōrdō m.
rove vi errāre, vagārī.
rover n vagus m; (*sea*) pīrāta m.
row n (*line*) ōrdō m; (*noise*) turba f, rixa f ♦ vi (*boat*) rēmigāre ♦ vt rēmīs incitāre.
rowdy adj turbulentus.
rower n rēmex m.
rowing n rēmigium nt.
royal adj rēgius, rēgālis.
royally adv rēgiē, rēgāliter.
royalty n (*power*) rēgnum nt; (*persons*) rēgēs mpl, domus rēgia f.
rub vt fricāre, terere; **~ away** conterere; **~ hard** dēfricāre; **~ off** dētergēre; **~ out** dēlēre; **~ up** expolīre.
rubbing n trītus m.
rubbish n quisquiliae fpl; (*talk*) nūgae fpl.
rubble n rūdus nt.
rubicund adj rubicundus.

rudder n gubernāculum nt, clāvus m.
ruddy adj rubicundus, rutilus.
rude adj (*uncivilized*) barbarus, dūrus, inurbānus; (*insolent*) asper, importūnus.
rudely adv horridē, rusticē; petulanter.
rudeness n barbariēs f; petulantia f, importūnitās f.
rudiment n elementum nt, initium nt.
rudimentary adj prīmus, incohātus.
rue n (*herb*) rūta f ♦ vt: **I ~ mē** paenitet (gen).
rueful adj maestus.
ruffian n grassātor m.
ruffle vt agitāre; (*temper*) sollicitāre, commovēre.
rug n strāgulum nt.
rugged adj horridus, asper.
ruggedness n asperitās f.
ruin n ruīna f; (*fig*) exitium nt, perniciēs f; **go to ~** pessum īre, dīlābī ♦ vt perdere, dēperdere, pessum dare; (*moral*) corrumpere, dēprāvāre; **be ~ed** perīre.
ruined adj ruīnōsus.
ruinous adj exitiōsus, damnōsus.
rule n (*instrument*) rēgula f, amussis f; (*principle*) nōrma f, lēx f, praeceptum nt; (*government*) dominātiō f, imperium nt; **ten-foot ~** decempeda f; **as a ~** ferē; **lay down ~s** praecipere; **make it a ~ to** īnstituere (*inf*); **~ of thumb** ūsus m ♦ vt regere, moderārī ♦ vi rēgnāre, dominārī; (*judge*) ēdīcere; (*custom*) obtinēre; **~ over** imperāre (*dat*).
ruler n (*instrument*) rēgula f; (*person*) dominus m, rēctor m.
ruling n ēdictum nt.
rumble vi mūgīre.
rumbling n mūgītus m.
ruminate vi rūminārī.
rummage vi: **~ through** rīmārī.
rumour n fāma f, rūmor m.
rump n clūnis f.
run vi currere; (*fluid*) fluere, mānāre; (*road*) ferre; (*time*) lābī ♦ n cursus m; **~ about** discurrere, cursāre; **~ across** incidere in (*acc*); **~ after** sectārī; **~ aground** offendere; **~ away** aufugere, terga vertere; (*from*) fugere, dēfugere; **~ down** dēcurrere, dēfluere ♦ vt (*in words*) obtrectāre; **~ high** (*fig*) glīscere; **~ into** incurrere in (*acc*), īnfluere in (*acc*); **~ off with** abripere, abdūcere; **~ on** pergere; **~ out** (*land*) excurrere; (*time*) exīre; (*supplies*) dēficere; **~ over** vt (*with car*) obterere; (*details*) percurrere; **~ riot** luxuriārī; **~ through** (*course*) dēcurrere; (*money*) disperdere; **~ short** dēficere; **~ up to** adcurrere ad; **~ up against** incurrere in (*acc*); **~ wild** lascīvīre ♦ vt gerere, administrāre.
runaway adj fugitīvus.
rung n gradus m.
runner n cursor m.
running n cursus m ♦ adj (*water*) vīvus.
rupture n (*fig*) dissidium nt ♦ vt dīrumpere.
rural adj rūsticus, agrestis.

ruse n fraus f, dolus m.
rush n (_plant_) cārex f, iuncus m; (_movement_)
impetus m ♦ vi currere, sē incitāre, ruere; ~
forward sē prōripere; prōruere; ~ in inruere,
incurrere; ~ out ēvolāre, sē effundere ♦ _adj_
iunceus.
russet _adj_ flāvus.
rust n (_iron_) ferrūgō f; (_copper_) aerūgō f ♦ vi
rōbīginem trahere.
rustic _adj_ rūsticus, agrestis.
rusticate vi rūsticārī ♦ vt relēgāre.
rusticity n mōrēs rūsticī mpl.
rustle vi increpāre, crepitāre ♦ n crepitus m.
rusty _adj_ rōbīginōsus.
rut n orbita f.
ruthless _adj_ inexōrābilis, crūdēlis.
ruthlessly _adv_ crūdēliter.
rye n secāle nt.

_S, s_

sabbath n sabbata ntpl.
sable _adj_ āter, niger.
sabre n acīnacēs m.
sacerdotal _adj_ sacerdōtālis.
sack n saccus m; (_MIL_) dīreptiō f ♦ vt dīripere,
expīlāre; spoliāre.
sackcloth n cilicium nt.
sacred _adj_ sacer, sanctus.
sacredly _adv_ sanctē.
sacredness n sanctitās f.
sacrifice n sacrificium nt, sacrum nt; (_act_)
immolātiō f; (_victim_) hostia f; (_fig_) iactūra f ♦
vt immolāre, sacrificāre, mactāre; (_fig_)
dēvovēre, addīcere ♦ vi sacra facere; (_give
up_) prōicere.
sacrificer n immolātor m.
sacrilege n sacrilegium nt.
sacrilegious _adj_ sacrilegus.
sacristan n aedituus m.
sacrosanct _adj_ sacrōsanctus.
sad _adj_ maestus, tristis; (_thing_) tristis.
sadden vt dolōre adficere.
saddle n strātum nt ♦ vt sternere; (_fig_)
impōnere.
saddlebags n clītellae fpl.
sadly _adv_ maestē.
sadness n tristitia f, maestitia f.
safe _adj_ tūtus; (_out of danger_) incolumis,
salvus; (_to trust_) fīdus. ~ and sound salvus ♦
n armārium nt.
safe-conduct n fidēs pūblica f.
safeguard n cautiō f, prōpugnāculum nt ♦ vt
dēfendere.
safely _adv_ tūtō, impūne.
safety n salūs f, incolumitās f;

seek ~ in flight salutem fugā petere.
saffron n crocus m ♦ _adj_ croceus.
sag vi dēmittī.
sagacious _adj_ prūdēns, sagāx, acūtus.
sagaciously _adv_ prūdenter, sagāciter.
sagacity n prūdentia f, sagācitās f.
sage n sapiēns m; (_herb_) salvia f ♦ _adj_ sapiēns.
sagely _adv_ sapienter.
sail n vēlum nt; set ~ vēla dare, nāvem solvere;
shorten ~ vēla contrahere ♦ vi nāvigāre; ~
past legere, praetervehī.
sailing n nāvigātiō f.
sailor n nauta m.
sail yard n antenna f.
saint n vir sanctus m.
sainted _adj_ beātus.
saintly _adj_ sanctus.
sake n: for the ~ of grātiā (_gen_), causā (_gen_),
propter (_acc_); (_behalf_) prō (_abl_).
salacious _adj_ salāx.
salad n morētum nt.
salamander n salamandra f.
salary n mercēs f.
sale n vēnditiō f; (_formal_) mancipium nt;
(_auction_) hasta f; for ~ vēnālis; be for ~
prōstāre; offer for ~ vēnum dare.
saleable _adj_ vēndibilis.
salient _adj_ ēminēns; ~ points capita ntpl.
saline _adj_ salsus.
saliva n salīva f.
sallow _adj_ pallidus.
sally n ēruptiō f; (_wit_) facētiae fpl ♦ vi
ērumpere, excurrere.
salmon n salmō m.
salon n ātrium nt.
salt n sal m ♦ _adj_ salsus.
saltcellar n salīnum nt.
saltpetre n nitrum nt.
salt-pits n salīnae fpl.
salty _adj_ salsus.
salubrious _adj_ salūbris.
salubriously _adv_ salūbriter.
salubriousness n salūbritās f.
salutary _adj_ salūtāris, ūtilis.
salutation n salūs f.
salute vt salūtāre.
salvage vt servāre, ēripere.
salvation n salūs f.
salve n unguentum nt.
salver n scutella f.
same _adj_ īdem; ~ as īdem ac; all the ~
nihilōminus; one and the ~ūnus et īdem;
from the ~ place indidem; in the ~ place
ibīdem; to the ~ place eōdem; at the ~ time
simul, eōdem tempore; (_adversative_) tamen;
it is all the ~ to me meā nōn interest.
Samnites n Samnītēs, Samnītium mpl.
sample n exemplum nt, specimen nt ♦ vt
gustāre.
sanctify vt cōnsecrāre.
sanctimony n falsa rēligiō f.
sanction n comprobātiō f, auctōritās f ♦ vt
ratum facere.

sanctity n sanctitās f.
sanctuary n fānum nt, dēlubrum nt; (for men) asӯlum nt.
sand n harēna f.
sandal n (outdoors) crepida f; (indoors) solea f.
sandalled adj crepidātus, soleātus.
sandpit n harēnāria f.
sandstone n tōfus m.
sandy adj harēnōsus; (colour) flāvus.
sane adj sānus.
sangfroid n aequus animus m.
sanguinary adj cruentus.
sanguine adj laetus.
sanitary adj salūbris.
sanity n mēns sāna f.
sap n sūcus m ♦ vt subruere.
sapience n sapientia f.
sapient adj sapiēns.
sapling n surculus m.
sapper n cunīculārius m.
sapphire n sapphīrus f.
sarcasm n aculeī mpl, dicācitās f.
sarcastic adj dicāx, acūleātus.
sardonic adj amārus.
sash n cingulum nt.
satchel n loculus m.
sate vt explēre, satiāre.
satellite n satelles m.
satiate vt explēre, satiāre, saturāre.
satiety n satietās f.
satire n satura f; (pl, of Horace) sermōnēs mpl.
satirical adj acerbus.
satirist n saturārum scrīptor m.
satirize vt perstringere, notāre.
satisfaction n (act) explētiō f; (feeling) voluptās f; (penalty) poena f; **demand ~** rēs repetere.
satisfactorily adv ex sententiā.
satisfactory adj idōneus, grātus.
satisfied adj: **be ~** satis habēre, contentum esse.
satisfy vt satisfacere (dat); (desire) explēre.
satrap n satrapēs m.
saturate vt imbuere.
satyr n satyrus m.
sauce n condīmentum nt; (fish) garum nt.
saucer n patella f.
saucily adv petulanter.
saucy adj petulāns.
saunter vi ambulāre.
sausage n tōmāculum nt, hīllae fpl.
savage adj ferus, efferātus; (cruel) atrōx, inhūmānus; saevus.
savagely adv ferōciter, inhūmānē.
savagery n ferōcitās f, inhūmānitās f.
savant n vir doctus m.
save vt servāre; **~ up** reservāre ♦ prep praeter (acc).
saving adj parcus; **~ clause** exceptiō f ♦ n compendium nt; **~s** pl peculium nt.
saviour n līberātor m.
savory n thymbra f.
savour n sapor m; (of cooking) nīdor m ♦ vi

sapere; **~ of** olēre, redolēre.
savoury adj condītus.
saw n (tool) serra f; (saying) prōverbium nt ♦ vt serrā secāre.
sawdust n scobis f.
say vt dīcere; **~ that ... not** negāre; **~ no** negāre; **he ~s** (quoting) inquit; **he ~s yes** āit; **they ~** ferunt (+ acc and infin).
saying n dictum nt.
scab n (disease) scabiēs f; (over wound) crusta f.
scabbard n vāgīna f.
scabby adj scaber.
scaffold, scaffolding n fala f.
scald vt ūrere.
scale n (balance) lanx f; (fish, etc) squāma f; (gradation) gradūs mpl; (music) diagramma nt ♦ vt scālīs ascendere.
scallop n pecten m.
scalp n capitis cutis f.
scalpel n scalpellum nt.
scamp n verberō m.
scamper vi currere.
scan vt contemplārī; (verse) mētīrī.
scandal n īnfāmia f, opprobrium nt; (talk) calumnia f.
scandalize vt offendere.
scandalous adj flāgitiōsus, turpis.
scansion n syllabārum ēnārrātiō f.
scant adj exiguus, parvus.
scantily adv exiguē, tenuiter.
scantiness n exiguitās f.
scanty adj exiguus, tenuis, exīlis; (number) paucus.
scapegoat n piāculum nt.
scar n cicātrīx f.
scarce adj rārus; **make oneself ~** sē āmovēre, dē mediō recēdere ♦ adv vix, aegrē.
scarcely adv vix, aegrē; **~ anyone** nēmō ferē.
scarcity n inopia f, angustiae fpl.
scare n formīdō f ♦ vt terrēre; **~ away** absterrēre.
scarecrow n formīdō f.
scarf n fōcāle nt.
scarlet n coccum nt ♦ adj coccinus.
scarp n rūpēs f.
scathe n damnum nt.
scatter vt spargere; dispergere, dissipāre; (violently) disicere ♦ vi diffugere.
scatterbrained adj dēsipiēns.
scattered adj rārus.
scene n spectāculum nt; (place) theātrum nt.
scenery n locī faciēs f, speciēs f; (beautiful) amoenitās f.
scent n odor m; (sense) odōrātus m; **keen ~** sagācitās f ♦ vt odōrārī; (perfume) odōribus perfundere.
scented adj odōrātus.
sceptic n Pyrrhōnēus m.
sceptical adj incrēdulus.
sceptre n scēptrum nt.
schedule n tabulae fpl, ratiō f.
scheme n cōnsilium nt, ratiō f ♦ vt māchinārī,

mōlīrī.
schemer n māchinātor m.
schism n discidium nt, sēcessiō f.
scholar n vir doctus m, litterātus m; (pupil) discipulus m.
scholarly adj doctus, litterātus.
scholarship n litterae fpl, doctrīna f.
scholastic adj umbrātilis.
school n (elementary) lūdus m; (advanced) schola f; (high) gymnasium nt; (sect) secta f, domus f ♦ vt īnstituere.
schoolboy n discipulus m.
schoolmaster n magister m.
schoolmistress n magistra f.
science n doctrīna f, disciplīna f, ars f.
scimitar n acīnacēs m.
scintillate vi scintillāre.
scion n prōgeniēs f.
Scipio n Scīpiō, Scīpiōnis m.
scissors n forfex f.
scoff vi irrīdēre; ~ **at** dērīdēre.
scoffer n irrīsor m.
scold vt increpāre, obiūrgāre.
scolding n obiūrgātiō f.
scoop n trulla f ♦ vt: ~ **out** excavāre.
scope n (aim) fīnis m; (room) locus m, campus m; **ample** ~ laxus locus.
scorch vt exūrere, torrēre.
scorched adj torridus.
score n (mark) nota f; (total) summa f; (reckoning) ratiō f; (number) vīgintī ♦ vt notāre ♦ vi vincere.
scorn n contemptiō f ♦ vt contemnere, spernere.
scorner n contemptor m.
scornful adj fastīdiōsus.
scornfully adv contemptim.
scorpion n scorpiō m, nepa f.
scot-free adj immūnis, impūnītus.
scoundrel n furcifer m.
scour vt (clean) tergēre; (range) percurrere.
scourge n flagellum nt; (fig) pestis f ♦ vt verberāre, virgīs caedere.
scout n explōrātor m, speculātor m ♦ vi explōrāre, speculārī ♦ vt spernere, repudiāre.
scowl n frontis contractiō f ♦ vi frontem contrahere.
scraggy adj strigōsus.
scramble vi: ~ **for** certātim captāre; ~ **up** scandere.
scrap n frūstum nt.
scrape vt rādere, scabere; ~ **off** abrādere.
scraper n strigilis f.
scratch vt rādere; (head) perfricāre; ~ **out** exsculpere, ērādere.
scream n clāmor m, ululātus m ♦ vi clāmāre, ululāre.
screech n ululātus m ♦ vi ululāre.
screen n obex m/f; (from sun) umbra f; (fig) vēlāmentum nt ♦ vt tegere.
screw n clāvus m; (of winepress) cochlea f.
scribble vt properē scrībere.

scribe n scrība m.
script n scrīptum nt; (handwriting) manus f.
scroll n volūmen nt.
scrub vt dētergēre, dēfricāre.
scruple n rēligiō f, scrūpulus m.
scrupulous adj rēligiōsus; (careful) dīligēns.
scrupulously adv rēligiōsē, dīligenter.
scrupulousness n rēligiō f; dīligentia f.
scrutinize vt scrūtārī, intrōspicere in (acc), excutere.
scrutiny n scrūtātiō f.
scud vi volāre.
scuffle n rixa f.
scull n calvāria f; (oar) rēmus m.
scullery n culīna f.
sculptor n fictor m, sculptor m.
sculpture n ars fingendī f; (product) statuae fpl ♦ vt sculpere.
scum n spūma f.
scurf n porrīgō f.
scurrility n maledicta ntpl.
scurrilous adj maledicus.
scurvy adj (fig) turpis, improbus.
scythe n falx f.
sea n mare nt; aequor nt; **open** ~ altum nt; **put to** ~ solvere; **be at** ~ nāvigāre; (fig) in errōre versārī ♦ adj marīnus; (coast) maritimus.
seaboard n lītus nt.
seafaring adj maritimus, nauticus.
seafight n nāvāle proelium nt.
seagull n larus m.
seal n (animal) phōca f; (stamp) signum nt ♦ vt signāre; ~ **up** obsignāre.
seam n sūtūra f.
seaman n nauta m.
seamanship n scientia et ūsus nauticārum rērum.
seaport n portus m.
sear vt adūrere, torrēre.
search n investigātiō f ♦ vi investīgāre, explōrāre ♦ vt excutere, scrūtārī; **in** ~ **of** causa (+ gen); ~ **for** quaerere, exquīrere, investīgāre; ~ **into** inquīrere, anquīrere; ~ **out** explōrāre, indāgāre.
searcher n inquīsītor m.
searching adj acūtus, dīligēns.
seashore n litus nt.
seasick adj: **be** ~ nauseāre.
seasickness n nausea f.
seaside n mare nt.
season n annī tempus nt, tempestās f; (right time) tempus nt, opportūnitās f; **in** ~ tempestīvē ♦ vt condīre.
seasonable adj tempestīvus.
seasonably adv tempestīvē.
seasoned adj (food) condītus; (wood) dūrātus.
seasoning n condīmentum nt.
seat n sēdēs f; (chair) sedīle nt; (home) domus f, domicilium nt; **keep one's** ~ (riding) in equō haerēre ♦ vt collocāre; ~ **oneself** īnsidēre.
seated adj: **be** ~ sedēre.
seaweed n alga f.
seaworthy adj ad nāvigandum ūtilis.

secede–send

secede *vi* sēcēdere.
secession *n* sēcessiō *f*.
seclude *vt* sēclūdere, abstrūdere.
secluded *adj* sēcrētus, remōtus.
seclusion *n* sōlitūdō *f*, sēcrētum *nt*.
second *adj* secundus, alter; **a ~ time** iterum ♦
  n temporis pūnctum *nt*; (*person*) fautor *m*; ~
  sight hariolātiō *f* ♦ *vt* favēre (*dat*), adesse
  (*dat*).
secondary *adj* īnferior, dēterior.
seconder *n* fautor *m*.
second-hand *adj* aliēnus, trītus.
secondly *adv* deinde.
secrecy *n* sēcrētum *nt*, silentium *nt*.
secret *adj* secrētus; occultus, arcānus;
  (*stealth*) fūrtīvus ♦ *n* arcānum *nt*; **keep ~**
  dissimulāre, cēlāre; **in ~** clam; **be ~** latēre.
secretary *n* scrība *m*, ab epistolīs, ā manū.
secrete *vt* cēlāre, abdere.
secretive *adj* tēctus.
secretly *adv* clam, occultē, sēcrētō.
sect *n* secta *f*, schola *f*, domus *f*.
section *n* pars *f*.
sector *n* regiō *f*.
secular *adj* profānus.
secure *adj* tūtus ♦ *vt* (*MIL*) firmāre, ēmūnīre;
  (*fasten*) religāre; (*obtain*) parāre, nancīscī.
securely *adj* tūtō.
security *n* salūs *f*, impūnitās *f*; (*money*) cautiō
  f, pignus *nt*, spōnsiō *f*; **sense of ~** sēcūritās *f*;
  give good ~ satis dare; **on good ~** (*loan*)
  nōminibus rēctis cautus; **stand ~ for**
  praedem esse prō (*abl*).
sedan *n* lectīca *f*.
sedate *adj* placidus, temperātus, gravis.
sedately *adv* placidē.
sedateness *n* gravitās *f*.
sedge *n* ulva *f*.
sediment *n* faex *f*.
sedition *n* sēditiō *f*, mōtus *m*.
seditious *adj* sēditiōsus.
seditiously *adv* sēditiōsē.
seduce *vt* illicere, pellicere.
seducer *n* corruptor *m*.
seduction *n* corruptēla *f*.
seductive *adj* blandus.
seductively *adv* blandē.
sedulity *n* dīligentia *f*.
sedulous *adj* dīligēns, sēdulus.
sedulously *adv* dīligenter, sēdulō.
see *vt* vidēre, cernere; (*suddenly*) cōnspicārī;
  (*performance*) spectāre; (*with mind*)
  intellegere; **go and ~** vīsere, invīsere; ~ **to**
  vidēre, cōnsulere (*dat*); curare (*+ acc and
  gerundive*); ~ **through** dīspicere; ~ **that you
  are** vidē ut sīs, fac sīs; ~ **that you are not** vidē
  nē sīs, cavē sīs.
seed *n* sēmen *nt*; (*in a plant*) grānum *nt*; (*in fruit*)
  acinum *nt*; (*fig*) stirps *f*, prōgeniēs *f*.
seedling *n* surculus *m*.
seed-time *n* sēmentis *f*.
seeing that *conj* quōniam, siquidem.
seek *vt* petere, quaerere.

seeker *n* indāgātor *m*.
seem *vi* vidērī.
seeming *adj* speciōsus ♦ *n* speciēs *f*.
seemingly *adv* ut vidētur.
seemly *adj* decēns, decōrus; **it is ~** decet.
seep *vi* mānāre, percōlārī.
seer *n* vātēs *m/f*.
seethe *vi* fervēre.
segregate *vt* sēcernere, sēgregāre.
segregation *n* sēparātiō *f*.
seize *vt* rapere, corripere, adripere,
  prehendere; (*MIL*) occupāre; (*illness*) adficere;
  (*emotion*) invādere, occupāre.
seizure *n* ēreptiō *f*, occupātiō *f*.
seldom *adv* rārō.
select *vt* ēligere, excerpere, dēligere ♦ *adj*
  lēctus, ēlēctus.
selection *n* ēlēctiō *f*, dēlēctus *m*; (*LIT*) ecloga *f*.
self *n* ipse; (*reflexive*) sē; **a second ~** alter īdem.
self-centred *adj* glōriōsus.
self-confidence *n* cōnfīdentia *f*, fidūcia *f*.
self-confident *adj* cōnfīdēns.
self-conscious *adj* pudibundus.
self-control *n* temperantia *f*.
self-denial *n* abstinentia *f*.
self-evident *adj* manifestus; **it is ~** ante pedēs
  positum est.
self-governing *adj* līber.
self-government *n* lībertās *f*.
self-important *adj* adrogāns.
self-interest *n* ambitiō *f*.
selfish *adj* inhūmānus, avārus; **be ~** suā causā
  facere.
selfishly *adv* inhūmānē, avārē.
selfishness *n* inhūmānitās *f*, incontinentia *f*,
  avāritia *f*.
self-made *adj* (*man*) novus.
self-possessed *adj* aequō animō.
self-possession *n* aequus animus *m*.
self-reliant *adj* cōnfīdēns.
self-respect *n* pudor *m*.
self-restraint *n* modestia *f*.
self-sacrifice *n* dēvōtiō *f*.
selfsame *adj* ūnus et īdem.
sell *vt* vēndere; (*in lots*) dīvēndere; **be sold**
  vēnīre.
seller *n* vēnditor *m*.
selvage *n* limbus *m*.
semblance *n* speciēs *f*, imāgō *f*.
semicircle *n* hēmicyclium *nt*.
senate *n* senātus *m*; **hold a meeting of the ~**
  senātum habēre; **decree of the ~** senātus
  cōnsultum *nt*.
senate house *n* cūria *f*.
senator *n* senātor *m*; (*provincial*) decuriō *m*; ~**s**
  pl patrēs *mpl*.
senatorial *adj* senātōrius.
send *vt* mittere; ~ **across** trānsmittere;
  ~ **ahead** praemittere; ~ **away** dīmittere; ~
  back remittere; ~ **for** accersere; (*doctor*)
  adhibēre; ~ **forth** ēmittere; ~ **forward**
  praemittere; ~ **in** immittere, intrōmittere; ~
  out ēmittere; (*in different directions*)

dīmittere; ~ **out of the way** ablēgāre; ~ **up**
submittere.
senile _adj_ senīlis.
senility _n_ senium _nt._
senior _adj_ nātū māior; (_thing_) prior.
sensation _n_ sēnsus _m_; (_event_) rēs nova _f_; **lose** ~
obtorpēscere; **create a** ~ hominēs
obstupefacere.
sensational _adj_ novus, prōdigiōsus.
sense _n_ (_faculty_) sēnsus _m_; (_wisdom_) prūdentia
_f_; (_meaning_) vis _f_, sententia _f_; **common** ~
prūdentia _f_; **be in one's ~s** apud sē esse,
mentis suae esse; **out of one's ~s** dēmēns;
recover one's ~s resipīscere; **what is the** ~ **of**
quid sibī vult? ◆ _vt_ sentīre.
senseless _adj_ absurdus, ineptus, īnsipiēns.
senselessly _adv_ īnsipienter.
senselessness _n_ īnsipientia _f._
sensibility _n_ sēnsus _m._
sensible _adj_ prūdēns, sapiēns.
sensibly _adv_ prūdenter, sapienter.
sensitive _adj_ mollis, inrītābilis, patibilis.
sensitiveness _n_ mollitia _f._
sensual _adj_ libīdinōsus.
sensuality _n_ libīdō _f_, voluptās _f._
sensually _adv_ libīdinōsē.
sentence _n_ (_judge_) iūdicium _nt_, sententia _f_;
(_GRAM_) sententia _f_; **pass** ~ iūdicāre; **execute** ~
lēge agere ◆ _vt_ damnāre; ~ **to death** capitis
damnāre.
sententious _adj_ sententiōsus.
sententiously _adv_ sententiōsē.
sentient _adj_ patibilis.
sentiment _n_ (_feeling_) sēnsus _m_; (_opinion_)
sententia _f_; (_emotion_) mollitia _f._
sentimental _adj_ mollis, flēbilis.
sentimentality _n_ mollitia _f._
sentimentally _adv_ molliter.
sentries _npl_ statiōnēs _fpl_, excubiae _fpl._
sentry _n_ custōs _m_, vigil _m_; **be on** ~ **duty** in
statiōne esse.
separable _adj_ dīviduus, sēparābilis.
separate _vt_ sēparāre, dīvidere, disiungere;
(_forcibly_) dīrimere, dīvellere ◆ _vi_ dīgredī ◆
adj sēparātus, sēcrētus.
separately _adv_ sēparātim, seōrsum.
separation _n_ sēparātiō _f_; (_violent_) discidium
_nt._
September _n_ mēnsis September _m_; **of** ~
September.
sepulchral _adj_ fūnebris.
sepulchre _n_ sepulcrum _nt._
sepulture _n_ sepultūra _f._
sequel _n_ exitus _m_, quae sequuntur.
sequence _n_ seriēs _f_, ōrdō _m._
sequestered _adj_ sēcrētus.
serenade _vt_ occentāre.
serene _adj_ tranquillus, sēcūrus.
serenely _adv_ tranquillē.
serenity _n_ sēcūritās _f._
serf _n_ servus _m._
serfdom _n_ servitūs _f._
sergeant _n_ signifer _m._

series _n_ seriēs _f_, ōrdō _m._
serious _adj_ gravis, sērius, sevērus.
seriously _adv_ graviter, sēriō, sevērē.
seriousness _n_ gravitās _f._
sermon _n_ ōrātiō _f._
serpent _n_ serpēns _f._
serpentine _adj_ tortuōsus.
serrated _adj_ serrātus.
serried _adj_ cōnfertus.
servant _n_ (_domestic_) famulus _m_, famula _f_;
(_public_) minister _m_, ministra _f_; **family ~s**
familia _f._
servant maid _n_ ancilla _f._
serve _vt_ servīre (_dat_); (_food_) ministrāre,
adpōnere; (_interest_) condūcere (_dat_) ◆ _vi_ (_MIL_)
stīpendia merēre, mīlitāre; (_suffice_)
sufficere; ~ **as** esse prō (_abl_); ~ **in the cavalry**
equō merēre; ~ **in the infantry** pedibus
merēre; **having ~d one's time** ēmeritus; ~ **a**
sentence poenam subīre; ~ **well** bene merērī
dē (_abl_).
service _n_ (_status_) servitium _nt_, famulātus _m_;
(_work_) ministerium _nt_; (_help_) opera _f_; (_by an_
equal) meritum _nt_, beneficium _nt_; (_MIL_) mīlitia
_f_, stīpendia _ntpl_; **be of** ~ **to** prōdesse (_dat_),
bene merērī dē; **I am at your** ~ adsum tibī;
complete one's ~ stīpendia ēmerērī.
serviceable _adj_ ūtilis.
servile _adj_ servīlis; (_fig_) abiectus, humilis.
servility _n_ adūlātiō _f._
servitude _n_ servitūs _f._
session _n_ conventus _m_; **be in** ~ sedēre.
sesterce _n_ sēstertius _m_; **10 ~s** decem sēstertiī;
10,000 ~s dēna sēstertia _ntpl_; **1,000,000 ~s**
deciēs sēstertium.
set _vt_ pōnere, locāre, statuere, sistere; (_bone_)
condere; (_course_) dīrigere; (_example_) dare;
(_limit_) impōnere; (_mind_) intendere; (_music_)
modulārī; (_sail_) dare; (_sentries_) dispōnere;
(_table_) īnstruere; (_trap_) parāre ◆ _vi_ (_ASTRO_)
occidere; ~ **about** incipere; ~ **against**
oppōnere; ~ **apart** sēpōnere; ~ **aside**
sēpōnere; ~ **down** (_writing_) perscrībere; ~
eyes on cōnspicere; ~ **foot on** ingredī; ~ **forth**
expōnere, ēdere; ~ **free** līberāre; ~ **in motion**
movēre; ~ **in order** compōnere, dispōnere; ~
off (_decoration_) distinguere; (_art_) illūmināre;
~ **on** (_to attack_) immittere; ~ **on foot**
īnstituere; ~ **on fire** incendere; ~ **one's heart**
on exoptāre; ~ **out** _vi_ proficīscī; ~ **over**
praeficere, impōnere; ~ **up** statuere; (_fig_)
cōnstituere.
set _adj_ (_arrangement_) status; (_purpose_) certus;
(_rule_) praescrīptus; (_speech_) compositus; **of** ~
purpose cōnsultō ◆ _n_ (_persons_) numerus _m_;
(_things_) congeriēs _f_; (_current_) cursus _m._
setback _n_ repulsa _f._
settee _n_ lectulus _m._
setting _n_ (_ASTRO_) occāsus _m_; (_event_) locus _m._
settle _n_ sella _f_ ◆ _vt_ statuere; (_annuity_)
praestāre; (_business_) trānsigere; (_colony_)
dēdūcere; (_debt_) exsolvere; (_decision_)
cōnstituere; (_dispute_) dēcīdere, compōnere

◆ *vi* (*abode*) cōnsīdere; (*agreement*)
cōnstituere, convenīre; (*sediment*) dēsīdere;
~ **in** īnsidēre (*dat*).
settled *adj* certus, explōrātus.
settlement *n* (*of a colony*) dēductiō *f*; (*colony*)
colōnia *f*; (*of dispute*) dēcīsiō *f*, compositiō *f*;
(*to wife*) dōs *f*.
settler *n* colōnus *m*.
set to *n* pugna *f*.
seven *num* septem; ~ **each** septēnī; ~ **times**
septiēns.
seven hundred *num* septingentī.
seven hundredth *adj* septingentēsimus.
seventeen *num* septendecim.
seventeenth *adj* septimus decimus.
seventh *adj* septimus; **for the** ~ **time**
septimum.
seventieth *adj* septuāgēsimus.
seventy *num* septuāgintā; ~ **each** septuāgēnī; ~
times septuāgiēns.
sever *vt* incīdere, sēparāre, dīvidere.
several *adj* complūrēs, aliquot.
severally *adv* singulī.
severe *adj* gravis, sevērus, dūrus; (*style*)
austērus; (*weather*) asper; (*pain*) ācer,
gravis.
severely *adv* graviter, sevērē.
severity *n* gravitās *f*; asperitās *f*; sevēritās *f*.
sew *vt* suere; ~ **up** cōnsuere; ~ **up in** īnsuere in
(*acc*).
sewer *n* cloāca *f*.
sex *n* sexus *m*.
shabbily *adv* sordidē.
shabbiness *n* sordēs *fpl*.
shabby *adj* sordidus.
shackle *n* compēs *f*, vinculum *nt* ◆ *vt* impedīre,
vincīre.
shade *n* umbra *f*; (*colour*) color *m*; ~**s** *pl* mānēs
mpl; **put in the** ~ officere (*dat*) ◆ *vt* opācāre,
umbram adferre (*dat*).
shadow *n* umbra *f*.
shadowy *adj* obscūrus; (*fig*) inānis.
shady *adj* umbrōsus, opācus.
shaft *n* (*missile*) tēlum *nt*, sagitta *f*; (*of spear*)
hastīle *nt*; (*of cart*) tēmō *m*; (*of light*) radius *m*;
(*excavation*) puteus *m*.
shaggy *adj* hirsūtus.
shake *vt* quatere, agitāre; (*structure*)
labefacere, labefactāre; (*belief*) īnfīrmāre;
(*resolution*) labefactāre, commovēre; ~
hands with dextram dare (*dat*) ◆ *vi* quatī,
agitārī, tremere, horrēscere; ~ **off** dēcutere,
excutere; ~ **out** excutere.
shaking *n* tremor *m*.
shaky *adj* īnstābilis, tremebundus.
shall *aux vb = fut indic*.
shallot *n* caepa Ascalōnia *f*.
shallow *adj* brevis, vadōsus; (*fig*) levis.
shallowness *n* vada *ntpl*; (*fig*) levitās *f*.
shallows *n* brevia *ntpl*, vada *ntpl*.
sham *adj* fictus, falsus, fūcōsus ◆ *n* simulātiō *f*,
speciēs *f* ◆ *vt* simulāre.
shambles *n* laniēna *f*.

shame *n* (*feeling*) pudor *m*; (*cause*) dēdecus *nt*,
ignōminia *f*; **it** ~**s** pudet (+ *acc of person, gen of
thing*); **it is a** ~ flāgitium est ◆ *vt* rubōrem
incutere (*dat*) ◆ *interj* prō pudor!
shamefaced *adj* verēcundus.
shameful *adj* ignōminiōsus, turpis.
shamefully *adv* turpiter.
shameless *adj* impudēns.
shamelessly *adv* impudenter.
shamelessness *n* impudentia *f*.
shank *n* crūs *nt*.
shape *n* fōrma *f*, figūra *f* ◆ *vt* fōrmāre, fingere;
(*fig*) īnfōrmāre ◆ *vi*: ~ **well** prōficere.
shapeless *adj* īnfōrmis, dēfōrmis.
shapelessness *n* dēfōrmitās *f*.
shapeliness *n* fōrma *f*.
shapely *adj* fōrmōsus.
shard *n* testa *f*.
share *n* pars *f*; (*plough*) vōmer *m*; **go** ~**s with**
inter sē partīrī ◆ *vt* (*give*) partīrī, impertīre;
(*have*) commūnicāre, participem esse (*gen*).
sharer *n* particeps *m/f*, socius *m*.
shark *n* volpēs marīna *f*.
sharp *adj* acūtus; (*fig*) ācer, acūtus; (*bitter*)
amarus.
sharpen *vt* acuere; (*fig*) exacuere.
sharply *adv* ācriter, acūtē.
sharpness *n* aciēs *f*; (*mind*) acūmen *nt*,
argūtiae *fpl*; (*temper*) acerbitās *f*.
shatter *vt* quassāre, perfringere, adflīgere;
(*fig*) frangere.
shave *vt* rādere; ~ **off** abrādere.
shavings *n* rāmenta *ntpl*.
she *pron* haec, ea, illa.
sheaf *n* manipulus *m*.
shear *vt* tondēre, dētondēre.
shears *n* forficēs *fpl*.
sheath *n* vāgīna *f*.
sheathe *vt* recondere.
shed *vt* fundere; (*blood*) effundere; (*one's
own*) profundere; (*tears*) effundere;
(*covering*) exuere; ~ **light on** (*fig*) lūmen
adhibēre (*dat*).
sheen *n* nitor *m*.
sheep *n* ovis *f*; (*flock*) pecus *nt*.
sheepfold *n* ovīle *nt*.
sheepish *adj* pudibundus.
sheepishly *adv* pudenter.
sheer *adj* (*absolute*) merus; (*steep*) praeruptus.
sheet *n* (*cloth*) linteum *nt*; (*metal*) lāmina *f*;
(*paper*) carta *f*, scheda *f*; (*sail*) pēs *m*; (*water*)
aequor *nt*.
shelf *n* pluteus *m*, pēgma *nt*.
shell *n* concha *f*; (*egg*) putāmen *nt*; (*tortoise*)
testa *f*.
shellfish *n* conchȳlium *nt*.
shelter *n* suffugium *nt*, tegmen *nt*; (*refuge*)
perfugium *nt*, asȳlum *nt*; (*lodging*) hospitium
nt; (*fig*) umbra *f* ◆ *vt* tegere, dēfendere;
(*refugee*) excipere ◆ *vi* latēre; ~ **behind** (*fig*)
dēlitēscere in (*abl*).
sheltered *adj* (*life*) umbrātilis.
shelve *vt* differre ◆ *vi* sē dēmittere.

shelving *adj* dēclīvis.
shepherd *n* pastor *m*.
shield *n* scūtum *nt*; clipeus *m*; (*small*) parma *f*;
(*fig*) praesidium *nt* ♦ *vt* prōtegere,
dēfendere.
shift *n* (*change*) mūtātiō *f*; (*expedient*) ars *f*,
dolus *m*; **make ~ to** efficere ut; **in ~s** per vicēs
♦ *vt* mūtāre; (*move*) movēre ♦ *vi* mūtārī;
discēdere.
shiftless *adj* iners, inops.
shifty *adj* vafer, versūtus.
shilling *n* solidus *m*.
shimmer *vi* micāre ♦ *n* tremulum lūmen *nt*.
shin *n* tībia *f*.
shine *vi* lūcēre, fulgēre; (*reflecting*) nitēre; (*fig*)
ēminēre; **~ forth** ēlūcēre, ēnitēre; effulgēre;
~ upon adfulgēre (*dat*) ♦ *n* nitor *m*.
shingle *n* lapillī *mpl*, glārea *f*.
shining *adj* lūcidus, splendidus; (*fig*) illūstris.
shiny *adj* nitidus.
ship *n* nāvis *f*; **admiral's ~** nāvis praetōria;
decked ~ nāvis tēcta, nāvis cōnstrāta ♦ *vt*
(*cargo*) impōnere; (*to a place*) nāvī invehere.
shipowner *n* nāviculārius *m*.
shipping *n* nāvēs *fpl*.
shipwreck *n* naufragium *nt*; **suffer ~**
naufragium facere.
shipwrecked *adj* naufragus.
shirk *vt* dēfugere, dētrectāre.
shirt *n* subūcula *f*.
shiver *n* horror *m* ♦ *vi* horrēre, tremere ♦ *vt*
perfringere, comminuere.
shivering *n* horror *m*.
shoal *n* (*fish*) exāmen *nt*; (*water*) vadum *nt*; **~s** *pl*
brevia *ntpl*.
shock *n* impulsus *m*; (*battle*) concursus *m*,
cōnflīctus *m*; (*hair*) caesariēs *f*; (*mind*)
offēnsiō *f* ♦ *vt* percutere, offendere.
shocking *adj* atrōx, dētestābilis, flāgitiōsus.
shoddy *adj* vīlis.
shoe *n* calceus *m*.
shoemaker *n* sūtor *m*.
shoot *n* surculus *m*; (*vine*) pampinus *m* ♦ *vi*
frondēscere; (*movement*) volāre; **~ up**
ēmicāre ♦ *vt* (*missile*) conicere, iaculārī;
(*person*) iaculārī, trānsfīgere.
shop *n* taberna *f*.
shore *n* lītus *nt*, ōra *f* ♦ *vt* fulcīre.
short *adj* brevis; (*broken*) curtus; (*amount*)
exiguus; **for a ~ time** parumper, paulisper; **~
of** (*number*) intrā (*acc*); **be ~ of** indigēre (*abl*);
cut ~ interpellāre; **in ~** ad summam, dēnique;
very ~ perbrevis; **fall ~ of** nōn pervenīre ad,
abesse ab; **run ~** dēficere; **to cut a long story
~** nē multīs morer, nē multa.
shortage *n* inopia *f*.
shortcoming *n* dēlictum *nt*, culpa *f*.
short cut *n* via compendiāria *f*.
shorten *vt* curtāre, imminuere, contrahere;
(*sail*) legere.
shorthand *n* notae *fpl*.
shorthand writer *n* āctuārius *m*.
short-lived *adj* brevis.

shortly *adv* (*time*) brevī; (*speak*) breviter; **~
after** paulō post, nec multō post.
shortness *n* brevitās *f*, exiguitās *f*; (*difficulty*)
angustiae *fpl*.
short-sighted *adj* (*fig*) imprōvidus,
imprūdēns.
short-sightedness *n* imprūdentia *f*.
short-tempered *adj* īrācundus.
shot *n* ictus *m*; (*range*) iactus *m*.
should *vi* (*duty*) dēbēre.
shoulder *n* umerus *m*; (*animal*) armus *m* ♦ *vt*
(*burden*) suscipere.
shout *n* clāmor *m*, adclāmātiō *f* ♦ *vt*, *vi*
clāmāre, vōciferārī; **~ down** obstrepere
(*dat*); **~ out** exclāmāre.
shove *vt* trūdere, impellere.
shovel *n* rutrum *nt*.
show *n* speciēs *f*; (*entertainment*) lūdī *mpl*,
spectāculum *nt*; (*stage*) lūdicrum *nt*; **for ~ in**
speciem; **put on a ~** spectācula dare ♦ *vt*
mōnstrāre, indicāre, ostendere, ostentāre;
(*point out*) dēmōnstrāre; (*qualities*) praestāre;
~ off *vi* sē iactāre ♦ *vt* ostentāre.
shower *n* imber *m* ♦ *vt* fundere, conicere.
showery *adj* pluvius.
showiness *n* ostentātiō *f*.
showing off *n* iactātiō *f*.
showy *adj* speciōsus.
shred *n* fragmentum *nt*; **in ~s** minūtātim; **tear
to ~s** ♦ *vt* concīdere.
shrew *n* virāgō *f*.
shrewd *adj* acūtus, ācer, sagāx.
shrewdly *adv* acūtē, sagāciter.
shrewdness *n* acūmen *nt*, sagācitās *f*.
shriek *n* ululātus *m* ♦ *vi* ululāre.
shrill *adj* acūtus, argūtus.
shrine *n* fānum *nt*, dēlubrum *nt*.
shrink *vt* contrahere ♦ *vi* contrahī; **~ from**
abhorrēre ab, refugere ab, dētrectāre.
shrivel *vt* corrūgāre ♦ *vi* exārēscere.
shroud *n* integumentum *nt*; **~s** *pl* rudentēs *mpl*
♦ *vt* involvere.
shrub *n* frutex *m*.
shrubbery *n* fruticētum *nt*.
shudder *n* horror *m* ♦ *vi* exhorrēscere; **~ at**
horrēre.
shuffle *vt* miscēre ♦ *vi* claudicāre; (*fig*)
tergiversārī.
shun *vt* vītāre, ēvītāre, dēfugere.
shut *vt* claudere; (*with cover*) operīre; (*hand*)
comprimere; **~ in** inclūdere; **~ off**
interclūdere; **~ out** exclūdere; **~ up**
inclūdere.
shutter *n* foricula *f*, lūmināre *nt*.
shuttle *n* radius *m*.
shy *adj* timidus, pudibundus, verēcundus.
shyly *adv* timidē, verēcundē.
shyness *n* verēcundia *f*.
sibyl *n* sibylla *f*.
sick *adj* aeger, aegrōtus; **be ~** aegrōtāre; **feel ~**
nauseāre; **I am ~ of** mē taedet (*gen*).
sicken *vt* fastīdium movēre (*dat*) ♦ *vi*
nauseāre, aegrōtāre.

sickle *n* falx *f*.
sickly *adj* invalidus.
sickness *n* nausea *f*; (*illness*) morbus *m*, aegritūdō *f*.
side *n* latus *nt*; (*direction*) pars *f*; (*faction*) partēs *fpl*; (*kin*) genus *nt*; **on all ~s** undique; **on both ~s** utrimque; **on one ~** unā ex parte; **on our ~** ā nōbis; **be on the ~ of** stāre ab, sentīre cum; **on the far ~ of** ultrā (*acc*); **on this ~** hīnc; **on this ~ of** cis (*acc*), citrā (*acc*) ♦ *vi*: **~ with** stāre ab, facere cum.
sideboard *n* abacus *m*.
sidelong *adj* oblīquus.
sideways *adv* oblīquē, in oblīquum.
sidle *vi* oblīquō corpore incēdere.
siege *n* obsidiō *f*, oppugnātiō *f*; **lay ~ to** obsidēre.
siege works *n* opera *ntpl*.
siesta *n* merīdiātiō *f*; **take a ~** merīdiāre.
sieve *n* crībrum *nt*.
sigh *n* suspīrium *nt*; (*loud*) gemitus *m* ♦ *vi* suspīrāre, gemere.
sight *n* (*sense*) vīsus *m*; (*process*) aspectus *m*; (*range*) cōnspectus *m*; (*thing seen*) spectāculum *nt*, speciēs *f*; **at ~** ex tempore; **at first ~** prīmō aspectū; **in ~** in cōnspectū; **come into ~** in cōnspectum sē dare; **in the ~ of** in oculīs (*gen*); **catch ~ of** cōnspicere; **lose ~ of** ē cōnspectū āmittere; (*fig*) oblīvīscī (*gen*) ♦ *vt* cōnspicārī.
sightless *adj* caecus.
sightly *adj* decōrus.
sign *n* signum *nt*, indicium *nt*; (*distinction*) īnsigne *nt*; (*mark*) nota *f*; (*trace*) vestīgium *nt*; (*proof*) documentum *nt*; (*portent*) ōmen *nt*; (*Zodiac*) signum *nt*; **give a ~** innuere ♦ *vi* signum dare, innuere ♦ *vt* subscrībere (*dat*); (*as witness*) obsignāre.
signal *n* signum *nt*; **give the ~ for retreat** receptuī canere ♦ *vi* signum dare ♦ *adj* īnsignis, ēgregius.
signalize *vt* nōbilitāre.
signally *adv* ēgregiē.
signature *n* nōmen *nt*, manus *f*, chīrographum *nt*.
signet *n* signum *nt*.
signet ring *n* anulus *m*.
significance *n* interpretātiō *f*, significātiō *f*, vīs *f*; (*importance*) pondus *nt*.
significant *adj* gravis, clārus.
signification *n* significātiō *f*.
signify *vt* significāre, velle; (*omen*) portendere; **it does not ~** nōn interest.
silence *n* silentium *nt*; **in ~** per silentium ♦ *vt* comprimere; (*argument*) refūtāre.
silent *adj* tacitus; (*habit*) taciturnus; **be ~** silēre, tacēre; **be ~ about** silēre, tacēre; **become ~** conticēscere.
silently *adv* tacitē.
silhouette *n* adumbrātiō *f*.
silk *n* bombȳx *m*; (*clothes*) sērica *ntpl* ♦ *adj* bombȳcinus, sēricus.
silken *adj* bombycinus.

sill *n* līmen *nt*.
silliness *n* stultitia *f*, ineptiae *fpl*.
silly *adj* fatuus, ineptus; stultus; **be ~** dēsipere.
silt *n* līmus *m*.
silver *n* argentum *nt* ♦ *adj* argenteus.
silver mine *n* argentāria *f*.
silver plate *n* argentum *nt*.
silver-plated *adj* argentātus.
silvery *adj* argenteus.
similar *adj* similis.
similarity *n* similitūdō *f*.
similarly *adv* similiter.
simile *n* similitūdō *f*.
simmer *vi* lēniter fervēre.
simper *vi* molliter subrīdēre.
simple *adj* simplex; (*mind*) fatuus; (*task*) facilis.
simpleton *n* homō ineptus *m*.
simplicity *n* simplicitās *f*; (*mind*) stultitia *f*.
simplify *vt* faciliōrem reddere.
simply *adv* simpliciter; (*merely*) sōlum, tantum.
simulate *vt* simulāre.
simulation *n* simulātiō *f*.
simultaneously *adv* simul, ūnā, eōdem tempore.
sin *n* peccātum *nt*, nefās *nt*, dēlictum *nt* ♦ *vi* peccāre.
since *adv* abhinc; **long ~** iamdūdum ♦ *conj* (*time*) ex quō tempore, postquam; (*reason*) cum (+ *subj*), quōniam; **~ he** quippe quī ♦ *prep* ab (*abl*), ex (*abl*), post (*acc*); **ever ~** usque ab.
sincere *adj* sincērus, simplex, apertus.
sincerely *adv* sincērē, ex animō.
sincerity *n* fidēs *f*, simplicitās *f*.
sinew *n* nervus *m*.
sinewy *adj* nervōsus.
sinful *adj* improbus, impius, incestus.
sinfully *adv* improbē, impiē.
sing *vt* canere, cantāre; **~ of** canere.
singe *vt* adūrere.
singer *n* cantor *m*.
singing *n* cantus *m* ♦ *adj* canōrus.
single *adj* ūnus, sōlus, ūnicus; (*unmarried*) caelebs ♦ *vt*: **~ out** ēligere, excerpere.
single-handed *adj* ūnus.
singly *adv* singillātim, singulī.
singular *adj* singulāris; (*strange*) novus.
singularly *adv* singulāriter, praecipuē.
sinister *adj* īnfaustus, malevolus.
sink *vi* dēsīdere; (*in water*) dēmergī; **~ in** inlābī, īnsīdere ♦ *vt* dēprimere, mergere; (*well*) fodere; (*fig*) dēmergere.
sinless *adj* integer, innocēns, castus.
sinner *n* peccātor *m*.
sinuous *adj* sinuōsus.
sip *vt* gustāre, lībāre.
siphon *n* siphō *m*.
sir *n* (*to master*) ere; (*to equal*) vir optime; (*title*) eques *m*.
sire *n* pater *m*.
siren *n* sīrēn *f*.

sirocco *n* Auster *m*.
sister *n* soror *f*; ~'s sorōrius.
sisterhood *n* germānitās *f*; (*society*) sorōrum
societās *f*.
sister-in-law *n* glōs *f*.
sisterly *adj* sorōrius.
sit *vi* sedēre; ~ **beside** adsidēre (*dat*); ~ **down**
cōnsīdere; ~ **on** īnsidēre (*dat*); (*eggs*)
incubāre; ~ **at table** accumbere; ~ **up** (*at
night*) vigilāre.
site *n* situs *m*, locus *m*; (*for building*) ārea *f*.
sitting *n* sessiō *f*.
situated *adj* situs.
situation *n* situs *m*; (*CIRCS*) status *m*, condiciō *f*.
six *num* sex; ~ **each** sēnī; ~ **or seven** sex
septem; ~ **times** sexiēns.
six hundred *num* sēscentī; ~ **each** sēscēnī; ~
times sēscentiēns.
six hundredth *adj* sēscentēsimus.
sixteen *num* sēdecim; ~ **each** sēnī dēnī; ~ **times**
sēdeciēns.
sixteenth *adj* sextus decimus.
sixth *adj* sextus; **for the** ~ **time** sextum.
sixtieth *adj* sexāgēsimus.
sixty *num* sexāgintā; ~ **each** sexāgēnī; ~ **times**
sexāgiēns.
size *n* māgnitūdō *f*, amplitūdō *f*; (*measure*)
mēnsūra *f*, fōrma *f*.
skate *vi* per glaciem lābī; ~ **on thin ice** (*fig*)
incēdere per ignēs suppositōs cinerī dolōsō.
skein *n* glomus *nt*.
skeleton *n* ossa *ntpl*.
sketch *n* adumbrātiō *f*, dēscrīptiō *f* ♦ *vt*
adumbrāre, īnfōrmāre.
skewer *n* verū *nt*.
skiff *n* scapha *f*, lēnunculus *m*.
skilful *adj* perītus, doctus, scītus; (*with hands*)
habilis.
skilfully *adv* perītē, doctē; habiliter.
skill *n* ars *f*, perītia *f*, sollertia *f*.
skilled *adj* perītus, doctus; ~ **in** perītus (+ *gen*).
skim *vt* dēspūmāre; ~ **over** (*fig*) legere,
perstringere.
skin *n* cutis *f*; (*animal*) pellis *f* ♦ *vt* pellem
dētrahere (*dat*).
skinflint *n* avārus *m*.
skinny *adj* macer.
skip *vi* exsultāre ♦ *vt* praeterīre.
skipper *n* magister *m*.
skirmish *n* leve proelium *nt* ♦ *vi* vēlitārī.
skirmisher *n* vēles *m*, excursor *m*.
skirt *n* īnstita *f*; (*border*) limbus *m* ♦ *vt*
contingere (*dat*); (*motion*) legere.
skittish *adj* lascīvus.
skulk *vi* latēre, dēlitēscere.
skull *n* caput *nt*.
sky *n* caelum *nt*; **of the** ~ caelestis.
skylark *n* alauda *f*.
slab *n* tabula *f*.
slack *adj* remissus, laxus; (*work*) piger,
neglegēns.
slacken *vt* remittere, dētendere ♦ *vi* laxārī.
slackness *n* remissiō *f*; pigritia *f*.

slag *n* scōria *f*.
slake *vt* restinguere, sēdāre.
slam *vt* adflīgere.
slander *n* maledicta *ntpl*, obtrectātiō *f*; (*law*)
calumnia *f* ♦ *vt* maledīcere (*dat*), īnfāmāre,
obtrectāre (*dat*).
slanderer *n* obtrectātor *m*.
slanderous *adj* maledicus.
slang *n* vulgāria verba *ntpl*.
slant *vi* in trānsversum īre.
slanting *adj* oblīquus, trānsversus.
slantingly *adv* oblīquē, ex trānsversō.
slap *n* alapa *f* ♦ *vt* palmā ferīre.
slapdash *adj* praeceps, temerārius.
slash *vt* caedere ♦ *n* ictus *m*.
slate *n* (*roof*) tēgula *f*; (*writing*) tabula *f* ♦ *vt*
increpāre.
slatternly *adj* sordidus, incōmptus.
slaughter *n* caedēs *f*, strāgēs *f* ♦ *vt* trucīdāre.
slaughterhouse *n* laniēna *f*.
slave *n* servus *m*; (*domestic*) famulus *m*; (*home-
born*) verna *m*; **be a** ~ **to** īnservīre (*dat*);
household ~**s** familia *f*.
slave girl *n* ancilla *f*.
slavery *n* servitūs *f*.
slavish *adj* servīlis.
slavishly *adv* servīliter.
slay *vt* interficere, occīdere.
slayer *n* interfector *m*.
sleek *adj* nitidus, pinguis.
sleep *n* somnus *m*; **go to** ~ obdormīscere ♦ *vi*
dormīre; ~ **off** *vt* ēdormīre.
sleeper *n* dormītor *m*.
sleepiness *n* sopor *m*.
sleepless *adj* īnsomnis, vigil.
sleeplessness *n* īnsomnia *f*.
sleepy *adj* somniculōsus; **be** ~ dormītāre.
sleeve *n* manica *f*.
sleight of hand *n* praestīgiae *fpl*.
slender *adj* gracilis, exīlis.
slenderness *n* gracilitās *f*.
slice *n* frūstum *nt* ♦ *vt* secāre.
slide *n* lāpsus *m* ♦ *vi* lābī.
slight *adj* levis, exiguus, parvus ♦ *n*
neglegentia *f* ♦ *vt* neglegere, offendere.
slightingly *adv* contemptim.
slightly *adv* leviter, paululum.
slightness *n* levitās *f*.
slim *adj* gracilis.
slime *n* līmus *m*.
slimness *n* gracilitās *f*.
slimy *adj* līmōsus, mūcōsus.
sling *n* funda *f* ♦ *vt* mittere, iaculārī.
slinger *n* funditor *m*.
slink *vi* sē subdūcere.
slip *n* lāpsus *m*; (*mistake*) offēnsiuncula *f*;
(*plant*) surculus *m* ♦ *vi* lābī; ~ **away** ēlābī,
dīlābī; ~ **out** ēlābī; (*word*) excidere; **give the**
~ **to** ēlūdere; **let** ~ āmittere, ēmittere;
(*opportunity*) ōmittere; **there's many a** ~ **twixt
the cup and the lip** inter ōs et offam multa
interveniunt.
slipper *n* solea *f*.

slippery *adj* lūbricus.
slipshod *adj* neglegēns.
slit *n* rīma *f* ♦ *vt* findere, incīdere.
sloe *n* spīnus *m*.
slope *n* dēclīve *nt*, clīvus *m*; (*steep*) dēiectus *m* ♦ *vi* sē dēmittere, vergere.
sloping *adj* dēclīvis, dēvexus; (*up*) adclīvis.
slot *n* rīma *f*.
sloth *n* inertia *f*, segnitia *f*, dēsidia *f*, ignāvia *f*.
slothful *adj* ignāvus, iners, segnis.
slothfully *adv* ignāvē, segniter.
slouch *vi* languidē incēdere.
slough *n* (*skin*) exuviae *fpl*; (*bog*) palūs *f*.
slovenliness *n* ignāvia *f*, sordēs *fpl*.
slovenly *adj* ignāvus, sordidus.
slow *adj* tardus, lentus; (*mind*) hebes.
slowly *adv* tardē, lentē.
slowness *n* tarditās *f*.
sludge *n* līmus *m*.
slug *n* līmāx *f*.
sluggard *n* homō ignāvus *m*.
sluggish *adj* piger, segnis; (*mind*) hebes.
sluggishly *adv* pigrē, segniter.
sluggishness *n* pigritia *f*, inertia *f*.
sluice *n* cataracta *f*.
slumber *n* somnus *m*, sopor *m* ♦ *vi* dormīre.
slump *n* vīlis annōna *f*.
slur *n* nota *f*; **cast ~ on** dētrectāre ♦ *vt*: **~ words** balbūtīre.
sly *adj* astūtus, vafer, callidus; **on the ~** ex opīnātō.
slyly *adv* astūtē, callidē.
slyness *n* astūtia *f*.
smack *n* (*blow*) ictus *m*; (*with hand*) alapa *f*; (*boat*) lēnunculus *m*; (*taste*) sapor *m* ♦ *vt* ferīre ♦ *vi*: **~ of** olēre, redolēre.
small *adj* parvus, exiguus; **how ~** quantulus, quantillus; **so ~** tantulus; **very ~** perexiguus, minimus; **a ~ meeting of** īnfrequēns.
smaller *adj* minor.
smallest *adj* minimus.
smallness *n* exiguitās *f*, brevitās *f*.
small talk *n* sermunculus *m*.
smart *adj* (*action*) ācer, alacer; (*dress*) concinnus, nitidus; (*pace*) vēlōx; (*wit*) facētus, salsus ♦ *n* dolor *m* ♦ *vi* dolēre; (*fig*) ūrī, mordērī.
smartly *adv* ācriter; nitidē; vēlōciter; facētē.
smartness *n* alacritās *f*; (*dress*) nitor *m*; (*wit*) facētiae *fpl*, sollertia *f*.
smash *n* ruīna *f* ♦ *vt* frangere, comminuere.
smattering *n*: **get a ~ of** odōrārī, prīmīs labrīs attingere; **with a ~ of** imbūtus (*abl*).
smear *vt* oblinere, ungere.
smell *n* (*sense*) odōrātus *m*; (*odour*) odor *m*; (*of cooking*) nīdor *m* ♦ *vt* olfacere, odōrārī ♦ *vi* olēre.
smelly *adj* olidus.
smelt *vt* fundere.
smile *n* rīsus *m* ♦ *vi* subrīdēre; **~ at** adrīdēre (*dat*); **~ upon** rīdēre ad; (*fig*) secundum esse (*dat*).
smiling *adj* laetus.

smirk *vi* subrīdēre.
smith *n* faber *m*.
smithy *n* fabrica *f*.
smock *n* tunica *f*.
smoke *n* fūmus *m* ♦ *vi* fūmāre.
smoky *adj* fūmōsus.
smooth *adj* lēvis; (*skin*) glaber; (*talk*) blandus; (*sea*) placidus; (*temper*) aequus; (*voice*) lēvis, teres ♦ *vt* sternere, līmāre.
smoothly *adv* lēviter, lēniter.
smoothness *n* lēvitās *f*, lēnitās *f*.
smother *vt* opprimere, suffocāre.
smoulder *vi* fūmāre.
smudge *n* macula *f*.
smug *adj* suī contentus.
smuggle *vt* fūrtim importāre.
smugness *n* amor suī *m*.
smut *n* fūlīgō *f*.
snack *n* cēnula *f*; **take a ~** gustāre.
snag *n* impedīmentum *nt*, scrūpulus *m*.
snail *n* cochlea *f*.
snake *n* anguis *m*, serpēns *f*.
snaky *adj* vīpereus.
snap *vt* rumpere, praerumpere; **~ the fingers** digitīs concrepāre ♦ *vi* rumpī, dissilīre; **~ at** mordēre; **~ up** corripere.
snare *n* laqueus *m*, plaga *f*, pedica *f* ♦ *vt* inrētīre.
snarl *n* gannītus *m* ♦ *vi* gannīre.
snatch *vt* rapere, ēripere, adripere, corripere; **~ at** captāre.
sneak *n* perfidus *m* ♦ *vi* conrēpere; **~ in** sē īnsinuāre; **~ out** ēlābī.
sneaking *adj* humilis, fūrtīvus.
sneer *n* irrīsiō *f* ♦ *vi* irrīdēre, dērīdēre.
sneeze *n* sternūtāmentum *nt* ♦ *vi* sternuere.
sniff *vt* odōrārī.
snip *vt* praecīdere, secāre.
snob *n* homō ambitiōsus *m*.
snood *n* mitra *f*.
snooze *vi* dormītāre.
snore *vi* stertere.
snoring *n* rhoncus *m*.
snort *n* fremitus *m* ♦ *vi* fremere.
snout *n* rōstrum *nt*.
snow *n* nix *f* ♦ *vi* ningere; **~ed under** nive obrutus; **it is ~ing** ningit.
snowy *adj* nivālis; (*colour*) niveus.
snub *vt* neglegere, praeterīre.
snub-nosed *adj* sīmus.
snuff *n* (*candle*) fungus *m*.
snug *adj* commodus.
snugly *adv* commodē.
so *adv* (*referring back*) sīc; (*referring forward*) ita; (*with adj and adv*) tam; (*with verb*) adeō; (*consequence*) ergō, itaque, igitur; **~** itaque; **~ great** tantus; **so-so** sīc; **~ as to** ut; **~ be it** estō; **~ big** tantus; **~ far** usque adeō, adhūc; **~ far as** quod; **~ far from** adeō nōn; **~ little** tantillus; **~ long as** dum; **~ many** tot; **~ much** *adj* tantus ♦ *adv* tantum; (*with compar*) tantō; **~ often** totiēns; **~ that** ut (+ *subj*); **~ that ... not** (*purpose*) nē; (*result*) ut nōn; **and ~ on** deinceps; **not ~ very** haud ita; **say ~** id dīcere.

soak *vt* imbuere, madefacere.
soaking *adj* madidus.
soap *n* sapō *m.*
soar *vi* in sublīme ferrī, subvolāre; ~ **above** superāre.
sob *n* singultus *m* ♦ *vi* singultāre.
sober *adj* sobrius; (*conduct*) modestus; (*mind*) sānus.
soberly *adv* sobriē, modestē.
sobriety *n* modestia *f*, continentia *f.*
so-called *adj* quī dīcitur.
sociability *n* facilitās *f.*
sociable *adj* facilis, cōmis.
sociably *adv* faciliter, cōmiter.
social *adj* sociālis, commūnis.
socialism *n* populāris ratiō *f.*
socialist *n* homō populāris *m/f.*
society *n* societās *f*; (*class*) optimātēs *mpl*; (*being with*) convīctus *m*; **cultivate the ~ of** adsectārī; **secret ~** sodālitās *f.*
sod *n* caespes *m*, glaeba *f.*
soda *n* nitrum *nt.*
sodden *adj* madidus.
soever *adv* -cumque.
sofa *n* lectus *m.*
soft *adj* mollis; (*fruit*) mītis; (*voice*) submissus; (*character*) dēlicātus; (*words*) blandus.
soften *vt* mollīre; (*body*) ēnervāre; (*emotion*) lēnīre, mītigāre ♦ *vi* mollēscere, mītēscere.
soft-hearted *adj* misericors.
softly *adv* molliter, lēniter; blandē.
softness *n* mollitia *f*, mollitiēs *f.*
soil *n* sōlum *nt*, humus *f* ♦ *vt* inquināre, foedāre.
sojourn *n* commorātiō *f*, mānsiō *f* ♦ *vi* commorārī.
sojourner *n* hospes *m*, hospita *f.*
solace *n* sōlātium *nt*, levātiō *f* ♦ *vt* sōlārī, cōnsōlārī.
solar *adj* sōlis.
solder *n* ferrūmen *nt* ♦ *vt* ferrūmināre.
soldier *n* mīles *m*; **be a ~** mīlitāre; **common ~** manipulāris *m*, gregārius mīles *m*; **fellow ~** commīlitō *m*; **foot ~** pedes *m*; **old ~** veterānus *m* ♦ *vi* mīlitāre.
soldierly *adj* mīlitāris.
soldiery *n* mīles *m.*
sole *adj* sōlus, ūnus, ūnicus ♦ *n* (*foot*) planta *f*; (*fish*) solea *f.*
solecism *n* soloecismus *m.*
solely *adv* sōlum, tantum, modō.
solemn *adj* gravis; (*religion*) sanctus.
solemnity *n* gravitās *f*, sanctitās *f.*
solemnize *vt* agere.
solemnly *adv* graviter; ritē.
solicit *vt* flāgitāre, obsecrāre.
solicitation *n* flāgitātiō *f.*
solicitor *n* advocātus *m.*
solicitous *adj* anxius, trepidus.
solicitously *adv* anxiē, trepidē.
solicitude *n* cūra *f*, anxietās *f.*
solid *adj* solidus; (*metal*) pūrus; (*food*) firmus; (*argument*) firmus; (*character*) cōnstāns,

spectātus; **become ~** concrēscere; **make ~** cōgere.
solidarity *n* societās *f.*
solidify *vt* cōgere ♦ *vi* concrēscere.
solidity *n* soliditās *f.*
solidly *adv* firmē, cōnstanter.
soliloquize *vi* sēcum loquī.
soliloquy *n* ūnīus ōrātiō *f.*
solitary *adj* sōlus, sōlitārius; (*instance*) ūnicus; (*place*) dēsertus.
solitude *n* sōlitūdō *f.*
solo *n* canticum *nt.*
solstice *n* (*summer*) sōlstitium *nt*; (*winter*) brūma *f.*
solstitial *adj* sōlstitiālis, brūmālis.
soluble *adj* dissolūbilis.
solution *n* (*of puzzle*) ēnōdātiō *f.*
solve *vt* ēnōdāre, explicāre.
solvency *n* solvendī facultās *f.*
solvent *adj*: **be ~** solvendō esse.
sombre *adj* obscūrus; (*fig*) tristis.
some *adj* aliquī; (*pl*) nonnullī, aliquot; ~ **people** sunt quī (+ *subj*); ~ ... **other** alius ... alius; **for ~ time** aliquamdiū; **with ~ reason** nōn sine causā ♦ *pron* aliquis; (*pl*) nonnullī, sunt quī (*subj*), erant quī (*subj*).
somebody *pron* aliquis; ~ **or other** nescioquis.
somehow *adv* quōdammodō, nescio quōmodō.
someone *pron* aliquis; (*negative*) quisquam; ~ **or other** nescioquis; ~ **else** alius.
something *pron* aliquid; ~ **or other** nescioquid; ~ **else** aliud.
sometime *adv* aliquandō; (*past*) quondam.
sometimes *adv* interdum, nonnumquam; ~ ... ~ **modo** ... modo.
somewhat *adv* aliquantum, nōnnihil, paulum; (*with compar*) paulō, aliquantō.
somewhere *adv* alicubi; (*to*) aliquō; ~ **else** alibī; (*to*) aliō; **from ~** alicunde; **from ~ else** aliunde.
somnolence *n* somnus *m.*
somnolent *adj* sēmisomnus.
son *n* fīlius *m*; **small ~** fīliolus *m.*
song *n* carmen *nt*, cantus *m.*
son-in-law *n* gener *m.*
sonorous *adj* sonōrus, canōrus.
soon *adv* mox, brevi, citō; **as ~ as** ut prīmum, cum prīmum (+ *fut perf*), simul āc/atque (+ *perf indic*); **as ~ as possible** quam prīmum; **too ~** praemātūrē, ante tempus.
sooner *adv* prius, mātūrius; (*preference*) libentius, potius; ~ **or later** sērius ōcius; **no ~ said than done** dictum factum.
soonest *adv* mātūrissimē.
soot *n* fūlīgō *f.*
soothe *vt* dēlēnīre, permulcēre.
soothing *adj* lēnis, blandus.
soothingly *adv* blandē.
soothsayer *n* hariolus *m*, vātēs *m/f*, haruspex *m.*
sooty *adj* fūmōsus.
sop *n* offa *f*; (*fig*) dēlēnīmentum *nt.*

sophism *n* captiō *f*.
sophist *n* sophistēs *m*.
sophistical *adj* acūleātus, captiōsus.
sophisticated *adj* lepidus, urbānus.
sophistry *n* captiō *f*.
soporific *adj* sopōrifer, somnifer.
soprano *adj* acūtus.
sorcerer *n* veneficus *m*.
sorceress *n* venefica *f*, saga *f*.
sorcery *n* venēficium *nt*; (*means*) venēna *ntpl*, carmina *ntpl*.
sordid *adj* sordidus; (*conduct*) illīberālis.
sordidly *adv* sordidē.
sordidness *n* sordēs *fpl*; illīberālitās *f*.
sore *adj* molestus, gravis, acerbus; **feel ~** dolēre ♦ *n* ulcus *nt*.
sorely *adv* graviter, vehementer.
sorrel *n* lapathus *f*, lapathum *nt*.
sorrow *n* dolor *m*, aegritūdō *f*; (*outward*) maeror *m*; (*for death*) lūctus *m* ♦ *vi* dolēre, maerēre, lūgēre.
sorrowful *adj* maestus, tristis.
sorrowfully *adv* maestē.
sorry *adj* paenitēns; (*poor*) miser; **I am ~ for** (*remorse*) mē paenitet, mē piget (*gen*); (*pity*) mē miseret (*gen*).
sort *n* genus *nt*; **a ~ of** quīdam; **all ~s of** omnēs; **the ~ of** tālis; **this ~ of** huiusmodī; **the common ~** plēbs *f*; **I am not the ~ of man to** nōn is sum quī (+ *subj*); **I am out of ~s** mihī displiceō ♦ *vt* dīgerere, compōnere; (*votes*) diribēre.
sortie *n* excursiō *f*, excursus *m*, ēruptiō *f*; **make a ~** ērumpere, excurrere.
sot *n* ēbriōsus *m*.
sottish *adj* ēbriōsus, tēmulentus.
sottishness *n* vīnolentia *f*.
soul *n* anima *f*, animus *m*; (*essence*) vīs *f*; (*person*) caput *nt*; **not a ~** nēmō ūnus; **the ~ of** (*fig*) medulla *f*.
soulless *adj* caecus, dūrus.
sound *n* sonitus *m*, sonus *m*; (*articulate*) vōx *f*; (*confused*) strepitus *m*; (*loud*) fragor *m*; (*strait*) fretum *nt* ♦ *vt* (*signal*) canere; (*instrument*) īnflāre; (*depth*) scrūtārī, temptāre; (*person*) animum temptāre (*gen*) ♦ *vi* canere, sonāre; (*seem*) vidērī; **~ a retreat** receptuī canere ♦ *adj* sānus, salūbris; (*health*) firmus; (*sleep*) artus; (*judgment*) exquīsītus; (*argument*) vērus; **safe and ~** salvus, incolumis.
soundly *adv* (*beat*) vehementer; (*sleep*) artē; (*study*) penitus, dīligenter.
soundness *n* sānitās *f*, integritās *f*.
soup *n* iūs *nt*.
sour *adj* acerbus, amārus, acidus; **turn ~** acēscere; (*fig*) coacēscere ♦ *vt* (*fig*) exacerbāre.
source *n* fōns *m*; (*river*) caput *nt*; (*fig*) fōns *m*, orīgō *f*; **have its ~ in** orīrī ex; (*fig*) proficīscī ex.
sourness *n* acerbitās *f*; (*temper*) mōrōsitās *f*.
souse *vt* immergere.

south *n* merīdiēs *f* ♦ *adj* austrālis ♦ *adv* ad merīdiem.
south-east *adv* inter sōlis ortum et merīdiem.
southerly *adj* ad merīdiem versus.
southern *adj* austrālis.
south-west *adv* inter occāsum sōlis et merīdiem.
south wind *n* auster *m*.
souvenir *n* monumentum *nt*.
sovereign *n* rēx *m*, rēgīna *f* ♦ *adj* prīnceps, summus.
sovereignty *n* rēgnum *nt*, imperium *nt*, prīncipātus *m*; (*of the people*) māiestās *f*.
sow *n* scrōfa *f*, sūs *f*.
sow *vt* serere; (*field*) cōnserere ♦ *vi* sementem facere.
sower *n* sator *m*.
sowing *n* sēmentis *f*.
spa *n* aquae *fpl*.
space *n* (*extension*) spatium *nt*; (*not matter*) ināne *nt*; (*room*) locus *m*; (*distance*) intervallum *nt*; (*time*) spatium *nt*; **open ~** ārea *f*; **leave a ~ of** intermittere ♦ *vt*: **~ out** dispōnere.
spacious *adj* amplus, capāx.
spaciousness *n* amplitūdō *f*.
spade *n* pāla *f*, rūtrum *nt*.
span *n* (*measure*) palmus *m*; (*extent*) spatium *nt* ♦ *vt* iungere.
spangle *n* bractea *f*.
spangled *adj* distinctus.
spar *n* tignum *nt*.
spare *vt* parcere (*dat*); (*to give*) suppeditāre; **~ time for** vacāre (*dat*) ♦ *adj* exīlis; (*extra*) subsecīvus.
sparing *adj* parcus.
sparingly *adv* parcē.
spark *n* scintilla *f*, (*fig*) igniculus *m*.
sparkle *vi* scintillāre, nitēre, micāre.
sparrow *n* passer *m*.
sparse *adj* rārus.
spasm *n* convulsiō *f*.
spasmodically *adv* interdum.
spatter *vt* aspergere.
spawn *n* ōva *ntpl*.
speak *vt*, *vi* loquī; (*make speech*) dīcere, contiōnārī, ōrātiōnem habēre; **~ out** ēloquī; **~ to** adloquī; (*converse*) colloquī cum; **~ well of** bene dīcere (*dat*); **it ~s for itself** rēs ipsa loquitur.
speaker *n* ōrātor *m*.
speaking *n*: **art of ~** dīcendī ars *f*; **practise public ~** dēclāmāre ♦ *adj*: **likeness ~** vīvida imāgō.
spear *n* hasta *f*.
spearman *n* hastātus *m*.
special *adj* praecipuus, proprius.
speciality *n* proprium *nt*.
specially *adv* praecipuē, praesertim.
species *n* genus *nt*.
specific *adj* certus.
specification *n* dēsignātiō *f*.
specify *vt* dēnotāre, dēsignāre.

specimen _n_ exemplar _nt_, exemplum _nt_.
specious _adj_ speciōsus.
speciously _adv_ speciōsē.
speciousness _n_ speciēs _f_.
speck _n_ macula _f_.
speckled _adj_ maculīs distinctus.
spectacle _n_ spectāculum _nt_.
spectacular _adj_ spectābilis.
spectator _n_ spectātor _m_.
spectral _adj_ larvālis.
spectre _n_ larva _f_.
speculate _vi_ cōgitāre, coniectūrās facere;
  (_comm_) forō ūtī.
speculation _n_ cōgitātiō _f_, coniectūra _f_; (_comm_)
  ālea _f_.
speculator _n_ contemplātor _m_; (_comm_) āleātor
  _m_.
speech _n_ ōrātiō _f_; (_language_) sermō _m_, lingua _f_;
  (_to people or troops_) cōntiō _f_; **make a ~**
  ōrātiōnem/cōntiōnem habēre.
speechless _adj_ ēlinguis, mūtus.
speed _n_ celeritās _f_, cursus _m_, vēlōcitās _f_; **with**
  all ~ summa celeritate; **at full ~** māgnō cursū,
  incitātus; (_riding_) citātō equō ♦ _vt_
  adcelerāre, mātūrāre ♦ _vi_ properāre,
  festīnāre.
speedily _adv_ celeriter, citō.
speedy _adj_ celer, vēlōx, citus.
spell _n_ carmen _nt_.
spellbound _adj_: **be ~** obstipēscere.
spelt _n_ far _nt_.
spend _vt_ impendere, īnsūmere; (_public money_)
  ērogāre; (_time_) agere, cōnsūmere, terere;
  (_strength_) effundere; **~ itself** (_storm_)
  dēsaevīre; **~ on** īnsūmere (_acc_ & _dat_).
spendthrift _n_ nepōs _m_, prōdigus _m_.
sphere _n_ globus _m_; (_of action_) prōvincia _f_.
spherical _adj_ globōsus.
sphinx _n_ sphinx _f_.
spice _n_ condīmentum _nt_; **~s** _pl_ odōrēs _mpl_ ♦ _vt_
  condīre.
spicy _adj_ odōrātus; (_wit_) salsus.
spider _n_ arānea _f_; **~'s web** arāneum _nt_.
spike _n_ dēns _m_, clāvus _m_.
spikenard _n_ nardus _m_.
spill _vt_ fundere, profundere ♦ _vi_ redundāre.
spin _vt_ (_thread_) nēre, dēdūcere; (_top_) versāre;
  ~ out (_story_) prōdūcere ♦ _vi_ circumagī,
  versārī.
spindle _n_ fūsus _m_.
spine _n_ spīna _f_.
spineless _adj_ ēnervātus.
spinster _n_ virgō _f_.
spiral _adj_ intortus ♦ _n_ spīra _f_.
spire _n_ cōnus _m_.
spirit _n_ (_life_) anima _f_; (_intelligence_) mēns _f_; (_soul_)
  animus _m_; (_vivacity_) spīritus _m_, vigor _m_, vīs _f_;
  (_character_) ingenium _nt_; (_intention_) voluntās _f_;
  (_of an age_) mōrēs _mpl_; (_ghost_) anima _f_; **~s** _pl_
  mānēs _mpl_; **full of ~** alacer, animōsus.
spirited _adj_ animōsus, ācer.
spiritless _adj_ iners, frāctus, timidus.
spiritual _adj_ animī.

spit _n_ verū _nt_ ♦ _vi_ spuere, spūtāre; **~ on**
  cōnspūtāre; **~ out** exspuere.
spite _n_ invidia _f_, malevolentia _f_, līvor _m_; **in ~ of**
  me mē invītō; **in ~ of the difficulties** in his
  angustiīs ♦ _vt_ incommodāre, offendere.
spiteful _adj_ malevolus, malignus, invidus.
spitefully _adv_ malevolē, malignē.
spitefulness _n_ malevolentia _f_.
spittle _n_ spūtum _nt_.
splash _n_ fragor _m_ ♦ _vt_ aspergere.
spleen _n_ splēn _m_; (_fig_) stomachus _m_.
splendid _adj_ splendidus, lūculentus; īnsignis;
  (_person_) amplus.
splendidly _adv_ splendidē, optimē.
splendour _n_ splendor _m_, fulgor _m_; (_fig_) lautitia
  _f_, adparātus _m_.
splenetic _adj_ stomachōsus.
splice _vt_ iungere.
splint _n_ ferula _f_.
splinter _n_ fragmentum _nt_, assula _f_ ♦ _vt_ findere.
split _vt_ findere ♦ _vi_ dissilīre ♦ _adj_ fissus ♦ _n_
  fissum _nt_; (_fig_) dissidium _nt_.
splutter _vi_ balbūtīre.
spoil _n_ praeda _f_ ♦ _vt_ (_rob_) spoliāre; (_mar_)
  corrumpere ♦ _vi_ corrumpī.
spoiler _n_ spoliātor _m_; corruptor _m_.
spoils _npl_ spolia _ntpl_, exuviae _fpl_.
spoke _n_ radius _m_; **put a ~ in one's wheel**
  inicere scrūpulum (_dat_).
spokesman _n_ interpres _m_, ōrātor _m_.
spoliation _n_ spoliātiō _f_, dīreptiō _f_.
spondee _n_ spondēus _m_.
sponge _n_ spongia _f_.
sponsor _n_ spōnsor _m_; (_fig_) auctor _m_.
spontaneity _n_ impulsus _m_, voluntās _f_.
spontaneous _adj_ voluntārius.
spontaneously _adv_ suā sponte, ultrō.
spoon _n_ cochlear _nt_.
sporadic _adj_ rārus.
sporadically _adv_ passim.
sport _n_ lūdus _m_; (_in Rome_) campus _m_; (_fun_)
  iocus _m_; (_ridicule_) lūdibrium _nt_; **make ~ of**
  illūdere (_dat_) ♦ _vi_ lūdere.
sportive _adj_ lascīvus.
sportiveness _n_ lascīvia _f_.
sportsman _n_ vēnātor _m_.
sportsmanlike _adj_ honestus, generōsus.
spot _n_ macula _f_; (_place_) locus _m_; (_dice_)
  pūnctum _nt_; **on the ~** īlicō ♦ _vt_ maculāre;
  (_see_) animadvertere.
spotless _adj_ integer, pūrus; (_character_) castus.
spotted _adj_ maculōsus.
spouse _n_ coniunx _m/f_.
spout _n_ (_of jug_) ōs _nt_; (_pipe_) canālis _m_ ♦ _vi_
  ēmicāre.
sprain _vt_ intorquēre.
sprawl _vi_ sē fundere.
sprawling _adj_ fūsus.
spray _n_ aspergō _f_ ♦ _vt_ aspergere.
spread _vt_ pandere, extendere; (_news_)
  dīvulgāre; (_infection_) vulgāre ♦ _vi_ patēre;
  (_rumour_) mānāre, incrēbrēscere; (_feeling_)
  glīscere.

spreadeagle vt dispandere.
spreading adj (tree) patulus.
spree n cōmissātiō f.
sprig n virga f.
sprightliness n alacritās f.
sprightly adj alacer, hilaris.
spring n (season) vēr nt; (water) fōns m; (leap) saltus m ♦ vi (grow) crēscere, ēnāscī; (leap) salīre; ~ **from** orīrī ex, proficīscī ex; ~ **on to** īnsilīre in (acc); ~ **up** exorīrī, exsilīre ♦ vt: ~ **a leak** rīmās agere; ~ **a surprise on** admīrātiōnem movēre (dat) ♦ adj vērnus.
springe n laqueus m.
sprinkle vt aspergere; ~ **on** īnspergere (dat).
sprint vi currere.
sprout n surculus m ♦ vi fruticārī.
spruce adj nitidus, concinnus.
sprung adj ortus, oriundus.
spume n spūma f.
spur n calcar nt; ~ **of a hill** prōminēns collis; **on the** ~ **of the moment** ex tempore ♦ vt incitāre; ~ **the willing horse** currentem incitāre; ~ **on** concitāre.
spurious adj falsus, fūcōsus, fictus.
spurn vt spernere, aspernārī, respuere.
spurt vi ēmicāre; (run) sē incitāre ♦ n impetus m.
spy n speculātor m, explōrātor m ♦ vi speculārī ♦ vt cōnspicere; ~ **out** explōrāre.
squabble n iūrgium nt ♦ vi rixārī.
squad n (MIL) decuria f.
squadron n (cavalry) āla f, turma f; (ships) classis f.
squalid adj sordidus, dēfōrmis.
squall n procella f.
squally adj procellōsus.
squalor n sordēs fpl, squālor m.
squander vt dissipāre, disperdere, effundere.
squanderer n prōdigus m.
square n quadrātum nt; (town) area f ♦ vt quadrāre; (account) subdūcere ♦ vi cōnstāre, congruere ♦ adj quadrātus.
squash vt conterere, contundere.
squat vi subsīdere ♦ adj brevis atque obēsus.
squatter n (on land) agripeta m.
squawk vi crōcīre.
squeak n strīdor m ♦ vi strīdēre.
squeal n vāgītus m ♦ vi vāgīre.
squeamish adj fastīdiōsus; **feel** ~ nauseāre, fastīdīre.
squeamishness n fastīdium nt, nausea f.
squeeze vt premere, comprimere; ~ **out** exprimere.
squint adj perversus ♦ n: **person with a** ~ strabō m ♦ vi strabō esse.
squinter n strabō m.
squinting adj paetus.
squire n armiger m; (landed) dominus m.
squirm vi volūtārī.
squirrel n sciūrus m.
squirt vt ēicere, effundere ♦ vi ēmicāre.
stab n ictus m, vulnus nt ♦ vt fodere, ferīre, percutere.

stability n stabilitās f, firmitās f, cōnstantia f.
stabilize vt stabilīre, firmāre.
stable adj firmus, stabilis ♦ n stabulum nt, equīle nt; **shut the** ~ **door after the horse is stolen** clipeum post vulnera sūmere.
stack n acervus m ♦ vt congerere, cumulāre.
stadium n spatium nt.
staff n scīpiō m, virga f; (augur's) lituus m; (officers) contubernālēs mpl.
stag n cervus m.
stage n pulpitum nt, proscēnium nt; (theatre) scēna f, theātrum nt; (scene of action) campus m; (of journey) iter nt; (of progress) gradus m ♦ adj scēnicus ♦ vt (play) dare, docēre.
stage fright n horror m.
stagger vi titubāre ♦ vt obstupefacere.
stagnant adj iners.
stagnate vi (fig) cessāre, refrīgēscere.
stagnation n cessātiō f, torpor m.
stagy adj scēnicus.
staid adj sevērus, gravis.
stain n macula f, lābēs f; (fig) dēdecus nt, ignōminia f ♦ vt maculāre, foedāre, contāmināre; ~ **with** īnficere (abl).
stainless adj pūrus, integer.
stair n scālae fpl, gradus mpl.
staircase n scālae fpl.
stake n pālus m, stīpes m; (pledge) pignus nt; **be at** ~ agī, in discrīmine esse ♦ vt (wager) dēpōnere.
stale adj obsolētus, effētus; (wine) vapidus.
stalemate n: **reach a** ~ ad incitās redigī.
stalk n (corn) calamus m; (plant) stīpes m ♦ vi incēdere ♦ vt vēnārī, īnsidiārī (dat).
stall n (animal) stabulum nt; (seat) subsellium nt; (shop) taberna f ♦ vt stabulāre.
stallion n equus m.
stalwart adj ingēns, rōbustus, fortis.
stamina n patientia f.
stammer n haesitātiō f ♦ vi balbūtīre.
stammering adj balbus.
stamp n fōrma f; (mark) nota f, signum nt; (of feet) supplōsiō f ♦ vt imprimere; (coin) ferīre, signāre; (fig) inūrere; ~ **one's feet** pedem supplōdere; ~ **out** exstinguere.
stampede n discursus m; (fig) pavor m ♦ vi discurrere; (fig) expavēscere.
stance n status m.
stanchion n columna f.
stand n (position) statiō f; (platform) suggestus m; **make a** ~ resistere, restāre ♦ vi stāre; (remain) manēre; (matters) sē habēre ♦ vt statuere; (tolerate) ferre, tolerāre; ~ **against** resistere (dat); ~ **aloof** abstāre; ~ **by** adsistere (dat); (friend) adesse (dat); (promise) praestāre; ~ **convicted** manifestum tenērī; ~ **down** concēdere; ~ **fast** cōnsistere; ~ **one's ground** in locō perstāre; ~ **for** (office) petere; (meaning) significāre; (policy) postulāre; ~ **in awe of** in metū habēre; ~ **in need of** indigēre (abl); ~ **on** īnsistere in (abl); ~ **on end** horrēre; ~ **on one's dignity** gravitātem suam tuērī; ~ **out** ēminēre, exstāre; (against)

resistere (*dat*); (*to sea*) in altum prōvehī; ~
out of the way of dēcēdere (*dat*); ~ over
(*case*) ampliāre; ~ still cōnsistere, īnsistere;
~ to reason sequī; ~ trial reum fierī; ~ up
surgere, cōnsurgere; ~ up for dēfendere,
adesse (*dat*); ~ up to respōnsāre (*dat*).

standard *n* (*MIL*) signum *nt*; (*measure*) nōrma *f*;
~ author scrīptor classicus *m*; up to ~ iūstus;
judge by the ~ of referre ad.

standard-bearer *n* signifer *m*.

standing *adj* perpetuus ♦ *n* status *m*; (*social*)
locus *m*, ōrdō *m*; of long ~ inveterātus; be of
long ~ inveterāscere.

stand-offish *adj* tēctus.

standstill *n*: be at a ~ haerēre, frīgēre; bring
to a ~ ad incitās redigere; come to a ~
īnsistere.

stanza *n* tetrastichon *nt*.

staple *n* uncus *m* ♦ *adj* praecipuus.

star *n* stēlla *f*, astrum *nt*; sīdus *nt*; shooting ~s
acontiae *fpl*.

starboard *adj* dexter.

starch *n* amylum *nt*.

stare *n* obtūtus *m* ♦ *vi* intentīs oculīs intuērī,
stupēre; ~ at contemplārī.

stark *adj* rigidus; simplex ♦ *adv* plānē, omnīnō.

starling *n* sturnus *m*.

starry *adj* stēllātus.

start *n* initium *nt*; (*movement*) saltus *m*;
(*journey*) profectiō *f*; by fits and ~s carptim;
have a day's ~ on diē antecēdere ♦ *vt*
incipere, īnstituere; (*game*) excitāre;
(*process*) movēre ♦ *vi* (*with fright*) resilīre;
(*journey*) proficīscī; ~ up exsilīre.

starting place *n* carcerēs *mpl*.

startle *vt* excitāre, terrēre.

starvation *n* famēs *f*.

starve *vi* fame cōnficī; (*cold*) frīgēre ♦ *vt* fame
ēnecāre.

starveling *n* famēlicus *m*.

state *n* (*condition*) status *m*, condiciō *f*; (*pomp*)
adparātus *m*; (*POL*) cīvitās *f*, rēs pūblica *f*; the
~ of affairs is ita sē rēs habet; I know the ~ of
affairs quō in locō rēs sit sciō; of the ~
pūblicus ♦ *adj* pūblicus ♦ *vt* adfirmāre,
expōnere, profitērī; ~ one's case causam
dīcere.

stateliness *n* māiestās *f*, gravitās *f*.

stately *adj* gravis, grandis, nōbilis.

statement *n* adfirmātiō *f*, dictum *nt*; (*witness*)
testimōnium *nt*.

state of health *n* valētūdō *f*.

state of mind *n* adfectiō *f*.

statesman *n* vir reī pūblicae gerendae
perītus *m*, cōnsilī pūblicī auctor *m*.

statesmanlike *adj* prūdēns.

statesmanship *n* cīvīlis prūdentia *f*.

static *adj* stabilis.

station *n* locus *m*; (*MIL*) statiō *f*; (*social*) locus *m*,
ōrdō *m* ♦ *vt* collocāre, pōnere; (*in different
places*) dispōnere.

stationary *adj* immōtus, statārius, stabilis.

statistics *n* cēnsus *m*.

statuary *n* fictor *m*.

statute *n* statua *f*, signum *nt*, imāgō *f*.

statuette *n* sigillum *nt*.

stature *n* fōrma *f*, statūra *f*.

status *n* locus *m*.

status quo *n*: restore the ~ ad integrum
restituere.

statutable *adj* lēgitimus.

statute *n* lēx *f*.

staunch *vt* (*blood*) sistere ♦ *adj* fīdus,
cōnstāns.

stave *vt* perrumpere, perfringere; ~ off
arcēre.

stay *n* firmāmentum *nt*; (*fig*) columen *nt*;
(*sojourn*) mānsiō *f*, commorātiō *f* ♦ *vt* (*prop*)
fulcīre; (*stop*) dētinēre, dēmorārī ♦ *vi*
manēre, commorārī.

stead *n* locus *m*; stand one in good ~ prōdesse
(*dat*).

steadfast *adj* firmus, stabilis, cōnstāns; ~ at
home tenēre sē domī.

steadfastly *adv* cōnstanter.

steadfastness *n* firmitās *f*, cōnstantia *f*.

steadily *adv* firmē, cōnstanter.

steadiness *n* stabilitās *f*; (*fig*) cōnstantia *f*.

steady *adj* stabilis, firmus; (*fig*) gravis,
cōnstāns.

steak *n* offa *f*.

steal *vt* surripere, fūrārī ♦ *vi*: ~ away sē
subdūcere; ~ over subrēpere (*dat*); ~ into sē
īnsinuāre in (*acc*); ~ a march on occupāre.

stealing *n* fūrtum *nt*.

stealth *n* fūrtum *nt*; by ~ fūrtim, clam.

stealthily *adv* fūrtim, clam.

stealthy *adj* fūrtīvus, clandestīnus.

steam *n* aquae vapor *m*, fūmus *m* ♦ *vi* fūmāre.

steed *n* equus *m*.

steel *n* ferrum *nt*, chalybs *m* ♦ *adj* ferreus ♦ *vt*
dūrāre; ~ oneself obdūrēscere.

steely *adj* ferreus.

steelyard *n* statēra *f*.

steep *adj* arduus, praeceps, praeruptus;
(*slope*) dēclīvis ♦ *vt* imbuere.

steeple *n* turris *f*.

steepness *n* arduum *nt*.

steer *vi* gubernāre, regere, dīrigere ♦ *n*
iuvencus *m*.

steering *n* gubernātiō *f*.

steersman *n* gubernātor *m*; rector *m*.

stellar *adj* stēllārum.

stem *n* stīpes *m*, truncus *m*; (*ship*) prōra *f* ♦ *vt*
adversārī (*dat*); ~ the tide of (*fig*) obsistere
(*dat*).

stench *n* foetor *m*.

stenographer *n* exceptor *m*, āctuārius *m*.

stenography *n* notae *fpl*.

stentorian *adj* (*voice*) ingēns.

step *n* gradus *m*; (*track*) vestīgium *nt*; (*of stair*)
gradus *m*; ~ by ~ gradātim; flight of ~s
gradus *mpl*; take a ~ gradum facere; take ~s
to ratiōnem inīre ut, vidēre ut; march in ~ in
numerum īre; out of ~ extrā numerum ♦ *vi*
gradī, incēdere; ~ aside dēcēdere; ~ back

regredī; **~ forward** prōdīre; **~ on** insistere (*dat*).

stepdaughter *n* prīvīgna *f*.

stepfather *n* vītricus *m*.

stepmother *n* noverca *f*.

stepson *n* prīvīgnus *m*.

stereotyped *adj* trītus.

sterile *adj* sterilis.

sterility *n* sterilitās *f*.

sterling *adj* integer, probus, gravis.

stern *adj* dūrus, sevērus; (*look*) torvus ♦ *n* puppis *f*.

sternly *adv* sevērē, dūriter.

sternness *n* sevēritās *f*.

stew *vt* coquere.

steward *n* prōcūrātor *m*; (*of estate*) vīlicus *m*.

stewardship *n* prōcūrātiō *f*.

stick *n* (*for beating*) fūstis *m*; (*for walking*) baculum *nt* ♦ *vi* haerēre; **~ at nothing** ad omnia dēscendere; **~ fast in** inhaerēre (*dat*), inhaerēscere in (*abl*); **~ out** ēminēre; **~ to** adhaerēre (*dat*); **~ up** ēminēre; **~ up for** dēfendere ♦ *vt* (*with glue*) conglūtināre; (*with point*) fīgere; **~ into** īnfīgere; **~ top on** praefīgere.

stickler *n* dīligēns (*gen*).

sticky *adj* lentus, tenāx.

stiff *adj* rigidus; (*difficult*) difficilis; **be ~** rigēre.

stiffen *vt* rigidum facere ♦ *vi* rigēre.

stiffly *adv* rigidē.

stiff-necked *adj* obstinātus.

stiffness *n* rigor *m*.

stifle *vt* suffocāre; (*fig*) opprimere, restinguere.

stigma *n* nota *f*.

stigmatize *vt* notāre.

stile *n* saepēs *f*.

still *adj* immōtus, tranquillus, quiētus; tacitus ♦ *vt* lēnīre, sēdāre ♦ *adv* etiam, adhūc, etiamnum; (*past*) etiam tum; (*with compar*) etiam; (*adversative*) tamen, nihilōminus.

stillness *n* quiēs *f*; silentium *nt*.

stilly *adj* tacitus.

stilted *adj* (*language*) īnflātus.

stilts *n* grallae *fpl*.

stimulant *n* stimulus *m*.

stimulate *vt* stimulāre, acuere, exacuere, excitāre.

stimulus *n* stimulus *m*.

sting *n* aculeus *m*; (*wound*) ictus *m*; (*fig*) aculeus *m*, morsus *m* ♦ *vt* pungere, mordēre.

stingily *adv* sordidē.

stinginess *n* avāritia *f*, sordēs *fpl*, tenācitās *f*.

stinging *adj* (*words*) aculeātus, mordāx.

stingy *adj* sordidus, tenāx.

stink *n* foetor *m* ♦ *vi* foetere; **~ of** olēre.

stinking *adj* foetidus.

stint *n* modus *m*; **without ~** abundē ♦ *vt* circumscrībere.

stipend *n* mercēs *f*.

stipulate *vt* pacīscī, stipulārī.

stipulation *n* condiciō *f*, pactum *nt*.

stir *n* tumultus *m* ♦ *vt* movēre, agitāre; (*fig*)

commovēre; **~ up** excitāre, incitāre ♦ *vi* movērī.

stirring *adj* impiger, tumultuōsus; (*speech*) ārdēns.

stitch *vt* suere ♦ *n* sūtūra *f*; (*in side*) dolor *m*.

stock *n* stirps *f*, genus *nt*, gēns *f*; (*equipment*) īnstrūmenta *ntpl*; (*supply*) cōpia *f*; (*investment*) pecūniae *fpl*; **live~** rēs pecuāria *f* ♦ *vt* īnstruere ♦ *adj* commūnis, trītus.

stockade *n* vallum *nt*.

stock dove *n* palumbēs *m/f*.

stock in trade *n* īnstrūmenta *ntpl*.

stocks *n* (*ship*) nāvālia *ntpl*; (*torture*) compedēs *fpl*.

stock-still *adj* plānē immōtus.

stocky *adj* brevis atque obēsus.

stodgy *adj* crūdus, īnsulsus.

stoic *n* Stōicus *m* ♦ *adj* Stōicus.

stoical *adj* dūrus, patiēns.

stoically *adv* patienter.

stoicism *n* Stōicōrum ratiō *f*, Stōicōrum disciplīna *f*.

stoke *vt* agitāre.

stole *n* stola *f*.

stolid *adj* stolidus.

stolidity *n* īnsulsitās *f*.

stolidly *adv* stolidē.

stomach *n* stomachus *m*; venter *m* ♦ *vt* patī, tolerāre.

stone *n* lapis *m*, saxum *nt*; (*precious*) gemma *f*, lapillus *m*; (*of fruit*) acinum *nt*; **leave no ~ unturned** omnia experīrī; **kill two birds with one ~** ūnō saltū duōs aprōs capere; **hewn ~** saxum quadrātum; **unhewn ~** caementum *nt* ♦ *vt* lapidibus percutere ♦ *adj* lapideus; **~ blind** plānē caecus; **~ deaf** plānē surdus.

stonecutter *n* lapicīda *m*.

stony *adj* (*soil*) lapidōsus; (*path*) scrūpōsus; (*feeling*) dūrus, ferreus.

stool *n* sēdēcula *f*.

stoop *vi* sē dēmittere; **~ to** dēscendere in (*acc*).

stop *n* mora *f*; (*punctuation*) pūnctum *nt*; **come to a ~** īnsistere; **put a ~ to** comprimere, dirimere ♦ *vt* sistere, inhibēre, fīnīre; (*restrain*) cohibēre; (*hole*) obtūrāre; **~ up** occlūdere, interclūdere ♦ *vi* dēsinere, dēsistere; (*motion*) īnsistere.

stopgap *n* tībīcen *m*.

stoppage *n* interclūsiō *f*, impedīmentum *nt*.

stopper *n* obtūrāmentum *nt*.

store *n* cōpia *f*; (*place*) horreum *nt*; (*for wine*) apothēca *f*; **be in ~ for** manēre; **set great ~ by** māgnī aestimāre ♦ *vt* condere, repōnere; **~ away** recondere; **~ up** repōnere, congerere.

storehouse *n* (*fig*) thēsaurus *m*.

storekeeper *n* cellārius *m*.

storeship *n* nāvis frūmentāria *f*.

storey *n* tabulātum *nt*.

stork *n* cicōnia *f*.

storm *n* tempestās *f*, procella *f*; **take by ~** expugnāre ♦ *vt* (*MIL*) expugnāre ♦ *vi* saevīre; **~ at** īnsectārī, invehī in (*acc*).

stormbound *adj* tempestāte dētentus.
stormer *n* expugnātor *m*.
storming *n* expugnātiō *f*.
stormy *adj* turbidus, procellōsus; (*fig*) turbulentus.
story *n* fābula *f*, nārrātiō *f*; (*short*) fābella *f*; (*untrue*) mendācium *nt*.
storyteller *n* nārrātor *m*; (*liar*) mendāx *m*.
stout *adj* pinguis; (*brave*) fortis; (*strong*) validus, rōbustus; (*material*) firmus.
stouthearted *adj* māgnanimus.
stoutly *adv* fortiter.
stove *n* camīnus *m*, fornāx *f*.
stow *vt* repōnere, condere; ~ **away** *vi* in nāvī dēlitēscere.
straddle *vi* vāricāre.
straggle *vi* deerrāre, pālārī.
straggler *n* pālāns *m*.
straggling *adj* dispersus, rārus.
straight *adj* rēctus, dīrēctus; (*fig*) apertus, vērāx; **in a ~ line** rēctā, ē regiōne; **set ~** dīrigere ♦ *adv* dīrēctō, rēctā.
straighten *vt* corrigere, extendere.
straightforward *adj* simplex, dīrēctus; (*easy*) facilis.
straightforwardness *n* simplicitās *f*.
straightness *n* (*fig*) integritās *f*.
straightway *adv* statim, extemplō.
strain *n* contentiō *f*; (*effort*) labor *m*; (*music*) modī *mpl*; (*breed*) genus *nt* ♦ *vt* intendere, contendere; (*injure*) nimiā contentiōne dēbilitāre; (*liquid*) dēliquāre, percōlāre ♦ *vi* ēnītī, vīrēs contendere.
strained *adj* (*language*) arcessītus.
strainer *n* cōlum *nt*.
strait *adj* angustus ♦ *n* fretum *nt*; **~s** *pl* angustiae *fpl*.
straiten *vt* coartāre, contrahere; **~ed circumstances** angustiae *fpl*.
strait-laced *adj* tristis, sevērus.
strand *n* lītus *nt*; (*of rope*) fīlum *nt* ♦ *vt* (*ship*) ēicere.
strange *adj* novus, īnsolitus; (*foreign*) peregrīnus; (*another's*) aliēnus; (*ignorant*) rudis, expers.
strangely *adv* mīrē, mīrum in modum.
strangeness *n* novitās *f*, īnsolentia *f*.
stranger *n* (*from abroad*) advena *f*; peregrīnus *m*; (*visiting*) hospes *m*, hospita *f*; (*not of the family*) externus *m*; (*unknown*) ignōtus *m*.
strangle *vt* strangulāre, laqueō gulam frangere.
strap *n* lōrum *nt*, habēna *f*.
strapping *adj* grandis.
stratagem *n* cōnsilium *nt*, fallācia *f*.
strategic *adj* (*action*) prūdēns; (*position*) idōneus.
strategist *n* artis bellicae perītus *m*.
strategy *n* ars imperātōria *f*, cōnsilia *ntpl*.
straw *n* (*stalk*) culmus *m*; (*collective*) strāmentum *nt*; **not care a ~ for** floccī nōn facere ♦ *adj* strāmenticius.
strawberry *n* frāgum *nt*.

strawberry tree *n* arbutus *m*.
stray *vt* aberrāre, deerrāre; vagārī ♦ *adj* errābundus.
streak *n* līnea *f*, macula *f*; (*light*) radius *m*; (*character*) vēna *f* ♦ *vt* maculāre.
stream *n* flūmen *nt*, fluvius *m*; **down ~** secundō flūmine; **up ~** adversō flūmine ♦ *vi* fluere, sē effundere; **~ into** īnfluere in (*acc*).
streamlet *n* rīvus *m*, rīvulus *m*.
street *n* via *f*, platea *f*.
strength *n* vīrēs *fpl*; (*of material*) firmitās *f*; (*fig*) rōbur *nt*, nervī *mpl*; (*MIL*) numerus *m*; **know the enemy's ~** quot sint hostēs scīre; **on the ~ of** frētus (*abl*).
strengthen *vt* firmāre, corrōborāre; (*position*) mūnīre.
strenuous *adj* impiger, strēnuus, sēdulus.
strenuously *adv* impigrē, strēnuē.
strenuousness *n* industria *f*.
stress *n* (*words*) ictus *m*; (*meaning*) vīs *f*; (*importance*) mōmentum *nt*; (*difficulty*) labor *m*; **lay great ~ on** in māgnō discrīmine pōnere ♦ *vt* exprimere.
stretch *n* spatium *nt*, tractus *m*; **at a ~** sine ullā intermissiōne ♦ *vt* tendere, intendere; (*length*) prōdūcere, extendere; (*facts*) in māius crēdere; **~ a point** indulgēre; **~ before** obtendere; **~ forth** porrigere; **~ oneself** (*on ground*) sternī; **~ out** porrigere, extendere ♦ *vi* extendī, patēscere.
strew *vt* (*things*) sternere; (*place*) cōnsternere.
stricken *adj* saucius.
strict *adj* (*defined*) ipse, certus; (*severe*) sevērus, rigidus; (*accurate*) dīligēns.
strictly *adv* sevērē; dīligenter; **~ speaking** scīlicet, immo.
strictness *n* sevēritās *f*; dīligentia *f*.
stricture *n* vītuperātiō *f*.
stride *n* passus *m*; **make great ~s** (*fig*) multum prōficere ♦ *vi* incēdere, ingentēs gradūs ferre.
strident *adj* asper.
strife *n* discordia *f*, pugna *f*.
strike *vt* ferīre, percutere; (*instrument*) pellere, pulsāre; (*sail*) subdūcere; (*tent*) dētendere; (*mind*) venīre in (*acc*); (*camp*) movēre; (*fear into*) incutere in (*acc*); **~ against** offendere; **~ out** dēlēre; **~ up** (*music*) incipere; **~ a bargain** pacīscī; **be struck** vāpulāre ♦ *vi* (*work*) cessāre.
striking *adj* īnsignis, īnsignītus, ēgregius.
strikingly *adv* īnsignītē.
string *n* (*cord*) resticula *f*; (*succession*) seriēs *f*; (*instrument*) nervus *m*; (*bow*) nervus *m*; **have two ~s to one's bow** duplicī spē ūtī ♦ *vt* (*bow*) intendere; (*together*) coniungere.
stringency *n* sevēritās *f*.
stringent *adj* sevērus.
strip *vt* nūdāre, spoliāre, dēnūdāre; **~ off** exuere; (*leaves*) stringere, dēstringere ♦ *n* lacinia *f*.
stripe *n* virga *f*; (*on tunic*) clāvus *m*; **~s** *pl* verbera *ntpl*.

striped *adj* virgātus.
stripling *n* adulescentulus *m*.
strive *vi* nītī, ēnītī, contendere; (*contend*)
  certāre.
stroke *n* ictus *m*; (*lightning*) fulmen *nt*; (*oar*)
  pulsus *m*; (*pen*) līnea *f*; ~ **of luck** fortūna
  secunda *f* ♦ *vt* mulcēre, dēmulcēre.
stroll *vi* deambulāre, spatiārī.
strong *adj* fortis, validus; (*health*) rōbustus,
  firmus; (*material*) firmus; (*smell*) gravis;
  (*resources*) pollēns, potēns; (*feeling*) ācer,
  māgnus; (*language*) vehemēns, probrōsus; **be**
  ~ valēre; **be twenty** ~ vīgintī esse numerō.
strongbox *n* arca *f*.
stronghold *n* arx *f*.
strongly *adv* validē, vehementer, fortiter,
  ācriter, graviter.
strong-minded *adj* pertināx, cōnstans.
strophe *n* stropha *f*.
structure *n* aedificium *nt*; (*form*) structūra *f*;
  (*arrangement*) compositiō *f*.
struggle *n* (*effort*) cōnātus *m*; (*fight*) pugna *f*,
  certāmen *nt* ♦ *vi* nītī; certāre, contendere;
  (*fight*) luctārī; ~ **upwards** ēnītī.
strut *vi* māgnificē incēdere.
stubble *n* stipula *f*.
stubborn *adj* pertināx, pervicāx.
stubbornly *adv* pertināciter, pervicāciter.
stubbornness *n* pertinācia *f*, pervicācia *f*.
stucco *n* gypsum *nt*.
stud *n* clāvus *m*; (*horses*) equī *mpl*.
studded *adj* distinctus.
student *n* discipulus *m*; **be a ~ of** studēre (*dat*).
studied *adj* meditātus, accūrātus; (*language*)
  exquīsītus.
studio *n* officīna *f*.
studious *adj* litterīs dēditus, litterārum
  studiōsus; (*careful*) attentus.
studiously *adv* dē industriā.
study *vt* studēre (*dat*); (*prepare*) meditārī; ~
  under audīre ♦ *n* studium *nt*; (*room*)
  bibliothēca *f*.
stuff *n* māteria *f*; (*cloth*) textile *nt* ♦ *vt* farcīre,
  refercīre; (*with food*) sagīnāre.
stuffing *n* sagina *f*; (*of cushion*) tōmentum *nt*.
stultify *vt* ad inritum redigere.
stumble *vi* offendere; ~ **upon** incidere in
  (*acc*), offendere.
stumbling block *n* offēnsiō *f*.
stump *n* stīpes *m*.
stun *vt* stupefacere; (*fig*) obstupefacere,
  cōnfundere.
stunned *adj* attonitus.
stunt *vt* corporis auctum inhibēre.
stunted *adj* curtus.
stupefaction *n* stupor *m*.
stupefied *adj*: **be** ~ stupēre, obstupefacere.
stupefy *vt* obstupefacere.
stupendous *adj* mīrus, mīrificus.
stupid *adj* stultus, hebes, ineptus.
stupidity *n* stultitia *f*.
stupidly *adv* stultē, ineptē.
stupor *n* stupor *m*.

sturdily *adv* fortiter.
sturdiness *n* rōbur *nt*, firmitās *f*.
sturdy *adj* fortis, rōbustus.
sturgeon *n* acipēnser *m*.
stutter *vi* balbūtīre.
stuttering *adj* balbus.
sty *n* hara *f*.
style *n* (*kind*) genus *nt*, ratiō *f*; (*of dress*) habitus
  m; (*of prose*) ēlocūtiō *f*, ōrātiō *f*; (*pen*) stilus *m*
  ♦ *vt* appellāre.
stylish *adj* ēlegāns, lautus, expolītus.
stylishly *adv* ēleganter.
suasion *n* suāsiō *f*.
suave *adj* blandus, urbānus.
suavity *n* urbānitās *f*.
subaltern *n* succenturiō *m*.
subdivide *vt* dīvidere.
subdivision *n* pars *f*, mōmentum *nt*.
subdue *vt* subigere, dēvincere, redigere,
  domāre; (*fig*) cohibēre.
subdued *adj* dēmissus, summissus.
subject *n* (*person*) cīvis *m/f*; (*matter*) rēs *f*;
  (*theme*) locus *m*, argūmentum *nt* ♦ *adj*
  subiectus; ~ **to** obnoxius (*dat*) ♦ *vt* subicere;
  obnoxium reddere.
subjection *n* servitūs *f*.
subjective *adj* proprius.
subject matter *n* māteria *f*.
subjoin *vt* subicere, subiungere.
subjugate *vt* subigere, dēbellāre, domāre.
sublime *adj* sublīmis, ēlātus, excelsus.
sublimely *adv* excelsē.
sublimity *n* altitūdō *f*, ēlātiō *f*.
submarine *adj* submersus.
submerge *vt* dēmergere; (*flood*) inundāre ♦ *vi*
  sē dēmergere.
submersed *adj* submersus.
submission *n* obsequium *nt*, servitium *nt*; (*fig*)
  patientia *f*.
submissive *adj* submissus, docilis,
  obtemperāns.
submissively *adv* submissē, oboedienter,
  patienter.
submit *vi* sē dēdere; ~ **to** pārēre (*dat*),
  obtemperāre (*dat*), patī, subīre ♦ *vt*
  (*proposal*) referre.
subordinate *adj* subiectus, secundus ♦ *vt*
  subiungere, subicere.
suborn *vt* subicere, subōrnāre.
subpoena *vt* testimōnium dēnūntiāre (*dat*).
subscribe *vt* (*name*) subscrībere; (*money*)
  cōnferre.
subscription *n* collātiō *f*.
subsequent *adj* sequēns, posterior.
subsequently *adv* posteā, mox.
subserve *vt* subvenīre (*dat*), commodāre.
subservience *n* obsequium *nt*.
subservient *adj* obsequēns; (*thing*) ūtilis,
  commodus.
subside *vi* dēsīdere, resīdere; (*fever*)
  dēcēdere; (*wind*) cadere; (*passion*)
  dēfervēscere.
subsidence *n* lābēs *f*.

subsidiary _adj_ subiectus, secundus.
subsidize _vt_ pecūniās suppeditāre (_dat_).
subsidy _n_ pecūniae _fpl_, vectīgal _nt_.
subsist _vi_ cōnstāre, sustentārī.
subsistence _n_ vīctus _m_.
substance _n_ (_matter_) rēs _f_, corpus _nt_; (_essence_) nātūra _f_; (_gist_) summa _f_; (_reality_) rēs _f_; (_wealth_) opēs _fpl_.
substantial _adj_ solidus; (_real_) vērus; (_important_) gravis; (_rich_) opulentus, dīves.
substantially _adv_ rē; māgnā ex parte.
substantiate _vt_ cōnfirmāre.
substitute _vt_ subicere, repōnere, substituere ♦ _n_ vicārius _m_.
substratum _n_ fundāmentum _nt_.
subterfuge _n_ latebra _f_, perfugium _nt_.
subterranean _adj_ subterrāneus.
subtle _adj_ (_fine_) subtīlis; (_shrewd_) acūtus, astūtus.
subtlety _n_ subtīlitās _f_; acūmen _nt_, astūtia _f_.
subtly _adv_ subtīliter; acūtē, astūte.
subtract _vt_ dētrahere, dēmere; (_money_) dēdūcere.
subtraction _n_ dētractiō _f_, dēductiō _f_.
suburb _n_ suburbium _nt_.
suburban _adj_ suburbānus.
subvention _n_ pecūniae _fpl_.
subversion _n_ ēversiō _f_, ruīna _f_.
subversive _adj_ sēditiōsus.
subvert _vt_ ēvertere, subruere.
subverter _n_ ēversor _m_.
succeed _vi_ (_person_) rem bene gerere; (_activity_) prosperē ēvenīre; ~ **in obtaining** impetrāre ♦ _vt_ īnsequī, excipere, succēdere (_dat_).
success _n_ bonus ēventus _m_, rēs bene gesta _f_.
successful _adj_ fēlīx; (_thing_) secundus; **be ~** rem bene gerere; (_play_) stāre.
successfully _adv_ fēlīciter, prosperē, bene.
succession _n_ (_coming next_) successiō _f_; (_line_) seriēs _f_, ōrdō _m_; **alternate ~** vicissitūdō _f_; **in ~** deinceps, ex ōrdine.
successive _adj_ continuus, perpetuus.
successively _adv_ deinceps, ex ōrdine; (_alternately_) vicissim.
successor _n_ successor _m_.
succinct _adj_ brevis, pressus.
succinctly _adv_ breviter, pressē.
succour _n_ auxilium _nt_, subsidium _nt_ ♦ _vt_ subvenīre (_dat_), succurrere (_dat_), opem ferre (_dat_).
succulence _n_ sūcus _m_.
succulent _adj_ sūcidus.
succumb _vi_ succumbere, dēficere.
such _adj_ tālis, ēiusmodī, hūiusmodī; (_size_) tantus; **at ~ a time** id temporis; **~ great** tantus.
suchlike _adj_ hūiusmodī, ēiusdem generis.
suck _vt_ sūgere; **~ in** sorbēre; **~ up** exsorbēre, ēbibere.
sucker _n_ surculus _m_.
sucking _adj_ (_child_) lactēns.
suckle _vt_ nūtrīcārī, mammam dare (_dat_).
suckling _n_ lactēns _m/f_.

sudden _adj_ subitus, repentīnus.
suddenly _adv_ subitō, repente.
sue _vt_ in iūs vocāre, lītem intendere (_dat_); **~ for** rogāre, petere, ōrāre.
suffer _vt_ patī, ferre, tolerāre; (_injury_) accipere; (_loss_) facere; (_permit_) patī, sinere ♦ _vi_ dolōre adficī; **~ defeat** cladem accipere; **~ from** labōrāre ex, adficī (_abl_); **~ for** poenās dare (_gen_).
sufferable _adj_ tolerābilis.
sufferance _n_ patientia _f_, tolerantia _f_.
suffering _n_ dolor _m_.
suffice _vi_ sufficere, suppetere.
sufficiency _n_ satis.
sufficient _adj_ idōneus, satis (_gen_).
sufficiently _adv_ satis.
suffocate _vt_ suffocāre.
suffrage _n_ suffrāgium _nt_.
suffuse _vt_ suffundere.
sugar _n_ saccharon _nt_.
suggest _vt_ admonēre, inicere, subicere; **~ itself** occurrere.
suggestion _n_ admonitiō _f_; **at the ~ of** admonitū (_gen_); **at my ~** mē auctōre.
suicidal _adj_ fūnestus.
suicide _n_ mors voluntāria _f_; **commit ~** mortem sibī cōnscīscere.
suit _n_ (_law_) līs _f_, āctiō _f_; (_clothes_) vestītus _m_ ♦ _vt_ convenīre (_dat_), congruere (_dat_); (_dress_) sedēre (_dat_), decēre; **it ~s** decet; **to ~ me** dē meā sententiā.
suitability _n_ convenientia _f_.
suitable _adj_ aptus (+ _acc_), idōneus (+ _acc_).
suitably _adv_ aptē, decenter.
suite _n_ comitēs _mpl_, comitātus _m_.
suitor _n_ procus _m_, amāns _m_.
sulk _vi_ aegrē ferre, mōrōsum esse.
sulky _adj_ mōrōsus, tristis.
sullen _adj_ tristis, mōrōsus.
sullenness _n_ mōrōsitās _f_.
sully _vt_ īnfuscāre, contāmināre.
sulphur _n_ sulfur _nt_.
sultriness _n_ aestus _m_.
sultry _adj_ aestuōsus.
sum _n_ summa _f_; **~ of money** pecūnia _f_ ♦ _vt_ subdūcere, computāre; **~ up** summātim dēscrībere; **to ~ up** ūnō verbō, quid plūra?
summarily _adv_ strictim, summātim; sine morā.
summarize _vt_ summātim dēscrībere.
summary _n_ summārium _nt_, epitomē _f_ ♦ _adj_ subitus, praesēns.
summer _n_ aestās _f_ ♦ _adj_ aestīvus; **of ~** aestīvus.
summit _n_ vertex _m_, culmen _nt_; (_fig_) fastīgium _nt_; **the ~ of** summus.
summon _vt_ arcessere; (_meeting_) convocāre; (_witness_) citāre; **~ up courage** animum sūmere.
summons _n_ (_law_) vocātiō _f_ ♦ _vt_ in iūs vocāre, diem dīcere (_dat_).
sumptuary _adj_ sūmptuārius.
sumptuous _adj_ sūmptuōsus, adparātus,

māgnificus, lautus.
sumptuously *adv* sūmptuōsē, māgnificē.
sun *n* sōl *m* ♦ *vt*: ~ **oneself** aprīcārī.
sunbeam *n* radius *m*.
sunburnt *adj* adūstus.
sunder *vt* sēparāre, dīvidere.
sundial *n* sōlārium *nt*.
sundry *adj* dīversī, complūrēs.
sunlight *n* sōl *m*.
sunlit *adj* aprīcus.
sunny *adj* aprīcus, serēnus.
sunrise *n* sōlis ortus *m*.
sunset *n* sōlis occāsus *m*.
sunshade *n* umbella *f*.
sunshine *n* sōl *m*.
sup *vi* cēnāre.
superabundance *n* abundantia *f*.
superabundant *adj* nimius.
superabundantly *adv* satis superque.
superannuated *adj* ēmeritus.
superb *adj* māgnificus.
superbly *adv* māgnificē.
supercilious *adj* adrogāns, superbus.
superciliously *adv* adroganter, superbē.
superciliousness *n* adrogantia *f*, fastus *m*.
supererogation *n*: **of ~** ultrō factus.
superficial *adj* levis; **acquire a ~ knowledge of** prīmīs labrīs gustāre.
superficiality *n* levitās *f*.
superficially *adv* leviter, strictim.
superfluity *n* abundantia *f*.
superfluous *adj* supervacāneus, nimius; **be ~** redundāre.
superhuman *adj* dīvīnus, hūmānō māior.
superimpose *vt* superimpōnere.
superintend *vt* prōcūrāre, praeesse (*dat*).
superintendence *n* cūra *f*.
superintendent *n* cūrātor *m*, praefectus *m*.
superior *adj* melior, amplior; **be ~** praestāre, superāre ♦ *n* prīnceps *m*, praefectus *m*.
superiority *n* praestantia *f*; **have the ~** superāre; (*in numbers*) plūrēs esse.
superlative *adj* ēgregius, optimus.
supernatural *adj* dīvīnus.
supernaturally *adv* dīvīnitus.
supernumerary *adj* adscrīptīcius; **~ soldiers** accēnsī *mpl*.
superscription *n* titulus *m*.
supersede *vt* succēdere (*dat*), in locum succēdere (*gen*); **~ gold with silver** prō aurō argentum suppōnere.
superstition *n* rēligiō *f*, superstitiō *f*.
superstitious *adj* rēligiōsus, superstitiōsus.
supervene *vi* īnsequī, succēdere.
supervise *vt* prōcūrāre.
supervision *n* cūra *f*.
supervisor *n* cūrātor *m*.
supine *adj* supīnus; (*fig*) neglegēns, segnis.
supinely *adv* segniter.
supper *n* cēna *f*; **after ~** cēnātus.
supperless *adj* iēiūnus.
supplant *vt* praevertere.
supple *adj* flexibilis, mollis.

supplement *n* appendix *f* ♦ *vt* amplificāre.
supplementary *adj* additus.
suppleness *n* mollitia *f*.
suppliant *n* supplex *m/f*.
supplicate *vt* supplicāre, obsecrāre.
supplication *n* precēs *fpl*.
supplies *npl* commeātus *m*.
supply *n* cōpia *f* ♦ *vt* suppeditāre, praebēre; (*loss*) supplēre.
support *n* firmāmentum *nt*; (*help*) subsidium *nt*, adiūmentum *nt*; (*food*) alimenta *ntpl*; (*of party*) favor *m*; (*of needy*) patrōcinium *nt*; **I ~** subsidio sum (*dat*); **lend ~ to rumours** alimenta rūmōribus addere ♦ *vt* fulcīre; (*living*) sustinēre, sustentāre; (*with help*) adiuvāre, opem ferre (*dat*); (*at law*) adesse (*dat*).
supportable *adj* tolerābilis.
supporter *n* fautor *m*; (*at trial*) advocātus *m*; (*of proposal*) auctor *m*.
supporting cast *n* adiūtōrēs *mpl*.
suppose *vi* (*assume*) pōnere; (*think*) existimāre, opīnārī, crēdere; **~ it is true** fac vērum esse.
supposedly *adv* ut fāma est.
supposing *conj* sī; (*for the sake of argument*) sī iam.
supposition *n* opīniō *f*; **on this ~** hōc positō.
supposititious *adj* subditus, subditīvus.
suppress *vt* opprimere, comprimere; (*knowledge*) cēlāre, reticēre; (*feelings*) coercēre, reprimere.
suppression *n* (*of fact*) reticentia *f*.
supremacy *n* imperium *nt*, dominātus *m*, prīncipātus *m*.
supreme *adj* summus; **be ~** domināri; **~ command** imperium *nt*.
supremely *adv* ūnicē, plānē.
sure *adj* certus; (*fact*) explōrātus; (*friend*) fīdus; **be ~ of** compertum habēre; **feel ~** persuāsum habēre, haud scīre an; pro certō habēre; **make ~ of** (*fact*) comperīre; (*action*) efficere ut; **to be ~** quidem; **~ enough** rē vērā.
surely *adv* certō, certē, nonne; (*tentative*) scīlicet, sānē; **~ you do not think?** num putās?; **~ not** num.
surety *n* (*person*) vās *m*, praes *m*, spōnsor *m*; (*deposit*) fīdūcia *f*; **be ~ for** spondēre prō.
surf *n* fluctus *m*.
surface *n* superficiēs *f*; **~ of the water** summa aqua.
surfeit *n* satietās *f* ♦ *vt* satiāre, explēre.
surge *n* aestus *m*, fluctus *m* ♦ *vi* tumēscere.
surgeon *n* chīrūrgus *m*.
surgery *n* chīrūrgia *f*.
surlily *adv* mōrōsē.
surliness *n* mōrōsitās *f*.
surly *adj* mōrōsus, difficilis.
surmise *n* coniectūra *f* ♦ *vi* suspicārī, conicere, augurārī.
surmount *vt* superāre.
surmountable *adj* superābilis.
surname *n* cognōmen *nt*.
surpass *vt* excellere, exsuperāre, antecēdere.

surpassing *adj* excellēns.
surplus *n* reliquum *nt*; (*money*) pecūniae residuae *fpl*.
surprise *n* admīrātiō *f*; (*cause*) rēs inopīnāta *f*; **take by** ~ dēprehendere ♦ *adj* subitus ♦ *vt* dēprehendere; (*MIL*) opprimere; **be ~d** dēmīrārī; **be ~d at** admīrārī.
surprising *adj* mīrus, mīrābilis.
surprisingly *adv* mīrē, mīrābiliter.
surrender *vt* dēdere, trādere, concēdere ♦ *vi* sē dēdere; ~ **unconditionally to** sē suaque omnia potestāti permittere (*gen*) ♦ *n* dēditiō *f*; (*legal*) cessiō *f*; **unconditional** ~ permissiō *f*.
surreptitious *adj* fūrtīvus.
surreptitiously *adv* fūrtim, clam; **get in** ~ inrēpere in (*acc*).
surround *vt* circumdare, cingere, circumvenīre, circumfundere.
surrounding *adj* circumiectus; ~**s** *n* vīcīnia *f*.
survey *vt* contemplārī, cōnsīderāre; (*land*) mētārī ♦ *n* contemplātiō *f*; (*land*) mēnsūra *f*.
surveyor *n* fīnītor *m*, agrīmēnsor *m*, mētātor *m*.
survival *n* salūs *f*.
survive *vt* superāre ♦ *vt* superesse (*dat*).
survivor *n* superstes *m/f*.
susceptibility *n* mollitia *f*.
susceptible *adj* mollis.
suspect *vt* suspicārī; **be ~ed** in suspiciōnem venīre.
suspend *vt* suspendere; (*activity*) differre; (*person*) locō movēre; **be ~ed** pendēre.
suspense *n* dubitātiō *f*; **be in** ~ animī pendēre, haerēre.
suspicion *n* suspiciō *f*; **direct** ~ **to** suspiciōnem adiungere ad.
suspicious *adj* (*suspecting*) suspiciōsus; (*suspected*) dubius, anceps.
sustain *vt* (*weight*) sustinēre; (*life*) alere, sustentāre; (*hardship*) ferre, sustinēre; (*the part of*) agere.
sustenance *n* alimentum *nt*, vīctus *m*.
sutler *n* lixa *m*.
suzerain *n* dominus *m*.
swaddling clothes *n* incūnābula *ntpl*.
swagger *vi* sē iactāre.
swaggerer *n* homō glōriōsus *m*.
swallow *n* hirundō *f* ♦ *vt* dēvorāre; ~ **up** absorbēre.
swamp *n* palūs *f* ♦ *vt* opprimere.
swampy *adj* ūlīginōsus.
swan *n* cycnus *m*; ~**'s** cycnēus.
swank *vi* sē iactāre.
sward *n* caespes *m*.
swarm *n* exāmen *nt*; (*fig*) nūbēs *f* ♦ *vi*: ~ **round** circumfundī.
swarthy *adj* fuscus, aquilus.
swathe *vt* conligāre.
sway *n* dīciō *f*, imperium *nt*; **bring under one's** ~ suae dīciōnis facere ♦ *vt* regere ♦ *vi* vacillāre.
swear *vi* iūrāre; ~ **allegiance to** iūrāre in verba (*gen*).

sweat *n* sūdor *m* ♦ *vi* sūdāre.
sweep *vt* verrere; ~ **away** rapere; ~ **out** ēverrere.
sweet *adj* dulcis, suāvis.
sweeten *vt* dulcem reddere.
sweetheart *n* dēliciae *fpl*.
sweetly *adv* dulciter, suāviter.
sweetness *n* dulcitūdō *f*, suāvitās *f*.
sweet-tempered *adj* suāvis, cōmis.
swell *n* tumor *m* ♦ *vi* tumēre, tumēscere; (*fig*) glīscere ♦ *vt* īnflāre.
swelling *adj* tumidus ♦ *n* tumor *m*.
swelter *vi* aestū labōrāre.
swerve *vi* dēclīnāre, dēvertere ♦ *n* dēclīnātiō *f*.
swift *adj* celer, vēlōx, incitātus.
swiftly *adv* celeriter, vēlōciter.
swiftness *n* celeritās *f*, vēlōcitās *f*.
swill *vt* (*rinse*) colluere; (*drink*) ēpōtāre.
swim *vi* nāre, innāre; (*place*) natāre; ~ **across** trānāre; ~ **ashore** ēnāre; ~ **to** adnāre.
swimming *n* natātiō *f*.
swindle *vt* circumvenīre, verba dare (*dat*) ♦ *n* fraus *f*.
swine *n* sūs *m/f*.
swineherd *n* subulcus *m*.
swing *n* (*motion*) oscillātiō *f* ♦ *vi* oscillāre ♦ *vt* lībrāre.
swinish *adj* obscēnus.
swirl *n* vertex *m* ♦ *vi* volūtārī.
switch *n* virga *f* ♦ *vt* flectere, torquēre.
swivel *n* cardō *f*.
swollen *adj* tumidus, turgidus, īnflātus.
swoon *n* dēfectiō *f* ♦ *vi* intermorī.
swoop *n* impetus *m* ♦ *vi* lābī; ~ **down on** involāre in (*acc*).
sword *n* gladius *m*; **put to the** ~ occīdere; **with fire and** ~ ferrō ignīque.
swordsman *n* gladiātor *m*.
sworn *adj* iūrātus.
sybarite *n* dēlicātus *m*.
sycophancy *n* adsentātiō *f*, adūlātiō *f*.
sycophant *n* adsentātor *m*, adūlātor *m*.
syllable *n* syllaba *f*.
syllogism *n* ratiōcinātiō *f*.
sylvan *adj* silvestris.
symbol *n* signum *nt*, īnsigne *nt*.
symmetrical *adj* concinnus, aequus.
symmetry *n* concinnitās *f*, aequitās *f*.
sympathetic *adj* concors, misericors.
sympathetically *adv* misericorditer.
sympathize *vi* cōnsentīre; ~ **with** miserērī (*gen*).
sympathy *n* concordia *f*, cōnsēnsus *m*; misericordia *f*.
symphony *n* concentus *m*.
symptom *n* signum *nt*, indicium *nt*.
syndicate *n* societās *f*.
synonym *n* verbum idem dēclārāns *nt*.
synonymous *adj* idem dēclārāns.
synopsis *n* summārium *nt*.
syringe *n* clystēr *m*.
system *n* ratiō *f*, fōrmula *f*; (*PHILOS*) disciplīna *f*.

systematic *adj* ōrdinātus, cōnstāns.
systematically *adv* ratiōne, ōrdine.
systematize *vt* in ōrdinem redigere.

T, t

tabernacle *n* tabernāculum *nt*.
table *n* mēnsa *f*; (*inscribed*) tabula *f*; (*list*) index *m*; **at ~** inter cēnam; **turn the ~s on** pār parī referre.
tablet *n* tabula *f*, tabella *f*.
taboo *n* rēligiō *f*.
tabulate *vt* in ōrdinem redigere.
tacit *adj* tacitus.
tacitly *adv* tacitē.
taciturn *adj* taciturnus.
taciturnity *n* taciturnitās *f*.
tack *n* clāvulus *m*; (*of sail*) pēs *m* ♦ *vt:* **~ on** adsuere ♦ *vi* (*ship*) reciprocārī, nāvem flectere.
tackle *n* armāmenta *ntpl* ♦ *vt* adgredī.
tact *n* iūdicium *nt*, commūnis sēnsus *m*, hūmānitās *f*.
tactful *adj* prūdēns, hūmānus.
tactfully *adv* prūdenter, hūmāniter.
tactician *n* reī mīlitāris perītus *m*.
tactics *n* rēs mīlitāris *f*, bellī ratiō *f*.
tactless *adj* ineptus.
tactlessly *adv* ineptē.
tadpole *n* rānunculus *m*.
tag *n* appendicula *f*.
tail *n* cauda *f*; **turn ~** terga vertere.
tailor *n* vestītor *m*.
taint *n* lābēs *f*, vitium *nt* ♦ *vt* inquināre, contāmināre, īnficere.
take *vt* capere, sūmere; (*auspices*) habēre; (*disease*) contrahere; (*experience*) ferre; (*fire*) concipere; (*meaning*) accipere, interpretārī; (*in the act*) dēprehendere; (*person*) dūcere; **~ after** similem esse (*dat, gen*); **~ across** trānsportāre; **~ arms** arma sūmere; **~ away** dēmere, auferre, adimere, abdūcere; **~ back** recipere; **~ by storm** expugnāre; **~ care that** curāre ut/ne (+ *subj*); **~ down** dētrahere; (*in writing*) exscrībere; **~ for** habēre prō; **~ hold of** prehendere; **~ in** (*as guest*) recipere; (*information*) percipere, comprehendere; (*with deceit*) dēcipere; **~ in hand** incipere, suscipere; **~ off** dēmere; (*clothes*) exuere; **~ on** suscipere; **~ out** eximere, extrahere; (*from store*) prōmere; **~ over** excipere; **~ place** fierī, accidere; **~ prisoner** capere; **~ refuge in** cōnfugere ad (+ *infin*); **~ the field** in aciem dēscendere; **~ to** sē dēdere (*dat*), amāre; **~ to oneself** suscipere; **~ up** sūmere,

tollere; (*task*) incipere, adgredī ad; (*in turn*) excipere; (*room*) occupāre; **~ upon oneself** recipere, sibī sūmere.
taking *adj* grātus ♦ *n* (MIL) expugnātiō *f*.
tale *n* fābula *f*, fābella *f*.
talent *n* (*money*) talentum *nt*; (*ability*) ingenium *nt*, indolēs *f*.
talented *adj* ingeniōsus.
talk *n* sermō *m*; (*with another*) colloquium *nt*; **common ~** fāma *f*; **be the ~ of the town** in ōre omnium esse ♦ *vi* loquī; (*to one*) colloquī cum; **~ down to** ad intellectum audientis dēscendere; **~ over** cōnferre, disserere dē.
talkative *adj* loquāx.
talkativeness *n* loquācitās *f*.
tall *adj* prōcērus, grandis.
tallness *n* prōcēritās *f*.
tallow *n* sēbum *nt*.
tally *n* tessera *f* ♦ *vi* congruere.
talon *n* unguis *m*.
tamarisk *n* myrīca *f*.
tambourine *n* tympanum *nt*.
tame *vt* domāre, mānsuēfacere ♦ *adj* mānsuētus; (*character*) ignāvus; (*language*) īnsulsus, frīgidus.
tamely *adv* ignāvē, lentē.
tameness *n* mānsuētūdō *f*; (*fig*) lentitūdō *f*.
tamer *n* domitor *m*.
tamper *vi:* **~ with** (*person*) sollicitāre; (*writing*) interpolāre.
tan *vt* imbuere.
tang *n* sapor *m*.
tangible *adj* tāctilis.
tangle *n* nōdus *m* ♦ *vt* implicāre.
tank *n* lacus *m*.
tanned *adj* (*by sun*) adūstus.
tanner *n* coriārius *m*.
tantalize *vt* lūdere.
tantamount *adj* pār, īdem.
tantrum *n* īra *f*.
tap *n* epitonium *nt*; (*touch*) plāga *f* ♦ *vt* (*cask*) relinere; (*hit*) ferīre.
tape *n* taenia *f*.
taper *n* cēreus *m* ♦ *vi* fastīgārī.
tapestry *n* aulaea *ntpl*.
tar *n* pix *f*.
tardily *adv* tardē, lentē.
tardiness *n* tarditās *f*, segnitia *f*.
tardy *adj* tardus, lentus.
tare *n* lolium *nt*.
targe *n* parma *f*.
target *n* scopus *m*.
tariff *n* portōrium *nt*.
tarn *n* lacus *m*.
tarnish *vt* īnfuscāre, inquināre ♦ *vi* īnfuscārī.
tarry *vi* morārī, commorārī, cunctārī.
tart *adj* acidus, asper ♦ *n* scrīblīta *f*.
tartly *adv* acerbē.
tartness *n* asperitās *f*.
task *n* pēnsum *nt*, opus *nt*, negōtium *nt*; **take to ~** obiūrgāre.
taskmaster *n* dominus *m*.
tassel *n* fimbriae *fpl*.

taste n (*sense*) gustātus m; (*flavour*) sapor m; (*artistic*) iūdicium nt, ēlegantia f; (*for rhetoric*) aurēs fpl; of ~ doctus; in good ~ ēlegāns ♦ vt gustāre, dēgustāre ♦ vi sapere; ~ of resipere.
tasteful adj ēlegāns.
tastefully adv ēleganter.
tastefulness n ēlegantia f.
tasteless adj īnsulsus, inēlegāns.
tastelessly adv īnsulsē, inēleganter.
tastelessness n īnsulsitās f.
taster n praegustātor m.
tasty adj dulcis.
tattered adj pannōsus.
tatters n pannī mpl.
tattoo vt compungere.
taunt n convīcium nt, probrum nt ♦ vt exprobrāre, obicere (*dat of pers, acc of charge*).
taunting adj contumēliōsus.
tauntingly adv contumēliōsē.
taut adj intentus; **draw ~** addūcere.
tavern n taberna f, hospitium nt.
tawdry adj vīlis.
tawny adj fulvus.
tax n vectīgal nt, tribūtum nt; **a 5 per cent ~** vīcēsima f; **free from ~** immūnis ♦ vt vectīgal impōnere (*dat*); (*strength*) contendere; ~ **with** (*charge*) obicere (*acc & dat*), īnsimulāre.
taxable adj vectīgālis.
taxation n vectīgālia ntpl.
tax collector n exāctor m.
tax farmer n pūblicānus m.
taxpayer n assiduus m.
teach vt docēre, ērudīre, īnstituere; (*thoroughly*) ēdocēre; (*pass*) discere; ~ **your grandmother** sūs Minervam.
teachable adj docilis.
teacher n magister m, magistra f, doctor m; (*PHILOS*) praeceptor m; (*of literature*) grammaticus m; (*of rhetoric*) rhētor m.
teaching n doctrīna f, disciplīna f.
team n (*animals*) iugum nt.
tear n lacrima f; **shed ~s** lacrimās effundere ♦ vt scindere; ~ **down** revellere; ~ **in pieces** dīlaniāre, discerpere, lacerāre; ~ **off** abscindere, dēripere; ~ **open** rescindere; ~ **out** ēvellere; ~ **up** convellere.
tearful adj flēbilis.
tease vt lūdere, inrītāre.
teat n mamma f.
technical adj (*term*) proprius.
technique n ars f.
tedious adj longus, lentus, odiōsus.
tediously adv molestē.
tedium n taedium nt, molestia f.
teem vi abundāre.
teeming adj fēcundus, refertus.
teens n: in one's ~ adulescentulus.
teethe vi dentīre.
tell vt (*story*) nārrāre; (*person*) dīcere (*dat*); (*number*) ēnumerāre; (*inform*) certiōrem facere; (*difference*) intellegere; (*order*) iubēre (+ acc and infin), imperare (+ ut/ne and subj);

~ **the truth** vēra dīcere; ~ **lies** mentior ♦ vi valēre; ~ **the difference between** discernere; **I cannot** ~ nesciō.
telling adj validus.
temerity n temeritās f.
temper n animus m, ingenium nt; (*bad*) īra f, īrācundia f; (*of metal*) temperātiō f ♦ vt temperāre; (*fig*) moderārī (*dat*).
temperament n animī habitus m, animus m.
temperamental adj incōnstāns.
temperance n temperantia f, continentia f.
temperate adj temperātus, moderātus, sobrius.
temperately adv moderātē.
temperature n calor m, frīgus nt; **mild ~** temperiēs f.
tempest n tempestās f, procella f.
tempestuous adj procellōsus.
temple n templum nt, aedēs f; (*head*) tempus nt.
temporal adj hūmānus, profānus.
temporarily adv ad tempus.
temporary adj brevis.
temporize vi temporis causā facere, tergiversārī.
tempt vt sollicitāre, pellicere, invītāre.
temptation n illecebra f.
tempter n impulsor m.
ten num decem; ~ **each** dēnī; ~ **times** deciēns.
tenable adj inexpugnābilis, stabilis, certus.
tenacious adj tenāx, firmus.
tenaciously adv tenāciter.
tenacity n tenācitās f.
tenant n inquilīnus m, habitātor m; (*on land*) colōnus m.
tenantry n colōnī mpl.
tend vi spectāre, pertinēre ♦ vt cūrāre, colere.
tendency n inclīnātiō f, voluntās f.
tender adj tener, mollis ♦ vt dēferre, offerre.
tenderhearted adj misericors.
tenderly adv indulgenter.
tenderness n indulgentia f, mollitia f.
tendon n nervus m.
tendril n clāviculus m.
tenement n habitātiō f; **block of ~s** īnsula f.
tenet n dogma nt, dēcrētum nt.
tennis court n sphaeristērium nt.
tenor n (*course*) tenor m; (*purport*) sententia f.
tense adj intentus ♦ n tempus nt.
tension n intentiō f.
tent n tabernāculum nt; (*general's*) praetōrium nt.
tentacle n bracchium nt.
tentatively adv experiendō.
tenterhooks n: on ~ animī suspēnsus.
tenth adj decimus; **for the ~ time** decimum; **men of the ~ legion** decumānī mpl.
tenuous adj rārus.
tenure n possessiō f.
tepid adj tepidus; **be ~** tepēre.
tergiversation n tergiversātiō f.
term n (*limit*) terminus m; (*period*) spatium nt; (*word*) verbum nt ♦ vt appellāre, nuncupāre.

terminate *vt* termināre, fīnīre ♦ *vi* dēsinere; (*words*) cadere.
termination *n* fīnis *m*, terminus *m*.
terminology *n* vocābula *ntpl*.
terms *npl* condiciō *f*, lēx *f*; **propose ~** condiciōnem ferre; **be on good ~ in** grātiā esse; **we come to ~** inter nōs convenit.
terrain *n* ager *m*.
terrestrial *adj* terrestris.
terrible *adj* terribilis, horribilis, horrendus.
terribly *adv* horrendum in modum.
terrific *adj* formīdolōsus; vehemēns.
terrify *vt* terrēre, perterrēre, exterrēre.
terrifying *adj* formīdolōsus.
territory *n* ager *m*, fīnēs *mpl*.
terror *n* terror *m*, formīdō *f*, pavor *m*; **object of ~** terror *m*; **be a ~ to** terrōrī esse (*dat*).
terrorize *vt* metum inicere (*dat*).
terse *adj* pressus, brevis.
tersely *adv* pressē.
terseness *n* brevitās *f*.
tessellated *adj* tessellātus.
test *n* experīmentum *nt*, probātiō *f*; (*standard*) obrussa *f*; **put to the ~** experīrī, perīclitārī; **stand the ~** spectārī ♦ *vt* experīrī, probāre, spectāre.
testament *n* testāmentum *nt*.
testamentary *adj* testāmentārius.
testator *n* testātor *m*.
testify *vt* testificārī.
testifying *n* testificātiō *f*.
testily *adv* stomachōsē.
testimonial *n* laudātiō *f*.
testimony *n* testimōnium *nt*.
testy *adj* difficilis, stomachōsus.
tether *n* retināculum *nt*, vinculum *nt* ♦ *vt* religāre.
tetrarch *n* tetrarchēs *m*.
tetrarchy *n* tetrarchia *f*.
text *n* verba *ntpl*.
textbook *n* ars *f*.
textile *adj* textilis.
textual *adj* verbōrum.
texture *n* textus *m*.
than *conj* quam *abl*; **other ~** alius ac.
thank *vt* grātiās agere (*dat*); **~ you** bene facis; **no, ~ you** benīgnē.
thankful *adj* grātus.
thankfully *adv* grātē.
thankfulness *n* grātia *f*.
thankless *adj* ingrātus.
thanklessly *adv* ingrātē.
thanks *n* grātiae *fpl*, grātēs *fpl*; **return ~** grātiās agere, grātēs persolvere; **~ to you** operā tuā, beneficiō tuō; **it is ~ to sb that . . .** not per aliquem stat quominus (+ *subj*).
thanksgiving *n* grātulātiō *f*; (*public*) supplicātiō *f*.
that *pron* (*demonstrative*) ille; (*relat*) quī ♦ *conj* (*statement*) *acc & infin*; (*command, purpose, result*) ut; (*fearing*) nē; (*emotion*) quod; **oh ~** utinam.
thatch *n* culmus *m*, strāmenta *ntpl* ♦ *vt* tegere,

integere.
thaw *vt* dissolvere ♦ *vi* liquēscere, tabēscere.
the *art not expressed*; (*emphatic*) ille; (*with compar*) quō . . . eō.
theatre *n* theātrum *nt*.
theatrical *adj* scēnicus.
theft *n* fūrtum *nt*.
their *adj* eōrum; (*ref to subject*) suus.
theme *n* māteria *f*, argūmentum *nt*.
themselves *pron* ipsī; (*reflexive*) sē.
then *adv* (*time*) tum, tunc; (*succession*) deinde, tum, posteā; (*consequence*) igitur, ergō; **now and ~** interdum; **only ~** tum dēmum.
thence *adv* inde.
thenceforth *adv* inde, posteā, ex eō tempore.
theologian *n* theologus *m*.
theology *n* theologia *f*.
theorem *n* prōpositum *nt*.
theoretical *adj* contemplātīvus.
theory *n* ratiō *f*; **~ and practice** ratiō atque ūsus.
there *adv* ibī, illīc; (*thither*) eō, illūc; **from ~** inde, illinc; **here and ~** passim; **~ is** est; (*interj*) ecce.
thereabout(s) *adv* circā, circiter, prope.
thereafter *adv* deinde, posteā.
thereby *adv* eā rē, hōc factō.
therefore *adv* itaque, igitur, ergō, idcircō.
therein *adv* inibī, in eō.
thereof *adv* ēius, ēius reī.
thereon *adv* īnsuper, in eō.
thereupon *adv* deinde, statim, inde, quo facto.
therewith *adv* cum eō.
thesis *n* prōpositum *nt*.
thews *n* nervī *mpl*.
they *pron* iī, hī, illī.
thick *adj* dēnsus; (*air*) crassus.
thicken *vt* dēnsāre ♦ *vi* concrēscere.
thickening *n* concrētiō *f*.
thicket *n* dūmētum *nt*.
thickheaded *adj* stupidus, hebes.
thickly *adv* dēnsē; **~ populated** frequēns.
thickness *n* crassitūdō *f*.
thickset *adj* brevis atque obēsus.
thick-skinned *adj*: **be ~** callēre; **become ~** occallēscere.
thief *n* fūr *m*.
thieve *vt* fūrārī, surripere.
thievery *n* fūrtum *nt*.
thievish *adj* fūrāx.
thigh *n* femur *nt*.
thin *adj* exīlis, gracilis, tenuis; (*attendance*) īnfrequēns ♦ *vt* attenuāre, extenuāre; **~ out** rārēfacere; **~ down** dīluere.
thine *adj* tuus.
thing *n* rēs *f*; **as ~s are** nunc, cum haec ita sint.
think *vi* cōgitāre; (*opinion*) putāre, existimāre, arbitrārī, rērī, crēdere; **as I ~** meā sententiā; **~ about** cōgitāre dē; **~ highly of** māgnī aestimāre; **~ nothing of** nihilī facere; **~ out** excōgitāre; **~ over** reputāre, in mente agitāre.
thinker *n* philosophus *m*.

thinking *adj* sapiēns ♦ *n* cōgitātiō *f*; ~ **that** ratus, arbitratus.

thinly *adv* exīliter, tenuiter; rārē.

thinness *n* exīlitās *f*, gracilitās *f*; (*person*) maciēs *f*; (*number*) exiguitās *f*, īnfrequentia *f*; (*air*) tenuitās *f*.

thin-skinned *adj* inrītābilis.

third *adj* tertius; **for the ~ time** tertium ♦ *n* tertia pars *f*, triēns *m*; **two ~s** duae partēs, bēs *m*.

thirdly *adv* tertiō.

thirst *n* sitis *f* ♦ *vi* sitīre; ~ **for** sitīre.

thirstily *adv* sitienter.

thirsty *adj* sitiēns.

thirteen *num* tredecim; ~ **each** ternī dēnī; ~ **times** terdeciēs.

thirteenth *adj* tertius decimus.

thirtieth *adj* trīcēsimus.

thirty *num* trīgintā; ~ **each** trīcēnī; ~ **times** trīciēns.

this *pron* hīc.

thistle *n* carduus *m*.

thither *adv* eō, illūc.

thole *n* scalmus *nt*.

thong *n* lōrum *nt*, habēna *f*.

thorn *n* spīna *f*, sentis *m*.

thorny *adj* spīnōsus.

thorough *adj* absolūtus, germānus; (*work*) accūrātus.

thoroughbred *adj* generōsus.

thoroughfare *n* via *f*.

thoroughly *adv* penitus, omnīnō, funditus.

thoroughness *n* cūra *f*, diligentia *f*.

thou *pron* tū.

though *conj* etsī, etiamsī, quamvīs (+ *subj*), quamquam all (+ *indic*).

thought *n* (*faculty*) cōgitātiō *f*, mēns *f*, animus *m*; (*an idea*) cōgitātum *nt*, nōtiō *f*; (*design*) cōnsilium *nt*, prōpositum *nt*; (*expressed*) sententia *f*; (*heed*) cautiō *f*, prōvidentia *f*; (*RHET*) inventiō *f*; **second ~s** posteriōrēs cōgitātiōnēs.

thoughtful *adj* cōgitābundus; prōvidus.

thoughtfully *adv* prōvidē.

thoughtless *adj* incōnsīderātus, incōnsultus, imprōvidus, immemor.

thoughtlessly *adv* temerē, incōnsultē.

thoughtlessness *n* incōnsīderantia *f*, imprūdentia *f*.

thousand *num* mīlle; **~s** *pl* mīlia (+ *gen*) *ntpl*; ~ **each** mīllēnī; ~ **times** mīlliēns; **three ~** tria mīlia.

thousandth *adj* mīllēsimus.

thrall *n* servus *m*.

thraldom *n* servitūs *f*.

thrash *vt* verberāre.

thrashing *n* verbera *ntpl*.

thread *n* fīlum *nt*; **hang by a ~** (*fig*) fīlō pendēre ♦ *vt*: ~ **one's way** sē īnsinuāre.

threadbare *adj* trītus, obsolētus.

threat *n* minae *fpl*, minātiō *f*.

threaten *vt* minārī (*dat of pers*), dēnūntiāre ♦ *vi* imminēre, impendēre.

threatening *adj* mināx, imminēns.

threateningly *adv* mināciter.

three *num* trēs; ~ **each** ternī; ~ **times** ter; ~ **days** triduum *nt*; ~ **years** triennium *nt*; ~ **quarters** trēs partēs *fpl*, dōdrāns *m*.

three-cornered *adj* triangulus, triquetrus.

threefold *adj* triplex.

three hundred *num* trecentī; ~ **each** trecēnī; ~ **times** trecentiēns.

three hundredth *adj* trecentēsimus.

three-legged *adj* tripēs.

three-quarters *n* dōdrāns *m*, trēs partēs *fpl*.

thresh *vt* terere, exterere.

threshing floor *n* ārea *f*.

threshold *n* līmen *nt*.

thrice *adv* ter.

thrift *n* frūgālitās *f*, parsimōnia *f*.

thriftily *adv* frūgāliter.

thrifty *adj* parcus, frūgī.

thrill *n* horror *m* ♦ *vt* percellere, percutere ♦ *vi* trepidāre.

thrilling *adj* mīrābilis.

thrive *vi* vigēre, valēre, crēscere.

thriving *adj* valēns, vegetus; (*crops*) laetus.

throat *n* faucēs *fpl*, guttur *nt*; **cut the ~ of** iugulāre.

throaty *adj* gravis, raucus.

throb *vi* palpitāre, micāre ♦ *n* pulsus *m*.

throe *n* dolor *m*; **be in the ~s** of labōrāre ex.

throne *n* solium *nt*; (*power*) rēgnum *nt*.

throng *n* multitūdō *f*, frequentia *f* ♦ *vt* celebrāre; ~ **round** stīpāre, circumfundī (*dat*).

throttle *vt* strangulāre.

through *prep* per (*acc*); (*cause*) propter (*acc*), *abl* ♦ *adv*: ~ **and** ~ penitus; **carry** ~ exsequī, peragere; **go** ~ trānsīre; **run** ~ percurrere; **be** ~ **with** perfūnctum esse (*abl*).

throughout *adv* penitus, omnīnō ♦ *prep* per (*acc*).

throw *n* iactus *m*, coniectus *m* ♦ *vt* iacere, conicere; ~ **about** iactāre; ~ **across** trāicere; ~ **away** abicere; (*something precious*) prōicere; ~ **back** rēicere; ~ **down** dēturbāre, dēicere; ~ **into** inicere; ~ **into confusion** perturbāre; ~ **off** excutere, exsolvere; ~ **open** patefacere; ~ **out** ēicere, prōicere; ~ **over** inicere; (*fig*) dēstituere; ~ **overboard** iactūram facere (*gen*); ~ **to** (*danger*) obicere; ~ **up** ēicere; (*building*) exstruere; ~ **a bridge over** pontem inicere (*dat*), pontem faciendum cūrāre in (*abl*); ~ **light on** (*fig*) lūmen adhibēre (*dat*); ~ **a rider** equitem excutere.

throwing *n* coniectiō *f*, iactus *m*.

thrum *n* līcium *nt*.

thrush *n* turdus *m*.

thrust *vt* trūdere, pellere, impingere; ~ **at** petere; ~ **away** dētrūdere; ~ **forward** prōtrūdere; ~ **home** dēfīgere; ~ **into** īnfīgere, impingere; ~ **out** extrūdere.

thud *n* gravis sonitus *m*.

thug *n* percussor *m*, sīcārius *m*.

thumb n pollex m; **have under one's ~** in potestāte suā habēre.
thump n plāga f ♦ vt tundere, pulsāre.
thunder n tonitrus m ♦ vi tonāre, intonāre; **it ~s** tonāt.
thunderbolt n fulmen nt.
thunderer n tonāns m.
thunderstruck adj attonitus.
thus adv (referring back) sīc; (referring forward) ita; **~ far** hāctenus.
thwack vt verberāre.
thwart vt obstāre (dat), officere (dat), remorārī, frustrārī ♦ n (boat's) trānstrum nt.
thy adj tuus.
thyme n thymum nt; (wild) serpyllum nt.
tiara n diadēma nt.
ticket n tessera f.
tickle vt titillāre.
tickling n titillātiō f.
ticklish adj lūbricus.
tidal adj: **~ waters** aestuārium nt.
tide n aestus m; (time) tempus nt; **ebb ~** aestūs recessus m; **flood ~** aestūs accessus m; **turn of the ~** commūtātiō aestūs; **the ~ will turn** (fig) circumagētur hīc orbis.
tidily adv concinnē, mundē.
tidiness n concinnitās f, munditia f.
tidings n nūntius m.
tidy adj concinnus, mundus.
tie n (bond) vinculum nt, cōpula f; (kin) necessitūdō f ♦ vt ligāre; (knot) nectere; **~ fast** dēvincīre, cōnstringere; **~ on** illigāre; **~ to** adligāre; **~ together** colligāre; **~ up** adligāre; (wound) obligāre.
tier n ōrdō m.
tiff n dissēnsiō f.
tiger n tigris m, more usu f.
tight adj strictus, astrictus, intentus; (close) artus; **draw ~** intendere, addūcere.
tighten vt adstringere, contendere.
tightly adv artē, angustē.
tightrope n extentus fūnis; **~ walker** n fūnambulus m.
tigress n tigris f.
tile n tegula f, imbrex f, later nt.
till conj dum, dōnec ♦ prep usque ad (acc), in (acc); **not ~** dēmum ♦ n arca f ♦ vt colere.
tillage n cultus m.
tiller n (AGR) cultor m; (ship) clāvus m, gubernāculum nt.
tilt vt inclīnāre.
tilth n cultus m, arvum nt.
timber n (for building) māteria f; (firewood) lignum nt.
timbrel n tympanum nt.
time n tempus nt; (lifetime) aetās f; (interval) intervallum nt, spatium nt; (of day) hōra f; (leisure) ōtium nt; (rhythm) numerus m; **another ~** aliās; **at ~s** aliquandō, interdum; **at all ~s** semper; **at any ~** umquam; **at one ~** ... at another aliās ... aliās; **at that ~** tunc, id temporis; **at the right ~** ad tempus, mātūrē, tempestīvē; **at the same ~** simul; tamen; **at**

the wrong ~ intempestīvē; **beating ~** percussiō f; **convenient ~** opportūnitās f; **for a ~** aliquantisper, parumper; **for a long ~** diū; **for some ~** aliquamdiū; **for the ~ being** ad tempus; **from ~ to ~** interdum, identidem; **have a good ~** geniō indulgēre; **have ~ for** vacāre (dat); **in ~** ad tempus, tempore; **in a short ~** brevī; **in good ~** tempestīvus; **in the ~ of** apud (acc); **keep ~** (marching) gradum cōnferre; (music) modulārī; **many ~s** saepe, saepenumerō; **pass, spend ~** tempus sūmere, dēgere; **several ~s** aliquotiēns; **some ~** aliquandō; **waste ~** tempus terere; **what is the ~?** quota hōra est?; **~ expired** ēmeritus.
time-honoured adj antīquus.
timeliness n opportūnitās f.
timely adj opportūnus, tempestīvus, mātūrus.
timid adj timidus.
timidity n timiditās f.
timidly adv timidē.
timorous adj timidus.
timorously adv timidē.
tin n stannum nt, plumbum album nt ♦ adj stanneus.
tincture n color m, sapor m ♦ vt īnficere.
tinder n fōmes m.
tinge vt imbuere, īnficere, tingere.
tingle vi horrēre.
tingling n horror m.
tinkle vi tinnīre ♦ n tinnītus m.
tinsel n bractea f; (fig) speciēs f, fūcus m.
tint n color m ♦ vt colōrāre.
tiny adj minūtus, pusillus, perexiguus.
tip n apex m, cacūmen nt, extrēmum nt; **the ~ of** prīmus, extrēmus ♦ vt praefīgere; **~ over** invertere.
tipple vi pōtāre.
tippler n pōtor m, ēbrius m.
tipsy adj tēmulentus.
tiptoes n: **on ~** suspēnsō gradū.
tirade n obiūrgātiō f, dēclāmātiō f.
tire vt fatīgāre; **~ out** dēfatīgāre ♦ vi defetīscī, fatīgārī; **I ~ of** mē taedet (gen); **it ~s** taedet (+ acc of person, gen of thing).
tired adj (dē)fessus, lassus; **~ out** dēfessus; **I am ~ of** mē taedet.
tiresome adj molestus, difficilis.
tiring adj labōriōsus, operōsus.
tiro n tīrō m, rudis m.
tissue n textus m.
tit n: **give ~ for tat** pār parī respondēre.
Titan n Tītān m.
titanic adj immānis.
titbit n cuppēdium nt.
tithe n decuma f.
tithe gatherer n decumānus m.
titillate vt titillāre.
titillation n titillātiō f.
title n (book) īnscrīptiō f, index m; (inscription) titulus m; (person) nōmen nt, appellātiō f; (claim) iūs nt, vindiciae fpl; **assert one's ~ to** vindicāre; **give a ~ to** īnscrībere.
titled adj nōbilis.

title deed *n* auctōritās *f*.
titter *n* rīsus *m* ♦ *vi* rīdēre.
tittle-tattle *n* sermunculus *m*.
titular *adj* nōmine.
to *prep* ad (*acc*), in (*acc*); (*attitude*) ergā (*acc*); (*giving*) *dat*; (*towns, small islands*, domus, rūs) *acc* ♦ *conj* (*purpose*) ut ♦ *adv*: **come ~** animum recipere; **~ and fro** hūc illūc.
toad *n* būfō *m*.
toady *n* adsentātor *m*, parasītus *m* ♦ *vt* adsentārī (*dat*).
toadyism *n* adsentātiō *f*.
toast *n*: **drink a ~** propīnāre ♦ *vt* torrēre; (*drink*) propīnāre (*dat*).
today *adv* hodiē; **~'s** hodiernus.
toe *n* digitus *m*; **big ~** pollex *m*.
toga *n* toga *f*.
together *adv* ūnā, simul; **bring ~** cōgere, congerere; **come ~** convenīre, congregārī; **put ~** cōnferre, compōnere.
toil *n* labor *m*; (*snare*) rēte *nt* ♦ *vi* labōrāre; **~ at** ēlabōrāre in (*abl*).
toilet *n* (*lady's*) cultus *m*.
toilsome *adj* labōriōsus, operōsus.
toil-worn *adj* labōre cōnfectus.
token *n* īnsigne *nt*, signum *nt*, indicium *nt*.
tolerable *adj* tolerābilis, patibilis; (*quality*) mediocris; (*size*) modicus.
tolerably *adv* satis, mediocriter.
tolerance *n* patientia *f*, tolerantia *f*.
tolerant *adj* indulgēns, tolerāns.
tolerantly *adv* indulgenter.
tolerate *vt* tolerāre, ferre, indulgēre (*dat*).
toleration *n* patientia *f*; (*freedom*) lībertās *f*.
toll *n* vectīgal *nt*; (*harbour*) portōrium *nt*.
toll collector *n* exāctor *m*; portitor *m*.
tomb *n* sepulcrum *nt*.
tombstone *n* lapis *m*.
tome *n* liber *m*.
tomorrow *adv* crās; **~'s** crāstinus; **the day after ~** perendiē; **put off till ~** in crāstinum differre.
tone *n* sonus *m*, vōx *f*; (*painting*) color *m*.
tongs *n* forceps *m/f*.
tongue *n* lingua *f*; (*shoe*) ligula *f*; **on the tip of one's ~** in prīmōribus labrīs.
tongue-tied *adj* ēlinguis, īnfāns.
tonnage *n* amphorae *fpl*.
tonsils *n* tōnsillae *fpl*.
tonsure *n* rāsūra *f*.
too *adv* (*also*) etiam, īnsuper, quoque; (*excess*) nimis ♦ *compar adj*: **~ far** extrā modum; **~ much** nimium; **~ long** nimium diū; **~ great to** māior quam quī (*subj*); **~ late** sērius; **~ little** parum (+ *gen*).
tool *n* īnstrūmentum *nt*; (*AGR*) ferrāmentum *nt*; (*person*) minister *m*.
tooth *n* dēns *m*; **~ and nail** tōtō corpore atque omnibus ungulīs; **cast in one's teeth** exprobrāre, obicere; **cut teeth** dentīre; **in the teeth of** obviam (*dat*), adversus (*acc*); **with the teeth** mordicus.
toothache *n* dentium dolor *m*.

toothed *adj* dentātus.
toothless *adj* ēdentulus.
toothpick *n* dentiscalpium *nt*.
toothsome *adj* suāvis, dulcis.
top *n* vertex *m*, fastīgium *nt*; (*tree*) cacūmen *nt*; (*toy*) turbō *m*; **from ~ to toe** ab īmīs unguibus usque ad verticem summum; **the ~ of** summus ♦ *vt* exsuperāre; **~ up** supplēre ♦ *adj* superior, summus.
tope *vi* pōtāre.
toper *n* pōtor *m*.
topiary *adj* topiārius. ♦ *n* topiārium opus *nt*.
topic *n* rēs *f*; (*RHET*) locus *m*; **~ of conversation** sermō *m*.
topical *adj* hodiernus.
topmost *adj* summus.
topography *n* dēscrīptiō *f*.
topple *vi* titubāre; **~ over** prōlābī.
topsail *n* dolō *m*.
topsyturvy *adv* praeposterē; **turn ~** sūrsum deōrsum versāre, permiscēre.
tor *n* mōns *m*.
torch *n* fax *f*, lampas *f*.
torment *n* cruciātus *m*; (*mind*) angor *m* ♦ *vt* cruciāre; (*mind*) discruciāre, excruciāre, angere.
tormentor *n* tortor *m*.
tornado *n* turbō *m*.
torpid *adj* torpēns; **be ~** torpēre; **grow ~** obtorpēscere.
torpor *n* torpor *m*, inertia *f*.
torrent *n* torrēns *m*.
torrid *adj* torridus.
torsion *n* tortus *m*.
torso *n* truncus *m*.
tortoise *n* testūdō *f*.
tortoiseshell *n* testūdō *f*.
tortuous *adj* flexuōsus.
torture *n* cruciātus *m*, supplicium *nt*; **instrument of ~** tormentum *nt* ♦ *vt* torquēre, cruciāre, excruciāre.
torturer *n* tortor *m*, carnifex *m*.
toss *n* iactus *m* ♦ *vt* iactāre, excutere; **~ about** agitāre; **be ~ed** (*at sea*) fluitāre.
total *adj* tōtus, ūniversus ♦ *n* summa *f*.
totality *n* ūniversitās *f*.
totally *adv* omnīnō, plānē.
totter *vi* lābāre, titubāre; **make ~** labefactāre.
tottering *n* titubātiō *f*.
touch *n* tāctus *m*; **a ~ of** aliquantulum (*gen*); **finishing ~** manus extrēma *f* ♦ *vt* tangere, attingere; (*feelings*) movēre, tangere ♦ *vi* inter sē contingere; **~ at** nāvem appellere ad; **~ on** (*topic*) attingere, perstringere; **~ up** expolīre.
touch-and-go *adj* anceps ♦ *n* discrīmen *nt*.
touching *adj* (*place*) contiguus; (*emotion*) flexanimus ♦ *prep* quod attinet ad (*acc*).
touchstone *n* (*fig*) obrussa *f*.
touchy *adj* inrītābilis, stomachōsus.
tough *adj* dūrus.
toughen *vt* dūrāre.
toughness *n* dūritia *f*.

tour n iter nt; (abroad) peregrīnātiō f.
tourist n viātor m, peregrīnātor m.
tournament n certāmen nt.
tow n stuppa f; **of ~** stuppeus ♦ vt adnexum trahere, remulcō trahere.
toward(s) prep ad (acc), versus (after noun, acc); (feelings) in (acc), ergā (acc); (time) sub (acc).
towel n mantēle nt.
tower n turris f ♦ vi ēminēre.
towered adj turrītus.
town n urbs f, oppidum nt; **country ~** mūnicipium nt ♦ adj urbānus.
town councillor n decuriō m.
townsman n oppidānus m.
townspeople npl oppidānī mpl.
towrope n remulcum nt.
toy n crepundia ntpl ♦ vi lūdere.
trace n vestīgium nt, indicium nt ♦ vt investīgāre; (draw) dēscrībere; **~ out** dēsignāre.
track n (mark) vestīgium nt; (path) callis m, sēmita f; (of wheel) orbita f; (of ship) cursus m ♦ vt investīgāre, indāgāre.
trackless adj invius.
tract n (country) tractus m, regiō f; (book) libellus m.
tractable adj tractābilis, facilis, docilis.
trade n mercātūra f, mercātus m; (a business) ars f, quaestus m; **freedom of ~** commercium nt ♦ vi mercātūrās facere, negōtiārī; **~ in** vēndere, vēnditāre.
trader n mercātor m, negōtiātor m.
tradesman n opifex m.
tradition n fāma f, mōs māiōrum m, memoria f.
traditional adj ā māiōribus trāditus, patrius.
traditionally adv mōre māiōrum.
traduce vt calumniārī, obtrectāre (dat).
traducer n calumniātor m, obtrectātor m.
traffic n commercium nt; (on road) vehicula ntpl ♦ vi mercātūrās facere; **~ in** vēndere, vēnditāre.
tragedian n (author) tragoedus m; (actor) āctor tragicus m.
tragedy n tragoedia f; (fig) calamitās f, malum nt.
tragic adj tragicus; (fig) tristis.
tragically adv tragicē; male.
tragicomedy n tragicocōmoedia f.
trail n vestīgia ntpl ♦ vt trahere ♦ vi trahī.
train n (line) agmen nt, ōrdō m; (of dress) īnstita f; (army) impedīmenta ntpl; (followers) comitēs mpl, satellitēs mpl, cohors f ♦ vt īnstituere, īnstruere, docēre, adsuēfacere; exercēre; (weapon) dīrigere.
trainer n (sport) lanista m, aliptēs m.
training n disciplīna f, īnstitūtiō f; (practice) exercitātiō f.
trait n līneāmentum nt.
traitor n prōditor m.
traitorous adj perfidus, perfidiōsus.
traitorously adv perfidiōsē.

trammel vt impedīre.
tramp n (man) planus m; (of feet) pulsus m ♦ vi gradī.
trample vi: **~ on** obterere, prōterere, prōculcāre.
trance n stupor m; (prophetic) furor m.
tranquil adj tranquillus, placidus, quiētus, sēdātus.
tranquility n tranquillitās f, quiēs f, pāx f.
tranquillize vt pācāre, sēdāre.
tranquilly adv tranquillē, placidē, tranquillō animō.
transact vt agere, gerere, trānsigere.
transaction n rēs f, negōtium nt.
transactor n āctor m.
transalpine adj trānsalpīnus.
transcend vt superāre, excēdere.
transcendence n praestantia f.
transcendent adj eximius, ēgregius, excellēns.
transcendental adj dīvīnus.
transcendentally adv eximiē, ēgregiē, ūnicē.
transcribe vt dēscrībere, trānscrībere.
transcriber n librārius m.
transcript n exemplar nt, exemplum nt.
transfer n trānslātiō f; (of property) aliēnātiō f ♦ vt trānsferre; (troops) trādūcere; (property) abaliēnāre; (duty) dēlēgāre.
transference n trānslātiō f.
transfigure vt trānsfōrmāre.
transfix vt trānsfīgere, trāicere, trānsfodere; (mind) obstupefacere; **be ~ed** stupēre, stupēscere.
transform vt commūtāre, vertere.
transformation n commūtātiō f.
transgress vt violāre, perfringere ♦ vi dēlinquere.
transgression n dēlictum nt.
transgressor n violātor m.
transience n brevitās f.
transient adj fluxus, cadūcus, brevis.
transit n trānsitus m.
transition n mūtātiō f; (speech) trānsitus m.
transitory adj brevis, fluxus.
translate vt vertere, reddere; **~ into Latin** Latīnē reddere.
translation n: **a Latin ~ of Homer** Latīnē redditus Homērus.
translator n interpres m.
translucent adj perlūcidus.
transmarine adj trānsmarīnus.
transmission n missiō f.
transmit vt mittere; (legacy) trādere, prōdere.
transmutable adj mūtābilis.
transmutation n mūtātiō f.
transmute vt mūtāre, commūtāre.
transom n trabs f.
transparency n perlūcida nātūra f.
transparent adj perlūcidus; (fig) perspicuus.
transparently adv perspicuē.
transpire vi (get known) ēmānāre, dīvulgārī; (happen) ēvenīre.
transplant vt trānsferre.

transport n vectūra f; (_ship_) nāvis onerāria f; (_emotion_) ēlātiō f, summa laetitia f ♦ vt trānsportāre, trānsvehere, trānsmittere; **be ~ed** (_fig_) efferrī, gestīre.
transportation n vectūra f.
transpose vt invertere; (_words_) trāicere.
transposition n (_words_) trāiectiō f.
transverse adj trānsversus, oblīquus.
transversely adv in trānsversum, oblīquē.
trap n laqueus m; (_fig_) īnsidiae fpl ♦ vt dēcipere, excipere; (_fig_) inlaqueāre.
trappings n ōrnāmenta ntpl, īnsignia ntpl; (_horse's_) phalerae fpl.
trash n nūgae fpl.
trashy adj vīlis.
Trasimene n Trasimēnus m.
travail n labor m, sūdor m; (_woman's_) puerperium nt ♦ vi labōrāre, sūdāre; parturīre.
travel n itinera ntpl; (_foreign_) peregrīnātiō f ♦ vi iter facere; (_abroad_) peregrīnārī; **~ through** peragrāre; **~ to** contendere ad, in (_acc_), proficīscī in (_acc_).
traveller n viātor m; (_abroad_) peregrīnātor m.
traverse vt peragrāre, lūstrāre; **~ a great distance** multa mīlia passuum iter facere.
travesty n perversa imitātiō f ♦ vt perversē imitārī.
tray n ferculum nt.
treacherous adj perfidus, perfidiōsus; (_ground_) lūbricus.
treacherously adv perfidiōsē.
treachery n perfidia f.
tread vi incēdere, ingredī; **~ on** īnsistere (_dat_) ♦ n gradus m, incessus m.
treadle n (_loom_) īnsilia ntpl.
treadmill n pistrīnum nt.
treason n māiestās f, perduelliō f; **be charged with ~** māiestātis accūsārī; **be guilty of high ~ against** māiestātem minuere, laedere (_gen_).
treasonable adj perfidus, perfidiōsus.
treasure n gāza f, thēsaurus m; (_person_) dēliciae fpl ♦ vt māximī aestimāre, dīligere, fovēre; **~ up** condere, congerere.
treasure house n thēsaurus m.
treasurer n aerārī praefectus m; (_royal_) dioecētēs m.
treasury n aerārium nt; (_emperor's_) fiscus m.
treat n convīvium nt; dēlectātiō f ♦ vt (_in any way_) ūtī (_abl_), habēre, tractāre, accipere; (_patient_) cūrāre; (_topic_) tractāre; (_with hospitality_) invītāre; **~ with** agere cum; **~ as a friend** amīcī locō habēre.
treatise n liber m.
treatment n tractātiō f; (_MED_) cūrātiō f.
treaty n foedus nt; **make a ~** foedus ferīre.
treble adj triplus; (_voice_) acūtus ♦ n acūtus sonus m ♦ vt triplicāre.
tree n arbor f.
trek vi migrāre ♦ n migrātiō f.
trellis n cancellī mpl.
tremble vi tremere, horrēre.

trembling n tremor m, horror m ♦ adj tremulus.
tremendous adj immānis, ingēns, vastus.
tremendously adv immāne quantum.
tremor n tremor m.
tremulous adj tremulus.
trench n fossa f.
trenchant adj ācer.
trenchantly adv ācriter.
trend n inclīnātiō f ♦ vi vergere.
trepidation n trepidātiō f.
trespass n dēlictum nt ♦ vi dēlinquere; **~ on** (_property_) invādere in (_acc_); (_patience, time, etc_) abūtī (_abl_).
trespasser n quī iniussū dominī ingreditur.
tress n crīnis m.
trial n (_essay_) experientia f; (_test_) probātiō f; (_law_) iūdicium nt, quaestiō f; (_trouble_) labor m, aerumna f; **make ~ of** experīrī, perīculum facere (_gen_); **be brought to ~** in iūdicium venīre; **put on ~** in iūdicium vocāre; **hold a ~ on** quaestiōnem habēre dē (_abl_).
triangle n triangulum nt.
triangular adj triangulus, triquetrus.
tribe n tribus m; gēns f; (_barbarian_) nātiō f.
tribulation n aerumna f.
tribunal n iūdicium nt.
tribune n tribūnus m; (_platform_) rōstra ntpl.
tribuneship, tribunate n tribūnātus m.
tribunician adj tribūnicius.
tributary adj vectīgālis ♦ n: **be a ~ of** (_river_) īnfluere in (_acc_).
tribute n tribūtum nt, vectīgal nt; (_verbal_) laudātiō f; **pay a ~ to** laudāre.
trice n: **in a ~** mōmentō temporis.
trick n dolus m, fallācia f, fraus f, īnsidiae fpl, ars f; (_conjurer's_) praestīgiae fpl; (_habit_) mōs m ♦ vt fallere, dēcipere, ēlūdere; (_with words_) verba dare (_dat_); **~ out** ōrnāre, distinguere.
trickery n dolus m, fraus f, fallāciae fpl.
trickle n guttae fpl ♦ vi mānāre, dēstillāre.
trickster n fraudātor m, veterātor m.
tricky adj lūbricus, difficilis.
trident n tridēns m, fuscina f.
tried adj probātus, spectātus.
triennial adj trietēricus.
triennially adv quārtō quōque annō.
trifle n nūgae fpl, paululum nt ♦ vi lūdere, nūgārī; **~ with** lūdere.
trifling adj levis, exiguus.
triflingly adv leviter.
trig adj lepidus, concinnus.
trigger n manulea f.
trim adj nitidus, concinnus ♦ vt putāre, tondēre; (_lamp_) oleum īnstillāre (_dat_) ♦ vi temporibus servīre.
trimly adv concinnē.
trimness n nitor, munditia f.
trinket n crepundia ntpl.
trip n iter nt ♦ vt supplantāre ♦ vi lābī, titubāre; **~ along** currere; **~ over** incurrere in (_acc_).
tripartite adj tripartītus.

tripe n omāsum nt.
triple adj triplex, triplus ♦ vt triplicāre.
triply adv trifāriam.
tripod n tripus m.
trireme n trirēmis f.
trite adj trītus.
triumph n triumphus m; (victory) victōria f ♦ vi triumphāre; vincere; ~ **over** dēvincere.
triumphal adj triumphālis.
triumphant adj victor; laetus.
triumvir n triumvir m.
triumvirate n triumvirātus m.
trivial adj levis, tenuis.
triviality n nūgae fpl.
trochaic adj trochaicus.
trochee n trochaeus m.
Trojan n Trōiānus m.
troop n grex f, caterva f; (cavalry) turma f ♦ vi cōnfluere, congregārī.
trooper n eques m.
troops npl cōpiae fpl.
trope n figūra f, trānslātiō f.
trophy n tropaeum nt; **set up a** ~ tropaeum pōnere.
tropic n sōlstitiālis orbis m; ~**s** pl loca fervida ntpl.
tropical adj tropicus.
trot vi tolūtim īre.
troth n fidēs f.
trouble n incommodum nt, malum nt, molestia f, labor m; (effort) opera f, negōtium nt; (disturbance) turba f, tumultus m; **take the** ~ **to** operam dare ut; **be worth the** ~ operae pretium esse ♦ vt (disturb) turbāre; (make uneasy) sollicitāre, exagitāre; (annoy) incommodāre, molestiam exhibēre (dat); ~ **oneself about** cūrāre, respicere; **be** ~**d with** labōrāre ex.
troubler n turbātor m.
troublesome adj molestus, incommodus, difficilis.
troublesomeness n molestia f.
troublous adj turbidus, turbulentus.
trough n alveus m.
trounce vt castīgāre.
troupe n grex f, caterva f.
trousered adj brācātus.
trousers n brācae fpl.
trow vi opīnārī.
truant adj tardus ♦ n cessātor m; **play** ~ cessāre, nōn compārēre.
truce n indutiae fpl.
truck n carrus m; **have no** ~ **with** nihil commercī habēre cum.
truckle vi adsentārī.
truculence n ferōcia f, asperitās f.
truculent adj truculentus, ferōx.
truculently adv ferōciter.
trudge vi rēpere, pedibus incēdere.
true adj vērus; (genuine) germānus, vērus; (loyal) fīdus, fidēlis; (exact) rēctus, iūstus.
truism n verbum trītum nt.
truly adv rēvērā, profectō, vērē.

trumpery n nūgae fpl ♦ adj vīlis.
trumpet n tuba f, būcina f.
trumpeter n būcinātor m, tubicen m.
trump up vt ēmentīrī, cōnfingere.
truncate vt praecīdere.
truncheon n fustis m, scīpiō m.
trundle vt volvere.
trunk n truncus m; (elephant's) manus f; (box) cista f.
truss n fascia f ♦ vt colligāre.
trust n fidēs f, fīdūcia f; **breach of** ~ mala fidēs; **held in** ~ fīdūciārius; **put** ~ **in** fidem habēre (dat) ♦ vt cōnfīdere (dat), crēdere (dat); (entrust) committere, concrēdere.
trustee n tūtor m.
trusteeship n tūtēla f.
trustful adj crēdulus, fīdēns.
trustfully adv fīdenter.
trustily adv fidēliter.
trustiness n fidēs f, fidēlitās f.
trusting adj fīdēns.
trustingly adv fīdenter.
trustworthily adv fidēliter.
trustworthiness n fidēs f, integritās f.
trustworthy adj fīdus, certus; (witness) locuplēs; (authority) certus, bonus.
trusty adj fīdus, fidēlis.
truth n vēritās f, vērum nt; **in** ~ rē vērā.
truthful adj vērāx.
truthfully adv vērē.
truthfulness n fidēs f.
try vt (attempt) cōnārī; (test) experīrī, temptāre; (harass) exercēre; (judge) iūdicāre, cognōscere; ~ **for** petere, quaerere.
trying adj molestus.
tub n alveus m, cūpa f.
tubby adj obēsus.
tube n fistula f.
tufa n tōfus m.
tuft n crista f.
tug vt trahere, tractāre.
tuition n īnstitūtiō f.
tumble vi concidere, corruere, prōlābī ♦ n cāsus m.
tumbledown adj ruīnōsus.
tumbler n pōculum nt.
tumid adj tumidus, īnflātus.
tumour n tūber nt.
tumult n tumultus m, turba f; (fig) perturbātiō f.
tumultuous adj tumultuōsus, turbidus.
tumultuously adv tumultuōsē.
tumulus n tumulus m.
tun n dolium nt.
tune n modī mpl, carmen nt; **keep in** ~ concentum servāre; **out of** ~ absonus, dissonus; (strings) incontentus ♦ vt (strings) intendere.
tuneful adj canōrus.
tunefully adv numerōsē.
tunic n tunica f; **wearing a** ~ tunicātus.
tunnel n cunīculus m.
tunny n thunnus m.

turban n mitra f, mitella f.
turbid adj turbidus.
turbot n rhombus m.
turbulence n tumultus m.
turbulent adj turbulentus, turbidus.
turbulently adv turbulentē, turbidē.
turf n caespes m.
turgid adj turgidus, īnflātus.
turgidity n (_RHET_) ampullae fpl.
turgidly adv īnflātē.
turmoil n turba f, tumultus m; (_mind_)
   perturbātiō f.
turn n (_motion_) conversiō f; (_bend_) flexus m,
   ānfrāctus m; (_change_) commūtātiō f,
   vicissitūdō f; (_walk_) spatium nt; (_of mind_)
   adfectus m; (_of language_) sententia f,
   cōnfōrmātiō f; ~ **of events** mutātiō rērum f;
   bad ~ iniūria f; **good ~** beneficium nt; ~ **of the**
   scale mōmentum nt; **take a ~ for the worse** in
   pēiōrem partem vertī; **in ~s** invicem,
   vicissim, alternī; **in one's ~** locō ōrdine ♦ vt
   vertere, convertere, flectere; (_change_)
   vertere, mūtāre; (_direct_) intendere, dīrigere;
   (_translate_) vertere, reddere; (_on a lathe_)
   tornāre; ~ **the edge of** retundere; ~ **the head**
   mentem exturbāre; ~ **the laugh against**
   rīsum convertere in (_acc_); ~ **the scale** (_fig_)
   mōmentum habēre; ~ **the stomach** nauseam
   facere; ~ **to account** ūtī (_abl_), in rem suam
   convertere ♦ vi versārī, circumagī; (_change_)
   vertere, mūtārī; (_crisis_) pendēre; (_direction_)
   convertī; (_scale_) prōpendēre; ~ **king's/**
   queen's evidence indicium profitērī; ~
   against vt aliēnāre ab ♦ vi dēscīscere ab; ~
   around (se) circumvertere; ~ **aside** vt
   dēflectere, dēclīnāre ♦ vi dēvertere, sē
   dēclīnāre; ~ **away** vt āvertere, dēpellere ♦ vi
   āversārī, discēdere; ~ **back** vi revertī; ~
   down vt invertere; (_proposal_) rēicere; ~ **into**
   vi vertere in (_acc_), mūtārī in (_acc_); ~ **out** vt
   ēicere, expellere ♦ vi cadere, ēvenīre,
   ēvādere; ~ **outside in** excutere; ~ **over** vt
   ēvertere; (_book_) ēvolvere; (_in mind_) volūtāre,
   agitāre; ~ **round** vt circumagere ♦ vi
   convertī; ~ **up** vt retorquēre; (_earth_) versāre;
   (_nose_) corrūgāre ♦ vi adesse, intervenire; ~
   upside down invertere.
turncoat n trānsfuga m.
turning n flexus m, ānfrāctus m.
turning point n discrīmen nt, mēta f.
turnip n rāpum nt.
turpitude n turpitūdō f.
turquoise n callais f ♦ adj callainus.
turret n turris f.
turreted adj turrītus.
turtle n testūdō f; **turn ~** invertī.
turtle dove n turtur m.
tusk n dēns m.
tussle n luctātiō f ♦ vi luctārī.
tutelage n tūtēla f.
tutelary adj praeses.
tutor n praeceptor m, magister m ♦ vt docēre,
   praecipere (_dat_).

tutorship n tūtēla f.
twaddle n nūgae fpl.
twang n sonus m ♦ vi increpāre.
tweak vi vellicāre.
tweezers n forceps m/f, volsella f.
twelfth adj duodecimus ♦ n duodecima pars f,
   ūncia f; **eleven ~s** deūnx m; **five ~s** quīncūnx
   m; **seven ~s** septūnx m.
twelve num duodecim; ~ **each** duodēnī; ~ **times**
   duodeciēns.
twelvemonth n annus m.
twentieth adj vīcēsimus ♦ n vīcēsima pars f;
   (_tax_) vīcēsima f.
twenty num vīgintī; ~ **each** vīcēnī; ~ **times**
   vīciēns.
twice adv bis; ~ **as much** duplus, bis tantō; ~ **a**
   day bis diē, bis in diē.
twig n virga f, rāmulus m.
twilight n (_morning_) dīlūculum nt; (_evening_)
   crepusculum nt.
twin adj geminus ♦ n geminus m, gemina f.
twine n resticula f ♦ vt nectere, implicāre,
   contexere ♦ vi sē implicāre; ~ **round**
   complectī.
twinge n dolor m.
twinkle vi micāre.
twirl vt intorquēre, contorquēre ♦ vi
   circumagī.
twist vt torquēre, intorquēre ♦ vi torquērī.
twit vt obicere (_dat_).
twitch vt vellicāre ♦ vi micāre.
twitter vi pīpilāre.
two num duo; ~ **each** bīnī; ~ **days** biduum nt; ~
   years biennium nt; ~ **years old** bīmus; ~ **by** ~
   bīnī; ~ **feet long** bipedālis; **in ~ parts**
   bifāriam, bipartītō.
two-coloured adj bicolor.
two-edged adj anceps.
twofold adj duplex, anceps.
two-footed adj bipēs.
two-headed adj biceps.
two-horned adj bicornis.
two hundred num ducentī; ~ **each** ducēnī; ~
   times ducentiēns.
two hundredth adj ducentēsimus.
two-oared adj birēmis.
two-pronged adj bidēns, bifurcus.
two-way adj bivius.
type n (_pattern_) exemplar nt; (_kind_) genus
   nt.
typhoon n turbō m.
typical adj proprius, solitus.
typically adv dē mōre, ut mōs est.
typify vt exprimere.
tyrannical adj superbus, crūdēlis.
tyrannically adv superbē, crūdēliter.
tyrannize vi dominārī, rēgnāre.
tyrannous adj see **tyrannical**
tyrannously adv see **tyrannically**.
tyranny n dominātiō f, rēgnum nt.
tyrant n rēx m, crūdēlis dominus m; (_Greek_)
   tyrannus m.
tyro n tīrō m, rudis m.

U, u

ubiquitous *adj* omnibus locīs praesēns.
ubiquity *n* ūniversa praesentia *f.*
udder *n* ūber *nt.*
ugliness *n* foedītās *f*, dēfōrmitās *f*, turpitūdō *f.*
ugly *adj* foedus, dēfōrmis, turpis.
ulcer *n* ulcus *nt*, vomica *f.*
ulcerate *vi* ulcerārī.
ulcerous *adj* ulcerōsus.
ulterior *adj* ulterior.
ultimate *adj* ultimus, extrēmus.
ultimately *adv* tandem, ad ultimum.
umbrage *n* offēnsiō *f*; **take ~ at** indignē ferre, patī.
umbrageous *adj* umbrōsus.
umbrella *n* umbella *f.*
umpire *n* arbiter *m*, disceptātor *m.*
unabashed *adj* intrepidus, impudēns.
unabated *adj* integer.
unable *adj* impotēns; **be ~** nōn posse, nequīre.
unacceptable *adj* ingrātus.
unaccompanied *adj* sōlus.
unaccomplished *adj* īnfectus, imperfectus; (*person*) indoctus.
unaccountable *adj* inexplicābilis.
unaccountably *adv* sine causā, repentē.
unaccustomed *adj* īnsuētus, īnsolitus.
unacquainted *adj* ignārus (*gen*), imperītus (*gen*).
unadorned *adj* inōrnātus, incōmptus; (*speech*) nūdus, ēnucleātus.
unadulterated *adj* sincērus, integer.
unadvisedly *adv* imprūdenter, incōnsultē.
unaffected *adj* simplex, candidus.
unaffectedly *adv* simpliciter.
unaided *adj* sine auxiliō, nūdus.
unalienable *adj* proprius.
unalloyed *adj* pūrus.
unalterable *adj* immūtābilis.
unaltered *adj* immūtātus.
unambiguous *adj* apertus, certus.
unambitious *adj* humilis, modestus.
unanimity *n* cōnsēnsiō *f*, ūnanimitās *f.*
unanimous *adj* concors, ūnanimus; **be ~** idem omnēs sentīre.
unanimously *adv* ūnā vōce, omnium cōnsēnsū.
unanswerable *adj* necessārius.
unanswerably *adv* sine contrōversiā.
unappreciative *adj* ingrātus.
unapproachable *adj* inaccessus; (*person*) difficilis.
unarmed *adj* inermis.
unasked *adj* ultrō, suā sponte.
unassailable *adj* inexpugnābilis.
unassailed *adj* intāctus, incolumis.

unassuming *adj* modestus, dēmissus; **~ manners** modestia *f.*
unassumingly *adv* modestē.
unattached *adj* līber.
unattempted *adj* intentātus; **leave ~** praetermittere.
unattended *adj* sōlus, sine comitibus.
unattractive *adj* invenustus.
unauthentic *adj* incertō auctōre.
unavailing *adj* inūtilis, inānis.
unavenged *adj* inultus.
unavoidable *adj* necessārius.
unavoidably *adv* necessāriō.
unaware *adj* īnscius, ignārus.
unawares *adv* inopīnātō, dē imprōvīsō; incautus.
unbalanced *adj* turbātus.
unbar *vt* reserāre.
unbearable *adj* intolerābilis, intolerandus.
unbearably *adv* intoleranter.
unbeaten *adj* invictus.
unbecoming *adj* indecōrus, inhonestus; **it is ~** dēdecet.
unbeknown *adj* ignōtus.
unbelief *n* diffīdentia *f.*
unbelievable *adj* incrēdibilis.
unbelievably *adv* incrēdibiliter.
unbelieving *adj* incrēdulus.
unbend *vt* remittere, laxāre ♦ *vi* animum remittere, aliquid dē sevēritāte remittere.
unbending *adj* inexōrābilis, sevērus.
unbiassed *adj* integer, incorruptus, aequus.
unbidden *adj* ultrō, sponte.
unbind *vt* solvere, resolvere.
unblemished *adj* pūrus, integer.
unblushing *adj* impudēns.
unblushingly *adv* impudenter.
unbolt *vt* reserāre.
unborn *adj* nōndum nātus.
unbosom *vt* patefacere, effundere.
unbound *adj* solūtus.
unbounded *adj* īnfīnītus, immēnsus.
unbridled *adj* īnfrēnātus; (*fig*) effrēnātus, indomitus, impotēns.
unbroken *adj* integer; (*animal*) intractātus; (*friendship*) inviolātus; (*series*) perpetuus, continuus.
unburden *vt* exonerāre; **~ oneself of** aperīre, patefacere.
unburied *adj* inhumātus, īnsepultus.
unbusinesslike *adj* iners.
uncalled-for *adj* supervacāneus.
uncanny *adj* mīrus, mōnstruōsus.
uncared-for *adj* neglectus.
unceasing *adj* perpetuus, adsiduus.
unceasingly *adv* perpetuō, adsiduē.
unceremonious *adj* agrestis, inurbānus.
unceremoniously *adv* inurbānē.
uncertain *adj* incertus, dubius, anceps; **be ~** dubitāre, pendēre.
uncertainly *adv* incertē, dubitanter.
uncertainty *n* incertum *nt*; (*state*) dubitātiō *f.*
unchangeable *adj* immūtābilis; (*person*)

cōnstāns.
unchanged adj immūtātus, īdem; **remain ~**
permanēre.
uncharitable adj inhūmānus, malignus.
uncharitableness n inhūmānitās f.
uncharitably adv inhūmānē, malignē.
unchaste adj impudīcus, libīdinōsus.
unchastely adv impudīcē.
unchastity n incestus m, libīdō f.
unchecked adj līber, indomitus.
uncivil adj inurbānus, importūnus,
inhūmānus.
uncivilized adj barbarus, incultus, ferus.
uncivilly adv inurbānē.
uncle n (paternal) patruus m; (maternal)
avunculus m.
unclean adj immundus; (fig) impūrus,
obscēnus.
uncleanly adv impūrē.
uncleanness n sordēs fpl; (fig) impūritās f,
obscēnitās f.
unclose vt aperīre.
unclothe vt nūdāre, vestem dētrahere (dat).
unclothed adj nūdus.
unclouded adj serēnus.
uncoil vt explicāre, ēvolvere.
uncomely adj dēfōrmis, turpis.
uncomfortable adj incommodus, molestus.
uncomfortably adv incommodē.
uncommitted adj vacuus.
uncommon adj rārus, īnsolitus, inūsitātus;
(eminent) ēgregius, singulāris, eximius.
uncommonly adv rārō; ēgregiē, ūnicē.
uncommonness n īnsolentia f.
uncommunicative adj tēctus, taciturnus.
uncomplaining adj patiēns.
uncompleted adj imperfectus.
uncompromising adj dūrus, rigidus.
unconcern n sēcūritās f.
unconcerned adj sēcūrus, ōtiōsus.
unconcernedly adv lentē.
uncondemned adj indemnātus.
unconditional adj absolūtus.
unconditionally adv nullā condiciōne.
uncongenial adj ingrātus.
unconnected adj sēparātus, disiūnctus;
(style) dissolūtus.
unconquerable adj invictus.
unconquered adj invictus.
unconscionable adj improbus.
unconscionably adv improbē.
unconscious adj: **~ of** īnscius (gen), ignārus
(gen); **become ~** sōpīrī, animō linquī.
unconsciousness n sopor m.
unconsecrated adj profānus.
unconsidered adj neglectus.
unconstitutional adj illicitus.
unconstitutionally adv contrā lēgēs, contrā
rem pūblicam.
uncontaminated adj pūrus, incorruptus,
integer.
uncontrollable adj impotēns, effrēnātus.
uncontrollably adv effrēnātē.

uncontrolled adj līber, solūtus.
unconventional adj īnsolitus, solūtus.
unconvicted adj indemnātus.
unconvincing adj incrēdibilis, nōn vērī
similis.
uncooked adj crūdus.
uncorrupted adj incorruptus, integer.
uncouple vt disiungere.
uncouth adj horridus, agrestis, inurbānus.
uncouthly adv inurbānē.
uncouthness n inhūmānitās f, rūsticitās f.
uncover vt dētegere, aperīre, nūdāre.
uncritical adj indoctus, crēdulus.
uncultivated adj incultus; (fig) agrestis,
rūsticus, impolītus.
uncultured adj agrestis, rudis.
uncut adj intōnsus.
undamaged adj integer, inviolātus.
undaunted adj intrepidus, fortis.
undecayed adj incorruptus.
undeceive vt errōrem tollere (dat), errōrem
ēripere (dat).
undecided adj dubius, anceps; (case) integer.
undecked adj (ship) apertus.
undefended adj indēfēnsus, nūdus.
undefiled adj integer, incontāminātus.
undemonstrative adj taciturnus.
undeniable adj certus.
undeniably adv sine dubiō.
undependable adj inconstāns, mōbilis.
under adv īnfrā, subter ♦ prep sub (abl), īnfrā
(acc); (number) intrā (acc); (motion) sub (acc);
~ arms in armīs; **~ colour** (pretext of) speciē
(gen), per speciem (gen); **~ my leadership** mē
duce; **~ the circumstances** cum haec ita sint;
labour ~ labōrāre ex; **~ the eyes of** in
cōnspectū (+ gen); **~ the leadership of** abl +
duce.
underage adj impūbēs.
undercurrent n: **an ~ of** lātens.
underestimate vt minōris aestimāre.
undergarment n subūcula f.
undergo vt subīre, patī, ferre.
underground adj subterrāneus ♦ adv sub
terrā.
undergrowth n virgulta ntpl.
underhand adj clandestīnus, fūrtīvus ♦ adv
clam, fūrtim.
underline vt subscrībere.
underling n minister m, satelles m/f.
undermine vt subruere; (fig) labefacere,
labefactāre.
undermost adj īnfimus.
underneath adv īnfrā ♦ prep sub (abl), īnfrā
(acc); (motion) sub (acc).
underprop vt fulcīre.
underrate vt obtrectāre, extenuāre, minōris
aestimāre.
understand vt intellegere, comprehendere;
(be told) accipere, comperīre; (in a sense)
interpretārī; **~ Latin** Latīnē scīre.
understandable adj crēdibilis.
understanding adj sapiēns, perītus ♦ n

intellegentia *f*; (*faculty*) mēns *f*, intellectus *m*; (*agreement*) cōnsēnsus *m*; (*condition*) condiciō *f*.
undertake *vt* suscipere, sūmere, adīre ad; (*business*) condūcere; (*case*) agere, dēfendere; (*promise*) recipere, spondēre.
undertaker *n* dissignātor *m*.
undertaking *n* inceptum *nt*, inceptiō *f*.
undervalue *vt* minōris aestimāre.
underwood *n* virgulta *ntpl*.
underworld *n* īnferī *mpl*.
undeserved *adj* immeritus, iniūstus.
undeservedly *adv* immeritō, indignē.
undeserving *adj* indignus.
undesigned *adj* fortuītus.
undesignedly *adv* fortuītō, temerē.
undesirable *adj* odiōsus, ingrātus.
undeterred *adj* immōtus.
undeveloped *adj* immātūrus.
undeviating *adj* dīrēctus.
undigested *adj* crūdus.
undignified *adj* levis, inhonestus.
undiminished *adj* integer.
undiscernible *adj* invīsus, obscūrus.
undisciplined *adj* lascīvus, immoderātus; (*MIL*) inexercitātus.
undiscovered *adj* ignōtus.
undisguised *adj* apertus.
undisguisedly *adv* palam, apertē.
undismayed *adj* impavidus, intrepidus.
undisputed *adj* certus.
undistinguished *adj* ignōbilis, inglōrius.
undisturbed *adj* tranquillus, placidus.
undo *vt* (*knot*) expedīre, resolvere; (*sewing*) dissuere; (*fig*) īnfectum reddere.
undoing *n* ruīna *f*.
undone *adj* īnfectus; (*ruined*) perditus; **be ~** perīre, disperīre; **hopelessly ~** dēperditus.
undoubted *adj* certus.
undoubtedly *adv* sine dubiō, plānē.
undress *vt* exuere, vestem dētrahere (*dat*).
undressed *adj* nūdus.
undue *adj* nimius, immoderātus, inīquus.
undulate *vi* fluctuāre.
undulation *n* spīra *f*.
unduly *adv* nimis, plūs aequō.
undutiful *adj* impius.
undutifully *adv* impiē.
undutifulness *n* impietās *f*.
undying *adj* immortālis, aeternus.
unearth *vt* ēruere, dētegere.
unearthly *adj* mōnstruōsus, dīvīnus, hūmānō māior.
uneasily *adv* aegrē.
uneasiness *n* sollicitūdō *f*, perturbātiō *f*.
uneasy *adj* sollicitus, anxius, inquiētus.
uneducated *adj* illitterātus, indoctus, rudis; **be ~** litterās nescīre.
unemployed *adj* ōtiōsus.
unemployment *n* cessātiō *f*.
unencumbered *adj* expedītus, līber.
unending *adj* perpetuus, sempiternus.
unendowed *adj* indōtātus.

unendurable *adj* intolerandus, intolerābilis.
unenjoyable *adj* iniūcundus, molestus.
unenlightened *adj* rudis, inērudītus.
unenterprising *adj* iners.
unenviable *adj* nōn invidendus.
unequal *adj* impār, dispār.
unequalled *adj* ūnicus, singulāris.
unequally *adv* inaequāliter, inīquē.
unequivocal *adj* apertus, plānus.
unerring *adj* certus.
unerringly *adv* certē.
unessential *adj* adventīcius, supervacāneus.
uneven *adj* impār; (*surface*) asper, inīquus, inaequābilis.
unevenly *adv* inīquē, inaequāliter.
unevenness *n* inīquitās *f*, asperitās *f*.
unexamined *adj* (*case*) incognitus.
unexampled *adj* inaudītus, ūnicus, singulāris.
unexceptionable *adj* ēmendātus; (*authority*) certissimus.
unexpected *adj* imprōvīsus, inopīnātus, īnsperātus.
unexpectedly *adv* dē imprōvīsō, ex īnspērātō, inopīnātō, necopīnātō.
unexplored *adj* inexplōrātus.
unfading *adj* perennis, vīvus.
unfailing *adj* perennis, certus, perpetuus.
unfailingly *adv* semper.
unfair *adj* inīquus, iniūstus.
unfairly *adv* inīquē, iniūstē.
unfairness *n* inīquitās *f*, iniūstitia *f*.
unfaithful *adj* īnfidēlis, īnfīdus, perfidus.
unfaithfully *adv* īnfidēliter.
unfaithfulness *n* īnfidēlitās *f*.
unfamiliar *adj* novus, ignōtus, īnsolēns; (*sight*) invīsitātus.
unfamiliarity *n* īnsolentia *f*.
unfashionable *adj* obsolētus.
unfasten *vt* solvere, refīgere.
unfathomable *adj* īnfīnītus, profundus.
unfavourable *adj* inīquus, adversus, importūnus.
unfavourably *adv* inīquē, male; **be ~ disposed** āversō animō esse.
unfed *adj* iēiūnus.
unfeeling *adj* dūrus, crūdēlis, ferreus.
unfeelingly *adv* crūdēliter.
unfeigned *adj* sincērus, vērus, simplex.
unfeignedly *adv* sincērē, vērē.
unfilial *adj* impius.
unfinished *adj* īnfectus, imperfectus.
unfit *adj* inūtilis, incommodus, aliēnus.
unfix *vt* refīgere.
unflinching *adj* impavidus, firmus.
unfold *vt* explicāre, ēvolvere; (*story*) expōnere, ēnārrāre.
unfolding *n* explicātiō *f*.
unforeseen *adj* imprōvīsus.
unforgettable *adj* memorābilis.
unforgiving *adj* implācābilis.
unformed *adj* īnfōrmis.
unfortified *adj* immūnītus, nūdus.

unfortunate _adj_ īnfēlīx, īnfortūnātus.
unfortunately _adv_ īnfēlīciter, male; ~ **you did not come** male accidit quod nōn vēnistī.
unfounded _adj_ inānis, vānus.
unfrequented _adj_ dēsertus.
unfriendliness _n_ inimīcitia _f_.
unfriendly _adj_ inimīcus, malevolus; **in an ~ manner** inimīcē.
unfruitful _adj_ sterilis; (_fig_) inānis, vānus.
unfruitfulness _n_ sterilitās _f_.
unfulfilled _adj_ īnfectus, inritus.
unfurl _vt_ explicāre, pandere.
unfurnished _adj_ nūdus.
ungainly _adj_ agrestis, rūsticus.
ungallant _adj_ inurbānus, parum cōmis.
ungenerous _adj_ illīberālis; ~ **conduct** illīberālitās _f_.
ungentlemanly _adj_ illīberālis.
ungirt _adj_ discinctus.
ungodliness _n_ impietās _f_.
ungodly _adj_ impius.
ungovernable _adj_ impotēns, indomitus.
ungovernableness _n_ impotentia _f_.
ungraceful _adj_ inconcinnus, inēlegāns.
ungracefully _adv_ inēleganter.
ungracious _adj_ inhūmānus, petulāns, importūnus.
ungraciously _adv_ acerbē.
ungrammatical _adj_ barbarus; **be ~** soloecismum facere.
ungrateful _adj_ ingrātus.
ungrudging _adj_ largus, nōn invītus.
ungrudgingly _adv_ sine invidiā.
unguarded _adj_ intūtus; (_word_) incautus, incōnsultus.
unguardedly _adv_ temerē, incōnsultē.
unguent _n_ unguentum _nt_.
unhallowed _adj_ profānus, impius.
unhand _vt_ mittere.
unhandy _adj_ inhabilis.
unhappily _adv_ īnfēlīciter, miserē.
unhappiness _n_ miseria _f_, tristitia _f_, maestitia _f_.
unhappy _adj_ īnfēlix, miser, tristis.
unharmed _adj_ incolumis, integer, salvus.
unharness _vt_ disiungere.
unhealthiness _n_ valētūdō _f_; (_climate_) gravitās _f_.
unhealthy _adj_ invalidus, aeger; (_climate_) gravis, pestilens.
unheard _adj_ inaudītus; (_law_) indictā causā.
unheard-of _adj_ inaudītus.
unheeded _adj_ neglectus.
unheeding _adj_ immemor, sēcūrus.
unhelpful _adj_ difficilis, invītus.
unhesitating _adj_ audāx, prōmptus.
unhesitatingly _adv_ sine dubitātiōne.
unhewn _adj_ rudis.
unhindered _adj_ expedītus.
unhinged _adj_ mente captus.
unhistorical _adj_ fictus, commentīcius.
unholiness _n_ impietās _f_.
unholy _adj_ impius.

unhonoured _adj_ inhonōrātus.
unhoped-for _adj_ īnspērātus.
unhorse _vt_ excutere, equō dēicere.
unhurt _adj_ integer, incolumis.
unicorn _n_ monocerōs _m_.
uniform _adj_ aequābilis, aequālis ♦ _n_ īnsignia _ntpl_; (_MIL_) sagum _nt_; **in ~** sagātus; **put on ~** saga sūmere.
uniformity _n_ aequābilitās _f_, cōnstantia _f_.
uniformly _adv_ aequābiliter, ūnō tenōre.
unify _vt_ coniungere.
unimaginative _adj_ hebes, stolidus.
unimpaired _adj_ integer, incolumis, illībātus.
unimpeachable _adj_ (_character_) integer; (_style_) ēmendātus.
unimportant _adj_ levis, nullīus mōmentī.
uninformed _adj_ indoctus, ignārus.
uninhabitable _adj_ inhabitābilis.
uninhabited _adj_ dēsertus.
uninitiated _adj_ profānus; (_fig_) rudis.
uninjured _adj_ integer, incolumis.
unintelligent _adj_ īnsipiēns, tardus, excors.
unintelligible _adj_ obscūrus.
unintelligibly _adv_ obscūrē.
unintentionally _adv_ imprūdēns, temerē.
uninteresting _adj_ frīgidus, āridus.
uninterrupted _adj_ continuus, perpetuus.
uninterruptedly _adv_ continenter, sine ullā intermissiōne.
uninvited _adj_ invocātus; ~ **guest** umbra _f_.
uninviting _adj_ iniūcundus, invenustus.
union _n_ coniūnctiō _f_; (_social_) cōnsociātiō _f_, societās _f_; (_POL_) foederātae cīvitātes _fpl_; (_agreement_) concordia _f_, cōnsēnsus _m_; (_marriage_) coniugium _nt_.
unique _adj_ ūnicus, ēgregius, singulāris.
unison _n_ concentus _m_; (_fig_) concordia _f_, cōnsēnsus _m_.
unit _n_ ūniō _f_.
unite _vt_ coniungere, cōnsociāre, cōpulāre ♦ _vi_ coīre; cōnsentīre, cōnspīrāre; (_rivers_) cōnfluere.
unity _n_ (_concord_) concordia _f_, cōnsēnsus _m_.
universal _adj_ ūniversus, commūnis.
universally _adv_ ūniversus, omnis; (_place_) ubīque.
universe _n_ mundus _m_, rērum nātūra _f_.
university _n_ acadēmia _f_.
unjust _adj_ iniūstus, inīquus.
unjustifiable _adj_ indignus, inexcūsābilis.
unjustly _adv_ iniūstē, iniūriā.
unkempt _adj_ horridus.
unkind _adj_ inhūmānus, inīquus.
unkindly _adv_ inhūmānē, asperē.
unkindness _n_ inhūmānitās _f_.
unknowingly _adv_ imprūdēns, īnscius.
unknown _adj_ ignōtus, incognitus; (_fame_) obscūrus.
unlawful _adj_ vetitus, iniūriōsus.
unlawfully _adv_ iniūriōsē, iniūriā.
unlearn _vt_ dēdiscere.
unlearned _adj_ indoctus, inērudītus.
unless _conj_ nisī.

unlettered *adj* illitterātus.
unlike *adj* dissimilis (+ *gen or dat*), dispār.
unlikely *adj* nōn vērīsimilis.
unlimited *adj* īnfīnītus, immēnsus.
unload *vt* exonerāre, deonerāre; (*from ship*) expōnere.
unlock *vt* reserāre, reclūdere.
unlooked-for *adj* īnspērātus, inexpectātus.
unloose *vt* solvere, exsolvere.
unlovely *adj* invenustus.
unluckily *adv* īnfēlīciter.
unlucky *adj* īnfēlīx, īnfortūnātus; (*day*) āter.
unmake *vt* īnfectum reddere.
unman *vt* mollīre, frangere, dēbilitāre.
unmanageable *adj* inhabilis.
unmanly *adj* mollis, ēnervātus, muliebris.
unmannerliness *n* importūnitās *f*, inhūmānitās *f*.
unmannerly *adj* importūnus, inhūmānus.
unmarried *adj* (*man*) caelebs; (*woman*) vidua.
unmask *vt* nūdāre, dētegere.
unmatched *adj* ūnicus, singulāris.
unmeaning *adj* inānis.
unmeasured *adj* īnfīnītus, immoderātus.
unmeet *adj* parum idōneus.
unmelodious *adj* absonus, absurdus.
unmentionable *adj* īnfandus.
unmentioned *adj* indictus; **leave ~** ōmittere.
unmerciful *adj* immisericors, inclēmēns.
unmercifully *adv* inclēmenter.
unmerited *adj* immeritus, indignus.
unmindful *adj* immemor.
unmistakable *adj* certus, manifestus.
unmistakably *adv* sine dubiō, certē.
unmitigated *adj* merus.
unmixed *adj* pūrus.
unmolested *adj* intāctus.
unmoor *vt* solvere.
unmoved *adj* immōtus.
unmusical *adj* absonus, absurdus.
unmutilated *adj* integer.
unnatural *adj* (*event*) mōnstruōsus; (*feelings*) impius, inhūmānus; (*style*) arcessītus, pūtidus.
unnaturally *adv* contrā nātūram; impiē, inhūmānē; pūtidē.
unnavigable *adj* innāvigābilis.
unnecessarily *adv* nimis.
unnecessary *adj* inūtilis, supervacāneus.
unnerve *vt* dēbilitāre, frangere.
unnoticed *adj*: **be ~** latēre, fallere.
unnumbered *adj* innumerus.
unobjectionable *adj* honestus, culpae expers.
unobservant *adj* tardus.
unobserved *adj*: **be ~** latēre, fallere.
unobstructed *adj* apertus, pūrus.
unobtrusive *adj* verēcundus; **be ~** fallere.
unobtrusiveness *n* verēcundia *f*.
unoccupied *adj* vacuus, ōtiōsus.
unoffending *adj* innocēns.
unofficial *adj* prīvātus.
unorthodox *adj* abnōrmis.
unostentatious *adj* modestus, verēcundus.

unostentatiously *adv* nullā iactātiōne.
unpaid *adj* (*services*) grātuītus; (*money*) dēbitus.
unpalatable *adj* amārus; (*fig*) iniūcundus, īnsuāvis.
unparalleled *adj* ūnicus, inaudītus.
unpardonable *adj* inexcūsābilis.
unpatriotic *adj* impius.
unpitying *adj* immisericors, ferreus.
unpleasant *adj* iniūcundus, ingrātus, īnsuāvis, gravis, molestus.
unpleasantly *adv* iniūcundē, ingrātē, graviter.
unpleasantness *n* iniūcunditās *f*, molestia *f*.
unpleasing *adj* ingrātus, invenustus.
unploughed *adj* inarātus.
unpoetical *adj* pedester.
unpolished *adj* impolītus; (*person*) incultus, agrestis, inurbānus; (*style*) inconditus, rudis.
unpopular *adj* invidiōsus, invīsus.
unpopularity *n* invidia *f*, odium *nt*.
unpractised *adj* inexercitātus, imperītus.
unprecedented *adj* īnsolēns, novus, inaudītus.
unprejudiced *adj* integer, aequus.
unpremeditated *adj* repentīnus, subitus.
unprepared *adj* imparātus.
unprepossessing *adj* invenustus, illepidus.
unpretentious *adj* modestus, verēcundus.
unprincipled *adj* improbus, levis, prāvus.
unproductive *adj* īnfēcundus, sterilis.
unprofitable *adj* inūtilis, vānus.
unprofitably *adv* frustrā, ab rē.
unpropitious *adj* īnfēlīx, adversus.
unpropitiously *adv* malīs ōminibus.
unprotected *adj* indēfēnsus, intūtus, nūdus.
unprovoked *adj* ultrō (*adv*).
unpunished *adj* impūnītus ♦ *adv* impūne.
unqualified *adj* nōn idōneus; (*unrestricted*) absolūtus.
unquestionable *adj* certus.
unquestionably *adv* facile, certē.
unquestioning *adj* crēdulus.
unravel *vt* retexere; (*fig*) ēnōdāre, explicāre.
unready *adj* imparātus.
unreal *adj* falsus, vānus.
unreality *n* vānitās *f*.
unreasonable *adj* inīquus, importūnus.
unreasonableness *n* inīquitās *f*.
unreasonably *adv* inīquē.
unreasoning *adj* stolidus, temerārius.
unreclaimed *adj* (*land*) incultus.
unrefined *adj* impolītus, inurbānus, rudis.
unregistered *adj* incēnsus.
unrelated *adj* aliēnus.
unrelenting *adj* implācābilis, inexōrābilis.
unreliable *adj* incertus, levis.
unreliably *adv* leviter.
unrelieved *adj* perpetuus, adsiduus.
unremitting *adj* adsiduus.
unrequited *adj* inultus, inānis.
unreservedly *adv* apertē, sine ullā exceptiōne.

unresponsive _adj_ hebes.
unrest _n_ inquiēs _f_, sollicitūdō _f_.
unrestrained _adj_ līber, impotēns, effrēnātus, immoderātus.
unrestricted _adj_ līber, absolūtus.
unrevenged _adj_ inultus.
unrewarded _adj_ inhonōrātus.
unrewarding _adj_ ingrātus, vānus.
unrighteous _adj_ iniūstus, impius.
unrighteously _adv_ iniūstē, impiē.
unrighteousness _n_ impietās _f_.
unripe _adj_ immātūrus, crūdus.
unrivalled _adj_ ēgregius, singulāris, ūnicus.
unroll _vt_ ēvolvere, explicāre.
unromantic _adj_ pedester.
unruffled _adj_ immōtus, tranquillus.
unruliness _n_ licentia _f_, impotentia _f_.
unruly _adj_ effrēnātus, impotēns, immoderātus.
unsafe _adj_ perīculōsus, dubius; (_structure_) īnstābilis.
unsaid _adj_ indictus.
unsatisfactorily _adv_ nōn ex sententiā, male.
unsatisfactory _adj_ parum idōneus, malus.
unsatisfied _adj_ parum contenus.
unsavoury _adj_ īnsuāvis, taeter.
unscathed _adj_ incolumis, integer.
unschooled _adj_ indoctus, inērudītus.
unscrupulous _adj_ improbus, impudēns.
unscrupulously _adv_ improbē, impudenter.
unscrupulousness _n_ improbitās _f_, impudentia _f_.
unseal _vt_ resignāre, solvere.
unseasonable _adj_ intempestīvus, importūnus.
unseasonableness _n_ incommoditās _f_.
unseasonably _adv_ intempestīvē, importūnē.
unseasoned _adj_ (_food_) nōn condītus; (_wood_) viridis.
unseat _vt_ (_rider_) excutere.
unseaworthy _adj_ īnfirmus.
unseeing _adj_ caecus.
unseemly _adj_ indecōrus.
unseen _adj_ invīsus; (_ever before_) invīsitātus.
unselfish _adj_ innocēns, probus, līberālis.
unselfishly _adv_ līberāliter.
unselfishness _n_ innocentia _f_, līberālitās _f_.
unserviceable _adj_ inūtilis.
unsettle _vt_ ad incertum revocāre, turbāre, sollicitāre.
unsettled _adj_ incertus, dubius; (_mind_) sollicitus, suspēnsus; (_times_) turbidus.
unsew _vt_ dissuere.
unshackle _vt_ expedīre, solvere.
unshaken _adj_ immōtus, firmus, stabilis.
unshapely _adj_ dēfōrmis.
unshaven _adj_ intōnsus.
unsheathe _vt_ dēstringere, stringere.
unshod _adj_ nūdis pedibus.
unshorn _adj_ intōnsus.
unsightliness _n_ dēfōrmitās _f_, turpitūdō _f_.
unsightly _adj_ foedus, dēfōrmis.
unskilful _adj_ indoctus, īnscītus, incallidus.

unskilfully _adv_ indoctē, īnscītē, incallide.
unskilfulness _n_ īnscītia _f_, imperītia _f_.
unskilled _adj_ imperītus, indoctus; ~ **in** imperitus (+ _gen_).
unslaked _adj_ (_lime_) vīvus; (_thirst_) inexplētus.
unsociable _adj_ īnsociābilis, difficilis.
unsoiled _adj_ integer, pūrus.
unsolicited _adj_ voluntārius ♦ _adv_ ultrō.
unsophisticated _adj_ simplex, ingenuus.
unsound _adj_ īnfirmus; (_mind_) īnsānus; (_opinion_) falsus, perversus.
unsoundness _n_ īnfirmitās _f_, īnsānitās _f_, prāvitās _f_.
unsparing _adj_ inclēmēns, immisericors; (_lavish_) prōdigus.
unsparingly _adv_ inclēmenter; prōdigē.
unspeakable _adj_ īnfandus, incrēdibilis.
unspeakably _adv_ incrēdibiliter.
unspoilt _adj_ integer.
unspoken _adj_ indictus, tacitus.
unspotted _adj_ integer, pūrus.
unstable _adj_ īnstabilis; (_fig_) incōnstāns, levis.
unstained _adj_ pūrus, incorruptus, integer.
unstatesmanlike _adj_ illīberālis.
unsteadily _adv_ incōnstanter; **walk** ~ titubāre.
unsteadiness _n_ (_fig_) incōnstantia _f_.
unsteady _adj_ īnstabilis; (_fig_) incōnstāns.
unstitch _vt_ dissuere.
unstring _vt_ retendere.
unstudied _adj_ simplex.
unsubdued _adj_ invictus.
unsubstantial _adj_ levis, inānis.
unsuccessful _adj_ īnfēlīx; (_effort_) inritus; **be** ~ offendere; **I am** ~ mihī nōn succēdit.
unsuccessfully _adv_ īnfēlīciter, rē īnfectā.
unsuitable _adj_ incommodus, aliēnus, importūnus; **it is** ~ dēdecet.
unsuitableness _n_ incommoditās _f_.
unsuitably _adv_ incommodē, ineptē.
unsuited _adj_ parum idōneus.
unsullied _adj_ pūrus, incorruptus.
unsure _adj_ incertus, dubius.
unsurpassable _adj_ inexsuperābilis.
unsurpassed _adj_ ūnicus, singulāris.
unsuspected _adj_ latēns, nōn suspectus; **be** ~ latēre, in suspiciōnem nōn venīre.
unsuspecting _adj_ imprōvidus, imprūdēns.
unsuspicious _adj_ nōn suspicāx, crēdulus.
unswerving _adj_ cōnstāns.
unsworn _adj_ iniūrātus.
unsymmetrical _adj_ inaequālis.
untainted _adj_ incorruptus, integer.
untamable _adj_ indomitus.
untamed _adj_ indomitus, ferus.
untaught _adj_ indoctus, rudis.
unteach _vt_ dēdocēre.
unteachable _adj_ indocilis.
untenable _adj_ inānis, īnfirmus.
unthankful _adj_ ingrātus.
unthankfully _adv_ ingrātē.
unthankfulness _n_ ingrātus animus _m_.
unthinkable _adj_ incrēdibilis.
unthinking _adj_ incōnsīderātus, imprōvidus.

unthriftily *adv* prōdigē.
unthrifty *adj* prōdigus, profūsus.
untidily *adv* neglegenter.
untidiness *n* neglegentia *f*.
untidy *adj* neglegēns, inconcinnus, squālidus.
untie *vt* solvere.
until *conj* dum, dōnec ♦ *prep* usque ad (*acc*), in (*acc*); ~ **now** adhūc.
untilled *adj* incultus.
untimely *adj* intempestīvus, immātūrus, importūnus.
untiring *adj* impiger; (*effort*) adsiduus.
unto *prep* ad (*acc*), in (*acc*).
untold *adj* innumerus.
untouched *adj* intāctus, integer.
untoward *adj* adversus, malus.
untrained *adj* inexercitātus, imperītus, rudis.
untried *adj* intemptātus, inexpertus; (*trial*) incognitus.
untrodden *adj* āvius.
untroubled *adj* tranquillus, placidus, quiētus; (*mind*) sēcūrus.
untrue *adj* falsus, fictus; (*disloyal*) īnfīdus, īnfidēlis.
untrustworthy *adj* infīdus, mōbilis.
untruth *n* mendācium *nt*, falsum *nt*.
untruthful *adj* mendāx, falsus.
untruthfully *adv* falsō, falsē.
untuneful *adj* absonus.
unturned *adj*: **leave no stone** ~ nihil intemptātum relinquere, omnia experīrī.
untutored *adj* indoctus, incultus.
unused *adj* (*person*) īnsuētus, īnsolitus; (*thing*) integer.
unusual *adj* īnsolitus, inūsitātus, īnsolēns, novus.
unusually *adv* īnsolenter, praeter cōnsuētūdinem.
unusualness *n* īnsolentia *f*, novitās *f*.
unutterable *adj* īnfandus, inēnārrābilis.
unvarnished *adj* (*fig*) simplex, nūdus.
unveil *vt* (*fig*) aperīre, patefacere.
unversed *adj* ignārus (*gen*), imperītus (*gen*).
unwanted *adj* supervacāneus.
unwarily *adv* imprudenter, incautē, incōnsultē.
unwariness *n* imprūdentia *f*.
unwarlike *adj* imbellis.
unwarrantable *adj* inīquus, iniūstus.
unwarrantably *adv* iniūriā.
unwary *adj* imprūdēns, incautus, incōnsultus.
unwavering *adj* stabilis, immōtus.
unwearied, unwearying *adj* indēfessus, adsiduus.
unweave *vt* retexere.
unwedded *adj* (*man*) caelebs; (*woman*) vidua.
unwelcome *adj* ingrātus.
unwell *adj* aeger, aegrōtus.
unwept *adj* indēflētus.
unwholesome *adj* pestilēns, gravis.
unwieldy *adj* inhabilis.
unwilling *adj* invītus; **be** ~ nolle.
unwillingly *adv* invītus.

unwind *vt* ēvolvere, retexere.
unwise *adj* stultus, īnsipiēns, imprūdēns.
unwisely *adv* īnsipienter, imprūdenter.
unwittingly *adv* imprūdēns, īnsciēns.
unwonted *adj* īnsolitus, inūsitātus.
unworthily *adv* indignē.
unworthiness *n* indignitās *f*.
unworthy *adj* indignus (+ *abl*).
unwounded *adj* intāctus, integer.
unwrap *vt* ēvolvere, explicāre.
unwritten *adj* nōn scrīptus; ~ **law** mōs *m*.
unwrought *adj* īnfectus, rudis.
unyielding *adj* dūrus, firmus, inexōrābilis.
unyoke *vt* disiungere.
up *adv* sūrsum; ~ **and down** sūrsum deōrsum; ~ **to** usque ad (*acc*), tenus (*abl, after noun*); **bring** ~ subvehere; (*child*) ēducāre; **climb** ~ ēscendere; **come** ~ **to** aequāre; **lift** ~ ērigere, sublevāre; **from childhood** ~ ā puerō; **it is all** ~ **with** āctum est dē; **well** ~ **in** gnārus (*gen*), perītus (*gen*); **what is he** ~ **to?** quid struit? ♦ *prep* (*motion*) in (*acc*) ♦ *n*: ~**s and downs** (*fig*) vicissitūdinēs *fpl*.
upbraid *vt* exprobrāre (*dat pers, acc charge*); obicere (*dat and acc*), increpāre, castīgāre.
upbringing *n* ēducātiō *f*.
upheaval *n* ēversiō *f*.
upheave *vt* ēvertere.
uphill *adj* acclīvis ♦ *adv* adversō colle, in adversum collem.
uphold *vt* sustinēre, tuērī, servāre.
upholstery *n* supellex *f*.
upkeep *n* impēnsa *f*.
upland *adj* montānus.
uplift *vt* extollere, sublevāre.
upon *prep* in (*abl*), super (*abl*); (*motion*) in (*acc*), super (*acc*); (*dependence*) ex (*abl*); ~ **this** quō factō.
upper *adj* superior; **gain the** ~ **hand** superāre, vincere.
uppermost *adj* suprēmus, summus.
uppish *adj* superbus.
upright *adj* rēctus, ērēctus; (*character*) integer, probus, honestus.
uprightly *adv* rēctē; integrē.
uprightness *n* integritās *f*.
upriver *adj, adv* adversō flūmine.
uproar *n* tumultus *m*; clāmor *m*.
uproarious *adj* tumultuōsus.
uproariously *adv* tumultuōsē.
uproot *vt* ērādīcāre, exstirpāre, ēruere.
upset *vt* ēvertere, invertere, subvertere; ~ **the apple cart** plaustrum percellere ♦ *adj* (*fig*) perturbātus.
upshot *n* ēventus *m*.
upside-down *adv*: **turn** ~ ēvertere, invertere; (*fig*) miscēre.
upstart *n* novus homō *m* ♦ *adj* repentīnus.
upstream *adj, adv* adversō flūmine.
upward(s) *adv* sūrsum; ~ **of** (*number*) amplius.
urban *adj* urbānus, oppidānus.
urbane *adj* urbānus, cōmis.
urbanely *adv* urbānē, cōmiter.

V, v

urbanity n urbānitās f.
urchin n (boy) puerulus m; (animal) echīnus m.
urge vt urgēre, impellere; (speech) hortārī,
incitāre; (advice) suādēre; (request)
sollicitāre; ~ **on** incitāre ♦ n impulsus m;
dēsīderium nt.
urgency n necessitās f.
urgent adj praesēns, gravis; **be ~** instāre.
urgently adv graviter.
urn n urna f.
usage n mōs m, īnstitūtum nt, ūsus m.
use n ūsus m; (custom) mōs m, cōnsuētūdō f; **be
of ~** ūsuī esse, prōdesse, condūcere; **out of ~**
desuētus; **go out of ~** exolēscere; **in common
~** ūsitātus; **it's no ~** nīl agis, nīl agimus ♦ vt
ūtī (abl); (improperly) abūtī; (for a purpose)
adhibēre; (word) ūsurpāre; **~ up** cōnsūmere,
exhaurīre; **~d to** adsuētus (dat); solēre (+
infin); **I ~d to do** faciebam.
useful adj ūtilis; **be ~** ūsuī esse.
usefully adv ūtiliter.
usefulness n ūtilitās f.
useless adj inūtilis; (thing) inānis, inritus; **be ~**
nihil valēre.
uselessly adv inūtiliter, frustrā.
uselessness n inānitās f.
usher n (court) apparitor m; (theatre)
dēsignātor m ♦ vt: ~ **in** indūcere,
intrōdūcere.
usual adj ūsitātus, solitus; **as ~** ut adsolet, ut
fert cōnsuētūdō, ex cōnsuētūdine; **out of the
~** īnsolitus, extrā ōrdinem.
usually adv ferē, plērumque; **he ~ comes**
venīre solet.
usufruct n ūsus et fructus m.
usurer n faenerātor m.
usurp vt occupāre, invādere in (acc),
ūsurpāre.
usurpation n occupātō f.
usury n faenerātiō f, ūsūra f; **practise ~**
faenerārī.
utensil n īnstrūmentum nt, vās nt.
utility n ūtilitās f, commodum nt.
utilize vt ūtī (abl); (for a purpose) adhibēre.
utmost adj extrēmus, summus; **at the ~**
summum; **do one's ~** omnibus vīribus
contendere.
utter adj tōtus, extrēmus, summus ♦ vt
ēmittere, ēdere, ēloquī, prōnūntiāre.
utterance n dictum nt; (process) prōnūntiātiō f.
utterly adv funditus, omnīnō, penitus.
uttermost adj extrēmus, ultimus.

vacancy n inānitās f; (office) vacuitās f; **there is
a ~** locus vacat; **elect to fill a ~** sufficere.
vacant adj inānis, vacuus; **be ~** vacāre.
vacate vt vacuum facere.
vacation n fēriae fpl.
vacillate vi vacillāre, dubitāre.
vacillation n dubitātiō f.
vacuity n inānitās f.
vacuous adj vacuus.
vacuum n ināne nt.
vagabond n grassātor m ♦ adj vagus.
vagary n libīdō f.
vagrancy n errātiō f.
vagrant n grassātor m, vagus m.
vague adj incertus, dubius.
vaguely adv incertē.
vain n vānus, inānis, inritus; (person)
glōriōsus; **in ~** frustrā.
vainglorious adj glōriōsus.
vainglory n glōria f, iactantia f.
vainly adv frustrā, nēquīquam.
vale n vallis f.
valet n cubiculārius m.
valiant adj fortis, ācer.
valiantly adv fortiter, ācriter.
valid adj ratus; (argument) gravis, firmus.
validity n vīs f, auctōritās f.
valley n vallis f.
valorous adj fortis.
valour n virtūs f.
valuable adj pretiōsus.
valuation n aestimātiō f.
value n pretium nt; (fig) vīs f, honor m ♦ vt
aestimāre; (esteem) dīligere; ~ **highly** magnī
aestimāre; ~ **little** parvī aestimāre, parvī
facere.
valueless adj vīlis, minimī pretī.
valuer n aestimātor m.
van n (in battle) prīma aciēs f; (on march)
prīmum agmen nt.
vanguard n prīmum agmen nt.
vanish vi diffugere, ēvānēscere, dīlābī.
vanity n (unreality) vānitās f; (conceit) glōria f.
vanquish vt vincere, superāre, dēvincere.
vanquisher n victor m.
vantage n (ground) locus superior m.
vapid adj vapidus, īnsulsus.
vapidly adv īnsulsē.
vaporous adj nebulōsus.
vapour n vapor m, nebula f; (from earth)
exhālātiō f.
variable adj varius, mūtābilis.
variableness n mūtābilitās f, incōnstantia f.
variance n discordia f, dissēnsiō f,
discrepantia f; **at ~** discors; **be at ~** dissidēre,

variant–vesture

inter sē discrepāre; **set at ~** aliēnāre.
variant *adj* varius.
variation *n* varietās *f*, vicissitūdō *f*.
variegate *vt* variāre.
variegated *adj* varius.
variety *n* varietās *f*; (*number*) multitūdō *f*;
(*kind*) genus *nt*; **a ~ of** dīversī.
various *adj* varius, dīversus.
variously *adv* variē.
varlet *n* verberō *m*.
varnish *n* pigmentum *nt*; (*fig*) fūcus *m*.
varnished *adj* (*fig*) fūcātus.
vary *vt* variāre, mūtāre; (*decorate*) distinguere
♦ *vi* mūtārī.
vase *n* vās *nt*.
vassal *n* ambāctus *m*; (*fig*) cliēns *m*.
vast *adj* vastus, immānis, ingēns, immēnsus.
vastly *adv* valdē.
vastness *n* māgnitūdō *f*, immēnsitās *f*.
vat *n* cūpa *f*.
vault *n* (ARCH) fornix *f*; (*jump*) saltus *m* ♦ *vi*
salīre.
vaulted *adj* fornicātus.
vaunt *vt* iactāre, ostentāre ♦ *vi* sē iactāre,
glōriārī.
vaunting *n* ostentātiō *f*, glōria *f* ♦ *adj*
glōriōsus.
veal *n* vitulīna *f*.
vedette *n* excursor *m*.
veer *vi* sē vertere, flectī.
vegetable *n* holus *nt*.
vehemence *n* vīs *f*, violentia *f*; (*passion*) ārdor
m, impetus *m*.
vehement *adj* vehemēns, violentus, ācer.
vehemently *adv* vehementer, ācriter.
vehicle *n* vehiculum *nt*.
Veii *n* Veiī, Vēiorum *mpl*.
veil *n* rīca *f*; (*bridal*) flammeum *nt*; (*fig*)
integumentum *nt* ♦ *vt* vēlāre, tegere.
vein *n* vēna *f*.
vellum *n* membrāna *f*.
velocity *n* celeritās *f*, vēlōcitās *f*.
venal *adj* vēnālis.
vend *vt* vēndere.
vendetta *n* simultās *f*.
vendor *n* caupō *m*.
veneer *n* (*fig*) speciēs *f*, fūcus *m*.
venerable *adj* gravis, augustus.
venerate *vt* colere, venerārī.
veneration *n* venerātiō *f*, cultus *m*.
venerator *n* cultor *m*.
vengeance *n* ultiō *f*, poena *f*; **take ~ on** ulcīscī,
vindicāre in (*acc*); **take ~ for** ulcīscī,
vindicāre.
vengeful *adj* ultor.
venial *adj* ignōscendus.
venison *n* dāma *f*, ferīna *f*.
venom *n* venēnum *nt*; (*fig*) vīrus *nt*.
venomous *adj* venēnātus.
vent *n* spīrāculum *nt*; (*outlet*) exitus *m*; **give ~
to** profundere, ēmittere ♦ *vt* ēmittere;
(*feelings on*) profundere in (*acc*), ērumpere
in (*acc*).

ventilate *vt* perflāre; (*opinion*) in medium
prōferre, vulgāre.
ventilation *n* perflāre.
venture *n* perīculum *nt*; (*gamble*) ālea *f*; **at a ~**
temerē ♦ *vi* audēre ♦ *vt* perīclitārī, in āleam
dare.
venturesome *adj* audāx, temerārius.
venturesomeness *n* audācia *f*, temeritās *f*.
veracious *adj* vērāx, vēridicus.
veracity *n* vēritās *f*, fidēs *f*.
verb *n* verbum *nt*.
verbally *adv* per colloquia; (*translate*) ad
verbum, verbum prō verbo.
verbatim *adv* ad verbum, totidem verbīs.
verbiage *n* verba *ntpl*.
verbose *adj* verbōsus.
verbosity *n* loquendī prōfluentia *f*.
verdant *adj* viridis.
verdict *n* sententia *f*, iūdicium *nt*; **deliver a ~**
sententiam prōnūntiāre; **give a ~ in favour of**
causam adiūdicāre (*dat*).
verdigris *n* aerūgō *f*.
verdure *n* viriditās *f*.
verge *n* ōra *f*; **the ~ of** extrēmus; **on the ~ of**
(*fig*) prope (*acc*) ♦ *vi* vergere.
verification *n* cōnfirmātiō *f*.
verify *vt* cōnfirmāre, comprobāre.
verily *adv* profectō, certē.
verisimilitude *n* vērī similitūdō *f*.
veritable *adj* vērus.
veritably *adv* vērē.
verity *n* vēritās *f*.
vermilion *n* sandīx *f*.
vermin *n* bestiolae *fpl*.
vernacular *adj* patrius ♦ *n* patrius sermō *m*.
vernal *adj* vērnus.
versatile *adj* versūtus, varius.
versatility *n* versātile ingenium *nt*.
verse *n* (*line*) versus *m*; (*poetry*) versus *mpl*,
carmina *ntpl*.
versed *adj* īnstructus, perītus, exercitātus.
versification *n* ars versūs faciendī.
versify *vt* versū inclūdere ♦ *vi* versūs facere.
version *n* (*of story*) fōrma *f*; **give a Latin ~ of**
Latīnē reddere.
vertex *n* vertex *m*, fastīgium *nt*.
vertical *adj* rēctus, dīrēctus.
vertically *adv* ad līneam, rēctā līneā, ad
perpendiculum.
vertigo *n* vertīgō *f*.
vervain *n* verbēna *f*.
verve *n* ācrimōnia *f*.
very *adj* ipse ♦ *adv* admodum, valdē,
vehementer ♦ *superl*: **at that ~ moment** tum
māximē; **not ~** non ita.
vessel *n* (*receptacle*) vās *nt*; (*ship*) nāvigium *nt*.
vest *n* subūcula *f* ♦ *vt*: **~ power in** imperium
dēferre (*dat*); **~ed interests** nummī locātī *mpl*.
vestal *adj* vestālis ♦ *n* virgō vestālis *f*.
vestibule *n* vestibulum *nt*.
vestige *n* vestīgium *nt*, indicium *nt*.
vestment *n* vestīmentum *nt*.
vesture *n* vestis *f*.

vetch *n* vicia *f.*
veteran *adj* veterānus ♦ *n* (*MIL*) veterānus *m*; (*fig*) veterātor *m.*
veto *n* interdictum *nt*; (*tribune's*) intercessiō *f* ♦ *vt* interdīcere (*dat*); (*tribune*) intercēdere (*dat*).
vex *vt* vexāre, sollicitāre, stomachum movēre (*dat*); **be ~ed** aegrē ferre, stomachārī.
vexation *n* (*caused*) molestia *f*; (*felt*) dolor *m*, stomachus *m.*
vexatious *adj* odiōsus, molestus.
vexatiously *adv* molestē.
vexed *adj* īrātus; (*question*) anceps.
via *prep* per (*acc*).
viaduct *n* pōns *m.*
viands *n* cibus *m.*
vibrate *vi* vībrāre, tremere.
vibration *n* tremor *m.*
vicarious *adj* vicārius.
vice *n* (*general*) prāvitās *f*, perditī mōrēs *mpl*; (*particular*) vitium *nt*, flāgitium *nt*; (*clamp*) fībula *f.*
viceroy *n* prōcūrātor *m.*
vicinity *n* vīcīnia *f*, vīcīnitās *f.*
vicious *adj* prāvus, vitiōsus, flāgitiōsus; (*temper*) contumāx.
viciously *adv* flāgitiōsē; contumāciter.
vicissitude *n* vicissitūdō *f*; **~s** *pl* vicēs *fpl.*
victim *n* victima *f*, hostia *f*; (*fig*) piāculum *nt*; (*exploited*) praeda *f*; **be the ~ of** labōrāre ex; **fall a ~ to** morī (*abl*); (*trickery*) circumvenīrī (*abl*).
victimize *vt* nocēre (*dat*), circumvenīre.
victor *n* victor *m.*
victorious *adj* victor *m*, victrīx *f*; **be ~** vincere.
victory *n* victōria *f*; **win a ~** victōriam reportāre; **win a ~ over** vincere, superāre.
victory message *n* laureātae litterae *fpl.*
victory parade *n* triumphus *m.*
victual *vt* rem frūmentāriam suppeditāre (*dat*).
victualler *n* caupō *m*; (*MIL*) frūmentārius *m.*
victuals *n* cibus *m*; (*MIL*) frūmentum *nt*, commeātus *m.*
vie *vi* certāre, contendere; **~ with** aemulārī.
view *n* cōnspectus *m*; (*from far*) prōspectus *m*; (*from high*) dēspectus *m*; (*opinion*) sententia *f*; **exposed to ~** in mediō; **entertain a ~** sentīre; **in ~ of** propter (*acc*); **in my ~** meā sententiā, meō iūdiciō; **end in ~** prōpositum *nt*; **have in ~** spectāre; **point of ~** iūdicium *nt*; **with a ~ to** eō cōnsiliō ut ♦ *vt* īnspicere, spectāre, intuērī.
vigil *n* pervigilium *nt*; **keep a ~** vigilāre.
vigilance *n* vigilantia *f*, dīligentia *f.*
vigilant *adj* vigilāns, dīligēns.
vigilantly *adv* vigilanter, dīligenter.
vigorous *adj* ācer, vegetus, integer; (*style*) nervōsus.
vigorously *adv* ācriter, strēnuē.
vigour *n* vīs *f*, nervī *mpl*, integritās *f.*
vile *adj* turpis, impūrus, abiectus.
vilely *adv* turpiter, impūrē.

vileness *n* turpitūdō *f*, impūritās *f.*
vilification *n* obtrectātiō *f*, calumnia *f.*
vilify *vt* obtrectāre, calumniārī, maledīcere (*dat*).
villa *n* vīlla *f.*
village *n* pāgus *m*, vīcus *m*; **in every ~** pāgātim.
villager *n* pāgānus *m*, vīcānus *m.*
villain *n* furcifer *m*, scelerātus *m.*
villainous *adj* scelestus, scelerātus, nēquam.
villainously *adv* scelestē.
villainy *n* scelus *nt*, nēquitia *f.*
vindicate *vt* (*right*) vindicāre; (*action*) pūrgāre; (*belief*) arguere; (*person*) dēfendere, prōpugnāre prō (*abl*).
vindication *n* dēfēnsiō *f*, pūrgātiō *f.*
vindicator *n* dēfēnsor *m*, prōpugnātor *m.*
vindictive *adj* ultor, ulcīscendī cupidus.
vine *n* vītis *f*; **wild ~** labrusca *f.*
vinedresser *n* vīnitor *m.*
vinegar *n* acētum *nt.*
vineyard *n* vīnea *f*, vīnētum *nt.*
vintage *n* vindēmia *f.*
vintner *n* vīnārius *m.*
violate *vt* violāre.
violation *n* violātiō *f.*
violator *n* violātor *m.*
violence *n* violentia *f*, vīs *f*, iniūria *f*; **do ~ to** violāre; **offer ~ to** vim īnferre (*dat*).
violent *adj* violentus, vehemēns; (*passion*) ācer, impotēns; **~ death** nex *f.*
violently *adv* vehementer, per vim.
violet *n* viola *f.*
viper *n* vīpera *f.*
viperous *adj* (*fig*) malignus.
virgin *n* virgō *f* ♦ *adj* virginālis.
virginity *n* virginitās *f.*
virile *adj* virīlis.
virility *n* virtūs *f.*
virtually *adv* rē vērā, ferē.
virtue *n* virtūs *f*, honestum *nt*; (*woman's*) pudīcitia *f*; (*power*) vis *f*, potestās *f*; **by ~ of** ex (*abl*).
virtuous *adj* honestus, probus, integer.
virtuously *adv* honestē.
virulence *n* vīs *f*, vīrus *nt.*
virulent *adj* acerbus.
virus *n* vīrus *nt.*
visage *n* ōs *n*, faciēs *f.*
vis-à-vis *prep* exadversus (*acc*).
viscosity *n* lentor *m.*
viscous *adj* lentus, tenāx.
visible *adj* ēvidēns, cōnspicuus, manifestus; **be ~** appārēre.
visibly *adv* manifestō.
vision *n* (*sense*) vīsus *m*; (*power*) aspectus *m*; (*apparition*) vīsum *nt*, vīsiō *f*; (*whim*) somnium *nt.*
visionary *adj* vānus ♦ *n* somniāns *m.*
visit *n* adventus *m*; (*formal*) salūtātiō *f*; (*long*) commorātiō *f*; **pay a ~ to** invīsere ♦ *vt* vīsere; **~ occasionally** intervīsere; **go to ~** invīsere.
visitation *n* (*to inspect*) recēnsiō *f*; (*to punish*) animadversiō *f.*

visitor n hospes m, hospita f; (formal) salūtātor m.
visor n buccula f.
vista n prōspectus m.
visual adj oculōrum.
visualize vt animō cernere, ante oculōs pōnere.
visually adv oculīs.
vital adj (of life) vītālis; (essential) necessārius, māximī mōmentī.
vitality n vīs f; (style) sanguis m.
vitally adv praecipuē, imprīmīs.
vitals n viscera ntpl.
vitiate vt corrumpere, vitiāre.
vitreous adj vitreus.
vitrify vt in vitrum excoquere.
vituperate vt vituperāre, obiūrgāre.
vituperation n vituperātiō f, maledicta ntpl.
vituperative adj maledicus.
vivacious adj alacer, vegetus, hilaris.
vivaciously adv hilare.
vivacity n alacritās f, hilaritās f.
vivid adj vīvidus, ācer.
vividly adv ācriter.
vivify vt animāre.
vixen n vulpēs f.
vocabulary n verbōrum cōpia f.
vocal adj: ~ **music** vōcis cantus m.
vocation n officium nt, mūnus nt.
vociferate vt, vi vōciferārī, clāmāre.
vociferation n vōciferātiō f, clāmor m.
vociferous adj vōciferāns.
vociferously adv māgnīs clāmōribus.
vogue n mōs m; **be in** ~ flōrēre, in honōre esse.
voice n vōx f ♦ vt exprimere, ēloquī.
void adj inānis, vacuus; ~ **of** expers (gen); **null and** ~ inritus ♦ n ināne nt ♦ vt ēvomere, ēmittere.
volatile adj levis, mōbilis.
volatility n levitās f.
volition n voluntās f.
volley n imber m.
volubility n volūbilitās f.
voluble adj volūbilis.
volume n (book) liber m; (mass) mōlēs f; (of sound) māgnitūdō f.
voluminous adj cōpiōsus.
voluntarily adv ultrō, suā sponte.
voluntary adj voluntārius; (unpaid) grātuītus.
volunteer n (MIL) ēvocātus m ♦ vt ultrō offerre ♦ vi (MIL) nōmen dare.
voluptuary n dēlicātus m, homō voluptārius m.
voluptuous adj voluptārius, mollis, dēlicātus, luxuriōsus.
voluptuously adv molliter, dēlicātē, luxuriōsē.
voluptuousness n luxuria f, libīdō f.
vomit vt vomere, ēvomere; ~ **up** ēvomere.
voracious adj vorāx, edāx.
voraciously adv avidē.
voracity n edācitās f, gula f.
vortex n vertex m, turbō m.

votary n cultor m.
vote n suffrāgium nt; (opinion) sententia f; ~ **for** (candidate) suffrāgārī (dat); (senator's motion) discēdere in sententiam (gen) ♦ vi (election) suffrāgium ferre; (judge) sententiam ferre; (senator) cēnsēre; **take a** ~ (senate) discessiōnem facere ♦ vt (senate) dēcernere; ~ **against** (bill) antīquāre.
voter n suffrāgātor m.
votive adj vōtīvus.
vouch vi spondēre; ~ **for** praestāre, testificārī.
voucher n (person) auctor m; (document) auctōritās f.
vouchsafe vt concēdere.
vow n vōtum nt; (promise) fidēs f ♦ vt vovēre; (promise) spondēre.
vowel n vōcālis f.
voyage n nāvigātiō f, cursus m ♦ vi nāvigāre.
vulgar adj (common) vulgāris; (low) plēbēius, sordidus, īnsulsus.
vulgarity n sordēs fpl, īnsulsitās f.
vulgarly adv vulgō; īnsulsē.
vulnerable adj nūdus; (fig) obnoxius; **be** ~ vulnerārī posse.
vulture n vultur m; (fig) vulturius m.

W, w

wad n massa f.
wade vi per vada īre; ~ **across** vadō trānsīre.
waft vt ferre, vehere.
wag n facētus homō m, ioculātor m ♦ vt movēre, mōtāre, agitāre ♦ vi movērī, agitārī.
wage n mercēs f; (pl) mercēs f, manupretium nt; (fig) pretium nt, praemium nt ♦ vt gerere; ~ **war on** bellum īnferre (dat)/gerere.
wager n spōnsiō f ♦ vi spōnsiōnem facere ♦ vt dēpōnere, oppōnere.
waggery n facētiae fpl.
waggish adj facētus, rīdiculus.
waggle vt agitāre, mōtāre.
wagon n plaustrum nt, carrus m.
waif n inops m/f.
wail n ēiulātus m ♦ vi ēiulāre, dēplōrāre, lāmentārī.
wailing n plōrātus m, lāmentātiō f.
waist n medium corpus nt; **hold by the** ~ medium tenēre.
wait n: **have a long** ~ diū exspectāre; **lie in** ~ īnsidiārī ♦ vi manēre, opperīrī, exspectāre; ~ **for** exspectāre; ~ **upon** (accompany) adsectārī, dēdūcere; (serve) famulārī (dat); (visit) salūtāre.
waiter n famulus m, minister m.

waive *vt* dēpōnere, remittere.
wake *vt* excitāre, suscitāre ♦ *vi* expergīscī.
wake *n* vestīgia *ntpl*; **in the ~** pōne, ā tergō; **follow in the ~ of** vestīgiīs instāre (*gen*).
wakeful *adj* vigil.
wakefulness *n* vigilantia *f*.
waken *vt* excitāre ♦ *vi* expergīscī.
walk *n* (*act*) ambulātiō *f*, deambulātiō *f*; (*gait*) incessus *m*; (*place*) ambulātiō *f*, xystus *m*; **~ of life** status *m*; **go for a ~** spatiārī, deambulāre ♦ *vi* ambulāre, īre, gradī; (*with dignity*) incēdere; **~ about** inambulāre; **~ out** ēgredī.
wall *n* mūrus *m*; (*indoors*) pariēs *m*; (*afield*) māceria *f*; **~s** *pl* (*of town*) moenia *ntpl* ♦ *vt* mūnīre, saepīre; **~ up** inaedificāre.
wallet *n* pēra *f*.
wallow *vi* volūtārī.
walnut *n* iūglāns *f*.
wan *adj* pallidus.
wand *n* virga *f*.
wander *vi* errāre, vagārī; (*in mind*) ālūcinārī; **~ over** pervagārī.
wanderer *n* errō *m*, vagus *m*.
wandering *adj* errābundus, vagus ♦ *n* errātiō *f*, error *m*.
wane *vi* dēcrēscere, senēscere.
want *n* inopia *f*, indigentia *f*, egestās *f*, pēnūria *f*; (*craving*) dēsīderium *nt*; **in ~** inops; **be in ~** egēre ♦ *vt* (*lack*) carēre (*abl*), egēre (*abl*), indigēre (*abl*); (*miss*) dēsīderāre; (*wish*) velle.
wanting *adj* (*missing*) absēns; (*defective*) vitiōsus, parum idōneus; **be ~** deesse, dēficere ♦ *prep* sine (*abl*).
wanton *adj* lascīvus, libīdinōsus ♦ *vi* lascīvīre.
wantonly *adv* lascīvē, libīdinōsē.
war *n* bellum *nt*; **regular ~** iūstum bellum; **fortunes of ~** fortūna bellī; **outbreak of ~** exortum bellum; **be at ~ with** bellum gerere cum; **declare ~** bellum indīcere; **discontinue ~** bellum dēpōnere; **end ~** (*by agreement*) compōnere; (*by victory*) cōnficere; **enter ~** bellum suscipere; **give the command of a ~** bellum mandāre; **make ~** bellum īnferre; **prolong a ~** bellum trahere; **provoke ~** bellum movēre; **wage ~** bellum gerere; **wage ~ on** bellum īnferre (*dat*) ♦ *vi* bellāre.
warble *vi* canere, cantāre.
warbling *adj* garrulus, canōrus ♦ *n* cantus *m*.
war cry *n* clāmor *m*.
ward *n* custōdia *f*; (*person*) pupillus *m*, pupilla *f*; (*of town*) regiō *f* ♦ *vt*: **~ off** arcēre, dēfendere, prōpulsāre.
warden *n* praefectus *m*.
warder *n* custōs *m*.
wardrobe *n* vestiārium *nt*.
wardship *n* tūtēla *f*.
warehouse *n* apothēca *f*.
wares *n* merx *f*, merces *fpl*.
warfare *n* bellum *nt*.
warily *adv* prōvidenter, cautē.
wariness *n* circumspectiō *f*, cautiō *f*.

warlike *adj* ferōx, bellicōsus.
warm *adj* calidus; (*fig*) ācer, studiōsus; **be ~** calēre; **become ~** calefierī, incalēscere; **keep ~ fovēre; ~ baths** thermae *fpl* ♦ *vt* calefacere, tepefacere, fovēre ♦ *vi* calefierī.
warmly *adv* (*fig*) ferventer, studiōsē.
warmth *n* calor *m*.
warn *vt* monēre, admonēre.
warning *n* (*act*) monitiō *f*; (*particular*) monitum *nt*; (*lesson*) documentum *nt*, exemplum *nt*.
warp *n* stāmina *ntpl* ♦ *vt* dēprāvāre, īnflectere.
warped *adj* (*fig*) prāvus.
warrant *n* auctōritās *f* ♦ *vt* praestāre.
warranty *n* cautiō *f*.
warrior *n* bellātor *m*, bellatrīx *f*, mīles *m*.
warship *n* nāvis longa *f*.
wart *n* verrūca *f*.
wary *adj* prōvidus, cautus, prūdēns.
wash *vt* lavāre; (*of rivers, sea*) adluere; **~ away** dīluere; **~ clean** abluere; **~ out** (*fig*) ēluere ♦ *vi* lavārī.
washbasin *n* aquālis *m*.
washing *n* lavātiō *f*.
wasp *n* vespa *f*.
waspish *adj* acerbus, stomachōsus.
waste *n* dētrīmentum *nt*, intertrīmentum *nt*; (*extravagance*) effūsiō *f*; (*of time*) iactūra *f*; (*land*) sōlitūdō *f*, vastitās *f* ♦ *adj* dēsertus, vastus; **lay ~** vastāre, populārī ♦ *vt* cōnsūmere, perdere, dissipāre; (*time*) terere, absūmere; (*with disease*) absūmere ♦ *vi*: **~ away** tābēscere, intābēscere.
wasteful *adj* prōdigus, profūsus; (*destructive*) damnōsus, perniciōsus.
wastefully *adv* prōdigē.
wasting *n* tābēs *f*.
wastrel *n* nebulō *m*.
watch *n* (*being awake*) vigilia *f*; (*sentry*) statiō *f*, excubiae *fpl*; **keep ~** excubāre; **keep ~ on, over** custōdīre, invigilāre (*dat*); **set ~** vigiliās dispōnere; **at the third ~** ad tertiam būcinam ♦ *vt* (*guard*) custōdīre; (*observe*) intuērī, observāre, spectāre ad (+ *acc*); **~ for** observāre, exspectāre; (*enemy*) īnsidiārī (*dat*); **~ closely** adservāre.
watcher *n* custōs *m*.
watchful *adj* vigilāns.
watchfully *adv* vigilanter.
watchfulness *n* vigilantia *f*.
watchman *n* custōs *m*, vigil *m*.
watchtower *n* specula *f*.
watchword *n* tessera *f*, signum *nt*.
water *n* aqua *f*; **deep ~** gurges *m*; **fresh ~** aqua dulcis; **high ~** māximus aestus; **running ~** aqua prōfluēns; **still ~** stagnum *nt*; **fetch ~** aquārī; **fetching ~** aquātiō *f*; **cold ~** frīgida *f*; **hot ~** calida *f*; **troubled ~s** (*fig*) turbidae rēs ♦ *vt* (*land*) inrigāre; (*animal*) adaquāre.
water carrier *n* aquātor *m*; (*Zodiac*) Aquārius *m*.
water clock *n* clepsydra *f*.
waterfall *n* cataracta *f*.
watering *n* aquātiō *f*; **~ place** *n* (*spa*) aquae *fpl*.

water pipe *n* fistula *f*.
watershed *n* aquārum dīvortium *nt*.
water snake *n* hydrus *m*.
water spout *n* prēstēr *m*.
watery *adj* aquōsus, ūmidus.
wattle *n* crātēs *f*.
wave *n* unda *f*, fluctus *m* ♦ *vt* agitāre, iactāre ♦ *vi* fluctuāre.
waver *vi* dubitāre, fluctuārī, nūtāre, vacillāre, labāre, inclīnāre.
wavering *adj* dubius, incōnstāns ♦ *n* dubitātiō *f*, fluctuātiō *f*.
wavy *adj* undātus; (*hair*) crispus.
wax *n* cēra *f* ♦ *vt* cērāre ♦ *vi* crēscere.
waxen *adj* cēreus.
waxy *adj* cērōsus.
way *n* via *f*; (*route*) iter *nt*; (*method*) modus *m*, ratiō *f*; (*habit*) mōs *m*; (*ship's*) impetus *m*; **all the ~ to, from** usque ad, ab; **by the ~** (*parenthesis*) etenim; **get in the ~ of** intervenīre (*dat*), impedīre; **get under ~** nāvem solvere; **give ~** (*structure*) labāre; (*MIL*) cēdere; **give ~ to indulgēre** (*dat*); **go out of one's ~ to do** ultrō facere; **have one's ~** imperāre; **in a ~** quōdam modō; **in this ~** ad hunc modum; **it is not my ~ to** nōn meum est (*infin*); **lose one's ~** deerrāre; **make ~** dē viā dēcēdere; **make ~ for** cēdere (*dat*); **make one's ~ into** sē īnsinuāre in (*acc*); **on the ~** inter viam, in itinere; **out of the ~** āvius, dēvius; (*fig*) recondītus; **pave the ~ for** praeparāre; **put out of the ~** tollere; **right of ~** iter; **stand in the ~ of** obstāre (*dat*); **that ~** illāc; **this ~** hāc; **~s and means** opēs *fpl*, reditūs *mpl*.
wayfarer *n* viātor *m*.
waylay *vt* īnsidiārī (*dat*).
wayward *adj* protervus, incōnstāns, levis.
waywardness *n* libīdō *f*, levitās *f*.
we *pron* nōs.
weak *adj* dēbilis, īnfirmus, imbēcillus; (*health*) invalidus; (*argument*) levis, tenuis; (*senses*) hebes.
weaken *vt* dēbilitāre, īnfirmāre; (*resistance*) frangere, labefactāre ♦ *vi* imminuī, labāre.
weakling *n* imbēcillus *m*.
weakly *adj* invalidus, aeger ♦ *adv* īnfirmē.
weak-minded *adj* mollis.
weakness *n* dēbilitās *f*, īnfirmitās *f*; (*of argument*) levitās *f*; (*of mind*) mollitia *f*, imbēcillitās *f*; (*flaw*) vitium *nt*; **have a ~ for** dēlectārī (*abl*).
weal *n* salūs *f*, rēs *f*; (*mark of blow*) vībex *f*; **the common ~** rēs pūblica *f*.
wealth *n* dīvitiae *fpl*, opēs *fpl*; **a ~ of** cōpia *f*, abundantia *f*.
wealthy *adj* dīves, opulentus, locuplēs, beātus; **make ~** locuplētāre, dītāre; **very ~** praedīves.
wean *vt* lacte dēpellere; (*fig*) dēdocēre.
weapon *n* tēlum *nt*.
wear *n* (*dress*) habitus *m*; **~ and tear** intertrīmentum *nt* ♦ *vt* gerere, gestāre; (*rub*)

terere, conterere; **~ out** cōnficere ♦ *vi* dūrāre; **~ off** minuī.
wearily *adv* cum lassitūdine, languidē.
weariness *n* fatīgātiō *f*, lassitūdō *f*; (*of*) taedium *nt*.
wearisome *adj* molestus, operōsus, labōriōsus.
weary *adj* lassus, fessus, dēfessus, fatīgātus ♦ *vt* fatīgāre; **I am weary of** me taedet (+ *gen*).
weasel *n* mustēla *f*.
weather *n* tempestās *f*, caelum *nt*; **fine ~** serēnitās *f* ♦ *vt* superāre.
weather-beaten *adj* tempestāte dūrātus.
weave *vt* texere.
weaver *n* textor *m*, textrix *f*.
web *n* (*on loom*) tēla *f*; (*spider's*) arāneum *nt*.
wed *vt* (*a wife*) dūcere; (*a husband*) nūbere (*dat*).
wedding *n* nūptiae *fpl*.
wedge *n* cuneus *m* ♦ *vt* cuneāre.
wedlock *n* mātrimōnium *nt*.
weed *n* inūtilis herba *f* ♦ *vt* runcāre.
weedy *adj* exīlis.
week *n* hebdomas *f*.
ween *vt* arbitrārī, putāre.
weep *vi* flēre, lacrimārī; **~ for** dēflēre, dēplōrāre.
weeping *n* flētus *m*, lacrimae *fpl*.
weevil *n* curculiō *m*.
weft *n* subtēmen *nt*; (*web*) tēla *f*.
weigh *vt* pendere, exāmināre; (*anchor*) tollere; (*thought*) ponderāre; **~ down** dēgravāre, opprimere; **~ out** expendere ♦ *vi* pendere.
weight *n* pondus *nt*; (*influence*) auctōritās *f*, mōmentum *nt*; (*burden*) onus *nt*; **have great ~** (*fig*) multum valēre; **he is worth his ~ in gold** aurō contrā cōnstat.
weightily *adv* graviter.
weightiness *n* gravitās *f*.
weighty *adj* gravis.
weir *n* mōlēs *f*.
weird *adj* mōnstruōsus ♦ *n* fātum *nt*.
welcome *adj* grātus, exspectātus, acceptus ♦ *n* salūtātiō *f* ♦ *vt* excipere, salvēre iubēre ♦ *interj* salvē, salvēte.
welfare *n* salūs *f*.
well *n* puteus *m*; (*spring*) fōns *m* ♦ *vi* scatēre ♦ *adj* salvus, sānus, valēns; **be ~** valēre ♦ *adv* bene, probē; (*transition*) age ♦ *interj* (*concession*) estō; (*surprise*) heia; **~ and good** estō; **~ begun is half done** dīmidium factī quī coepit habet; **~ done!** probē!; **~ met** opportūnē venis; **~ on in years** aetāte prōvectus; **all is ~** bene habet; **as ~** etiam; **as ~ as** cum ... tum, et ... et; **let ~ alone** quiēta nōn movēre; **take ~** in bonam partem accipere; **wish ~** favēre (*dat*); **you may ~ say** iūre dīcis; **you might as ~ say** illud potius dīcās.
well-advised *adj* prūdēns.
well-behaved *adj* modestus.
wellbeing *n* salūs *f*.
well-bred *adj* generōsus, līberālis.

well-disposed *adj* benevolus, amīcus.
well-informed *adj* ērudītus.
well-judged *adj* ēlegāns.
well-knit *adj* dēnsus.
well-known *adj* nōtus, nōbilis; (*saying*) trītus.
well-nigh *adv* paene.
well-off *adj* beātus, fortūnātus; **you are ~** bene est tibī.
well-read *adj* litterātus.
well-timed *adj* opportūnus.
well-to-do *adj* beātus, dīves.
well-tried *adj* probātus.
well-turned *adj* rotundus.
well-versed *adj* perītus, expertus.
well-wisher *n* amīcus *m*, benevolēns *m*.
well-worn *adj* trītus.
welter *n* turba *f* ♦ *vi* miscērī, turbārī; (*wallow*) volūtārī.
wench *n* muliercula *f*.
wend *vt*: **~ one's way** īre, sē ferre.
west *n* occidēns *m*, sōlis occāsus *m* ♦ *adj* occidentālis.
westerly, western *adj* occidentālis.
westwards *adv* ad occidentem.
west wind *n* Favōnius *m*.
wet *adj* ūmidus, madidus; **be ~** madēre; **~ weather** pluvia *f* ♦ *vt* madefacere.
wether *n* vervēx *m*.
wet nurse *n* nūtrīx *f*.
whack *n* ictus *m*, plāga *f* ♦ *vt* pulsāre, verberāre.
whale *n* bālaena *f*.
wharf *n* crepīdō *f*.
what *pron* (*interrog*) quid; (*adj*) quī; (*relat*) id quod, ea quae; **~ kind of?** qualis.
whatever, whatsoever *pron* quidquid, quodcumque; (*adj*) quīcumque.
wheat *n* trīticum *nt*.
wheaten *adj* trīticeus.
wheedle *vt* blandīrī, pellicere.
wheedling *adj* blandus ♦ *n* blanditiae *fpl*.
wheel *n* rota *f* ♦ *vt* flectere, circumagere ♦ *vi* sē flectere, circumagī.
wheelbarrow *n* pabō *m*.
wheeze *vi* anhēlāre.
whelm *vt* obruere.
whelp *n* catulus *m*.
when *adv* (*interrog*) quandō, quō tempore ♦ *conj* (*time*) cum (+ *subj*), ubī (+ *indic*).
whence *adv* unde.
whenever *conj* quotiēns, utcumque, quandocumque, cum (+ *perf/pluperf indic*); (*as soon as*) simul āc.
where *adv* ubī; (*to*) quō; **~ ... from** unde; **~ to** quo (*interrog and relat*).
whereabouts *n* locus *m*; **your ~** quō in locō sīs.
whereas *conj* quōniam; (*contrast*) *not expressed*.
whereby *adv* quō pāctō, quō.
wherefore *adv* (*interrog*) quārē, cūr; (*relat*) quamobrem, quāpropter.
wherein *adv* in quō, in quā.
whereof *adv* cūius, cūius reī.

whereon *adv* in quō, in quā.
whereupon *adv* quō factō.
wherever *conj* ubiubī, quācumque.
wherewith *adv* quī, cum quō.
wherry *n* linter *f*.
whet *vt* acuere; (*fig*) exacuere.
whether *conj* (*interrog*) utrum; (*single question*) num; (*condition*) sīve, seu; **~ ... or** utrum ... an (*in indir question*); (*in cond clauses*) seu (sive) ... seu (sive); **~ ... not** utrum ... necne (*in indir question*).
whetstone *n* cōs *f*.
whey *n* serum *nt*.
which *pron* (*interrog*) quis; (*of two*) uter; (*relat*) quī ♦ *adj* quī; (*of two*) uter.
whichever *pron* quisquis, quīcumque; (*of two*) utercumque.
whiff *n* odor *m*.
while *n* spatium *nt*, tempus *nt*; **for a ~** parumper; **a little ~** paulisper; **a long ~** diū; **it is worth ~** expedit, operae pretium est; **once in a ~** interdum ♦ *conj* dum + *pres indic* (= *during the time that*); + *imperf indic* (= *all the time that*) ♦ *vt*: **~ away** dēgere, fallere.
whilst *conj* dum.
whim *n* libīdō *f*, arbitrium *nt*.
whimper *n* vāgītus *m* ♦ *vi* vāgīre.
whimsical *adj* facētus, īnsolēns.
whimsically *adv* facētē.
whimsy *n* dēliciae *fpl*, facētiae *fpl*.
whine *n* quīritātiō *f* ♦ *vi* quīritāre.
whinny *n* hinnītus *m* ♦ *vi* hinnīre.
whip *n* flagellum *nt*, flagrum *nt* ♦ *vt* flagellāre, verberare.
whirl *n* turbō *m* ♦ *vt* intorquēre contorquēre ♦ *vi* contorquērī.
whirlpool *n* vertex *m*, vōragō *f*.
whirlwind *n* turbō *m*.
whisper *n* susurrus *m* ♦ *vt*, *vi* susurrāre, īnsusurrāre; **~ to** ad aurem admonēre, in aurem dīcere.
whistle *n* (*instrument*) fistula *f*; (*sound*) sībilus *m* ♦ *vi* sībilāre.
white *adj* albus; (*shining*) candidus; (*complexion*) pallidus; (*hair*) cānus; **turn ~** exalbēscere ♦ *n* album *nt*; (*egg*) albūmen *nt*.
white-hot *adj*: **to be ~** excandēscere.
whiten *vt* dealbāre ♦ *vi* albēscere.
whiteness *n* candor *m*.
whitewash *n* albārium *nt* ♦ *vt* dealbāre.
whither *adv* quō; **~soever** quōcumque.
whitish *adj* albulus.
whizz *n* strīdor *m* ♦ *vi* strīdere, increpāre.
who *pron* quis; (*relat*) quī.
whoever *pron* quisquis, quīcumque.
whole *adj* tōtus, cūnctus; (*unhurt*) integer, incolumis; (*healthy*) sānus ♦ *n* tōtum *nt*, summa *f*, ūniversitās *f*; **on the ~** plērumque.
wholehearted *adj* studiōsissimus.
wholeheartedly *adv* ex animō.
wholesale *adj* māgnus, cōpiōsus; **~ business** negōtiātiō *f*; **~ dealer** mercātor *m*, negōtiātor *m*.

wholesome adj salūtāris, salūbris.
wholesomeness n salūbritās f.
wholly adv omnīnō, tōtus.
whoop n ululātus m ♦ vi ululāre.
whose pron cūius.
why adv cūr, quārē, quamobrem, qua de causa.
wick n mergulus m.
wicked adj improbus, scelestus; (to gods, kin, country) impius.
wickedly adv improbē, scelestē, impiē.
wickedness n improbitās f, scelus nt, impietās f.
wicker adj vīmineus ♦ n vīmen nt.
wide adj lātus, amplus; **be ~ of** aberrāre ab ♦ adv lātē; **far and ~** longē lātēque.
widely adv lātē; (among people) vulgō.
widen vt laxāre, dilātāre.
widespread adj effūsus, vulgātus.
widow n vidua f.
widowed adj viduus, orbus.
widower n viduus m.
widowhood n viduitās f.
width n lātitūdō f, amplitūdō f.
wield vt tractāre, gestāre, ūtī (abl).
wife n uxor f.
wifely adj uxōrius.
wig n capillāmentum nt.
wild adj ferus, indomitus, saevus; (plant) agrestis; (land) incultus; (temper) furibundus, impotens, āmēns; (shot) temerārius; **~ state** ferītās f.
wild beast n fera f.
wilderness n sōlitūdō f, loca dēserta ntpl.
wildly adv saevē.
wildness n ferītās f.
wile n dolus m, ars f, fraus f.
wilful adj pervicāx, contumāx; (action) cōnsultus.
wilfully adv contumāciter; cōnsultō.
wilfulness n pervicācia f, libīdō f.
wilily adv astūtē, vafrē.
wiliness n astūtia f.
will n (faculty) voluntās f, animus m; (intent) cōnsilium nt; (decision) arbitrium nt; (of gods) nūtus m; (document) testāmentum nt; **~ and pleasure** libīdō f; **against one's ~** invītus; **at ~** ad libīdinem suam; **good ~** studium nt; **ill ~** invidia f; **with a ~** summō studiō; **without making a ~** intestātus, intestātō ♦ vt velle, fut; (legacy) lēgāre; **as you ~** ut libet.
willing adj libēns, parātus; **be ~** velle; **not be ~** nōlle.
willingly adv libenter.
willingness n voluntās f.
willow n salix f ♦ adj salignus.
willowy adj gracilis.
wilt vi flaccēscere.
wily adj astūtus, vafer, callidus.
wimple n mitra f.
win vt ferre, obtinēre, adipisci; (after effort) auferre; (victory) reportāre; (fame) cōnsequī, adsequī; (friends) sibī conciliāre; **~ the day**

vincere; **~ over** dēlēnīre, conciliāre ♦ vi vincere.
wince vi resilīre.
winch n māchina f, sucula f.
wind n ventus m; (north) aquilō m; (south) auster m; (east) eurus m; (west) favōnius m; **I get ~ of** subolet mihī; **run before the ~** ventō sē dare; **take the ~ out of one's sails** suō sibī gladiō iugulāre; **there is something in the ~** nescioquid olet; **which way the ~ blows** quōmodo sē rēs habeat.
wind vt torquēre; **~ round** intorquēre ♦ vi flectī, sinuāre; **~ up** (speech) perōrāre.
windbag n verbōsus m.
winded adj anhēlāns.
windfall n repentīnum bonum nt.
winding adj flexuōsus, tortuōsus ♦ n flexiō f, flexus m; **~s** pl (speech) ambāgēs fpl.
windlass n māchina f, sucula f.
window n fenestra f.
windpipe n aspera artēria f.
windward adj ad ventum conversus ♦ adv: **to ~** ventum versus.
windy adj ventōsus.
wine n vīnum nt; (new) mustum nt; (undiluted) merum nt.
winebibber n vīnōsus m.
wine cellar n apothēca f.
wine merchant n vīnārius m.
wine press n prēlum nt.
wing n āla f; (MIL) cornū nt, āla f; (of bird) penna f; **take ~** ēvolāre; **take under one's ~** patrōnus fierī (gen), clientem habēre, in custōdiam recipere.
winged adj ālātus, pennātus, volucer.
wink n nictus m ♦ vi nictāre; **~ at** cōnīvēre (dat).
winner n victor m.
winning adj blandus, iūcundus.
winningly adv blandē, iūcundē.
winning post n mēta f.
winnings n lucra ntpl.
winnow vt ventilāre; (fig) excutere.
winnowing-fan n vannus f.
winsome adj blandus, suāvis.
winter n hiems f; (mid) brūma f ♦ adj hiemālis, hībernus ♦ vi hībernāre.
winter quarters n hīberna ntpl.
wintry adj hiemālis, hībernus.
wipe vt dētergēre; **~ away** abstergēre; **~ dry** siccāre; **~ off** dētergēre; **~ out** dēlēre; **~ the nose** ēmungere.
wire n fīlum aēneum nt.
wiry adj nervōsus.
wisdom n sapientia f; (in action) prūdentia f; (in judgment) cōnsilium nt.
wise adj sapiēns, prūdēns.
wisely adv sapienter, prūdenter.
wish n optātum nt, vōtum nt; (for something missing) dēsīderium nt; **~es** pl (greeting) salūs f ♦ vt optāre, cupere, velle; **~ for** exoptāre, expetere, dēsīderāre; **~ good-day** salvēre iubēre; **as you ~** ut libet; **I ~ I could** utinam

possim.
wishful *adj* cupidus.
wishing n optātiō f.
wisp n manipulus m.
wistful *adj* dēsīderī plenus.
wistfully *adv* cum dēsīderiō.
wistfulness n dēsīderium nt.
wit n (*humour*) facētiae *fpl*, salēs *mpl*; (*intellect*)
argūtiae *fpl*, ingenium *nt*; **caustic** ~ dicācitās
f; **be at one's wits' end** valdē haerēre; **be out
of one's ~s** dēlīrāre; **have one's ~s about one**
prūdens esse; **to** ~ nempe, dīcō.
witch n sāga f, strīga f.
witchcraft n veneficium nt, magicae artēs *fpl*.
with *prep* (*person*) cum (*abl*); (*thing*) *abl*; (*in
company*) apud (*acc*); (*fight*) cum (*abl*), contrā
(*acc*); **be angry** ~ īrāscī (*dat*); **begin** ~ incipere
ab; **rest** ~ esse penes (*acc*); **end** ~ dēsinere in
(*acc*); **what do you want** ~ **me?** quid mē vis?
withdraw *vt* dēdūcere, dētrahere; (*fig*)
āvocāre; (*words*) retractāre ♦ *vi* discēdere,
abscēdere, sē recipere, sē subdūcere.
withdrawal n (*MIL*) receptus m.
wither *vt* torrēre ♦ *vi* dēflōrēscere.
withered *adj* marcidus.
withhold *vt* abstinēre, retinēre, supprimere.
within *adv* intus, intrā; (*motion*) intrō ♦ *prep*
intrā (*acc*), in (*abl*).
without *adv* extrā, forīs; **from** ~ extrīnsecus;
be ~ vacāre (*abl*), carēre (*abl*) ♦ *prep* sine
(*abl*), expers (*gen*); **I admire ~ fearing** ita
laudō ut nōn timeam; ~ **breaking the law**
salvīs lēgibus; **you cannot see ~ admiring**
vidēre nōn potes quīn laudēs; **you cannot
appreciate ~ seeing for yourself** aestimāre
nōn potes nisī ipse vīderis; ~ **doubt** sine
dubio; ~ **the order of iniūssū** (*gen*); ~ **striking
a blow** rē integrā
withstand *vt* resistere (*dat*), obsistere (*dat*);
(*attack*) ferre, sustinēre.
withy n vīmen nt.
witless *adj* excors, ineptus, stultus.
witness n (*person*) testis *m/f*; (*to a document*)
obsignātor m; (*spectator*) arbiter m; (*evidence*)
testimōnium nt; **call as** ~ antestārī; **bear** ~
testificārī; **call to** ~ testārī ♦ *vt* testificārī;
(*see*) vidēre, intuērī.
witnessing n testificātiō f.
witticism n dictum nt; ~**s** *pl* facētiae *fpl*.
wittily *adv* facētē, salsē.
wittingly *adv* sciēns.
witty *adj* facētus, argūtus, salsus; (*caustic*)
dicāx.
wizard n magus m, veneficus m.
wizardry n magicae artēs *fpl*.
wizened *adj* marcidus.
woad n vitrum nt.
wobble *vi* titubāre; (*structure*) labāre.
woe n luctus m, dolor m, aerumna f; ~**s** *pl* mala
ntpl, calamitātēs *fpl*; ~ **to** vae (*dat*).
woeful *adj* tristis, maestus, aerumnōsus.
woefully *adv* triste, miserē.
wolf n lupus m, lupa f; ~**'s** lupīnus.

woman n fēmina f, mulier f; **old** ~ anus f;
married ~ mātrōna f; ~**'s** muliebris.
womanish *adj* muliebris, effēminātus.
womanly *adj* muliebris.
womb n uterus m.
wonder n admīrātiō f; (*of a thing*)
admīrābilitās f; (*thing*) mīrāculum nt, mīrum
nt, portentum nt ♦ *vi* mīrārī; ~ **at** admīrārī,
dēmīrārī.
wonderful *adj* mīrus, mīrābilis, admīrābilis; ~
to relate mīrābile dictu.
wonderfully *adv* mīrē, mīrābiliter, mīrum
quantum.
wonderfulness n admīrābilitās f.
wondering *adj* mīrābundus.
wonderment n admīrātiō f.
wondrous *adj* mīrus, mīrābilis.
wont n mōs m, cōnsuētūdō f.
wonted *adj* solitus.
woo *vt* petere.
wood n silva f, nemus nt; (*material*) lignum nt;
gather ~ lignārī; **touch ~!** absit verbō invidia
♦ *adj* ligneus.
woodcutter n lignātor m.
wooded *adj* silvestris, saltuōsus.
wooden *adj* ligneus.
woodland n silvae *fpl* ♦ *adj* silvestris.
woodman n lignātor m.
wood nymph n dryas f.
woodpecker n pīcus m.
wood pigeon n palumbēs *m/f*.
woodwork n tigna *ntpl*.
woodworker n faber tignārius m.
woody *adj* silvestris, silvōsus.
wooer n procus m.
woof n subtēmen nt.
wool n lāna f.
woollen *adj* lāneus.
woolly *adj* lānātus.
word n verbum nt; (*spoken*) vōx f; (*message*)
nūntius m; (*promise*) fidēs f; (*term*)
vocābulum nt; ~ **for** ~ ad verbum, verbum ē
verbō; **a** ~ **with you!** paucīs tē volō!; **break
one's** ~ fidem fallere; **bring back** ~
renūntiāre; **by** ~ **of mouth** ōre; **fair ~s**
blanditiae *fpl*; **give one's** ~ fidem dare; **have a
~ with** colloquī cum; **have ~s with** iūrgāre
cum; **have a good ~ for** laudāre; **in a** ~ ūnō
verbō, dēnique; **keep one's** ~ fidem
praestāre; **of few ~s** taciturnus; **take at one's
~** crēdere (*dat*).
wording n verba *ntpl*.
wordy *adj* verbōsus.
work n (*energy*) labor m, opera f; (*task*) opus nt;
(*thing done*) opus nt; (*book*) liber m; (*trouble*)
negōtium nt; ~**s** (*MIL*) opera *ntpl*; (*mechanism*)
māchinātiō f; (*place*) officīna f ♦ *vi* labōrāre ♦
vt (*men*) exercēre; (*metal*) fabricārī; (*soil*)
subigere; (*results*) efficere; ~ **at** ēlabōrāre; ~
in admiscēre; ~ **off** exhaurīre; ~ **out**
ēlabōrāre; ~ **up** (*emotion*) efferre; ~ **one's
way up** prōficere ♦ *vi* gerī.
workaday *adj* cottīdiānus.

workhouse *n* ergastulum *nt*.
working *n* (*mechanism*) māchinātiō *f*; (*soil*)
cultus *m*.
workman *n* (*unskilled*) operārius *m*; (*skilled*)
opifex *m*, faber *m*; **workmen** operae *fpl*.
workmanship *n* ars *f*, artificium *nt*.
workshop *n* fabrica *f*, officīna *f*.
world *n* (*universe*) mundus *m*; (*earth*) orbis
terrārum *m*; (*nature*) rērum nātūra *f*;
(*mankind*) hominēs *mpl*; (*masses*) vulgus *nt*; **of
the ~** mundānus; **man of the ~** homō urbānus
m; **best in the ~** rērum optimus, omnium
optimus; **where in the ~** ubī gentium.
worldliness *n* quaestūs studium *nt*.
worldly *adj* quaestuī dēditus.
worm *n* vermis *m* ♦ *vi*: **~ one's way** sē
īnsinuāre.
worm-eaten *adj* vermiculōsus.
wormwood *n* absinthium *nt*.
worn *adj* trītus.
worried *adj* sollicitus, anxius.
worry *n* cūra *f*, sollicitūdō *f* ♦ *vi* sollicitārī ♦ *vt*
vexāre, sollicitāre; (*of dogs*) lacerāre.
worse *adj* pēior, dēterior; **grow ~**
ingravēscere; **make matters ~** rem
exasperāre ♦ *adv* pēius, dēterius.
worsen *vi* ingravēscere, dēterior fierī.
worship *n* venerātiō *f*, deōrum cultus *m*; (*rite*)
sacra *ntpl*, rēs dīvīnae *fpl* ♦ *vt* adōrāre,
venerārī, colere.
worst *adj* pessimus, dēterrimus; **~ enemy**
inimīcissimus *m*; **endure the ~** ultima patī;
vincere.
worsted *n* lāna *f*.
worth *n* (*value*) pretium *nt*; (*moral*) dignitās *f*,
frūgālitās *f*, virtūs *f*; (*prestige*) auctōritās *f* ♦
adj dignus; **for all one's ~** prō virīlī parte;
how much is it ~? quanti vēnit?; **it is ~ a lot**
multum valet; **it is ~ doing** operae pretium
est.
worthily *adv* dignē, meritō.
worthiness *n* dignitās *f*.
worthless *adj* (*person*) nēquam; (*thing*) vīlis,
inānis.
worthlessness *n* levitās *f*, nēquitia *f*; vīlitās *f*.
worthy *adj* dignus; (*person*) frūgī, honestus; **~
of** dignus (*abl*).
wound *n* vulnus *nt* ♦ *vt* vulnerāre; (*feelings*)
offendere.
wounded *adj* saucius.
wrangle *n* iūrgium *nt*, rixa *f* ♦ *vi* iūrgāre,
rixārī, altercārī.
wrap *vt* involvere, obvolvere; **~ round**
intorquēre; **~ up** involvere.
wrapper *n* involucrum *nt*.
wrapping *n* integumentum *nt*.
wrath *n* īra *f*, īrācundia *f*.
wrathful *adj* īrātus.
wrathfully *adv* īrācundē.
wreak *vt*: **~ vengeance on** saevīre in (*acc*),
ulcīscī.
wreath *n* corōna *f*, sertum *nt*.
wreathe *vt* (*garland*) torquēre; (*object*)
corōnāre.
wreck *n* naufragium *nt* ♦ *vt* frangere; (*fig*)
perdere; **be ~ed** naufragium facere.
wreckage *n* fragmenta *ntpl*.
wrecked *adj* (*person*) naufragus; (*ship*)
frāctus.
wrecker *n* perditor *m*.
wren *n* rēgulus *m*.
wrench *vt* intorquēre, extorquēre; **~ away**
ēripere; **~ open** effringere.
wrest *vt* extorquēre.
wrestle *vi* luctārī.
wrestler *n* luctātor *m*, athlēta *m*.
wrestling *n* luctātiō *f*.
wretch *n* scelerātus *m*, nēquam homō *m*; **poor
~** miser homō *m*.
wretched *adj* īnfēlīx, miser; (*pitiful*) flēbilis.
wretchedly *adv* miserē.
wretchedness *n* miseria *f*; maestitia *f*.
wriggle *vi* sē torquēre.
wriggling *adj* sinuōsus.
wright *n* faber *m*.
wring *vt* torquēre; **~ from** extorquēre.
wrinkle *n* rūga *f* ♦ *vt* corrūgāre.
wrinkled *adj* rūgōsus.
wrist *n* prīma palmae pars *f*.
writ *n* (*legal*) auctōritās *f*.
write *vt* scrībere; (*book*) cōnscrībere; **~ off**
indūcere; **~ on** īnscrībere (*dat*); **~ out**
exscrībere, dēscrībere; **~ out in full**
perscrībere.
writer *n* (*lit*) scrīptor *m*, auctor *m*; (*clerk*)
scrība *m*.
writhe *vi* torquērī.
writing *n* (*act*) scrīptiō *f*; (*result*) scrīptum *nt*.
wrong *adj* falsus, perversus, prāvus; (*unjust*)
iniūstus, inīquus; **be ~, go ~** errāre ♦ *n*
iniūria *f*, culpa *f*, noxa *f*, malum *nt*; **do ~**
peccāre, dēlinquere; **right and ~** (*moral*)
honesta ac turpia *ntpl* ♦ *vt* laedere, nocēre
(*dat*); (*by deceit*) fraudāre.
wrongdoer *n*, maleficus *m*, scelerātus *m*.
wrongdoing *n* scelus *nt*.
wrongful *adj* iniūstus, iniūriosus, inīquus.
wrongfully *adv* iniūriā, iniūstē, inīquē.
wrong-headed *adj* perversus.
wrong-headedness *n* perversitās *f*.
wrongly *adv* falsō, dēprāvātē, male,
perperam.
wroth *adj* īrātus.
wrought *adj* factus.
wry *adj* dētortus; **make a ~ face** ōs dūcere.
wryness *n* prāvitās *f*.

Y, y

yacht n phasēlus m.
yard n (court) ārea f; (measure) trēs pedēs.
yardarm n antenna f.
yarn n fīlum nt; (story) fābula f.
yawn n hiātus m ♦ vi hiāre, ōscitāre; (chasm) dehiscere.
ye pron vōs.
yean vt parere.
year n annus m; **every ~** quotannīs; **for a ~ in** annum; **half ~** sēmēstre spatium nt; **this ~'s** hōrnus; **twice a ~** bis annō; **two ~s** biennium nt; **three ~s** triennium nt; **four ~s** quadriennium nt; **five ~s** quinquennium nt.
yearly adj annuus, anniversārius ♦ adv quotannīs.
yearn vi: **~ for** dēsīderāre, exoptāre.
yearning n dēsīderium nt.
yeast n fermentum nt.
yell n clāmor m; (of pain) ēiulātiō f ♦ vi clāmāre, eiulāre.
yellow adj flāvus; (pale) gilvus; (deep) fulvus; (gold) luteus; (saffron) croceus.
yelp n gannītus m ♦ vi gannīre.
yeoman n colōnus m.
yes adv ita vērō (est), māximē; (correcting) immo.
yesterday adv herī ♦ n hesternus diēs m; **~'s** hesternus; **the day before ~** nudius tertius.
yet adv (contrast) tamen, nihilōminus, attamen; (time) adhūc, etiam; (with compar) etiam; **and ~** atquī, quamquam; **as ~** adhūc; **not ~** nōndum.
yew n taxus f.
yield n fructus m ♦ vt (crops) ferre, efferre; (pleasure) adferre; (concession) dare, concēdere; (surrender) dēdere ♦ vi cēdere; (surrender) sē dēdere, sē trādere; **~ to the**

wishes of mōrem gerere (dat), obsequī (dat).
yielding adj (person) facilis, obsequēns; (thing) mollis ♦ n cessiō f; dēditiō f.
yoke n iugum nt ♦ vt iungere, coniungere.
yokel n agrestis m.
yolk n vitellus m.
yonder adv illīc ♦ adj ille, iste.
yore n: **of ~** quondam, ōlim.
you pron tū, vōs.
young adj iuvenis, adulēscēns; (child) parvus; **~er** iūnior, nātū minor; **~est** nātū minimus ♦ n fētus m, pullus m, catulus m.
young man n iuvenis m; adulēscēns m.
youngster n puer m.
your adj tuus, vester.
yourself pron ipse.
youth n (age) iuventūs f, adulescentia f; (person) iuvenis m, adulēscēns m; (collective) iuventūs f.
youthful adj iuvenīlis, puerīlis.
youthfully adv iuvenīliter.

Z, z

zeal n studium nt, ārdor m.
zealot n studiōsus m, fautor m.
zealous adj studiōsus, ārdēns.
zealously adv studiōsē, ārdenter.
zenith n vertex m.
zephyr n Favōnius m.
zero n nihil nt.
zest n (taste) sapor m; (fig) gustātus m, impetus m.
zigzag n ānfrāctus m ♦ adj tortuōsus.
zither n cithara f.
zodiac n signifer orbis m.
zone n cingulus m.

Grammar and Verb Tables

This book is designed to help pupils and students of Latin to understand the grammar of the language. For beginners, the book provides an introduction to and explanation of the basic forms. More advanced students will find it an invaluable guide for reference and revision.

All parts of speech (nouns, pronouns, adjectives etc) are treated separately and clearly explained for the benefit of learners. Differences in usages are illustrated by extensive examples from many Latin authors. *American students and teachers, please note: this book is designed for use by students around the world, many of whom use British case ordering (Nom, Voc, Acc, Gen, Dat, Abl).*

A special section on word order in Latin, one of the greatest problems for students and pupils, has been included to guide the learner through both simple and compound sentences.

For ease of reference, all necessary structures, such as Indirect Statement, Conditional Sentences etc, have been listed under Contents. Each is then explained, for both English and Latin usage, to show the learner how to recognize the structure and translate it into English. Further examples of all structures are provided, for practice.

Handy, practical hints are given in the section on Translation Guidelines, to highlight the more common problems that confront students, and to assist in translation.

The final part of the grammar section lists the many "false friends" or confusable words that often lead students and pupils astray when translating from Latin. This section is of particular importance for examination candidates.

Tables of regular verbs provide information on verb formation and usage, while unique verbs are given in full with their meanings. A special feature of the grammar is a list of the 400 most common verbs, both regular and irregular. Irregular parts of verbs are highlighted and the conjugation number of each listed, so that by referring to the table indicated by this number, any part of the verb may be deduced.

6 CONTENTS

Abbreviations used

abl	ablative	**m, masc**	masculine
acc	accusative	**nt, neut**	neuter
adv	adverb	**nom**	nominative
conj	conjunction	**pl**	plural
dat	dative	**plup**	pluperfect
dep	deponent	**p(p)**	page(s)
f, fem	feminine	**prep**	preposition
gen	genitive	**pron**	pronoun
indic	indicative	**sing**	singular
intrans	intransitive	**voc**	vocative

NOUNS 7

Nouns

A noun is the name of a person, thing or quality.

- In Latin, as in English, the gender of nouns, representing persons or living creatures, is decided by meaning. Nouns denoting male people and animals are masculine

vir	a man
Gaius	Gaius
cervus	stag

- Nouns denoting female people and animals are feminine

femina	a woman
Cornelia	Cornelia
cerva	doe/hind

- However, the gender of things or qualities in Latin is decided by the ending of the noun.

anulus (ring)	*masc*	
sapientia (wisdom)		*fem*
barba (beard)	*fem*	
gaudium (joy)		*nt*

Number

- Nouns may be singular, denoting one, or plural, denoting two or more. This is shown by change of ending

sing	pl
terra (land)	terrae
modus (way)	modi
opus (work)	opera

Cases

- There are six cases in Latin, expressing the relationship of the noun to the other words in the sentence.

Nominative
the subject of the verb: **Caesar** died

Vocative
addressing someone/thing: Welcome, **Alexander**

Accusative
the object of the verb: The cat ate **the mouse**

Genitive
belonging to someone/thing: The home of **my friend**

Dative
the indirect object of the verb: I gave the book **to my son**

Ablative
says by, with or from whom/what: This was agreed **by the Senate**

Declensions

- Latin nouns are divided into five groups or declensions by the ending of their stems. Each declension has six cases, both singular and plural, denoted by different endings. The endings of the genitive singular case help to distinguish the different declensions.

	STEMS	GENITIVE SINGULAR
1st Declension	-a	-ae
2nd Declension	-o or u	-ī
3rd Declension	-i, u, consonant	-is
4th Declension	-ŭ	-ūs
5th Declension	-ē	-ēi

First Declension

- All nouns end in -a in the nominative case and all are feminine except when the noun indicates a male, eg **poēta** (a poet), **agricola** (a farmer), etc.

	SINGULAR		PLURAL	
Nom	fēmina	the woman	fēminae	women
Voc	fēmina	o woman	fēminae	o women
Acc	fēminam	the woman	fēminās	women
Gen	fēminae	of the woman	fēminārum	of the women
Dat	fēminae	to/for the woman	fēminīs	to/for the women
Abl	fēminā	by/with/ from the woman	fēminīs	by/with/ from the women

- Note that **dea** (goddess) and **filia** (daughter), have their dative and ablative plurals **deābus** and **filiābus**

Declensions (contd)

Second Declension

• Nouns of the second declension end in **-us**, or a few in **-er** or **-r**. All are masculine. Those few which end in **-um** are neuter.

	SINGULAR	*slave*	PLURAL	*slaves*
Nom	servus		servī	
Voc	serve		servī	
Acc	servum		servōs	
Gen	servī		servōrum	
Dat	servō		servīs	
Abl	servō		servīs	

	SINGULAR	*boy*	PLURAL	*boys*
Nom	puer		puerī	
Voc	puer		puerī	
Acc	puerum		puerōs	
Gen	puerī		puerōrum	
Dat	puerō		puerīs	
Abl	puerō		puerīs	

	SINGULAR	*war*	PLURAL	*wars*
Nom	bellum		bella	
Voc	bellum		bella	
Acc	bellum		bella	
Gen	bellī		bellōrum	
Dat	bellō		bellīs	
Abl	bellō		bellīs	

• Note that proper names ending in **-ius** have vocative in **-ī**, o Vergilī – o Virgil!!

• **deus** (god), has an alternative vocative **deus**, and plural forms **dī** in nominative and **dīs** in dative and ablative.

Third Declension

This is the largest group of nouns and may be divided into two broad categories, stems ending in a consonant and those ending in -ī. All genders in this declension must be learnt.

Consonant Stems

• ending in **-l**

consul, -is *m* (consul)

	SINGULAR	PLURAL
Nom	cōnsul	cōnsulēs
Voc	cōnsul	cōnsulēs
Acc	cōnsulem	cōnsulēs
Gen	cōnsulis	cōnsulum
Dat	cōnsulī	cōnsulibus
Abl	cōnsule	cōnsulibus

• ending in **-n**

legio, -onis *f* (legion)

	SINGULAR	PLURAL
Nom	legiō	legiōnēs
Voc	legiō	legiōnēs
Acc	legiōnem	legiōnēs
Gen	legiōnis	legiōnum
Dat	legiōnī	legiōnibus
Abl	legiōne	legiōnibus

Continued

Declensions (contd)

flumen, -inis *nt* (river)

	SINGULAR	PLURAL
Nom	flūmen	flūmina
Voc	flūmen	flūmina
Acc	flūmen	flūmina
Gen	flūminis	flūminum
Dat	flūminī	flūminibus
Abl	flūmine	flūminibus

- Note that the genitive plural of these nouns ends in **-um.**

- Stems ending in **-i**

civis, -is *m/f* (citizen)

	SINGULAR	PLURAL
Nom	civis	civēs
Voc	civis	civēs
Acc	civem	civēs
Gen	civis	civium
Dat	civī	civibus
Abl	cive	civibus

- Note that these nouns have genitive plural in **-ium.**

Neuter Nouns

mare, -is *nt* (sea)

	SINGULAR	PLURAL
Nom	mare	maria
Voc	mare	maria
Acc	mare	maria
Gen	maris	marium
Dat	marī	maribus
Abl	marī	maribus

animal, -is *nt* (animal)

	SINGULAR	PLURAL
Nom	animal	animālia
Voc	animal	animālia
Acc	animal	animālia
Gen	animālis	animālium
Dat	animālī	animālibus
Abl	animālī	animālibus

- Note that the ablative singular of these neuter nouns ends in **-ī.**

- Nominative, vocative and accusative singular endings of neuter nouns are identical.

- Nominative, vocative and accusative plural endings of neuter nouns in **all** declensions end in **-ă.**

Continued

14 NOUNS

Declensions (contd)

Monosyllabic Consonant Stems

The following have their genitive plural in -ium:

arx, arcis f (citadel) — arcium (of citadels)
gēns, gentis f (race) — gentium (of races)
mōns, montis m (mountain) — montium (of mountains)
nox, noctis f (night) — noctium (of nights)
pōns, pontis m (bridge) — pontium (of bridges)
urbs, urbis f (city) — urbium (of cities)

Fourth Declension

Nouns in this declension end in -us in the nominative singular and are mainly masculine. A few end in -u and are neuter.

exercitus, -ūs m (army)

	SINGULAR	PLURAL
Nom	exercitus	exercitūs
Voc	exercitus	exercitūs
Acc	exercitum	exercitūs
Gen	exercitūs	exercituum
Dat	exercituī	exercitibus
Abl	exercitū	exercitibus

genū, -ūs nt (knee)

	SINGULAR	PLURAL
Nom	genū	genua
Voc	genū	genua
Acc	genū	genua
Gen	genūs	genuum
Dat	genū	genibus
Abl	genū	genibus

- Note that a few common nouns are feminine, eg domus (house), manus (hand), Īdus (Ides or 15th of the month).

- The form domī (at home) is an old form called locative. domō (from home) abl sing, domōs acc pl and domōrum gen pl are also used besides the fourth declension forms of domus (house).

Fifth Declension

There are only a few nouns in this declension. All end in -ēs in the nominative case. Most are feminine, but diēs (day) and merīdiēs (midday) are masculine.

diēs, -diēī m (day)

	SINGULAR	PLURAL
Nom	diēs	diēs
Voc	diēs	diēs
Acc	diem	diēs
Gen	diēī	diērum
Dat	diēī	diēbus
Abl	diē	diēbus

Cases

Use Of Cases

Nominative Case

The nominative case is used where:

- the noun is the **subject** of the verb (→**1**)
- the noun is a **complement** (→**2**)
- the noun is in **apposition** to the subject (→**3**)

Accusative Case

The accusative case is used:

- for the **direct object** of the verb (→**4**)
- with verbs of teaching and asking which take accusative of person and thing (→**5**)
- Verbs of naming, making *etc* take two accusatives for the same person or thing (→**6**)
- in exclamations (→**7**)
- to show extent of space (→**8**)
- to show extent of time (→**9**)
- to show motion to a place or country usually with a preposition (→**10**)
- to show motion towards, without a preposition, before names of towns and small islands (→**11**)

  Note also: **domum** (home), **rus** (to the country), **foras** (outside)

- for an object with similar meaning to the verb (*cognate*) (→**12**)

Continued

---

1 **Sextus** ridet
Sextus laughs

2 Romulus **rex** factus est
Romulus was made king

3 Marcus Annius, **eques Romanus**, hoc dicit
Marcus Annius, a Roman businessman, says this

4 canis **baculum** petit
the dog fetches the stick

5 **puerum litteras** docebo
I shall teach the boy literature

6 **Ancum Martium regem** populus creavit
The people made Ancus Martius king

7 o **tempora**, o **mores**
what times, what conduct!

8 murus decem **pedes** altus est
the wall is 10 foot high

9 Troia decem **annos** obsessa est
Troy was under siege for 10 years

10 **ad Hispaniam** effugerunt
they escaped to Spain

11 **Athenas** legati missi sunt
Ambassadors were sent to Athens

12 **vitam** bonam **vixit**
he lived a good life

Cases (contd)

Dative Case

- Indirect object (*ie* to or for whom an action is performed) (→**1**)

- used with verbs of obeying (**parēre**), resisting (**resistere**), pleasing (**placēre**), ordering (**imperāre**) *etc* (→**2**)

- verb compounds (beginning **ad-**, **ob-**, **prae-**, **sub-**) denoting helping or hindering take dative (→**3**)

  adesse – come to help
  subvenire – help

- indicates possession (→**4**)

- is used with adjectives meaning "like" (**similis**), "fit" (**aptus**), "near" (**proximus**) (→**5**)

- indicates a purpose (known as *predicative dative*) (→**6**)

- shows the agent of gerund/gerundive (→**7**)

Examples

1 pecuniam **domino** dedit
he gave the money to his master

2 maria terraeque **Deo** parent
land and sea obey God

3 Pompeius **hostibus** obstitit
Pompey opposed the enemy

4 Poppaea amica est **Marciae**
Poppaea is Marcia's friend

5 feles **tigri similis** est
the cat is like a tiger

6 nemo mihi **auxilio** est
there is no-one to help me

7 omnia erant agenda **nobis**
everything had to be done by us

Continued

Cases (contd)

Genitive Case

- Indicates possession (→**1**)

- Denotes part of a whole (→**2**)

- Indicates a quality, always with an adjective (→**3**)

- Is used as a predicate, where a person represents a quality (→**4**)

- Is used with superlatives (→**5**)

- Precedes **causa** and **gratia** (for the sake of) (→**6**)

- Is used after certain adjectives (→**7**)

sciens	(knowing)
inscius	(ignorant of)
cupidus	(desiring)
particeps	(sharing) *etc*

- Is used with verbs of remembering (**memini**) and forgetting (**obliviscor**) (→**8**)

- Follows verbs of accusing, convicting *etc* (→**9**)

- Represents value or worth (→**10**)

Continued

Examples

1 domus **regis**
the king's house

uxor **Augusti**
the wife of Augustus

2 quid **novi**
what news?

plus **cibi**
more food

3 magnae **auctoritatis** es
your reputation is great

4 **stulti est** hoc facere
it is the mark of a fool to do this

5 Indus est **omnium fluminum maximum**
the Indus is the greatest of all rivers

6 tu me **amoris causa** servavisti
you saved me for love's sake

7 Verres, **cupidus pecuniae,** ex hereditate praedatus est
Verres, greedy for money, robbed the estate

8 **mortis** memento
remember death

9 ante **actarum rerum** Antonius accusatus est
Antony was accused of previous offences

10 frumentum **minimi** vendidit
he sold corn at the lowest price

flocci non facio
I don't care at all

Cases (contd)

Ablative Case

- Indicates place, usually with the preposition "in" (→**1**)
  Note, however: **totā Asiā** – throughout Asia
  terrā marīque – by land and sea

- Indicates motion from, or down from a place, usually with prepositions **ex**, **de**, **a(b)** (→**2**)

- Note prepositions are omitted before names of towns, small islands and **domo** (from home), **rure** (from the country), **foris** (from outside) (→**3**)

- Represents time when or within which something happens (→**4**)

- Indicates origin, sometimes with prepositions **in**, **ex**, **a(b)** (→**5**)

- Is used to show material from which something is made (→**6**)

- Indicates manner (how something is done), usually with **cum** when there is no adjective, and without **cum** when there is an adjective (→**7**)

- Is used with verbs of depriving, filling, needing and with **opus est** (→**8**)

- Is used with deponent verbs **utor** (use), **abutor** (abuse), **fungor** (accomplish), **potior** (gain possession of) (→**9**)

- States cause (→**10**)

- To form **ablative absolute**, where a noun in the ablative is combined with a participle or another noun or adjective in the same case, to form an idea independent of the rest of the sentence. This is equivalent to an adverbial clause (→**11**)

1 Milo **in urbe** mansit
Milo remained in the city

2 **de equo** cecidit
He fell down from his horse

praedam **ex urbe ornatissima** sustulit
He stole booty from the rich city

3 **domo** cucurrerunt servi
The slaves ran from the house

4 **hac nocte** Agricola obiit
Agricola died on this night

decem annis Lacedaimonii non haec confecerunt
The Spartans did not complete this task within 10 years

5 Romulus et Remus, **Marte nati**
Romulus and Remus, sons of Mars

flumina **in Caucaso monte** orta
Rivers rising in the Caucasus mountains

6 statua **ex auro** facta est
The statue was made of gold

7 mulieres **cum virtute** vixerunt
The women lived virtuously

summa celeritate Poeni regressi sunt
The Carthaginians retreated at top speed

8 aliquem **vita** privare
to deprive someone of life

opus est mihi **divitiis**
I need wealth

9 **vi et armis** usus est
He used force of arms

10 leo **fame** decessit
The lion died of hunger

11 **exigua parte aestatis reliqua**, Caesar in Britanniam proficisci contendit
Although only a little of the summer remained, Caesar hurried to set out for Britain

Adjectives

An adjective adds a quality to the noun. It usually follows the noun but sometimes comes before it for emphasis. The adjective agrees with its noun in number, case and gender.

Gender
vir bonus (*masc*)   a good man
fēmina pulchra (*fem*)   a beautiful woman
bellum longum (*neut*)   a long war

Number
virī bonī (*pl*)   good men
fēminae pulchrae (*pl*)   beautiful women
bella longa (*pl*)   long wars

Case
virō bonō (*dat sing*)   for a good man
fēminās pulchrās (*acc pl*)   beautiful women
bellī longī (*gen sing*)   of a long war

- Adjectives are declined like nouns and usually arranged in two groups:
  1 those with endings of the first and second declensions
  2 those with endings of the third declension

First and Second Declensions

bonus, bona, bonum (good)

	Masc	Fem	Neut
SINGULAR			
Nom	bonus	bona	bonum
Voc	bone	bona	bonum
Acc	bonum	bonam	bonum
Gen	bonī	bonae	bonī
Dat	bonō	bonae	bonō
Abl	bonō	bonā	bonō
PLURAL			
Nom	bonī	bonae	bona
Voc	bonī	bonae	bona
Acc	bonōs	bonās	bona
Gen	bonōrum	bonārum	bonōrum
Dat	bonīs	bonīs	bonīs
Abl	bonīs	bonīs	bonīs

Declensions (contd)

miser, misera, miserum (unhappy)

	Masc	Fem *SINGULAR*	Neut
Nom	miser	misera	miserum
Voc	miser	misera	miserum
Acc	miserum	miseram	miserum
Gen	miserī	miserae	miserī
Dat	miserō	miserae	miserō
Abl	miserō	miserā	miserō

	Masc	Fem *PLURAL*	Neut
Nom	miserī	miserae	misera
Voc	miserī	miserae	misera
Acc	miserōs	miserās	misera
Gen	miserōrum	miserārum	miserōrum
Dat	miserīs	miserīs	miserīs
Abl	miserīs	miserīs	miserīs

- **liber** (free) and **tener** (tender) are declined like **miser**

pulcher, pulchra, pulchrum (beautiful)

	Masc	Fem *SINGULAR*	Neut
Nom	pulcher	pulchra	pulchrum
Voc	pulcher	pulchra	pulchrum
Acc	pulchrum	pulchram	pulchrum
Gen	pulchrī	pulchrae	pulchrī
Dat	pulchrō	pulchrae	pulchrō
Abl	pulchrō	pulchrā	pulchrō

	Masc	Fem *PLURAL*	Neut
Nom	pulchrī	pulchrae	pulchra
Voc	pulchrī	pulchrae	pulchra
Acc	pulchrōs	pulchrās	pulchra
Gen	pulchrōrum	pulchrārum	pulchrōrum
Dat	pulchrīs	pulchrīs	pulchrīs
Abl	pulchrīs	pulchrīs	pulchrīs

- **aeger** (sick), **crēber** (frequent), **integer** (whole), **niger** (black), **piger** (slow) and **sacer** (sacred) are declined like **pulcher**

Declensions (contd)

● The following group of adjectives form their genitive singular in **-ius** and dative singular in **-i**:

alius, -a, -ud	another
alter, altera, alterum	one of two
neuter, neutra, neutrum	neither
nūllus, -a, -um	none
sōlus, -a, -um	alone
tōtus, -a, -um	whole
ūllus, -a, -um	any
ūnus, -a, -um	one
uter, utra, utrum	which of two?

solus (alone)

SINGULAR

	Masc	Fem	Neut
Nom	solus	sola	solum
Acc	solum	solam	solum
Gen	solius	solius	solius
Dat	soli	soli	soli
Abl	solo	sola	solo

PLURAL

	Masc	Fem	Neut
Nom	soli	solae	sola
Acc	solos	solas	sola
Gen	solorum	solarum	solorum
Dat	solis	solis	solis
Abl	solis	solis	solis

Third Declension

Adjectives of the third declension, like nouns, may be divided into two broad types, those with consonant stems and those with vowel stems in **-i**.

Consonant Stems

These have **one** ending in nominative singular.

prūdēns (wise)

SINGULAR

	Masc	Fem	Neut
Nom	prūdēns	prūdēns	prūdēns
Voc	prūdēns	prūdēns	prūdēns
Acc	prūdentem	prūdentem	prūdēns
Gen	prūdentis	prūdentis	prūdentis
Dat	prūdentī	prūdentī	prūdentī
Abl	prūdentī	prūdentī	prūdentī

PLURAL

	Masc	Fem	Neut
Nom	prūdentēs	prūdentēs	prūdentia
Voc	prūdentēs	prūdentēs	prūdentia
Acc	prūdentēs	prūdentēs	prūdentia
Gen	prūdentium	prūdentium	prūdentium
Dat	prūdentibus	prūdentibus	prūdentibus
Abl	prūdentibus	prūdentibus	prūdentibus

● **dīligēns** (careful), **innocēns** (innocent), **potēns** (powerful), **frequēns** (frequent), **ingēns** (huge) are declined like **prūdēns**

Declensions (contd)

amāns (loving)

SINGULAR

	Masc	Fem	Neut
Nom	amāns	amāns	amāns
Voc	amāns	amāns	amāns
Acc	amantem	amantem	amāns
Gen	amantis	amantis	amantis
Dat	amantī	amantī	amantī
Abl	amante	amante	amante

PLURAL

	Masc	Fem	Neut
Nom	amantēs	amantēs	amantia
Voc	amantēs	amantēs	amantia
Acc	amantēs	amantēs	amantia
Gen	amantium	amantium	amantium
Dat	amantibus	amantibus	amantibus
Abl	amantibus	amantibus	amantibus

- All Present participles are declined like **amans,** although Present participles of the other conjugations end in **-ēns**

- When participles are used as adjectives **-ī** is used instead of **-e** in ablative singular case

fēlix (lucky)

SINGULAR

	Masc	Fem	Neut
Nom	fēlix	fēlix	felix
Voc	fēlix	fēlix	felix
Acc	fēlicem	fēlicem	felix
Gen	fēlicis	fēlicis	fēlicis
Dat	fēlicī	fēlicī	fēlicī
Abl	fēlicī	fēlicī	fēlicī

PLURAL

	Masc	Fem	Neut
Nom	fēlicēs	fēlicēs	fēlicia
Voc	fēlicēs	fēlicēs	fēlicia
Acc	fēlicēs	fēlicēs	fēlicia
Gen	fēlicium	fēlicium	fēlicium
Dat	fēlicibus	fēlicibus	fēlicibus
Abl	fēlicibus	fēlicibus	fēlicibus

audāx (bold) and **ferōx** (fierce) are declined like **fēlix**

- Note that all the above adjectives have the same case endings in all genders except for the neuter accusative singular and the neuter nominative, vocative and accusative plural.

Declensions (contd)

Vowel Stems

The following adjectives have **two** endings in nominative singular, one for masculine and feminine, one for neuter.

fortis, forte (brave)

SINGULAR

	Masc	Fem	Neut
Nom	fortis	fortis	forte
Voc	fortis	fortis	forte
Acc	fortem	fortem	forte
Gen	fortis	fortis	fortis
Dat	fortī	fortī	fortī
Abl	fortī	fortī	fortī

PLURAL

	Masc	Fem	Neut
Nom	fortēs	fortēs	fortia
Voc	fortēs	fortēs	fortia
Acc	fortēs	fortēs	fortia
Gen	fortium	fortium	fortium
Dat	fortibus	fortibus	fortibus
Abl	fortibus	fortibus	fortibus

● **brevis** (short), **facilis** (easy), **gravis** (heavy), **levis** (light), **omnis** (all), **tristis** (sad), **turpis** (disgraceful), **talis** (of such a kind), and **qualis** (of which kind), are declined like **fortis**.

The following adjectives have **three** endings in nominative singular.

ācer, ācris, ācre (sharp)

SINGULAR

	Masc	Fem	Neut
Nom	ācer	ācris	ācre
Voc	ācer	ācris	ācre
Acc	ācrem	ācrem	ācre
Gen	ācris	ācris	ācris
Dat	ācrī	ācrī	ācrī
Abl	ācrī	ācrī	ācrī

PLURAL

	Masc	Fem	Neut
Nom	ācrēs	ācrēs	ācria
Voc	ācrēs	ācrēs	ācria
Acc	ācrēs	ācrēs	ācria
Gen	ācrium	ācrium	ācrium
Dat	ācribus	ācribus	ācribus
Abl	ācribus	ācribus	ācribus

● **alacer** (lively), **equester** (of cavalry), and **volucer** (winged), are declined like **ācer**, and **celer** (swift), declines similarly, but keeps -e- throughout (*eg* **celer, celeris, celere**)

Use of Adjectives

There are two ways of using adjectives.

- They can be used **attributively**, where the adjective in English comes before the noun: the new car

- An attributive adjective in Latin usually follows its noun but may sometimes come before it with a change of meaning (→**1**)

- They can be used **predicatively**, where the adjective comes after the verb: the car is new (→**2**)

- If an adjective describes two nouns, it agrees in gender with the nearer (→**3**)

- When an adjective describes two subjects of different sex it is often masculine plural (→**4**)

- When an adjective describes two subjects representing things without life it is often neuter plural (→**5**)

1 res **parvae**
     small things

   in parvis rebus
     in unimportant matters

   civis **Romanus** sum
     I am a Roman citizen

2 Servi erant **fideles**
     The slaves were faithful

3 Antonius, vir consilii **magni** et prudentiae
     Antony, a man of great wisdom and prudence

4 frater et soror sunt **timidi**
     Brother and sister are frightened

5 Calor et ventus per artus **praesentia** erant
     Warmth and wind were present in the limbs

Comparative and Superlative

Adjectives also have comparative forms *eg* I am **luckier** than you, and superlative forms *eg* the **noblest** Roman of them all.

Formation

● The comparative is formed by adding **-ior** (*masc and fem*) and **-ius** (*neut*) to the consonant stem of the adjective and the superlative by adding **-issimus, -a, -um** to the stem:

POSITIVE	**altus**	high
	audāx	bold
	brevis	short
	prūdēns	wise
COMPARATIVE	**altior**	higher
	audācior	bolder
	brevior	shorter
	prūdentior	wiser
SUPERLATIVE	**altissimus**	highest
	audācissimus	boldest
	brevissimus	shortest
	prūdentissimus	wisest

Continued

● If the adjective ends in **-er** (*in masc nom sing*) add **-rimus** to form the superlative.

POSITIVE	**ācer**	sharp
	celer	swift
	miser	unhappy
	pulcher	beautiful
COMPARATIVE	**ācrior**	sharper
	celerior	swifter
	miserior	more unhappy
	pulchrior	more beautiful
SUPERLATIVE	**ācerrimus**	sharpest
	celerrimus	swiftest
	miserrimus	most unhappy
	pulcherrimus	most beautiful

● Six adjectives ending in **-ilis** (*in masc nom sing*) add **-limus** to the stem to form the superlative.

POSITIVE	**facilis**	easy
	difficilis	difficult
	similis	like
	dissimilis	unlike
	gracilis	slight
	humilis	low
COMPARATIVE	**facilior**	easier
	difficilior	more difficult
	similior	more like
	dissimilior	more unlike
	gracilior	more slight
	humilior	lower
SUPERLATIVE	**facillimus**	easiest
	difficillimus	most difficult
	simillimus	most like
	dissimillimus	most unlike
	gracillimus	most slight
	humillimus	lowest

Comparative and Superlative (contd)

Irregular comparison

● Some adjectives have irregular comparative and superlative forms:

POSITIVE	
bonus	good
malus	bad
parvus	small
magnus	big
multus	much
multi	many

COMPARATIVE	
melior	better
pēior	worse
minor	smaller
māior	bigger
plūs	more
plūrēs	more

SUPERLATIVE	
optimus	best
pessimus	worst
minimus	smallest, least
māximus	biggest
plūrimus	most
plūrimī	most

● Note that all adjectives ending in **-us** preceded by a vowel (except those ending in **-quus**) form comparative and superlative thus:

idōneus	suitable
magis idōneus	more suitable
māximē idōneus	most suitable

but

antiquus	old
antiquior	older
antiquissimus	oldest

● Note the following comparatives and superlatives where there is no positive form:

exterior	outer	**extrēmus** furthest
inferior	lower	**infimus** or **īmus** lowest
superior	upper, higher	**suprēmus** or **summus** highest
posterior	later	**postrēmus** latest

Continued

Comparative and Superlative (contd)

Declension of Comparative and Superlative

- All comparatives decline like adjectives of the third declension.

	SINGULAR		*PLURAL*	
	Masc/Fem	Neut	Masc/Fem	Neut
Nom	altior	altius	altiōrēs	altiōra
Voc	altior	altius	altiōrēs	altiōra
Acc	altiōrem	altius	altiōrēs	altiōra
Gen	altiōris	altiōris	altiōrum	altiōrum
Dat	altiōrī	altiōrī	altiōribus	altiōribus
Abl	altiōre	altiōre	altiōribus	altiōribus

- Note ablative singular in -e.
- All superlatives decline like adjectives of first and second declensions (*eg* bonus, bona, bonum).

Use

- The comparative is often followed by **quam** (than), or the thing or person compared is given in the ablative case (→**1**)

- Sometimes the comparative can be translated by "rather" or "quite" (→**2**)

- The comparative is often strengthened by **"multo"** (→**3**)

- Sometimes the superlative can be translated by "very", or even as a positive adjective in English (→**4**)

- **"quam"** with the superlative means "as ... as possible" (→**5**)

1 Marcus est **altior quam soror**
Marcus est **altior sorore**
Marcus is taller than his sister

2 Gallus erat **fortior**
the Gaul was rather brave

3 **multo carior**
much dearer

4 **vir sapientissimus**
a very wise man
integerrima vita
of virtuous life

5 **quam paucissimi**
as few people as possible

Adverbs

An adverb modifies a verb, adjective, another adverb or a noun. It answers questions such as "how?", "when?", "why?", "where?", "to what extent?".

Formation

- Some are formed from nouns *eg* **furtim** (stealthily) or pronouns **aliās** (at other times) but most are formed from adjectives.

- Accusative singular neuter of adjectives of extent:

multum	much	**nimium**	too much
paulum	a little	**aliquantum**	somewhat
prīmum	first	**cēterum**	for the rest

- Adjectives in **-us** and **-er** change to **-e**:

altē	highly	**miserē**	wretchedly

- Ablative forms of these adjectives in **-o** or **-a**:

certē *or* **certō**	certainly	**vērē**	in truth
dextrā	on the right	**vērō**	certainly

- Adjectives of the third declension add **-ter**/**-iter**:

audacter	boldly	**celeriter**	quickly
prudenter	wisely		

Position

- An adverb comes before the verb, adjective, adverb or noun that it modifies (→**1**)

- However adverbs of time often come at the beginning of the sentence (→**2**)

Continued

1 **vehementer** errabas, Verres
   you were making a big mistake, Verres

   nimium libera respublica
   too free a state

   bis consul
   twice consul

2 **cras mane** putat se venturum esse
   He thinks he will come tomorrow morning

   saepe hoc mecum cogitavi
   I often thought this over by myself

Common Adverbs

● **Manner** – "how?"

ita	thus	**crudeliter**	cruelly
sīc	thus	**iustē**	justly
aliter	otherwise	**liberē**	freely
fortē	by chance	**repentē**	suddenly
magnoperē	greatly		

● **Time** – "when?"

iam, nunc	now	**(n)umquam**	(n)ever
simul	at the same time	**iterum**	again
anteā	before	**saepe**	often
posteā	afterwards	**hodiē**	today
cōtīdiē	every day	**herī**	yesterday
diū	for a long time	**crās**	tomorrow
mox	soon	**postrīdiē**	next day
interim or -ea	meanwhile	**statim**	immediately
tum	then		

● **Place** – "where?"

ubi?	where?	**unde?**	where from
ibi	there	**inde**	from there
hīc	here	**hinc**	from here
usquam	any-where	**nusquam**	nowhere

quō?	where to?		
eō	to there		
hūc	to here		

Others

etiam	also	**fortasse**	perhaps
quoque	also	**consultō**	on purpose
quidem	indeed	**scīlicet**	no doubt

Comparison of Adverbs

The comparative form of the adverb is the nominative singular neuter of the comparative adjective. The superlative of the adverb is formed by changing -us of the superlative adjective to -e.

POSITIVE	COMPARATIVE	SUPERLATIVE
altē highly	**altius** more highly	**altissimē** most highly
audācter boldly	**audācius** more boldly	**audācissimē** most boldly
bene well	**melius** better	**optimē** best
breviter briefly	**brevius** more briefly	**brevissimē** most briefly
diū for a long time	**diūtius** longer	**diūtissimē** longest
facile easily	**facilius** more easily	**facillimē** most easily
magnoperē greatly	**magis** more	**maximē** most
male badly	**peius** worse	**pessimē** worst
miserē wretchedly	**miserius** more wretchedly	**miserrimē** most wretchedly
multum much	**plūs** more	**plūrimum** most
paulum a little	**minus** less	**minimē** least
prope near	**propius** nearer	**proximē** nearest
saepe often	**saepius** more often	**saepissimē** most often

- Notes on use of the comparative adjective may be applied also to the comparative adverb (*see p 40*).

Examples

rem totam brevius cognōscite
Find out about the whole matter more briefly

magis cōnsiliō quam virtūte vīcit
He won more because of his strategy than his courage

legiōnēs diūtius sine cōnsule fuērunt
The legions were too long without a consul

multō plus
much more

optimē
very well

mihi placēbat Pompōnius maximē vel minimē
I liked Pompōnius the most or disliked him the least

optimus quisque id optimē facit
All the best people do it best

quam celerrimē as quickly as possible

Pronouns

Personal Pronouns

The pronouns **ego** (I), **nōs** (we), **tū** (you, *sing*), **vōs** (you, *pl*) decline as follows:

SINGULAR

Nom	**ego**	I
Acc	**mē**	me
Gen	**mei**	of me
Dat	**mihi**	to/for me
Abl	**mē**	by/with/ from me

	tū	you
	tē	you
	tui	of you
	tibi	to/for you
	tē	by/with/from you

PLURAL

Nom	**nōs**	we
Acc	**nōs**	us
Gen	**nostrum**	of us
Dat	**nōbis**	to/for us
Abl	**nōbis**	by/with/ from us

	vōs	you
	vōs	you
	vestrum	of you
	vobis	to/for you
	vōbis	by/with/from you

Possessive

meus, -a, -um	my	**tuus, -a, -um** your
noster, -ra, -rum	our	**vester, -ra, -rum** your

- **nostri** and **vestri** are alternative forms of genitive plural.

- Possessives are sometimes used instead of the genitive of personal pronouns:

odium tuum
hatred of you

- For the third person pronoun, he/she/it, Latin uses **is, ea, id**:

SINGULAR

	Masc		Fem		Neut	
Nom	**is**	he	**ea**	she	**id**	it
Acc	**eum**	him	**eam**	her	**id**	it
Gen	**ēius**	of him	**ēius**	of her	**ēius**	of it
Dat	**eī**	to him	**eī**	to her	**eī**	to it
Abl	**eō**	by him	**eā**	by her	**eō**	by it

PLURAL

Nom	**eī**	they	**eae**	they	**ea**	they
Acc	**eōs**	them	**eās**	them	**ea**	them
Gen	**eōrum**	of them	**eārum**	of them	**eōrum**	of them
Dat	**eīs**	to them	**eīs**	to them	**eīs**	to them
Abl	**eīs**	by them	**eīs**	by them	**eīs**	by them

Use

- Pronouns as subjects (I, you) are not usually used in Latin. The person of the verb is indicated by the ending (*eg* **misimus** – we sent). **ego**, **nos** *etc* are used only for emphasis:

ego vulgus odi; tū amas
I hate crowds, you love them

- The genitive forms **nostrum** and **vestrum** are used partitively:

multi nostrum
many of us
pauci vestrum
a few of you

Reflexive Pronouns

Acc	**mē**	myself	
Gen	**meī**		
Dat	**mihi**		
Abl	**mē**		
Acc	**tē**		yourself
Gen	**tuī**		
Dat	**tibi**		
Abl	**tē**		
Acc	**nōs**	ourselves	
Gen	**nostrum**		
Dat	**nōbis**		
Abl	**nōbis**		
Acc	**vōs**	yourselves	
Gen	**vestrum**		
Dat	**vōbis**		
Abl	**vōbis**		

● These are identical in form to personal pronouns.

Acc	**sē**	himself/herself/itself/themselves
Gen	**suī**	
Dat	**sibi**	
Abl	**sē**	

● Reflexive pronouns are used to refer to the subject of the sentence:

quisque **se** amat
everybody loves themselves

me lavo
I wash myself

Determinative Pronouns

● **is** – he/that, **ea** – she, **id** – it: as above
● **idem** (the same)

	SINGULAR		
	Masc	Fem	Neut
Nom	**īdem**	**eadem**	**idem**
Acc	**eundem**	**eandem**	**idem**
Gen	**ēiusdem**	**eiusdem**	**eiusdem**
Dat	**eīdem**	**eīdem**	**eīdem**
Abl	**eōdem**	**eādem**	**eōdem**

	PLURAL		
Nom	**eīdem**	**eaedem**	**eadem**
Acc	**eōsdem**	**eāsdem**	**eadem**
Gen	**eōrundem**	**eārundem**	**eōrundem**
Dat	**eīsdem**	**eīsdem**	**eīsdem**
Abl	**eīsdem**	**eīsdem**	**eīsdem**

● **ipse** (himself/herself/itself/themselves)

	SINGULAR		
	Masc	Fem	Neut
Nom	**ipse**	**ipsa**	**ipsum**
Acc	**ipsum**	**ipsam**	**ipsum**
Gen	**ipsīus**	**ipsīus**	**ipsīus**
Dat	**ipsī**	**ipsī**	**ipsī**
Abl	**ipsō**	**ipsā**	**ipsō**

	PLURAL		
Nom	**ipsī**	**ipsae**	**ipsa**
Acc	**ipsōs**	**ipsās**	**ipsa**
Gen	**ipsōrum**	**ipsārum**	**ipsōrum**
Dat	**ipsīs**	**ipsīs**	**ipsīs**
Abl	**ipsīs**	**ipsīs**	**ipsīs**

Demonstrative Pronouns

- **hic** (this/these)

	Masc	*SINGULAR* Fem	Neut
Nom	hic	haec	hōc
Acc	hunc	hanc	hōc
Gen	hūius	hūius	hūius
Dat	huic	huic	huic
Abl	hōc	hāc	hōc

		PLURAL	
Nom	hī	hae	haec
Acc	hōs	hās	haec
Gen	hōrum	hārum	hōrum
Dat	hīs	hīs	hīs
Abl	hīs	hīs	hīs

- **ille** (that/those)

	Masc	*SINGULAR* Fem	Neut
Nom	ille	illa	illud
Acc	illum	illam	illud
Gen	illīus	illīus	illīus
Dat	illī	illī	illī
Abl	illō	illā	illō

		PLURAL	
Nom	illī	illae	illa
Acc	illōs	illās	illa
Gen	illōrum	illārum	illōrum
Dat	illīs	illīs	illīs
Abl	illīs	illīs	illīs

- Note that **īdem**, **hīc**, **ille** and all their parts may be adjectives as well as pronouns

---

1 **eadem** femina
the same woman

hīc puer
this boy

tu autem **eadem** ages?
Are you going to do the same things?

2 patria est cārior quam **nos ipsi**
Our native land is dearer than ourselves

3 **hac** remota, quomodo **illum** aestimemus?
When she is removed, how are we to judge him?

4 **nos** oportet opus conficere
We must complete the task

5 accusatores dicunt **te ipsam** testem **eius** criminis esse
The prosecutors claim that you yourself are the witness of that crime

6 sed **haec** omitto; ad **illa** quae **me** magis moverunt respondeo
But I pass over these matters; I reply to those which have affected me more deeply

7 pax **vobiscum**
Peace be with you!

8 puella intravit; **ea mihi** litteras dedit
The girl came in; she gave me a letter

Relative Pronouns

SINGULAR

	Masc		Fem	
Nom	qui	who	quae	who
Acc	quem	whom	quam	whom
Gen	cūius	whose	cūius	whose
Dat	cui	to whom	cui	to whom
Abl	quō	by whom	quā	by whom

	Neut	
Nom	quod	which/that
Acc	quod	which/that
Gen	cūius	of which
Dat	cui	to which
Abl	quō	by which

PLURAL

	Masc		Fem	
Nom	qui	who	quae	who
Acc	quōs	whom	quās	whom
Gen	quōrum	whose	quārum	whose
Dat	quibus	to whom	quibus	to whom
Abl	quibus	by whom	quibus	by whom

	Neut	
Nom	quae	which
Acc	quae	which
Gen	quōrum	of which
Dat	quibus	to which
Abl	quibus	by which

- A relative pronoun attaches a subordinate clause to a word preceding it (its antecedent). It agrees with this word in number and gender but takes its case from its own clause (→**1**)

- **quidam, quaedam, quoddam** (a certain, somebody) **quicumque, quaecumque, quodcumque** (whoever/ whatever), decline in the same way as the relative above (→**2**)

Examples

1 **iuvenis cuius librum Sextus legit laetus erat**
The young man, whose book Sextus read, was happy

Fortunata, quae erat uxor Trimalchionis, saltare coeperat
Fortunata, who was Trimalchio's wife, had begun to dance

tum duo crotalia protulit quae Fortunatae consideranda dedit
Then she brought out a pair of earrings which she gave to Fortunata to look at

2 **quidam ex legatis**
a certain ambassador

tu, quicumque es
you, whoever you are

Interrogative Pronouns

SINGULAR

	Masc	Fem	Neut	
Nom	quis	quis/quae	who?	
Acc	quem	quam	whom?	
Gen	cūius	cūius	whose?	
Dat	cui		to whom?	
Abl	quō	quā	by whom?	

	Neut			
Nom	quid		what?	
Acc	quid	Dat	cui	to what?
Gen	cūius	Abl	quō	by what?

PLURAL

	Masc	Fem	Neut	
Nom	quī	quae	who?	
Acc	quōs	quās	whom?	
Gen	quōrum	quārum	whose?	
Dat	quibus	quibus	to whom?	
Abl	quibus	quibus	by whom?	

	Neut			
Nom	quae		what?	
Acc	quae	Dat	quibus	to what?
Gen	quōrum	Abl	quibus	by what?

- The interrogative pronoun is used to ask questions and usually is the first word in the sentence (→1)

- quisquis, quisquid, quidquid (whoever, whatever)
  quisque, quisque, quidque (each)
  quisquam, quisquam, quicquam (anyone, anything)
  aliquis, aliquis, aliquid (someone, something)
  These pronouns decline in the same way as **quis** above
  (→2)

Examples

1 quae fuit enim causa quamobrem isti mulieri
venenum dare vellet Caelius?
What was the reason why Caelius wanted to give that
woman poison?

quid agam, iudices?
What am I to do, men of the jury?

quos ad cenam invitavisti?
Whom did you invite for dinner?

quorum agros Galli incenderunt?
Whose fields did the Gauls burn?

2 quisque is est
whoever he is

si quemquam video
if I see anyone

liber alicuius
someone's book

Prepositions

A preposition expresses the relationship of one word to another. Each Latin preposition governs a noun or pronoun in the accusative or ablative case. Some prepositions govern both cases. Some may also be used as adverbs *eg* **prope** (near).

Position

- Prepositions generally come before the noun, or an adjective or equivalent qualifying the noun *eg*

  ad villam
  to the house

  ad Ciceronis villam
  to Cicero's house

- **cum** follows a personal pronoun *eg*

  mēcum
  with me

Prepositions governing the Accusative

On the following pages you will find some of the most frequent uses of prepositions in Latin. In the list below, the broad meaning is given on the left, with examples of usage following. Prepositions are given in alphabetical order.

ad

to/towards (*a place or person*)	**oculos ad caelum sustulit** he raised his eyes to heaven
at, in the direction of, with regard to	**ad Capuam profectus sum** I set out in the direction of Capua
	ad portas at the gates
	ad duo milia occisi about 2000 were killed
	nil ad me attinet it means nothing to me

adversum (-us)

opposite	**sedens adversus te** sitting opposite you
towards	**adversus Italiam** towards (*ie* facing) Italy
against	**adversum flumen** against the stream

Continued

Prepositions governing the Accusative (contd)

ante

before (*of place and time*), used with ordinal number in dates	**ante meridiem** before midday
	ante limen before the doorway
	ante diem quintum Kalendas Ianuarias 28th December (*ie* 5th before Kalends of January)

apud

at/near (*usually with persons*)	**Crassus apud eum sedet** Crassus is sitting near him
in the writing of	**apud Platonem** in Plato's writings
before (*authorities*)	**apud pontifices** before the high priests

circum (circa)

around, about (*of place, people*)	**circum forum** around the forum
	circum Hectorem around Hector
	circa montes around the mountains
	circa decem milia Gallorum about ten thousand Gauls

contra

against	**contra hostes** against the enemy
	contra ventos against the wind
opposite	**contra Britanniam** facing Britain

extra

outside of	**extra muros** outside the walls
beyond (*of place and time*)	**extra iocum** beyond a joke

inter

between	**inter oppositos exercitus** between the opposing armies
	amans inter se loving each other
among	**inter saucios** among the wounded
	inter manus within reach
during	**inter hos annos** during these years

Continued

Prepositions governing the Accusative (contd)

intra

within (*of place and time*)

intra parietes
within the walls

intra quattuor annos
within four years

ob

on account of

quam ob rem
therefore

ob stultitiam
on account of your foolishness

per

through

per noctem
through the night

by means of

per vos
by means of you

per aetatem periit
he died of old age

per deos iuro
I swear by the gods

---

post

after (*of time and place*)

post urbem conditam
after the foundation of the city

post tergum
behind your back

praeter

beyond

praeter naturam
beyond nature

besides

praeter se tres alios adduxit
he brought three others besides himself

except for

praeter paucos
except for a few

prope

near

prope me habitavit
he lived near me

propter

on account of

propter metum mortis
on account of fear of death

Continued

64 PREPOSITIONS

Prepositions governing the Accusative (contd)

secundum

along (of place)	**secundum flumen** along the river
immediately after (time)	**secundum quietem** on waking from sleep
according to	**secundum naturam** according to nature

trans

across	**vexillum trans vallum traicere** to take the standard across the rampart **trans Rhenum** across the Rhine

ultra

beyond (of time, degree etc)	**ultra vires** beyond one's power

PREPOSITIONS 65

Prepositions governing the Ablative

Those which are spatial represent the idea of rest in a place or motion from a place.

a(b)

from (of place, people, direction, time)	**ab arce hostes deiecti sunt** the enemy were driven from the citadel **a nobis abesse** to be distant from us **a dextrā** from the right **a tertiā horā** from the third hour
by (agent)	**ab amicis desertus** abandoned by friends

cum

with	**vade mecum** go with me! **cum curā loqui** to speak with care **cum Augusto coniurare** to conspire with Augustus **summa cum laude** with distinction

Continued

Prepositions governing the Ablative (contd)

dē

down from	**dē caelō dēmittere** to send down from heaven
away from	**dē trīclīniō exīre** to go away from the dining room
about	**cōgitāre dē hāc rē** to think about this matter
	dē industriā on purpose
during *or* at (*of time*)	**dē nocte** at night, during the night

ē(x)

out of (*from*)	**ē carcere effūgērunt** they escaped from prison
	ex equīs dēsilīre to jump from their horses
	quīdam ex Hispāniā someone from Spain
	statua ex argentō facta a statue made of silver
immediately after	**ex cōnsulātū** immediately after his consulship
from	**ex hōc diē** from that day
	ex aequō equally

pro

for/on behalf of	**pro se quisque** each one for himself/herself
	pro patriā morī to die for one's country
according to	**pro vīribus agere** to act according to one's ability
in front of	**pro rostrīs** in front of the rostrum

sine

without	**sine spē** without hope
	sine pecūniā without money

Prepositions governing Accusative and Ablative

in

with accusative

into

in hanc urbem venire
to come into the city

till

in primam lucem dormivit
he slept till dawn

against

in rem publicam aggredi
to attack the state

with ablative

in

puella in illā domō laetē vivebat
the girl lived happily in that house

on

in capite coronam gerebat
he wore a crown on his head

in animo habere
to intend (to have in one's mind)

within (of time)

in omni aetate
within every age

in (of condition)

in parte facilis, in parte difficilis
easy in parts, difficult in others

sub

with accusative

beneath

sub iugum mittere
to send beneath the yoke
(*ie* into slavery)

below (*with verb of motion*)

sub ipsum murum
just below the wall

before (*of time*)

sub vesperum
just before nightfall

with ablative

under (*of place and power*)

sub montibus constituere
to station under the mountains

sub Nerone
under the power of Nero

super

with accusative

over, above (*of place*), in addition

super capita hostium
over the heads of the enemy

alii, super alios, advenerunt
they arrived one after the other

with ablative

concerning/about

super his rebus scribam
I shall write about these matters

Numerals

Cardinal and Ordinal Numbers

		CARDINAL	ORDINAL
1	I	ūnus, -a, -um	prīmus, -a, -um
2	II	duo, -ae, -o	secundus, -a, -um
3	III	trēs, tria	tertius, -a, -um
4	IV	quattuor	quartus, -a, -um
5	V	quīnque	quīntus, -a, -um
6	VI	sex	sextus, -a, -um
7	VII	septem	septimus, -a, -um
8	VIII	octō	octāvus, -a, -um
9	IX	novem	nōnus, -a, -um
10	X	decem	decimus, -a, -um
11	XI	ūndecim	ūndecimus, -a, -um
12	XII	duodecim	duodecimus, -a, -um
13	XIII	tredecim	tertius decimus, -a, -um
14	XIV	quattuordecim	quartus decimus, -a, -um
15	XV	quīndecim	quīntus decimus, -a, -um
16	XVI	sēdecim	sextus decimus, -a, -um
17	XVII	septendecim	septimus decimus, -a, -um
18	XVIII	duodēvigintī	duodēvicēsimus, -a, -um
19	XIX	ūndēvigintī	ūndēvicēsimus, -a, -um
20	XX	vigintī	vicēsimus, -a, -um
21	XXI	vigintī ūnus	vicēsimus prīmus
30	XXX	trīgintā	trīcēsimus
40	XL	quadrāgintā	quadrāgēsimus
50	L	quīnquāgintā	quīnquāgēsimus
60	LX	sexāgintā	sexāgēsimus
70	LXX	septuāgintā	septuāgēsimus
80	LXXX	octōgintā	octōgēsimus
90	XC	nōnāgintā	nōnāgēsimus
100	C	centum	centēsimus

		CARDINAL	ORDINAL
200	CC	ducentī, -ae, -a	ducentēsimus
300	CCC	trecentī, -ae, -a	trecentēsimus
400	CCCC	quadringentī, -ae, -a	quadringentēsimus
500	D (IƆ)	quīngentī, -ae, -a	quīngentēsimus
600	DC	sescentī, -ae, -a	sescentēsimus
700	DCC	septingentī, -ae, -a	septingentēsimus
800	DCCC	octingentī, -ae, -a	octingentēsimus
900	DCCCC	nōngentī, -ae, -a	nōngentēsimus
1000	M (CIƆ)	mīlle	mīllēsimus
2000	MM	duo mīlia	bis mīllēsimus
1,000,000		deciēs centēna (centum)	mīlia

- Fractions are expressed as follows:

dīmidia pars	1/2
tertia pars	1/3
quārta pars	1/4

Continued

Cardinal and Ordinal Numbers (contd)

- Ordinal numbers (→**1**) decline like 1st and 2nd declension adjectives

- Cardinal numbers (→**2**) do not decline except for **ūnus**, **duo**, **trēs** and hundreds (**ducentī** etc)

- **ūnus** declines as 1st and 2nd declension adjectives except that the genitive singular ends in **-ius** and the dative in **-i**

- **duo** (two) declines as follows:

	Masc	Fem	Neut
Nom	**duo**	**duae**	**duo**
Acc	**duōs**	**duās**	**duo**
Gen	**duōrum**	**duārum**	**duōrum**
Dat	**duōbus**	**duābus**	**duōbus**
Abl	**duōbus**	**duābus**	**duōbus**

ambō, -ae, -a (both) declines in the same way

- **trēs** (three) declines as follows:

	Masc	Fem	Neut
Nom	**trēs**	**trēs**	**tria**
Acc	**trēs**	**trēs**	**tria**
Gen	**trium**	**trium**	**trium**
Dat	**tribus**	**tribus**	**tribus**
Abl	**tribus**	**tribus**	**tribus**

- Genitive of hundreds, *eg* **trecentī** ends **-um** (→**3**)

- **mīlia** (thousands) declines as follows:

Nom	**mīlia**	Dat	**mīlibus**
Acc	**mīlia**	Abl	**mīlibus**
Gen	**mīlium**		

- **mīlle** (thousand) does not decline.

---

1 coquus **secundam** mensam paraverat
The cook had prepared the second course

legionis **nonae** milites magnam partem hostium interfecerunt
Soldiers of the ninth legion killed a large number of the enemy

2 **decem milia** passuum exercitus progressus est
The army advanced 10 miles

Cerberus, qui **tria** capita habebat, in antro recubuit
Cerberus, who had three heads, crouched in the cave

Stellae **novem** orbes confecerunt
The stars completed nine orbits

duodeviginti onerariae naves huc accedebant
Eighteen cargo ships were approaching

Caesar **trecentos** milites trans Padanum traiecit
Caesar transported three hundred soldiers across the River Po

da mi basia **mille**
Give me a thousand kisses

3 **trecentum militum**
of three hundred soldiers

4 **duo milia passuum** (*gen*)
2000 paces *or* 2 miles

Distributive Numerals

These are used when repetition is involved as when multiplying (→1)

1	singulī, -ae, -a	*one each*
2	bīnī, -ae, -a	*two each*
3	ternī (trīnī)	
4	quaternī	
5	quīnī	
6	sēnī	
7	septēnī	
8	octōnī	
9	novēnī	
10	dēnī	

Numeral Adverbs

1	semel	*once*
2	bis	*twice*
3	ter	
4	quater	
5	quīnquiēs	
6	sexiēs	
7	septiēs	
8	octiēs	
9	noviēs	
10	deciēs	

(→2)

1 **bīnī** gladiatores
(*describing pairs of gladiators*)

bīna castra
two camps

quaternos denarios in **singulas** vini amphoras
4 denarii each for a bottle of wine

2 non plus quam **semel**
not more than once

deciēs centēna milia sestertium *or* **deciēs** sestertium
1,000,000 sesterces

ter quattuor
twelve (*three times four*)

Dates

- Events of the year were usually recorded by using the names of the consuls holding office that year (→**1**)

- From the late republic the date of the foundation of Rome was established – 753 BC and time was calculated from this date (→**2**)

- The four seasons were: (→**3**)

vēr, vēris (nt)	spring
aestās, -ātis (f)	summer
autumnus, -ī (m)	autumn
hiems, -is (f)	winter

- The months were reformed by Julius Caesar (7 of 31 days, 4 of 30, 1 of 28, and an extra day each leap year). Each month (**mensis, -is,** m) was identified by the following adjectives:

Iānuārius	January
Februārius	February
Martius	March
Aprīlis	April
Māius	May
Iūnius	June
Iūlius (Quintīlis)	July
Augustus (Sextīlis)	August
September	September
Octōber	October
November	November
December	December

- Three important days each month were:

Kalendae, -ārum (fpl)	Kalends or 1st
Nōnae, -ārum (fpl)	Nones or 5th/7th
Īdūs, -uum (fpl)	Ides or 13th/15th

Continued

1 **Nerōne iterum L. Pīsōne consulibus** pauca memoria digna evēnērunt
Few incidents worth recording took place during the year when Nero and Lucius Piso were consuls (AD 57)

Lentulō Gaetulicō C. Calvisiō consulibus decreta sunt triumphī insignia Poppaeō Sabīnō
A triumph was voted to Poppaeus Sabinus during the consulship of Lentulus Gaetulicus and Gaius Calvisius

2 **ab urbe conditā**
since the foundation of Rome

ante urbem conditam
before the foundation of the city

post urbem conditam
after the foundation of the city

3 ineunte **aestāte**
in the beginning of summer

media **aestāte**
midsummer

iam **hieme confectā**
when winter was already over

vere ineunte Antōnius Tarentum nāvigāvit
At the beginning of spring, Antony sailed to Tarentum

Dates (contd)

- In March, July, October and May, Nones fall on the 7th and Ides on the 15th day (5th and 13th in all other months).

- To refer to these dates, the ablative is used (→1)

- To refer to the day before these dates, use **pridiē** (→2)

- All other days were reckoned by counting (inclusively) the days before the next main date. "ante diem" + accusative of ordinal numbers and the next main date were used:
9th of February is 5 days before the 13th of February (counting inclusively). 28th April is 4 days before 1st May (→3)

- An easy way to work out such dates is to add one to Nones and Ides and subtract the Latin number. Add two to the number of days in the month before the Kalends, again subtracting the given Latin number. You will then have the date in English.

- The day was divided into twelve hours **horae, -ārum** (fpl). The hours of darkness into four watches of three hours each, **vigiliae, -ārum** (fpl), from 6–9 pm, 9–12 pm, 12–3 pm, 3–6 am

- Other ways of expressing time:

primā luce	at dawn
solo orto	at sunrise
solis occasu	at sunset
media nocte	at midnight
noctu, nocte	at night
mane	in the morning
meridie	at midday
sub vesperum	towards evening
vespere	in the evening (→4)

Examples

1 **Kalendis Martiis**
on the 1st of March

Idibus Decembribus
on the 13th of December

Idibus Martiis Caesar a Bruto interfectus est
Caesar was killed by Brutus on the 15th of March

2 **pridiē Nonas Ianuarias (Non. Ian.)**
4th January

3 **ante diem quintum Idus Februarias**
9th February

ante diem quartum Kalendas Maias
28th April

4 **prima hora**
at the first hour (6–7 am)

tertia vigilia
during the third watch (midnight–3 am)

tertia fere vigilia navem solvit
He set sail after midnight (during the third watch)

ipse **hora circiter quarta diei** cum primis navibus Britanniam attigit
He himself reached Britain with the first ships around 10 o'clock in the morning

vespere vinum optimum convivae bibunt
In the evening, the guests drink vintage wine

Word Order

Simple Sentences

Word order in English is stricter than in Latin. The usual English order – subject + verb + object – differentiates the meaning of sentences such as, "The cat caught the mouse" and "The mouse caught the cat". Latin order is more flexible since the endings of words clearly show their function, whatever their position in the sentence.

Compare the following:

feles murem cepit   the cat caught the mouse
murem cepit feles   it was the cat that caught the mouse

The sentences are identical in meaning, although the emphasis is different. This difference in word order often makes it difficult for English translators to unravel long Latin sentences. However there are certain principles to help:

- The normal *grammatical* word order in Latin is:

  Subject first, Predicate after (by Predicate understand "verb")

- Expressions qualifying the subject (*ie* adjectives) must be near the subject

- Expressions qualifying the predicate (*eg* objects, adverbs, prepositional phrases) must be near the verb

Thus the usual word order of a simple sentence is:

(Connecting Word)
Subject
(Adjective)
Object
Adverbs *or* Prepositional Phrases
Predicate (verb) (→**1**)

Continued

1 at **hostes** magnam virtutem in extrema spe salutis **praestiterunt**
But the enemy showed great courage, finally hoping to save themselves

Ariovistus ad postulata Caesaris pauca **respondit**
Ariovistus briefly replied to Caesar's demands

iste **Hannibal** sic hanc Tertiam **dilexit**
Thus that Hannibal loved this Tertia

Simple Sentences (contd)

- Another principle is *emphasis*, where the words are in an unusual order, eg subject last, predicate first (→**1**)

- Questions usually begin with interrogatives (→**2**)

- Adjectives may precede or follow nouns. Check agreement of endings (→**3**)

- Genitives usually follow the governing word (→**4**)

- Words in apposition usually follow one another, although "rex" often comes first (→**5**)

- Adverbs usually come before their verb, adjective or adverb (→**6**)

- Prepositions usually come before their nouns (→**7**) but note, magna **cum** cura (with great care).

- Finally, watch out for the omission of words, particularly parts of **esse** (to be) (→**8**)

Examples

1 horum adventu **redintegratur** | **seditio** (subject last)
On their arrival trouble broke out once more

confecerunt me | **infirmitates** meorum (verb first)
I have been upset by the illnesses of my slaves

2 **quid** hoc loco potes dicere, homo amentissime?
What can you say at this point, you madman?

quis clarior in Graecia Themistocle?
Who (is) more famous in Greece than Themistocles?

3 **bello magno** victus   **magna domus**
conquered in a great war   a large house

4 multi **nostrum**   filius **Augusti**
many of us   Augustus' son

5 Cicero, **consul**
Cicero, the consul

rex Tarquinius
King Tarquinius

6 **vix** cuiquam persuadebatur
hardly anyone could be persuaded

multo carius
much dearer

7 in villam
into the house

sub monte
under the mountain

8 **pudor inde et miseratio et patris Agrippae, Augusti avi memoria (est)**
A feeling of pity and shame came over them and they remembered her father Agrippa and her grandfather Augustus

Compound Sentences

A compound sentence is one with a main clause and one or more subordinate clauses. In Latin this is called a **period**, where the most important idea is kept to the end.

- conservate parenti filium, parentem filio, (1) ne aut senectutem iam prope desperatam contempsisse aut adulescentiam plenam spei|maximae non modo non aluisse vos verum etiam perculisse atque adflixisse videamini (2). (Cic. – Pro Caelio 32.80)

  1. Main clause
     save a son for his father, a father for his son.

  2. Negative purpose clause
     lest you appear either to have cast aside an old man near despair or that you have failed to sustain a young man full of the highest hopes, but have even struck him down and ruined him.

  Note that this sentence builds towards a climax at the end. The most important verbs here are **perculisse** and **adflixisse** rather than **videamini** (you may seem). Notice also the rhythm of the last two words. Repetition of similar phrases is common – **parenti filium, parentem filio**. This sentence is a good illustration of an orator's style.

- Historical style is much simpler, often a subordinate clause followed by a main clause:

  cum equites nostri funditoribus sagittariisque flumen transgressi essent (1), cum equitatu proelium commiserunt

1. Subordinate adverbial clause of time
   when our cavalry had crossed the river with slingers and archers

2. Main clause
   they joined battle with the cavalry

- Participle phrase followed by the **main clause** and **subordinate** clause:

  nec patrum cognitionibus satiatus iudiciis (1), adsidebat in cornu tribunalis (2), ne praetorem curuli depelleret (Tac Ann I 75)

  1. Participle phrase
     nor was he (the emperor) satisfied with taking part in Senate trials

  2. Main clause
     he used to sit in the ordinary lawcourts

  3. Subordinate clause of purpose
     in case he pushed the praetor from his curule chair

Many other combinations of clauses are possible. It is important to relate the sentence to its context and to the passage as a whole as Latin sentences are linked logically. It is often helpful when translating a long sentence to pick out subjects and verbs in order to recognize the structure of the clauses and grasp the overall meaning of the sentence.

Simple Sentences

Direct Statement

The basic patterns involved in direct statement have been illustrated under **Word Order** (*see* p 80).

Direct Questions

In Latin a direct question can be expressed as follows by:

● an interrogative pronoun (→**1**)

   quis? (who?), **quid?** (what?), **cur?** (why?)

● adding **-ne** to the first word, where no definite answer is indicated (→**2**)

● **nonne**, when the expected answer is YES (→**3**)

● **num**, when the expected answer is NO (→**4**)

● **utrum ... an(non)**
   -ne ...an(non)   } (whether) ... or (not)
   ... an(non)
   in double questions (→**5**)

Examples

1 **quis** est?
      Who is it?

   quid dicit?
      What is he saying?

   cur lacrimas?
      Why are you crying?

2 timesne Verrem?
      Are you scared of Verres?

3 **nonne** cladem audivisti?
      Surely you heard of the defeat?
   or You heard of the defeat, didn't you?

4 **num** heri venisti?
      Surely you didn't come yesterday?
   or You didn't come yesterday, did you?

5 utrum has condiciones accepistis **annon**?
      Have you accepted these conditions or not?

Continued

Simple Sentences (contd)

Direct Command

- A direct command in Latin is expressed in the second person by the imperative if positive, by **noli(te)** with the present infinitive if negative (→**1**)

- A direct command in the first or third persons is expressed by the present subjunctive, with **nē** if negative (→**2**)

Wishes

- Wishes are expressed in Latin by **utinam** with the subjunctive, **utinam nē** when negative (→**3**)

- **vellem** may also be used with imperfect or pluperfect subjunctive to express wishes (→**4**)

Examples

1 **venite** mecum
come with me

noli me tangere
don't touch me

2 **vivamus** atque **amemus**
let us live and let us love

ne **fiat** lux
let there not be light

3 **utinam** frater redeat
I wish my brother would return (*future*)

utinam ne vere scriberem
I wish I were not writing the truth (*present*)

utinam brevi moratus esses
I wish you had stayed a little (*past*)

4 **vellem** me ad cenam **invitavisses**
I wish you had invited me to dinner

Compound Sentences

Indirect Statement

"You are making a mistake" is a *direct statement.* "I think that you are making a mistake" is an *indirect statement.*

● The indirect statement is the object clause of "I think". In indirect statement in Latin, the subject of the clause (*eg* te) goes into the accusative case, the verb is an infinitive (errare):

Puto **te errare**
I think that you are making a mistake

● This pattern is used after verbs of saying, thinking, perceiving, knowing (→**1**)

Examples

1				
audire	hear	**negare**	say ... not
cognoscere	discover	**nescire**	not to know
credere	believe	**putare**	think
dicere	say	**scire**	know
intellegere	understand	**sentire**	perceive
meminisse	remember	**videre**	see
narrare	tell		

Continued

Indirect Statement (contd)

Translation

- The *present infinitive* refers to actions happening at the same time and may be translated – is, are, was, were.

- The *perfect infinitive* refers to prior action and may be translated – has, have, had.

- The *future infinitive* refers to future action and may be translated – will, would.

putamus	te errāre	that you are making a mistake
	te errāvisse	that you have made a mistake
We think	te errātūrum esse	that you will make a mistake

putabāmus	te errāre	that you were making a mistake
	te errāvisse	that you had made a mistake
We thought	te errātūrum esse	that you would make a mistake

- Notice that when the main verb is *past* tense, translate the present infinitive – "was, were", the past infinitive – "had", the future infinitive – "would".

- The reflexive pronoun **sē** is used to refer to the subject of the main verb (→**1**)

- Translate **negō** – I say that ... not (→**2**)

- Verbs of promising, hoping, threatening or swearing (*eg* **promittō, polliceor, spērō, minor, iuro**) are followed by an accusative and future infinitive (→**3**)

Examples

1   senex dixit **se** thesaurum invenisse
The old man said that he had found treasure

2   **negavit** servum domum venturum esse
He said that the slave would not come home

3   **promisi me festinaturum esse**
I promised that I would hurry

sperabat se hoc confecturum esse
He hoped that he could complete this
or He hoped to complete this

Further Examples

creditores existimabant **eum** totam pecuniam **perdidisse**
His creditors thought that he had lost all his money

memini **simulacra** deorum de caelo **percussa esse**
I remember that the gods' statues were struck down from the heavens

vidistine **Catonem** in bibliotheca **sedere**?
Did you see Cato sitting in the library?

iuro **me** pro patria fortiter **pugnaturum esse**
I swear that I shall fight bravely for my country

iam ego credo **vos** verum **dixisse**
I now believe that you spoke the truth

negavit **nihil** umquam pulchrius statua **fuisse**
He said that nothing had ever been more beautiful than that statue

94 SENTENCES

Indirect Question

"Where did he come from?" is a *direct question.* "I asked where he had come from" is an *indirect question.* Latin uses the same interrogative words (**quis** – who, **quid** – what *etc*) and the verb in indirect questions is always subjunctive

rogavi unde venisset
  I asked where he had come from

● Latin uses six different forms of the subjunctive in this construction in a precise sequence depending on the main verb (→**1**)

Examples

1 rogo	I ask	**unde veniat**	(present)
		unde venerit	(perfect)
		unde venturus sit	(future)

		where he comes from	(present)
		where he has come from	(perfect)
		where he will come from	(future)

	rogavi	**unde veniret**	(imperfect)
		unde venisset	(pluperfect)
		unde venturus esset	(future perfect)

	I asked	where he was coming from	(imperfect)
		where he had come from	(pluperfect)
		where he would come from	(future perfect)

Continued

Indirect Question (contd)

Translation

Translation of tenses in indirect question is *easy*, because English uses the same tenses as Latin, as can be seen on page 94.

- The reflexive pronoun **se** is used to refer to the subject of the main verb (→**1**)

- **utrum ... an** (if ... or), **utrum ... necne** (whether ... or not) are also used in indirect questions (→**2**)

- **num** is used to mean "if" in indirect questions (→**3**)

Examples

1 rogavit **quando se visuri essemus**
He asked when we would see him

2 roga **utrum** iverit **an** manserit
Ask whether he went or stayed

roga **utrum** manserit **necne**
Ask whether he stayed or not

rogavit **utrum** Scylla infestior **esset** Charybdis **necne**
He asked whether Charybdis was more dangerous than Scylla or not

3 nescio **num** venturi sint
I don't know if they will come

Further Examples

nescimus **quid facturi simus**
We don't know what we shall do

mirum est **quanta sit Roma**
It is amazing how big Rome is
or The size of Rome is amazing

exploratores cognoverunt **quanti essent** Poeni
Scouts discovered what the numbers of the Carthaginians were

incredibile est **quomodo** talia facere **potuerit**
It is incredible how he was able to do such things

nemo audivit **quid** rex **constituisset**
No one heard what the king had decided
or No one heard the king's decision

Indirect Command

"Come here" is a *direct command*. "I ordered you to come here" is an *indirect command*. Indirect commands in Latin are expressed by **ut** (when positive) or **nē** (when negative) and have their verbs in the subjunctive (→**1**)

- Latin uses two tenses of the subjunctive, present or imperfect, in this construction. It uses the present subjunctive if the main verb is present or future tense and imperfect subjunctive if the main verb is in the past tense. (→**2**)

Translation

- The English translation of the indirect command is the same, whichever tense is used in Latin – the infinitive (*eg* to come)

- The reflexive **se** is used to refer to the subject of the main verb (→**3**)

- Common verbs introducing indirect command are:

hortor	encourage
moneo	warn
oro	beg
persuadeo	persuade
rogo	ask

- *Only* **iubeo** (to order), **veto** (to tell … not), are usually used with the infinitive in Latin (→**4**)

Examples

1 tibi imperavi **ut venīrēs**
I ordered you to come

tibi imperavi **ne venires**
I forbade you to come

milites oravit **ne** in castris diutius **manerent**
He begged his soldiers not to stay in camp any longer

hoc rogo, mi Tiro, **ne** temere **naviges**
I beg you, my dear Tiro, not to sail carelessly

2 tibi **impero ut venias**   (*present*)
I order you to come

tibi **imperavi ut venires**   (*imperfect*)
I ordered you to come

deos precor **ut nobis parcant**
I beg the gods to spare us

amicos roga **ut veniant**, operamque **dent**, et messim hanc nobis **adiuvent**
Ask your friends to come and lend a hand and help us with this harvest

3 nos oravit ut **sibi** cibum daremus
He begged us to give him food

4 **iubeo** eos navigare
I order them to sail

veto eos **navigare**
I tell them not to sail

mater me **vetuit** in murum **ascendere**
Mother forbade me to climb on the wall

Antonius eos **iussit** adventum **suum exspectare**
Antony told them to await his arrival

Purpose or Final Clauses

There are two ways of expressing purpose in English:

I am hurrying to the city to see the games
or I am hurrying to the city so that I may see the games

- In Latin **ut** is used with the present or imperfect subjunctive, to express purpose. The present subjunctive is used if the main verb is in the present or future tense and the imperfect subjunctive if the main verb is in the past tense (→**1**)

- Negative purpose clauses are introduced by **ne** which can be translated "so that … not", "in case", "to avoid", "lest" etc (→**2**)

- If there is a comparative adjective or adverb in the Latin sentence **quō** is used instead of **ut** (→**3**)

- The relative **qui, quae, quod** may be used instead of **ut**, if it refers to an object in the main clause (→**4**)

- After negative **ne**, **quis** is used instead of **aliquis** to mean "anyone"

- Note that **se** is used to refer to the subject of the main verb (→**5**)

- **ad** is used with the gerundive to express purpose (→**6**)

- The supine **-um** is used after verbs of motion to express purpose (→**7**)

1 ad urbem festino **ut** ludos **videam**
I am hurrying to the city to see the games
ad urbem festinavi **ut** ludos **viderem**
I hurried to the city to see the games
filium multo cum fletu complexus, pepulit **ut abiret**
Embracing his son tearfully, he drove him to leave

2 Tiberius hoc recusavit **ne** Germanicus imperium **haberet**
Tiberius refused this lest Germanicus had power
pontem resciderunt **ne** hostes flumen **transirent**
They broke down the bridge in case the enemy crossed the river

3 puellae cantabant **quo** laetiores essent **hospites**
The girls sang to make their guests happier

4 rex sex milites delegit **qui** ad Graeciam **proficiscerentur**
The king chose six soldiers to set off for Greece

5 in silvis se abdidit **ne quis se** videret
He hid in the woods lest anyone should see him
sed **ut** venenum manifesto comprehendi **posset**, constituit locum iussit, **ut** eo **mitteret** amicos, **qui laterent**, cum venisset Licinius, venenumque traderet, comprehenderent
But *so that the poison could be seized openly*, he ordered that a place be appointed, *to send friends there, to hide.* When Licinius came to hand over the poison they could arrest him.

6 Verres ad Siciliam venit **ad urbes diripiendas**
Verres came to Sicily to plunder its cities

7 veniunt **spectatum**
They come to see

Result or Consecutive Clauses

The road is so long that I am tired
It was so hot that we could not work

In both these sentences, a result or consequence is expressed in English by using words such as

so … that (positive)
so that … not (negative)

- In Latin the following words are frequently used in the main clause

adeo	to such an extent
ita	thus, so
talis	of such a kind
tam	so
tantus	so great
tot	so many

- In the result clause, **ut** (so that) and **ut … non** (so that … not) are used with the present or imperfect subjunctive. Present subjunctive is used where the main verb is in the present and the imperfect subjunctive is used where the main verb is past (→**1**)

- **Note** that **eum** is used to refer to "him" instead of **se** when referring to the subject of the main clause as in the first example (→**1**)

---

1 Gallus **tam** ferox est **ut** omnes Romani eum **timeant**
The Gaul is so fierce that all the Romans are scared of him

tanta erat tempestas **ut** nautae navem **non solverent**
So great was the storm that the sailors could not set sail

nemo est **adeo** stultus **ut non** discere **possit**
No one is so stupid that he can't learn

tot sententiae erant **ut** nemo **consentiret**
There were so many opinions that no one could agree

tales nos esse putamus **ut** ab omnibus **laudemur**
We think that we are the sort of people to be praised by everyone

Verbs of Fearing

In Latin, verbs of fearing (**timeo, metuo, paveo, vereor**) are followed by **nē, nē non** or **ut** with the present and perfect, imperfect and pluperfect subjunctive according to sequence of tenses:

- The present subjunctive represents present and future tenses in English

  I am afraid he is coming
  I am afraid he will come

- The perfect subjunctive represents the past tense in English

  I am afraid that he has come

- When the verb of fearing is in the past tense, imperfect and pluperfect subjunctive are used in Latin instead (→**1**)

- **nē** is used if the fear is expressed in a positive sentence (*ie* I am afraid he will come). **nē nōn, ut** is used if the fear is expressed negatively (*ie* I am afraid that he won't come) (→**2**)

- As in English, the infinitive can follow a verb of fearing, provided that the subjects of both are the same (→**3**)

Examples

1 veritus sum **ne veniret**
I was afraid he was coming

veritus sum **ne venisset**
I was afraid that he had come

2 **vereor ne** amicus **veniat**
I am afraid lest my friend comes
or lest my friend will come

vereor ne amicus **non veniat**
I am afraid that my friend won't come

vereor ut amicus **venerit**
I am afraid that my friend has not come

verebar ne amicus **non venisset**
I was afraid that my friend had not come

metuo ne virtutis maiorum nostrum **obliviscamur**
I am afraid that we shall forget the courage of our ancestors

paves ne ducas tu illam
You are afraid to marry her

Verres, **veritus ne** servi bellum in Sicilia **facerent**, multos in vincula coniecit
Verres, fearing that slaves might revolt in Sicily, threw many into prison

Romani **verebantur ne** fortiter **non pugnavissent**
The Romans were afraid that they had not fought bravely

3 timeo **abire**
I am afraid to go away

mulier **timebat manere** sola
The woman was scared to remain alone

Conditional Sentences

Compare the following two sentences in English:

(a) If I tell you a lie, you will be angry
(b) If I were to tell you a lie, you would be angry

The first is a *logical statement of fact*, stating what *will* happen, the second is a *hypothesis*, stating what *would* happen.

For the first type of sentence, Latin uses the indicative mood in both main and conditional clauses. For the second type, Latin uses the subjunctive mood in both main and conditional clauses.

Translate type (a) as follows:

si hoc **dicis,** sapiens **es**
if you say this, you are wise

si hoc **dicebas,** sapiens **eras**
if you were saying this, you were wise

si hoc **dixisti,** erravisti
if you said this, then you made a mistake

si hoc **dixeris,** errabis
if you say this, you will make a mistake

Notice that the same tenses in English are used as in Latin except in the last sentence. Latin is more precise – you *will have said* this, before you make a mistake, therefore Latin uses the *future perfect* tense.

Continued

● Consider also the following sentence:

si me **amabis,** mecum **manebis**
If you love me, you will stay with me

Latin uses the *future* tense in both clauses, English uses the *present* tense in the "if" clause. Both actions, "loving" and "remaining" *logically* refer to the *future*.

Translate type (b) as follows:

(*present*)
si hoc **dicas, erres**
if you were to say this, you would be making a mistake

(*imperfect*)
si hoc **diceres, errares**
if you said (*or* were saying) that, you would be making a mistake

(*pluperfect*)
si hoc **dixisses, erravisses**
if you had said that, you would have made a mistake

Notice that both tenses of the subjunctive are the same in the above examples. Sometimes an imperfect may be used in one clause and the pluperfect in the other:

si pudorem **haberes,** Roma **abiisses**
if you had any sense of shame, you would have left Rome

Conditional Sentences (contd)

Negative Conditional Sentences

- **nisi** (unless) is the negative of **si** (if). (→**1**)

- **si non** (if not), is less common and negates *one* word, or is used when the same verb is repeated (→**2**)

1 **nisi** id statim **feceris**, ego te **tradam** magistratui
Unless you do this immediately, I shall hand you over
to the magistrate

nisi utilem **crederem**, non pacem **peterem**
Unless I thought it useful, I would not be seeking
peace

2 **si** me **adiuveris**, laeta **ero**; **si** me **non adiuveris**, tristis
ero
If you help me, I shall be happy; if you don't help me,
I shall be sad

si navigatio **non morabitur**, mox te **videbo**
If my sailing is not delayed, I shall see you soon

Further Examples

(b) quis illum sceleratum fuisse **putavisset**, **si tacuisset**?
Who would have thought he was a rascal, if he had
kept quiet?

(b) multi **agerent** et **pugnarent si** rei publicae **videretur**
Many would act and fight, if the state decided

(a) **gaudemus si** liberi in horto **ludunt**
We are happy if the children play in the garden

(b) **si quis** in caelum **ascendisset**, pulchritudinem side-
rum **conspexisset**
If anyone had gone up to heaven, he would have seen
the beauty of the stars

Concessive Clauses

In English, Concessive clauses usually begin with "although":

Although he is rich, he is not happy
I shall succeed although it is difficult

- **quamquam** (although) is followed by the indicative (→**1**)

    Note that **tamen** (however) is often used in the main clause in concessive sentences

- **quamvis** (although) is always followed by the subjunctive (→**2**)

- **cum** in the sense "although" is always followed by the subjunctive (→**3**)

- **etsi** (although) takes the indicative or subjunctive according to the same rules as **si** (see p 106). The indicative is more common (→**4**)

Examples

1 medici **quamquam intellegunt,** numquam **tamen** aegris de morbo dicunt
Although doctors know, they never tell their patients about their illness

quamquam Aeneas dicere **volebat,** Dido solo fixos oculos aversa tenebat
Although Aeneas wished to speak, Dido turned away and kept her eyes fixed on the ground

2 **quamvis** frater **esset** molestus, Marcus eum amavit
Although his brother was a nuisance, Marcus loved him

feminae, **quamvis** in periculo **essent,** tamen liberos servaverunt
Although the women were in danger, yet they saved their children

3 **cum non didicissem** geometrias, litteras sciebam
Although I had not learnt geometry, I knew my letters

non poterant, **cum vellent,** Lucium liberare
They were not able, although they wished, to free Lucius

4 **etsi** servus **est,** certe persona est
Although he is a slave, he is a person

etsi victoriam non **reportavissetis,** tamen vos contentos esse oportebat
Although you had not won a victory, yet you should have been content

etsi domi **esset filius iuvenis,** agros ipse colebat
Although he had a young son at home, he cultivated the fields by himself

112 SENTENCES

Causal Clauses

Clauses which begin with the words "because" or "since" and give a reason for something are often called causal clauses in English.

- Causal clauses have their verbs in the indicative when the *actual* cause is stated. They are introduced by **quod**, **quia** (because), and **quoniam** (since) (→**1**)

- **quod** is used with the subjunctive when the cause is only *suggested* (→**2**)

- **non quod** (+ *subj*) ... **sed quia** (+ *indic*) not because ... but because ..., is used when the first reason is discarded. The true reason is expressed in the indicative (→**3**)

- **cum** (since, as) is always followed by the subjunctive (→**4**)

- **qui** with the subjunctive can be used to mean "since" (→**5**)

SENTENCES 113

Examples

1 non iratus sum **quod** in me **fuisti** asperior
I am not angry because you were too harsh towards me

in crypta Neapolitana vecti, timebamus **quia** longior et obscurior carcere **erat**
Travelling in the Naples tunnel, we were afraid because it was longer and darker than a prison

quoniam ita tu **vis**, ego Puteolos tecum proficiscar
Since you wish this, I shall set off with you to Pozzuoli

2 templa spoliare non poterant **quod** religione im-**pedirentur**
They could not plunder the temples because (they said) they were prevented by religious feelings

3 mater semper maxime laboravit **non quod** necessarium **esset sed quia** honestum esse **videbatur**
Mother always worked very hard, not because it was necessary but because it seemed proper

4 quae **cum** ita **sint**, Catilina, egredere ex urbe!
Since this is so, Catilina, leave the city!

Caesar, **cum** in continente hiemare **constituisset**, ad Galliam rediit
Since Caesar had decided to spend the winter on the mainland, he returned to Gaul

5 sapiens erat **qui** studiis totos annos **dedisset**
He was wise since he had devoted all his years to study

Temporal Clauses

Clauses denoting time are introduced by conjunctions, *eg* **ubi** (when) followed by verbs in the indicative. **Some conjunctions**, *eg* **cum** (when) may also take the subjunctive. (→**1**)

Conjunctions followed by the indicative:

ut	when, as
ubi	when
cum primum	
ubi primum	as soon as
ut primum	
simul ac	as soon as
simul atque	
quotiens	as often as, whenever
quamdiu	as long as, while
ex quo (tempore)	ever since
postquam	after (**post** or **postea**
posteaquam	may be separated from **quam**)

Continued

1 **ut** valetudo Germanici Romae **nuntiata est**, magna ira
erat
When Germanicus' state of health was announced in
Rome, there was great anger
ubi primum classis visa est, **complentur** non modo
portus sed moenia ac tecta
As soon as the fleet was seen, not only the harbour
but the walls and rooftops were filled (with people)
quod **ubi cognitum est** hostibus, universi nonam legi-
onem nocte aggressi sunt
When this was discovered by the enemy, all of them
attacked the ninth legion at night
quotiens proficiscor, pluit
Every time I set out, it rains
manebat **quamdiu poterat**
He stayed as long as he could
septimus annus est, milites, **ex quo** Britanniam **vicistis**
It is seven years, soldiers, since you conquered Britain
postquam vallum **intravit,** portas stationibus con-
firmavit
After entering the fortification, he strengthened the
gates with guards
post tertium diem **quam redierat,** mortuus est
He died three days after his return

Temporal Clauses (contd)

Conjunctions which take the indicative or subjunctive:

cum

- **when** with indicative and often **tum** in the main clause (→**1**)

- **whenever** with the following pattern of tenses in the indicative: (→**2**)

  + **perfect** followed by **present** tense
  + **future perfect** followed by **future** tense
  + **pluperfect** followed by **imperfect** tense

- **when, as** with the imperfect or pluperfect subjunctive narrative (→**3**)

dum

- **while** with indicative

  the present tense is used when **dum** means "during the time that" (→**4**)

- Note that where the same tense (here, the future) is used in both clauses, **dum** means "all the time that". Latin uses future **vivam** more accurately than English "live" (→**5**)

Continued

---

1 **cum** tu Romae **eras, tum** ego domi eram
   When you were in Rome, I was then at home

2 **cum surrexerat, cadebat**
   Whenever he got up, he fell down

   cum domum **veni**, amicum **visito**
   Whenever I come home, I visit my friend

3 Socrates, **cum** triginta tyranni **essent**, non exibat
   Socrates didn't go out when there were 30 tyrants

   cum id Caesari **nuntiatum esset** ab urbe profectus est
   When that message had been given to Caesar, he set out from the city

4 **dum** haec **geruntur** sex milia hominum ad Rhenum contenderunt
   While this was going on, 6000 men marched to the Rhine

5 **dum vivam**, laeta **ero**
   While I live, I shall be happy

Temporal Clauses (contd)

Clauses which take Indicative or Subjunctive (contd)

dum, donec

- **until** with subjunctive, often with the sense of purpose or suspense (→**1**)

antequam, priusquam

- **before** with indicative (→**2**)

- **ante** and **prius** may be separated from **quam** especially in negative sentences (→**3**)

- **before** with subjunctive, usually with a sense of purpose or limit (→**4**)

1 multa Antonio concessit **dum** interfectores patris **ulcisceretur**
He made many concessions to Antony until he could avenge his father's killers

Haterius in periculo erat **donec** Augustam auxilium **oraret**
Haterius was in danger until he begged for Augusta's help

2 **antequam finiam**, hoc dicam
Before I finish, I shall say this

priusquam gallus **cantabit**, ter me negabis
Before the cock crows, you will deny me three times

3 neque **prius** fugere destiterunt **quam** ad castra **pervenerunt**
They didn't stop running away before reaching their camp

4 consul Romam festinavit **antequam** Hannibal eo **perveniret**
The consul hurried to Rome before Hannibal could reach it

ita cassita nidum migravit **priusquam** agricola frumentum **meteret**
And so the lark abandoned her nest before the farmer could reap the corn

120 SENTENCES

Comparative Clauses

- These are adverbial clauses which express likeness, agreement (or the opposite) with what is stated in the main clause. (→1)

- When the comparative clause states a fact (as above) the verb is in the **indicative**. The commonest words of comparison are (→2)

ut (as), **sicut** (just as), **aliter ac, aliter ut** (different from), **idem ac, idem atque, qui** etc (the same as)

- When the comparative clause is purely **imaginary**, the verb is **subjunctive**. The commonest words used with this type of clause are (→3)

velut(si), quasi, tamquam (si) (as if)

Examples

1   eadem dixi ac prius dixeram
I said the same as I had said before

2   **ego ita ero, ut me esse oportet**
I shall be as I should be

sicut lupus agnos rapit, ita mater liberos servat
Just as the wolf snatches the lamb, so the mother saves her children

haud aliter se gerebat ac solebat
He behaved as he usually did

or He behaved no differently from usual

idem abierunt qui venerant
The same men vanished as came

3   **velutsi haec res nihil ad se pertinuisset, tacebat**
He remained silent, as if this thing had nothing to do with him

hic flammae Aetnae minantur quasi ad caelum sublatae sint
Here Aetna's flames threaten, as if raised to the heavens

Cleopatram salutaverunt **tamquam si esset** regina
They greeted Cleopatra as if she were queen

Relative Clauses

- Relative clauses are more common in Latin than in English. They are introduced by the following:

qui, quae, quod	which, who, that
ubi	where, in which
unde	from where, from which

- These relatives come at the beginning of the clause but after prepositions.

- The relative agrees with a word which precedes it – its *antecedent* – in gender and number, but takes its case from its own clause (→**1**)

  qui is masculine plural agreeing with antecedent **Romani**, nominative because it is the subject of **incenderunt**

- **quā** is feminine singular agreeing with **regio**, ablative after preposition **in** (→**2**)

- **quos** is masculine plural agreeing with **servos**, accusative because it is the object of **iudicavit** (→**3**)

- The relative **quod** refers to a sentence, and **id** is omitted (**id quod** – that which). This is often used in parenthesis, and not attached grammatically to the rest of the sentence

- After **cuius** (of, concerning which) the noun **laudationis** is repeated (→**4**)

- The relative sometimes agrees with the following word, especially with the verb **esse** (→**5**)

Continued

Examples   SENTENCES 123

1 hi sunt Romani **qui** libros incenderunt
These are the Romans who burnt the books

2 haec est regio **in qua** ego sum natus
This is the region in which I was born

3 servos **quos** ipse iudicavit, eos sua sponte liberavit
He willingly freed those slaves whom he himself had judged

4 deinde, **quod** alio loco antea dixi, quae est ista tandem laudatio, **cuius laudationis** legati et principes et publice tibi navem aedificatam, et privatim se ipsos abs te spoliatos esse dixerunt? (**Cicero**, Verres V 58)
Well then, as I said earlier elsewhere, what does that praise consist of, namely that publicly the ambassadors and chief citizens said a ship had been built for you, but privately that they themselves had been robbed by you?

5 iusta gloria **qui** fructus virtutis est, bello quaeritur
True glory, which is the reward of courage, is looked for in war

Relative Clauses (contd)

Use Of Subjunctive In Relative Clauses

- The subjunctive is used in relative clauses dependent on infinitives or subjunctives (→1)

- When **qui** is used with the subjunctive, it may express cause (→2)

- **quippe** is sometimes used with **qui** in this sense

- When **qui** *etc* is used with the present or imperfect subjunctive, it may express purpose (→3)

- **qui** with the subjunctive is used with the following (→4)

dignus est qui	he is worthy of
idoneus est qui	he is fit to
sunt qui	there are people who
nemo est qui	there is no one who

- At the beginning of a sentence, any part of **qui, quae, quod** may be used as a connective (instead of the demonstrative) with the previous sentence. Translate it in English by "this" or "that" (→5)

1 quis sit **cui** vita talis **placeat**?
Who is there that likes such a life?

2 multa de mea sententia questus est Caesar (**quippe**) **qui** Ravennae Crassum ante **vidisset**
Caesar complained a lot about my decision since he had seen Crassus at Ravenna previously

3 legatos misit **qui** pacem **peterent**
He sent ambassadors to ask for peace

4 **Sunt qui** dicere **timeant**
There are some who are afraid to speak

nemo **idoneus** aderat **qui responderet**
There was nobody there capable of replying

5 **quod** cum **audivisset**, soror lacrimas fudit
When she heard this, my sister shed tears

quae cum ita **sint**, Vatinium defendam
Since this is so, I shall defend Vatinius

Negatives

There are several ways of forming a negative in Latin.

non

- This is the common negative in the indicative and usually stands before the verb, although it may be put in front of any word for emphasis (→**1**)

- Two negatives in the same sentence make an affirmative (→**2**)

haud

- This makes a single word negative, usually an adjective or an adverb (→**3**)

- It is also used in expressions such as **haud scio an** (I don't know whether), and **haud dubito** (I don't doubt) (→**4**)

- **haudquaquam** means not at all (→**5**)

Continued

---

1 ante horam tertiam noctis de foro non **discedit**
   He didn't leave the forum before nine o'clock at night

   Ambarri Caesarem certiorem faciunt se, vastatis agris, **non facile** vim hostium ab oppidis prohibere
   The Ambarri informed Caesar that it was **not easy** for them, since their territory was destroyed, to keep the enemy force away from their towns

   Caesar **non exspectandum** sibi statuit dum Helvetii pervenirent
   Caesar decided **not to wait** till the Swiss arrived

2 non possum non facere
   I must do

   non sumus ignari
   We are well aware

3 haud magnus
   not great

   haud procul
   not far away

4 haud scio an ire mihi liceat
   I don't know whether I am allowed to go

5 homo bonus, haudquaquam eloquens
   A good man but not at all a good speaker

128 SENTENCES

Negatives (contd)

ne

- This is the negative of the imperative and subjunctive. It is also used in many subordinate clauses where the verb is in the subjunctive (→1)

- Wishes (→2)
- Purpose (→3)
- Indirect command (→4)
- Fearing (→5)

Examples   SENTENCES 129

1 **ne** diutius **vivamus**
   Let us **not live** any longer

2 utinam **ne** id **accidisset**
   I wish that it **had not happened**

3 agnus celeriter fugit **ne** lupi se **caperent**
   The lamb ran away quickly **in case** the wolves caught it

4 pater mihi imperavit **ne** abirem
   Father told me **not to go away**

5 cives metuebant **ne** Tiberius libertatem sibi **non redderet**
   The citizens were afraid that Tiberius **would not give** them **back** their freedom

   veritus sum **ne** id quod accidit **adveniret**
   I was afraid that what did in fact happen **might take place**

Negatives (contd)

Other Negatives

- **neque ... neque** neither ... nor (→**1**)
- **neque ... quisquam** neither anyone *or* and no one
- **neque ... quidquam** neither anything *or* and nothing
- **neque ... umquam** neither ever *or* and never
- **nemo ... umquam** no one ever *or* never anyone
- **nihil ... umquam** nothing ever *or* never anything (→**2**)

- Notice the following combinations:

nonnulli	some	*but* **nulli ... non** all
nonnihil	somewhat	*but* **nihil ... non** everything (→**3**)

- **non solum ... sed etiam** } not only ... but also
  non solum ... sed quoque } (→**4**)

- Roman authors repeat negatives for effect (→**5**)

---

1 **neque** illo adit **quisquam neque** eis ipsis **quidquam** praeter oram maritimam notum est
Neither did anyone approach that place, nor did they themselves know anything except the coast

2 **neque** post id tempus **umquam** summis nobiscum copiis hostes contenderunt
And after that the enemy never engaged in battle with us at full strength

ego **nihil umquam** feci solus
I never did anything alone

3 **nonnulli** amici
some friends

nulli amici **non** venerunt
all my friends came

4 Herennius Pontius, iam gravis annis, **non solum** militaribus **sed quoque** civilibus muneribus abscesserat
Herennius Pontius, now old, had withdrawn not only from military but also from civic duties

5 **nihil** audio quod audisse, **nihil** dico quod dixisse paeniteat; **nemo** apud me quemquam sinistris sermonibus carpit, **neminem** ipse reprehendo, **nisi** tamen me cum parum commode scribo; **nulla** spe, **nullo** timore sollicitor, **nullis** rumoribus inquietor; mecum tantum et cum libellis loquor (**Pliny Ep** 1, 9)
I hear nothing that I would regret having heard, I say nothing that I would regret having said; at home nobody nags me with vicious remarks, I don't blame anyone except myself when I write badly; no hope or fear worries me, no idle talk disturbs me; I speak only to myself and to my books

Translation Guidelines

Translating from Latin into English can be both a challenge and a pleasure. The word order of both languages is different: word order shows the relationship of words in English, in Latin it is shown by word endings. Sentences are generally shorter in English, structures simpler. Latin sentences often contain more subordinate clauses, sometimes embedded in other clauses, and often build up to form a long periodic sentence. Subject matter is two thousand years distant in time, although many ideas are still familiar to us today. The following guidelines are suggested to help in translation.

Guidelines

- *Establish the context* of the passage to be translated. Read the introduction in English carefully, find out *who* or *what* is being discussed, *when* and *where* the action took place.

- *Read through the whole passage* fairly quickly to gain some general understanding of the passage, however incomplete.

- *Focus on each sentence*, either taking each word as it comes, or establishing subject/verb/object according to your normal approach. Many find it helpful to pick out the verbs and work out the structure of the clauses. Watch for agreement of adjectives with nouns and how prepositional phrases fit in.

- *Watch conjunctions* **et**, **sed** *etc* and connectives such as **tamen** (however), and **igitur** (therefore). These help explain the logic of the passage as a whole.

- *Note punctuation.* It can be helpful in isolating clauses within the sentences, or marking off an ablative absolute.

- *Be open-minded.* Does **cum**, for example, mean "when", "since", or "although"? Don't decide till the whole sentence is worked out.

- *Use dictionaries carefully.* Check words of similar spelling, check endings. Once you have found the right Latin word, check all of its meanings before deciding on the correct translation.

- *Watch out for features of style eg* use of two adjectives with same meaning *etc*.

- Finally, *check your translation.* Does the narrative or logic of the passage seem consistent? Does your English sound natural? Does it represent the tone or style of the Latin passage? At this stage, fill in any blanks or make corrections.

Translation Problems

Finding the subject

- Look for a noun with a nominative ending. Check with verb ending for agreement. **If there is no nominative, the subject will be indicated by the verb ending.** Remember that, in Latin, the subject is continued from the previous sentence unless there is clear indication otherwise (→1)

Adjective agreement

- Check which adjective agrees with which noun in number, case and gender. Remember that it may be separated from its noun.

    a   b   b   a

te **flagrantis atrox hora Caniculae** nescit tangere
The blazing Dog Star's fierce daytime heat can't touch you

Passive

- Often it is better to turn a Latin passive verb into an active verb in English (→2)

Tense

- English is not so precise as Latin in its use of tenses. Use the tense that seems most natural in English, for example, English past tense for historic present in Latin, or English present tense for Latin future perfect in a conditional clause (→3)

Continued

---

1 consules et armare plebem et inermem pati timebant. **sedabant** tumultum, sedando interdum movebant.
The consuls were afraid both to arm the people and to leave them unarmed. **They quelled** the riot, but sometimes, in quelling it, **they stirred it up again.**

2 hoc a tu **demonstrari** et **probari** volo
I wish you to demonstrate and prove this
or I wish this to be demonstrated and proved by you

3 hoc faciam si **potuero** (*future perfect*)
I shall do this if I can (*present*)

136 TRANSLATION

Translation Problems (contd)

Ablative absolute

hostibus victis can be translated:

when the enemy had been beaten
after beating the enemy
they beat the enemy and ...
although the enemy were beaten

Choose the version that makes most sense within the context of the passage.

Omission of esse

- Parts of **esse** (to be) are often omitted and have to be supplied in English (→**1**)

Omission of small words (ut, id, eo, hic etc)

- Check that you do not omit to translate these words – they are often very important (→**2**)

Neuter plurals

- **omnia** (everything) and **multa** (many things) are often mistranslated.

Impersonal passives

- It is worthwhile learning these (→**3**)

Continued

Examples   TRANSLATION 137

1 sed Germanicus quanto (**erat**) summae spei propior, tanto impensius pro Tiberio niti
But the nearer Germanicus **was** to succeeding, the more strenuously he exerted himself on behalf of Tiberius

2 **eo**   to there (*adv*), by, with *or* from
                     him (*abl of pronoun*)
id ... quod   that which
hic   this (*pron*), here (*adv*)
fit ... ut   it happens ... that

3 **allatum est**   it was announced
cognitum est   it was discovered
pugnatum est   a battle was fought
traditum est   it was recorded
visum est   it seemed

Translation Problems (contd)

Similarity of English/Latin Words

A higher percentage of English words are derived from Latin than from any other source. This can be helpful when trying to deduce the meaning of a Latin word, *eg* **portus** (port). But **porta** (gate) may cause confusion. The following examples taken from actual examination scripts provide a cautionary note. The correct translation follows in brackets:

prima luce nuntius hic **Ameriam** venit
At dawn the messenger came to America
(*At dawn the messenger came to Ameria*)

sex et quinquaginta **milia passuum** in cisio pervolavit
56 thousand flew past in a chariot
(*He quickly travelled fifty-six miles in a chariot*)

ut mori **mallet**
He would rather be killed by a mallet
(*To prefer to die*)

legati **crediderunt**
The embassy got credit
(*The ambassadors believed*)

False Friends/Confusables

ad (+ acc)	to, towards
ab (+ abl)	from, by, with
adeo	to such an extent
adeō	I approach
aestās	summer
aestus	heat, tide
aetas	age
aura	breeze
aurēs (pl)	ears
aurum	gold
avis	bird
avus	grandfather
cado	I fall
caedō	I cut, kill
cēdō	I go, yield
campus	plain
castra (pl)	camp
cēterum	but
cēterī (pl)	the rest
coepī	I began
coēgi	I forced
constituō	I decide
consistō	I stop

Continued

crīmen	charge
scelus	crime
cum (prep)	with
cum (conj)	when, since, although
dominus	master
domus	house
equitēs (pl)	horsemen
equus	horse
fama	fame, report
fames	hunger
forte	by chance
fortis	brave (not strong)
fugāre	to put to flight
fugere	to flight, escape
hōra	hour
hōrum (gen pl)	of these
iaceō	I lie
iaciō	I throw
imperātor	general (not emperor)
imperātus	ordered (past participle)
inveniō	I find (not come in)
invītō	I invite
invītus	unwilling
iter, -ineris	journey
iterum	again
lātus, -a, -um	broad
lātus, -a, -um	brought
lātus, -eris	side

False Friends/Confusables (contd)

liber, -ri	book
liber, -a, -um	free
liberi, -orum (pl)	children
libertus, -i	freedman
magister, -ri	master
magistratus	magistrate
malus, -a, -um	bad
malum, -i	apple
malo, malle	I prefer
manus, -us	hand, band
manes, -ium	spirits of dead
miser, -a, -um	unhappy
miseram	I had sent (plup of mitto)
morior, -i	I die
moror, -ari	I delay
nauta	sailor
navis	ship
nemo	no one
nimium	too much
occasio	opportunity
occasus (solis)	setting (of sun)
occidere	to fall, set
occidere	to kill
opem	help
opera, -ae	work
opus, -eris	task
opus est	it is necessary

Continued

ora, -ae	coast
oro, -are	I pray, beg
os, oris	face
os, ossis	bone
parco, -ere	I spare
pareo, -ere	I obey
pario, -ere	I give birth to
paro, -are	I prepare
passus, -us	a pace
passus, -a, -um	suffered (past participle of patior)
porta, -ae	gate
portus, -us	port
porto, -are	I carry
quaero, -ere	I seek
queror, -i	I complain
quidam	a certain (person)
quidem	indeed
reddo, -ere	I give back
redeo, -ire	I go back
servio, -ire	I serve
servo, -are	I save
sol, -is	sun
soleo, -ere	I am accustomed
solitus sum	
solum, -i	soil
solus, -a, -um	alone

False Friends/Confusables (contd)

tamen	however
tandem	at last
ut(ī)	in order that, as, when
utī (*dep*)	to use
vallis, -is	valley
vallum, -ī	wall, rampart
victor	winner
victus (*past part*)	beaten
vinctus (*past part*)	bound
vīs	force
vīres, -ium	strength
vir, -ī	man
virga, -ae	stick
virgō, -inis	girl
vīta, -ae	life
vītō, -āre	I avoid

VERB TABLES

Conjugations

There are four patterns of regular Latin verbs called conjugations. Each can be identified by the ending of the **present infinitive**:

- First conjugation verbs end in -**āre** (*eg* amāre – to love)

- Second conjugation verbs end in -**ēre** (*eg* habēre – to have)

- Third conjugation verbs end in -**ere** (*eg* mittere – to send)

- Fourth conjugation verbs end in -**īre** (*eg* audīre – to hear)

Each regular verb has three **stems**:

- A **present stem** which is found by cutting off -**re** from the present infinitive (*eg* amāre, habēre, mittere, audīre).

- A **perfect stem** which is formed by adding -**v** to the present stem in the first and fourth conjugations (*eg* amāvī, audīvī), and by adding -**u** to the present stem in the second conjugation (*eg* habuī).

  In the third conjugation there are several possible endings (*eg* scrīpsī, dīxī).

  Some short verbs lengthen the stem vowel (*eg* lēgī), others double the first consonant and vowel (*eg* cucurrī).

- A **supine stem** which is formed by cutting off -**um** from the supine forms (*eg* amātum, habitum, missum, audītum).

Tenses

These forms of the verb show when an action takes place, in the present, in the past or in the future.

In Latin there are six tenses:

1 Present
2 Imperfect } formed from the **present** stem
3 Future

4 Perfect
5 Pluperfect } formed from the **perfect** stem
6 Future Perfect

Tenses Formed from the Present Stem

The following endings are added to the stem:

	PRESENT	IMPERFECT	FUTURE Conj 1&2	Conj 3&4
sing				
1st person	-ō	-bam	-bō	-am
2nd person	-s	-bas	-bis	-ēs
3rd person	-t	-bat	-bit	-et
pl				
1st person	-mus	-bāmus	-bimus	-ēmus
2nd person	-tis	-bātis	-bitis	-ētis
3rd person	-nt	-bant	-bunt	-ent

Note that the above endings show the number and person of the subject of the verb. Subject pronouns are therefore not normally necessary in Latin.

Continued

Conjugations

	1	2	3	4
INFINITIVE	amāre	habēre	mittere	audīre
PRESENT STEM	amā-	habē-	mitte-	audī-
PRESENT				
	amō	habeō	mittō	audiō
	amās	habēs	mittis	audīs
	amat	habet	mittit	audit
	amāmus	habēmus	mittimus	audīmus
	amātis	habētis	mittitis	audītis
	amant	habent	mittunt	audiunt
IMPERFECT				
	amābam	habēbam	mittēbam	audiēbam
	amābās	habēbās	mittēbās	audiēbās
	amābat	habēbat	mittēbat	audiēbat
	amābāmus	habēbāmus	mittēbāmus	audiēbāmus
	amābātis	habēbātis	mittēbātis	audiēbātis
	amābant	habēbant	mittēbant	audiēbant
FUTURE				
	amābō	habēbō	mittam	audiam
	amābis	habēbis	mittēs	audiēs
	amābit	habēbit	mittet	audiet
	amābimus	habēbimus	mittēmus	audiēmus
	amābitis	habēbitis	mittētis	audiētis
	amābunt	habēbunt	mittent	audient

Tenses (contd)

Use:

The Present

In Latin, the present tense expresses what is going on now and can be translated into English in two ways (*eg laborat* – he works, he is working)

- The present is often used in Latin instead of a past tense to make the action more exciting (→**1**)

- Sometimes the Latin present tense is used to describe an action begun in the past and and still continuing (→**2**)

The Imperfect

- Describes what went on or continued for a time (→**3**)

- Denotes an action repeated in the past (→**4**)

- Is used when an action is intended or interrupted (→**5**)

- Is sometimes translated "had" when used with **iam** (→**6**)

The Future

- Is used in Latin as in English to denote what will or is going to be or to happen (→**7**)

- Is occasionally used as a command (→**8**)

- After "**si**" (if) in conditional sentences, it is sometimes translated as present tense in English (→**9**)

Examples

1 **prima luce Caesar Gallos oppugnat**
Caesar attacked the Gauls at dawn

2 **Alexander iam tres annos regit**
Alexander has been ruling for three years now

3 **pluebat** – it was raining

4 **fortiter pugnabant**
They used to fight bravely
or They kept fighting bravely

5 **Romam intrabam**
I was about to enter Rome

6 **multos iam dies villam habitabat**
He had already lived in the house for many days

7 **hoc faciemus**
We shall do this
or We are going to do this

erit gloria
There will be glory

8 **non me vocabis**
Don't call me

9 **si id credes, errabis**
If you believe this, you will be making a mistake

152 VERBS

Tenses (contd)

Tenses Formed from the Perfect Stem

To the appropriate perfect stem add the following endings:

	PERFECT	PLUPERFECT	FUTURE PERFECT
sing			
1st person	-ī	-eram	-erō
2nd person	-istī	-erās	-eris
3rd person	-it	-erat	-erit
pl			
1st person	-imus	-erāmus	-erimus
2nd person	-istis	-erātis	-eritis
3rd person	-ērunt	-erant	-erint

Continued

VERBS 153

Conjugations

	1	2	3	4
PERFECT STEM	amāv-	habu-	mīs-	audī-
PERFECT				
	amāvī	habuī	mīsī	audīvī
	amāvistī	habuistī	mīsistī	audīvistī
	amāvit	habuit	mīsit	audīvit
	amāvimus	habuimus	mīsimus	audīvimus
	amāvistis	habuistis	mīsistis	audīvistis
	amāvērunt	habuērunt	mīsērunt	audīvērunt
PLUPERFECT				
	amāveram	habueram	mīseram	audīveram
	amāverās	habuerās	mīserās	audīverās
	amāverat	habuerat	mīserat	audīverat
	amāverāmus	habuerāmus	mīserāmus	audīverāmus
	amāverātis	habuerātis	mīserātis	audīverātis
	amāverant	habuerant	mīserant	audīverant
FUTURE PERFECT				
	amāverō	habuerō	mīserō	audīverō
	amāveris	habueris	mīseris	audīveris
	amāverit	habuerit	mīserit	audīverit
	amāverimus	habuerimus	mīserimus	audīverimus
	amāveritis	habueritis	mīseritis	audīveritis
	amāverint	habuerint	mīserint	audīverint

Tenses (contd)

Use:

The Perfect

- In Latin, the perfect tense is equivalent to the simple past tense (*eg* **vīdī** – I saw) and the perfect tense (*eg* **vīdī** – I have seen) in English.

- It states past action particularly in narrative (→**1**)

- Expresses an action completed in the past which still has effect in the present (→**2**)

The Pluperfect

- Denotes an action completed in the past before another past action (→**3**)

The Future Perfect

- Denotes completing something in the future (→**4**)

- Is often used with **volō, possum, nolō** *etc* (→**5**)

- Denotes an action which precedes another action in the future, often in a subordinate clause (→**6**)

Examples

1. **veni, vidi, vici**
   I came, I saw, I conquered

2. **spem in fide alicuius habuerunt**
   They place their hope in someone's good faith

3. **Mithridates urbem Asiae clarissimam obsederat quam L. Lucullus virtute liberavit**
   Mithridates had besieged the most famous city in Asia that Lucius Lucullus freed by his courage

4. **id fecero**
   I shall have done it

5. **si potuero, faciam**
   If I can, I shall do it

6. **qui prior venerit, prior discedet**
   First to come will be first to go

The Passive

Verbs may be active or passive. In **active** forms of the verb, the subject carries out the action (*eg* Brutus **killed** Caesar). In **passive** forms of the verb, the subject receives the action (*eg* Caesar **was killed** by Brutus).

Conjugation

To form the passive tenses of regular verbs, substitute the following endings for those of the present, imperfect and future active tenses (conjugated on page 148):

- In the present 1st person sing the ending is **-or**.
- In the imperfect, the endings are added to **-ba**.
- In the future (conjugations 1 and 2), the endings are added to **-bo** (*1st person sing*), **-be** (*2nd person sing*), and **-bi** for other persons. In conjugations 3 and 4, the 1st person *sing* ending is **-ar**.

Continued

---

sing	1st person	-r
	2nd person	-ris
	3rd person	-tur
pl	1st person	-mur
	2nd person	-mini
	3rd person	-ntur

Conjugations

	1	2	3	4
PRESENT PASSIVE				
	amor	habeor	mittor	audior
	amāris	habēris	mitteris	audīris
	amātur	habētur	mittitur	audītur
	amāmur	habēmur	mittimur	audīmur
	amāmini	habēmini	mittimini	audīmini
	amantur	habentur	mittuntur	audiuntur
IMPERFECT PASSIVE				
	amābar	habēbar	mittēbar	audiēbar
	amābāris	habēbāris	mittēbāris	audiēbāris
	amābātur	habēbātur	mittēbātur	audiēbātur
	amābāmur	habēbāmur	mittēbāmur	audiēbāmur
	amābāmini	habēbāmini	mittēbāmini	audiēbāmini
	amābantur	habēbantur	mittēbantur	audiēbantur
FUTURE PASSIVE				
	amābor	habēbor	mittar	audiar
	amāberis	habēberis	mittēris	audiēris
	amābitur	habēbitur	mittētur	audiētur
	amābimur	habēbimur	mittēmur	audiēmur
	amābimini	habēbimini	mittēmini	audiēmini
	amābuntur	habēbuntur	mittentur	audientur

The Passive (contd)

Translation

Present Passive

1 I am loved
you (*sing*) are loved
he/she/it is loved

we are loved
you (*pl*) are loved
they are loved

2 I am held *etc*

3 I am sent *etc*

4 I am heard *etc*

Imperfect Passive

1 I was loved
you (*sing*) were loved
he/she/it was loved

we were loved
you (*pl*) were loved
they were loved

2 I was held *etc*

3 I was sent *etc*

4 I was heard *etc*

Future Passive

1 I shall be loved
you (*sing*) will be loved
he/she/it will be loved

we shall be loved
you (*pl*) will be loved
they will be loved

2 I shall be held *etc*

3 I shall be sent *etc*

4 I shall be heard *etc*

● "going to be" may also be used to translate the future.
Continued

The Passive (contd)

Perfect, Pluperfect and Future Perfect Passive

These tenses consist of the past participle (formed from the supine stem) and tenses of the verb **sum** (to be). The past participle endings agree in number and gender with the subject of the verb.

Conjugations

	1	2	3	4	
PERFECT PASSIVE					
	amātus -a, -um	habitus -a, -um	missus -a, -um	audītus -a, -um	sum es est
	amātī -ae, -a	habitī -ae, -a	missī -ae, -a	audītī -ae, -a	sumus estis sunt
PLUPERFECT PASSIVE					
	amātus	habitus	missus	audītus	eram erās erat
	amātī	habitī	missī	audītī	erāmus erātis erant
FUTURE PERFECT PASSIVE					
	amātus	habitus	missus	audītus	erō eris erit
	amātī	habitī	missī	audītī	erimus eritis erunt

The Passive (contd)

Translation

Perfect Passive

1 I have been loved   we have been loved
   you (*sing*) have been   you (*pl*) have been loved
   loved   they have been loved
   he/she/it has been loved

2 I have been held *or* I was held *etc*
3 I have been sent *or* I was sent *etc*
4 I have been heard *or* I was heard *etc*

Pluperfect Passive

1 I had been loved   we had been loved
   you (*sing*) had been loved   you (*pl*) had been loved
   he/she/it had been loved   they had been loved

2 I had been held *etc*
3 I had been sent *etc*
4 I had been heard *etc*

Future Perfect Passive

1 I shall have been loved   we shall have been loved
   you (*sing*) will have been   you (*pl*) will have been
   loved   loved
   he/she/it will have been   they will have been loved
   loved

2 I shall have been held *etc*
3 I shall have been sent *etc*
4 I shall have been heard *etc*

Examples

1 **milites a populo occisi sunt**
   The soldiers were killed by the people

2 **populus milites occidit**
   The people killed the soldiers

- Note that the subject of the passive verb in (1) becomes the object of the active verb in (2).

- Often in English it is better to translate the meaning actively as in (2).

- The **agent** of the action is translated by **a(b)** with the ablative case as in a **populo** (1) – by the people.

- The **thing** causing the action is translated by the ablative case alone

   saxo percussus erat
   He had been struck by a rock

The Subjunctive

So far all verbs described have belonged to the indicative mood, which states facts. The subjunctive mood represents ideas, possibilities or necessities and is often translated by auxiliary verbs such as **may**, **might**, **could**, **would**, **should** or **must**. There are four tenses active and passive – present, imperfect, perfect and pluperfect.

Formation of Active

The present subjunctive active is formed from the present stem, the imperfect from the infinitive. To these add the endings

-m, -s, -t, -mus, -tis, -nt.

- Note that in first conjugation present the preceding vowel is **-e**, and in all others **-a**.
- The present subjunctive active is sometimes translated by using **"may"** (→**1**)
- The imperfect subjunctive active is sometimes trans-lated by using **"might"** (→**2**)

Conjugations

	1	2	3	4
PRESENT SUBJUNCTIVE ACTIVE				
	amem	habeam	mittam	audiam
	amēs	habeās	mittās	audiās
	amet	habeat	mittat	audiat
	amēmus	habeāmus	mittāmus	audiāmus
	amētis	habeātis	mittātis	audiātis
	ament	habeant	mittant	audiant
IMPERFECT SUBJUNCTIVE ACTIVE				
	amārem	habērem	mitterem	audīrem
	amārēs	habērēs	mitterēs	audīrēs
	amāret	habēret	mitteret	audīret
	amārēmus	habērēmus	mitterēmus	audīrēmus
	amārētis	habērētis	mitterētis	audīrētis
	amārent	habērent	mitterent	audīrent

1 amem – I may love
mittās – you (*sing*) may send
habeat – he may have
audiant – they may hear

2 mitterētis – you (*pl*) might send
habērem – I might have
amāret – she might love
audīrent – they might hear

Continued

The Subjunctive (contd)

Formation of Passive

The passive of the present and imperfect subjunctive is easily formed by substituting the normal passive endings (-r, -ris, -tur, -mur, -mini, -ntur) for the active ones.

Conjugation

	1	2	3	4
PRESENT SUBJUNCTIVE PASSIVE	amer	habear	mittar	audiar
	amēris	habeāris	mittāris	audiāris
	amētur	habeātur	mittātur	audiātur
	amēmur	habeāmur	mittāmur	audiāmur
	amēminī	habeāminī	mittāminī	audiāminī
	amentur	habeantur	mittantur	audiantur
IMPERFECT SUBJUNCTIVE PASSIVE	amārer	habērer	mitterer	audīrer
	amārēris	habērēris	mitterēris	audīrēris
	amārētur	habērētur	mitterētur	audīrētur
	amārēmur	habērēmur	mitterēmur	audīrēmur
	amārēminī	habērēminī	mitterēminī	audīrēminī
	amārentur	habērentur	mitterentur	audīrentur

- The present subjunctive passive is sometimes translated by using "**may be**" (→**1**)

- The imperfect subjunctive passive is sometimes translated by using "**might be**" (→**2**)

Continued

Examples

1 **habeamur** – we may be held
  amer – I may be loved
  mittaminī – you (*pl*) may be sent
  audiantur – they may be heard

2 **audirēminī** – you (*pl*) might be heard
  amārētur – he might be loved
  haberentur – they might be held
  mitterer – I might be sent

The Subjunctive (contd)

Perfect and Pluperfect Subjunctive Active

Both perfect and pluperfect subjunctive active are formed from the perfect stem as follows:

Conjugation

1	**2**	**3**	**4**
PERFECT SUBJUNCTIVE ACTIVE			
amāverim	habuerim	mīserim	audīverim
amāveris	habueris	mīseris	audīveris
amāverit	habuerit	mīserit	audīverit
amāverimus	habuerimus	mīserimus	audīverimus
amāveritis	habueritis	mīseritis	audīveritis
amāverint	habuerint	mīserint	audīverint
PLUPERFECT SUBJUNCTIVE ACTIVE			
amāvissem	habuissem	mīsissem	audīvissem
amāvissēs	habuissēs	mīsissēs	audīvissēs
amāvisset	habuisset	mīsisset	audīvisset
amāvissēmus	habuissēmus	mīsissēmus	audīvissēmus
amāvissētis	habuissētis	mīsissētis	audīvissētis
amāvissent	habuissent	mīsissent	audīvissent

- The Perfect subjunctive active is sometimes translated by using **"may have"** with the past participle in English (→1)

- The Pluperfect subjunctive active is sometimes translated by using **"might have"** with the past participle in English (→2)

Continued

Examples

1 **miserit** – he may have sent
habuerint – they may have had
audiveris – you (*sing*) may have heard
amaveritis – you (*pl*) may have loved

2 **amavissemus** – we might have loved
habuisset – he might have had
audivissent – they might have heard
misissem – I might have sent

The Subjunctive (contd)

Perfect and Pluperfect Subjunctive Passive

Both perfect and pluperfect subjunctive passive are formed from the supine stem and the present and imperfect subjunctive of **sum** respectively:

Conjugation

1

PERFECT SUBJUNCTIVE PASSIVE

amátus	habitus	sim
		sīs
		sit

pl

amátī	habitī	sīmus
		sītis
		sint

PLUPERFECT SUBJUNCTIVE PASSIVE

amátus	habitus	essem
		essēs
		esset

pl

amátī	habitī	essēmus
		essētis
		essent

2

PERFECT SUBJUNCTIVE PASSIVE

	sim
	sīs
	sit

	sīmus
	sītis
	sint

PLUPERFECT SUBJUNCTIVE PASSIVE

	essem
	essēs
	esset

	essēmus
	essētis
	essent

Conjugation

3

PERFECT SUBJUNCTIVE PASSIVE

missus	sim
	sīs
	sit

pl

missī	sīmus
	sītis
	sint

PLUPERFECT SUBJUNCTIVE PASSIVE

missus	essem
	essēs
	esset

pl

missī	essēmus
	essētis
	essent

4

auditus	sim
	sīs
	sit

audītī	sīmus
	sītis
	sint

auditus	essem
	essēs
	esset

audītī	essēmus
	essētis
	essent

Continued

The Subjunctive (contd)

- The perfect subjunctive passive is sometimes translated by using **"may have been"** with the past participle in English (→**1**)

- The pluperfect subjunctive passive is sometimes translated by using **"might have been"** with the past participle in English (→**2**)

1 **habitus sis** – you (*sing*) may have been held
missi simus – we may have been sent
auditus sim – I may have been heard
amati sint – they may have been loved

2 **amati essemus** – we might have been loved
habiti essent – they might have been held
missus esses – you (*sing*) might have been sent
auditus essem – I might have been heard

The Imperative

This is the mood of command. It has two forms, 2nd person *sing* and *pl*, active (→**1**) and passive: (→**2**)

Conjugations

	1	2	3	4
IMPERATIVE ACTIVE				
sing	amā	habē	mitte	audī
pl	amāte	habēte	mittite	audīte
IMPERATIVE PASSIVE				
sing	amāre	habēre	mittere	audīre
pl	amāminī	habēminī	mittīminī	audīminī

1 **pecuniam mittite, o cives**
Citizens, send money! (active)

spem habe
Have hope! (active)

2 **in curia audimini**
Be heard in the senate! (passive)

ab omnibus semper amare, Romule
Always be loved by everyone, Romulus (passive)

The Infinitive

The infinitive was originally a noun and can be used in this way in Latin (*eg* amāre – to love *or* loving). There are three types, present, future and perfect, both active and passive, formed as follows:

Active

	1	**2**
PRESENT	amāre	habēre
FUTURE	amātūrus esse	habitūrus esse
PERFECT	amāvisse	habuisse

	3	**4**
PRESENT	mittere	audīre
FUTURE	missūrus esse	auditūrus esse
PERFECT	mīsisse	audīvisse

Translation

to love
to be going to love
to have loved

to have
to be going to have
to have had

to send
to be going to send
to have sent

to hear
to be going to hear
to have heard

Continued

Passive

	1	**2**
PRESENT	amārī	habērī
FUTURE	amātum īrī	habitum īrī
PERFECT	amātus esse	habitus esse

	3	**4**
PRESENT	mittī	audīrī
FUTURE	missum īrī	auditum īrī
PERFECT	missus esse	audītus esse

Translation

to be loved
to be going to be loved
to have been loved

to be had
to be going to be had
to have been had

to be sent
to be going to be sent
to have been sent

to be heard
to be going to be heard
to have been heard

- In the future active -**urus**, -**a**, -**um** and in the perfect passive -**us**, -**a**, -**um** agree in number and gender with the noun or pronoun in indirect speech.

The Infinitive (contd)

Uses of the Infinitive

- It can be used as a neuter noun

- As the subject of the sentence (→**1**)

- With certain nouns such as **fas** (right), **nefas** (wrong) (→**2**)

- As the object of the following verbs: (→**3**)

volō	I wish	**cupiō**	I desire
nōlō	I do not wish	**sinō**	I allow
possum	I am able to, can	**cogō**	I force
sciō	I know (how)	**audeō**	I dare
nesciō	I do not know	**conor**	I try
debeō	I ought	**desinō**	I stop
soleō	I am accustomed	**dubitō**	I hesitate
incipiō	I begin	**coepi**	I begin

- It can be used to describe a rapid series of events instead of using the perfect tense (→**4**)

Examples

1 **errare est humanum**
To err is human

2 **nefas est templa destruere**
It is wrong to destroy temples

3 **volo domum redire**
I wish to return home

desine mortuos commemorare
Stop remembering the dead

Romam exstinctam esse cupit
He wishes Rome blotted out

4 **ille non tollere oculos, non remittere stilum, tum fragor adventare et intra limen audiri**
He did not raise his eyes nor put down his pen, then the noise came closer and could be heard inside the door.

Participles

There are three participles (or verbal adjectives) in Latin: the present active, the perfect passive and the future active.

The Present Participle

This is formed from the present stem by adding -ns and lengthening the previous vowel. The genitive ending is -ntis.

Conjugation

1	2	3	4
amāns	habēns	mittēns	audiēns
loving	having	sending	hearing

- Note that these decline like group 3 adjectives ending in -ns with ablative singular, in -i when used as an adjective and in -e when used as a verb. They agree in number, case and gender with nouns or pronouns in the sentence.

Use

- It denotes an action going on at the same time as the main verb (→1)

- It can be used as a noun (→2)

Continued

Examples

1   **pro patria pugnantes iuvenes mortui sunt**
    The young men died *while fighting* for their country
    Romulo regnante, Roma urbs parva erat
    While Romulus was ruling, Rome was a small city

2   **lacrimae adstantium**
    the tears of *people standing by*

Participles (contd)

The Perfect Participle

This is formed from the supine stem by adding the endings -us, -a, -m. It declines like first and second declension adjectives (see pages 25–28)

Conjugation

1	2	3	4
amātus (having been) loved	habitus (having been) held	missus (having been) sent	audītus (having been) heard

Use

• It denotes an action that is completed before that of the main verb (→1)

• English is less precise in the use of tenses and frequently uses a present to translate a Latin past participle.

The Future Participle

This is formed by adding -ūrus, -a, -um to the supine stem. It declines like first and second declension adjectives.

Conjugation

1	2	3	4
amātūrus going to love	habitūrus going to have	missūrus going to send	audītūrus going to hear

Use

• It denotes an action that is going to take place (→2)

• The forms futūrus (going to be) and ventūrus (going to come) are often used as adjectives.

---

1 **equites Romani auditi ad senatum adducti sunt**
   The Roman businessmen *were heard* and then were brought before the Senate

   castra capta incendimus
   We *captured* the camp and burnt it
   or *Capturing* the camp, we burnt it

2 **nos morituri te salutamus**
   We who are *about to die* salute you

Gerunds and Gerundives

The **gerund** is a **verbal noun** and is active.

The **gerundive** is a **verbal adjective** and is passive.

The gerund is formed by adding -**ndum** to the present stem. It declines like a neuter noun -**ndum**, -**ndī**, -**ndō**, -**ndō**.

The gerundive declines like first and second declension adjectives -**us**, -**a**, -**um** (A)

Conjugation

	1	2	3	4
GERUND	amandum loving	habendum having	mittendum sending	audiendum hearing
GERUNDIVE	amandus requiring to be loved	habendus requiring to be held	mittendus requiring to be sent	audiendus requiring to be heard

Gerunds and Gerundives (contd)

Use of Gerund and Gerundive

- The gerund is often used with the accusative case to express **purpose** (→**1**)

- If the verb has a direct object, the gerundive is used instead (→**2**)

- The gerund is used in the genitive case with nouns and adjectives (→**3**) such as

  ars (art), **spes** (hope), **cupidus** (eager), **peritus** (skilled)

- Both the gerund and the gerundive can be used in the genitive with **causa** to express **purpose** (→**4**)

- The gerundive can be used to imply **obligation** and the person is expressed by the dative case (→**5**)

- If the verb cannot take a direct object, the impersonal form is used (→**6**)

- Both the gerund and the gerundive can be used in the ablative case (→**7**)

Examples

1   **venit ad regnandum**
He came to rule

2   **venit ad pacem petendam**
He came to make peace

3   **spes videndi**
Hope of seeing

     peritus equitandi
Skilled in riding

4   **dicendi causa**
to speak

     pacis petendae causa
For the sake of making peace

5   **poenae nobis timendae sunt**
Punishment must be feared by us
or We must fear punishment

6   **mihi parendum est**
You must obey me

7   **docendo discimus**
We learn by teaching

     me puniendo effugit
By punishing me he escaped

186 VERBS: IMPERSONAL

Impersonal Verbs

Impersonal verbs are used in the third person singular only

- To describe the weather (→1)

- To express feeling. The person affected appears in the accusative case and the cause in the genitive case (→2)

- To express permission or pleasure. The person affected appears in the dative case. The verb is often followed by a present infinitive (→3)

- To express happening, following etc. These are followed by **ut** with the subjunctive mood (→4)

  fit ut   it happens that
  accidit ut   it happens that
  sequitur ut   it follows that

- Certain intransitive verbs are used impersonally in the passive (→5)

- Verbs of saying, believing etc are used impersonally in the perfect passive tense (→6)

- The verbs, **interest** (it is of importance), and **refert** (it is of concern), are followed usually by **meâ, tuâ, nostrâ, vestrâ** (→7)

- Sometimes **interest** is followed by genitive of the person (→8)

- The following verbs are followed by a present infinitive. The person involved appears in the accusative case (→9)

  me decet   it is fitting for me
  me oportet   I must/ought

Examples VERBS: IMPERSONAL 187

1 **pluit**
it is raining
tonat
there is thunder

fulgurat
there is lightning
ningit
it is snowing

2 **me miseret**
I am sorry for
me paenitet
I repent of

me miseret sociorum
I am sorry for my comrades

3 **mihi licet**
I am allowed to
tibi videtur
it seems good to you
or you decide

nobis placet
it is pleasing to us
or we like

4 **fit ut**
it happens that
accidit ut
it happens that

fit ut fallar
it happens that I am mistaken

5 **pugnatum est in mari**
the battle was fought at sea
vivitur in oculis omnium
life is lived in the sight of everyone

6 **nuntiatum est**
it has been announced
mihi dictum est Germanos transiisse Rhenum
I was told that the Germans had crossed the Rhine

7 **nihil mea refert**
it is of no interest to me

8 **Caesaris interest**
it is important to Caesar

9 **nos morari oportuit**
we ought to have waited

Deponent Verbs

Deponent verbs are passive in form but active in meaning. They also have present and future participles and future infinitive which are active in meaning. The perfect participle is also active in meaning. Otherwise the conjugation is similar to that of regular verbs.

1st Conjugation

conārī (to try)

INDICATIVE		SUBJUNCTIVE	
PRESENT	I try etc		I may try etc
conor		coner	
conāris		conēris	
conātur		conētur	
conāmur		conēmur	
conāminī		conēminī	
conantur		conentur	
IMPERFECT	I was trying etc		I might try etc
conābar		conārer	
conābāris		conārēris	
conābātur		conārētur	
conābāmur		conārēmur	
conābāminī		conārēminī	
conābantur		conārentur	
FUTURE	I shall try etc		
conābor			
conāberis			
conābitur			
conābimur			
conābiminī			
conābuntur			

Continued

PERFECT					
conātus	sum	I tried	conātus	sim	I may have tried
-a, -um	es	you tried etc	-a, -um	sīs	you may have tried etc
PLUPERFECT					
conātus	eram	I had tried	conātus	essem	I might have tried
-a, -um	erās	you had tried etc	-a, -um	essēs	you might have tried etc
FUTURE PERFECT					
conātus	erō	I shall have tried			
-a, -um	eris	you will have tried etc			

IMPERATIVE

conāre	sing	try
conāminī	pl	try

INFINITIVES

present	conārī	to try
future	conātūrus esse	to be going to try
perfect	conātus esse	to have tried

PARTICIPLES

present	conāns	trying
future	conātūrus	going to try
perfect	conātus	having tried

GERUND

conāndum	trying

GERUNDIVE

conāndus	requiring to be tried

Second, Third, Fourth Conjugations

These are conjugated like the passive form of verbs of the corresponding conjugations. A summary is provided as follows:

Second Conjugation

verērī (to fear, be afraid)

INDICATIVE		
Present	**vereor**	I am afraid
Imperfect	**verēbar**	I was afraid
Future	**verēbor**	I shall be afraid
Perfect	**veritus sum**	I was afraid
Pluperfect	**veritus eram**	I had been afraid
Future Perfect	**veritus erō**	I shall have been afraid

SUBJUNCTIVE		
Present	**verear**	I may be afraid
Imperfect	**verērer**	I might be afraid
Perfect	**veritus sim**	I may have been afraid
Pluperfect	**veritus essem**	I might have been afraid

IMPERATIVE		
Singular	**verēre**	be afraid
Plural	**verēminī**	be afraid

Continued

INFINITIVES		
Present	**verērī**	to be afraid
Future	**veritūrus esse**	to be going to be afraid
Perfect	**veritus esse**	to have been afraid

PARTICIPLES		
Present	**verēns**	fearing, being afraid
Future	**veritūrus**	going to fear or be afraid
Perfect	**veritus**	having feared or been afraid (active)

GERUND	**verendum**	fearing
GERUNDIVE	**verendus**	requiring to be feared

Second, Third, Fourth Conjugations (contd)

Third Conjugation

sequī (to follow)

INDICATIVE		
Present	sequor	I follow
Imperfect	sequēbar	I was following
Future	sequar	I shall follow
Perfect	secūtus sum	I followed
Pluperfect	secūtus eram	I had followed
Future Perfect	secūtus erō	I shall have followed
SUBJUNCTIVE		
Present	sequar	I may follow
Imperfect	sequerer	I might follow
Perfect	secūtus sim	I may have followed
Pluperfect	secūtus essem	I might have followed
IMPERATIVE		
Singular	sequere	follow
Plural	sequiminī	follow
INFINITIVES		
Present	sequī	to follow
Future	secūtūrus esse	to be going to follow
Perfect	secūtus esse	to have followed
PARTICIPLES		
Present	sequēns	following
Future	secūtūrus	going to follow
Perfect	secūtus	having followed
GERUND	sequendum	following
GERUNDIVE	sequendus	requiring to be followed

Fourth Conjugation

mentīrī (to lie)

INDICATIVE		
Present	mentior	I lie
Imperfect	mentiēbar	I was lying
Future	mentiar	I shall lie
Perfect	mentītus sum	I lied
Pluperfect	mentītus eram	I had lied
Future Perfect	mentītus erō	I shall have lied
SUBJUNCTIVE		
Present	mentiar	I may lie
Imperfect	mentīrer	I might lie
Perfect	mentītus sim	I may have lied
Pluperfect	mentītus essem	I might have lied
IMPERATIVE		
Singular	mentīre	lie
Plural	mentīminī	lie
INFINITIVES		
Present	mentīrī	to lie
Future	mentītūrus esse	to be going to lie
Perfect	mentītus esse	to have lied
PARTICIPLES		
Present	mentiēns	lying
Future	mentītūrus	going to lie
Perfect	mentītus	having lied
GERUND	mentiendum	lying
GERUNDIVE	mentiendus	requiring to be lied to

Semi-deponent Verbs

A few verbs are passive in form and active in meaning in only the perfect tenses. All other tenses are active in form and meaning. These are:

audēre	to dare	
gaudēre	to be glad	
solēre	to be accustomed	
confīdere	to trust	

INDICATIVE		
Present	audeō	I dare
Imperfect	audēbam	I was daring
Future	audēbo	I shall dare

SUBJUNCTIVE		
Present	audeam	I may dare
Imperfect	audērem	I might dare

IMPERATIVE		
Singular	audē	dare
Plural	audēte	dare

INFINITIVE		
Present	audēre	to dare

PRES PARTICIPLE	audēns	daring
GERUND	audendum	daring
GERUNDIVE	audendus	requiring to be dared

All other parts are **passive** in form:

INDICATIVE		
Perfect	ausus **sum**	I dared
Pluperfect	ausus **eram**	I had dared
Future Perfect	ausus **erō**	I shall have dared

SUBJUNCTIVE		
Perfect	ausus **sim**	I may have dared
Pluperfect	ausus **essem**	I might have dared

PARTICIPLES		
Perfect	ausus	having dared
Future	ausūrus	going to dare

INFINITIVES		
Perfect	ausus **esse**	to have dared
Future	ausūrus **esse**	to be going to dare

Unique Verbs

The following verbs are different from the conjugations described so far:

esse (to be)

Indicative

PRESENT

sum	I am
es	you (*sing*) are
est	he/she/it is
sumus	we are
estis	you (*pl*) are
sunt	they are

IMPERFECT

eram	I was
erās	you (*sing*) were
erat	he/she/it was
erāmus	we were
erātis	you (*pl*) were
erant	they were

FUTURE

erō	I shall be
eris	you (*sing*) will be
erit	he/she/it will be
erimus	we shall be
eritis	you (*pl*) will be
erunt	they will be

Subjunctive

PRESENT

sim	I may be
sīs	you (*sing*) may be
sit	he/she/it may be
sīmus	we may be
sītis	you (*pl*) may be
sint	they may be

IMPERFECT

essem	I might be
essēs	you (*sing*) might be
esset	he/she/it might be
essēmus	we might be
essētis	you (*pl*) might be
essent	they might be

Continued

esse (to be) (contd)

Indicative

PERFECT

fuī	I have been, was
fuistī	you (*sing*) have been/were
fuit	he/she/it has been/was
fuimus	we have been/were
fuistis	you (*pl*) have been/were
fuērunt	they have been/were

PLUPERFECT

fueram	I had been
fuerās	you (*sing*) had been
fuerat	he/she/it had been
fuerāmus	we had been
fuerātis	you (*pl*) had been
fuerant	they had been

FUTURE PERFECT

fuerō	I shall have been
fueris	you (*sing*) will have been
fuerit	he/she/it will have been
fuerimus	we shall have been
fueritis	you (*pl*) will have been
fuerint	they will have been

Subjunctive

PERFECT

fuerim	I may have been
fueris	you (*sing*) may have been
fuerit	he/she/it may have been
fuerīmus	we may have been
fuerītis	you (*pl*) may have been
fuerint	they may have been

PLUPERFECT

fuissem	I might have been
fuissēs	you (*sing*) might have been
fuisset	he/she/it might have been
fuissēmus	we might have been
fuissētis	you (*pl*) might have been
fuissent	they might have been

Imperative

Singular	es	be
Plural	este	be

Infinitives

Present	esse	to be
Future	futūrus esse / fore	to be going to be
Perfect	fuisse	to have been

Participle

	futūrus	going to be

● Compounds of **esse** are listed in the principal parts page 220.

posse (to be able)

● This verb is formed from **pot-** and **-esse**. Note that **t** becomes **s** before another **s**.

Indicative

PRESENT

possum	I am able
potes	you (*sing*) are able
potest	he/she/it is able
possumus	we are able
potestis	you (*pl*) are able
possunt	they are able

IMPERFECT

poteram	I was able *etc*
poterās	
poterat	
poterāmus	
poterātis	
poterant	

FUTURE

poterō	I shall be able *etc*
poteris	
poterit	
poterimus	
poteritis	
poterunt	

Subjunctive

PRESENT

possim	I may be able *etc*
possis	
possit	
possīmus	
possītis	
possint	

IMPERFECT

possem	I might be able *etc*
possēs	
posset	
possēmus	
possētis	
possent	

Continued

posse (to be able) (contd)

Indicative

PERFECT
potuī
potuistī
potuit
potuimus
potuistis
potuērunt

I have been able *etc*

PLUPERFECT
potueram
potuerās
potuerat
potuerāmus
potuerātis
potuerant

I had been able *etc*

FUTURE PERFECT
potuerō
potueris
potuerit
potuerimus
potueritis
potuerint

I shall have been able *etc*

Subjunctive

PERFECT
potuerim
potueris
potuerit
potuerimus
potueritis
potuerint

I may have been able *etc*

PLUPERFECT
potuissem
potuissēs
potuisset
potuissēmus
potuissētis
potuissent

I might have been able *etc*

Infinitives

posse   to be able
potuisse   to have been able

ferre (to bear)

Active

Indicative

PRESENT
ferō	I bear *etc*
fers	
fert	
ferimus	
fertis	
ferunt	

IMPERFECT
ferēbam I was bearing

FUTURE
feram I shall bear

PERFECT
tulī I bore

PLUPERFECT
tuleram I had borne

FUTURE PERFECT
tulerō I shall have borne

Subjunctive

PRESENT
feram	I may bear *etc*
ferās	
ferat	
ferāmus	
ferātis	
ferant	

IMPERFECT
ferrem I might bear

PERFECT
tulerim I may have borne

PLUPERFECT
tulissem I might have borne

Infinitives
Present	**ferre**	to bear
Future	**lātūrus esse**	to be going to bear
Perfect	**tulisse**	to have borne

Imperatives
Singular	**fer**	bear
Plural	**ferte**	bear

Supine
lātum

Continued

ferre (to bear) (contd)

Passive

Indicative

PRESENT
feror I am borne *etc*
ferris
fertur
ferimur
feriminī
feruntur

IMPERFECT
ferēbar I was being borne

FUTURE
ferar I shall be borne

PERFECT
lātus sum I was borne

PLUPERFECT
lātus eram I had been borne

FUTURE PERFECT
lātus erō I shall have been borne

Subjunctive

PRESENT
ferar I may be borne *etc*
ferāris
ferātur
ferāmur
ferāminī
ferantur

IMPERFECT
ferrer I might be borne

PERFECT
lātus sim I may have been borne

PLUPERFECT
lātus essem I might have been borne

Infinitives
Present	**ferrī**	to be borne
Future	**lātum īrī**	to be going to be borne
Perfect	**lātus esse**	to have been borne

Imperatives
Singular	**ferre**	be borne
Plural	**feriminī**	be borne

Participles
Present	**ferēns**	bearing
Future	**lātūrus**	going to bear
Perfect	**lātus**	having been borne/carried

Gerund	**ferendum**	bearing
Gerundive	**ferendus**	requiring to be borne

Continued

fieri (to become, be made)

● This verb is the passive form of **facere** – to make.

Indicative

PRESENT
fiō	I become
fis	you (*sing*) become
fit	he/she/it becomes
(fimus)	
(fitis)	
fiunt	

IMPERFECT
fiēbam I was becoming

FUTURE
fiam I shall become

PERFECT
factus sum I became

PLUPERFECT
factus eram I had become

FUTURE PERFECT
factus erō I shall have become

Subjunctive

PRESENT
fiam	I may become *etc*
fiās	
fiat	
fiāmus	
fiātis	
fiant	

IMPERFECT
fierem I might become

PERFECT
factus sim I may have become

PLUPERFECT
factus essem I might have become

Infinitives
Present	**fierī**	to become
Future	**factum īrī**	to be going to become
Perfect	**factus esse**	to have become

Participle
Perfect	**factus**	having become

Gerundive **faciendus** becoming

īre (to go)

- The stem is **i-**. Before **a, o, u,** it changes to **e-**.

Indicative

PRESENT

eo	I go *etc*
īs	
it	
īmus	
ītis	
eunt	

IMPERFECT
ībam   I was going

FUTURE
ībō   I shall go

PERFECT
īvī or iī   I went/have gone

PLUPERFECT
īveram   I had gone

FUTURE PERFECT
īverō   I shall have gone

Subjunctive

PRESENT

eam	I may go *etc*
eās	
eat	
eāmus	
eātis	
eant	

IMPERFECT
īrem   I might go

PERFECT
īverim   I may have gone

PLUPERFECT
īvissem   I might have gone

Infinitives

Present	**īre**	to go
Future	**ītūrus esse**	to be going to go
Perfect	**īvisse** *or* **īsse**	to have gone

Imperative

Singular	**ī**	go
Plural	**īte**	go

Participles

Present	**iēns** (*gen* **euntis**)	going
Future	**ītūrus**	going to go

Gerund	**eundum**	going

velle (to wish)

Indicative

PRESENT
volō   I wish/am willing *etc*
vīs
vult
volumus
vultis
volunt

IMPERFECT
volēbam   I was wishing
volēbās
volēbat
volēbāmus
volēbātis
volēbant

FUTURE
volam   I shall wish

PERFECT
voluī   I wished/have wished

PLUPERFECT
volueram   I had wished

FUTURE PERFECT
voluerō   I shall have wished

Subjunctive

PRESENT
velim   I may wish
velīs
velit
velīmus
velītis
velint

IMPERFECT
vellem   I might wish
vellēs
vellet
vellēmus
vellētis
vellent

PERFECT
voluerim   I may have wished

PLUPERFECT
voluissem   I might have wished

Infinitives
Present   **velle**   to wish
Perfect   **voluisse**   to have wished

Participle   **volēns, -entis**   wishing

Continued

214 VERBS: UNIQUE

nōlle (not to wish, to be unwilling)

- This verb was originally **nōn volo**.

Indicative

PRESENT

nolō	I do not wish *etc*
nōn vīs	
nōn vult	
nōlumus	
nōn vultis	
nōlunt	

IMPERFECT

nōlēbam	I was not wishing
nōlēbās	
nōlēbat	
nōlēbāmus	
nōlēbātis	
nōlēbant	

FUTURE

nōlam	I shall not wish

PERFECT

nōluī	I have not wished

PLUPERFECT

nōlueram	I had not wished

FUTURE PERFECT

nōluerō	I shall not have wished

Continued

Subjunctive

PRESENT

nōlim	I may not wish
nōlīs	
nōlit	
nōlīmus	
nōlītis	
nōlint	

IMPERFECT

nōllem	I might not wish
nōllēs	
nōllet	
nōllēmus	
nōllētis	
nōllent	

PERFECT

nōluerim	I may not have wished

PLUPERFECT

nōluissem	I might not have wished

Infinitives

Present	nōlle	not to wish
Perfect	nōluisse	not to have wished

Participle

nōlēns, -entis	not wishing

mālle (to prefer)

- This verb is formed from **ma volō** or **magis volō** (I wish more).

Indicative

PRESENT
mālō   I prefer
māvis
māvult
mālumus
māvultis
mālunt

IMPERFECT
mālēbam   I was preferring
mālēbās
mālēbat
malēbamus
mālēbātis
mālēbant

FUTURE
mālam   I shall prefer

PERFECT
mālui   I preferred

PLUPERFECT
mālueram   I had preferred

FUTURE PERFECT
māluerō   I shall have preferred

Subjunctive

PRESENT
mālim   I may prefer
mālīs
māiit
mālīmus
mālītis
mālint

IMPERFECT
māllem   I might prefer
māllēs
māllet
māllēmus
māllētis
māllent

PERFECT
māluerim   I may have preferred

PLUPERFECT
māluissem   I might have preferred

Infinitives
Present   mālle   to prefer
Perfect   māluisse   to have preferred

Defective Verbs

The following verbs have only a few forms which are used. These are shown below.

inquam (I say)

PRESENT

inquam
inquis
inquit
inquimus
inquitis
inquiunt

This verb is mainly used in the third person singular

inquiēbat	he said
inquiet	he will say
inquit	he said

avēre	to hail, say "hello"
salvēre	to hail
valēre	to say goodbye

• These verbs are found mainly in infinitives as above or imperatives:

avē, salvē	hello (*sing*)
avēte, salvēte	hello (*pl*)
valē (*sing*), valēte (*pl*)	goodbye

• Four verbs, **ōdī, meminī, coepī, nōvī** are found only in the perfect stem but are translated as follows:

ōdī	I hate
ōderam	I hated
ōderō	I shall hate
ōdisse	to hate

meminī	I remember
memineram	I remembered
meminerō	I shall remember
meminisse	to remember

coepī	I begin
coeperam	I began
coeperō	I shall begin
coepisse	to begin

nōvī	I know
nōveram	I knew
nōverō	I shall know
nōvisse	to know

Likewise subjunctive:

| ōderim | I may hate |
| ōdissem | I might hate |

| meminerim | I may remember |
| meminissem | I might remember |

| coeperim | I may begin |
| coepissem | I might begin |

| nōverim | I may know |
| nōvissem | I might know |

Principal Parts of Common Verbs

Latin verbs are most usefully listed under four principal parts, from which all other tenses *etc* may be formed or recognized

	1ST PERSON PRESENT ACTIVE	PRESENT INFINITIVE	1ST PERSON PERFECT ACTIVE	SUPINE
1st Conjugation	amō	amāre	amāvī	amātum
2nd Conjugation	habeō	habēre	habuī	habitum
3rd Conjugation	mittō	mittere	mīsī	missum
4th Conjugation	audiō	audīre	audīvī	audītum

400 of the most common verbs in Latin are listed below. Included are the following:

- 120 regular verbs. Their conjugations are indicated by numbers 1-4. All parts of these verbs can be deduced from the model conjugations on pp 148–185.

- Nearly 300 verbs which are irregular in parts (highlighted in bold), mainly in the perfect and supine. Again their conjugation is indicated by the number of the group to which they belong. Regular parts of these verbs and person endings etc may be deduced from the models of conjugations 1-4. Many compound verbs are included (*eg* afficio from ad-facio).

- Eight unique verbs and their compounds. These are marked bold throughout and a page reference is given *in italics* for these.

- Defective verbs which are shown in full in the main text. Again a page reference *in italics* is provided.

Principal Parts		Conj / Page
abdō, abdere, **abdidī, abditum**	hide	3
abeō, abire, abiī, abitum	go away	3
abicio, abicere, **abiēcī, abiectum**	throw away	3
absum, abesse, afui	be away	3
accēdō, accēdere, **accessī, accessum**	approach	1
accidō, accidere, **accidī**	happen	3
accipiō, accipere, **accēpī, acceptum**	receive	3
accūsō, accūsāre, accūsāvī, accūsātum	accuse	1
addō, addere, **addidī, additum**	add	3
adeō, adire, adiī, aditum	approach	3
adimō, adimere, **adēmī, ademptum**	take away	3
adiuvō, adiuvare, **adiūvī, adiūtum**	help	1
administrō, administrāre, administrāvī, administrātum	administer	1
adsum, adesse, adfui	be present	1
adveniō, advenire, **advēnī, adventum**	reach	4
aedificō, aedificāre, aedificāvī, aedificātum	build	1
afferō, afferre, attulī, allātum	bring to	1
afficiō, afficere, **affēcī, affectum**	affect	3
aggredior, aggredi, **aggressus sum**	attack	3
agnōscō, agnōscere, **agnōvī, agnitum**	recognize	3
agō, agere, **ēgī, āctum**	do/drive	3
alō, alere, **aluī, altum**	feed	3
ambulō, ambulāre, ambulāvī, ambulātum	walk	1
āmittō, āmittere, **āmisī, āmissum**	lose	3
amō, amāre, amāvī, amātum	love	1

	Conj *Page*
animadvertō, animadvertere, animadvertī, **animadversum** — notice	3
aperiō, aperīre, **aperuī, apertum** — open	4
appāreō, appārēre, appāruī, appāritum — appear	2
appellō, appellāre, appellāvī, appellātum — call	1
appropinquō, appropinquāre, appropinquāvī, appropinquātum — approach	1
arbitror, arbitrārī, arbitrātus sum — think	1
arcessō, arcessere, **arcessīvī, arcessītum** — send for	3
ārdeō, ārdēre, **ārsī, ārsum** — burn	2
armō, armāre, armāvī, armātum — arm	1
ascendō, ascendere, **ascendī, ascēnsum** — climb up	3
aspiciō, aspicere, **aspexī, aspectum** — look at	3
attingō, attingere, **attigī, attāctum** — touch	3
audeō, audēre, **ausus sum** — dare	2
audiō, audīre, audīvī, audītum — hear	4
auferō, auferre, abstulī, ablātum — take away	
augeō, augēre, **auxī, auctum** — increase	2
bibō, bibere, **bibī** — drink	3
cadō, cadere, **cecidī, cāsum** — fall	3
caedō, caedere, **cecīdī, caesum** — cut/kill	3
canō, canere, **cecinī, cantum** — sing	3
capiō, capere, **cēpī, captum** — take	3
careō, carēre — lack	2
carpō, carpere, **carpsī, carptum** — pick	3
caveō, cavēre, **cāvī, cautum** — beware	2
cēdō, cēdere, **cessī, cessum** — go/give way	3

	Conj *Page*
cēlō, cēlāre, cēlāvī, cēlātum — hide	1
cernō, cernere, **crēvī, crētum** — perceive	3
cieō, ciēre, **cīvī, cītum** — rouse	2
cingō, cingere, **cīnxī, cīnctum** — surround	3
circumdō, circumdāre, **circumdedī, circumdātum** — place round	1
clāmō, clāmāre, clāmāvī, clāmātum — shout	1
claudō, claudere, **clausī, clausum** — close	3
coepī, coeptus — begin	*219*
cōgitō, cōgitāre, cōgitāvī, cōgitātum — think	1
cōgnōscō, cōgnōscere, **cōgnōvī, cōgnitum** — find out	3
cōgō, cōgere, **coēgī, coāctum** — collect/compel	3
colō, colere, **coluī, cultum** — look after/worship	3
collocō, collocāre, collocāvī, collocātum — place	1
commoveō, commovēre, **commōvī, commōtum** — upset	2
comparō, comparāre, comparāvī, comparātum — get ready	1
comperiō, comperīre, **comperī, compertum** — discover	4
compleō, complēre, **complēvī, complētum** — fill	2
comprehendō, comprehendere, **comprehendī, comprehēnsum** — grasp	3
concurrō, concurrere, **concurrī, concursum** — run together	3
condō, condere, **condidī, conditum** — found	3
conficiō, conficere, **confēcī, confectum** — finish	3
confīdō, confīdere, **confīsus sum** — trust	3

		Conj Page
confirmō, confirmāre, confirmāvī, confirmātum	strengthen	1
confiteor, confitērī, confessus sum	confess	2
congredior, congredī, congressus sum	meet	3
coniciō, conicere, coniēcī, coniectum	throw	3
coniungō, coniungere, coniūnxī, coniūnctum	join	3
coniūrō, coniūrāre, coniūrāvī, coniūrātum	conspire	1
conor, conārī, conātus sum	try	1
consentiō, consentīre, consēnsī, consēnsum	agree	4
consistō, consistere, constitī, constitum	stop	3
conspiciō, conspicere, conspexī, conspectum	catch sight of	3
constō, constāre, constitī	agree	1
constituō, constituere, constituī, constitūtum	decide	3
construō, construere, constrūxī, constructum	construct	3
consulō, consulere, consuluī, consultum	consult	3
consūmō, consūmere, consūmpsī, consūmptum	use up	3
contemnō, contemnere, contempsī, contemptum	despise	3
contendō, contendere, contendī, contentum	strive/hurry	3
contingō, contingere, contigī, contactum	touch	3

		Conj Page
conveniō, convenīre, convēnī, conventum	meet	4
corripiō, corripere, corripuī, correptum	seize	3
crēdō, crēdere, crēdidī, crēditum	believe	3
crescō, crescere, crēvī, crētum	grow	3
culpō, culpāre, culpāvī, culpātum	blame	1
cupiō, cupere, cupīvī, cupītum	desire	1
cūrō, cūrāre, cūrāvī, cūrātum	look after	1
currō, currere, cucurrī, cursum	run	3
custōdiō, custōdīre, custōdīvī, custōdītum	guard	4
damnō, damnāre, damnāvī, damnātum	condemn	1
dēbeō, dēbēre, dēbuī, dēbitum	have to/owe	2
dēdō, dēdere, dēdidī, dēditum	hand over/yield	3
dēdūcō, dēdūcere, dēdūxī, dēdūctum	bring/escort	3
dēfendō, dēfendere, dēfendī, dēfensum	defend	3
dēficiō, dēficere, dēfēcī, dēfectum	revolt/fail	3
dēiciō, dēicere, dēiēcī, dēiectum	throw down	3
dēlectō, dēlectāre, dēlectāvī, dēlectatum	delight	1
dēleō, dēlere, dēlēvī, dēlētum	destroy	2
dēligō, dēligere, dēlēgī, dēlectum	choose	3
dēmonstrō, dēmonstrāre, dēmonstrāvī, dēmonstrātum	show	1
dēpōnō, dēpōnere, dēposuī, dēpositum	lay down	3

		Conj	Page
dēscendō, dēscendere, dēscendī, dēscensum	go down	3	
dēserō, dēserere, dēseruī, dēsertum	desert	3	
dēsīderō, dēsīderāre, dēsīderāvī, dēsīderātum	long for	1	
dēsiliō, dēsilīre, dēsiluī, dēsultum	jump down	3	
dēsinō, dēsinere, dēsiī, dēsitum	stop/leave off	3	
dēsistō, dēsistere, dēstitī	stop/leave off	3	
dēspērō, dēspērāre, dēspērāvī, dēspērātum	despair	1	
dēstruō, dēstruere, dēstrūxī, dēstructum	destroy	3	
dīcō, dīcere, dīxī, dictum	tell/say	3	
dīligō, dīligere, dīlēxī, dīlēctum	love	3	
dīmittō, dīmittere, dīmīsī, dīmissum	send away	3	
discēdō, discēdere, discessī, discessum	go away	3	
discō, discere, didicī	learn	3	
dīvidō, dīvidere, dīvīsī, dīvīsum	divide	3	
dō, dāre, dedī, datum	give	1	
doceō, docēre, docuī, doctum	teach	2	
doleō, dolēre, doluī, dolitum	grieve	2	
dormiō, dormīre, dormīvī, dormītum	sleep	4	
dubitō, dubitāre, dubitāvī, dubitātum	doubt	1	
dūcō, dūcere, dūxī, ductum	lead	3	
edō, edere, ēdī, ēsum	eat	3	
efficiō, efficere, effēcī, effectum	complete	3	
effugiō, effugere, effūgī	escape	3	
ēgredior, ēgredī, ēgressus sum	go out	3	
emō, emere, ēmī, ēmptum	buy	3	
eō, īre, īvī, ītum	go		210

		Conj	Page
errō, errāre, errāvī, errātum	wander/be wrong	1	
ērumpō, ērumpere, ērūpī, ēruptum	burst out	3	
excitō, excitāre, excitāvī, excitātum	arouse	1	
exeō, exīre, exiī, exitum	go out	2	
exerceō, exercēre, exercuī, exercitum	exercise/train	2	
exīstimō, exīstimāre, exīstimāvī, exīstimātum	think	1	
expellō, expellere, expulī, expulsum	drive out	3	
experior, experīrī, expertus sum	try/test	4	
exspectō, exspectāre, exspectāvī, exspectātum	wait for	1	
exuō, exuere, exuī, exūtum	take off	3	
faciō, facere, fēcī, factum	do/make	3	
fallō, fallere, fefellī, falsum	deceive	3	
faveō, favēre, fāvī, fautum	favour	2	
ferō, ferre, tulī, lātum	bring/bear		204
festīnō, festīnāre, festīnāvī, festīnātum	hurry	1	
fīgō, fīgere, fīxī, fīxum	fix	3	
fingō, fingere, finxī, fictum	invent	3	
fīō, fierī, factus sum	become/happen		208
flectō, flectere, flexī, flexum	bend	3	
fleō, flēre, flēvī, flētum	weep	2	
fluō, fluere, flūxī, flūxum	flow	3	
frangō, frangere, frēgī, frāctum	break	3	
fruor, fruī, frūctus or fruitus sum	enjoy	3	
fugiō, fugere, fūgī, fugitum	flee/escape	3	
fugō, fugāre, fugāvī, fugātum	put to flight	1	
fundō, fundere, fūdī, fūsum	pour	3	
fungor, fungī, fūnctus sum	perform	3	

		Conj / Page
gaudeō, gaudēre, **gāvīsus sum**	be glad	2
gemō, gemere, **gemuī, gemitum**	groan	3
gerō, gerere, **gessī, gestum**	carry on/wear	3
gignō, gignere, **genuī, genitum**	produce	3
habeō, habēre, habuī, habitum	have/keep	2
habitō, habitāre, habitāvī, habitātum	live (in)	1
haereō, haerēre, **haesī, haesum**	stick	2
hauriō, haurīre, **hausī, haustum**	drain away	4
horreō, horrēre, horruī	stand on end	2
hortor, hortārī, hortātus sum	encourage	1
iaceō, iacēre, iacuī	lie down	2
iaciō, iacere, **iēcī, iactum**	throw	3
ignōscō, ignōscere, **ignōvī, ignōtum**	forgive	3
immineō, imminēre	threaten	2
impediō, impedīre, impedīvī, impedītum	hinder	4
impellō, impellere, **impulī, impulsum**	drive on	3
imperō, imperāre, imperāvī, imperātum	order	1
incendō, incendere, **incendī, incēnsum**	burn	3
incipiō, incipere, **coepī, coeptum**	begin	3
incitō, incitāre, incitāvī, incitātum	drive on	1
inclūdō, inclūdere, **inclūsī, inclūsum**	include	3
incolō, incolere, incoluī	live (in)	3
inferō, **inferre, intulī, illātum**	bring against	3
ingredior, ingredī, **ingressus sum**	enter	3

		Conj / Page
īnstituō, īnstituere, **īnstituī, īnstitūtum**	set up	3
īnstruō, īnstruere, **īnstrūxī, īnstrūctum**	set/draw up	3
intellegō, intellegere, **intellēxī, intellēctum**	realize	3
interficiō, interficere, **interfēcī, interfectum**	kill	3
intersum, interesse	be among/be important	(impers)
intrō, intrāre, intrāvī, intrātum	enter	1
inveniō, invenīre, **invēnī, inventum**	come upon/find	4
invītō, invītāre, invītāvī, invītātum	invite	1
irrumpō, irrumpere, **irrūpī, irruptum**	rush into	3
iubeō, iubēre, **iussī, iussum**	order	2
iūdicō, iūdicāre, iūdicāvī, iūdicātum	judge	1
iungō, iungere, **iūnxī, iūnctum**	join	3
iūrō, iūrāre, iūrāvī, iūrātum	swear	1
iuvō, iuvāre, **iūvī, iūtum**	help	1
labor, lābī, **lāpsus sum**	slip	3
labōrō, labōrāre, labōrāvī, labōrātum	work	1
lacessō, lacessere, **lacessīvī, lacessītum**	harass	3
lacrimō, lacrimāre, lacrimāvī, lacrimātum	weep	1
laedō, laedere, **laesī, laesum**	hurt	3
lateō, latēre, latuī	lie hidden	2
laudō, laudāre, laudāvī, laudātum	praise	1
lavō, lavāre, **lāvī, lautum/lavātum/ lōtum**	wash	1
legō, legere, **lēgī, lēctum**	read/choose	3

		Conj Page
levō, levāre, levāvī, levātum	lighten	1
liberō, liberāre, liberāvī, liberātum	free	1
licet, licēre, licuit	it is allowed	2
locō, locāre, locāvī, locātum	place	1
loquor, loquī, **locūtus sum**	speak	3
lūdō, lūdere, **lūsī, lūsum**	play	3
lustrō, lustrāre, lustrāvī, lustrātum	purify/scan	1
mālō, mālle, māluī	prefer	216
mandō, mandāre, mandāvī, mandātum	command/trust	1
maneō, manēre, **mānsī, mānsum**	remain/stay	2
meminī, meminisse	remember	219
mentior, mentīrī, mentītus sum	tell lies	4
metuō, metuere, **metuī**	fear	3
minor, minārī, minātus sum	threaten	1
minuō, minuere, **minuī, minūtum**	lessen	3
miror, mirārī, mirātus sum	wonder (at)	1
misceō, miscēre, **miscuī, mixtum**	mix	2
misereor, miserērī, miseritus sum / misereō, miserēre, miseruit (*eg* me miseret tuī – I am sorry for you)	pity	2
mittō, mittere, **mīsī, missum**	send	3
mōlior, mōlīrī, mōlītus sum	strive/toil	4
moneō, monēre, monuī, monitum	advise/warn	2
morior, morī, **mortuus sum**	die	3
moror, morārī, morātus sum	delay/loiter	1
moveō, movēre, **mōvī, mōtum**	move	2
mūniō, mūnīre, mūnīvī/mūniī, mūnītum	fortify	4
mūtō, mūtāre, mūtāvī, mūtātum	change	1
nancīscor, nancīscī, **na(n)ctus sum**	obtain	3
nārrō, nārrāre, nārrāvī, nārrātum	tell	1

		Conj Page
nāscor, nāscī, **nātus sum**	be born	3
nāvigō, nāvigāre, nāvigāvī, nāvigātum	sail	1
necō, necāre, necāvī, necātum	kill	1
negō, negāre, negāvī, negātum	refuse/deny	1
neglegō, neglegere, **neglēxī, neglēctum**	neglect	3
nesciō, nescīre, nescīvī or iī, nescītum	not to know	4
noceō, nocēre, nocuī, nocitum	harm	2
nōlō, nōlle, nōluī	not to wish/be unwilling	214
nōscō, nōscere, **nōvī, nōtum** (in perfect tenses translate as "know")	get to know	3
nūntiō, nūntiāre, nūntiāvī, nūntiātum	announce	1
obeō, obīre, obīvī or iī, obitum	die	
obiciō, obicere, **obiēcī, obiectum**	throw to/oppose	3
oblīvīscor, oblīvīscī, **oblītus sum**	forget	3
obsideō, obsidēre, **obsēdī, obsessum**	besiege	2
obtineō, obtinēre, obtinuī, **obtentum**	hold/obtain	2
occidō, occidere, **occidī, occāsum**	fall	3
occīdō, occīdere, **occīdī, occīsum**	kill	3
occupō, occupāre, occupāvī, occupātum	seize	1
occurrō, occurrere, **occurrī, occursum**	meet	3
ōdī, ōdisse	hate	219
offerō, offerre, obtulī, oblātum	present	219

		Conj / Page
oportet, oportēre, oportuit	be proper/ought	2
opprimō, opprimere, **oppressī, oppressum**	crush	3
oppugnō, oppugnāre, oppugnāvī, oppugnātum	attack	1
optō, optāre, optāvī, optātum	wish	1
orior, orīrī, **ortus sum**	arise	4
ōrō, ōrāre, ōrāvī, ōrātum	beg/plead	1
ōrnō, ōrnāre, ōrnāvī, ōrnātum	decorate/equip	1
ostendō, ostendere, **ostendī, ostentum**	show	3
pācō, pācāre, pācāvī, pācātum	pacify	1
paenitet, paenitēre, paenituit	repent of	2
pandō, pandere, **pandī, passum**	spread out	3
parcō, parcere, **pepercī, parsum**	spare	3
pāreō, parēre, paruī	obey	2
pariō, parĕre, **peperī, partum**	give birth to	3
parō, parāre, parāvī, parātum	prepare	1
pāscō, pāscere, **pāvī, pāstum**	feed	3
patefaciō, patefacere, **patefēcī, patefactum**	open	3
pateō, patēre, patuī	be open	2
patior, patī, **passus sum**	suffer/allow	3
paveō, pavēre, **pāvī**	fear	2
pellō, pellere, **pepulī, pulsum**	drive	3
pendeō, pendēre, **pependī** (intrans)	hang	2
pendō, pendēre, **pependī, pēnsum**	weigh/pay	3
perdō, perdere, **perdidī, perditum**	lose/destroy	3
pereō, **perīre, periī, peritum**	perish	1
perficiō, perficere, **perfēcī, perfectum**	complete	3

		Conj / Page
pergō, pergere, **perrēxī, perrēctum**	proceed	3
permittō, permittere, **permīsī, permissum**	allow	3
persuadeō, persuadēre, **persuāsī, persuāsum**	persuade	2
pertineō, pertinēre, pertinuī	concern	2
perturbō, perturbāre, perturbāvī, perturbātum	confuse	1
perveniō, pervenīre, **pervēnī, perventum**	arrive at	4
petō, petere, **petīvī, petītum**	seek/ask	3
placeō, placēre, placuī, placitum	please	2
placet, placēre, placuit	it seems good	2
polliceor, pollicērī, **pollicitus sum**	promise	2
pōnō, pōnere, **posuī, positum**	place/put	3
portō, portāre, portāvī, portātum	carry	1
poscō, poscere, **poposcī**	ask for/demand	3
possum, posse, potuī	to be able	200
postulō, postulāre, postulāvī, postulātum	demand	1
potior, potīrī, potītus sum	gain possession of	4
praebeō, praebēre, praebuī, praebitum	show	2
praeficiō, praeficere, **praefēcī, praefectum**	put in command of	3
praestō, praestāre, **praestitī, praestatum**	stand out	1
premō, premere, **pressī, pressum**	press	3
prōcēdō, prōcēdere, **prōcessī, prōcessum**	advance	3

		Conj Page
prōdō, prōdere, **prōdidī**, **prōditum**	betray	3
proficīscor, proficīscī, **profectus sum**	set out	3
prōgredior, prōgredī, **progressus sum**	advance	3
prohibeō, prohibēre, prohibuī, prohibitum	prevent	2
prōmittō, prōmittere, **prōmīsī**, **prōmissum**	promise	3
prōvideō, prōvidēre, **prōvīdī**, **prōvīsum**	take precautions	3
pugnō, pugnāre, pugnāvī, pugnātum	fight	1
pūniō, pūnīre, pūnīvī or iī, pūnītum	punish	4
putō, putāre, putāvī, putātum	think	1
quaerō, quaerere, **quaesīvī**, **quaesītum**	ask/seek	3
queror, querī, **questus sum**	complain	3
quiēscō, quiēscere, **quiēvī**, **quiētum**	keep quiet	3
rapiō, rapere, **rapuī**, **raptum**	snatch/seize	3
recipiō, recipere, **recēpī**, **receptum**	receive/recover	3
recūsō, recūsāre, recūsāvī, recūsātum	refuse	1
reddō, reddere, **reddidī**, **redditum**	give back/return	3
redeō, **redīre**, **rediī**, **reditum**	come back/return	
redūcō, redūcere, **redūxī**, **reductum**	bring back	3
regō, regere, **rēxī**, **rēctum**	rule	3
regredior, regredī, **regressus sum**	retreat	3
relinquō, relinquere, **relīquī**, **relictum**	leave	3

		Conj Page
remittō, remittere, **remīsī**, **remissum**	send back	3
reor, rērī, **ratus sum**	think	2
repellō, repellere, **reppulī**, **repulsum**	drive back	3
reperiō, reperīre, **repperī**, **repertum**	find	4
resistō, resistere, **restitī**	resist	3
respiciō, respicere, **respexī**, **respectum**	look back	3
respondeō, respondēre, **respondī**, **respōnsum**	answer	2
restō, restāre, **restitī**	remain	1
restituō, restituere, restituī, **restitūtum**	restore	3
retineō, retinēre, retinuī, **retentum**	hold back	2
rīdeō, rīdēre, **rīsī**, **rīsum**	laugh	2
rogō, rogāre, rogāvī, rogātum	ask	1
rumpō, rumpere, **rūpī**, **ruptum**	burst	3
ruō, ruere, **ruī**, **rutum** (ruitūrus – *fut part*)	rush/fall	3
sciō, scīre, **scīvī/iī**, **scītum**	know	4
scrībō, scrībere, **scrīpsī**, **scriptum**	write	3
sēcernō, sēcernere, **secrēvī**, **secrētum**	set apart	3
secō, secāre, **secuī**, **sectum**	cut	1
sedeō, sedēre, **sēdī**, **sessum**	sit	2
sentiō, sentīre, **sēnsī**, **sēnsum**	feel/perceive	4
sepeliō, sepelīre, sepelīvī, **sepultum**	bury	4
sequor, sequī, **secūtus sum**	follow	3
serō, serere, **sēvī**, **satum**	sow	3
serviō, servīre, servīvī, servītum	serve/be a slave	4
servō, servāre, servāvī, servātum	save	1

		Conj/Page
simulō, simulāre, simulāvī, simulātum	pretend	1
sinō, sinere, **sīvī, situm**	allow	3
sistō, sistere, **stitī, statum**	set up	3
soleō, solēre, **solitus sum**	be used to	2
sollicitō, sollicitāre, sollicitāvī, sollicitātum	worry	1
solvō, solvere, **solvī, solūtum**	loosen	3
sonō, sonāre, **sonuī, sonitum**	sound	1
spargō, spargere, **sparsī, sparsum**	scatter/sprinkle	3
spectō, spectāre, spectāvī, spectātum	look at	1
spērō, spērāre, spērāvī, spērātum	hope	1
spoliō, spoliāre, spoliāvī, spoliātum	rob/plunder	1
statuō, statuere, **statuī, statūtum**	set up	3
sternō, sternere, **strāvī, strātum**	cover/ overthrow	3
stō, stāre, **stetī, statum**	stand	1
struō, struere, **strūxī, strūctum**	build	3
studeō, studēre, studuī	study	2
suādeō, suādēre, **suāsī, suāsum**	advise	2
subeō, subīre, subiī, subitum	undergo	
succēdō, succēdere, successī, **successum**	go up/relieve	3
succurrō, succurrere, succurrī, succursum	help	3
sum, esse, fuī, futūrus		196
sūmō, sūmere, **sūmpsī, sūmptum**	take	3
superō, superāre, superāvī, superātum	overcome	1
supersum, superesse, superfuī	survive	
surgō, surgere, **surrēxī, surrēctum**	rise/get up	3
suscipiō, suscipere, **suscēpī, susceptum**	undertake	3

		Conj/Page
suspicor, suspicārī, suspicātus sum	suspect	1
sustineō, sustinēre, sustinuī, **sustentum**	sustain	2
taceō, tacēre, tacuī, tacitum	be silent	2
taedet, taedēre, taeduit, **taesum est**	be tired of	2
tangō, tangere, **tetigī, tāctum**	touch	3
tegō, tegere, **tēxī, tēctum**	cover	3
tendō, tendere, **tetendī, tentum** or **tēnsum**	stretch	3
teneō, tenēre, tenuī, **tentum**	hold	2
terreō, terrēre, terruī, territum	terrify	2
timeō, timēre, timuī	fear	2
tollō, tollere, **sustulī, sublātum**	raise/remove	3
tonō, tonāre, tonuī	thunder	1
torqueō, torquēre, **torsī, tortum**	twist	2
trādō, trādere, **trādidī, trāditum**	hand over	3
trahō, trahere, **trāxī, tractum**	drag	3
trāiciō, trāicere, **trāiēcī, trāiectum**	take across	3
trānseō, trānsīre, trānsiī, trānsitum	cross over	
tueor, tuērī, tuitus sum	look at	2
ulcīscor, ulcīscī, **ultus sum**	punish/avenge	3
urgeō, urgēre, **ursī**	press/urge	2
ūrō, ūrere, ussī, ustum	burn	3
ūtor, ūtī, **ūsus sum**	use	3
valeō, valēre, valuī, valitum	be strong	2
vāstō, vāstāre, vāstāvī, vāstātum	destroy	1
vehō, vehere, **vēxī, vectum**	carry	3
vendō, vendere, **vendidī, venditum**	sell	3
veniō, venīre, **vēnī, ventum**	come	4
vereor, verērī, veritus sum	fear	2

		Conj *Page*
vertō, vertere, **vertī, versum**	turn	**3**
vescor, vescī	feed on	3
vetō, vetāre, **vetuī, vetitum**	forbid	**1**
videō, vidēre, **vīdī, vīsum**	see	**2**
vigilō, vigilāre, vigilāvī, vigilātum	stay awake	1
vinciō, vincīre, **vīnxī, vīnctum**	bind	**4**
vincō, vincere, **vīcī, victum**	defeat/conquer	**3**
vitō, vitāre, vitāvī, vitātum	avoid	1
vīvō, vīvere, **vīxī, victum**	live	**3**
vocō, vocāre, vocāvī, vocātum	call/invite	1
volō, velle, voluī	wish/want	*212*
volvō, volvere, **volvī, volūtum**	roll	**3**
voveō, vovēre, **vōvī, vōtum**	vow	**2**

The following index lists comprehensively both grammatical terms and key words in English and Latin.

Latin

Dictionary

Plus Grammar

Collins

An Imprint of HarperCollins*Publishers*

first published in this format 1997

© HarperCollins Publishers 1997

latest reprint 2003

HarperCollins Publishers
Westerhill Road, Bishopbriggs, Glasgow G64 2QT
Great Britain

www.collinsdictionaries.com

Collins® is a registered trademark of
HarperCollins Publishers Limited

ISBN 0-00-472092-X

HarperCollins Publishers, Inc
10 East 53rd Street, New York, NY 10022

ISBN 0-06-053690-X

Library of Congress Cataloging-in-Publication Data has been applied for

www.harpercollins.com

First HarperCollins edition published 2003

Dictionary based on the Collins Latin Gem © 1957 by
Professor D.A. Kidd
Canterbury University

Grammar text and dictionary supplements by
Mary Wade

Editorial coordinator
Joyce Littlejohn

Latin consultants
Ian Brookes
Denis Bruce   Michael D. Igoe

Series editor
Lorna Sinclair

Editorial management
Vivian Marr

All rights reserved

A catalogue record for this book is available from the British Library

Dictionary text typeset by Tradespools Ltd, Somerset
Grammar typeset by Latimer Trend Ltd, Plymouth

Printed by Legoprint S.P.A.